Women's Voices, Feminist Visions

Women's Voices, Feminist Visions

Classic and Contemporary Readings

Second Edition

SUSAN M. SHAW AND JANET LEE

Oregon State University

Boston Burr Ridge, IL Dubuque, IA Madison, WI New York
San Francisco St. Louis Bangkok Bogotá Caracas Kuala Lumpur
Lisbon London Madrid Mexico City Milan Montreal New Delhi
Santiago Seoul Singapore Sydney Taipei Toronto

Higher Education

WOMEN'S VOICES, FEMINIST VISIONS: CLASSIC AND CONTEMPORARY READINGS
Published by McGraw-Hill, a business unit of The McGraw-Hill Companies, Inc., 1221 Avenue of the Americas,
New York, NY, 10020. Copyright © 2004, 2001, by The McGraw-Hill Companies, Inc. All rights reserved. No
part of this publication may be reproduced or distributed in any form or by any means, or stored in a database
or retrieval system, without the prior written consent of The McGraw-Hill Companies, Inc., including, but not
limited to, in any network or other electronic storage or transmission, or broadcast for distance learning.

Some ancillaries, including electronic and print components, may not be available to customers outside the
United States.

This book is printed on acid-free paper.

1 2 3 4 5 6 7 8 9 0 FGR/FGR 0 9 8 7 6 5 4 3

ISBN 0-07-282242-2

Publisher: Phillip A. Butcher
Sponsoring editor: Sherith H. Pankratz
Senior marketing manager: Dan Loch
Senior project manager: Christina Thornton-Villagomez
Production supervisor: Janean Utley
Associate designer: George Kokkonas
Lead supplement producer: Marc Mattson
Manager, photo research: Brian Pecko
Art editor: Cristin Yancey
Permissions: Marty Granahan
Cover design: Mary Spanburg
Cover image: "Prismes électriques" by Sonia Delaunay courtesy of L&M Services.
Interior design: Kiera Pohl
Typeface: 10/12 Minion
Compositor: G&S Typesetters
Printer: Quebecor World Fairfield Inc.

Library of Congress Cataloging-in-Publication Data
Women's voices, feminist visions : classic and contemporary readings / [edited by] Susan M. Shaw and Janet Lee.
     p.   cm.
     Includes bibliographical references and index.
     ISBN 0-07-282242-2 (softcover : alk. paper)
     1. Women's studies.   2. Feminism.   I. Shaw, Susan M. (Susan Maxine), 1960–   II. Lee, Janet, 1954–
HQ1180.W689 2004
305.42—dc21
                                                                                    2003043034

Dedicated to all our WS 223 "Women: Self and Society" students
with thanks for all they have taught us.

About the Authors

SUSAN M. SHAW is director of women studies at Oregon State University. Her research interests are in women and rock 'n' roll, women and HIV/AIDS, and women in religion, and she teaches courses in systems of oppression, women and sexuality, feminist theology, and women and pop culture. She is author of *Storytelling in Religious Education* (Religious Education Press, 1999) and coauthor of a forthcoming book on women and rock music (University Press of Kentucky), and she serves on the board of the Center Against Rape and Domestic Violence (CARDV). She is an avid racquetball player, gardener, and reader of murder mysteries.

JANET LEE is professor of women studies at Oregon State University where she teaches a variety of courses on gender and feminism. Research interests include women's history and biography, feminist theories and pedagogy, and issues concerning women and the body. She is author of *Comrades and Partners: The Shared Lives of Grace Hutchins and Anna Rochester* (Rowman and Littlefield, 2000), and coauthor of *Blood Stories: Menarche and the Politics of the Female Body in Contemporary U.S. Society* (Routledge, 1996). Her new book *War Girls: The First Aid Nursing Yeomanry (FANY) in the Great War* is forthcoming with Manchester University Press. She trains horses, loves to ride, and enjoys playing tennis.

Contents

CHAPTER 5: INSCRIBING GENDER ON THE BODY   199

CHAPTER 12: RELIGION AND SPIRITUALITY IN WOMEN'S LIVES   516

Preface

We decided to create this book after finding our students were increasingly not reading the assigned material in our introductory women's studies course. Our students found the texts to be mostly inaccessible, or alternatively, they enjoyed reading the more testimonial first-person accounts included in some texts but were not getting the theoretical framework necessary to make sense of these more experiential readings. We were tired of creating packets of readings, and students were tired of having to access alternative readings on top of purchasing a textbook. This book was crafted to include a balance of recent contemporary readings with historical and classic pieces as well as both testimonial and more theoretical essays that would speak to the diversity of women's experiences. Each chapter has an introduction that provides an overview of the topic and provides a framework for the readings that follow. Additionally, each chapter provides a variety of learning activities, activist profiles, ideas for activism, and other sidebars that can engage students with the material in various ways.

Although students of women's studies in the early 2000s are in many ways like the students who have preceded them, they are also characterized by certain distinctions from the students of the 1980s and 1990s. Many of today's students come to our classes believing the goals of the women's movement have already been accomplished, and, although most will say they believe in gender equity of some sort, few identify with feminism as a political theory or social movement. Even among students who are supportive of feminist thought, there is a distinct sense of a "third wave" of feminism that reflects the interests of young women who have come of age benefiting from the gains made by their feminist foremothers. Moreover, as women's studies has become institutionalized on college campuses and is fulfilling baccalaureate core requirements, more students are being exposed to women's studies than ever before. Many of these students "choose" women's studies from a menu of options and come to the discipline with varying levels of misunderstanding and resistance. Some of these students have been influenced by the backlash efforts of the 1980s and 1990s and by conservative religious ideologies that seek a return to traditional gender relations. All of these distinctions call for a new, relevant, and accessible introductory women's studies text.

As is typical of contemporary students, students in women's studies today are the kind of visual learners who often prefer reading and interacting in front of a computer screen or watching video clips to reading traditional texts. They are unlikely to wade through long, dense, theoretical readings because they deem them "boring" and "irrelevant." We know from experience that a large percentage of students in introductory women's studies classes only read a fragment of the required readings and that our required readings end up as "fragmented texts."

Our intention in this book is to address these challenges by presenting a student-friendly text that provides short, accessible readings reflecting the diversity of women's experiences and offering a balance of classic/contemporary and theoretical/experiential pieces. The goal is to start where students are rather than where we hope they might be and to provide a text that enriches their thinking, encourages them to read, and relates to their everyday experiences. We have chosen accessible articles that we hope are readable. They are relatively short, to the point, and interesting in terms of both topics and writing styles. Although most articles are quite contemporary, we have also included several earlier classic articles that are "must-reads." And although the articles we have chosen cover the breadth of issues and eras in women's studies, we hope students will read them and enjoy reading them because of their accessibility, style of presentation, and relevance to their lives. Many are written by young feminists, many are testimonial in format, and, on the whole, they avoid dense, academic theorizing. The cartoons, we hope, bring humor to this scholarship.

We also structure opportunities for students to reflect on their learning throughout the text, and, in this sense, the book is aimed at "teaching itself." It includes not only articles and introductions but also a number of features designed to engage students in active learning around the content. For example, we address students' tendencies to lose interest by creating a format that presents smaller, self-contained, more manageable pieces of knowledge that hold together through related fields and motifs that are woven throughout the larger text as boxes. This multiple positioning of various forms of scholarship creates independent but related pieces that enable students to read each unit in its entirety and make connections between the individual units and the larger text. We see this subtext as a way to address students' familiarity and comfort with contemporary design, multiple windows (as on web pages), and "sound bytes." By also presenting material in these familiar formats, we intend to create a student-friendly text that will stimulate their interest. We encourage them to actually read the text and then be actively engaged with the material.

Pedagogy is embedded within the text itself. In addition to the textual narrative, we include in each chapter learning activities, questions for discussion that help students explore chapter themes critically, activism ideas that provide students with examples and opportunities for the practical implementation of the content, and suggestions for further reading. Instructors will be able to utilize the various pedagogical procedures suggested in the text itself to develop teaching plans for their class sessions. By embedding the pedagogy within the text, we are creating a classroom tool that enables a connection between content and teaching procedure, between assigned readings and classroom experience. Thus, students and instructors should experience the text as both a series of manageable units of information and a holistic exploration of the larger topics.

We hope that this text will address the needs and concerns of students and instructors alike by speaking to students where they are in relation to feminist issues. Our hope is that the innovations included in this book will invite students into productive dialogue with feminist ideas and encourage personal engagement in feminist work.

Like other women's studies text-readers, this book covers the variety of issues that we know instructors address in the introductory course. We do not isolate race and racism and other issues of difference and power as separate topics, but thoroughly integrate them throughout the text into every issue addressed. We have also chosen not to present groups of chapters in parts or sections but to let the individual chapters stand alone. Pragmatically, this facilitates instructors being able to decide how they want to organize their own courses. At the same time, however, the chapters do build on each other. For example, after introducing students to women's studies, Chapter 2 presents the systems of privilege and inequality that form the context of women's lives and then Chapter 3 explores the social construction of gender, building on the previous chapter by introducing the plurality of sex/gender systems. The following chapters then examine how sex/gender systems are expressed and maintained in social institutions.

For this new edition, we have made a few changes based on the feedback of our reviewers and our own experience using the book in our classes. First, we've added a "Historical Moment" sidebar to each chapter to provide students with at least a small peek into some of the important events in the history of the women's movement. We've also added more global information to help students develop a sense of women's issues around the world. We kept most of the readings, but we did take out some that either were dated or didn't seem to work well with introductory students, and we added a few new articles that should help keep the book fresh and contemporary.

ACKNOWLEDGMENTS

Writing a textbook is inevitably a community project, and without the assistance of a number of people this project would have been impossible. We would particularly like to thank our graduate assistant Dawn M. C. Cuellar for the many hours of tedious library and Internet research she put into this book. Our office coordinator, Lisa Lawson, also provided invaluable help with the clerical tasks of preparing a manuscript. Additionally, we thank our graduate teaching assistants for their input at various stages throughout the writing and editing process—Janet Armentor, Sriyanthi Gunewardena, Fabiola Sanchez-Sandoval, Susan Wood, Tracy Clow, Rebecca Farrow, Evy Cowan, and Michelle Kilkenny.

We also would like to acknowledge the work of the many reviewers who provided insights and suggestions that strengthened our work:

Lisa M. Anderson, Arizona State University
Amber Ault, Oakland University
Suzanne Bergeron, University of Michigan, Dearborn
Jill Bystydzienski, Iowa State University
Suzanne Cherrin, University of Delaware
Mary C. Cook, Western Michigan University
Carolyn DiPalma, University of South Florida

Susan Goldstein, Diablo Valley College
Patricia L. Hartman, California University of Pennsylvania
Mazie Hough, University of Maine
John Kellermeier, Plattsburgh State University
Patricia Langley, University of Illinois, Springfield
Amy Lind, Arizona State University
Sujata Moorti, Old Dominion University
Carol O. Perkins, Minnesota State University, Mankato
Dian Ulner, Clark College

Finally, we want to thank Serina Beauparlant, our initial editor at Mayfield Publishing Company. Serina pushed, supported, challenged, and cajoled us at every step along the way to create an innovative, accessible, and useful introductory text. She is a wonderful editor, whose constant encouragement was key to the completion of this book. We would also like to thank our subsequent editors at McGraw-Hill, Katherine Bates and Sherith Pankratz.

CHAPTER ONE

Women's Studies: Perspectives and Practices

WHAT IS WOMEN'S STUDIES?

Women's studies is the examination of women's experiences that recognizes our achievements and addresses our status in society. Women's studies puts women (in all our diversity) at the center of inquiry and focuses on our reality as subjects of study. This is different than the traditional enterprise of women as objects of study. Being the objects of study means that researchers theorize about women's lives without women's input, placing women in a subordinate position to men. Instead, women as subjects of study implies both active agency on women's part and a challenge to male domination and other systems of inequality like racism and classism. In other words, when we are subjects of study as in women's studies courses, our experiences and voices have informed analyses about our lives. This means that all women, across all our differences, are included. It also means that traditional notions regarding men as "humans" and women as "others" must be challenged and transcended. This confusion of maleness with humanity, which puts men at the center and relegates women to outsiders in society, is called *androcentrism*. By making women the subjects of study, we assume that our opinions and thoughts about our own experiences are central in understanding human society generally. Adrienne Rich's "Claiming an Education" articulates this demand for women as subjects of study. It also encourages you as a student to take seriously your right to be taken seriously.

Women's studies also involves the study of gender as a central aspect of human existence. Gender concerns what it means to be a woman or a man in society. Gender involves the way society creates, patterns, and rewards our understandings of femininity and masculinity. In other words, *gender* can be defined as the way society organizes understandings of sexual difference. Women's studies explores our gendered existence: what it means to be feminine and masculine and how this interacts with other aspects of our identity, such as our race, ethnicity, socio-economic status, and sexuality.

HOW DID WOMEN'S STUDIES COME ABOUT?

Women's studies emerged as women and concerned men noticed the absence, misrepresentation, and trivialization of women in the higher education curriculum as well as the ways women were systematically excluded from many positions of power and authority as college faculty and administrators. This was especially true for women of color. In the late 1960s and early 1970s, students and faculty began demanding that the knowledge learned and shared in colleges around the country be more inclusive of women's issues, and they

Reprinted with permission.

asked to see more women in leadership positions on college campuses. It was not unusual, for example, for entire courses in English or American literature to include not one novel written by a woman. Literature was full of men's ideas about women—ideas that often continued to stereotype women and justify their subordination. History courses often taught only about men in wars and as leaders, and sociology courses primarily addressed women in the context of marriage and the family. Similarly, entire departments often consisted exclusively of men with perhaps a small minority of (usually White) women in junior or part-time positions. Although there have been important changes on most college campuses as women's issues are slowly integrated into the curriculum and advances have been made in terms of women in leadership positions, these problems still do, unfortunately, exist in higher education today.

It is important to note that making women subjects of study involves two strategies that together resulted in changes in how colleges do business. First, it rebalanced the curriculum. Women as subjects of study were integrated into existing curricula, and whole courses about women were offered. This shifted the focus on men and men's lives in the traditional academic curriculum and gave some attention to women's lives and concerns. Second, it resulted in a transformation of the existing curriculum. People began questioning the nature of knowledge, how knowledge is produced, and the applications and consequences of knowledge in wider society. Although the first strategy was an "add women and stir" approach, the second involved a serious challenge to traditional knowledge and its claims to truth. In this way, women's studies aimed not only to create programs of study where students might focus on women's issues and concerns but also to integrate a perspective for looking at things that would challenge previously unquestioned knowledge. This perspective questions how such knowledge reflects women's lives and concerns, how it maintains patterns of male privilege and power, and how the consequences of such knowledge affect women.

Women's studies as a discipline has its origins in the women's movement and is often named as its academic wing. The demand to include women as subjects of study in higher education in the late 1960s and early 1970s was facilitated by a broad societal movement in which organizations and individuals (both women and men) focused on such issues as work and employment, family and parenting, sexuality, reproductive rights, and violence against

HISTORICAL MOMENT:
THE FIRST WOMEN'S STUDIES DEPARTMENT

Following the activism of the 1960s, feminists in the academy worked to begin establishing a place for the study of women. In 1970, women faculty at San Diego State University (SDSU) taught five upper-division women's studies classes on a voluntary overload basis. In the fall of that year, the SDSU senate approved a women's studies department, the first in the United States, and a curriculum of 11 courses. The school hired one full-time instructor for the program. Other instructors included students and faculty from several existing departments. Quickly, many other colleges and universities around the nation followed suit, establishing women's studies courses, programs, and departments. In 1977 academic and activist feminists formed the National Women's Studies Association (NWSA) to further the development of the discipline. NWSA held its first convention in 1979. Presently, more than 600 women's studies programs, departments, research centers, and libraries exist in the United States.

women. The objective was to improve women's status in society and therefore the conditions of women's lives. The women's movement emerged at a moment of widespread social turmoil as various social movements questioned traditional social and sexual values, racism, poverty and other inequities, and U.S. militarism. These social movements, including the women's movement and the civil rights movement, struggled for the rights of people of color, women, the poor, gays and lesbians, the aged and the young, and the disabled.

■ THE WORLD'S WOMEN 2000: EDUCATION

- The gender gap in primary and secondary schooling is closing, but women still lag behind men in some countries of Africa and Southern Asia.
- Two thirds of the world's 876 million illiterates are women, and the number of illiterates is not expected to decrease significantly in the next twenty years.
- Women have made significant gains in higher education enrollment in most regions of the world; in some regions, women's enrollment now equals or surpasses that of men.
- More women than men lack the basic literacy and computer skills needed to enter "new media" professions.
- In many countries, women represent a rapidly increasing share of Internet users.

Source: The World's Women 2000: Trends and Statistics. Obtained from *http://unstats.un.org/unsd/demographic/ww2000/edu2000.htm*, August 2002.

Two aspects of the women's movement—a commitment to personal change and to societal change—have helped establish women's studies. In terms of the personal, the women's movement involved women asking questions about the cultural meanings of being a woman in U.S. society. Intellectual perspectives that became central to women's studies as a discipline were created from the everyday experiences of women both inside and outside the movement. Through consciousness-raising groups and other situations where women came together to talk about their lives, women realized that they were not alone in their experiences. Problems they thought to be personal (like working outside the home all day and then coming home to work another full day taking care of the domestic tasks that are involved with being a wife and mother) were actually part of a much bigger picture of masculine privilege and female subordination. Women began to make connections and coined the notion "*the personal is political*" to explain how things taken as personal or idiosyncratic have broader social, political, and economic causes and consequences. In other words, situations that we are encouraged to view as personal are actually part of broader cultural patterns and arrangements. Note that the idea that the personal is political has relevance for men's lives too. In his essay "Shame, Guilt, and Responsibility," Allan Johnson discusses the issue of masculine privilege and entitlement. He emphasizes that men need to understand the connections between patterns of gender in societal institutions and their personal experience of privilege and entitlement. The term *patriarchy* can be defined as a system in which men dominate because power and authority are in the hands of adult men. However, it is important to remember that many men are supporters of women's rights and that many of the goals of the women's movement do benefit men as well.

In terms of societal change, the women's movement continues to be successful in bringing about various legal and political changes that increase women's status in society. These changes have laid the foundation for the increased power of women in higher education. Remember that although women have been present on college campuses since the nineteenth century, they have been a small minority of faculty and administrators. Not until the 1960s did political and legal changes improve women's status in society and help remove legal obstacles to their full participation in higher education as faculty and students. This struggle continues today.

These legal changes include the passage of the Equal Pay Act in 1963 that sought equal pay for individuals performing the same work, Title VII of the 1964 Civil Rights Act that forbade workplace discrimination, and the creation of the Equal Employment Opportunity Commission (EEOC) to enforce antidiscrimination laws in the early 1970s. Affirmative action as a legal mechanism to combat discrimination was first utilized in 1961 and was extended to women in 1967. In terms of legal changes directly aimed at higher education, Title IX of the Education Amendments Act of 1972 supported equal education and forbade gender discrimination in schools. This included women's access to sports in the context of schooling.

These legal changes were accompanied by a small, although significant, increase in women running for political office and taking positions of authority in government, business, education, science, and the arts. Women were becoming visible and active in all societal institutions. In addition, the gains women were making in U.S. society were being mirrored by women's gains in other Western societies. These societal changes strengthened the demand for alternative educational models: Not only was it the right thing to include women in college life, but it was illegal to prevent their participation.

EDUCATIONAL ATTAINMENT OF THE POPULATION 25 YEARS AND OVER BY SEX: MARCH 2000

EDUCATIONAL ATTAINMENT	Total		Male		Female	
	NUMBER*	PERCENT	NUMBER*	PERCENT	NUMBER*	PERCENT
Total	175,230	100.0	83,611	100.0	91,620	100.0
Less than 9th grade	12,179	7.0	5,918	7.1	6,261	6.8
9th to 12th grade (no diploma)	15,675	8.9	7,298	8.7	8,377	9.1
High school graduate	58,086	33.1	26,651	31.9	31,435	34.3
Some college or associate degree	44,445	25.4	20,493	24.5	23,952	26.1
Bachelor's degree	29,840	17.0	14,909	17.8	14,931	16.3
Advanced degree	15,006	8.6	8,342	10.0	6,664	7.3
Less than high school diploma	27,853	15.9	13,215	15.8	14,638	16.0
High school graduate or more	147,377	84.1	70,395	84.2	76,982	84.0
Less than bachelor's degree	130,384	74.4	60,359	72.2	70,025	76.4
Bachelor's degree or more	44,846	25.6	23,251	27.8	21,595	23.6

* Numbers in thousands.
Source: U.S. Census Bureau, Current Population Survey, March 2000, Special Populations Branch, Population Division. Obtained from http://www.census.gov/population/socdemo/gender/ppl-121/tab07.txt, August 2002.

Born in Massachusetts in 1820, Susan B. Anthony grew up in a Quaker family in which she learned justice and activism. In the 1840s she became involved with the temperance movement, campaigning for stricter liquor laws to address the ill effects of drunkenness on families. In 1853, she was denied the right to speak at the New York Sons of Temperance meeting because she was a woman. That year she joined with Elizabeth Cady Stanton in founding the Women's State Temperance Society. The society gathered 28,000 signatures urging the state legislature to pass a law limiting the sale of liquor, but, because most of the signatures were from women and children, the legislature rejected the petition. As a result of this experience, Anthony realized that women needed the vote in order to have political influence.

From that point on, Anthony campaigned vigorously for women's suffrage. In 1866, she and Stanton founded the American Equal Rights Association and in 1868 began to publish *The Revolution,* with the masthead "Men, their rights, and nothing more; women, their rights, and nothing less." In 1872, Anthony was arrested in Rochester, New York, for voting. At her trial, the judge ordered the jury to find her guilty, and then he fined her $100 plus court fees. Although she refused to pay, he did not imprison her, thereby denying her the opportunity to appeal and force the issue before the Supreme Court.

In 1877 she gathered 10,000 signatures from twenty-six states, but Congress ignored them. She appeared before every Congress from 1869 to 1906 to ask for passage of a suffrage amendment. Even in her senior years, Anthony remained active in the cause of suffrage, presiding over the National American Women Suffrage Association from 1892 to 1900. Anthony died in 1906, fourteen years before American women won the vote with the Nineteenth Amendment, also known as the Susan B. Anthony Amendment.

WHAT WERE THE ORIGINS OF WOMEN'S RIGHTS ACTIVISM IN THE UNITED STATES?

Although the women's movement of the 1960s and 1970s (often termed the *second wave*) facilitated women's studies on college campuses, earlier in the nineteenth century there was a first wave of activity organized around women's issues. Women had few legal, social, and economic rights in nineteenth-century U.S. society. They had no direct relationship to the law outside of their relationships as daughters or wives; in particular, married women lost property rights upon marriage. Women were also mostly barred from higher education until women's colleges started opening later in the nineteenth century.

Most early women's rights activists (then it was referred to as "woman's" rights) in the United States had their first experience with social activism in the abolition movement, the struggle to free slaves. These activists included such figures as Elizabeth Cady Stanton, Lucretia Mott, Susan B. Anthony, Sojourner Truth, Sarah M. and Angelina Grimké, Henry Blackwell, Frederick Douglass, and Harriet Tubman. Many abolitionists became aware of inequities elsewhere in society. Some realized that to improve women's status a separate social movement was required. In this way, for many abolitionists, their experiences with abolition inspired their desire to improve the conditions of women's lives.

Although English philosopher Mary Wollstonecraft's book *A Vindication of the Rights of Woman* (1792) is seen as the first important expression of the demand for women's equality, the beginning of the women's movement in the United States is usually dated to the Seneca Falls Convention of 1848. This convention was conceived as a response to the experience of Lucretia Mott and Elizabeth Cady Stanton, who, as delegates to the world Anti-Slavery Convention in London in 1840, were refused seating, made to sit behind a curtain, and not allowed to voice their opinions because they were women. Their experience fueled the need for an independent women's movement in the United States and facilitated the convention at Seneca Falls, New York, in July 1848. An important document, the "Declaration of Sentiments and Resolutions," came out of this convention. Authored primarily by Elizabeth Cady Stanton, it used the language of the U.S. Declaration of Independence and included a variety of demands to improve women's status in the family and in society. Woman's suffrage, the right of women to vote, was included. Other conventions occurred across the country, and national organizations were organized to promote women's rights generally and suffrage in particular. These organizations included the National Woman Suffrage Association (NWSA) formed in 1869 and the National American Woman Suffrage Association

LEARNING ACTIVITY: ■ THE NATIONAL WOMEN'S HALL OF FAME

How many significant American women can you name? Most students cannot name 20 women from American history. To learn more about some of the women who have made important contributions in the United States, visit the National Women's Hall of Fame at *www.greatwomen.org*. What is the mission of the Hall of Fame? Who are this year's inductees and why were they inducted? What do you think is the significance of having a National Women's Hall of Fame?

Reprinted with permission.

(NAWSA) in 1890. NAWSA was formed from the merging of NWSA and the American Woman Suffrage Association. These organizations fought for women's political person-hood—a struggle that continues today. The "Anthony Amendment," the women's suffrage amendment, was introduced into Congress in 1878; it took another 42 years for this amendment to be ratified as the Nineteenth Amendment in 1920, granting women the right to vote.

WHAT IS THE STATUS OF WOMEN'S STUDIES ON COLLEGE CAMPUSES TODAY?

Over the past 25 or 30 years women's studies has steadily become institutionalized, or established as a regular custom, on many college campuses. From a scattering of courses (often taught for free by committed faculty when colleges did not want to spend money on these courses) have come whole programs and departments with minors and majors of study and graduate degrees at both the master's and doctorate levels. Although most campuses have adopted women's studies, some have gone with gender studies and others with feminist studies. These different names reflect different perspectives concerning knowledge about and for women.

Professors of women's studies might only teach women's studies, or they might do most of their work in another department like anthropology or history. This illustrates the multidisciplinary nature of women's studies: It can be taught from the point of view of many different disciplines. For the most part, however, women's studies is *interdisciplinary;* that is, it combines knowledge from and methodologies of disciplines across the humanities and the social and biological sciences in its analysis.

A list of the goals or objectives of women's studies might look like this:

- To understand the social construction of gender and the intersection of gender with other systems of inequality in women's lives
- To learn about the status of women in society and ways to improve that status through individual and collective action for social change.
- To experience how institutions in society affect individual lives and to be able to think critically about the role of patterns of privilege and discrimination in women's lives
- To improve writing and speaking skills, gain new insights, and empower self and others

WHAT DOES WOMEN'S STUDIES HAVE TO DO WITH FEMINISM?

Women's studies is generally associated with feminism as a paradigm for understanding self and society. Although there are many definitions of feminism and some disagreement concerning a specific definition, there is agreement on two core principles underlying any concept of feminism. First, feminism concerns equality and justice for all women, and it seeks to eliminate systems of inequality and injustice in all aspects of women's lives. Because feminism is politics of equality, it anticipates a future that guarantees human dignity and equality for all people, women and men. Second, feminism is inclusive and affirming of women; it celebrates women's achievements and struggles and works to provide a positive and affirming stance toward women and womanhood. Feminism is a personal perspective as well as a social movement.

Put this way, feminism is hardly a radical notion. Indeed, a recent study found that a large number of women (more than 90 percent who were asked) said they believed women should be paid comparably to men for the work that they do, that women deserve equal rights in society, and that sexism still exists. However, very few of these same women (only 16 percent) said they considered themselves feminists.

Other kinds of feminism, although they embrace the two core concepts listed above, vary in terms of their explanations for understanding the social organization of gender and their solutions for the problem. Rosalyn Baxandall and Linda Gordon mention these in their article and make the distinction between the liberal feminism and radical feminism of the women's movement. Liberal feminists believe in the viability of the present system and work within this context for change in such public areas as education and employment. Liberal feminists attempt to remove obstacles to women's full participation in public life. Strategies include education, federal and state policies, and legal statutes.

Although liberal feminists want a piece of the pie, radical feminists (sometimes known as cultural feminists or difference feminists) want a whole new pie. Radical feminists recognize the oppression of women as a fundamental political oppression wherein women are categorized as inferior based upon their gender. It is not enough to remove obstacles; rather, deeper, more transformational changes need to be made in societal institutions (like the government or media) as well as in people's heads. Patriarchy, radical feminists believe, shapes how women and men think about the world, their place in it, and their relationships with one another as well as the social institutions in which it is embedded. Radical feminists assert that reformist solutions like those liberal feminism would enact are problematic because they work to maintain rather than undermine the system. Not surprisingly, although the focus of liberal feminism is on the public sphere, the focus of this radical approach is the private sphere of everyday individual consciousness and change. Radical feminist offshoots include lesbian feminism, which focuses on how compulsory heterosexuality (the cultural norm that assumes and requires heterosexuality) and heterosexual privilege (the rights and privileges of heterosexuality, such as legal marriage and being intimate in public) affect women's lives. It also includes ecofeminism, a perspective that focuses on the association of women with nature and the environment and the simultaneous relationships among patriarchy, global economic expansion, and environmental degradation.

In addition, Baxandall and Gordon write about Marxist feminism, a perspective that uses economic explanations from traditional Marxist theory to understand women's oppression. For Marxist feminists, the socio-economic inequities of the class system are the major

THANK A FEMINIST

Thank a feminist if you agree that . . .

- Women should have the right to vote.
- Women should have access to contraceptives.
- Women should have the right to work outside the home.
- Women should receive equal pay for equal work.
- Women should have the right to refuse sex, even with their husbands.
- Women should be able to receive a higher education.
- Women should have access to safe, legal abortion.
- Women should be able to participate in sports.
- Women should be able to hold political office.
- Women should be able to choose any career that interests them.
- Women should be free from sexual harassment in the workplace.
- Women should be able to enter into legal and financial transactions.
- Women should be able to study issues about women's lives and experiences.

One hundred years ago, none of these statements was possible for women in the United States. Only through the hard work and dedication of women in each decade of the twentieth century did these rights become available to women.

Imagine a world without feminism. If you are a woman, you would not be in college. You would not be able to vote. You could not play sports. Contraception is illegal. So is abortion. You're expected to marry and raise a family. If you must work, the only jobs available to you are in cleaning or clerical services. And you have no legal protection on the job if your boss pressures you for sex or makes lewd comments. Your husband can force you to have sex, and, if you were sexually abused as a child, most likely no one will believe you if you tell. If you are sexually attracted to women, you are considered mentally ill and may be subjected to an array of treatments for your illness.

Today, young women who claim, "I'm not a feminist, but . . . " benefit from the many gains made by feminists through the twentieth century. So, the next time you go to class or vote or play basketball, thank a feminist!

issues. Baxandall and Gordon also mention socialist feminism, a perspective that integrates both Marxist and radical feminism. Socialist feminists use the insights of class analysis alongside radical feminist explanations of gender oppression. Socialist feminists seek to understand the workings of capitalist patriarchal institutions and societies. All these feminist approaches have been critiqued by the perspectives of women of color, who require that these approaches be inclusive of *all* women's lives. Similarly, some feminists have utilized a postmodern perspective to emphasize that truth is a relative concept and that identity is more multifaceted than we often imagine. This approach pays attention to differences among women and avoids using the term *woman* because that may imply that all women share similar or universal characteristics. It emphasizes that women actively construct or shape their lives in the context of various social systems and often in the face of serious constraints.

Feminists recognize both the similarities and differences in women's status worldwide. Women's status in developing and nonindustrialized countries is often very low, especially

■ IDEAS FOR ACTIVISM: TWO-MINUTE ACTIVIST

Many important legislative issues related to women come before elected officials regularly. You can make your voice to support women heard by contacting your senators and representative. To become a two-minute activist ("one minute to read, one minute to act"), visit the website of the American Association of University Women (AAUW) at www.aauw.org. Follow the "Issues" link to find the Two-Minute Activist link. There, you'll find links to information about the latest issues before Congress and to prewritten AAUW messages that you can personalize and send to your representatives.

in societies where strict religious doctrines govern gendered behaviors. Although women in various countries around the world tend to be in subordinate positions, the form this subordination takes varies. As a result, certain issues, like the ability of women to maintain subsistence agriculture and feed their families—matters of personal survival—take priority over the various claims to autonomy that characterize women's issues in the West. What are considered feminist issues in the United States are not necessarily the most important concerns of women in other parts of the world. It is important to understand this in order to avoid overgeneralizing about feminism's usefulness globally, even though the notion of global feminism is real and useful for political alliances across national borders. Nonetheless, global feminism underscores the similarities women share across the world and seeks strategies that take into account the interdependence of women globally. And, as communication technologies have advanced, the difficulties of organizing women in all parts of the world have lessened. International feminist groups have worked against militarism, global capitalism, and racism, and they have worked for issues identified by local women. This action culminated in the United Nations Fourth World Conference on Women held in Beijing, China, in 1995. More than 30,000 women attended the Beijing conference, and 181 governments signed the "Platform for Action." This platform is a call for concrete action to include the human rights of women and girls as part of universal human rights, thus eradicating poverty of women, removing the obstacles to women's full participation in public life and decision making, eliminating all forms of violence against women, ensuring women's access to educational and health services, and promoting actions for women's economic autonomy.

Many writers now refer to a current "third wave" of feminist activity that has its origins in the early 1990s. Third wave feminists are typically young adults who are part of generation X, those born after 1960. Coming of age during the Reagan years of the 1980s, they grew up with feminism as well as the resistance or backlash to it. Indeed, many third wave feminists are the children of second wave parents (activists of the 1960s and 1970s). Third wave issues focus on sexuality and identity and tend not to have arisen from a mass-based social movement. For these reasons, many believe that third wave feminism is better understood as a generational aspect of contemporary feminism (that is, young adults responding to what they see as the outdated issues of the second wave) and that it represents a transitional period in the movement rather than a new feminist perspective as such. Nonetheless, contemporary third wave activity has been important in fueling feminist activism, especially through "riot grrl" punk rock band performances and other musical and artistic forms, various "rags" or "zines" (consciousness-raising magazines produced locally and usually shared electronically), and the use of electronic information and entertainment technologies generally. Third wave feminists understand the need for theory and practice that take into account the globalization of economic markets, technologies, and the workplace as well as global information systems. Jennifer Baumgardner and Amy Richards' article, "A Day without Feminism," is written from this perspective. They are actively claiming feminism as relevant to their lives and are appreciative of the work of second wave feminists.

WHAT ARE THE MYTHS ASSOCIATED WITH FEMINISM?

Feminism suffers from an image problem, one that has grown in proportion to feminist progress, and there has been an institutionalized backlash to the gains feminism has achieved. For example, certain groups who believe they would lose from a redistribution of power have worked hard to discredit and destroy the feminist movement and brand feminists in negative ways. This perspective is known as anti-feminism. Although such anti-feminist activity includes conservative groups and politicians, it also involves women who claim to be feminists yet are resistant to its core principles. These women include such successful female academics as Christina Hoff Summers, Camille Paglia, and Daphne Patai, and such third wave "feminist" voices as Katie Roiphe and Rene Denfield. The reading by Deborah Rhode, an excerpt from *Speaking of Sex: The Denial of Gender Inequality,* focuses on the backlash that denies the existence of gender inequality despite the concrete realities of women's lives.

One result of this backlash has been the coining of the term *postfeminism* by those who recognize feminism as an important perspective but believe its time has passed, and it is now obsolete. "We're already liberated" is the stance they take. Like other broad generalizations, there is some truth to this: Things have improved for some women in some areas. Although generally it is accurate to say that women's status in the United States at the end of the twentieth century is markedly improved, we still have a long way to go to reach equality. In terms of the issues of poverty, violence, pornography, and HIV/AIDS (to name just a few), things are worse for many women than they ever have been. There are still many areas in which women's status might be enhanced, and, for the majority of the world's women, life is very difficult indeed.

The idea that women have achieved equality is reinforced by the capitalist society in which we live. Surrounded by consumer products, we are encouraged to confuse liberation with the freedom to purchase these products or to choose among a relatively narrow range of choices. Often personal style is mistaken for personal freedom as the body becomes a focus for fashion, hair, piercing, exercise, and so forth. We are often encouraged to confuse such freedoms of expression with freedom in the sense of equality and social justice. Of course, popular culture and the mass media play a large part in this. We are encouraged to enjoy the freedoms that, in part, feminism has brought, without recognition of this struggle or allegiance to maintaining such freedoms.

Many people, groups, and institutions have attempted to discredit feminism (and therefore women's studies) in other ways. Feminism has been associated with (1) angry, whiny women who have an axe to grind, no sense of humor, and who exaggerate discrimination against women; (2) it is declared that feminists hate men or want to be like men and selfishly want to create new systems of power *over* men; (3) all feminists are said to be lesbians, women who choose romantic relationships with other women; (4) feminists are said to reject motherhood, consider children a burden, and have rejected all things feminine;

LEARNING ACTIVITY: THE DINNER PARTY

In *Manifesta: Young Women, Feminism, and the Future,* Jennifer Baumgardner and Amy Richards tell the story of a dinner party they had, reminiscent of the consciousness-raising meetings of the 1970s during which women shared the stories and frustrations of their lives, most of which were directly related to sexism. The point of consciousness raising was to radicalize women, to help them develop the consciousness and motivation needed to make personal and political change in the world. One night in 1999, Jennifer and Amy brought together six of their friends around a dinner table to talk about current issues for women and directions needed for the contemporary women's movement. They found that the conversation wound its way around personal experiences and stories and their political implications and strategies. Their dinner party offered the beginnings of a revolution. They write, "Every time women get together around a table and speak honestly, they are embarking on an education that they aren't getting elsewhere in our patriarchal society. And that's the best reason for a dinner party a feminist could hope for."

Have a dinner party! Invite five or six of your friends over for dinner to discuss issues related to women. What are the experiences of the people around the table in terms of sexuality, work, family, body image, media, religion? What are the political implications of these experiences? What can be done to make the world better around these issues?

After your dinner party, write about what happened. What issues came up? What did various guests have to say about the issues? What strategies for change did the group identify? What plans for action did the group make? What did you learn from the experience?

and (5) feminism is dismissed as a White, middle-class movement that draws energy away from attempts to correct social and economic problems and discourages coalition building.

While several of these myths contain a grain of truth, as a whole they can easily be shattered. First, although there are some feminists who respond, some would say rightly, to societal injustices with anger, most feminists work patiently with little resentment. Men as a social group demonstrate much more anger than women, feminists included. Even though men's rage comes out in numerous acts of violence, wars, school shootings, and so on, men's anger is seen merely as a human response to circumstance. Note the androcentrism at work here. Because a few angry feminists get much more publicity than the majority of those resigned to the status quo, a better question might be why women are not more angry, given the levels of injustice against women both in the United States and worldwide. Feminists do not exaggerate this injustice; injustice is a central organizing principle of contemporary society. We should also ask why women's anger provokes such a negative response. The cause of the relatively intense reaction to women's anger is grounded in a societal mandate against female anger that works to keep women from resisting their subordination—that is, it keeps them passive. Anger is seen as destructive and inappropriate, going against what we imagine to be feminine. As a result, organized expressions of anger are interpreted as hostile.

Second, it is often said that feminists hate men. It is accurate to say that, in their affirmation of women and their desire to remove systems of inequality, feminists ask that men un-

YES, I AM

"I'm proud to be a lifelong [feminist]. It's as natural as breathing, feeling, and thinking. Never go back, never apologize, and never forget we're half the human race."
—Bella Abzug, former congresswoman

"It is from feminism that all of the many other things that I am flow. I am a mother and a mate, an activist, a mistake-maker, rule-breaker, Gloria-worshipping, Oprah-loving, risk-taker. I am a feminist, and my God and my feminism are compatible and powerful. I am a feminist, and sometimes I disappoint my feminism, and sometimes I walk hand in hand with it. I celebrate every feminist who stood strong, who took the chance, risked, and leapt."
—Kathy Najimy, actor

"This is what comes to mind when I think about feminism: a female infant placed in a wooden bucket, floating down the river. Slowly, the bucket sinks. A peasant couple in Northern China were discovered to have drowned five of their daughters this way. The victims' only fault was that they were girls."
—Anchee Min, author

"I'm not ashamed of [being feminist]. A lot of women are. It's difficult to be in the work-force, in any position of power, and not be a feminist. We have to be twice as intelli-gent to be in the same positions as men. On top of that, I'm a Black woman, so in my career, I've had to walk a very thin line. When I am assertive, men equate that with be-ing antimale. Strongmindedness intimidates most men. I've had many brothers say, 'You're a helluva woman. I hope you can find a man who can deal with you!' So much of the support I've gotten has been from women. Women have the spine, they feel where I'm coming from."
—Sandra St. Victor, vocalist

"In my native Dominican Republic, I run into women who shake their heads disapprov-ingly and say, 'Yo no soy feminista, pero, sí creo . . .' The subtext of the phrase is: I am a feminist, but I don't want to have to fight for what I believe in. By refusing to claim their feminism openly, these women make the burden all the harder for the rest of us who are willing to pay the price."
—Julia Alvarez, author

"Feminism saved my life. It's a simple fact. If there had not been a women's movement and a lesbian and gay rights movement, there's no question I'd be dead. I was on my way as it was. I deeply believe that I got picked up by a wave of history that had the possibility of allowing me to see my life in a different way and survive. There was no other voice that could say to you, 'Yes, you're an incest survivor, but you're not a mon-ster.' There was no other voice that could say to you, 'Yes, you come out of this enor-mous, broken, working-class family, and that is not the problem.' There was no other voice that could say, 'Yes, you're a lesbian, but you're not crazy.' The women's move-ment was it. That's where my source of sanity originated. I can still remember the feel-ing of being lifted up out of this confusion and despair and self-destruction—just lifted up. It's been the fuel of my life."
—Dorothy Allison, author

"Every woman who has achieved success in the working world in the last quarter cen-tury owes that success in some measure to the feminist movement. My mother taught us to respect and pay homage to those whose efforts benefited us. My life has been indelibly marked by the civil rights and feminist movements, so in addition to acknowledging my debt to the civil rights movement, I am a feminist out of respect for the efforts of those who fought for equal rights for women in every sphere.

"There are few monuments to the early feminists who revolutionized society. Their most important and enduring monument should be the gratitude of women whose minds, lives, and futures were made safe by feminists. We owe them our gratitude and a commitment to continue the equal rights struggle."
—Ruth Simmons, president, Smith College

derstand how gender privilege works in men's lives. Many men are more than willing to do this because the same social constructions of masculinity that privilege men also limit them. The demand for the examination of gender privilege is not synonymous with hating men, and thus we might ask why these different concepts are so easily conflated. A more interesting question is why men are not accused more often of hating women. Certainly the world is full of *misogyny,* the hatred of women, and every day we see examples of the ways misogyny influences, and sometimes destroys, the lives of women. The reality, of course, is that most feminists are in relationships with men, and some feminists *are* men. Some men eagerly call themselves pro-feminist because feminism is a perspective on life (even though some would argue that just as people of color are better prepared to understand racial inequality, so women are in a better place to understand how gender works). Nonetheless, the man-hating myth works to prevent many women who want to be in relationships with men from claiming feminism. They are encouraged to avoid a political stance that suggests antagonism toward men.

Feminists often respond to the declaration that they hate men with the observation that the statement illustrates a hypersensitivity about the possibility of exclusion and loss of power on the part of men. Only in a patriarchal society would the inclusion of women be interpreted as a potential threat or loss of men's power. It is a reflection of the fact that we live in a competitive patriarchal society that it is assumed that the feminist agenda is one that seeks to have power over men. And only in an androcentric society where men and their reality is center stage would it be assumed that an inclusion of one group must mean the exclusion of another. In other words, male domination encourages the idea that affirming women means hating men and interprets women's request for power sharing as a form of taking over. This projection of patriarchal mentality equates someone's gain with another's loss.

In response to the assertion that feminists want to be men, it is true to say that feminists might like to share some of the power granted to men in society. However, feminism is not about encouraging women to be like men but valuing women for being women. People opposed to feminism often confuse *sameness* and *equality* and say that women will never be equal to men because they are different (less physically strong, more emotional, etc.) or they say that equality is dangerous because women will start being like men. Feminism of course affirms and works to maintain difference; it merely asks that these differences are valued equally.

Third, feminists are accused of being lesbians in an effort to discredit feminism and prevent women both from joining the movement and from taking women's studies classes. The term for this is *lesbian baiting.* Feminism affirms women's choices to be and love whomever they choose. Although some lesbians are feminists, many lesbians are not feminists, and many feminists are heterosexual. Feminists do not interpret an association with lesbianism as an insult. Nonetheless, *homophobia,* the societal fear or hatred of lesbians and gay men, functions to maintain this as an insult. There is considerable fear associated with being called a lesbian, and this declaration that all feminists are lesbians serves to keep women in line, apart from one another, and suspicious of feminism and women's studies. Note that this myth is related to the above discussion on men-hating because it is assumed that lesbians hate men too. Again, although lesbians love women, this does not necessitate a dislike of men.

Fourth, feminism has never rejected motherhood but instead has attempted to improve the conditions under which women mother. They have rejected some of the constraints associated with femininity such as corsets and hazardous beauty products and practices but mostly strive to claim back femininity as a valuable construct that should be respected.

Fifth, feminism has been critiqued as a White, middle-class perspective that has no relevance to the lives of women of color. The corollary of this is that women's studies is only about the lives of White, bourgeois young women. This critique is important because throughout the history of the women's movement there have been examples of both blatant and subtle racism, and White women have been the ones to hold most of the positions of power and authority. Similarly, working-class women have been underrepresented. This is also reflected in the discipline of women's studies as faculty and students have often been disproportionately White and economically privileged. Much work has been done to transform the women's movement into an inclusive social movement that has relevance for all people's lives. Women's studies departments and programs today are often among the most diverse units on college campuses, although most still have work to do. It is absolutely crucial that the study of women as subjects both recognizes and celebrates diversity and works to transform all systems of oppression in society. In "Feminist Politics" bell hooks claims back feminism as the movement to do just that. She emphasizes that any call to sisterhood must involve a commitment on the part of White women to examine White privilege and understand the interconnections among gender, race, and class domination.

bell hooks's essay is followed by JeeYeun Lee's "Beyond Bean Counting." Lee shares her experience of women's studies and her observations about inclusion. She recalls how she lamented the absence of information about Asian American women in her first feminist studies course but at the same time was profoundly exhilarated by the class. She recognizes the efforts feminists have made to deal with issues of race even though work remains to be done. She also notes how social movements that affirm struggles over race and ethnicity can still be exclusionary in terms of sexual orientation. She uses the term *queer* in this essay as a way to affirm and celebrate her lesbianism. Her hope is for solidarity among all groups.

The first and second waves of the women's movement have had a profound impact on the lives of American women, and, although great strides have been made toward equality, real problems remain. Women continue to face discrimination and harassment in the workplace, domestic violence, rape and abuse, inequities in education, poverty, racism, and homophobia. Women's studies provides a forum for naming the problems women face, analyzing the root causes of these problems, envisioning a just and equitable world, and developing strategies for change. As you read the following articles, keep these questions in mind: What does the author identify as problems women face? What does the author suggest is the root of these problems? What strategies does the author suggest for bringing about change to improve the lives of women?

1792	British author Mary Wollstonecraft argues for the equality of the sexes in her book, the *Vindication of the Rights of Women*.
1840	The World's Anti-Slavery Convention is held in London, England. When the women delegates from the United States are not allowed to participate, Lucretia Mott and Elizabeth Cady Stanton determine to have a women's rights convention when they return home.
1845	Margaret Fuller publishes Woman in the Nineteenth Century, which has a profound influence on the development of American feminist theory.
1848 July 19:	The first woman's rights convention is called by Mott and Stanton. It is held on July 20 at the Wesleyan Chapel in Seneca Falls, NY.
August 2:	A reconvened session of the woman's rights convention is held at the Unitarian Church in Rochester, NY. Amelia Bush is chosen chair, and becomes the first woman to preside over a meeting attended by both men and women. New York State Legislature passes a law which gives women the right to retain possession of property they owned prior to their marriage.
1851	Elizabeth Cady Stanton and Susan B. Anthony meet and begin their fifty-year collaboration to win for women their economic, educational, social, and civil rights.
	Sojourner Truth delivers her "And Ain't I a Woman Speech" at the Woman's Rights Convention in Akron, OH.

(continued)

1855	Elizabeth Cady Stanton makes an unprecedented appearance before the New York State Legislature to speak in favor of expanding the Married Woman's Property Law.
1863	Stanton and Anthony organize the Women's Loyal National League and gather 300,000 signatures on a petition demanding that the Senate abolish slavery by constitutional amendment.
1866	The American Equal Rights Association is founded with the purpose to secure for all Americans their civil rights irrespective of race, color, or sex. Lucretia Mott is elected president. To test women's constitutional right to hold public office, Stanton runs for Congress receiving 24 of 12,000 votes cast.
1867	Stanton, Anthony, and Lucy Stone address a subcommittee of the New York State Constitutional Convention requesting that the revised constitution include woman suffrage. Their efforts fail.
	Kansas holds a state referendum on whether to enfranchise blacks and/or women. Lucy Stone, Susan B. Anthony, and Elizabeth Cady Stanton traverse the state speaking in favor of women suffrage. Both black and women suffrage is voted down.
1868	Stanton and Anthony launch their women's rights newspaper, *The Revolution,* in New York City.
	Anthony organizes the Working Women's Association, which encourages women to form unions to win higher wages and shorter hours.
	The 14th amendment to the U.S. Constitution is adopted. The amendment grants suffrage to former male African-American slaves, but not to women. Anthony and Stanton bitterly oppose the amendment, which for the first time explicitly restricts voting rights to "males." Many of their former allies in the abolitionist movement, including Lucy Stone, support the amendment.
1869	National Woman Suffrage Association is founded with Elizabeth Cady Stanton as president.
	American Woman Suffrage Association is founded with Henry Ward Beecher as president.
	Wyoming Territory grants suffrage to women.
1870	Utah Territory grants suffrage to women.
	First issue of the *Woman's Journal* is published with Lucy Stone and her husband Henry Blackwell as editors.
1871	Victoria Woodhull addresses the Judiciary Committee of the House of Representatives arguing that women have the right to vote under the 14th amendment. The Committee issues a negative report.
1872	In Rochester, NY, Susan B. Anthony registers and votes contending that the 14th amendment gives her that right. Several days later she is arrested.

1873	At Anthony's trial the judge does not allow her to testify on her own behalf, dismisses the jury, rules her guilty, and fines her $100. She refuses to pay.
1874	In *Minor v. Happersett,* the Supreme Court decides that citizenship does not give women the right to vote and that women's political rights are under the jurisdiction of each individual state.
1876	Stanton writes a *Declaration and Protest of the Women of the United States* to be read at the centennial celebration in Philadelphia. When the request to present the Declaration is denied, Anthony and four other women charge the speakers' rostrum and thrust the document into the hands of Vice-President Thomas W. Ferry.
1880	New York state grants school suffrage to women.
1882	The House of Representatives and the Senate appoint Select Committees on Woman Suffrage.
1887	The first three volumes of the *History of Woman Suffrage,* edited by Susan B. Anthony, Matilda Joslyn Gage and Elizabeth Cady Stanton, are published.
1890	After several years of negotiations, the NWSA and the AWSA merge to form the National American Woman Suffrage Association (NAWSA) with Elizabeth Cady Stanton, Susan B. Anthony and Lucy Stone as officers.
	Wyoming joins the union as the first state with voting rights for women. By 1900 women also have full suffrage in Utah, Colorado and Idaho.
	New Zealand is the first nation to give women suffrage.
1892	Susan B. Anthony becomes president of the NAWSA.
1895	Elizabeth Cady Stanton publishes *The Woman's Bible,* a critical examination of the Bible's teaching about women. The NAWSA censures the work.
1900	Anthony resigns as president of the NAWSA and is succeeded by Carrie Chapman Catt.
1902 October 26:	Elizabeth Cady Stanton dies.
	Women of Australia are enfranchised.
1903	Carrie Chapman Catt resigns as president of the NAWSA and Anna Howard Shaw becomes president.
1906 March 13:	Susan B. Anthony dies. Women of Finland are enfranchised.
1907	Harriet Stanton Blatch, daughter of Elizabeth Cady Stanton, founds the Equality League of Self-Supporting Women, later called the Women's Political Union.

(continued)

1910	The Women's Political Union holds its first suffrage parade in New York City.
1911	National Association Opposed to Woman Suffrage is founded.
1912	Suffrage referendums are passed in Arizona, Kansas, and Oregon.
1913	Alice Paul organizes a suffrage parade in Washington, DC, the day of Woodrow Wilson's inauguration.
1914	Montana and Nevada grant voting rights to women.
	Alice Paul and Lucy Burns organize the Congressional Union for Woman Suffrage. It merges in 1917 with the Woman's Party to become the National Woman's Party.
1915	Suffrage referendum in New York State is defeated.
	Carrie Chapman Catt is elected president of the NAWSA.
	Women of Denmark are enfranchised.
1916	Jeannette Rankin, a Republican from Montana, is elected to the House of Representatives and becomes the first woman to serve in Congress.
	President Woodrow Wilson addresses the NAWSA.
1917	Members of the National Woman's Party picket the White House. Alice Paul and ninety-six other suffragists are arrested and jailed for "obstructing traffic." When they go on a hunger strike to protest their arrest and treatment, they are force-fed.
	Women win the right to vote in North Dakota, Ohio, Indiana, Rhode Island, Nebraska, Michigan, New York, and Arkansas.
1918	Women of Austria, Canada, Czechoslovakia, Germany, Hungary, Ireland, Poland, Scotland, and Wales are enfranchised.
	House of Representatives passes a resolution in favor of a woman suffrage amendment. The resolution is defeated by the Senate.
1919	Women of Azerbaijan Republic, Belgium, British East Africa, Holland, Iceland, Luxembourg, Rhodesia, and Sweden are enfranchised.
	The Nineteenth Amendment to the Constitution granting women the vote is adopted by a joint resolution of Congress and sent to the states for ratification.
	New York and twenty-one other states ratify the Nineteenth Amendment.
1920	Henry Burn casts the deciding vote that makes Tennessee the thirty-sixth, and final state, to ratify the Nineteenth Amendment.
August 26:	The Nineteenth Amendment is adopted and the women of the United States are finally enfranchised.

Source: Anthony Center for Women's Leadership: US Suffrage Movement Timeline, *prepared by Mary M. Huth, Department of Rare Books and Special Collections, University of Rochester Libraries, February 1995. Obtained from http://www.rochester.edu/SBA/timeline1.html, August 2002.*

TITLE IX AT 30:
REPORT CARD ON GENDER EQUITY

Thirty years after the enactment of Title IX, while educational opportunities for girls and women have increased, there is much room for improvement in the enforcement of Title IX. . . . While some gains have been made in many areas—such as higher education, athletics programming, and math and science—many barriers remain. Too many girls and women still confront sex discrimination in their education programs. Girls and women are severely underrepresented in the critical area of technology. Sex segregation is persistent in vocational training programs, with girls and women clustered in programs that are traditional for their sex and that lead to low-wage jobs. Colleges and universities continue to spend the lion's share of athletics money on men's programming. Scoring gaps persist in high-stakes standardized testing across all races and ethnicities, limiting women's access to education institutions, financial aid, and careers. Employment numbers for women at colleges and universities tend to decrease as the rank in the career ladder or the prestige of the institution increases. Women still lag behind men in earning doctoral and professional degrees. Sexual harassment continues to undermine equal opportunity for male and female students. Gender bias continues to permeate the learning environment. Schools continue to brush aside pregnant and parenting students. And little has been done to address the multiple barriers faced by girls of color, girls with disabilities, and girls from poor backgrounds—all of whom experience a disproportionate number of inequities.

The [highlights] that follow examine these obstacles through the lens of 30 years of Title IX. The reports assess how far we have come in making Title IX's goal of equal opportunity a reality—and how far the United States as a nation has yet to go.

ACCESS TO HIGHER EDUCATION

B

Since its passage in 1972, Title IX has dramatically expanded women's access to higher education. The increased representation of women in degree-granting programs has contributed to the economic progress of women and their families. Title IX has helped reduce sex discrimination, most notably in admissions standards, to the benefit of women and men alike. But other barriers to higher education persist, including sex segregation by academic subject and disparities in financial aid awards.

. . .

- Women still lag behind men in earning doctoral and professional degrees.
- Some scholarships still are reserved for men.
- Women are underrepresented in math and science, in large part because of the hostile environment many confront in these fields.
- Education institutions are moving to dismantle affirmative action programs that have increased access for women and students of color.
- Low-income women have lost an avenue to higher education under the new welfare law.

(continued)

ATHLETICS

C+

For many people, Title IX is synonymous with expanded opportunities in athletics. Women's and girls' increased participation in sports, the impressive achievements of the nation's female athletes, their stunning advances in summer and winter Olympic Games, and the creation of nationally televised professional women's basketball and soccer leagues demonstrate Title IX's success. . . .

Research studies commissioned by the Women's Sports Foundation in 1998 and 2000 found that girls who play sports enjoy greater physical and emotional health and are less likely to engage in a host of risky health behaviors (i.e., drug use, smoking, and drinking) than nonparticipants. Other studies have linked sports participation to reduced incidences of breast cancer and osteoporosis later in life. Yet compared to boys, girls enjoy 30 percent fewer opportunities to participate in high school and college sports and are twice as likely to be inactive. Much distance remains between the current status of women and girls in sports and the ultimate goal of gender equity.

Participation Rates and Resource Allocation

Prior to 1972, women and girls looking for opportunities for athletic competition were more likely to try out for cheerleading or secure places in the bleachers as spectators. In 1971 fewer than 295,000 girls participated in high school varsity athletics, accounting for just 7 percent of all high school varsity athletes. The outlook for college women was equally grim: Fewer than 30,000 females competed in intercollegiate athletics. Low participation rates reflected the lack of institutional commitment to providing athletics programming for women. Before Title IX, female college athletes received only 2 percent of overall athletic budgets, and athletic scholarships for women were virtually nonexistent. . . .

- By 2001 nearly 2.8 million girls participated in athletics, representing 41.5 percent of varsity athletes in U.S. high schools—an increase of more than an 847 percent from 1971. . . .
- Today 150,916 women compete in intercollegiate sports, accounting for 43 percent of college varsity athletes—an increase of more than 403 percent from 1971.
- Contrary to media reports, men's participation levels at both the high school and college level have also increased. . . .
- In 1999–2000 female students represented about 54 percent of the student body at four-year colleges, yet only 23 percent of all NCAA Division I colleges provided women with athletic opportunities within five percentage points of female student enrollment. . . .
- In the past four years, for every new dollar going into athletics at the Division I and Division II levels, male sports received 58 cents while female sports received 42 cents.
- Each year male athletes receive $133 million or 36 percent more than female athletes in college athletic scholarships at NCAA member institutions.
- In Division I, colleges spent an average of $2,983 per female athlete compared to $3,786 for male athletes. . . .
- In the early 1970s women head coaches led 90 percent of women's collegiate teams. By the 2001–02 school year, female head coaches led only 44 percent of women's intercollegiate athletic teams, the lowest total since the passage of Title IX. . . .

- Since 2000, 90 percent of the available head coaching positions in women's athletics have gone to men. . . .
- At the Division I level, men's basketball head coaches average $149,700. By contrast, women's basketball head coaches average just $91,300: 61 cents to every dollar paid to men. . . .

CAREER EDUCATION

D

Title IX has made training for nontraditional careers possible for girls and women. This option clearly was off limits to female students before 1972, when schools routinely denied girls the opportunity to take classes in shop, manufacturing, architectural drafting, and ceramics or to attend certain vocational schools. Girls were directed to classes where they would learn to cook and sew. Title IX's passage meant that schools no longer could shut the doors to certain courses on the basis of gender. Thirty years later, however, patterns of sex segregation persist, and vocational education opportunities for women and girls remain largely separate and unequal.

. . .

- Sex segregation persists in vocational education: Male students predominate in high-skill, high-wage career tracks, while female students are clustered in the low-skilled, low-wage tracks.
- Programs where male students predominate are being updated with new technology opportunities while traditionally female programs receive no technology updates.
- Female students in programs that are traditional for their gender have limited access to high-level academic courses.
- The vocational education law no longer requires targeted support for programs that have helped women gain access to and succeed in nontraditional occupations.

EMPLOYMENT

C-

The hearings leading up to the passage of Title IX were replete with statistical and anecdotal information highlighting the second-class status of women working in education institutions. At that time, employment for women in education was characterized by—

- Lack of tenure in colleges and universities, particularly elite institutions
- Nepotism rules that locked a woman out of a teaching position where her husband was employed
- Slower promotion rates than those for their male counterparts
- Smaller salaries than those of their male colleagues
- Little access to high-level administrative positions
- Virtually no opportunities to head colleges and universities, even women's institutions

After 30 years of Title IX and a Supreme Court decision declaring that this law prohibits employment discrimination in education based on sex, there is progress but much room for improvement. Notably, a pattern evident at the time lawmakers debated Title

(continued)

IX persists: Women's numbers tend to decrease as the rank in the career ladder or the prestige of the education institution increases. Women still have far to go to attain full equality with men in employment in education institutions.

. . .

- Less than 35 percent of school principals are women.
- Just 21 percent of full professors are women and 2.4 percent are women of color.
- Women are least represented at elite education institutions, making up just 26.2 percent of the faculty.
- Students and colleagues evaluate female faculty more harshly than male faculty.
- Women head only 19 percent of colleges and universities.
- Women full professors earn 88 percent of the salaries their male counterparts receive; women elementary school teachers earn 92 percent of the salaries their male counterparts receive.

LEARNING ENVIRONMENT

C-

. . .

While the 1970s and 1980s witnessed clear progress in freeing students from the limits of gender stereotypes in the learning environment, the 1990s ushered in a new era challenging the progress to date. Critics of gender equity and Title IX now propose a return to many of these past practices. Some critics write that efforts to create equal learning opportunities for females detract from the educational quality provided boys. Recommendations range from creating different learning climates for boys and girls based on their "biological" differences to using textbooks that feature more males. One of the more startling suggestions is to abandon coeducation and return to the single-sex schools popular in the 1800s. While these suggestions pose blatant challenges to gender equity, more subtle gender bias still permeates learning climates, limiting the potential of both girls and boys.

. . .

- A study tracking the college progress of high school valedictorians found that while a significant number of male valedictorians continued to describe themselves as substantially brighter than their peers, female valedictorians actually lose self-esteem during their college years. By college graduation day, one in four male valedictorians rated himself at the top of his peer group in intelligence; not a single female valedictorian in this study rated herself this way. . . .
- A 1970 study of history texts found that students had to read more than 500 pages before they read one page of information about women. In most history texts, the contributions of women are still minimized, with newer texts devoting only 2 to 3 percent of book space to the experiences or contributions of women. Through these books, both boys and girls learn erroneously that women were of little importance in creating our nation. When asked, most students cannot name 20 famous women from American history. Typically, they list fewer than five. . . .
- A 1990s study of elementary mathematics software revealed that when gender-identifiable characters were present (about 40 percent of the time), only 12 percent of the characters were female. Reinforcing stereotypes, the software portrayed female

characters passively as mothers and princesses while male characters were shown as active and as "heavy equipment operators, factory workers, shopkeepers, mountain climbers, hang gliders, garage mechanics, and as a genie providing directions." . . .

- Two decades ago, teacher education textbooks gave less than 1 percent of content coverage to the experiences of women, the issue of sexism in schools, and curricular resources or teaching strategies for overcoming such bias. Today, that figure is only 3 percent. . . .

MATH AND SCIENCE

B-

The enactment of Title IX 30 years ago removed many gender barriers in the nontraditional fields of math and science, areas critical to success in an increasingly technological world. Disparities still exist, however, in achievement and participation rates in these disciplines. Gender differences in math and science start small and grow as students reach secondary school, where boys outperform girls on standardized tests and participate in math and science classes at higher rates. In postsecondary schools, men major in math and the sciences at rates that exceed those of women, shutting women out of the career opportunities these fields can provide.

. . .

- Although decreasing, the gender gap persists in girls' science and math achievement, starting small in elementary school and increasing in high school.
- On high-stakes tests, such as the math SAT, scoring gaps persist, with girls scoring 3 points below boys.
- Women continue to be underrepresented in math and science in higher education, with their representation decreasing as the degree level increases.

SEXUAL HARASSMENT

C

Although some gains have been made in this area . . . , sexual harassment continues to plague our nation's schools and students—both boys and girls. Sexual harassment is unwanted and unwelcome sexual behavior that creates a hostile environment, limiting full access to education and work. Legal developments . . . confirm that schools have an obligation under Title IX to respond to sexual harassment in school. But in too many cases, sexual harassment continues to undermine equal opportunity for students and school employees.

. . .

- Eight in 10 students experience some form of harassment during their school lives, and more than one-quarter of them experience it often.
- Girls are more likely than boys to experience harassment, but boys today are more likely to be harassed than boys in 1993.
- Six in 10 students experience physical sexual harassment at some point in their school lives, one-third often or occasionally.

(continued)

- The most common forms of sexual harassment in school span the nonphysical and physical:
    - ✔ Making sexual comments, jokes, gestures, or looks
    - ✔ Claiming that a person is gay or lesbian
    - ✔ Spreading sexual rumors about a person
    - ✔ Touching, grabbing, or pinching in a sexual way
    - ✔ Intentionally brushing up against someone in a sexual way
    - ✔ Flashing or "mooning"

STANDARDIZED TESTING

C

. . .

A substantial record of disparities in scoring between male and female students on many standardized tests date from before Title IX's enactment and continue over the last 30 years. These gaps have had a harmful impact on educational and economic opportunities available to women and girls as well as students of color. Under Title IX, tests must be valid predictors of success in the areas being tested and must measure what they purport to measure. If a test does not meet this standard, and if it produces a scoring deficit for one sex, it has a discriminatory impact on the members of that sex and is unlawful. Despite these requirements, most standardized tests used in K-12 classrooms and for university admissions continue to show gender gaps and underpredict the abilities of females.

. . .

- The increasingly high stakes attached to many standardized tests compound the problems associated with the longstanding gender gap. The lower test scores of African American, Latina, and Native American females compared to their white and Asian peers remain a serious educational divide.
- Scholarship programs, such as the National Merit contest, continue to use test scores as a qualifying criteria. Such use leads to disproportionately fewer females receiving the valuable awards.
- Rigid use of test scores in university admissions underestimates the potential achievement of women, who score lower on the exams but perform comparably to their male peers once enrolled.

TECHNOLOGY

D+

. . .

While Title IX opened paths for girls and women in fields such as math and science, girls and women are now severely underrepresented in this new field of technology and face barriers that must be addressed. Unless women and girls achieve greater parity in technology, they will continue to be underrepresented and earn less in these fields.

. . .

- Fewer girls than boys enroll in computer science, feel self-confident with computers, and use computers outside the classroom.

- According to a 2000 study by the Department of Labor, nearly 75 percent of future jobs will require the use of computers, but less than 33 percent of participants in computer courses and related activities are girls. Girls take approximately half of all AP exams but only 17 percent of the AP computer science exams. Further, women receive only 34 percent of math and computer science degrees—a number that has decreased 25 percent since 1984.
- Although teenage girls use computers and the Internet at rates similar to their male peers, girls are five times less likely to consider a technology-related career path or plan on taking postsecondary technology classes. According to a 1996 study of SAT test takers, female students are less likely to have experience using computers to solve math problems but more likely to have used a computer for word processing, a skill that will not lead to high-paying, high-tech jobs.

Title IX at 30
Report Card on Gender Equity

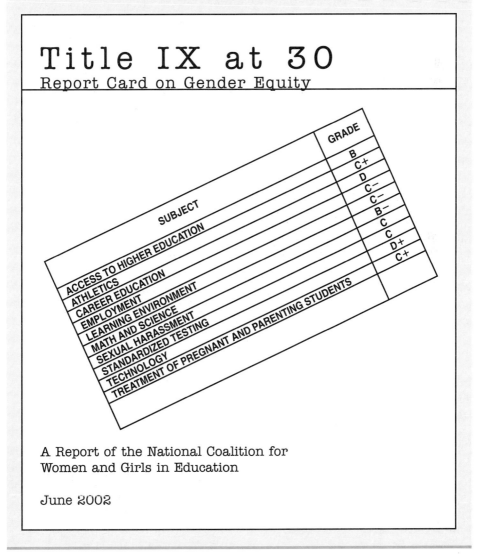

SUBJECT	GRADE
ACCESS TO HIGHER EDUCATION	B
ATHLETICS	C+
CAREER EDUCATION	D
EMPLOYMENT	C−
LEARNING ENVIRONMENT	C−
MATH AND SCIENCE	B−
SEXUAL HARASSMENT	C
STANDARDIZED TESTING	C
TECHNOLOGY	D+
TREATMENT OF PREGNANT AND PARENTING STUDENTS	C+

A Report of the National Coalition for Women and Girls in Education

June 2002

READING 1

Claiming an Education

Adrienne Rich

For this convocation, I planned to separate my remarks into two parts: some thoughts about you, the women students here, and some thoughts about us who teach in a women's college. But ultimately, those two parts are indivisible. If university education means anything beyond the processing of human beings into expected roles, through credit hours, tests, and grades (and I believe that in a women's college especially it *might* mean much more), it implies an ethical and intellectual contract between teacher and student. This contract must remain intuitive, dynamic, unwritten; but we must turn to it again and again if learning is to be reclaimed from the depersonalizing and cheapening pressures of the present-day academic scene.

The first thing I want to say to you who are students, is that you cannot afford to think of being here to *receive* an education; you will do much better to think of yourselves as being here to *claim* one. One of the dictionary definitions of the verb "to claim" is: *to take as the rightful owner; to assert in the face of possible contradiction.* "To receive" is *to come into possession of; to act as receptacle or container for; to accept as authoritative or true.* The difference is that between acting and being acted-upon, and for women it can literally mean the difference between life and death.

One of the devastating weaknesses of university learning, of the store of knowledge and opinion that has been handed down through academic training, has been its almost total erasure of women's experience and thought from the curriculum, and its exclusion of women as members of the academic community. Today, with increasing numbers of women students in nearly every branch of higher learning,

we still see very few women in the upper levels of faculty and administration in most institutions. Douglass College itself is a women's college in a university administered overwhelmingly by men, who in turn are answerable to the state legislature, again composed predominantly of men. But the most significant fact for you is that what you learn here, the very texts you read, the lectures you hear, the way your studies are divided into categories and fragmented one from the other—all this reflects, to a very large degree, neither objective reality, nor an accurate picture of the past, nor a group of rigorously tested observations about human behavior. What you can learn here (and I mean not only at Douglass but any college in any university) is how *men* have perceived and organized their experience, their history, their ideas of social relationships, good and evil, sickness and health, etc. When you read or hear about "great issues," "major texts," "the mainstream of Western thought," you are hearing about what men, above all white men, in their male subjectivity, have decided is important.

Black and other minority peoples have for some time recognized that their racial and ethnic experience was not accounted for in the studies broadly labeled human; and that even the sciences can be racist. For many reasons, it has been more difficult for women to comprehend our exclusion, and to realize that even the sciences can be sexist. For one thing, it is only within the last hundred years that higher education has grudgingly been opened up to women at all, even to white, middle-class women. And many of us have found ourselves poring eagerly over books with titles like *The Descent of Man; Man and His Symbols; Irrational Man; The Phenomenon of Man; The Future of Man; Man and the Machine; From Man to Man; May Man Prevail?; Man, Science and Society;* or *One-Dimensional Man*—books pretending to describe a "human" reality that does not include over one-half the human species.

This talk was given at the Douglass College Convocation, September 6, 1977, and first printed in *The Common Woman*, a feminist literary magazine founded by Rutgers University women in New Brunswick, New Jersey.

Less than a decade ago, with the rebirth of a feminist movement in this country, women students and teachers in a number of universities began to demand and set up women's studies courses—to *claim* a woman-directed education. And, despite the inevitable accusations of "unscholarly," "group therapy," "faddism," etc., despite backlash and budget cuts, women's studies are still growing, offering to more and more women a new intellectual grasp on their lives, new understanding of our history, a fresh vision of the human experience, and also a critical basis for evaluating what they hear and read in other courses, and in the society at large.

But my talk is not really about women's studies, much as I believe in their scholarly, scientific, and human necessity. While I think that any Douglass student has everything to gain by investigating and enrolling in women's studies courses, I want to suggest that there is a more essential experience that you owe yourselves, one which courses in women's studies can greatly enrich, but which finally depends on you, in all your interactions with yourself and your world. This is the experience of *taking responsibility toward your selves.* Our upbringing as women has so often told us that this should come second to our relationships and responsibilities to other people. We have been offered ethical models of the self-denying wife and mother; intellectual models of the brilliant but slapdash dilettante who never commits herself to anything the whole way, or the intelligent woman who denies her intelligence in order to seem more "feminine," or who sits in passive silence even when she disagrees inwardly with everything that is being said around her.

Responsibility to yourself means refusing to let others do your thinking, talking, and naming for you; it means learning to respect and use your own brains and instincts; hence, grappling with hard work. It means that you do not treat your body as a commodity with which to purchase superficial intimacy or economic security; for our bodies and minds are inseparable in this life, and when we allow our bodies to be treated as objects, our minds are in mortal danger. It means insisting that those to whom you give your friendship and love are able to respect your mind. It means being able to say, with Charlotte Brontë's *Jane Eyre:* "I have an inward treasure born

with me, which can keep me alive if all the extraneous delights should be withheld or offered only at a price I cannot afford to give."

Responsibility to yourself means that you don't fall for shallow and easy solutions—predigested books and ideas, weekend encounters guaranteed to change your life, taking "gut" courses instead of ones you know will challenge you, bluffing at school and life instead of doing solid work, marrying early as an escape from real decisions, getting pregnant as an evasion of already existing problems. It means that you refuse to sell your talents and aspirations short, simply to avoid conflict and confrontation. And this, in turn, means resisting the forces in society which say that women should be nice, play safe, have low professional expectations, drown in love and forget about work, live through others, and stay in the places assigned to us. It means that we insist on a life of meaningful work, insist that work be as meaningful as love and friendship in our lives. It means, therefore, the courage to be "different"; not to be continuously available to others when we need time for ourselves and our work; to be able to demand of others—parents, friends, roommates, teachers, lovers, husbands, children—that they respect our sense of purpose and our integrity as persons. Women everywhere are finding the courage to do this, more and more, and we are finding that courage both in our study of women in the past who possessed it, and in each other as we look to other women for comradeship, community, and challenge. The difference between a life lived actively, and a life of passive drifting and dispersal of energies, is an immense difference. Once we begin to feel committed to our lives, responsible to ourselves, we can never again be satisfied with the old, passive way.

Now comes the second part of the contract. I believe that in a women's college you have the right to expect your faculty to take you seriously. The education of women has been a matter of debate for centuries, and old, negative attitudes about women's role, women's ability to think and take leadership, are still rife both in and outside the university. Many male professors (and I don't mean only at Douglass) still feel that teaching in a women's college is a second-rate career. Many tend to eroticize their women students—to treat them as sexual objects—instead of demanding the best of their minds. (At Yale a legal suit [*Alexander* v. *Yale*] has been brought against the university by a group of women students demanding a stated policy against sexual advances toward female students by male professors.) Many teachers, both men and women, trained in the male-centered tradition, are still handing the ideas and texts of that tradition on to students without teaching them to criticize its antiwoman attitudes, its omission of women as part of the species. Too often, all of us fail to teach the most important thing, which is that clear thinking, active discussion, and excellent writing are all necessary for intellectual freedom, and that these require *hard work*. Sometimes, perhaps in discouragement with a culture which is both antiintellectual and antiwoman, we may resign ourselves to low expectations for our students before we have given them half a chance to become more thoughtful, expressive human beings. We need to take to heart the words of Elizabeth Barrett Browning, a poet, a thinking woman, and a feminist, who wrote in 1845 of her impatience with studies which cultivate a "passive recipiency" in the mind, and asserted that "women want to be made to *think actively*: their apprehension is quicker than that of men, but their defect lies for the most part in the logical faculty and in the higher mental activities." Note that she implies a defect which can be remedied by intellectual training; *not* an inborn lack of ability.

I have said that the contract on the student's part involves that you demand to be taken seriously so that you can also go on taking yourself seriously. This means seeking out criticism, recognizing that the most affirming thing anyone can do for you is demand that you push yourself further, show you the range of what you *can* do. It means rejecting attitudes of "take-it-easy," "why-be-so-serious," "why-worry-you'll-probably-get-married-anyway."   It means assuming your share of responsibility for what happens in the classroom, because that affects the quality of your daily life here. It means that the student sees herself engaged *with* her teachers in an active, ongoing struggle for a real education. But for her to do this, her teachers must be committed to the belief that women's minds and experience are intrinsically valuable and indispensable to any civilization worthy [of] the name; that there is no more exhilarating and intellectually fertile place in the academic world today than a women's college—*if* both students and teachers in large enough numbers are trying to fulfill this contract. The contract is really a pledge of mutual seriousness about women, about language, ideas, methods, and values. It is our shared commitment toward a world in which the inborn potentialities of so many women's minds will no longer be wasted, raveled-away, paralyzed, or denied.

READING 2

A Day Without Feminism

Jennifer Baumgardner and Amy Richards

We were both born in 1970, the baptismal moment of a decade that would change dramatically the lives of American women. The two of us grew up thousands of miles apart, in entirely different kinds of families, yet we both came of age with the awareness that certain rights had been won by the women's movement. We've never doubted how important feminism is to people's lives—men's and women's. Both of our mothers went to consciousness-raising-

type groups. Amy's mother raised Amy on her own, and Jennifer's mother, questioning the politics of housework, staged laundry strikes.

With the dawn of not just a new century but a new millennium, people are looking back and taking stock of feminism. Do we need new strategies? Is feminism dead? Has society changed so much that the idea of a feminist movement is obsolete? For us, the only way to answer these questions is to imagine what our lives would have been if the women's movement had never happened and the conditions for women had remained as they were in the year of our births.

Imagine that for a day it's still 1970, and women have only the rights they had then. Sly and the Family Stone and Dionne Warwick are on the radio, the kitchen appliances are Harvest Gold, and the name of your Whirlpool gas stove is Mrs. America. What is it like to be female?

Babies born on this day are automatically given their father's name. If no father is listed, "illegitimate" is likely to be typed on the birth certificate. There are virtually no child-care centers, so all preschool children are in the hands of their mothers, a baby-sitter, or an expensive nursery school. In elementary school, girls can't play in Little League and almost all of the teachers are female. (The latter is still true.) In a few states, it may be against the law for a male to teach grades lower than the sixth, on the basis that it's unnatural, or that men can't be trusted with young children.

In junior high, girls probably take home ec; boys take shop or small-engine repair. Boys who want to learn how to cook or sew on a button are out of luck, as are girls who want to learn how to fix a car. *Seventeen* magazine doesn't run feminist-influenced current columns like "Sex + Body" and "Trauma-rama." Instead the magazine encourages girls not to have sex; pleasure isn't part of its vocabulary. Judy Blume's books are just beginning to be published, and *Free to Be . . . You and Me* does not exist. No one reads much about masturbation as a natural activity; nor do they learn that sex is for anything other than procreation. Girls do read mystery stories about Nancy Drew, for whom there is no sex, only her blue roadster and having "luncheon." (The real mystery is how Nancy gets along without a purse and manages to meet only white people.) Boys read about the Hardy Boys, for whom there are no girls.

In high school, the principal is a man. Girls have physical-education class and play half-court basketball, but not soccer, track, or cross country; nor do they have any varsity sports teams. The only prestigious physical activity for girls is cheerleading, or being a drum majorette. Most girls don't take calculus

or physics; they plan the dances and decorate the gym. Even when girls get better grades than their male counterparts, they are half as likely to qualify for a National Merit Scholarship because many of the test questions favor boys. Standardized tests refer to males and male experiences much more than to females and their experiences. If a girl "gets herself pregnant," she loses her membership in the National Honor Society (which is still true today) and is expelled.

Girls and young women might have sex while they're unmarried, but they may be ruining their chances of landing a guy full-time, and they're probably getting a bad reputation. If a pregnancy happens, an enterprising gal can get a legal abortion only if she lives in New York or is rich enough to fly there, or to Cuba, London, or Scandinavia. There's also the Chicago-based Jane Collective, an underground abortion-referral service, which can hook you up with an illegal or legal termination. (Any of these options are going to cost you. Illegal abortions average $300 to $500, sometimes as much as $2,000.) To prevent pregnancy, a sexually active woman might go to a doctor to be fitted for a diaphragm, or take the high-dose birth-control pill, but her doctor isn't likely to inform her of the possibility of deadly blood clots. Those who do take the Pill also may have to endure this contraceptive's crappy side effects: migraine headaches, severe weight gain, irregular bleeding, and hair loss (or gain), plus the possibility of an increased risk of breast cancer in the long run. It is unlikely that women or their male partners know much about the clitoris and its role in orgasm unless someone happens to fumble upon it. Instead, the myth that vaginal orgasms from penile penetration are the only "mature" (according to Freud) climaxes prevails.

Lesbians are rarely "out," except in certain bars owned by organized crime (the only businessmen who recognize this untapped market), and if lesbians don't know about the bars, they're less likely to know whether there are any other women like them. Radclyffe Hall's depressing early-twentieth-century novel *The Well of Loneliness* pretty much indicates their fate.

The Miss America Pageant is the biggest source of scholarship money for women. Women can't be students at Dartmouth, Columbia, Harvard, West Point, Boston College, or the Citadel, among other all-male institutions. Women's colleges are referred to as "girls' schools." There are no Take Back the Night marches to protest women's lack of safety after dark, but that's okay because college girls aren't allowed out much after dark anyway. Curfew is likely to be midnight on Saturday and 9 or 10 p.m. the rest of the week. Guys get to stay out as late as they want. Women tend to major in teaching, home economics, English, or maybe a language—a good skill for translating someone else's words. The women's studies major does not exist, although you can take a women's studies course at six universities, including Cornell and San Diego State College. The absence of women's history, black history, Chicano studies, Asian-American history, queer studies, and Native American history from college curricula implies that they are not worth studying. A student is lucky if he or she learns that women were "given" the vote in 1920, just as Columbus "discovered" America in 1492. They might also learn that Sojourner Truth, Mary Church Terrell, and Fannie Lou Hamer were black abolitionists or civil-rights leaders, but not that they were feminists. There are practically no tenured female professors at any school, and campuses are not racially diverse. Women of color are either not there or they're lonely as hell. There is no nationally recognized Women's History Month or Black History Month. Only 14 percent of doctorates are awarded to women. Only 3.5 percent of MBAs are female.

Only 2 percent of everybody in the military is female, and these women are mostly nurses. There are no female generals in the U.S. Air Force, no female naval pilots, and no Marine brigadier generals. On the religious front, there are no female cantors or rabbis, Episcopal canons, or Catholic priests. (This is still true of Catholic priests.)

Only 44 percent of women are employed outside the home. And those women make, on average, fifty-two cents to the dollar earned by males. Want ads are segregated into "Help Wanted Male" and "Help Wanted Female." The female side is preponderantly for secretaries, domestic workers, and other low-wage service jobs, so if you're a female lawyer you must look under "Help Wanted Male." There are female doctors, but twenty states have only five female

gynecologists or fewer. Women workers can be fired or demoted for being pregnant, especially if they are teachers, since the kids they teach aren't supposed to think that women have sex. If a boss demands sex, refers to his female employee exclusively as "Baby," or says he won't pay her unless she gives him a blow job, she either has to quit or succumb—no pun intended. Women can't be airline pilots. Flight attendants are "stewardesses"—waitresses in the sky —and necessarily female. Sex appeal is a job requirement, wearing makeup is a rule, and women are fired if they exceed the age or weight deemed sexy. Stewardesses can get married without getting canned, but this is a new development. (In 1968 the Equal Employment Opportunity Commission —EEOC—made it illegal to forcibly retire stewardesses for getting hitched.) Less than 2 percent of dentists are women; 100 percent of dental assistants are women. The "glass ceiling" that keeps women from moving naturally up the ranks, as well as the sticky floor that keeps them unnaturally down in low-wage work, has not been named, much less challenged.

When a woman gets married, she vows to love, honor, and obey her husband, though he gets off doing just the first two to uphold his end of the bargain. A married woman can't obtain credit without her husband's signature. She doesn't have her own credit rating, legal domicile, or even her own name unless she goes to court to get it back. If she gets a loan with her husband—and she has a job—she may have to sign a "baby letter" swearing that she won't have one and have to leave her job.

Women have been voting for up to fifty years, but their turnout rate is lower than that for men, and they tend to vote right along with their husbands, not with their own interests in mind. The divorce rate is about the same as it is in 2000, contrary to popular fiction's blaming the women's movement for divorce. However, divorce required that one person be at fault, therefore if you just want out of your marriage, you have to lie or blame your spouse. Property division and settlements, too, are based on fault. (And at a time when domestic violence isn't a term, much less a crime, women are legally encouraged to remain in abusive marriages.) If fathers ask for custody of the children, they get it in 60 to 80 percent of the cases. (This is still true.) If a husband or a lover hits his partner, she has no shelter to go to unless she happens to live near the one in northern California or the other in upper Michigan. If a woman is downsized from her role as a housewife (a.k.a. left by her husband), there is no word for being a displaced homemaker. As a divorcée, she may be regarded as a family disgrace or as easy sexual prey. After all, she had sex with one guy, so why not *all* guys?

If a woman is not a Mrs., she's a Miss. A woman without makeup and a hairdo is as suspect as a man with them. Without a male escort she may be refused service in a restaurant or a bar, and a woman alone is hard-pressed to find a landlord who will rent her an apartment. After all, she'll probably be leaving to get married soon, and, if she isn't, the landlord doesn't want to deal with a potential brothel.

Except among the very poor or in very rural areas, babies are born in hospitals. There are no certified midwives, and women are knocked out during birth. Most likely, they are also strapped down and lying down, made to have the baby against gravity for the doctor's convenience. If he has a schedule to keep, the likelihood of a cesarean is also very high. *Our Bodies, Ourselves* doesn't exist, nor does the women's health movement. Women aren't taught how to look at their cervixes, and their bodies are nothing to worry their pretty little heads about; however, they are supposed to worry about keeping their little heads pretty. If a woman goes under the knife to see if she has breast cancer, the surgeon won't wake her up to consult about her options before performing a Halsted mastectomy (a disfiguring radical procedure, in which the breast, the muscle wall, and the nodes under the arm, right down to the bone, are removed). She'll just wake up and find that the choice has been made for her.

Husbands are likely to die eight years earlier than their same-age wives due to the stress of having to support a family and repress an emotional life, and a lot earlier than that if women have followed the custom of marrying older, authoritative, paternal men. The stress of raising kids, managing a household, and being undervalued by society doesn't seem to kill off women at the same rate. Upon a man's death, his beloved gets a portion of his Social Security. Even if she has worked outside the home for her entire adult life, she is probably better off with that portion than with hers in its entirety, because she has earned less and is likely to have taken time out for such unproductive acts as having kids.

Has feminism changed our lives? Was it necessary? After thirty years of feminism, the world we inhabit barely resembles the world we were born into. And there's still a lot left to do.

READING 3

Dear Sisters

Rosalyn Baxandall and Linda Gordon

Social Roots of Women's Liberation

Women's liberation was a movement long overdue. By the mid-1950s a majority of American women found themselves expected to function as full economic, social, and political participants in the nation while still burdened with handicaps. As wage-earners, as parents, as students, as citizens, women were denied equal opportunity and, often, even minimal rights and respect. Many women experienced sharp conflict among the expectations placed on them—education, employment, wife- and motherhood. Looking back at the beginning of the twenty-first century, we can see feminism as a necessary modernizing force and, not surprisingly, one which rapidly became global. Within the U.S., the movement gained widespread support so quickly because it met real needs, because the great majority of women stood to benefit from reducing discrimination, harassment, and prejudice against them. A movement that might at first have seemed to promise to rationalize the current political and economic system by integrating women into it quickly took off—as many social movements do—into uncharted territory, exposing the degree to which basic social structures had rested on a traditional gender system. The radical challenge to these fundamental structures can be measured by the virulence of the later worldwide backlash, from the Taliban to the Christian Coalition.

How did an apparently arch-conservative decade like the 1950s produce a movement so radical? To answer that we have to look beneath a veneer that concealed discomforts and discontents. The period between the end of World War II and the birth of women's liberation at the end of the 1960s has usually been described as an era of prosperity, stability, and peace, leading to the conclusion that it was also an era of satisfaction and little change. An intensely controlled and controlling official and commercial culture seemed to provide evidence for that conclusion. The domestic correlate of the cold war and the Korean War was the hysterical anticommunism that stigmatized nonconformity, including that related to family, sex, and gender. Anxiety about the Soviet threat made family stability seem critical and linked women's domestic roles to the nation's security. Just as schoolchildren were drilled in ducking under their desks and covering their heads to protect themselves from atomic bombs, so teenage girls were taught the imperatives of beauty and domesticity. Far from interpreting these women's obligations as constraints, cold war American culture regarded them as freedom. That American middle-class women did not seem to need jobs and enjoyed an expanding array of household appliances demonstrated the superiority of American institutions over Soviet society, where dowdy women grew heavily muscled from their hard labor and could shop only for a narrow array of dreary clothes and consumer goods. In the early 1960s future feminist Betty Friedan was to name this view of women's appropriate destiny the "feminine mystique," a term now used by historians to describe the domestic gendered face of the cold war. Twenty years later historian Elaine Tyler May observed that

the concept of containment, first used to characterize the U.S. policy of preventing Soviet expansion, could characterize equally well the stifling of female ambitions, the endorsement of female subordination, and the promotion of domesticity by cold war gender culture. Resistance to these norms was un-American, and that label became a heavy club with which to beat misfits and dissidents.

. . .

Girls grew up in this cold war era barred from wearing blue jeans or sneakers to school, required to sit with their knees together and to set their hair in pin curls. Nothing in the culture encouraged them to become strong or competitive. Girls grew to hate athletics and dread physical education in school, where they were required to wear unfashionable tunics or bloomers. Girls were not encouraged to fantasize about careers, about what they would "become" when they grew up. They were expected to break a date with a girlfriend if a boy asked for a date. They watched movies and TV in which married couples slept in twin beds and mothers were full-time housewives. The people of color on TV were stereotypes, comic or worse: step-and-fetch-it black servants, marauding Apaches, or fat lazy Mexicans. Rape, illegitimacy, abortion—some of women's real problems—were among many tabooed subjects, whispered about but rarely seriously or openly discussed.

But this official feminine-mystique culture obscured an unofficial but probably more widespread reality that was, ironically, designated as deviant. A small band of historians has been uncovering the story of what turns out to be the majority of American women who did not, and often could not, conform. We belonged to that majority. Neither of our families was like *Leave It to Beaver* or *Father Knows Best.* Our mothers "worked," which meant, of course, employment for wages, and we thought they were unusual. In fact, in contrast to official norms, women's labor-force participation climbed rapidly throughout the fifties and by 1954 women's employment had equaled that during World War II. Most women displaced from well-paid, industrial jobs at the war's end did not return to domesticity but found work in traditionally female low-paying jobs in the expanding service and clerical sectors. As has long been true in American history, African American women and poor women of all colors had particularly high rates of employment, so that the domesticity myth was in part a racist assumption that elite white norms were universal. Women in "pink colar" employment swelled the membership of unions, such as the Hotel Employees and Restaurant Employees and the National Federation of Telephone Workers. And these working women were not only young and single: By 1960, 30 percent of married women were employed, and 39 percent of mothers with school-age children were in the labor force. By 1955, 3 million women belonged to unions, constituting 17 percent of union members. In unions in which women made up a significant part of the membership, they wielded considerable power, especially at the local level.

The number of married women seeking employment rose fastest in the middle class. Women benefited from an enormous expansion in higher education after World War II. Government investment in universities after the war had multiplied educational opportunity, especially in public institutions. In 1940, 26 percent of American women completed college; in 1970, 55 percent. These relatively privileged American women faced a particular dilemma: educated with men and often achieving, despite discrimination, the same levels of knowledge, discipline, and sophistication as the men of their social class, they were still expected to forego professional or intellectual pursuits after college to become full-time housewives and mothers. Those who resisted this directive and sought employment, through choice or economic necessity, usually found themselves limited to clerical or low-level administrative jobs.

In part as a response to this restriction, many women, like both our mothers, defied the limits of domesticity through community and political activism. Even in the suburbs, where women seemed to be conforming to the "feminine mystique" by staying home with small children, many were active in churches, schools, libraries, and parks. New forms of organizing appeared: In 1956, for example, the first all-female La Leche group met to encourage breast feeding. Other groups, alarmed by Rachel Carson's studies of the dangers of pesticides like DDT, had the audacity to challenge official science. Women Strike for Peace, composed largely of left-wing women, at-

tacked military spending priorities, raised an alarm about strontium-90 fallout in milk, and directly challenged the cold war and American military buildup by contesting U.S. government propaganda about the threat of Soviet expansionism. Even conservative women, while paying official homage to the ideal of women's domesticity, were organizing in the Ku Klux Klan, White Citizen's Councils, John Birch Society, and Republican Party.

. . .

Dissidence in the 1950s was, of course, particularly pronounced in youth culture. Rebellious adolescent voices competed with homogenized "Archie" comic book people and Disney's cute, servile Annette Funicello. Young people identified as "rebels without a cause," the phrase sent reverberating through America by James Dean, Hollywood's symbol of alienated middle-class youth. The idea that they didn't have "a cause" came from their affluence, the fact that they "had everything." But these rebels did have a cause—they just couldn't name it—and the affluence of their parents only heightened their discontent. They rejected the false facades of family, the suburbs, and corporate careers, the measurement of success by large houses and consumer goods. They sought authenticity instead among male outsider figures—cowboys, hoods, oddballs, delinquents, but also blacks and Latinos. As with the beats, women remained followers, but some were choosing geeks or boys on motorcycles instead of jocks. Rebellion among less privileged groups took different forms, less covered by the mainstream media and less shocking to middle-class whites, who considered the norms of poor people and people of color outside established culture anyway. But the protest was there, among young Chicanos dressing in flashy "zoot suits" and "low-riding" their jazzed-up cars, among the hoods and rockers with their greased ducktail hairdos.

Nowhere was the youth rebellion as intense or as contagious as in music, and the transcendence of race segregation was the proximate cause. The officially dominant 1950s white sound (Peggy Lee, Jo Stafford, Rosemary Clooney, and Pat Boone) combined inane lyrics, like "How Much Is That Doggie in the Window," with soothing melodies, bland orchestration, and ballad rhythms. Yet this is the decade that produced rock and roll, a revolution in popular music. The term was first applied to black rhythm and blues by Alan Freed, the white disk jockey who promoted black music to white audiences. The breakthrough singer was Elvis Presley, the "white boy who could sing black." Not only did whites start to buy records by black artists but they also attended huge concerts where for the first time white and black youth mingled and danced. In Los Angeles, for example, racially mixed rock concerts were busted up by the police. Conservatives considered rock and roll the music of the devil, dangerous, degenerate, mongrel, oversexualized, and in a way they were right: it is difficult to overestimate the impact of rock and roll on the men and women who moved from the inchoate, half-conscious alienation of rebels without a cause to the organized radical movements that began with the civil rights movement.

Political Roots
of Women's Liberation

From the vantage point of the new century, the women's liberation movement appears extravagant, immoderate, impatient, as well as young and naive. It was all those and more, but how one weighs its radicalism, positively or negatively, and how one measures its naivete depend on understanding its historical context. Thirty years later our culture has been so transformed, the expectations of young women so altered, that it is hard to grasp the unique combination of anger and optimism that made second-wave feminism so determined to change so much so fast.

Women coming into adulthood at the end of the 1960s, both middle- and working-class, faced an economy that was producing an ever larger number of jobs for women and for the men they might marry. Even more important, women had unprecedented access to education. But many were disappointed in the jobs they could get. They went from being the equals or even the superiors of men in educational achievement to working as secretaries or "administrative assistants" for the same class of men. Although they faced discrimination in their colleges and universities, they also encountered professors who recognized and challenged their intelligence.

Yet their studies, no matter how rigorous, offered them no way to escape the cultural imperative that directed them toward marriage and family as their fundamental and often exclusive source of identity and satisfaction.

If economic and educational abundance opened windows for the women who began women's liberation in 1968, the passionate new social activism of the 1950s and 1960s opened doors and invited women in. But these movements, like the economy as a whole, also sent women a double message. Whenever there have been progressive social change movements in modern history, women's movements have arisen within them, and for similar reasons: in the crucible of activism for civil rights, for peace, for the environment, for free speech, for social welfare, women have been valued participants who gained skills and self-confidence. At the same time they have been thwarted, treated as subordinates, gophers, even servants, by the men in charge—including men who considered themselves partisans of democracy and equality. Within these movements women learned to think critically about social structures and ideologies, to talk the language of freedom and tyranny, democracy and domination, power and oppression. Then they applied these concepts to question their own secondary status. It is precisely this combination of raised aspirations and frustration that gives rise to rebellion.

. . .

By the mid-1960s, the more ideologically Left currents within the movement were called the New Left, because they differed fundamentally from the older Lefts: communism, socialism, and New Deal progressivism. At least a decade earlier, the civil rights movement had been the first to break with conventional politics, helped by its high proportion of student activists, ability to stimulate mass participation, decentralized and pluralist organization, and commitment to direct but nonviolent action. Like all mass movements, the civil rights movement had no defined beginning, although the 1955 Montgomery bus boycott announced to the country that something big was happening. Thousands of African Americans were challenging three hundred years of apartheid, demonstrating unprecedented discipline, solidarity, and bravery against brutal retaliation.

Their courage forced racist viciousness into the open; journalists and their cameras then brought into living rooms the high-power water hoses turned on peaceful protesters, the grown men who spat on first-graders, the dogs who charged at protesters singing gospel hymns. The news brought a heightened appreciation of the possibility of making change from the bottom up. In contrast to the bitter liberal-versus-conservative national division in the 1980s and 1990s, the civil rights struggles seemed to galvanize, at least among the most articulate citizenry, broad majority approval for social change in the direction of greater democracy and equality. (There may have been a "silent majority" that did not approve.) While any individual battle might be won or lost, it seemed to supporters that their cause was unstoppable, so great was the groundswell of desire for the long-overdue racial equality and respect.

. . .

In the late 1950s, another kind of rebellion was developing, primarily among the more privileged whites: a cultural rebellion. Discovering and inventing unconventional art, music, and poetry; exploring a variety of intoxicants; and signaling defiance in the way they dressed, adherents of this new cultural revolution soon grew visible enough to draw mainstream media attention. The press created popular icons—"flower children" and "hippies"—whose values resembled those of the earlier 1950s beatnik rebels. The influence of this lifestyle dissent can be measured by how quickly it was picked up by commercial interests and sold back to a broader public: the new fashion included beards, long straight hair, psychedelic design, granny dresses, and beads. Handmade, patched, and embroidered clothing and jeans once bought at Sears Roebuck or Goodwill were soon being mass-produced in Hong Kong and sold in department stores. For its most zealous participants, counterculture iconoclasm and adventurousness meant such an extreme rejection of the work ethic, temperance, and discipline that it horrified many observers, including some in the movement. Excessive use of drugs, promiscuous sexuality, and irresponsibility were sometimes destructive to participants, some of whom later rebounded into conventionality. Women suffered particular exploitation, as the counterculture's gender ideology reaf-

firmed that of the conventional culture, but now with a twist, lauding "free" and "natural" heterosexual relations between women who were sexually open and "giving" and men who could not be tied down. Women were to be earth mothers, seeking fulfillment by looking after men and children, while guys needed freedom from marital or paternal responsibilities in order to find and express themselves.

This cultural rebellion had transformative potential and gave rise to some serious political challenges. When civil rights and the counterculture intersected on campuses, the result was a college students' movement for free speech that would ultimately create the New Left and women's liberation. The first major student revolt, at the University of California at Berkeley in 1964, arose in reaction to the administration's attempt to prevent students from recruiting civil rights volunteers on campus. This protest movement spread to campuses late in the 1960s throughout the U.S., producing a series of protests against *in loco parentis* rules that treated students like children.

Campus protests soon expanded to include national issues and nonstudents. Sensitized to injustice and convinced of the potential of grassroots activism by what they learned from civil rights, more and more Americans began to see the Vietnam War as immoral and undemocratic. In the name of stopping communism, the U.S. was defending a flagrantly corrupt regime that had canceled elections when it seemed likely to lose to a popular, nationalist liberation movement that promised land reform in the interests of the poor peasantry. The most powerful nation in the world was attacking a tiny nation that had demonstrated not the slightest aggression toward Americans. The U.S. employed some of the cruelest weapons and tactics yet developed: shooting down unarmed peasants because of fear that they might be supporting the liberation movement; bulldozing villages; spraying herbicides from planes to deprive the guerrilla fighters of their jungle cover; dropping napalm, a jellied gasoline antipersonnel weapon that stuck to the skin and burned people alive. There was not yet extensive censorship of the press, so Americans routinely witnessed these atrocities on the evening news. American soldiers of color and of the working class were killed and injured in disproportionate numbers. Hundreds of young men began resisting or dodging the draft while scores of soldiers deserted and defied orders. So widespread, vocal, and convincing were the protests at home, including several massive national demonstrations, that by its end the Vietnam War become the only war in U.S. history to be opposed by a majority of the population.

The Vietnamese revolution was part of a wave of nationalist struggles of Third World countries against Western imperial domination, and these also influenced American domestic politics. Many of these emerging nations and movements took socialist forms, as Third World nationalists observed that the introduction of capitalism increased inequality and impoverishment. But many of these newly independent countries fell under Soviet domination as the price of the aid they so desperately needed, and leading parts of the American New Left, already angry at the stultifying domestic culture of the cold war, neglected to subject Soviet control to the same critique. U.S. interventions against communism, both military and covert, had the ironic effect of making the New Left less critical of Soviet and Chinese communism than it might have been otherwise.

. . .

Activism spread throughout the U.S., creating civil rights movements among other racial/ethnic groups, including Chicanos, Asian Americans, Native Americans; movements to protect the environment; a movement for the rights of the disabled; and renewed labor struggles for a fair share of the prosperity. Among whites there soon arose a national student organization that was to become central to the white New Left, Students for a Democratic Society (SDS), established in 1962. With a membership reaching about 100,000 at its peak in the late 1960s, and with many times that number of students—including high school students—who considered themselves a part of the movement, SDS changed the attitudes of a considerable part of a generation. New Leftists and counterculture activists created institutions that spread progressive ideas still further: radical bookstores, a few national magazines, and many local underground newspapers. These were produced by amateurs working in scruffy offices, offering critical perspectives on everything from U.S. foreign policy to the local police to the latest films. Many of these underground newspapers combined

words and graphics in innovative ways, inspired in part by the street art of 1968 in France where the *beaux arts* students had considerable influence.

Although the movement (civil rights and the New Left) had no unified ideology—its members included anarchists, social democrats, Marxist-Leninists, black nationalists—it bequeathed identifiable legacies to feminism. Most important among these were anti-authoritarianism and irreverence. Favorite buttons and T-shirts read "Question Authority" and "Never Trust Anyone Over 30." Arrogant and disrespectful, yes, but also understandably rebellious. The movement's message was: look beneath formal legal and political rights to find other kinds of power, the power of wealth, of race, of violence.

Following this instruction, some women began in the mid-1960s to examine power relations in areas that the movement's male leaders had not considered relevant to radical politics. The women's preliminary digging uncovered a buried deposit of grievances about men's power over women within the movement. Women in civil rights and the New Left were on the whole less victimized, more respected, and less romanticized than they were in the mainstream culture or the counterculture. Despite women's passionate and disciplined work for social change, however, they remained far less visible and less powerful than the men who dominated the meetings and the press conferences. Women came into greater prominence wherever there was grassroots organizing, as in voter registration in the South and the SDS community projects in northern cities. Throughout the civil rights and the student movements, women proved themselves typically the better organizers, better able than men to listen, to connect, to reach across class and even race lines, to empower the previously diffident, to persevere despite failure and lack of encouragement. Still, the frustrations and humiliations were galling. In every organization women were responsible for keeping records, producing leaflets, telephoning, cleaning offices, cooking, organizing social events, and catering to the egos of male leaders, while the men wrote manifestos, talked to the press, negotiated with officials, and made speeches. This division of labor did not arise from misogyny or acrimony. It was "natural" and had always been so, until it began to seem not natural at all.

The Rise of Second-Wave Feminism

Although women's liberation had foremothers, the young feminists of the late 1960s did not usually know about this heritage because so little women's history had been written. Feminist historians have now made us aware that a continuing tradition of activism stretched from "first-wave" feminism, which culminated in winning the right to vote in 1920, to the birth of the "second wave" in 1968. Some women of unusual longevity bridged the two waves. Florence Luscomb, who had traveled the state of Massachusetts speaking for women suffrage during World War I, also spoke for women's liberation in Boston in the early 1970s. Within many progressive social movements, even at the nadir of the conservative 1950s, there were discontented women agitating against sex discrimination and promoting female leadership. Within the Communist and Socialist Parties there had been women's caucuses and demands to revise classic socialist theory to include sex inequality: for example, folksinger Melvina Reynolds, the women of the Jeannette Rankin Brigade. Some women spanned the older progressive causes and the new feminism—Ella Baker, Judy Collins, Ruby Dee, Eleanor Flexner, Fanny Lou Hamer, Flo Kennedy, Coretta Scott King, Gerda Lerner, Amy Swerdlow.

Liberal women had continued to be politically active between feminism's two waves. They were mainly Democrats but there were some Republicans, such as Oveta Culp Hobby, who became the first secretary of the Department of Health, Education and Welfare, established in 1953. In 1961 this women's political network persuaded President Kennedy, as payback for their support in the close election of 1960, to establish a Presidential Commission on the Status of Women. It was chaired by Eleanor Roosevelt, embodying continuity with first-wave feminism and the New Deal, and Women's Bureau head Esther Peterson served as vice-chair. Kennedy may have expected this commission to keep the women diverted and out of his hair. But the commission produced substantive recommendations for a legislative agenda and set in motion a continuing process. Its report, issued in 1963, called for equal pay for *comparable* work (understanding that equal pay for *equal* work would not be adequate because women so rarely did the same work as men), as well as child care services, paid maternity leave, and many other measures still not achieved. Determined not to let its momentum stall or its message reach only elite circles, the commission built a network among women's organizations, made special efforts to include black women, and got Kennedy to establish two ongoing federal committees. Most consequentially, it stimulated the creation of state women's commissions, created in every state by 1967. The network that formed through these commissions enabled the creation of the National Organization for Women (NOW) in 1966.

NOW's history has been often misinterpreted, especially by the radical women's liberationists, who denounced it, as the radicals of SNCC criticized their elders and the New Left criticized the Old Left, as stodgy and "bourgeois." At first NOW included more working-class and minority leadership than women's liberation did. Many of its leaders identified strongly with civil rights and defined NOW as pursuing civil rights for women. Former Old Leftist Betty Friedan and black lawyer and poet Pauli Murray were centrally involved in the East, while in the Midwest, labor union women like Dorothy Haener of the United Auto Workers and Addie Wyatt of the Amalgamated Meatcutters were prime movers. NOW's first headquarters was provided by the UAW. NOW concentrated heavily on employment issues, reflecting its close ties to the U.S. Women's Bureau and the unions, and NOW's membership was composed largely of employed women. NOW refused to endorse reproductive rights, which the majority considered too controversial, but it rejected the idea that gender was immutable and called for "equitable sharing of responsibilities of home and children and of the economic burdens of their support." This position marked a decisive break with earlier women's rights agitation, which had primarily accepted the traditional division of labor—breadwinner husbands and housewives—as inevitable and desirable. And this position was to give rise to tremendous advances in feminist theory in the next decades.

NOW represented primarily adult professional women and a few male feminists, and at first it did not attempt to build a mass movement open to all women. Although only thirty women had attended its founding conference, and 300 its second conference, NOW demonstrated political savvy in creating the impression that it spoke for a mass power base. It had no central office of its own for three years—networking among a relatively small group did not require one. Its members used their professional and political skills to exert pressure on elected officials.

NOW concentrated on lobbying, using its ties to the few women in influential positions in government; its program focused on governmental action against sex discrimination. Its members met with the attorney general, the secretary of labor, the head of the Civil Service commission. Its board of directors read like entries from a "Who's Who" of professional women and their male supporters. Its initial impetus was anger that the Equal Employment Opportunity Commission (EEOC) was not enforcing the sex-discrimination provisions of the Civil Rights Act of 1965, and it got immediate results: in 1967 President Johnson issued Executive Order 11375, prohibiting sex discrimination by federal contractors. In the same year NOW forced the EEOC to rule that sex-segregated want ads were discriminatory (although newspapers ignored this ruling with impunity for years). NOW's legal committee, composed of four high-powered Washington lawyers, three of them federal employees, brought suits against protective legislation that in the name of protecting women's fragility in fact kept them out of better jobs. (In arguing one case the five-foot, 100-pound lawyer picked up the equipment the company claimed was too heavy for women and carried it around with one hand as she argued to the jury.)

Women's liberation derided NOW's perspective and tactics as "liberal"—not in the 1990s pejorative sense, coined by the Right, of permissive, but in the 1960s sense, used by the Left, as legalistic and compromising. When a mass women's movement arose, it was not liberal but radical in the sense of seeking out the roots of problems and working for structural change at a level more fundamental than law. It wanted not just to redistribute wealth and power in the existing society, but to challenge the sources of male dominance: the private as well as the public, the psychological as well as the economic, the cultural as well as the legal. Given this radical agenda it was hard for women's liberation to become a player in the political process, and it tended to make purist and moralistic judgments of those who chose to work within the system.

The mass women's movement arose independently of NOW and the government commissions, and its members had a different style: they were younger, typically in their twenties, and less professional. Most importantly, it generated groups consisting of women only. The new women's liberation movement insisted that women needed a woman-only space in which they could explore their grievances and define their own agenda. They observed that women frequently censored not only what they said but even what they thought when men were around. Arriving directly from male-dominated, grassroots social-justice movements, these women longed for a space where they could talk freely with other women. First in Chicago, then in several other cities such as Gainesville, Florida; Chapel Hill, North Carolina; Washington, D.C.; and New York City, women's liberation groups formed in 1967 and 1968. At a 1968 antiwar demonstration in Washington organized by the Jeannette Rankin Brigade, 500 women gathered as a women's liberation counter-conference and then spread the movement to other towns and cities. In August 1968 twenty of them met in Sandy Springs, Maryland, to plan a larger conference. Everyone present was disturbed by the fact that they were all white. But identifying this problem did not mean they could solve it: when over 200 women from thirty-seven states and Canada met in Chicago at Thanksgiving, black women's groups were not represented, because they had not been invited or because they were not interested.

The first women's liberation groups were founded by veteran activists, but soon women with no previous movement experience joined. The decentralization of the movement was so great, despite the few early national conferences and women's frequent travel and relocation, that different geographic locations developed different agendas and organizational structures. In Iowa City, a university town, the movement began with college students and concentrated much of its energies on publishing a newspaper, *Ain't I a Woman?* In Gainesville, Florida, another university town, the movement originated in civil rights networks. In several large cities—Baltimore, Chicago, Boston, Los Angeles—single city-wide organizations brought different groups together; in New York City an original group, New York Radical Women, gave birth to several smaller groups with divergent ideologies. Small-town feminists had to hang together despite their differences, while in big cities there was room to elaborate various political positions. Different cities had different ideological personalities: Washington, D.C., was best known for The Furies, a lesbian separatist group, while Chapel Hill, North Carolina, was noted for its socialist-feminist orientation.

The movement developed so widely and quickly that it is impossible to trace a chronology, impossible to say who led, what came first, who influenced whom. This lack of a clear narrative, and the sense that participants across great distances were making some of the same breakthroughs simultaneously, are characteristic of all mass social movements. In this case, though, we can outline some of the major political factions. We are identifying not the various theoretical positions in feminist intellectual debates today, but the theory that informed the practices of women's liberation groups in the early 1970s.

Women's Liberation Develops

The movement's characteristic form of development was consciousness-raising (CR), a form of structured discussion in which women connected their personal experiences to larger structures of gender. . . . These discussion groups, usually small, sprung up starting in 1968–70 throughout the country among women of all ages and social positions. They were simultaneously supportive and transformative. Women formed these groups by the hundreds, then by the thousands. In Cambridge/Boston where a core group offered to help other women form CR groups, a hundred *new* women attended weekly for several months. The mood was exhilarating. Women came to understand that many of their "personal" problems—insecurity about ap-

pearance and intelligence, exhaustion, conflicts with husbands and male employers—were not individual failings but a result of discrimination. The mood became even more electric as women began to create collective ways of challenging that discrimination. At first there was agitprop: spreading the word through leaflets, pamphlets, letters to newspapers; pasting stickers onto sexist advertisements; verbally protesting being called "girl" or "baby" or "chick"; hollering at guys who made vulgar proposals on the streets. Soon action groups supplemented and, in some cases, replaced CR groups. Women pressured employers to provide day care centers; publicized job and school discrimination; organized rape crisis hot lines; opened women's centers, schools, and credit unions; built unions for stewardesses and secretaries; agitated for women's studies courses at colleges; published journals and magazines.

Soon different groups formulated different theoretical/political stands. But the clarity and discreteness of these positions should not be exaggerated; there was cross-fertilization, none was sealed off from others, the borderlines and definitions shifted, and there were heated debates *within* tendencies. Liberal feminists were at first associated with NOW and similar groups, although these tended to merge with women's liberation by the end of the 1970s. Those who remained committed to a broad New Left agenda typically called themselves socialist feminists (to be distinguished from Marxist feminists, who remained convinced that Marxist theory could explain women's oppression and were not committed to an autonomous women's movement). Socialist feminists weighed issues of race and class equally with those of gender and tried to develop an integrated, holistic theory of society. Radical feminists, in contrast, prioritized sexual oppression, but by no means ignored other forms of domination. Our research suggests that the radical/socialist opposition was overstated, but small theoretical differences seemed very important at the time because the early feminists were in the process of developing new political theory, not yet making political alliances to achieve concrete objectives. A few separatists, often but not exclusively lesbians, attempted to create self-sustaining female communities and to withdraw as much as possible from contact with men. By the late 1970s, some women had become cultural feminists, celebrating women's specialness and difference from men and retreating from direct challenges to sexist institutions; they believed that change could come about through building new exemplary female communities. But despite this proliferation of ideological groupings, most members of women's liberation did not identify with any of these tendencies and considered themselves simply feminists, unmodified.

Racial/ethnic differences were more significant. Feminists of different racial/ethnic groups established independent organizations from the beginning and within those organizations created different feminisms: black, Chicana, Asian American, Native American. Feminists of color emphasized the problems with universalizing assumptions about women and with identifying gender as a category autonomous from race and class. But here too we found that these *theoretical* differences are sometimes overstated; and feminists of color were not more unanimous than white feminists—there were, for example, black liberal feminists, black socialist feminists, black radical feminists, black cultural feminists. These complexities do not negate the fact that feminists of color experienced racism within the women's movement. The majority of feminists, white women from middle-class backgrounds, were often oblivious to the lives of women from minority and working-class families. Feminists of color faced the additional problems that certain women's issues, such as reproductive rights, had been historically tainted by racism; and that feminist criticisms of men were experienced differently, often as betraying racial solidarity when the men were themselves victims of racism.

Lesbians sometimes created separate feminist groups, but the gay-straight conflict has also been exaggerated. Ironically, while some accused women's liberation of homophobia, others accused it of being a lesbian conspiracy. As lesbians became more open and vocal, they protested the heterosexual assumptions of straight feminists, but they also experienced discrimination from the male-dominated gay movement. For the most part lesbians continued to be active in women's liberation and made impor-

tant contributions to feminist theory. Lesbians even led campaigns of primary concern to heterosexual women, such as campaigns for reproductive rights.

At the beginning of the movement, feminists tended to create multi-issue organizations, which in turn created committees to focus on single issues, such as day care, rape, or running a women's center. One of the fundamental tenets of early feminist theory was the interconnectedness of all aspects of women's oppression. As political sophistication grew and activists grasped the difficulties of making sweeping changes, feminists settled for piecemeal, fragmented activism. By the mid-1970s feminist politics often occurred in single-issue organizations focussed on, for example, reproductive rights, employment discrimination, health, domestic violence, female unions, women's studies. Single-issue politics de-emphasized theory, which reduced divisions; it had the advantage of making coalitions easier but the disadvantage of turning theory construction over to academics, who were usually divorced from activism. The coalitions and compromises necessitated by single-issue politics made the movement less radical and more practical. Single-issue politics also lessened the movement's coherence as its activists became specialized and professionalized.

Organizational Principles of Women's Liberation

In sharp opposition to its liberal feminist sisters in NOW, women's liberation preferred radical decentralization. In addition to following New Left principles of direct democracy and anti-authoritarianism, these young feminists had their own woman-centered reasons for lack of interest in, even hostility toward, creating a large national organization. Women, whose voices had been silenced and whose actions had been directed by others, were loath to have anyone telling them what to think or do. They understood that central organization would produce principles, programs, and priorities they would be required to follow. They also sensed that a movement growing at such velocity could not be contained by central organizations, which would only inhibit creative growth. Without formal rules of membership, any group of women could declare themselves a women's liberation organization, start a newspaper or a women's center, issue a manifesto. The resulting diversity then made it all the harder to keep track of, let alone unify, the many groups.

Not only was there no formal structure bringing groups together, there was very little structure within groups, and this was, again, by choice. Feminists could dispense with Roberts' Rules of Order because the groups were small and the members usually knew each other well. But they were often also hostile in principle to formal procedures, which they saw as arbitrary and not organic. This attitude was part of the feminist critique of the public/private distinction, and it was a way of making the public sphere accessible to women who were traditionally more experienced with a personal, familial form of conversing. In small meetings, especially in the consciousness-raising groups that were the essence of women's liberation, the informal "rapping" style was nurturant, allowing women to speak intimately and risk self-exposure, and therefore to come up with rich new insights into the workings of male dominance. When there were large meetings and/or sharp disagreements, the sessions often became tediously long, unable to reach decisions, and even chaotic. As a result, small groups of women or strong-minded and charismatic individuals sometimes took charge, and others, exhausted by the long aimless discussions, grudgingly relinquished power to these unelected leaders.

Women's liberation faced a major dilemma with respect to leadership. Its search for direct democracy led the movement to revere the principle of "every woman a leader" and to imagine that collectives could speak with one voice. Consequently the movement empowered thousands of women who had never dreamt they could write a leaflet, speak in public, talk to the press, chair a meeting, assert unpopular points of view, or make risky suggestions. The emphasis on group leadership meant that many important statements were unsigned, written anonymously or collectively, or signed with first names only, indicating the degree to which theory and strategy were being developed democratically. But the

bias against leadership hindered action, decision-making, and coherent communication beyond small groups. More problematically, the movement did create leaders, but they were frequently unacknowledged and almost always unaccountable because they were essentially self-appointed rather than chosen by the members. This led to widespread, sometimes intense resentment of leaders. The hostility, usually covert, sometimes escalated to stimulate open attacks, as women publicly criticized or "trashed" leaders in meetings. One result was that individuals who had worked hard and made personal sacrifices felt betrayed and embittered. Another was that women's liberation groups became vulnerable to takeovers by highly organized sectarian groups (mainly the Marxist-Leninist sects) or obstruction by disturbed individuals who could not be silenced. Perhaps the most deleterious result was that many women became reluctant to assert leadership and thus deprived the movement of needed talent. The leadership problem involved the movement's denial of internal inequalities, its refusal to recognize that some women were more articulate and self-confident; had more leisure time, connections, and access to power; or were simply more forceful personalities. These inequalities mainly derived, as the feminists' own analysis showed, from the class and race hierarchy of the larger society. This is an example of utopian hopes becoming wishful thinking: feminists so badly wanted equality that they pretended it was already here.

Despite decentralization and structurelessness, women's liberation created a shared culture, theory, and practice. In an era before e-mail, even before xeroxing, printed publications were vital and feminists spent a significant proportion of their energy, resources, and ingenuity producing them. Mimeographed pages stapled together into pamphlets were the common currency of the early years of the movement, and soon a few feminist publishing houses, such as KNOW in Pittsburgh, Lollipop Inc. in Durham, and the Feminist Press in New York, were printing and selling feminist writings for prices ranging from a nickel to a quarter. These were widely discussed, debated, and answered in further publications. By the mid-1970s over 500 feminist magazines and newspapers appeared throughout the country, such as *Women, A Journal of Liberation* from Baltimore, *It Ain't Me Babe* from the San Francisco Bay Area, *Off Our Backs* from Washington, D.C., *Everywoman* from Los Angeles. The male-dominated New Left underground press, like the New England Free Press in Boston or Liberation News Service, a left-wing news syndicate, also published a great deal of women's liberation news and position papers.

Unlike *Ms.,* a mass-circulation advertisement-supported liberal feminist magazine established in 1972, women's liberation publications struggled along without funds or paid staff, featuring not-quite-aligned layouts, sometimes poorly written pieces, and amateur poetry and drawings. Many articles were signed simply "Susan" or "Randy," or not signed at all, because the movement was hostile to the idea of intellectual private property. The papers sometimes forgot to print dates of publication, addresses, and subscription information. Women worked hard at producing these publications but, unfortunately, less hard at financing and distributing them, so many were irregularly published and short-lived. Nevertheless, it was in these homespun rags that you could find the most creative and cutting-edge theory and commentary.

What Women's Liberation Accomplished

. . .

Judicial and legislative victories include the legalization of abortion in 1973, federal guidelines against coercive sterilization, rape shield laws that encourage more women to prosecute their attackers, affirmative action programs that aim to correct past discrimination—but not, however, the Equal Rights Amendment, which failed in 1982, just three states short of the required two-thirds. There are many equally important but less obvious accomplishments: not only legal, economic, and political gains, but also changes in the way people live, dress, dream of their future, and make a living. In fact, there are few areas of contemporary life untouched by feminism. As regards health care, for example, many physicians and hospitals have made major improve-

ments in the treatment of women; about 50 percent of medical students are women; women successfully fought their exclusion from medical research; diseases affecting women, such as breast and ovarian cancer, now receive more funding thanks to women's efforts. Feminists insisted that violence against women, previously a well-kept secret, become a public political issue; made rape, incest, battering, and sexual harassment understood as crimes; and got public funding for shelters for battered women. These gains, realized in the 1980s and 1990s, are the fruits of struggles fought in the 1970s.

Feminist pressure generated substantial changes in education: curricula and textbooks have been rewritten to promote equal opportunity for girls, more women are admitted and funded in universities and professional schools, and a new and rich feminist scholarship in many disciplines has won recognition. Title IX, passed in 1972 to mandate equal access to college programs, has worked a revolution in sports. Consider the many women's records broken in track and field, the expanding number of athletic scholarships for women, professional women's basketball, and the massive popularity of girls' and women's soccer.

Campaigning to support families, feminists organized day care centers, developed standards and curricula for early childhood education, demanded day care funding from government and private employers, fought for parental leave from employers and a decent welfare system. They also struggled for new options for women in employment. They won greater access to traditionally male occupations, from construction to professions and business. They joined unions and fought to democratize them, and they succeeded in organizing previously nonunion workers such as secretaries, waitresses, hospital workers, and flight attendants. As the majority of American women increasingly need to work for wages throughout their lives, the feminist movement tried to educate men to share in house work and child raising. Although women still do the bulk of the housework and child rearing, it is common today to see men in the playgrounds, the supermarkets, and at the PTA meetings.

Feminism changed how women look and what is considered attractive, although the original feminist impulse toward simpler, more comfortable, and less overtly sexual clothing is being challenged by another generation of women at the turn of the century. As women's-liberation influence spread in the 1970s, more and more women refused to wear the constricting, uncomfortable clothes that were required in the 1950s—girdles, garter belts, and stockings; tight, flimsy, pointed, and high-heeled shoes; crinolines and cinch belts; tight short skirts. Women wearing pants, loose jackets, walking shoes, and no makeup began to feel attractive and to be recognized by others as attractive. By the 1980s, however, younger women began to feel that feminist beauty standards were repressive, even prudish, and developed a new, more playful, ornate, and multicultural fashion sensibility that may signal a "third wave" of feminism. Women's newfound passion for athletics has made a look of health and strength fashionable, sometimes to an oppressive degree as women feel coerced to reach a firm muscular, spandex thinness. At the same time, a conservative antifeminist backlash is also influencing fashion, trying to reestablish an allegedly lost femininity. The politics of feminism is being fought out on the fashion front.

Other aspects of the culture also reveal feminism's impact. Finally some older movie actresses, such as Susan Sarandon, Olympia Dukakis, and Meryl Streep, are recognized as desirable, and women entertainers in many media and art forms are rejecting simplistic, demeaning, and passive roles, despite the reemergence of misogynist and hypersexualized entertainments. Soap operas, sitcoms, even cop shows now feature plots in which lesbianism, abortion, rape, incest, and battering are portrayed from women's perspectives. In the fine arts, women's progress has been slower, illustrating the fallacy of assuming that the elite is less sexist than those of lesser privilege. The way we speak has been altered: new words have been coined—"sexist" and "Ms." and "gender"; many Americans are now self-conscious about using "he" to mean a human, and textbooks and even sacred texts are being rewritten in inclusive language. Women now expect to be called "women" instead of "ladies" or "girls."

Some of the biggest transformations are personal and familial, and they have been hotly contested. Indeed, even from a feminist perspective not all of them are positive. Women's relationships with other women are more publicly valued and celebrated and lesbianism is more accepted. People are marrying later and some are choosing not to marry. Most women today enter marriage or other romantic relationships with the expectation of equal partnership; since they don't always get this, they seem more willing to live as single people than to put up with domineering or abusive men. Conservatives argue that the growth of divorce, out-of-wedlock childbirth, and single motherhood is a sign of social deterioration, and certainly the growing economic inequality in the U.S. has rendered many women and especially single mothers and their children impoverished, depressed, and angry. But, feminists retort, is being poor in a destructive marriage really better than being poor on one's own? Even the growth of single motherhood reflects an element of women's choice: in different circumstances both poor and prosperous women are refusing to consider a bad marriage the price of motherhood, and are giving birth to or adopting children without husbands. More women think of marriage as only one possible option, aware that singleness and lesbianism are reasonable alternatives. Even women who do marry increasingly consider marriage only one aspect of life, supplementing motherhood and work. There is a growing sentiment that families come in a variety of forms.

By the mid-1970s an antifeminist backlash was able to command huge funding from right-wing corporate fortunes, fervent support from religious fundamentalists, and considerable media attention. The intensity of the reaction is a measure of how threatened conservatives were by popular backing for women's liberation and the rapid changes it brought about. Even with their billions of dollars, their hundreds of lobbyists and PR men, their foundations and magazines dishing out antifeminist misinformation, as compared to the puny amounts of money and volunteer labor available to women's liberation, the striking fact is that public opinion has not shifted much. Polls show overwhelming support for what feminism stands for: equal rights, respect, opportunity, and access for women.

That there is still a long way to go to reach sexual equality should not prevent us from recognizing what has been achieved. If there is disappointment, it is because women's liberation was so utopian, even apocalyptic, emerging as it did in an era of radical social movements and grand optimism. Unrealistic? Perhaps. But without utopian dreams, without anger, without reaching for the moon and expecting to get there by express, the movement would have achieved far less. In fact, without taking risks, feminists would never have been able to imagine lives of freedom and justice for women.

Feminism is by no means dead. Feminist groups continue to work on specific issues such as reproductive rights, rape, violence against women, sweatshops, sexism in the media, union organizing, and welfare rights. Nevertheless, the mass social movement called women's liberation did dissolve by the end of the 1970s. This is not a sign of failure. All social movements are short-lived because of the intense personal demands they make; few can sustain the level of energy that they require at their peak of activity. Moreover, as people age, most put more energy into family, employment, and personal life. Equally important, women's liberation could not survive outside the context of the other progressive social movements that nurtured hope and optimism about social change. As the Left declined, the right-wing backlash grew stronger. It did not convert many feminists to conservatism but it moved the mainstream far to the right. Given this change in mainstream politics, it is all the more striking that so few feminist gains have been rolled back and many have continued and even increased their momentum. Although the word "feminist" has become a pejorative term to some American women, most women (and most men as well) support a feminist program: equal education, equal pay, child care, freedom from harassment and violence, shared housework and child rearing, women's right to self-determination.

READING 4

Feminist Politics
Where We Stand

bell hooks

Simply put, feminism is a movement to end sexism, sexist exploitation, and oppression. This was a definition of feminism I offered in *Feminist Theory: From Margin to Center* more than 10 years ago. It was my hope at the time that it would become a common definition everyone would use. I liked this definition because it did not imply that men were the enemy. By naming sexism as the problem it went directly to the heart of the matter. Practically, it is a definition which implies that all sexist thinking and action is the problem, whether those who perpetuate it are female or male, child or adult. It is also broad enough to include an understanding of systemic institutionalized sexism. As a definition it is open-ended. To understand feminism it implies one has to necessarily understand sexism.

As all advocates of feminist politics know, most people do not understand sexism, or if they do, they think it is not a problem. Masses of people think that feminism is always and only about women seeking to be equal to men. And a huge majority of these folks think feminism is anti-male. Their misunderstanding of feminist politics reflects the reality that most folks learn about feminism from patriarchal mass media. The feminism they hear about the most is portrayed by women who are primarily committed to gender equality—equal pay for equal work, and sometimes women and men sharing household chores and parenting. They see that these women are usually white and materially privileged. They know from mass media that women's liberation focuses on the freedom to have abortions, to be lesbians, to challenge rape and domestic violence. Among these issues, masses of people agree with the idea of gender equity in the workplace—equal pay for equal work.

Since our society continues to be primarily a "Christian" culture, masses of people continue to believe that god has ordained that women be subordinate to men in the domestic household. Even though masses of women have entered the workforce, even though many families are headed by women who are the sole breadwinners, the vision of domestic life which continues to dominate the nation's imagination is one in which the logic of male domination is intact, whether men are present in the home or not. The wrongminded notion of feminist movement which implied it was anti-male carried with it the wrongminded assumption that all female space would necessarily be an environment where patriarchy and sexist thinking would be absent. Many women, even those involved in feminist politics, chose to believe this as well.

There was indeed a great deal of anti-male sentiment among early feminist activists who were responding to male domination with anger. It was that anger at injustice that was the impetus for creating a women's liberation movement. Early on most feminist activists (a majority of whom were white) had their consciousness raised about the nature of male domination when they were working in anti-classist and anti-racist settings with men who were telling the world about the importance of freedom while subordinating the women in their ranks. Whether it was white women working on behalf of socialism, black women working on behalf of civil rights and black liberation, or Native American women working for indigenous rights, it was clear that men wanted to lead, and they wanted women to follow. Participating in these radical freedom struggles awakened the spirit of rebellion and resistance in progressive females and led them towards contemporary women's liberation.

As contemporary feminism progressed, as women realized that males were not the only group in our society who supported sexist thinking and behavior—that females could be sexist as well—anti-male sentiment no longer shaped the movement's consciousness. The focus shifted to an all-out effort to create gender justice. But women could not band together to further feminism without confronting our sexist thinking. Sisterhood could not be powerful as long as women were competitively at war with one another. Utopian visions of sisterhood based solely on the awareness of the reality that all women were in some way victimized by male domination were disrupted by discussions of class and race. Discussions of class differences occurred early on in contemporary feminism, preceding discussions of race. Diana Press published revolutionary insights about class divisions between women as early as the mid-'70s in their collection of essays *Class and Feminism.* These discussions did not trivialize the feminist insistence that "sisterhood is powerful," they simply emphasized that we could only become sisters in struggle by confronting the ways women—through sex, class, and race—dominated and exploited other women, and created a political platform that would address these differences.

Even though individual black women were active in contemporary feminist movement from its inception, they were not the individuals who became the "stars" of the movement, who attracted the attention of mass media. Often individual black women active in feminist movement were revolutionary feminists (like many white lesbians). They were already at odds with reformist feminists who resolutely wanted to project a vision of the movement as being solely about women gaining equality with men in the existing system. Even before race became a talked about issue in feminist circles it was clear to black women (and to their revolutionary allies in struggle) that they were never going to have equality within the existing white supremacist capitalist patriarchy.

From its earliest inception feminist movement was polarized. Reformist thinkers chose to emphasize gender equality. Revolutionary thinkers did not want simply to alter the existing system so that women would have more rights. We wanted to transform that system, to bring an end to patriarchy and sexism. Since patriarchal mass media was not interested in the more revolutionary vision, it never received attention in mainstream press. The vision of "women's liberation" which captured and still holds the public imagination was the one representing women as wanting what men had. And this was the vision that was easier to realize. Changes in our nation's economy, economic depression, the loss of jobs, etc., made the climate ripe for our nation's citizens to accept the notion of gender equality in the workforce.

Given the reality of racism, it made sense that white men were more willing to consider women's rights when the granting of those rights could serve the interests of maintaining white supremacy. We can never forget that white women began to assert their need for freedom after civil rights, just at the point when racial discrimination was ending and black people, especially black males, might have attained equality in the workforce with white men. Reformist feminist thinking focusing primarily on equality with men in the workforce overshadowed the original radical foundations of contemporary feminism which called for reform as well as overall restructuring of society so that our nation would be fundamentally anti-sexist.

Most women, especially privileged white women, ceased even to consider revolutionary feminist visions, once they began to gain economic power within the existing social structure. Ironically, revolutionary feminist thinking was most accepted and embraced in academic circles. In those circles the production of revolutionary feminist theory progressed, but more often than not that theory was not made available to the public. It became and remains a privileged discourse available to those among us who are highly literate, well-educated, and usually materially privileged. Works like *Feminist Theory: From Margin to Center* that offer a liberatory vision of feminist transformation never receive mainstream attention. Masses of people have not heard of this book. They have not rejected its message; they do not know what the message is.

While it was in the interest of mainstream white supremacist capitalist patriarchy to suppress visionary feminist thinking which was not anti-male or concerned with getting women the right to be like men, reformist feminists were also eager to silence these forces. Reformist feminism became their route to class mobility. They could break free of male domination in the workforce and be more self-determining in their lifestyles. While sexism did not end, they could maximize their freedom within the existing system. And they could count on there being a lower class of exploited subordinated women

to do the dirty work they were refusing to do. By accepting and indeed colluding with the subordination of working-class and poor women, they not only ally themselves with the existing patriarchy and its concomitant sexism, they give themselves the right to lead a double life, one where they are the equals of men in the workforce and at home when they want to be. If they choose lesbianism they have the privilege of being equals with men in the workforce while using class power to create domestic lifestyles where they can choose to have little or no contact with men.

Lifestyle feminism ushered in the notion that there could be as many versions of feminism as there were women. Suddenly the politics was being slowly removed from feminism. And the assumption prevailed that no matter what a woman's politics, be she conservative or liberal, she too could fit feminism into her existing lifestyle. Obviously this way of thinking has made feminism more acceptable because its underlying assumption is that women can be feminists without fundamentally challenging and changing themselves or the culture. For example, let's take the issue of abortion. If feminism is a movement to end sexist oppression, and depriving females of reproductive rights is a form of sexist oppression, then one cannot be anti-choice and be feminist. A woman can insist she would never choose to have an abortion while affirming her support of the right of women to choose and still be an advocate of feminist politics. She cannot be anti-abortion and an advocate of feminism. Concurrently there can be no such thing as "power feminism" if the vision of power evoked is power gained through the exploitation and oppression of others.

Feminist politics is losing momentum because feminist movement has lost clear definitions. We have those definitions. Let's reclaim them. Let's share them. Let's start over. Let's have T-shirts and bumper stickers and postcards and hip-hop music, television and radio commercials, ads everywhere and billboards, and all manner of printed material that tells the world about feminism. We can share the simple yet powerful message that feminism is a movement to end sexist oppression. Let's start there. Let the movement begin again.

READING 5

Beyond Bean Counting

JeeYeun Lee

I came out as a woman, an Asian American and a bi-sexual within a relatively short span of time, and ever since then I have been guilty of the crime of bean counting, as Bill Clinton oh-so-eloquently phrased it. Every time I am in a room of people gathered for any reason, I automatically count those whom I can identify as women, men, people of color, Asian Americans, mixed-race people, whites, gays and lesbians, bisexuals, heterosexuals, people with disabilities. So when I received the call for submissions for this anthology, I imagined opening up the finished book to the table of contents and counting beans; I then sent the call for submissions to as many queer Asian/Pacific American women writers as I knew.

Such is the nature of feminism in the 1990s: an uneasy balancing act between the imperatives of outreach and inclusion on the one hand, and the risk of tokenism and further marginalization on the other. This dynamic has indelibly shaped my personal experiences with feminism, starting from my very first encounter with organized feminism. This encounter happened to be, literally, Feminist Studies 101 at the university I attended. The content of the class was divided into topics such as family, work, sexuality and so forth, and for each topic we studied what various feminist paradigms said about it: "liberal feminism," "social feminism," "radical feminism" and "feminism and women of color."

Taking this class was an exhilarating, empowering and very uneasy experience. For the first time I found people who articulated those murky half-formed feelings that I could previously only express incoherently as "But that's not fair!" People who agreed, sympathized, related their own experiences, theorized, helped me form what I had always known. In seventh grade, a teacher made us do a mock debate, and I ended up arguing with Neil Coleman about whether women or men were better cooks. He said more men were professional chefs, therefore men were better. I responded that more women cooked in daily life, therefore women were better. He said it was quality that mattered, not quantity, and left me standing there with nothing to say. I knew there was something wrong with his argument, something wrong with the whole issue as it was framed, and felt extremely betrayed at being made to consent to the inferiority of my gender, losing in front of the whole class. I could never defend myself when arguments like this came up, invariably with boys who were good at debates and used to winning. They left me seething with resentment at their manipulations and frustrated at my speechlessness. So to come to a class that addressed these issues directly and gave me the words for all those pent-up feelings and frustrations was a tremendously affirming and empowering experience.

At the same time, it was an intensely uncomfortable experience. I knew "women of color" was supposed to include Asian American women, but I could not find any in the class readings. Were there no Asian American feminists? Were there none who could write in English? Did there even exist older Asian American women who were second or third generation? Were we Asian American students in the class the first to think about feminism? A class about women, I thought, was a class about me, so I looked for myself everywhere and found nothing. Nothing about Asian American families, immigrant women's work patterns, issues of sexuality and body image for Asian women, violence against Asian American women, Asian American women in the seventies feminist movement, nothing anywhere. I wasn't fully conscious then that I was searching for this, but this absence came out in certain feelings. First of all, I felt jealous of African American and Chicana feminists. Their work was present at least to some degree in the readings: They had research and theories, they were eloquent and they *existed*. Black and Chicana women in the class could claim them as role models, voices, communities—I had no one to claim as my own. My emerging identification as a woman of color was displaced through the writings of black and Chicana women, and I had to read myself, create my politics, through theirs; even now, to a certain extent, I feel more familiar with their issues than those of Asian American women. Second, I felt guilty. Although it was never expressed outright, I felt that there was some pressure on me to represent Asian American issues, and I could not. I felt estranged from the Asian American groups on campus and Asian American politics and activism in general, and guilty about this ignorance and alienation.

Now mind you, I'm still grateful for this class. Feminism was my avenue to politics: It politicized me; it raised my consciousness about issues of oppression, power and resistance in general. I learned a language with which I could start to explain my experiences and link them to larger societal structures of oppression and complicity. It also gave me ways that I could resist and actively fight back. I became interested in Asian American politics, people of color politics, gay/lesbian/bisexual politics and other struggles because of this exposure to feminism. But there is no excuse for this nearly complete exclusion of Asian/Pacific American women from the class. Marginalization is not simply a politically correct buzzword, it is a material reality that affects people's lives—in this case, my own. I would have been turned off from feminism altogether had it not been for later classes that dealt specifically with women of color. And I would like to name names here: I went to Stanford University, a bastion of privilege that pretends to be on the cutting edge of "multiculturalism." Just under twenty-five percent of the undergraduate population is Asian/Pacific American, but there was no mention of Asian/Pacific American women in Feminist Studies 101. All the classes I took on women of color were taught by graduate students and visiting professors. There was, at that time, only one woman of color on the feminist studies faculty. I regret that I realized the political import of these facts only after I left Stanford.

I understand that feminists in academia are caught between a rock and a hard place—not too many of us hold positions of decision-making power in universities. And I must acknowledge my gratitude for their struggles in helping to establish feminist studies programs and produce theories and research about women, all of which create vital opportunities and affirmation. But other women's organizations that are not constrained by such explicit forces are also lily-white. This obviously differs from group to group, and I think many of them are very conscientious about outreach to historically marginalized women. But, for instance, in 1992 and 1993, at the meetings I attended of the Women's Action Coalition (WAC) in New York City, out of approximately two hundred women usually fewer than twenty women of color were present.

But this is not a diatribe against feminism in general. I want to emphasize that the feminism that I and other young women come to today is one that is at least sensitive to issues of exclusion. If perhaps twenty years ago charges of racism, classism and homophobia were not taken seriously, today they are the cause of extreme anguish and soul-searching. I am profoundly grateful to older feminists of color and their white allies who struggled to bring U.S. feminist movements to this point. At the same time, I think that this current sensitivity often breeds tokenism, guilt, suspicion and self-righteousness that have very material repercussions on women's groups. I have found these uneasy dynamics in all the women's groups I've come across, addressed to varying degrees. At one extreme, I have seen groups that deny the marginalizing effects of their practices, believing that issues of inclusion really have nothing to do with their specific agendas. At the other extreme, I have seen groups ripped apart by accusations of political correctness, immobilized by guilt, knowing they should address a certain issue but not knowing how to begin, and still wondering why "women of color just don't come to our meetings." And tokenism is alive and well in the nineties. Those of us who have been aware of our tokenization often become suspicious and tired of educating others, wondering if we are invested enough to continue to do so, wondering if the overall goal is worth it.

In this age when "political correctness" has been appropriated by conservative forces as a derogatory term, it is extremely difficult to honestly discuss and confront any ideas and practices that perpetuate dominant norms—and none of us is innocent of such collusion. Many times, our response is to become defensive, shutting down to constructive critiques and actions, or to individualize our collusion as solely a personal fault, as if working on our individual racist or classist attitudes would somehow make things better. It appears that we all have a lot of work to do still.

And I mean *all*. Issues of exclusion are not the sole province of white feminists. I learned this very vividly at a 1993 retreat organized by the Asian Pacifica Lesbian Network. It has become somewhat common lately to speak of "Asian and Pacific Islanders" or "Asian/Pacific Americans" or, as in this case, "Asian Pacifica." This is meant to be inclusive, to recognize some issues held in common by people from Asia and people from the Pacific Islands. Two women of Native Hawaiian descent and some Asian American allies confronted the group at this retreat to ask for more than lip service in the organization's name: If the group was seriously committed to being an inclusive coalition, we needed to educate ourselves about and actively advocate Pacific Islander issues. And because I don't want to relegate them to a footnote, I will mention here a few of these issues: the demand for sovereignty for Native Hawaiians, whose government was illegally overthrown by the U.S. in 1893; fighting stereotypes of women and men that are different from those of Asian people; decrying U.S. imperialist possession and occupation of the islands of Guam, the Virgin Islands, American Samoa, the Marshall Islands, Micronesia, the Northern Mariana Islands and several others.

This was a retreat where one would suppose everyone had so much in common—after all, we were all queer API women, right? Any such myth was effectively destroyed by the realities of our experiences and issues: We were women of different ethnic backgrounds, with very different issues among East Asians, South Asians, Southeast Asians and Pacific Islanders; women of mixed race and heritage; women who identified as lesbians and those who identified as bisexuals; women who were immigrants, refugees, illegal aliens or second generation or more; older women, physically challenged women, women adopted by white families, women from the Midwest. Such tangible differences brought home the

fact that no simplistic identity politics is *ever* possible, that we had to conceive of ourselves as a coalition first and foremost; as one woman on a panel said, our identity as queer API women must be a *coalitional* identity. Initially, I thought that I had finally found a home where I could relax and let down my guard. This was true to a certain degree, but I discovered that this was the home where I would have to work the hardest because I cared the most. I would have to be committed to push myself and push others to deal with all of our differences, so that we *could* be safe for each other. And in this difficult work of coalition, one positive action was taken at the retreat: We changed the name of the organization to include "bisexual," thus becoming the Asian Pacifica Lesbian and Bisexual Network, a name that people started using immediately.

All this is to say that I and other young women have found most feminist movements today to be at this point, where there is at least a stated emphasis on inclusion and outreach with the accompanying risk of tokenism. I firmly believe that it is always the margins that push us further in our politics. Women of color do not struggle in feminist movements simply to add cultural diversity, to add the viewpoints of different kinds of women. Women of color feminist theories challenge the fundamental premises of feminism, such as the very definition of "women," and call for recognition of the constructed racial nature of *all* experiences of gender. In the same way, heterosexist norms do not oppress solely lesbians, bisexuals and gay men, but affect all of our choices and nonchoices; issues posed by differently abled women question our basic assumptions about body image, health care, sexuality and work; ecofeminists challenge our fundamental ideas about living on and with the earth, about our interactions with animals, plants, food, agriculture and industry. Many feminists seem to find the issues of class the most difficult to address; we are always faced with the fundamental inequalities inherent to late-twentieth-century multinational capitalism and our unavoidable implication in its structures. Such an overwhelming array of problems can numb and immobilize us, or make us concentrate our energies too narrowly. I don't think that we have to address everything fully at the same time, but we *must* be fully aware of the limitations of our specific agendas. Progressive activists cannot afford to do the masters' work for them by continuing to carry out oppressive assumptions and exclusions.

These days, whenever someone says the word "women" to me, my mind goes blank. What "women"? What is this "women" thing you're talking about? Does that mean me? Does that mean my mother, my roommates, the white woman next door, the checkout clerk at the supermarket, my aunts in Korea, half of the world's population? I ask people to specify and specify, until I can figure out exactly what they're talking about, and I try to remember to apply the same standards to myself, to deny myself the slightest possibility of romanticization. Sisterhood may be global, but who is in that sisterhood? None of us can afford to assume anything about anybody else. This thing called "feminism" takes a great deal of hard work, and I think this is one of the primary hallmarks of young feminists' activism today: We realize that coming together and working together are by no means natural or easy.

READING 6

Shame, Guilt, and Responsibility

Allan G. Johnson

With just enough exceptions to prove the rule,[1] men have taken almost no responsibility for patriarchy. Some men confuse taking responsibility with being sensitive to women. They offer emotional support and tolerate women's anger and frustration around gender issues. Men can be sensitive, however, without doing anything to challenge or undermine their male privilege or to define gender issues as *men's* issues, especially to other men. Even sensitive men can be drawn to the path of least resistance that defines problems such as housework, workplace discrimination, sexual harassment, and violence as women's issues. This makes it easy for men to see themselves as "good guys"—loving helpers, loyal supporters, or valiant defenders who help women in a patient and caring way. What these men often don't do is the work of taking the initiative: of deciding what needs to be said, asked, listened to, discussed, fought over, attended to, and cared for; of overcoming the status quo's foot-dragging inertia. When women get tired or confused or distracted by the everyday details of their lives, the responsibility these men take often lies dormant until the next time a woman feels compelled to risk making trouble by raising a "women's issue." And when women express anger at always having to carry the burden of figuring out patriarchy and doing something about it, these sensitive and supportive men often react as if they're being unfairly criticized or even attacked, their exceptional and seemingly generous efforts unappreciated, their supposed immunity from reproach unfairly snatched away.

. . . What's going on here, however, isn't men taking responsibility and being punished for their trouble. In my experience, men who take responsibility for patriarchy are the last men most feminist women want to attack. More often than not, [these] men present the appearance of taking responsibility without the substance, *because they don't have a clear sense of what taking responsibility actually means or what there is to take responsibility for.* They may claim to be on women's side because doing the right thing makes them feel good about themselves or because they value their relationships with women and fear women's displeasure and anger, but this merely avoids taking responsibility. It's a stance that dominant groups often take, and women and other minorities rightly distrust it and feel insulted by its implicit condescension.

Why do men avoid taking responsibility for patriarchy? In the simplest sense, most men don't realize that patriarchy exists and therefore don't know there's any responsibility for them to take in the first place. Also, the path of least resistance for members of any dominant group is to see themselves as not *having* to do anything. The status quo is organized in their image and in their gender interests. It reflects maleness in its highest ideals and images. Why, then, change it? Why question, much less give up, what they've got and risk *men's* disapproval, anger, and rejection, not to mention feeling disempowered, diminished, and "softened" to a position of equality with women? And why should they do this when they may not feel terribly good about their own lives in the first place?

Many men feel threatened by the idea of taking responsibility not only because they would have to give up a great deal of what they've been taught to value, but also because they would have to confront what they have given up *already* in order to participate in an oppressive system. There is among men in modern industrial patriarchies an enormous pool of loss, pain, and grief, some of which . . . is tied to the lost relationship between younger and older men. But this reflects a much deeper loss traceable to the portion of men's humanity that they give up as part of their *solidarity* with older men and the patriarchal society whose interests they both identify with. For men to feel their deep and deadening disconnection from their own and other people's lives is potentially so painful and frightening that most men simply don't want to know about it.

Perhaps the most important barrier to men taking responsibility, however, is their reluctance to expose themselves to the ocean of guilt and shame they believe awaits them if they acknowledge that patriarchy and male privilege exist.[2] The negative power of guilt and shame is especially significant for men who are otherwise most sympathetic to women and most likely to oppose patriarchy. These are the men who are most aware of male privilege and the price women pay in order for men to have it, which also makes them most prone to feeling blameworthy. They're in this trap because . . . both women and men often confuse individuals with systems and often place blame where it doesn't belong. Add to this the fact that men routinely confuse guilt and blame with taking responsibility, and it's understandable why

even men sympathetic to gender justice avoid going very far down the road of taking responsibility.

. . .

Dominant groups typically show the least tolerance for allowing themselves to feel guilt and shame. I suspect that women, for example, are more likely to feel guilty over criticizing a man for his male privilege and making him feel bad than he is for being criticized. Privilege, after all, should exempt one from having to feel such things. This means that sooner or later, dominant groups experience reminders of their potential for feeling guilt as an affront that infringes on their sense of entitlement to a life unplagued by concern for how their privilege affects other people. The right to deny that privilege exists is an integral part of privilege itself. So men can be quick to complain about "being made to feel guilty" without actually *feeling guilty*. . . .

. . . [F]ighting social oppression with blame and guilt psychologizes and individualizes something that's rooted in *systems*. The individualistic model relies on the false notion that systems produce bad consequences solely because bad people with bad motives participate in them. The vast majority of men, like women, were born into patriarchy and have grown up knowing little else. They are not, individually or collectively, patriarchy; they do *participate* in it, however, and that's where both the responsibility for how things are and the power to do something about it lie.

The guilt strategy also doesn't work because it disempowers people to act for change. Fear can get people to look at what's going on as a way to survive. Guilt, on the other hand, typically has just the opposite effect. For every man whose guilt has spurred him to dig deeper into the reality of patriarchy, there are thousands more who'd rather dig a deep hole of denial to hide in. To make men feel guilty simply because they are men puts them in a box with no way out, which all but ensures they'll never make a move toward changing themselves or anything else. They're far more likely to detach themselves from whatever the guilt is about ("I wasn't there; I never knew; it never even happened"); or angrily defend themselves against the unfairness of being blamed simply for being male; or get off the hook by saying they're sorry; or seem to change their ways, promising to be more careful in the future.

. . .

To take responsibility for patriarchy, men will have to claim, embrace, and own it without guilt or shame. Men can't hide behind arguments that patriarchy is about someone else, that others benefit from it more or suffer from it less, or that we're the exceptional nice guys who never hurt anyone. We can't pass off the enormous complexity of patriarchy to bad parenting or flawed personalities. We can't hide behind the damage we do to ourselves as we participate in patriarchy ("Leave me alone; it hurts me, too"), for how we damage our own lives doesn't remove responsibility for how patriarchy destroys the lives of others. Suicide doesn't balance homicide, just as men's abuse of themselves and one another doesn't balance men's abuse of women. Men can't hold out until women agree to take care of men's wounds along with their own or even to stop blaming men individually or collectively, fairly or not. And we can't take refuge in issues of race or class by reducing patriarchy to the power of upper-class white males. Men privileged by race and class are in a better position to benefit from core patriarchal values, but they don't have a monopoly on identifying with and defending them. Patriarchy is about all of us.

. . .

. . . To the extent that feminist work is about *patriarchy,* men have the potential to contribute a great deal of experience and analytical perspective. In this sense, feminist work has as much to do with men as it does with women. This doesn't mean that men should presume to tell women how to liberate themselves from gender oppression, but it does mean that men have something to say to other men—and occasionally to women—about *male* privilege and the male-dominated, male-centered, male-identified system that underlies and enforces it.

. . .

. . . It's hard work, not only because no one likes to focus on human suffering or give up privilege or risk feeling guilty, but also because the path of least resistance in a male-centered system is for men to focus on themselves and their own needs and concerns, not on women and gender oppression.

. . .

The tendency of men to focus on themselves as victims rather than on patriarchy is nowhere more evident than in the mythopoetic men's movement.[3] This is most closely associated with the work of Robert Bly, Sam Keen, and various Jung-inspired writers and activists . . . .

As such, the mythopoetic men's movement does more harm than good by encouraging men to pursue private solutions to what are social problems. Drumming, chanting, and storytelling may help men feel more connected to one another and to a mythic essence of manhood, but it does nothing to illuminate or transform the patriarchal system that creates the wounds they want to heal. . . .

. . .

A key step for men who want to participate in change is to connect their inner lives to the outer reality of patriarchy, to go beyond vague attributions to "society" to a clearer understanding of how social systems work and how our participation affects them. If the new men's movement is to be part of the solution rather than merely a self-absorbed, increasingly entrenched part of the problem, men are going to have to learn how to take responsibility for this social system that bears their name. Becoming part of the solution involves a fundamental moral choice about whether to use gender privilege to further that privilege or to join women in taking responsibility for the patriarchal legacy. Either men empower themselves to move toward taking their share of responsibility or they make way for those who will. Until men begin to share seriously in the emotional, intellectual, and practical aspects of struggling with our legacy, not only will change be seriously limited, but men and women will continue to feel at odds with one another, because in fact they *will be* at odds.

Men's alternatives aren't appealing, but neither are the alternatives for women or racial and ethnic minorities trying to deal with oppression. Like all dominant groups, men are often stuck in a state of arrested development that can wrap them in an almost childlike obliviousness, grandiosity, and sense of entitlement in relation to women.[4] This insulates them from the adult responsibility to know what's going on and to move toward doing something about it, a responsibility that includes coming to terms with the reality of privilege and the oppression that supports it. Gender oppression has forced many women to grow up in order to survive and work for something better for us all. It demands nothing less from men.

NOTES

1. See, for example, the work of Arthur Brittan, Harry Brod, Robert Connell, Michael Kaufman, Michael Kimmel, Joseph Pleck, Jon Snodgrass, and John Stoltenberg.

2. See, for example, Robert Bly, *Iron John: A Book About Men* (Reading, Mass.: Addison-Wesley, 1990); Farrell, *Myth of Male Power;* and Sam Keen, *Fire in the Belly: On Being a Man* (New York: Bantam, 1991).

3. See Kay Leigh Hagan, ed., *Women Respond to the Men's Movement* (San Francisco: HarperCollins, 1992); and Michael S. Kimmel, ed., *The Politics of Manhood: Profeminist Men Respond to the Mythopoetic Movement (And the Mythopoetic Leaders Respond)* (Philadelphia: Temple University Press, 1995).

4. See Ellyn Kaschak, *Engendered Lives* (New York: Basic Books, 1992), 74.

READING 7

Denials of Inequality

Deborah L. Rhode

Americans' most common response to gender inequality is to deny its dimensions. A widespread perception is that once upon a time, women suffered serious discrimination, but those days are over. Barriers have been coming down, women have been moving up, and full equality is just around the corner. If anything, many men believe that women are now getting undeserved advantages. In a series of recent articles with titles like "The Decline and Fall of the White Male," commentators air their view that "merit is out," "special privileges" are in, and the only group that can't claim equal protection under law is white men. "Pale males eat it again," announces a character in Michael Crichton's popular film *Disclosure*. This perspective is widely shared. According to recent polls, close to half of all men think that they are subject to unfair penalties for advantages that others had in the past. Two-thirds of men and three-quarters of male business leaders do not believe that women encounter significant discrimination for top positions in business, professions, or government.

Such views are difficult to square with the facts. White males account for about 40 percent of the population but about 95 percent of senior managers, 90 percent of newspaper editors, 80 percent of the *Forbes* list of richest Americans, and 80 percent of congressional legislators. Significant sex-based disparities in employment salaries and status persist, even when researchers control for objective factors such as education, experience, and hours worked. As *Newsweek's* article "White Male Paranoia" points out, the pale male certainly appears to be "holding his own (and most of everybody else's) in the world of hard facts"; it's only in the "world of images and ideas . . . [that] he's taking a clobbering."

What explains this gap between popular perceptions and concrete data on gender inequality? Part of the explanation lies with selective perception. Men often deny bias because they fail to recognize it. They usually don't need to, it does not significantly affect their lives. As with race, part of the privilege of dominance is the privilege of accepting without noticing its benefits.

. . .

For obvious reasons, women are more sensitive to gender inequality than men are, but some perceptual blinders persist among both sexes. Not all women encounter all forms of bias, and those who lack personal experience sometimes fail to appreciate collective problems. What sociologists label the "Queen Bee Syndrome" is common among some professionally successful women. Their attitude is, "I managed, why can't you?"

Many women also are unable to see patterns of discrimination because important parts of the picture are missing or murky. Salary, hiring, and promotion data that compare similarly qualified men and women are hard to come by, and the most overt sexism has gone underground. As a 1989 Supreme Court case revealed, male employers may still penalize a woman who they think needs courses in "charm school." But that is no longer what they say in mixed company or in personnel records. Moreover, gender is only one of the characteristics, and not always the most important one, that disadvantages women. Race, ethnicity, class, disability, and sexual orientation often overshadow or interact with gender.

. . .

Self-interest complicates the process. For some men, the increasing unacceptability of sexism, coupled with the inconvenience of eliminating it, encourages various strategies of self-deception. These techniques frequently surface on issues of household work. Employed men, who average only half as much time as employed women on family tasks, generally manage not to notice the disparity. In one recent poll, over two-thirds of surveyed husbands reported that they shared childrearing duties equally with their wives, an assessment wildly inconsistent with that of most wives and virtually all reported research.

Moreover, even men who acknowledge disparities often view women's extra tasks as matters of personal choice, not joint responsibility. Rather than accept an equal division of cleaning, cooking, or childcare obligations, some men redefine their share as unnecessary; they don't mind a little mess or a fast-food dinner, and their infants will do just fine with extra time among their "friends" at daycare. Other men seem not to notice when some of their assigned tasks need doing, or else mismanage key parts of the job. Rather than broadcast constant reminders of complaints, many women simply pick up pieces that their partners don't even realize have been dropped. As one wife wearily noted, "I do my half, I do half of [my husband's half], and the rest doesn't get done."

. . .

Part of what keeps men, and often women, from recognizing that gap is their choice of reference groups. Where gender appears to be a relevant characteristic, most individuals compare themselves to members of their own sex. In assessing domestic burdens, husbands look to other husbands or their own fathers rather than to wives. From this perspective, unequal divisions of labor become easy to rationalize because they remain the norm rather than the exception.

Women also tend to compare their family burdens to those of members of their own sex. As a result, many wives deny that their husbands do less than their "fair share" around the home, even when responsibilities are grossly unequal. Cultural attitudes reinforce such perceptions. As Anna Quindlen notes, "When men do the dishes it's called helping. When women do dishes, that's called life." Most women are not fully aware of how much time they or their partners spend on family work and generally believe that their arrangements are far more equal than they truly are.

This is not to imply that women totally fail to notice gender inequalities in household burdens. How much help they receive (or don't receive) from their male partners shows up in opinion surveys as one of the greatest sources of resentment. Yet even women who are most resentful often do not expect an equal division of household work. It is only their partner's refusal to help with particular jobs or his inability to justify refusing, that triggers conflict. And for many women, avoiding conflict is more important than achieving equality. They, like their male counterparts, use selective perception as a form of self-protection.

Similar patterns operate in other contexts. According to workplace surveys, even when women recognize gender discrimination as a problem or where objective evidence points to that conclusion, most individuals still do not believe that they personally have been targets. Although many critics denounce feminism for encouraging women to exaggerate their own victimization, recent research finds that individuals generally are reluctant to see themselves in that light. Acknowledging vulnerability carries a cost: it erodes individuals' sense of control and self-esteem, and involves the unpleasantness of identifying a perpetrator. Many women understandably are unwilling to alienate men whose approval is important personally and professionally.

Although some individuals enjoy nursing grievances and claiming the moral leverage of victim status, most do not. As Hillary Clinton once noted, "Who wants to walk around constantly with clenched fists?" Particularly where women feel powerless to avoid inequality, they are likely to avoid acknowledging it.

DISCUSSION QUESTIONS FOR CHAPTER ONE

1. Why are you taking a women's studies course?

2. What are your expectations, fears, anxieties, and hopes about taking a women's studies class?

3. Why did women's studies emerge in the academic community?

4. What are negative stereotypes of feminism? Where do they come from? How do these stereotypes serve to perpetuate the dominant social order?

5. Do you think on the whole equality has been achieved? Why or why not? Are there places where you see room for improvement or the need for drastic change?

SUGGESTIONS FOR FURTHER READING

Douglas, Susan J. "I'm Not a Feminist, But . . . ." *Where the Girls Are: Growing Up Female with the Mass Media.* New York: Times Books, 1995.

Hernandez, Daisy, and Bushra Rheman, eds. *Colonize This! Young Women of Color on Today's Feminism.* New York, Avalon, 2002.

hooks, bell. *Feminism Is for Everybody: Passionate Politics.* Boston: South End, 2000.

—. *Teaching to Transgress: Education as the Practice of Freedom.* New York: Routledge, 1994.

MacDonald, Amie, and Susan Sanchez, eds. *Twenty-First Century Feminist Classrooms: Pedagogies of Identity and Difference.* New York: St. Martin's, 2002.

Maher, Frances A., and Mary Kay Thompson Tetreault. *The Feminist Classroom: An Inside Look at How Professors and Students Are Transforming Higher Education for a Diverse Society.* New York: Basic Books, 1994.

Messer-Davidow, Ellen. *Disciplining Feminism: How Women's Studies Transformed the Academy and Was Transformed by It.* Durham, NC: Duke University Press, 2002.

Rogers, Mary F., and C. D. Garrett. *Who's Afraid of Women's Studies? Feminisms in Everyday Life.* Walnut Creek, CA: Alta Mira Press, 2002.

CHAPTER TWO

Systems of Privilege and
Inequality in Women's Lives

As women, we are as different as we are alike. Although we share some conditions, including having primary responsibility for children and being victims of male violence, our lives are marked by difference. This is a result of the varying conditions of women's existence in communities around the world and the societies in which these communities are embedded. We inhabit different cultures whose norms or cultural expectations prescribe different ways of acting as women and different sanctions if these norms are broken. It is therefore important to recognize difference and avoid using "woman" as a universal or homogeneous category that assumes sameness.

In the United States, women's lives are also marked by difference. This difference is illustrated by the material conditions of our lives, the values and cultures of the communities in which we live, and even the geographic region of the country we inhabit. In particular, we are different in terms of race and ethnicity, religion, age, looks, sexual orientation, socioeconomic status, and ability. Just as it is important to question the homogenizing notions of sameness in terms of the category "woman" across societies, it is also important to understand that these universalizing tendencies work against our understanding of women in the United States as well. Often we tend to think of women in comparison to a *mythical norm:* White, middle-class, heterosexual, abled, thin, and a young adult. Women not fitting these categories often tend to be considered different. The important question to ask, however, is, different from what? Such a question reveals how difference gets constructed against what people think of as normal. And what is perceived as normal is that which those in power are able to define as normal.

It is important to recognize that the meanings associated with differences are socially constructed. These social constructions would not be problematic were they not created against the notion of the mythical norm. Being a lesbian would not be a "difference" that invoked cultural resistance if it were not for *compulsory heterosexuality,* the notion that everyone should be heterosexual and have relationships with the opposite sex. This concept is illustrated in "The Social Construction of Disability" by Susan Wendell. She makes the case that *ableism,* discrimination against the mentally and physically disabled, is a direct result of social factors that actively create standards of normality against which ability/disability is constructed. In this chapter we focus on differences among women and explore the ways systems of privilege and inequality are created out of these differences.

Figure 2.1 Intersecting Axes of Privilege, Domination, and Oppression

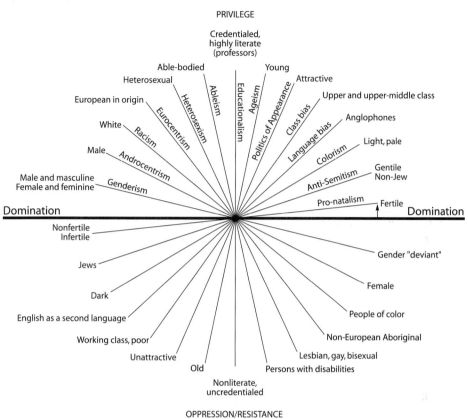

Source: Kathryn Pauly Morgan, "Describing the Emperor's New Clothes: Three Myths of Educational (In)Equality." *The Gender Question in Education: Theory, Pedagogy & Politics,* Ann Diller et al., Boulder, CO: Westview, 1996.

DIFFERENCE, HIERARCHY, AND SYSTEMS OF OPPRESSION

Society recognizes the ways people are different and assigns group membership based upon these differences; at the same time society also ranks the differences (fig. 2.1). Male is placed above female, thin above fat, economically privileged above poor, and so forth. These rankings of groups and their members create a hierarchy where some ways of being, like being abled or heterosexual, are valued more than others, like being disabled or gay or lesbian. In this way, rankings occur against societal notions of the mythical norm.

The hierarchical ranking of these differences is constructed through social processes such that patterns of difference become systems of inequality and privilege. Inequality for some and privilege for others is the consequence of these processes. *Privilege* can be defined as special advantages people have by virtue of their status or position in society. In "White Privilege and Male Privilege," Peggy McIntosh writes that White privilege is the "invisible package of unearned assets" that White people can count on cashing in every day. And, as McIntosh explains, it is easier to grant that others are disadvantaged than to admit being overprivileged. Men might be supportive of women's rights but balk at the suggestion that their personal behavior is in need of modification. Whites might be horrified by the stories of racial injustice but still not realize that taken-for-granted White privilege is part of the problem.

Systems that facilitate privilege and inequality, subordination and domination, include *racism* based upon racial/ethnic group membership (African American, Asian American, Latino/a, Native American—note this also includes anti-Semitism, or discrimination against Jews and those of Semitic descent), *sexism* based upon gender, *classism* associated with socio-economic status, *heterosexism,* concerning sexual orientation, *ageism* relating to age, *looksism,* concerning body size and looks, and *ableism,* about physical and mental ability. Systems of oppression can be defined as systems that discriminate and privilege based upon perceived or real differences among people. Given this, sexism discriminates and privileges on the basis of gender, resulting in gender stratification, racism discriminates and privileges on the basis of racial and ethnic differences, and so forth for classism, heterosexism, ageism, looksism, and ableism.

Every woman is in multiple places vis-à-vis these systems. She might not have access to race and gender privilege because she is African American and a woman; she might have access to heterosexual privilege because she is heterosexual and class privilege because she lives in a family that is financially secure. This is the *confluence,* the flowing together of various identities. As Patricia Hill Collins explains in "Toward a New Vision," it is not as useful to think of these various identities as being stacked or arranged in a cumulative manner. Lives are not experienced as "Here I'm a woman, here I'm abled, here I'm poor," as if all our various statuses are all stacked up; we experience ourselves as ordinary people who struggle daily with the inequities in our lives and who usually take the privileges for granted. Various identities concerning these systems of equality and privilege are usually thoroughly blended.

Systems of inequality like racism, sexism, and classism interconnect and work together to enforce inequality and privilege, each mostly supporting the other. As Babba Copper explains in her article on ageism, age discrimination is very much connected to sexism as well as to looksism. Women learn to "age pass"; that is, we do not want to be mistaken for 40 when we are in our 30s, or mistaken for 70 when only 60. This is part of the pursuit for

LEARNING ACTIVITY:
UNPACK YOUR KNAPSACK

Peggy McIntosh lists a number of ways that she experiences White privilege. Based on your various nontarget statuses, make lists of the ways you experience the following categories of privilege:

White	Male	Heterosexual
Middle or upper class	Young	Able-bodied

LEARNING ACTIVITY: TEST FOR HIDDEN BIAS

Go to the Southern Poverty Law Center's Teaching Tolerance website at *www.tolerance .org*. Click on "Explore your hidden biases" to take a series of tests to uncover unconscious biases you may have. Even though most of us believe we view everyone equally, we still may hold stereotypes and biases of which we are unaware. These tests can check and see if perhaps you hold hidden biases of race, sexual orientation, age, gender, or body image. After you finish the tests, take a few minutes to write about what you learned about yourself. Were there any surprises? Do you hold hidden biases? How do you feel about your test results? Now that you know about your hidden biases, what can you do?

youth and beauty that encourages women to participate as agents of ageism as we fulfill the expectations of gender. Similarly, Suzanne Pharr writes about the ways homophobia functions as a weapon of sexism. *Homophobia* is the fear and dislike of lesbians and gay men. Pharr emphasizes that homophobia functions as a threat to keep women apart from one another and under male power, thus reinforcing sexism.

Another way that systems of inequality and privilege are maintained is by coercion and force. The best example of this is *hate crimes,* crimes whose motive is hate and bigotry and whose perpetrators are most likely heterosexual White males. There has been a substantial increase in hate crimes in the last decade, especially against people of color and lesbians and gay men, although it may be that improved reporting systems are also increasing our awareness of hate crimes. It is important to emphasize that gender as a category is omitted from many hate crime statutes despite the fact that women suffer from crimes of misogyny. Women are often hurt and killed because they are women. Hate crimes against women also involve a form of *sexual terrorism,* the threat of rape and sexual assault that controls a woman's life whether or not she is actually raped or assaulted.

Although hate crimes vary in the amount of terror and violence they involve, all leave women feeling vulnerable and victimized. Here are some examples. In 1994 the White neighbors of a Black woman in a Los Angeles suburb burned a cross on her lawn, kicked her children, hanged and gassed her pets, and placed "White power" signs on her property. In Oklahoma City, following the bombing of the federal building, an Iraqi refugee in her mid-20s miscarried her near-term baby after an attack on her home in which assailants pounded on her door, broke windows, and screamed anti-Islamic epithets. In Minneapolis in 1996, an African American lesbian found a note reading "Hate Nigger Faggots" at her door. After a burned cross was left outside her door, she decided to move. These are just a few examples of a widespread problem.

INSTITUTIONS

Institutions are social organizations that involve established patterns of behavior organized around particular purposes. They function through social norms and established rules and/ or laws. Major institutions in our society include the family, marriage, the economy, government and criminal justice systems, religion, education, science, health and medicine,

■ CHALLENGING YOUR ASSUMPTIONS

Read the following sentences and identify the assumptions inherent in each regarding age, ability, appearance, ethnicity, gender, race, religion, sexual orientation, and socioeconomic power or status.

Identify the "norm" (a standard of conduct that should or must be followed; a typical or usual way of being or behaving, usually said of a certain group) and discuss how the assumptions reflect this norm.

Discuss how these assumptions operate in your cultural situation. How are you affected by cultural assumptions about the "norm"?

Our founding fathers carved this great state out of the wilderness.
Mrs. Imoto looks remarkably good for her age.
Fashion Tights are available in black, suntan, and flesh color.
Someday I intend to visit the third world.
We need more manpower.
Our facilities all provide handicapped access.
I'm just a person.
The network is down again. We'd better get Kevin in here to do his voodoo on it.
Our boys were having a rough time of it, and the black regiment was, too.
How Neandertal man existed for so long is a mystery. He must have had the ability
    to adapt to his environment.
I see she forgot to sign her time sheet. She's acting a little blond today.
Mitochondrial DNA testing should help us determine when our race split off from the
    lower creatures.
Confined to a wheelchair, Mr. Garcia still manages to live a productive life.
Pat really went on the warpath when the budget figures came out.
I won't be associated with you and your pagan behaviors!
The Academy now admits women and other minorities.
We have a beautiful daycare center where women can leave their children while
    they work.
See if you can Jew him down to $50.
Personally, I don't think it's right that the foreign students come in here before term
    and buy up all the insignia bags. Our kids don't get a chance at them.
I completely forgot where I put my car keys. I must be having a senior moment.
Win a fabulous lovers' weekend in Hawaii! Prizes include a day at the spa for her
    and a relaxing game of golf for him.
That is not a very Christian attitude.
We welcome all guests, their wives, and their children.
May I speak to Mr. or Mrs. Williams?

Source: Janet Lockhart and Susan Shaw, *Writing for Change: Raising Awareness of Issues of Difference, Power, and Discrimination,* www.teachingtolerance.org.

■ LEARNING ACTIVITY: COMBATING HATE

Many web pages provide valuable information about hate, hate crimes, and hate groups in the United States. Go to the Southern Poverty Law Center's homepage at *www.splcenter.org*. Click on "Intelligence Project" and then on "Hate Incidents." Put in your state to see a list of hate crimes where you live. You may also want to visit these websites as well: *www.wiesenthal.com*, *www.adl.org*, *www.stopthehate.org*, *www.hrc .org*, and *www.hatewatch.org*. Using information from these sites, make a list of ways you can help stop hate.

mass media, the military, and sports. Usually patterns of rules and practices implicit in major societal institutions have a historical component and reflect political, military, legal, and socio-economic decisions made over decades and centuries. Although institutions are intended to meet the needs of society generally, or people in particular, they meet some people's needs better than others. These social organizations are central in creating systems of inequality and privilege because they pattern and structure differences among women in relatively organized ways. Institutions are important channels for the perpetuation of what Hill Collins calls "structures of domination and subordination."

Marilyn Frye focuses on the institutional aspect of systems of inequality and privilege in her article "Oppression." She emphasizes that people who suffer under systems of inequality are oppressed by these systems. Frye goes on to explain the difference between being oppressed and being limited and writes that a fundamental aspect of oppression is the double bind: All potential options have limitations. She uses the metaphor of a birdcage to explain the networks of related barriers that function in systems of oppression. One wire might be like an individual-level prejudice; a bird could just move around it and escape. But a birdcage involves patterns of wires, systematically arranged so that escape is thwarted. The wires of the cage symbolically become institutionalized into a system of oppression.

Institutions encourage the channeling of various systems of gendered inequality to all aspects of women's lives. In terms of the patterning of resources and practices, three institutional functions support systems of inequality and privilege. First, institutions assign various roles to women and men and are also places of employment where people perform gendered work. Educational institutions, for example, employ a considerable number of women. However, as the prestige of the teaching position increases, the number of White males in these positions increases, along with higher salaries. Also, it is very difficult for openly lesbian teachers to find employment in schools, and many states are attempting to pass laws preventing lesbians and gay men from teaching in state-funded educational establishments.

Second, institutions distribute resources and extend privileges differentially to different groups. Sports are a good example of this. As an institution, athletics has traditionally been male dominated. Men's sports are more highly valued than women's sports and are a major focus for sports entertainment. Compared to men's professional sports, women's are grossly underrepresented. Despite Title IX of the 1972 Educational Amendments Act, which barred discrimination in education, many colleges still are not in compliance and spend considerably more money on men's sports than on women's. Female athletes on some campuses complain that men receive better practice times in shared gymnasiums and more

HISTORICAL MOMENT:
WOMEN OF COLOR FEMINISM

Acutely aware of the intersections of gender, race, sexual orientation, and social class were women of color who daily experienced the material realities of the confluence of oppressions. From the beginning of the women's movement, women of color participated actively, although their specific concerns were often overlooked by some of the middle-class White women in the movement. In the early 1970s, women of color spoke out about their experiences of racism, sexism, and heterosexism. Barbara Smith cofounded the Combahee River Collective, a Black feminist group that confronted racism and homophobia in the women's, gay, and Black movements. The Collective took its name from a river in South Carolina where Harriet Tubman led a military action that freed hundreds of slaves.

In the late 1970s, Smith joined forces with Cherríe Moraga to found Kitchen Table/ Women of Color Press when Moraga and Gloria Anzaldua could not find a publisher for *This Bridge Called My Back: Writings by Radical Women of Color*. Kitchen Table/ Women of Color Press was the first independent press to publish exclusively works by feminists of color. *This Bridge Called My Back* won an American Book Award from the Columbus Foundation.

In 1983 poet and novelist Alice Walker coined the term *womanism* to describe Black feminism in contrast to *feminism* which has generally been associated with White women. Walker situates womanists in a long line of Black women who have struggled for social change and liberation. Womanists are, in her words, "outrageous, audacious, courageous, and willful, responsible, in charge, serious." They love Black women's culture, Black women's beauty, and themselves.

up-to-date equipment. And, within women's sports, some are more "White" than others. Examples that immediately come to mind are gymnastics, ice skating, equestrian sports, tennis, and golf (all relatively expensive sports). In addition, most women's sports—outside of basketball, volleyball, and track—are dominated by White women. In this way, sports and athletics are an example of an institution where resources are inequitably distributed.

Another blatant example of inequitable distribution concerns the economic system. Other than inherited wealth, the major way our economic system distributes resources is in terms of remuneration for the work that we do. Women tend to work in jobs that are heavily occupied by women; examples include clerical work, service and retail sales, and semiprofessional occupations like teaching and nursing. These jobs are undervalued in our society, contributing to the fact that a woman's average salary generally for all occupations is about 77 percent of a man's wage. Some women work under deplorable conditions at minimum wage levels; some work with hazardous chemicals or have to breathe secondhand smoke throughout their workday. Old women and women of color own a tiny percentage of the wealth in this society—another example of the inequitable distribution of resources.

Third, major institutions in society are interconnected and work to support and maintain one another. Often this means that personnel are shared among major institutions; more likely it means that these institutions mutually support one another in terms of the ways they fulfill (or deny) the needs of people in society. For example, close ties to economic institutions include the military (through the military-industrial complex), the government (corporate leaders often have official positions in government and rely on legislative loopholes and taxation systems to maintain corporate profits), health and medicine (with important ties to pharmaceutical companies), the media (whose content is controlled in part by advertising), and sports (through corporate sponsorship).

STARK INTERSECTIONS: GENDER, RACE, CLASS, AND HIV/AIDS

"We must address power imbalances in every single policy, strategy, and programme related to prevention, treatment and care if we seriously want to tackle this global challenge. [Gender] equality is not simply a matter of justice or fairness. Gender inequality is fatal."
—*Noeleen Heyzer, UNIFEM*

Gender inequality is fuelling the HIV/AIDS epidemic: it deprives women of the ability to say no to risky practices, leads to coerced sex and sexual violence, keeps women uninformed about prevention, puts them last in line for care and life-saving treatment, and imposes an overwhelming burden for the care of the sick and dying. These fundamental threats to women's lives, health, and well-being are critical human rights issues—when women's human rights are not promoted, protected, and fulfilled, gender inequality is the dangerous result. Guaranteeing women's human rights is an indispensable component of the international struggle to combat HIV/AIDS. To combat today's scourge, we must understand the multiple intersections between gender, racial and ethnic discrimination, and the epidemiology of HIV/AIDS.

This intersectional approach derives from the realization that discriminations based on gender, race, ethnicity, caste, and class are not discrete phenomena, but compound one another in almost all socio-economic circumstances.[1] Nine points are critical with regard to HIV/AIDS:

- Economic dependence and social subordination limit the ability of women and members of racial and ethnic minorities to demand safe and responsible sexual practices, including the use of condoms.
- Groups already subject to socio-economic discrimination—including racial and ethnic minorities, migrant populations, and refugees—rank high among those most vulnerable to HIV infection. In all these groups, women are hardest hit.
- Racial and ethnic identities operate in complicated ways to increase women's vulnerability to sex trafficking, a major factor in women's growing infection rates.
- The culture of silence that surrounds female sexuality in many societies prevents women and girls from accessing information and services for protection or treatment.
- In many countries, especially among racial and ethnic minorities, men receive preferential treatment in anti-retroviral therapies.
- Gender-based violence, both inside and outside the household, increases women's vulnerability to HIV/AIDS. HIV-positive women are frequently shunned by families and communities—and often subjected to further violence.
- This vulnerability mounts because of practices such as polygamy and wife-inheritance, as well as mistaken beliefs, such as that sex with a virgin can cure AIDS.

(continued)

- Because women are primarily responsible for care-giving, caring for people with HIV/AIDS typically falls to widows and grandmothers or older girl children. Care-giving responsibilities increase as health and social services decrease and increasingly privatized services require a higher proportion of household income.
- Because women often care for communities as well as families, their illness or absorption in sheer survival activities weakens the vital informal support systems on which poor and marginalized communities depend, deepening and perpetuating poverty.[2]

These intersections are more alarming in light of the gender dimensions of HIV/AIDS:[3]

- Worldwide, of the 17.5 million adults who have died of the disease, 9 million have been women. Approximately 47 percent of all new adult infections afflict women.
- In Sub-Saharan Africa, 55 percent of HIV-positive adults are women. In Mozambique, HIV infection is twice as prevalent among girls as boys.[4]
- Of the 1.3 million cases in Eastern Europe and Central Asia reported in 2000, at least half are estimated to be female.
- In parts of Latin America and the Caribbean, the proportion has reached 45 percent, a rapidly rising figure.

Moreover, these statistics represent underestimations due to the personal reluctance to report the disease as well as government reluctance to acknowledge its extent. In addition, medical studies often do not disaggregate data according to race and gender, nor do they examine the specific health issues affecting women from racial and ethnic minorities or indigenous women as a matter of course. Thus, they may fail to uncover medical problems specific to particular groups of women.[5]

[1] For discussion of the concept of intersectionality, see *Gender and Racial Discrimination: Report of the Expert Group Meeting*, November 2000, Zagreb. UN Division for the Advancement of Women, 2001.
[2] Mercedes González de la Rocha and Alejandro Grinspun, "Private Adjustments: Household, Crisis and Work," in Grinspun, ed., *Choices for the Poor: Lessons from National Poverty Strategies*. New York: UNDP, 2001.
[3] Unless otherwise noted, statistics are taken from the UNAIDS *AIDS Epidemic Update*, December, 2000 or the UNAIDS *Report on the Global HIV Epidemic*, June, 2000.
[4] Dr. Pascoal Macumbi, prime minister of Mozambique, quoted in *Conference News Daily*, UN Special Session on HIV/AIDS, June 25, 2001.
[5] UNIFEM, 2000. "Integrating Gender into the Third World Conference against Racism, Racial Discrimination, Xenophobia and Related Intolerance." Background Paper prepared for the *Gender and Racial Discrimination: Report of the Expert Group Meeting*, November 2000, Zagreb, Croatia.
Source: www.undp.org/unifem/hrights.htm.

IDEOLOGY AND LANGUAGE

In addition to distributing resources and practices, institutions produce messages that shape our understandings of gender. Importantly, ideas and values (like stereotypes and jokes) or sets of beliefs (often called ideologies) provide the rationale for injustice. Hill Collins calls this the "symbolic dimension" of systems of domination and subordination. For example, the media often reinforce stereotypes about women like dumb blondes, passive Asian Americans, or pushy African Americans. Another example of gendered messages comes from the institution of religion. This institution is especially powerful because it implies the notion of divine sanction. Traditional religious texts tell stories (for example, Eve's behavior that led to the banishment from the Garden of Eden or the chaste role of the Virgin Mary) that convey important messages about moral thought and behavior as well as women's place in society. These messages tend to be strongly gendered and often support different behaviors for women and men. A central code of much religious teaching is that women should be subordinate to men in their spiritual and everyday lives.

An example of an ideology that is supported by various institutions and that affects women's lives is the bootstrap myth concerning economic success. Propagated by the economic system, it paints economic success as a result of hard work and ambition. All people, if properly motivated and willing to work hard, can pull themselves up by their bootstraps. Given this set of ideas, those individuals who are not able to provide for their families must have deficiencies. Perhaps they were unmotivated, did not work hard enough, or were not smart enough. Such ideas encourage blaming the poor for their poverty rather than understanding the wider societal forces that shape people's existence and maintain classism. Notice that a particular ideology need not be supported unanimously for it to influence society. Many would disagree vehemently with the bootstrap myth; yet, still, this is a key part of the ideology of capitalist countries. In this way, institutions perpetuate sets of ideas and practices and use them to justify the institution.

Classism is also addressed in the article by Donna Langston titled "Tired of Playing Monopoly?" Here she explains how class is not just about socio-economic status, that is, how much wealth you have access to or how much you earn. She writes,

> Class is also culture. As a result of the class you were born into and raised in, class is your understanding of the world and where you fit in; it's composed of ideas, attitudes, values, and language; class is how you think, feel, act, look, dress, talk, move, walk; class is what stores you shop at, restaurants you eat in; class is the schools you attend, the education you attain; class is the jobs you will work at throughout your adult life. Class even determines when we marry and become mothers.

Stereotypes and ideologies that support systems of inequality involve prejudices. *Prejudice* means, literally, to prejudge and involves making premature judgments without adequate information or with inaccurate information. Often these ideas support systems of inequality and privilege because prejudice is often adopted when there is no other basis for understanding. For example, many White people have little contact with people of color, and many young people do not interact on an everyday basis with old people. As a result, there is a lack of accurate information, and stereotypes or images from television or the movies are used instead. This kind of ignorance and misinformation breeds prejudice. In "Something About the Subject Makes It Hard to Name," Gloria Yamato writes about different kinds of prejudice: aware/blatant, aware/covert, unaware/unintentional, and unaware/self-righteous. In this article she emphasizes that much prejudice comes from misinformation and is very often unintentional. She also notes that social norms against racism have pushed some racism underground.

Prejudices are *internalized* (assimilated, integrated, or incorporated into our thoughts and behavior) by all of us. If we are members of the target group, the group against whom the prejudice is aimed, it can lead to low self-esteem, self-loathing, and shame. Sadly, it can mean individuals are encouraged to believe they are not worthy of social justice and therefore are less likely to seek equality. Although members of target groups may internalize negative messages, members of nontarget groups, groups (often part of the mythical norm) against whom the prejudice is not aimed, also internalize these messages as well as messages about their own privilege. This can encourage or justify hostility against target groups.

ACTIVIST PROFILE: FANNIE LOU HAMER

She began life in Mississippi in 1917 as the granddaughter of slaves and the daughter of sharecroppers, but Fannie Lou Hamer was to become one of the most important leaders of the civil rights movement in the United States. Although Hamer became a sharecropper herself, by 1962 she'd had enough of the second-class life of the segregated South. She joined 17 other African Americans taking a bus to the county seat to register to vote. On the way home, they were stopped by police and arrested. After Hamer returned home, she was visited by the plantation owner, who told her that if she insisted on voting, she would have to get off his land, which she did that same day.

The next year, when Hamer joined other civil rights workers in challenging the "Whites only" policy at a bus terminal diner, she was arrested and jailed. The police ordered two other African American prisoners to beat her with a metal-spiked club. Hamer was blinded in one eye from the beating and suffered permanent kidney damage.

In 1964, Hamer helped organize the Mississippi Freedom Democratic Party (MFDP) to challenge the all-White Mississippi delegation to the Democratic Convention. Hamer spoke to the credentials committee of the convention, and although her live testimony was preempted by a presidential press conference, it was aired by national networks in its entirety later that evening. The MFDP and the credentials committee reached a compromise, giving voting and speaking rights to two MFDP delegates and seating the others as honored guests. Hamer responded, "We didn't come all this way for two seats when all of us is tired." In 1968 the Mississippi Democratic Party did seat an integrated delegation.

Throughout her life, Hamer continued to work for justice, supporting Head Start for Black schools and jobs for poor African Americans, opposing the Vietnam War, and helping to convene the National Women's Political Caucus in the 1970s.

Hamer died in 1977 and was buried in Mississippi. Her tombstone reads, "I am sick and tired of being sick and tired."

IDEAS FOR ACTIVISM

- Find out how your university ensures access for people with disabilities. If some structures on your campus are inaccessible, advocate with your administration to create accessibility.
- Plan a celebration of Black women during Black History Month.
- Find out what programs your university offers to recruit and retain students and faculty of color. If programs are not in place, advocate with your administration to develop such programs.
- Find out if your university's antidiscrimination policy includes sexual orientation as a protected classification, and find out if your university provides benefits for domestic partners. If not, advocate with your administration to include sexual orientation in its policy and/or to provide domestic partner benefits.

Internalizing oppression means that we not only police ourselves, but also police one another, encouraging compliance with institutions that may oppress. When individuals direct the resentment and anger they have about their situation onto those who are of equal or of lesser status, this process is called *horizontal hostility.* As a strategy, it is similar to the military notion of "divide and conquer" where groups are encouraged to fight with one another in order to avoid alliances that might collaboratively overpower an enemy. Babba Copper remarks on this horizontal conflict when she writes about woman-to-woman ageism and the ways women compete "for the crumbs of social power."

Language, or the symbolic means by which we communicate, is a central aspect of what makes us human. It is an incredibly sophisticated process of symbols that we learn at an early age and mostly take for granted unless we are confronted with trying to communicate in a language not our own. Because language allows us not only to name the objects of our experience but also to typify them (experience them as similar to something of a similar type), it creates as well as reflects our reality. It shapes as well as expresses thought. And because language helps us sort and anticipate our experiences, it has a primary influence on our lives.

The English language is structured in such a way that it maintains sexism and racism. Lois Keith's poem "Tomorrow I'm Going to Rewrite the English Language" suggests how the English language helps shape our understandings of gender and limits women's options for self-definition. This article encourages us to think about the ways that language shapes our reality and helps structure the everyday realities of women's lives. When you grow up knowing 20 different words synonymous with *slut,* you learn something powerful about gender. The English language also maintains racism. For example:

> Some may blackly (angrily) accuse me of trying to blacken (defame) the English language, to give it a black eye (a mark of shame) by writing such black words (hostile). They may denigrate (to cast aspersions; to darken) me by accusing me of being black hearted (malevolent), of having a black outlook (pessimistic, dismal) on life, of being a blackguard (scoundrel)—which will certainly be a black mark (detrimental act) against me. Some may black-brow (scowl) at me and hope that a black cat crosses in front of me because of this black deed. I may become a black sheep (one who causes shame or embarrassment because of deviation

CHALLENGING THE PSEUDOGENERIC "MAN"

Examine the following phrases that use male nouns as "generic." Describe the mental image created for you by each phrase. Do you see yourself and people like you in the images?

Next, choose a term representing a group of people of a specific age, religion, class, or ethnicity, and substitute that term for the male noun (example: "childkind"). Does use of the new, specific term sound incongruous or unusual? Why?

Describe the mental images created by using the substitute terms. Do you see yourself and people like you in the images?

Finally, suggest a gender-free, inclusive term for each (ex: for "mankind," "humanity" or "people").

For the benefit of all mankind
"All men are created equal"
May the best man win
Prehistoric man
Man the pumps!
The first manned mission to Mars
Chairman of the Board
We need more manpower
Not fit for man or beast
The relationship between men and machines
Man's best friend
"To boldly go where no man has gone before"
Man of the Year
"Peace on Earth, goodwill toward men"
The founding fathers
"Crown thy good with brotherhood"
"Friends, Romans, countrymen; lend me your ears"

Source: Janet Lockhart and Susan M. Shaw, *Writing for Change: Raising Awareness of Difference, Power, and Discrimination,* www.teachingtolerance.org.

from the expected standards), who will be black-balled (ostracized) by being placed on a black list (list of undesirables) in an attempt to blackmail (to force or coerce into a particular action) me to retract my words. . . . The preceding is of course a white lie (not intended to cause harm), meant only to illustrate some examples of racist terminology in the English language.*

In this chapter we focus on the social construction of difference and how systems of inequality and privilege based upon these differences function and are maintained. A next

---

* Robert B. Moore, "Racism in the English Language." Excerpted in *Experiencing Race, Class, and Gender in the U.S.,* Virginia Cyrus, ed. (Mountain View, CA: Mayfield, 1993), p. 152.

step is to consider how to effect change to improve the conditions of women's lives. Several of the readings focus on this. In particular, Peggy McIntosh suggests we recognize our privilege and work on our internalized prejudices and privileges. Babba Copper writes about identifying and acknowledging sources of inequality and specifically the ways we have been taught to hate old women and deny them power. She hopes for alliances across our differences. Patricia Hill Collins echoes this and writes about the necessity of developing empathy for others as well as creating coalitions around common causes. Suzanne Pharr points out the homophobia of the women's movement and its failure to achieve solidarity when the rights of all women are not recognized. Donna Langston presents ways to challenge classism that involve confronting the behavior in ourselves, making demands on behalf of poor communities, and learning from the skills and strengths of working-class people. Similarly, Gloria Yamato has good ideas for Whites who want to be allies to people of color. The message in all these articles is the need to recognize difference, to understand how the meanings associated with difference get translated into privilege and inequality, and to celebrate those differences through coalitions and other expressions of personal and social concern.

READING 8

Toward a New Vision
Race, Class, and Gender as Categories of Analysis and Connection

Patricia Hill Collins

The true focus of revolutionary change is never merely the oppressive situations which we seek to escape, but that piece of the oppressor which is planted deep within each of us.

—Audre Lorde, *Sister Outsider*, 123

Audre Lorde's statement raises a troublesome issue for scholars and activists working for social change. While many of us have little difficulty assessing our own victimization within some major system of oppression, whether it be by race, social class, religion, sexual orientation, ethnicity, age or gender, we typically fail to see how our thoughts and actions uphold someone else's subordination. Thus, white feminists routinely point with confidence to their oppression as women but resist seeing how much their white skin privileges them. African-Americans who possess eloquent analyses of racism often persist in viewing poor White women as symbols of white power. The radical left fares little better. "If only people of color and women could see their true class interests," they argue, "class solidarity would eliminate racism and sexism." In essence, each group identifies the type of oppression with which it feels most comfortable as being fundamental and classifies all other types as being of lesser importance.

Oppression is full of such contradictions. Errors in political judgment that we make concerning how we teach our courses, what we tell our children, and which organizations are worthy of our time, talents and financial support flow smoothly from errors in theoretical analysis about the nature of oppression and activism. Once we realize that there are few pure victims or oppressors, and that each one of us derives varying amounts of penalty and privilege from the multiple systems of oppression that frame our lives, then we will be in a position to see the need for new ways of thought and action.

. . .

[This discussion] addresses this need for new patterns of thought and action. I focus on two basic questions. First, how can we reconceptualize race, class and gender as categories of analysis? Second, how can we transcend the barriers created by our experiences with race, class and gender oppression in order to build the types of coalitions essential for social exchange? To address these question[s] I contend that we must acquire both new theories of how race, class and gender have shaped the experiences not just of women of color, but of all groups. Moreover, we must see the connections between these categories of analysis and the personal issues in our everyday lives, particularly our scholarship, our teaching and our relationships with our colleagues and students. As Audre Lorde points out, change starts with self, and relationships that we have with those around us must always be the primary site for social change.

How Can We Reconceptualize Race, Class and Gender as Categories of Analysis?

To me, we must shift our discourse away from additive analyses of oppression (Spelman 1982; Collins 1989). Such approaches are typically based on two key premises. First, they depend on either/or, dichotomous thinking. Persons, things and ideas are conceptualized in terms of their opposites. For example, Black/White, man/woman, thought/feeling, and fact/opinion are defined in oppositional terms. Thought and feeling are not seen as two different and interconnected ways of approaching truth that can coexist in scholarship and teaching. Instead, feeling is defined as antithetical to reason, as its opposite. In spite of the fact that we all have "both/and" identities, (I am both a college professor and a mother—I don't stop being a mother when I drop my child off at school, or forget everything I learned while scrubbing the toilet), we persist in trying to classify each other in either/or categories. I live each day as an African-American woman—a race/gender specific experience. And I am not alone. Everyone has a race/gender/class specific identity. Either/or, dichotomous thinking is especially troublesome when applied to theories of oppression because every individual must be classified as being either oppressed or not oppressed. The both/and position of simultaneously being oppressed and oppressor becomes conceptually impossible.

A second premise of additive analyses of oppression is that these dichotomous differences must be ranked. One side of the dichotomy is typically labeled dominant and the other subordinate. Thus, Whites rule Blacks, men are deemed superior to women, and reason is seen as being preferable to emotion. Applying this premise to discussions of oppression leads to the assumption that oppression can be quantified, and that some groups are oppressed more than others. I am frequently asked, "Which has been most oppressive to you, your status as a Black person or your status as a woman?" What I am really being asked to do is divide myself into little boxes and rank my various statuses. If I experience oppression as a both/and phenomenon, why should I analyze it any differently?

Additive analyses of oppression rest squarely on the twin pillars of either/or thinking and the necessity to quantify and rank all relationships in order to know where one stands. Such approaches typically see African-American women as being more oppressed than everyone else because the majority of Black women experience the negative effects of race, class and gender oppression simultaneously. In essence, if you add together separate oppressions, you are left with a grand oppression greater than the sum of its parts.

I am not denying that specific groups experience oppression more harshly than others—lynching is certainly objectively worse than being held up as a sex object. But we must be careful not to confuse this issue of the saliency of one type of oppression in people's lives with a theoretical stance positing the interlocking nature of oppression. Race, class and gender may all structure a situation but may not be equally visible and/or important in people's self-definitions. In certain contexts, such as the antebellum American South and contemporary South America, racial oppression is more visibly salient, while in other contexts, such as Haiti, El Salvador and Nicaragua, social class oppression may be more apparent. For middle class White women, gender may assume experiential primacy unavailable to poor Hispanic women struggling with the ongoing issues of low paid jobs and the frustrations of the welfare bureaucracy. This recognition that one category may have salience over another for a given time and place does not minimize the theoretical importance of assuming that race, class and gender as categories of analysis structure all relationships.

In order to move toward new visions of what oppression is, I think that we need to ask new questions. How are relationships of domination and subordination structured and maintained in the American political economy? How do race, class and gender function as parallel and interlocking systems that shape this basic relationship of domination and subordination? Questions such as these promise to move us away from futile theoretical struggles concerned with ranking oppressions and towards analyses that assume race, class and gender are all present in any given setting, even if one appears more visible and salient than the others. Our task becomes redefined as one of reconceptualizing oppression by uncovering the connections among race, class and gender as categories of analysis.

1. Institutional Dimension of Oppression

Sandra Harding's contention that gender oppression is structured along three main dimensions—the institutional, the symbolic, and the individual—offers a useful model for a more comprehensive analysis encompassing race, class and gender oppression (Harding 1986). Systemic relationships of domination and subordination structured through social institutions such as schools, businesses, hospitals, the work place, and government agencies represent the institutional dimension of oppression. Racism, sexism and elitism all have concrete institutional locations. Even though the workings of the institutional dimension of oppression are often obscured with ideologies claiming equality of opportunity, in actuality, race, class and gender place Asian-American women, Native American men, White men, African-American women, and other groups in distinct institutional niches with varying degrees of penalty and privilege.

Even though I realize that many . . . would not share this assumption, let us assume that the institutions of American society discriminate, whether by design or by accident. While many of us are familiar with how race, gender and class operate separately to structure inequality, I want to focus on how these three systems interlock in structuring the institutional dimension of oppression. To get at the interlocking nature of race, class and gender, I want you to think about the antebellum plantation as a guiding metaphor for a variety of American social institutions. Even though slavery is typically analyzed as a racist institution, and occasionally as a class institution, I suggest that slavery was a race, class, gender specific institution. Removing any one piece from our analysis diminishes our understanding of the true nature of relations of domination and subordination under slavery.

. . .

A brief analysis of key American social institutions most controlled by elite White men should convince us of the interlocking nature of race, class and gender in structuring the institutional dimension of oppression. For example, if you are from an American college or university, is your campus a modern plantation? Who controls your university's political economy? Are elite White men over represented among the upper administrators and trustees controlling your university's finances and policies? Are elite White men being joined by growing numbers of elite White women helpmates? What kinds of people are in your classrooms grooming the next generation who will occupy these and other decision-making positions? Who are the support staff that produce the mass mailings, order the supplies, fix the leaky pipes? Do African-Americans, Hispanics or other people of color form the majority of the invisible workers who feed you, wash your dishes, and clean up your offices and libraries after everyone else has gone home?

If your college is anything like mine, you know the answers to these questions. You may be affiliated with an institution that has Hispanic women as vice-presidents for finance, or substantial numbers of Black men among the faculty. If so, you are fortunate. Much more typical are colleges where a modified version of the plantation as a metaphor for the institutional dimension of oppression survives.

2. The Symbolic Dimension of Oppression

Widespread, societally-sanctioned ideologies used to justify relations of domination and subordination comprise the symbolic dimension of oppression. Central to this process is the use of stereotypical or controlling images of diverse race, class and gender groups. In order to assess the power of this dimension of oppression, I want you to make a list, either on paper or in your head, of "masculine" and "feminine" characteristics. If your list is anything like that compiled by most people, it reflects some variation of the following:

Masculine	*Feminine*
aggressive	passive
leader	follower
rational	emotional
strong	weak
intellectual	physical

Not only does this list reflect either/or dichotomous thinking and the need to rank both sides of the dichotomy, but ask yourself exactly which men and women you had in mind when compiling these characteristics. This list applies almost exclusively to middle class White men and women. The allegedly "masculine" qualities that you probably listed are only acceptable when exhibited by elite White men, or when used by Black and Hispanic men against each other or against women of color. Aggressive Black and Hispanic men are seen as dangerous, not powerful, and are often penalized when they exhibit any of the allegedly "masculine" characteristics. Working class and poor White men fare slightly better and are also denied the allegedly "masculine" symbols of leadership, intellectual competence, and human rationality. Women of color and working class and poor White women are also not represented on this list, for they have never had the luxury of being "ladies." What appear to be universal categories representing all men and women instead are unmasked as being applicable to only a small group.

It is important to see how the symbolic images applied to different race, class and gender groups interact in maintaining systems of domination and subordination. If I were to ask you to repeat the same assignment, only this time, by making separate lists for Black men, Black women, Hispanic women and Hispanic men, I suspect that your gender symbolism would be quite different. In comparing all of the lists, you might begin to see the interdependence of symbols applied to all groups. For example, the elevated images of White womanhood need devalued images of Black womanhood in order to maintain credibility.

. . .

Assuming that everyone is affected differently by the same interlocking set of symbolic images allows us to move forward toward new analyses. Women of color and White women have different relationships to White male authority and this difference explains the distinct gender symbolism applied to both groups. Black women encounter controlling images such as the mammy, the matriarch, the mule and the whore, that encourage others to reject us as fully human people. Ironically, the negative nature of these images simultaneously encourages us to reject them. In contrast, White women are offered seductive images, those that promise to reward them for supporting the status quo. And yet seductive images can be equally controlling. Consider, for example, the views of Nancy White, a 73-year old Black woman, concerning images of rejection and seduction:

My mother used to say that the black woman is the white man's mule and the white woman is his dog. Now, she said that to say this: we do the heavy work and get beat whether we do it well or not. But the white woman is closer to the master and he pats

them on the head and lets them sleep in the house, but he ain't gon' treat neither one like he was dealing with a person. (Gwaltney, 148)

Both sets of images stimulate particular political stances. By broadening the analysis beyond the confines of race, we can see the varying levels of rejection and seduction available to each of us due to our race, class and gender identity. Each of us lives with an allotted portion of institutional privilege and penalty, and with varying levels of rejection and seduction inherent in the symbolic images applied to us. This is the context in which we make our choices. Taken together, the institutional and symbolic dimensions of oppression create a structural backdrop against which all of us live our lives.

3. The Individual Dimension of Oppression

Whether we benefit or not, we all live within institutions that reproduce race, class and gender oppression. Even if we never have any contact with members of other race, class and gender groups, we all encounter images of these groups and are exposed to the symbolic meanings attached to those images. On this dimension of oppression, our individual biographies vary tremendously. As a result of our institutional and symbolic statuses, all of our choices become political acts.

Each of us must come to terms with the multiple ways in which race, class and gender as categories of analysis frame our individual biographies. I have lived my entire life as an African-American woman from a working class family and this basic fact has had a profound impact on my personal biography. Imagine how different your life might be if you had been born Black, or White, or poor, or of a different race/class/gender group than the one with which you are most familiar. The institutional treatment you would have received and the symbolic meanings attached to your very existence might differ dramatically from what you now consider to be natural, normal and part of everyday life. You might be the same, but your personal biography might have been quite different.

I believe that each of us carries around the cumulative effect of our lives within multiple structures of oppression. If you want to see how much you have been affected by this whole thing, I ask you one simple question—who are your close friends? Who are the people with whom you can share your hopes, dreams, vulnerabilities, fears and victories? Do they look like you? If they are all the same, circumstance may be the cause. For the first seven years of my life I saw only low income Black people. My friends from those years reflected the composition of my community. But now that I am an adult, can the defense of circumstance explain the patterns of people that I trust as my friends and colleagues? When given other alternatives, if my friends and colleagues reflect the homogeneity of one race, class and gender group, then these categories of analysis have indeed become barriers to connection.

I am not suggesting that people are doomed to follow the paths laid out for them by race, class and gender as categories of analysis. While these three structures certainly frame my opportunity structure, I as an individual always have the choice of accepting things as they are, or trying to change them. As Nikki Giovanni points out, "we've got to live in the real world. If we don't like the world we're living in, change it. And if we can't change it, we change ourselves. We can do something" (Tate 1983, 68). While a piece of the oppressor may be planted deep within each of us, we each have the choice of accepting that piece or challenging it as part of the "true focus of revolutionary change."

How Can We Transcend the Barriers Created by Our Experiences with Race, Class and Gender Oppression in Order to Build the Types of Coalitions Essential for Social Change?

Reconceptualizing oppression and seeing the barriers created by race, class and gender as interlocking categories of analysis is a vital first step. But we must transcend these barriers by moving toward race, class and gender as categories of connection, by building relationships and coalitions that will bring about so-

cial change. What are some of the issues involved in doing this?

1. Differences in Power and Privilege

First, we must recognize that our differing experiences with oppression create problems in the relationships among us. Each of us lives within a system that vests us with varying levels of power and privilege. These differences in power, whether structured along axes of race, class, gender, age or sexual orientation, frame our relationships. African-American writer June Jordan describes her discomfort on a Caribbean vacation with Olive, the Black woman who cleaned her room:

> . . . even though both "Olive" and "I" live inside a conflict neither one of us created, and even though both of us therefore hurt inside that conflict, I may be one of the monsters she needs to eliminate from her universe and, in a sense, she may be one of the monsters in mine (1985, 47).

Differences in power constrain our ability to connect with one another even when we think we are engaged in dialogue across differences. . . .

In extreme cases, members of privileged groups can erase the very presence of the less privileged. When I first moved to Cincinnati, my family and I went on a picnic at a local park. Picnicking next to us was a family of White Appalachians. When I went to push my daughter on the swings, several of the children came over. They had missing, yellowed and broken teeth, they wore old clothing and their poverty was evident. I was shocked. Growing up in a large eastern city, I had never seen such awful poverty among Whites. The segregated neighborhoods in which I grew up made White poverty all but invisible. More importantly, the privileges attached to my newly acquired social class position allowed me to ignore and minimize the poverty among Whites that I did encounter. My reactions to those children made me realize how confining phrases such as "well, at least they're not Black," had become for me. In learning to grant human subjectivity to the Black victims of poverty, I had simultaneously learned to demand White victims of poverty. By applying categories of race to the objective conditions confronting me, I was quantifying and ranking oppressions and missing the very real suffering which, in fact, is the real issue.

One common pattern of relationships across differences in power is one that I label "voyeurism." From the perspective of the privileged, the lives of people of color, of the poor, and of women are interesting for their entertainment value. The privileged become voyeurs, passive onlookers who do not relate to the less powerful, but who are interested in seeing how the "different" live. Over the years, I have heard numerous African-American students complain about professors who never call on them except when a so-called Black issue is being discussed. The students' interest in discussing race or qualifications for doing so appear unimportant to the professor's efforts to use Black students' experiences as stories to make the material come alive for the White student audience. Asking Black students to perform on cue and provide a Black experience for their White classmates can be seen as voyeurism at its worst.

Members of subordinate groups do not willingly participate in such exchanges but often do so because members of dominant groups control the institutional and symbolic apparatuses of oppression. Racial/ethnic groups, women, and the poor have never had the luxury of being voyeurs of the lives of the privileged. Our ability to survive in hostile settings has hinged on our ability to learn intricate details about the behavior and world view of the powerful and adjust our behavior accordingly. I need only point to the difference in perception of those men and women in abusive relationships. Where men can view their girlfriends and wives as sex objects, helpmates and a collection of stereotyped categories of voyeurism—women must be attuned to every nuance of their partners' behavior. Are women "naturally" better in relating to people with more power than themselves, or have circumstances mandated that men and women develop different skills? . . .

Coming from a tradition where most relationships across difference are squarely rooted in relations of domination and subordination, we have much less experience relating to people as different

but equal. The classroom is potentially one powerful and safe space where dialogues among individuals of unequal power relationships can occur. . . .

2. Coalitions Around Common Causes

A second issue in building relationships and coalitions essential for social change concerns knowing the real reasons for coalition. Just what brings people together? One powerful catalyst fostering group solidarity is the presence of a common enemy. African-American, Hispanic, Asian-American, and women's studies all share the common intellectual heritage of challenging what passes for certified knowledge in the academy. But politically expedient relationships and coalitions like these are fragile because, as June Jordan points out:

> It occurs to me that much organizational grief could be avoided if people understood that partnership in misery does not necessarily provide for partnership for change: When we get the monsters off our backs all of us may want to run in very different directions (1985, 47).

Sharing a common cause assists individuals and groups in maintaining relationships that transcend their differences. Building effective coalitions involves struggling to hear one another and developing empathy for each other's points of view. The coalitions that I have been involved in that lasted and that worked have been those where commitment to a specific issue mandated collaboration as the best strategy for addressing the issue at hand.

. . .

None of us alone has a comprehensive vision of how race, class and gender operate as categories of analysis or how they might be used as categories of connection. Our personal biographies offer us partial views. Few of us can manage to study race, class and gender simultaneously. Instead, we each know more about some dimensions of this larger story and less about others. . . . Just as the members of the school had special skills to offer to the task of building the school, we have areas of specialization and expertise, whether scholarly, theoretical, pedagogical or within areas of race, class or gender. We do not all have to do the same thing in the same way. Instead, we must support each other's efforts, realizing that they are all part of the larger enterprise of bringing about social change.

3. Building Empathy

A third issue involved in building the types of relationships and coalitions essential for social change concerns the issue of individual accountability. Race, class and gender oppression form the structural backdrop against which we frame our relationship —these are the forces that encourage us to substitute voyeurism . . . for fully human relationships. But while we may not have created this situation, we are each responsible for making individual, personal choices concerning which elements of race, class and gender oppression we will accept and which we will work to change.

One essential component of this accountability involves developing empathy for the experiences of individuals and groups different than ourselves. Empathy begins with taking an interest in the facts of other people['s] lives, both as individuals and as groups. If you care about me, you should want to know not only the details of my personal biography but a sense of how race, class and gender as categories of analysis created the institutional and symbolic backdrop for my personal biography. How can you hope to assess my character without knowing the details of the circumstances I face?

Moreover, by taking a theoretical stance that we have all been affected by race, class and gender as categories of analysis that have structured our treatment, we open up possibilities for using those same constructs as categories of connection in building empathy. For example, I have a good White woman friend with whom I share common interests and beliefs. But we know that our racial differences have provided us with different experiences. So we talk about them. We do not assume that because I am Black, race has only affected me and not her or that because I am a Black woman, race neutralizes the effect of gender in my life while accenting it in hers.

We take those same categories of analysis that have created cleavages in our lives, in this case, categories of race and gender, and use them as categories of connection in building empathy for each other's experiences.

Finding common causes and building empathy is difficult, no matter which side of privilege we inhabit. Building empathy from the dominant side of privilege is difficult, simply because individuals from privileged backgrounds are not encouraged to do so. For example, in order for those of you who are White to develop empathy for the experiences of people of color, you must grapple with how your white skin has privileged you. This is difficult to do, because it not only entails the intellectual process of seeing how whiteness is elevated in institutions and symbols, but it also involves the often painful process of seeing how your whiteness has shaped your personal biography. Intellectual stances against the institutional and symbolic dimensions of racism are generally easier to maintain than sustained self-reflection about how racism has shaped all of our individual biographies. Were and are your fathers, uncles, and grandfathers really more capable than mine, or can their accomplishments be explained in part by the racism members of my family experienced? Did your mothers stand silently by and watch all this happen? More importantly, how have they passed on the benefits of their whiteness to you?

These are difficult questions, and I have tremendous respect for my colleagues and students who are trying to answer them. Since there is no compelling reason to examine the source and meaning of one's own privilege, I know that those who do so have freely chosen this stance. They are making conscious efforts to root out the piece of the oppressor planted within them. To me, they are entitled to the support of people of color in their efforts. Men who declare themselves feminists, members of the middle class who ally themselves with antipoverty struggles, heterosexuals who support gays and lesbians, are all trying to grow, and their efforts place them far ahead of the majority who never think of engaging in such important struggles.

Building empathy from the subordinate side of privilege is also difficult, but for different reasons.

Members of subordinate groups are understandably reluctant to abandon a basic mistrust of members of powerful groups because this basic mistrust has traditionally been central to their survival. As a Black woman, it would be foolish for me to assume that White women, or Black men, or White men or any other group with a history of exploiting African-American women have my best interests at heart. These groups enjoy varying amounts of privilege over me and therefore I must carefully watch them and be prepared for a relation of domination and subordination.

Like the privileged, members of subordinate groups must also work toward replacing judgments by category with new ways of thinking and acting. Refusing to do so stifles prospects for effective coalition and social change. Let me use another example from my own experiences. When I was an undergraduate, I had little time or patience for the theorizing of the privileged. My initial years at a private, elite institution were difficult, not because the course work was challenging (it was, but that wasn't what distracted me) or because I had to work while my classmates lived on family allowances (I was used to work). The adjustment was difficult because I was surrounded by so many people who took their privilege for granted. Most of them felt entitled to their wealth. That astounded me.

I remember one incident of watching a White woman down the hall in my dormitory try to pick out which sweater to wear. The sweaters were piled up on her bed in all the colors of the rainbow, sweater after sweater. She asked my advice in a way that let me know that choosing a sweater was one of the most important decisions she had to make on a daily basis. Standing knee-deep in her sweaters, I realized how different our lives were. She did not have to worry about maintaining a solid academic average so that she could receive financial aid. Because she was in the majority, she was not treated as a representative of her race. She did not have to consider how her classroom comments or basic existence on campus contributed to the treatment her group would receive. Her allowance protected her from having

to work, so she was free to spend her time studying, partying, or in her case, worrying about which sweater to wear. The degree of inequality in our lives and her unquestioned sense of entitlement concerning that inequality offended me. For a while, I categorized all affluent White women as being superficial, arrogant, overly concerned with material possessions, and part of my problem. But had I continued to classify people in this way, I would have missed out on making some very good friends whose discomfort with their inherited or acquired social class privileges pushed them to examine their position.

Since I opened with the words of Audre Lorde, it seems appropriate to close with another of her ideas. . . .

> Each of us is called upon to take a stand. So in these days ahead, as we examine ourselves and each other, our works, our fears, our differences, our sisterhood and survivals, I urge you to tackle what is most difficult for us all, self-scrutiny of our complacencies, the idea that since each of us believes she is on the side of right, she need not examine her position (1985).

I urge you to examine your position.

REFERENCES

Collins, Patricia Hill. 1989. "The Social Construction of Black Feminist Thought." *Signs*. Summer 1989.

Gwaltney, John Langston. 1980. *Drylongso: A Self-Portrait of Black America*. New York: Vintage.

Harding, Sandra. 1986. *The Science Question in Feminism*. Ithaca, New York: Cornell University Press.

Jordan, June. 1985. *On Call: Political Essays*. Boston: South End Press.

Lorde, Audre. 1984. *Sister Outsider*. Trumansberg, New York: The Crossing Press.

———. 1985 "Sisterhood and Survival." Keynote address, conference on the Black Woman Writer and the Diaspora, Michigan State University.

Spelman, Elizabeth. 1982. "Theories of Race and Gender: The Erasure of Black Women." *Quest* 5: 36–32.

Tate, Claudia, ed. 1983. *Black Women Writers at Work*. New York: Continuum.

READING 9

Oppression

Marilyn Frye

It is a fundamental claim of feminism that women are oppressed. The word 'oppression' is a strong word. It repels and attracts. It is dangerous and dangerously fashionable and endangered. It is much misused, and sometimes not innocently.

The statement that women are oppressed is frequently met with the claim that men are oppressed too. We hear that oppressing is oppressive to those who oppress as well as to those they oppress. Some men cite as evidence of their oppression their much-advertised inability to cry. It is tough, we are told, to be masculine. When the stresses and frustrations of being a man are cited as evidence that oppressors are oppressed by their oppressing; the word 'oppression' is being stretched to meaninglessness; it is treated as though its scope includes any and all human experience of limitation or suffering, no matter the cause, degree or consequence. Once such usage has been put over on us, then if ever we deny that any person or group is oppressed, we seem to imply that we think they never suffer and have no feelings. We are accused of insensitivity; even of bigotry. For women, such accusation is particularly intimidating, since sensitivity is one of the few virtues that has been assigned to us. If we are found insensitive, we may fear we have no redeeming traits at all and perhaps are not real women. Thus are we silenced before we begin: the name of our situation drained of meaning and our guilt mechanisms tripped.

But this is nonsense. Human beings can be miserable without being oppressed, and it is perfectly consistent to deny that a person or group is oppressed without denying that they have feelings or that they suffer. . . .

The root of the word 'oppression' is the element 'press.' *The press of the crowd; pressed into military service; to press a pair of pants; printing press; press the button.* Presses are used to mold things or flatten them or reduce them in bulk, sometimes to reduce them by squeezing out the gasses or liquids in them. Something pressed is something caught between or among forces and barriers which are so related to each other that jointly they restrain, restrict or prevent the thing's motion or mobility. Mold. Immobilize. Reduce.

The mundane experience of the oppressed provides another clue. One of the most characteristic and ubiquitous features of the world as experienced by oppressed people is the double bind—situations in which options are reduced to a very few and all of them expose one to penalty, censure or deprivation. For example, it is often a requirement upon oppressed people that we smile and be cheerful. If we comply, we signal our docility and our acquiescence in our situation. We need not, then, be taken note of. We acquiesce in being made invisible, in our occupying no space. We participate in our own erasure. On the other hand, anything but the sunniest countenance exposes us to being perceived as mean, bitter, angry or dangerous. This means, at the least, that we may be found "difficult" or unpleasant to work with, which is enough to cost one one's livelihood; at worst, being seen as mean, bitter, angry or dangerous has been known to result in rape, arrest, beating and murder. One can only choose to risk one's preferred form and rate of annihilation.

Another example: It is common in the United States that women, especially younger women, are in a bind where neither sexual activity nor sexual inactivity is all right. If she is heterosexually active, a woman is open to censure and punishment for being loose, unprincipled or a whore. The "punishment" comes in the form of criticism, snide and embarrassing remarks, being treated as an easy lay by men, scorn from her more restrained female friends. She may have to lie and hide her behavior from her parents. She must juggle the risks of unwanted pregnancy and dangerous contraceptives. On the other hand, if she refrains from heterosexual activity, she is fairly constantly harassed by men who try to persuade her into it and pressure her to "relax" and "let her hair down"; she is threatened with labels like "frigid," "uptight," "man-hater," "bitch" and "cocktease." The same parents who would be disapproving of her sexual activity may be worried by her inactivity because it suggests she is not or will not be popular, or is not sexually normal. She may be charged with lesbianism. If a woman is raped, then if she has been heterosexually active she is subject to the presumption that she liked it (since her activity is presumed to show that she likes sex), and if she has not been heterosexually active, she is subject to the presumption that she liked it (since she is supposedly "repressed and frustrated"). Both heterosexual activity and heterosexual nonactivity are likely to be taken as proof that you wanted to be raped, and hence, of course, weren't *really* raped at all. You can't win. You are caught in a bind, caught between systematically related pressures.

Women are caught like this, too, by networks of forces and barriers that expose one to penalty, loss or contempt whether one works outside the home or not, is on welfare or not, bears children or not, raises children or not, marries or not, stays married or not, is heterosexual, lesbian, both or neither. Economic necessity; confinement to racial and/or sexual job ghettos; sexual harassment; sex discrimination; pressures of competing expectations and judgments about *women, wives* and *mothers* (in the society at large, in racial and ethnic subcultures and in one's own mind); dependence (full or partial) on husbands, parents or the state; commitment to political ideas; loyalties to racial or ethnic or other "minority" groups; the demands of self-respect and responsibilities to others. Each of these factors exists in complex tension with every other, penalizing or prohibiting all of the apparently available options. And nipping at one's heels, always, is the endless pack of little things. If one dresses one way, one is subject to the assumption that one is advertising one's sexual availability; if one dresses another way, one appears to "not care about oneself" or to be "unfeminine." If one uses "strong language," one invites categorization as a whore or slut; if one does not, one invites

categorization as a "lady"—one too delicately constituted to cope with robust speech or the realities to which it presumably refers.

The experience of oppressed people is that the living of one's life is confined and shaped by forces and barriers which are not accidental or occasional and hence avoidable, but are systematically related to each other in such a way as to catch one between and among them and restrict or penalize motion in any direction. It is the experience of being caged in: all avenues, in every direction, are blocked or booby trapped.

Cages. Consider a birdcage. If you look very closely at just one wire in the cage, you cannot see the other wires. If your conception of what is before you is determined by this myopic focus, you could look at that one wire, up and down the length of it, and be unable to see why a bird would not just fly around the wire any time it wanted to go somewhere. Furthermore, even if, one day at a time, you myopically inspected each wire, you still could not see why a bird would have trouble going past the wires to get anywhere. There is no physical property of any one wire, *nothing* that the closest scrutiny could discover, that will reveal how a bird could be inhibited or harmed by it except in the most accidental way. It is only when you step back, stop looking at the wires one by one, microscopically, and take a macroscopic view of the whole cage, that you can see why the bird does not go anywhere; and then you will see it in a moment. It will require no great subtlety of mental powers. It is perfectly *obvious* that the bird is surrounded by a network of systematically related barriers, no one of which would be the least hindrance to its flight, but which, by their relations to each other, are as confining as the solid walls of a dungeon.

It is now possible to grasp one of the reasons why oppression can be hard to see and recognize: one can study the elements of an oppressive structure with great care and some good will without seeing the structure as a whole, and hence without seeing or being able to understand that one is looking at a cage and that there are people there who are caged, whose motion and mobility are restricted, whose lives are shaped and reduced.

. . .

As the cageness of the birdcage is a macroscopic phenomenon, the oppressiveness of the situations in which women live our various and different lives is a macroscopic phenomenon. Neither can be *seen* from a microscopic perspective. But when you look macroscopically you can see it—a network of forces and barriers which are systematically related and which conspire to the immobilization, reduction and molding of women and the lives we live.

READING 10

Tomorrow I'm Going to Rewrite the English Language

Lois Keith

Tomorrow I am going to rewrite the English
    Language.
I will discard all those striving ambulist metaphors
of power and success
And construct new ways to describe my strength.
My new, different strength.

Then I won't have to feel dependent
Because I can't stand on my own two feet.
And I'll refuse to feel a failure
When I don't stay one step ahead.
I won't feel inadequate if I can't
Stand up for myself
Or illogical when I don't
Take it one step at a time.

I will make them understand that it is a very male
    way
To describe the world.
All this walking tall
And making great strides.

Yes, tomorrow I am going to rewrite the English
    Language
Creating the world in my own image.
Mine will be a gentler, more womanly way
To describe my progress.
I will wheel, cover and encircle.
Somehow I will learn to say it all.

READING 11

Homophobia
A Weapon of Sexism

Suzanne Pharr

Homophobia—the irrational fear and hatred of those who love and sexually desire those of the same sex. Though I intimately knew its meaning, the word homophobia was unknown to me until the late 1970s, and when I first heard it, I was struck by how difficult it is to say, what an ugly word it is, equally as ugly as its meaning. Like racism and anti-Semitism, it is a word that calls up images of loss of freedom, verbal and physical violence, death.

In my life I have experienced the effects of homophobia through rejection by friends, threats of loss of employment, and threats upon my life; and I have witnessed far worse things happening to other lesbian and gay people: loss of children, beatings, rape, death. Its power is great enough to keep ten to twenty percent of the population living lives of fear (if their sexual identity is hidden) or lives of danger (if their sexual identity is visible) or both. And its power is great enough to keep the remaining eighty to ninety percent of the population trapped in their own fears.

. . .

Homophobia works effectively as a weapon of sexism because it is joined with a powerful arm, heterosexism. Heterosexism creates the climate for homophobia with its assumption that the world is and must be heterosexual and its display of power and privilege as the norm. Heterosexism is the systemic display of homophobia in the institutions of society. Heterosexism and homophobia work together to enforce compulsory heterosexuality and that bastion of patriarchal power, the nuclear family. The central focus of the rightwing attack against women's liberation is that women's equality, women's self-determination, women's control of our own bodies and lives will damage what they see as the crucial societal institution, the nuclear family. The attack has been led by fundamentalist ministers across the country. The two areas they have focused on most consistently are abortion and homosexuality, and their passion has led them to bomb women's clinics and to recommend deprogramming for homosexuals and establishing camps to quarantine people with AIDS. To resist marriage and/or heterosexuality is to risk severe punishment and loss.

It is not by chance that when children approach puberty and increased sexual awareness they begin to taunt each other by calling these names: "queer," "faggot," "pervert." It is at puberty that the full force of society's pressure to conform to heterosexuality and prepare for marriage is brought to bear. Children know what we have taught them, and we have given clear messages that those who deviate from standard expectations are to be made to get back in line. The best controlling tactic at puberty is to be treated as an outsider, to be ostracized at a time when it feels most vital to be accepted. Those who are different must be made to suffer loss. It is also at puberty that misogyny begins to be more apparent, and girls are pressured to conform to societal norms that do not permit them to realize their full potential. It is at this time that their academic achievements begin to decrease as they are coerced into compulsory heterosexuality and trained for dependency upon a man, that is, for economic survival.

There was a time when the two most condemning accusations against a woman meant to ostracize and disempower her were "whore" and "lesbian." The sexual revolution and changing attitudes about heterosexual behavior may have led to some lessening of the power of the word *whore,* though it still has strength as a threat to sexual property and prostitutes are stigmatized and abused. However, the word *lesbian* is still fully charged and carries with it the full threat of loss of power and privilege, the threat of being cut asunder, abandoned, and left outside society's protection.

To be a lesbian is to be *perceived* as someone who has stepped out of line, who has moved out of sexual/economic dependence on a male, who is woman-identified. A lesbian is perceived as someone who can live without a man, and who is therefore (however illogically) against men. A lesbian is perceived as being outside the acceptable, routinized order of things. She is seen as someone who has no societal institutions to protect her and who is not privileged to the protection of individual males. Many heterosexual women see her as someone who stands in contradiction to the sacrifices they have made to conform to compulsory heterosexuality. A lesbian is perceived as a threat to the nuclear family, to male dominance and control, to the very heart of sexism.

Gay men are perceived also as a threat to male dominance and control, and the homophobia expressed against them has the same roots in sexism as does homophobia against lesbians. Visible gay men are the objects of extreme hatred and fear by heterosexual men because their breaking ranks with male heterosexual solidarity is seen as a damaging rent in the very fabric of sexism. They are seen as betrayers, as traitors who must be punished and eliminated. In the beating and killing of gay men we see clear evidence of this hatred. When we see the fierce homophobia expressed toward gay men, we can begin to understand the ways sexism also affects males through imposing rigid, dehumanizing gender roles on them. The two circumstances in which it is legitimate for men to be openly physically affectionate with one another are in competitive sports and in the crisis of war. For many men, these two experiences are the highlights of their lives, and they think of them again and again with nostalgia. War and sports offer a cover of all-male safety and dominance to keep away the notion of affectionate openness being identified with homosexuality. When gay men break ranks with male roles through bonding and affection outside the arenas of war and sports, they are perceived as not being "real men," that is, as being identified with women, the weaker sex that must be dominated and that over the centuries has been the object of male hatred and abuse. Misogyny gets transferred to gay men with a vengeance and is increased by the fear that their sexual identity and behavior will bring down the entire system of male dominance and compulsory heterosexuality.

If lesbians are established as threats to the status quo, as outcasts who must be punished, homophobia can wield its power over all women through lesbian baiting. Lesbian baiting is an attempt to control women by labeling us as lesbians because our behavior is not acceptable, that is, when we are being independent, going our own way, living whole lives, fighting for our rights, demanding equal pay, saying no to violence, being self-assertive, bonding with and loving the company of women, assuming the right to our bodies, insisting upon our own authority, making changes that include us in society's decision-making; lesbian baiting occurs when women are called lesbians because we resist male dominance and control. And it has little or nothing to do with one's sexual identity.

To be named as lesbian threatens all women, not just lesbians, with great loss. And any woman who steps out of role risks being called a lesbian. To understand how this is a threat to all women, one must understand that any woman can be called a lesbian and there is no real way she can defend herself: there is no way to credential one's sexuality. ("The Children's Hour," a Lillian Hellman play, makes this point when a student asserts two teachers are lesbians and they have no way to disprove it.) She may be married or divorced, have children, dress in

the most feminine manner, have sex with men, be celibate—but there are lesbians who do all those things. *Lesbians look like all women and all women look like lesbians.* There is no guaranteed method of identification, and as we all know, sexual identity can be kept hidden. (The same is true for men. There is no way to prove their sexual identity, though many go to extremes to prove heterosexuality.) Also, women are not necessarily born lesbian. Some seem to be, but others become lesbians later in life after having lived heterosexual lives. Lesbian baiting of heterosexual women would not work if there were a definitive way to identify lesbians (or heterosexuals).

We have yet to understand clearly how sexual identity develops. And this is disturbing to some people, especially those who are determined to discover how lesbian and gay identity is formed so that they will know where to start in eliminating it. (Isn't it odd that there is so little concern about discovering the causes of heterosexuality?) There are many theories: genetic makeup, hormones, socialization, environment, etc. But there is no conclusive evidence that indicates that heterosexuality comes from one process and homosexuality from another.

We do know, however, that sexual identity can be in flux, and we know that sexual identity means more than just the gender of people one is attracted to and has sex with. To be a lesbian has as many ramifications as for a woman to be heterosexual. It is more than sex, more than just the bedroom issue many would like to make it: it is a woman-centered life with all the social interconnections that entails. Some lesbians are in long-term relationships, some in short-term ones, some date, some are celibate, some are married to men, some remain as separate as possible from men, some have children by men, some by alternative insemination, some seem "feminine" by societal standards, some "masculine," some are doctors, lawyers and ministers, some laborers, housewives and writers: what all share in common is a sexual/affectional identity that focuses on women in its attractions and social relationships.

If lesbians are simply women with a particular sexual identity who look and act like all women, then the major difference in living out a lesbian sexual identity as opposed to a heterosexual identity is that as lesbians we live in a homophobic world that threatens and imposes damaging loss on us for being *who we are,* for choosing to live whole lives. Homophobic people often assert that homosexuals have the choice of not being homosexual; that is, we don't have to act out our sexual identity. In that case, I want to hear heterosexuals talk about their willingness not to act out their sexual identity, including not just sexual activity but heterosexual social interconnections and heterosexual privilege. It is a question of wholeness. It is very difficult for one to be denied the life of a sexual being, whether expressed in sex or in physical affection, and to feel complete, whole. For our loving relationships with humans feed the life of the spirit and enable us to overcome our basic isolation and to be interconnected with humankind.

. . .

What does a woman have to do to get called a lesbian? Almost anything, sometimes nothing at all, but certainly anything that threatens the status quo, anything that steps out of role, anything that asserts the rights of women, anything that doesn't indicate submission and subordination. Assertiveness, standing up for oneself, asking for more pay, better working conditions, training for and accepting a non-traditional (you mean a man's?) job, enjoying the company of women, being financially independent, being in control of one's life, depending first and foremost upon oneself, thinking that one can do whatever needs to be done, but above all, working for the rights and equality of women.

In the backlash to the gains of the women's liberation movement, there has been an increased effort to keep definitions man-centered. Therefore, to work on behalf of women must mean to work against men. To love women must mean that one hates men. A very effective attack has been made against the word *feminist* to make it a derogatory word. In current backlash usage, *feminist* equals *man-hater* which equals *lesbian.* This formula is created in the hope that women will be frightened away from their work on behalf of women. Consequently, we now have women who believe in the rights of women and work for those rights while from fear deny that they are feminists, or refuse to use the word because it is so "abrasive."

So what does one do in an effort to keep from being called a lesbian? She steps back into line, into the role that is demanded of her, tries to behave in such a way that doesn't threaten the status of men, and if she works for women's rights, she begins modifying that work. When women's organizations begin doing significant social change work, they inevitably are lesbian-baited; that is, funders or institutions or community members tell us that they can't work with us because of our "man-hating attitudes" or the presence of lesbians. We are called too strident, told we are making enemies, not doing good.

The battered women's movement has seen this kind of attack: the pressure has been to provide services only, without analysis of the causes of violence against women and strategies for ending it. To provide only services without political analysis or direct action is to be in an approved "helping" role; to analyze the causes of violence against women is to begin the work toward changing an entire system of power and control. It is when we do the latter that we are threatened with the label of man-hater or lesbian. For my politics, if a women's social change organization has not been labeled lesbian or communist, it is probably not doing significant work; it is only "making nice."

Women in many of these organizations, out of fear of all the losses we are threatened with, begin to modify our work to make it more acceptable and less threatening to the male-dominated society which we originally set out to change. The work can no longer be radical (going to the root cause of the problem) but instead must be reforming, working only on the symptoms and not the cause. Real change for women becomes thwarted and stopped. The word *lesbian* is instilled with the power to halt our work and control our lives. And we give it its power with our fear.

In my view, homophobia has been one of the major causes of the failure of the women's liberation movement to make deep and lasting change. (The other major block has been racism.) We were fierce when we set out but when threatened with the loss of heterosexual privilege, we began putting on brakes. Our best-known nationally distributed women's magazine was reluctant to print articles about lesbians, began putting a man on the cover several times a year, and writing articles about women who succeeded in a man's world. We worried about our image, our being all right, our being "real women" despite our work. Instead of talking about the elimination of sexual gender roles, we stepped back and talked about "sex role stereotyping" as the issue. Change around the edges for middleclass white women began to be talked about as successes. We accepted tokenism and integration, forgetting that equality for all women, for all people—and not just equality of white middleclass women with white men—was the goal that we could never put behind us.

But despite backlash and retreats, change is growing from within. The women's liberation movement is beginning to gain strength again because there are women who are talking about liberation for all women. We are examining sexism, racism, homophobia, classism, anti-Semitism, ageism, ableism, and imperialism, and we see everything as connected. This change in point of view represents the third wave of the women's liberation movement, a new direction that does not get mass media coverage and recognition. It has been initiated by women of color and lesbians who were marginalized or rendered invisible by the white heterosexual leaders of earlier efforts. The first wave was the 19th and early 20th century campaign for the vote; the second, beginning in the 1960s, focused on the Equal Rights Amendment and abortion rights. Consisting of predominantly white middleclass women, both failed in recognizing issues of equality and empowerment for all women. The third wave of the movement, multi-racial and multi-issued, seeks the transformation of the world for us all. We know that we won't get there until everyone gets there; that we must move forward in a great strong line, hand in hand, not just a few at a time.

We know that the arguments about homophobia originating from mental health and Biblical/religious attitudes can be settled when we look at the sexism that permeates religious and psychiatric history. The women of the third wave of the women's liberation movement know that *without the existence of sexism, there would be no homophobia.*

Finally, we know that as long as the word lesbian can strike fear in any woman's heart, then work on behalf of women can be stopped; the only successful work against sexism must include work against homophobia.

READING 12

White Privilege and Male Privilege

Peggy McIntosh

Through work to bring materials and perspectives from Women's Studies into the rest of the curriculum, I have often noticed men's unwillingness to grant that they are overprivileged in the curriculum, even though they may grant that women are disadvantaged. Denials that amount to taboos surround the subject of advantages that men gain from women's disadvantages. These denials protect male privilege from being fully recognized, acknowledged, lessened, or ended.

Thinking through unacknowledged male privilege as a phenomenon with a life of its own, I realized that since hierarchies in our society are interlocking, there was most likely a phenomenon of white privilege that was similarly denied and protected, but alive and real in its effects. As a white person, I realized I had been taught about racism as something that puts others at a disadvantage, but had been taught not to see one of its corollary aspects, white privilege, which puts me at an advantage.

I think whites are carefully taught not to recognize white privilege, as males are taught not to recognize male privilege. So I have begun in an untutored way to ask what it is like to have white privilege. This paper is a partial record of my personal observations and not a scholarly analysis. It is based on my daily experiences within my particular circumstances.

I have come to see white privilege as an invisible package of unearned assets that I can count on cashing in each day, but about which I was "meant" to remain oblivious. White privilege is like an invisible weightless knapsack of special provisions, assurances, tools, maps, guides, codebooks, passports, visas, clothes, compass, emergency gear, and blank checks.

Since I have had trouble facing white privilege, and describing its results in my life, I saw parallels here with men's reluctance to acknowledge male privilege. Only rarely will a man go beyond acknowledging that women are disadvantaged to acknowledging that men have unearned advantage, or that unearned privilege has not been good for men's development as human beings, or for society's development, or that privilege systems might ever be challenged and *changed.*

I will review here several types or layers of denial that I see at work protecting, and preventing awareness about, entrenched male privilege. Then I will draw parallels, from my own experience, with the denials that veil the facts of white privilege. Finally, I will list forty-six ordinary and daily ways in which I experience having white privilege, by contrast with my African American colleagues in the same building. This list is not intended to be generalizable. Others can make their own lists from within their own life circumstances.

Writing this paper has been difficult, despite warm receptions for the talks on which it is based.[1] For describing white privilege makes one newly accountable. As we in Women's Studies work [to] reveal male privilege and ask men to give up some of their power, so one who writes about having white privilege must ask, "Having described it, what will I do to lessen or end it?"

The denial of men's overprivileged state takes many forms in discussions of curriculum change work. Some claim that men must be central in the curriculum because they have done most of what is important or distinctive in life or in civilization. Some recognize sexism in the curriculum but deny that it makes male students seem unduly important in life. Others agree that certain *individual* thinkers are male oriented but deny that there is any *systemic* tendency in disciplinary frameworks or epistemology to overempower men as a group. Those men who do grant that male privilege takes institutionalized and embedded forms are still likely to deny that

male hegemony has opened doors for them personally. Virtually all men deny that male overreward alone can explain men's centrality in all the inner sanctums of our most powerful institutions. Moreover, those few who will acknowledge that male privilege systems have overempowered them usually end up doubting that we could dismantle these privilege systems. They may say they will work to improve women's status, in the society or in the university, but they can't or won't support the idea of lessening men's. In curricular terms, this is the point at which they say that they regret they cannot use any of the interesting new scholarship on women because the syllabus is full. When the talk turns to giving men less cultural room, even the most thoughtful and fair-minded of the men I know will tend to reflect, or fall back on, conservative assumptions about the inevitability of present gender relations and distributions of power, calling on precedent or sociobiology and psychobiology to demonstrate that male domination is natural and follows inevitably from evolutionary pressures. Others resort to arguments from "experience" or religion or social responsibility or wishing and dreaming.

After I realized, through faculty development work in Women's Studies, the extent to which men work from a base of unacknowledged privilege, I understood that much of their oppressiveness was unconscious. Then I remembered the frequent charges from women of color that white women whom they encounter are oppressive. I began to understand why we are justly seen as oppressive, even when we don't see ourselves that way. At the very least, obliviousness of one's privileged state can make a person or group irritating to be with. I began to count the ways in which I enjoy unearned skin privilege and have been conditioned into oblivion about its existence, unable to see that it put me "ahead" in any way, or put my people ahead, overrewarding us and yet also paradoxically damaging us, or that it could or should be changed.

My schooling gave me no training in seeing myself as an oppressor, as an unfairly advantaged person, or as a participant in a damaged culture. I was taught to see myself as an individual whose moral state depended on her individual moral will. At school, we were not taught about slavery in any depth; we were not taught to see slaveholders as damaged people. Slaves were seen as the only group at risk of being dehumanized. My schooling followed the pattern which Elizabeth Minnich has pointed out: whites are taught to think of their lives as morally neutral, normative, and average, and also ideal, so that when we work to benefit others, this is seen as work that will allow "them" to be more like "us." I think many of us know how obnoxious this attitude can be in men.

After frustration with men who would not recognize male privilege, I decided to try to work on myself at least by identifying some of the daily effects of white privilege in my life. It is crude work, at this stage, but I will give here a list of special circumstances and conditions I experience that I did not earn but that I have been made to feel are mine by birth, by citizenship, and by virtue of being a conscientious law-abiding "normal" person of goodwill. I have chosen those conditions that I think in my case *attach somewhat more to skin-color privilege* than to class, religion, ethnic status, or geographical location, though these other privileging factors are intricately intertwined. As far as I can see, my Afro-American co-workers, friends, and acquaintances with whom I come into daily or frequent contact in this particular time, place, and line of work cannot count on most of these conditions.

1. I can, if I wish, arrange to be in the company of people of my race most of the time.
2. I can avoid spending time with people whom I was trained to mistrust and who have learned to mistrust my kind or me.
3. If I should need to move, I can be pretty sure of renting or purchasing housing in an area which I can afford and in which I would want to live.
4. I can be reasonably sure that my neighbors in such a location will be neutral or pleasant to me.
5. I can go shopping alone most of the time, fairly well assured that I will not be followed or harassed by store detectives.
6. I can turn on the television or open to the front page of the paper and see people of my race widely and positively represented.

7. When I am told about our national heritage or about "civilization," I am shown that people of my color made it what it is.
8. I can be sure that my children will be given curricular materials that testify to the existence of their race.
9. If I want to, I can be pretty sure of finding a publisher for this piece on white privilege.
10. I can be fairly sure of having my voice heard in a group in which I am the only member of my race.
11. I can be casual about whether or not to listen to another woman's voice in a group in which she is the only member of her race.
12. I can go into a book shop and count on finding the writing of my race represented, into a supermarket and find the staple foods that fit with my cultural traditions, into a hairdresser's shop and find someone who can deal with my hair.
13. Whether I use checks, credit cards, or cash, I can count on my skin color not to work against the appearance that I am financially reliable.
14. I could arrange to protect our young children most of the time from people who might not like them.
15. I did not have to educate our children to be aware of systemic racism for their own daily physical protection.
16. I can be pretty sure that my children's teachers and employers will tolerate them if they fit school and workplace norms; my chief worries about them do not concern others' attitudes toward their race.
17. I can talk with my mouth full and not have people put this down to my color.
18. I can swear, or dress in secondhand clothes, or not answer letters, without having people attribute these choices to the bad morals, the poverty, or the illiteracy of my race.
19. I can speak in public to a powerful male group without putting my race on trial.
20. I can do well in a challenging situation without being called a credit to my race.
21. I am never asked to speak for all the people of my racial group.

22. I can remain oblivious to the language and customs of persons of color who constitute the world's majority without feeling in my culture any penalty for such oblivion.

23. I can criticize our government and talk about how much I fear its policies and behavior without being seen as a cultural outsider.

24. I can be reasonably sure that if I ask to talk to "the person in charge," I will be facing a person of my race.

25. If a traffic cop pulls me over or if the IRS audits my tax return, I can be sure I haven't been singled out because of my race.

26. I can easily buy posters, postcards, picture books, greeting cards, dolls, toys, and children's magazines featuring people of my race.

27. I can go home from most meetings of organizations I belong to feeling somewhat tied in, rather than isolated, out of place, outnumbered, unheard, held at a distance, or feared.

28. I can be pretty sure that an argument with a colleague of another race is more likely to jeopardize her chances for advancement than to jeopardize mine.

29. I can be fairly sure that if I argue for the promotion of a person of another race, or a program centering on race, this is not likely to cost me heavily within my present setting, even if my colleagues disagree with me.

30. If I declare there is a racial issue at hand, or there isn't a racial issue at hand, my race will lend me more credibility for either position than a person of color will have.

31. I can choose to ignore developments in minority writing and minority activist programs, or disparage them, or learn from them, but in any case, I can find ways to be more or less protected from negative consequences of any of these choices.

32. My culture gives me little fear about ignoring the perspectives and powers of people of other races.

33. I am not made acutely aware that my shape, bearing, or body odor will be taken as a reflection on my race.

34. I can worry about racism without being seen as self-interested or self-seeking.

35. I can take a job with an affirmative action employer without having my co-workers on the job suspect that I got it because of my race.

36. If my day, week, or year is going badly, I need not ask of each negative episode or situation whether it has racial overtones.

37. I can be pretty sure of finding people who would be willing to talk with me and advise me about my next steps, professionally.

38. I can think over many options, social, political, imaginative, or professional, without asking whether a person of my race would be accepted or allowed to do what I want to do.

39. I can be late to a meeting without having the lateness reflect on my race.

40. I can choose public accommodation without fearing that people of my race cannot get in or will be mistreated in the places I have chosen.

41. I can be sure that if I need legal or medical help, my race will not work against me.

42. I can arrange my activities so that I will never have to experience feelings of rejection owing to my race.

43. If I have low credibility as a leader, I can be sure that my race is not the problem.

44. I can easily find academic courses and institutions that give attention only to people of my race.

45. I can expect figurative language and imagery in all of the arts to testify to experiences of my race.

46. I can choose blemish cover or bandages in "flesh" color and have them more or less match my skin.

I repeatedly forgot each of the realizations on this list until I wrote it down. For me, white privilege has turned out to be an elusive and fugitive subject. The pressure to avoid it is great, for in facing it I must give up the myth of meritocracy. If these things are true, this is not such a free country; one's life is not what one makes it; many doors open for certain people through no virtues of their own. These perceptions mean also that my moral condition is not what I had been led to believe. The appearance of being a good citizen rather than a troublemaker comes in large part from having all sorts of doors open automatically because of my color.

A further paralysis of nerve comes from literary silence protecting privilege. My clearest memories of finding such analysis are in Lillian Smith's unparalleled *Killers of the Dream* and Margaret Andersen's review of Karen and Mamie Fields' *Lemon Swamp.* Smith, for example, wrote about walking toward black children on the street and knowing they would step into the gutter; Andersen contrasted the pleasure that she, as a white child, took on summer driving trips to the south with Karen Fields' memories of driving in a closed car stocked with all necessities lest, in stopping, her black family should suffer "insult, or worse." Adrienne Rich also recognizes and writes about daily experiences of privilege, but in my observation, white women's writing in this area is far more often on systemic racism than on our daily lives as light-skinned women.[2]

In unpacking this invisible knapsack of white privilege, I have listed conditions of daily experience that I once took for granted, as neutral, normal, and universally available to everybody, just as I once thought of a male-focused curriculum as the neutral or accurate account that can speak for all. Nor did I think of any of these perquisites as bad for the holder. I now think that we need a more finely differentiated taxonomy of privilege, for some of these varieties are only what one would want for everyone in a just society, and others give license to be ignorant, oblivious, arrogant, and destructive. Before proposing some more finely tuned categorization, I will make some observations about the general effects of these conditions on my life and expectations.

In this potpourri of examples, some privileges make me feel at home in the world. Others allow me to escape penalties or dangers that others suffer. Through some, I escape fear, anxiety, insult, injury, or a sense of not being welcome, not being real. Some keep me from having to hide, to be in disguise, to feel sick or crazy, to negotiate each transaction from the position of being an outsider or, within my group, a person who is suspected of having too close links with a dominant culture. Most keep me from having to be angry.

I see a pattern running through the matrix of white privilege, a pattern of assumptions that were passed on to me as a white person. There was one main piece of cultural turf; it was my own turf, and I was among those who could control the turf. I could measure up to the cultural standards and take advantage of the many options I saw around me to make what the culture would call a success of my life. *My skin color was an asset for any move I was educated to want to make.* I could think of myself as "belonging" in major ways and of making social systems work for me. I could freely disparage, fear, neglect, or be oblivious to anything outside of the dominant cultural forms. Being of the main culture, I could also criticize it fairly freely. My life was reflected back to me frequently enough so that I felt, with regard to my race, if not to my sex, like one of the real people.

Whether through the curriculum or in the newspaper, the television, the economic system, or the general look of people in the streets, I received daily signals and indications that my people counted and that others *either didn't exist or must be trying, not very successfully, to be like people of my race.* I was given cultural permission not to hear voices of people of other races or a tepid cultural tolerance for hearing or acting on such voices. I was also raised not to suffer seriously from anything that darker-skinned people might say about my group, "protected," though perhaps I should more accurately say *prohibited,* through the habits of my economic class and social group, from living in racially mixed groups or being reflective about interactions between people of differing races.

In proportion as my racial group was being made confident, comfortable, and oblivious, other groups were likely being made unconfident, uncomfortable, and alienated. Whiteness protected me from many kinds of hostility, distress, and violence, which I was being subtly trained to visit in turn upon people of color.

For this reason, the word "privilege" now seems to me misleading. Its connotations are too positive to fit the conditions and behaviors which "privilege systems" produce. We usually think of privilege as being a favored state, whether earned, or conferred by birth or luck. School graduates are reminded they are privileged and urged to use their (enviable) assets well. The word "privilege" carries the connotation of being something everyone must want. Yet some of the conditions I have described here work to systemically overempower certain groups. Such privilege simply *confers dominance,* gives permission to control, because of one's race or sex. The kind of privilege that gives license to some people to be, at best, thoughtless and, at worst, murderous should not continue to be referred to as a desirable attribute. Such "privilege" may be widely desired without being in any way beneficial to the whole society.

Moreover, though "privilege" may confer power, it does not confer moral strength. Those who do not depend on conferred dominance have traits and qualities that may never develop in those who do. Just as Women's Studies courses indicate that women survive their political circumstances to lead lives that hold the human race together, so "underprivileged" people of color who are the world's majority have survived their oppression and lived survivors' lives from which the white global minority can and must learn. In some groups, those dominated have actually become strong through *not* having all of these unearned advantages, and this gives them a great deal to teach the others. Members of so-called privileged groups can seem foolish, ridiculous, infantile, or dangerous by contrast.

I want, then, to distinguish between earned strength and unearned power conferred systemically. Power from unearned privilege can look like strength when it is, in fact, permission to escape or to dominate. But not all of the privileges on my list are inevitably damaging. Some, like the expectation that neighbors will be decent to you, or that your race will not count against you in court, should be the norm in a just society and should be considered as the entitlement of everyone. Others, like the privilege not to listen to less powerful people, distort the humanity of the holders as well as the ignored groups. Still others, like finding one's staple foods everywhere, may be a function of being a member of a numerical majority in the population. Others have to do with not having to labor under pervasive negative stereotyping and mythology.

We might at least start by distinguishing between positive advantages that we can work to spread, to the point where they are not advantages at all but simply part of the normal civic and social fabric, and negative types of advantage that unless rejected will always reinforce our present hierarchies. For example, the positive "privilege" of belonging, the feeling that one belongs within the human circle, as Native Americans say, fosters development and should not be seen as privilege for a few. It is, let us say, an entitlement that none of us should have to earn; ideally it is an *unearned entitlement.* At present, since only a few have it, it is an *unearned advantage* for them. The negative "privilege" that gave me cultural permission not to take darker-skinned Others seriously can be seen as arbitrarily conferred dominance and should not be desirable for anyone. This paper results from a process of coming to see that some of the power that I originally saw as attendant on being a human being in the United States consisted in *unearned advantage* and *conferred dominance,* as well as other kinds of special circumstance not universally taken for granted.

In writing this paper I have also realized that white identity and status (as well as class identity and status) give me considerable power to choose whether to broach this subject and its trouble. I can pretty well decide whether to disappear and avoid and not listen and escape the dislike I may engender in other people through this essay, or interrupt, answer, interpret, preach, correct, criticize, and control to some extent what goes on in reaction to it. Being white, I am given considerable power to escape many kinds of danger or penalty as well as to choose which risks I want to take.

There is an analogy here, once again, with Women's Studies. Our male colleagues do not have a great deal to lose in supporting Women's Studies, but they do not have a great deal to lose if they oppose it either. They simply have the power to decide whether to commit themselves to more equitable distributions of power. They will probably feel few penalties whatever choice they make; they do not seem, in any obvious short-term sense, the ones at risk, though they and we are all at risk because of the behaviors that have been rewarded in them.

Through Women's Studies work I have met very few men who are truly distressed about systemic, unearned male advantage and conferred dominance. And so one question for me and others like me is whether we will be like them, or whether we will get truly distressed, even outraged, about unearned race advantage and conferred dominance and if so, what we will do to lessen them. In any case, we need to do more work in identifying how they actually affect our daily lives. We need more down-to-earth writing by people about these taboo subjects. We need more understanding of the ways in which white "privilege" damages white people, for these are not the same ways in which it damages the victimized. Skewed white psyches are an inseparable part of the picture, though I do not want to confuse the kinds of damage done to the holders of special assets and to those who suffer the deficits. Many, perhaps most, of our white students in the United States think that racism doesn't affect them because they are not people of color; they do not see "whiteness" as a racial identity. Many men likewise think that Women's Studies does not bear on their own existences because they are not female; they do not see themselves as having gendered identities. Insisting on the universal "effects" of "privilege" systems, then, becomes one of our chief tasks, and being more explicit about the *particular* effects in particular contexts is another. Men need to join us in this work.

In addition, since race and sex are not the only advantaging systems at work, we need to similarly examine the daily experience of having age advantage, or ethnic advantage, or physical ability, or advantage related to nationality, religion, or sexual orientation. Professor Marnie Evans suggested to me that in many ways the list I made also applies directly to heterosexual privilege. This is a still more taboo subject than race privilege: the daily ways in which heterosexual privilege makes some persons comfortable or powerful, providing supports, assets, approvals, and rewards to those who live or expect to live in heterosexual pairs. Unpacking that content is still more difficult, owing to the deeper imbeddedness of heterosexual advantage and dominance and stricter taboos surrounding these.

But to start such an analysis I would put this observation from my own experience: the fact that I live under the same roof with a man triggers all kinds of societal assumptions about my worth, politics, life, and values and triggers a host of unearned advantages and powers. After recasting many elements

from the original list I would add further observations like these:

1. My children do not have to answer questions about why I live with my partner (my husband).
2. I have no difficulty finding neighborhoods where people approve of our household.
3. Our children are given texts and classes that implicitly support our kind of family unit and do not turn them against my choice of domestic partnership.
4. I can travel alone or with my husband without expecting embarrassment or hostility in those who deal with us.
5. Most people I meet will see my marital arrangements as an asset to my life or as a favorable comment on my likability, my competence, or my mental health.
6. I can talk about the social events of a weekend without fearing most listeners' reactions.
7. I will feel welcomed and "normal" in the usual walks of public life, institutional and social.
8. In many contexts, I am seen as "all right" in daily work on women because I do not live chiefly with women.

Difficulties and dangers surrounding the task of finding parallels are many. Since racism, sexism, and heterosexism are not the same, the advantages associated with them should not be seen as the same. In addition, it is hard to isolate aspects of unearned advantage that derive chiefly from social class, economic class, race, religion, region, sex, or ethnic identity. The oppressions are both distinct and interlocking, as the Combahee River Collective statement of 1977 continues to remind us eloquently.[3]

One factor seems clear about all of the interlocking oppressions. They take both active forms that we can see and embedded forms that members of the dominant group are taught not to see. In my class and place, I did not see myself as racist because I was taught to recognize racism only in individual acts of meanness by members of my group, never in invisible systems conferring racial dominance on my group from birth. Likewise, we are taught to think that sexism or heterosexism is carried on only through intentional, individual acts of discrimination, meanness, or cruelty, rather than in invisible systems conferring unsought dominance on certain groups. Disapproving of the systems won't be enough to change them. I was taught to think that racism could end if white individuals changed their attitudes; many men think sexism can be ended by individual changes in daily behavior toward women. But a man's sex provides advantage for him whether or not he approves of the way in which dominance has been conferred on his group. A "white" skin in the United States opens many doors for whites whether or not we approve of the way dominance has been conferred on us. Individual acts can palliate, but cannot end, these problems. To redesign social systems, we need first to acknowledge their colossal unseen dimensions. The silences and denials surrounding privilege are the key political tool here. They keep the thinking about equality or equity incomplete, protecting unearned advantage and conferred dominance by making these taboo subjects. Most talk by whites about equal opportunity seems to me now to be about equal opportunity to try to get into a position of dominance while denying that *systems* of dominance exist.

Obliviousness about white advantage, like obliviousness about male advantage, is kept strongly inculturated in the United States so as to maintain the myth of meritocracy, the myth that democratic choice is equally available to all. Keeping most people unaware that freedom of confident action is there for just a small number of people props up those in power and serves to keep power in the hands of the same groups that have most of it already. Though systemic change takes many decades, there are pressing questions for me and I imagine for some others

like me if we raise our daily consciousness on the perquisites of being light-skinned. What will we do with such knowledge? As we know from watching men, it is an open question whether we will choose to use unearned advantage to weaken invisible privilege systems and whether we will use any of our arbitrarily awarded power to try to reconstruct power systems on a broader base.

NOTES

I have appreciated commentary on this paper from the Working Papers Committee of the Wellesley College Center for Research on Women, from members of the Dodge seminar, and from many individuals, including Margaret Andersen, Sorel Berman, Joanne Braxton, Johnnella Butler, Sandra Dickerson, Marnie Evans, Beverly Guy-Sheftall, Sandra Harding, Eleanor Hinton Hoytt, Pauline Houston, Paul Lauter, Joyce Miller, Mary Norris, Gloria Oden, Beverly Smith, and John Walter.

1. This paper was presented at the Virginia Women's Studies Association conference in Richmond in April 1986, and the American Educational Research Association conference in Boston in October 1986, and discussed with two groups of participants in the Dodge seminars for Secondary School Teachers in New York and Boston in the spring of 1987.

2. Andersen, Margaret, "Race and the Social Science Curriculum: A Teaching and Learning Discussion." *Radical Teacher*, November 1984, pp. 17–20. Smith, Lillian, *Killers of the Dream*, New York: W. W. Norton, 1949.

3. "A Black Feminist Statement," The Combahee River Collective, pp. 13–22 in G. Hull, P. Scott, B. Smith, Eds., *All the Women Are White, All the Blacks Are Men, But Some of Us Are Brave: Black Women's Studies*, Old Westbury, NY: The Feminist Press, 1982.

READING 13

Something About the Subject Makes It Hard to Name

Gloria Yamato

Racism—simple enough in structure, yet difficult to eliminate. Racism—pervasive in the U.S. culture to the point that it deeply affects all the local town folk and spills over, negatively influencing the fortunes of folk around the world. Racism is pervasive to the

point that we take many of its manifestations for granted, believing "that's life." Many believe that racism can be dealt with effectively in one hellifying workshop, or one hour-long heated discussion. Many actually believe this monster, racism, that has had at least a few hundred years to take root, grow, invade our space and develop subtle variations . . . this mind-funk that distorts thought and action, can be merely wished away. I've run into folks who really think that we can beat this devil, kick this habit, be healed of this disease in a snap. In a sincere blink of a well-intentioned eye, presto—poof—racism disappears. "I've dealt with my racism . . . (envision a laying on of hands) . . . Hallelujah! Now I can go to the beach." Well, fine. Go to the beach. In fact, why don't we all go to the beach and continue to work on the sucker over there? Cuz you can't even shave a little piece off this thing called racism in a day, or a weekend, or a workshop.

When I speak of *oppression,* I'm talking about the systematic, institutionalized mistreatment of one group of people by another for whatever reason. The oppressors are purported to have an innate ability to access economic resources, information, respect, etc., while the oppressed are believed to have a corresponding negative innate ability. The flip side of oppression is *internalized oppression.* Members of the target group are emotionally, physically, and spiritually battered to the point that they begin to actually believe that their oppression is deserved, is their lot in life, is natural and right, and that it doesn't even exist. The oppression begins to feel comfortable, familiar enough that when mean ol' Massa lay down de whip, we got's to pick up and whack ourselves and each other. Like a virus, it's hard to beat racism, because by the time you come up with a cure, it's mutated to a "new cure-resistant" form. One shot just won't get it. Racism must be attacked from many angles.

The forms of racism that I pick up on these days are (1) aware/blatant racism, (2) aware/covert racism, (3) unaware/unintentional racism, and (4) unaware/self-righteous racism. I can't say that I prefer any one form of racism over the others, because they all look like an itch needing a scratch. I've heard it said (and understandably so) that the aware/blatant form of racism is preferable if one must suffer it. Outright racists will, without apology or confusion, tell us that because of our color we don't appeal to them. If we so choose, we can attempt to get the hell out of their way before we get the sweat knocked out of us. Growing up, aware/covert racism is what I

heard many of my elders bemoaning "up north," after having escaped the overt racism "down south." Apartments were suddenly no longer vacant or rents were outrageously high, when black, brown, red, or yellow persons went to inquire about them. Job vacancies were suddenly filled, or we were fired for very vague reasons. It still happens, though the perpetrators really take care to cover their tracks these days. They don't want to get gummed to death or slobbered on by the toothless laws that supposedly protect us from such inequities.

Unaware/unintentional racism drives usually tranquil white liberals wild when they get called on it, and confirms the suspicions of many people of color who feel that white folks are just plain crazy. It has led white people to believe that it's just fine to ask if they can touch my hair (while reaching). They then exclaim over how soft it is, how it does not scratch their hand. It has led whites to assume that bending over backwards and speaking to me in high-pitched (terrified), condescending tones would make up for all the racist wrongs that distort our lives. This type of racism has led whites right to my doorstep, talking 'bout, "We're sorry/we love you and want to make things right," which is fine, and further, "We're gonna give you the opportunity to fix it while we sleep. Just tell us what you need. 'Bye!!"—which *ain't* fine. With the best of intentions, the best of educations, and the greatest generosity of heart, whites, operating on the misinformation fed to them from day one, will behave in ways that are racist, will perpetuate racism by being "nice" the way we're taught to be nice. You can just "nice" somebody to death with naïveté and lack of awareness of privilege. Then there's guilt and the desire to end racism and how the two get all tangled up to the point that people, morbidly fascinated with their guilt, are immobilized. Rather than deal with ending racism, they sit and ponder their guilt and hope nobody notices how awful they are. Meanwhile, racism picks up momentum and keeps on keepin' on.

Now, the newest form of racism that I'm hip to is unaware/self-righteous racism. The "good white" racist attempts to shame Blacks into being blacker, scorns Japanese-Americans who don't speak Japanese, and knows more about the Chicano/a community than the folks who make up the community.

They assign themselves as the "good whites," as opposed to the "bad whites," and are often so busy telling people of color what the issues in the Black, Asian, Indian, Latino/a communities should be that they don't have time to deal with their errant sisters and brothers in the white community. Which means that people of color are still left to deal with what the "good whites" don't want to . . . racism.

Internalized racism is what really gets in my way as a Black woman. It influences the way I see or don't see myself, limits what I expect of myself or others like me. It results in my acceptance of mistreatment, leads me to believe that being treated with less than absolute respect, at least this once, is to be expected because I am Black, because I am not white. "Because I am (*you fill in the color*), you think, "Life is going to be hard." The fact is life may be hard, but the color of your skin is not the cause of the hardship. The color of your skin may be used as an excuse to mistreat you, but there is no reason or logic involved in the mistreatment. If it seems that your color is the reason, if it seems that your ethnic heritage is the cause of the woe, it's because you've been deliberately beaten down by agents of a greedy system until you swallowed the garbage. That is the internalization of racism.

Racism is the systematic, institutionalized mistreatment of one group of people by another based on racial heritage. Like every other oppression, racism can be internalized. People of color come to believe misinformation about their particular ethnic group and thus believe that their mistreatment is justified. With that basic vocabulary, let's take a look at how the whole thing works together. Meet "the Ism Family," racism, classism, ageism, adultism, elitism, sexism, heterosexism, physicalism, etc. All these ism's are systematic, that is, not only are these parasites feeding off our lives, they are also dependent on one another for foundation. Racism is supported and reinforced by classism, which is given a foothold and a boost by adultism, which also feeds sexism, which is validated by heterosexism, and so it goes on. You cannot have the "ism" functioning without first effectively installing its flip-side, the internalized version of the ism. Like twins, as one particular form of the ism grows in potency, there is a corresponding increase in its internalized form within the popula-tion. Before oppression becomes a specific ism like racism, usually all hell breaks loose. War. People fight attempts to enslave them, or to subvert their will, or to take what they consider theirs, whether that is territory or dignity. It's true that the various elements of racism, while repugnant, would not be able to do very much damage, but for one generally overlooked key piece: power/privilege.

. . .

So, what can we do? Acknowledge racism for a start, even though and especially when we've struggled to be kind and fair, or struggled to rise above it all. It is hard to acknowledge the fact that racism circumscribes and pervades our lives. Racism must be dealt with on two levels, personal and societal, emotional and institutional. It is possible—and most effective—to do both at the same time. We must reclaim whatever delight we have lost in our own ethnic heritage or heritages. This so-called melting pot has only succeeded in turning us into fast-food gobbling "generics" (as in generic "white folks" who were once Irish, Polish, Russian, English, etc. and "black folks," who were once Ashanti, Bambara, Baule, Yoruba, etc.). Find or create safe places to actually *feel* what we've been forced to repress each time we were a victim of, witness to or perpetrator of racism, so that we do not continue, like puppets, to act out the past in the present and future. Challenge oppression. Take a stand against it. When you are aware of something oppressive going down, stop the show. At least call it. We become so numbed to racism that we don't even think twice about it, unless it is immediately life-threatening.

Whites who want to be allies to people of color: You can educate yourselves via research and observation rather than rigidly, arrogantly relying solely on interrogating people of color. Do not expect that people of color should teach you how to behave non-oppressively. Do not give into the pull to be lazy. Think, hard. Do not blame people of color for your frustration about racism, but do appreciate the fact that people of color will often help you get in touch with that frustration. Assume that your effort to be a good friend is appreciated, but don't expect or accept gratitude from people of color. Work on racism for your sake, not "their" sake. Assume that you are needed and capable of being a good ally. Know that you'll make mistakes and commit yourself to correcting them and continuing on as an ally, no matter what. Don't give up.

People of color, working through internalized racism: Remember always that you and others like you are completely worthy of respect, completely capable of achieving whatever you take a notion to do. Remember that the term "people of color" refers to a variety of ethnic and cultural backgrounds. These various groups have been oppressed in a variety of ways. Educate yourself about the ways different peoples have been oppressed and how they've resisted that oppression. Expect and insist that whites are capable of being good allies against racism. Don't give up. Resist the pull to give out the "people of color seal of approval" to aspiring white allies. A moment of appreciation is fine, but more than that tends to be less than helpful. Celebrate yourself. Celebrate yourself. Celebrate the inevitable end of racism.

READING 14

Tired of Playing Monopoly?

Donna Langston

I. Magnin, Nordstrom, The Bon, Sears, Penneys, K mart, Goodwill, Salvation Army. If the order of this list of stores makes any sense to you, then we've begun to deal with the first question which inevitably arises in any discussion of class here in the U.S.— huh? Unlike our European allies, we in the U.S. are reluctant to recognize class differences. This denial of class divisions functions to reinforce ruling class control and domination. America is, after all, the supposed land of equal opportunity where, if you just work hard enough, you can get ahead, pull yourself up by your bootstraps. What the old bootstraps theory overlooks is that some were born with silver shoe horns. Female-headed households, communities of color, the elderly, disabled and children find themselves, disproportionately, living in poverty. If hard work were the sole determinant of your ability to support yourself and your family, surely we'd have a different outcome for many in our society. We also, however, believe in luck and, on closer examination, it certainly is quite a coincidence that the "unlucky" come from certain race, gender and class backgrounds. In order to perpetuate racist, sexist and classist outcomes, we also have to believe that the current economic distribution is unchangeable, has always existed, and probably exists in this form throughout the known universe; i.e., it's "natural." Some people explain or try to account for poverty or class position by focusing on the personal and moral merits of an individual. If people are poor, then it's something they did or didn't do; they were lazy, unlucky, didn't try hard enough, etc. This has the familiar ring of blaming the victims. Alternative explanations focus on the ways in which poverty and class position are due to structural, systematic, institutionalized economic and political power relations. These power relations are based firmly on dynamics such as race, gender, and class.

In the myth of the classless society, ambition and intelligence alone are responsible for success. The myth conceals the existence of a class society, which serves many functions. One of the main ways it keeps the working class and poor locked into a class-based system in a position of servitude is by cruelly creating false hope. It perpetuates the false hope among the working class and poor that they can have different opportunities in life. The hope that they can escape the fate that awaits them due to the class position they were born into. Another way the rags-to-riches myth is perpetuated is by creating enough visible tokens so that oppressed persons believe they, too, can get ahead. The creation of hope through tokenism keeps a hierarchical structure in place and lays the blame for not succeeding on those who don't. This keeps us from resisting and changing the class-based system. Instead, we accept it as inevitable, something we just have to live with. If oppressed people believe in equality of opportunity, then they won't develop class consciousness and will internalize the blame for their economic position. If the working class and poor do not recognize the way false hope is used to control them, they won't get a chance to control their lives by acknowledging their class position, by claiming that identity and taking action as a group.

The myth also keeps the middle class and upper class entrenched in the privileges awarded in a class-based system. It reinforces middle- and upper-class beliefs in their own superiority. If we believe that anyone in society really can get ahead, then middle- and upper-class status and privileges must be deserved, due to personal merits, and enjoyed—and defended at all costs. According to this viewpoint, poverty is regrettable but acceptable, just the outcome of a fair game: "There have always been poor people, and there always will be."

Class is more than just the amount of money you have; it's also the presence of economic security. For the working class and poor, working and eating are matters of survival, not taste. However, while one's class status can be defined in important ways in terms of monetary income, class is also a whole lot more—specifically, class is also culture. As a result of the class you are born into and raised in, class is your understanding of the world and where you fit in; it's composed of ideas, behavior, attitudes, values, and language; class is how you think, feel, act, look, dress, talk, move, walk; class is what stores you shop at, restaurants you eat in; class is the schools you attend, the education you attain; class is the very jobs you will work at throughout your adult life. Class even determines when we marry and become mothers. Working-class women become mothers long before middle-class women receive their bachelor's degrees. We experience class at every level of our lives; class is who our friends are, where we live and work even what kind of car we drive, if we own one, and what kind of health care we receive, if any. . . .

Class affects what we perceive as and what we have available to us as choices. Upon graduation from high school, I was awarded a scholarship to attend any college, private or public, in the state of California. Yet it never occurred to me or my family that it made any difference which college you went to. I ended up just going to a small college in my town. It never would have occurred to me to move away from my family for school, because no one ever had and no one would. I was the first person in my family to go to college. I had to figure out from reading college catalogs how to apply—no one in my family could have sat down and said, "Well, you take this test and then you really should think about . . ." Although tests and high school performance had shown I had the ability to pick up white middle-class lingo, I still had quite an adjustment to make—it was lonely and isolating in college. I lost my friends from high school—they were at the community college, vo-tech school, working, or married. I lasted a year and a half in this foreign environment before I quit college, married a factory worker, had a baby and resumed living in a community I knew. . . .

If class is more than simple economic status but one's cultural background as well, what happens if you're born and raised middle class, but spend some of your adult life with earnings below a middle-class income bracket—are you then working-class? Probably not. If your economic position changes, you still have the language, behavior, educational background, etc., of the middle class, which you can bank on. You will always have choices. Men who consciously try to refuse male privilege are still male; whites who want to challenge white privilege are still white. I think those who come from middle-class backgrounds need to recognize that their class privilege does not float out with the rinse water. Middle-class people can exert incredible power just by being nice and polite. The middle-class way of doing things is the standard—they're always right, just by being themselves. Beware of middle-class people who deny their privilege. Many people have times when they struggle to get shoes for the kids, when budgets are tight, etc. This isn't the same as long-term economic conditions without choices. . . .

How about if you're born and raised poor or working class, yet through struggle, usually through education, you manage to achieve a different economic level: do you become middle class? Can you pass? I think some working-class people may successfully assimilate into the middle class by learning to dress, talk, and act middle class—to accept and adopt the middle-class way of doing things. It all depends on how far they're able to go. To succeed in the middle-class world means facing great pressures to abandon working-class friends and ways.

Contrary to our stereotype of the working class—white guys in overalls—the working class is not homogeneous in terms of race or gender. If you are a person of color, if you live in a female-headed household, you are much more likely to be working class or poor. The experience of Black, Latino, American Indian or Asian American working classes will differ significantly from the white working classes, which have traditionally been able to rely on white privilege to provide a more elite position within the working class. Working-class people are often grouped together and stereotyped, but distinctions can be made among the working class, working poor, and poor. Many working-class families are supported by unionized workers who possess marketable skills. Most working-poor families are supported by non-unionized, unskilled men and women. Many poor families are dependent on welfare for their income.

Attacks on the welfare system and those who live on welfare are a good example of classism in action. We have a "dual welfare" system in this country whereby welfare for the rich in the form of tax-free capital gain, guaranteed loans, oil depletion allowances, etc., is not recognized as welfare. Almost everyone in America is on some type of welfare; but, if you're rich, it's in the form of tax deductions for "business" meals and entertainment, and if you're poor, it's in the form of food stamps. The difference is the stigma and humiliation connected to welfare for the poor, as compared to welfare for the rich, which is called "incentives." . . . The "dual welfare" system also assigns a different degree of stigma to programs that benefit women and children, such as AFDC, and programs whose recipients are primarily male, such as veterans' benefits. The implicit assumption is that mothers who raise children do not work and therefore are not deserving of their daily bread crumbs.

Anti-union attitudes are another prime example of classism in action. At best, unions have been a very progressive force for workers, women and people of color. At worst, unions have reflected the same regressive attitudes which are out there in other social structures: classism, racism, and sexism. Classism exists within the working class. The aristocracy of the working class—unionized, skilled workers—have mainly been white and male and have viewed themselves as being better than unskilled workers, the unemployed, and the poor, who are mostly women and people of color. The white working class must commit itself to a cultural and ideological transformation of racist attitudes. The history of working people, and the ways we've resisted many types of oppressions, are not something we're taught in school. Missing from our education is information about workers and their resistance.

Working-class women's critiques have focused on the following issues:

Education: White middle-class professionals have used academic jargon to rationalize and justify classism. The whole structure of education is a classist system. Schools in every town reflect class divisions: like the store list at the beginning of this article, you can list schools in your town by what classes of kids attend, and in most cities you can also list by race. The classist system is perpetuated in schools with the tracking system, whereby the "dumbs" are tracked into homemaking, shop courses and vocational school futures, while the "smarts" end up in advanced math, science, literature, and college-prep courses. If we examine these groups carefully, the coincidence of poor and working-class backgrounds with "dumbs" is rather alarming. The standard measurement of supposed intelligence is white middle-class English. If you're other than white middle class, you have to become bilingual to succeed in the educational system. If you're white middle class, you only need the language and writing skills you were raised with, since they're the standard. To do well in society presupposes middle-class background, experiences and learning for everyone. The tracking system separates those from the working class who can potentially assimilate to the middle class from all our friends, and labels us "college bound."

After high school, you go on to vocational school, community college, or college—public or private—according to your class position. Apart from the few who break into middle-class schools, the classist stereotyping of the working class as being dumb and inarticulate tracks most into vocational and low-skilled jobs. A few of us are allowed to slip through to reinforce the idea that equal opportunity exists. But for most, class position is destiny—determining our educational attainment and employment. Since we must overall abide by middle-class rules to succeed, the assumption is that we go to college in order to "better ourselves"—i.e., become more like them. I suppose it's assumed we have "yuppie envy" and desire nothing more than to be upwardly mobile individuals. It's assumed that we want to fit into their world. But many of us remain connected to our communities and families. Becoming college educated doesn't mean we have to, or want to, erase our first and natural language and value system. It's important for many of us to remain in and return to our communities to work, live, and stay sane.

Jobs: Middle-class people have the privilege of choosing careers. They can decide which jobs they want to work, according to their moral or political commitments, needs for challenge or creativity. This is a privilege denied the working class and poor, whose work is a means of survival, not choice. . . . Working-class women have seldom had the luxury of choosing between work in the home or market. We've generally done both, with little ability to purchase services to help with this double burden. Middle- and upper-class women can often hire other women to clean their houses, take care of their children, and cook their meals. Guess what class and race those "other" women are? Working a double or triple day is common for working-class women. Only middle-class women have an array of choices such as: parents put you through school, then you choose a career, then you choose when and if to have babies, then you choose a support system of working-class women to take care of your kids and house if you choose to resume your career. After the birth of my second child, I was working two part-time jobs—one loading trucks at night—and going to school during the days. While I was quite privileged because I could take my colicky infant with me to classes and the day-time job, I was in a state of continuous semi-consciousness. I had to work to support my family; the only choice I had was between

school or sleep: Sleep became a privilege. A white middle-class feminist instructor at the university suggested to me, all sympathetically, that I ought to hire someone to clean my house and watch the baby. Her suggestion was totally out of my reality, both economically and socially. I'd worked for years cleaning other peoples' houses. Hiring a working-class woman to do the shit work is a middle-class woman's solution to any dilemma which her privileges, such as a career, may present her.

Mothering: The feminist critique of families and the oppressive role of mothering has focused on white middle-class nuclear families. This may not be an appropriate model for communities of class and color. Mothering and families may hold a different importance for working-class women. Within this context, the issue of coming out can be a very painful process for working-class lesbians. Due to the homophobia of working-class communities, to be a lesbian is most often to be excommunicated from your family, neighborhood, friends and the people you work with. If you're working class, you don't have such clearly demarcated concepts of yourself as an individual, but instead see yourself as part of a family and community that forms your survival structure. It is not easy to be faced with the risk of giving up ties which are so central to your identity and survival.

. . .

Ways to Avoid Facing Classism

Deny Deny Deny: Deny your class position and the privileges connected to it. Deny the existence or experience of the working class and poor. You can even set yourself up (in your own mind) as judge and jury in deciding who qualifies as working class by your white middle-class standards. So if someone went to college, or seems intelligent to you, not at all like your stereotypes, they must be middle class.

Guilt Guilt Guilt: "I feel so bad, I just didn't realize!" is not helpful, but is a way to avoid changing attitudes and behaviors. Passivity—"Well, what can I do about it, anyway?"—and anger—"Well, what do they want!"—aren't too helpful either. Again, with these responses, the focus is on you and absolving the white middle class from responsibility. A more helpful remedy is to take action. Donate your time and money to local foodbanks. Don't cross picket lines. Better yet, go join a picket line.

How to Challenge Classism

If you're middle class, you can begin to challenge classism with the following:

1. Confront classist behavior in yourself, others and society. Use and share the privileges, like time or money, which you do have.

2. Make demands on working-class and poor communities' issues—anti-racism, poverty, unions, public housing, public transportation, literacy and day care.

3. Learn from the skills and strength of working people—study working and poor people's history; take some Labor Studies, Ethnic Studies, Women Studies classes. Challenge elitism. There are many different types of intelligence: white middle-class, academic, professional intellectualism being one of them (reportedly). Finally, educate yourself, take responsibility and take action.

If you're working class, just some general suggestions (it's cheaper than therapy—free, less time-consuming and I won't ask you about what your mother said to you when you were five):

1. Face your racism! Educate yourself and others, your family, community, any organizations you belong to; take responsibility and take action. Face your classism, sexism, heterosexism, ageism, able-bodiness, adultism. . . .

2. Claim your identity. Learn all you can about your history and the history and experience of all working and poor peoples. Raise your children to be anti-racist, anti-sexist and anti-classist. Teach them the language and culture of working peoples. Learn to survive with a fair amount of anger and lots of humor, which can be tough when this stuff isn't even funny.

3. Work on issues which will benefit your community. Consider remaining in or returning to your communities. If you live and work in white middle-class environments, look for working-class allies to help you survive with your humor and wits intact. How do working-class people spot each other? We have antenna.

We need not deny or erase the differences of working-class cultures but can embrace their richness, their variety, their moral and intellectual heritage. We're not at the point yet where we can celebrate differences—not having money for a prescription for your child is nothing to celebrate. It's not time yet to party with the white middle class, because we'd be the entertainment ("Aren't they quaint? Just love their workboots and uniforms and the way they cuss!"). We need to overcome divisions among working people, not by ignoring the multiple oppressions many of us encounter; or by oppressing each other, but by becoming committed allies on all issues which affect working people: racism, sexism, classism, etc. An injury to one is an injury to all. Don't play by ruling-class rules, hoping that maybe you can live on Connecticut Avenue instead of Baltic, or that you as an individual can make it to Park Place and Boardwalk. Tired of Monopoly? Always ending up on Mediterranean Avenue? How about changing the game?

READING 15

Voices
On Becoming Old Women

Baba Copper

When we ask for a chance to live our old age in comfort, creativity and usefulness, we ask it not for ourselves alone, but for you. We are not a special interest group. We are your roots. You are our continuity. What we gain is your inheritance.

—Irene Pauli, *Some Ironies of Aging*

How can old women define the subjects of age and ageism so that false understanding of these issues does not dominate the interactions between women and keep us forever separate? Aging is a natural and universal personal experience that begins the day we are born. It is a process of challenge—not necessarily growth and development when we are young as opposed to loss and deterioration when we are old—but learning through change. Ageism is the negative social response to different stages in the process of aging and it is a political issue. The ageism that old women experience is firmly embedded in sexism—an extension of the male power to define, control values, erase, disempower, and divide. Woman-to-woman ageism is an aspect of the horizontal conflict that usurps the energies of the colonized—part of the female competition for the crumbs of social power.

How can the same word be used for the experience of teenagers, old women, and the most powerful men in the world? Yet we say that all these are subject to *ageist* attitudes—stereotyping and denigration because of age. But each age group—children, teens, midlife women, old women, old men—have radically different expectations of their due, their rightful social place. For an old woman, ageism is a killer, because her sense of worth has been eroded by a lifelong pursuit of youth/beauty. Age passing—passing for young enough—is part of all female experience. The foundation of lies built into passing and the fear and loathing of female aging are what keep the generations of women—decade by decade—divided from each other.

I believe that age passing is one of the primary learning arenas of female competition, as well as an apprenticeship to hatred of old women. When women pass easily, we gain comfort knowing that we do not have to identify with the woman who, in our view, is not passing. "I am not like her" translates easily into "I am better than her." In our thirties, we do not want to be mistaken for forty. In our forties, we do not want anyone to assume we are fifty. Somewhere in our fifties, the mass of anxieties about age, and the increase of rejection and invisibility we are experiencing, becomes critical. This is often a time when our trained inability to identify with women older than ourselves reaches its climax. Old women cannot rely upon the midlife woman as ally. The midlife woman, in her rage and fear, may unconsciously discharge all kinds of covert aggression against the old woman as the personification of what is threatening her.

Can women afford to ignore issues that surround the aging process? When I have asked younger women what they thought ageism was all about, they talked about the aura of death and decay which permeates age for them, the oppressive power/over of the mythic Mother figure, and the deplorable neglect exhibited by the authorities in making adequate institutional responses to age. None have seen ageism as a problem of prejudice or bigotry on their part. With a righteousness reminiscent of the anchorman on the evening news, most of my young informants have advocated more and better government support for the old. But government subsidies for medicine and institutional care have created a highly profitable industry of geriatric technology, with the elderly aid recipients captive to the modern Grail, longevity. Just staying alive is a false goal. Acceptance of age in women has not kept pace with our increasing life expectancy. It is the quality of that extra time that is important. As long as women allow themselves to be brainwashed into worshiping youth and plasticized beauty, increased life expectancy (and the institutionalized responses to it) will remain a burden for both the young and the old.

How can ageism be defined by women; how can we develop clear vocabulary and theory; can we afford to ignore it? For me these questions are more than rhetorical. I am an old woman living in a highly politicized community of women. I find struggle and change taking place in relation to all the differences between women except age. I need to divert some of that political consciousness toward ageism.

I am an *old* woman. I am sixty-six. Part of the reason I self-identify as *old* is a need to escape the prissy category of "older woman." This label claims descriptive power over women from eighteen to eighty, depending upon the age and consciousness of the user. . . . After lots of internal arguments, I found a rationalization that made me comfortable with the label. Calling myself an old woman was the radical way out of my dilemma. At sixty-six, it may be presumptuous of me to assume a label that is descriptive of women in their nineties, but I have noticed that many of them avoid the term. Like other words that feminists are reclaiming by proud usage, I would take to myself the word everyone seems to fear. My *real* circumstances would not suffer more than they have from the visual impact of my years. Nobody but radical women would stand there beside me, honest and angry about the distortions that surround the time of life all women dread. I would walk through the door-of-no-return and from the other side name the politics of age instead of waltzing around pretending I am just an "older woman." The lies of age passing would not save me from the stigma of age. In fact, it has been my experience that the invention and practice of feminine lies keep women forever in harness, laboring to be someone who fits in, who pleases, who is chosen, who earns (and therefore deserves) love. I have grown sick of the harness.

. . .

Young and midlife women tend to see ageism as a continuing oppression of women throughout their lives. The point of view I tried to voice as an old woman sprang from my new experience, which revealed abrupt changes in the degree or intensity of stigma, when, for whatever reasons, one could no longer pass as middle-aged. I am uncomfortable with the absence of differentiation between the kind of ageism I can remember experiencing as a teenager and what I am experiencing in my sixties.

I felt confused. I did not know how to integrate these concepts into my present circumstances. Was the pain over the ageism I experience intensified by the fact that my youth privilege had been augmented by the privileges of being white, able, thin, blond, tall, middle class? And how did all this relate to age passing, for many women try—and some even succeed by the use of repeated plastic surgery—to appear forever middle-aged? For instance, the small, thin old woman—especially one who plays the "cute" social role—does not receive the same direct hostility that big "motherly" women do. Was the pain of ageism relative also, or was there a pall that settled over an old woman (the year varying for different women) which was similar for all whether or not they had been pretty or middle-class?

. . .

Death is an extremely important subject that our culture has mystified, professionalized, sensationalized—and at the same time, made taboo. Everyone needs to make his or her peace with the meaning of death. However, the assumption that death is a preoccupation, or subject of expertise, of midlife or old women is ageist. I understood that we might want to talk about death. But the old should not be seen as standing with death at their elbow. Nor should they be expected to help others on the subject or allow the subject to be age segregated. Repeatedly, younger women make assumptions about my relationship to death. One woman said that she shared identity with me because she had had many losses of people close to her in her life. She assumed that I had too. In reality, other than the death of my mother when she was ninety-three, no one I loved has ever died.

. . .

Here it was, that virulent stereotype—the age/death connection. . . . Apparently only old people die. Death does not hover near the cradle, the motorcycle, the toxic workplace, high bridges, or battlefields. But around old women, everyone is reminded that they have given their own possible mortality insufficient attention. Death is a forbidden subject with all but the old, who are expected to bear the burden of this social suppression. Since my own demise is as distant from my conscious mind as it was when I was twenty, I have come to recognize that it is my looks that evoke the age/death connection in others. Death has become a private buzzword for me, warning me of the shoals of ageism before me.

Talking about choice in relation to dying always makes me very nervous. I reminded the group that we were at the beginning of a worldwide demographic boom of old women. It is easy to predict that our society will soon be subject to all kinds of "new looks" at death and dying. I read a clipping from a futurist magazine suggesting that a demise pill be available to the elderly (but not the young, of course). The old are seen as half dead already. Old women, like everyone else, buy into the prevailing concepts surrounding both worth and death—we are as easy to brainwash as the next. When one believes that one has done everything one wants to do, it may be a way of expressing the feeling that what one has to contribute from a wheelchair, for example, is not valuable.

. . .

How can old women begin to change this? First, we have to name our circumstances more clearly, identifying the root sources of our denigrated place in society. Feminist analysis and the concept of ageism are not used as tools by most old women to explain the increased negative content of our experience. Old women tend to see problems as personal —interpersonal or physical or economic—instead of political. The time of life that should be a final ripening, a meaningful summation, a last chance for all the risks and pleasures of corporeal existence, is all too often deadened by emotional isolation and self-doubts. As the average life expectancy for women keeps creeping upward—almost into the eighties now—the quality of that life-to-be-expected keeps deteriorating.

The "natural alliance" that old women have a right to expect with midlife women will not emerge until all women begin to recognize the pitfalls of age passing. Separating the perspective of the barely-passing older woman from some of my concerns as one-who-no-longer-is-able-to-pass has taken all my confidence and a great deal of hindsight. The midlife woman feels increasing pressure—internal and external—about aging as well as the rejections of ageism. It is natural that she rushes forward to define the problem. In asserting her power over the insights of the old woman—the complaints, the accusations of ageism, the naming of the universal hatred of the Old Woman—she unconsciously silences the inherent radicalism of the only one who can tell her how it really is.

The problem for old women is a problem of power. First, power over the circumstances and directions of our own lives and identity. Second, power as an influence upon the world we live in— the world we have served, in which we have such a large, unrecognized vested interest. This is, of course, the rub. Patriarchal institutions are, without exception, designed to exclude the vision of old women. Most old women have little experience in leadership, influence, or even respect. Mostly, old women know how to serve. The roles reserved and expected of women in old age—grandmothers, self-effacing volunteers to the projects and priorities designed by others, or caretakers of old men—are custom fit to our powerless status.

But there are ways that all women can begin to prepare the way for the empowerment of themselves in the future, when they are old. These changes can first be brought about in the women's community, among lesbians and political women. The first step is for women to recognize that they have been programmed to hate old women and to deny them power. This brainwashing is so subtle that its eradication will take an effort equal to that which we have made and still must expend upon sexism. Further, this brainwashing extends down through our lives, making us fear the processes of our own bodies within time, so that our energies and attention are constantly undermined by ageist competition and self-doubts. These are attitudes and expectations that we can change now, if we decide to. Empowerment of women will come when we identify with women older than we are and not before.

READING 16

The Social Construction of Disability

Susan Wendell

I maintain that the distinction between the biological reality of a disability and the social construction of a disability cannot be made sharply, because the biological and the social are interactive in creating disability. They are interactive not only in that complex interactions of social factors and our bodies affect health and functioning, but also in that social arrangements can make a biological condition more or less relevant to almost any situation. I call the interaction of the biological and the social to create (or prevent) disability "the social construction of disability."

Disability activists and some scholars of disability have been asserting for at least two decades that disability is socially constructed. Moreover, feminist scholars have already applied feminist analyses of the social construction of the experience of being female to their analyses of disability as socially constructed. Thus I am saying nothing new when I claim that disability, like gender, is socially constructed. Nevertheless, I understand that such an assertion may be new and even puzzling to many readers, and that not everyone who says that disability is socially constructed means the same thing by it. Therefore, I will explain what I mean in some detail.

I see disability as socially constructed in ways ranging from social conditions that straightforwardly create illnesses, injuries, and poor physical functioning, to subtle cultural factors that determine standards of normality and exclude those who do not meet them from full participation in their societies. I could not possibly discuss all the factors that enter into the social construction of disability here, and I feel sure that I am not aware of them all, but I will try to explain and illustrate the social construction of disability by discussing what I hope is a representative sample from a range of factors.

Social Factors That Construct Disability

First, it is easy to recognize that social conditions affect people's bodies by creating or failing to prevent sickness and injury. Although, since disability is relative to a person's physical, social, and cultural environment, none of the resulting physical conditions is necessarily disabling, many do in fact cause disability given the demands and lack of support in the environments of the people affected. In this direct sense of damaging people's bodies in ways that are disabling in their environments, much disability is created by the violence of invasions, wars, civil wars, and terrorism, which cause disabilities not only through direct injuries to combatants and noncombatants, but also through the spread of disease and the deprivations of basic needs that result from the chaos they create. In addition, although we more often hear about them when they cause death, violent crimes such as shootings, knifings, beatings, and rape all cause disabilities, so that a society's success or failure in protecting its citizens from injurious crimes has a significant effect on its rates of disability.

The availability and distribution of basic resources such as water, food, clothing, and shelter have major effects on disability, since much disabling physical damage results directly from malnutrition and indirectly from diseases that attack and do more lasting harm to the malnourished and those weakened by exposure. Disabling diseases are also contracted from contaminated water when clean water is not available. Here too, we usually learn more about the deaths caused by lack of basic resources than the (often lifelong) disabilities of survivors.

Many other social factors can damage people's bodies in ways that are disabling in their environments, including (to mention just a few) tolerance of high-risk working conditions, abuse and neglect of children, low public safety standards, the degradation of the environment by contamination of air, water, and food, and the overwork, stress, and daily grinding deprivations of poverty. The social factors that can damage people's bodies almost always affect some groups in a society more than others because of racism, sexism, heterosexism, ageism, and advantages of class background, wealth, and education.

Medical care and practices, traditional and Western-scientific, play an important role in both preventing and creating disabling physical damage. (They also play a role in defining disability, . . .) Lack of good prenatal care and dangerous or inadequate obstetrical practices cause disabilities in babies and in the women giving birth to them. Inoculations against diseases such as polio and measles prevent quite a lot of disability. Inadequate medical care of those who are already ill or injured results in unnecessary disablement. On the other hand, the rate of disability in a society increases with improved medical capacity to save the lives of people who are dangerously ill or injured in the absence of the capacity to prevent or cure all the physical damage they have incurred. Moreover, public health and sanitation measures that increase the average lifespan also increase the number of old people with disabilities in a society, since more people live long enough to become disabled.

The *pace of life* is a factor in the social construction of disability that particularly interests me, because it is usually taken for granted by non-disabled people, while many people with disabilities are acutely aware of how it marginalizes or threatens to marginalize us. I suspect that increases in the pace of life are important social causes of damage to people's bodies through rates of accident, drug and alcohol abuse, and illnesses that result from people's neglecting their needs for rest and good nutrition. But the pace of life also affects disability as a second form of social construction, the social construction of disability through expectations of performance.

When the pace of life in a society increases, there is a tendency for more people to become disabled, not only because of physically damaging consequences of efforts to go faster, but also because fewer people can meet expectations of 'normal' performance; the physical (and mental) limitations of those who cannot meet the new pace become conspicuous and disabling, even though the same limitations were inconspicuous and irrelevant to full participation in the slower-paced society. Increases in the pace of life can be counterbalanced for some people by improvements in accessibility, such as better transportation and easier communication, but for those who must move or think slowly, and for those whose energy is severely limited, expectations of pace can make work, recreational, community, and social activities inaccessible.

Let me give a straightforward, personal illustration of the relationship between pace and disability. I am currently just able (by doing very little else) to work as a professor three-quarter time, on one-quarter disability leave. There has been much talk recently about possible increases in the teaching duties of professors at my university, which would not be accompanied by any reduction in expectations for the other two components of our jobs, research and administration. If there were to be such an increase in the pace of professors' work, say by one additional course per term, I would be unable to work more than half-time (by the new standards) and would have to request half-time disability leave, even though there had been no change in my physical condition. Compared to my colleagues, I would be more work-disabled than I am now. Some professors with less physical limitation than I have, who now work full-time, might be unable to work at the new full-time pace and be forced to go on part-time disability leave. This sort of change could contribute to disabling anyone in any job.

Furthermore, even if a person is able to keep up with an increased pace of work, any increase in the pace of work will decrease the energy available for other life activities, which may upset the delicate balance of energy by which a person manages to participate in them and eventually exclude her/him from those activities. The pace of those other activities may also render them inaccessible. For example, the more the life of a society is conducted on the assumption of quick travel, the more disabling are those physical conditions that affect movement and travel, such as needing to use a wheelchair or having a kind of epilepsy that prevents one from driving a car, unless compensating help is provided. These disabling effects extend into people's family, social, and sexual lives and into their participation in recreation, religious life, and politics.

Pace is a major aspect of expectations of performance; non-disabled people often take pace so much for granted that they feel and express impatience with the slower pace at which some people with disabilities need to operate, and accommodations of pace are often crucial to making an activity accessible to people with a wide range of physical and mental abilities. Nevertheless, expectations of pace are not the only expectations of performance that contribute to disability. For example, expectations of individual productivity can eclipse the actual contributions of people who cannot meet them, making people unemployable when they can in fact do valuable work. There are often very definite expectations about *how* tasks will be performed (not the standards of performance, but the methods). For example, many women with disabilities are discouraged from having children because other people can only imagine caring for children in ways that are impossible for women with their disabilities, yet everything necessary could be done in other ways, often with minor accommodations. Furthermore, the expectation that many tasks will be performed by individuals on their own can create or expand the disability of those who can perform the tasks only in cooperative groups or by instructing a helper.

Expectations of performance are reflected, because they are assumed, in the social organization and physical structure of a society, both of which create disability. Societies that are physically constructed and socially organized with the unacknowledged assumption that everyone is healthy, non-disabled, young but adult, shaped according to cultural ideals, and, often, male, create a great deal of disability through sheer neglect of what most people need in order to participate fully in them.

Feminists talk about how the world has been designed for the bodies and activities of men. In many industrialized countries, including Canada and the United States, life and work have been structured as though no one of any importance in the public world, and certainly no one who works outside the home for wages, has to breast-feed a baby or look after a sick child. Common colds can be acknowledged publicly, and allowances are made for them, but men-struation cannot be acknowledged and allowances are not made for it. Much of the public world is also structured as though everyone were physically strong, as though all bodies were shaped the same, as though everyone could walk, hear, and see well, as though everyone could work and play at a pace that is not compatible with any kind of illness or pain, as though no one were ever dizzy or incontinent or simply needed to sit or lie down. (For instance, where could you rest for a few minutes in a supermarket if you needed to?) Not only the architecture, but the entire physical and social organization of life tends to assume that we are either strong and healthy and able to do what the average young, non-disabled man can do or that we are completely unable to participate in public life.

A great deal of disability is caused by this physical structure and social organization of society. For instance, poor architectural planning creates physical obstacles for people who use wheelchairs, but also for people who can walk but cannot walk far or cannot climb stairs, for people who cannot open doors, and for people who can do all of these things but only at the cost of pain or an expenditure of energy they can ill afford. Some of the same architectural flaws cause problems for pregnant women, parents with strollers, and young children. This is no coincidence. Much architecture has been planned with a young adult, non-disabled male paradigm of humanity in mind. In addition, aspects of social organization that take for granted the social expectations of performance and productivity, such as inadequate public transportation (which I believe assumes that no one who is needed in the public world needs public transportation), communications systems that are inaccessible to people with visual or hearing impairments, and inflexible work arrangements that exclude part-time work or rest periods, create much disability.

When public and private worlds are split, women (and children) have often been relegated to the private, and so have the disabled, the sick, and the old. The public world is the world of strength, the positive (valued) body, performance and production, the non-disabled, and young adults. Weakness, illness, rest and recovery, pain, death, and the negative (devalued) body are private, generally hidden, and often neglected. Coming into the public world with illness, pain, or a devalued body, people encounter resistance to mixing the two worlds; the split is vividly revealed. Much of the experience of disability and illness goes underground, because there is no socially acceptable way of expressing it and having the physical and psychological experience acknowledged. Yet acknowledgement of this experience is exactly what is required for creating accessibility in the public world. The more a society regards disability as a private matter, and people with disabilities as belonging in the private sphere, the more disability it creates by failing to make the public sphere accessible to a wide range of people.

Disability is also socially constructed by the failure to give people the amount and kind of help they need to participate fully in all major aspects of life in the society, including making a significant contribution in the form of work. Two things are important to remember about the help that people with disabilities may need. One is that most industrialized societies give non-disabled people (in different degrees and kinds, depending on class, race, gender, and other factors) a lot of help in the form of education, training, social support, public communication and transportation facilities, public recreation, and other services. The help that non-disabled people receive tends to be taken for granted and not considered help but entitlement, because it is offered to citizens who fit the social paradigms, who by definition are not considered dependent on social help. It is only when people need a different kind or amount of help than that given to 'paradigm' citizens that it is considered help at all, and they are considered socially dependent. Second, much, though not all, of the help that people with disabilities need is required because their bodies were damaged by social conditions, or because they cannot meet social expectations of performance, or because the narrowly-conceived physical structure and social organization of society have placed them at a disadvantage; in other words, it is needed to overcome problems that were created socially.

Thus disability is socially constructed through the failure or unwillingness to create ability among people who do not fit the physical and mental profile of 'paradigm' citizens. Failures of social support for people with disabilities result in inadequate rehabilitation, unemployment, poverty, inadequate personal and medical care, poor communication services, inadequate training and education, poor protection from physical, sexual, and emotional abuse, minimal opportunities for social learning and interaction, and many other disabling situations that hurt people with disabilities and exclude them from participation in major aspects of life in their societies.

. . .

Cultural Construction of Disability

Culture makes major contributions to disability. These contributions include not only the omission of experiences of disability from cultural representations of life in a society, but also the cultural stereotyping of people with disabilities, the selective stigmatization of physical and mental limitations and other differences (selective because not all limitations and differences are stigmatized, and different limitations and differences are stigmatized in different societies), the numerous cultural meanings attached to various kinds of disability and illness, and the exclusion of people with disabilities from the cultural meanings of activities they cannot perform or are expected not to perform.

The lack of realistic cultural representations of experiences of disability not only contributes to the 'Otherness' of people with disabilities by encouraging the assumption that their lives are inconceivable to non-disabled people but also increases non-disabled people's fear of disability by suppressing knowledge of how people live with disabilities. Stereotypes of disabled people as dependent, morally depraved, super-humanly heroic, asexual, and/or pitiful are still the most common cultural portrayals of people with disabilities. Stereotypes repeatedly get in the way of full participation in work and social life. For example, Francine Arsenault, whose leg was damaged by childhood polio and later by gangrene, describes the following incident at her wedding:

> When I got married, one of my best friends came to the wedding with her parents. I had known her par-

ents all the time I was growing up; we visited in each other's homes and I thought that they knew my situation quite well.

But as the father went down the reception line and shook hands with my husband, he said, "You know, I used to think that Francine was intelligent, but to put herself on you as a burden like this shows that I was wrong all along."

Here the stereotype of a woman with a disability as a helpless, dependent burden blots out, in the friend's father's consciousness, both the reality that Francine simply has one damaged leg and the probability that her new husband wants her for her other qualities. Moreover, the man seems to take for granted that the new husband sees Francine in the same stereotyped way (or else he risks incomprehension or rejection), perhaps because he counts on the cultural assumptions about people with disabilities. I think both the stigma of physical 'imperfection' (and possibly the additional stigma of having been damaged by disease) and the cultural meanings attached to the disability contribute to the power of the stereotype in situations like this. Physical 'imperfection' is more likely to be thought to 'spoil' a woman than a man by rendering her unattractive in a culture where her physical appearance is a large component of a woman's value; having a damaged leg probably evokes the metaphorical meanings of being 'crippled,' which include helplessness, dependency, and pitifulness. Stigma, stereotypes, and cultural meanings are all related and interactive in the cultural construction of disability. . . .

Social Deconstruction of Disability

In my view, then, disability is socially constructed by such factors as social conditions that cause or fail to prevent damage to people's bodies; expectations of performance; the physical and social organization of societies on the basis of a young, non-disabled, 'ideally shaped,' healthy adult male paradigm of citizens; the failure or unwillingness to create ability among citizens who do not fit the paradigm; and cultural representations, failures of representation, and ex-

pectations. Much, but perhaps not all, of what can be socially constructed can be socially (and not just intellectually) deconstructed, given the means and the will.

A great deal of disability can be prevented with good public health and safety standards and practices, but also by relatively minor changes in the built environment that provide accessibility to people with a wide range of physical characteristics and abilities. Many measures that are usually regarded as helping or accommodating people who are now disabled, such as making buildings and public places wheelchair accessible, creating and respecting parking spaces for people with disabilities, providing American Sign Language translation, captioning, and Telephone Devices for the Deaf, and making tapes and Descriptive Video services available for people who are visually impaired, should be seen as preventive, since a great deal of disability is created by building and organizing environments, objects, and activities for a too-narrow range of people. Much more could be done along the same lines by putting people with a wide variety of physical abilities and characteristics in charge of deconstructing disability. People with disabilities should be in charge, because people without disabilities are unlikely to see many of the obstacles in their environment. Moreover, they are likely not to see them *as obstacles* even when they are pointed out, but rather as 'normal' features of the built environment that present difficulties for 'abnormal' people.

Disability cannot be deconstructed by consulting a few token disabled representatives. A person with a disability is not likely to see all the obstacles to people with disabilities different from her/his own, although s/he is likely to be more aware of potential inaccessibility. Moreover, people with disabilities are not always aware of the obstacles in our environment *as obstacles*, even when they affect us. The cultural habit of regarding the condition of the person, not the built environment or the social organization of activities, as the source of the problem, runs deep. For example, it took me several years of struggling with the heavy door to my building, sometimes having to wait until someone stronger came along, to realize that the door was an accessibility problem, not only for me, but for others as well. And I did not notice, until one of my students pointed it out, that the lack of signs that could be read from a distance at my university forced people with mobility impairments to expend a lot of energy unnecessarily, searching for rooms and offices. Although I have encountered this difficulty myself on days when walking was exhausting to me, I interpreted it, automatically, as a problem arising from my illness (as I did with the door), rather than as a problem arising from the built environment having been created for too narrow a range of people and situations. One of the most crucial factors in the deconstruction of disability is the change of perspective that causes us to look in the environment for both the source of the problem and the solutions.

. . .

Obstacles to the Deconstruction of Disability

. . .

Attitudes that disability is a personal or family problem (of biological or accidental origin), rather than a matter of social responsibility, are cultural contributors to disability and powerful factors working against social measures to increase ability. The attitude that disability is a personal problem is manifested when people with disabilities are expected to overcome obstacles to their participation in activities by their own extraordinary efforts. The public adoration of a few disabled heroes who are believed to have 'overcome their handicaps' against great odds both demonstrates and contributes to this expectation. The attitude that disability is a family matter is manifested when the families of people with disabilities are expected to provide whatever they need, even at great personal sacrifice by other family members. Barbara Hillyer describes the strength of expectations that mothers and other caregivers will do whatever is necessary to 'normalize' the lives of family members, especially children, with disabilities—not only providing care, but often doing the work of two people to maintain the illusion that there is nothing 'wrong' in the family.

These attitudes are related to the fact that many modern societies split human concerns into public and private worlds. Typically, those with disabilities and illnesses have been relegated to the private realm, along with women, children, and the old. This worldwide tendency creates particularly intractable problems for women with disabilities; since they fit two 'private' categories, they are often kept at home, isolated and overprotected. In addition, the confinement of people with disabilities in the private realm exploits women's traditional caregiving roles in order to meet the needs of people with disabilities, and it hides the need for measures to make the public realm accessible to everyone.

There also seem to be definite material advantages for some people (people without disabilities who have no disabled friends or relatives for whom they feel responsible) to seeing disability as a biological misfortune, the bad luck of individuals, and a personal or family problem. Accessibility and creating ability cost time, energy, and/or money. Charities for people with disabilities are big businesses that employ a great many non-disabled professionals; these charities depend upon the belief that responding to the difficulties faced by people with disabilities is superogatory for people who are not members of the family—not a social responsibility to be fulfilled through governments, but an act of kindness. Moreover, both the charities and most government bureaucracies (which also employ large numbers of non-disabled professionals) hand out help which would not be needed in a society that was planned and organized to include people with a wide range of physical and mental abilities. The potential resistance created by these vested interests in disability should not be underestimated.

The 'personal misfortune' approach to disability is also part of what I call the 'lottery' approach to life, in which individual good fortune is hoped for as a substitute for social planning that deals realistically with everyone's capabilities, needs and limitations, and the probable distribution of hardship. In Canada and the United States, most people reject the 'lottery' approach to such matters as acute health care for themselves and their families or basic education for their children. We expect it to be there when we need it, and we are (more or less) willing to pay for it to be there. I think the lottery approach persists with respect to disability partly because *fear,* based on ignorance and false beliefs about disability, makes it difficult for most non-disabled people to identify with people with disabilities. If the non-disabled saw the disabled as potentially themselves or as their future selves, they would want their societies to be fully accessible and to invest the resources necessary to create ability wherever possible. They would feel that 'charity' is as inappropriate a way of thinking about resources for people with disabilities as it is about emergency medical care or basic education.

The philosopher Anita Silvers maintains that it is probably impossible for most non-disabled people to imagine what life is like with a disability, and that their own becoming disabled is unthinkable to them. Certainly many people without disabilities believe that life with a disability would not be worth living. This is reflected in the assumption that potential disability is a sufficient reason for aborting a fetus, as well as in the frequent statements by non-disabled people that they would not want to live if they had to use a wheelchair, lost their eyesight, were dependent on others for care, and so on. The belief that life would not be worth living with a disability would be enough to prevent them from imagining their own disablement. This belief is fed by stereotypes and ignorance of the lives of people with disabilities. For example, the assumption that permanent, global incompetence results from any major disability is still prevalent; there is a strong presumption that competent people either have no major physical or mental limitations or are able to hide them in public and social life.

It seems that the cultural constructions of disability, including the ignorance, stereotyping, and stigmatization that feed fears of disability, have to be at least partly deconstructed before disability can be seen by more people as a set of social problems and social responsibilities. Until that change in perspective happens, people with disabilities and their families will continue to be given too much individual responsibility for 'overcoming' disabilities, expectations for the participation of people with disabilities

in public life will be far too low, and social injustices that are recognized now (at least in the abstract), such as discrimination against people with disabilities, will be misunderstood.

To illustrate, let me look briefly at the problem of discrimination. Clearly, when considering whether some action or situation is an instance of discrimination on the basis of ability, the trick is to distinguish ability to do the relevant things from ability to do irrelevant things. But, given that so many places and activities are structured for people with a narrow range of abilities, telling the two apart is not always easy. No one has to walk to be a typist, but if a company is housed in a building that is inaccessible to wheelchairs, and therefore refuses to hire a competent typist who uses a wheelchair because it would be expensive to fix the building, has it discriminated against her on the basis of her disability? Laws may say yes, but people will resist the laws unless they can see that the typist's inability to work in that office is not solely a characteristic of her as an individual. Most people will be ready to recognize refusal to hire her to work in a wheelchair-accessible office, provided she is the most competent typist who applied, as discrimination against her because of her disability; they will regard her disability (like her race) as a personal characteristic irrelevant in the circumstances. But will they be ready to require a company to create wheelchair accessibility so that it can hire her? This is being tested now in the United States by the 1990 Americans with Disabilities Act. Although I expect the Act to have an invaluable educational function, I predict that it will be very difficult to enforce until more people see accessibility as a public responsibility. Only then will they be able to recognize inabilities that are created by faulty planning and organization as irrelevant.

Consider these sentiments expressed in the Burger King case, as described in *The Disability Rag and Resource:*

> When deaf actress Terrylene Sacchetti sued Burger King under the ADA for refusing to serve her when she handed the cashier a written order at the pickup window instead of using the intercom, Stan Kyker, executive vice-president of the California Restau-

rant Association, said that those "people (with disabilities) are going to have to accept that they are not 100 percent whole and they can't be made 100 percent whole in everything they do in life."

Had a woman been refused service because she used a cane to walk up to the counter, her treatment would, I think, have been recognized at once as discrimination. But since Ms. Sacchetti was refused service because she was unable to perform the activity (ordering food) in the way (orally) that the restaurant required it to be performed, the refusal to serve her was not immediately recognized as discrimination. Indeed, the representative of the restaurant association apparently felt comfortable defending it on the grounds that her individual characteristics were the obstacles to Ms. Sacchetti's being served.

When I imagine a society without disabilities, I do not imagine a society in which every physical and mental 'defect' or 'abnormality' can be cured. On the contrary, I believe the fantasy that someday everything will be 'curable' is a significant obstacle to the social deconstruction of disability. Instead I imagine a fully accessible society, the most fundamental characteristic of which is universal recognition that all structures have to be built and all activities have to be organized for the widest practical range of human abilities. In such a society, a person who cannot walk would not be disabled, because every major kind of activity that is accessible to

someone who can walk would be accessible to someone who cannot, and likewise with seeing, hearing, speaking, moving one's arms, working for long stretches of time without rest, and many other physical and mental functions. I do not mean that everyone would be able to do everything, but rather that, with respect to the major aspects of life in the society, the differences in ability between someone who can walk, or see, or hear, and someone who cannot would be no more significant than the differences in ability among people who can walk, see, or hear. Not everyone who is not disabled now can play basketball or sing in a choir, but everyone who is not disabled now can participate in sports or games and make art, and that sort of general ability should be the goal in deconstructing disability.

I talk about accessibility and ability rather than independence or integration because I think that neither independence nor integration is always an appropriate goal for people with disabilities. Some people cannot live independently because they will always need a great deal of help from caregivers, and some people with disabilities, for example the Deaf, do not want to be integrated into non-disabled society; they prefer their own, separate social life. Everyone should, however, have access to *opportunities* to develop their abilities, to work, and to participate in the full range of public and private activities available to the rest of society.

DISCUSSION QUESTIONS FOR CHAPTER TWO

1. How do different forms of prejudice affect your life?

2. How do ideologies undergird institutions? How do these ideologies show up in the institutions that most affect your life?

3. How do institutions maintain gender inequality? Have you experienced gender inequality in particular institutions?

4. How do institutions work together to support and maintain one another?

5. How do hate crimes help maintain systems of inequality? What images of hate crimes do you recall? What effects do these images have on you?

SUGGESTIONS FOR FURTHER READING

Allison, Dorothy. *Trash.* Ithaca, NY: Firebrand, 1989.

Anzaldúa, Gloria. *Borderlands/La Frontera: The New Mestiza.* San Francisco: Aunt Lute, 1987.

Blee, Kathleen M. *Inside Organized Racism: Women in the Hate Movement.* Berkeley: University of California Press, 2002.

Frankenberg, Ruth. *White Women, Race Matters: The Social Construction of Whiteness.* Minneapolis: University of Minnesota Press, 1993.

hooks, bell. *Where We Stand: Class Matters.* New York: Routledge, 2002.

Lorde, Audre. *Sister Outsider.* Freedom, CA: Crossing Press, 1984.

Penelope, Julia, and Susan J. Wolfe, eds. *The Original Coming Out Stories,* 2nd ed. Freedom, CA: Crossing Press, 1991.

Stein, Arlene. *The Stranger Next Door: The Story of a Small Community's Battle over Sex, Faith, and Civil Rights.* Boston: Beacon Press, 2002.

CHAPTER THREE

Learning Gender in a Diverse Society

Recently, while teaching a unit on the social construction of gender in a women's studies class, we asked how many among the large number of women students were identified as tomboys when they were growing up. A sea of hands responded as women remembered their early years as girls who resisted traditional notions of femininity. Then the male students were asked whether they had been called "sissies" when they were young. The whole group laughed as one lone male sheepishly raised his hand and remarked that he'd always been a sissy. Why is it so easy to say you were a tomboy and so difficult to admit to being a sissy? This has a lot to do with the meanings associated with masculinity and femininity and the ways these are ranked in society. In this chapter we focus specifically on gender and sexism, keeping in mind two important points: First, how gender is constructed in connection to other differences among women like race, ethnicity, and class, and second, how sexism as a system of oppression is related to other systems of inequality and privilege.

BIOLOGY AND CULTURE

In Chapter 1 we explained gender as the way society creates, patterns, and rewards our understandings of femininity and masculinity or the process by which roles and appropriate behaviors are ascribed to women and men. Gender, in other words, can be understood as the social organization of sexual difference. Although biological distinctions create female and male humans, society interprets these differences and gives us "feminine" and "masculine" people. These adjectives are intentionally placed in quotation marks to emphasize that notions of femininity and masculinity are socially constructed—created by social processes that reflect the various workings of power in society. Therefore these notions are culturally and historically changeable. There is nothing essential, intrinsic, or static about femininity or masculinity; rather they are social categories that might mean different things in different societies and in different historical periods. Society shapes notions of femininity and masculinity through the subtle interactions between nature and nurture.

The relationship between biology (female/male) and culture (feminine/masculine), however, is more complicated than the assertion that sex is a biological fact and gender is the societal interpretation of that fact. Although biology may imply some basic physiological facts, culture gives meaning to these in such a way that we must question whether biology can exist except within the society that gives it meaning in the first place. This implies that sex, in terms of raw male or female, is already gendered by the culture within which these physiological facts of biology exist. In other words, although many people make a distinction between biological sex (female/male) and learned gender (feminine/masculine), it

■ LEARNING ACTIVITY: TOMBOYS AND SISSIES

Take an informal poll on your campus. Ask the women if they ever wanted to be a boy when they were growing up. Note their reaction to the question. Then ask why or why not. Also ask the women if they were considered tomboys growing up and how they felt about it if they were. Record responses and observations in a research journal.

Ask men on your campus if they ever wanted to be a girl when they were growing up. Again, note their reaction to the question. Ask why or why not. Then ask if they were considered sissies growing up and, if so, how they felt about it. Record responses and observations.

Once you've completed your poll, compare and contrast the responses you received from women and men. What do you notice? Why do you think responses may have been the way they were? What do responses suggest about gender in American society?

is really impossible to speak of a fixed biological sex category outside of the sense that a culture makes of that category.

An example that highlights how biology is connected to culture concerns the processes by which ambiguous sex characteristics in children are handled. When hermaphrodites or "intersex" children are born without distinct genitalia to characterize them as either girls or boys, health professionals and the family make a sex determination. Hormone therapy and surgeries follow to make such a child fit the constructed binary categories our society has created, and gender is taught in accordance with this decision. This is an example of a breakdown in the taken-for-granted tight connection between natural biology and learned gender.

Gender is one of the most important features of a person's identity, shaping social life and informing attitudes, behavior, and the individual's sense of self. This is aptly revealed in Lois Gould's "X: A Fabulous Child's Story." "X" is neither obviously masculine nor feminine, and, as a result, s/he causes much confusion among people who just do not know what to do with an "X." The pervasiveness of gender is also a theme of Judith Lorber's article "The Social Construction of Gender." She explains that gender is a process that involves multiple patterns of interaction and is created and re-created constantly in human interaction. Lorber also makes the important point that because gender is so central in shaping our lives, much of what is gendered we do not even recognize; it's made normal and ordinary and occurs on a subconscious level. In other words, the differences between femininity (passive, dependent, intuitive, emotional) and masculinity (strong, independent, in control, out of touch emotionally) are made to seem natural and inevitable despite the fact that gender is a social script that individuals learn. Importantly, many of the skills and practices associated with gender involve privilege and entitlements. They also involve limitations.

In reality, gender is a practice in which all people engage; it is something we perform over and over in our daily lives. In this sense, gender is something that we "do" rather than "have." Through a process of *gender socialization,* we are taught and learn the appropriate thinking and behaviors associated with being a boy or girl in this culture. We actively learn the skills and practices of gender, and most of us become very accomplished in these various performances. For example, in sports, the way that girls tend naturally to throw a ball is often the object of derision. Throwing the way boys do, however, is actually an act that is learned, then performed again and again until it becomes a skill. Girls can learn to throw like boys if they are taught. As Mariah Burton Nelson contends, men are not necessarily better athletes than women; rather, sports as an institution has developed to reflect the particular athletic competencies of men. For example, if long-distance swimming or balance beam (activities where women generally outperform men) were popular national sports, then we might think differently about the athletic capabilities of women and men.

In addition to sports, there are many other major U.S. institutions that support gendered practices. You only need go to a toy store and cruise the very different girls' and boys'

LEARNING ACTIVITY: SPEAKING OF WOMEN AND MEN

Think about the adjectives we typically use to describe women and men and list these words in the columns below. A couple of examples are provided to get you started.

WOMEN	MEN
Passive	Active
Nurturing	Strong

What do you notice about the words we use to describe women and men? How does our language reinforce stereotypical notions about women and men?

Think about the words we use to designate women and list these names in the columns below. Also, try to find parallel names for women and men. And think about the profanities we use as well. Again, a couple of examples are provided.

WOMEN	MEN
Slut	Stud
Chick	

What do you notice here about the terms we use to name women and men? What is the significance of the words for which you could not identify parallels?

How do you think language plays a role in shaping the ways we think about and "do" gender?

aisles to witness the social construction of gender in contemporary U.S. society. What does it mean to get a child-size ironing board instead of a toy gun, and what kinds of behaviors and future roles do these toys help create and justify? In "Spiking the Punch," Natalie Angier contends that the social context limits how girls and women express their aggression; instead of using their bodies, they use words (as a direct form) and snubbing, sulking, and withdrawing (as indirect forms).

This discussion of gender identity and practices does not imply that all men are ambitious and independent and all women domestic and emotional. However, this discussion clarifies the social norms or shared values associated with the two kinds of human beings our society has created. Gender norms provide the standards or parameters through which thoughts and behaviors are molded. If we created a continuum with "feminine" on one end and "masculine" on the other, we would find mostly women on one end and mostly men on the other, and a mixture in between. This means that women and men learn the practices of gender, internalize the norms associated with masculinity and femininity, are rewarded for appropriate behaviors and sanctioned for inappropriate behaviors, and learn to perform the ones that are expected of them.

There are some people who consider themselves *transgendered.* Identifying oneself as transgendered involves resisting the social construction of gender into two distinct categories, masculinity and femininity, and working to break down these constraining categories. Transgendered people push at the boundaries of gender and help reveal its constructed nature. *Transsexuals* are transgendered people who believe that they are born with the bodies of the wrong sex. Usually they desire to be surgically altered to claim a sex different from the one into which they were born. The terms *transgendered* and *transsexual* are distinct from *transvestites*, people who dress in the other sex's attire. Being transgendered does not imply being gay. Transgendered identities are about gender performance, whereas homosexual identity is about the expression of sexuality. In "To Be or Not to Be," Leslie Feinberg writes about trans liberation and the necessity for *gender freedom:* the right of all individuals to be able to express their gender in any way they choose.

As a concept, transgendered is different from androgyny, although in practice some people who identify as transgendered may attempt to be androgynous as they push against gender boundaries. *Androgyny* can be defined as the lack of gender differentiation; androgynous people display a balanced mixture of recognizable feminine and masculine traits. X in Lois Gould's story is an androgynous child. Transgendered individuals do not want to be constrained by categories of masculinity and femininity and exhibit instead traits that are difficult to label as either masculine or feminine.

HISTORICAL MOMENT: GENDER TESTING

In 1966, the European Athletics Championships in Budapest required the first sex testing of women athletes. Earlier, charges had been leveled suggesting that some women competitors were really men. In 1966, the first sex test was a visual examination of the naked athletes. Later, this test was replaced by a test that detected the athletes' chromosomal pattern (XX for female and XY for male).

In 1967, Polish sprinter Ewa Klobukowska failed the sex test and was banned from competition. Later, doctors found that she had a condition that once identified would have allowed her to compete.

In 1985, Spanish hurdler Maria Patino expected to compete in the World University Games in Kobe, Japan. Patino had lived her entire life as a woman, and her body type and sex characteristics were typically female. Unfortunately, for Patino, however, her sex test revealed that she did not have two X chromosomes. She was barred from the competition. A few months later, she competed in Spain and won her event. Following her win, however, she was kicked off the Spanish national team, stripped of her titles, and banned from all future competition. Her fight to be reinstated by the International Amateur Athletics Federation took 2½ years.

While our society generally operates under the assumption that people are either male or female, variations from typical biological patterns are common. Some form of intersexuality may occur in as many as 1 in 100 births. Generally, 1 in 400 female athletes will fail the sex test. For many years, women athletes engaged in activism to stop the sex test. Finally, the test was suspended for the 2000 Olympics, although the Olympic Committee reserved the right to reinstate the test at any point in the future.

Notice that sex testing has only been used for female athletes. Why do you suppose this is true? How does the existence of people who do not fit neatly into one or the other of the biological categories of male and female disrupt notions of fixed sexes and fixed genders?

Calvin and Hobbes   by Bill Watterson

It is interesting to note that contemporary ideas about androgyny tend to privilege the "andro" more than the "gyny," with the presentation of androgyny looking a lot like a young male than a mature female. The trappings of femininity seem to be the first things that are shed when a body tries to redo itself as androgynous. This is related to androcentrism and the ways masculinity more closely approximates our understanding of "human."

MASCULINITY

In contemporary U.S. society, *masculinity* has been constructed from the classical traits of intelligence, courage, and honesty, with the addition of two other key dimensions. One of these revolves around potent sexuality and an affinity for violence: the machismo element. *Machismo* involves breaking rules, sexual potency contextualized in the blending of sex and violence, and contempt for women (*misogyny*). To be a man is to *not* be a woman. Weakness, softness, and vulnerability are to be avoided at all costs. It is no coincidence that the symbol of male ♂ represents Mars, the Roman god of war. Another dimension of masculinity is the *provider role, composed of ambition, confidence, competence, and strength.* Research by Deborah David and Robert Brannon characterizes four dictates of masculinity that encompass these key dimensions. The dictates include the following: (1) "no sissy stuff," the rejection of femininity; (2) the "big wheel," ambition and the pursuit of success, fame, and wealth; (3) the "sturdy oak," confidence, competence, stoicism, and toughness; and (4) "give 'em hell," the machismo element.* Although these scripts dictate masculinity in a broad sense, there are societal demands that construct masculinity differently for different kinds of men. Middle-class masculinity puts an emphasis on the big wheel dimension, the dictates of White masculinity often involve the sturdy oak, and men of color often become associated with the machismo element. The latter, however, tends not to apply to Asian or Asian American men who are often seen as feminized and less masculine.

---

*Deborah S. David and Robert Brannon, eds. *The Forty-Nine Percent Majority: The Male Sex Role* (Reading, MA: Addison-Wesley, 1976), pp. 13–35.

RITES OF PASSAGE

In almost every culture, adolescents participate in some rite of passage to mark entry into adulthood. Quite often, these rites reinforce gender distinctions. Most rites of passage share four basic elements: (1) separation from society, (2) preparation or instruction from an elder, (3) transition, and (4) welcoming back into society with acknowledgment of changed status.* Notice in the following examples how gender is reinforced through rites of passage:

• Among the Okrika of Africa, girls participate in the Iria, a rite that begins in the "fatting rooms" where the girls are fed rich foods to cause the body to "come out." The girls learn traditional songs from the elderly women, and these songs are used to free the girls from their romantic attachments to water spirits so they can become marriageable and receive mortal suitors. On the final day of their initiation, the water spirits are expected to try to seize the girls, but the Osokolo (a male) strikes the girls with sticks and drives them back to the village, ensuring their safety and future fertility.*

• The Tukuna of the Amazon initiate girls into womanhood at the onset of menstruation through the Festa das Mocas Novas. For several weeks, the girl lives in seclusion in a chamber in her family's home. The Tukuna believe that during this time, the girl is in the underworld and in increasing danger from demons, the Noo. Near the end of the initiation period, the girl is painted with black genipa dye for 2 days to protect her from the Noo, while guests arrive, some wearing masks to become incarnations of the Noo. On the third day, she leaves the chamber to dance with her family until dawn. The shaman gives her a firebrand to throw at the Noo to break the Noo's power and allow her to enter into womanhood.*

• In Ohafia in Nigeria, a father provides his son with a bow and arrows around age 7 or 8. The boy practices shooting at targets until he develops the skill to kill a small bird. When this task is accomplished, the boy ties the dead bird to the end of his bow and marches through his village singing that his peers who have not yet killed their first

(continued)

bird are cowards. His father, then, dresses him in finery and takes him to visit, often for the first time, his maternal family. His new social role distinguishes him from the "cowards" and marks his entrance into manhood.[†]

What are some rites of passage in the United States? How do these rites reinforce gender? How might rites of passage be developed that acknowledge entrance into adulthood without reinforcing gender distinctions?

[*] Cassandra Halle Delaney, "Rites of Passage in Adolescence," *Adolescence* 30 (1995): 891–987.
[†] www.siu.edu/~anthro/mccall/children.html.

LEARNING ACTIVITY: PERFORMING GENDER IN THE MOVIES

Many movies offer gender-bending performances. Choose one or more of the following movies to watch. During the movie, record your observations about how the various characters learn and perform gender.

- *Victor/Victoria*
- *Tootsie*
- *Mrs. Doubtfire*
- *To Wong Foo, Thanks for Everything! Julie Newmar*
- *The Adventures of Priscilla, Queen of the Desert*
- *Switch*
- *The Birdcage*
- *Orlando*
- *Shakespeare in Love*
- *Boys Don't Cry*
- *Big Momma's House*
- *Sorority Boys*
- *Nutty Professor*
- *Nutty Professor II: The Klumps*

Some changes in the social construction of contemporary masculinity have allowed for a downplaying of the machismo element without a loss of sexual potency or societal control: a few small steps made into the land of the feminine. Although the machismo element is still acted out by countless teenage boys and men, it is also avoided by many men who genuinely do not want to be constrained by its demands. Often these men have realized that moving away from the machismo does not necessarily imply a loss of power. In fact, it seems contemporary women may prefer men who are a little more sensitive and vulnerable. In part, these changes have come about as a result of the focus on gender provided by the women's movement. As feminist writer and activist Gloria Steinem once said, gender is a prison for both women and men. The difference, she said, is that for men it's a prison with wall-to-wall carpeting and someone to bring you coffee. Understanding the limitations associated with masculine social scripts has encouraged many men to transform these scripts into more productive ways of living. Many pro-feminist men and men's organizations have been at the forefront of this work.

Some men have responded to the limitations of masculinity and the advances of women brought about by feminism by focusing on themselves as victims. This is evident in the mytho-poetic men's movement, discussed in Allan Johnson's essay "Shame, Guilt, and Responsibility" in Chapter 1. Johnson suggests that it does

> more harm than good by encouraging men to pursue private solutions to social problems. Drumming, chanting, and storytelling may help men feel more connected to one another and to a mythic sense of manhood, but it does little to illuminate or transform the patriarchal system that created the wounds they want to heal.

Other men more overtly express their desire to take back the power they believe they have lost as a result of changes in contemporary notions of femininity and the gains of the women's movement. These include the Promise Keepers, a group of Christian-affiliated men who want to return men to their rightful place in the family and community through a strong re-assertion of traditional gender roles. They believe, that in the family, men are to rule and women are to serve.

FEMININITY

Adjectives associated with traditional notions of femininity include soft, passive, domestic, nurturing, emotional, dependent, sensitive, as well as delicate, intuitive, fastidious, needy, fearful, and so forth. These are the qualities that have kept women in positions of subordination and encouraged them to do the domestic and emotional work of society. Again, no surprise that the symbol of female ♀ represents Venus, the goddess of love. "Doing gender" in terms of femininity involves speaking, walking, looking, and acting in certain ways: in feminine ways. The performative quality involved in being a drag queen (a gay man who is acting out normative femininity) highlights and reveals the taken-for-granted (at least by women) affectations of femininity. Yet, femininity, like masculinity, varies across cultures and groups. For example, due to historical and cultural factors, many African American women have not internalized the association of femininity with passivity and dependence characteristic of White women. Asian American women, on the other hand, often have to deal with societal stereotypes that construct femininity very much in terms of passivity and dependence: the "exotic gardenia" or "oriental chick" described in Nellie Wong's poem "When I Was Growing Up."

A key aspect of femininity is its bifurcation or channeling into two opposite aspects. These aspects involve the chaste, domestic, caring mother or madonna and the sexy, seducing, fun-loving playmate or whore (known in popular mythology as women you marry and women with whom you have sex). These polar opposites cause tension as women navigate the implications of these aspects of femininity in their everyday lives. This is an example of the double bind that Marilyn Frye wrote about in her article "Oppression" included in Chapter 2. A woman often discovers that neither sexual activity nor sexual inactivity is quite right. If she is too sexually active, she will be censured for being too loose, the whore; if she refrains from sexual activity, she might similarly be censured for being a prude or frigid. Notice there are many slang words for both kinds of women: those who have too much sex

ACTIVIST PROFILE: GLORIA STEINEM

Gloria Steinem didn't set out to become one of the key spokespersons for feminism. Growing up in poverty and with a mentally ill mother, Steinem often found herself in the role of her mother's caretaker. Despite the difficulties at home, she succeeded at school and was eventually accepted to Smith College, where her interest in women's rights began to take hold. After graduating from Smith, Steinem received a fellowship to do graduate studies at the University of Delhi and University of Calcutta, India. While in India, she did some work as a freelance writer and, upon returning to the United States, began a career in journalism.

As a woman in journalism, Steinem was rarely given serious assignments. Her most famous article resulted from a 1963 undercover assignment as a Playboy Bunny. Steinem saw the article as an opportunity to expose sexual harassment, but following its publication she had a difficult time being taken seriously as a journalist, despite the excellent reviews the article received.

She finally got her chance for key political assignments in 1968 when she came on board *New York Magazine* as a contributing editor. One assignment sent her to cover a radical feminist meeting, and following that meeting she moved to the center of the women's movement, co-founding the National Women's Political Caucus and the Women's Action Alliance.

In 1972 she co-founded *Ms.* magazine. Although Steinem believed there should be a feminist magazine, she had not intended to start it herself. Originally, she had thought she'd turn over the editorship once the magazine got on its feet. But with the success of *Ms.*, Steinem became one of the nation's most visible and important proponents of feminism.

The first issue of *Ms.* featured Wonder Woman on the cover, and its entire first printing of 300,000 copies sold out in 8 days. Steinem remained editor for 15 years and is still involved with the magazine today.

THE PROBLEM WITH PROMISE KEEPERS

". . . sit down with your wife and say something like this, 'Honey, I've made a terrible mistake. . . . I gave up leading this family, and I forced you to take my place. Now I must reclaim that role.' . . . I'm not suggesting you ask for your role back; I'm urging you to take it back. . . . there can be no compromise here. If you're going to lead, you must lead. . . . Treat the lady gently and lovingly. But lead."
—Tony Evans, leader of Promise Keepers

Promise Keepers posits itself as a Christian men's movement intended to unite men through vital relationships to become godly influences in the world. Sounds great on the surface, doesn't it? Promise Keepers claims it has no political agenda and only desires to help men build meaningful relationships with God, their families, and one another. Admirable goals, no doubt.

But let's look a little deeper. According to a *Washington Post* poll conducted during a Promise Keepers rally in D.C., 60 percent had an unfavorable opinion of feminists, 69 percent favored making divorce harder to obtain, and 94 percent opposed allowing same-sex marriages.

Promise Keepers calls for wives to submit themselves to their husbands and urges husbands to take control of the family back from their wives. They oppose abortion and homosexuality. Promise Keepers founder Bill McCartney was instrumental in the success of Colorado's anti-lesbian and anti-gay legislation, which was eventually ruled unconstitutional by the Supreme Court. McCartney has also been a featured speaker at rallies of the extremist anti-abortion group, Operation Rescue.

At its core, Promise Keepers is about maintenance of patriarchy. Again, examine the words of Promise Keepers leader Tony Evans: "I believe that feminists of the more aggressive persuasion are frustrated women unable to find the proper male leadership. If a woman were receiving the right kind of love and attention and leadership, she would not want to be liberated from that."

Listen carefully and critically to the rhetoric of any group trying to influence people to its way of thinking. Although the rhetoric may suggest the group is doing one thing, the reality may be that the group's agenda is entirely something else. The problem with Promise Keepers is not that it wants to help men be good husbands. The problem is that Promise Keepers wants men to take control and women to submit. They may couch their ideas in language about honor and integrity, but their ideas are really about reinforcing male supremacy.

The National Organization for Women maintains a web page on Promise Keepers. Visit this site at *www.now.org/issues/right/pk.html.*

and those who do not have enough. This is the double bind: You're damned if you do and potentially damned if you don't. These contradictions and mixed messages serve to keep women in line.

Unlike contemporary masculinity, which is exhibiting very small steps into the realms of the feminine, femininity has boldly moved into areas that were traditionally off-limits. Today's ideal woman (perhaps from a woman's point of view) is definitely more androgy-

LEARNING ACTIVITY:
WALK LIKE A MAN, SIT LIKE A LADY

One of the ways we perform gender is by the way we use our bodies. Very early, children learn to act their gender in the ways they sit, walk, and talk.

Try this observation research:

- Observe a group of schoolchildren playing. Make notes about what you observe concerning how girls and boys act, particularly how they use their bodies in their play and communication.
- Find a place where you can watch people sitting or walking. A public park or mall may offer an excellent vantage point. Record your observations about the ways women and men walk and sit.

Also try this experiment: Ask a friend of the opposite sex to participate in an experiment with you. Take turns teaching each other to sit and to walk like the opposite sex. After practicing your newfound gender behaviors, write your reflections about the experience.

nous than the ideal woman of the past. The contemporary ideal woman might be someone who is smart, competent, and independent, beautiful, thin, and sexy, yet also loving, sensitive, competent domestically, and emotionally healthy. Note how this image has integrated characteristics of masculinity with traditional feminine qualities, at the same time that it has retained much of the feminine social script. The contemporary ideal woman is strong, assertive, active, and independent rather than soft, passive, fearful, delicate, and dependent. The assumption is that she is out in the public world rather than confined to the home. She has not completely shed her domestic, nurturing, and caring dimension, however, or her intuitive, emotional, and sensitive aspects. These attributes are important in her success as a loving and capable partner to a man, as indeed are her physical attributes concerning looks and body size.

To be a modern woman today (we might even say a "liberated woman") is to be able to do *everything*: the superwoman. It is important to ask who is benefiting from this new social script. Women work in the public world (often in jobs that pay less, thus helping employers and the economic system) and yet still are expected to do the domestic and emotional work of home and family as well as stay beautiful. In many ways contemporary femininity tends to serve both the capitalist economic system and individual men better than the traditional, dependent, domestic model.

GENDER RANKING

Gender encompasses not only the socially constructed differences prescribed for different kinds of human beings but also the values, associated with these differences. Recall the sissy/tomboy exercise at the beginning of this chapter. Those traits assigned as feminine are less valued than those considered masculine. It is okay to emulate the masculine and act like a boy, but it is not okay to emulate the feminine. We recently attended a baby shower where the expectant mother was opening gifts. As she pulled a blue sleeper suit from its wrapper, the person who had bought the gift explained that even though the baby's sex was not yet known, she hoped the gift was still appropriate because a girl could still wear blue. The implication was that because a boy ought not to wear pink, a blue sleeper was a more adaptable color and therefore a safer gift.

Gender ranking sets the stage for sexism. Judith Lorber writes, "When genders are ranked, the devalued genders have less power, prestige, and economic rewards than the valued genders." Just as White is valued above Brown or Black, and young (though not too young) above old, and heterosexual above homosexual, masculinity tends to be ranked higher than femininity. To be male is to have privileges vis-à-vis gender systems; to be female means to be a member of a target group. The social system here that discriminates and privileges on the basis of gender is sexism. It works by viewing the differences between women and men as important for determining access to social, economic, and political resources. As defined in Chapter 2, *sexism* is the system that discriminates and privileges on the basis of gender and that results in gender stratification. Given the ranking of gender in our society, sexism works to privilege men and limit women. In other words, men receive entitlements and privilege in a society that ranks masculinity over femininity.

DIVERSE GENDERED EXPERIENCES

Although all women are limited by sexism as a system of power that privileges men over women, the social category "woman," as you recall from Chapter 2, is hardly homogeneous. Gender shapes different women's lives in different ways; women are not affected by gender as a system of privilege and inequality in the same way. Other systems based upon class, race, sexual orientation, and so forth interact with gender to produce different experiences for individual women. In other words, the effects of gender and understandings of both femininity and masculinity are mediated by other systems of power. This is what Virginia Sapiro in "The Plurality of Gender-Based Realities" means when she says that forms of gender-based oppression and exploitation depend in part upon other social characteristics in people's lives. She also makes the important point that gender practices are often a way to enforce other types of inequalities.

For example, African American women are often characterized as promiscuous or matriarchal, and African American men are described as hyperathletic and sexually potent. Jewish women are painted as overly materialistic and overbearing, whereas Jewish men are

IDEAS FOR ACTIVISM

- Be a gender traitor for a day. Act/dress in ways that are not generally considered to be appropriate for your gender.
- Develop and perform on campus a street theater piece about gender performance.
- Plan, create, publish, and distribute a zine challenging traditional gender roles.
- Examine how masculinity is valued above femininity on your campus. Write a letter about your findings to your campus newspaper.

supposedly very ambitious, thrifty, good at business, yet still tied to their mothers' apron strings. Latinas and Chicanas are stereotyped as sexy and fun loving, and, likewise, Latinos and Chicanos are seen as oversexed, romantic, and passionate. Native American women are portrayed as silent and overworked or exotic and romantic, whereas Native American men are seen as aloof mystics, close to nature, or else as savages and drunks. Asian American women have also been typed as exotic, as well as passive and delicate, at the same time that Asian American men are seen as lacking in masculinity and feminized. All these problematic constructions are created against the norm of Whiteness and work to maintain the privileges of the mythical norm. This concept is illustrated in Nellie Wong's poem. She longed to be White, something she saw as synonymous with being a desirable woman. Although there are ethnic and regional stereotypes for White women (like the dizzy blonde, Southern belle, sexually liberated Scandinavian, or hot-tempered Irish), for the most part White women tend not to have discrete stereotypes associated with their race. This reflects the fact that White people are encouraged not to see White as a racial category although it is just as racialized as any other racial group. The fact that being White can be claimed the mythical norm strips Whiteness from the historical and political roots of its construction as a racial category.

Diverse gendered experiences (the title of this subsection) implies that the expression of femininity, or the parameters of femininity expected and allowed, is related to the confluence of gender with other systems. Historically, certain women (the poor and women of color) were regarded as carrying out appropriate womanhood when they fulfilled the domestic labor needs of strangers. Upper-class femininity meant that there were certain jobs such women could not perform. This demonstrates the interaction of gender with class and race systems. Old women endure a certain brand of femininity that tends to be devoid of the playmate role and is heavy on the mother aspect. Sexually active old women are violating the norms of femininity set up for them: This shows the influence of ageism in terms of shaping gender norms. Other stereotypes that reveal the interaction of gender with societal systems of privilege and inequality include disabled women's supposedly relatively low sexual appetite or lesbians' lack of femininity (they are presumed to want to be like men at the same time that they are said to hate them). In this way the expression of femininity is dependent upon other intersecting systems of inequality and privilege and the beliefs, stereotypes, and practices associated with these systems.

READING 17

X
A Fabulous Child's Story

Lois Gould

Once upon a time, a baby named X was born. This baby was named X so that nobody could tell whether it was a boy or a girl. Its parents could tell, of course, but they couldn't tell anybody else. They couldn't even tell Baby X, at first.

. . .

The day the Joneses brought their baby home, lots of friends and relatives came over to see it. None of them knew about the secret Xperiment, though. So the first thing they asked was what kind of a baby X was. When the Joneses smiled and said, "It's an X!" nobody knew what to say. They couldn't say, "Look at her cute little dimples!" And they couldn't say, "Look at his husky little biceps!" And they couldn't even say just plain "kitchy-coo." In fact, they all thought the Joneses were playing some kind of rude joke.

But, of course, the Joneses were not joking. "It's an X" was absolutely all they would say. And that made the friends and relatives very angry. The relatives all felt embarrassed about having an X in the family. "People will think there's something wrong with it!" some of them whispered. "There *is* something wrong with it!" others whispered back.

"Nonsense!" the Joneses told them all cheerfully. "What could possibly be wrong with this perfectly adorable X?"

. . .

Clearly, nothing at all was wrong. Nevertheless, none of the relatives felt comfortable about buying a present for a Baby X. The cousins who sent the baby a tiny football helmet would not come and visit any more. And the neighbors who sent a pink-flowered romper suit pulled their shades down when the Joneses passed their house.

. . .

Ms. and Mr. Jones had to be Xtra careful about how they played with little X. They knew that if they kept bouncing it up in the air and saying how *strong* and *active* it was, they'd be treating it more like a boy than an X. But if all they did was cuddle it and kiss it and tell it how *sweet* and *dainty* it was, they'd be treating it more like a girl than an X.

. . .

Meanwhile, the Joneses were worrying about other problems. Toys, for instance. And clothes. On his first shopping trip, Mr. Jones told the store clerk, "I need some clothes and toys for my new baby." The clerk smiled and said, "Well, now, is it a boy or a girl?" "It's an X," Mr. Jones said, smiling back. But the clerk got all red in the face and said huffily, "In *that* case, I'm afraid I can't help you, sir." So Mr. Jones wandered helplessly up and down the aisles trying to find what X needed. But everything in the store was piled up in sections marked "Boys" or "Girls." There were "Boys' Pajamas" and "Girls' Underwear" and "Boys' Fire Engines" and "Girls' Housekeeping Sets." Mr. Jones went home without buying anything for X. . . .

By the time X grew big enough to play with other children, the Joneses' troubles had grown bigger, too. Once a little girl grabbed X's shovel in the sandbox, and zonked X on the head with it. "Now, now, Tracy," the little girl's mother began to scold, "little girls mustn't hit little—" and she turned to ask X, "are you a little boy or a little girl, dear?"

Mr. Jones, who was sitting near the sandbox, held his breath and crossed his fingers.

X smiled politely at the lady, even though X's head had never been zonked so hard in its life. "I'm a little X," X replied.

"You're a *what?*" the lady exclaimed angrily. "You're a little b-r-a-t, you mean!"

"But little girls mustn't hit little Xes, either!" said X, retrieving the shovel with another polite smile. "What good does hitting do, anyway?"

X's father, who was still holding his breath, finally let it out, uncrossed his fingers, and grinned back at X.

But then it was time for X to start school. The Joneses were really worried about this, because school was even more full of rules for boys and girls, and there were no rules for Xes. The teacher would tell boys to form one line, and girls to form another line. There would be boys' games and girls' games, and boys' secrets and girls' secrets. The school library would have a list of recommended books for girls, and a different list of recommended books for boys. There would even be a bathroom marked BOYS and another one marked GIRLS. Pretty soon boys and girls would hardly talk to each other. What would happen to poor little X?

. . .

Nobody in X's class had ever known an X before. What would they think? How would X make friends?

You couldn't tell what X was by studying its clothes—overalls don't even button right-to-left, like girls' clothes, or left-to-right, like boys' clothes. And you couldn't guess whether X had a girl's short haircut or a boy's long haircut. And it was very hard to tell by the games X liked to play. Either X played ball very well for a girl or played house very well for a boy.

Some of the children tried to find out by asking X tricky questions, like "Who's your favorite sports star?" That was easy. X had two favorite sports stars: a girl jockey named Robyn Smith and a boy archery champion named Robin Hood. Then they asked, "What's your favorite TV program?" And that was even easier. X's favorite TV program was "Lassie," which stars a girl dog played by a boy dog.

When X said that its favorite toy was a doll, everyone decided that X must be a girl. But then X said that the doll was really a robot, and that X had computerized it, and that it was programmed to bake fudge brownies and then clean up the kitchen. After X told them that, the other children gave up guessing what X was. All they knew was they'd sure like to see X's doll.

After school, X wanted to play with the other children. "How about shooting some baskets in the gym?" X asked the girls, But all they did was make faces and giggle behind X's back.

"How about weaving some baskets in the arts and crafts room?" X asked the boys. But they all made faces and giggled behind X's back, too.

That night, Ms. and Mr. Jones asked X how things had gone at school. X told them sadly that the lessons were okay, but otherwise school was a horrible place for an X. It seemed as if the Other Children would never want an X for a friend.

. . .

X liked being itself. But X cried a lot that night, partly because it felt afraid. So X's father held X tight, and cuddled it, and couldn't help crying a little, too. And X's mother cheered them both up by reading an Xciting story about an enchanted prince called Sleeping Handsome, who woke up when Princess Charming kissed him.

The next morning, they all felt much better, and little X went back to school with a brave smile and a clean pair of red-and-white checked overalls.

There was a seven-letter-word spelling bee in class that day. And a seven-lap boys' relay race in the gym. And a seven-layer-cake baking contest in the girls' kitchen corner. X won the spelling bee. X also won the relay race. And X almost won the baking contest, except it forgot to light the oven. Which only proves that nobody's perfect.

One of the Other Children noticed something else, too. He said: "Winning or losing doesn't seem to count to X. X seems to have fun being good at boys' skills *and* girls' skills."

"Come to think of it," said another one of the Other Children, "maybe X is having twice as much fun as we are!"

So after school that day, the girl who beat X at the baking contest gave X a big slice of her prizewinning cake. And the boy X beat in the relay race asked X to race him home.

From then on, some really funny things began to happen. Susie, who sat next to X in class, suddenly refused to wear pink dresses to school any more. She insisted on wearing red-and-white checked overalls —just like X's. Overalls, she told her parents, were much better for climbing monkey bars.

Then Jim, the class football nut, started wheeling his little sister's doll carriage around the football field. He'd put on his entire football uniform, except for the helmet. Then he'd put the helmet *in* the carriage, lovingly tucked under an old set of shoulder pads. Then he'd start jogging around the field, pushing the carriage and singing "Rockabye Baby" to his football helmet. He told his family that X did the same thing, so it must be okay. After all, X was now the team's star quarterback.

Susie's parents were horrified by her behavior, and Jim's parents were worried sick about him. But the worst came when the twins, Joe and Peggy, decided to share everything with each other. Peggy used Joe's hockey skates, and his microscope, and took half his newspaper route. Joe used Peggy's needlepoint kit, and her cookbooks, and took two of her three babysitting jobs. Peggy started running the lawn mower, and Joe started running the vacuum cleaner.

Their parents weren't one bit pleased with Peggy's wonderful biology experiments, or with Joe's ter-rific needlepoint pillows. They didn't care that Peggy mowed the lawn better, and that Joe vacuumed the carpet better. In fact, they were furious. It's all that little X's fault, they agreed. Just because X doesn't know what it is, or what it's supposed to be, it wants to get everybody *else* mixed up, too!

Peggy and Joe were forbidden to play with X any more. So was Susie, and then Jim, and then *all* the Other Children. But it was too late; the Other Children stayed mixed up and happy and free, and re-fused to go back to the way they'd been before X.

. . .

READING 18

The Social Construction of Gender

Judith Lorber

Talking about gender for most people is the equiv-alent of fish talking about water. Gender is so much the routine ground of everyday activities that ques-tioning its taken-for-granted assumptions and pre-suppositions is like thinking about whether the sun will come up.[1] Gender is so pervasive that in our soci-ety we assume it is bred into our genes. Most people find it hard to believe that gender is constantly cre-ated and re-created out of human interaction, out of social life, and is the texture and order of that social life. Yet gender, like culture, is a human production that depends on everyone constantly "doing gender" (West and Zimmerman 1987).

And everyone "does gender" without thinking about it. Today, on the subway, I saw a well-dressed man with a year-old child in a stroller. Yesterday, on a bus, I saw a man with a tiny baby in a carrier on his chest. Seeing men taking care of small children in public is increasingly common—at least in New York City. But both men were quite obviously stared at—and smiled at, approvingly. Everyone was doing gen-der—the men who were changing the role of fathers and the other passengers, who were applauding them silently. But there was more gendering going on that probably fewer people noticed. The baby was wear-ing a white crocheted cap and white clothes. You couldn't tell if it was a boy or a girl. The child in the stroller was wearing a dark blue T-shirt and dark print pants. As they started to leave the train, the fa-ther put a Yankee baseball cap on the child's head. Ah, a boy, I thought. Then I noticed the gleam of tiny earrings in the child's ears, and as they got off, I saw the little flowered sneakers and lace-trimmed socks. Not a boy after all. Gender done.

. . .

For the individual, gender construction starts with assignment to a sex category on the basis of what the genitalia look like at birth.[2] Then babies are dressed or adorned in a way that displays the cat-egory because parents don't want to be constantly asked whether their baby is a girl or a boy. A sex category becomes a gender status through naming, dress, and the use of other gender markers. Once a child's gender is evident, others treat those in one gender differently from those in the other, and the children respond to the different treatment by feeling different and behaving differently. As soon as they can talk, they start to refer to themselves as members of their gender. Sex doesn't come into play again until puberty, but by that time, sexual feelings and desires and practices have been shaped by gendered norms and expectations. Adolescent boys and girls approach and avoid each other in an elaborately scripted and gendered mating dance. Parenting is gendered, with different expectations for mothers and fathers, and people of different genders work at different kinds of jobs. The work adults do as mothers and fathers and as low-level workers and high-level bosses, shapes women's and men's life experiences, and these experiences produce different feelings, consciousness, relationships, skills—ways of being that we call feminine or masculine.[3] All of these processes constitute the social construction of gender.

. . .

To explain why gendering is done from birth, constantly and by everyone, we have to look not only at the way individuals experience gender but at gender as a social institution. As a social institution, gender is one of the major ways that human beings organize their lives. Human society depends on a predictable division of labor, a designated allocation of scarce goods, assigned responsibility for children and others who cannot care for themselves, common values and their systematic transmission to new members, legitimate leadership, music, art, stories, games, and other symbolic productions. One way of choosing people for the different tasks of society is on the basis of their talents, motivations, and competence—their demonstrated achievements. The other way is on the basis of gender, race, ethnicity— ascribed membership in a category of people. Although societies vary in the extent to which they use one or the other of these ways of allocating people to work and to carry out other responsibilities, every society uses gender and age grades. Every society classifies people as "girl and boy children," "girls and boys ready to be married," and "fully adult women and men," constructs similarities among them and differences between them, and assigns them to different roles and responsibilities. Personality characteristics, feelings, motivations, and ambitions flow from these different life experiences so that the members of these different groups become different kinds of people. The process of gendering and its

outcome are legitimated by religion, law, science and the society's entire set of values.

Gender as Process, Stratification, and Structure

As a social institution, gender is a process of creating distinguishable social statuses for the assignment of rights and responsibilities. As part of a stratification system that ranks these statuses unequally, gender is a major building block in the social structures built on these unequal statuses.

As a *process,* gender creates the social differences that define "woman" and "man." In social interaction throughout their lives, individuals learn what is expected, see what is expected, act and react in expected ways, and thus simultaneously construct and maintain the gender order. . . .

Gendered patterns of interaction acquire additional layers of gendered sexuality, parenting, and work behaviors in childhood, adolescence, and adulthood. Gendered norms and expectations are enforced through informal sanctions of gender-inappropriate behavior by peers and by formal punishment or threat of punishment by those in authority should behavior deviate too far from socially imposed standards for women and men.

. . .

As part of a *stratification* system, gender ranks men above women of the same race and class. Women and men could be different but equal. In practice, the process of creating difference depends to a great extent on differential evaluation. . . . The dominant categories are the hegemonic ideals, taken so for granted as the way things should be that white is not ordinarily thought of as a race, middle class as a class, or men as a gender. The characteristics of these categories define the Other as that which lacks the valuable qualities the dominants exhibit.

In a gender-stratified society, what men do is usually valued more highly than what women do because men do it, even when their activities are very similar or the same. In different regions of southern India, for example, harvesting rice is men's work, shared work, or women's work: "Wherever a task is done by women it is considered easy, and where it is done by [men] it is considered difficult" (Mencher

1988, 104). A gathering and hunting society's survival usually depends on the nuts, grubs, and small animals brought in by the women's foraging trips, but when the men's hunt is successful, it is the occasion for a celebration. Conversely, because they are the superior group, white men do not have to do the "dirty work," such as housework; the most inferior group does it, usually poor women of color (Palmer 1989).

. . .

When gender is a major component of structured inequality, the devalued genders have less power, prestige, and economic rewards than the valued genders. In countries that discourage gender discrimination, many major roles are still gendered; women still do most of the domestic labor and child rearing, even while doing full-time paid work; women and men are segregated on the job and each does work considered "appropriate"; women's work is usually paid less than men's work. Men dominate the positions of authority and leadership in government, the military, and the law; cultural productions, religions, and sports reflect men's interests.

In societies that create the greatest gender difference, such as Saudi Arabia, women are kept out of sight behind walls or veils, have no civil rights, and often create a cultural and emotional world of their own (Bernard 1981). But even in societies with less rigid gender boundaries, women and men spend much of their time with people of their own gender because of the way work and family are organized. This spatial separation of women and men reinforces gendered differences, identity, and ways of thinking and behaving (Coser 1986).

Gender inequality—the devaluation of "women" and the social domination of "men"—has social functions and social history. It is not the result of sex, procreation, physiology, anatomy, hormones, or genetic predispositions. It is produced and maintained by identifiable social processes and built into the general social structure and individual identities deliberately and purposefully. The social order as we know it in Western societies is organized around racial, ethnic, class, and gender inequality. I contend, therefore, that the continuing purpose of gender as a modern social institution is to construct women as a group to be the subordinates of men as a group.

The Paradox of Human Nature

To say that sex, sexuality, and gender are all socially constructed is not to minimize their social power. These categorical imperatives govern our lives in the most profound and pervasive ways, through the social experiences and social practices of what Dorothy Smith calls the "everday/evernight world" (1990, 31–57). The paradox of human nature is that it is *always* a manifestation of cultural meanings, social relationships, and power politics; "not biology, but culture, becomes destiny" (J. Butler 1990, 8). Gendered people emerge not from physiology or sexual orientations but from the exigencies of the social order, mostly, from the need for a reliable division of the work of food production and the social (not physical) reproduction of new members. The moral imperatives of religion and cultural representations guard the boundary lines among genders and ensure that what is demanded, what is permitted, and what is tabooed for the people in each gender is well known and followed by most (C. Davies 1982). Political power, control of scarce resources, and, if necessary, violence uphold the gendered social order in the face of resistance and rebellion. Most people, however, voluntarily go along with their society's prescriptions for those of their gender status, because the norms and expectations get built into their sense of worth and identity as [the way we] think, the way we see and hear and speak, the way we fantasy, and the way we feel.

There is no core or bedrock in human nature below these endlessly looping processes of the social production of sex and gender, self and other, identity and psyche, each of which is a "complex cultural construction" (J. Butler 1990, 36). *For humans, the social is the natural. . . .*

NOTES

1. Gender is, in Erving Goffman's words, an aspect of *Felicity's Condition*: "any arrangement which leads us to judge an individual's . . . acts not to be a manifestation of strangeness. Behind Felicity's Condition is our sense of what it is to be sane" (1983:27). Also see Bem 1993; Frye 1983, 17–40; Goffman 1977.
2. In cases of ambiguity in countries with modern medicine, surgery is usually performed to make the genitalia more clearly male or female.

3. See J. Butler 1990 for an analysis of how doing gender is gender identity.

REFERENCES

Bem, Sandara Lipsitz. 1993. *The Lenses of Gender: Transforming the Debate on Sexual Inequality.* New Haven: Yale University Press.

Bernard, Jessie. 1981. *The Female World.* New York: Free Press.

Butler, Judith. 1990. *Gender Trouble: Feminism and the Subversion of Identity.* New York and London: Routledge.

Coser, Rose Laub. 1986. "Cognitive structure and the use of social space," *Sociological Forum* 1: 1–26.

Davies, Christie. 1982. "Sexual taboos and social boundaries," *American Journal of Sociology* 87: 1032–63.

Dwyer, Daisy, and Judith Bruce (eds.). 1988. *A Home Divided: Women and Income in the Third World.* Palo Alto, Calif.: Stanford University Press.

Frye, Marilyn. 1983. *The Politics of Reality: Essays in Feminist Theory.* Trumansburg, N.Y.: Crossing Press.

Goffman, Erving, 1977. "The arrangement between the sexes," *Theory and Society* 4:301–33.

Mencher, Joan. 1988. "Women's work and poverty: Women's contribution to household maintenance in South India," In *Dwyer and Bruce.*

Palmer, Phyllis. 1989. *Domesticity and Dirt: Housewives and Domestic Servants in the United States, 1920–1945.* Philadelphia: Temple University Press.

Smith, Dorothy. 1990. *The Conceptual Practices of Power: A Feminist Sociology of Knowledge.* Toronto: University of Toronto Press.

West, Candace, and Don Zimmerman. 1987. "Doing gender." *Gender & Society* 1: 125–51.

READING 19

The Plurality of Gender-Based Realities

Virginia Sapiro

In complex societies marked by stratification and gender divisions of labor, the sex/gender system is composed of a *plurality of gender-based stereotypes* and expectations that depend on other aspects of social position and identity. . . . [T]here may be a central, widely unattainable ideal that can be met only by women with the highest status, but the dominant society also develops stereotypes and expectations aimed specifically at women in different social positions. Despite the great variety of American Indian communities and the many different roles women play in those communities, White American society historically imagined Native American women either as silent, oppressed, laboring squaws or as romantic and noble princesses, described in the popular stories of Pocahontas. African-American women came to be characterized as either promiscuous, earthy women who could be used as beasts of burden, or as Mammy, a loyal member of a White household with a special knowledge of nature and children. The late 20th century has added another African-American female figure: the welfare cheat, placing burdens on the system through having uncontrollable numbers of children for whom she cannot care or provide.

Esther Ngan-Ling Chow has offered further examples from the stereotyped views of Asian-American women, defined in a variety of closely related roles: Suzie Wong, geisha, picture bride, and sexpot. In each case, the definition of the Asian-American woman depends on both race and sex. These stereotypes often come together with colonialist myths, fostering male fantasies that serve as the basis of the frightening racialized sexual harassment that Asian-American women receive. As a result, Asian-American women find themselves victims of education and employment discrimination *despite* the popular image of being the model minority. Jewish women have their choice of stereotypes: the domineering, stifling "Jewish mother," or the bitchy, self-centered "Jewish princess."

Neither gender nor race nor ethnicity alone is sufficient to understand most women's situation. In each case, scholars have noted, the special characters of the stereotypes are not just accidents. These stereotypes serve the ideological needs of both an androcentric structure of power relations and the racial/ethnic structure of power by not just *describing* these power relations but *justifying* them. The cast of subculturally differentiated female characters could be extended indefinitely by turning to depictions based on other ethnic/racial groups or on socioeconomic class, sexuality, geographic region, or other aspects of sociocultural diversity. Lillian Faderman and Donna Penn, among others, have written about the historical development of stereotypes of lesbian women during the 20th century, including the pervasive view that lesbians can either be categorized as "butch," in which case they are hypermasculine predators of other women, or "femme," the feminized victim who might be rescued from homosexuality if the right man came along. The construction of female (and male) gender is also partly determined by region, as in the case of the Southern belle, the Boston "bluestocking," the "gentle tamer" of the West, the "madonna of the Plains," or the "tall woman" and the "mountain belle" of Appalachia. . . .

Evelyn Nakano Glenn's research on service work offers an excellent example of the institutionalization of specific racial–ethnic norms of womanhood. She has reminded us that woman's central role has been defined as both physical and social reproduction, or the "creation and re-creation of people as cultural and social, as well as physical beings." This role means having responsibility for the care of (but not the financial provision for) the household and the people within it.

Glenn has pointed out, however, an important contradiction in the expectations placed on women, which arose from the 19th-century cult of womanhood: Domestic labor is, in many respects, dirty, difficult, labor-intensive work, especially in a society without electricity. The image of the "domestic angel," therefore, is largely inconsistent with the actual domestic labor that is required to keep homes in the preferred domestic order. It should be no surprise, therefore, that in the era of industrial development, when labor was both plentiful and cheap, families of any means employed servants to do much of the domestic labor. First, the work was intensive enough that most women probably welcomed any help; only

the most upper-class women tended to shift the entire burden of domestic labor to servants. Second, shifting the work to servants could reduce the contradiction within the gender role of the "lady" of the house.

This observation does not tell the whole story yet. This domestic labor was shifted from the hands of women to the hands of other women because it was gender-specified labor. Nonetheless, isn't there as much contradiction between the domestic-angel image and this dirty, laborious work for the women hired to do the labor as for the "lady" of the house? In the eyes of the employing class, there was not, because their gender norms depended not just on a woman's *gender,* but also on her *class* and *race/ethnicity.* Serving the domestic labor needs of strangers is entirely consistent with dominant culture definitions of appropriate womanhood for *some* types of women but not for others. As Glenn has pointed out, exactly which classification of women was supposed to perform these tasks changes historically and differs from geographic region to geographic region. In the northeastern United States at the turn of the century, recent European immigrants, especially Irish-American women, were thought to be specially fitted to doing domestic labor. White women in the South turned to African-American women; in the Southwest, Mexican-American women filled the service roles, as did Japanese-American women on the Pacific coast and in Hawaii.

These groups of women engaged in paid domestic service because they needed the money and they lived in those areas in large numbers. In each of these regions, however, these women came to be culturally reinterpreted as a servant class *by nature,* marked out and determined by their gender and their race/ethnicity. Glenn has argued that in each case, the women, marked by their race/ethnicity, were understood to have inherent traits suiting them for service, and they were not perceived as mothers and wives in their own right, but rather as servants. Thus, Glenn has shown, in each region, young women were institutionally tracked into fulfilling their presumed natural destiny. She found examples of how Mexican girls in the Southwest and Japanese girls in Hawaii were blocked from school programs other than those that would lead to domestic service. Even in the job programs run by the federal World Progress Administration (WPA) in the New Deal response to the Great Depression of the 1930s, Chicanas and African-American and Asian-American women were funneled into domestic service jobs and out of others.

. . .

For another example, consider the story of Pocahontas. To Euro-American society, the story of Pocahontas is a romantic tale of a beautiful Indian princess who falls in love with an Englishman, who generously marries her and takes her off to England, where she is the talk of the town. The story can be seen as symbolizing to the Euro-American the unique "marriage" of the civilized European with the wildness of nature on the new continent, with all living happily ever after as Indians and the wilderness are "tamed." American Indians are more likely to hear the rest of the story and, presumably, to take a different message from it. Pocahontas was offered to John Smith as part of a policy of alliance, much as European aristocrats and royalty intermarried to solidify international agreements. When she went to London, although she was displayed in society, neither her husband nor the society in which she was now isolated ever accepted her, and while longing to return home to America, she died before her 25th birthday.

Each of these subcultures, defined by race/ethnicity, class, and geography (among other things), has distinctive ways of understanding gender and different norms about how women and men should do gender to some degree. For communities defined by race/ethnicity, religion, or geography, distinctive rituals and practices, cultural figures, myths and stories, and graphic representations offer a way of understanding the specific subcultural constructions of male and female. The Navajo Changing Woman, for example, responsible for the growth of crops and the birth of new life, presents a model of the woman warrior and defender of her home that is a cultural ideal for Navajo women. Young Jewish girls dress up at Purim as Queen Esther, a savior of her people, as often as they might, like many other American children, appear as fairy princesses and witches at Halloween. Many Appalachian authors incorporate the locally well-known image of the "tall women," so

named because of the saying that "a tall woman casts a long shadow." This image of "strong women, who can manage the household and children as well as milk the cows and cultivate the fields" served as a positive cultural image of femininity for Appalachian women for whom the image of the Southern belle must have seemed foreign. From one part of the country to another, where the different flow of seasons and the different cultural traditions shape women's and men's lives differently, the understanding of women as women and men as men varies.

The more closely women's lives are scrutinized, the more clear it becomes that there is immense variation in the ways that gender is shaped and represented in a complex sex/gender system. Nevertheless, they are not completely independent. They are linked through the common social institutions that tie them all together into the larger society, including, for example, the government, the mass media, and the school and health-care systems. Thus, women (and men) do gender within sex/gender systems that often simultaneously demand different and sometimes conflicting things of them, in order to act in gender appropriate ways.

. . .

Rape would seem at first to offer a clear example of a form of oppression or violence based solely on gender. Slavery would seem at first to offer a clear example of a form of oppression or violence based solely on race. In fact, however, for a complete understanding of rape, it is necessary to look beyond gender, and for a complete understanding of slavery, it is necessary to look beyond race.

Gender is a crucial determinant of the degree to which women are regarded and treated as objects of sex and rape, but their race, ethnicity, class, and status as recent immigrants or native-born Americans are also important. The lower a woman's status is by almost any measure, the more likely she is to be a target of sexual violence. Some examples of how this works follow.

bell hooks offered a powerful analysis of the intertwined effects of race and gender on sexual oppression. Rape was an integral part of the female slave experience, beginning with the sea voyage, during which the slavers did what they could to break the Africans' spirits and make them passive and compliant. For the women, this process included rape. Neither race nor gender alone accounts for the experience of slavery because "while racism was clearly the evil that had decreed Black people would be enslaved, it was sexism that determined that the lot of the Black female would be harsher, more brutal than that of the Black male slave." Women were subjected to slavery because of their race, but they were also used as sexual objects and as breeders because of their sex. The same was true for the Native Americans held as slaves in the American Southwest. There are many other situations in which rape clearly depends not just on gender, but also on the race, ethnic, or class relations between perpetrator and victim. Susan Brownmiller's argument that rape has often been used as a tactic of war and imperialism depends on recognizing that rape does not occur just because of gender and sexual relations. A recent example in a long history may be found in the massive and systematic use of rape in Serbia against Muslim women in 1992–1993, during the civil war that followed the breakup of Yugoslavia.

Gender played other roles in differentiating the slave experience. For instance, bell hooks has pointed out that an important aspect of slavery in the United States was the requirement that women do labor regarded in America as men's work. Male slaves were less often subjected to the complementary treatment of being required to do women's work.

Race and gender also combined to affect the experience of slave owners in 19th-century America. White men could own slaves because of their race and gender. Their sex gave them the right to own property (married women could not own property), and their race gave them the right to own human beings (very few nonWhites owned slaves). In one sense, this gender difference among Whites is little more than a technical point. White women had great power over their husbands' slaves. Moreover, during the Civil War, about three quarters of White Southern men were in the military, so their wives had to take over the management of plantations, including the slaves. Drew Gilpin Faust's historical analysis shows that many of these women were especially uncomfortable with this role and were caught in a web

of conflicting social norms. They lived in a society based on violence, in which White people could hold Black people in bondage and enforce their power with violence against them; on the other hand, gender norms defined women as nurturant and nonviolent.

Gender distinguished among White slaveholders in one important respect: White women knew about their husbands', brothers', and sons' sexual treatment of their slaves. They knew that the children of some of the enslaved women were progeny of their "loved ones" through rape. This knowledge motivated some White women, such as the Grimké sisters, to become abolitionists, but many others simply stored their resentment or even blamed the victimized Black women. In addition, hooks has suggested another dimension to this complex picture of gender and race by speculating, "Surely it must have occurred to White women that were enslaved Black women not available to bear the brunt of such intense anti-woman male aggression, they themselves might have been the victims." White society in general has tried to ignore the massive scale of the rapes that occurred.

Blaming the victim plays an important role in all forms of sexual- and gender-based violence. However, just as enslaved women were often held responsible for their own victimization, women of low-status groups, especially those perceived as alien, have often been regarded as excessively sexual (and even animal-like) and thus have become special targets for sexual violence and exploitation. As bell hooks has explained, by defining Black women as initiators of the sexual relationships that were in fact rapes, Whites reinforced a stereotype of Black women as sexual savages who, in effect, could not be raped. The same principle applied to Hispanic and Native American women. Likewise, in the late 19th and early 20th centuries, native-born Whites often claimed that immigrant women—Irish, Italian, Jewish, or whatever—were especially promiscuous and likely to ruin the morals of innocent American men. Young immigrant women, especially those helping to support their families, were constantly subjected to sexual harassment and exploitation and then labeled promiscuous.

These examples demonstrate that the forms of gender-based oppression and exploitation people experience depend in part on their other social characteristics, and that racial/ethnic- or class-based forms of oppression and exploitation depend in part on gender. In fact, the exploitation of gender relations may often be seen as a means of enforcing other types of oppression. Some examples from the legal control of sexuality and marriage follow.

The state's control over marriage and sexual relations gives it leverage to pursue many different goals. . . . Among these goals is the preservation of particular racial or ethnic hierarchies. In order to preserve a particular racial/ethnic social order, societies must ensure that different races or ethnic groups cannot intermarry or develop the mutual loyalty and commitment owed to intimates and family members. Thus, nations with an apartheid history, such as the United States and South Africa, declared *miscegenation,* racial intermarriage, illegal during those eras.

Laws against interracial sexual relations or marriage may seem to fall equally on the shoulders of women and men, and on those of different races or ethnic groups, but in fact, they do not. Higher status men, however defined, tend to have sexual rights over lower-status women, or at least, they are not punished as severely as their partners in interracial sexual contact. In the American past, sexual relations between White women and nonWhite men were punished more severely than relations between White men and nonWhite women. The first American antimiscegenation law, passed in 1664 in Maryland, declared that a White woman who had sexual relations with an enslaved Black male must herself become a slave. No such law applied to White men.

These dynamics appear not just through law, but also in the way societies have often treated mixed-race, -ethnicity, or even -class couples and their ba-bies. If a low-status female becomes pregnant by a high-status male, it has little effect on their relative status. Patriarchal ideology keeps the male in control; if the woman makes too many claims, he can abandon and reject her with relatively little social cost, partly because he can accuse her of promiscuity. A situation involving a low-status male and a high-status female is very different. For example, a baby of mixed-race parentage born to a White woman has been regarded as a pollution of the White race. Because women are regarded as the property of male protectors in a patriarchal society, a nonWhite male who has sexual relations with a White woman is ultimately seen as taking something from White men. The effects of this dual system of racial and sexual oppression lasted long after the end of slavery. The rape of a White woman by a nonWhite man has usually been treated by White society as the most serious type of heterosexual rape, whereas rape of a nonWhite woman by a White man has not often been regarded as rape at all. False charges that a Black man raped a White woman were often used as excuses for lynching Black men.

Almost a generation ago, women's studies researchers began to emphasize the need to take gender into account to understand important social issues. In recent years, they have been demanding yet more sophistication and argue that gender analysis is not complete without integrating it with an understanding of other structural bases of social life. Maxine Baca Zinn has offered a good example in her writing on the family and poverty. She has shown that efforts to understand and solve the problems of poverty are doomed to failure if researchers look only at culture or race and class structures or gender structures. Society and social relations are constructed of all of these elements.

READING 20

When I Was Growing Up

Nellie Wong

I know now that once I longed to be white.
How? you ask.
Let me tell you the ways.

> when I was growing up, people told me
> I was dark and I believed my own darkness
> in the mirror, in my soul, my own narrow vision

>> when I was growing up, my sisters
>> with fair skin got praised
>> for their beauty, and in the dark
>> I fell further, crushed between high walls

> when I was growing up, I read magazines
> and saw movies, blonde movie stars, white skin,
> sensuous lips and to be elevated, to become
> a woman, a desirable woman, I began to wear
> imaginary pale skin

>> when I was growing up, I was proud
>> of my English, my grammar, my spelling
>> fitting into the group of small children
>> smart Chinese children, fitting in,
>> belonging, getting in line

> when I was growing up and went to high school,
> I discovered the rich white girls, a few yellow girls,
> their imported cotton dresses, their cashmere sweaters,
> their curly hair and I thought that I too should have
> what these lucky girls had

>> when I was growing up, I hungered
>> for American food, American styles,
>> coded: white and even to me, a child
>> born of Chinese parents, being Chinese
>> was feeling foreign, as limiting,
>> was unAmerican

> when I was growing up and a white man wanted
> to take me out, I thought I was special,
> an exotic gardenia, anxious to fit
> the stereotype of an oriental chick

when I was growing up, I felt ashamed
of some yellow men, their small bones,
their frail bodies, their spitting
on the streets, their coughing,
their lying in sunless rooms,
shooting themselves in the arms

when I was growing up, people would ask
if I were Filipino, Polynesian, Portuguese.
They named all colors except white, the shell
of my soul, but not my dark, rough skin

when I was growing up, I felt
dirty. I thought that god
made white people clean
and no matter how much I bathed,
I could not change, I could not shed
my skin in the gray water

when I was growing up, I swore
I would run away to purple mountains,
houses by the sea with nothing over
my head, with space to breathe,
uncongested with yellow people in an area
called Chinatown, in an area I later learned
was a ghetto, one of many hearts
of Asian America

I know now that once I longed to be white.
How many more ways? you ask.
Haven't I told you enough?

READING 21

Spiking the Punch
In Defense of Female Aggression

Natalie Angier

This study has been done many times. If you take a group of babies or young toddlers and dress them in nondescript, non-sex-specific clothes—yellow is always a good color—and make sure that their haircuts don't give them away, and if you put them in a room with a lot of adults watching, the adults will not be able to sex the children accurately. The adults will try, based on the behaviors of each child, but they will be right no more often than they would be if they flipped a coin. This has been shown again and again, but still we don't believe it. We think we can tell a boy or a girl by the child's behavior, specifically by its level of aggressiveness. If you show a person a videotape of a crying baby and tell her the baby is a boy, the observer will describe the baby as looking angry; if you tell the person the baby is a girl, she will say the child is scared or miserable.

I am at a party with my daughter, who is sixteen months old. A boy who is almost eighteen months comes into the room and takes a toy away from my daughter. I say something humorous to her about how she's got to watch out for those older kids, they'll always try to push you around. And the boy's mother says, It's also because he's a boy. That's what happens at this age, she says. The boys become very boyish. A little while later, a girl who is almost eighteen months old takes my daughter's cup of milk away from her. The mother of the other girl doesn't say, It's because she's a girl, she's becoming girlish. Of course she doesn't say that; it would make no sense, would it? An older girl taking a cup away from a younger girl has nothing to do with the girlness of either party. But taking the toy away is viewed as inherent to the older boy's boyness.

I felt very aggressive about the whole thing; alas, not being a toddler, I couldn't go and kick anybody in the kneecap. Which is the sort of thing that toddlers do, whatever their sex. They kick, they hit, they scream, they throw objects around, they act like pills past their expiration date. And we adults put up with it, and we subscribe to the myth of the helpless, innocent child, and it's a good thing we do and that children are cute, because otherwise we might well see the truth: that our children are born with astonishing powers, and with brains that seem by default to counsel aggression.

"Young children are like animals," says Kaj Björkqvist, of Turku Akademi University in Finland. "Before they have language, they have their bodies. And through their bodies they can be aggressive, and so that is what they do, that is how they are. They are physically aggressive—boys, girls, all of them." Björkqvist studies female aggression. He has done crosscultural comparisons of children in Europe, North America, the Middle East, and Asia. Everywhere he has found that young children are physically aggressive, and that before the age of three, there are no significant differences between girl aggression and boy aggression.

We grow into our sex-specific aggressions. We own the code of aggression from birth, and we perfect its idiom through experience and experimentation. Now I must do something artificial and divide aggression into two basic categories, "bad" aggression and "good" aggression. Earlier I said that context determines whether we see a behavior as good aggression or bad aggression and that even Lady Macbeth looks swell in Nordic gear. But for the sake of examining how female aggression evolves and what its multitudinous sources and expressions may be, it helps to do as researchers do and distinguish between the malign and the resolute. Henri Parens, a child psychiatrist at the Medical College of Pennsylvania, calls the two phyla of aggression "hostile aggression," which is "generated by excessive unpleasure and motivates fantasies and acts of anger, hostility and hate," and "nondestructive aggression," which is "inborn and fuels assertive and goal achieving behaviors." In the infant and toddler, the two aggressions are one, and they are of the reactive nervous system—anger, hate, assertiveness, whatever it takes, or whatever can be done, to maintain momentum and attract the attention of the parent, the intermediary between self and no self.

With the awakening of the mind, the child learns to channel aggressive impulses and to calculate and compare actions and responses. Children begin to learn the meaning of hurting another. A baby kicks you in the mouth and doesn't know she hurts you. By the age of two or three, a girl knows she can hurt other beings, and hurt them badly, and with that knowledge the distinctions between malign and resolute aggression become meaningful. The mainstream model posits that aggression is a public health crisis. Mainstream studies of female aggression focus on hostile aggression, the aggression aimed to hurt, with foreknowledge, with malice.

When the mind comes into its own and the child starts speaking fluently, purposefully, adults become less tolerant of physical aggression. Today, in most cultures, acceptance of physical aggression declines as the child gets older; by the time a person reaches puberty, the tendency to use physical force to wrest a desired object or behavior from another is considered frankly pathological. This is true for both sexes, but particularly for girls. Physical aggression is discouraged in girls in manifold and aggressive ways. Not only are they instructed against offensive fighting; they are rarely instructed in defensive fighting. Girls don't learn how to throw a punch. Humor is another form of aggression, and until recently humor has been used to squelch the very notion of a warrior female. Just the thought of a girl-fight, and people snicker and rub their hands with glee. Cat fight! Scratching, screeching, pulling hair, and falling on butt with skirt hiked in the air! Happily, the smirky parody of girl-fights has gotten a bit paunchy and dated of late, and instead we've been treated to images of GI Janes and bodiced Xenas wielding swords and Klingon women with brickbat fists, though whether the mass media's revisionist fighting female has been driven by attitudinal change or by the need to jolt a bored and distracted audience is unclear.

Whatever the media moment may be, girls still do not often engage in physical fights. The older children get, the less physically aggressive they become— though not always, and not everywhere— but the dropoff rate for the use of physical aggression in girls is much sharper than it is for boys. At least in the developed West, by the time girls and boys are in third grade, boys are about three times as likely as girls to kick or strike at somebody who makes them mad. What then do girls do with that aggressiveness, which in the bliss of preverbalism could speak through hands and feet? It does not go away. It finds a new voice. It finds words. Girls learn to talk hornet talk. Mastering curse words and barbed insults is an essential task of childhood. Girls also learn to use their faces as weapons. Expressions like sticking out your tongue or rolling your eyes or curling your lip all seem funny to adults, but studies show that they aren't funny to children, and that they can be effective in conveying anger and dislike or in ostracizing an undesirable. Aggression researchers initially thought that girls had the edge over boys in verbal aggression and that they were more likely than boys to belittle their peers with words and facial flexions, but a series of Finnish studies of eight- and eleven-year-olds suggested otherwise. The researchers sought to determine how children responded when they were angry. They asked the children to describe themselves and their reactions to being roused to rage; they asked teachers and parents to describe how the children reacted in conflict; and

they asked children to talk about each other, to rate each other's rileability and behaviors in a squall. The scientists found that boys and girls were equally likely to use verbal aggression against their cohorts, to call them nasty names to their faces, to yell, to mock, to try to make the despised ones look stupid And so boys kick and fight more than girls do, and the sexes argue and chide in equal amounts. We might then conclude, So boys *are* more aggressive, for they shout with their mouths and on occasion with their bodies, while the girls keep their fists to themselves.

There are other ways in which rage emerges among girls, though, ways that are roughly girl-specific. A girl who is angry often responds by stalking off, turning away, snubbing the offender, pretending she doesn't exist. She withdraws, visibly so, aggressively so. You can almost hear the thwapping of her sulk. Among eleven-year-olds, girls are three times more likely than boys to express their anger in the form of a flamboyant snub. In addition, girls at this age, more than boys, engage in a style of aggression called indirect aggression.

. . .

Indirect aggression is not pretty, nor is it much admired. To the contrary, it is universally condemned. When children and adults are asked to describe their feelings about the various methods of expressing anger, backstabbing behavior ranks at the bottom, below a good swift kick to the crotch. Yet there it is, with us, among us, not exclusively female by any means, but a recognizable hazard of girlhood. Part of the blame lies with the myth of the "good" girl, for the more girls are counseled against direct forms of aggression and the more geniality of temperament is prized, the greater is the likelihood that the tart girls will resort to hidden machinations to get what they want. In cultures where girls are allowed to be girls, to speak up and out, they are in fact more verbally, directly aggressive and less indirectly aggressive than in cultures where girls and women are expected to be demure. In Poland, for example, a good smart mouth is considered a female asset, and girls there rag each other and pull no punches and report feeling relatively little threat of intragroup skullduggery. Among female Zapotec Indians in Mexico, who are exceedingly subordinate to men, indirect aggression prevails. Among the Vanatinai of Papua New Guinea, one of the most egalitarian and least stratified societies known to anthropologists, women speak and move as freely as they please, and they sometimes use their fists and feet to demonstrate their wrath, and there is no evidence of a feminine edge in covert operations.

Another reason that girls may resort to indirect aggression is that they feel such extraordinary aggression toward their friends—lashing, tumbling, ever-replenishing aggression. Girl friendships are fierce and dangerous. The expression "I'll be your best friend" is not exclusively a girl phrase, but girls use it a lot. They know how powerful the words are, how significant the offer is. Girls who become good friends feel a compulsion to define the friendship, to stamp it and name it, and they are inclined to rank a close friend as a best friend, with the result that they often have many best friends. They think about their friends on a daily basis and try to figure out where a particular friend fits that day in their cosmology of friendships. Is the girl her best friend today, or a provisional best friend, pending the resolution of a minor technicality, a small bit of friction encountered the day before? The girl may want to view a particular girl as her best friend, but she worries how her previous best friend will take it—as a betrayal or as a potential benefit, a bringing in or a new source of strength to the pair. Girls fall in love with each other and feel an intimacy for each other that is hard for them to describe or understand.

When girls are in groups, they form coalitions of best friends, two against two, or two in edgy harmony with two. A girl in a group of girls who doesn't feel that she has a specific ally feels at risk, threatened, frightened. If a girl who is already incorporated into the group decides to take on a newcomer, to sponsor her, the resident girl takes on a weighty responsibility, for the newcomer will view her as (for the moment) her best friend, her only friend, the guardian of her oxygen mask.

When girls have a falling-out, they fall like Alice down the tunnel, convinced that it will never end, that they will never be friends again. The Finnish studies of aggression among girls found that girls hold grudges against each other much longer than boys do. "Girls tend to form dyadic relationships,

with very deep psychological expectations from their best friends," Björkqvist said. "Because their expectations are high, they feel deeply betrayed when the friendship falls apart. They become as antagonistic afterwards as they had been bonded before." If a girl feels betrayed by a friend, she will try to think of ways to get revenge in kind, to truly hurt her friend, as she has been hurt. Fighting physically is an unsatisfactory form of punishing the terrible traitor. It is over too quickly. To express anger might work if the betrayer accepts the anger and responds to it with respect. But if she doesn't acknowledge her friend's anger or sense of betrayal, if she refuses to apologize or admit to any wrongdoing, or if she goes further, walking away or mocking or snubbing her friend, at that point a girl may aim to hurt with the most piercing and persistent tools for the job, the psychological tools of indirect, vengeful aggression, with the object of destroying the girl's position, her peace of mind, her right to be. Indirect aggression is akin to a voodoo hex, an anonymous but obsessive act in which the antagonist's soul, more than her body, must be got at, must be penetrated, must be nullified.

The intensities of childhood friendships, dyads, coalitions, and jihads subside with age, but sometimes just barely. Women remain, through much of their lives, unsettled about other women. We feel drawn and repelled, desirous of a connection and at the same time aggressive toward those who register on our radar screen. . . .

Women bond with other women, and yet our strongest aggressions and our most frightening hostilities may be directed against other women. We hear about the war between the sexes, but surprisingly few of our aggressive impulses are aimed against men, the putative adversaries in that war. We don't consider men our competitors, even now, in the market free-for-all, when they often are. It is so much easier to feel competitive with another woman, to feel our nerves twitch with anxiety and hyperattentiveness when another woman enters our visual field. We dress women in fairy white, we dress them in mafia black. We want them around us. We want to be alone among men.

Men say they envy women the depth of their friendships, their ability to emote with and engage each other. Men are also stunned when they see the ferocity of a failed friendship between women, the staggering thickness of the anger and bile. "Picking a fight can actually be a way for men to relate to one another, check each other out, and take a first step toward friendship," Frans de Waal wrote in *Good Natured*. "This bonding function is alien to most women, who see confrontation as causing rifts." It's not because we are nice and want to make nicer. Women know, from their experience and from their harrowing girlhood, that rifts often are hard to heal, and can last, and can consume them.

The fierceness of female friendships and the unease with which we regard other women are in my view related phenomena, and are the legacy of dissonance between our ancient primate and our neo-hominid selves and of our inherent strategic plasticity, the desire to keep all options open. Other females are a potential source of strength, and other females can destroy us. Or flip it around, as the English salonist Elizabeth Holland did, when she wrote at the turn of the nineteenth century, "as nobody can do more mischief to a woman than a woman, so perhaps one might reverse the maxim and say nobody can do more good."

READING 22

Boys Will Be Boys and Girls Will Not

Mariah Burton Nelson

My aunts washed the dishes while the uncles
squirted each other on the lawn with
*   garden hoses. Why are we in here,*
I said, and they are out there?
*   that's the way it is,*
*   said Aunt Hetty, the shriveled-up one.*
                        —*Paulette Jiles, "Paper Matches"*

Two scientists recently made this forecast: The fastest woman may eventually outrun the fastest man. Their prediction appeared only as a letter to the editor in *Nature* magazine, yet it generated a stampede of interest from the media. *Time*, the *Chicago Tribune*, *USA Today*, the *New York Times*, the *Washington Post*, and *Sports Illustrated* printed stories. All quoted experts who ridiculed the conjecture as "ludicrous," "sheer ignorance," "a good laugh," "absurd," "asinine," "completely fallacious," and/or "laughable."

In one Associated Press report, the word ridiculous was used five times. *Science News* ran the headline "Women on the verge of an athletic showdown." *Runner's World* entitled its article "Battle of the Sexes." Unlike questionable projections that are dismissed without fanfare, this one seems to have struck a nerve.

The researchers, Brian Whipp and Susan Ward of the University of California, Los Angeles, calculated runners' average speeds during record-breaking races over the past seventy years, then compared the rates of increase. Noting that women's average speeds are increasing at a faster rate than are men's, they projected that in the future, the best women may catch up to and even surpass the best men at various distances.

Indisputably, neither women nor men will continue to improve at their current rates forever. Otherwise, humans would one day run the marathon in a matter of minutes But the very idea that women might someday beat men elicited passionate responses. *Runner's World* writers Amby Burfoot and Marty Post, as if verbally to stop women in their tracks, pointed out that in the past five years, women have made few improvements in world-record times.

This is a sure sign, they said, that women "have already stopped" improving.

When I appear on radio and television shows to discuss women's sports or my first book, *Are We Winning Yet? How Women Are Changing Sports and Sports Are Changing Women,* I encounter a similar fury. Female callers are not the problem; they brag about their triceps or gripe about male egos or ask for advice about discrimination. Some male callers tell stories about female martial artists or mountain climbers who taught them, in a way they could understand, about female strength. But at least half of the male callers act as if my views were heretical. Angry and antagonistic, they belittle me, my ideas, my book, and female athletes in general.

What seems to make them angriest is my observation that men are not better athletes than women are. In no sport are all men better than all women, I point out, and in many sports, women routinely defeat men. Although single-sex competitions are often appropriate, and men do have physical advantages in some sports, women should see themselves as men's peers, I suggest, rather than exclusively competing against women.

These men don't want to hear any of that. In voices I can only describe as high-pitched and hysterical, they say, "Yeah, but you're never going to see a woman play pro football!"

It is a taunt and, I think, a genuine fear. I'm not talking about football. I've never met a woman who aspires to play pro football. I'm talking about auto racing, horse racing, dog sled racing, equestrian events, rifle shooting, and marathon swimming, where women and men compete together at the elite levels. I'm talking about tennis, golf, racquetball, bowling, skiing, and other recreational sports, where a wife and husband or a female and male pair of friends are likely to find themselves evenly matched. In sports, as in the rest of life, women do compete with men on a daily basis, and often win.

So it intrigues me that in response to my discussion of women's athletic excellence, men change the subject to football. They try to assert football as the sine qua non of athleticism. Because "women could never play football," they imply, men are physically, naturally, biologically superior.

Most men can't play pro football themselves—but they can take vicarious comfort in the display of male physical competence and aggression.

They take comfort in professional baseball ("Women could never play pro baseball") and in professional basketball ("Women could never play pro basketball") and in boxing ("Women could never box") and in footraces ("Women could never win the marathon").

Here are a few more quotes from men on radio shows, on airplanes, at restaurants:

"Women can't dunk."

"OK, women can play golf, but they can't drive the ball as far as men can."

"OK, female jockeys win, but there's a horse involved."

"Women win at marathon swimming? Who cares? You call that a major sport? I'd like to see a 320-pound female linebacker. That's a laugh."

Most men are not 320-pound linebackers. But, identified with these hulks, average men take great pleasure in the linebackers' exploits (a revealing term). Football, baseball, basketball, boxing, and hockey are important to men in part *because* they seem to be all-male pursuits, because they seem to be activities that *only men can do.* When women demonstrate excellence in sports like running, tennis, and golf, men take great pains to describe that excellence as less important, less worthy, less of an achievement than male excellence.

Psychiatrist Arnold R. Beisser explains the phenomenon this way: "It is small wonder that the American male has a strong affinity for sports. He has learned that this is one area where there is no doubt about sexual differences and where his biology is not obsolete. Athletics help assure his difference from women in a world where his functions have come to resemble theirs."

Sports are about distinction. Who is better? One inch, one point, or one-hundredth of a second can differentiate winner from loser. One pound, one meal, one more set of two-hundred-meter sprints in practice can determine, or seem to determine, whether a person finishes first or last. Athletes may train for the sheer joy of moving their bodies through space, but eventually they grow curious to see how fast they can move, or how well they can perform, compared to others. They want to compare, to contrast, to differentiate. To know where they stand. To win.

It is in this comparative, competitive arena that we are repeatedly told that women and men are different. And men are better. Women may no longer be weak, granted, but they are still weak*er*. Weaker than men. Still the weaker sex.

Still, as de Beauvoir said, the second sex.

Actually, in many ways, men are the weaker sex. Men die on average seven years earlier than women. Women have a better sense of smell, taste, hearing, and sight (colorblindness affects one woman for every sixteen men). Women are more susceptible to migraines, arthritis, and depression, but men commit suicide more and have higher rates of heart attack and stroke. "Women are sick, but men are dead," Edward Dolnick wrote in his *In Health* magazine article on the subject.

Yet men keep pointing to one physical advantage —upper-body strength— to maintain their illusion of supremacy. Sports that depend on such strength— that, indeed, were designed to showcase that strength —bolster the myth.

Those who claim male sports superiority are not thinking of male gymnasts, who lack the flexibility to use some of the apparatus women use. Or male swimmers, who can't keep up with women over long distances. Or male equestrians, who gallop side by side with—or in the dust of—their female peers.

They are not considering how much women and men have in common: the human experience of sport. These same people would never think of comparing Sugar Ray Leonard to Muhammad Ali. One weighed sixty pounds more than the other. Clearly, they deserved to box in different classes. Yet the top female tennis player is often compared to the top male tennis player ("Yeah but, she could never beat *him*"), who usually outweighs her by sixty pounds.

Those who claim male superiority are not remembering jockstraps. Because men's genitals dangle precariously outside the pelvis, they are vulnerable to speeding baseballs and to angry fists or feet. In addition, "bikes with dropped handlebars bring the rider's legs close to the stomach, and the testicles can get squashed or twisted against the saddle," notes

sportswriter Adrianne Blue in *Faster, Higher, Further.* "This can lead to gangrene and amputation." Such cases have been noted in medical journals.

Blue also suggests that men's bigger bodies make more "dangerous missiles" that are more likely than women's bodies to cause injury when they collide. For this reason a case could be made, she says, for banning men from contact sports.

If women and men were to compete together in noncontact sports, a man would currently win at the elite levels of most existing events: running (as long as the race is under 100 miles); swimming (under about 22 miles); throwing shot, discus, or javelin. On average, men can carry and use more oxygen. They tend to be heavier—an advantage in football —and taller: handy in basketball and volleyball. Men have more lean muscle mass, convenient in sports requiring explosive power— which happens to include most of the sports men have invented.

Less muscle-bound, women generally have better flexibility, useful in gymnastics, diving, and skating. Our lower center of gravity can help in hockey, golf, tennis, baseball, and even basketball. We sweat better (less dripping, therefore better evaporation), which is critical since, like car engines, human bodies need to remain cool and well lubricated to function efficiently.

Physiologist Diane Wakat, associate professor of health education at the University of Virginia, tested athletes under various conditions of heat, humidity, exercise, and nutritional intake, and concluded that women are better able to adjust to the environmental changes. "In every case, females were better able to handle the stress," says Wakat.

The longer the race, the better women do. Women's superior insulation (fat) is, believe it or not, prized by some because it offers buoyancy, heat retention, and efficient use of fuel over long distances, whether by land or by sea.

Ann Trason, a California microbiology teacher, became in 1989 the first woman to win a coed national championship—the twenty-four-hour run —by completing 143 miles. The best male finisher completed four fewer miles. Of Ward and Whipp's prediction that women will one day hold the overall world record in the relatively short (26.2-mile) marathon, Trason says: "I'd be there and be really happy to see it, but it seems unlikely. I do think women will get closer."

Helen Klein's world-record distance in a twenty-four-hour race—109.5 miles—exceeds the best distance for an American man in her age group (65–69). She says of the possibility that a woman will one day set the overall marathon record, "I would not say no. There is hope. If I were younger, I might try it myself."

In marathon and long-distance cold-water swims, "women usually out-swim the men," says Bob Duenkel, curator of the International Swimming Hall of Fame. Penny Dean still holds the English Channel record she set in 1978. Diana Nyad is the only athlete to complete the swim from Bimini to Florida. Lynne Cox holds the records for swimming the Bering Strait and the Strait of Magellan. The first person to swim all five Great Lakes, and the first ever to cross Lake Superior (in 1988), was Vicki Keith.

Susan Butcher has been the overall winner of the 1,100-mile Iditarod dog sled race four times. A woman named Seana Hogan recently cycled the four hundred miles from San Francisco to Los Angeles in nineteen hours, forty-nine minutes, breaking the previous men's record by almost an hour.

But women's successes are rarely attributable to gender. In ultra-distance running, swimming, and cycling, as well as in equestrian events, horse racing, auto racing, and dog sled racing, success is determined primarily by physical and mental preparation, competitive spirit, self-discipline, or other non-gender-related factors. Because upper-body strength is not paramount in these sports, women and men become free to compete together as individuals, even at the highest levels of competition.

Men's strength advantage is actually marginal, meaning that there is more variation among individual men than between the average man and the average woman. It only becomes relevant when comparing trained, competitive athletes. On any recreational doubles tennis team, the female player might be stronger.

Age is also important. Men's strength advantage occurs primarily during the reproductive years. Before puberty, girls, who tend to mature faster, have a height and strength advantage which, if not nullified by institutional and cultural discrimination, would actually render the best of them superior to the best boys. In old age, there is little physical difference between female and male strength.

But we've so long been told that men are better athletes. I even catch myself thinking this way, despite daily evidence to the contrary. For instance, in my masters swimming program, the fastest athletes —including college competitors—swim in Lane 1, while the slowest—including fit, fast, white-haired folks in their seventies—swim in Lane 6. There are women and men in all the lanes.

I swim in Lane 3. In Lane 2 is Ken. Because he's about my age and height, I identify with him. We have the same stroke length, so we look at each other sometimes, his breathing to the left, my breathing to the right, as we windmill through the water. But eventually he pulls ahead. He's faster. At first, I attributed his greater speed to the fact that he is male. His shoulders are broader; his muscles are more prominent than mine.

But then I looked over at Lane 4. There swims Bruce. Also about my height and my age, Bruce is slower than I am. He's got those same broad shoulders and big muscles, but there he is anyway, poking along in Lane 4. I'm faster because I've trained longer, or I have better technique, or I'm in better shape, or I'm more competitive, or some combination of those factors—the same reasons Ken is faster than both Bruce and me, and the same reasons Susie, Karen, Diane, Denise, Lynn, and Martha are faster than Ken. It has nothing to do with gender.

. . .

Because "being masculine" has included access to diverse sporting opportunities and "being feminine" has not, it's shortsighted to postulate that current gaps between male and female athletic potential will not close, at least partially, in the future— or that, as Post and Burfoot asserted, women "have already stopped improving." Men prevented women from running marathons until 1967. The Olympics did not offer a women's marathon until 1984, and still doesn't offer a women's swimming event longer than eight hundred meters (the men swim fifteen hundred meters). For every college woman who gets a chance to play college sports, 2.24 men do. For every woman who receives a college scholarship, 2.26 men do. The more women run, the greater the likelihood that some of them will run fast. Increased numbers of female runners—along with female-focused training, coaching, scholarships, equipment, and even clothing—account for the historical improvements in women's times, and greater numbers in the future are likely to improve times further.

If marathon swimming were our national sport, as it is in Egypt—if there were a nationally televised Super Bowl of marathon swimming, and spectators packed college swim meets like sardines—we might think differently about women's and men's athletic capabilities. If men competed against women on the balance beam, or in synchronized swimming or in rhythmic gymnastics, we might rephrase the question about who might catch up to whom.

. . .

One reason male–female athletic comparisons are tempting to make, and hard to argue with, is that they seem natural. What could be more natural than human bodies? Sports seem to offer measurable, inarguable proof of human physical potential. Especially when no machines or animals are involved, sports seem to represent a raw, quintessentially fair contest between individuals or teams. *Ready? Set? Go. May the best man win.*

In fact, few professional athletes have "natural" bodies; otherwise we'd bump into pro football–sized men in the supermarkets. The linebacker has been shaped by many behavioral (nutrition, weight lifting) and often chemical (steroids, growth hormones) factors. Women who play or do not play sports have also been shaped by various factors, including restricted access to training opportunities, restrictive shoes and clothing, ridicule by peers, and cultural pressure to limit food intake for the sake of creating a thin, rather than strong, body. There's nothing natural about any of that.

But because sports seem natural, and because in the sports media we so often see men who are bigger and stronger than the biggest, strongest women, these men make a convincing subliminal case: not only are men better athletes, men are superior physical specimens. And because the men engaged in sporting events are so often enacting some form of mock combat, we receive the message: Men are inherently, naturally aggressive and, as a gender, dominant.

. . .

As every first-grader knows, there are physical differences between women and men, but these differences would be largely irrelevant except in matters of sex, reproduction, urination, and toupee purchases if it weren't for our culture's insistence on categorizing people first and foremost as "male" or "female." It is from these cultural categories—not from biological realities—that most "masculine" and "feminine" behaviors emerge. Cynthia Fuchs Epstein, author of *Deceptive Distinctions,* writes, "The overwhelming evidence created by the past decade of research on gender supports the theory that gender differentiation—as distinct of course from sexual differentiation—is best explained as a social construction rooted in hierarchy."

Here's where the hierarchy part comes in: we don't just say, boys shouldn't play with dolls and girls shouldn't play with pistols. Through our economic structure and through the media, we say that taking care of children—"women's work"—is less important than war—"men's work." We don't just say that football is for boys and cheerleading is for girls. We say that playing football is more valuable than cheerleading or field hockey or volleyball or Double Dutch jump rope or anything girls do—more important, more interesting, more newsworthy: better.

Thus boys have an incentive to cling religiously to "boy behaviors," and they do. Boys are more likely than girls to insist on sex-typed activities and toys, and with good reason—it cements their place in the dominant class. Boys also have an incentive to keep girls out of their tree forts and clubhouses and sports associations and military elite: like "undesirables" moving into a pricey neighborhood, females lower the property value. Women's participation challenges the entire concept of relevant differences between women and men. "To allow women into sport would be an ultimate threat to one of the last strongholds of male security and supremacy," write Mary A. Boutilier and Lucinda SanGiovanni in *The Sporting Woman.* To put it another way, if women can play sports then "men aren't really men."

Of course, it's too late to keep women out of sports. But they can be kept out of the public eye and kept out of key, visible, highly paid positions like a football or men's basketball coach. Their accomplishments can be ignored or trivialized or sexualized. They can be barred from "masculine" activities—a term having nothing, really, to do with who men are, and everything to do with what men want to claim as their own.

. . .

Female athletes, sweat soaking their muscled chests, aren't half-women, half-men. They aren't Lady Panthers or Lady Rams or Lady Cheetahs, trying in vain to catch up to Gentlemen Bulls. They're people in pursuit of perfection—a quest that human beings, in all their diversity, seem to enjoy.

READING 23

To Be or Not to Be

Leslie Feinberg

"You were born female, right?" The reporter asked me for the third time. I nodded patiently. "So do you identify as female now, or male?"

She rolled her eyes as I repeated my answer. "I am transgendered. I was born female, but my masculine gender expression is seen as male. It's not my sex that defines me, and it's not my gender expression. It's the fact that my gender expression appears to be at odds with my sex. Do you understand? It's the social contradiction between the two that defines me."

The reporter's eyes glazed over as I spoke. When I finished she said, "So you're a *third* sex?" Clearly, I realized, we had very little language with which to understand each other.

When I try to discuss sex and gender, people can only imagine woman or man, feminine or masculine. We've been taught that nothing else exists in nature. Yet, as I've shown, this has not been true in all cultures or in all historical periods. In fact, Western law took centuries to neatly partition the sexes into only two categories and mandate two corresponding gender expressions.

"The paradigm that there are two genders founded on two biological sexes began to predominate in western culture only in the early eighteenth century," historian Randolph Trumbach notes in his essay, "London's Sapphists: From Three Sexes to Four Genders in the Making of Modern Culture."[1] Trumbach explains that as late as the eighteenth century, in northwestern Europe, feminine men and masculine women—known as mollies and tommies respectively—were thought of as third and fourth genders.

But how many sexes and genders *do* exist? All too frequently, this question is presented as an abstract one, like how many angels can dance on the head of a pin? But the search for the answer to this question has to be understood within the context of oppression.

Those of us who cross the "man-made" boundaries of sex and gender run afoul of the law, are subject to extreme harassment and brutality, and are denied employment, housing, and medical care. We have grown up mostly unable to find ourselves represented in the dominant culture.

So how can we have a discussion of how much sex and gender diversity actually exists in society, when all the mechanisms of legal and extralegal repression render our lives invisible? Gender theorists can't just function as census takers who count how much sex and gender diversity exists; they must be part of the struggle to defend our right to exist, or most of us will be forced to remain underground.

The more inclusive the trans liberation movement becomes, and the more visible our movement is in society, the more clearly sex and gender variation will be seen. However, as the trans movement grows and develops, part of its impact has been to pose questions. What is the relationship between birth sex, gender expression, and desire? Does the body you are born with determine your sex for life? How many variations of sex and gender exist today?

The gradations of sex and gender self-definition are limitless. When I first opened an America Online account, I tried to establish the *nom de net* "stone butch" or "drag king." I discovered these names were already taken. As I later prowled through AOL and UNIX bulletin boards, I found a world of infinite sex and gender identities, which cyberspace has given people the freedom to explore with a degree of anonymity.

But although this fluidity and variation exists, there still aren't many more words to express sex and gender than there were when I was growing up. All of the complexity of my gender expression is reduced to looking "like a man." Since I'm not a man, what does it mean when people tell me I look like one? When I was growing up, other kids told me I pitched baseballs and shot marbles "like a boy." As a young adult, I suffered a torrent of criticism from adults who admonished me for standing, walking, and sitting "like a boy." Strangers felt free to stop me on the street to confront me with this observation. Something about me was inappropriate, but what?

The "gender theory" I learned in school, at home, in books, and at the movies was very simple. There are men and women. Men are masculine and women are feminine. End of subject. But clearly the subject didn't end there for me.

I had no words to discuss this with anyone. The way I expressed myself was wrong. There was no language to dispute this because the right way was assumed to be natural. Thank goodness, by the time I was sixteen years old the women's liberation movement was beginning to vocally denounce the outrageously separate and unequal indoctrination of girls and boys. For the first time, I was able to separate my birth sex from the gender education I received as a girl. Since sex and gender had always been seen as synonymous when I was growing up, disconnecting the two was a very important advance in my own thinking.

In addition, one of the gifts the women's movement gave me was a closer look at the values that have been attached to masculinity and femininity. In my social education, masculinity had been inaccurately contrasted as stronger, more analytical, more stable, and more rational than femininity.

But it was not until the rise of the movement for transgender liberation that I began to see the important distinction between the negative gender *values* attached to being masculine or feminine and my

right to my own gender *expression*. I am subjugated by the values attached to gender expression. But I am not oppressing other people by the way I express my gender when I wear a tie. Nor are other people's clothing or makeup crushing my freedom.

Both women's and trans liberation have presented me with two important tasks. One is to join the fight to strip away the discriminatory and oppressive values attached to masculinity and femininity. The other is to defend gender freedom—the right of each individual to express their gender in any way they choose, whether feminine, androgynous, masculine, or any point on the spectrum between. And that includes the right to gender ambiguity and gender contradiction.

It's equally important that each person have the right to define, determine, or change their sex in any way they choose—whether female, male, or any point on the spectrum between. And that includes the right to physical ambiguity and contradiction.

This struggle affects millions of people, because, as it turns out, sex and gender are a lot more complicated than woman and man, pink and blue. As the brochure of the Intersex Society of North America explains: "Our culture conceives sex anatomy as a dichotomy: humans come in two sexes, conceived of as so different as to be nearly different species. However, developmental embryology, as well as the existence of intersexuals, proves this to be a cultural construction. Anatomic sex differentiation occurs on a male/female continuum, and there are several dimensions."[2]

In an article entitled, "The Five Sexes: Why Male and Female Are Not Enough," geneticist Dr. Anne Fausto-Sterling stresses that "Western culture is deeply committed to the idea that there are only two sexes." But, she adds, "If the state and the legal system have an interest in maintaining a two-party sexual system, they are in defiance of nature. For biologically speaking, there are many gradations running from female to male; and depending on how one calls the shots, one can argue that along that spectrum lie at least five sexes—and perhaps even more."[3]

The right to physical ambiguity and contradiction are surgically and hormonally denied to newborn intersexual infants who fall between the "poles" of female and male. If doctors refrained from immediately "fixing" infants who don't fit the clear-cut categories of male and female, we would be spared the most commonly asked question: "What a beautiful baby! Is it a boy or a girl?"

And imagine what a difference it would make if parents replied, "We don't know, our child hasn't told us yet."

Why are infants being shoehorned into male or female? As Fausto-Sterling points out, "For questions of inheritance, legitimacy, paternity, succession to title, and eligibility for certain professions to be determined, modern Anglo-Saxon legal systems require that newborns be registered as either male or female." As a result, infants are surgically and hormonally manipulated into one sex or the other after birth, sometimes without even the parents' knowledge. Fausto-Sterling concludes that society, therefore, "mandates the control of intersexed bodies because they blur and bridge the great divide."[4]

Intersexuality is not news; it's been recorded since antiquity. Creation legends on every continent incorporate a sacred view of intersexuality. But with the rise of patriarchal, sex-segregated societies in Greece and Rome, for example, intersexual babies were burned alive, or otherwise murdered. In recent centuries, intersexuals were ordered to pick one sex in which to live, and were killed if they changed their minds.[5]

What's news is hearing courageous intersexual people voice their own demands. Day-old infants can't give informed consent to genital surgery. Intersexed babies have a right to grow up and make their own decisions about the body they will live in for the rest of their lives. Parents need counseling; intersexual youth need intersexual advisors. These are basic human rights, yet they are being violated every day. Cheryl Chase, founder of the Intersex Society of North America describes this nightmare:

> When an intersexual infant is born, the parents are confronted with a shocking fact that violates their understanding of the world. Physicians treat the birth of such an infant as a medical emergency. A medical team, generally including a surgeon and an endocrinologist, is roused from bed, if need be, and assembled to manage the situation. Intersexual bodies are rarely sick ones; the emergency here is culturally constructed. The team analyzes the genetic makeup, anatomy, and endocrine status of the infant, "assigns" it male or female, and informs the parents of their child's "true" sex. They then proceed to enforce this sex with surgical and hormonal intervention.
>
> The parents are so traumatized and shamed that they will not reveal their ordeal to anyone, including the child as he/she comes of age. The child is left genitally and emotionally mutilated, isolated, and without access to information about what has happened to them. The burden of pain and shame is so great that virtually all intersexuals stay deep in the closet throughout their adult lives.[6]

Even reactionaries might agree with the struggle against the surgical alteration of infants, but with a twist: Let no man put asunder what God has brought together. However, this argument must not be used as a weapon against the rights of transsexual adults who choose sex-reassignment surgery. Not all transsexuals want or can afford that elective. But for those who do, there's no contradiction between the rights of transsexuals and those of intersexuals. The heart of the struggle of both communities is the right of each individual to control their own body.

I can remember standing in front of an abortion clinic in Buffalo, my arms linked with others in the dim glint of dawn, with cold rain dripping off my face. We were defending the women's health clinic against a right-wing assault on the right of women to choose abortion. I certainly knew politically what I was supporting. But that morning, perhaps because I was so miserably cold and wet, I felt the intersection of the demands of the trans movement and the women's movement in my own body. The heart of both is the right of each individual to make decisions about our own bodies and to define ourselves.

That is a right of each woman, each intersexed person, each transsexual man or woman—each human being. I believe that people who don't identify as transsexual also have a right to hormones and surgery. There are many of us who have wanted to shape our bodies without changing our sex. Since sex-reassignment programs won't prescribe hormones or arrange surgery for a person who does not identify as a transsexual, we have to lie, buy hormones on the street, or go to quacks who sell prescriptions for a hefty fee.

Legions of people in this society do all sorts of things to make themselves more comfortable in their own bodies: myriad types of cosmetic surgery, nose jobs, piercing, tattooing, augmentation, liposuction, dieting, bodybuilding, circumcision, bleaching, coloring, and electrolysis. But many of the people who add, subtract, reshape, or adorn their bodies criticize those transsexuals who elect surgery for *their* life decisions. I believe that the centuries-old fears and taboos about genitalia, buried deep in the dominant Western cultures, make the subject of surgical sex-change highly sensational. Today some opponents of sex-reassignment argue that sex-change is merely a high-tech phenomenon, a consequence of people being squeezed into narrow cultural definitions of what it means to be a woman or a man because surgical and hormonal options are now available. It's true that the development of anesthesia, and the commercial synthesis of hormones, opened up new opportunities for sex-reassignment. However, the argument that transsexuals are merely escaping rigid sex roles doesn't take into account ancient surgical techniques of sex-change developed in communal societies that offered more flexible sex and gender choices.

It all comes down to this: Each person has the right to control their own body. If each individual doesn't have that right, then who gets to judge and make decisions? Should we hand over that power to the church or the state? Should we make these rights subject to a poll?

And equally important to me is the right of each person to express their gender in any way they choose. But currently, strangers don't have to ask a parent if their infant is a boy or a girl if the child is dressed in pink or blue. Even gender color-coded diapers are now marketed in the United States.

[I am] surprised to discover that this pink-for-girls, blue-for-boys gender assignment is a relatively recent development in the United States.[7] In the last century in this country, babies of all sexes wore little white dresses, which didn't seem to skew the gender expressions of these generations of children. Fur-

thermore, the pink-blue gender values used to be just the opposite.

"Gender-based color schemes were adopted only at the onset of the twentieth century, as plumbing, cloth diapers, and color-fast fabrics became more available," wrote historians Vern and Bonnie Bullough. "However, different countries adopted different color schemes. In fact, there were heated arguments in the American popular press that pink was a more masculine color than light blue."[8]

How did the current pink and blue finally get assigned? Pink became a "girl's" color and blue a "boy's" in the United States in the early twentieth century after a media circus surrounding the acquisition of Thomas Gainsborough's painting *Blue Boy* and Sir Thomas Lawrence's *Pinkie* by wealthy art aficionado Henry Edwards Huntington.[9]

But the problem with the binary categories of pink and blue is that I'm not so easily color-coded, and neither are a lot of people I know. I've been taught that feminine and masculine are two polar opposites, but when I ride the subways or walk the streets of New York City, I see women who range from feminine to androgynous to masculine and men who range from masculine to androgynous to feminine. That forms a circle—a much more liberating concept than two poles with a raging void in between. A circle has room on it for each person to explore, and it offers the freedom for people to move on that circle throughout their lives if they choose.

Even today, when sex and gender choices have been so narrowed, when there are such degrading and murderous social penalties for crossing the boundaries of sex and gender, many of us can't—and don't want to—fit. We have to fight for the right of each person to express their gender in any way they choose. Who says our self-expression has to match our genitals? Who has the right to tell anyone else how to define their identities? And who has the right to decide what happens to each of our bodies? We cannot let these fundamental freedoms be taken away from us.

But those rights can't be won and protected without a fight. Strong bonds between the women's and trans liberation movements would put even more muscle into that struggle.

NOTES

1. Randolph Trumbach, "London's Sapphists: From Three Sexes to Four Genders in the Making of Modern Culture," *Body-guards: The Cultural Politics of Gender Ambiguity*, eds. Julia Epstein and Kristina Straub (New York: Routledge, 1991) 112–13.
2. *What Is Intersexuality?* (San Francisco: Intersex Society of North America, n. d.).
3. Anne Fausto-Sterling, "The Five Sexes: Why Male and Female Are Not Enough," *The Sciences* March/April 1993: 20–21.
4. Ibid., 23–24.
5. The prevalence of intersexual myths is reflected in documentation as diverse as "Androgyne," *The Woman's Encyclopedia of Myths and Secrets*, ed. Barbara G. Walker (San Francisco: Harper & Row, 1983) 32–34; the Greek *androgyne* of Plato, *The Symposium*, trans. Walter Hamilton (London: Penguin Books, 1951) 58–65; the Japanese *Izanagi/Izanami* unity described in Mircea Eliade, *Myths, Dreams, and Mysteries: The Encounter between Contemporary Faiths and Archaic Realities*, trans. Philip Mairet (1957; New York: Harper & Row, 1975) 179–83; the Yoruban and Dahomean *Mawulisa* and *Seboulisa* of Audre Lorde, *The Black Unicorn* (New York: W. W. Norton, 1978), William Bascom, *The Yoruba of Southwestern Nigeria* (New York: Holt, Rinehart & Winston, 1969), and Melville Herskovits, *Dahomey*, 2 vols. (New York: J. J. Augustin, 1934); the "twofold gods" of Crete, Cyprus, Rome, Greece in Marie Delcourt, *Hermaphrodite: Myths and Rites of the Bisexual Figure in Classical Antiquity*, trans. Jennifer Nicholson (1956; London: Studio Books, 1961) 17–43; and the *Warharmi* of the Kamia of southwestern North America in Walter Williams, *The Spirit and the Flesh: Sexual Diversity in American Indian Culture* (Boston: Beacon Press, 1986) 18. For some information on persecution of hermaphrodites, see the original classical sources referenced in P. M. C. Forbes Irving, *Metamorphosis in Greek Myths* (Oxford: The Clarendon Press, 1990) 149–50, and the French sources in Eugene de Savitsch, *Homosexuality, Transvestism and Change of Sex* (Springfield, IL: Charles C. Thomas, 1958) 30.
6. Cheryl Chase, e-mail communication, 2 February 1995.
7. Sandra Salmans, "Objects and Gender: when an It Evolves into a He or a She," *New York Times* 16 November 1989: B1.
8. Vern L. Bullough and Bonnie Bullough, *Cross Dressing, Sex, and Gender* (Philadelphia: University of Pennsylvania Press, 1993) viii.
9. Ibid.

DISCUSSION QUESTIONS FOR CHAPTER THREE

1. How do notions of sex and gender take shape within a cultural context? In what ways has your cultural context shaped your notions of sex and gender?

2. How would you describe the dominant notions of masculinity and femininity in U.S. society? How do these dominant notions help maintain systems of inequality?

3. How do people learn to "do" gender? Can you think of ways you've learned to do gender? From what sources did you learn to do gender?

4. How does gender ranking reinforce sexism?

5. How is the experience of sexism shaped by the confluences of other systems of oppression?

SUGGESTIONS FOR FURTHER READING

Bornstein, Kate. *My Gender Workbook.* New York: Routledge, 1998.

Fausto-Sterling, Anne. *Sexing the Body: Gender Politics and the Construction of Sexuality.* New York: Basic Books, 2000.

Feinberg, Leslie. *Transgender Warriors.* Boston: Beacon, 1996.

Howey, Noelle. *Dress Codes: Of Three Girlhoods—My Mother's, My Father's, and Mine.* New York: St. Martin's Press, 2002.

Lorber, Judith. *Paradoxes of Gender.* New Haven, CT: Yale University Press, 1994.

Tavris, Carol. "The Mismeasure of Woman." *Feminism and Psychology* 3 (1993): 149–168.

West, Candace, and Don H. Zimmerman. "Doing Gender." *Gender and Society* 1 (1987): 125–151.

CHAPTER FOUR

Sex, Power, and Intimacy

Sexuality is a topic of great interest to most people. It entertains and intrigues and is a source of both personal happiness and frustration. Over the centuries men have struggled to control women's sexuality through a variety of physical and emotional means; controlling a woman's sexuality has often meant controlling her life. The flipside of this is that sexuality has the potential to be a liberating force in women's lives. To enjoy and be in control of one's sexuality and to be able to seek a mutually fulfilling sexual relationship can be an empowering experience. This chapter begins with a discussion of the social construction of sexuality and provides definitions for key terms. Following is a focus on two themes associated with sexuality: first, the politics of sexuality, and second, intimacy, romance, and communication.

THE SOCIAL CONSTRUCTION OF SEXUALITY

Human sexuality involves erotic attractions, identity, and practices, and it is constructed by and through societal sexual scripts. *Sexual scripts* reflect social norms, practices, and workings of power, and they provide frameworks and guidelines for sexual feelings and behaviors. There is often embarrassment, shame, and confusion associated with these sexual scripts, and they easily become fraught with potential misunderstandings. Misunderstandings associated with sexual scripts are humorously illustrated in the short excerpt by April Sinclair from *Coffee Will Make You Black*.

Sexual scripts vary across cultures and through time and are almost always heavily informed by societal understandings of gender. The article by Pepper Schwartz and Virginia Rutter, "Sexual Desire and Gender," emphasizes two key points: that sexuality is about society as much as it is about biological urges and that the most significant dimension of sexuality is gender. For example, as discussed in Chapter 3, feminine sexual scripts have often involved a double bind: to want sex is to risk being labeled promiscuous and not to want sex means potentially being labeled frigid and a prude. For many women, sexuality is shrouded in shame and fear, and, rather than seeing themselves as subjects in their own erotic lives, these women understand themselves as objects, seen through the eyes of others. In terms of masculinity, sexual potency is a key aspect of doing gender for many men in contemporary Western societies.

Within the context of sexual scripts, individuals develop their own sexual self-schemas. *Sexual self-schemas* can be defined as identities or cognitive generalizations about sexual aspects of the self that are established from past and present experiences and that guide sexual feelings and behavior. What is desirable or acceptable to one person may be unacceptable or even disgusting to another. Note that sexual scripts are societal-level guidelines for human sexuality, whereas sexual self-schemas are individual-level understandings of the self.

RAINBOW TRIVIA

1. At what New York bar did the modern gay liberation movement begin?
   a. Studio 54
   b. Stonewall
   c. Club 57
   d. Scandals

2. What were homosexuals required to wear to identify them in concentration camps during World War II?
   a. A yellow star
   b. A lavender H
   c. A pink star
   d. A pink triangle

3. What Greek letter symbolizes queer activism?
   a. Lambda
   b. Alpha
   c. Delta
   d. Sigma

4. What is the name of the religious organization that supports queer Catholics?
   a. Spirit
   b. Celebration
   c. Dignity
   d. Affirmation

5. What is the country's largest political organization working specifically for queer rights?
   a. Human Rights Campaign
   b. ACT-UP
   c. NOW
   d. Christian Coalition

6. What famous athlete came out at the 1993 March on Washington?
   a. Greg Louganis
   b. Reggie White
   c. Tonya Harding
   d. Martina Navritalova

7. What show made television history by having the first gay lead character?
   a. *Soap*
   b. *Roseanne*
   c. *Ellen*
   d. *All in the Family*

8. Who of the following is not a famous lesbian performer?
   a. Sarah McLachlan
   b. Melissa Etheridge
   c. k.d. lang
   d. Indigo Girls

9. Which of the following is a must-read for any good lesbian?
   a. *The Well of Loneliness* by Radclyffe Hall
   b. *Rubyfruit Jungle* by Rita Mae Brown
   c. Anything by Dorothy Allison
   d. All of the above

10. Which of the following movies did *not* have a lesbian character?
    a. *Boys on the Side*
    b. *Personal Best*
    c. *Desert Hearts*
    d. *None of the above*

Answers: 1. b 2. d 3. a 4. c 5. a 6. d 7. c 8. a 9. d 10. d

Sexual scripts vary across such differences as race, class, age, and ability. The short story by Emily Oxford, "Prue Shows Her Knickers," tells of the empowerment of an adolescent girl with disabilities as well as the constraints associated with her physical condition. The relentless youth-oriented culture of contemporary U.S. society sees "older" ("older than whom?" you may ask—note how this term encourages a mythical norm associated with young adulthood) people or people with disabilities as less sexual, or interprets their sexuality as humorous or out of place.

Likewise, there are class and race differences associated with interpersonal relationships that reflect the norms of specific communities. For example, Chicana lesbians have spoken out about intense homophobia that is related to the sexual scripts identifying women as wives and mothers in their communities. In "La Güera," Cherríe Moraga describes how coming out as a lesbian helped her connect with the inequities of race. She is a light-skinned Chicana who had learned to pass as White. She writes, "The joys of looking like a white girl haven't been so great since I realized I could be beaten on the street for being a dyke." Paula Gunn Allen's poem, "Some Like Indians Endure," also makes the connections between racism and heterosexism. Both Indians and lesbians have endured and survived oppression.

There have also been strong mandates in U.S. society (such as anti-miscegenation laws) that have maintained racial superiority by outlawing interracial dating and marriage. Carolyn Reyes and Eric DeMeulenaere write about their love and friendship across ethnic and class barriers and the ways respect and trust have enriched their lives in their essay "Compañeros."

Sexual orientation is a person's attraction to, or preference for, people of a given sex. It is an individual's romantic and/or sexual (also called erotic) identity and behavior toward other people. Note that sexual orientation does not necessarily require sexual experience. *Heterosexuality* is a sexual orientation where romantic and/or sexual attachments and identification are between people of the opposite sex (popularly termed *straight*). *Homosexuality* is a sexual orientation where romantic and/or sexual attachments and identification are between people of the same sex. Because the term *homosexual* is stigmatized and because the term seems to emphasize sexual behavior, homosexual communities have preferred the term *gay*. *Gay* and *homosexual* are terms inclusive of women, although they are used mainly to describe men. The term *lesbian* means the romantic and/or sexual attachment and identification between women, specifically.

WORLD REPORT 2002: LESBIAN, GAY, BISEXUAL, AND TRANSGENDER RIGHTS

Although the visibility of lesbian, gay, bisexual, and transgender people throughout the world continued to rise in 2001, their increased visibility was accompanied by attacks based on sexual orientation and gender identity. Human rights activists who sought to use the human rights framework to call to account states that participated in these rights abuses or condoned them also came under attack. In virtually every country in the world people suffered from de jure and de facto discrimination based on their actual or perceived sexual orientation. In some countries, sexual minorities lived with the very real threat of being deprived of their right to life and security of person. A small number of countries continued to impose the death penalty for private sexual acts between consenting adults. In several others, sexual minorities were targeted for extrajudicial executions. In many countries, police or other members of the security forces actively participated in the persecution of lesbians, gay, bisexual, and transgender people, including their arbitrary detention and torture. Pervasive bias within the criminal justice system in many countries effectively precluded members of sexual minorities from seeking redress.

. . .

[The following examples suggest the enormity of discrimination faced by lesbian, gay, bisexual, and transgender people worldwide:]

• In Namibia, President Samuel Nujoma continued to vilify gay men and lesbians, stating, "The Republic of Namibia does not allow homosexuality, lesbianism here. Police are ordered to arrest you, and deport you, and imprison you too." The nationally televised speech came just two weeks after the Namibian Supreme Court overturned a lower court ruling recognizing the right of one member of a same sex couple to confer permanent residency on the other. Soon after the speech, the Rainbow Project, a nongovernmental human rights organization working with sexual minorities, started receiving reports of harassment and beatings by the Special Field Forces, a security unit reporting directly to the president. Nujoma later clarified his statement, "Traditional leaders, governors, see to it that there are no criminals, gays and lesbians in your villages and regions. We . . . have not fought for an independent Namibia that gives rights to botsotsos [criminals], gays and lesbians to do their bad things here."

• In November, Malaysian Prime Minister Mahathir Mohamad also verbally attacked gays, announcing that he would expel any gay British government minister if he came to Malaysia with a partner. Mahathir explained in an interview with BBC radio, "the British people accept homosexual ministers. But if they ever come here bringing their boyfriend along, we will throw them out. We will not accept them."

. . .

• [In Egypt] fifty-three people [were] detained and charged with ["debauchery"-related] offenses after a crackdown in May against men presumed to be gay. . . . There were reports that the men were beaten and subjected to forensic examinations in order to ascertain if they had engaged in anal sex. They were prosecuted before an Emergency State Security Court, which reached a verdict on November 14. Twenty-three were sentenced to between one and five years of hard labor; twenty-nine were acquitted. Be cause the trial took place before an Emergency State Security Court, those convicted could not appeal their sentences.

. . .

• . . . In April, the National Human Rights Commission of India missed a significant opportunity to address this violation when it announced that it did "not want to take cognizance" of a case brought before the commission objecting to involuntary aversion therapy and other forms of psychiatric abuse aimed at "converting" homosexuals. The commission explained its decision by stating, "sexual minority rights did not fall under the purview of human rights."

• More than a year after the murder of transgender activist Dayana (Jose Luis Nieves), transgender people living in Venezuela continued to face unrelenting police harass-ment. The Commander of Police in the state of Carabobo announced, "homosexuals and prostitutes are to be ruled by the police code. They cannot move freely in the streets." . . .

• Seven years after the [U.S.] military's "Don't Ask, Don't Tell" policy was codified as law and implemented, the United States military's own surveys and investigations found that training on how to implement the law was deficient and that anti-gay harassment remained pervasive in the military. . . . Although the "Don't Ask, Don't Tell" policy was ostensibly intended to allow gay, lesbian, and bisexual service members to remain in the military, discharges increased significantly after the policy's adoption. From 1994 to 2000, more than 6,500 servicemembers were discharged under the policy, with a rec-ord number of 1,231 separations during 2000. Women were discharged at a dispro-portionately high rate, while the policy provided an additional means for men to harass women service members by threatening to "out" those who refused their advances or threatened to report them, thus ending their careers.

Source: http://www.hrw.org/wr2k2/lgbt.html.

To complicate matters, the term *queer* is also used by both gays and lesbians to describe gay sexual orientation. Originally an insult, gays and lesbians have claimed the term as a source of pride and positive identity. *Queer* is also inclusive of *bisexuality,* the sexual orien-tation where individuals have romantic and/or sexual attachments, identification, and ori-entation with both women and men. There are derogatory social connotations of bisexual-ity as hypersexualized: not only do these people have sex all the time, but they are doing it with both women and with men, simultaneously. Of course, to be bisexual does not imply this at all; it just means the choice of lover can be either a woman or a man. Nonetheless, these connotations reflect the fact that there are many stigmas associated with bisexuality from both the straight and the lesbian and gay communities. Marcia Deihl and Robyn Ochs write about bisexuality and the fears of both heterosexual and homosexual communities to-ward bisexuality in "Biphobia."

You might also hear the terms *dyke, butch,* and *femme. Dyke* is synonymous with *les-bian,* although it connotes a masculine or mannish lesbian. Like *queer, dyke* is a word that is used against lesbians as an insult and has been appropriated or reclaimed by lesbians with pride. This means that if you are not a member of the lesbian, gay, or queer communities,

LEARNING ACTIVITY:
TALKING ABOUT BEING "OUT"

Answer the following questions:

Do you know of any people in your school whose sexual orientation differs from
yours?
How do you know?
Are you comfortable with that person or those people? Why or why not?
Do you think that person or those people [are] comfortable with you? Why or why not?

[With your classmates,] discuss the following:

What are some factors that might encourage or discourage a person about being
"out" as homosexual or bisexual in this class or your school?
What are, or what do you think would be, the consequences of a person being
"out" as homosexual or bisexual in this class or your school?

Source: Janet Lockhart and Susan M. Shaw. *Writing for Change: Raising Awareness of Difference, Power, and
Discrimination, www.teachingtolerance.org.*

you should probably not use the terms *queer* and *dyke,* because they most likely will be taken
as insults. *Butch* and *femme* are roles associated with gender that have been adopted by some
lesbians, especially in the past. Butch means acting as the masculine partner, and femme
means acting in a feminine role. Although today many lesbians avoid these role types because there is little incentive to mimic traditional heterosexual relationships, others enjoy
these identities and appropriate them to suit themselves.

Finally, the term *coming out* refers to someone adopting a gay, lesbian, bisexual, or
queer identity. Coming out is a psychological process that tends to involve two aspects: first,
recognizing and identifying this to oneself, and second, declaring oneself in a public way. In
terms of this second aspect, individuals usually come out to affirming members in their own
community before they face a general public. Some never come out to families or coworkers for fear of rejection, reprisals, and retaliation. For some, coming out means becoming
part of an identifiable political community; for others, it means functioning for the most
part as something of an outsider in a straight world. The phrase *in the closet* means not being out at all. In the closet can imply that a person understands her/himself to be lesbian or
gay but is not out to others. It can also imply that a person is in denial about her/his own
sexual identity and is not comfortable claiming a homosexual orientation.

THE POLITICS OF SEXUALITY

The term *politics* used here implies issues associated with the distribution of power in sexual relationships. There are politics in sexual relationships because they occur in the context
of a society that assigns power based upon gender and other systems of inequality and privilege. As discussed in Chapter 1, the personal is political: Issues and problems taken as personal or idiosyncratic within sexuality or relationships have broader social, political, and
economic causes and consequences.

According to J. Edgar Hoover, she was one of the most dangerous women in America in the early twentieth century. Emma Goldman came to the United States from Russia as a teenager in 1885, but for a Jewish immigrant, America was not the land of opportunity she had envisioned. Rather, she found herself in slums and sweatshops, eking out a living. Goldman had witnessed the slaughter of idealist political anarchists in Russia, and in 1886 she saw the hangings of four Haymarket anarchists who had opposed Chicago's power elite. As a result of these experiences, Goldman was drawn to anarchism and became a revolutionary.

Goldman moved to New York, where she met anarchist Johann Most, who advocated the overthrow of capitalism. Most encouraged Goldman's public speaking, although she eventually began to distance herself from him, recognizing the need to work for practical and specific improvements such as higher wages and shorter working hours. In 1893, she was arrested and imprisoned for encouraging a crowd of unemployed men to take bread if they were starving.

In New York, Goldman also worked as a practical nurse in New York's ghettos where she witnessed the effects of lack of birth control and no access to abortion. She began a campaign to address this problem, and her views eventually influenced Margaret Sanger and Sanger's work to make contraception accessible. Goldman was even arrested for distributing birth control literature.

Goldman was particularly concerned about sexual politics within anarchism. She recognized that a political solution alone would not rectify the unequal relations between the sexes. Rather, she called for a transformation of values, particularly by women themselves—by asserting themselves as persons and not sex commodities, by refusing to give the right over her body to anyone, by refusing to have children unless she wants them.

Her involvement in no conscription leagues and rallies against World War I led to her imprisonment and subsequent deportation to Russia. There she witnessed the Russian Revolution and then saw the corruption of the Bolsheviks as they amassed power. Her experience led her to reassess her earlier approval of violence as a means to social justice. Instead, she argued that violence begets counterrevolution.

Goldman remained active in Europe and continued to exercise influence in the United States. In 1922 *Nation* magazine named her one of the 12 greatest living women. In 1934 she was allowed to lecture in the United States, and in 1936 she went to Spain to participate in the Spanish Revolution. Goldman died in 1940 and was buried in Chicago near the Haymarket martyrs.

■ LEARNING ACTIVITY: AS THE WORLD TURNS

Tune into your favorite soap opera each day for a week. As you watch, record observations about the depictions, roles, and interactions of women and men. If all anyone knew about heterosexual relationships was what she or he saw on the soaps, what would this person believe?

Work with one or two other people in your class to devise an episode of a feminist soap opera. Who would be the characters? What dilemmas would they face? How would they resolve them? What would you call your soap opera? Is feminist soap opera possible? Would anyone watch?

In terms of sexuality, when a woman and a man get together romantically, what results is more than the mingling of two idiosyncratic individuals. The politics of this relationship involves two issues: first, women and men bring the baggage of their gendered lives into relationships. They have negotiated gender and other systems of inequality and privilege, and these experiences have shaped who they are. Much of this baggage is so familiar that it's thoroughly normalized and seen as completely natural. Second, the baggage of differently gendered lives implies power in relationships. As many feminists have pointed out, heterosexuality is organized in such a way that the power men have in society gets carried into relationships and encourages women's subservience, sexually and emotionally. Practically, this might mean that a woman sees herself through the eyes of men, or a particular man, and strives to live up to his image of who she should be. It might mean that a woman feels that men, or again, a particular man, owns or has the right to control her body or sexuality, or that she should be the one to ease the emotional transitions of the household, or tend to a man's daily needs—preparing his meals, cleaning his home, washing his clothes, raising his children—while still working outside the home. Even though she might choose this life and enjoy the role she has, feminists would argue that this is still an example of male domination in the private sphere. Men benefit from this. They have their emotional and domestic needs filled by women and are left free to work or play at what they want. Of course, their part of the bargain for these services is that they should provide for women economically. This is an arrangement that many women choose rationally.

We know that heterosexual relationships are a source of support and strength for many women; it is not heterosexuality that is faulted but the context in which heterosexual coupling takes place. When heterosexual intimacies are grounded in unequal power relationships, it becomes more and more difficult for women and men to love in healthy ways. This point is underscored in bell hooks' article "The Search for Men Who Love."

The politics of sexuality also come into play in lesbian relationships. Women come together with the baggage of femininity to work out and often internalized homophobia as well. They also come together with few clear models for successful relationships. An example of this is the "Are we on a date?" syndrome that occurs as two women attempt to deal with the boundaries between being girlfriends and being romantically interested in each other. Lesbian relationships also occur in the context of *heteronormativity*, the way heterosexuality is constructed as the norm. A related concept is *compulsory heterosexuality*, as already discussed in previous chapters: that heterosexuality is the expected and desirable sexual orientation. For example, various institutions support and encourage heterosexual coupling and dating. Schools offer dances and proms, the entertainment industry generally assumes heterosexual dating, and there is a public holiday (Valentine's Day) that celebrates it. There are billboards, magazine covers, television shows and movies, public displays of heterosexual intimacy in the park, in the cinema, walking on the street, dancing close. And ultimately, there is marriage, an institution that does not legally (although there are increasingly challenges to this with various domestic partner legislation) recognize two committed people unless one is a woman and the other a man.

Lesbian couples often encounter obstacles when adopting children, raising their biological children (products of previous heterosexual relationships, planned heterosexual encounters with the goal of conception, or artificial insemination), as well as gaining custody of these children. This is because being a lesbian is often constructed as an immoral and abnormal "choice" that could have negative consequences on children. It has generally been assumed that children of homosexual parents will grow up to be homosexual, although all the evidence shows that this is indeed not the case. Despite research that suggests that lesbians make fine mothers and lesbian couples fine parents, there are strong social imperatives against lesbian child rearing. A related prejudice is the notion that homosexuals abuse or recruit children. These negative and uninformed stereotypes reinforce homophobia and help maintain heterosexism. Research shows overwhelmingly that it is heterosexual males who are the major predators of children. Nonetheless, because of these societal stigmas, lesbians and gay men encounter many obstacles concerning voluntary parenting, and, in addition, are often not welcome in occupations involving children. In this way, sexual self-schemas develop in a social context and are framed by the various workings of power in society.

LEARNING ACTIVITY:
HETERONORMATIVITY: IT'S EVERYWHERE

Heterosexism is maintained by the illusion that heterosexuality is the norm. This illusion is partly kept in place by the visibility of heterosexuality and the invisibility of other forms of sexuality. To begin to think about the pervasiveness of heterosexuality, grab a clipboard, pen, and paper and keep a tally.

- Go to a card store and peruse the cards in the "love" and "anniversary" sections. How many depict heterosexual couples? How many depict same-sex couples? What options are there for customers who wish to buy a card for a same-sex partner?
- Look at the advertisements in one of your favorite magazines. How many pictures of heterosexual couples do you find? How many pictures of same-sex couples? If a photo is of a man or woman alone, do you automatically assume the person is heterosexual? Or is that assumption so deep-seated that you don't even think about it at all?
- Watch the commercials during your favorite hour of television. How many images of heterosexual couples do you see? Of same-sex couples?
- Go to the mall or a park and people-watch for an hour. How many heterosexual couples holding hands do you see? How many same-sex couples?

■ LEARNING ACTIVITY: IT'S IN THE CARDS

Go to a local card shop and browse through the cards in the "love" or "romance" sections. What are their messages about heterosexual relationships? How do cards targeted toward women differ from cards targeted toward men?

Now get creative. Design a feminist romance greeting card. How does it differ from the ones you saw at the card shop? How do you think the recipient will feel about this card? Now, if you're really brave, mail it to the one you love.

INTIMACIES

Courtship is that period when two people are attracted to each other, develop intimacy, enjoy each other's company, and identify as a couple. In our society this period usually involves dating. An essential aspect of courtship and dating is the development of romantic love: a mainstay of our culture and one of the most important mythologies of our time. *Romantic love* is about a couple coming together, sharing the excitement of an erotic relationship, and feeling united with the other in such a way that the other is unique and irreplaceable. The clichés of love abound: Love is blind; love is painful; love means never having to say you're sorry; love conquers all; and so forth.

Although cultural constructions of love would have us believe that romantic love as we know it has always been around, it is possible to trace the history of romantic love in U.S. society as a cultural phenomenon. There is a tight relationship between romantic love as an ideology and consumer culture as an industrial development. Prior to the twentieth century, dating as we know it did not exist. As dating developed after the turn of the century, it quickly became associated with consuming products and going places. The emerging movie industry glamorized romance and associated it with luxury products; the automobile industry provided those who could afford it with the allure of travel, get-aways, and private intimacy; and dancehalls allowed close contact between men and women in public. Romance became a commodity that could be purchased, and it made great promises. Women were (and still are) encouraged to purchase certain products with the promise of romantic love. Fashion and makeup industries began revolving around the prospect of romantic love, and the norms associated with feminine beauty became tied to glamorous, romantic images. Romantic love came to be seen as women's special domain; women were encouraged to spend enormous emotional energy, time, and money in the pursuit and maintenance of romantic love.

Romantic love is fun; it can be the spice of life and one of the most entertaining features of women's lives. In particular, it often contrasts starkly with our working lives because romance is associated with leisure, entertainment, and escape. At the same time, however, romantic love and its pursuit have become the means by which women are encouraged to form relationships and the justification for tolerating inequities in interpersonal relationships.

When it comes to sexuality, romantic love plays a large part in feminine sexual scripts. Research suggests that women make sense of sexual encounters in terms of the amount of intimacy experienced; love becomes a rationale for sex. If I am in love, women often reason, sex is okay. Men more easily accept sex for its own sake, with no emotional strings necessarily attached. In this way, sexual scripts for men have involved more of an *instrumental* (sex for its own sake) approach, whereas for women it tends to be more *expressive* (sex involving emotional attachments). There is evidence to suggest that women are moving in the direction of sex as an end in itself without the normative constraints of an emotional relationship, although, by and large, women are still more likely than men to engage in sex as an act of love. In this way, romantic love serves to bind women sexually to men.

As romantic relationships develop, individuals may become physically intimate and sexually active. These sexual practices can include kissing, hugging, petting, snuggling, caressing, oral sex (oral stimulation of genital area), penis in vagina sex, and anal sex (sexual stimulation of the anus with fingers, penis, or other object). Lesbians do many of the same things as straight couples, although there is no penis-vagina sex. Some women, straight and lesbian, use dildos (penis-shaped objects that can be inserted into a bodily opening) when they are having sex or during masturbation (sexual self-stimulation).

In heterosexual relationships, sexual scripts tend to encourage men to be sexual initiators and sexually more dominant. Although this is not always the case, women who do initiate sex often run the risk of being labeled with terms that are synonymous with *slut*. Having one person in the relationship more sexually assertive and the other more passive is different from sado-masochistic sexual practices (S and M) where one person takes a domineering role and the other becomes dominated. There are both heterosexuals and homosexuals who enjoy sado-masochistic practices. Although usually consensual, S and M can also be coercive.

Emotional intimacy can be defined as sharing aspects of the self with others with the goal of mutual understanding. Intimacy can sometimes be a source of conflict in heterosexual relationships because women tend to be more skilled at intimacy than men, as the title of John Gray's popular book *Men Are from Mars, Women Are from Venus* suggests. Women have been socialized to be emotional and emotionally expressive, and men have been socialized to put their energy into shaping culture and society.

Although some scholars have suggested that women are inherently better at connecting with others and that this skill is rooted in early childhood psychosexual development, others have focused on the social context of childhood skill acquisition. They suggest that the interpersonal skills girls learn at an early age are a result of social learning. Certainly these skills are useful for women in terms of intimacy generally, and in terms of their role as keepers of heterosexual relationships in particular. For example, girls are more likely to play games that involve communication: talking and listening, as well as taking the role of the other through imaginary role-playing games. Boys, on the other hand, are more likely to play rule-bound games where the "rights" and "wrongs" of the game are predetermined rather than negotiated. As a result, girls learn to notice: They learn to be sensitive of others' feelings, and they are willing to do emotional work. Boys are often raised to repress and deny their inner thoughts and fears and learn not to notice them. Often they are taught that feelings are feminine or are for sissies. Girls become more comfortable with intimacy, and boys learn to shy away from it because intimacy is often seen as synonymous with weakness. Boys learn to camouflage feelings under a veneer of calm and rationality because fears are not manly. Importantly, as boys grow up they learn to rely on women to take care of their emotional needs, and girls learn that this request is part of being a woman.

Because emotional intimacy is about self-disclosure and revealing oneself to others, when people are intimate with each other, they open themselves to vulnerability. In the process of becoming intimate, one person shares feelings and information about her- / himself,

In the early days of the second wave of the Women's Movement, women gathered in small consciousness-raising groups to talk about their experiences as women, and, of course, sooner or later, the conversation turned to sex. What surprised most women as they began to talk openly was that they were not the only ones ever to fake orgasm. While the sexual revolution was rolling on for men, opening greater and greater access to sexual exploits with lots of women, women were finding themselves continuing to fall into the role prescribed by their gender—pleasing men sexually even when they themselves were not being satisfied. But as the Women's Movement began to have an impact, women came to expect to be equal partners in the sexual revolution . . . and that meant no longer faking orgasms.

In 1968, Anne Koedt wrote "The Myth of the Vaginal Orgasm," denouncing Freud's construction of the vaginal orgasm as the truly mature sexual response and denigrating the clitoral orgasm as "infantile." She argued that by marginalizing the clitoris, Freud and other doctors and scientists had controlled women's sexuality and had made women feel sexually inadequate for not achieving vaginal orgasm. Soon, the "faked orgasm" became a metaphor for women's sexual exploitation.

And feminists offered a variety of solutions, from sex toys to celibacy. In 1970, Shulamith Firestone argued that sex, not social class, was the root of all oppression. In *The Dialectic of Sex,* she argued that reproductive technologies should be pursued to deliver women from the tyranny of their biology.

Germaine Greer, author of *The Female Eunuch,* contended that all women should become sexually liberated, and she advocated a strike, the withdrawal of women from sexual labor. She said that women should have the same sexual freedom as men and, if need be, should use men for sexual pleasure.

The debate about sexuality swirled among feminists through the 70s, encompassing issues ranging from pornography to rape, abortion to prostitution. And while the question of the dangers and/or pleasures of sex remained an open one, the raising of the question itself had made an important mark on the consciousness of American women.

Source: Ruth Rosen, *The World Split Open.* New York: Viking, 2000.

Reprinted with permission from Nicole Hollander

and then the other person (if they want to maintain and develop intimacy) responds by sharing too. In turn each gives away little pieces of oneself, and, in return, mutual trust, understanding, and friendship develop. Given the baggage of gender, however, what can happen is that one person does more of the giving away, and the other reveals less; one opens up to being vulnerable, and the other maintains personal power. The first person also takes on the role of helping the other share, drawing that person out, translating ordinary messages for their hidden emotional meanings, and investing greater amounts of energy into interpersonal communication. The first person has taken the role prescribed by femininity and the latter the role that masculinity endorses. The important point here is that intimacy is about power. Men tend to be less able to open themselves up because of anxiety associated with being vulnerable and potentially losing personal power.

Central in understanding masculine sexual scripts and issues around emotional intimacy is the mandate against homosexuality. Because boys and men may play rough and work closely together—touching each other physically in sports and other masculine pursuits—there are lots of opportunities for *homoeroticism* (arousal of sexual feelings through contact with people of the same sex). In response to this, strong norms against homosexuality regulate masculine behavior—norms fed by homophobia and enforced by such institutions as education, sports, media, family, the military, and the state. These norms discourage men from showing affection with each other and thus discourage intimacy between men. As an aside, they also encourage male bonding where women may function as objects in order for men to assert sexual potency. Examples of this include women as entertainment

■ IDEAS FOR ACTIVISM

- Work with various women's groups on your campus to develop, publish, and distribute a "Check Up on Your Relationship" brochure. This brochure should contain a checklist of signs for emotional/physical/sexual abuse and resources to get help.
- Organize and present a forum on healthy dating practices.
- Organize a clothes drive for your local women's shelter.
- Research gay rights, such as protection against discrimination in employment or housing, domestic partner benefits, or hate crimes legislation in your city or state. If you find that gay, lesbian, bisexual, or transgender people in your area do not enjoy full civil rights, write your government officials to encourage them to enact policies providing civil rights for queer people.
- Organize a National Coming Out Day celebration on your campus.
- Organize an event on your campus in recognition of World AIDS Day, which is December 1.
- Become a member of the Human Rights Campaign. For more information see *www.hrc.org*.

for various kinds of stag parties, women as pinups in places where men live and/or work together, and, in the extreme, gang rape. Homophobia serves to keep women apart too, of course. In particular, women are encouraged to give up the love of other women in order to gain the approval of men.

A key aspect of intimacy, and thus sexuality, is interpersonal communication. Again, the ways we communicate in relationships have a lot to do with gender; these different styles help to maintain gender differences in status and power. Women and men tend to communicate differently in the following ways: First, in terms of speech patterns, women tend to use more polite speech, less profanity, and more standard forms. They use more fillers like "uhm," hedges like "sort of" and "I guess," and intensifiers like "really" and "very." They are more likely to tag questions on statements like "It's hot today, isn't it?" and to turn an imperative into a question: "Would you mind opening the door?" rather than "Open the door!" All these forms of speaking are less authoritative.

Second, women tend to use different intonations than men when they speak. Women have a higher pitch that is recognized as less assertive than a lower pitch. They tend to speak with more emotional affect than men and are more likely to end a sentence with a raised pitch. This sounds like a question and gives a more hesitant quality to women's speech.

Third, women and men use interruptions differently in speech. Although men and women interrupt at about the same rate in same-sex conversations, in mixed groups men interrupt more than women and are more likely to interrupt women than to interrupt men. Men are also more likely to change the subject in the process. Although there are cultural differences around interruptions, it is clear that who interrupts and who gets interrupted is about power.

Four, women tend to use more confirmations and reinforcements such as "Yes, go on" or "I hear you" or "uh-hums" during conversation. Examples of nonverbal confirmation of the speaker include leaning forward, eye contact, and nodding.

Finally, feminine and masculine speech fulfills different functions. Feminine speech tends to work toward maintaining relationships, developing rapport, avoiding conflict, and maintaining cooperation. Masculine speech, on the other hand, is more likely oriented toward attracting and maintaining an audience, asserting power and dominance, and giving information. Given these gendered differences in communication, it is easy to see how problems might arise in interpersonal interaction generally and in sexual relationships in particular, and how these issues are related to the give and take of interpersonal power.

In this way, sexual intimacy is as much about society as it is about physiology. Sexuality is wound up with our understandings of gender, and these norms channel our sense of ourselves as sexual persons. These social constructs encourage us to feel desire and enjoy certain sexual practices and relationships, and they guide the meanings we associate with our experiences.

READING 24

Sexual Desire and Gender

Pepper Schwartz and Virginia Rutter

The gender of the person you desire is a serious matter seemingly fundamental to the whole business of romance. And it isn't simply a matter of whether someone is male or female; how well the person fulfills a lover's expectations of masculinity or femininity is of great consequence. . . .

. . . Although sex is experienced as one of the most basic and biological of activities, in human beings it is profoundly affected by things other than the body's urges. Who we're attracted to and what we find sexually satisfying is not just a matter of the genital equipment we're born with. . . .

Before we delve into the whys and wherefores of sex, we need to come to an understanding about what sex is. This is not as easy a task as it may seem, because sex has a number of dimensions.

On one level, sex can be regarded as having both a biological and a social context. The biological (and physiological) refers to how people use their genital equipment to reproduce. In addition, as simple as it seems, bodies make the experience of sexual pleasure available—whether the pleasure involves other bodies or just one's own body and mind. It should be obvious, however, that people engage in sex even when they do not intend to reproduce. They have sex for fun, as a way to communicate their feelings to each other, as a way to satisfy their ego, and for any number of other reasons relating to the way they see themselves and interact with others.

Another dimension of sex involves both what we do and how we think about it. *Sexual behavior* refers to the sexual acts that people engage in. These acts involve not only petting and intercourse but also seduction and courtship. Sexual behavior also involves the things people do alone for pleasure and stimulation and the things they do with other people. *Sexual desire*, on the other hand, is the motivation to engage in sexual acts. It relates to what turns people on. A person's *sexuality* consists of both behavior and desire.

The most significant dimension of sexuality is *gender*. Gender relates both to the biological and social contexts of sexual behavior and desire. People tend to believe they know whether someone is a man or a woman not because we do a physical examination and determine that the person is biologically male or biologically female. Instead, we notice whether a person is masculine or feminine. Gender is a social characteristic of individuals in our society that is only sometimes consistent with biological sex. Thus, animals, like people, tend to be identified as male and female in accordance with the reproductive function, but only people are described by their gender, as a man or a woman.

When we say something is *gendered* we mean that social processes have determined what is appropriately masculine and feminine and that gender has thereby become integral to the definition of the phenomenon. For example, marriage is a gendered institution: The definition of marriage involves a masculine part (husband) and a feminine part (wife). Gendered phenomena, like marriage, tend to appear "naturally" so. But as recent debates about same-sex marriage underscore, the role of gender in marriage is the product of social processes and beliefs about men, women, and marriage. In examining how gender influences sexuality, moreover, you will see that gender rarely operates alone: Class, culture, race, and individual differences also combine to influence sexuality.

. . .

Desire: Attraction and Arousal

The most salient fact about sex is that nearly everybody is interested in it. Most people like to have sex, and they talk about it, hear about it, and think about it. But some people are obsessed with sex and willing to have sex with anyone or anything. Others are aroused only by particular conditions and hold exacting criteria. For example, some people will have sex only if they are positive that they are in love, that their partner loves them, and that the act is sanctified by marriage. Others view sex as not much different from eating a sandwich. They neither love nor hate the sandwich; they are merely hungry, and they want something to satisfy that hunger. What we are talking about here are differences of desire. As you have undoubtedly noticed, people differ in what they find attractive, and they are also physically aroused by different things.

Many people assume that differences in sexual desire have a lot to do with whether a person is female or male. In large representative surveys about sexual behavior, the men as a group inevitably report more frequent sex, with more partners, and in more diverse ways than the women as a group do . . . First, we should consider the approaches we might use to interpret it. Many observers argue that when it comes to sex, men and women have fundamentally different biological wiring. Others use the evidence to argue that culture has produced marked sexual differences among men and women. We believe, however, that it is hard to tease apart biological differences and social differences. As soon as a baby enters the world, it receives messages about gender and sexuality. In the United States, for example, disposable diapers come adorned in pink for girls and blue for boys. In case people aren't sure whether to treat the baby as masculine or feminine in its first years of life, the diaper signals them. The assumption is that girl babies really are different from boy babies and the difference ought to be displayed. This different treatment continues throughout life, and therefore a sex difference at birth becomes amplified into gender differences as people mature.

Gendered experiences have a great deal of influence on sexual desire. As a boy enters adolescence, he hears jokes about boys' uncontainable desire. Girls are told the same thing and told that their job is to resist. These gender messages have power not only over attitudes and behavior (such as whether a person grows up to prefer sex with a lover rather than a stranger) but also over physical and biological experience. For example, a girl may be discouraged from vigorous competitive activity, which will subse-quently influence how she develops physically, how she feels about her body, and even how she relates to the adrenaline rush associated with physical competition. Hypothetically, a person who is accustomed to adrenaline responses experiences sexual attraction differently from one who is not.

What follows are three "competing" explanations of differences in sexual desire between men and women: a biological explanation, sociobiological and evolutionary psychological explanations, and an explanation that acknowledges the social construction of sexuality. We call these competing approaches because each tends to be presented as a complete explanation in itself, to the exclusion of other explanations. Our goal, however, is to provide a clearer picture of how "nature" and "nurture" are intertwined in the production of sexualities.

The Biology of Desire: Nature's Explanation

Biology is admittedly a critical factor in sexuality. Few human beings fall in love with fish or sexualize trees. Humans are designed to respond to other humans. And human activity is, to some extent, organized by the physical equipment humans are born with. Imagine if people had fins instead of arms or laid eggs instead of fertilizing them during intercourse. Romance would look quite different.

Although biology seems to be a constant (i.e., a component of sex that is fixed and unchanging), the social world tends to mold biology as much as biology shapes humans' sexuality. Each society has its own rules for sex. Therefore, how people experience their biology varies widely. In some societies, women act intensely aroused and active during sex; in others, they have no concept of orgasm. In fact, women in some settings, when told about orgasm, do not even believe it exists, as anthropologists discovered in some parts of Nepal. Clearly, culture—not biology—is at work, because we know that orgasm is physically possible, barring damage to or destruction of the sex organs. Even ejaculation is culturally dictated. In some countries, it is considered healthy to ejaculate early and often; in others, men are told to conserve semen and ejaculate as rarely as possible.

The biological capacity may not be so different, but the way bodies behave during sex varies according to social beliefs.

Sometimes the dictates of culture are so rigid and powerful that the so-called laws of nature can be over-ridden. Infertility treatment provides an example: For couples who cannot produce children "naturally," a several billion dollar industry has provided technology that can, in a small proportion of cases, overcome this biological problem. Recently, in California, a child was born to a 63-year-old woman who had been implanted with fertilized eggs. The cultural emphasis on reproduction and parenthood, in this case, overrode the biological incapacity to produce children. Nevertheless, some researchers have focused on the biological foundations of sexual desire. They have examined the endocrine system and hormones, brain structure, and genetics. Others have observed the mechanisms of arousal. What all biological research on sex has in common is the proposition that many so-called sexual choices are not choices at all but are dictated by the body. A prominent example comes from the study of the biological origins of homosexuality. However, contradictory and debatable findings make conclusions difficult.

The Influence of Hormones

Biological explanations of sexual desire concentrate on the role of hormones. *Testosterone,* sometimes called the male sex hormone, appears to be the most important hormone for sexual function. Numerous research studies identify testosterone as an enabler for male sexual arousal. But we cannot predict a man's sexual tastes, desires, or behavior by measuring his testosterone. Although a low level of testosterone in men is sometimes associated with lower sexual desire, this is not predictably the case. Furthermore, testosterone level does not always influence sexual performance. Indeed, testosterone is being experimented with as a male contraceptive, thus demonstrating that desire and the biological goal of reproduction need not be linked to sexual desire.

Testosterone has also been implicated in nonsexual behaviors, such as aggression. Furthermore, male aggression sometimes crosses into male sexuality, generating sexual violence. But recent research on testosterone and aggression in men has turned the testosterone-aggression connection on its head: Low levels of testosterone have been associated with aggression, and higher levels have been associated with calmness, happiness, and friendliness.

Testosterone is also found in women, although at levels as little as one-fifth those of men. This discrepancy in levels of testosterone has incorrectly been used as evidence for "natural" gender differences in sex drives. However, women's testosterone receptors are simply more sensitive than men's to smaller amounts of testosterone.

Estrogen, which is associated with the menstrual cycle, is known as the female hormone. Like testosterone, however, estrogen is found in both women and men. Furthermore, estrogen may be the more influential hormone in human aggression. In animal research, male mice whose ability to respond to estrogen had been bred out of them lost much of their natural aggressiveness. Researchers are currently investigating the association between adolescents' moodiness and their levels of estrogen. Of course, many social factors—such as changes in parental behavior toward their teenagers—help explain moodiness among adolescents.

Some biological evidence indicates that a woman's sexual desire may be linked to the impact of hormones as levels change during her reproductive cycle. (No evidence shows men's sexual desire to be cyclical.) Some scientists believe that women's sexual arousal is linked to the fertile portion of their cycle. They believe that sexual interest in women is best explained as the product of thousands of years of natural selection. Natural selection would favor for survival those women who are sexually aroused during ovulation (the time women are most likely to become pregnant). These women would be reproductively successful and therefore pass on to their children the propensity for arousal during ovulation. Neat though this theory is, it doesn't fit all the data. Other research finds no evidence of increased sexual interest among women who are ovulating. Instead, the evidence suggests that women's sexual interest actually tends to peak well before ovulation. Still other evidence finds no variation in sexual desire or sexual activity in connection to the menstrual cycle.

. . . [T]estosterone and estrogen are not clearly linked to either men's desire or women's. Research shows a complicated relationship between hormones and sexuality. Hormonal fluctuations may not be the central cause of sexual behavior or any social acts; instead, social circumstances may be the cause of hormonal fluctuation. A famous series of experiments makes the point. One animal experiment took a dominant rhesus monkey out of his environment and measured [his] testosterone level. It was very high, suggesting that he had reached the top of the monkey heap by being hormonally superior. Then the monkey was placed among even bigger, more dominant monkeys than himself. When his testosterone was remeasured, it was much lower. One interpretation is that social hierarchy had influenced the monkey's biological barometer. His testosterone level had adjusted to his social status. In this case, the social environment shaped physiology.

. . .

Sociobiology and Evolutionary Psychology

The past few decades of research on sexuality have produced a new school of human behavior—*sociobiology* and a related discipline, *evolutionary psychology*—that explains most gender differences as strategies of sexual reproduction. According to evolutionary psychologist David Buss, "evolutionary psychologists predict that the sexes will differ in precisely those domains in which women and men have faced different sorts of adaptive problems." By "those domains," Buss refers to reproduction, which is the only human function that depends on a biological difference between men and women.

The key assumption of sociobiological/evolutionary theory is that humans have an innate, genetically triggered impulse to pass on their genetic material through successful reproduction: This impulse is called *reproductive fitness.* The human species, like other species that sociobiologists study, achieves immortality by having children who live to the age of reproductive maturity and produce children themselves. Sociobiologists and evolutionary psychologists seek to demonstrate that almost all male and fe-

male behavior, and especially sexuality, is influenced by this one simple but powerful proposition.

Sociobiologists start at the species level. Species are divided into *r* and *K reproductive categories.* Those with *r* strategies obtain immortality by mass production of eggs and sperm. The *r* species is best illustrated by fish. The female manufactures thousands of eggs, the male squirts millions of sperm over them, and that is the extent of parenting. According to this theory, the male and female fish need not pair up to nurture their offspring. Although thousands of fertilized fish eggs are consumed by predators, only a small proportion of the massive quantity of fertilized eggs must survive for the species to continue. In the *r* species, parents need not stay together for the sake of the kids.

In contrast, humans are a *K*-strategy species, which has a greater investment in each fertilized egg. Human females and most female mammals have very few eggs, especially compared to fish. Moreover, offspring take a long time to mature in the mother's womb and are quite helpless when they are born, with no independent survival ability. Human babies need years of supervision before they are independent. Thus, if a woman wants to pass on her genes (or at least the half her child will inherit from her), she must take good care of her dependent child. The baby is a scarce resource. Even if a woman is pregnant from sexual maturation until menopause, the number of children she can produce is quite limited. This limitation was particularly true thousands of years ago. Before medical advances of the nineteenth and twentieth centuries, women were highly unlikely to live to the age of menopause. Complications from childbirth commonly caused women to die in their 20s or 30s. Where the food supply was scarce, women were less likely to be successful at conceiving, further reducing the possibility of generating offspring.

Sociobiologists and evolutionary psychologists say that men inseminate, women incubate. The human female's reproductive constraints (usually one child at a time, not so many children over a life cycle, and a helpless infant for a long period of time) shape most of women's sexual and emotional approaches to men and mating. According to their theory, women have good reason to be more selective than men about potential mates. They want to find a man who will stick around and continue to provide resources and protection to this child at least until the child has a good chance of survival. Furthermore, because a woman needs to create an incentive for a man to remain with her, females have developed more sophisticated sexual and emotional skills specifically geared toward creating male loyalty and commitment to their mutual offspring.

Sociobiologists and evolutionary psychologists say that differences in reproductive capacity and strategy also shape sexual desire. Buss asserts that reproductive strategies form most of the categories of desire: Older men generally pick younger women because they are more fertile; younger women seek older men who have more status, power, and resources (a cultural practice known as *hypergamy*) because such men can provide for their children. Furthermore, health and reproductive capacity make youth generally sexier, and even certain shapes of women's bodies (such as an "ideal" hip-to-waist ratio epitomized by an hourglass figure, which correlate with ability to readily reproduce), are widely preferred—despite varying standards of beauty across cultures. Likewise, men who have demonstrated their fertility by producing children are more sought after than men who have not.

According to evolutionary psychologists, men's tastes for recreational sex, unambivalent lust, and a variety of partners are consistent with maximizing their production of children. Men's sexual interest is also more easily aroused because sex involves fewer costs to them than to women, and the ability for rapid ejaculation has a reproductive payoff. On the other hand, women's taste for relationship-based intimacy and greater investment in each sexual act is congruent with women's reproductive strategies.

In a field that tends to emphasize male's "natural" influence over reproductive strategies, evolutionary anthropologist Helen Fisher offers a feminist twist. Her study of hundreds of societies shows that divorce, or its informal equivalent, occurs most typically in the third or fourth year of a marriage and then peaks about every four years after that. Fisher hypothesizes that some of the breakups have to do with a woman's attempt to obtain the best genes and best survival chances for her offspring. In both agrar-

ian and hunter-gatherer societies, Fisher explains, women breast-feed their child for three or four years —a practice that is economical and sometimes helps to prevent further pregnancy. At the end of this period, the woman is ready and able to have another child. She reenters the mating marketplace and assesses her options to see if she can improve on her previous mate. If she can get a better guy, she will leave the previous partner and team up with a new one. In Fisher's vision, unlike the traditional sociobiological view . . . , different male and female reproductive strategies do not necessarily imply female sexual passivity and preference for lifelong monogamy.

Sociobiologists and evolutionary psychologists tell a fascinating story of how male and female reproductive differences might shape sexuality. To accept sociobiological arguments, one must accept the premise that most animal and human behavior is driven by the instinct to reproduce and improve the gene pool. Furthermore, a flaw of sociobiology as a theory is that it does not provide a unique account of sexual behavior with the potential to be tested empirically. Furthermore, other social science explanations for the same phenomena are supported by more immediate, close-range evidence.

Consider hypergamy, the practice of women marrying men slightly older and "higher" on the social status ladder than they are. Sociobiologists would say women marry "up" to ensure the most fit provider for their offspring. But hypergamy makes little sense biologically. Younger men have more years of resources to provide, and they have somewhat more sexual resources. Empirically, however, hypergamy is fact. It is also a fact that men, overall and in nearly every subculture, have access to more rewards and status than women do. Furthermore, reams of imagery—in movies, advertising, novels—promote the appeal of older, more resourceful men. Why not, when older, more resourceful men are generating the images? Social practice, in this case, overrides what sociobiologists consider the biological imperative.

The Social Origins of Desire

Your own experience should indicate that biology and genetics alone do not shape human sexuality. From the moment you entered the world, cues from the environment were telling you which desires and behaviors were "normal" and which were not. The result is that people who grow up in different circumstances tend to have different sexualities. Who has not had their sexual behavior influenced by their parents' or guardians' explicit or implicit rules? You may break the rules or follow them, but you can't forget them. . . .

The Social Construction of Sexuality

Social constructionists believe that cues from the environment shape human beings from the moment they enter the world. The sexual customs, values, and expectations of a culture, passed on to the young through teaching and by example, exert a powerful influence over individuals. When Fletcher Christian sailed into Tahiti in Charles Nordhoff's 1932 account, *Mutiny on the Bounty,* he and the rest of his nineteenth-century English crew were surprised at how sexually available, playful, guilt free, and amorous the Tahitian women were. Free from the Judeo-Christian precepts and straightlaced customs that inhibited English society, the women and girls of Tahiti regarded their sexuality joyfully and without shame. The English men were delighted and, small wonder, refused to leave the island. Such women did not exist in their own society. The women back in England had been socialized within their Victorian culture to be modest, scared of sex, protective of their reputation, and threatened by physical pleasure. As a result, they were unavailable before marriage and did not feel free to indulge in a whole lot of fun after it. The source of the difference was not physiological differences between Tahitian and English women; it was sexual *socialization* or the upbringing that they received within their differing families and cultures.

If we look back at the Victorian, nineteenth-century England that Nordhoff refers to, we can identify *social structures* that influenced the norms of women's and men's sexuality. A burgeoning, new, urban middle class created separate spheres in the division of family labor. Instead of sharing home and farm or small business, the tasks of adults in families became specialized: Men went out to earn money, women stayed home to raise children and take care of the home. Although this division of labor was not the norm in all classes and ethnicities in England at the time, the image of middle-class femininity and masculinity became pervasive. The new division of labor increased women's economic dependence on men, which further curbed women's sexual license but not men's. When gender organizes one aspect of life—such as men's and women's position in the economy—it also organizes other aspects of life, including sex.

In a heterogeneous and individualistic culture like North America, sexual socialization is complex. A society creates an "ideal" sexuality, but different families and subcultures have their own values. For example, even though contemporary society at large may now accept premarital sexuality, a given family may lay down the law: Sex before marriage is against the family's religion and an offense against God's teaching. A teenager who grows up in such a household may suppress feelings of sexual arousal or channel them into outlets that are more acceptable to the family. Or the teenager may react against her or his background, reject parental and community opinion, and search for what she or he perceives to be a more "authentic" self. Variables like birth order or observations of a sibling's social and sexual expression can also influence a person's development.

As important as family and social background are, so are individual differences in response to that background. In the abstract, people raised to celebrate their sexuality must surely have a different approach to enjoying their bodies than those who are taught that their bodies will betray them and are a venal part of human nature. Yet whether or not a person is raised to be at ease with physicality does not always help predict adult sexual behavior. Sexual sybarites and libertines may have grown up in sexually repressive environments, as did pop culture icon and Catholic-raised Madonna. Sometimes individuals whose families promoted sex education and free personal expression are content with minimal sexual expression.

. . .

To summarize, social constructionists believe that a society influences sexual behavior through its norms. Some norms are explicit, such as laws against adult sexual activity with minors. Others are implicit, such as norms of fidelity and parental responsibility. In a stable, homogeneous society, it is relatively easy to understand such rules. But in a changing, complex society like the United States, the rules may be in flux or indistinct. Perhaps this ambiguity is what makes some issues of sexuality so controversial today.

An Integrative Perspective on Gender and Sexuality

Social constructionist explanations of contemporary sexual patterns are typically pitted against the biology of desire and the evolutionary understanding of biological adaptations. Some social constructionists believe there is no inflexible biological reality; everything we regard as either female or male sexuality is culturally imposed. In contrast, *essentialists*—those who take a biological, sociobiological, or evolutionary point of view—believe people's sexual desires and orientations are innate and hard-wired and that social impact is minimal. Gender differences follow from reproductive differences. Men inseminate, women incubate. People are born with sexual drives, attractions, and natures that simply play themselves out at the appropriate developmental age. Even if social constraints conspire to make men and women more similar to each other (as in the 1990s, when the sensitive and nurturing new man [was] encouraged to get in touch with his so-called feminine, emotional side), people's essential nature is the same: Man is the hunter, warrior, and trailblazer, and woman is the gatherer, nurturer, and reproducer. To an essentialist, social differences, such as the different earning power of men and women, are the consequence of biological difference. In short, essentialists think the innate differences between women and men are the cause of gendered sexuality; social constructionists think the differences between men and women are the result of gendering sexuality through social processes.

Using either the social constructionist or essentialist approach to the exclusion of the other constrains understanding of sexuality. We believe the evidence shows that gender differences are more plausibly an outcome of social processes than the

other way around. But a social constructionist view is most powerful when it takes the essentialist view into account. . . . [W]e describe this view of gender differences in sexual desire as *integrative.* Although people tend to think of sex as primarily a biological function—tab B goes into slot A—biology is only one part of the context of desire. Such sociological factors as family relationships and social structure also influence sex. A complex mix of anatomy, hormones, and the brain provides the basic outline for the range of acts and desires possible, but biology is neither where sexuality begins nor where it ends. Social and biological contexts link to define human sexual possibilities.

The integrative approach follows from a great deal that sexuality researchers have observed. Consider the following example: A research project, conducted over three decades ago, advertised for participants stating that its focus was how physical excitement influences a man's preference for one woman over another. The researchers connected college men to a monitor that allowed them to hear their heartbeats as they looked at photographs of women models. The men were told that they would be able to hear their heartbeat when it surged in response to each photograph. A greater surge would suggest greater physical attraction. The participants were then shown a photograph of a dark-haired woman, then a blonde, then a redhead. Afterward, each man was asked to choose the picture that he would prefer to take home. In each case, the man chose the photograph of the woman who, as he believed from listening to his own speeding heartbeat, had most aroused him. Or at least the man thought he was choosing the woman who had aroused him most. In reality, the men had been listening to a faked heartbeat that was speeded up at random. The men thus actually chose the women whom they believed had aroused them most. In this case, the men's invented attraction was more powerful than their gut response. Their mind (a powerful sexual organ) told them their body was responding to a specific picture. The participants' physiological experience of arousal was eclipsed by the social context. When social circumstances influence sexual tastes, are those tastes real or sincere? Absolutely. The social world is as much a fact in people's lives as the biological world.

READING 25

The Search for Men Who Love

bell hooks

Looking for love and looking for a man are two very different agendas. Most women without male partners are looking for a man. And guess what? Men are easy to find. Finding a man is not the same as finding love. To find love with a male partner, women have to be clear that this is our desire. The feminist movement exposed the harsh truth of woman hating. More than at any other time in the history of this nation, the word "misogynist" became commonplace. It was the shortcut way to describe a sexist, patriarchal, woman-hating man. But the other reality that feminism exposed, which was more uncomfortable for women to talk about, was female hatred of men.

Years ago, in the heyday of the contemporary feminist movement, I remember lesbian women joking all the time about how wrong the world was in casting them in the role of man haters, because everyone knew that if you gathered a bunch of women together in a room and started talking about men, the most vicious man-hating sentiments would be expressed by women who were with men and who were planning to stay with men for the rest of their lives. Hearing these comments again and again, knowing firsthand the truth in these words, I searched my soul to see what my honest feelings about men were. I determined that if I looked inside and saw that I really held men in contempt, I would cease considering them as potential partners and lovers.

When I looked inside, I found my thinking about men dominated by three images: my patriarchal father, whom I feared, at times hated, and wished was dead; my eccentric, antipatriarchal grandfather, whom I never feared, loved at all times, and wanted to live forever; and my playful older brother. My father did not care for our souls. He worked hard to care for our material needs. I appreciated this, but I never felt he loved me, even when I tried to please him, to meet the conditions he set. Even though I was told that he had been "mad about me," thrilled

with his new baby girl when I was first born, taking me everywhere and showing me off, the dad I knew most intimately was cold, withholding, aloof, and emotionally shut down. Daddy Gus, my grandfather, was antimaterialistic and loved me unconditionally. Daddy was given to intense anger and now and then would throw a major violent fit. Our granddad was always kind and gentle, and he never spoke in anger. Our mother told us that he was not this way just with his grandchildren; he had been the same with his own children throughout their lives. She admired and loved him.

Then there was my brother, Kenneth. We looked like twins, even though he came first, eight months before me. Kenneth was everything a boy was not supposed to be: sweet, tender, playful, and fearful of being hurt. He charmed us with his humor. He was everything that Dad was not. His sisters loved him, and he loved us. We loved our brother, the eternal boy, ever Peter Pan, but we mostly feared grown men.

Honestly, had Mama's father, Daddy Gus, not been in my life, I believe I might easily have become a man-hating woman or at best a woman who just simply feared men. Lots of women fear men. And fear can lay the foundation for contempt and hatred. It can be a cover-up for repressed, killing rage. When girl children are learning what men are like within patriarchal culture and shaping our sense of them, we look to the male authority we know to teach us about masculinity. If the primary male figures in our lives are cruel, unkind, and in some cases violently abusive, this is the way we think men are. If the men in our lives—our fathers, uncles, grandfathers, brothers—stand idly by while elder women abuse us, then we lose respect for them. We do not forgive them their failure to protect us from harm.

I am grateful that the images of masculinity surrounding me as a child were varied. I knew that lots of men were "macho" like my dad, but I also knew there were men like my granddad—calm, gentle, and kind. These diverse images shaped my perspective. In my childhood there were men who were not ashamed to express their love of God openly and to shed ecstatic tears. These men were renegades, rebelling against the patriarchal norm. And they were the men I was destined to love, the sensitive, soulful, shy men who were looked down upon by the patriarchy. The men who inhabited my dreams were men of feeling.

When I entered wholeheartedly into the feminist movement, I had the full encouragement of my male partner, whose personality, as it turned out, was a mixture of my dad and granddad. At that moment in our lives we had not fallen into the gender strife that would later lead us to separate. Then he supported my efforts to become a liberated woman. He was not homophobic. At no time did he worry about all the time I was spending with lesbian feminists, as some men did. In our groups women confessed that the men in their lives did not want them to hang out with lesbians. Their partners believed that they would turn into lesbians just by sitting next to one. We laughed at those stories. And we felt sad for these men who were missing out on friendships that might have changed their perspective on love and life.

In those days we used the phrase "male-identified" to describe women who did not necessarily like men, though they usually pretended to, but who supported any standpoint men in their lives held, who let their own opinions go to please men. Some of these women were subordinated against their will, but many of them were artful manipulators, pretending to embody the sexist feminine ideal even as they were contemptuous of real men, whom they believed to be stupid and childlike. Retrospectively, I can see that our phrase was incomplete. These females were not simply male-identified, they were patriarchally male-identified. Even then the most radical feminist woman knew that not all men wanted to be patriarchs. Male-identified women espoused the same negative sexist notions about gender common to any sexist man. They were not interested in the perspectives of progressive male advocates of feminism. To them, these men were not "real" men.

In our feminist consciousness-raising groups, women involved with men often had the harshest stories to tell. Knowing men intimately, up close and personal, they also knew the immediacy of male-inflicted pain. They knew about emotional abuse and domestic violence. Their rage at men was intense and unrelenting. At times it was infectious. It was difficult to hear a woman describing being raped repeatedly by an angry dad as a child, then running away from home with the first guy who was nice to her, only to find out later that when he was angry she was the punching bag for his rage—and on and on—and not feel antimale. These stories were commonplace.

Sitting in intimate circles listening to so much pain made us want to get rid of abusive men. It was easy to fantasize about finding them, interrogating them to discover whether they had ever abused a female, lining up the abusers, and blowing them away. Afterward you would go to the women they had hurt and assure them, "He will never hurt you again—never again." These fantasies did not emerge from an irrational urge to bash men. They were the stuff of feminist dreams of ending male violence against women. They were the stuff of wanting to know what the world would be like if it were a safe place—a place where women could roam freely, where we could "take back the night." Of course there were women in these groups who hated men and wanted revenge, but most of them expressed their rage and then went home to nurture and care for the men in their lives. Rarely were they lesbians.

Women's disappointment with men is rarely given a public hearing in our society. The flip side of the feminist consciousness-raising group was the informal gathering of wives in any community who played cards, shopped, and shared, in between the gossip about this and that, their rage and anger at men. Unlike feminists, they did not want men to stop being patriarchs; they just wanted men to be kinder, gentler patriarchs. Using feminist terms, we called these men "benevolent patriarchs." They were men who believed themselves to be superior to women and therefore felt they should rule over us. They just thought they should be kind providers and protectors. Prior to major feminist shifts in gender roles in our society, men who were cruel and abusive, usually found male-identified women to help justify and legitimize their actions. However, as feminist thinking about ending male violence against women, however diluted, has trickled down to the larger culture, most women will speak against male domination, against male violence, but still support patriarchal culture.

Women, like my mother, who have stayed in marriages with unkind husbands for more than fifty years, will condemn acts of cruelty and unkindness that as late as ten years ago they would have sought to justify or explain away. Whenever I would speak harshly about my father, my mother would always speak positively, reminding me of how steady a provider he had been. In recent years she has become more critical of his acts of unkindness. And she has grown bitter. Nowadays, past the age of sixty, when she makes comments about men in general, they are more likely to be negative than positive. As a mother of six grown daughters, several of whom suffered at the hands of unkind, abusive men, she, a traditionally male-identified woman, has begun to change her perspective. Now she knows that women are not to be blamed when men are treating us in violent and/or cruel ways.

More than ever before in our nation's history, women in general feel free to speak their resentment and rage at men. My youngest sister wears a button reading SO MANY MEN, SO MANY REASONS NOT TO SLEEP WITH ANY OF THEM. In the wake of contemporary feminist movement, it has become harder to articulate what we like, desire, and love about men. In this world where so many women work, few females talk about the pleasure of being economically supported by a male partner's income. And even a woman like Jane Fonda, married to one of the richest men in the world, who freed her from work, now testifies that she felt she was losing her identity in her marriage, and she left and began to create her own work projects.

Overall, women seem to agree that unless one has pleasurable and engaging pursuits, staying home is no fun. As should be the case, many working women find it wonderful to be home when they have a newborn babe. But even newborns grow up. The feminist movement created the social space for men to choose to stay home and be "househusbands," and like housewives they suffer the same complaints if they are unable to use their time away from a paid job meaningfully. In Arlie Hochschild's book *The*

Time Bind: When Work Becomes Home and Home Becomes Work, women acknowledged that they prefer working low-paying jobs even if they must do a second shift at home. They would rather work than be financially dependent on men. They would rather leave home and work even if they do not earn enough money to be free. If wages for housework had become a reality, this might not be the case. A domestic revolution might occur if wages for homemakers (like child support in some states) were automatically deducted from the working partner's paycheck.

Whether they think of themselves as feminists or not, more women than ever before face the reality that we live in a male-dominated society. And many women like it like that, as long as they derive benefits from men and no negative side effects. The negative side effects—tyranny in the household or sexual violence—no woman likes or wants. What most women do not choose to face is the reality that if you support patriarchy, you get negative side effects. As Elizabeth Wurtzel puts it, "It still feels like men have all the power. They still seem to obey their impulses to run away while women are enslaved to their impulses to run toward. As long as men continually get messages about avoiding commitment while women are taught to desperately seek it out, the sexes will always be at odds with each other and nothing will work." Of course, many men in patriarchal relationships deploy emotional abuse and physical violence to avoid intimacy. Perpetuating this violence makes the system of patriarchy work. Without male violence blocking the door, men might be emotionally open, they might find their way to love.

The popularity of books like John Gray's *Men Are from Mars, Women Are from Venus* indicates that lots of folks want to believe that women are innately different from men in personality and habits of being and that these differences naturally maintain the social order. They choose denial over facing the reality that the gender differences we were once taught are innate are really mostly learned, that while biology is significant and should not be discounted, it is not destiny. Nowadays almost everyone knows that not all men are stronger than women, or smarter, or less emotional, and so on. Sexist notions of gender rarely hold up when we look at real life. And they hold up even less when we go outside the boundaries of this culture and look at males and females in other cultures. Living in the United States, people easily forget or remain ignorant of the reality that women in other parts of the world often do much more physically arduous labor than do their male counterparts. Or that a great majority of men in the world are suffering from malnutrition or starving and are nowhere near the physical equals of females eating three meals a day who are citizens of rich nations.

The aspect of patriarchy that most women want to change is the unkindness and cruelty of men, their contempt and dislike of women. It is a testament to the learned ignorance of political reality that so many females cannot accept that patriarchy requires of men cruelty to women, that the will to do violence defines heterosexual, patriarchal masculinity. Liberal, benevolent, patriarchal writers, like John Gray, offer women strategies for coping with male and female mutual dislike. In all his work Gray basically encourages women and men to accept their differences and find ways to avoid conflict and abusive behavior. Superficially, it may appear that the popularity of his work exposes women's passive acceptance of patriarchal thinking, but it is in fact women's dissatisfaction with negative aspects of patriarchy that creates an audience for this work. While it may help women to cope with patriarchal men, Gray's work does not call for an end to male domination. Instead it perpetuates the conventional sexist belief that it is natural for males to desire dominion over others.

Many women feel despair about patriarchy's ending and try to find ways to cope with male domination that will heighten their well-being. It is certainly clear that sexist men are not rushing out to buy literature that will help them unlearn sexist thinking. Patriarchal thinking keeps women and men separate, locked in the artificial differences that Gray and other thinkers choose to regard as natural. Nothing was more frightening to women who wanted to be with men than a feminist movement exposing the depths of male contempt and disregard for the female sex. Luckily, by changing the workforce, the feminist movement did alter in fundamental ways how men see women. Yet despite the feminist call to change patriarchal thinking that denies men access to emotional growth, most men continue to believe it is "natural" for them to behave as though emotions do not matter, as though all emotional work, including loving, is primarily a female task.

The first chapter of Shere Hite's report *Women and Love* cites "men's emotional withholding and distancing," their "reluctance to talk about personal thoughts and feelings," as a major problem. Hite reports, "Ninety-eight percent of the women in this study say that they would like more verbal closeness with the men they love; they want the men in their lives to talk more about their own personal thoughts, feelings, plans, and questions, and to ask them about theirs." I read this and remembered the card by the cartoonist Nicole Hollander that has an image on the cover of a woman sitting in front of a female psychic who stares into her crystal ball. The woman is saying, "Why won't he talk about his feelings?" And when you open the card, the caption reads, "At 2 A.M. men all over the world will talk about their feelings and women all over the world will be sorry." I purchased this card years ago and held on to it.

It reminded me of the occasions in therapy with my longtime partner when he would say that I always encouraged him to talk about his feelings, but when he did, everything he shared upset me. This made him want to remain silent. What he shared usually exposed that he was not the person I thought he was —that his values, ethics, and beliefs were radically different from mine. Try having a conversation with almost any man about whether it is best to cease sexual intercourse if a woman is uncomfortable. Most men want to continue coitus irrespective of what women feel. And if women talked to men about this openly, they would know that men feel this way before they engage in sexual activity with them. Much of what men have to say would be a turnoff, so no wonder many male seducers learn to keep their thoughts to themselves, the better to manipulate and con their female admirers.

Women are afraid to hear patriarchal men speak their thoughts and feelings when what they reveal expresses a reality vastly different from how we imagined them to be. Not only does this speaking expose our differences, the ways we do not connect, it exposes the possibility that we may not be *able* to connect. This is the possibility that the card alludes to. Patriarchal men seem to know this better than women. Their silence helps maintain patriarchy. When they speak thoughts and feelings that reveal pathological narcissism or negate a concern for love, it becomes clearer to the women they are speaking to that these men will not provide desired companionship or meet their emotional needs. Women do not want to talk to men about love, because we do not want to hear that most men are simply not interested in the subject. An honest patriarchal man will boldly proclaim that he pretends interest in love to get sex.

We all know relationships in which couples remain together for more than fifty years but seem to be total strangers. They really do seem to be on different planets. Yet all too often it is the male whose needs are met in these bonds, who feels no desire to communicate, and the female who anguishes. Long before we had books like Michael Vincent Miller's *Intimate Terrorism,* describing the underlying sado-masochism of such bonds, Tillie Olsen painted a moving and sad portrait of a marriage like this in her story "Tell Me a Riddle." In the story it is the patriarchal man whose values triumph and the woman whose spirit is broken. Victory for the man, however, does not mean happiness. Both parties are locked in a negative bond.

It has been hard for women to face that abusive men may wield power but not be happy. While my dad dominates Mom, he does not seem to be content with his power. He longs for connection. And as with many patriarchal men, womanizing allows him to conduct a secret search for love. Everyone imagines that the womanizing man is out there looking for sexual action when he may in fact just be searching for an honest emotional connection to ease the pain he feels as constantly as the pain felt by the woman he torments. Being sexual may allow him the space to let his guard down and receive emotional care. If patriarchal men talked to women openly, honestly, more women might want to bring an end to patriarchy. They might see more clearly the ways sexist thinking places women and men at odds with one another, creating and sustaining the conditions of gender warfare. Every female who has been in a relationship with a male who is emotionally withholding, who tries to connect with him, knows that when she communicates her desire, conflict ensues more often than not. Frequently, men are not particularly negative when asked to speak about their

feelings. They simply respond by saying, "I don't know the answer." This is a passive form of control, for it closes down all discussion.

Ironically, the feminist movement was and is often portrayed in mass media as creating gender warfare, when the truth remains that the conflict was already happening. Feminist thinking was a solution —a way to resolve differences between women and men. Nowadays folks like to believe that gender warfare has escalated because of the shift in gender roles, but in fact the warfare never stopped. Unquestionably, more women turn away from abusive men. This is a positive outcome of the feminist movement. If women turning away from abusive patriarchal violence enrages men, intensifying their misogyny, feminism is not to blame.

Hard-core patriarchal men rarely like women. Hard-core patriarchal women think like their male counterparts. And they both feel it's natural for these two different antagonistic groups to sexually mate with one another. It's clear that women who accept antagonism between the sexes as the "natural order" are happier in their relationships with men than are women who want an end to conflict. Shere Hite's report suggests that the vast majority of women want to see conflict end. Whether they are willing to give voice to it or not, this means that they want to see patriarchy end. As long as we live in a patriarchal culture, strife between women and men will be the norm. To some extent, changes created by the feminist movement that did not alter the underlying structure have made it possible for women and men to give voice to their discontent. It appears as though feminist thinking and practice made the conflict worse, when in reality had they been embraced by everyone, they would have resolved many conflicts.

It's hard for women to face the fact that patriarchy pits females and males against one another. When any woman first meets a man, she quickly decides, either consciously or subconsciously, whether he constitutes a threat. As long as the predominant response women have to men is initially fear, concern for our safety, then we will not have a world where women can wholeheartedly like men. Lots of women feel they need men in their lives, but far too many of them feel uncertain about whether they like men, because they do not really know who men are and what they think. Or if they do, they may confess to loving men but not liking them.

When women talk about what they find likable in a man, they name traits like kindness, strength of character, and integrity. As Harriet Lerner points out in *Life Preservers* in the section titled "Mr. Right and Mr. Wrong," "While individual taste varies, we want a partner who is mature and intelligent, loyal and trustworthy, loving and attentive, sensitive and open, kind and nurturant, competent and responsible. I've yet to meet a woman who says, 'Well, to be honest, I'm hoping to find an irresponsible, distant, ill-tempered sort of guy who sulks a lot and won't pick up after himself.'" Yet, she says, "Many women put more careful judgment into selecting a new toaster oven than they put into evaluating a prospective partner." Perhaps women suspend careful judgment because deep down they know that to exercise it might mean doing without male partnership for long periods of time.

Looking for a man who can love is a search that can take ages. Most men are still clinging to the rewards and forms of power patriarchy extends to them for not being loving. Since patriarchy wounds men in the place where they could be self-loving by imposing on them an identity that denies their wholeness, in order to know love, men must challenge patriarchy. And there are men who are rising to the challenge. These are the men women want to find.

I was way past thirty before I made that useful list of qualities I most desired in a partner. At the top of my list of ten qualities were honesty and openness. Had I applied this standard of evaluation, I would not have chosen the three talented, attractive men who had been my serious partners before I made this list. They were, all three, liars. And I knew from the beginning that they were liars. I liked other traits and believed the lying would stop, which it always did for a time. When I faced this discrepancy between what I desired and what I had chosen, I was actually stunned. Therapeutic discussion of the thinking that was motivating my choices revealed a deep-seated message learned in childhood: "Men never tell women the truth." While I desired truthfulness from a male partner, subconsciously I did not believe that this was a realistic expectation. Clearly the message I had learned in childhood reveals stereotypically sexist thinking women hold about men. Women who truly believe that men can never be truthful can never feel as though they really know their male partners. If we do not know someone well, then how can we know we like them? And on what basis do we choose to love them?

When women eliminate sexist attitudes toward men from our consciousness, we are better situated to evaluate and like the real men we encounter. While I would not choose them as partners, I like some men I know who are sexist in their thinking, men who are liberal, benevolent, patriarchs, because I see other qualities in them I value. This does not mean I accept or condone their sexism. Knowing that both women and men are socialized to accept patriarchal thinking should make it clear to everyone that men are not the problem. The problem is patriarchy.

Making the distinctions clear in *Fear of Fifty*, Erica Jong declares, "The truth is I don't blame individual men for this system. They carry it on mostly unknowingly. And women carry it on unknowingly, too. But more and more I wonder if it can ever be changed . . . I believe the world is full of men who are truly as perplexed and hurt by women's anger as women are perplexed by sexism, who only want to be loved and nurtured, who cannot understand how these desires have suddenly become so hard to fulfill." Patriarchy can be challenged and changed. We know this because many women and a few men have radically changed their lives. The men who are comrades in struggle search for love to find the communion that is needed to support their refusal to perpetuate patriarchal thinking. The men who are our comrades in struggle show us that they are willing to be challenged, that they are willing to change. As patriarchy changes, women are able to love men more, and men are better able to love us.

READING 26

Biphobia

Marcia Deihl and Robyn Ochs

I was in a feminist bookstore. As the woman rang up my purchase, she asked me if a "lesbian discount" was appropriate. I was somewhat taken aback, but I said (half in jest). "Well, I'm bisexual, so how about half?" She didn't smile and I didn't get a discount.

—*Marcia*

I came out to my brother several years ago and he seems on many levels to accept my bisexual identity. However, about a year ago I was visiting him and he took special care to request that I not discuss being bisexual in front of his roommates.

—*Robyn*

A friend of ours had been active in her lesbian community for several years. Then she fell in love with a man. When her lesbian "friends" found out, they ostracized her and held a "funeral" for her.

—*Robyn and Marcia*

I told a heterosexual male friend that I was bisexual. His response was to make repeated attempts to sexualize our relationship. He made the false assumption that since I was bi-SEX-ual. I was attracted to everybody.

—*Robyn*

Stories and Stereotypes

These are all stories that happen to bisexuals. Some of these mirror homophobia, others heterophobia, and still others are specifically "biphobic." All of them oppress bisexuals.

Biphobia: What is it? It is fear of the other and fear of the space between categories. Our sexual categories have long been founded on the illusion that there are two separate and mutually exclusive sexual identities: homosexual and heterosexual. The assumption is that you are either one or the other; those who are not like you are very different, and you

needn't worry about becoming like them. Biphobia, like homophobia, is prejudice based on negative stereotypes. It is often born of ignorance, but sometimes it is simply bigotry:

> Everybody knows about bisexuals—they're *confused* ("just a stage you're going through . . . you'll eventually choose . . . you're not secure in your mature heterosexuality yet . . . you're afraid of the other sex and the same sex is less threatening . . ."): they're '*sex maniacs*' ("They will do it with anyone, anytime") they're *shallow* ("They can't commit themselves to any one person or even any one sex for a long-term relationship. . . . They're typical swingers . . . they're fickle. . . . "). (Delhi in Blumenfeld and Raymond 1988, 81)

. . .

Fear from Heterosexual People

Homophobic heterosexual men and women alike react to bisexuality as they react to homosexuality. But with bisexuality, there is the added dimension of identification with the "straight half" of a bisexual person. They may be even more threatened, because they see that the "other" is not quite so different as they had believed. It could be a case of fantasy turning into a very real possibility.

Sigmund Freud and Alfred Kinsey agree that there is a spectrum of sexuality from "purely" gay to "purely" straight. (Freud 1938; Kinsey et al. 1948). Scholars working in other disciplines have made similar observations. Margaret Mead, for example, said "I think extreme heterosexuality is a perversion"; W. Somerset Maugham stated, "I tried to persuade myself that I was three-quarters normal and that only a quarter of me was queer . . . whereas it was the other way round" and Richard Aldington, biographer and friend of D. H. Lawrence, wrote, "I should say Lawrence was about eighty-five percent hetero and fifteen percent homo" (all quoted in Rutledge 1988: 20, 46, 142).

If internalized homophobia is keeping some heterosexual people from acting on their gay fantasies, they will probably be biphobic. If they are living a heterosexual life out of negative reasons (e.g., "I don't deserve what I really want"; "It's sick and perverse and sinful to act on these feelings"), then they will probably be threatened by others' bisexuality. If they are truly choosing to respond heterosexually for positive, clear, inner-directed reasons, their chances of being threatened are lessened.

We can't "convert" anyone. We don't have the right to come out for anyone else or to say that someone is "really bisexual." We don't have the right to judge another's reasons for avoiding intimacy with a given sex. We simply want it to be known that there is a third option, encompassing a wide range of variations. Some of our best allies are secure heterosexual people.

Heterosexual men and women will react slightly differently to bisexual men and bisexual women than they might react to gay men and lesbians. A homophobic straight man may respond similarly to a bisexual man as he does to a gay man (e.g., "Sissy!"). This sentiment may mask the outrage that men feel about other men renouncing their patriarchal prerogative of superiority to women. (Matteson 1989, 6). We have seen documentaries in which the Marines refer to recruits in basic training as "ladies" and "girls" in a derogatory sense. These names are considered the worst possible putdown for men who aren't being "masculine" enough. Similarly, taunting gay men with feminine names is a thinly veiled disrespect for all women. Another typical homophobic reaction is, "I just know he's going to make a pass at me." For the first time, a heterosexual man is in the position of potential "prey." Terrified and outraged, he may not be able to say "No!" safely.

Heterosexual women cannot write off bisexual men as "just friends" with no sexual undercurrents the way they might gay men. But, they cannot assume that these men are attracted to them either. Heterosexual women may see bisexual women as better "initiation" experiences than lesbians, or they may assume that bisexual women are after them.

Bisexuality defies old categories and evokes new responses. Bisexuals are relegated to a netherworld by heterosexuals and homosexuals alike. Our sexual minority status is simply one of nonexistence. What fears are expressed about us are largely based on ignorance rooted in our invisibility. (In the mainstream media, gay men and lesbians are becoming more visible.)

Bisexual women who are not middle class or rich, traditionally "beautiful," able-bodied, or white are invisible. Thus, it is hardly surprising that when *Newsweek* finally got around to publishing a feature story on bisexuality in 1995, the principal focus was on the secretive married bisexual men who are passing AIDS along to their wives. The gay community fares little better. We hear in conversation that bisexuals are "really lesbians who want access to heterosexual privilege" and that bisexuals were "really heterosexuals who want access to the support and excitement of the lesbian community."

Fear from Gay and Lesbian People

The early homophile (1950s and 1960s) and later (1970s) gay liberation movements have fought for the right of gay men and lesbians to exist, to love, and to be treated with dignity. Therefore, any perceived "regression" by gay people "converting" back to heterosexuality is considered a threat. This feeling is understandable. The gay and lesbian communities are under siege, especially in this age of AIDS; people under constant siege band together to form a united front. Thus formerly gay and lesbian people who "turn bi" are often met with feelings of betrayal and anger, but these reactions do not do justice to the truth of the situation.

Why are bisexuals perceived as such a threat to so many gay men and lesbians? We see a combination of society's homophobia and internalized biphobia at work here. A recurring theme in my [Robyn] lesbian relationships is the voiced fear on the part of my lover that I would choose to leave her for a man. After all, so much of our society is structured to encourage and support heterosexual relationships—families, the media, institutions such as marriage and corporations providing health insurance "family plans" are all based on the configuration of the heterosexual couple. Therefore, how could she possibly "compete" with the odds so stacked against us? There is no denying that the encouragement of heterosexuality and the discouragement of homosexuality is a very real fact. However, I also felt that there was a certain amount of internalized homophobia at work here, too: the feeling that whatever she had to offer me and whatever we had together couldn't possibly outweigh the external benefits of being in a heterosexual relationship. There's an underlying assumption there that anyone who has the choice will ultimately choose heterosexuality, that lesbians and gay men choose homosexual relationships because they are unable to be heterosexual. The number of bisexuals who have chosen homosexual relationships shows that this isn't necessarily so.

Some say that bisexuals are only half-oppressed. Yet we are not put on half-time when we are fired by a homophobic boss: we do not lose only half our children when we lose a custody battle; we cannot say to the gay-basher. "Oh! Please only beat me up on one side of my body."

We hear others stating that bisexual women dilute the power of the lesbian community. According to this reasoning, bisexual women should be banned from attending lesbian events despite the fact that bisexual women have greatly contributed to women's music and culture. Ironically, many lesbian organizers and performers downplay the lesbian energy in their own lives and in the history of feminism. For example, many performers who are or have been lesbians never use the "L-word" on stage. The brave ones acknowledge this problem, and address questions of privacy, expectations, and the right to change. Holly Near recently said at a concert, "I know that some of you are uncomfortable because you think I might be a lesbian. And there are others who are upset because I might not be one." Though not explicitly stated. Near seems to be referring to the ongoing and often angry controversy in the women's community over rumors of her involvement with a man.

After I [Marcia] was asked if I warranted the "lesbian discount," I thought seriously about it. I respected the woman's right to run her store the way she wanted. I loved the idea that there was such a

thing as a lesbian discount—a rare opportunity for lesbians to be rewarded, not made invisible or degraded. But, then I thought of my ten years of gay marches and my six years of playing in a feminist band that performed 25 to 50 percent lesbian material. I think I *did* deserve at least half of the discount!

Bisexuals should not automatically be categorized along with heterosexuals; bisexuals should not be excluded from the lesbian and gay community. Yet, it is generally only famous bisexual persons—reclassified as "gay" or "lesbian"—(e.g., Virginia Woolf, Sappho, Christopher Isherwood, James Baldwin, Vita Sackville-West, Colette, Kate Millet) who are embraced by lesbians and gay men; modern-day bisexuals working common jobs and bearing ordinary names are not. For example, if we want to put our name into an organization, we are often called "intruders."

We won't accept it both ways; the lesbian and gay community cannot have it both ways; either bisexuals are in or we're out. The feminist bookstore offering a lesbian discount was a store for *all* women, but, lesbians got a discount; heterosexual and bisexual women did not. It seemed in this instance we were *out* of the lesbian-gay community. We want to be in, but we are called "divisive" when we name ourselves as a third category. Such attitudes often keep us away and only reinforce the impression that we have "deserted the ranks."

Like heterosexual people who may be ignoring their homosexual inner signals, some gay men and lesbians may be repressing their bisexuality. They may fear the loss of their gay identity and their closest friends if they act on these desires. Others are happy. They have chosen positively to be gay or lesbian. These persons tend to be supportive of bisexuality in others; those who are threatened or unsure of themselves are less so.

A clear example of biphobia is the ostracism of some bisexuals from the lesbian and gay community. When women and men come out as bisexuals, their gay and lesbian friends often tell them that they can't really be bisexuals—that they are confused, or that they are waiting to reap the benefits of heterosexism. This is ironic where one considers that the lesbian and gay liberation movement in the United States is united around the right to love whomever we please, and to have our relationships validated and recognized, even when they do not conform to society's norms. Bisexuals are often pushed into a closet *within* a closet.

Our Vision: The Bisexual Artist/Citizen Today

Can you spot a bisexual when you meet one? Is there any hidden meaning to someone who is wearing one long earring and one short one, very short bangs with long hair in the back, dresses with hightops, or heels with pants (even the women!)? Perhaps. We come in every conceivable outer package—just like all other groups. What is important is what is inside. Our psyches are not split down the middle. We do not get up everyday and think. "Should I be straight or gay today?" We are, every day, in all situations, bisexual. We are like the mint breath freshener, Certs: "TWO . . . TWO . . . TWO sexualities in one." We are like the yin and yang symbol, perhaps emphasizing one aspect but with the seed of the other always present. We are simply a third option.

In sum, we are not defined by our behavior, but by our essence. If we walk down the street holding hands with a woman, people will assume we are lesbians. If we walk down the street holding hands with a man, people will assume we are heterosexual. We aren't shifting; others' perceptions are.

As public television's Mr. Rogers tells very young children, each of us is unique. We are all completely different from anyone else, with our own gifts and limitations. We are all artists; we are all queers; we are all "oddists." And lesbian, gay, bisexual, and transgender people have practically been forced to be creative. We experience a conflict between inner signals and outer demands that requires that we invent ourselves and think on our feet at every moment. Perhaps this is why we have contributed more than our share to the arts. As Fran Lebowitz quipped. "If you removed all of the homosexuals and homosexual influence from what is generally regarded as American culture, you would be pretty much left with *Let's Make a Deal* (quoted in Rutledge 1988, 93). We would do well to join some old Native American Indian cultures in considering differences in sexuality and gender expression as special, honored gifts, not as threatening deviations (Williams 1986).

Being bisexual and naming ourselves makes us special. Yet, we have our cultural work cut out for us. We must invent and create our own lives, music, theater, writing, and art, just as some of us did with women's culture. We need art that reflects, analyzes, reinvents, and inspires our daily lives. We must not simply react to biphobia, we must come together with others like ourselves to name and love ourselves.

Though we are unique, we are also like everyone else: we are citizens of this planet. We need to work in coalitions because we want to help clear up the many problems that face us and our children and grandchildren today. Problems of poverty, pollution, and violence are obvious to us all—female and male, gay, lesbian, bisexual, and straight. In order to solve these problems, action must be taken against heterosexism, sexism, racism, and class privilege. And since we are all minorities, we must work together on common projects in order to be effective. Bisexuals are natural leaders for uniting progressive men and women, and also gays and straights.

Bisexuals are not fence-sitters; there is no fence. Sexuality is a giant field in which mostly lesbian-and gay-identified people are clustered on one side and mostly heterosexual-identified people on the other. We are the middle; sometimes we travel toward one end or the other in a day, in a lifetime. We hereby declare a field day!

REFERENCES

Blumenfeld, W. J. and D. Raymond. (1988/1993). *Looking at Gay and Lesbian Life.* New York: Beacon Press.

Freud, S. (1938). "Infantile Sexuality." In *The Basic Writings of Sigmund Freud,* trans. A. Brel. New York: Modern Library.

Kinsey, A. W. Pomeroy, C. Martin, and R. Gebhard, (1948). *Sexual Behavior in the Human Male.* Philadelphia: Saunders.

Matteson, D. (1989). "Racism, Sexism, and Homophobia." *Empathy 1: 6.*

Rutledge, L. (1988). *Unnatural Quotations.* Boston: Alyson Publications.

Williams, W. (1986). *The Spirit and the Flesh.* Boston: Beacon Press.

READING 27

Coffee Will Make You Black

April Sinclair

"Mama, are you a virgin?"

I was practicing the question in my head as I set the plates with the faded roosters down on the shiny yellow table. When Mama came back into the kitchen to stir the rice or turn the fish sticks or check on the greens, I would ask her.

This afternoon at school a boy named Michael had passed a note with "Stevie" written on it; inside it had asked if I was a virgin.

My name is Jean Stevenson but the kids at school all call me Stevie counta there's been this other Jean in my class since the first grade. Now I am eleven and a half and in the sixth grade.

So, anyhow, I was really surprised to get this note from a boy like Michael Dunn, who's tall with muscles and has gray eyes, curly hair, skin the color of taffy apples, and wears Converse All-Stars even though they cost $10 a pair.

I'm not saying I look like homemade sin or anything. It's just that I'm taller than most of the other girls in my class and half of the boys. Mama says I'm at that awkward age, and that soon I won't just be arms and legs; I'll need a bra and a girdle. I can't picture myself needing a bra, as flat-chested as I am now. And to tell you the truth, I'm not too hot on having my behind all hitched up in a girdle. I have to help Mama into hers on Sunday mornings, and I feel sorry for her, all squeezed in so tight you wonder how she can even breathe.

I stirred the pitcher of cherry-flavored Kool-Aid. I loved Daylight Saving Time; it was after six o'clock and still light outside. The sunshine pouring in through the ruffled curtains made the flowers on the wallpaper look alive.

I studied my reflection in the pitcher of Kool-Aid. It wasn't like I wasn't cute. I had dimples and my features seemed right for my face. My straightened hair was long enough to make a ponytail. My skin was the color of Cracker Jacks. But most negroes didn't get excited over folks who were darker than a paper bag.

"Jean, turn off the oven!" Mama shouted from her bedroom.

"Okay."

I stared out the kitchen window at the row of gray back porches and dirt backyards. We had been in the middle of Social Studies when I had gotten Michael's note. I had lifted the lid of my wooden desk and felt behind the bag of old, wet sucked-on sunflower-seed shells and pulled out my hardcover dictionary. I'd snuck a peek inside and looked up the word "virgin." I'd seen the words "pure" and "spotless" and "like the Virgin Mary, mother of Jesus." I thought I was a good person for the most part. I didn't steal and I tried my best not to lie. I went to Sunday school, and when I stayed for church, I always put my dime in the collection plate. But I wasn't about to put myself up there with Jesus' mother. It seemed like Michael was asking me if I was a goody-two-shoes or something.

So I'd had no choice but to answer the note with the words "Not exactly" and pass it back to him. I wondered what Michael thought of my answer, I hadn't seen him after school. I hoped he would say something to me on Monday. I knew it wasn't my place as a girl to say anything to him. I would just have to wait and see what happened, I told myself.

Mama returned to the kitchen. She looked glad to be out of her girdle and work clothes. She was wearing her oldest print housedress, and the extra pounds showing around her waist didn't make her look fat, they just made her look like somebody's mother. Mama had tied a scarf around her hair so she wouldn't sweat it out, and she was wearing Daddy's old house slippers. It struck me how different Mama looked from June Cleaver or Donna Reed on TV, not just because of her pecan-colored skin but because they practically did their housework in pearls!

I turned facing Mama, and folded my arms across my chest. I watched her take the pan of fish sticks out of the oven and set them on a plate.

I cleared my throat. "Mama, are you a virgin?"

Mama lifted the top off the pot of collard greens and breathed in the steam. She glanced at me and turned off the gas. I could tell by the look on her face that she was trying to think up a good answer.

"Jean, where did you pick up that word, at church?" Mama asked, rearranging the pressing comb and the can of bacon grease on the stove.

I stared down at the yellowed gray linoleum.

"Well, no, not exactly . . . at school."

"Mrs. Butler brought it up?"

I pulled on the tie of my sailor blouse and twisted it around my fingers.

"No, Mama, Mrs. Butler ain't brought it up, this boy asked me if I was a virgin."

I had the nerve to glance at Mama. Her large dark eyes were arched up like she had seen a ghost.

"Don't say 'ain't'! Didn't I tell you to never say 'ain't'? I can run from 'ain't.'"

In my opinion, this was not time for an English lesson, so I just hunched my shoulders. "Mrs. Butler *didn't* bring it up, this boy asked me if I was a virgin." I repeated, correcting my English.

"Well, Jean Eloise, you should have told him he'll never get the chance to find out." Mama frowned as she stirred the rice. "Humph, you stay away from that boy; he's got his mind in the gutter." Mama pointed her finger in my face. "All men are dogs! Some are just more doggish than others. Do you hear me?"

"Mama, the dictionary said something about the word 'virgin' meaning pure and spotless, like the Virgin Mary. I don't understand why you say Michael's got his mind in the gutter then."

"'Cause he's a dog, that's why! I just got through telling you that."

I stuffed my hands into the pockets of my blue pedal pushers and looked Mama in the eye. "Mama, am I a virgin or not?"

"Lord, have mercy, I forgot about the cornbread." Mama opened the oven door and took out the pan of cornbread. It looked fine.

Mama let out a big breath. Maybe it was hard having a daughter at an awkward age, I thought. "Jean, all unmarried girls should be virgins."

"Mama, Michael knows I'm unmarried."

"You haven't even started your period yet, of course you're a virgin."

I stared down at my brown penny loafers. "Mama, what happens when you start your period?"

Mama patted her cornbread. "I don't think you're ready for this kind of discussion."

"Mama, I'll be twelve in four months."

"Jean Eloise, I'll tell you everything I want you to know when the time comes. Now, call your daddy and the boys for dinner, the fish sticks are gettin cold."

I groaned as I left the kitchen. Boy, I could've gotten more out of Beaver Cleaver's mother.

READING 28

La Güera

Cherríe Moraga

It requires something more than personal experience to gain a philosophy or point of view from any specific event. It is the quality of our response to the event and our capacity to enter into the lives of others that help us to make their lives and experiences our own.

—*Emma Goldman*[1]

I am the very well-educated daughter of a woman who, by the standards in this country, would be considered largely illiterate. My mother was born in Santa Paula, Southern California, at a time when much of the central valley there was still farm land. Nearly thirty-five years later, in 1948, she was the only daughter of six to marry an Anglo, my father.

I remember all of my mother's stories, probably much better than she realizes. She is a fine story-teller, recalling every event of her life with the vividness of the present, noting each detail right down to the cut and color of her dress. I remember her stories of her being pulled out of school at the ages of five, seven, nine, and eleven to work in the fields, along with her brothers and sisters; stories of her father drinking away whatever small profit she was able to make for the family; of her going the long way home to avoid meeting him on the street, staggering toward the same destination. I remember stories of my mother lying about her age in order to get a job as a hat-check girl at Agua Caliente Racetrack in Tijuana. At fourteen, she was the main support of the family. I can still see her walking home alone at 3 A.M., only to turn all of her salary and tips over to her mother, who was pregnant again.

The stories continue through the war years and on: walnut-cracking factories, the Voit Rubber factory, and then the computer boom. I remember my mother doing piecework for the electronics plant in our neighborhood. In the late evening, she would sit in front of the TV set, wrapping copper wires into the backs of circuit boards, talking about "keeping up with the younger girls." By that time, she was already in her mid-fifties.

Meanwhile, I was college-prep in school. After classes, I would go with my mother to fill out job applications for her, or write checks for her at the supermarket. We would have the scenario all worked out ahead of time. My mother would sign the check before we'd get to the store. Then, as we'd approach the checkstand, she would say—within earshot of the cashier—"Oh honey, you go 'head and make out the check," as if she couldn't be bothered with such an insignificant detail. No one asked any questions.

I was educated, and wore it with a keen sense of pride and satisfaction, my head propped up with the knowledge, from my mother, that my life would be easier than hers. I was educated; but more than this, I was *la güera:* 'fair-skinned.' Born with the features of my Chicana mother, but the skin of my Anglo father, I had it made.

No one ever quite told me this (that light was right), but I knew that being light was something valued in my family (who were all Chicano, with the exception of my father). In fact, everything about my upbringing (at least what occurred on a conscious level) attempted to bleach me of what color I did have. Although my mother was fluent in it, I was never taught much Spanish at home. I picked up what I did learn from school and from overheard snatches of conversation among my relatives and mother. She often called the other lower-income Mexicans *braceros,* or 'wet-backs,' referring to herself and her family as "a different class of people." And yet, the real story was that my family, too, had been poor (some still are) and farmworkers. My mother can remember this in her blood as if it were yesterday. But this is something she would like to forget (and rightfully), for to her, on a basic economic level, being Chicana meant being "less." It was through my mother's desire to protect her children from poverty and illiteracy that we became "Anglo-ized"; the more effectively we could pass in the white world, the better guaranteed our future.

From all of this, I experience daily a huge disparity between what I was born into and what I was to grow up to become. Because, as Goldman suggests, these stories my mother told me crept under my *güera* skin. I had no choice but to enter into the life of my mother. *I had no choice.* I took her life into my heart, but managed to keep a lid on it as long as I feigned being the happy, upwardly mobile heterosexual.

When I finally lifted the lid to my lesbianism, a profound connection with my mother was re-awakened in me. It wasn't until I acknowledged and confronted my own lesbianism in the flesh, that my heartfelt identification with and empathy for my mother's oppression—due to being poor, uneducated, and Chicana   was realized. My lesbianism is the avenue through which I have learned the most about silence and oppression, and it continues to be the most tactile reminder to me that we are not free human beings.

You see, one follows the other. I had known for years that I was a lesbian, had felt it in my bones, had ached with the knowledge, gone crazed with the knowledge, wallowed in the silence of it. Silence *is* like starvation, Don't be fooled. It's nothing short of that, and felt most sharply when one has had a full belly most of her life. When we are not physically starving, we have the luxury to realize psychic and emotional starvation. It is from this starvation that other starvations can be recognized—if one is willing to take the risk of making the connection—if one is willing to be responsible to the result of the connection. For me, the connection is an inevitable one.

What I am saying is that the joys of looking like a white girl haven't been so great since I realized I could be beaten on the street for being a dyke. If my sister's being beaten because she's black, it's pretty much the same principle. We're both getting beaten any way you look at it. The connection is blatant; and in the case of my own family, the differences in the privileges attached to looking white instead of brown are merely a generation apart.

In this country, lesbianism is poverty—as is being brown, as is being a woman, as being just plain poor. The danger lies in ranking the oppressions. *The danger lies in failing to acknowledge the specificity of the oppression.* The danger lies in attempting to deal with oppression purely from a theoretical base. Without an emotional, heartfelt grappling with the source of our own oppression, without naming the enemy within ourselves and outside of us, no authentic, nonhierarchical connection among oppressed groups can take place.

When the going gets rough, will we abandon our so-called comrades in a flurry of racist/heterosexist/what-have-you panic? To whose camp, then, should the lesbian of color retreat? Her very presence violates the ranking and abstraction of oppression. Do we merely live hand to mouth? Do we merely struggle with the "ism" that's sitting on top of our own heads?

The answer is: yes, I think first we do; and we must do so thoroughly and deeply. But to fail to move out from there will only isolate us in our own oppression—will only insulate, rather than radicalize us.

. . .

Within the women's movement, the connections among women of different backgrounds and sexual orientations have been fragile, at best. I think this phenomenon is indicative of our failure to seriously address ourselves to some very frightening questions: How have I internalized my own oppression? How have I oppressed? Instead, we have let rhetoric

do the job of poetry. Even the word *oppression* has lost its power. We need new language, better words that can more closely describe women's fear of and resistance to one another; words that will not always come out sounding like dogma.

I don't really understand first-hand what it feels like being shit on for being brown. I understand much more about the joys of it—being Chicana and having family are synonymous for me. What I know about loving, singing, crying, telling stories, speaking with my heart and hands, even having a sense of my own soul comes from the love of my mother, aunts, cousins. . . .

But at the age of twenty-seven, it is frightening to acknowledge that I have internalized a racism and classism, where the object of oppression is not only someone outside of my skin, but the someone inside my skin. In fact, to a large degree, the real battle with such oppression, for all of us, begins under the skin. I have had to confront the fact that much of what I value about being Chicana, about my family, has been subverted by Anglo culture and my own cooperation with it. This realization did not occur to me overnight. For example, it wasn't until long after my graduation from the private college I'd attended in Los Angeles, that I realized the major reason for my total alienation from and fear of my classmates was rooted in class and culture. *Click.*

Three years after graduation, in an apple-orchard in Sonoma, a friend of mine (who comes from an Italian working-class family), says to me, "Cherríe, no wonder you felt like such a nut in school. Most of the people there were white and rich." It was true. All along I had felt the difference, but not until I had put the words *class* and *culture* to the experience did my feelings make any sense. For years, I had berated myself for not being as "free" as my classmates. I completely bought that they simply had more guts than I did—to rebel against their parents and run around the country hitchhiking, reading books and studying "art." They had enough privilege to be atheists, for chrissake. There was no one around filling in the disparity for me between their parents, who were Hollywood filmmakers, and my parents, who wouldn't know the name of a filmmaker if their lives depended on it (and precisely because their lives didn't depend on it, they couldn't be bothered). But I knew nothing about "privilege" then. White was right. Period. I could pass. If I got educated enough, there would never be any telling.

Three years after that, another click. In a letter to a friend, I wrote:

> I went to a concert where Ntozake Shange was reading. There, everything exploded for me. She was speaking a language that I knew—in the deepest parts of me—existed, and that I had ignored in my own feminist studies and even in my own writing. What Ntozake caught in me is the realization that in my development as a poet, I have, in many ways, denied the voices of my brown mother—the brown in me. I have acclimated to the sound of a white language which, as my father represents it, does not speak to the emotions in my poems—emotions which stem from the love of my mother.
>
> The reading was agitating. Made me feel uncomfortable. Threw me into a week-long terror of how deeply I was affected. I felt that I had to start all over again. That I had turned only to the perceptions of white middle-class women to speak for me and all women. I am shocked by my own ignorance.

Sitting in that auditorium chair was the first time I had realized to the core of me that for years I had disowned the language I knew best—ignored the words and rhythms that were the closest to me. The sounds of my mother and aunts gossiping—half in English, half in Spanish—while drinking cerveza in the kitchen. And the hands—I had cut off the hands in my poems. But not in conversation; still the hands could not be kept down. Still they insisted on moving.

The reading had forced me to remember that I knew things from my roots. But to remember puts me up against what I don't know. Shange's reading agitated me because she spoke with power about a world that is both alien and common to me: "the capacity to enter into the lives of others." But you can't just take the goods and run. I knew that then, sitting in the Oakland auditorium (as I know in my poetry), that the only thing worth writing about is what seems to be unknown and therefore fearful.

The "unknown" is often depicted in racist literature as the "darkness" within a person. Similarly, sexist writers will refer to fear in the form of the vagina, calling it "the orifice of death." In contrast, it is a pleasure to read works such as Maxine Hong Kingston's *Woman Warrior,* where fear and alienation are described as "the white ghosts." And yet, the bulk of literature in this country reinforces the myth that what is dark and female is evil. Consequently, each of us—whether dark, female, or both—has in some way *internalized* this oppressive imagery. What the oppressor often succeeds in doing is simply *externalizing* his fears, projecting them into the bodies of women, Asians, gays, disabled folks, whoever seems most "other."

> call me
> roach and presumptuous
> nightmare on your white pillow
> your itch to destroy
> the indestructible
> part of yourself   —*Audre Lorde*[2]

But it is not really difference the oppressor fears so much as similarity. He fears he will discover in himself the same aches, the same longings as those of the people he has shit on. He fears the immobilization threatened by his own incipient guilt. He fears he will have to change his life once he has seen himself in the bodies of the people he has called different. He fears the hatred, anger, and vengeance of those he has hurt.

This is the oppressor's nightmare, but it is not exclusive to him. We women have a similar nightmare, for each of us in some way has been both the oppressed and the oppressor. We are afraid to see how we have taken the values of our oppressor into our hearts and turned them against ourselves and one another. We are afraid to admit how deeply "the man's" words have been ingrained in us.

To assess the damage is a dangerous act. I think of how, even as a feminist lesbian, I have so wanted to ignore my own homophobia, my own hatred of myself for being queer. I have not wanted to admit that my deepest personal sense of myself has not quite "caught up" with my "woman-identified" politics. I have been afraid to criticize lesbian writers who choose to "skip over" these issues in the name of feminism. In 1979, we talk of "old gay" and "butch and femme" roles as if they were ancient history. We toss them aside as merely patriarchal notions. And yet, the truth of the matter is that I have sometimes taken society's fear and hatred of lesbians to bed with me. I have sometimes hated my lover for loving me. I have sometimes felt "not woman enough" for her. I have sometimes felt "not man enough." For a lesbian trying to survive in a heterosexist society, there is no easy way around these emotions. Similarly, in a white-dominated world, there is little getting around racism and our own internalization of it. It's always there, embodied in some one we least expect to rub up against.

When we do rub up against this person, *there* then is the challenge. *There* then is the opportunity to look at the nightmare within us. But we usually shrink from such a challenge.

. . .

As Lorde suggests in the passage I cited earlier, it is in looking to the nightmare that the dream is found. There, the survivor emerges to insist on a future, a vision, yes, born out of what is dark and female. The feminist movement must be a movement of such survivors, a movement with a future.

NOTES

1. Alix Kates Shulman, ed., "Was My Life Worth Living?" *Red Emma Speaks* (New York: Random House, 1972), p. 388.
2. From "The Brown Menace or Poem to the Survival of Roaches," *The New York Head Shop and Museum* (Detroit: Broadside, 1974), p. 48.

■ READING 29

Prue Shows Her Knickers

Emily Oxford

Prue was just a teenager. She was skinny and lean but two budding breasts made faint bumps under her clothes. Boys teased her and Andy kept asking for a flash.

The once-soft face of childhood was harder now, her jaw jutted forward a little, a physical sign of her stubbornness. Circumstance had made her wilful, wary and nervous of the world she lived in, but somewhere the indomitable spirit of her optimism still burned.

She was not normal. She was a cripple, she was handicapped, she was a Special pre-pubescent.

Her legs were unique maps of her illness, stiff and unbending, her knees decorated with tiny craters and variously swelling bumps. She didn't walk on them much and used a wheelchair at times she called simply 'agony' days. Her neck, though rarely painful, bent to one side and stayed there. These were her bodily impairments which attracted the labels of doctors, and consequently categorised her neatly for the rest of the world.

The labels attached to her had done their work; her psyche suffered its own impairments as a result,

and as she approached adolescence, she found herself nervous about a world which had once seemed a dazzling dance of magic.

She never thought much about her situation, she just accepted that she was these things other people placed on her, and if it kept the peace with her anxious, fretting mother, then she played by the rules that meant she saw lots of white-coats, went to a Special school in a Special bus and didn't expect to do a whole array of things in the hostile, anti-cripple world.

But even these rules had begun to change of late.

Now she was expected to play the Independence game—a game with a particular definition. Lectures on 'Personal Independence' featured in her life these days with growing regularity. She had to go to 'Buttons and Bows' classes, where groups of bored teenagers were grilled about how to tie shoe laces; tackle buckles, poppers, buttons, zips; pull this on, pull that off; and sundry other activities. With her twig-like fingers curving at bulbous joints that neither bent very far nor had the strength to stay straight, most of these tasks were to Prue a punishment in ritualised boredom. She knew her own limits, just as she knew what challenges were worth taking on. These activities were pointless and demoralising as she failed at every attempt. The 'teachers'—in fact blue-coats serving under the Head's baleful glare—would tut at her and admonish her to try harder.

The enforced ideas about Independence were suffocating shadows closing in on her life. She had to be taught to do everything in her life herself, absolutely, in readiness for adulthood when there would be no kind mum to wait on you, no teachers and Care ladies, oh no. It seemed to Prue it was the sort of Independence you might only need if you were the only person left alive on some fantastic, civilised desert island; and it was the sort of Independence which she knew she could never actually achieve.

What being Independent meant, of course, was being able to present to their real world an approximation of Normality. You wouldn't ever have to bother a nice Normal person with your nasty difficulties, you'd never have to ask for anything. It didn't matter how many hopeless hours of pain and toil were involved.

But who was she to argue? She was just a cripple kid, told every day that she didn't know what was best for herself, in her Special situation . . .

If you didn't play the game of Independence by their rules, they made fearful threats about putting you in a Home when you reached sixteen. It was up to you, they would shrug, as if they had no say in the decision. If you tried your hardest and were Independent, then you didn't have to worry. You would be allowed into their world.

. . .

Prue had to draw on every ounce of her hard-won reserve of strength today because two traumas were facing her at school. The white-coat prodders had decided to send her away to a new place for 'better treatment', so this was her last day for God knows how long. She would be going to another hospital. They all kept insisting that it wasn't hospital—even her mother—but a special residential centre for children and young adults with arthritis; just what she needed. But Prue was not calmed by their explanations. She had grown weary and resigned towards their soothing platitudes and downright lies. With a

churning in her stomach, she braced herself for the worst.

But although this imminent event lay in her mind like a heavy, dulling ache, there was a more pressing engagement awaiting her at school.

She had been half dared, half coaxed into promising Andy Easter a look down her knickers—as long as she was allowed a look down his. She and Sally had giggled over the prospect all week, and in high bravado she had announced the forthcoming exploit for days. Now the whole class knew about it, and boys and girls alike laughed and chattered expectantly as she entered the classroom.

Sally was excited and anxious, a great bubbling jitter of worry.

'What if you're caught? What if they tell your mum?'

'Mum won't care, she knows I'm not stupid. I'd say it was just a silly game. Anyway, we won't get caught—he's only getting a few seconds look! That's the dare!'

Sammy Smith, one of their gang, a small compact tomboy of a girl with twisting wiry hair, pulled a face.

'You'll have to watch him, 'e's a bugger! Don't let him touch nothin'! If 'e does I'll whack him for year!'

Sammy was tough, renowned for hurtling down the corridors on her three-wheeled walking frame, scattering unwary younger pupils as she went.

'Oh blimey, no touching, course not!' Prue laughed, hiding the lurch in her stomach which reminded her suddenly not only of the present embarrassing scrape she was in, but also of her appointment with new white-coats tomorrow. She could hardly believe that she was leaving all her friends, Miss Tobin, and her mum and brother, for who knew how long. And thoughts of her mum brought back the painful scene at breakfast.

Andy was grinning at her across the classroom, tapping his flies with the palm of his hand, a swanking display for his sniggering mates. She pulled a disgusted face at him before turning back to the gang. At least there was a morning full of lessons before she had to Do It.

No one was allowed to watch, they both insisted on that, meeting inside the stationery cupboard, at the edge of the assembly hall. Their friends waited outside, giggling and hushing each other, keeping a sharp watch for teachers or prowling Snotty Scott.

Prue had worked herself up into a perfect state of arrogant devilry, deciding this was the only way she could get through the ordeal. Anyhow, her mother had taught her not to be ashamed of anything to do with her private parts (although she didn't like Prue to display her bumpy lumpy legs), saying that they were hers and she should be proud to be a woman.

Now here she was, wearing her best pink knickers, facing Andy and staring him in the eye, allowing him no chance to renege on his part of the dare. He looked up at her, sheepish now the door was shut, his grin not so swanky.

'Well?' said Prue, keen to get it over with. Mum might have told her to be proud of her 'Miss Mary' but at this instant she felt silly and embarrassed.

'Who's going to go first, then?' he asked uncertainly, playing with the top of his trousers.

'We'll do it together. Let's count to three, then— then show ourselves—only for five seconds—we'll count together.'

Her stomach was doing somersaults. A tiny voice somewhere asked her why she was being so childish. It was too late to answer that.

Andy had his hands ready at his zip. Prue hooked her stiff fingers with some difficulty into her knickers. Looking down at him, a pang of pity hit her. What a sorrowful sight he was. He was terrified! But being a boy he couldn't let on, could he? She felt strong and in charge. Why was she afraid? She'd seen a willy, on Rory and in books. His couldn't be any more peculiar or strange. She decided to display herself with a flourish.

'Right then . . . get ready, let's count together . . . one . . . two . . . three!'

A quick extra second of struggle with unwieldy clothes and there they stood.

'One chim-pan-zee, TWO chim-pan-zee . . .' Prue stared hard at the grey-pink length of flesh that lay limp and wrinkled in Andy's hand. She wanted to laugh but managed a less insulting smile instead, noticing that Andy was avidly looking down as she held her dress under her chin. She stepped back slightly, her legs moving apart. His willy looked like a sagging sausage that was going off she decided, and those straggles of hair around it, yuck!

' . . . FIVE chim-pan-zee!' they chorused together before hastily covering themselves. Outside the others were growing restless. Andy still looked nervous.

'Er . . . it's not very big, is it? I mean, my brother has got a really huge one.'

Prue wanted to laugh out loud. She was going away from all this tomorrow, and she knew how much she would miss it. She would even miss Andy.

'Well, I don't really know. It looked just the same as the others I've seen,' Prue remarked airily, amazed at how timid he had become in displaying his prized part to her. 'How did I do?'

She didn't actually care much what he thought but was interested in what he might say.

He looked up at her, taller as she was, and smiled shyly.

'You're great, Prue. I really like you. You're pretty.'

Prue was flabbergasted by this response, expecting something rude and smart. But she was in control and she knew it. She also knew now that the great, bragging, flashy bugger Andy Easter had never seen a woman's private part before. She glowed and smiled.

'You're all right too, mate.' There was a little devil suddenly inside her. Tomorrow this would all be gone . . . for a long time, she just knew it.

'Give us a kiss, then.' The words came out of her mouth, a dancing request half-filled with laughter, half with blank nerve. She bent down to him, put her hand on his shoulder, and pressed her lips against his.

She didn't want him to forget her in a hurry while she was away.

READING 30

Compañeros

Carolyn Reyes and Eric DeMeulenaere

[E.D.] . . . I am known as someone who smiles a lot, but the truth is that it is Carolyn who keeps me smiling. We have always struggled with what to call each other not only for political reasons, but because wife, spouse and partner simply do not capture who we are to each other. The term I like best, both politically and emotionally, is *compañera*. Its flavor is more soulful than its English counterpart: companion. Carolyn is *mi compañera*. And I cannot imagine life without her.

[C.R.] Eric had been smiling way before he met me. I could tell he was no novice. It was that smile that I first noticed about him and that lit my journey through my adulthood. Everything I love about Eric can be found in that smile. In his smile lies compassion—his immense capacity to enter into and share in the suffering of others and to be moved to action on their behalf. This is coupled by his deep love for justice—a commitment to a vision of the world as a safe place for all people and to participation in the realization of such a vision. . . . Eric is a most faithful friend and lover. I could ask for no better companion through life.

. . .

[E.D.] We met at what may be the most unlikely of places—a small religious liberal arts college in the suburbs of Chicago. I came from a white upper-middle class politically conservative and religious home. I began my youthful rebellion (which continues still) by registering as a Democrat and expressing my disbelief in God. Yet my background had enough momentum to propel me into the college my parents and church thought suitable. I never really felt like I belonged in the college environment in which I found myself, so I took pride in a relentless critique I waged against the school and all that I felt it stood for.

But if mentally I did not belong in that institution, at least my socio-economic class and race matched the unwritten standard. I looked like and spoke like the vast majority of the student body. Carolyn's story was much different. Coming from a low-income Latino family from Miami, she looked, spoke and thought very differently. Racism and sexism on campus slowly worked to push her to the social, political and spiritual edges of the campus. It was here that we found each other and our friendship developed as we vented our frustrations with the ultra-conservative, racist and sexist environment in which we existed.

[C.R.] Back then it didn't occur to me that we would have to negotiate racial or class differences or gender roles. I was aware of many of those differences but had given little thought to the idea that they could play a significant role in our relationship. I had no idea that the power dynamics that were at play at the wider societal level could have a bearing on our micro-level relationship. Neither had I given much thought to the possible social and political statements our relationship would make to the communities to which we belong and to society-at-large. It would be several years before we would hear my sister-in-law's father say to me in congratulatory fashion, *"Estás blanqueando la raza"* (You're whitening the race) when meeting Eric for the first time. It would be quite some time before I would face the disapproving looks from progressive people of color who count me as yet another traitor who is "sleeping with the enemy." It would take a lot less time for Eric to gain status among white liberals who believe his being in a relationship with a woman of color is an admirable and "down" reality.

[E.D.] Yet society affects even the most personal areas of our lives. We have clearly rejected societal expectations for our relationship in terms of gender roles, but in so doing we have often been just as controlled by those expectations when we try to live in opposition to them. It is fine for Carolyn to handle the finances and for me to do the laundry, for instance. But Carolyn's enjoyment of washing dishes and my greater knowledge about automotive mechanics often makes us feel uneasy. Whenever we notice ourselves or each other acting in traditional ways in terms of sex roles, we pause to critically examine why we're doing what we're doing. Are we sure we really want to be doing this or are we somehow giving in to societal pressures and expectations? The time and energy expended in this process reminds us that those forces continue to have some power in our lives—to some degree controlling us even though we are explicitly trying to break free from their constraints.

[C.R.] No place do we face societal constraints more directly than in our families. A pattern has evolved during our visits to Miami, and always in Eric's presence, in which both my sisters-in-law publicly bemoan being married to Latino men. During these visits when Eric cooks or washes the dishes, my sisters-in-law will often comment on my luck in finding such a helpful and supportive white man because they believe Latino men don't help much around the house. They praise Eric profusely for "helping" me and explain, "Eric, you just don't understand Latino men. They just don't do that," completely unaware of their internalized sexism and racism. They later go on to comment, "American [read "white"] men are the best!" Eric and I try to explain the dangers of generalizing from their experiences, but regardless of our words, these experiences fit their preconceived ideas and they continue to fail to see that sexism knows no ethnic boundaries and that there are men from all backgrounds who attempt to defy the stereotypical roles into which they have been socialized.

While my mother shares my sisters-in-law's perceptions, our relationship also makes her uncomfortable. She agrees that I am lucky to have such a helpful and caring man in my life but fears that I am too controlling and not supportive enough of him. When either of us goes out, whether to dance clubs or school events, unaccompanied by the other partner, my mother criticizes me for not supporting him. Eric is a high-school history teacher and I am finishing up my Masters degree in Social Work. There is something about our independence—and mine in particular—that does not sit well with her. In fact, it is my independence, in thought and action, that has caused her to label me *de carácter fuerte* (of

strong character—not a positive characteristic for a woman) and *dominante* (domineering). While my assertiveness is labeled domineering, Eric's more easy-going attitude makes him seem "wrapped-around my finger." *No hay nada mas feo que una mujer que domine a un hombre* (There's nothing uglier than a woman who dominates a man), I can hear her say. We're both quite certain that if the opposite were true it would go unchallenged.

[E.D.] In addition to our families expecting us to live out traditional gender roles, they also confront us with issues regarding race. Most of Carolyn's family's stereotypes about my whiteness, although unfair and restricting, are nevertheless intended to be positive. Such positive intentions are often lacking on the part of my family, however. My aunt's grimace at our bringing black beans for a Christmas dinner is just one of the many ways that Carolyn's culture is devalued in my family.

While my relatives seek to embrace Carolyn as part of the family, they fail to see why she might be reluctant to fully accept the welcome. My brother, in particular, believes that Carolyn and I are overly sensitive about issues of race and gender and feels frustrated that he has to be careful about everything he says. He has frequently argued that if Carolyn is offended by his words or actions it is because she is "hypersensitive." He accepts that he says things at times that we might find inappropriate, but he never intends to be hurtful. "Why can't you guys let anything slide?" he challenges when our frequent confrontations lead to tension and bitterness. While he has matured and changed in his level of consideration for Carolyn and people of color in general, problems still arise and both Carolyn and he continue to be hurt. This raises an important question for me. My brother wants very badly that we do not challenge him on everything he says that we find problematic. Carolyn and I want very badly that my brother stop saying—and more importantly, thinking—sexist and racist things. Given my relationship to Carolyn, what should my relationship to my brother be?

If Carolyn met someone like my brother in a different context, she would not choose to develop a relationship with him. But because he is my family it makes it very difficult. Holidays are very difficult times for us. Carolyn would prefer to avoid my family because even if nothing inappropriate is said, her ethnic and class background make her feel like an outsider. More importantly, she experiences a sense of otherness which no one understands nor even recognizes. And although she recognizes that my family is friendly and generous to her, this creates an incredible tension for her and makes her visits with my family miserable. I, however, am an insider and remain close to my family. I feel very comfortable with them, and I look forward to seeing them. How do I support and protect Carolyn while at the same time maintaining my relationship with my family? I see that Carolyn feels like an outsider in my family. Yet I also understand how her reluctance to accept my family's embrace hurts them. If both are my community, whose pain do I embrace? What does my stand against racism mean if the person closest to me has to struggle with her status in my own family?

These questions troubled me in an incident with my uncle. He and my aunt live in a small town, predominantly white, and align themselves with the religious Right. In the first interaction Carolyn had with my uncle, the subject of race came up. Speaking from his military experience, he boldly argued that "Blacks are okay one on one; it's when you get them in groups that they're a problem." Since then, Carolyn has understandably avoided virtually all contact with my uncle and his family. But my brother will be having a wedding in their town soon, and my parents are planning to move there after retirement. What are my responsibilities in dealing with these situations?

Such unanswered questions affect us because we are both isolated from each other's experiences. In these situations, I am an insider while Carolyn feels like an outsider. We are also isolated from each other in our individual struggles with identity. I cannot give Carolyn a sense of what it means to be Cuban. Her ethnic identity is best affirmed and supported, obviously, by people within her own ethnic community. More recently, I have also come to realize that Carolyn can be of limited assistance to me in my struggle to understand how I should live in the world as a white man who seeks to be anti-sexist and anti-racist. Developing an awareness of this reality was painful because we realized that we could not meet a very major need for each other. We came to understand the value of sharing our lives with people whose identities more closely resemble our own. Thus we have been forced to think seriously about what it means to share our lives together as people whose backgrounds and identities are very different. While there are insights to be gained from our differences, it is clear that our differences have their disadvantages as well.

[C.R.] Given the difficulties we have experienced in loving across the boundaries of race, class and gender, why do we bother? Why continue to struggle? My initial response to these questions is to explain that I have never been a stranger to struggle. I am reminded of my grandmother, who raised me, and who when asked how she was doing on any given day, would often respond, "*Aqui, en la lucha.*" (Here, in the struggle.) Her statement was, to me, a declaration that life is, in essence, a struggle. It was less a statement of resignation than a recognition of her position in the world and a testament to her survival. Struggle, I learned early on, is not to be feared or avoided at any cost; rather it is to be embraced as a part of living.

. . .

READING 31

Some Like Indians Endure

Paula Gunn Allen

i have it in my mind that
dykes are indians

they're a lot like indians
they used to live as tribes
they owned tribal land
it was called the earth

they were massacred
lots of times
they always came back
like the grass
like the clouds
they got massacred again

they thought caringsharing
about the earth and each other
was a good thing
they rode horses
and sang to the moon

but i don't know
about what was so longago
and it's now that dykes
make me think i'm with indians
when i'm with dykes

because they bear
witness bitterly
because they reach
and hold
because they live every day
with despair laughing
in cities and country places
because earth hides them
because they know
the moon
because they gather together
enclosing
and spit in the eye of death

indian is an idea
some people have

of themselves
dyke is an idea some women
have of themselves
the place where we live now
is idea
because whiteman took
all the rest
because father
took all the rest
but the idea which
once you have it
you can't be taken
for somebody else
and have nowhere to go
like indians you can be
stubborn

the idea might move you on,
ponydrag behind
taking all your loves and
children maybe downstream

maybe beyond the cliffs
but it hangs in there
an idea
like indians
endures

it might even take your
whole village with it
stone by stone
or leave the stones
and find more
to build another village
someplace else

like indians
dykes have fewer and fewer
someplace elses to go
so it gets important
to know
about ideas and

to remember or uncover
the past
and how the people
traveled
all the while remembering
the idea they had
about who they were
indians, like dykes
do it all the time

dykes know all about dying
and that everything belongs
to the wind
like indians
they do terrible things
to each other
out of sheer cussedness
out of forgetting
out of despair
so dykes
are like indians
because everybody is related
to everybody
in pain
in terror
in guilt
in blood
in shame
in disappearance
that never quite manages
to be disappeared
we never go away

even if we're always
leaving

because the only home
is each other
they've occupied all
the rest
colonized it; an
idea about ourselves is all
we own

and dykes remind me of indians
like indians dykes
are supposed to die out
or forget
or drink all the time
or shatter
go away
to nowhere
to remember what will happen
if they don't

they don't anyway—even
though the worst happens

they remember and they
stay
because the moon remembers
because so does the sun
because the stars
remember
and the persistent stubborn grass
of the earth

DISCUSSION QUESTIONS FOR CHAPTER FOUR

1. In what ways is the personal political for you in your relationships?

2. How is the personal political in heterosexual relationships generally?

3. How does socialization into gender affect intimacy in relationships?

4. How does homophobia discourage intimacy? Have there been instances in your life when homophobia has prevented you from developing intimacy with someone?

5. How would you describe women's and men's different ways of communicating? How do women's and men's different ways of communicating affect relationships?

6. How is romantic love related to consumerism? Give some examples.

SUGGESTIONS FOR FURTHER READING

Bright, Susie, ed. *Herotica: A Collection of Women's Erotic Fiction,* 2nd ed. San Francisco: Down There Press, 1998.

Collins, Patricia Hill. "Sexual Politics and Black Women's Relationships." *Black Feminist Thought.* New York: Routledge, 1991.

Kamen, Paula. *Her Way: Young Women Remake the Sexual Revolution.* New York: Broadway Books, 2002.

Snitow, Ann, Christine Stansell, and Sharon Thompson, eds. *Powers of Desire: The Politics of Sexuality.* New York: Monthly Review Press, 1983.

Stoltenberg, John. *Refusing to Be a Man: Essays on Sex and Justice,* revised ed. London: UCL Press, 1999.

Wolf, Naomi. *Promiscuities: A Secret History of Female Desire.* London: Random House, 2000.

CHAPTER FIVE

Inscribing Gender on the Body

In contemporary U.S. society we are surrounded by images of beautiful, thin, young, White, smiling women. These images set standards for appearance and beauty that are internalized—standards that affect how we feel about our own bodies. As a result, most of us grow up disliking our bodies, or some parts of them. We are especially troubled by those parts of our bodies that we see as larger than societal ideals.

It is distressing that women often experience their bodies as sources of despair rather than joy and celebration. This is especially true as we age and measure our bodies against notions of youthful beauty. These images of perfect bodies are fabricated by a male-dominated culture and are reinforced by multi-billion-dollar industries that serve to maintain both corporate profits and patriarchal social relations. The images we are given are flawless and give the illusion of absolute perfection. In reality these images tend to be airbrushed and computer-enhanced; often even the models themselves do not look like their pictures. Fashion models today weigh more than 20 percent less than the average woman, with only about 5 percent of the female population in our society weighing in at the average fashion model's weight given her height. Obviously, real women come in all shapes and sizes. Our diversity is part of our beauty!

Although the body is an incredibly sophisticated jumble of physiological events, our understanding of the body cannot exist outside of the society that gives it meaning. Even though bodies are biophysical entities, what our bodies mean and how they are experienced is intimately connected to the meanings and practices of the society in which we reside. In this way, bodies are like cultural artifacts; culture becomes embodied and is literally inscribed or represented through the body at the same time that the *objectification* of women's bodies (seeing the body as an object and separate from its context) is supported by the media and entertainment industries. Note how these norms about the body rely on a notion of the healthy and/or abled body.

Bodies, however, are not only reflections of social norms and practices but also sites of *identity* and *self-expression*. It has been suggested that as our lives become more complex and we have less power over the way we live our lives, we are encouraged to focus more on the body as something we *can* control and as something we can use to express our identity. As a result, the body becomes something to be fashioned and controlled; at the same time, this control over body—and the ability to shape, clothe, and express it—becomes synonymous with personal freedom.

Perhaps the current trend for tattoos and piercing among young women is an example of this trend toward self-expression in the context of mass-market consumerism. Having a tattoo, or multiple tattoos—traditionally a masculine or an outlaw, rebellious act—is increasingly a form of self-expression for women. Similarly, the current fad of multiple pierc-

LEARNING ACTIVITY: CONSIDERING BODY SIZE, SHAPE, AND MOVEMENT

Take a tour examining the public facilities of your school or campus, which may include:

Telephone booths or stalls

Drinking fountains

Bleachers

Sinks and stalls in public restrooms

Curbs, ramps, and railings

Chairs and tables

Turnstiles

Elevators and escalators

Stairs and staircases

Vending machines

Doors and doorways

Fire alarm boxes

Answer the following questions:

What assumptions about the size and shape of the users (height, weight, proportionate length of arms and legs, width of hips and shoulders, hand preference, mobility, etc.) are incorporated into the designs?

How do these design assumptions affect the ability of you and people you know to use the facilities satisfactorily?

How would they affect you if you were significantly:

Wider or narrower than you are?

Shorter or taller?

Heavier or lighter?

Rounder or more angular?

More or less mobile/ambulatory?

Identify any access or usage barriers to people with physical disabilities. Answer the following questions:

Are classrooms accessible to people who can't walk up or down stairs?

Are emergency exit routes usable by people with limited mobility?

Are amplification devices or sign language interpreters available for people with hearing impairments?

Are telephones and fire alarms low enough to be reached by people who are seated in wheelchairs or who are below average height?

Are audio-visual aids appropriate for people with hearing or vision impairments?

Describe the experience of a person in your class or school who has a mobility, vision, speech, or hearing impairment.

Variation 1. Identify one assumption incorporated into the design of one of the facilities (drinking fountain, phone booth, etc.). Gather formal or informal data about the number of people on campus that might not be able to use the facility satisfactorily, based on the design assumption. Suggest one or two ways to make the facility more useful to those people.

Variation 2. Choose one of the access or usage barriers you have identified and suggest a way to remove the barrier. Research the cost involved. Identify one or two ways of funding the access strategy you have suggested.

Source: Janet Lockhart and Susan M. Shaw, *Writing for Change: Raising Awareness of Difference, Power, and Discrimination, www.teachingtolerance.org.*

ing of many body parts, including erogenous and sexually charged areas of the body, can be seen as a form of rebellion against the constraints of gender. Both tattooing and piercing can also be interpreted as reactionary trends and as examples of the many ways women are encouraged to mutilate and change parts of their bodies. Note that these "rebellious" practices have now been appropriated as relatively ordinary fashion practices. You can buy nose and belly button rings, for example, that clip on without ever having to pierce anything, just as you can buy fake tattoos. In fact, the self-consciousness involved in the parody of the real thing is now a form of self-expression all its own. This issue of body image and its consequences for women's lives is a central issue for third wave feminism, mobilizing many young feminists. Amy Richards writes about this in "Body Image: Third Wave Feminism's Issue?"

Although men are taught to be concerned with their bodies and looks (and increasingly so given the advertising industry's desire to create a new market for beauty products), women are particularly vulnerable to the cultural preoccupation with the body. There is a *double standard* of beauty for women and men: Physical appearance is more important in terms of the way women are perceived and treated. This is especially true in terms of the aging body where there is a much stronger mandate for women to keep their bodies looking young.

We want to focus on two issues associated with the cultural preoccupation of women and the body: (1) the close relationship between women and nature and bodily functions, and (2) norms associated with appearance and beauty that help determine women's identity and worth. We examine these two issues next and then discuss eating disorders and methods for resisting the beauty ideal.

BODIES, NATURE, AND WOMEN

Although both women and men have bodies, an obvious aspect of the social construction of the body is that what female and male bodies stand for or signify implies different things in most cultures. Women have been associated with *nature:* the body, earth, and the do-

ACTIVIST PROFILE: MAGGIE KUHN

Most people are getting ready to retire at 65. Maggie Kuhn began the most important work of her life at that age. In 1970, Kuhn was forced to retire from her career with the Presbyterian Church. In August of that year, she convened a group of five friends, all of whom were retiring, to talk about the problems faced by retirees—loss of income, loss of social role, pension rights, age discrimination. Finding new freedom and strength in their voices, they also concerned themselves with other social issues, such as the Vietnam War.

The group gathered in Philadelphia with college students opposed to the war at the Consultation of Older and Younger Adults for Social Change. A year later, more than 100 people joined the Consultation. As this new group began to meet, a New York television producer nicknamed the group the Gray Panthers, and the name stuck.

In 1972, Kuhn was asked at the last minute to fill in for someone unable to speak during the 181st General Assembly of the United Presbyterian Church. Her stirring speech launched the Gray Panthers into national prominence, and calls began to flood the organization's headquarters. Increased media attention came as the Gray Panthers became activists. They co-sponsored the Black House Conference on Aging to call attention to the lack of African Americans at the first White House Conference on Aging, and they performed street theater at the American Medical Association's 1974 conference, calling for health care as a human right. At the core of Panther activities was the belief that older people should seize control of their lives and actively campaign for causes in which they believe.

The Gray Panthers have been instrumental in bringing about nursing home reform, ending forced retirement provisions, and combating fraud against the elderly in health care. Kuhn, who was active with the Panthers until her death at age 89, offered this advice to other activists: "Leave safety behind. Put your body on the line. Stand before the people you fear and speak your mind—even if your voice shakes. When you least expect it, someone may actually listen to what you have to say. Well-aimed slingshots can topple giants."

BODY ART

Across practically all times and cultures, humans have practiced various forms of body modification for such differing reasons as warding off or invoking spirits, attracting sexual partners, indicating social or marital status, identifying with a particular age or gender group, and marking a rite of passage (Lemonick et al.). People all over the world have pierced, painted, tattooed, reshaped, and adorned their bodies, turning the body itself into an artistic canvas.

The earliest records of tattoos were found in Egypt around the time of the building of the pyramids. Later, the practice was adopted in Crete, Greece, Persia, Arabia, and China. The English word *tattoo* comes from the Polynesian *tatau*, a practice observed by James Cook when he visited Tahiti on his first voyage around the world. In the Marquesas, Cook noted that the men were marked from head to foot, and, while the men had their entire bodies tattooed, women only tattooed their hands, lips, shoulders, ankles, and the area behind the ears.

Today, many of the Maori men of New Zealand are returning to the practice of wearing the elaborate tattoos of their ancestors. In Morocco, henna designs on the hands and feet are an integral part of significant celebrations, such as weddings and religious holidays. In Ethiopia, Hamar men earn raised scars made by cutting with a razor and then rubbing ash into the wounds for killing a dangerous animal or enemy. Surma girls have their earlobes stretched by clay plates and paint their faces during courtship season.

As you may have noted, body art is a gendered practice. Tattooing, piercing, painting, and reshaping the body also serve the purpose of marking gender. What are common body modification practices in the United States? How do these practices express and reinforce gender?

Sources: Monica Desai, "Body Art: A History." *Student BMJ* 10 (2002):196–197. Michael Lemonick et al. "Body Art." *Time South Pacific* (12/13/99), 66–68. Pravina Shukla, "The Human Canvas." *Natural History* 108 (1999): 80.

mestic, whereas men, because of historical and mythological associations with the spirit and sky, have been associated with *culture:* the mind rather than the body and abstract reason rather than earthly mundane matters. Importantly, Western civilizations have incorporated not only a distinction between nature and culture but also a domination of culture and mind over nature and body. In particular, Western societies' notions of progress have involved the taming and conquering of nature in favor of civilization. As a result, the female/nature side of this dichotomy is valued less and often denigrated.

A prime example of this is the way the normal processes of the female body have been seen as smelly, taboo, and distasteful. Menstruation is regarded negatively and described with a multitude of derogatory euphemisms like "the curse" and "on the rag," and girls are still taught to conceal menstrual practices from others (and men in particular). As Gloria Steinem suggests in the reading, "If Men Could Menstruate," the experience would be something entirely different if it was men who menstruated. Advertisements abound in magazines and on television about tampons, pads, douches, feminine hygiene sprays, and yeast infection medicines that give the message that women's bodies are constantly in need of hygienic attention. Notice we tend not to get ads for jock itch during prime-time television like

■ LEARNING ACTIVITY: ON THE RAG

Collect a wide variety of women's magazines such as *Cosmopolitan, Glamour, Vogue, Elle, Mirabella,* and so on. Identify advertisements for "feminine hygiene products"— tampons, pads, douches, feminine hygiene sprays, yeast infection medicines. What do the visual images in the ads suggest? What do the words tell readers? What messages do these advertisements send about women's bodies? Now collect a variety of men's magazines such as *GQ, Maxim, Men's Journal.* Identify advertisements for "masculine hygiene products." What do you find? What does the difference imply about women's bodies in contrast to men's bodies? How does this implication reinforce structures of gender subordination?

we do ads for feminine "ailments." In this way, there is a strange, very public aspect to feminine bodily processes at the same time that they are coded as very private.

These notions about women and the body have helped shape gender ideologies and reinforce *biological determinism,* a tendency that sees women in terms of their reproductive and biological selves. Male bodies are not so marked by these earthly reminders, and men have been able to imagine their bodies free of such constraints. And, as feminist scholars have reminded us, men as a group have been able to project their fears and anxieties about frailty and mortality onto women's flesh. Although these notions affect all of us in Western societies, women and men, it is important to understand that the body and its expressions have stronger repercussions in women's lives.

THE BEAUTY IDEAL

In this section we discuss four points associated with the beauty ideal. First, contemporary images of female beauty are changeable. What was considered beautiful or feminine for an aristocratic Elizabethan woman in Tudor England involved whitening the face, plucking eyelashes, and shaving back the hairline to show a prominent forehead—hardly beauty practices that would help you get a date in contemporary U.S. society. Some societies consider large women especially attractive and see their fat as evidence of prosperity; again, in most contemporary Western societies, thin is closer to standards of ideal beauty, although there are differences within specific ethnic communities within the United States. In other words, what is considered beautiful is culturally produced and therefore changes across time and across cultures.

A look at standards of female beauty over time reveals that in the nineteenth century White, privileged women were encouraged to adopt a delicate, thin, and fragile appearance and wear bone-crushing (literally) corsets that not only gave them the hourglass figure but also cramped and ruptured vital organs. These practices made women faint, appear frail, delicate, dependent, and passive—responses to nineteenth-century notions of middle-class femininity. Victorian furniture styles accommodated this ideal with special swooning chairs. Standards for weight and body shape changed again in the early twentieth century when a sleek, boyish look was adopted by the flappers of the 1920s. Women bound their breasts to hide their curves. Although more curvaceous and slightly heavier bodies were encouraged

HISTORICAL MOMENT: PROTESTING MISS AMERICA

In 1921, a group of hotel owners in Atlantic City came up with the idea to stage a bathing beauty contest to get tourists to stay in town after the Labor Day holiday. Eight finalists were chosen from photo entries in newspapers, and Margaret Gorman, representing Washington, DC, was crowned the first "Miss America" at the age of 16.

Throughout the rest of the twentieth century, the Miss America pageant continued to reinforce norms of the ideal woman. By 1968, the women's movement had begun to challenge beauty ideals and the ways women were judged by their appearance. In the days leading up to the 1968 pageant, members of the New York Radical Women made known their intentions to protest the oppressive image of the beauty queen. On September 7, as the winner paraded onstage, activists in the auditorium unfurled a women's liberation banner and chanted slogans. While people in the hall barely noticed the protest, network TV picked it up and broadcast it to the nation.

Outside the hall, 200 women protested. In a mock mini-pageant, protestors led out a sheep which they crowned as Miss America. Into a "Freedom Trash Can," they threw "instruments of torture"—girdles, curlers, false eyelashes, cosmetics, issues of *Cosmopolitan* and *Playboy*, and bras. While they had originally planned to set a fire in the can, they chose to comply with local fire regulations and did not. When a reporter asked Robin Morgan why, she explained that the mayor had been concerned about fire safety. She added, "We told him we wouldn't do anything dangerous—just a symbolic bra-burning." While the *New York Times* correctly reported no fire had been lit, only a few weeks later the paper referred to "bra-burning" as if it had actually taken place. The image caught on with the media, and, without reference to any reality, the media promoted the myth of the bra-burning feminist.

Source: Ruth Rosen, The World Split Open: How the Modern Women's Movement Changed America. New York: Viking, 2000.

through the next decades, body maintenance came to dominate many women's lives. Fueled by an emerging multi-million-dollar fashion industry, the 1960s gave us a return to a more emaciated, long-legged look, but with very short skirts and long hair. At the beginning of this new century, we see a more eclectic look and a focus on health and fitness, but norms associated with ideal female beauty still construct the thin, White (tanned, but not too brown) body as the beautiful body.

A second point concerning the beauty ideal is that the ideal reflects various relations of power in society. Culture is constructed in complex ways, and groups with more power and influence tend to set the trends, create the options, and enforce the standards. Standards tend not to be created by the ordinary women whose lives these beauty ideals affect. In our culture, beauty standards are very much connected to the production and consumption of various products, and, indeed, the beauty product and fashion industries are multi-billion-dollar enterprises. As the reading excerpted from Joan Jacobs Brumberg's *The Body Project* explains, garment industries in the United States helped sexualize women's breasts through their development of the bra. Corporate powers, advertising, and the fashion, cosmetics, and entertainment industries all help create standards for us and help reinforce gender relations. Even the "natural look" is sold to us as something to be tried on, when obviously the real natural look is devoid of marketing illusions in the first place. Most of these industries are controlled by White males or by other individuals who have accepted what many scholars call ruling-class politics. The main point is that most of us get offered beauty and fashion options constructed by other people. Although we have choices and can reject them, lots of resources are involved in encouraging us to adopt the standards created by various industries.

In this way, the beauty ideal offered to us reflects social power in that these standards tend to be White and middle class. White standards of beauty can humiliate fat or non-White women as well as the poor, the aged, and the disabled. In this way the norms help enforce racism, classism, ableism, ageism, and fat oppression, as well as sexism generally. Many ethnic communities, however, have alternative notions of feminine beauty and actively resist the normalizing standards of Anglo culture. Lisa Miya-Jervis understands the racial politics of appearance and explains in "Hold That Nose" why she avoided surgery to change the shape of her nose.

The third point concerning beauty practices is that standards are enforced in complex ways. Of course, "enforcement" does not mean, as Sandra Bartky has said, that someone marches you off to electrolysis at gunpoint. Instead, we adopt various standards, integrate them as choices we make for ourselves, and police one another in a general sense. Norms are internalized, and we receive various positive and negative responses for complying with or resisting them. It is interesting to think about the everyday practices we engage in to maintain the body: the seemingly trivial routines, rules, and practices. Some scholars call these *disciplinary practices*. They are "practices" because they involve such taken-for-granted routinized behaviors as shaving legs, applying makeup, or curling/straightening/coloring hair; and they are "disciplinary" because they involve social control in the sense that we spend time, money, effort, and imbue meaning in these practices. Again, disciplinary practices are connected to the production and consumption of various products. Of particular concern is the connection between weight control and smoking. A recent study from the National Institutes of Health reported that weight concerns and a "drive for thinness" among both Black and White girls at ages 11 to 12 were the most important factors leading to subsequent daily smoking (*www.nih.gov*).

BODY IMAGE QUIZ

INTRODUCTION

When was the last time you looked in the mirror and liked what you saw? Most women have to think long and hard before answering this question. Whether or not we admit it, women are active players in the beauty game, which requires us to think looks and body weight are the true sources of our happiness. The truth is women are their own worst critics when it comes to their bodies. Yet, experts tell us that self-esteem is closely tied to body image, even more so than our actual physical appearance. Take this quiz to learn more about body image and self-esteem.

1. In a national survey in which 200 women were asked, "If you could change one thing about your body, what would it be?" How many women said they would leave their bodies unchanged?
   a. 50
   b. 25
   c. 10
   d. 0

2. What percentage of American women overestimate their body size?
   a. 20 percent
   b. 35 percent
   c. 50 percent
   d. 95 percent

3. Which of the following do psychologists call "eating disorder breeding grounds" for women?
   a. Sports teams
   b. Dance troupes
   c. High schools and colleges
   d. Commercial weight loss programs
   e. All of the above

4. In a national survey, women were asked what they thought was the "peak age" for attractiveness. Which was the most frequent age answer from the following choices?
   a. 16
   b. 22
   c. 33
   d. 45

5. How many women in the United States suffer from eating disorders?
   a. 200,000
   b. 2 million
   c. 4 million
   d. 5 million
   e. 12 million

ANSWERS

1. d. 0. In a body image survey, conducted by Rita Freeman, Ph.D., the author of *Body-love: Learning to Like Our Looks—And Ourselves,* not a single woman out of 200

(continued)

was willing to leave her body alone. Body areas and/or conditions that women seem most dissatisfied with run from head to toe. Some of the body changes women wish for include wider eyes, freckles, longer legs, smaller feet, better posture, firmer thighs, thinner ankles, longer nails, and bigger breasts. Above all else, American women want to lose weight. Two-thirds of the women surveyed wanted to drop weight, particularly in the area between their waist and knees. Why such an obsession with weight loss? Psychologists say the reasons abound. Obviously American society sets unrealistic, even ridiculous standards by glorifying models who are dangerously thin. Psychologists say there is also a social tendency to associate good looks and thinness with success. It's called "looksism," and it is a form of stereotyping.

2. d. 95 percent. The condition of not being satisfied with one's weight is far more prevalent in women than men, and it includes American women of all races, ethnic groups, religions, professions, and economic classes. Most women who weigh in the normal, healthy range for their age and height still tend to consider themselves overweight. Many remain in a lifelong, futile diet mentality, thinking that life would be bliss if only they could lose 10 pounds. Two-thirds of all American women list fear of getting fat on their list of life's worst fears. Finally, women over age 60 report that gaining weight is their second most serious concern, with losing their memory as first.

   Many health care experts believe that women have a poor notion of what a healthy weight should be for themselves. Health care providers say that a healthy weight is based on several factors, including weight history (your weight, age, and activity level over several years), genetic factors, age, activity level, as well as other factors such as hormonal changes, stress, and use of nicotine and/or alcohol.

3. c. High schools and colleges. It is during the teenage years that many women first begin their unhealthy preoccupation with their body and appearance. On the brink of puberty, many girls describe a tremendous pressure to be feminine, which, sadly, often equates to being beautiful like a movie star and having an emaciated look. For this reason, eating disorders, such as anorexia and bulimia, are detected more frequently in high school girls and college women than in any other group.

4. c. 33. The good news in the results of this survey is that most women didn't check off the earliest age. Still, 33 is less than half the age expectancy for most women, and psychologists say that women should strive to accept themselves at every age and to see themselves as continuously attractive in a different, more mature way.

   A couple of myths exist on women and aging. Dispelling these myths may help women come to a better acceptance of themselves and their bodies.

   Myth 1: As time passes, more women become increasingly unhappy with their bodies. In reality, a survey showed that women in their 20s, 30s, and 40s said they felt no different about their bodies than they had earlier in life.

   Myth 2: With age women become even more self-conscious of their looks and minor imperfections. In reality, women become less self-conscious. Again, good news!

5. d. 5 million. Eating disorders are devastating mental illnesses that affect more than 5 million American women. Ninety percent of the people who suffer from anorexia nervosa and bulimia nervosa are women, according to the National Association of Anorexia Nervosa and Associated Disorders. Although they revolve around eating and body weight, eating disorders aren't about food, but about feelings and self-

expression. Women with eating disorders use food and dieting as ways of coping with life's stresses. For some, food becomes a source of comfort and nurturing or a way to control or release stress. For others, losing weight is a way to gain the approval of friends and family. Eating disorders are not diets, signs of personal weakness, or problems that will go away without treatment. And although the teenage years are considered a high-risk period for these eating disorders, women of all ages can experience the problem or have a relapse later in life.

Anorexia is a condition of self-induced starvation. The desire to lose weight becomes an obsession because the woman has a distorted body image and cannot see herself as anything but fat. Ten percent of women with anorexia die from it.

Bulimia is an eating disorder that involves binging and purging. A bulimic woman will eat a large quantity of food and then take separate measures to purge herself of the food by vomiting, taking laxatives, or heavy exercising.

If you think you may have an eating disorder, you should consult a health care provider. Eating disorders are complex medical and psychological conditions, but with therapy and medical intervention, they can be treated.

Source: www.electra.com/electraquiz/admin/Body_Image_Quiz.html.

You can probably think of many disciplinary practices that you or your friends take part in. Men have their practices too, although these tend to be simpler and involve a narrower range of products. Alongside fashion and various forms of cosmetics and body sculpting, women are more likely to get face-lifts, eye tucks, nose jobs, collagen injections to plump up lips, liposuction, tummy tucks, stomach stapling, and, of course, breast implants as well as breast reductions. By the early 1990s, more than 150,000 women a year were paying for breast implants, with about 80 percent for nonmedical reasons. The FDA (Food and Drug Administration) now requires women receiving silicone-gel breast implants to sign a "known risks" (leaking and rupture, loss of sensation in the nipples) and "possible risks" (fibrositis or pain and stiffness of muscles, ligaments, and tendons) clause. In considering these practices—from following fashion and buying clothes and accessories to makeup application to breast enhancement and all the other practices in between—it is important to keep in mind how much they cost, how they channel women's energies away from other, perhaps more productive, pursuits, and how they may affect health and well-being.

The body and the various practices associated with maintaining the female body are probably the most salient aspects of what we understand as femininity and are crucial in social expressions of sexuality. Note how many of these bodily practices that are so wound up with contemporary femininity encourage women to stay small, not take up space, and stay young. Maturity in the form of body hair is unacceptable; we are encouraged to keep our bodies sleek, soft, and hairless—traits that some scholars identify with youth and powerlessness.

The final point regarding the beauty ideal is that while it shapes women's bodies and lives, it is a huge aspect of corporate capitalism and U.S. consumerism. Enormous profits result from fashion, cosmetics, beauty, and entertainment industries yearly. It is important to remember that gendered beauty practices are related to specific products and commodities that women are encouraged to purchase. And, of course, the underlying message is that women are not good enough the way they are but need certain products to improve their looks or their relationships. This is not good for women's self-esteem in many cases. In addition, there is also a huge weight-loss industry in the United States. Millions of dollars are spent every year by people who seek to cram their bodies into smaller sizes. Of course, many individuals want to make their bodies smaller out of a concern for better health and mobility, and the weight and exercise industries help them attain these goals. But many have learned to despise flesh and fat and participate in these industries' profits out of a desire to more closely fit the cultural standard. Again, there is a double standard here whereby fat women have a harder time than fat men in our culture. This is not to say that fat men have an easy time; certainly prejudice against large-sized people is one of the last bulwarks of oppression in our society. Many people have no qualms about blatantly expressing their dislike and disgust for fat people even when they might keep sexist or racist attitudes hidden. However, fat women have an especially difficult time because of the interaction between sexism and fat phobia. In this way the beauty ideal supports the weight-loss industry and encourages lookism and fat oppression.

EATING DISORDERS

Contemporary eating disorders are compulsive behaviors that include *anorexia nervosa* (self-starvation) and *bulimia* (binge eating with self-induced vomiting and/or laxative use). They are serious problems with serious health consequences that can include death. Women with eating disorders tend to have a distorted body image and see themselves as fat and ugly irrespective of their weight and appearance. These problems are particularly rampant among young women aged 15 to 25 years and are especially prevalent on college campuses.

Many students who live in dorms and sororities report a high incidence of eating disorders; perhaps you have struggled with an eating disorder yourself or have had a close friend or sister similarly diagnosed. If the huge number of women who have various issues with food—always on a diet, overly concerned with weight issues, compulsive about what they do or do not eat—are also included in the figures on eating disorders, then the number of women with these problems increases exponentially. Indeed, one study has suggested that 80 percent of fifth-grade girls report being on a diet. Although this does not mean that 80 percent of these girls really *are* on a diet, it does highlight the way the discourses of dieting and bodily control are being internalized even by 10-year-old girls. Food and bodies are central preoccupations in so many women's lives. We need to ask, why women and why food?

First, women have long been associated with food and domestic pursuits; food preparation and focus on food is a socially accepted part of female cultural training. Given that women have been relegated to the private sphere of the home more than the public world, food consumption is easily accessible and unquestioned. Second, food is something that nourishes and gives pleasure. In our culture food has been associated with comfort and celebration, and it is easy to see how eating can be a way of dealing with the anxieties and unhappiness of life. Put these two together, and we get food as the object of compulsion; when we add the third factor, the beauty ideal, with all the anxieties associated with closely monitoring the size and shape of women's bodies, the result can be eating disorders.

Scholars also emphasize that eating disorders might reflect the ways that women desire self-control in the context of little power and autonomy. In other words, young women turn to controlling their bodies and attempt to sculpt them to perfection because they are denied

IDEAS FOR ACTIVISM

- Organize an eating disorders awareness event. Provide information about eating disorders and resources for help. Invite a therapist who specializes in treating eating disorders to speak. Create awareness posters to hang around your campus.
- Organize a letter-writing campaign to protest the representation of such a small range of women's shapes and sizes in a particular women's magazine.
- Organize a speak-out about beauty ideals.
- Organize a tattoo and piercing panel to discuss the politics of tattooing and piercing. Have a tattoo and piercing fashion show and discuss the meaning of the various tattoos/piercings.

power and control in other areas of their lives. Central in understanding eating disorders, however, is the pressure in our society for women to measure up to cultural standards of beauty and attractiveness, what Becky Wangsgaard Thompson in the reading "A Way Outa No Way" calls the "culture of thinness." These standards infringe on all our lives whether we choose to comply with them or resist them. Messages abound telling women that they are not good enough or beautiful enough, encouraging us to constantly change ourselves, often through the use of various products. The result is that girls learn early on that they must aspire to some often-unattainable standard of physical perfection. Such a bombardment affects girls' self-esteem and constantly assaults women's psyches as we age. In this way, eating disorders can be read as cultural statements about gender.

RESISTING THE BEAUTY IDEAL

Although many women strive to attain the beauty ideal on an ongoing, daily basis, some actively resist such cultural norms. These women are choosing to not participate in the beauty rituals, not support the industries that produce both images and products, and create other definitions of beauty. Some women are actively appropriating these standards by highlighting and/or exaggerating the very norms and standards themselves. They are carving out their own notions of beauty through their use of fashion and cosmetics. For them, empowerment involves playing with existing cultural standards. In "Dancing Toward Redemption," for example, Meredith McGhan shares her story of empowerment and acceptance as a topless dancer. Her story expresses the contradictions associated with gaining self-esteem in the midst of masculine entitlements and misogyny. In "Dreadlocked," another essay on identity and the body, Veronica Chambers explores the social meanings associated with hair and, in particular, how her dreadlocks came to help her form her own identity. Most women comply with some standards associated with the beauty ideal and resist others. We find a place that suits us, criticize some standards and practices and yet conform to others, usually learning to live with the various contradictions that this implies.

A question that might be raised in response to ideas about resisting beauty ideals and practices is, What's wrong with being beautiful? In response, feminists say that it is not beauty that is a problem, but rather the way that beauty has been constructed. This con-

LEARN TO LOVE YOUR BODY

Do you ever stand in front of the mirror dreaming about where you'd get a few nips and tucks? Or feeling like life would be better if only you had smaller thighs, a flatter tummy, or there was simply less of you? These are all signs of a not-so-hot body image.

It's important that you feel good about who you are. And until you like yourself as is, trying to change your body shape will be a losing proposition. High self-esteem is important for a healthy, balanced lifestyle—and it's a definite must if successful weight loss is one of your goals. So it's time to smile back at that image in the mirror and value all the wonderful characteristics about the person reflected there. Try these techniques:

1. *Recognize your special qualities.* Make a list of all your positive qualities—not including your physical traits. Are you kind? Artistic? Honest? Good in business? Do you make people laugh? Post your list near the mirror or another place where you'll see it every day.

2. *Put your body back together.* Most of us with negative body images have dissected our bodies into good and bad parts. "I hate my thighs and butt." "My butt's okay, but my stomach is fat and my arms are flabby." Reconnect with your body by appreciating how it all works to keep you going. Try stretching or yoga—the fluid movements are great for getting in touch with the wonders of the human body.

3. *Remember the kid inside you.* Give yourself permission not to be perfect. Inside all of us is the kid we used to be—the kid who didn't have to be perfect and worry about everything. Remember that kid, and give yourself a break. Place a photo of yourself as a child in your bedroom or at your desk at work, so you can see it each day and remember to nurture yourself and laugh a little.

4. *Enjoy your food.* Eating is pleasurable. So enjoy it! Food gives us energy and sustains life. Don't deprive yourself or consider eating an evil act. If you allow yourself to enjoy some of the foods you like, you'll be less likely to overeat. In turn, your body won't feel bloated and uncomfortable.

5. *Indulge in body pleasures.* One step toward being kind to your body, and inevitably yourself, is to indulge yourself. Get a massage, take a long, hot bath, use lotions that smell good, or treat yourself to a manicure or pedicure.

6. *Speak positively.* Pay attention to your self-talk. It's amazing how often we put ourselves down throughout the day. Each time you catch yourself making critical comments, fight back by immediately complimenting yourself.

7. *See the world realistically.* It's common to compare ourselves to people in magazines or movies, but this can make you feel self-conscious. If you want to compare yourself to others, look at the real people around you. They come in different shapes and sizes—and none of them are airbrushed or highlighted.

8. *Dress in clothes that fit.* When we feel badly about our bodies, we often dress in shabby clothes, waiting until we lose weight before we buy something we like. But why? Feel good now! Find attractive clothes that fit your current size. Treating yourself will make you feel renewed.

9. *Be active.* Movement and exercise can make you and your body feel terrific. Not only does exercise help boost your mood, it stimulates your muscles, making you feel more alive and connected to your body.

10. *Thrive!* Living well will help you feel better about who you are and how you look. Strive to make your personal and professional lives fulfilling. You are a unique, amazing person. A healthy, happy life can be all yours!

Source: www.thriveonline.com/shape/countdown/countdown.feature2.week7.html.

struction excludes many beautiful women and helps maintain particular (and very restricted) notions of femininity. Maya Angelou's poem "Phenomenal Woman" celebrates female beauty and encourages women to rejoice in themselves and their looks.

Another common question is, Can you wear makeup and enjoy the adornments associated with femininity and still call yourself a feminist? Most feminists answer with a resounding yes. In fact, you can claim back these trappings and go ultra-femme in celebration of your femininity and your right to self-expression. What is important from a feminist perspective is that these practices are *conscious*. In other words, when women take part in various reproductions of femininity, it is important to understand the bigger picture and be aware of the ways the beauty ideal works to limit women, encourages competitiveness (Is she better looking than me? Who is the cutest woman here? How do I measure up?), and ultimately tends to lower women's self-esteem. Understand also how many beauty products are tested on animals, how the packaging of cosmetics and other beauty products encourages the use of resources that end up polluting the environment, and how many fashion items are made by child and/or sweatshop global labor. The point is for us to make conscious and informed choices about our relationships to the beauty ideal and to love and take care of our bodies.

READING 32

Breast Buds and the "Training" Bra

Joan Jacobs Brumberg

In every generation, small swellings around the nipples have announced the arrival of puberty. This development, known clinically as "breast buds," occurs before menarche and almost always provokes wonder and self-scrutiny. "I began to examine myself carefully, to search my armpits for hairs and my breasts for signs of swelling," wrote Kate Simon about coming of age in the Bronx at the time of World War I. Although Simon was "horrified" by the rapidity with which her chest developed, many girls, both in literature and real life, long for this important mark of maturity. In Jamaica Kincaid's fictional memoir of growing up in Antigua, *Annie John*, the main character regarded her breasts as "treasured shrubs, needing only the proper combination of water and sunlight to make them flourish." In order to get their breasts to grow, Annie and her best friend, Gwen, lay in a pasture exposing their small bosoms to the moonlight.

Breasts are particularly important to girls in cultures or time periods that give powerful meaning or visual significance to that part of the body. Throughout history, different body parts have been eroticized in art, literature, photography, and film. In some eras, the ankle or upper arm was the ultimate statement of female sexuality. But breasts were the particular preoccupation of Americans in the years after World War II, when voluptuous stars, such as Jayne Mansfield, Jane Russell, and Marilyn Monroe, were popular box-office attractions. The mammary fixation of the 1950s extended beyond movie stars and shaped the experience of adolescents of both genders. In that era, boys seemed to prefer girls who were "busty," and American girls began to worry about breast size as well as about weight. This elaboration of the ideal of beauty raised expectations about what adolescent girls should look like. It also required them to put even more energy and resources into their body projects, beginning at an earlier age.

The story of how this happened is intertwined with the history of the bra, an undergarment that came into its own, as separate from the corset, in the early twentieth century. In 1900, a girl of twelve or thirteen typically wore a one-piece "waist" or camisole that had no cups or darts in front. As her breasts developed, she moved into different styles of the same garment, but these had more construction, such as stitching, tucks, and bones, that would accentuate the smallness of her waist and shape the bosom. In those days, before the arrival of the brassiere, there were no "cups." The bosom was worn low; there was absolutely no interest in uplift, and not a hint of cleavage.

The French word *brassière*, which actually means an infant's undergarment or harness, was used in *Vogue* as early as 1907. In the United States, the first boneless bra to leave the midriff bare was developed in 1913 by Mary Phelps Jacobs, a New York City debutante. Under the name Caresse Crosby, Jacobs marketed a bra made of two French lace handkerchiefs suspended from the shoulders. Many young women in the 1920s, such as Yvonne Blue, bought their first bras in order to achieve the kind of slim, boyish figure that the characteristic chemise (or flapper) dress required. The first bras were designed simply to flatten, but they were superseded by others intended to shape and control the breasts. Our current cup sizes (A, B, C, and D), as well as the idea of circular stitching to enhance the roundness of the breast, emerged in the 1930s.

Adult women, not adolescents, were the first market for bras. Sexually maturing girls simply moved into adult-size bras when they were ready—and if their parents had the money. Many women and girls in the early twentieth century still made their own underwear at home, and some read the advertisements for bras with real longing. When she began to develop breasts in the 1930s, Malvis Helmi, a midwestern farm girl, remembered feeling embarrassed whenever she wore an old summer dimity that pulled and gaped across her expanding chest. As a result, she spoke to her mother, considered the brassieres in the Sears, Roebuck catalog, and decided to purchase two for twenty-five cents. However, when her hardworking father saw the order form, he vetoed the idea and declared, "Our kind of people can't afford to spend money on such nonsense." Although her mother made her a makeshift bra, Malvis vowed that someday she would have store-bought brassieres. Home economics teachers in the interwar years tried to get high school girls to make their own underwear because it saved money, but the idea never caught on once mass-produced bras became widely available.

The transition from homemade to mass-produced bras was critical in how adolescent girls thought about their breasts. In general, mass-produced clothing fostered autonomy in girls because it took matters of style and taste outside the dominion of the mother, who had traditionally made and supervised a girl's wardrobe. But in the case of brassieres, buying probably had another effect. So long as clothing was made at home, the dimensions of the garment could be adjusted to the particular body intended to wear it. But with store-bought clothes, the body had to fit instantaneously into standard sizes that were constructed from a pattern representing a norm. When clothing failed to fit the body, particularly a part as intimate as the breasts, young women were apt to perceive that there was something wrong with their bodies. In this way, mass-produced bras in standard cup sizes probably increased, rather than diminished, adolescent self-consciousness about the breasts.

Until the 1950s, the budding breasts of American girls received no special attention from either bra manufacturers, doctors, or parents. Girls generally wore undershirts until they were sufficiently developed to fill an adult-size bra. Mothers and daughters traditionally handled this transformation in private, at home. But in the gyms and locker rooms of postwar junior high schools, girls began to look around to see who did and did not wear a bra. Many of these girls had begun menstruating and developing earlier than their mothers had, and this visual information

was very powerful. In some circles, the ability to wear and fill a bra was central to an adolescent girl's status and sense of self. "I have a figure problem," a fourteen-year-old wrote to *Seventeen* in 1952: "All of my friends are tall and shapely while my figure still remains up-and-down. Can you advise me?"

In an era distinguished by its worship of full-breasted women, interest in adolescent breasts came from all quarters: girls who wanted bras at an earlier age than ever before; mothers who believed that they should help a daughter acquire a "good" figure; doctors who valued maternity over all other female roles; and merchandisers who saw profits in convincing girls and their parents that adolescent breasts needed to be tended in special ways. All of this interest coalesced in the 1950s to make the brassiere as critical as the sanitary napkin in making a girl's transition into adulthood both modern and successful.

The old idea that brassieres were frivolous or unnecessary for young girls was replaced by a national discussion about their medical and psychological benefits. "My daughter who is well developed but not yet twelve wants to wear a bra," wrote a mother in Massachusetts to *Today's Health* in 1951. "I want her to wear an undervest instead because I think it is better not to have anything binding. What do you think about a preadolescent girl wearing a bra?" That same year a reader from Wilmington, Delaware, asked *Seventeen*: "Should a girl of fourteen wear a bra? There are some older women who insist we don't need them." The editor's answer was an unequivocal endorsement of early bras: "Just as soon as your breasts begin to show signs of development, you should start wearing a bra." By the early 1950s, "training" or "beginner" bras were available in AAA and AA sizes for girls whose chests were essentially flat but who wanted a bra nonetheless. Along with acne creams, advertisements for these brassieres were standard fare in magazines for girls.

Physicians provided a medical rationale for purchasing bras early. In 1952, in an article in *Parents' Magazine*, physician Frank H. Crowell endorsed bras for young girls and spelled out a theory and program of teenage breast management. "Unlike other organs such as the stomach and intestines which have ligaments that act as guywires or slings to hold them in place," Crowell claimed, the breast was simply "a growth developed from the skin and held up only by the skin." An adolescent girl needed a bra in order to prevent sagging breasts, stretched blood vessels, and poor circulation, all of which would create problems in nursing her future children. In addition, a "dropped" breast was "not so attractive," Crowell said, so it was important to get adolescents into bras early, before their breasts began to sag. The "training" that a training bra was supposed to accomplish was the first step toward motherhood and a sexually alluring figure, as it was defined in the 1950s.

In the interest of both beauty and health, mothers in the 1950s were encouraged to check their daughters' breasts regularly to see if they were developing properly. This was not just a matter of a quick look and a word of reassurance. Instead, Crowell and others suggested systematic scrutiny as often as every three months to see if the breasts were positioned correctly. One way to chart the geography of the adolescent bustline was to have the girl stand sideways in a darkened room against a wall covered with white paper. By shining a bright light on her and having her throw out her chest at a provocative angle, a mother could trace a silhouette that indicated the actual shape of her daughter's bosom. By placing a pencil under her armpit, and folding the arm that held it across the waist, mothers could also determine if their daughter's nipples were in the right place. On a healthy breast, the nipple was supposed to be at least halfway above the midway point between the location of the pencil and the hollow of the elbow.

Breasts were actually only one part of a larger body project encouraged by the foundation garment industry in postwar America. In this era, both physicians and entrepreneurs promoted a general philosophy of "junior figure control." Companies such as Warners, Maidenform, Formfit, Belle Mode, and Perfect Form (as well as popular magazines like *Good Housekeeping*) all encouraged the idea that young women needed both lightweight girdles and bras to "start the figure off to a beautiful future."

The concept of "support" was aided and abetted by new materials—such as nylon netting and two-way stretch fabrics—developed during the war but applied afterward to women's underwear. By the early 1950s, a reenergized corset and brassiere industry

was poised for extraordinary profits. If "junior figure control" became the ideal among the nation's mothers and daughters, it would open up sales of bras and girdles to the largest generation of adolescents in American history, the so-called baby boomers. Once again, as in the case of menstruation and acne, the bodies of adolescent girls had the potential to deliver considerable profit.

There was virtually no resistance to the idea that American girls should wear bras and girdles in adolescence. Regardless of whether a girl was thin or heavy, "junior figure control" was in order, and that phrase became a pervasive sales mantra. "Even slim youthful figures will require foundation assistance," advised *Women's Wear Daily* in 1957. In both *Seventeen* and *Compact*, the two most popular magazines for the age group, high school girls were urged to purchase special foundation garments such as "Bobbie" bras and girdles by Formfit and "Adagio" by Maidenform that were "teen-proportioned" and designed, allegedly, with the help of adolescent consultants. The bras were available in pastel colors in a variety of special sizes, starting with AAA, and they were decorated with lace and ribbon to make them especially feminine. In addition to holding up stockings, girdles were intended to flatten the tummy and also provide light, but firm, control for hips and buttocks. The advertisements for "Bobbie," in particular, suggested good things about girls who controlled their flesh in this way; they were pretty, had lots of friends, and drank Coca-Cola. As adults, they would have good figures and happy futures because they had chosen correct underwear in their youth.

By the mid-1950s, department stores and specialty shops had developed aggressive educational programs designed to spread the gospel of "junior figure control." In order to make young women "foundation conscious," Shillito's, a leading Cincinnati department store, tried to persuade girls and their mothers of the importance of having a professional fitting of the first bra. Through local newspaper advertisements, and also programs in home economics classes, Shillito's buyer, Edith Blincoe, promoted the idea that the purchase of bras and girdles required special expertise, which only department stores could provide. (*Seventeen* echoed her idea and advised a "trained fitter" for girls who wanted a "prettier" bosom and a "smoother" figure.) Blincoe acknowledged that teenage girls were already "100% bra conscious," and she hoped to develop the same level of attention to panty girdles. In order to attract junior customers and get them to try on both items, she had the corset department place advertising cards on the walls of dressing rooms in sections of the store where teenagers and their mothers shopped. Strapless bras were suggested on cards in the dress and formal wear departments; light-weight girdles were suggested in the sportswear and bathing suit sections.

In home economics classes, and also at the local women's club, thousands of American girls saw informational films such as *Figure Forum* and *Facts About Your Figure,* made by the Warner Brassiere Company in the 1950s. Films like these stressed the need for appropriate foundation garments in youth and provided girls with scientific principles for selecting them. They also taught young women how to bend over and lean into their bras, a maneuver that most of us learned early and still do automatically. Most middle-class girls and their mothers embraced the code of "junior figure control" and spent time and money in pursuit of the correct garments. Before a school dance in 1957, Gloria James, a sixteen-year-old African-American girl, wrote in her diary: "Mommy and I rushed to Perth Amboy [New Jersey] to get me some slacks, bras and a girdle. I don't even know how to get it [the girdle] on."

In the postwar world, the budding adolescent body was big business. Trade publications, such as *Women's Wear Daily,* gave special attention to sales strategies and trends in marketing to girls. In their reports from Cincinnati, Atlanta, and Houston, one thing was clear: wherever American girls purchased bras, they wanted to be treated as grown-ups, even if they wore only a AAA or AA cup. In Atlanta, at the Redwood Corset and Lingerie Shop, owner Sally Blye and her staff spoke persuasively to young customers about the importance of "uplift" in order "not to break muscle tissue." And at Houston's popular Teen Age Shop, specially trained salesgirls allowed young customers to look through the brassieres on their own, and then encouraged them to try on items in the dressing room without their mothers. Although many girls were shy at first, by the age of fourteen and

fifteen most had lost their initial self-consciousness. "They take the merchandise and go right in [to the dressing room]," Blincoe said about her teenage clientele. Girls who could not be reached by store or school programs could send away to the Belle Mode Brassiere Company for free booklets about "junior figure control" with titles such as "The Modern Miss—Misfit or Miss Fit" and "How to Be Perfectly Charming." In the effort to help girls focus on their figures, Formfit, maker of the popular "Bobbies," offered a free purse-size booklet on calorie counting.

Given all this attention, it's not surprising that bras and breasts were a source of concern in adolescents' diaries written in the 1950s. Sandra Rubin got her first bra in 1951, when she was a twelve-year-old in Cleveland, but she did not try it on in a department store. Instead, her mother bought her a "braziere" while she was away on a trip and sent it home. "It's very fancy," Sandra wrote. "I almost died! I ran right upstairs to put it on." When she moved to New York City that September and entered Roosevelt Junior High School, Sandra got involved with a clique of seven girls who called themselves the "7Bs." Their name was not about their homeroom; it was about the cup size they wanted to be. "Flat, Flat! The air vibrates with that name as my friends and I walk by," Sandra wrote in a humorous but self-deprecating manner. By the time she was sixteen, Sandra had developed amply, so that her breasts became a source of pride. One night she had an intimate conversation with a male friend about the issue of chests: "We talked about flat-chested women (of which, he pointed out, I certainly am not [one])."

Breasts, not weight, were the primary point of comparison among high school girls in the 1950s. Although Sandra Rubin called herself a "fat hog" after eating too much candy, her diary reportage was principally about the bosoms, rather than the waistlines, she saw at school. Those who had ample bosoms seemed to travel through the hallways in a veritable state of grace, at least from the perspective of girls who considered themselves flat-chested. "Busty" girls made desirable friends because they seemed sophisticated, and they attracted boys. In December 1959, when she planned a Friday-night pajama party, thirteen-year-old Ruth Teischman made a courageous move by inviting the "gorgeous" Roslyn, a girl whom she wrote about frequently but usually only worshiped from afar. After a night of giggling and eating with her junior high school friends, Ruth revealed in her diary the source of Roslyn's power and beauty: "Roslyn is very big. (Bust of course.) I am very flat. I wish I would get bigger fast." Many girls in the 1950s perused the ads, usually in the back of women's magazines, for exercise programs and creams guaranteed to make their breasts grow, allegedly in short order.

The lament of the flat-chested girl—"I must, I must, I must develop my bust"—was on many private hit parades in the 1950s. There was a special intensity about breasts because of the attitudes of doctors, mothers, and advertisers, all of whom considered breast development critical to adult female identity and success. Although "junior figure control" increased pressure on the entire body, and many girls wore waist cinches as well as girdles, it was anxiety about breasts, more than any other body part, that characterized adolescent experience in these years. As a result, thousands, if not millions, of girls in early adolescence jumped the gun and bought "training bras" at the first sight of breast buds, or they bought padded bras to disguise their perceived inadequacy. In the 1950s, the bra was validated as a rite of passage: regardless of whether a girl was voluptuous or flat, she was likely to purchase her first bra at an earlier age than had her mother. This precocity was due, in part, to biology, but it was also a result of entrepreneurial interests aided and abetted by medical concern. By the 1950s, American society was so consumer-oriented that there were hardly any families, even among the poor, who would expect to make bras for their daughters the way earlier generations had made their own sanitary napkins.

Training bras were a boon to the foundation garment industry, but they also meant that girls' bodies were sexualized earlier. In contemporary America, girls of nine or ten are shepherded from undershirts into little underwear sets that come with tops that are protobrassieres. Although this may seem innocuous and natural, it is not the same as little girls "dressing up" in their mother's clothing. In our culture, traditional distinctions between adult clothing and juvenile clothing have narrowed considerably, so that mature women dress "down," in the garments of kids, just as often as little girls dress "up." While the age homogeneity of the contemporary wardrobe helps adult women feel less matronly, dressing little girls in adult clothing can have an insidious side effect. Because a bra shapes the breasts in accordance with fashion, it acts very much like an interpreter, translating functional anatomy into a sexual or erotic vocabulary. When we dress little girls in brassieres or bikinis, we imply adult behaviors and, unwittingly, we mark them as sexual objects. The training bras of the 1950s loom large in the history of adolescent girls because they foreshadowed the ways in which the nation's entrepreneurs would accommodate, and also encourage, precocious sexuality.

READING 33

If Men Could Menstruate

Gloria Steinem

A white minority of the world has spent centuries conning us into thinking that a white skin makes people superior—even though the only thing it really does is make them more subject to ultraviolet rays and to wrinkles. Male human beings have built whole cultures around the idea that penis-envy is "natural" to women—though having such an unprotected organ might be said to make men vulnerable, and the power to give birth makes womb-envy at least as logical.

In short, the characteristics of the powerful, whatever they may be, are thought to be better than the characteristics of the powerless—and logic has nothing to do with it.

What would happen, for instance, if suddenly, magically, men could menstruate and women could not?

The answer is clear—menstruation would become an enviable, boast-worthy, masculine event:

Men would brag about how long and how much.

Boys would mark the onset of menses, the longed-for proof of manhood, with religious ritual and stag parties.

Congress would fund a National Institute of Dysmenorrhea to help stamp out monthly discomforts.

Sanitary supplies would be federally funded and free. (Of course, some men would still pay for the prestige of commercial brands such as John Wayne Tampons, Muhammad Ali's Rope-a-dope Pads, Joe Namath Jock Shields—"For Those Light Bachelor Days," and Robert "Barretta" Blake Maxi-Pads.)

Military men, right-wing politicians, and religious fundamentalists would cite menstruation ("*men*struation") as proof that only men could serve in the Army ("you have to give blood to take blood"), occupy political office ("can women be aggressive without that stead-fast cycle governed by the planet Mars?"), be priests and ministers ("how could a woman give her blood for our sins?"), or rabbis ("without the monthly loss of impurities, women remain unclean").

Male radicals, left-wing politicians, and mystics, however, would insist that women are equal, just different; and that any woman could enter their ranks if only she were willing to self-inflict a major wound every month ("you *must* give blood for the revolution"), recognize the preeminence of menstrual issues, or subordinate her selfness to all men in their Cycle of Enlightenment.

Street guys would brag ("I'm a three-pad man") or answer praise from a buddy ("Man, you lookin' *good!*") by giving fives and saying, "Yeah, man, I'm on the rag!"

TV shows would treat the subject at length. ("Happy Days": Richie and Potsie try to convince Fonzie that he is still "The Fonz," though he has missed two periods in a row.) So would newspapers. (SHARK SCARE THREATENS MENSTRUATING MEN. JUDGE CITES MONTHLY STRESS IN PARDONING RAPIST.) And movies. (Newman and Redford in "Blood Brothers"!)

Men would convince women that intercourse was *more* pleasurable at "that time of the month." Lesbians would be said to fear blood and therefore life itself—though probably only because they needed a good menstruating man.

Of course, male intellectuals would offer the most moral and logical arguments. How could a woman master any discipline that demanded a sense of time, space, mathematics, or measurement, for instance, without that in-built gift for measuring the cycles of the moon and planets—and thus for measuring anything at all? In the rarefied fields of philosophy and religion, could women compensate for missing the rhythm of the universe? Or for their lack of symbolic death-and-resurrection every month?

Liberal males in every field would try to be kind: the fact that "these people" have no gift for measuring life or connecting to the universe, the liberals would explain, should be punishment enough.

And how would women be trained to react? One can imagine traditional women agreeing to all these arguments with a staunch and smiling masochism. ("The ERA would force housewives to wound themselves every month": Phyllis Schlafly. "Your husband's blood is as sacred as that of Jesus—and so sexy, too!": Marabel Morgan.) Reformers and Queen Bees would try to imitate men, and *pretend* to have a monthly cycle. All feminists would explain endlessly that men, too, needed to be liberated from the false idea of Martian aggressiveness, just as women needed to escape the bonds of menses-envy. Radical feminists would add that the oppression of the nonmenstrual was the pattern for all other oppressions. ("Vampires were our first freedom fighters!") Cultural feminists would develop a bloodless imagery in art and literature. Socialist feminists would insist that only under capitalism would men be able to monopolize menstrual blood. . . . In fact, if men could menstruate, the power justifications could probably go on forever.

If we let them.

•

READING 34

Body Image
Third Wave Feminism's Issue?

Amelia (Amy) Richards

In the United States, each wave of feminism has fought its own battles with body image. The suffragists of the late nineteenth and early twentieth centuries rebelled against corsets and fought the characterization of women's-righters as unfeminine, homely and pretentious "blue-stockings." In the 1960s and '70s, the second wave of feminists fought stereotyping that pegged them as humorless, ugly and anti-sex. Women struggled to be taken seriously, to be more than just pretty faces and pin-up girls. They wanted to be defined by their minds rather than their bodies.

In the late 1990s, among the rising third wave of feminists, image and body are at the center of feminist analysis. For many women, our bodies have become the canvasses upon which our struggles paint themselves. Body image, in fact, may be the pivotal third wave issue—the common struggle that mobilizes the current feminist generation.

The first two waves of feminism were organized movements, with clearly defined goals. The first wave fought to establish women's right to be citizens—to vote, own property, divorce and inherit money. The second wave's agenda was to elevate women's status to that of men.

In the third wave, we've expanded the fight for equal status. We are aware of the need to express our various identities—racial, ethnic, sexual, political, religious and class—as well as our feminist identity. This individuality is necessary, but it also poses a challenge. Because we now have many different paths to—and definitions of—empowerment, it's become difficult to organize a unified movement. In this wave of feminism, you're as likely to run into women who defend, enjoy and create pornography as you are to come across feminists who see pornography as the ultimate oppressor. You are also likely to find women who are tired of the pressure to act and look "perfect." Others pack their feminist toolkits

with lipstick and nail polish, forgetting that while lipstick and nail polish aren't feminist concerns, the right to choose—or not choose—them is.

It's also difficult to unite everyone under an umbrella term like feminism when the third wave feminist vocabulary has been co-opted by the media. For example, "girl power" has been transformed from an expression of individuality and empowerment to a slick marketing slogan. And many women have taken the bait, assuming that the "girl power" label comes complete with feminist securities such as reproductive freedom, freedom from violence and other issues played out on women's bodies.

To unite today's young women, we need to focus on a particular issue and then bring together the diverse feminist opinions on the matter to create a rich, complex dialogue. Better to disagree than to be silent, to fill out feminism rather than trim it down.

Second wave feminists named our struggles—domestic violence, sexual harassment, equal pay for work of equal value, which had lain silenced until then—and lobbied for laws that would protect us. Now, our generation has turned the focus inward. Tellingly, our relationships with our bodies often signal how far we still have to go. It is evident not only in how we treat them, but in how their role continues to permeate our existence and dictate our lives.

So where do we begin? Although "body image" won't make it into Congress, related issues will—for instance, sports, reproductive rights and affirmative action. As young feminists, we can point out how these individual and personal issues are linked to a larger political agenda.

Body image is significant as a rallying focus because it speaks not only to the converted but also to the "I'm not a feminist, but . . . I'm tired of measuring myself against an impossible-to-achieve beauty standard" contingent. It can catalyze our dormant or displaced activism, primarily because it's both a cultural and a political issue—and we are a pop culture–driven generation. Mention teen magazines, for example, and many young women react viscerally, offering stories of how fat/ugly/ethnic/misfitting/self-hating the magazines made them feel. Even young women who don't identify as feminists offer heartfelt and complex emotions on the topic.

Perhaps that's why much of third wave feminism has centered on pop culture, rather than legal and political strategies. Our activism is directed at our most visible "oppressors"—the media and entertainment industries. Rather than holding marches or rallies, many young women create zines, websites, music, films and videos that counter images we deem insulting or dangerous.

In the visual world of the late twentieth century, however, the outside counts as well as the inside. We use our appearance—bodies, clothing, style—to express our inner convictions, our pride, our affiliations, our identities, our insecurities and our weaknesses. In a generation focused on identity issues—and unafraid to show them to the public—our bodies, and how we adorn them, can express who we are.

But, as young women redesign feminism, we run the risk of being misinterpreted as all image, no substance—as having no collective agenda. Too often, image becomes a convenient cover-up for issues we haven't resolved, just as eating disorders often manifest more deeply rooted problems such as childhood abuse.

We have to be careful not to fall into the trap of only having our bodies and our images speak for who we are—what we think, what we feel, what we do. Images and slogans are too easily co-opted and robbed of the substance they have the potential to convey. Instead, we must take this opportunity to seize control of our bodies and the forces that manipulate them—mostly the advertising and entertainment industries.

A feminist world is often where women find themselves when they get fed up with the representation of women in the media. It's a place to express all the rage, realization and healing that follow—and to find a support community of people who have had similar experiences. Once feminists reach a point of understanding that we are not these images—that we don't have to look like Claudia Schiffer to be beautiful—then what? The silence, at that point, is deafening. We're supposed to go out and educate other women about loving their bodies, to save them from eating disorders. But if, as leaders, we dare to expose our own unresolved body image issues, we have to worry about tarnishing our feminist credibility. We're not supposed to have those problems anymore.

But we do. I do. As a feminist, I feel helpless at times, caught in a double standard. At "Ask Amy," my online feminist advice column, I confront painfully honest letters from young women who are dealing with their own eating disorders or body issues. What do I tell them? I could ignore the fact that the women we see thriving are those who fall under the rubric of athletic, attractive, slim, good-looking, fit, healthy. I could forget that, statistically, thin women have a greater chance of being accepted to elite colleges than heavier women do even if their credentials are identical; and that it isn't poverty that causes obesity, but obesity that causes poverty. But I see it as my responsibility to be honest with my correspondents. Body image issues, like most any other painful life experience, become less difficult once an open dialogue begins. So my advice usually includes my own experience. I tell them how I struggled with bulimia and how I eventually realized that developing my own identity is more important than pleasing other people.

The road to a solution is certainly a feminist one. It includes women creating our own beauty standards rather than following those dictated by corporations. It includes pointing out that this problem affects men, too. (Men are only slightly less likely to be concerned about their body image than women are, and a reported 10 percent of those suffering from eating disorders are men.) It means better sex education and more forums to talk about body image. But we can't stop there. We must create a dialogue that extends beyond these forums and into our daily lives, a dialogue that leads us to less shame, less denial and more room for individuality. It's up to the third wave of feminism to make sure this conversation continues and that a support network exists.

READING 35

"A Way Outa No Way"
Eating Problems Among African–American, Latina, and White Women

Becky Wangsgaard Thompson

Bulimia, anorexia, binging, and extensive dieting are among the many health issues women have been confronting in the last 20 years. Until recently, however, there has been almost no research about eating problems among African–American, Latina, Asian–American, or Native American women, working-class women, or lesbians.[1] In fact, according to the normative epidemiological portrait, eating problems are largely a white, middle-, and upper-class heterosexual phenomenon. Further, while feminist research has documented how eating problems are fueled by sexism, there has been almost no attention to how other systems of oppression may also be implicated in the development of eating problems.

In this article, I reevaluate the portrayal of eating problems as issues of appearance based in the "culture of thinness." I propose that eating problems begin as ways women cope with various traumas including sexual abuse, racism, classism, sexism, heterosexism, and poverty. Showing the interface between these traumas and the onset of eating problems explains why women may use eating to numb pain and cope with violations to their bodies. This theoretical shift also permits an understanding of the economic, political, social, educational, and cultural resources that women need to change their relationship to food and their bodies.

. . .

Methodology

I conducted 18 life history interviews and administered lengthy questionnaires to explore eating problems among African–American, Latina, and White women. I employed a snowball sample, a method in which potential respondents often first learn about the study from people who have already participated. This method was well suited for the study since it enabled women to get information about me and the interview process from people they already knew. Typically, I had much contact with the respondents prior to the interview. This was particularly important given the secrecy associated with this topic (Russell 1986; Silberstein, Striegel-Moore, and Rodin 1987), the necessity of women of color and lesbians to be discriminating about how their lives are studied, and the fact that I was conducting across-race research.

. . .

Demographics of the Women in the Study

The women I interviewed included 5 African–American women, 5 Latinas, and 8 White women. Of these women, 12 are lesbian and 6 are heterosexual. Five women are Jewish, 8 are Catholic, and 5 are Protestant. Three women grew up outside of the United States. The women represented a range of class backgrounds (both in terms of origin and current class status) and ranged in age from 19 to 46 years old (with a median age of 33.5 years).

The majority of the women reported having had a combination of eating problems (at least two of the following: bulimia, compulsive eating, anorexia, and/or extensive dieting). In addition, the particular types of eating problems often changed during a woman's life span. (For example, a woman might have been bulimic during adolescence and anorexic as an adult.) Among the women, 28 percent had been bulimic, 17 percent had been bulimic and anorexic, and 5 percent had been anorexic. All of the women who had been anorexic or bulimic also had a history of compulsive eating and extensive dieting. Of the women, 50 percent were compulsive eaters and dieters (39 percent) or compulsive eaters (11 percent) but had not been bulimic or anorexic.

Two-thirds of the women have had eating problems for more than half of their lives, a finding that contradicts the stereotype of eating problems as transitory. The weight fluctuation among the women varied from 16 to 160 pounds, with an average fluctuation of 74 pounds. This drastic weight change illustrates the degree to which the women adjusted to major changes in body size at least once during their lives as they lost, gained, and lost weight again. The average age of onset was 11 years old, meaning that most of the women developed eating problems prior to puberty. Almost all of the women (88 percent) consider themselves as still having a problem with eating, although the majority believe they are well on the way to recovery.

The Interface of Trauma and Eating Problems

One of the most striking findings in this study was the range of traumas the women associated with the origins of their eating problems, including racism, sexual abuse, poverty, sexism, emotional or physical abuse, heterosexism, class injuries, and acculturation.[2] The particular constellation of eating problems among the women did not vary with race, class, sexuality, or nationality. Women from various race and class backgrounds attributed the origins of their eating problems to sexual abuse, sexism, and emotional and/or physical abuse.

Among some of the African–American and Latina women, eating problems were also associated with poverty, racism, and class injuries. Heterosexism was a key factor in the onset of bulimia, compulsive eating, and extensive dieting among some of the lesbians. These oppressions are not the same nor are the injuries caused by them. And certainly, there are a variety of potentially harmful ways that women respond to oppression (such as using drugs, becoming a workaholic, or committing suicide). However,

for all these women, eating was a way of coping with trauma.

Sexual Abuse

Sexual abuse was the most common trauma that the women related to the origins of their eating problems. Until recently, there has been virtually no research exploring the possible relationship between these two phenomena. Since the mid-1980s, however, researchers have begun identifying connections between the two, a task that is part of a larger feminist critique of traditional psychoanalytical symptomatology (DeSalvo 1989; Herman 1981; Masson 1984). Results of a number of incidence studies indicate that between one-third and two-thirds of women who have eating problems have been abused (Oppenheimer et al. 1985; Root and Fallon 1988). . . .

Among the women I interviewed, 61 percent were survivors of sexual abuse (11 of the 18 women), most of whom made connections between sexual abuse and the beginning of their eating problems. Binging was the most common method of coping identified by the survivors. Binging helped women "numb out" or anesthetize their feelings. Eating sedated, alleviated anxiety, and combated loneliness. Food was something that they could trust and was accessible whenever they needed it. . . .

Extensive dieting and bulimia were also ways in which women responded to sexual abuse. Some women thought that the men had abused them because of their weight. They believed that if they were smaller, they might not have been abused. For example when Elsa, an Argentine woman, was sexually abused at the age of 11, she thought her chubby size was the reason the man was abusing her. Elsa said, "I had this notion that these old perverts liked these plump girls. You heard adults say this too. Sex and flesh being associated." Looking back on her childhood, Elsa believes she made fat the enemy partly due to the shame and guilt she felt about the incest. Her belief that fat was the source of her problems was supported by her socialization. Raised by strict German governesses in an upper-class family, Elsa was taught that a woman's weight was a primary criterion for judging her worth. Her mother "was socially conscious of walking into places with a fat daughter and maybe people staring at her." Her father often referred to Elsa's body as "shot to hell." When asked to describe how she felt about her body when growing up, Elsa described being completely alienated from her body. . . .

As is true for many women who have been abused, the split that Elsa described between her body and soul was an attempt to protect herself from the pain she believed her body caused her. In her mind her fat body was what had "bashed in her dreams." Dieting became her solution, but, as is true for many women in the study, this strategy soon led to cycles of binging and weight fluctuation. . . .

These women's experiences suggest many reasons why women develop eating problems as a consequence of sexual abuse. Most of the survivors "forgot" the sexual abuse after its onset and were unable to retrieve the abuse memories until many years later. With these gaps in memory, frequently they did not know why they felt ashamed, fearful, or depressed. When sexual abuse memories resurfaced in dreams, they often woke feeling upset but could not remember what they had dreamed. These free floating, unexplained feelings left the women feeling out of control and confused. Binging or focusing on maintaining a new diet were ways women distracted or appeased themselves, in turn, helping them regain a sense of control. As they grew older, they became more conscious of the consequences of these actions. Becoming angry at themselves for binging or promising themselves they would not purge again was a way to direct feelings of shame and self-hate that often accompanied the trauma.

Integral to this occurrence was a transference process in which the women displaced onto their bodies painful feelings and memories that actually derived from or were directed toward the persons who caused the abuse. Dieting became a method of trying to change the parts of their bodies they hated, a strategy that at least initially brought success as they lost weight. Purging was a way women tried to reject the body size they thought was responsible for the abuse. Throwing up in order to lose the weight they thought was making them vulnerable to the abuse was a way to try to find the body they had lost when the abuse began.

Poverty

Like sexual abuse, poverty is another injury that may make women vulnerable to eating problems. One woman I interviewed attributed her eating problems directly to the stress caused by poverty. Yolanda is a Black Cape Verdean mother who began eating compulsively when she was 27 years old. After leaving an abusive husband in her early 20s, Yolanda was forced to go on welfare. As a single mother with small children and few financial resources, she tried to support herself and her children on $539 a month. Yolanda began binging in the evenings after putting her children to bed.

Eating was something she could do alone. It would calm her, help her deal with loneliness, and make her feel safe. Food was an accessible commodity that was cheap. She ate three boxes of macaroni and cheese when nothing else was available. As a single mother with little money, Yolanda felt as if her body was the only thing she had left. . . . When she was eating, Yolanda felt a momentary reprieve from her worries. Binging not only became a logical solution because it was cheap and easy but also because she had grown up amid positive messages about eating. In her family, eating was a celebrated and joyful act. However, in adulthood, eating became a double-edged sword. While comforting her, binging also led to weight gain. During the three years Yolanda was on welfare, she gained seventy pounds.

Yolanda's story captures how poverty can be a precipitating factor in eating problems and highlights the value of understanding how class inequalities may shape women's eating problems. As a single mother, her financial constraints mirrored those of most female heads of households. The dual hazards of a race- and sex-stratified labor market further limited her options (Higginbotham 1986). . . .

The fact that many women use food to anesthetize themselves, rather than other drugs (even when they gained access to alcohol, marijuana, and other illegal drugs), is partly a function of gender socialization and the competing demands that women face. One of the physiological consequences of binge eating is a numbed state similar to that experienced by drinking. Troubles and tensions are covered over as a consequence of the body's defensive response to massive food intake. When food is eaten in that way, it effectively works like a drug with immediate and predictable effects. Yolanda said she binged late at night rather than getting drunk because she could still get up in the morning, get her children ready for school, and be clearheaded for the college classes she attended. By binging, she avoided the hangover or sickness that results from alcohol or illegal drugs. In this way, food was her drug of choice since it was possible for her to eat while she continued to care for her children, drive, cook, and study. Binging is also less expensive than drinking, a factor that is especially significant for poor women. Another woman I interviewed said that when her compulsive eating was at its height, she ate breakfast after rising in the morning, stopped for a snack on her way to work, ate lunch at three different cafeterias, and snacked at her desk throughout the afternoon. Yet even when her eating had become constant, she was still able to remain employed. While her patterns of eating no doubt slowed her productivity, being drunk may have slowed her to a dead stop.

Heterosexism

The life history interviews also uncovered new connections between heterosexism and eating problems. One of the most important recent feminist contributions has been identifying compulsory heterosexuality as an institution which truncates opportunities for heterosexual and lesbian women (Rich 1986). All of the women interviewed for this study, both lesbian and heterosexual, were taught that heterosexuality was compulsory, although the versions of this enforcement were shaped by race and class. Expectations about heterosexuality were partly taught through messages that girls learned about eating and their bodies. In some homes, boys were given more food than girls, especially as teenagers, based on the rationale that girls need to be thin to attract boys. As the girls approached puberty, many were told to stop being athletic, begin wearing dresses, and watch their weight. For the woman who weighed more than was considered acceptable, threats about their need to diet were laced with admonitions that being fat would ensure becoming an "old maid."

While compulsory heterosexuality influenced all of the women's emerging sense of their bodies and eating patterns, the women who linked heterosexism directly to the beginning of their eating problems were those who knew they were lesbians when very young and actively resisted heterosexual norms. One working-class Jewish woman, Martha, began compulsively eating when she was 11 years old, the same year she started getting clues of her lesbian identity. In junior high school, as many of her female peers began dating boys, Martha began fantasizing about girls, which made her feel utterly alone. Confused and ashamed about her fantasies, Martha came home every day from school and binged. Binging was a way she drugged herself so that being alone was tolerable. Describing binging, she said, "It was the only thing I knew. I was looking for a comfort." Like many women, Martha binged because it softened painful feelings. Binging sedated her, lessened her anxiety, and induced sleep.

Martha's story also reveals ways that trauma can influence women's experience of their bodies. Like many other women, Martha had no sense of herself as connected to her body. When I asked Martha whether she saw herself as fat when she was growing up she said, "I didn't see myself as fat. I didn't see myself. I wasn't there. I get so sad about that because I missed so much." In the literature on eating problems, *body image* is the term that is typically used to describe a woman's experience of her body. This term connotes the act of imagining one's physical appearance. Typically, women with eating problems are assumed to have difficulties with their body image. However, the term body image does not adequately capture the complexity and range of bodily responses to trauma experienced by the women. Exposure to trauma did much more than distort the women's visual image of themselves. These traumas often jeopardized their capacity to consider themselves as having bodies at all.

Given the limited connotations of the term body image, I use the term *body consciousness* as a more useful way to understand the range of bodily responses to trauma.[3] By body consciousness I mean the ability to reside comfortably in one's body (to see oneself as embodied) and to consider one's body as connected to oneself. The disruptions to their body consciousness that the women described included leaving their bodies, making a split between their body and mind, experiencing being "in" their bodies as painful, feeling unable to control what went in and out of their bodies, hiding in one part of their bodies, or simply not seeing themselves as having bodies. Binging, dieting, or purging were common ways women responded to disruptions to their body consciousness.

Racism and Class Injuries

For some of the Latinas and African-American women, racism coupled with the stress resulting from class mobility related to the onset of their eating problems. Joselyn, an African-American woman, remembered her White grandmother telling her she would never be as pretty as her cousins because they were lighter skinned. Her grandmother often humiliated Joselyn in front of others, as she made fun of Joselyn's body while she was naked and told her she was fat. As a young child, Joselyn began to think that although she could not change her skin color, she could at least try to be thin. When Joselyn was young, her grandmother was the only family member who objected to Joselyn's weight. However, her father also began encouraging his wife and daughter to be thin as the family's class standing began to change. When the family was working class, serving big meals, having chubby children, and keeping plenty of food in the house was a sign the family was doing well. But, as the family became mobile, Joselyn's father began insisting that Joselyn be thin. She remembered, "When my father's business began to bloom and my father was interacting more with White businessmen and seeing how they did business, suddenly thin became important. If you were a truly well-to-do family, then your family was slim and elegant."

As Joselyn's grandmother used Joselyn's body as territory for enforcing her own racism and prejudice about size, Joselyn's father used her body as the territory through which he channeled the demands he faced in the white-dominated business world. However, as Joselyn was pressured to diet, her father still served her large portions and bought treats for her and the neighborhood children. These contradictory messages made her feel confused about her body. As

was true for many women in this study, Joselyn was told she was fat beginning when she was very young even though she was not overweight. And, like most of the women, Joselyn was put on diet pills and diets before even reaching puberty, beginning the cycles of dieting, compulsive eating, and bulimia.

. . .

The fact that some of the African-American and Latina women associated the ambivalent messages about food and eating to their family's class mobility and/or the demands of assimilation while none of the eight White women expressed this (including those whose class was stable and changing) suggests that the added dimension of racism was connected to the imperative to be thin. In fact, the class expectations that their parents experienced exacerbated standards about weight that they inflicted on their daughters.

Eating Problems as Survival Strategies

Feminist Theoretical Shifts

My research permits a reevaluation of many assumptions about eating problems. First, this work challenges the theoretical reliance on the culture-of-thinness model. . . .

Establishing links between eating problems and a range of oppressions invites a rethinking of both the groups of women who have been excluded from research and those whose lives have been the basis of theory formation. The construction of bulimia and anorexia as appearance-based disorders is rooted in a notion of femininity in which White middle- and upper-class women are portrayed as frivolous, obsessed with their bodies, and overly accepting of narrow gender roles. This portrayal fuels women's tremendous shame and guilt about eating problems—as signs of self-centered vanity. This construction of White middle- and upper-class women is intimately linked to the portrayal of working-class White women and women of color as their opposite: as somehow exempt from accepting the dominant standards of beauty or as one step away from being hungry and therefore not susceptible to eating problems. Identifying that women may binge to cope with poverty contrasts the notion that eating problems are class bound. Attending to the intricacies of race, class, sexuality, and gender pushes us to rethink the demeaning construction of middle-class femininity and establishes bulimia and anorexia as serious responses to injustices.

Understanding the link between eating problems and trauma also suggests much about treatment and prevention. Ultimately, their prevention depends not simply on individual healing but also on changing the social conditions that underlie their etiology. As Bernice Johnson Reagon sings in Sweet Honey in the Rock's song "Oughta Be a Woman," "A way outa no way is too much to ask/too much of a task for any one woman" (Reagon 1980).[4] Making it possible for women to have healthy relationships with their bodies and eating is a comprehensive task. Beginning steps in this direction include insuring that (1) girls can grow up without being sexually abused, (2) parents have adequate resources to raise their children, (3) children of color grow up free of racism, and (4) young lesbians have the chance to see their reflection in their teachers and community leaders. Ultimately, the prevention of eating problems depends on women's access to economic, cultural, racial, political, social, and sexual justice.

NOTES

Author's Note The research for this study was partially supported by an American Association of University Women Fellowship in Women's Studies. An earlier version of this article was presented at the New England Women's Studies Association Meeting in 1990 in Kingston, Rhode Island. I am grateful to Margaret Andersen, Liz Bennett, Lynn Davidman, Mary Gilfus, Evelynn Hammonds, and two anonymous reviewers for their comprehensive and perceptive comments on earlier versions of this article.

1. I use the term *eating problems* as an umbrella term for one or more of the following: anorexia, bulimia, extensive dieting, or binging. I avoid using the term eating disorder because it categorizes the problems as individual pathologies, which deflects attention away from the social inequalities underlying them (Brown 1985). However, by using the term *problem* I do not wish to imply blame. In fact, throughout, I argue that the eating strategies that women develop begin as logical solutions to problems, not problems themselves.

2. By trauma I mean a violating experience that has long-term emotional, physical, and/or spiritual consequences that may have immediate or delayed effects.

One reason the term *trauma* is useful conceptually is its association with the diagnostic label Post Traumatic Stress Disorder (PTSD) (American Psychological Association 1987). PTSD is one of the few clinical diagnostic categories that recognizes social problems (such as war or the Holocaust) as responsible for the symptoms identified (Trimble 1985). This concept adapts well to the feminist assertion that a woman's symptoms cannot be understood as solely individual, considered outside of her social context, or prevented without significant changes in social conditions.

3. One reason the term *consciousness* is applicable is its intellectual history as an entity that is shaped by social context and social structures (Delphy 1984; Marx 1964). This link aptly applies to how the women described their bodies because their perceptions of themselves as embodied (or not embodied) directly relate to their material conditions (living situations, financial resources, and access to social and political power).

4. Copyright © 1980. Used by permission of Songtalk Publishing.

REFERENCES

American Psychological Association. 1987. *Diagnostic and statistical manual of mental disorders.* 3rd ed. rev. Washington, DC: American Psychological Association.

Brown, Laura S. 1985. Women, weight and power: Feminist theoretical and therapeutic issues. *Women and Therapy* 4:61–71.

Delphy, Christine. 1984. *Close to home: A materialist analysis of women's oppression.* Amherst: University of Massachusetts Press.

DeSalvo, Louise. 1989. *Virginia Woolf: The impact of childhood sexual abuse on her life and work.* Boston, MA: Beacon.

Herman, Judith. 1981. *Father-daughter incest.* Cambridge, MA: Harvard University Press.

Higginbotham, Elizabeth. 1986. We were never on a pedestal: Women of color continue to struggle with poverty, racism and sexism. In *For crying out loud,* edited by Rochelle Lefkowitz and Ann Withorn, Boston, MA: Pilgrim Press.

Marx, Karl. 1964. *The economic and philosophic manuscripts of 1844.* New York: International.

Masson, Jeffrey. 1984. *The assault on the truth: Freud's suppression of the seduction theory.* New York: Farrar, Strauss & Giroux.

Oppenheimer, R., K. Howells, R. L. Palmer, and D. A. Chaloner. 1985. Adverse sexual experience in childhood and clinical eating disorders: A preliminary description. *Journal of Psychiatric Research* 19:357–61.

Reagon, Bernice Johnson. 1980. Oughta be a woman. On Sweet Honey in the Rock's album, *Good News.* Music by Bernice Johnson Reagon; lyrics by June Jordan. Washington, DC: Songtalk.

Rich, Adrienne. 1986. Compulsory heterosexuality and lesbian existence. In *Blood, bread and poetry.* New York: Norton.

Root, Maria P. P., and Patricia Fallon. 1988. The incidence of victimization experiences in a bulimic sample. *Journal of Interpersonal Violence* 3:161–73.

Russell, Diana E. 1986. *The secret trauma: Incest in the lives of girls and women.* New York: Basic Books.

Silberstein, Lisa, Ruth Striegel-Moore, and Judith Rodin. 1987. Feeling fat: A woman's shame. In *The role of shame in symptom formation,* edited by Helen Block Lewis. Hillsdale, NJ: Lawrence Erlbaum.

Trimble, Michael. 1985. Post-traumatic stress disorder: History of a concept. In *Trauma and its wake: The study and treatment of post-traumatic stress disorder* edited by C. R. Figley. New York: Brunner/Mazel.

READING 36

Dreadlocked

Veronica Chambers

I have two relationships with the outside world: One is with my hair, and the other is with the rest of me. Sure, I have concerns and points of pride with my body. I like the curve of my butt but dislike my powerhouse thighs. My breasts, once considered too small, have been proclaimed perfect so often that not only am I starting to believe the hype, but also am booking my next vacation to a topless resort in Greece. But my hair. Oh my hair.

I have reddish brown dreadlocks that fall just below shoulder length. Eventually, they will cover my aforementioned breasts, at which time I will give serious thought to nude modeling at my local art school. I like my hair—a lot. But over the last eight years my dreadlocks have conferred upon me the following roles: rebel child, Rasta mama, Nubian princess, drug dealer, unemployed artist, rock star, world-famous comedienne, and nature chick. None of which is true. It has occurred to me more than once that my hair is a whole lot more interesting than I am.

Because I am a black woman, I have always had a complicated relationship with my hair. Here's a quick primer on the politics of hair and beauty aesthetics in the black community vis-à-vis race and class in the late 20th century: "Good" hair is straight and, preferably, long. Think Naomi Campbell. Diana Ross. For that matter, think RuPaul. "Bad" hair is thick and coarse, aka "nappy," and, often, short. Think Buckwheat in *The Little Rascals.* Not the more recent version, but the old one in which Buckwheat looked like Don King's grandson.

Understand that these are stereotypes: broad and imprecise. Some will say that the idea of "good" hair and "bad" hair is outdated. And it is less prevalent than in the '70s when I was growing up. Sometimes I see little girls with their hair in braids and Senegalese twists sporting cute little T-shirts that say HAPPY TO BE NAPPY and I get teary-eyed. I was born between the black power Afros of the '60s and the blue contact lenses and weaves of the '80s; in my childhood, no one seemed happy to be nappy at all.

I knew from the age of 4 that I had "bad" hair because my relatives and family friends discussed it as they might discuss a rare blood disease. "Something must be done," they would cluck sadly. "I think I know someone," an aunt would murmur, referring to a hairdresser as if she were a medical specialist. Some of my earliest memories are of Brooklyn apartments where women did hair for extra money. These makeshift beauty parlors were lively and loud, the air thick with the smell of lye from harsh relaxer, the smell of hair burning as the hot straightening comb did its job.

When did I first begin to desire hair that bounced? Was it because black Barbie wasn't, and still isn't, happy to be nappy? Was it Brenda, the redhead, my best friend in second grade? Every time she flicked her hair to the side, she seemed beyond sophistication. My hair bounced the first day back from the hairdresser's, but not much longer. "Don't sweat out that perm," my mother would call. But I found it impossible to sit still. Hairdressers despaired like cowardly lion tamers at the thought of training my kinky hair. "This is some hard hair," they would say. I knew that I was not beautiful and I blamed it on my hair.

The night I began to twist my hair into dreads, I was 19 and a junior in college. It was New Year's Eve and the boy I longed for had not called. A few months before, Alice Walker had appeared on the cover of *Essence,* her locks flowing with all the majesty of a Southern American Cleopatra. I was inspired. It was my family's superstition that the hours between New Year's Eve and New Year's Day were the time to cast spells. "However New Year's catches you is how you'll spend the year," my mother always reminded me.

I decided to use the hours that remained to transform myself into the vision I'd seen on the magazine. Unsure of how to begin, I washed my hair, carefully and lovingly. I dried it with a towel, then opened a jar of hair grease. Using a comb to part the sections, I began to twist each section into baby dreads. My hair, at the time, couldn't have been longer than an inch. I twisted for two hours, and in the end was far from smitten with what I saw: My full cheeks dominated my face now that my hair lay in flat twists around my head. My already short hair seemed shorter. I did not look like the African goddess I had imagined. I emerged from the bathroom and ran into my aunt Diana, whose luxuriously long, straight black hair always reminded me of Diahann Carroll on *Dynasty.* "Well, Vickie," she said, shaking her head. "Well, well." I knew that night my life would begin to change. I started my dreadlocks and began the process of seeing beauty where no one had ever seen beauty before.

There are, of course, those who see my hair and still consider it "bad." A family friend touched my hair recently, then said, "Don't you think it's a waste? All that lovely hair twisted in those things?" I have been asked by more than one potential suitor if I had any pictures of myself before "you did that to your hair." A failure at small talk and countless other social graces, I sometimes let my hair do the talking for me. At a cocktail party, I stroll though the room, silently, and watch my hair tell white lies. In literary circles, it brands me "interesting, adventurous." In black middle-class circles, I'm "rebellious" or, more charitably, "Afrocentric." In predominantly white circles, my hair doubles my level of exotica. My hair says, "Unlike the black woman who reads you the evening news, I'm not even trying to blend in."

For those ignorant enough to think that they can read hair follicles like tea leaves, my hair says a lot of things it doesn't mean. Taken to the extreme, it says that I am a pot-smoking Rastafarian wannabe who in her off-hours strolls through her house in an African dashiki, lighting incense and listening to Bob Marley. I don't smoke pot. In my house, I wear Calvin Klein nightshirts, and light tuberose candles that I buy from Diptyque in Paris. I play tennis in my off-hours and, while I love Bob Marley, I mostly listen to jazz vocalists like Ella Fitzgerald and Diana Krall.

Once after a dinner party in Beverly Hills, a white colleague of mine lit up a joint. Everyone at the table passed and when I passed too, the man cajoled me relentlessly. "Come on," he kept saying. "Of all people, I thought you'd indulge." I shrugged and said nothing. As we left the party that night, he kissed me good-bye. "Boy, were you a disappointment," he said, as if I had been a bad lay. But I guess I had denied him a certain sort of pleasure. It must have been his dream to smoke a big, fat spliff with a real live Rastafarian.

As much as I hate to admit it, I've been trained to turn my head to any number of names that aren't mine. I will answer to "Whoopi." I will turn when Jamaican men call out "Hey, Rasta" on the street. I am often asked if I am a singer, and I can only hope that I might be confused with the gorgeous Cassandra Wilson, whose dreadlocks inspired me to color my hair a jazzy shade of red. Walking through the streets of Marrakesh, I got used to trails of children who would follow me, trying to guess which country I came from. "Jamaica!" they would shout. "Ghana!

Nigeria!" I shook my head no to them all. They did not believe me when I said I was from America; instead, they called me "Mama Africa" all day long. It's one of my favorite memories of the trip.

Once, after the end of a great love affair, I watched a man cut all of his dreadlocks off and then burn them in the backyard. This, I suspect, is the reason that might tempt me to change my hair. After all, a broken heart is what started me down this path of twisting hair. Because I do not cut my hair, I carry eight years of history on my head. One day, I may tire of this history and start anew. But one thing is for sure, whatever style I wear my hair in, I will live happily—and nappily—ever after.

READING 37

Hold That Nose

Lisa Miya-Jervis

I'm a Jew. I'm not even slightly religious. Aside from attending friends' bat mitzvahs, I've been to temple maybe twice. I don't know Hebrew; my junior-high self, given the option of religious education, easily chose to sleep in on Sunday mornings. My family skips around the Passover Haggadah to get to the food faster. Before I dated someone from an observant family, I wouldn't have known a mezuzah if it bit me on the butt. I was born assimilated.

But still, I'm a Jew, an ethnic Jew of a very specific variety: a godless, New York City–raised, neurotic middle-class girl from a solidly liberal-Democratic family, who attended largely Jewish, "progressive" schools. When I was growing up, almost everyone around me was Jewish; I was stunned when I found out that Jews make up only 2 percent of the American population. For me, being Jewish meant that on Christmas Day my family went out for Chinese food and took in the new Woody Allen movie. It also meant that I had a big honkin' nose.

And I still do. By virtue of my class and its sociopolitical trappings, I always knew I had the option to have my nose surgically altered. From adolescence on, I've had a standing offer from my mother to pay for a nose job.

"It's not such a big deal."

"Doctors do such individual-looking noses these days, it'll look really natural."

"It's not too late, you know," she would say to me for years after I flat-out refused to let someone break my nose, scrape part of it out, and reposition it into a smaller, less obtrusive shape. "I'll still pay." As if money were the reason I was resisting.

My mother thought a nose job was a good idea. See, she hadn't wanted one either. But when she was 16, her parents demanded that she get that honker "fixed," and they didn't take no for an answer. She insists that she's been glad ever since, although she usually rationalizes that it was good for her social life. (She even briefly dated a guy she met in the surgeon's waiting room, a boxer having his deviated septum corrected.)

Even my father is a believer. He says that without my mother's nose job, my sister and I wouldn't exist, because he never would have gone out with Mom. I take this with an entire salt lick. My father thinks that dressing up means wearing dark sneakers; that pants should be purchased every 20 years—and then only if the old ones are literally falling apart; and that haircuts should cost $10 and take as many minutes. The only thing he says about appearances is, "You have some crud . . ." as he picks a piece of lint off your sleeve. But he cared about the nose? Whatever.

Even though my mother is happy with her tidy little surgically altered nose, she wasn't going to put me through the same thing, and for that I am truly grateful. I'm also unspeakably glad that her comments stayed far from the "you'd be so pretty if you did" angle. I know a few people who weren't so lucky. Not that they were dragged kicking and screaming to the doctor's office; no, they were coerced and shamed into it. Seems it was their family's decision more than their own—usually older female relatives: mothers, grandmothers, aunts.

What's the motivation for that kind of pressure? Can it be that for all the strides made against racism and anti-Semitism, Americans still want to expunge their ethnicity from their looks? Were these mothers and grandmothers trying to fit their offspring into a more white, gentile mode? Possibly. Well, definitely. But on purpose? Probably not. Their lust for the button nose is probably more a desire for a typical femininity than for any specific de-ethnicizing. But given the society in which we live, the proximity of WASPy white features to the ideal of beauty is no coincidence. I think that anyone who opts for a nose job today (or who pressures her daughter to get one) would say that the reason for the surgery is to look "better" or "prettier." But when we scratch the surface of what "prettier" means, we find that we might as well be saying "whiter" or "more gentile" (I would add "bland," but that's my personal opinion).

Or perhaps the reason is to become unobtrusive. The stereotypical Jewish woman is loud and pushy —qualities girls really aren't supposed to have. So is it possible that the nose job is supposed to usher in not only physical femininity but a psychological, traditional femininity as well? Bob your nose, and become feminine in both mind and body. (This certainly seems to be the way it has worked with Courtney Love, although her issue is class more than ethnicity. But it's undeniable that her new nose comes with a Versace-shilling, tamed persona, in stark contrast to her old messy, outspoken self.)

Even though I know plenty of women with their genetically determined schnozzes still intact, sometimes I still feel like an oddity. From what my mother tells me, nose jobs were as compulsory a rite of passage for her peers as multiple ear-piercings were for mine. Once, when I was still in high school, I went with my mother to a Planned Parenthood fundraiser, a cocktail party in a lovely apartment, with

lovely food and drink, and a lovely short speech by Wendy Wasserstein. But I was confused: We were at a lefty charity event in Manhattan, and all the women had little WASP noses. (Most of them were blond, too, but that didn't really register. I guess hair dye is a more universal ritual.)

"Why are there no Jewish women here?" I whispered to my mother. She laughed, but I think she was genuinely shocked. "What do you mean?" she asked. "All of these women are Jewish." And then it hit me: It was wall-to-wall rhinoplasties. And worse, there was no reason to be surprised. These were women my mother's age or older who came of age in the late '50s or before, when anti-Semitism in this country was much more overt than it is today. Surface assimilation was practically the norm back then, and those honkers were way too, ahem, big a liability on the dating and social scenes. Nose jobs have declined since then. They're no longer among the top five plastic surgeries, edged out by liposuction and laser skin resurfacing.

I don't think it's a coincidence that, growing up in New York, I didn't consider my nose an "ethnic" feature. Almost everyone around me had that ethnicity, too. It wasn't until I graduated from college and moved to California that I realized how marked I was. I also realized how much I like being instantly recognizable to anyone who knows how to look. I once met another Jewish woman at a conference in California. In the middle of our conversation, she randomly asked, "You're Jewish, right?" I replied, "With this nose and this hair, you gotta ask?" We both laughed. The question was just a formality, and we both knew it.

Only once did I feel uneasy about being "identified." At my first job out of college, my boss asked, after I mentioned an upcoming trip to see my family, "So, are your parents just like people in Woody Allen movies?" I wondered if I had a sign on my forehead reading "Big Yid Here." His comment brought up all those insecurities American Jews have that, not coincidentally, Woody Allen loves to emphasize for comic effect: Am I *that* Jewish? I felt conspicuous, exposed. Still, I'm glad I have the sign on my face, even if it's located a tad lower than my forehead.

Judaism is the only identity in which culture and religion are supposedly bound closely: If you're Irish and not a practicing Catholic, you can still be fully Irish; being Buddhist doesn't specify race or ethnicity. To me, being a Jew is cultural, but it's tied only marginally—even hypothetically—to religion, and mostly to geography (New York Jews are different from California Jews, lemme tell ya). So what happens when identity becomes untied from religion? I don't know for sure. And that means I'll grab onto anything I need to keep that identity—including my nose.

READING 38

Dancing Toward Redemption

Meredith McGhan

When I remove my top during the second song, the audience claps and cheers. I look at them now, not really afraid anymore, just a little nervous. I recognize genuine lust in some of the men's eyes. I can hardly believe it — they think I'm sexy, me. These men are strangers— strangers who typify The American Male and what he wants. These are the men who hide Playboy *under their beds. They're clapping, cheering and coming up to the stage to tuck bills into my thong. Exhilarated, I walk off-stage, wanting more of their attention, more of their money. I count the bills in my waistband—ten dollars for a ten-minute routine. I had done it! I had guts. I had nerve. I had power.*

And so began my career as a topless dancer.

When I tell people that I used to strip for a living, they're always surprised. "What? You, a feminist?" There's an immediate, visceral association. Exotic dancers are supposed to be hard, jaded and, well, not exactly bright. Aside from supporting our various drug addictions, we dance because we're so economically oppressed we can't recognize our own exploitation. We're tall, bleached-blond bimbos with breast implants, who occasionally appear on *Jerry Springer* to reveal our "secret" occupations to shocked parents and boyfriends, followed by a gratis studio performance.

I don't fit the expectation. I've never had a guy beg me to "quit the profession" on national TV. I'm also a middle-class white chick with a master's degree in women's studies, a woman who's far shorter and heavier than the buff Demi Moore in *Striptease* or the lean, leggy Elizabeth Berkley of *Showgirls*. And I'm neither blonde nor tan. But I often think that my not being a Demi or an Elizabeth propelled me into the sex industry, where, ironically or not, I pieced together a new self-image.

The women's movement has always faltered when feminist sex workers bring their voices to the discourse. There's a hesitation to support the premise that women can *choose* to do this work, that feminism should advocate for women's rights to use sexual power in a professional way. Many feminists strongly disagree that sex work offers women an element of choice at all—and to an extent that may be true. After all, we live in a system that makes it difficult for women to earn as much money in jobs that don't involve their beauty or their sexuality.

Still, I never got the impression that any of my co-workers felt trapped in their jobs, unable to leave or forced into dancing—at least not anymore than anyone else working in the blue or white-collar worlds. The dancers I met came from a variety of situations. Some, like me, were artists or students looking for a part-time job that paid a lot and left them with time to pursue their interests. Others were single mothers who needed the free time to look after their children. For the most part, they enjoyed or tolerated their jobs like anyone.

Besides the money, why did I choose the sex industry? To answer that, I have to go back to the stash of soft-core porn magazines I discovered in my father's study when I was nine years old. *Playboy, Penthouse, Oui* and the occasional *Hustler* were my first exposure to what adult women supposedly looked like naked. I didn't know that photographers used tricks to make models look like fantasy women—airbrushing, soft focus, strategic posing (any woman's breasts look perky when her arms are raised and her chest is pushed out like a pigeon's). And it didn't occur to me that I wouldn't resemble those images when I grew up.

Not long after finding the magazines, my breasts started to develop. In fourth grade, my mother was urging me to wear a bra. I was terrified. It was too early. No one else in my class wore one yet, and I felt like a freak—I couldn't even bring myself to say the word *bra*. I wore layers of clothing to hide my chest, but my breasts grew rapidly. By the end of the school year, I was getting different looks from men on the street, and it frightened me. At school, boys would tease me and try to grab my breasts or snap my bra strap, and other girls would remark, "Wow, you have big boobs." By fifth grade, I was wearing a 34B and had reached my full height of five feet nothing. I thought there was something wrong with me. Why did I have to be short and curvy, when it was obvious even to a fifth grader that only the tall and willowy were considered beautiful? And if you weren't beautiful, you weren't anything, right?

I begged my mother to take me to the doctor to find out if, indeed, something was wrong with me. My mother didn't have much time or patience for this. She told me that early development ran in the family and I should just deal with it. The doctor agreed. So I dealt with it. I dealt with it by deciding that my body was a traitor and I hated it. I dealt with it by ignoring most of the other kids at school (who needed friends? I could always read a book instead of play). And I dealt with it by deciding that I had better start overcompensating for being a freak by being perfect in every other way.

So when my father suggested I stop eating desserts and take smaller portions, I began dieting in earnest, turning my precocious reading skills to weight-loss books. The books told me that a five-foot-tall woman should weigh a hundred pounds, and for each inch over five feet, five more pounds were permissible.

My overcompensation kicked in, and I decided to beat the hundred-pound standard and try for ninety-five. I drank a lot of diet soda to fill my empty stomach, ignoring the head rushes and tremors. But even as I hovered just below a hundred pounds, my curves were still obvious. By the time I was twelve, my war against my body was firmly entrenched. I was convinced I was a fat, ugly freak, and I was miserable.

Imagine my surprise when I turned eighteen and met a guy who was genuinely attracted to me. Though I still saw a disproportionate dwarf in the mirror, I began to hold male opinion as an article of faith. I told myself that as long as I was attractive to men, the ugliness I saw in the mirror must be a delusion. That was as close as I could get to feeling good about my body.

The topless dancing seed was planted when I noticed that a few women from my hometown were driving across the border to strip in Canada three nights a week—and raking in the money. I was intrigued but disdainful. Why would they want to exploit themselves that way? Wasn't it dangerous and humiliating?

The idea crept closer to home, though, when my friend Jen began dancing at the local Déjà Vu strip club. One night, a couple of guys I knew convinced me to go to a show—just to see what it was like. Jen wasn't working that night, but we stayed for a couple hours anyway. To my surprise, I wasn't really offended. As I watched the dancers grind their hips and gyrate in men's laps, I was captivated. Their bodies were vastly different from what I had expected—and far from perfect. They had sagging breasts, stretch marks, cellulite on their thighs. Some were unabashedly plump. And they were all getting money—and compliments—from men.

I turned to my friend and whispered, "I thought you had to be a super-skinny model type to do this kind of work."

"Some clubs you do, but not here," he answered; then he teasingly nudged my shoulder. "Why—you thinking of doing it?"

"No way," I said. "I'd feel exploited."

"The men are the ones getting exploited," he argued deftly. "The women are in control. I mean, they're making all the money."

I wasn't sure I agreed, but the idea stayed in my mind.

A few years later, I met a woman named Katie at a party. We got to talking, and she told me she danced at a local club that was owned and operated by women. "I make about $300 a week for twenty hours of work," she told me. "The rest of the time I spend writing and going to college. It's great."

What a luxury, I mused, reflecting on the gamut of dull, low-wage temp jobs I'd worked since graduation. After forty hours a week, I was usually too tired to find much inspiration for my writing. I confessed to Katie I was looking for an easy, part-time gig that would pay my bills without draining my creativity.

"Oh, it's a *perfect* job for a writer," Katie gushed. "You should totally try it."

"Yeah, well, there's one problem," I said, waving a dispassionate hand at myself. "I hardly have the body for it."

"Are you kidding?" she laughed, patting my arm. "Just come to my club sometime and see what you think. If you want a job, I'll get you in."

A week later, I gathered up my courage and asked a male friend to drive me to Katie's club. We parked on a rundown street, below a painted sign of a dancing, bikini-clad woman. "I don't know," my friend looked at me. "It looks like a dive." I pulled him through the doorway.

The club made no pretense at classiness. Its squat, shabby tables and chairs were mostly empty that afternoon, and a woman danced on stage to an audience of one disheveled, hooting old man. The place reeked of the cigarette smoke hanging visibly in the air and an undertone of sweat. A sweetness touched the air, too, the scent of the dancers' many mingled perfumes and lotions and shampoos.

My friend, uncomfortable with the scene, averted his eyes. I watched avidly, taking stock of the scene, measuring out a place for myself in this foreign terrain. I spied Katie across the room, doing a table dance. She picked up her breasts, leaned toward a guy and shook them in his face. Another dancer rubbed her small breasts surreptitiously against a man's cheek. "Oh, baby," he groaned, and tucked a twenty-dollar bill into the elastic of her fuschia thong.

Katie finished her table dance and headed my way. I covertly checked out her body as she walked. She was a little taller than I was, with large breasts and a thick waist. We were shaped differently, but neither of us fit my image of topless dancers. A glance around the room showed me that the other dancers didn't either. A few were what some might call fat. Some were bone-thin. Only a couple were, by society's standards, drop-dead gorgeous. And their work didn't look that difficult. Since there were hardly any customers, most of the dancers were sitting at a table near the DJ booth, talking and sipping water. No one had any fancy moves. No one was sweating. The atmosphere was almost comfortable. It certainly wasn't intimidating.

"What do you think?" Katie asked, plopping down next to me.

"It looks pretty easy," I said, trying not to stare at her breasts. "But do I have to touch the customers?"

"You're not supposed to," she answered, twisting her hair into a ponytail. "And they're not supposed to touch you. I've smacked people before for trying stuff."

The small-breasted dancer had obviously been playing against the rules. Katie didn't, though, and she made just as much money.

"So when are you going to audition?" she asked.

"I don't know. I have to think it over," I said. But I already knew I would. I had spent over half my life hating my body. I wanted redemption. I wanted to be someone's fantasy for once. Just long enough to prove that I could be. If it was too hard to reconcile with my feminist principles, I could always quit. But I'd never know unless I tried.

The next morning, I called Katie. "I want to audition," I said. She volunteered to come over and help me practice. In my basement, Katie demonstrated a few moves on the thick, floor-to-ceiling pipes, showing me how to remove skimpy clothing as part of the dance. I mimicked her, feeling self-conscious as she adjusted my hips and stepped back to appraise my performance. But after a while, she said I had gotten the gist, so were drove to Woolworth's to shop for cheap lingerie. "You're going to need a few thongs," she directed, dumping a handful of them into our shopping basket. "Get some matching bras, too, and a couple of lacy tops."

The next day I went to the club, already dressed and made up "for the stage," as Katie had advised. I introduced myself to the other dancers, who were friendly and encouraging. One even rushed off to get me a shot of liquor. "Drink this," she patted my shoulder. "Then just get up there and dance. Pretend you're all alone in the room. Don't look at anyone. The men don't care, and they're going to hire you anyway."

When the DJ called my name, my walk was surprisingly steady in my three-inch heels. I felt as if someone else was taking over—someone on the brink of tasting a new kind of power. A glance in the mirror behind the *barre* showed me that the heels slowed me down, made me sway my hips, elongated my legs. I held the *barre* for balance, gyrating and bending as I had seen the other dancers do. I didn't dare look at the audience during the first song, but I could hear their primal hoots and inarticulate pleas. As I continued to dance, I grew more comfortable under their gaze. It was all context. I began to relax and enjoy the music and the movement. And when the manager told me that I could start tomorrow, I felt good about my body for the first time in my life.

During my six-month stay at the club, at least two men would tell me I was beautiful every day. I was surrounded by women of different shapes, sizes, ages and ethnicities, all of whom had their particular admirers, as did I. Some men would come into the club, ignore the tall, thin, blond dancers and be all over me. I can't count the compliments I got. "Your legs look so strong," one guy told me. "You must work out." My friend Kitty, considered among the dancers as the most attractive with her waist-length blonde hair and willowy figure, said she envied my legs and wished her own "weren't so damn skinny." Twenty hours a week for six months, I got positive reinforcement for my body—and a paycheck to boot. I had put myself in an environment where I was saturated with praise for my looks, and my old self-image was eroded there, little by little, until I became proud of my appearance. Even my severely distorted perception could not withstand the power of the relentless compliments—and the money I made responding to them.

At the time, I didn't analyze the drastic way my self-confidence rose when I stepped on the platform.

I was drunk with the validation, the thrill that I had faced my inner demons and walked away victorious. There were no disparaging "fat" remarks, no eyes scanning me with disapproval. The men there were as delighted by my body as I was with their attention. I made them weak with desire, like the pictures in my father's magazines. The mere sight of me flipped on a primal switch in these men, as though I held some mysterious power.

And all it took was a simple dance number. Reveling in the movements of my body, the sight of my own skin, freed me from a lifetime of self-hatred. Never had I imagined that my body—my despicable body—could grant me so much control. Once I discovered it, I was willing to go to extremes, to put politics aside, to keep that feeling alive.

Yes, there were things I wanted to be other than just a body—a poet, an editor, a student. But more than anything, I wanted to be beautiful. My body hatred had superseded all I wanted for myself spiritually, intellectually and ethically. I had friends in the fat acceptance movement, but my own body obsession drove a wedge between us. I felt terrible about my own hypocrisy, but I felt even worse when I looked in the mirror and didn't see what the men at the club did, a body that could command the power of lust and desire.

When the initial glow of realizing that I was as attractive as anyone else wore off, the men at the club became annoying. I started to feel cheapened and objectified, and I became increasingly aware of the inherent danger tingeing my new position. The fantasy realm began to spill into the safety of my outside reality. Customers began asking me for my phone number and wanting to see me off the job. A couple of the other dancers had stalkers. I was worried; the place was in a rough neighborhood, and I couldn't even walk to my car alone.

I finally quit when the bar made lap dances legitimate. Once the owners relaxed the rules, the dancers who didn't allow a little feel-copping wouldn't get tipped. My earnings fell off, and the customers' out-of-line behavior got worse. Work became a dangerous place.

For the first time in my life, I felt that being attractive could make one vulnerable. When I had believed I was ugly, I imagined that beauty would make me safe—acceptable, not a reject. I hadn't bargained that beauty would make me into an object, an object that some men believed belonged to them. I knew I had truly crossed the line then—when I was so sure that I was attractive that I could afford to wish, sometimes, that I wasn't.

Dancing convinced me that I'm physically attractive to many men. To a degree, that will always matter to me. Feel like your body is unattractive—even unacceptable? Take it all off onstage, and you'll hear a different story.

Yet, I realize the irony of my experience. My original body hatred was the result of our society's appropriation of the female body as an object of consumerism. Had there been no *Playboy* standard with which to compare my developing figure, no father who told me I was gaining weight, there would have been no obsession with looking perfect. I conquered much of that body hatred by proving to myself that my body was an adequate object of consumerism, that it wasn't too much worse than the standard. What if I had not been able to do that? What if, instead of a bad body *image,* I had a body that truly could not, in our society, conform to the norm? I like to think I would have somehow been able to love my body anyway. I like to think I would have found a way.

There are so many contradictions in the sex industry. My sense of empowerment from dancing was bound on all sides by not only the glass ceiling, but the glass floor and walls, which keep women from having easy access to well-paying jobs. And I wonder how my self-image would change if I suddenly no longer fit the norms of attractiveness. My body image, though now fairly good, is still dependent upon outside forces.

I can't deny that I feel better after dancing, but I also can't deny the irony. I haven't become a person who can accept her body unconditionally—not yet. I have become a person who is tremendously relieved to discover that she really does look okay to her oppressors. Thus, I tacitly admit that my oppressors have the right to define who I am, and I tacitly betray my sisters who are crusading for a new standard of beauty. How do I live with this? I want to resolve these contradictions. But perhaps they can never be resolved in our culture. However, by owning my struggle with them, I can begin.

■ # READING 39

Phenomenal Woman

Maya Angelou

Pretty women wonder where my secret lies.
I'm not cute or built to suit a fashion model's size
But when I start to tell them,
They think I'm telling lies.
I say,
It's in the reach of my arms,
The span of my hips,
The stride of my step,
The curl of my lips.
I'm a woman
Phenomenally.
Phenomenal woman,
That's me.

I walk into a room
Just as cool as you please,
And to a man,
The fellows stand or
Fall down on their knees.
Then they swarm around me,
A hive of honey bees.
I say,
It's the fire in my eyes,
And the flash of my teeth,
The swing in my waist,
And the joy in my feet.
I'm a woman

Phenomenally.
Phenomenal woman,
That's me.

Men themselves have wondered
What they see in me.
They try so much
But they can't touch
My inner mystery.
When I try to show them
They say they still can't see.
I say,
It's in the arch of my back,
The sun of my smile,
The ride of my breasts,
The grace of my style.
I'm a woman
Phenomenally.
Phenomenal woman,
That's me.

Now you understand
Just why my head's not bowed.
I don't shout or jump about
Or have to talk real loud.
When you see me passing
It ought to make you proud.
I say,
It's in the click of my heels,
The bend of my hair,
The palm of my hand,
The need for my care.
Cause I'm a woman
Phenomenally.
Phenomenal woman,
That's me.

DISCUSSION QUESTIONS FOR CHAPTER FIVE

1. How are power relations reflected and reinforced in beauty norms?

2. How do beauty norms affect women and men differently? How have beauty norms affected you?

3. Two of your readings talk about women's connections with particular aspects of their bodies—dreadlocked hair and a big nose. What aspects of your body reflect key elements of your sense of self?

4. What are some of the connections between beauty standards and women's health?

5. How can women resist the beauty ideal?

SUGGESTIONS FOR FURTHER READING

Gimlin, Debra L. *Body Work: Beauty and Self-Image in American Culture.* Berkeley: University of California Press, 2002.

Grogan, Sarah. *Body Image: Understanding Body Dissatisfaction in Men, Women, and Children.* New York: Routledge, 1999.

Hesse-Biber, Sharon. *Am I Thin Enough Yet?: The Cult of Thinness and the Commercialization of Identity.* New York: Oxford University Press, 1997.

Holmlund, Chris. *Impossible Bodies: Femininity and Masculinity at the Movies.* New York: Routledge, 2002.

Karp, Michelle. *The Bust Guide to the New Girl Order.* New York: Penguin, 1999.

Solovay, Sondra. *Tipping the Scales of Justice: Fighting Weight Based Discrimination.* Amherst, NY: Prometheus, 2000.

CHAPTER SIX

Health and Reproductive Rights

HEALTH AND WELLNESS

Health is a central issue in women's lives. Ask parents what they wish for their newborns and they speak first about hoping the baby is healthy; quiz people about their hopes for the new year and they speak about staying healthy; listen to politicians debate their positions before an election and health care is almost always a key issue. In contemporary U.S. society, good health is generally understood as a requirement for happy and productive living at the same time that medical institutions provide different levels of service based upon health insurance status and general ability to pay. In other words, although health is a central aspect of everyday life, not all individuals are able to rely upon access to health and medical services.

Health is not just about medical services. Health conditions are related to such factors as poverty, diet, malnutrition and hunger, violence, stress, housing, and education. In essence, health is related to many aspects of our everyday lives as women. Heart disease, osteoporosis, migraine headaches, psychiatric disorders, substance abuse, and other health problems are closely related to gender. As suggested in "How Far We've Come," strides have been made in dealing with many health issues that affect women, but we still need activism to ensure optimal health care for women.

Two prominent health issues highlighted in the readings are breast cancer and AIDS. As the article "Breast Cancer: Is It the Environment?" suggests, breast cancer research has focused on finding a cure, when in reality a focus on environmental contributors could work more effectively to prevent breast cancer. Certainly the impact of the AIDS epidemic on women has concretely demonstrated the ways gender, race, and class intersect to affect women's lives in different ways. For example, women's manifestations of opportunistic infections were excluded from the definition of AIDS until 1993, most research is done on men and the findings are generalized to women, women are diagnosed later (often postmortem) than men, treated later, and die sooner after diagnosis. In addition, women of color are greatly overrepresented among AIDS patients, accounting for over 75 percent of AIDS cases among U.S. women. As Lisa Collier Cool argues in "Forgotten Women: How Minorities Are Underserved by Our Health Care System," racial discrimination complicates minority women's experiences in the health care system, resulting in inadequate care.

Because women are prominent as both providers and consumers of health care, health issues and the health care system affect us on many levels. To make sense of the complexities of women's relationship to health care systems, we will discuss three concepts: androcentrism, medicalization, and gender stereotyping.

First, men's bodies have been seen as the norm, and much medical research has focused on men (mostly White men) and then been overgeneralized to women and people of color.

THE WORLD'S WOMEN 2000: HEALTH

- Life expectancy continues to increase for women and men in most developing regions but has decreased dramatically in Southern Africa as a result of AIDS.
- Infant mortality is generally higher for boys than for girls, except for some countries in Asia where gender-based discrimination outweighs girls' biological advantage.
- Where women are sexually active at a young age, they are at risk of suffering short- and long-term consequences of sexually transmitted infections (including HIV), early pregnancy and unsafe abortion.
- Data on maternal mortality and other causes of death are often unavailable or, where available, are unreliable due to deficiencies in vital statistics registration systems.
- Women now account for almost half of all cases of HIV/AIDS, and in countries with high HIV prevalence, young women are at higher risk than young men of contracting HIV.
- New efforts are being made to measure health expectancy—not just life expectancy—of the world's aging population.

Source: http://unstats.un.org/unsd/demographic/ww2000/health2000.htm.

LEARNING ACTIVITY:
OBSESSED WITH BREASTS

Go to the Web page of the Breast Cancer Fund's "Obsessed with Breasts" ad campaign at *www.breastcancerfund.org/campaign.htm.* What are the goals of the campaign? Why is the campaign necessary? Now go to the Fund's "Facts, News, and Opinions" page. Identify five facts about breast cancer that are new to you.

For Better or For Worse®   **by Lynn Johnston**

HEALTH CONSEQUENCE OF TOBACCO USE AMONG WOMEN

MORTALITY

- Cigarette smoking plays a major role in the mortality of U.S. women. Since 1980, when the Surgeon General's Report on Women and Smoking was released, about three million women have died prematurely of smoking-related diseases.
- In 1997, about 165,000 U.S. women died of smoking-related diseases, including lung and other cancers, heart disease, stroke, and chronic lung diseases such as emphysema.
- Each year throughout the 1990s, about 2.1 million years of the potential life of U.S. women were lost prematurely because of smoking-attributable diseases. Women smokers who die of a smoking-related disease lose on average 14 years of potential life.
- Women who stop smoking greatly reduce their risk of dying prematurely. The relative benefits of smoking cessation are greater when women stop smoking at younger ages, but smoking cessation is beneficial at all ages.

LUNG CANCER

- Cigarette smoking is the major cause of lung cancer among women. About 90% of all lung cancer deaths among U.S. women smokers are attributable to smoking.
- In 1950, lung cancer accounted for only 3% of all cancer deaths among women; however, by 2000, it accounted for an estimated 25% of cancer deaths.
- Since 1950, lung cancer mortality rates for U.S. women have increased an estimated 600%. In 1987, lung cancer surpassed breast cancer to become the leading cause of cancer death among U.S. women. In 2000, about 27,000 more women died of lung cancer (about 68,000) than breast cancer (about 41,000).

OTHER CANCERS

- Smoking is a major cause of cancer of the oropharynx and bladder among women. Evidence is also strong that women who smoke have increased risk for cancer of the pancreas and kidney. For cancer of the larynx and esophagus, evidence that smoking increases the risk among women is more limited but consistent with large increases in risk.
- Women who smoke may have a higher risk for liver cancer and colorectal cancer than women who do not smoke.
- Smoking is consistently associated with an increased risk for cervical cancer. The extent to which this association is independent of human papillomavirus (tumor caused by virus) infection is uncertain.
- Several studies suggest that exposure to environmental tobacco smoke is associated with an increased risk for breast cancer; however, this association remains uncertain. More research is needed.

CARDIOVASCULAR DISEASE

- Smoking is a major cause of coronary heart disease among women. Risk increases with the number of cigarettes smoked and the duration of smoking.

(continued)

- Women who smoke have an increased risk for ischemic stroke (blood clot in one of the arteries supplying the brain) and subarachnoid hemorrhage (bleeding in the area surrounding the brain).
- Women who smoke have an increased risk for peripheral vascular atherosclerosis.
- Smoking cessation reduces the excess risk of coronary heart disease, no matter at what age women stop smoking. The risk is substantially reduced within 1 or 2 years after they stop smoking.
- The increased risk for stroke associated with smoking begins to reverse after women stop smoking. About 10 to 15 years after stopping, the risk for stroke approaches that of a woman who never smoked.

CHRONIC OBSTRUCTIVE PULMONARY DISEASE (COPD) AND LUNG FUNCTION

- Cigarette smoking is the primary cause of COPD in women, and the risk increases with the amount and duration of cigarette use.
- Mortality rates for COPD have increased among women for the past 20 to 30 years. About 90% of mortality from COPD among U.S. women is attributed to smoking.
- Exposure to maternal smoking is associated with reduced lung function among infants, and exposure to environmental tobacco smoke during childhood and adolescence may be associated with impaired lung function among girls.
- Smoking by girls can reduce their rate of lung growth and the level of maximum lung function. Women who smoke may experience a premature decline of lung function.

MENSTRUAL FUNCTION

- Some studies suggest that cigarette smoking may alter menstrual function by increasing the risks for painful menstruation, secondary amenorrhea (abnormal absence of menstrual), and menstrual irregularity.
- Women smokers have natural menopause at a younger age than do nonsmokers, and they may experience more severe menopausal symptoms.

REPRODUCTIVE OUTCOMES

- Women who smoke have increased risk for conception delay and for both primary and secondary infertility.
- Women who smoke during pregnancy risk pregnancy complications, premature birth, low-birth-weight infants, stillbirth, and infant mortality.
- Women who smoke may have a modest increase in risks for ectopic pregnancy (fallopian tube or peritoneal cavity pregnancy) and spontaneous abortion.
- Studies show a link between smoking and the risk of sudden infant death syndrome (SIDS) among the offspring of women who smoke during pregnancy.

BONE DENSITY AND FRACTURE RISK

- Postmenopausal women who smoke have lower bone density than women who never smoked.
- Women who smoke have an increased risk for hip fracture than women who never smoked.

OTHER CONDITIONS

- Women who smoke may have a modestly elevated risk for rheumatoid arthritis.
- Women smokers have an increased risk for cataract, and may have an increased risk for age-related macular degeneration.
- The prevalence of smoking generally is higher for women with anxiety disorders, bulimia, depression, attention deficit disorder, and alcoholism; it is particularly high among patients with diagnosed schizophrenia. The connection between smoking and these disorders requires additional research.

HEALTH CONSEQUENCES OF ENVIRONMENTAL TOBACCO SMOKE (ETS)

- Exposure to ETS is a cause of lung cancer among women nonsmokers.
- Studies support a causal relationship between exposure to ETS and coronary heart disease mortality among women nonsmokers.
- Infants born to women who are exposed to ETS during pregnancy may have a small decrement in birth weight and a slightly increased risk for intrauterine growth retardation.

This is an example of *androcentrism* (male-centeredness and the confusion of maleness with humanity) in the context of health care. Fortunately, due to new guidelines with the Food and Drug Administration (FDA) now half of all subjects in large-scale drug studies are female. However, less than a quarter of subjects in small-scale safety trials are female and a third of new drug applications do not include separate safety and efficiency data for men and women as required by the FDA. In addition, more money has been spent on diseases that are more likely to afflict men. Related to this is the notion of "anatomy is destiny" where female physiology, and especially reproductive anatomy, is seen as central in understanding behavior. Social norms about femininity have come to guide medical and scientific ideas about women's health, and female genital organs have long been seen as sources of special emotional and physical health problems. Furthermore, in "Man-Made Threats to Women's Health," Adrienne Germaine contends that men's political and social domination over women worldwide in itself constitutes a health threat for women.

In terms of women as health care providers, androcentrism has supported sexism and encouraged systems where men have more positions of power and influence in the health care system. Although nursing is still overwhelmingly a feminine occupation, increasingly more women are becoming physicians, even though most prestigious specialties are still dominated by men. It remains to be seen whether this increase in female physicians will change the face of medicine as we know it.

Medicalization is the process whereby normal functions of the body come to be seen as indicative of disease. This tends to be the model by which modern medicine works. This affects women in two ways. One, because women have more episodic changes in their bodies as a result of childbearing (for example, menstruation, pregnancy, childbirth, lactation, and menopause), they are more at risk for medical personnel interpreting these natural processes as problematic. Note how this tends to reinforce the argument that biology is destiny. Two, medicalization supports business and medical technologies. It tends to work against preventive medicine and encourages sophisticated medical technologies to "fix" problems after they occur. Medical services are dominated by drug treatments and surgery,

LEARNING ACTIVITY:
TEST YOUR KNOWLEDGE OF HIV/AIDS

TRUE OR FALSE?

1. HIV stands for human immunodeficiency virus.
2. AIDS stands for acquired immunodeficiency syndrome.
3. HIV is airborne.
4. HIV can be transmitted through saliva.
5. HIV can be transmitted through blood, semen, and breast milk.
6. Women were not initially infected with HIV in the 1980s when the disease was primarily a problem for gay men.
7. Injection drug use is not a significant cause of HIV infection among women.
8. Poverty increases a woman's risk for contracting HIV.
9. HIV can be transmitted from a pregnant woman to her baby.
10. HIV is transmitted more easily from women to men than from men to women.
11. AIDS manifests through the same opportunistic infections in both women and men.
12. Heterosexual transmission is the most rapidly increasing transmission category among women with HIV.
13. Black and Latina women are disproportionately represented in AIDS cases.
14. A history of childhood sexual abuse is a risk factor for HIV infection.
15. Gender norms (for example, women are passive and submissive; nice women don't talk about sex) often make HIV prevention among women difficult.

ANSWERS

1. T	6. F	11. F
2. T	7. F	12. T
3. F	8. T	13. T
4. F	9. T	14. T
5. T	10. F	15. T

LEARNING ACTIVITY: WOMEN, HEART
DISEASE, AND CANCER IN YOUR STATE

- To learn more about the prevalence of heart disease among women in your state, visit the Centers for Disease Control's website at *ww.cdc.gov/nccdphp/cvd/ womensatlas/factsheets/index.htm* and click on your state's name.
- To learn about the prevalence of cancer in your state, go to *www.cdc.gov/cancer/ dbdata.htm* and select your state.

ALCOHOL ABUSE

Alcohol abuse and alcohol dependence are complicated illnesses that present unique threats to women's health. Women who abuse alcohol may develop addictions and substance abuse–related health problems faster than men. Ultimately medical research is showing that women are just more vulnerable. Recent surveys show that drinking is most common for:

- Women who are between the ages of 26 and 34
- Women who are divorced or separated

Binge drinking (consumption of five or more drinks) is most common among women who are ages 18 to 25. And drinking among women is more prevalent among Caucasians, although African American women are more likely to drink heavily.

All these statistics aside, the latest word from the National Institute on Alcohol Abuse and Alcoholism is that all women are more vulnerable to alcohol-related organ damage, trauma, and interpersonal difficulties:

- Liver damage: Women develop alcohol-induced liver disease in a shorter time period than men even if they consume less alcohol. And, women are more likely to develop alcohol hepatitis and die from cirrhosis (liver disease).
- Brain damage: Studies of brains (as seen via magnetic resonance imaging) show that women may be more vulnerable to brain damage due to alcohol consumption than men.
- Heart disease: Among heavy drinkers, women develop heart disease at the same rate as men, despite the fact that women use alcohol 60 percent less than men over their lifetimes.
- Breast cancer: Some studies have shown a link between moderate or heavy alcohol consumption and an increased risk for breast cancer.
- Violence: College women who drink are more likely to be the victims of sexual abuse. And high school girls who use alcohol are more likely to be the victims of dating violence.
- Traffic crashes: Although women are less likely than men to drive after drinking, they have a higher risk of dying.
- Women are more likely than men to use a combination of alcohol and prescription drugs.
- Women may begin to abuse alcohol and drugs following depression, to relax on dates, to feel more adequate, to lose weight, to decrease stress, or to help them sleep at night.

Poor self-esteem is a major issue for most women who develop problems with drugs and alcohol. The following conditions may also increase your risk for developing alcohol abuse problems:

- A history of physical or sexual abuse. Physical and sexual violence against women is common when one or both partners have been drinking or using drugs. Women also are more likely to drink or use drugs when their partners use.
- Depression, panic disorders, and posttraumatic stress disorders.

(continued)

Researchers now know that there is a strong family component to addiction. If you have a family history of addiction, you should be aware of the risk for developing dependency, especially during stressful periods in your life.

Because very few women who abuse alcohol or drugs fit the addict stereotype, it is difficult for the addicted woman to see herself as an addict. It is also common for health care professionals to overlook substance abuse in women patients. If you suspect you may have an addiction problem, you might want to ask yourself the following questions, known as the CAGE Questionnaire: *

- Have you ever felt you should **c**ut down on your drinking or drug use?
- Have people **a**nnoyed you by criticizing your drinking or drug use?
- Have you ever felt bad or **g**uilty about your drinking or drug use?
- Have you ever had a drink or drug first thing in the morning to steady your nerves or to get rid of a hangover (**e**ye opener)?

Responses are scored 0 or 1, with a higher score an indication of alcohol problems. A total score of 2 or greater is considered clinically significant. If you scored greater than a 2 or if any of your answers bother you, it is time to talk to a health care professional about getting help.

* CAGE was developed by John Ewing, MD, founding Director of the Bowles Center for Alcohol Studies, University of North Carolina at Chapel Hill. CAGE is an internationally used assessment instrument for identifying alcoholics.
Source: National Women's Health Resource Center, *www.healthywomen.org.*

and controlled by pharmaceutical companies, health maintenance organizations, and such professional organizations as the American Medical Association.

Third, *gender stereotyping* encompasses how notions about femininity and masculinity inform everyday understanding of health care occupations and influence how medical practitioners treat their patients. For example, patients often assume white-coated white male orderlies to be doctors and call women doctors "nurse." Furthermore, as Patti Watkins and Diane Whaley suggest, women interact differently with the health care system and are treated differently, often to the detriment of women's health. For example, research suggests that physicians generally are more likely to consider emotional factors when diagnosing women's problems, and they are more likely to assume that the cause of illness is psychosomatic when the patient involved is female. It is well known that physicians also prescribe more mood-altering medication for women than they do for men. In addition, physicians attribute stereo-typical notions of ethnicity, as well as gender, to patients, expecting Latinas/os, for example, to be more nervous and excitable.

REPRODUCTIVE CHOICE

Reproductive choice involves being able to have safe and affordable birthing and parenting options; reliable, safe, and affordable birth control technologies; freedom from forced sterilization; and the availability of abortion. In other words, a key aspect of reproductive rights is the extent to which women can control their reproduction and therefore shape the quality and character of their lives. This choice is increasingly under attack in contemporary society.

Sterilization Practices

Female sterilization includes tubal ligation, a surgical procedure where the fallopian tubes are blocked, and hysterectomy, where the uterus is removed. Recently a noninvasive alternative to tubal ligation, the springlike device called *Essure* which blocks the fallopian tubes, has been marketed. Although hysterectomies are usually performed for medical reasons not associated with a desire for sterilization, this procedure results in sterilization. Countless women freely choose sterilization as a form of permanent birth control, and it is a useful method of family planning for many. "Freely choose," however, assumes a range of options not available to some women. In other words, "freely choose" is difficult in a racist, class-

HISTORICAL MOMENT:
THE WOMEN'S HEALTH MOVEMENT

From the beginnings of the medical industry, women often suffered from the humiliation and degradation of medical practitioners who treated women as hysterical and hypochondriac, who medicalized normal female body functions, and who prevented women from controlling their own health. In 1969, as the women's movement heightened consciousness about other issues, women also began to examine the ways they had been treated and the ways women's biology and health had been largely unexplored. In the spring of that year, several women participated in a workshop on "women and their bodies" at a Boston conference. As they vented their anger at the medical establishment, they also began to make plans to take action. Although most of them had no medical training, they spent the summer studying all facets of women's health and the health care system. Then they began giving courses on women's bodies wherever they could find an audience. These women became known as the Boston Women's Health Collective and published their notes and lectures in what would eventually be known as *Our Bodies, Our Selves.*

Their efforts resulted in a national women's health movement. In March 1971, 800 women gathered for the first women's health conference in New York. Women patients began to question doctors' authority and to bring patient advocates to their medical appointments to take notes on their treatment by medical professionals. Feminists questioned established medical practices such as the gendered diagnosis and treatment of depression, the recommendation for radical mastectomies whenever breast cancer was found, and the high incidence of cesarean deliveries and hysterectomies.

While the original members of the women's health movement tended to be well-educated, middle-class, white women, the movement quickly expanded to work with poor women and women of color to address the inequities caused by the intersections of gender with race and social class. Together, these women worked on reproductive rights, recognizing that for many poor women and women of color, the right to abortion was not as paramount as the right to be free from forced sterilization. Their work shaped the agenda of the National Women's Health Network, founded in 1975 and dedicated to advancing the health of women of all races and social classes.

Source: Ruth Rosen, *The World Split Open: How the Modern Women's Movement Changed America.* New York: Viking, 2000.

based, and sexist society that does not provide all women with the same options from which to choose. As a result, women on welfare are more likely to be sterilized than women who are not on welfare, and women of color and Third World women are disproportionately more likely to receive this procedure. Although Medicaid pays for sterilization, it does not pay for some other birth control options. Lingering here is the racist and classist idea that certain groups have more right to reproduce than others, a belief and social practice called *eugenics.* Policies providing support for sterilization that make it free or very accessible obviously do not force women to be sterilized. Rather, policies like these make the option attractive at a time when other options are limited.

One of the unfortunate legacies of reproductive history has been that some women have been sterilized against their will, usually articulated as "against their full, informed consent." In the 1970s it was learned that many poor women—especially women of color, and Native American women in particular, as well as women who were mentally retarded or incarcerated—had undergone forced sterilization. Situations varied, but often they included women not giving consent at all, not knowing what was happening, believing they were having a different procedure, being strongly pressured to consent, or being unable to read or understand the options told to them. The latter was especially true for women who did not speak or read English. Forced sterilization is now against the law, although problems still remain.

Parenting Options

In considering reproductive choice, it is important to think about the motivations for having children as well as the motivations for limiting fertility. Most people, women and men, assume they will have children at some point in their lives, and, for some, reproduction and parenting are less of a choice than something that people just do. Although in many nonindustrial and developing societies children can be economic assets, in contemporary U.S. society, for the most part, children consume much more than they produce. Some women do see children as insurance in their old age, but generally today we have children for emotional reasons such as personal and marital fulfillment, and for social reasons like carrying on the family name and fulfilling religious mandates.

Childbirth is an experience that has been shared by millions of women the world over. Women have historically helped other women at this time, strengthening family and kinship bonds and the ties of friendship. As the medical profession gained power and status and developed various technologies (forceps, for example), women's traditional authority associated with birthing became eclipsed by an increasing medicalization of birthing. Again, the medicalization of childbirth regards birthing as an irregular episode that requires medical procedures, often including invasive forms of "treatment." Women who could afford it started going to hospitals to birth their children instead of being attended at home by relatives, friends, or midwives. Unfortunately, in these early days, hospitals were relatively dangerous places where sanitation was questionable and women in childbirth were attended by doctors who knew far less about birthing than did midwives. As the century progressed and birthing in hospitals became routine, women gave birth lying down in the pelvic exam position with their feet in stirrups, sometimes with their arms strapped down; they were given drugs, episiotomies (an incision from the vagina toward the anus to prevent tearing), and were routinely shaved in the pubic area. More recently, thanks to a strong consumer move-

ment, women give birth under more humane conditions. Birthing centers now predominate in most hospitals, and doctors no longer perform the routine procedures and administer the drugs that they used to. Nonetheless, a large number of pregnant women do not receive any health care at all, and a larger number still receive inadequate health care. Women
of color are especially underserved.

Why might women want to control their fertility? The first and obvious answer concerns health. Over a woman's reproductive life, she could potentially birth many children
and be in a constant state of pregnancy and lactation. Such a regimen compromises maximum health. Second, birthing unlimited numbers of children might be seen as irresponsible in the context of a society and an earth with finite resources. Third, birthing is expensive and the raising of children even more expensive. Fourth, given that in contemporary
Western societies women have primary responsibility for childcare and that the organization of mothering tends to isolate women in their homes, it is important to consider the
emotional effects of constant child rearing. And, finally, if women had unlimited children,
the constant care taking of these children would preempt women's ability to be involved in
other productive work outside the home. This "indirect cost" concept involves the loss or
limitation of financial autonomy, work-related or professional identity, and creative and ego
development.

Although today women are as likely to have children as they ever were, three facts stand
out. First, the average family size decreased as the twentieth century progressed. Second,
women are having children later in life than they did in earlier times in our society. Both of
these trends are related to changes in health care technologies that have raised health care
standards and encouraged parenting at later ages, the availability of birth control and abortion, and the increase in women's education and participation in paid labor with subsequent
postponement of marriage and child rearing. Third, there has been a large increase in the
number of children born to single women, especially among non-White populations. A
little over 17 percent of family households are headed by single women and less than 6 percent headed by single men (U. S. Census, 2000). This increase in households headed by
single women can be attributed to lack of knowledge about reproduction and contraception
in the context of an increasingly sexually active population, poverty and lack of opportunities for work and employment, failure of family and school systems to keep young people in
school, and increased use of alcohol and other drugs. Some girls see motherhood as a rite
of passage into adulthood, as a way to escape their families of origin, or as a way to connect
with another human being who will love them unconditionally. The rise in the number of
babies born to single women also reflects changing norms, at least among middle-class populations, that it is okay to raise a child alone rather than "having to get married."

Birth control technologies have been around for a long time. Many preindustrial societies used suppositories coated in various substances that blocked the cervix or functioned
as spermicides; the condom was used originally to prevent the spread of syphilis, although
it was discovered that it functioned as a contraceptive; and the concept of the intrauterine
device was first used by bedouins who hoped to prevent camels from conceiving during
long treks across the desert by inserting small pebbles into the uterus. Nineteenth-century
couples in the United States used "coitus interruptus" (withdrawal before ejaculation), the
rhythm method (sexual intercourse only during nonfertile times), condoms, and absti-
nence. Although technologies of one kind or another have been around for generations, the
issue for women has been the control of and access to these technologies. Patriarchal socie-

ties have long understood that to control women's lives it is necessary to control women's reproductive options. In this way, information about, access to, and denial of birth control technologies are central aspects of women's role and status in society.

In the 1880s, the Comstock Law (statutes supposed to control pornography) limited contraception because these technologies were considered obscene. At the same time, however, women realized that the denial of contraception kept them in the domestic sphere and, more importantly, exposed them to repetitive and often dangerous pregnancies. In response, a social movement emerged that was organized around reproductive choice. Called "voluntary motherhood," this movement not only involved giving women access to birth control, but also worked to facilitate reproduction and parenting under the most safe, humane, and dignified conditions. Margaret Sanger was a leader of this movement and writes about her decision to become involved in "My Fight for Birth Control."

One unfortunate aspect, however, was the early birth control movement's affiliation with an emerging eugenics movement. Following Charles Darwin's theory of the survival of the fittest, eugenics argued that only the "fit" should be encouraged to reproduce and that birth control was necessary to prevent the "unfit" from unlimited reproduction. The "unfit" included poor and immigrant populations, the "feeble-minded," and criminals. Using a rationale grounded in eugenics, birth control proponents were able to argue their case while receiving the support of those in power in society. Nonetheless, although contraceptive availability varied from state to state, it was not until a Supreme Court decision (*Griswold v. Connecticut*) in the mid-1960s that married couples were allowed rights to birth control. The Court's ruling said that the prohibition of contraceptive use by married people was unconstitutional in that it violated the constitutional right to privacy. This right was extended to single people in 1972 and to minors in 1977.

Today there are a variety of contraceptive methods available. Their accessibility is limited by the availability of information about them, by cost, and by health care providers' sponsorship. As you read about these technologies, consider the following questions: Whose body is being affected? Who gets to deal with the side effects? Who is paying for these methods? Who will pay if these methods fail? Who will be hurt if these side effects become more serious? These questions are framed by gender relations and the context of the U.S. economy and its health organizations. For example, since hitting the market in 1998, prescriptions for Viagra (a male impotence medication) were covered by more than half of health insurance plans whereas most plans did not cover birth control pills. Fury over this has created bills passed in over 20 states to date to require insurers to provide contraceptive coverage. A federal bill is in the works.

Other than tubal ligation where women are surgically sterilized and vasectomy where men are surgically sterilized, birth control methods include, first, the intrauterine device (IUD), a small piece of plastic with copper inside it that is inserted into the uterus. It prevents the implantation of a fertilized egg. One trade name is the ParaGard; the Progestasert is another IUD that contains hormones. IUDs generally last up to 10 years, can result in heavier periods, and may increase risk of pelvic inflammatory disease among women with multiple sexual partners. The Dalkon Shield was an IUD that caused infection, infertility, and death among women in the 1970s and was subsequently banned in the United States. (It was then exported for use by women overseas.)

Second are the hormone regulation methods. The pill is an oral contraceptive that contains two hormones: progestin and estrogen. It became widely available in the United States in the 1960s and quickly became the most popular means of contraception despite such side

ACTIVIST PROFILE: MARGARET SANGER

Margaret Sanger completed her nursing training in 1900 at the age of 21. Following her marriage and the birth of three children, Sanger returned to work as a visiting nurse in some of the worst slums in New York City. A great deal of her work involved assisting poor women in giving birth, and she began to see the impact of bearing too many children on the health and welfare of these women. She also saw the suffering and near fatality of many women who obtained unsafe, illegal abortions to avoid having even more children. Often these women would beg Sanger to tell them how to prevent pregnancy, but by law Sanger was forbidden to share this knowledge with them. When at last a young woman who had pleaded with Sanger for this information died from giving birth to yet another baby, Sanger decided to take action.

Convinced that women had a right to know how to prevent pregnancy and that the improvement of women's lives depended on family planning, Sanger began to educate herself about birth control. Armed with her newfound information, Sanger began her real life's work. Her plan was to educate the public about birth control, form a birth control organization to help raise awareness and money, seek to overturn the Comstock Law, which prevented sending birth control information through the U.S. mail, and lobby Congress to allow doctors to prescribe birth control devices, which were illegal even for married couples.

In 1914, Sanger started the *Woman Rebel,* a magazine encouraging women to think for themselves and promoting family planning. Under the Comstock Law, the magazine was banned by the U.S. Postal Service, and Sanger was charged with nine counts of obscenity. She fled to England for 2 years until the charges were dropped. Upon her re-

(continued)

turn to New York, she founded the National Birth Control League, which later became Planned Parenthood. In 1916, she opened a birth control clinic in a poor section of Brooklyn. After only 9 days in operation, the clinic was raided and shut down. Sanger was sentenced to 30 days in a workhouse. Upon her release, Sanger reopened the clinic out of her home.

In 1921, Sanger moved her battle to the national level and started *The Birth Control Review.* During the first 5 years of its publication, she received more than a million letters from women detailing the horrors of poverty and unwanted pregnancy. In 1928, Sanger organized 500 of the letters into a book, *Mothers in Bondage,* which became highly influential in the fight for birth control. Throughout the 1930s Sanger continued her fight, speaking and lobbying. At last, the Supreme Court overturned the Comstock Law in 1936, and the American Medical Association (AMA) reversed its position, giving doctors the right to distribute birth control devices. After her victory, Sanger persisted in her work for affordable and effective contraceptives. Her tireless efforts to secure research funding at last led to the development of the most significant contraceptive of the century—the birth control pill. Only a few months before Sanger died in 1966, the U.S. Supreme Court, in *Griswold v. Connecticut,* made birth control legal for married couples.

effects as nausea, weight gain, breast tenderness, and headaches. The minipill contains no estrogen and a small dose of progestin and has fewer side effects than the regular pill. Norplant is a contraceptive device that lasts 5 years. Six flexible capsules are inserted beneath the skin on the upper arm where they release progestin to suppress ovulation. It can cause irregular bleeding and the possibility of pain and scarring upon removal. Depo-provera is an injection of synthetic hormones that suppresses ovulation for 11 to 13 months. There are similar side effects as the pill, including depression and heavier, more frequent periods. In addition, the effects are not easily reversible, and it may take up to a year before a woman is fertile again. Some groups have questioned the safety of Norplant and depo-provera. A new device marketed under the name NuvaRing was approved in 2001. It is a flexible, transparent ring about 3 inches in diameter that women insert vaginally once a month. The ring releases a continuous dose of estrogen and progesterone. The ring remains in the vagina for 21 days and is then removed and discarded and a new ring inserted. It is interesting to note that in a news media interview the FDA was reported as saying that about 14 percent of women in the NuvaRing clinical trials had vaginal infections or symptoms "but that some of them would have had them anyway." Other hormone regulation methods include hormone patches that must be changed weekly and hormone-releasing intrauterine devices (IUDs) that can stay in place for 5 years.

Next are the barrier methods. The diaphragm and cervical cap are barrier methods that are inserted into the vagina before sexual intercourse, fit over the cervix, and prevent sperm from entering the uterus. They work in conjunction with spermicidal jelly that is placed along the rim of the device. Some women use them in conjunction with spermicidal foam that is inserted into the vagina with a small plunger. Unlike the other methods, spermicides are available at any drugstore. Also available at drugstores are vaginal sponges that are coated with spermicide, inserted into the vagina, and work to block the cervix and absorb sperm. All these barrier methods work best when used in conjunction with a condom and are much

SEXUALLY TRANSMITTED DISEASES

Every year more than 12 million cases of sexually transmitted diseases (STDs) are reported in the United States. These infections result in billions of dollars in preventable health care spending. In addition, the health impact of STDs is particularly severe for women. Because the infections often cause few or no symptoms and may go untreated, women are at risk for complications from STDs, including ectopic (tubal) pregnancy, infertility, chronic pelvic pain, and poor pregnancy outcomes.

CHLAMYDIA

Chlamydia is the most common bacterial sexually transmitted disease in the United States. It causes an estimated 4 million infections annually, primarily among adolescents and young adults. In women, untreated infections can progress to involve the upper reproductive tract and may result in serious complications. About 75 percent of women infected with chlamydia have few or no symptoms, and without testing and treatment the infection may persist for as long as fifteen months. Without treatment, 20–40 percent of women with chlamydia may develop pelvic inflammatory disease (PID). An estimated one in ten adolescent girls and one in twenty women of reproductive age are infected.

PELVIC INFLAMMATORY DISEASE

PID refers to upper reproductive tract infection in women, which often develops when STDs go untreated or are inadequately treated. Each year, PID and its complications affect more than 750,000 women. PID can cause chronic pelvic pain or harm to the reproductive organs. Permanent damage to the fallopian tubes can result from a single episode of PID and is even more common after a second or third episode. Damage to the fallopian tubes is the only preventable cause of infertility. As much as 30 percent of infertility in women may be related to preventable complications of past STDs.

One potentially fatal complication of PID is ectopic pregnancy, an abnormal condition that occurs when a fertilized egg implants in a location other than the uterus, often in a fallopian tube. It is estimated that ectopic pregnancy has increased about fivefold over a twenty-year period. Among African American women, ectopic pregnancy is the leading cause of pregnancy-related deaths. The economic cost of PID and its complications is estimated at $4 billion annually.

GONORRHEA

Gonorrhea is a common bacterial STD that can be treated with antibiotics. Although gonorrhea rates among adults have declined, rates among adolescents have risen or remained unchanged. Adolescent females aged 15–19 have the highest rates of gonorrhea. An estimated 50 percent of women with gonorrhea have no symptoms. Without early screening and treatment, 10–40 percent of women with gonorrhea will develop PID.

HUMAN IMMUNODEFICIENCY VIRUS

Human immunodeficiency virus (HIV) is the virus that causes AIDS. The risk of a woman acquiring or transmitting HIV is increased by the presence of other STDs. In particular, the presence of genital ulcers, such as those produced by syphilis and herpes, or the

(continued)

presence of an inflammatory STD, such as chlamydia or gonorrhea, may make HIV transmission easier.

HERPES SIMPLEX VIRUS (HSV)

Genital herpes is a disease caused by herpes simplex virus (HSV). The disease may recur periodically and has no cure. Scientists have estimated that about 30 million persons in the United States may have genital HSV infection. Most infected persons never recognize the symptoms of genital herpes; some will have symptoms shortly after infection and never again. A minority of those infected will have recurrent episodes of genital sores. Many cases of genital herpes are acquired from people who do not know they are infected or who had no symptoms at the time of the sexual contact. Acyclovir is a drug that can help to control the symptoms of HSV, but it is not a cure. HSV is frequently more severe in people with weakened immune systems, including people with HIV infection.

HUMAN PAPILLOMA VIRUS (HPV)

HPV is a virus that sometimes causes genital warts but in many cases infects people without causing noticeable symptoms. Concern about HPV has increased in recent years after several studies showed that HPV infection is associated with the development of cervical cancer. Approximately twenty-five types of HPV can infect the genital area. These types are divided into high-risk and low-risk groups based on whether they are associated with cancer. Infection with a high-risk type of HPV is one risk factor for cervical cancer, which causes 4,500 deaths among women each year. No cure for HPV infection exists.

SYPHILIS

Syphilis is a bacterial infection that can be cured with antibiotics. Syphilis cases increased dramatically from 1985 to 1990 among women of all ages. Data from 1993 show that female adolescents were twice as likely to have syphilis as male adolescents. African American women have syphilis rates that are seven times greater than the female population as a whole.

More than 3,000 cases of congenital syphilis were reported in 1993. Such infections among infants are largely preventable if women receive appropriate diagnosis and treatment during prenatal care. Death of the fetus or newborn infant occurs in up to 40 percent of pregnant women who have untreated syphilis.

CONDOM EFFECTIVENESS AND RELIABILITY

When used consistently and correctly, latex condoms are very effective in preventing a variety of STDs, including HIV infection. Multiple studies have demonstrated a strong protective effect of condom use. Because condoms are regulated as medical devices, they are subject to random testing by the Food and Drug Administration. Every latex condom manufactured in the United States is tested electronically for holes before packaging. Condom breakage rates are low in the United States—no higher than two per 100 condoms used. Most cases of condom failure result from incorrect or inconsistent use.

For further information, contact the Office of Women's Health, Centers for Disease Control and Prevention, 1600 Clifton Road, MS: D-51, Atlanta, GA 30033; phone: (404) 639-7230.

Source: www.cdc.gov/od/owh/whstd.htm.

less effective when used alone. The male condom is a latex rubber tube that comes rolled up and is unrolled on the penis. The female condom is a floppy polyurethane tube with an inner ring at the closed end that fits over the cervix and an outer ring at the open end that hangs outside the vagina. Condoms block sperm from entering the vagina and, when used properly in conjunction with other barrier methods, are highly effective in preventing pregnancy. Another very important aspect of condoms is that they are the only form of contraception that offers prevention against sexually transmitted diseases (STDs) generally and HIV/AIDS in particular. All health care providers emphasize that individuals not in a mutually monogamous sexual relationship should always use condoms.

Abortion

Although induced abortion, the removal of the fertilized ovum or fetus from the uterus, is only one aspect of reproductive choice, it has dominated discussion of this topic. This is unfortunate because there is more to reproductive rights than abortion. Nonetheless, this is one topic that generates unease and often heated discussion. *Pro-choice* advocates believe abortion is women's choice, women should not be forced to have children against their will, a fertilized ovum should not have all the legal and moral rights of personhood, and all children should be wanted children. Pro-choice advocates tend to believe in a woman's right to have an abortion even though they might not make that decision for themselves. *Pro-life* advocates believe that human personhood begins at conception and a fertilized ovum or fetus has the right to full moral and legal rights of personhood. These rights about the sanctity of human life outweigh the rights of mothers. Some pro-life advocates see abortion as murder and doctors and other health care workers who assist in providing abortion services as accomplices to a crime.

Although there are exceptions (most notably the Feminists for Life of America organization whose motto is "Pro Woman Pro Life"—they advocate opposition to all forms of violence and characterize abortion as violence), most people who consider themselves feminists are pro-choice. There are several issues raised by this perspective. The first issue is the moral responsibilities associated with requiring the birth of unwanted children, because the forces attempting to deny women safe and legal abortions are the very same ones that call for reductions in the social, medical, educational, and economic support of poor children. Does "pro-life" include being "for life" of these children once they are born? "Pro-life" politicians often tend to vote against increased spending for services for women and families. The second issue raised includes the moral responsibilities involved in requiring women to be mothers against their will. If you do grant full personhood rights to a fertilized ovum or fetus, then at what point do these rights take priority over the rights of another fully established full person, the mother? What of fathers' rights? Third, several studies have shown that between two-thirds and three-quarters of all women accessing abortions would have an illegal abortion if abortion were illegal. Illegal abortions have high mortality rates; issues do not go away just by making them illegal.

A 1996 poll reported over 50 percent of registered voters as "pro-choice" (defined as in favor of women's choice to access abortion services) and 36 percent as "pro-life" (defined as against abortion), with the rest uncertain. Here are some other statistics: Approximately 1.5 million abortions take place in the United States annually, with about 15,000 of these occurring after rape or incest. More than 50 percent of pregnancies among U.S. women are unintended, and about half of these pregnancies are terminated by abortion. At current

■ LEARNING ACTIVITY: WALK IN HER SHOES

Go to the California Abortion Rights Action League (CARAL) homepage at *www.caral .org* and follow the links to "Walk in the Shoes" of a woman deciding about having an abortion in the time before choice was legal. Explore the barriers women faced in seeking an abortion before *Roe v. Wade*. Now go to the homepage of the International Planned Parenthood Federation (IPPF) at *www.ippf.org*. Follow the links to resources and then country profiles. Click on a country to find out the status of women's reproductive rights in that nation. Return to the IPPF homepage and follow the links to resources and then the IPPF Charter on Sexual and Reproductive Rights to learn what basic rights IPPF is demanding for women. Go to the homepage for the National Abortion Rights Action League (NARAL) at *www.naral.org* and click on "100 Ways to Fight 4 Choice" under "Take Action" to discover things you can do to help protect freedom to choose. To find out about your state's abortion and reproductive rights, select "Access to Abortion & Reproductive Rights" under "Get Informed About Reproductive Rights Issues." Then under "Facts and Information" select "NARAL Report: Who Decides? A State-by-State Review of Abortion and Reproductive Rights."

rates, about 43 percent of women will have an abortion by the time they are 45 years old. Among women obtaining abortions, about half of these are younger than 25 years, and women aged 20 to 24 years obtain about a third of all abortions. African American and Latina women have higher rates of abortion than White women. Approximately two-thirds of all abortions are obtained by never-married women, and the same number (although not necessarily the same women) intend to have children in the future.

In the United States abortion was not limited by law or even opposed by the church until the nineteenth century. Generally, abortion was allowed before "quickening," understood as that time when the fetus's movements could be felt by the mother (usually between 3 and 4 months). In the 1820s, however, laws in New England declared abortion of an unquickened fetus a misdemeanor and a quickened fetus, second-degree manslaughter. As the century progressed, more restrictive laws were passed in various states, and in 1860 the Catholic Church officially ruled against abortion. Nonetheless, abortion rates continued. By the early twentieth century, abortion of any kind was illegal in the United States. In "Caught in the Crossfire," Cynthia Gorney describes the experiences of a group of people who provided illegal abortion services in the late 1960s.

The major abortion decision came in January 1973 with the Supreme Court ruling of *Roe v. Wade*. Although some states such as California and New York had reformed their abortion laws before this time, the Supreme Court ruling overturned all states' bans on abortion. The ruling used the *Griswold v. Connecticut* decision in arguing that abortion must be considered part of privacy rights in deciding whether to have children. It did not, however, attempt to decide the religious or philosophical decisions about when life begins. The Court did agree that, under the law, a fetus is not treated as a legal person with civil rights. The ruling went on to divide pregnancy into three equal stages or trimesters and explained the differential interventions that the state could make during these different periods. During the first trimester, women have the right to an abortion upon demand and the state cannot interfere. During the second trimester, the state is allowed to regulate abortion in order to preserve maternal health and well-being, and in the third trimester, similarly, the state has full right to regulate abortion as well as ban it completely, unless the life of the mother is in jeopardy.

Although there has been a general chipping away of women's rights to abortion since *Roe v. Wade,* there has been no ruling that says life begins at conception and therefore no complete overturning of *Roe v. Wade.* In terms of the various nibblings at this legislation, they include, first the Hyde Amendment, sponsored by Henry Hyde, a Republican senator from Illinois. It was an amendment to the 1977 Health, Education, and Welfare Appropriations Act and gave states the right to prohibit the use of Medicaid funds for abortion, thus limiting abortion to those women who could afford to pay. Note that this was accompanied by Supreme Court rulings (*Beal v. Doe,* 1977) that said that states could refuse to use Med-

FACTS ABOUT ABORTION, CHOICE, AND WOMEN'S HEALTH

- Between 1973, when abortion was made legal in the United States, and 1990, the number of deaths per 100,000 legal abortion procedures declined tenfold. By 1990, the risk of death from legal abortion had declined to 0.3 deaths per 100,000. (This rate is half the risk of a tonsillectomy and one-hundredth the risk of an appendectomy.)
- The mortality rate associated with childbirth is ten times higher than for legal abortion.
- Worldwide, 125,000 to 200,000 women die each year from complications related to unsafe and illegal abortions.
- In 84 percent of the counties in the United States, no physicians are willing or able to provide abortions.
- Only 12 percent of ob-gyn residency programs in the United States offer routine training in abortion procedures.
- Eighty-eight percent of abortions are performed before the end of the first trimester of pregnancy.
- Sixty-four percent of states prohibit most government funding for abortion, making access to the procedure impossible for many poor women.
- Thirty-eight states have enacted parental consent or notice requirements for minors seeking abortions.
- Abortion has no overall effect on the risk of breast cancer.
- Abortion does not increase the risk of complications during future pregnancies or deliveries.
- Emergency contraceptives reduce a woman's chance of becoming pregnant by 75 percent when taken within 72 hours of unprotected sex with a second dose 12 hours after the first.
- Emergency contraceptives do not cause abortions; they inhibit ovulation, fertilization, or implantation before a pregnancy occurs.
- Use of emergency contraceptives could reduce the number of unintended pregnancies and abortions by half annually.
- Eighty-nine percent of women aged 18 to 44 have not heard of or do not know the key facts critical to the use of emergency contraceptives.

Sources: NARAL Publications: *www.naral.org;* Reproductive Health and Rights Center: *www.choice.org.*

IDEAS FOR ACTIVISM: TEN THINGS
YOU CAN DO TO PROTECT CHOICE

1. *Volunteer for a pro-choice organization.* Pro-choice organizations need volunteers. There are dozens of organizations working in various ways to help women get the services they need. For pro-choice organizations nationwide, check *www .choice.org.*

2. *Write a letter to a local clinic or abortion provider thanking them for putting themselves on the line for women.* Doctors and clinic workers hear vociferously from those opposed to abortion. Hearing a few words of thanks goes a long way.

3. *Monitor your local paper for articles about abortion.* Write a letter to the editor thanking them for accurate coverage or correcting them if coverage is biased.

4. *Find out how your elected representatives have voted on abortion.* Call and ask for their voting records, not just on bills relating to legality of abortion, but also on related issues such as funding for poor women, restrictions meant to impede a woman's access to services (such as waiting periods and informed consent), and contraceptives funding and/or insurance coverage. Whether or not you agree with the votes of your elected officials, write and let them know that this is an issue on which you make voting decisions. Anti-choice activists don't hesitate to do this; you should do it too.

5. *Talk to your children now about abortion.* Explain why you believe it's a decision only a woman can make for herself.

6. *If you have had an abortion, legal or illegal, consider discussing it with people in your life.* Over 40 percent of American women will have at least one abortion sometime during their lives. More openness about the subject might lead to less judgment, more understanding, and fewer attempts to make it illegal.

7. *Volunteer for a candidate whom you know to be pro-choice.*

8. *Be an escort at a clinic that provides abortions.*

9. *Vote!*

10. *Hold a house meeting to discuss choice with your friends.* You could show one or all of Dorothy Fadiman's excellent documentaries from the trilogy, *From the Back Alleys to the Supreme Court and Beyond. When Abortion Was Illegal* is a good conversation starter. For information on obtaining these videos, contact the CARAL Pro-Choice Education Fund or *Concentric Media.*

Source: www.choice.org.

icaid funds to pay for abortions and that Congress could forbid states to use federal funds (including Medicaid) to pay for abortion services (*Harris v. McRae,* 1980). The latter ruling also allowed states to deny funds even for medically necessary abortions.

Second, the 1989 *Webster v. Reproductive Health Services,* sponsored by Missouri State Attorney William Webster, upheld a state's right to prevent public facilities or public employees from assisting with abortions, to prevent counseling concerning abortion if public funds were involved, and to allow parental notification rights. Third, *Planned Parenthood v. Casey,* although upholding *Roe v. Wade* in 1992, also upheld the state's right to restrict abortion in various ways: parental notification, mandatory counseling and waiting periods, and limitations on public spending for abortion services. As Rachel Roth notes in "How Women Pay for Fetal Rights," the more rights given a fetus, the more rights are stripped from women.

The situation at the turn of the century is that abortion is legal at the same time that its availability and accessibility have been limited. One piece of legislation, however, was passed in 1994 to safeguard women's right to access their legal rights. After the public outcry associated with the public harassment, wounding, and death of abortion services providers, and the vandalism and bombing of various clinics, the Supreme Court ruled in *Madsen et al. v. Women's Health Center, Inc.* to allow a buffer zone around clinics to allow patients and employees access and to control noise around the premises. The same year the Freedom of Access to Clinic Entrances (FACE) Act made it a federal crime to block access, harass, or incite violence in the context of abortion services.

READING 40

How Far We've Come

Harvard Women's Health Watch

With the new millennium only weeks away, authorities in every field of science are marveling at the accomplishments in their fields over the last 1,000 years. When it comes to women's health, it isn't necessary to look back to 1000 to see how dramatically things have changed. The idea of providing medical care that is based on the assumption that women are different from men isn't much older than this decade.

In 1990, women were largely irrelevant to medical training. When the subject wasn't pregnancy, childbirth, or diseases of the reproductive organs, everything medical students learned was based on the male anatomy. Little wonder that doctors trained this way often miss heart disease and other disorders in women, whose symptoms are different from men's —and routinely dismiss as trivial premenstrual syndrome and conditions more prevalent in women, such as chronic fatigue syndrome.

Not only were women being ignored in medical training, but they were also excluded from clinical trials to test new drugs, including early trials of female hormones. Being banned from studies was said to be in premenopausal women's best interests. The birth defects that arose from thalidomide used by pregnant women in the 1960s were often cited as an example of the harm that could come from experimental treatments. Women were also deemed unreliable subjects because hormonal fluctuations might skew study results. When postmenopausal women participated in studies, their results were usually lumped together with those in men so it was impossible to determine whether men and women had different reactions to a particular procedure or drug.

Those days are over. One needs only to turn on the TV to see that women's health is now one of the most talked about subjects of our time. Newscasts bring the latest developments in breast-cancer treatments; magazine programs showcase infertility, PMS, and menopause; a commercial for a cholesterol-lowering drug depicts a woman at risk for heart disease; and announcements for screening opportunities, medical studies, and prevention programs abound. Middle-aged women, once deemed demographically undesirable, are aggressively sought by health plans, medical centers, and drug companies.

A Brief History of Women's Health

This turn-about was no overnight phenomenon; it had been in the making for more than 30 years. The availability of oral contraceptives in the 1960s and legalized abortion in the 1970s had given women a new sense of control over their reproductive lives. The 1973 publication of *Our Bodies, Ourselves* had demystified their physiology. The traditional, paternalistic model of medical care was overturned as women demanded partnerships in which they shared information and decision-making with their doctors.

Yet, at the same time, doctors who wanted to better serve their female patients found themselves without answers to many of their patients' questions. There just wasn't much data on women. In 1989, a coalition of female scientists and health professionals decided to go after the data. They founded the Society for the Advancement of Women's Health Research with the principal goal of effecting the changes that would deliver the information doctors needed and headed for Congress.

The activists were instrumental in initiating a 1990 General Accounting Office investigation, which verified that women had been overlooked with regard to health research. As a result, the Office of Research on Women's Health was established within the National Institutes of Health. The office launched the Women's Health Initiative, a study of 150,000 postmenopausal women—the largest to date. The Food and Drug Administration followed suit, abolishing a long-held policy that excluded fertile women from clinical trials and directing gender-specific investigations of subsequent study results.

By the mid-1990s the floodgates had opened.

By the end of the decade there were several major research efforts in the works, each with a government-issue acronym—PEPI, SWAN, HERS, WELL-HART, STAR, RUTH. All represent NIH-funded studies of measures to reduce health risks in older women. The fields of research that follow have been the beneficiaries.

Menopause

Silent no more, this passage is one of the most loudly heralded events of a woman's lifetime. The World Health Organization weighed in on menopause and has proclaimed that it is actually a construct—the point at which a year has passed since our last menstrual period. It's a marker between perimenopause—the stage when estrogen and progesterone levels fluctuate wildly and then drop—and postmenopause—when the ovaries have pretty much stopped producing either hormone.

As a result, perimenopause is not considered a transition that for some women is characterized by a host of symptoms, including hot flashes and insomnia. Postmenopause—the open-ended era that begins after menopause—is now known as the time when women become vulnerable to heart disease, osteoporosis, breast cancer, and other conditions. Drug companies, supplement manufacturers, and noncommercial interests are bending over backwards to provide new approaches to symptom relief and risk reduction.

The question for most women is: "Which among the burgeoning field of methods for relieving symptoms and reducing risk is best—or best for *me?*" It's a question fit for a multiple-choice test—with a long list of potential answers. The list would certainly begin with estrogen, in all its myriad forms and doses. While it reduces the risk of osteoporosis and lowers some of the risk factors for cardiovascular disease, it increases the risk of endometrial and breast cancers.

Include a natural or synthetic progesterone, and the excess uterine cancer risk disappears, but the trade-off can be side effects that resemble PMS.

The dietary approach—relying on generous helpings of phytoestrogens from soy, flax, and herbs—would have a prominent place among potential answers. It may alleviate symptoms, but there are few data on its preventive effects.

Evista (raloxifene), a selective estrogen receptor modulator, or SERM, is one of the newest additions to the list. Like other SERMs being evaluated, Evista performs as an estrogen-mimic in some tissues and as an estrogen-block in others. It reduces fractures, lowers serum LDL (bad) cholesterol levels, and, according to early reports, may cut the risk of breast cancer.

Farther down on the list are other hormones under evaluation as supplements. These include testosterone, dehydroepiandrosterone (DHEA), human growth hormone, and melatonin.

The list terminates, of course, with "none of the above." Many still believe that if our grandmothers made it through this transition unaided, we can too.

The introduction of so many new approaches during the last decade has made postmenopause management a moving target. If your aim is to decide on an approach, the good news is that the Nurses' Health Study and others have indicated that the first five years of estrogen use are, in essence, a free trial period. You can take it to see how you like it without incurring an increased risk of breast cancer. You can see if it makes enough difference in your bone density to protect you from osteoporosis and whether it improves your cholesterol enough to protect you from heart disease. Meanwhile, you can await newer and potentially safer options.

Advances

- *An information explosion.* The last decade has seen the publication of hundreds of books, countless articles in periodicals and on the Internet, and immense coverage in scientific journals on research relating to menopause.
- *New interest in the psychosocial aspects of menopause.* Interest has grown exponentially. The gov-

ernment, nonprofit foundations, and pharmaceutical companies are sponsoring scores of new studies on midlife women. Among the most innovative is the Study of Women Across the Nation (SWAN), which is chronicling the midlife medical and social experiences of women in several ethnic groups.

- *New options for hormone replacement therapy.* These include natural progesterone in oral form (Prometrium), patch (CombiPatch), and vaginal gel (Crinone). New formulations and doses of estrogen continue to appear. Among the latest entrants are a vaginal ring (Estring) and conjugated estrogens from plants (Cenestin).

Heart Disease

Heart disease, the number one cause of death in women, is a paradigm of gender differences in health.

Epidemiologic studies have shown women do not develop heart disease until 10 years after their male counterparts do. Nonetheless, when women are stricken, they are more likely to die, and survivors are more likely to have another heart attack or go on to have a stroke than are men.

This outcome gap reflects a treatment gulf. Because women's symptoms aren't as likely to be recognized, women may not be diagnosed as rapidly or treated as aggressively as men. Chest pain is less likely to signal coronary-artery disease in women, probably because women are more likely to have other conditions that can produce similar sensations, such as mitral-valve prolapse, vessel spasms, costochondritis (an inflamation of the ribs), or pleurisy. Women are more likely to experience nausea and vomiting, which are often interpreted as the flu, food poisoning, or indigestion. When heart disease is suspected, traditional nuclear imaging tests, such as gallium scintigraphy, are less informative in women because breast tissue can obstruct the signal from the radioactive agent.

Moreover, the track record for therapeutic procedures, such as angioplasty and bypass surgery, is worse in women than in men. Recent research indicates, however, that age, extent of disease, and physical condition—rather than gender—account for

the difference. Women tend to be older and in poorer health than men when they undergo such procedures. When other factors are equal, women tend to fare as well as men do.

Because heart attacks tend to occur a decade later in women than in men, researchers assumed that the protective effect of estrogen was responsible. Observational studies added credence to that theory, but clinical trials have been less supportive. The Postmenopausal Estrogen/Progestin Intervention (PEPI) trial suggested that estrogen lessened many risk factors for heart disease, yet the Heart Attack and Estrogen Replacement Study (HERS) failed to show estrogen use protected against heart attacks in women with existing heart disease. The Women's Health Initiative, among other studies currently in progress, is expected to provide more definitive answers.

[Editors' note: 2003 data from the Nurses' Health Study stopped research trials on postmenopausal hormones. The reason for halting the trials was twofold: first, women on estrogen plus progestin were found to have a higher rate of breast cancer than those women taking the placebo, and second it became clear to the researchers that the benefits of estrogen plus progestin did not outweigh the risks. See www.NursesHealthStudy.org for more information on these data.]

Advances

- *New studies.* The Women's Health Initiative and several other research projects will provide more information on the factors that increase a woman's risk of heart disease.
- *Better understanding.* In the last decade, researchers better defined the role of HDL cholesterol and suggested that women need higher levels of the good cholesterol for protection against heart disease. Research has also indicated that other blood markers, like serum triglycerides and homocysteine, may play more meaningful roles in defining women's heart disease risk.
- *Treatment.* Cholesterol-lowering drugs, such as Mevacor (lovastatin), are now suggested for women at a much earlier stage than previously

and are being suggested as an alternative to estrogen for postmenopausal women at risk.

Breast Cancer

We hear so much about the growing epidemic of breast cancer that the good news is often lost. In fact, the likelihood that a woman will die of breast cancer is decreasing steadily. For example, about a quarter of tumors are now spotted while they're still precancerous, that is, they haven't broken out of the mammary ducts or lobules. Ninety-five percent of women who undergo lumpectomy and radiation for these cancers are still alive five years later. This treatment, while still no picnic, is much more palatable than it once was. Biopsies employing stereotactic and ultrasound-guided techniques (in which a needle removes the required sample) produce less damage and scarring. Women who have small tumors can opt for lumpectomy and radiation rather than mastectomies. Those who choose to undergo mastectomy can now have reconstructive surgery at the same time. Sentinel-node biopsy and more precise surgical lymph-node sampling have emerged as promising new approaches that can improve the detection rate for metastases and reduce lymphedema in the affected arm.

Chemotherapy is easier to stomach thanks to new anti-nausea drugs. Women who have recurrences or metastatic disease also have more options for treatment. Herceptin—which employs an antibody that homes in on breast cancer cells—and Taxol have boosted survival rates in women with more advanced disease.

The treatment experience has also changed in other ways. In the past, it was routine to send patients from one medical facility to another to receive radiation, chemotherapy, and other tests. Comprehensive breast centers are springing up around the country. They provide all necessary forms of therapy and other services, such as support groups and nutritional counseling, under one roof.

Perhaps most importantly, breast cancer has come out of the closet; it is no longer kept a secret. Breast-cancer activist groups, such as the National Alliance of Breast Cancer Organizations, Y-Me, and the National Breast Cancer Coalition, have made the disease one that women can talk openly about and thus receive support. There is a much more active involvement of patients in decision-making and more emphasis on nutrition, exercise, and other lifestyle factors for women undergoing treatment.

However, the greatest advances in the last decade have come not in treatment, but in prevention. The introduction of tests for the BRCA1 and BRCA2 genes allows physicians to forecast with reasonable accuracy some women's risk of developing breast cancer, but it has also opened a Pandora's box of issues that require genetic counseling. Mathematical modeling has made risk estimation possible for women who aren't interested in genetic testing. Prophylactic mastectomy, albeit a drastic measure, has been demonstrated to reduce the expected rate of breast cancer by at least 90% in high-risk women. The pharmaceutical approach, tamoxifen, reduced the rate of breast cancer 40–50% in high-risk women in clinical trials, and raloxifene showed promise in reducing breast-cancer risk in women who were taking it to prevent osteoporosis. These two drugs will be tested head to head in the federally funded STAR trial, which plans to enroll 23,000 postmenopausal women in centers throughout the country.

Advances

- *Activism.* By bringing breast cancer to the forefront, activist groups have brought more research dollars to bear against the disease, established wide-reaching support networks for patients, and increased the flow of information.
- *Detection.* The Mammography Quality Standardization Act has ensured that all women have access to the same standard of mammography and that they are notified of the results within a week.
- *Treatment.* New surgery spares more tissue, both in the breast and under the arm. New chemotherapy procedures are more effective and have fewer side effects.
- *Prevention.* Drugs such as tamoxifen (and possibly raloxifene) can reduce risk over the short term. Prophylactic mastectomy has proven to be extremely effective for motivated women who are at high-risk.

Osteoporosis

Osteoporosis—which once went undetected until a fractured hip, forearm, or vertebra uncovered its presence—has been flushed out of hiding. Thanks to the widespread availability of bone density measurement, doctors can now identify women with osteoporosis well ahead of symptoms such as a broken bone. New drugs have allowed women to rebuild porous bone.

Dual-energy x-ray absorptiometry (DXA), the state-of-the-art technology for measuring bone density, is emerging as a reliable tool for pinpointing women who are at risk for osteoporotic bone fractures. The number of DXA machines in the nation has grown from 750 in 1994 to 4,000 today. The use of ultrasound to measure bone density at the heel is also increasing. These devices, which don't involve x-rays, are used in the doctor's office to flag women with very low bone density for further testing.

The availability of options for treatment has also expanded. At the beginning of the decade, the only approved choices were estrogen and calcitonin injections. Since then two new oral drugs—alendronate (Fosamax) and raloxifene (Evista)—and a nasal spray form of calcitonin have come on the market. Numerous studies over the decade have shown how valuable those drugs, taken with calcium and vitamin D, can be to increase or maintain bone density in patients with postmenopausal osteoporosis. Sodium fluoride, parathyroid hormone, and several new SERMs are being studied for approval.

A new treatment for painful vertebral compression fractures, a common consequence of osteoporosis, has been undertaken by interventional radiologists. The procedure, called vertebroplasty, involves injecting a surgical cement into the fractured bone to strengthen it and alleviate pain.

Advances

- *Diagnostics.* The growth of DXA testing and the availability of ultrasound for determining heel fractures has made it possible to identify women with low bone density long before fractures occur.

- *Treatment.* The approval of three new drugs, and several more in the pipeline, increases the options for women who have low bone density.

Mental Health

The recognition of depression as one of the greatest health risks to women resulted in a number of new studies not only of major depression, but also of related disorders like dysthymia, premenstrual syndrome (PMS), and seasonal affective disorder (SAD). The National Institute of Mental Health produced a white paper, *Depression in Women,* noting the urgency and recommending increased screening programs and studies.

However, epidemiologic studies have indicated that depression is not as prevalent at certain life stages as once thought. For example, researchers have found no evidence that menopause is associated with an elevated rate of depression, which is a surprise to those who assumed women were prone to depression when their childbearing capacity—their perceived principal source of power in society—ceased.

If there is one factor that characterizes the change in treating depression, it may well be in the widespread use of a new generation of antidepressants, which, although not entirely free of side effects, are generally easier to tolerate than earlier classes were. The selective serotonin reuptake inhibitors (SSRIs) in particular have emerged as a class of drugs that is helpful in treating most of the depressive disorders, although some drugs are more effective than others for certain conditions. The mood-elevating effects of estrogen are also under study. There is some evidence that the hormone can enhance the work of SSRIs.

Treatment for depression is now successful in 80% of patients. Although the new antidepressants have contributed to this statistic, there's evidence that a combined treatment of drugs and psychotherapy provide the fastest relief.

Yet, there is also evidence that biology isn't exclusively responsible for depression in women. Studies have also pointed to the role of life experiences, particularly those of being in an abusive relationship, experiencing poverty, raising children without support, and having a lack of control over one's fate, as contributing to depression in women.

Anxiety disorders, which also affect women in greater numbers than men, became another focus during the 1990s. The recognition of the increasing incidence of eating disorders—anorexia, bulimia, and binge eating—spurred not only research into the causes, but also initiatives designed to prevent, detect, and develop effective treatments beginning in young girls.

Advances

- *New data.* Defining societal factors that increase the risk of depression in women.
- *Initiatives.* Awareness has led to initiatives, such as National Depression Screening Day and eating disorders awareness programs, that help identify these conditions in women.
- *New treatment approaches.* New medications and multidisciplinary approaches to eating disorders and depression have emerged.

READING 41

Gender Role Stressors and Women's Health

Patti Lou Watkins and Diane Whaley

Women's Health Problems

Unarguably, significant gender differences exist in the experience of health problems. For instance, morbidity rates of musculoskeletal and connective tissue diseases such as osteoporosis are much greater for women. Women, more often than men, also experience neurologic disorders, including migraine headaches, as well as psychiatric disorders, particularly affective, anxiety, and eating disorders (Litt, 1993). In the keynote address at the Society of Behavioral Medicine's annual meeting, Chesney (1997) implored those assembled to add domestic violence to the list of women's health problems. The Midcourse Review of the Healthy People 2000 goals (U.S. Department of Health & Human Services [USDHHS], 1995) acknowledged that, "Women are frequent targets of both physical and sexual assault often perpetrated by spouses, intimate partners, or others known to them" (p. 60). Unfortunately, this report also states that homicides, weapons-related violent deaths, and assault injuries have increased

since 1990. As such, women account for nearly two thirds of the medical visits and are recipients of most medications prescribed (Hoffman, 1995).

Chronic disease risk factors, such as smoking, have increased dramatically among women in recent years (Litt, 1993). Furthermore, the USDHHS (1995) reported that although the general public has made progress toward smoking cessation goals, the inverse is true for pregnant women and women without a high school education. Obesity rates have also increased since health objectives were established in 1990, especially for women. The Surgeon General's Report on Physical Activity and Health (USDHHS, 1996) implicated women's relative lack of exercise in explanation of this trend. Gender differences in mortality rates are fast disappearing as cardiovascular disease (CVD) is now the leading cause of death among women as well as men. Cancer mortality rates are also roughly equivalent, with women's lung cancer death rate rising rapidly over the past 30 years.

Finally, women are developing AIDS at a faster pace than men (Litt, 1993).

Given these patterns, it is little wonder that women consistently perceive themselves as having worse health than men (Verbrugge, 1989). Although women currently live approximately 7 years longer than men, the quality of their lives may be vastly diminished. Verbrugge (1989) contended that gender differences in health status transcend biological predispositions, resulting more from sociocultural forces such as well-documented employment inequities (Amott & Matthaie, 1996). Contributing to the problem, women are also less likely than men to have adequate health insurance coverage (Stanton & Gallant, 1995). Indeed, Anson, Paran, Neumann, and Chernichovsky (1993) found that gender differences in health perceptions disappeared when they controlled for risks embedded in the social construction of gender and gender roles, leading the authors to suggest that women's socialization results in less successful coping with the "inevitable stressors faced in human life" (p. 426). A feminist perspective, however, might argue that the stressors for women are not inevitable. Rather, many are socially constructed, and perpetuated through existing power structures.

In summary, contemporary women are suffering and dying from disorders that the lay public, along with the medical profession itself, have long considered diseases of men—and in the case of AIDS, gay men. Additionally, women experience debilitating, although not imminently life-threatening, medical problems more than men. In conjunction with relatively greater psychological distress, deteriorating health habits, and frequent victimization, women's quality of life may be severely compromised as they negotiate their life spans. The next section explores the influence of gender roles on these problems.

Gender Roles: Interpersonal Communication

Women interact with the health-care system differently than men do, with increased visits and different types of complaints. In turn, the health-care system responds to women and men in a different fashion, often to the detriment of women's health. Studies have shown that medical practitioners treat CVD less aggressively in women relative to men. In fact, across conditions, treatment protocols are based on a male model of medicine, with women's health problems viewed as deviations from a male-defined norm (Hoffman, 1995). Lee and Sasser-Cohen (1996) contended that the medical profession has, in fact, pathologized women's normal biological processes and body structure.

In a recent study, Chiaramonte and Friend (1997) asked medical students to review cases of women and men with either only symptoms of heart disease or heart disease symptoms accompanied by anxiety. When presented with unambiguous cases, students were able to detect heart disease in both genders. However, when presented with cases evidencing both cardiac and anxiety symptoms, they correctly detected heart disease among the male cases, referring them to cardiologists. Conversely, they more often misdiagnosed heart disease among the female cases, referring them instead to psychologists. Advanced medical students were more likely to make this error, suggesting that medical school training serves to increase gender biases in diagnostic and treatment decisions. Russo, Denious, Keita, and Koss (1997) asserted that battered women also escape detection when they are in medical settings. Like women with CVD symptoms, they are likely to receive psychiatric diagnoses along with tranquilizing medication.

Communication of diagnostic information and treatment recommendations by medical practitioners represents another area of concern for the female patient. Smith (1996) saw physicians' failure to interact with patients in a courteous, informative fashion as a breach of ethics, rather than a case of poor "bedside manner." In her view, most medical encounters constitute interviews in which patient-initiated questions are discouraged, thereby establishing the practitioner's position of power. Such interactions prevent patients from taking charge of their health. Smith contrasts this to a model in which practitioners might interact with patients as participants in a shared project, with mutual understanding as the goal. As such, patients should have the right "to speak, to question, to challenge, and to express themselves" (p. 202). Smith contends that women, particularly women of color and those of lower socioeconomic status (SES), receive less information than male patients. In a survey of Black women who had been physically and sexually abused, Russo et al. (1997) found that lower income participants, indeed, perceived physicians as "patronizing and unhelpful" (p. 340). Although the FGRS construct suggests that women may be less inclined to assert themselves in such situations, Smith notes that practitioners dub women "difficult patients" when they ask questions during the medical interview. A female patient "may be taken as hostile, uncooperative, and confrontative, whereas a male patient might be viewed as rational and actively involved in his own treatment" (p. 194). Roter and Hall (1992) disagreed, noting that in some studies, female patients received relatively more information from practitioners. In fact, women's communication styles may make them "more savvy users of their time with doctors" (p. 44). These authors admit that exploration of gender differences in patient–practitioner communication is a relatively new endeavor, with many questions remaining unanswered at this point.

Indirect support for Smith's (1996) claims, however, may come from studies of individuals who present to medical settings with symptoms of anxiety and depression. A number of researchers (e.g., Agras, 1993) agree that these patients, predominantly women, leave the medical setting with a limited understanding of their complaints. Watkins, Nock, Champion, and Lidren (1996) found that practitioners typically spent less than 5 minutes explaining diagnostic information to individuals with panic disorder (PD). In only a few cases were patients actually provided with an accurate diagnosis. Rather, they received a variety of vague explanations such as "some strange flu" and "hidden problems" (p. 180). One participant remarked, "First few times he suggested it was 'just' stress, then, later, after a few months, he said it was depression, then later, without much concern, he suggested it was anxiety" (p. 184). This broad array of unclear explanations resulted in low levels of patient understanding and satisfaction, perhaps best summarized by one patient's experience of "resentment" toward the practitioner "for not being as sympathetic and respectful of this being a real and true experience for me" (p. 184). Watkins et al. (1996) found that partic-

ipants rarely received referrals, although most received pharmacological treatment. Compared to cognitive-behavioral therapy (CBT) for PD, medications have a higher relapse rate (Gould, Otto, & Pollack, 1995). This difference may be due to the superior ability of CBT to enhance self-efficacy, the belief that one can successfully manage a situation, in this case panic attacks (PA) and the circumstances that surround them. Finally, the high cost of medications compared to various forms of CBT (Gould et al., 1995) may present a greater problem for women whose economic resources are generally less than those of their male peers.

Roter and Hall (1992) agreed that physicians often substitute medications for effective communication. In terms of gender differences, [it was] observed that physicians prescribe psychotropic medications to women relatively more often and that these prescriptions extend for longer periods of time than those provided for men. She asserts that medicating women without attempting to impart coping skills, or more importantly, to resolve the inequities that women suffer at home and in the workplace, equates to oppression. This practice prompts women to nurture others at the expense of their own health. When physicians prescribe psychotropic medications, they may be abetting dysfunctional, possibly abusive, social arrangements as well as fostering women's self-blame.

Practitioner communication most assuredly warrants further research. Russo et al. (1997) suggested that such work address diversity issues within, as well as across, gender. Their findings also suggest that various presenting complaints may elicit specific types of problem behavior from practitioners. In their study, women who had been sexually abused reported that physicians had acted in sexually inappropriate ways toward them. Concurrent examination of practitioners' gender might enhance understanding of communication problems in the medical setting. Hall, Irish, Roter, Ehrlich, and Miller (1994) conducted a study in which they found female physicians to be more nurturant, expressive, and interpersonally oriented than males. This, along with Gross's (1992) finding that male physicians encounter more interpersonal difficulties with patients, aligns with the concepts of gender role stressors outlined here. Although organized efforts are underway to improve the communication skills of medical practitioners (e.g., Levinson & Roter, 1993), many Americans, especially women, are turning to treatment strategies that minimize practitioner contact...

REFERENCES

Agras, W. S. (1993). The diagnosis and treatment of panic disorder. *Annual Review of Medicine, 4,* 39–51.

Ammott, T., & Matthaei, J. (1996). *Race, gender, and work: A multicultural economic history of women in the United States.* Boston: South End Press.

Anson, O., Paran, E., Neumann, L., & Chernichovsky, D. (1993). Gender differences in health perceptions and their predictors. *Social Science and Medicine, 36,* 419–427.

Chesney, M. A. (1997, March). *Unanswered challenges to behavioral medicine: Broadening the agenda.* Paper presented at the Society of Behavioral Medicine annual meeting, San Francisco.

Chiaramonte, G., & Friend, R. (1997, March). *Do medical schools reinforce gender bias in diagnosing CHD?* Paper presented at the annual meeting of the Society of Behavioral Medicine, San Francisco.

Gould, R. A., Otto, M. W., & Pollack, M. H. (1995). A meta-analysis of treatment outcome for panic disorder. *Clinical Psychology Review, 15,* 819–844.

Gross, E. B. (1992). Gender differences in physician stress. *Journal of the American Medical Women's Association, 47,* 107–112.

Hall, J. A., Irish, J. T., Roter, D. L., Ehrlich, C. M., & Miller, L. (1994). Gender in medical encounters: An analysis of physician and patient communication in a primary care setting. *Health Psychology, 13,* 384–392.

Hoffman, E. (1995). *Our health, our lives: A revolutionary approach to health care for women.* New York: Simon & Schuster.

Lee, J., & Sasser-Cohen, J. (1996). *Blood stories: Menarche and the politics of the female body in contemporary U. S. society.* New York: Routledge.

Levinson, W., & Roter, D. (1993). The effects of two continuing medical education programs on communication skills of practicing primary care physicians. *Journal of General Internal Medicine, 8,* 318–324.

Litt, I. (1993). Health issues for women in the 1990s. In S. Matteo (Ed.), *American women in the nineties: Today's critical issues* (pp. 139–157). Boston: Northeastern University Press.

Roter, D. L., & Hall, J. A. (1992). *Doctors talking with patients/patients talking with doctors: Improving communication in medical visits.* Westport, CT: Auburn House.

Russo, N. F., Denious, J. E., Keita, G. P., & Koss, M. P. (1997). Intimate violence and Black women's health. *Women's Health: Research on Gender, Behavior, and Policy, 3,* 335–348.

Smith, J. F. (1996). Communicative ethics in medicine: The physician–patient relationship. In S. M. Wolf (Ed.), *Feminism and bioethics: Beyond reproduction* (pp. 184–215). New York: Oxford University Press.

Stanton, A. L., & Gallant, S. J. (1995). Psychology of women's health: Challenges for the future. In A. L. Stanton & S. J. Gallant (Eds.), *The psychology of women's health: Progress and challenges in research and application* (pp. 567–582). Washington, DC: American Psychological Association.

U.S. Department of Health and Human Services (1995). *Healthy people 2000: Midcourse review and 1995 revisions.* Washington, DC: Public Health Service.

U.S. Department of Health and Human Services (1996). *Physical activity and health: A report of the Surgeon General.* Atlanta, GA. USDHHS, Centers for Disease Prevention and Health Promotion.

Verbrugge, L. (1989). The twain meet: Empirical explanations of sex differences in health and mortality. *Journal of Health and Social Behavior, 30,* 282–304.

Watkins, P. L., & Lee, J. (1997). A feminist perspective on panic disorder and agoraphobia: Etiology and treatment. *Journal of Gender, Culture, & Health, 2,* 65–87.

Watkins, P. L., Nock, C., Champion, J., & Lidren, D. M. (1996). Practitioner–patient communication in the presentation of panic symptoms. *Mind/Body Medicine, 4,* 177–189.

READING 42

Forgotten Women
How Minorities Are Underserved by Our Health Care System

Lisa Collier Cool

Imagine living in a place where going to a doctor involves a difficult or even dangerous trek to a distant, overcrowded clinic where you wait hours for a few minutes of questionable medical care—a place where preventive treatment is so lacking that breast tumors sometimes protrude through the skin before they are diagnosed.

You might expect these conditions in a third world country, but actually they're faced every day by minority women in some parts of the U.S. Statistics show that "an African-American woman born in Harlem today has less chance of surviving to age 65 than a woman from Bangladesh, one of the poorest nations on earth," say Colin McCord, M.D., associate director of surgery at Harlem Hospital in New York City.

Although you might think that poverty is to blame, the truth is that even affluent minority women—whether black, Hispanic, Asian-American or Native American—fare poorly in our medical system. "An African-American woman who earns triple what a Euro-American female earns still has a greater chance of mortality from disease like breast cancer," says Faye Gary, Ed.D., distinguished service professor at the College of Nursing of the University of Florida in Gainesville.

What makes this all the more shocking is that even as progress has been made in women's health as a whole, the health disparities between black and white women have remained. Mortality from heart disease and cancer has fallen among white women, yet is unchanged in blacks. At every age, "African-American, Native American, Hispanic and Asian-American women suffer from poorer health and greater risk of premature death," says Dr. Gary.

Deadly Discrimination

Socioeconomic factors explain only some of these inequities. While it's true that black women have triple the rate of poverty of white women and are slightly less likely to be insured, research reveals that they're also the victims of subtle but potentially fatal medical bias. A recent study at Boston University found that at every income level, black women over age 64 are only half as likely as whites to have a mammogram ordered for them by a doctor, even if they see a primary-care physician just as often. Mammography rates are even lower for Native American women. The result is that black and Native American women have 30% higher risk of dying of breast cancer, despite the fact that the disease is much less common in these groups than in whites.

The same pattern of prejudice prevails in hospital care: A study at Beth Israel Hospital in Boston found that doctors order $1\frac{1}{2}$ times as much surgery and other high-tech treatment for whites as for equally ill blacks. It's not just costly procedures these patients are shortchanged on, either: 20% of Latinas and 65% of Korean Americans have never had a pap smear, yet lab costs start at $16.

Even in the emergency room, your race or ethnicity can have more impact on your care than your condition, says Jane Delgado, Ph.D., president and CEO of the National Coalition of Hispanic Health and Human Services Organizations in Washington. "A study of people treated for a broken leg showed that the single greatest predictor of who got pain-killers was whether they were Hispanic," she says. "The doctors often withheld painkillers from Hispanic patients even though Hispanic and non-Hispanic patients rated their pain as equally severe." This reminds Dr. Gary of the segregated care she received growing up in the south in the '50s. "My parents had to drive 100 miles to take me to the only white dentist who would see black people," she recalls. "I remember feeling grateful when he yanked out my teeth at his kitchen table, because I wasn't allowed into his office."

Deep-Rooted Stereotypes

Not only are minorities' medical needs dangerously neglected, but doctor prejudice can also result in substandard care for those who get treated, says Claudia R. Baquet, M.D., associate dean for policy and planning at University of Maryland School of Medicine in Baltimore. "In focus groups," she says, "minority women say that doctors assume they have multiple partners or start having sex at an early age. Racial and ethnic stereotyping is still rampant and a barrier to quality care."

Minority women are doubly disadvantaged because they may be subjected to sexism in addition to racial bias, notes Aida Giachello, Ph.D., director of the Midwest Latino Health Research, Training and Policy Center at the University of Illinois in Chicago. Many Latinas report that doctors dismiss their complaints. "The stereotype is that Latinas overuse the health system," says Dr. Giachello. "But when we did a focus group with these women, the reality was that they had to go to the doctors over and over with the same symptoms, because the physicians would say it was stress while the real problem went undiagnosed, sometimes causing serious complications."

Equally damaging are the assumptions physicians may make if they judge a patient's ethnicity based on her skin color or surname. "If a Native American woman from the Southwest has a Latino last name, a doctor may misclassify her and not test for gallbladder disease, which is epidemic in that population," says Dr. Baquet. Others question the medical value of determining ethnicity at all. "Asking someone what race she considers herself to be doesn't tell you what her genetics are," points out Olivia Carter-Pokras, Ph.D., an epidemiologist and public health analyst at the Office of Minority Health in Washington. "Even sickle-cell anemia, thought of as a 'black' disorder, also appears in white people of Mediterranean origin."

Research Bias

More serious still is the situation in clinical trials, where scientists develop the medicine of the future by testing new drugs, diagnostic techniques and other treatments. Despite laws mandating the inclusion of women and minorities in trials sponsored by the National Institutes of Health, many doctors don't seem to have gotten the message, reports Dr. Carter-Pokras, who says she constantly sees unconscious or even overt prejudice on the part of researchers. "A doctor may decide to recruit from her own clinic, never stopping to think that since her patients are 80% white, she needs to be aggressive about finding minority cases," she says. Investigators often try to recruit Spanish speakers with no translators or bilingual materials. Not only do such attitudes reduce minority women's access to state-of-the-art care, but also underrepresentation in studies ensures that the second-class medical care will continue for decades to come.

Increasing the number of women of color participating in medical studies is important, but Dr. Gary feels it doesn't go far enough. "There also needs to be better representation of ethnic groups among the people who do the studies," she says. Despite doctors' best intentions, subtle biases and cultural differences can still interfere with good research.

Constructive Changes

The outrage from women of color is finally starting to be heard on Capitol Hill. The U.S. Public Health Service's Office on Women's Health is developing a culturally sensitive women's health curriculum for medical and nursing schools, and has stated programs to recruit more minority women in to health careers and as participants in clinical trials.

Other federal agencies are creating their own initiatives. The Centers for Disease Control and Prevention is funding studies of chronic diseases that affect women of color disproportionately. But it's still up to women to help alert doctors to the potential for bias in diagnosis and treatment and to become more attuned to how our racial or ethnic background may affect our health. Each of these efforts shares the same crucial goal: to create a healthier tomorrow for *all* women.

READING 43

Man-made Threats to Women's Health

Adrienne Germain

The expression "man-made threats" to women's health probably brings to mind environmental and occupational hazards that cause medical problems ranging from cancers to genetic defects. These are certainly important concerns for people everywhere, but the vast majority of the world's women face graver and more insidious dangers of man's making, dangers that lurk in their bedrooms, in the streets and in the corridors of power. What is the source of these perils? The age-old domestic, social and political dominion that men have over the lives—bodies and minds—of women.

A woman's well-being begins at home, yet home is hardly the healthy haven it is thought to be. Men routinely beat women for any number of reasons—for failing to have dinner on the table, for asking to use condoms during sex, or expressing their own opinions—and frequently for no reason at all. In the United States alone, as many as 4 million women each year are seriously battered by their male partners; in more than 20 countries where reliable, large-scale studies have been done, 16 to 52 per cent of women had been assaulted by an intimate partner. The vast majority of women beaten by their men almost never have a forum for redress or a place of refuge, not even the homes of their own parents. In South Asia, for example, women who are beaten by their husbands and seek shelter with their parents are told such violence is a part and parcel of marriage. More often than not, they are ordered to be "obedient" wives and return to their assailants.

Other dangers stemming from the power imbalance between the sexes have just as much potential to injure and kill. Men who refuse to use contraception or who prevent female partners from using it put women at risk for unwanted pregnancies. In too many cases, husbands also prevent their pregnant wives from seeking health care or skilled help to give birth, often with fatal consequences. World-wide, botched abortions and unsafe childbirth claim the lives of some 600,000 women each year.

When men shirk their sexual responsibility by having sex with multiple partners and by refusing to use condoms, the women in their lives often end up with sexually transmitted diseases, including the human immunodeficiency virus (HIV). A recent study shows that young married women in India are being infected with HIV by their prostitute-visiting husbands at alarming rates. In Uganda, a country with a high prevalence of HIV, women are infected at far younger ages than men because men seek out virgins with whom to have safe sex, although their definition of safe does not mean they use condoms. Outside the home, in the community and the nation, the threat to women comes from man-made norms and social policies. Mass media, increasingly pervasive around the world, reduces women to sex objects and promotes male ownership and even violence against women's bodies.

Sexual harassment degrades and threatens girls and women in school and at work. Almost defying belief, rejected suitors in one country commonly throw acid in the faces of the women they desire so that no other men will want them. In some parts of another region, male "honour" is justification for murdering wives and sisters who commit adultery. Across a great part of the world, male privilege is reflected in the preference for sons in health care, in sex-selective abortion, and even in female infanticide. At least 2 million girls and young women each year are subjected to female genital mutilation to ensure their chastity and marriageability, with serious emotional and health consequences, including death. Trafficking in girls and women now crosses virtually all borders.

Women's relegation to second-class citizens in the name of religion seriously jeopardizes their health. A recent—and extreme—example of this was the Taliban's system of medical apartheid in Afghanistan: women patients were to be seen only by female health professionals, of which there were very few, in segregated facilities with nothing like the medical equipment and supplies available for men. Around the world, other proscriptions on women's access to health care—opposition to contraception and safe induced abortion on the one hand; forced pregnancy, forced abortion and forced sterilization on the other—result in untold suffering and countless deaths. Some 12 Latin American countries exonerate rapists if they marry their victims.

The attitudes and beliefs that drive such practices on every continent also express themselves in social policies. In general, these man-made measures don't make women's health a priority; sometimes, it seems, their aim is quite the reverse. For one particular example, one need look no farther than the United States Congress. In recent months, a single American Congressman—one who relentlessly opposes a woman's right to protect her health and control her reproduction—has held hostage payment of United States dues to the United Nations and contributions to the International Monetary Fund in order to deny women access to safe, legal abortions and related information and services.

Bleak as it might appear, this picture is not one of utter darkness, and each day brings new hope. By organizing at the grassroots level, women all over the globe are now playing an increasingly vocal, visible and vital role in helping to shape the policies and programmes that determine their well-being. Significantly, these women are joined every day by more and more men who have begun to realize that they and their communities will benefit. Governments, too, are coming around: in Vienna in 1993, in Cairo in 1994, and in Beijing in 1995, the nations of the world committed themselves to action to promote the sexual and reproductive health of women. Major United Nations agencies and programmes have pledged to assist Governments to meet these commitments. While these are surely important steps, lasting improvements in women's well-being will come only when many more men change their ways —starting with how they behave at home.

READING 44

Breast Cancer
Is It the Environment?

Ms.

"For too long now breast cancer research has been dominated by the elusive search for the cure," says Andrea Martin, founder and executive director of the Breast Cancer Fund, a San Francisco–based group that has launched a major campaign to draw attention to the links between the environment and breast cancer. Citing the fact that only 5 to 10 percent of breast cancer cases are genetically caused and that the number of women with breast cancer nearly doubled between 1970 and 1990, the fund has teamed up with the Susan G. Komen Breast Cancer Founda-

tion to urge the public to agitate for more research into environmental causes of the disease. Last October the two groups rallied 70 individuals and organizations (including local breast cancer groups, the Coalition of Labor Union Women, and the YWCA) to sign a letter to President Clinton. The letter called for increased funding for research examining environmental links; monitoring by the Centers for Disease Control (CDC) of what chemicals are in our bodies and in what amounts; full funding for the Environmental Protection Agency's (EPA) program to screen for environmental toxins; and a cross-agency committee to oversee government funding for environmental health research.

The following is excerpted from the Breast Cancer Fund's publication *Examining the Environmental Links to Breast Cancer.*

Since 1971, the year President Richard Nixon declared a "war on cancer," more than $35 billion has been committed to research. Yet we still cannot pinpoint with certainty the causes behind the vast majority of breast cancer cases, nor have treatment options changed or improved much over the years. Women still must choose from surgery, radiation, and/or chemotherapy.

In addition, some in the medical establishment have misleadingly focused on mammography as a prevention measure, with the assumption that early detection can prevent serious illness. Mammography, however, is *not* prevention. It can only detect cancer that already exists and may have been present for eight to ten years. It fails to detect breast cancer 20 percent of the time in women over 50, and as much as 40 percent of the time in younger women.

What We Know

Hundreds of scientific studies of laboratory animals and wildlife have drawn links between exposure to toxic chemicals and cancer. Emerging science suggests that synthetic chemicals in the environment pose a risk to the human reproductive system, the endocrine system, and to human growth and development both *in utero* and after birth.

A rapidly evolving field of research involves the study of "endocrine disrupters" or "hormone mimickers"—synthetic chemicals found in pesticides like DDT, some fuels, plastics, detergents, and pharmaceutical drugs. We know that estrogen binds with receptors in mammary glands, signaling cells to grow. In 1993, scientists at Cornell University cautioned that growing evidence seemed to indicate that exposure to estrogen-mimicking chemicals, called xenoestrogens, can cause cells to rapidly grow out of control and form tumors. It has been postulated that xenoestrogens may be responsible for increasing a

woman's chances of getting breast cancer. Researchers at Tufts University Medical School have demonstrated that xenoestrogens make human breast cancer cells grow in the laboratory, just as natural estrogen does.

There are also studies that show drastic changes in development, particularly in the reproductive system, when laboratory mice are exposed to estrogen mimickers during critical windows of vulnerability *in utero.* When cells are rapidly developing and proliferating, there can be a key period of vulnerability during which damaging or altering cell development can lead to cancer. Other windows of vulnerability include puberty and a woman's first pregnancy.

Studies tracking patterns of breast cancer development in humans also strongly suggest the influence of environmental factors. In Asia, women are four to seven times less likely to develop breast cancer than women in the U.S. Yet when Asian women migrate to the U.S., their risk of breast cancer rises over a two-generation span. Women who live in the U.S. for a decade or more have an 80 percent higher risk of developing breast cancer than more recent immigrants, and those whose grandparents were born in the U.S. have a 60 percent greater risk than women whose grandparents were born overseas.

Estrogen mimickers may be either beneficial or detrimental. Estrogen-mimicking compounds found in foods such as broccoli, soy products, and cauliflower may act as "good" estrogens, providing some protection against the effects of estradiol, the chief "bad" estrogen, made naturally by our bodies. Critics of the "xenoestrogen theory" argue that these beneficial compounds found in foods can balance possible hazards posed by human-made chemicals. Other scientists point out that the human body has been fine-tuned to handle plant estrogens through thousands of years of evolution, while human-made estrogen mimickers have been in the environment only since the 1940s. Since we do not yet understand how women's natural estrogen affects breast cancer, it is difficult to predict how estrogen mimickers might behave, even at low doses.

Studies have identified the presence of more than 200 foreign chemicals in women's breast milk, including significant levels of dioxin, a carcinogen that has been shown to disrupt children's hormone systems. Within six months of being breast-fed, a baby in the U.S. or Europe receives the maximum recommended lifetime dose of dioxin.

More Research Needed

Chemicals that are persistent in the environment accumulate in body fat and are carried by women in their breast tissue. Thus far, human data about the link between these chemicals and breast cancer are inconclusive. For example, some studies have shown that women with breast cancer have the same or lower levels of pesticide residue in their system than women without the disease.

However, other studies, by U.S. and Canadian scientists, have found that women with higher levels of organochlorines in their blood have four to ten times the risk of breast cancer than those with lower levels. [Organochlorines are hydrocarbon-based chemicals containing chlorines like DDT. Many of these compounds break down very slowly in the environment and can be stored in the fat of animals, fish, and humans.] These seemingly inconsistent results point to the need for long-term prospective studies on this issue.

There are only two recognized causes of breast cancer: exposure to ionizing radiation and inherited genetic defects in breast cells. Other factors, though they have not been shown to *cause* the disease, are associated with higher risk: beginning menstruation before age 12, onset of menopause after 55, bearing children late in life or not at all, not breast-feeding, and prolonged use of estrogen after menopause.

More research is needed to examine why the established risk factors increase a woman's vulnerability. However, additional and different research is needed to determine which of the thousands of chemicals in the environment cause the disease, and how. Most important, we must conduct long-term prospective studies that measure exposures to chemicals during critical windows of breast development.

Research Priorities

For many years the focus of the National Cancer Institute (NCI), the largest single government funding source for cancer investigations, has been on earlier detection with mammography, improved radiation and chemotherapy, and improved surgical techniques designed to help women survive the disease and live longer. Much research continues to be focused on the role of inherited gene defects. Currently, there is no breast cancer prevention research strategy at the NCI except for chemo-prevention through the use of raloxifene and tamoxifen in high-risk, healthy women.

The federal government has funded one multi-million-dollar, multiyear environment research study, the Long Island Breast Cancer Study Project, to determine whether environmental contaminants increase breast cancer risk. But overall, funding for environmental research represents only a tiny fraction of the government's budget for disease research. Of the National Institutes of Health's $15.7 billion budget last year, just $382 million, or 2.4 percent, went to the National Institute of Environmental Health Sciences, the primary agency conducting research on environmental health. Similarly, the CDC's National Center for Environmental Health received just $172 million for 1999.

A Call for Action

Over the years, a growing movement has emerged calling for prevention-based research.

Breast cancer advocates and researchers have identified three important types of research currently underfunded by the federal government: testing and screening of industrial chemicals and pesticides for their toxicity and hormone-mimicking effects; measuring the levels of these chemicals in our bodies—a process known as "bio-monitoring"; and learning how girls and women are exposed to these chemicals, so we can study health effects and ultimately reduce health risks.

In 1996, an advisory committee of scientists and experts established by the EPA recommended the creation of a program to test the toxicity and hormonal effects of 9,000 chemicals, as required under the Food Quality Protection Act. However, this program has been grossly underfunded. Development of the tests alone will cost $50 million over a period of several years. The program's proposed 2000 budget is only $12 million. Further, as currently devised, the tests do not screen for toxicity during the prenatal and early development period when chemicals have been known to have different and often more harmful effects.

To fully understand the impact of environmental contaminants on humans, the EPA's data on the toxicity of these chemicals must be completed and complemented by an ongoing systematic program of bio-monitoring data to identify what chemicals exist in our bodies and at what levels.

Unfortunately, the CDC's National Environmental Health Laboratory, the agency that spearheads bio-monitoring research, is also severely underfunded. The Breast Cancer Fund is calling for more broad-based testing as well as testing on breast milk, a fluid that absorbs chemicals differently, and, in some cases, at higher and potentially more dangerous levels. Not only do women have the right to know what chemicals are in their breasts and breast milk, but investing in this kind of research is also a critical step to developing public policies and prevention strategies that will effectively address the breast cancer epidemic and other serious illnesses.

Yet research into the environmental causes of breast cancer remains a low priority among leading cancer organizations and government agencies. Ad-vocates have attributed this lack of commitment, in part, to pressure from industry. Pharmaceutical companies, in particular, have a vested interest in keeping breast cancer research focused on drug therapies and away from environmental pollution. Breast Cancer Awareness Month was initiated by the pharmaceutical giant Zeneca, the maker of tamoxifen. [Activists often note Zeneca's link to Imperial Chemical Industries (ICI), the maker of pesticides, plastics, pharmaceutical, and paper. Zeneca was a spin-off company of ICI, which was sued in 1990 by state and federal agencies for dumping DDT and PCBs in California harbors.] In 1999, Zeneca merged with the Swedish pharmaceutical company Astra to become the world's third-largest drug concern. AstraZeneca continues to be the primary sponsor of Breast Cancer Awareness Month.

A Matter of Life and Death

If exposure to chemicals in the environment was shown to be associated with only 10 to 20 percent of breast cancer cases, and the U.S. acted to reduce or eliminate these hazardous chemicals, we would be able to prevent between 9,000 and 36,000 women from contracting the disease each year.

READING 45

My Fight for Birth Control

Margaret Sanger (1931)

Mrs. Sacks was only twenty-eight years old; her husband, an unskilled worker, thirty-two. Three children, aged five, three and one, were none too strong nor sturdy, and it took all the earnings of the father and the ingenuity of the mother to keep them clean, provide them with air and proper food, and give them a chance to grow into decent manhood and womanhood.

Both parents were devoted to these children and to each other. The woman had become pregnant and had taken various drugs and purgatives, as advised by her neighbors. Then, in desperation, she had used some instrument lent to her by a friend. She was found prostrate on the floor amidst the crying children when her husband returned from work. Neighbors advised against the ambulance, and a friendly doctor was called. The husband would not hear of her going to a hospital, and as a little money had been saved in the bank a nurse was called and the battle for that precious life began.

It was in the middle of July. The three-room apartment was turned into a hospital for the dying patient. Never had I worked so fast, never so concentratedly as I did to keep alive that little mother. Neighbor women came and went during the day doing the odds and ends necessary for our comfort. The children were sent to friends and relatives and the doctor and I settled ourselves to outdo the force and power of an outraged nature.

Never had I known such conditions could exist. July's sultry days and nights were melted into a torpid inferno. Day after day, night after night, I slept only in brief snatches, ever too anxious about the condition of that feeble heart bravely carrying on, to stay long from the bedside of the patient. . .

At the end of two weeks recovery was in sight, and at the end of three weeks I was preparing to leave the fragile patient to take up the ordinary duties of her life, including those of wifehood and motherhood. Everyone was congratulating her on her recovery. All the kindness of sympathetic and understanding neighbors poured in upon her in the shape of convalescent dishes, soups, custards, and drinks. Still she appeared to be despondent and worried. She seemed to sit apart in her thoughts as if she had no part in these congratulatory messages and endearing welcomes. I thought at first that she still retained some of her unconscious memories and dwelt upon them in her silences.

But as the hour of my departure came nearer, her anxiety increased, and finally with trembling voice she said: "Another baby will finish me, I suppose."

"It's too early to talk about that," I said, and resolved that I would turn the question over to the doctor for his advice. When he came I said: "Mrs. Sacks is worried about having another baby."

"She well might be," replied the doctor, and then he stood before her and said: "Any more such capers, young woman, and there will be no need to call me."

"Yes, yes—I know, Doctor," said the patient with trembling voice, "but," and she hesitated as if it took all of her courage to say it, "*what* can I do to prevent getting that way again?"

"Oh ho!" laughed the doctor good naturedly, "You want your cake while you eat it too, do you? Well, it can't be done." Then, familiarly slapping her on the back and picking up his hat and bag to depart, he said: "I'll tell you the only sure thing to do. Tell Jake to sleep on the roof!"

With those words he closed the door and went down the stairs, leaving us both petrified and stunned.

Tears sprang to my eyes, and a lump came in my throat as I looked at the face before me. It was stamped with sheer horror. I thought for a moment she might have gone insane, but she conquered her feelings, whatever they may have been, and turning to me in desperation said: "He can't understand, can he?—he's a man after all—but you do, don't you? You're a woman and you'll tell me the secret and I'll never tell it to a soul."

She clasped her hands as if in prayer, she leaned over and looked straight into my eyes and beseechingly implored me to tell her something—something *I really did not know.* It was like being on a rack and tortured for a crime one had not committed. To plead guilty would stop the agony; otherwise the rack kept turning.

I had to turn away from that imploring face. I could not answer her then. I quieted her as best I could. She saw that I was moved by the tears in my eyes. I promised that I would come back in a few days and tell her what she wanted to know. The few simple means of limiting the family like *coitus interrupts* or the condom were laughed at by the neighboring women when told these were the means used by men in the well-to-do families. That was not believed, and I knew such an answer would be swept aside as useless were I to tell her this at such a time.

A little later when she slept I left the house, and made up my mind that I'd keep away from those cases in the future. I felt helpless to do anything at all, I seemed chained hand and foot, and longed for an earthquake or a volcano to shake the world out of its lethargy into facing these monstrous atrocities.

The intelligent reasoning of the young mother— how to *prevent* getting that way again—how sensible, how just she had been—yes, I promised myself I'd go back and have a long talk with her and tell her more, and perhaps she would not laugh but would believe that those methods were all that were really known.

But time flew past, and weeks rolled into months. That wistful, appealing face haunted me day and night. I could not banish from my mind memories of that trembling voice begging so humbly for knowledge she had a right to have. I was about to retire one night three months later when the telephone rang and an agitated man's voice begged me to come at once to help his wife who was sick again. It was the husband of Mrs. Sacks, and I intuitively knew before I left the telephone that it was almost useless to go.

I dreaded to face that woman. I was tempted to send someone else in my place. I longed for an accident on the subway, or on the street—anything to prevent my going into that home. But on I went just the same. I arrived a few minutes after the doctor, the same one who had given her such noble advice. The woman was dying. She was unconscious. She died within ten minutes after my arrival. It was the same result, the same story told a thousand times before—death from abortion. She had become pregnant, had used drugs, had then consulted a five-dollar professional abortionist, and death followed.

The doctor shook his head as he rose from listening for the heart beat. I knew she had already passed on; without a groan, a sigh or recognition of our belated presence she had gone into the Great Beyond as thousands of mothers go every year. I looked at that drawn face now stilled in death. I placed her thin hands across her breast and recalled how hard they had pleaded with me on that last memorable occasion of parting. The gentle woman, the devoted mother, the loving wife had passed on leaving behind her a frantic husband, helpless in his loneliness, bewildered in his helplessness as he paced up and down the room, hands clenching his head, moaning "My God! My God! My God!"

The Revolution came—but not as it has been pictured nor as history relates that revolutions have come. It came in my own life. It began in my very being as I walked home that night after I had closed the eyes and covered with a sheet the body of that little helpless mother whose life had been sacrificed to ignorance.

After I left that desolate house I walked and walked and walked; for hours and hours I kept on, bag in hand, thinking, regretting, dreading to stop; fearful of my conscience, dreading to face my own accusing soul. At three in the morning I arrived home still clutching a heavy load the weight of which I was quite unconscious.

I entered the house quietly, as was my custom, and looked out the window down upon the dimly lighted, sleeping city. As I stood at the window and looked out, the miseries and problems of that sleeping city arose before me in a clear vision like a panorama: crowded homes, too many children; babies dying in infancy; mothers overworked; baby nurseries; children neglected and hungry—mothers so nervously wrought they would not give the little things the comfort nor care they needed; mothers half sick most of their lives—"always ailing, never failing"; women made into drudges; children working in cellars; children aged six and seven pushed into the labor market to help earn a living; another baby on the way; still another; yet another; a baby born dead—great relief; an older child dies—sorrow, but nevertheless relief—insurance helps; a mother's death—children scattered into institutions; the father, desperate, drunken; he slinks away to become an outcast in a society which has trapped him. . . .

. . . For hours I stood, motionless and tense, expecting something to happen. I watched the lights go out, I saw the darkness gradually give way to the first shimmer of dawn, and then a colorful sky heralded the rise of the sun. I knew a new day had come for me and a new world as well.

It was like an illumination. I could now see clearly the various social strata of our life; all its mass problems seemed to be centered around uncontrolled breeding. There was only one thing to be done: call out, start the alarm, set the heather on fire! Awaken the womanhood of America to free the motherhood of the world! I released from my almost paralyzed hand the nursing bag which unconsciously I had clutched, threw it across the room, tore the uniform from my body, flung it into a corner, and renounced all palliative work forever.

I would never go back again to nurse women's ailing bodies while their miseries were as vast as the stars. I was now finished with superficial cures, with doctors and nurses and social workers who were brought face to face with this overwhelming truth of women's needs and yet turned to pass on the other side. They must be made to see these facts. I resolved that women should have knowledge of contracep-tion. They have every right to know about their own bodies. I would strike out—I would scream from the housetops. I would tell the world what was going on in the lives of these poor women. I *would* be heard. No matter what it should cost. *I would be heard.*

READING 46

Caught in the Crossfire

Cynthia Gorney

What happened in Sedalia was not a thing that Rob-ert Duemler talked about: not the place, nor the smell, nor the low sick feeling that came to his stom-ach when he thought about it afterward. Doctors see things they wish they had not seen, he understood that, and Duemler was a quiet man who delivered babies for a living at a big Catholic hospital where they were cordial to him even though he belonged to the United Church of Christ. The hospital was out-side St. Louis, which people liked to call a Catholic city, and when Duemler was at work, nurses in nuns' habits bustled down the corridors and nodded in their deferential nurses' way: Good morning, doctor.

Among the obstetrical nurses was a big, smart, opinionated woman named Judith Widdicombe, and sometimes after deliveries Duemler and Widdi-combe would lean against a wall in their scrubs and talk. Duemler, in his 30s then, was older than she was, and it amused him to see her point out when and where she thought the senior physicians had bungled their work. She was not deferential. There was some undiplomatic clarity of vision to Judy Widdicombe that Duemler admired. They might be attending the birth of a patient's sixth or seventh child and know, without exactly saying it, that some-times this felt like bringing forth the miracle of life and sometimes it felt like handing a small squalling package to a tired woman who was not interested in receiving it.

Widdicombe would say casually, "I bet she doesn't really want that kid." Maybe not, Duemler would say. And they would talk about something else. But he understood that Widdicombe, who was not a nun, was signaling him. There was a code at work, and Duemler knew that he was in on it somehow, and that it had to do with ideas that might be dan-gerous to discuss in a public place.

After a while, he told her what had happened in Sedalia in 1962.

He was a young Air Force doctor, the first obste-trician on the base in central Missouri. Sometimes patients would call him in the middle of the night, and he would need to hurry to help them. That was when this call came, and when Duemler walked into the emergency room, what he saw, in more places than he would have thought possible, was blood. Blood on the walls. On the floor. On the gurney and on the towels and on the hands and arms of the emergency crew. Beneath them lay a woman whose skin had gone slack, and when Duemler lifted her legs into the stirrups, he saw that someone had pushed inside her vagina with a sharp instrument and aimed it toward the cervix and thrust straight up. The blood vessels to either side had emptied all over the emergency room and the car in which this woman's husband had driven her 20 miles, the dis-tance between the abortionist and the hospital.

The husband told Duemler they had five children already.

Duemler remembered that for a long time after-ward, when he was no longer able to summon up any-thing except the bewildered look on the husband's face as his wife was pronounced dead on the exam-ining table.

Duemler had learned in medical school that you pull down the shade when you have to, that you cannot climb into the life of every patient; but after it was over he would think about Sedalia, and the words *stupid, stupid* would press up inside him. It was a stupid death. When he was a resident, an older doctor had asked him to assist at a dilation and curettage in the sterile operating room of a fine St. Louis hospital. The patient was a nice young woman whose boyfriend had come from a family of high social standing, and they had all invented a plausible diagnosis requiring termination of pregnancy to save her life. Duemler understood that his job was to hold the dilators and shut up, but when he thought about Sedalia he always thought about this other woman, the one with the fancy boyfriend. So he told Judy Widdicombe that story, too.

Then she knew she had been right about Bob Duemler, and she came to him one day and said: There is a group of us, and we are doing something illegal. We need your help.

In 1968, the year Judith McWhorter Widdicombe began recruiting medical doctors into a conspiracy to commit repeated felonies in the state of Missouri, she was 30 years old and lived in a modest house with her children and her husband, Arthur. At that time she had three occupations, each of which interested her deeply. From morning until early afternoon she cared for her two sons and other children who needed baby-sitting; from early afternoon until 11 at night she worked the hospital swing shift; and one evening each week she stayed home answering telephone calls from people threatening to commit suicide.

The phone work was a volunteer job, coordinated through a program called St. Louis Suicide Prevention, run by Gwyndolyn Harvey, a local psychologist. At first Widdicombe worked the phones in Suicide Prevention's office, but eventually the calls that came during her shift were routed to a telephone on the Widdicombes' back porch. She was very good at it. She liked sitting out there on the porch at night, leading her caller carefully away from harm, just as she might do up in the hospital wards.

As the service was publicized, pregnant women began to call, too. But they were not suicidal—not the way others were. They were direct. They would say: This is a telephone number for desperate people, right? I am desperate. I want an abortion.

Sometimes they would add, as though in deference to the name: If I don't get an abortion, I will kill myself.

Widdicombe didn't know what to say.

Call your doctor, she said at first, feeling foolish. If their doctors had been able to get these women abortions, the women would not have been calling Suicide Prevention. Widdicombe had never read the Missouri statute book, Section 559, where abortion was described as "felony manslaughter," but she knew it was illegal and, in the hospital where she worked, unspeakable. "In retrospect, I know that through the years there were women who'd come in for 'diagnostic D&Cs' who were really pregnant. But nobody talked about it," she recalls.

Gwyn Harvey told her that the other volunteers were reporting abortion callers too, even though nobody at Suicide Prevention had any useful information. When Harvey listened to the detailed accounts of these calls, it seemed to her that most of these women were not really looking for crisis intervention or a referral to a psychologist. What they wanted was an abortionist.

douches: Lysol, Hexol, bleach, green soap and glycerine, powdered kitchen mustard, hydrogen peroxide
potassium permanganate corrosive tablets
intrauterine installation of kerosene and vinegar
gauze packing
artist's paintbrush
curtain rod
slippery elm stick
garden hose
tubes: rubber or polyethylene
glass cocktail stirrer
ear syringe
wires: telephone, copper, coat hanger
nut pick
pencil
cotton swabs
clothespin
knitting needle
catheters: rubber, woven silk, or with stylette
chopsticks
bicycle pump and tube
football pump and plastic straw

plastic tube with soap solution
gramophone needle
bulb syringe
by mouth: castor oil, quinine, ergot, Humphries
No. 11 tablets, turpentine

A roster of terrible specificity accumulated, before the late 1960s, in American medical journals. This was what she did it with, the examining physicians must have murmured. Sometimes a woman could be persuaded to describe the device that had been used; sometimes the doctors could look inside the vaginal area, or open an abdomen at autopsy, and recognize the markers left behind.

Air pumped into the uterus left the large blood vessels distended. Turpentine, ingested or introduced by douche, gave the urine an odor reminiscent of violets. Lower abdominal tenderness was a sign that soap or detergent might have been forced up the cervix. Potassium permanganate tablets, pushed into the vagina to stimulate bleeding that emergency-room doctors might misidentify as a miscarriage, left craters of corroded tissue along the vaginal walls; suturing them was like trying to put fine surgical stitches into softened butter.

There was no practical way to document the number of American women who ended their own pregnancies, or tried to. For some years the figure of 681,600 a year was used; this was a 1936 statistic from Frederick J. Taussig, a St. Louis professor whose book was for two decades the only serious reference work on abortion. He spent five pages explaining his calculations and extrapolations. Directly attributable to these abortions, Taussig asserted, were 8,179 deaths.

On a national scale, there was little else to go by. "The desire to avoid any public record of an event so often tied up with the moral life of the individual is bound to result in failure to get accurate information." Taussig wrote. "The same lack of honesty appears in our mortality records, where we find cases of abortion death registered as pneumonia, kidney disease, or heart failure."

By 1955, when the Planned Parenthood Federation of America medical director, Mary Steichen Calderone, convened a national conference, estimates of illegal abortions in this country ranged from 200,000 to 1.2 million a year. . . .

The very notion of a national conference was sufficiently alarming in 1955 that the participants were anxious that the press not get wind of it. It was a kind of declaration of intent, men and women with worthy institutions attached to their names, all discussing the problem of induced abortion. It was a problem because nobody could obtain respectable data. It was a problem because illegal abortion made a lot of women sick. It was a problem because there were urban public hospitals in which entire wards had been ceded to patients trying to recover from illegal abortions; at Los Angeles County, on any given afternoon, 50 to 100 women were separated off into what the doctors referred to as Infected OB.

. . .

By the mid-1960s, every state harbored at least a scattering of doctors . . . who had come to believe that something was wrong with American abortion law. Many of them traced their moment of conversion not to the battlefield of a hospital ward but instead to a single patient, a single detail, a single moment of helplessness or rage.

. . .

By 1968 a new form of civil disobedience had begun, its spiritual and organizational center lodged in a 19th-century brick Baptist church, called Judson Memorial, in Greenwich Village, in New York City. A lot of unusual activity went on there under the Reverend Howard Moody's supervision. Civil rights marchers, Vietnam War protesters, and local Democratic Club organizers all mingled and argued at Moody's church, which was regarded less as a temple of God than as a stewpot for liberal politics.

In 1967 a young Jewish woman named Arlene Carmen was hired as a church administrator. Moody asked for her help with one project in particular: He had the idea that women looking for abortions should be able to receive detailed information from a minister who could counsel them first and help them find what they were looking for.

Such a minister would almost certainly be acting in violation of state abortion laws. Moody and Carmen both knew that. Publicly the stance was to be at once truculent and gravely ministerial. When in May

1967 Moody and others organized the first formal clergymen's counseling service, they used the word *abortion* in the name, declining euphemisms, and called *The New York Times*. The article appeared on the front page. "Twenty-one Protestant ministers and rabbis have announced the establishment of a Clergyman's Consultation Service on Abortion to assist women seeking abortions," began the story. "The clergymen cited 'higher laws and moral obligations transcending legal codes,' and said that it was their 'pastoral responsibility and religious duty to give aid and assistance to all women with problem pregnancies.'"

The telephone began to ring the day the story appeared. Within a week, distraught female voices had backed up on the answering-machine tape, and Moody was spending seven hours a day ushering women in and out of his office. The sheer volume astonished him, but more startling were the women who had telephoned Manhattan and then gotten on airplanes in places hundreds of miles away. There were so many of them that the clergymen's abbreviated lists of abortion doctors were inadequate. They had a doctor in Puerto Rico, a polite man whose patients came back with reports of scrubbed tile floors and attentive nurses; they had a doctor in Louisiana, a Tulane-educated gynecologist who worked alone out of a New Orleans hotel and put pot holders on the examining table stirrups to keep the metal from chilling the women's feet. But they needed more, and Carmen began visiting abortionists herself. She took notes. "Code: Nina." "Call & ask for Dr. SOS." "On probation for three years; slum area; filthy; bad procedure." "Butcher, avoid at all costs."

The list kept growing; Moody traveled to places like Cleveland and Chicago, working social webs laid out by the civil rights movement and Vietnam War protest. He would instruct the ministers he met that this was to be a counseling service, not a hand-over-the-address service; they should remain alert to ambivalence, should encourage women to keep their babies or give them up for adoption if the idea of abortion disturbed them. There was a famous story about a woman who called Judson Memorial in the early months, when Moody assumed their telephones were tapped.

"Is this where you can get an abortion?" she asked.

Moody explained that she had called a church, but could come in for abortion counseling.

"I don't need the Sermon on the Mount, Reverend," she said. "I need an abortion." And she hung up.

Within a year of its debut. Moody's office was ferrying information to and from the quiet regional abortion network headquartered on the Washington University campus in St. Louis. Compared to some of its more ambitious counterparts, this operation in 1967 was still modest in scope and discreet in its public presence. John Vavra, a medical professor, had enlisted medical students to examine and interview women before and after their abortions, but there was no letterhead or telephone listing. The service did not even have a name. It was simply known that Dr. Vavra and Reverend Ewing helped women find abortionists.

And when Gwyndolyn Harvey set out to learn about abortionists, she was directed to Vavra, who received her in his office. He was soft-spoken, scholarly, and calm—"unflappable," Harvey recalls. "He looked as far from anybody doing anything radical as you could possibly imagine."

Vavra was careful about what he would and would not say; he offered up no names or telephone numbers, but when Harvey told him about the Suicide Prevention callers, he was interested at once. There was no conversation at all, that day or later, about why such a service might be justifiable, about what it was in their backgrounds or philosophies that might prompt two well-educated professionals to sit in a university office and make arrangements for the ongoing violation of state law. "We didn't have to discuss it," Harvey recalls. "There were people getting hurt."

Among her colleagues and from her volunteer roster, Harvey selected her initial recruits: a Washington University psychiatric social worker, and Judy Widdicombe. The model for her program already existed, Harvey explained: counselors, ministers, abortionists, and doctors, all linked together by a telephone network that would serve as each woman's initial point of contact. Vavra would lead them to the abortionists; Harvey and Widdicombe would assemble a medical and pastoral corps to attend to the women beforehand and afterward.

Widdicombe thought about what she was going to say to these doctors, and how best to say it, and approached Dr. Melvin Schwartz and Dr. Robert Duemler and Dr. George Wulff, who taught at the hospital where she had trained as a nurse and who had worked the Infected OB ward, and who had learned as an intern to recognize the caustic blackened stain of a self-administered potassium permanganate douche, and who answered her, like the others, without hesitation: Yes.

READING 47

How Women Pay for Fetal Rights

Rachel Roth

For months, David was a victim of torture. He was kept in a small darkened room. His food was poisoned and his brain severely damaged. And then one day he was born.

—*Minnesota fetal alcohol syndrome public awareness poster*

As government-sponsored materials depict fetuses as tortured prisoners, so do prosecutors hear fetal voices, psychologists dispense advice on behalf of fetal patients, factories exclude women lest they bring fetal visitors, legislators craft public policy for fetuses, and judges issue rulings based on fetuses' preferences, including one judge who denied a "surrogate mother" custody of a child she bore because there was "no evidence whatsoever" that the fetus had bonded with her. These are but a few developments in the expanding terrain of reproductive and gender politics that has come to be known as the politics of fetal rights.

People must commonly associate the term "fetal rights" with efforts to curtail legal abortion. Yet as the right-to-life movement's success in restricting women's access to abortion waxed and waned throughout the 1970s and 1980s, other targets of scrutiny and regulation in the name of fetal rights emerged: women who would be carrying their pregnancies to term and women who were not pregnant at all, but merely fertile.

The struggles over these women's lives are the ones explored here . . . .

. . . When institutions assert or accept rights claims on behalf of fetuses, their stated reasons usually involve protecting fetuses from potential harm and enhancing their chances of healthy birth and survival. As I show, however, the strategy of creating fetal rights is not necessary to achieve those goals, is often counterproductive to these goals, and always undermines women's equal standing as citizens.

Fetal rights do not come free. When courts, legislatures, or other political and social institutions decide to award rights to fetuses, the award translates into costs of others. Women currently bear a disproportionate share of the costs of ensuring fetal health, relative to the rest of society. This unequal distribution burdens women and fails to provide a clear pattern of benefit to fetuses or to society as a whole.

American ideology and social arrangements assign to women the primary responsibility for reproduction. When I speak of primary responsibility for reproduction, I refer to women's disproportionate responsibility for the entire reproductive process, which includes timing pregnancies and rearing children as well as gestating fetuses and giving birth. Because all women are perceived as potentially pregnant for much of their lives, they are susceptible to having restrictions imposed on them because of what others think about that potential. . . . This is most often done according to class, race, or culture. By culture, I mean a range of influences on someone's life, including religion, national origin, or first language.

In addition, the ideological message of fetal rights politics—that women are not entitled to be as self-determining as men because they can become pregnant—exacts a high price from women as a class. Taken together, the many forms of fetal advocacy politics place a heavy burden on all women's opportunities and pursuit of equality.

Because rights claims resonate so deeply with American political and cultural values, fetal rights claims have been taken seriously in the political arena, and courts and legislatures have granted rights to fetuses. Although she does not address fetal advocacy politics in her book *Making All the Difference: Inclusion, Exclusion, and American Law*, Martha Minow offers some insights about the power of establishing rights for fetuses. When people make rights claims, they assert their identity as individuals entitled to equality and liberty, and emphasize their essential sameness to others as persons and as members of the polity. Rights analysis further "treats each individual as a separate unit, related only to the state rather than to a group or to social bonds." Fetal rights claims, then, present a rhetorically powerful strategy by giving the fetus an individual identity, asserting its equality with the woman, and establishing its independent relationship with the state that bypasses the pregnant women.

The logic of fetal rights depends on certain rhetorical constructions. First, proponents of fetal rights oppose them rhetorically to women's rights, constructing a contest of equal antagonists with only one possible winner. Consider these representative titles of journal and newspaper articles: "Fetal versus Maternal Rights: Medical and Legal Perspectives"; "When the Rights of Mother and Fetus Collide"; "Maternal versus Fetal Rights: A Clinical Dilemma"; and "Fetal Patients and Conflicts with Their Mothers." All set up a conflict between woman and fetus: a zero-sum choice.[1]

A second frequent formulation opposes fetal rights to women's responsibilities, as in this 1989 article in a medical journal: "Fetal Therapy and Surgery: Fetal Rights and Maternal Obligations." This title suggests that it is incumbent upon the pregnant woman to honor the right to surgery and medical treatment that doctors believe fetuses hold; in other words, women can be forcibly subjected to unwanted medical procedures. This kind of right is an entitlement enforceable against the pregnant woman. Its logic dictates that social institutions hold pregnant women accountable for the fulfillment of fetal rights. In this case, that means that pregnant women are responsible for ensuring the fetus's access to medical treatment, even though they themselves have no right to medical care.

These formulations have become so pervasive that supposedly objective news reporters use them freely. On National Public Radio's *All Things Considered*, news anchor Linda Wertheimer described a criminal charge of attempted murder against a woman who drank heavily during pregnancy as the latest chapter in the debate over how "to balance the rights of the woman against those of the fetus." This concept gains legitimacy through constant repetition in scholarly journals, popular media, and public discourse.

Creating individual fetal identities that are hostile to women's identities is not the only thing that rights rhetoric accomplishes. Rights rhetoric is also powerful because it obscures the question of costs. Both of the constructions I just described—maternal rights versus fetal rights and maternal responsibilities versus fetal rights—obscure the way that fetal rights function to distribute social costs. When a court or other institution decides to award rights, it has to assign the costs of those rights to some individual or group. That assignment—who should bear the costs of fetal rights—is a political question that has received very little direct public debate. It is the central concern of this study. The answer, explicit or implicit, has been to impose the costs of fetal rights on women.

These costs are tangible. They can't be measured solely in terms of money, although that is certainly at stake. Women also incur costs to their free, physical and mental security, identity, and privacy when they are denied jobs because they are fertile, when they are subjected to court-ordered medical operations against their will, and when they are given additional civil and criminal penalties for using drugs or alcohol during pregnancy that are never imposed on women who are not pregnant or on men. Women are assigned responsibility for taking care of fetuses without being given the resources they need to do so, and then penalized for falling short.

"There seems to be a qualitative difference between an invasion of privacy by your government and an invasion by a stranger," explain Ellen Alderman and Caroline Kennedy in their analysis of a class-action lawsuit women brought against the city of Chicago's policy to strip search every single woman brought to the jail, regardless of the circumstances of her arrest or the reason she was booked. "The women spoke of an abuse of a basic trust. They felt they had been violated by the very people who were supposed to be their protectors and expressed a sense of betrayal and vulnerability. All of them said they dreaded any future contact with the police." The feelings of abuse and subsequent loss of trust that characterized the Chicago women's experiences also characterize the experiences of women whose privacy and bodies are invaded in the name of fetal rights. When forced to submit to unwanted surgery such as a cesarean or sterilization, or when jailed without due process, women may come to mistrust the medical and legal institutions that they rely on for care and protection.[2] Their mistrust, and that of their families and friends, in turn creates costs for all of society.

Women inevitably bear some of the costs of reproducing the species. They bear the physical, emotional, and time costs associated with pregnancy and birth. The Centers for Disease Control (CDC) reports that the maternal death ratio has held steadily at 7 or 8 deaths per 100,000 births since 1982, and that half of these deaths are preventable. The United States lags behind 20 other countries and has made no progress toward its goal of cutting deaths to 3.3 per 100,000 by the year 2000. The causes of death include ectopic pregnancy, hemorrhage, infection, blood clots, and pregnancy-induced high blood pressure. The CDC also estimates that for every woman who dies as a result of pregnancy, 3,100 women are hospitalized for complications each year. In addition, there may be severe long-term consequences for some women. Women who have borne children appear much more likely than other women or men to get such autoimmune diseases as systemic sclerosis.

Women also *evitably* bear a disproportionate share of the physical, emotional, and time costs in rearing children. Although new trends in paternal involvement in child-rearing make headlines, studies overwhelmingly show that women continue to shoulder most of the child care, as well as homemaking, even when they work the same number of hours outside the home as men.

What is so troubling about fetal rights claims is that they make women bear almost all the costs, instead of distributing them more evenly across society. Consider, as an alternative model, how the demands of disabled people to participate fully in American life have led to newly articulated rights of access to education, housing, transportation, and work. In this case, when government actors and institutions decided that the rights claims of disabled Americans had merit, they distributed the attendant costs broadly to taxpayers, employers, and consumers. Rather than requiring disabled people to pay for their own access, Congress decided that society must share the burden, and enacted a series of laws culminating in the Americans with Disabilities Act (ADA) of 1990.[3]

Reproductive costs can also be distributed. . . . Moreover, the burdens that have been imposed on women in the name of fetal rights do not produce clear evidence of benefits to fetuses, calling into question the motives underlying fetal rights policy. By contrast, we can have more confidence that—if fully enforced—the ADA will improve the lives of its intended beneficiaries.

The notion of fetal rights is linked to another important rhetorical construct prevalent in public discourse—that of "maternal-fetal conflict." This notion is used to focus attention on women's behavior as the source of risk to fetal health and away from other factors. This study critically examines this construct, which rests simultaneously on two assumptions: (1) that all pregnant women are already mothers and (2) that they are bad mothers, for if they were good mothers they wouldn't be having conflicts with their fetuses.

Maternal-fetal conflict erases all other aspects of a pregnant woman's identity. All pregnant women are *expectant* mothers (unless they plan to place their future children up for adoption), but only some pregnant women are already rearing children. Referring to pregnant women as "mothers" before they give birth evokes the qualities of selflessness and duty associated with motherhood and suggests that pregnant women have failed to demonstrate these important qualities. It also turns the fetus into a child. Cultural expectations and legal standards of parental duty then apply to pregnant women, and the fetus gains an independent identity that enables it to engage rhetorically in conflict with the pregnant woman ("mother"). Again, this serves to focus attention on the pregnant woman and away from her environment and the responsibilities that other individuals or institutions might have.

These rhetorical constructions are complemented by images that depict fetuses as independent. As Barbara Duden's book *Disembodying Women* aptly suggests, the politics of fetal rights has disembodied fetuses from pregnant women in visual culture and public discourse. From Lennart Nilsson's famous *Life* magazine photographs of "the drama of life before birth" to prime time ultrasound scans, images of disembodied fetuses abound. Rosalind Petchesky explains how ultrasound imaging of fetuses presents the fetus "as though removed from the pregnant woman's body, as though suspended in space." A 1991 Volvo ad does just this: A huge sonogramlike image of a fetus hovers above a tiny car at the bottom of the page; the text asks, "Is something inside telling you to buy a Volvo?" In the television version of the ad, a voice off-camera asks the same question. Janelle Taylor explains that fetal images "gain whatever power and meaning they may have precisely upon the strength of the ideological status of photographs as purely denotative, transparent representations of reality." Political movements can deploy these supposedly neutral, self-evident images in a variety of ways.[4]

Even a recent collection of feminist essays called *Expecting Trouble: Surrogacy, Fetal Abuse, and New Reproductive Technologies* recapitulates this problem on its cover. The cover design features the profile of a pregnant woman in front of the Supreme Court; she is merely a dark blue silhouette, while the fetus is rendered in intricate detail, its tiny features and fingers giving it the distinct human appearance the pregnant woman lacks. (Never mind that the term *fetal abuse* is not in quotation marks, implying it is an acceptable and unproblematic category.) As all of these examples show, the more the fetus is aggrandized, the more women tend to be diminished.

NOTES

1. All the titles also cast the pregnant woman in the role of mother. In our society, mothering connotes women's selfless devotion to children, a connotation that is at odds with any action that could potentially jeopardize the health of a fetus. I address this point later in this chapter.
2. The poor treatment many women receive when they bring rape charges to the criminal justice system is perhaps the paradigmatic experience of such institutional betrayal. Women who press charges often speak of being raped twice: once by the accused, and again by the state.
3. I would like to thank Eve Weinbaum for suggesting this contrast. Laura Rothstein's book *Disabilities and the Law* describes the requirements of the ADA, signed into law in 1990.
4. Echoing the idea that fetal rights politics and the construct of "maternal-fetal conflict" locate problems of fetal safety within pregnant women themselves, Taylor argues that the ad presents the pregnant woman "as potentially dangerous to the fetus, [whose] safety can be ensured only by enclosing it (and her) within a car. The Volvo ad implicitly suggests that the pregnant woman is herself a sort of transport vehicle, and a relatively unsafe one at that: the steel body of a Volvo is needed to encase her, if the fetus is to remain safe."

DISCUSSION QUESTIONS FOR CHAPTER SIX

1. How do patriarchal norms constitute a threat to women's health?
2. How are women treated differently in the health care system? What is the effect of this differential treatment? How does racism have an impact on the gendered

experiences of women of color in the health care system? Have you ever had a negative experience based on gender in the health care system?

3. Why is reproductive choice important for women?

4. What have been the consequences of women's loss of control of their reproductive processes?

5. How does the chipping away of abortion rights threaten the achievements of *Roe v. Wade?*

SUGGESTIONS FOR FURTHER READING

Boston Women's Health Book Collective, *Our Bodies, Our Selves for the New Century.* New York: Simon & Schuster, 1998.

Eisenstein, Zillah. *Manmade Breast Cancers.* Ithaca, NY: Cornell University Press, 2001.

Farmer, Paul, Margaret Connors, and Janie Simmons, eds. *Women, Poverty, and AIDS: Sex, Drugs, and Structural Violence.* Monroe, ME: Common Courage, 1996.

Gorney, Cynthia. *Articles of Faith: A Frontline History of the Abortion Wars.* New York: Touchstone, 2000.

Morgen, Sandra. *Into Our Own Hands: The Women's Health Movement in the United States, 1969–1990.* New Brunswick, NJ: Rutgers University Press, 2002.

Solinger, Rickie, ed. *Abortion Wars: A Half Century of Struggle, 1950–2000.* Los Angeles: University of California Press, 1998.

Weddington, Sarah. *A Question of Choice.* New York: Penguin, 1993.

CHAPTER SEVEN

Family Systems, Family Lives

The title of this chapter, "Family Systems, Family Lives," reflects the reality of the family as both a major societal institution and a place where individuals experience intimate relationships. At the institutional level, the family maintains patterns of privilege and inequity and is intimately connected to other institutions in society such as the economy, the political system, religion, and education. At the level of experience, the family fulfills basic human needs and provides most of us with our first experiences of love and relationship as well as power and conflict. A focus of recent scholarship on the family has demonstrated that family forms are historically and culturally constructed and that family is a place for the reproduction of power relations in society. In this way, the family is a primary social unit that maintains other institutions and reinforces existing patterns of domination. At the same time, however, family networks provide support systems that can reduce the indignities and/or challenge the inequities produced by various systems of inequality in society.

DEFINITIONS OF FAMILY

Families are part of what social scientists call kinship systems or patterns of relationships that define family forms. Kinship systems vary widely around the world, although they tend to pattern such features as the meaning of marriage, the number of marriage partners permitted at one time (monogamy involves one husband and one wife and polygamy is multiple spouses, the most common form being polygyny or multiple wives), norms about marriageability, determination of descent, and distribution of property. In the United States, there is no "normal" family even though it tends to be constructed as the nuclear family of the middle-class, White, married, heterosexual couple with children. Nuclear family implies a married couple residing together with their children, and it can be distinguished from an extended family in which a group of related kin, in addition to parents and children, live together in the same household. The nuclear family arose as a result of Western industrialization that separated the home from productive activities. In pre- and early-industrial America, the family was relatively self-sufficient in producing goods for family consumption and exchange with other families. As industrial capitalism developed, family members increasingly worked outside the home for wages that were spent on goods for family consumption.

Traditional myths about the normative family are rampant in the United States, and they hide the reality of the wide diversity of family life: single parents, extended and multi-generational families, lesbian and gay families with and without children, people (single or not and with or without children) living in community with other adults, grandparents raising grandchildren or nieces and nephews, and so forth. And, of course, these families

■ FACTS ABOUT U.S. FAMILIES

- Fifty-two percent of American households are maintained by married couples (54.5 million households).
- The second most common type of American household consists of people living alone (27.2 million households).
- Family households increased from 64.5 million in 1990 to 105.5 million in 2000.
- Nonfamily households increased from 27.4 million to 33.7 million during the same period.
- The highest proportion (63 percent) of married-couple households are in Utah.
- Households headed by women with children under 18 years old increased from 6 million in 1990 to 7.6 million in 2000, from 6.6 percent of all households to 7.2 percent.
- Multigenerational families (made up of more than two generations) numbered 3.9 million or 3.7 percent of all households.
- Of all families 9.3 percent live below the poverty level.
- Of all households headed by women 27.8 percent are below the poverty level.
- Although children represent only about 26 percent of the population, children under age 18 represent nearly 40 percent of people living in poverty.
- Eighteen percent of all children live in families with incomes below the poverty line.
- Nearly a third of Black and Latino children live in poverty. Ten percent of White children live in poverty.
- Seniors are the fastest growing population group in the United States. There are currently about 35 million people age 65 and older, 13 percent of the population, but that number is expected to double by 2030 and represent 20 percent of the population.

Source: U.S. Census Bureau; Centers for Disease Control.

■ THE WORLD'S WOMEN 2000: WOMEN AND FAMILIES

Some important findings:

- Women are generally marrying later but more than a quarter of women aged 15 to 19 are married in 22 countries — all in developing regions.
- Informal unions are common in developed regions and in some countries of the developing regions.
- Birthrates continue to decline in all regions of the world.
- Births to unmarried women have increased dramatically in developed regions.
- More people are living alone in the developed regions, and the majority are women.
- In many countries of the developed regions, more than half of mothers with children under age 3 are employed.

Source: http://unstats.un.org/unsd/demographic/ww2000/wm2000.htm.

MYTHS AND FACTS
ABOUT LESBIAN FAMILIES

Myth 1: Lesbians don't have lasting relationships.

Fact: Many lesbians are in long-term partnerships. Unfortunately, social supports and civil rights are not accorded to lesbian partnerships as they are to heterosexual marriages. No state in the country recognizes gay marriage, although in 1999 the Vermont Supreme Court ruled that denying lesbian and gay couples the benefits of marriage was unconstitutional and ordered the legislature to develop a form of civil union to allow lesbian and gay partnerships the same rights and responsibilities as married couples in Vermont.

Myth 2: Lesbians don't have children.

Fact: The American Bar Association estimates that at least 6 million American children have lesbian or gay parents. Many lesbians have children from previous heterosexual relationships before they came out. Others have children through artificial insemination, and others adopt children. Unfortunately, because the courts may believe stereotypes about lesbians, lesbian mothers often lose custody of their children in a divorce, despite research indicating the fitness of lesbian mothers. In many states, adoption is difficult for lesbians, and rarely can both partners in a lesbian relationship legally adopt a child together.

Myth 3: Children of lesbian parents develop psychological disorders.

Fact: Research indicates that there is no difference in the development or frequency of pathologies between children of heterosexual or homosexual parents. In fact, study after study suggests that children in lesbian families are more similar than different from children in heterosexual families. Studies of separation-individuation, behavior problems, self-concept, locus of control, moral judgment, and intelligence have revealed no major differences between children of lesbian mothers versus children of heterosexual mothers.

Myth 4: Children of lesbian parents become gay themselves.

Fact: Research indicates no difference between children raised in lesbian families and children raised in heterosexual families with respect to gender identity, gender role behavior, and sexual orientation. Studies suggest that children in lesbian families develop along the same lines as children in heterosexual families; they are as likely to be happy with their gender, exhibit gender role behaviors, and be heterosexual as children of heterosexual mothers.

LEARNING ACTIVITY:
WHAT MAKES A FAMILY?

Conduct an informal survey of the people on your dorm floor or in an organization to which you belong about the structure of their family of origin. Whom do they consider to be in their family? What relation do these people have to them? Did all of these people live in the same house? Who had primary responsibility for caring for them as children? Who was primarily responsible for the financial well-being of the family? For the emotional well-being of the family? Was the family closely connected to extended family? If so, which extended family members and in what ways?

Compare your findings with those of your classmates. What do your findings lead you to surmise about what makes a family? How closely do the families of your interviewees resemble the dominant notion of the nuclear family—a husband and wife (in their first marriage) and their two or three children? What do you think is the impact of our stereotype of the nuclear family on social policy? How do you think this stereotype affects real families dealing with the real problems of everyday family life?

represent all social classes and all racial and ethnic groups. Even though some families are not legally recognized, they are still part of the diversity among America's families. In the reading "What We Call Each Other," Anndee Hochman writes about how the English language is devoid of words to adequately describe relationships and families outside of this norm.

The recent political debate concerning "family values" illustrates how supporters of the *status quo* (or existing power relations) in society have made the term *family values* synonymous with traditional definitions of the family and its role in society. This includes seeing women defined in terms of their domestic and reproductive roles and men as the rightful sources of power and authority in the family. Many people are offended by this narrow construction of family and its association with a repressive political agenda, and they reject these values as *their* family values. Determining what kinds of families get to be counted as "real" families and determining whose "family values" are used as standards for judging others have become heated debate topics in the United States.

The notion of family—with all its connotations of love, security, connectedness, and nurturing—is a prime target for nostalgia in the twenty-first century. As economic forces have transformed the ways that families function, we yearn for a return to the traditional family, with its unconditional love and acceptance, to escape from the complexities and harsh realities of society. Although many families do provide this respite, dominant ideologies about the family have idealized and sometimes glorified the family, and women's roles in the family, in ways that hide underlying conflict and violence. In addition, these ideologies present a false dichotomization between public (society) and private (family) spheres. Poor and non-White families have rarely enjoyed the security and privacy assumed in this split between family and society. For example, the state, in terms of both social welfare policies and criminal justice statutes, has stronger impact and more consequences on poor families than middle-class families. This is the topic of the next section: the connections between the family and other social institutions.

INSTITUTIONAL CONNECTIONS

The family interacts with other institutions in society and provides various experiences for family members. For example, economic forces shape women's family roles and help construct the balance between work and family responsibilities. As discussed in Chapter 8, women perform over two-thirds of household labor—labor that is constructed as family work and often not seen as work. In addition, the family work that women do in the home is used to justify the kinds of work women are expected to perform in the labor force. It is no coincidence that women are congregated in a small number of occupations known for their care taking, educating, and servicing responsibilities. In addition, the boundaries are more fluid between women's paid work and home life than men's. This is structured into the very kinds of jobs women tend to perform, as well as part of the expectations associated with hiring women. These assumptions can be used against women very easily as women attempt to advance in their careers. At the same time, the more rigid boundaries between work and home for male-dominated jobs mean that men have a more difficult time with parenting responsibilities when they want to be more actively involved in their children's lives.

The economic system impacts families in many ways; in turn, families support and impact economic systems. Women care for and maintain male workers as well as socialize future generations of workers, thus supporting economic institutions that rely on workers to be fed, serviced, and able to fulfill certain work roles. Although in contemporary U.S. society some families are still productive units in that they produce goods directly for family consumption or for exchange on the market, most families are consumptive units in that they participate in the market economy through goods purchased for family consumption. As a result, advertisers target women as family shoppers. The family is a consumptive unit that provides the context for advertising, media, and other forms of entertainment. In these ways family systems are intimately connected to economic forces in society.

The impact of shifting economies and changing technologies on families varies considerably by gender, class, and race, such that a family's placement in the larger political economy directly influences diverse patterns of family organization. Economic factors impact single-headed families such that over 52 percent of families headed by a woman, compared to 29 percent headed by a man, earn under $25,000 a year. The number of single-headed households earning over $50,000 a year is more than double for those headed by men compared to women (U.S. Census, 2000). Race impacts this such that households headed by women of color are the most likely to experience poverty. In this way families are shaped by their relationship to systems of inequality in society. This means, for example, that working-class women's lack of flexible work scheduling affects how families are able to meet their needs, as does the lower pay of working-class women, making them less able to afford quality daycare. Similarly, higher unemployment among men of color as compared to White men impacts families and pushes women in family relationships with unemployed men to work outside the home full time while also taking care of young children. As Betty Holcomb explains in the reading "Friendly for Whose Family?" jobs with different incomes and levels of authority and seniority affect access to such family-friendly benefits as flextime, on-site childcare, and company-sponsored tax breaks for childcare. Parenting leave is a legal right of all U.S. employees, but many companies provide better family benefits for their higher level and better paid employees than they do for the lower level employees.

The family experience is also affected by the state and its legal and political systems. The government closely regulates the family and provides certain benefits to legally married

■ LEARNING ACTIVITY: FAMILIES AND POVERTY

Go to the website of the 2000 U.S. Census at *www.census.gov/main/www/cen2000 .html*. Click on the link to the American FactFinder. In the "Basic Facts" box, select "Economic Characteristics: Employment, Income, Poverty, and more." Select your state and town to find out more information about income and families in poverty where you live.

couples. Couples need a license from the state to marry, and the government says they may file a joint tax return. Lesbian and gay couples who jointly own property and share income and expenses do not have the privileges of marriage (although this is now hotly contested), joint tax filing, and, in many situations, domestic partner benefits. Benefits accrue to certain family members but not to people who, even though they might see themselves as family, are not recognized as such by the state. In addition, although an advanced industrial society, the United States has no national funding of daycare centers, and this affects the social organization of the family and the experience of parenting. Federal and state policies also impact the family through legal statutes that regulate marriage and divorce legislation, reproductive choice, and violence in families.

Indeed, the family has connections to all societal institutions, and these connections help shape the kind and quality of experiences that we have as family members. Religion and the family are closely tied as social institutions. Religious socialization of children occurs in the family through religious and moral teachings, and religious institutions often shape societal understandings of families as well as provide rituals that help symbolize family and kin relations (such as baptisms, weddings, and funerals). Educational institutions rely on the family as a foundation for socialization and care and maintenance of children, and health systems rely on parents (and women in particular) to nurse and care for sick family members as well as provide adequate nutrition and cleanliness to prevent disease. Military institutions need the family as a foundation for ideologies of combat and for socialization and support of military personnel. Sports and athletics are tied to the family through gender socialization, the purchase of certain equipment and opportunities, and the consumption and viewing of professional sports in the home.

POWER AND FAMILY RELATIONSHIPS

At the direct level of experience, the family is the social unit where most people are raised, learn systems of belief, experience love, perhaps abuse and neglect, and generally grow to be a part of communities and society. It is in the family where most of us internalize messages about ourselves, about others, and our place in the world. Some of us learn that love comes with an abuse of power as large people hit little people, all in the name of love. Others learn that love means getting our own way without responsibility—a lesson that may detract from the hopes of a civil society where individuals care about one another and the communities of which they are a part.

Family is where many of us first experience gender because societal understandings of the differences between girls and boys are transferred through early teachings by family

ACTIVIST PROFILE: HANNAH SOLOMON

Hannah Greenbaum Solomon believed that "woman's sphere is the whole wide world" and her first responsibility was to her family. Solomon worked tirelessly in turn-of-the-century Chicago for social reform. Laboring alongside Jane Addams at Hull House, Solomon worked to improve child welfare. She reformed the Illinois Industrial School for Girls, established penny lunch stations in the public schools, and led efforts for slum clearance, low-cost housing, child labor laws, mothers' pensions, and public health measures.

In 1876 Solomon became the first Jewish member of the Chicago Woman's Club, where she developed a sense of women's ability to work together for social good. In 1893, she organized the Jewish Women's Congress at the Chicago World's Fair, which led to her founding the National Council of Jewish Women (NCJW) to enhance social welfare and justice. Solomon saw her commitment to justice as a part of her responsibility as a Jew, a woman, and an American.

Under Solomon's leadership, the National Council of Jewish Women sponsored programs for the blind, formed the Port and Dock Department to assist immigrant women in finding housing and jobs, established a permanent immigrant aid station on Ellis Island, supported Margaret Sanger's National Birth Control League, raised relief dollars during World War I, and participated in the presidential effort to create jobs during the Depression.

Solomon's legacy has continued in the NCJW since her death in 1942. Following World War II, the NCJW provided assistance to Holocaust survivors in Europe and Israel. During the McCarthy era, NCJW organized the Freedom Campaign to protect civil liberties. Additionally, the organization was the first national group to sponsor Meals on Wheels, built the Hebrew University High School in Jerusalem, helped establish the Court Appointed Advocate Project (CASA) to protect the rights of children in court cases, and launched a national campaign to try to ensure that children were not harmed by changes in welfare law.

Currently, the National Council of Jewish Women has 90,000 members and continues the work of Hannah Solomon by bringing her vision of justice to bear in the world.

members. Parents bring home baby girls and boys, dress them in gender "appropriate" colors, give them different toys, and decorate their bedrooms in different ways. As Chapter 3 emphasized, the family is a primary institution for teaching about gender. Experiences of gender are very much shaped by the gender composition of family members. A girl growing up in a family of brothers or a boy with only women and girls in his family have different experiences of gender. This is illustrated in the reading by Sandra Cisneros titled "Only Daughter."

Central in any discussion of family is a focus on power. Power in families is understood as access to resources (tangible or intangible) that allows certain family members to define

■
LEARNING ACTIVITY: DIVORCE LAW: WHO BENEFITS IN MY STATE?

Research your state's divorce laws. How is property divided in a divorce? How is custody determined? How are alimony and child support determined? How do these laws affect women and children in actuality in your state? What are the poverty rates for divorced women and their children in your state? How many fathers do not pay child support as ordered by the court? How does your state deal with nonpaying fathers? What can you do to challenge the legal system in your state to be more responsive to women and children's needs following divorce?

■
IDEAS FOR ACTIVISM

- Become a Court Appointed Special Advocate (CASA) for children.
- Offer to babysit for free for a single mother one evening a month.
- Lobby your state lawmakers to enact legislation recognizing lesbian and gay unions.
- Organize an educational activity on your campus around alternative family models.

the reality of others, have their needs met, and experience more resources. In most U.S. families today, power is distributed according to age and gender. Older family members (although not the aged, who often lose power in late life) tend to have more power than children and young people who are often defined as "dependents." Men have more power in the family than women do if this is measured in resource management and allocation and decision-making authority. Women, however, do have power if this is defined as day-to-day decisions about the running of the household and how certain household chores get done. Sociologists, however, tend to emphasize that this latter sort of "power" is vulnerable to changes in broader family dynamics and subject to decisions by men in positions as major economic providers or heads of household.

The United States has the highest marriage and the highest divorce rates of any industrialized country. Although a large number of people get divorced, this does not seem to indicate disillusionment with marriage because large numbers of people remarry. As Michael Kimmel emphasizes in the reading "The 'Constructed Problems' of Family Life" remarriage constitutes about half of all marriages yearly. Marriage traditionally has been based upon gender relations that prescribe authority of husbands over wives and that entail certain norms and expectations that are sanctioned by the state. The traditional marriage contract assumes the husband will be the head of household with responsibilities to provide a family wage and the wife will take primary responsibility for the home and the raising of children and integrate her personal identity with that of her husband. As in "Mrs. John Smith" and "Dr. and Mrs. John Smith," Mrs. Smith easily can become someone who loses her identity to her husband. The declaration of "man and wife" in the traditional marriage ceremony illustrates how men continue to be men under this contract and women become wives. The rituals of marriage ceremonies also illustrate normative gender relations: the father "giving away" his daughter, representing the passage of the woman from one man's house to another; the wearing of white to symbolize purity and virginity; the engagement ring representing a woman already spoken for; and the throwing of rice to symbolize fertility and the woman's obligation to bear and raise children.

It is especially in the family where many girls and women experience gender oppression. Where women and girls are in close relationship with men, they often experience

HISTORICAL MOMENT:
THE FEMININE MYSTIQUE

In 1963 Betty Friedan, a housewife and former labor activist, published the results of a series of interviews she had conducted with women who had been educated at Smith College. Despite their picture-perfect lives, these women reported extreme despair and unhappiness and, unaware that others shared this experience, blamed themselves. To deal with this "problem that has no name," these women turned to a variety of strategies, ranging from using tranquilizers to having affairs to volunteering with church, school, and charitable organizations.

What had happened to these educated women? Following World War II, when women had found a prominent role in the workforce, a national myth emerged that the place for (middle-class, White) women was in the home. To conform to this ideal, women sublimated their dreams and desires and fell in line with "the feminine mystique."

When Friedan's book, *The Feminine Mystique,* appeared in 1963, it spoke loudly to the unspoken misery of millions of American housewives. In its first year, it sold 3 million copies. Unfortunately, during the era just immediately following the repressive, anti-Communist McCarthy years, Friedan feared that were she to push the envelope in her book to include an analysis of race and social class, her work would be discredited. So, rather than choosing to address the more complex problems of working-class women and women of color and likely be dismissed, she chose to be heard and addressed the safer topic of middle-class housewives.

Despite its shortcomings, *The Feminine Mystique* found a readership that needed to know that they were not alone in believing that something was seriously wrong with their lives. Friedan suggested that that something wrong was a conspiracy of social institutions and culture that limited the lives of women. Friedan challenged women to find meaningful and purposeful ways of living, particularly through careers.

While Friedan did not go so far as to question the need for men to move into equitable work in the home as she was encouraging women to move out into the workforce or to examine the social and economic, as well as psychological, forces at work in limiting women's lives, she did bring to national attention the problem of women's circumscribed existence and offered a call for women to begin to examine the limitations imposed on them.

Source: Ruth Rosen, *The World Split Open: How the Modern Women's Movement Changed America.* New York: Viking, 2000.

*"Yes, this is a two career household.
Unfortunately I have both careers."*

Reprinted with permission from Carol Simpson Productions.

gender domination. In other words, in the home and family many girls and women feel the consequences of masculine power and privilege. Writing in 1910, socialist anarchist Emma Goldman saw marriage as an economic transaction that binds women into subservience to men (through love and personal and sexual services) and society (through unpaid housework). In the reading "Marriage and Love," she advocates "free love" that is unconstrained by marriage and relations with the state. Goldman believed love found in marriages occurred in spite of the institution of marriage and not because of it.

Sexism in interpersonal relationships among family members reduces female autonomy and lowers women's and girls' self-esteem. Consequences of masculine privilege in families can mean that men dominate women in relationships in subtle or not-so-subtle ways, expecting or taking for granted personal and sexual services, making and/or vetoing important family decisions, controlling money and expenditures, and so forth. In addition, power in family and marital relationships may lead to psychological, sexual, and/or physical abuse against women and children. Often the double standard of sexual conduct allows boys more freedom and autonomy compared to girls. Also, girls are very often expected to perform more household duties than boys, duties that often include cleaning up after their brothers or father.

In particular, the balance of power in marriage (or any domestic partnership) depends in part upon how couples negotiate paid labor and family work in their relationships. Marriages or domestic partnerships can be structured according to different models that promote various ways that couples live and work together. These models include "head–complement," "junior partner/senior partner," and "equal partners"—relationships that each have different ways of negotiating paid work and family work, and, as a result, provide different balances of power within these relationships.

The "head–complement" model reflects the traditional marriage contract as discussed previously where the head / husband has responsibilities to provide a family wage and the complement / wife takes primary responsibility for the home and the raising of children. In addition the complement sees (usually her) role as complementing the head's role by being supportive and encouraging in both emotional and material ways. The balance of power in this family system is definitely tilted in the direction of the "head" of the head–complement couple. Power for the complement is to a large extent based upon the goodwill of the head as well as the resources (educational and financial in particular) that the complement brings into the relationship. Although the complement does tend to have control over the day-to-day running of the household, this power may disappear with divorce or other internal family disruption. It is estimated that heterosexual head–complement families make up only about 14 percent of all families in the United States.

The "junior partner/senior partner" model is where the traditional marriage contract has been modified. Both members of the couple work outside the home, although one member (usually wife or female domestic partner) considers her work to be secondary to the senior partner's job. She also takes primary responsibility for the home and childcare. This means that the junior partner has taken on some of the provider role while still maintaining responsibility for the domestic role. In practice this might mean that if the senior partner is transferred or relocated because of (usually his) work, the junior partner experiences a disruption in her work to follow. If someone is contacted when the children come home from school sick, it is the junior partner. She might enter and leave the labor force based upon the needs of the children and family. This model, the most frequently occurring structure for marriage or domestic partnerships today, encourages the double day of work for women where they work both inside and outside the home.

In terms of power, there is a more equitable sharing in this model because the junior partner is bringing resources into the family and has control over the day-to-day running of the household. Note in both models described here, the head and senior partner loses out to a greater or lesser degree on the joys associated with household work—especially the raising of children. Junior partners tend to fare better after divorce than the "complements" of the head–complement model. But junior partners do have the emotional stress and physical burdens of working two jobs. These stresses and burdens are affected by how much the senior partner helps out in the home.

The "equal partners" model is one where the traditional marriage contract is completely disrupted. Neither partner is more likely to perform provider or domestic roles. In practice this might mean both jobs or careers are valued equally such that one does not take priority over the other and domestic responsibilities are shared equally. Alternatively, it might mean an intentional sharing of responsibilities such that one partner agrees to be the economic provider for a period of time and the other agrees to take on domestic responsibilities, although neither is valued more than the other, and this is negotiated rather than implied. In this model financial power is shared, and the burdens and joys of domestic work and childcare are also shared. Although this arrangement gives women the most power in marriage or domestic partnerships, not surprisingly it is a relatively infrequent arrangement among contemporary couples. This is because first, most men in domestic relationships have been socialized to expect the privileges associated with having women service their everyday needs or raise their children, and most women expect to take on these responsibilities. Both men and women rarely question this taken-for-granted gendered division of labor. Second, men's jobs are more likely to involve a separation of home and work, and it is more difficult for them to integrate these aspects of their lives. Third, men tend to earn more money than women do on the average, and although it might be relatively easy to value women's paid work equally in theory, it is difficult to do so in practice if one job brings in a much higher salary than the other. For example, imagine an equal partner relationship between a dentist and a dental hygienist. These occupations are very gender segregated, with the majority of dentists being men and dental hygienists women. Although the couple may value each other's work equally, it might be difficult for a family to make decisions concerning relocation and so forth in favor of the one partner who works as the dental hygienist because she makes a small percentage of her partner's salary as a dentist.

It is important to emphasize that despite these various arrangements and the differential balance of power in marriage or domestic partnerships, for many women the family is where they feel most empowered. Many women find the responsibilities of maintaining a household or the challenges of child rearing fulfilling and come to see the family as a source of their competency and happiness. Sometimes this involves living in traditional family forms, and sometimes it means devising new ways of living in families. In this way the family is a positive source of connection, community, and/or productive labor. These diverse experiences associated with family life suggest how family relationships are a complex tangle of compliance to and resistance against various forms of inequities. Mothering, in particular, is one experience that often brings women great joy and shapes their experiences of family relations. This is the topic to which we now turn.

MOTHERING

Although the meaning and practice of motherhood is culturally constructed, it tends to be conflated with notions of innate, biologically programmed behavior and expectations of unconditional love and nurturance. In other words, even though the meanings associated with motherhood vary historically and culturally, women are expected to want to be mothers, and mothers are expected to take primary responsibility for the nurturing of children. Unlike the assumptions associated with "to father," "to mother" implies nurturing, comforting, and care taking. You might mother a kitten or a friend without the assumption of having given birth to them. To have fathered a kitten implies paternity: you are its parent; you did not cuddle and take care of it. Similarly, to father a friend makes no sense in this context. In contemporary U.S. society there is a cultural construction of "normal motherhood" that is class and race based and which sees mothers as devoted to and sacrificing for their children. Deborah R. Connolly addresses this issue by looking at the experience of homeless mothers in "Motherly Things."

This primary association between women and the nurturing aspects of mothering has brought joys and opportunities for empowerment as well as problems and hardship. It has justified the enormous amount of work we do in the home and encouraged girls to set their sights on babies rather than on other forms of productive work. It has justified the type of labor women have traditionally done in the labor force as well as justified lower pay, it has kept women out of specific positions such as in the military where they might be involved in taking life rather than giving life, and it has encouraged all kinds of explanations for why

CHILDREN WITH SINGLE PARENTS—
HOW THEY FARE

Children living at home with both parents grow up with more financial and educational advantages than youngsters raised by one parent, as U.S. Census Bureau statistics have long shown. But even for those children living in single-parent homes, the marital status of the parent can affect the quality of life. More than a quarter of America's children now live with one parent.

Children living with a divorced parent typically have a big edge over those living with a parent who has never married—an even bigger edge if that parent is the father.

Never-married parents are significantly younger than divorced parents and on average tend to have fewer years of school completed and lower levels of income. Nonetheless, although age does have an effect, the differences remain.

DIVORCED PARENTS ARE MORE EDUCATED

About 85 percent of children living with either a divorced mother or father in 1995 were living with a parent who had finished high school. In contrast, among children living with a never-married parent, fewer than two-thirds had parents who had completed high school.

CHILDREN OF DIVORCED PARENTS ARE LESS LIKELY TO LIVE IN RENTAL HOMES

Of the 19 million children of single parents, two-thirds lived in rented homes. In 1995, about 78 percent of children living with never-married parents, and one-half (52 percent) of children living with divorced parents, lived in rented homes.

CHILDREN OF DIVORCED PARENTS ARE LESS LIKELY TO BE POOR

Nearly 6 of 10 children living with only their mother were near (or below) the poverty line. About 45 percent of children raised by divorced mothers and 69 percent of those raised by never-married mothers lived in or near poverty. Children living with their father (particularly if he was divorced) were more likely to be part of a family with a higher median income than those living with a single mom.

Employment was an important reason for this poverty. Although many single parents had jobs, there were 7.4 million children living with single moms who were unemployed or not in the labor force. Children of never-married mothers were twice as likely (59 percent) to have their moms unemployed or not in the labor force as children whose mothers were divorced (29 percent).

men are, and should be, in control in society. In addition, the close relationship between womanhood and mothering has caused pain for women who are not able to have children as well as for those who have intentionally chosen to not have any.

Contemporary constructions of mothering, like the family, tend to be created around a mythical norm that reflects a White, abled, middle-class, heterosexual, and young adult experience. But, of course, mothers come in all types and reflect the wide diversity of women in the United States. Their understandings of their roles and their position within systems of inequality and privilege are such that mothering is a diverse experience. This is because society has different expectations of mothers depending upon class and culture and other differences at the same time that these differences create different attitudes toward the experience of mothering. For example, although society often expects poor mothers to work outside the home rather than accept welfare, middle-class mothers might be made to feel guilty for "abandoning" their babies to daycare centers. Because of class, ethnicity, and/or religious orientation, some women experience more ambivalence than others when it comes to combining work and family roles. Differently abled women often experience little support and encouragement when it comes to their decision to raise an abled child. A little over one-quarter of all births in the United States are to single mothers, and many more women become single in the process of raising children. Motherhood for single mothers is often constructed through societal notions of stigma, and, as Michael Kimmel explains in his article, because fatherlessness is often seen as a major cause of social problems, single mothers are blamed. He emphasizes that a correlation (relation between factors) does not imply causality and suggests that both social problems and fatherlessness are products of poverty.

Interracial or lesbian couples or people who adopt a child of another race are often accused of not taking into account the best interests of their children. Of course, it is society that has these problems and the families are doing their best to cope. Lesbian mothers in particular have to deal with two mutually exclusive categories that have been constructed as contradictory: mother and lesbian. This illustrates the narrow understandings of motherhood as well as the stereotypes associated with being a mother and with being a lesbian. In addition, in most states lesbian mothers, although often mothering with a female partner who also parents, are legally understood as single mothers: women parenting with an absent father. As a result, they must deal with that stigma too.

In this way, American families are increasingly diverse forms of social organization that are intricately connected to other institutions in society. The family is a basic social unit around which much of society is built; it is fundamental to the processes of meeting individual and social needs. The centrality of the family in U.S. society encourages us to think about the way the family reproduces and resists gender relations and what it means to each of us in our everyday lives.

READING 48

The "Constructed Problems" of Contemporary Family Life

Michael Kimmel

. . . Without a concerted national policy to assist working women and men to balance work and family obligations, we continue to put such enormous strains on two sets of bonds, between husbands and wives and between parents and children, and virtually guarantee that the "crisis" of the family will continue. And we will also continue to face a series of "constructed problems"—problems that stem from the strain felt by individual families as they negotiate the increased pressures of sustaining dual-career couples and dividing housework and child care in the absence of help from the outside.

In the 1950s, the government stepped in where once the community and extended kinship networks had sustained family life, and created an infrastructure (schools, hospitals, roads, and suburban homes) that supported and sustained family life. Today, we expect families to accomplish far more—expect them, for example, to support children often beyond high school and college and to provide for virtually all of an adult's emotional needs—on far less. It is from this widening chasm between what we expect from our families and what support we offer them that several "constructed problems" emerge. These problems are also the result of gender inequality—both its persistence and the efforts by women to remedy it. Only when we develop a sustained national effort—both individually and politically—to reduce the gender inequality in both the home and the workplace, will these constructed problems begin to ease.

The "Problem" of Day Care

Take, for example, the "problem" of day care. Many Americans are reluctant to place their children in day care, and the government has no national funding for day-care centers. Yet the most common conclusion from the research on the impact of day care on children's development is that there are no negative psychological, intellectual, developmental, or emotional consequences to being in day care. And a 1996 National Institutes of Health study found that children's attachment to their mothers is not affected by whether or not they are in day care, what age they enter, or how many hours they spend there.

Despite these findings, we seem to be bombarded daily with headlines that remind us of such negative consequences, including child sexual abuse at day-care centers. The implication of such terrifying stories is that if these children were home with their mothers, where they "belong," such terrible things would not be happening to them. The "problem" of day care turns out to be a debate about whether or not women should be working outside the home. "Having a nanny read you a story isn't the same as having your mother do so," writes William R. Mattox, a senior writer for the conservative Family Research Council. "A mother's worth cannot be reduced to the cost of what a paid substitute might command. To suggest that it can is like saying that the value of a woman making love to her husband is equal to the going rate for prostitutes in the area."

To ask whether or not women should work outside the home is, of course, to ask the wrong question. For one thing, it poses a class-based contradiction, since we encourage poor women to leave the home and go to work, and middle-class women to leave the workplace and return home. The landmark Welfare Reform legislation of 1996 requires that welfare recipients start working within two years of going on welfare. "It is difficult to argue that poor mothers should find jobs but that middle-class mothers should stay home," writes family researcher Andrew Cherlin. And when they can find jobs, working-class and middle-class women are simply not going to stop working.

Nor is there any reason that they should, since there is no evidence whatsoever that mothers working outside the home adversely affects children. In fact, most of the evidence indicates that both direct and indirect benefits accrue to children of working mothers. Such children tend to have expanded role models, more egalitarian gender role attitudes, and more positive attitudes toward women and women's employment. Daughters of employed women are more likely to be employed, and in jobs similar to those of their mothers, than daughters of non-employed women. Moreover, adolescent children of working mothers assume more responsibility around the home, which increases their self-esteem.

Working outside the home also increases women's self-esteem and sense of personal efficacy and well-being, so working mothers tend to be happier in their marriages—which makes divorce less likely. One study found that the happier wives were in their jobs, the happier they were in their marriages. In a four-year study sponsored by the National Institute for Mental Health, Rosalind Barnet observed three hundred dual-career families, and found that the women were neither depressed nor stressed out, but said they had good marriages and good relationships with their children. Another survey of more than eight hundred two-career couples found similar results.

Not only *will* women continue to work outside the home, but they *should* work outside the home, argues Joan Peters. "If they do not, they cannot preserve their identities or raise children" who are able to be both independent and family oriented. But, "women can do so successfully only if men take half the responsibility for child care." Again, the "solution" turns out to be social and political. Only one-third of all employees in large and midsize U.S. companies can even receive unpaid parental leave. Both nationally and in each family, the solution turns out to be greater gender equality—not women working less outside the home, but men working more inside it.

. . .

The "Problem" of Fatherlessness

The question of men's responsibility also surfaces in the debates about fatherlessness. In recent years, commentators have noticed that fathers are not around, having left their children either through divorce or cavalier indifference. Recent works such as David Blankenhorn's *Fatherless America* or David Popenoe's *Life without Father* have credited absent fathers with causing myriad social problems, ranging from juvenile delinquency, crime, and violence to unemployment. We read, for example, that 70 percent of all juveniles in state reform institutions come from fatherless homes. This bodes especially ill for young boys, because without a father, we are told, these young boys will grow up without secure foundation in their manhood. "In families where the father is absent, the mother faces an impossible task: She cannot raise a boy into a man. He must bond with a man as he grows up," writes psychologist Frank Pittman. It is a mistake to believe that "a mother is able to show a male child how to be a man." "Boys raised by traditionally masculine fathers generally do not commit crimes," adds David Blankenhorn. "Fatherless boys commit crimes." In a home without a father, Robert Bly writes somewhat more poetically, "the demons have full permission to rage." This has consequences for both the fathers and the boys, creating in one moment two sets of unattached and unconstrained males roaming around the streets. "Every society must be wary of the unattached male," family researcher David Popenoe reminds us, "for he is universally the cause of numerous social ills."

It is true that more children of both sexes are being raised in single-parent homes, and that the "single parent" doing that child raising is more often than not a woman. Whereas just over one in ten (11 percent) children were being raised by unmarried mothers in 1970, nearly one-fourth (24 percent) are being raised that way as of 1996. More than one in four (26 percent) of all births are to single women. And it is also true that the other side of the "feminization of poverty" coin is the "masculinization of irresponsibility"—the refusal of fathers to provide economically for their children. What is less certain, however, is the impact of fathers on the myriad social problems with which their absence seems to be correlated. Though father involvement may provide some benefits to children, family researchers Paul Amato and Alan Booth note that the effects are "far from overwhelming" and certainly are not decisive for the well-being of their children. Remember, also, that correlation is not causation, and though fatherlessness may be correlated with high crime rates, that does not mean that fatherlessness *caused* the criminality. In fact, it might just be the other way around. It turns out that high crime rates and fatherlessness are *both* products of a larger and more overwhelming problem: poverty.

The National Academy of Sciences reports that the single best predictor of violent crime is not fatherlessness but "personal and neighborhood income." And, it turns out, fatherlessness also varies with income; the higher the income bracket, the more likely the father is home—which suggests that the crisis of fatherlessness is actually a crisis of poverty. In his impressive ethnographic research on street gangs in Los Angeles, Martin Sanchez-Jankowski found "as many gang members from homes where the nuclear family was intact as there were from families where the father was absent" and "as many members who claimed close relationships with their families as those who denied them." Clearly something other than the mere presence or absence of a father is at work here.

The confusion of correlation and causation also reveals a deeper confusion of consequence and cause. Fatherlessness may be a consequence of those larger, deeper, more structural forces that drive fathers from the home and keep them away—such as unemployment or increased workplace demands to maintain a standard of living. Pundits often attempt to transform the problem of fatherlessness into another excuse to blame feminism, and specifically women working outside the home. They yearn for a traditional nuclear family, with traditional gender inequality. For example, David Popenoe writes nostalgically about the family form of the 1950s —"heterosexual, monogamous, life-long marriage in which there is a sharp division of labor, with the female as the full-time housewife and the male as primary provider and ultimate authority"— without pausing to underscore that such a family form was also dramatically unequal when viewed from a gender perspective. Such a vision substitutes form for content, apparently under the impression that if only the family conformed to a specific form, then the content of family life would dramatically improve.

The "Problem" of Divorce

It is hard to deny that divorce is a real problem. The divorce rate in the United States is astonishingly high, around half of all marriages. This is considerably higher than in other industrialized countries, more than double the rates in Germany and France, and nearly double the rate in Sweden and Britain, countries where individuals remain supported by national health care and children specifically benefit from adequate access to education and health care, while their custodial parents receive regular governmental stipends. (These, of course, ameliorate the harsh economic impact of divorce.) According to the Census Bureau, the number of divorced people had more than quadrupled from 4.3 million in 1970 to 19.3 million in 1997. This represents 10 percent of all adults aged eighteen or over, up from 3 percent in 1970.

Divorce may be a serious social problem, but not exactly for the reasons that many political commentators claim it is. First, these high divorce rates are not shattering the family. Rates of marital dissolution are roughly the same as they have been for a very long time. Looked at historically, high rates of divorce are merely accomplishing by conscious action what higher mortality rates had accomplished in an earlier period. As historian Lawrence Stone put it, "the median duration of marriage today is almost exactly the same as it was a hundred years ago. Divorce, in short, now acts as a functional substitute for death: Both are means of terminating marriage at a premature stage." (Of course, he adds that the psychological effects are not the same.) Nor does the number of divorces necessarily indicate a loss of faith in marriage. Ninety five percent of men and 94 percent of women between the ages of forty-five and fifty-four have been married. In fact, writes sociologist Constance Ahrons, author of *The Good Divorce*, "we like marriage so much that many of us will do it two, three, or more times." Remarriages now comprise about half of all marriages every year.

The problem with divorce is more accurately linked to the constructed problem of fatherlessness and the real problem of gender inequality. Divorce reform was promoted, after all, by feminist women at the turn of the century to provide some legal recourse to women who wanted to escape marriages that were desperately unhappy, and others brutally, even, violently oppressive. The option of divorce loosened the marital knot to keep it from choking women. Like birth control and abortion, both of which have also generated heated debates, divorce undermined men's power over women and reduced gender inequality in the family.

Although liberalizing divorce laws may have reduced gender inequality within marriage, they seem neither to have reduced it entirely nor reduced it after the marriage is dissolved. One recent study found that three of four women listed pathological behaviors by male partners (adultery, violence, substance abuse, abandonment) as their reason for divorce. Just as there are "his" and "her" marriages, there are also "his" and "her" divorces because divorce affects wives and husbands differently. Divorce exaggerates gender differences in the marriage, exacerbating gender inequality. In the mid-1980s, family researcher Leonore Weitzman calculated that following divorce, the woman's income drops a precipitous 73 percent, while her ex-husband's income increases 42 percent. In recent years, these data have been revised as overly dramatic, but no research suggests that the economic and social statuses of women and men after divorce are equivalent, and researchers still agree that women's resources decline somewhat even as men's improve. As sociologist Paul Amato writes, "the greater the inequality between men and women in a given society, the more detrimental the impact of divorce on women."

. . .

The "Problem" of Child Custody

Whether or not divorce has simply accomplished by social policy what high mortality rates used to accomplish "naturally," there is one significant difference between the two methods to dissolve a marriage. With a divorce often comes the problem of child custody. Before the Industrial Revolution, children were seen as an economic "good," and courts used an economic means test to determine who would receive custody, and custody was regularly and routinely given to fathers. In the early years of the twentieth century, though, children came to be seen as a luxury, and so a new test, based on care and nurture, was used to determine custody arrangements, a policy that favored mothers. Today, the "best interest of the child" is the criterion employed to provide the foundation for custody decisions, although in practice, the best interests of the child are presumed to be better served by staying with the mother not the father, since the presumption is that mothers provide better child care, especially for young children, than do fathers.

Such a policy makes a certain amount of sense, since women perform most of the tasks that provide the care and nurture that children most need. And yet, in the late 1970s, 63 percent of fathers who requested custody received it, a significant increase from the 35 percent and 37 percent who requested and received it in 1968 and 1972 respectively. In a recent study of one thousand divorces in two California counties, psychologist Eleanor Maccoby and law professor Robert Mnookin found that a majority of mothers and fathers wanted joint legal custody, while those that didn't preferred that they, and not their spouses, be given custody. Nearly 82 percent of mothers and 56 percent of fathers requested the custody arrangement they wanted, while 6.7 percent of women and 9.8 percent of men requested more than they wanted and 11.5 percent of women and 34.1 percent of men requested less than they wanted. This suggests that "gender still matters" in what parents ask for and what they do to get it. That mothers were more likely to act on their desires by filing for a specific request also indicates that men need to ask for more up front to avoid feeling bitter later.

Maccoby and Mnookin's research is notable for another finding. Children living with mothers generally did as well as children living with fathers, that "the welfare of kids following a divorce did not depend a lot on who got custody," Maccoby told a journalist, "but rather on how the household was managed and how the parents cooperated." But one consequence of current custody arrangements is paternal withdrawal. Whether this is because the father is bereft at being kept from regular contact with his children or because once the marital bond is severed he experiences a euphoria of "freedom" and considers himself to have escaped from a conflict-ridden family situation, it appears that many men "see parenting and marriage as part of the same bargain—a package deal," write sociologists Frank Furstenberg and Andrew Cherlin. "It is as if they stop being fathers as soon as the marriage is over." In one nationally representative sample of 11- to 16-year-old children living with their mothers, almost half had not seen their fathers in the previous twelve months. Nearly half of all divorced fathers in the United States pay no child support; in Europe the comparable number is about one-fourth.

Paternal withdrawal, it turns out, actually affects the father-daughter relationship most significantly, even more than the much-touted father-son relationship, whereas the mother-daughter relationship seems to be the most resilient to divorce and custody disputes. This may surprise those who believe that the father-son bond is the most fragile and most hard-hit by postdivorce fatherlessness, but it illustrates how frequently daughters are ignored in that literature, and how both boys and girls benefit from paternal responsibility and continued presence in their children's lives.

In recent years, postdivorce fatherhood has become a political issue, as "father's rights" organizations have sprouted up, declaring men to be the victims of inequality in custody decisions. It is true, of course, that most court decisions grant custody to the mother, based on the "best interest of the child" standard. Father's rights groups challenge this assumption, and claim that, invariably, joint custody is preferable for children. Sometimes, it appears that their rhetoric substitutes these aggrieved fathers' vindictiveness against ex-wives, or their bewilderment at the entire divorce proceeding, for the "best interests" of children, but it also appears to be the case that all things being equal, joint physical and legal custody ought to be the norm in custody decisions. Here, of course, "all things being equal" means that there is no discernible danger to the child of sexual or physical abuse; that the parents can manage to contain their own postdivorce conflict and prevent the children from becoming pawns in a parental power struggle; and that the parents agree to equally support the children financially and emotionally. Such arrangements may be more difficult for parents than for children, who often report "a sense of being loved by both parents," as well as "feeling strongly attached to two psychological parents, in contrast to feeling close to just one primary parent." Contrary to some popular opinion, joint custody "does not create uncertainty or confusion," and seems to benefit children, who say they are more satisfied with the arrangement than those in single-custody homes and consider having two homes advantageous.

We know, too, that joint custody will benefit men, who will, by maintaining a legal connection to their children, be far more likely to continue to share financial responsibilities for their development. What's more, joint custody may relieve the deep sense of loss, disengagement, and depression often experienced by men who are cut loose from continued involvement with their families. On the other hand, mandated joint legal custody may not be so good for women. Feminist legal theorist Martha Fineman argues that mandated joint legal custody may appear to be gender neutral, but gender "neutrality" in one arena in an overall system of gender inequality may perpetuate gender discrimination, much the way the abandonment of affirmative action sounds race- or gender-neutral, but actually favors white males over others by withdrawal from explicit challenge to historical discrimination. As Fineman writes:

> What may have started out as a system which, focusing on the child's need for care, gave women a preference *solely* because they had usually been the child's primary caretaker, is evolving into a system which, by devaluing the content of necessity of such care, gives men more than an equal chance to gain the custody of their children after divorce if they choose to have it, because biologically equal parents are considered as equal in expressive regards. Non-nurturing factors assume importance which often favor men.

Perhaps the most judicious system of child custody will be one that recognizes the difference in "inputs" between fathers and mothers in the actual experiences of the children—time spent in child care, level of parental involvement in child development —while at the same time presuming that both parents are capable of and interested in (absent any evidence to the contrary) continued committed and involved relationships with their children. Men's increased involvement in predivorce child care ought to be reflected in custody arrangements, as should women's continuing to shoulder the overwhelming majority of such care, despite their commitments to work. Fathers' "rights" following divorce will come more readily if the fathers have recognized their responsibilities during the marriage.

The "Problem" of Gay and Lesbian Families

Another recent constructed problem is that of gay and lesbian families. I often find it ironic that the same political commentators who fret about the decline of the family are the very people who would prevent gay men and lesbians from creating them. But the problems of gay families—marriage, child rearing—are actually less about families, and more about the legal status of homosexuals. As soon as the Hawaii state Supreme Court indicated the likelihood that it would recognize gay and lesbian marriages in 1997, for example, several states rescinded their adherence to the "full faith and credit" clause of the U.S. Constitution, the provision that requires one state to recognize contracts concluded in another state, such as marriage, voting, education, or driving. Soon thereafter, the U.S. Congress passed the Defense of Marriage Act, as if the institution of marriage were under attack by those who seek to enter it. It is expressly legal for gay men and lesbians to adopt children in only ten states and the District of Columbia (Alaska, California, Minnesota, Oregon, Washington, Massachusetts, New Jersey, New York, Pennsylvania, and Vermont).

One reason that many gay and lesbian couples want to marry is because so many benefits accrue to married couples—benefits that heterosexual couples often take for granted. These include the right to inherit from a spouse who dies without a will; the right to consult with doctors and make crucial medical decisions if the partner is incapacitated; the right of residency of a foreign spouse; the right to Social Security benefits; the right to include a spouse on one's health plan; the right to visit a spouse in a government institution like a prison or hospital; and the

right to immunity from having to testify against one's spouse in a legal proceeding.

It is true that gay male relationships are more fragile than heterosexual relationships and that gay men are more "promiscuous" (have a greater number of different sexual partners) than heterosexuals, though neither of these statements is true of lesbians. Some of the reasons for this disparity can be found in masculine gender socialization, which discourages men from commitment to domestic life in the first place; exclusion from formal legal marriage, which cements heterosexual relationships and increases the couple's likelihood of staying together despite disagreement; lack of children, who are often the reason that heterosexual couples continue to work on their relationships; and social disapproval and institutionalized homophobia, which can destabilize any couple. "It is paradoxical that mainstream America perceives gays and lesbians as unable to maintain long-term relationships while at the same time denying them the very institutions that stabilize such relationships" argued Craig Dean, executive director of the Marriage Rights Fund.

Marriage is more than a legal right, more than a relationship. It is an institution, the bedrock institution of our ideal of the family. Without the right to marry, it is codified into law that gay relationships are less valuable, less important, than heterosexual ones. Such a devaluation leads to the very promiscuity that is used as the rationale for denying the right to marry in the first place.

In many cases, gay and lesbian couples provide a model of family life. For one thing, gay and lesbian couples are "less likely to fall into patterns of inequality" that define heterosexual marriages. By bringing together two people of the same gender, gender inequality is neutralized and gender difference eliminated. Compared with heterosexual couples, gay and lesbian couples are more likely to share housework; lesbian couples are the most egalitarian of all couple arrangements. And, it turns out, gay men and lesbians often make excellent parents. In the late 1960s, one woman lamented her position, not as a lesbian, but as a nonparent:

> One of my mother's big disappointments was the fact that there would be no grandchildren. I love

both of my parents a great deal, and I would do almost anything for their happiness, but I couldn't do that. I think I was saddened too, when, . . . I knew that I wasn't ever going to have children. And I would like to have some . . . for myself.

Just as heterosexual women once felt they were forced to choose between having a career and having a family, many gay men and lesbians felt forced to choose between acknowledging their sexuality and having a family. And just as women today are unwilling to make that choice, wanting to "have it all," so too are gays and lesbians, who have decided that their homosexuality ought not to disqualify them as good parents. In 1976, there were between 300,000 and 500,000 gay and lesbian parents; today there are an estimated 1.5 million to 5 million lesbian mothers, and between 1 million and 3 million gay fathers. Currently, between 6 million and 14 million children (about 5 percent of all children in the United States) are being raised by at least one gay parent.

None of the feared consequences of gay parenting has materialized. There is no evidence that gay fathers or lesbian mothers exert any special negative influence on child development or that they sexually abuse their children. In fact, the few studies that have been conducted show that "the outcomes for children in these families tend to be better than average." For example, when fathers come out to their children, even if they are not raising the children themselves, it tends to relieve family stress and strengthen the bond between father and child. The research on lesbian mothers suggests that their children, both boys and girls, have similar patterns of gender identity development to children of heterosexual parents at comparable ages, and display no differences in intelligence or adjustment. "Quality of mothering" rather than sexual orientation is the crucial determinant of children's development. . . .

The Real Problem of Family Violence

For too many Americans, children and parents alike, the family bears only a passing resemblance to the "haven in a heartless world" of nostalgic myth. Far from shielding their members from the cold and violent world outside its doors, the family *is* that cold and violent world. Violence tears at the fabric of the family. . . . Family violence is remarkably gendered, reproducing and reinforcing gender inequality. The overwhelming amount of family violence is perpetrated by males: husbands beating wives, fathers hitting children, or sons hitting their parents, boys hitting their brothers or their sisters. "The actual or implicit threat of physical coercion is one of many factors underlying male dominance in the family," writes sociologist Murray Straus.

Violence against children by parents is among the most controversial types of family violence. Although widespread support exists for corporal punishment—over three-fourths of Americans believe that it is all right for a parent to spank a child—that support disappears when such violent behaviors by parents against children become systematic or extreme. Although most Americans have hit their children, and most children have been hit by their parents, we nightly gasp at news reports of parental violence against children. The most common forms of parental violence against children are spanking or slapping, though one in five parents have hit their child with an object, almost 10 percent have kicked, bit, or hit their children with their fist, and almost one in twenty families have experienced a parent beating up a child. Though mothers as well as fathers commit this violence, they are not equivalent. In one study, Bergman and his colleagues found that men are more than ten times more likely to inflict serious harm on their children, and that every perpetrator of the death of a child in this limited sample was either a father or a father surrogate.

The most evident consequence of parental violence against children is observed in the behaviors of children. Children see that violence is a legitimate way to resolve disputes, and learn to use it themselves. Violence against siblings is ubiquitous in American families. As Straus writes:

> Violence between siblings often reflects what children see their parents doing to each other, as well as what the child experiences in the form of discipline. Children of non-violent parents also tend to use non-violent methods to deal with their siblings and

later with their spouses and children. If violence, like charity, begins at home, so does non-violence.

(Parents wondering how to discourage violence among their children might begin by resisting the temptation to hit them, and settling marital problems without resorting to violence.)

The long-term consequences of parental violence against children are also evident. The greater the corporal punishment experienced by the child, the greater the probability that the child will hit a spouse as an adult. And the likelihood is also higher that children hit by their parents will strike back. Child-to-parent violence is also serious; nearly one in ten (9 percent) of all parents of children aged ten to seventeen are victims of violence perpetrated by their

own children. Mothers are more likely to be victims of such violence, especially in the more severe cases.

The antecedent causes of children hitting their parents, and especially their mothers, are directly related to the severity of the violence experienced by the child and the severity of the spousal violence the child observes. Children see their mothers hit by their fathers, and they "learn that mothers are an appropriate and acceptable target for intrafamily violence," writes sociologist Richard Gelles. Nowhere is the gender inequality of the family more evident than when a young boy hit his mother because he has learned by watching his father that violence against women is acceptable behavior for a boy coming into manhood.

READING 49

Marriage and Love

Emma Goldman (1910)

The popular notion about marriage and love is that they are synonymous, that they spring from the same motives, and cover the same human needs. Like most popular notions this also rests not on actual facts, but on superstition.

Marriage and love have nothing in common; they are as far apart as the poles; are, in fact, antagonistic to each other. No doubt some marriages have been the result of love. Not, however, because love could assert itself only in marriage; much rather is it because few people can completely outgrow a convention. There are today large numbers of men and women to whom marriage is naught but a farce, but who submit to it for the sake of public opinion. At any rate, while it is true that some marriages are based on love, and while it is equally true that in some cases love continues in married life, I maintain that it does so regardless of marriage, and not because of it.

On the other hand, it is utterly false that love results from marriage. On rare occasions one does hear of a miraculous case of a married couple falling in love after marriage, but on close examination it

will be found that it is a mere adjustment to the inevitable. Certainly the growing-used to each other is far away from the spontaneity, the intensity, and beauty of love, without which the intimacy of marriage must prove degrading to both the woman and the man.

Marriage is primarily an economic arrangement, an insurance pact. It differs from the ordinary life insurance agreement only in that it is more binding, more exacting. Its returns are insignificantly small compared with the investments. In taking out an insurance policy one pays for it in dollars and cents, always at liberty to discontinue payments. If, however, woman's premium is a husband, she pays for it with her name, her privacy, her self-respect, her very life, "until death doth part." Moreover, the marriage insurance condemns her to life-long dependency, to parasitism, to complete uselessness, individual as well as social. Man, too, pays his toll, but as his sphere is wider, marriage does not limit him as much as woman. He feels his chains more in an economic sense.

Thus Dante's motto over Inferno applies with equal force to marriage. "Ye who enter here leave all hope behind."

. . .

From infancy, almost, the average girl is told that marriage is her ultimate goal; therefore her training and education must be directed towards that end. Like the mute beast fattened for slaughter, she is prepared for that. Yet, strange to say, she is allowed to know much less about her function as wife and mother than the ordinary artisan of his trade. It is indecent and filthy for a respectable girl to know anything of the marital relation. Oh, for the inconsistency of respectability, that needs the marriage vow to turn something which is filthy into the purest and most sacred arrangement that none dare question or criticize. Yet that is exactly the attitude of the average upholder of marriage. The prospective wife and mother is kept in complete ignorance of her only asset in the competitive field—sex. Thus she enters into life-long relations with a man only to find herself shocked, repelled, outraged beyond measure by the most natural and healthy instinct, sex. It is safe to say that a large percentage of the unhappiness, misery, distress, and physical suffering of matrimony is due to the criminal ignorance in sex matters that is being extolled as a great virtue. Nor is it at all an exaggeration when I say that more than one home has been broken up because of this deplorable fact.

If, however, woman is free and big enough to learn the mystery of sex without the sanction of State or Church, she will stand condemned as utterly unfit to become the wife of a "good" man, his goodness consisting of an empty brain and plenty of money. Can there be anything more outrageous than the idea that a healthy, grown woman, full of life and passion, must deny nature's demand, must subdue her most intense craving, undermine her health and break her spirit, must stunt her vision, abstain from the depth and glory of sex experience until a "good" man comes along to take her unto himself as a wife? That is precisely what marriage means. How can such an arrangement end except in failure? This is one, though not the least important, factor of marriage, which differentiates it from love.

Ours is a practical age. The time when Romeo and Juliet risked the wrath of their fathers for love, when Gretchen exposed herself to the gossip of her neighbors for love, is no more. If, on rare occasions, young people allow themselves the luxury of romance, they are taken in care by the elders, drilled and pounded until they become "sensible."

The moral lesson instilled in the girl is not whether the man has aroused her love, but rather is it, "How much?" The important and only God of practical American life: Can the man make a living? Can he support a wife? That is the only thing that justifies marriage. Gradually this saturates every thought of the girl; her dreams are not of moonlight and kisses, of laughter and tears; she dreams of shopping tours and bargain counters. This soul poverty and sordidness are the elements inherent in the marriage institution. The State and the Church approve of no other ideal, simply because it is the one that necessitates the State and Church control of men and women.

Doubtless there are people who continue to consider love above dollars and cents. Particularly is this true of that class whom economic necessity has forced to become self-supporting. The tremendous change in woman's position, wrought by that mighty factor, is indeed phenomenal when we reflect that it is but a short time since she has entered the industrial arena. Six million women wage workers; six million women, who have the equal right with men to be exploited, to be robbed, to go on strike; aye, to starve even. Anything more, my lord? Yes, six million wage workers in every walk of life, from the highest brain work to the mines and railroad tracks; yes, even detectives and policemen. Surely the emancipation is complete.

Yet with all that, but a very small number of the vast army of women wage workers look upon work as a permanent issue, in the same light as does man. No matter how decrepit the latter, he has been taught to be independent, self-supporting. Oh, I know that no one is really independent in our economic treadmill; still, the poorest specimen of a man hates to be a parasite; to be known as such, at any rate.

The woman considers her position as worker transitory, to be thrown aside for the first bidder. That is why it is infinitely harder to organize women than men. "Why should I join a union? I am going to get married, to have a home." Has she not been taught from infancy to look upon that as her ultimate calling? She learns soon enough that the home, though not so large a prison as the factory, has more solid doors and bars. It has a keeper so faithful that naught can escape him. The most tragic part, however, is that the home no longer frees her from wage slavery; it only increases her task.

According to the latest statistics submitted before a Committee "on labor and wages, and congestion of population," ten per cent of the wage workers in New York City alone are married, yet they must continue to work at the most poorly paid labor in the world. Add to this horrible aspect the drudgery of housework, and what remains of the protection and glory of the home? As a matter of fact, even the middle-class girl in marriage can not speak of her home, since it is the man who creates her sphere. It is not important whether the husband is a brute or a darling. What I wish to prove is that marriage guar-

antees woman a home only by the grace of her husband. There she moves about in *his* home, year after year, until her aspect of life and human affairs becomes as flat, narrow, and drab as her surroundings. Small wonder if she becomes a nag, petty, quarrelsome, gossipy, unbearable, thus driving the man from the house. She could not go, if she wanted to; there is no place to go. Besides, a short period of married life, of complete surrender of all faculties, absolutely incapacitates the average woman for the outside world. She becomes reckless in appearance, clumsy in her movements, dependent in her decisions, cowardly in her judgment, a weight and a bore, which most men grow to hate and despise. . . .

The institution of marriage makes a parasite of woman, an absolute dependent. It incapacitates her for life's struggle, annihilates her social consciousness, paralyzes her imagination, and then imposes its gracious protection, which is in reality a snare, a travesty on human character.

READING 50

Motherly Things

Deborah R. Connolly

Mythical Mothers: The Susan Smith Case

Dichotomies of the moralized poles of the good virtuous mother and the evil neglectful one are carefully maintained in the public imagination and in public policies (Tsing 1990; Fineman and Karpin 1995; Roberts 1991; Mink 1995; Ladd-Taylor and Umansky 1998). For example, consider a case that helped to solidify and illustrate this dichotomy— the Susan Smith case. This case took place in 1994 when a white South Carolina woman claimed that a Black man carjacked her and abducted her two young sons. She was later found guilty of their murders, having pushed her car into a lake. The children both drowned.

The Susan Smith case holds a special fascination for me because it sparks one of those debates where the crevice between liberals and conservatives deepens and where many from both sides fall into the canyon together, making a host of unlikely companions. When analyzing the media reactions to this case, one cannot fail to note the public horror toward the image of two children victimized by the same person expected to devote and sacrifice her life for them. How could anyone be so heartless, cruel, selfish, and calculating? Or alternatively, if somewhat less common, how could someone be so unstable and pathological without being detected until after the tragedy occurred?

My goal is not to attempt an explanation of Susan Smith's behavior, nor to contribute to the cultural preoccupation with her punishment. What I am doing is to ponder the role that conceptions of motherhood play in portraying Susan Smith either as a monster or as a victim of mental instability. My work with homeless mothers has led me to consider how motherhood is associated with a complex set of traits that are represented as universal (nurturing, sacrifice, nonviolence). The "naturalness" of motherhood makes any deviation from that identity uniquely abhorrent (Scheper-Hughes 1992).

Susan Smith was tried not simply as a murderer but as a white mother who killed. Middle- and upper-class white women in the United States are bound more closely to the cult of perfect mothering, while Black women are more readily assumed to be deviant mothers and their children viewed as less socially valuable (Roberts 1995; Solinger 1992). Thus, the transgression of motherhood norms by white women is a particularly rich metaphor for understanding how race politics contribute to the cultural fascination with "bad" mothers (Ladd-Taylor and Umansky 1998; Mink 1995). Mothers who are bad or deemed to be "monsters" (Tsing 1990) or "Other" (Polakow 1993) legitimate social enforcement of good-mother codes of conduct by offering an allegedly dangerous antimodel. This process of normalization negates the continuum of behavior that more adequately represents how women live their lives. In effect, the model of normal motherhood is produced and enforced even though it does not adequately represent the experiences of mothers—even those purported to embody the ideal. Thus, a fiction is generated that is potentially destructive to all mothers and children. Furthermore, the model of the normal mother creates a series of intense difficulties and binds for homeless mothers living in circumstances far removed from those implicitly assumed to surround normal mothers.

When Susan Smith was at the center of public attention and hostility, she became an icon of antimaternity. And through her representation of all that good motherhood is not, she thereby reinforced an idealized version of good motherhood. The romanticization of the "good mother" is so pervasive that it impacts women in all social strata—for example, women who work and leave their children in the care of others; or women who cannot afford or find adequate housing for their children; or women whose lives are so full of pain, violence, sickness, and/or poverty that their children are not at its center.

Consider how the cultural staging of normal motherhood might affect someone like Sally, a thirty-three-year-old white woman and client at Westside Community Center (WCC).

"I wanted kids . . . but [then again] I didn't," said Sally, looking over at me from her cramped kitchen table. Behind her there was an American flag on the wall. "But my perfect ideal life was I wanted to be married and have kids." Sally has never been married. She has three boys from three different fathers. The first father ran a nude modeling agency that employed her; the second never knew she was pregnant; and the last one is now in prison:

> He stabbed some guy several times in the chest and it took the other guy's life. If the guy hadn't have died, then he wouldn't have got so severe [a sentence]. . . . Me and him, we will eventually be married. . . . I've moved with my kids . . . to protect my kids, even though it might look bad on their school records. . . . I did it to protect my kids 'cause if I'd stayed, my kids woulda kept getting abused or myself, and I was always in fear.
>
> At one time I had to give my kids up temporarily because I was afraid I was gonna hurt them. I was really close to my first breakdown. I had such a breakdown I couldn't even remember if I had kids or not. . . . Like I said, it's been extremely hectic, really spastic sometimes, being a single parent for what I've gone through. . . . My life or death don't mean nothing to me. . . . I would give my life, whatever, in a heartbeat for my kids. No problem.

The distance between "I wanted kids but I didn't" and "I would give my life in a heartbeat for my kids" reflects an ambivalence that haunts Sally and, as I have discovered, many homeless mothers. Sally expresses other motherly ambivalences and contradictions:

> Me and my kids have been through so much. And I know they love me with all their heart. And I love them. But . . . I just wish I didn't have the part—what they consider abuse. I'm working on it at least.

I'm so afraid of losing my kids and I don't want to lose my kids. They would have to kill me to take my kids, whether I accidentally hurt them or not. . . . I don't care if it's the law or not, nobody will get my kids after what I've encountered and had to go through. That's the one thing I can say is mine. The good Lord gave them to me, and He's the only one that's gonna take them from me. I feel like that with all my heart. 'Cause like I said, at least I did have my kids when we went through what we did. At least I have something that I can say that's part of me, you know?

Sally is defensive about her parenting, warning that even if she hurts her kids "accidentally," she still will not consent to their removal. To Sally, to hurt her children accidentally is to hurt them without explicitly or consciously meaning to. Her language is testimony to the ways in which she feels out of control in her parenting, even while feeling protective of her right to parent. Sally stresses her love for her children but also her need for them as witnesses and for companionship through tumultuous life events. Yet Sally's children have not just endured tribulations with her; they are part of what she has endured, and therefore, "nobody will get my kids after what I've encountered and had to go through."

Even though Sally's own lived experiences of parenting are at odds with the larger cultural model of the good mother—that is, a woman who is devoted to and sacrifices for her children—she nonetheless subscribes to this model. Yet it is this model that presses women to erase any ambivalence accompanying their efforts to raise their children under difficult conditions. Sally's self-presentation clearly maintains the tensions between the good mother model drawn from the larger culture and the actual circumstances of her mothering.

One route to thinking about cultural models of motherhood is to explore sites where such norms are produced and enforced. Social service settings are just such arenas. Indeed, social services have taken on the role of regulating mothers for a long time (Ladd-Taylor and Umansky 1998; Appell 1998; Gordon 1994; Skocpol 1992; Mink 1995). As Linda Gordon points out, in the early 1900s the kind of intervention promoted to help poor single mothers

changed. Previously, the emphasis had been on providing charity and moral reform. However, in the early 1900s single motherhood was recast as a more pressing social problem, and social service agencies were employed to not only provide relief for the impoverished but to bring diverse parenting practices into conformity with middle-class norms of the time (Gordon 1994; Mink 1995).

These paradigms continue to resonate through social service programs today. Indeed, at WCC [Westside Community Center] staff members take seriously the position of evaluating families and breaking patterns of violence, abuse, and neglect. While such issues are not limited to low-income people, their lives are so often entwined with social service systems that such labels get attached to them easily (Roberts 1991, 1434). Thus, part of the project of serving families becomes teaching and enforcing particular familial codes to clients. For example, WCC has a "no-hitting" policy, which means that while you are in the program you are not allowed to discipline your children harshly. (Subsumed under this policy is a dictate against all other forms of harsh punishment, including yelling.) The staff see clients' time in the program as an "opportunity" for them to learn nonabusive disciplinary techniques. As is the case with rules in general, this one is enforced to different degrees depending on the individual client and caseworker.

The program director, Margaret, explains the policy, saying that staff should not be in the position of distinguishing between "appropriate" spanking and child abuse. Therefore, they must insist that no physical punishment be used in order to avoid confusion. While the no-hitting policy is designed to protect children, it also functions to protect staff. As Margaret admitted to me one day, she just does not want to be around such dynamics. Furthermore, staff do not want to be held accountable by other staff or external agencies for not addressing neglectful or abusive behaviors.

The no-hitting and no-yelling mandates are challenging for many clients to adhere to—if not impossible for some. They are thrust into new environments (here I refer particularly to the day and night shelters where these rules are the easiest to enforce), and they are surrounded by other families and staff, all of whom are potentially watching their behavior.

Since children tend to experience high levels of stress in shelters, it often produces disciplinary issues in an environment where many of the tools that they have relied on to control their children are deemed inappropriate and potentially abusive. Clients also know, partly from street knowledge but also from the many forms they must sign when they come into the program, that WCC staff are "mandatory reporters." This means that staff members are obligated to report any signs or incidences of child abuse to the Children's Services Division, a federal agency that has a reputation of acting inconsistently and sometimes arbitrarily (Appell 1998).

Many clients complained about the no-hitting and no-yelling policy. They said they needed to yell at or spank their children in order to get them to mind. Many implied, and others outright asserted, that since I do not have children, I do not understand the nature of discipline. Michelle, a white twenty-year-old pregnant mother of one, looked me straight in the eye after I asked her to lower her voice with her daughter in the day shelter, saying, "Debbie, sometimes you *have* to yell at your kids or spank them. Otherwise, they don't hear you."

While I am sometimes uncomfortable, frustrated, and even indignant when I witness parents being particularly harsh with their children, it is worth considering the ways in which agency policies dictate norms of motherhood. Implicit in the no-hitting policy are certain standards that automatically place mothers at WCC under a cloud of suspicion. The very existence of the rule suggests to clients, staff, and outsiders a "problem" in parenting, a need for regulation and control. It also makes mothers feel that they are being parented themselves.

In a session with a client in which we were discussing discipline, I asked this mom if she ever hit her child.

"I don't abuse him, if that's what you mean," she replied, bristling with obvious defensiveness. "I've spanked him before, but I don't *beat* him!" She kept her eyes turned away from me as she said this, the anger in her voice apparent. What this client understood, and took offense at, was that my questioning of her disciplinary practices called into question the very nature of her role as a mother. My query implied to her that I viewed her as a person who was in

fact capable of abuse and furthermore that I might expose her as such, thereby placing her under additional control.

The mothers I worked with at WCC resented any implication that their "proper" maternity was being called into question. However, simultaneously they had complex and sometimes paradoxical relationships to their children, to their identities as mothers, and to outside representations of motherhood. For example, without any prompting from me, Sally said this about the Susan Smith case, which was receiving heavy media attention at the time of our interviews:

> And then you hear this thing, this lady finally admitted to killing those two boys. And I'm sitting there, man, I just started crying this morning when I heard that. I said, "Man, I hope they throw the book at you, lady." But yet, I shouldn't feel that, because maybe there was . . . maybe she's got . . . you know? I try to think of other people, too, but it's just, something I just cannot see, you know? And because especially where I've hurt my kids sometimes. Where there's been a couple times where I've lost control with the kids. But I turned myself in and they worked with me.

Sally is horrified by the crime and feels Smith should be punished severely. In this way Sally distances herself from Smith. Smith lost control completely, committing the ultimate sin. While Sally can look down on Smith with a punitive gaze, she also struggles with her identifications with Smith. She suggests, not quite finishing her sentences, that "maybe there was [a reason], maybe she's got [a reason]." Sally knows that for her mothering is a struggle, and she wants that aspect of mothering to be more widely acknowledged. One can imagine that she stutters because she does not want to convey the impression that it is acceptable to let her violent impulses win out, yet she simultaneously recognizes that those impulses do exist:

> I hope and pray to God that I never lose my temper again. And before I feel like I'm gonna do that again, and I hate to say this, I'll get something where I can calm myself completely down. . . . That's part of the reason why I got on a lot of downer drugs, so that way I wouldn't lose it. Because there's been a lot of

times when I've thought, "God, I'm gonna kill my kids." That's a horrible thought! It's horrible! But the only way I would not get that out is to pop some downers, drink a bottle of Jack, no problem. I drink that stuff like Kool-Aid. I could drink a couple of fifths or pints in a day. . . . My kids, they think, "Oh wow, mommy, she's not mad." They didn't realize a lot of times it's because I was in my own little world on drugs. . . . But I still managed to do a lot of the motherly things. . . . I didn't know how else to do it. . . . Because a lot of times I just feel like I'm going to lose control completely. I hate feeling that way because I feel helpless when I feel that way.

Sally's relationship to her children is an ambivalent one, a combination of love, resentment, and the sense of being overwhelmed. She also struggles with a terrifying acknowledgment that she is not always in control of herself. She uses desperate strategies to protect her children from her—strategies that deviate from mainstream standards of positive parenting and that place her own life and the custody of her children in further jeopardy. But, she argues, these strategies keep her children relatively safe.

Sally claims to use drugs and alcohol to diffuse her anger. "I hate to say this," she says and then confesses that she would use drugs and alcohol again if she felt as though she needed to protect her kids from herself. Of course, one should be wary of an addict's claim that drugs and alcohol help her maintain positive parenting. While drug and alcohol use might at times calm a person down, such behaviors are just as likely, if not more so, to promote violence and a sense of being out of control. Further, Sally's own version of why she uses them could provide an excuse for future use.

It may be that drugs and alcohol provide at least a temporary numbing against the hatred inside of Sally, hatred that was instilled in her during her own upbringing and that continues to wreak havoc on her life and the lives of her children. Yet these kinds of negotiations between anger, violence, and drug use are precisely what is erased from idealized versions of motherhood. Mythical mothers do not experience rage at their children; they never lose control; they do not use drugs (at least not illicit ones) to keep themselves from lashing out at their families.

The erasure of these paradoxes and negotiations from discourses on the normal family pushes to the margin those unable to fulfill the ideal [and] intensifies support for regulatory and penal systems as the only solutions, leaving mothers like Sally with bleak options.

> I know what I'm capable of doing in a really bad time, and that part scares me. I hate myself for that part, but [also] that's the part I hate my stepparents for. I will probably go to hell for the hate I have. And I hope it doesn't end up killing me, because I'm not a hateful person really. . . . But the hate, it just gets to me so bad. . . . I mean, that's just how I survive— by lying, stealing, doing drugs. I've done jobs that most women wouldn't even think of doing in their lives—just to survive.

Earlier, when Sally talked about "turning herself in," she was referring to an incident when she had beaten all of her boys bloody with a switch and then had turned herself in to the Children's Services Division. At that time, a time she describes as a nervous breakdown, she gave up her children to foster care while she tried to address her mental health issues. Perhaps it is this kind of personal experience that prompts Sally to both relate to and distinguish herself from Smith. Unlike Smith, Sally was able to acknowledge that her behavior was dangerous, even life threatening, and she took steps to contain it. Smith did not—perhaps could not.

The Smith murders, as well as other forms of child abuse or endangerment, are intolerable. However, one of the questions that its media coverage poses is how good motherhood is constructed antithetically to "monster mothers" (Tsing 1990). Susan Smith did not just commit the social crime of murder. Susan Smith revealed, to quote *Newsweek,* just "how much evil can lurk in even a mother's heart" (1995, 28). The heart, according to *Newsweek*'s imagery, is the place where maternal love is supposed to reside. It is the embodiment of care and nurturance. Yet Susan Smith's heart is instead tainted with "evil" —an evil so dark that it can lurk in even a mother's heart.

While one could view this statement through the simple lens of media exploitation, I believe it reveals a great deal more about cultural norms. These representations of antimothers, monster mothers, and

Other mothers can be understood as one facet of a cultural drive to monitor mothers, regulate them intensively, and steer them toward fictive models of normality. The population most affected by such regulatory trends is women who are already marginalized—those who are already suspect because their poverty, their lack of education, and their immersion in pain render them unable to act out the middle-class ideal.

NOTES

1. For further discussion of idealized portrayals of family life and corresponding repercussions on contemporary families in the United States, see Coontz (1992).

2. Only 16 percent of the families I worked with at WCC had a biological father present in the family. This picture mirrors the national situation, in which the overwhelming majority of homeless families are headed by single mothers (Homes for the Homeless 1998).

3. Giving the "gift of life" is a notion about maternity and reproduction that has been used in a variety of ideologies. Rickie Solinger in *Wake Up Little Susie: Single Pregnancy and Race before Roe v. Wade* (1992) discusses how between 1945 and 1965 white teens were indoctrinated into the idea that they did not have the right to their illegitimate children. Social services, in alignment with wider cultural ideologies, pressured them to believe that they wanted to give up their children in retribution for their "mistake" of getting pregnant. In return, supposedly, these girls get the "gift" of a second chance at normal middle-class life. Furthermore, antiabortion activists have dramatized the "miracle of life," effectively casting women as having the responsibility to provide this gift to their unborn fetuses.

More currently, Helena Ragoné, in *Surrogate Motherhood: Conception in the Heart* (1994), discusses the cultural narrative propagated by agencies and internalized by surrogate mothers of choosing to devote themselves to bearing a child for a couple as an ultimate act of gift giving.

4. Luker emphasizes that adoption rates have gone down significantly in the past forty years. She notes that from 1965 to 1972, 20 percent of all white babies and 2 percent of all Black babies were given up for adoption. However, from 1982 to 1988 the figures were 3 percent and 1 percent, respectively.

5. For more detailed accounts of abuses such as forced sterilization and their impacts on particular communities, see *Women, Race and Class* by Angela Davis (1983); *Women under Attack: Victories, Backlash, and the Fight for Reproductive Freedom* edited by Susan Davis (1988); Dorothy Robert's essay "Punishing Drug Addicts Who Have Babies: Women of Color, Equality, and the Right to Privacy" (1991); and several essays in *Mothering: Ideology, Experience, and Agency* (notably those by Evelyn Nakano Glenn, Patricia Hill Collins, and Rickie Solinger), edited by Evelyn Nakano Glenn et al. (1994).

For contemporary discussions about legislation designed to regulate women's childbearing by such means as mandating the implant of the contraceptive Norplant, see Hartouni 1997 (105).

READING 51

Friendly for Whose Family?

Betty Holcomb

One might assume that Lynnell Minkins, a single mother of three, would be thrilled to work for Marriott International. Last year, Marriott made *Working Mother* magazine's list of the 100 best companies for working mothers, largely because it offers flexible work schedules, hot lines to help employees deal with child-care emergencies, and three on-site child-care centers. Minkins, a food server at the San Francisco Marriott, could use that sort of help. But it's not available to her. Instead, she never knows from week to week what her hours will be, making it hard to find and hold on to decent child care, let alone make plans. "How can I get doctor appointments if I don't know when I'll be working?" she asks. "A month ahead, the clinic says there are only these days. I take them, and then I have to work."

When her kids were younger, she relied on a neighbor, paying a flat rate to send them over whenever she had to work. But now that they're in school, she has to figure out how to get them there on days she has to be at work early. A simple schedule change could solve everything, but she hasn't asked for one. "I don't dare bring it up. I'm afraid I'll get written up." A write-up means getting disciplined, and too many write-ups can lead to losing her job.

The irony is that, at least officially, Marriott offers flextime to its approximately 135,000 U.S. employees. Yet the one time Minkins tried it, her supervisors constantly pressed her to fix the "problem," and in her annual performance review that year she was described as being "challenged" by time management. "I should have called them on it, but I let it go," she says. "People who work in these jobs, they need the money. So you don't tell anybody what's going on." Senior managers, says Minkins, don't seem to suffer the same scrutiny. "It doesn't look like their job is being challenged. The lower people, the people in the back of the house, they're having the problems."

So it goes for hundreds of thousands of lower-level workers at companies widely recognized for their "family-friendly" policies. In fact, the research conducted by the Families and Work Institute exclusively for this article shows that the workers who most need benefits such as child care and flexible hours are the least likely to get them.

Consider these facts from the study. Workers in low-wage jobs are

- half as likely as managers and professionals to have flextime;
- less likely to have on-site child care;
- more likely to lose a day's pay when they must stay home to care for a sick child;
- three times less likely to get company-sponsored tax breaks to help pay for child care.

In addition, other studies show that workers in entry-level, low-paying, or low-status jobs are much less likely to be offered a paid maternity leave than managers are, and in the case of unpaid leave, they are less likely to get as much time off after having a baby.

"It's clear that more advantaged workers have more access to certain benefits," says Ellen Galinsky, president of the Families and Work Institute. Put another way, some families seem to count more than others. "You ask yourself if people really care about the family benefits of people who clean the toilets, who clean the office buildings after everyone else leaves," says Netsy Firestein, director of the Labor Project for Working Families in Berkeley, California. "Who's taking care of their kids? Often it's older children putting younger ones to bed, while the parents struggle to make wages and get health insurance paid."

The types of benefits currently offered are also skewed toward higher-paid workers. Child-care help, for example, comes most often in the form of company-sponsored tax breaks or "resource and referral" hot lines. Both are useless to workers like Minkins, who don't make enough to pay much in taxes and can't afford the licensed child care the hot line refers them to. "Most of it is as much as $100 a week just to watch my kids before and after school. Maybe I could afford $50, but not $100!" Minkins says. Her problem is far from unique. According to the *Wall Street Journal,* a huge 85 percent of Marriott's U.S. employees are hourly workers—meaning low-wage. Its "core hourly employees simply couldn't afford paid care, the cost of which can easily exceed 50 percent of gross income," reports the *Journal.*

The rare companies that offer on-site child care —about 5,000 of the nation's millions of employers—often do so only at headquarters, where managers and executives work, and the fees may still be too high for the clerical and office support staff. Just as much of a problem is that many benefits are offered only at the discretion of supervisors—who expect lower-level workers to stick to unbending schedules.

. . .

Perhaps the biggest irony behind family-friendly benefits is that the workers most likely to get them don't need the help. Last year, the Hyatt Regency San Diego touted the success of a job-sharing initiative. Six women out of a workforce of 800 were sharing three jobs, and each of the women said they could afford to stop working if they had to.

. . .

It's not that corporate leaders haven't confronted the issue of equity. Most trumpet their efforts to make benefits universally available. In presentations, Marriott officials stress that family-friendly benefits are meant for everyone, from the most senior manager to the busboy in the company's restaurants.

"We have a firm stake in the sand in seeing to it that our hourly employees are served well," says Donna Klein, vice president for diversity and workforce effectiveness, and chief architect of many of Marriott's family-friendly benefits. "We have master's-level social workers dedicated to Marriott callers 24 hours a day. We help with everything from finding child care, child-care subsidies, even immigration and housing issues."

But for Minkins, that's just a lot of talk if she can't afford the benefits. Meanwhile, Marriott has refused to contribute to a fund created by hotel workers' unions to help pay for care, saying they won't contribute to something that involves employees from other companies. If Marriott participated in the union/management effort, Minkins could receive a child-care subsidy based on need—just the opposite of the way most companies dole out benefits.

The central question is whether management thinks of lower-wage workers as important to their companies, and therefore deserving of benefits. This was the issue that a group of human resource executives from the nation's leading corporations found themselves asking at a conference on the family-friendly workplace in New York City back in April of 1995. Wining and dining at the luxurious Waldorf-Astoria, they began to talk about a problem emerging in the field. They'd broken ground by introducing flextime, part-time work with benefits, job-sharing, and on-site child care at their companies. And they were getting plenty of attention for their efforts. But now, in an attack of conscience, they turned their attention to the workers who made their beds, served their food, and cleared their tables while they set workplace policies. "What about the chambermaids?" asked Arlene Johnson, a leading researcher on work-family conflict who was chairing the plenary session. "How are we meeting their needs?"

J. Thomas Bouchard, a senior vice president of IBM, who had championed the growing visibility of family-friendly benefits a few minutes earlier, now sounded a more somber note. "I don't see how we can or will. Who's going to pay for it if we try to make these things universal?" In fact, he insisted, it was probably best to not even suggest that all workers might someday have access to child care and flex-

ible schedules via their employers. "There's nothing worse than false hope," he insisted. Better to simply acknowledge that most companies don't want to add costly new benefits or change the way people work.

. . .

Finding solutions isn't easy. Many advocates of family-friendly benefits say we have to challenge the notion that work and family are separate spheres; the workplace has to bend to the demands of the home. But those are long-range goals. In the short term, advocates are trying to win over executives by making a business case for these benefits. They are trying to disprove the ideas of people like IBM's J. Thomas Bouchard that companies can't afford benefits for all. The data is most assuredly there. Studies have shown again and again that family-friendly policies help the bottom line. Xerox, for example, improved productivity in its call centers simply by letting workers devise their own schedules.

In the end, the question is really one of power and privilege. Who has the power to change things, on what terms, and for whom? For the moment, the most progressive innovations arise out of the goodwill and good vision of a few corporate leaders. But even they are hesitant to challenge the notion that family-benefit funds could be better spent. If you ask them, "If there isn't enough money to provide benefits for everyone, why not spend what is available on the people who need it most?" they look at you as though you were speaking a foreign language. The truth is that professional, skilled workers are the ones corporations are trying to keep, and they do it with expensive benefits packages, among other things. Nonprofessional staff is more easily replaced, they believe, and thus not worth the financial investment. At the moment most employers see no need for dramatic change. "The companies sure do like getting on the lists and getting publicity," says Paul Ruppert of WFD, one of the leading consulting firms on work-family conflict in the U.S. "But you have to wonder how much change they really want to make."

The most lasting victories have come through collective action. The 40-hour work week, paid vacations, antidiscrimination laws, and, recently, the Family and Medical Leave Act were won by feminists, organized labor, and progressives working together. At long last, the labor movement has begun to take up the mantle of family-friendliness.

"The unions are finally getting religion on this," says Donna Dolan, director of work-family issues for the Communications Workers of America. Dolan has worked since the early 1980s to win pacts that include paid leave for childbirth, time off to care for sick family members, and subsidies for child care. She and other union activists helped create the first big family-friendly pact in 1989, when NYNEX agreed to create a $6 million fund to help develop and pay for child care.

In recent years, Dolan has been heartened to see the AFL-CIO take up the cause in earnest. "When you hear John Sweeney [president of the AFL-CIO] on the stump on these issues, you know we're getting somewhere," she says. Indeed, a growing number of unions have bargained for and won funds to help pay for family-friendly benefits. And there is a move afoot to help push for a paid family leave, one that replicates the sort of parental leave that workers in all other industrialized countries already have.

It is this sort of victory that gives Lynnell Minkins hope. Minkins has worked for Marriott for three years, and the stress has worn her down. "I have stomach problems, and I'm sure it's the tension of all this," she says. But she's not about to go elsewhere. "We've been fighting for three long years to get Marriott to give us regular schedules and to do what's right for people's families, to do the things that the other hotels are doing," she says. "I'm not going to quit until we win that fight for everybody."

■ READING 52

What We Call Each Other

Anndee Hochman

My eighty-nine-year-old grandfather and I had covered all the routine subjects—the weather in Portland, the weather on the New Jersey shore (it was summer in both places). I'd thanked him for sending me a paperback copy of *The Joys of Yiddish.* Then he asked, "So, how's your lady friend?"

I gulped. It was possible he meant my roommate, Rachael, and "lady friend" was a quaint attempt to cover up the fact that he'd forgotten her name. But I'd never heard him use that phrase, with its tinge of old-fashioned, coy romance, to describe an acquaintance of mine.

Finally, I mumbled that she was just fine, thanks. There was no response. Later, I told my "lady friend" about the comment, and we both laughed. But I still don't know if my grandfather knew what he asked, if he grasped what he heard. Words are like that. They can swab the air clean of illusion, or they can fog the truth in a comfy, opaque veil.

So many of the words for romantic or sexual partners make women mere appendages of men, extend a long-standing power imbalance. What is the term to describe a relationship of equals, two adults trying to make a life together? I like "partner," with its hints of adventure and readiness, the idea of moving together through a love affair or a life. Most of my friends, gay or straight, use it to describe their romantic associates.

But even "partner" isn't perfect. For one thing, it conveys a sense of stability that doesn't apply to all relationships, especially brand new ones. Heterosexual couples have a whole vocabulary that hints at changing degrees of intimacy and intention. First "lovers" or "boyfriend/girlfriend"; then "fiancée"; finally "spouse." But unmarried or gay partners have no language to describe those shifts.

The words commonly used in such cases are designed to mask the truth rather than tell it. The euphemisms for gay and lesbian lovers—"constant companion" or "very special friend"—hide the true nature of the relationship under a cloak of decorum. But it's a cloak made to be seen through; everyone knows it's a cover for something else. It indicates that the real thing is too scandalous even for discourse; the word itself can't go out of doors unclad.

One lesbian couple I know dislikes "partner" for the same reasons I'm drawn to it—because it is democratic, gender-neutral. These women refer to each other as "girlfriends," refusing, even in casual conversation, to pass.

Slowly, slowly, names gather a new history; the weight of a word can shift. When lesbians and gay men appropriate the language of the mainstream, filling in their partners' names where government forms say "spouse," insisting that they deserve a "family" membership to the YMCA, they force others to reorder their mental maps. Those maps would change even faster if heterosexual couples boycotted marriage and its honorifics, if they, too combed the language for words that more precisely describe their bonds.

Girlfriend. Boyfriend. Mistress. Beau. Old man. Lady friend. Steady. Helpmate. Fiancé/e. Lover. Paramour. Spouse. Domestic partner. Soul mate. Significant other. Homeslice. Sweetie. Co-habitant. Ally. Longtime companion. Live-in. Partner. Collaborator. Consort. Intimate. Confidant/e. Familiar. Alter ego. Mainstay. Second self. Complement. Mate.

Even words that don't carry a gender bias can be suspect, quiet enforcers of the status quo. I used the word "single" to describe women without intimate partners until the irony of the term struck me. I was writing about these women precisely because they'd built networks of support through work, friends, housemates, yet my easy description of them conveyed someone alone and unconnected, with no important social ties.

"Are you in a relationship?" people inquire euphemistically, when what they mean is "Are you sexually involved with someone?" The notion of *a* relationship—primary, intimate, more weighty than the rest— doesn't fit the lives of people who choose celibacy, or who are in nonmonogamous relationships involving two or more significant "others."

Then there's "friend," which doesn't begin to cover enough ground. It describes everyone from the colleague I chat with once a month at a writers'

meeting to the woman I've known since infancy but haven't seen for a decade, to Rachael, whom I lived with for more than five years. The word, forced to stand for such a range of connections, erases distinction, implies all friendships are the same.

Names wake us to the particulars of a thing. If I call Diana my mainstay, Pattie my soul mate, and Rachael my sister, I remember that these women have different qualities, that my friendship with each is unique.

I say Rachael is my "sister," and then pause. Why is that the only term that seems to fit? I struggle to describe closeness and am left holding a simile, a stand-in phrase that only gropes at description. "He's like a brother to me," we say, revealing not only the assumed potency of sibling bonds but the dearth of words to describe intense, nonsexual attachments.

There's a level of intimacy that "friend" seems too small to contain. Then we make it even smaller, often denigrating it with the qualifier "just." They're "just friends," we concede, as if friendship were automatic and uninteresting, less full of potential than any romantic pairing. In fact, the vast majority of people in our lives fall into that maligned category; friendship deserves a vocabulary of its own.

Acquaintance. Colleague. Buddy. Bosom-buddy. Sidekick. Chum. Amiga. Compadre. Homegirl. Mate. Pal. Sister. Fellow. Right-hand man. Companion. Compañera. Associate. Cohort. Crony. Aficionado. Compeer. Confrere. Ally. Comrade. Familiar. Accomplice. Mainstay. Primary. Neighbor. Friend.

I've wrestled, too, with "childless." It's a gender-weighted word—we don't refer, with quite the same sense of anomaly and pity, to "childless" men. And it assumes childbearing is the norm and *not* childbearing a lesser version of life; it defines an existence by what it lacks. "Nonparent" makes the same mistake.

I've seen women use "child-free," which seems tipped in the other direction—as though children were a burden and only people without them have liberty. Besides, many women who choose not to be parents include children in their lives as nieces and nephews, neighbors, clients, friends. I thought about words like "adult-based" or "adult-centered" for women who don't have much to do with children.

But I've yet to find a term that expresses, without judgment, the facets of this complicated choice.

And there are relationships, existences we scarcely have language to describe. The words for an unmarried woman—maiden aunt, spinster—are all pejorative. "Old maid," in particular, holds layers of judgment—a woman who contradicts her own nature, at once old and young, a perpetual servant. Thanks to Mary Daly and others, feminists are reclaiming "spinster" as a source of creative pride; one woman I know named her sewing business "Spinster Textiles."

Few terms exist to describe former lovers who now are good friends, or nonbiological parents, or relationships between the childhood families of a gay couple. I've heard a woman explain to her child, conceived through alternative (as opposed to "artificial") insemination, that there are "seed daddies" as well as the kind of daddies who live at home, and a lesbian friend coined "sister-outlaws" to describe her lover's siblings.

The contemporary women's movement and gay and lesbian liberation helped prompt people to create new honorifics, such as "Ms.," and reclaim old names, taking them back from the domain of those who hate. Queer. Dyke. Crone. Cripple. Faggot. Fat person. Fairy. When we use these words for ourselves, we become powerful, filled with the awesome responsibility that is naming. We print the words on buttons, shout them in parades. We repossess the names and, in the process, repossess ourselves.

Language changes from the edges; new terms ripple back to the center. Gradually, I have seen "partner" replace "longtime companion" in news stories about gay men and lesbians. Several papers even have begun listing gay commitment ceremonies. As such events become more popular and public, terms unimagined as yet may enter the lexicon.

Coupling. Espousals. Union. Match. Bond. Pairing. Knot. Joining. Dovetailing. Commitment ceremony. Intentional. Dedication. Webbing. Mingling. Intertwining. Weaving. Blending. Braiding. Concord. Alignment. Alchemy. Convergence. Handfasting. Tryst.

What we call each other—how we refer to lovers and friends, partnerships and families—is more than a matter of etiquette. The words tell us who is owned and who is free, who really counts and who is merely secondary.

The language of the nuclear family continues to sway our speech, crowd out equally valid models of living. Homeless teenagers I worked with took the words of the families that failed them and applied them to each other. I heard them use "sister" and "brother" for their friends, but also "mother" and "kid," outlining large and intricate networks of street kin.

The actual people represented by those terms may have abused or abandoned these teenagers, but the words themselves seem to carry an infinitely renewable potency, a hope that someday someone will grow into the legend that is "mother," "sister," or "son."

"Blood family" itself carries that mythic power— "blood," with its symbolism of oath and source, a magical connection that cannot be undone. "Biological family" is less poetic but equally weighted. Married couples aren't related genetically, nor are adopted children. In families formed through remarriage, in foster families and extended families, "blood" connections have little to do with linkage.

I've toyed with "first family," "original family," and "childhood family" to describe the groups we grow up with, and "present family," "chosen family," or "adult family" for those we have now.

But the word "family" itself is loaded. The term can help justify secrecy ("let's keep it in the family") or serve as an argument for public hands-off ("that's a family matter"). And it is used disingenuously, as in "We're all one big happy family here" by businesses that want to promote childlike docility from employees and avuncular rule from bosses.

No mere noun, it's a way of categorizing society, even allocating resources, with "family" memberships and "family" fares on airlines and trains. "Family values" is political shorthand, evoking marriage, patriotism, and obedient children, a code aimed to halt a changing world.

Imagination is larger than language. The names claim who we already are and who we wish to become. We don't require them in order to live, but they make our living known, translatable, turn it into something we can talk about. There is room for more words, for the finest of distinctions, for as many possibilities as our minds can shape.

Someday, [my parents'] white house in New Jersey will be mine. I cannot imagine selling it. I want it to remain in the family. Families. Meaning me, my cousins, our parents, our children, if we have them. And more than that. The partners and compatriots, lovers and allies, cronies and intimates, all those who share the everyday acts of our lives.

I can see it. Someone will tap on the glass between the front stairs and the kitchen. I will look up, out the window, through the house and the window beyond it, straight out to the ocean we all come from. I will recognize the face, and I will wave.

Welcome, I might say, to my tribe. My group. Cabal. Circle. Club. Nucleus. Team. Neighborhood. Community. Affinity group. Kin. Karass. People. Coalition. League. Assemblage. Confederation. Gang. Clique. Coterie. Set. Crew. Crowd. Cadre. We-group. Affiliates. Relations. Folk. Household. Brood. Collection. Cronies. Network.

Welcome to my company, my clan.

READING 53

Only Daughter

Sandra Cisneros

Once, several years ago, when I was just starting out my writing career, I was asked to write my own contributor's note for an anthology I was part of. I wrote: "I am the only daughter in a family of six sons. *That* explains everything."

Well, I've thought about that ever since, and yes, it explains a lot to me, but for the reader's sake I should have written: "I am the only daughter in a *Mexican* family of six sons." Or even: "I am the only daughter of a Mexican father and a Mexican-American mother." Or: "I am the only daughter of a working-class family of nine." All of these had everything to do with who I am today.

I was/am the only daughter and *only* a daughter. Being an only daughter in a family of six sons forced me by circumstance to spend a lot of time by myself because my brothers felt it beneath them to play with a *girl* in public. But that aloneness, that loneliness, was good for a would-be writer—it allowed me time to think and think, to imagine, to read and prepare myself.

Being only a daughter for my father meant my destiny would lead me to become someone's wife. That's what he believed. But when I was in the fifth grade and shared my plans for college with him, I was sure he understood. I remember my father saying, "*Que bueno, mi'ja,* that's good." That meant a lot to me, especially since my brothers thought the idea hilarious. What I didn't realize was that my father thought college was good for girls—good for finding a husband. After four years in college and two more in graduate school, and still no husband, my father shakes his head even now and says I wasted all that education.

In retrospect, I'm lucky my father believed daughters were meant for husbands. It meant it didn't matter if I majored in something silly like English. After all, I'd find a nice professional eventually, right? This allowed me the liberty to putter about embroidering my little poems and stories without my father interrupting with so much as a "What's that you're writing?"

But the truth is, I wanted him to interrupt. I wanted my father to understand what it was I was scribbling, to introduce me as "My only daughter, the writer." Not as "This is only my daughter. She teaches." *Es maestra*—teacher. Not even *profesora.*

In a sense, everything I have ever written has been for him, to win his approval even though I know my father can't read English words, even though my father's only reading includes the brown-ink *Esto* sports magazines from Mexico City and the bloody *!Alarma!* magazines that feature yet another sighting of *La Virgen de Guadalupe* on a tortilla or a wife's revenge on her philandering husband by bashing his skull in with a *molcajete* (a kitchen mortar made of volcanic rock). Or the *fotonovelas,* the little picture paperbacks with tragedy and trauma erupting from the characters' mouths in bubbles.

My father represents, then, the public majority. A public who is disinterested in reading, and yet one whom I am writing about and for, and privately trying to woo.

When we were growing up in Chicago, we moved a lot because of my father. He suffered bouts of nostalgia. Then we'd have to let go of our flat, store the furniture with mother's relatives, load the station wagon with baggage and bologna sandwiches and head south. To Mexico City.

We came back, of course. To yet another Chicago flat, another Chicago neighborhood, another Catholic school. Each time, my father would seek out the parish priest in order to get a tuition break, and complain or boast: "I have seven sons."

He meant *siete hijos,* seven children, but he translated it as "sons." "I have seven sons." To anyone who would listen. The Sears Roebuck employee who sold us the washing machine. The short-order cook where my father ate his ham-and-eggs breakfasts. "I have seven sons." As if he deserved a medal from the state.

My papa. He didn't mean anything by that mistranslation, I'm sure. But somehow I could feel myself being erased. I'd tug my father's sleeve and whisper: "Not seven sons. Six! and *one daughter.*"

When my oldest brother graduated from medical school, he fulfilled my father's dream that we study hard and use this—our heads, instead of this—our hands. Even now my father's hands are thick and yellow, stubbed by a history of hammer and nails and twine and coils and springs. "Use this," my father said, tapping his head, "and not this," showing us those hands. He always looked tired when he said it.

Wasn't college an investment? And hadn't I spent all those years in college? And if I didn't marry, what was it all for? Why would anyone go to college and then choose to be poor? Especially someone who had always been poor?

Last year, after ten years of writing professionally, the financial rewards started to trickle in. My second National Endowment for the Arts Fellowship. A guest professorship at the University of California, Berkeley. My book, which sold to a major New York publishing house.

At Christmas, I flew home to Chicago. The house was throbbing, same as always: hot tamales and sweet tamales hissing in my mother's pressure cooker, and everybody—my mother, six brothers, wives, babies, aunts, cousins—talking too loud and at the same time. Like in a Fellini film, because that's just how we are.

I went upstairs to my father's room. One of my stories had just been translated into Spanish and published in an anthology of Chicano writing and I wanted to show it to him. Ever since he recovered from a stroke two years ago, my father likes to spend his leisure hours horizontally. And that's how I found him, watching a Pedro Infante movie on Galavisión and eating rice pudding.

There was a glass filled with milk on the bedside table. There were several vials of pills and balled Kleenex. And on the floor, one black sock and a plastic urinal that I didn't want to look at but looked at anyway. Pedro Infante was about to burst into song, and my father was laughing.

I'm not sure if it was because my story was translated into Spanish, or because it was published in Mexico, or perhaps because the story dealt with Tepeyac, the *colonia* my father was raised in and the house he grew up in, but at any rate, my father punched the mute button on his remote control and read my story.

I sat on the bed next to my father and waited. He read it very slowly. As if he were reading each line over and over. He laughed at the right places and read lines he liked out loud. He pointed and asked questions: "Is this So-and-so?" "Yes," I said. He kept reading.

When he was finally finished, after what seemed like hours, my father looked up and asked: "Where can we get more copies of this for the relatives?"

Of all the wonderful things that happened to me last year, that was the most wonderful.

■

DISCUSSION QUESTIONS FOR CHAPTER SEVEN

1. What are some myths about the normative U.S. family? To what degree does your family reflect this norm? Has your family experienced discrimination in any ways based on deviation from this norm? What are some of the realities of the diversity of U.S. families?

2. How are families both places of comfort, security, and nurture and at the same time places of domination, conflict, and violence?

3. How do social institutions reinforce power relations in the family? How does the family often reflect power relations of the dominant social order? How do power relations operate in your family?

4. How does the difference between mothering and fathering reflect dominant social norms for women and men?

5. What tasks do various members of your family do within the home? Do these tasks reflect typical social norms?

SUGGESTIONS FOR FURTHER READING

Bem, Sandra Lipsitz. *An Unconventional Family.* New Haven, CT: Yale University Press, 2001.

Coontz, Stephanie. *The Way We Never Were: American Families and the Nostalgia Trap,* reprint. Austin, TX: Basic, 2000.

———. *The Way We Really Are: Coming to Terms with America's Changing Families.* Austin, TX: Basic, 1998.

Lehr, Valerie. *Queer Family Values: Debunking the Myth of the Nuclear Family (Queer Politics, Queer Theories).* Philadelphia: Temple University Press, 1999.

Mason, Mary Ann, Arlene Skolnick, and Stephen D. Sugarman, eds. *All Our Families: New Policies for a New Century.* 2nd ed. New York: Oxford University Press, 2002.

Stacey, Judith. *In the Name of the Family: Rethinking Family Values in the Postmodern Age.* Boston: Beacon, 1997.

CHAPTER EIGHT

Women's Work Inside and Outside the Home

There is an important truth in the saying "women's work is never done." In the United States and around the world, women work longer hours than men because work for women often involves unpaid domestic labor and care of dependent family members as well as paid labor. In addition, when they do get paid for their work, women tend to earn lower wages compared to men and are less likely to have control over the things they produce and the wages they receive. When the United Nations World Conference on Women met in Beijing, China, in 1995, the Platform for Action prioritized strategies to promote economic autonomy for women, ensure their access to productive resources, and encourage equitable sharing of family responsibilities. In this chapter we examine both women's domestic unpaid labor and their employment in the labor force. In the latter the focus is on the global economy and the changing nature and patterns of women's labor force participation and remuneration. We close the chapter with a discussion of comparable worth.

UNPAID LABOR IN THE HOME

The work women do in the home is often not considered work at all: It is something women do for love, or because they are women, and it is the natural thing for women to do. On the *Roseanne* situation comedy, Roseanne Barr was asked by a family member whether she knew the location of a lost item. "How should I know," she responded. "What do you think a uterus is, a tracking device?" Her point was that there is nothing natural about the fact that women on the average do over two-thirds of all household work. The fact that they may be better at it is only because of years of practice. Gender norms that associate women, the home, and domesticity reinforce the assumption that housework and childcare is women's work.

The reading by Barbara Ehrenreich, "Maid to Order," explains the politics of housework in contemporary U.S. society. She emphasizes that housework is not degrading because it involves manual labor, but instead because it is embedded in degrading relationships that have the potential to reproduce male domination from one generation to the next. She suggests that a contemporary solution to the housework problem among those who can afford it is to hire someone else to do the work. That "someone" is most likely a woman and very often a woman of color. Domestic work is one occupation traditionally held by women of color; it is also an occupation that is usually nonunionized, has low pay, little power, and few or no benefits. In addition, individuals who used to contract services directly with employers are now being replaced by corporate cleaning services that control a good portion of the housecleaning business. Because this new relationship between cleaners and those

WOMEN AND AGRICULTURE

- Women make up 51 percent of the agricultural labor force worldwide.
- A study of the household division of labor in Bangladeshi villages found that women worked almost 12 hours a day—compared with the eight to ten hours a day worked by men in the same villages.
- In many regions, women spend up to five hours a day collecting fuelwood and water and up to four hours preparing food.
- In Africa and Asia, women work about 13 hours more than men each week.
- In Southeast Asia, women provide up to 90 percent of the labor for rice cultivation.
- In Africa, 90 percent of the work of gathering water and wood, for the household and for food preparation, is done by women.
- In Pakistan, 50 percent of rural women cultivate and harvest wheat.
- In the world's least developed countries, 23 percent of rural households are headed by women.
- In sub-Saharan Africa, women produce up to 80 percent of basic foodstuffs both for household consumption and for sale.
- Women perform from 25 to 45 percent of agricultural field tasks in Colombia and Peru.
- Women constitute 53 percent of the agricultural labor in Egypt.
- Fewer than 10 percent of women farmers in India, Nepal, and Thailand own land.
- An analysis of credit schemes in five African countries found that women received less than 10 percent of the credit awarded to male smallholders.
- Only 15 percent of the world's agricultural extension agents are women.

Sources: www.fao.org/gender/en/labb2-e.htm and www.fao.org/gender/en/agrib4-e.htm.

who can afford to employ them abolishes the traditional "mistress-maid" relationship, it allows middle-class people who are sensitive to the political issues involved with hiring servants to avoid confronting these issues.

Most researchers who study household labor define it as all tasks involved in household maintenance, purchasing and preparing food, taking care of children, garden and yard work, and routine care and maintenance of vehicles. Three major findings emerge in this area, summarized as follows. First, women perform more household work than men do, with the figure averaging out at around two-thirds. The other third tends to be shared by men and children, with female children performing a greater amount of housework than male children. In addition, men tend to overestimate the work they do in the home and women underestimate it.

The second major finding is that women and men do different kinds of work in the home. Women tend to do the repetitive, ongoing, daily kinds of tasks, and men are more likely to perform the less repetitive or seasonal tasks. This is called the gender division of household work. Some tasks are seen as more masculine and some as more feminine. Note that if household labor were defined solely as housework, the amount of male participation would decrease. Because the definition generally includes fixing things and yard and garage work, men's contributions tend to increase. These tasks are often (though not always) more

Reprinted with permission.

interesting, require more skills, and have a higher status than the repetitive household cleaning tasks that women are more likely to perform. Also, in terms of the gender division of labor, it is important not to forget the emotional and behind-the-scenes kind of work that women do that is so crucial to family functioning. These include such activities as calling the baby-sitter, remembering somebody needs his or her math book or school lunch, corresponding with family and friends, and organizing holidays and vacations. These activities are difficult to measure in a quantitative sense.

Third, it seems that when women and men perform various tasks they tend to do so in different ways. Women are much more likely to "multitask" or perform a series of tasks simultaneously. This means, for example, that they might be folding laundry at the same time that they are feeding the baby, or are cooking dinner at the same time that they are vacuuming. Men are less likely to do this; they tend to focus on one task at a time.

Many readers are probably remembering their father doing the housework or have a partner who shares equally in domestic labor. Although there have been changes over the past decades with some men taking on greater household responsibilities and some assuming an equal share, unfortunately this averages out across men generally as a matter of an increase in minutes per day. For every ten men who do little to no housework, there is a large group who "help" to a greater or lesser extent, and less than one who takes equal responsibility. Note how the term *helping* assumes that it is someone else's responsibility. Nonetheless, it is important to state that housework, although often dreary and repetitive, can also be creative and more interesting than some paid labor. And, although raising children is among the hardest work of all, it is also full of rewards. Men who do not participate in household work and childcare miss the joys associated with this work even while they have the privilege of being free to do other things.

LEARNING ACTIVITY: WHO DOES THE WORK AT YOUR SCHOOL AND IN YOUR HOME?

Use the following charts to discover who does various kinds of work at your school and in your home. Discuss your findings with your classmates. What patterns do you notice? What do your findings suggest about how systems of inequality function in the institution of work, both inside and outside the home?

WHO DOES THE WORK AT YOUR SCHOOL?

JOB DESCRIPTION	WHITE MEN	WHITE WOMEN	MEN OF COLOR	WOMEN OF COLOR
Top administration				
Teaching				
Secretarial				
Groundskeeping				
Electrical/carpentry				
Janitorial				
Food preparation				
Security				
Intercollegiate coaching				

WHO DOES THE WORK IN YOUR HOME?

JOB DESCRIPTION	PERSON IN THE FAMILY WHO GENERALLY DOES THIS JOB	SEX OF PERSON WHO GENERALLY DOES THIS JOB	HOURS PER WEEK SPENT IN DOING THIS JOB
Laundry			
Mowing the lawn			
Maintaining the car			
Buying the groceries			
Cooking			
Vacuuming			
Washing dishes			
Making beds			
Cleaning bathroom			

HISTORICAL MOMENT:
WAGES FOR HOUSEWORK

Women do two-thirds of the world's work but only receive 5 percent of the world's income. Worldwide, women's unpaid labor is estimated at $11 trillion. Early in the women's movement feminists made the connection between women's unpaid labor and the profits accumulated by the businesses that relied on women's household and child-rearing work to support the waged laborers that produced goods and capital. They argued, then, that women should be compensated for the domestic labor that is taken for granted and yet depended on to maintain capitalist economy.

Several groups agitated for wages for housework, and in 1972 the International Wages for Housework (WFH) Campaign was organized by women in developing and industrialized countries to agitate for compensation for the unpaid work women do. They argued that this goal could best be reached by dismantling the military-industrial complex. In 1975, the International Black Women for Wages for Housework (IBWWFH) Campaign, an international network of women of color, formed to work for compensation for unwaged and low-waged work and to ensure that challenging racism was not separated from challenging sexism and other forms of discrimination.

Few American feminists advocated this position, although it constituted a significant position for feminists in Europe. Some feminists opposed the campaign, arguing that to pay women for housework would reinforce women's role in the home and strengthen the existing gendered division of labor.

Both the WFH and IBWWFH campaigns are still active, advocating change in the ways women's work is valued and rewarded. They have been involved in a campaign for pay equity and a global women's strike. For more information, check out these websites:

www.ourworld.compuserve.com/homepages/crossroadswomenscentre/WFH.html

www.payequity.net/WFHCampaign/wfhcpgn.htm

www.crossroadswomen.net/BWWFH/BWWHF.html

PAID LABOR

Trends and Legalities

The reading "A Brief History of Working Women" by Sharlene Hesse-Biber and Gregg Lee Carter overviews the changes in women's labor force participation over the past centuries for different groups of women. Briefly, as U.S. society became industrialized in the nineteenth century, the traditional subsistence economies of producing what families needed to survive from the home, taking in work (like spinning or washing), or working in others' homes or on their land was changed in favor of a more distinct separation between work and home. Factories were established, employees were congregated under one roof (and thus more easily controlled), and emerging technologies started producing mass-produced goods. Instead of making products in the home for family consumption, people were working outside the home and spending their earnings on these mass-produced goods. Urban centers grew up around these sites of production, and ordinary people tended to work long hours in often very poor conditions. In *Women and Economics,* written in 1898, Charlotte Perkins Gilman explains that the harsh conditions associated with women's wage labor coincided with continuing domestic servitude in the home. This double day of work was recognized by scholars such as Gilman over a hundred years ago and is still a central aspect of women's lives today. For example, Michelle Sidler, writing about the agenda of third wave feminism, ponders the way this agenda can meet gendered economic disparities in "Living in McJobdom: Third Wave Feminism and Class Inequity."

At the same time that working-class women and children were working in factories, mines, and sweatshops, the middle-class home came to be seen as a haven from the cruel world, and middle-class women were increasingly associated with this sphere. From this developed the "cult of true womanhood"—prescriptions for femininity that included piety, purity, and domesticity. Although these notions of femininity could only be achieved by privileged White women, these norms came to influence women generally. At the same time, some women were starting to enter higher education. With the founding of Oberlin Collegial Institute in 1833, other women's colleges like Mount Holyoke, Bryn Mawr, and Wellesley were established as the century progressed. In addition, state universities (beginning with Utah in 1850) started admitting women. By the turn of the century, there were cohorts of (mostly privileged White) women who were educated to be full political persons and who helped shape the Progressive Era with a focus on reform and civic leadership. These women entered the labor force in relatively large numbers and many chose a career over marriage and the family.

As the twentieth century progressed, more women entered the public sphere. The years of the Great Depression slowed women's advancement, and it was not until World War II that women were seen working in traditionally male roles in unprecedented numbers. The government encouraged this transition, and many women were, for the first time, enjoying decent wages. All this would end after the war as women were encouraged or forced to return to the home so that men could claim their jobs in the labor force. Childcare centers were dismantled, and the conservative messages of the 1950s encouraged women to stay home and partake in the rapidly emerging consumer society. The social and cultural upheavals of the 1960s and the civil rights and women's movements fought for legislation to help women gain more power in the workplace.

The most important legislative gains included, first, the Equal Pay Act of 1963 that made it illegal to pay women and men different salaries for the same job. Next came Title VII of the 1964 Civil Rights Act (which went into effect in 1965) banning discrimination in employment. It made it illegal to discriminate in hiring, firing, compensation, terms, conditions, or privileges of employment. Title VII said gender could not be used as a criterion in employment except where there is a "bona fide occupational qualification," meaning it is illegal unless an employer can prove that gender is crucial to job performance. For the most part, the law had little influence until the establishment of the Equal Employment Opportunity Commission in the early 1970s to enforce the law. The courts have fine-tuned Title VII over the years, and it remains the most important legislation that protects working women and people of color.

In 1976 the Supreme Court expanded the interpretation of Title VII to include discrimination on the basis of pregnancy as sex discrimination, and 10 years later it declared that sexual harassment is also a form of sex discrimination. In 1993 the Supreme Court then broadened this ruling by stating that women suing on the basis of sexual harassment did not

DETAILED OCCUPATION GROUP OF THE EMPLOYED CIVILIAN POPULATION 16 YEARS AND OVER BY SEX: MARCH 2000 *

| DETAILED OCCUPATION GROUP | Total | | Sex | | | |
| | | | Male | | Female | |
	NUMBER	PERCENT	NUMBER	PERCENT	NUMBER	PERCENT
Total	134,338	100.0	71,237	100.0	63,102	100.0
Executive, administrators, and managerial	19,764	14.7	10,877	15.3	8,888	14.1
Professional speciality	20,729	15.4	9,420	13.2	11,309	17.9
Technical and related support	4,384	3.3	2,060	2.9	2,324	3.7
Sales	16,138	12.0	8,207	11.5	7,931	12.6
Administrative support, including clerical	19,020	14.2	3,908	5.5	15,112	23.9
Precision production, craft, and repair	14,386	10.7	12,975	18.2	1,410	2.2
Machine operators, assemblers, and inspectors	7,352	5.5	4,775	6.7	2,576	4.1
Transportation and material moving	5,340	4.0	4,786	6.7	554	0.9
Handlers, equipment cleaners, helpers, and laborers	5,310	4.0	4,254	6.0	1,056	1.7
Service workers, private household	884	0.7	40	0.1	843	1.3
Service workers, except private household	17,787	13.2	7,419	10.4	10,369	16.4
Farming, forestry, and fishing	3,245	2.4	2,515	3.5	729	1.2

* Numbers are in thousands.
Source: U.S. Census Bureau, Current Population Survey, March 2000, Special Populations Branch, Population Division.

have to prove that they had suffered "concrete psychological harm." Sexual harassment legislation made a distinction between "quid pro quo" (sexual favors are required in return for various conditions of employment) and "hostile work environment" (no explicit demand for an exchange of sexual acts for work-related conditions but being subjected to a pattern of harassment as part of the work environment). In "Hey, Why Don't You Wear a Shorter Skirt?" Jackie Krasas Rogers and Kevin D. Henson focus on the gendered and racialized work settings of temporary clerical workers and their vulnerability in terms of sexual harassment.

Affirmative action policies that encouraged employers to take gender and race into account in terms of hiring were first initiated by President Kennedy in the 1960s. Since that time, affirmative action has helped diversify the workplace and encouraged the hiring of women and people of color. However, there is a lot of misunderstanding as well as serious hostility associated with affirmative action, as evidenced by the dismantling of affirmative action guidelines in many states. Basically, affirmative action requests that employers take

Sexual harassment is legally defined as unwelcome sexual advances or requests for sexual favors. It also includes any verbal or physical conduct of a sexual nature when the following criteria are met:

- Submission is made explicitly or implicitly a term or condition of an individual's employment.
- Submission to or rejection of such conduct by an individual is used as the basis for employment decisions affecting such individual.
- Such conduct has the purpose or effect of substantially interfering with an individual's work performance or creating an intimidating, hostile, or offensive working environment.

Sexual harassment may include physical conduct, verbal conduct, or nonverbal conduct such as sexual gestures or pornographic pictures.

TWO TYPES OF SEXUAL HARASSMENT

Quid Pro Quo

Unwelcome sexual advances, requests for sexual favors, and other verbal or physical conduct of a sexual nature constitute quid pro quo sexual harassment when:

Submission to such conduct is made either explicitly or implicitly a term or condition of an individual's employment or submission to or rejection of such conduct by an individual is used as the basis for employment decisions affecting such individual.

Hostile Work Environment

In determining whether or not an environment is hostile, it must be determined whether or not the conduct unreasonably interfered with an individual's work performance or created an intimidating, hostile, or offensive work environment.

The Equal Employment Opportunity Commission (EEOC) suggests that the courts look at the following criteria:

- Whether the conduct was verbal, physical, or both
- How frequently the conduct was repeated
- Whether the conduct was hostile or patently offensive
- Whether the alleged harasser was a coworker or a supervisor
- Whether others joined in perpetrating the harassment
- Whether the harassment was directed at more than one individual
- Whether the remarks were hostile and derogatory
- Whether the harasser singled out the charging party
- Whether the charging party participated in the exchange
- The relationship between the charging party and alleged harasser

The Supreme Court established a two-pronged test for determining a hostile environment:

1. The conduct must "be severe or pervasive enough to create an objectively hostile or abusive environment that a reasonable person would find hostile or abusive."
2. The victim must "subjectively perceive the environment to be abusive."

Bernice Sandler of the National Association of Women in Education reports that surveys indicate that up to 30 percent of female college students and 70 percent of women in the workplace have been sexually harassed.

IDEAS FOR ACTIVISM

- Advocate with your elected representatives for an increase in the minimum wage.
- Encourage your school to analyze pay equity and to make corrections where needed.
- Write your elected representatives to encourage legislation and funding for childcare.
- Investigate exploitative employment practices of major national and multinational corporations and launch boycotts to demand improved conditions for workers.
- Encourage your elected representatives to support affirmative action.

gender and race into account to correct the historical discrimination against these groups. Affirmative action encourages the diversification of the job pool, but it does not encourage the hiring of unqualified women or people of color. It is a misunderstanding of these policies to think that White males now have a hard time getting jobs because they are being undercut by unqualified women or people of color.

At the turn of the twenty-first century, it is important to understand the changing nature of the workplace in the United States and the connection between U.S. corporate capitalism and the global economy. Electronic communications have revolutionized the marketplace; they have also made it increasingly possible for corporations to cross national boundaries. Multinational corporations have grown in size and influence, and various mergers have resulted in a smaller number of corporations controlling a larger part of the market. Because many U.S.-based corporations rely on the cheaper, nonunionized labor force and looser environmental restrictions outside the United States, much manufacturing is done overseas. In addition, the military has close ties to the economy, creating what some scholars call the military-industrial complex. The presence of various international military forces in developing countries serves in part to "stabilize" these nations and protect foreign business interests. These issues are discussed in the reading, "The Globetrotting Sneaker" by Cynthia Enloe.

The effects of the global economy often include profound inequalities between rich and poor nations as well as between rich and poor citizens within individual countries. Often these inequalities are based upon older inequities resulting from nineteenth- and early twentieth-century colonization and imperialism. For individual women, although multinational corporations do give women a wage, they often upset subsistence economies, cause increasing consumerism, encourage sex trading and cultural dislocation, and pollute fragile environments. Women often work in poor and unhealthy conditions for little pay. In addition, many thousands of U.S. workers have lost their jobs as corporations have moved productive processes overseas. These events are not random but part of a broader pattern of capitalist expansion.

Horizontal and Vertical Segregation

The major change in terms of trends in women's workforce participation has been the increase in the number of women who are in paid employment as the last century progressed. The U.S. Bureau of Labor Statistics reports that this number has grown from 5.3 million in 1900 to 18.4 million in 1950 and 65 million in 1999. About three-quarters of all working women work full-time. Women made up 18 percent of the labor force in 1900, almost 30 percent in 1950, 46 percent in 1999, and are expected to constitute 48 percent of the labor force by 2005. The Women's Bureau of the U.S. Department of Labor reports that 60 percent of women aged 16 years and over were labor force participants in 1999, with African American women having the highest participation rates at 65 percent.

Another major change is the number of women with preschool-aged children in the labor force. In 1999, 61 percent of women with children under 3 years old were employed in the labor force. Historically, although mothers have always worked outside the home, they have been less likely to work when they had babies and small children. The increase in paid labor participation among this group of women can be explained by several factors: One, there is a strong need among families for the money married women earn; two, the increase in single, female-headed households has meant that women have had no choice but to work outside the home; three, societal norms about gender have changed as well as the expectations for how individual women should live their lives; four, there has been an increase in women's education; and, finally, legislative changes to protect working women have resulted in the increased labor force participation of these women.

Given the large number of women working in the labor force, what kinds of work are they doing? The answer is everything. Women are doing all kinds of work and can be found in all segments of the labor force. At the same time, however, women are much more likely to be found in some sectors than others and are crowded into a small number of fields. The Women's Bureau reports that the largest share of employed women is in technical, sales, and clerical and administrative support positions. In addition, more women work as teachers (excluding postsecondary), secretaries, and cashiers than any other line of work, with one out of every five employed women working in these occupations. This phenomenon of segregating women and men into different jobs is termed *occupational segregation by gender* or *horizontal segregation* (meaning segregation *across* jobs). Not only are women crowded into certain fields, but these types of horizontal segregation have been relatively continuous

■ THE WORLD'S WOMEN 2000: WORK

Some important findings:

- Women now constitute an increasing share of the world's labor force—at least one third in all regions except northern Africa and western Asia.
- Self-employment and part-time and home-based work have expanded opportunities for women's participation in the labor force but are characterized by lack of security, lack of benefits, and low income.
- The informal sector is a larger source of employment for women than for men.
- More women than before are in the labor force throughout their reproductive years, though obstacles to combining family responsibilities with employment persist.
- Women, especially younger women, experience more unemployment than men and for a longer period of time than men.
- Women remain at the lower end of a segregated labor market and continue to be concentrated in a few occupations, to hold positions of little or no authority, and to receive less pay than men.
- Available statistics are still far from providing a strong basis for assessing both quantitative and qualitative changes in women's employment.

Source: http://unstats.un.org/unsd/demographic/ww2000/work2000.htm.

ACTIVIST PROFILE: DOLORES HUERTA

Dolores Huerta is one of the most powerful and influential labor leaders in the United States. Born in Dawson, New Mexico, in 1930, Huerta grew up in Stockton, California, and eventually earned a teaching certificate from Stockton College. After one year of teaching, however, she quit to work with Community Service Organization (CSO) because she thought she could do more to help the hungry children she saw at school by helping organize their farmworker parents.

While with CSO, she met César Chavez, and in 1962 they founded the United Farm Workers of America (UFW). Although Chavez was more comfortable in the fields organizing workers, Huerta became the voice of the union, becoming the first woman and first Chicana negotiator in labor history. The UFW met with great success in the 1965 Delano Grape Strike, which won the first collective bargaining agreement for farmworkers, and Huerta was instrumental in the negotiations. She also became consciously involved with the feminist movement when she met Gloria Steinem in 1968, although she had always focused on issues specific to women farmworkers.

In 1972 she co-chaired the California delegation to the Democratic Convention, and she led the struggle for unemployment insurance, collective bargaining rights, and immigration rights for farmworkers under the 1985 amnesty legalization program. She was the first Latina inducted into the National Women's Hall of Fame, and she received the National Organization for Women's Woman of Courage Award and the American Civil Liberties Union's Bill of Rights Award. She continues to struggle for farmworkers through the UFW and serve as a role model for Chicanas in their fight against discrimination.

throughout the twentieth century. These jobs are often called pink-collar jobs and can be understood as an extension of women's work in the home. One of the most female-segregated jobs is sex work such as prostitution, where women workers have often struggled to control the conditions of their work against the demoralization and abuse by customers, pimps, and police. Priscilla Alexander's article, "Prostitution: A Difficult Issue for Feminists," discusses prostitution, the legalities surrounding it, and the necessity for prostitutes to have some say in deciding the future of their profession.

The term *blue collar* implies working class or involved with industrial, production, and factory work and can be contrasted with *white collar,* which means office or professional work and is often characterized as middle-class occupations. Note the slippage between industrial work and male-segregated work such that blue collar means working class but also implies male-segregated work with its use of the word *blue* as opposed to *pink.* The Bureau of Labor Statistics reports the following occupations as the most male segregated: engineers, mechanics and drivers, carpenters and construction trades, firefighters, airline pilots and navigators, and forestry and logging work. You will note the obvious ways feminine jobs involve working with people, children, cleaning, and administrative support, whereas masculine employment tends to involve working with machines and inanimate objects. There are other differences too, such as the wages for the heavily male-segregated jobs tend to be higher than wages for the female-segregated, pink-collar work. That is because these jobs are

SELECTED NONTRADITIONAL OCCUPATIONS FOR WOMEN IN 2001 *

OCCUPATION	EMPLOYED, BOTH SEXES	EMPLOYED, FEMALE	PERCENT FEMALE
Police and detectives (supervisors)	111,000	11,000	9.9
Dentists	170,000	34,000	20
Architects	214,000	50,000	23.4
Forestry and logging	90,000	7,000	7.8
Truck drivers	3,156,000	167,000	5.3
Airplane pilots and navigators	136,000	5,000	3.7
Firefighters	250,000	7,000	2.8
Automobile mechanics	837,000	12,000	1.4
Garbage collectors	56,000	3,000	5.4
Construction trades	6,253,000	153,000	2.4
Taxicab drivers and chauffeurs	305,000	38,000	12.5
Air traffic controllers	28,000	2,000	7.1

* Nontraditional occupations are any that women constitute 25 percent or less of the total employed.
Source: U.S. Department of Labor.

LEARNING ACTIVITY: WORKING WOMEN AND UNIONS

Visit the web page of the AFL-CIO at *www.aflcio.org* to learn more about women in the workforce. What are some of the key issues for working women identified by the AFL-CIO? What legislative issues does the AFL-CIO identify that would be beneficial to working women? What is a union? What benefits do unions provide? Why are unions important for working women? What steps would people take to form a union at their workplace?

valued more, and they are more likely to be unionized, which tends to pay more. Indeed, if you compare the median weekly earnings of unionized versus nonunionized women in 1997, the union members earned on the average almost $150 a week more than nonunion women and also received better health and pension benefits.

An important aspect of occupational segregation by gender is that there is gender segregation even within the same job classification. This is termed *vertical segregation* (segregation *within* jobs), and, like horizontal segregation, it functions as a result of sexism in society. For example, although the number of women physicians is increasing, women are still overwhelmingly found in such specialties as pediatrics, dermatology, and public health work, and less likely to be found in surgical specialties, orthopedics, and more entrepreneurial positions. Female physicians on the average make only 77 percent of what male physicians make. Similarly, female lawyers are less likely to be in criminal law and are more likely to practice family law and make about 70 percent of male lawyers' salaries. Male teachers are more

20 LEADING OCCUPATIONS OF EMPLOYED WOMEN

2001 Annual Averages (Employment in thousands)

OCCUPATION	TOTAL EMPLOYED WOMEN	TOTAL EMPLOYED (MEN AND WOMEN)	PERCENT WOMEN	WOMEN'S MEDIAN USUAL WEEKLY EARNINGS[1]	RATIO OF WOMEN'S EARNINGS TO MEN'S EARNINGS
Total, 16 years and older	62,992	135,073	46.6	$511	76
Managers and administrators, n.e.c.[2]	2,486	8,018	31	762	65.6
Secretaries	2,366	2,404	98.4	475	N.A.
Cashiers[3]	2,288	2,974	76.9	292	89.3
Registered nurses	2,013	2,162	93.1	820	87.9
Sales supervisors and proprietors	1,990	4,836	41.1	502	70.5
Nursing aides, orderlies, and attendants	1,874	2,081	90	356	89.7
Elementary school teachers	1,828	2,216	82.5	731	94.9
Bookkeepers, accounting, and auditing clerks	1,506	1,621	92.9	474	93.7
Waiters and waitresses	1,029	1,347	76.4	317	87.3
Sales workers, retail and personal services[3]	1,023	2,311	44.3	N.C.	N.C.
Receptionists	1,015	1,047	96.9	401	N.A.
Accountants and auditors	975	1,657	58.8	687	72
Sales workers, other commodities[4,5]	925	1,426	64.9	351	82
Cooks	881	2,073	42.5	305	87.9
Investigators and adjusters, excluding insurance	878	1,171	75	487	89.4
Janitors and cleaners	779	2,166	36	318	81.7
Administrative support occupations, n.e.c.[2]	779	1,020	76.4	512	82.3
Hairdressers and cosmetologists	772	854	90.4	374	N.A.
Secondary school teachers	763	1,304	58.5	759	91.9
General office clerks	756	903	83.7	462	96

[1] Wage and salary for full-time workers.
[2] Not elsewhere classified.
[3] Excludes cashiers and sales workers, other commodities.
[4] Not included in sales workers, personal and retail services.
[5] Includes foods, drugs, health, and other commodities.
N.A.: Median not available where base is less than 50,000 male workers.
N.C.: Not calculable.
Source: U.S. Department of Labor, Bureau of Labor Statistics, Unpublished data, Annual Averages 2001.

likely to teach sciences and are more likely to be with older children; female professors are more typically in the humanities and the social sciences and found in smaller number in the physical and applied sciences and technical fields. Usually the specialties and fields that men occupy are more prestigious and the salaries are higher. In this way, women and men do not just tend to perform different jobs, but the jobs that they do are valued differently and have different levels of status and power. This differential is related to sexism in society generally.

Barriers to advancement in the labor force (what is often called the *glass ceiling*) have been challenged by women, by the courts, and by the women's movement. And, although these barriers are beginning to come down, they are still holding strong in many areas. Women tend not to be promoted at the same rate as men and they continue to face obstacles when trying to enter the most prestigious and best-paid occupations. A 1996 study found that women hold only 2 percent of powerful positions in the corporate world and almost 20 percent of the Fortune 500 have no top women directors. These figures get worse if you focus on the advancement of women of color.

Finally, it is interesting to look at how the development of certain occupations as female segregated has affected the status and conditions of work. For example, clerical work, although low prestige, was definitely a man's job until the turn of the twentieth century when women quickly became associated with this work. This was due to the following factors: there was a large pool of women with few other opportunities; clerical work's low status made it easier for women to be accepted; typewriter manufacturers began promoting the typewriter as something women used; and the personal service aspect of the work fit gender norms about the feminine aspect of secretarial work. As more women entered this profession, the gap between clerical wages and blue-collar wages generally increased, and the status of the clerical profession fell. A more recent example is the field of pharmacy. Two trends—the increasing number of pharmacies attached to chain drugstores and the increasing number of female pharmacists—have been seen as the reasons why the status of pharmacy has fallen as a profession.

Wages and Comparable Worth

Currently, women earn about 77 percent of the earnings of men: a difference of $144 a week between the median earnings of women and men. For women of color, this figure drops to 64 percent. Men of color also earn less than White men. The U.S. Bureau of Labor Statistics reports that although in 1999 the median weekly earnings of men and women generally were $612 and $468, respectively, White men's median weekly earnings were $629. Black men's median weekly earnings were $483, White women's were $477, Black women's were $408, Latino/Hispanic men's were $407, and Latina/Hispanic women's were the lowest at $348. Overall, these figures have risen significantly in the last couple of decades. In 1982, on average, women earned 59 cents for every dollar a man earned. Despite the increase to 77 cents in recent years, the Institute for Policy Research reports that over a lifetime of work, the average 25-year-old woman who works full-time, year-round until she retires at age 65 will earn on the average $523,000 less than the average working man. Currently 24 percent of men and only 13 percent of women earn over $50,000 a year, while a little more than 9 percent of men and less than 4 percent of women earn over $75,000 a year. As you might imagine, there are more women in the United States living in poverty (at about $17,000 a year for a family of four) than men. While almost 12 percent of the population is below the poverty level, 10 percent of adult men and 13 percent of women live in poverty. As life earn-

Reprinted with permission from Nicole Hollander.

ings are calculated, the number of women over 65 years of age in poverty is almost double that of men (U.S. Census, 2000).

Statistics on the wage gap do not include part-time or seasonal workers and only compare year-round, full-time male and female workers. Because a larger number of women work part-time jobs, the inclusion of part-time workers in this statistic would most likely result in a lowering of the above figures because part-time work is often lower status, less stable, and has fewer job-related benefits like health insurance.

So why do women earn less money than men on the average? Because of both horizontal and vertical segregation. In terms of horizontal segregation, women tend to be crowded into different jobs than men, and these jobs are more likely to be paid less. Recall that although the Equal Pay Act of 1963 said that men and women working in the *same* job could not receive different compensation, this does not help women who are in *different,* less-valued jobs. In terms of vertical segregation, even within the same fields there are forces to keep women in positions that are less prestigious and poorer paid. The equal pay legislation tends not to apply to distinctions within the same field where women and men are in different subspecialties. Traditional norms about gender, race, social class, and age work to create patterns of institutionalized inequalities that reinforce ideas concerning women's and men's worth and the kind of work various people can do. These forces maintain both horizontal and vertical segregation.

Comparable worth, also known as pay equity, is one means to pay women and men in different occupations comparably. Basically, comparable worth works to compare different jobs on experience, skill, training, and job conditions and assigns relative points on these indices in order to determine their worth. There is no federal-level comparable worth legislation, although many states have enacted laws demanding comparable worth comparisons in determining pay for state workers. In addition, the courts have ruled both for and against workers who have brought comparable worth suits against various corporations. When the courts have ruled in favor of plaintiffs, it has often meant a considerable amount of money in back pay to compensate female workers for years of financial inequities.

In this way gender inequality in women's work lives has important consequences for gender inequality in other spheres of life. Because most women work both inside and outside the home and spend a considerable part of their lives working, it is of central importance to understand the conditions under which women work as well as to strive for equality in the workplace.

READING 54

Women and Economics

Charlotte Perkins Gilman (1898)

... Because of her maternal duties, the human female is said to be unable to get her own living. As the maternal duties of other females do not unfit them for getting their own living and also the livings of their young, it would seem that the human maternal duties require the segregation of the entire energies of the mother to the service of the child during her entire adult life, or so large a proportion of them that not enough remains to devote to the individual interests of the mother. . . .

Is this the condition of human motherhood? Does the human mother, by her motherhood, thereby lose control of brain and body, lose power and skill and desire for any other work? Do we see before us the human race, with all its females segregated entirely to the uses of motherhood, consecrated, set apart, specially developed, spending every power of their nature on the service of their children?

We do not. We see the human mother worked far harder than a mare, laboring her life long in the service, not of her children only, but of men; husbands, brothers, fathers, whatever male relatives she has; for mother and sister also; for the church a little, if she is allowed; for society, if she is able; for charity and education and reform,—working in many ways that are not the ways of motherhood.

It is not motherhood that keeps the housewife on her feet from dawn till dark; it is house service, not child service. Women work longer and harder than most men, and not solely in maternal duties. . . . Many mothers, even now, are wage-earners for the family, as well as bearers and rearers of it. And the women who are not so occupied, the women who belong to rich men,—here perhaps is the exhaustive devotion to maternity which is supposed to justify an admitted economic dependence. But we do not find it even among these. Women of ease and wealth provide for their children better care than the poor woman can; but they do not spend more time upon it themselves, nor more care and effort. They have other occupation.

In spite of her supposed segregation to maternal duties, the human female, the world over, works at extra-maternal duties for hours enough to provide her with an independent living, and then is denied independence on the ground that motherhood prevents her working!

READING 55

A Brief History of Working Women

Sharlene Hesse-Biber and Gregg Lee Carter

Women Workers in Pre-Industrial America

Seven hundred and fifty thousand Europeans came to America between 1600 and 1700. The bulk of them were from Britain, but the colonies also saw significant numbers from Holland, France, and Germany. Many came as indentured servants, exchanging their labor for the cost of passage to the American colonies. Indentured servants often worked from five to ten years to pay back their creditors. As early as the 1600s, prior to the slave trade, some Africans also came to the colonies as indentured servants; they often worked side by side with white indentured servants. Women's lives in this country differed drastically, depending on their race, class, and marital status.

White Women

European women usually arrived in the New World with their families, as daughters and wives, under the auspices of fathers or husbands. In the pre-industrial economy of the American colonial period (from the seventeenth century to the early eighteenth century), work was closely identified with home and family life. The family was the primary economic unit, and family members were dependent on one another for basic sustenance. Men performed the agricultural work, while women's work was done chiefly in the home, which was a center of production in colonial America. In addition to cooking, cleaning, and caring for children, women did spinning and weaving, and made lace, soap, candles, and shoes. Indeed, they manufactured nearly all articles used in daily life. This work was highly valued, and the colonies relied on the production of these "cottage industries."

Single women remained within the domestic sphere, living with relatives, often as "assistant homemakers." For married women, the nature of their work depended on the economic circumstances of their husbands:

> In cash-poor homes and among frontier families, women bore the burden of filling most of the family's basic needs. They worked to reduce cash expenditures by growing vegetables in the kitchen garden and making the family's clothes, candles, soap and household furnishings. If a husband were a craftsman or the proprietor of a shop or tavern, his wife and children might also work in the business, in addition to all the other tasks. In contrast, the wife of a successful farmer, plantation owner, or merchant did little actual work; instead, she supervised household servants and slaves who purchased or made the goods the family needed, cooked the meals, and maintained the house.

The social codes of colonial America did not exclude a woman from working outside the home, and many did so. Colonial women engaged in a great range of occupations, and as old documents are discovered and new histories of women's work are written, that range appears greater still. Women were innkeepers, shopkeepers, crafts workers, nurses, printers, teachers, and landholders. In the city of Boston during 1690, for example, women ran approximately 40 percent of all taverns. During that year, city officials also granted more than thirty women the right to saw lumber and manufacture potash. Women acted as physicians and midwives in all the early settlements, producing medicines, salves, and ointments. Many of the women who worked outside their homes were widows with dependent children, who took their husbands' places in family enterprises. It seems that at one time or another, colonial women engaged in many of the occupations practiced by men. Indeed, most models of the "patriarchal family economy" ill fit the historical evidence; for example, eighteenth-century diaries describe "a world in which wives as well as husbands traded with their neighbors" and "young women felt themselves responsible for their own support." Not surprisingly, however, women's wages in this period were significantly lower than those of men.

For poor women, there were special incentives to work outside the home. Local poor laws encouraged single poor women to work rather than become recipients of relief. The choice of jobs was much more limited, and many poor women became laundresses, house servants, or cooks. Again, however, female laborers were paid approximately 30 percent less than the lowest-paid unskilled, free, white male workers and 20 percent less than hired-out male slaves.

The fact that some women worked in so-called "masculine fields"—that they were merchants, tavern owners, shopkeepers, and so on—has sometimes been interpreted to mean that the colonial period was a "golden age of equality" for women. Contemporary historians argue instead, however, that these jobs were exceptions to the rule, and that in fact "colonial times were characterized by a strict and simple division of labor between men and women, which assigned them to fields and house, or to the public and private spheres, respectively." The dominant ideology was still that a woman's place was at home, raising children. . . .

Women of Color

Historically, the experiences of women of color have differed dramatically from those of white women. If we consider only the present time period, it may appear that women of color and white women have certain experiences in common—relatively low economic position, being the target of discriminatory practices in education and in work, and overall marginality in the power structure. But women of color and white women have reached their present circumstances through very different histories. Although white women's status was clearly inferior to that of white men, they were treated with deference, and they shared in the status privileges of their husbands. African American women almost never had the option of choosing between work and leisure, as did some white women. They were not included in the image of the "colonial housewife." African American women were not considered "weak" females, but were treated more like beasts of burden. Thus these women of color suffered a double oppression of sexism and racism.

Nowhere is this double oppression more clearly demonstrated than within the institution of slavery, which became established in late seventeenth- and early eighteenth-century colonial society—largely as a result of the demand for cheap agricultural labor, especially within the Southern plantation economy. Historians estimate the slave population in the United States, Caribbean, and Brazil consisted of 9.5 million blacks. More than double that number are estimated to have died in transit to the New World. Slave women in the Southern colonies were without doubt the most exploited of all women. They were exploited not only as workers but as breeders of slaves. The following advertisement was typical of the time:

Negroes for Sale: A girl about twenty years of age (raised in Virginia) and her two female children, four and the other two years old—remarkably strong and healthy. Never having had a day's sickness with the exception of the smallpox in her life. She is prolific in her generating qualities and affords a rare opportunity to any person who wishes to raise a family of strong and healthy servants for their own use.

Slave women were also sometimes exploited as sex objects for white men. Like male slaves, they were considered intrinsically inferior. Slaves were property, not people. They faced severe cultural and legal restrictions: their family lives were controlled by their owners, their children were not their own, and their educational opportunities were almost nonexistent.

Sojourner Truth, formerly a slave and an activist in the abolitionist and women's rights movements, eloquently expressed the differences in treatment, under slavery, of black and white women: "That man over there says that women need to be helped into carriages and lifted over ditches, and to have the best place everywhere. Nobody ever helped me into carriages, or over mud puddles, or gives me any best place . . . and ain't I a woman?"

Before the Civil War, a black woman in one of the "cotton states," working on one of the larger plantations, would have been either a house servant or one of several million field hands who produced major cash crops. In the Southern plantation economy, we thus find a "bifurcated" concept of woman. The European woman became "the guardian of civilization," while the African American woman was "spared neither harsh labor nor harsh punishment," though the experience of slaves differed depending on the economic status and individual personality of the slave owner. Even pregnancy did not deter some slavemasters from cruel treatment: "One particular method of whipping pregnant slaves was used throughout the South; they were made to lie face down in a specially dug depression in the ground, a practice that provided simultaneously for the protection of the fetus and the abuse of its mother."

Some white women benefited from such slave labor and shared with their husbands the role of oppressor, although the slave-mistress relationship was psychologically complex: "In their role as labor managers, mistresses lashed out at slave women not only to punish them, but also to vent their anger on victims even more wronged than themselves. We may speculate that, in the female slave, the white woman saw the source of her own misery, but she also saw herself—a woman without rights or recourse, subject to the whims of an egotistical man." Conflict between white and African American women often resulted in violence, in which "mistresses were likely to attack with any weapon available—knitting needles, tongs, a fork, butcher knife, ironing board, or pan of boiling water." Yet, while the relationship was often filled with strife, white and African American women "also shared a world of physical and emotional intimacy that is uncommon among women of antagonistic classes and different races."

Slavery was justified by notions of race involving the "biological superiority" of the colonists. It was assumed that Europeans in the colonies made up an easily identifiable and discrete biological and social entity; a "natural" community of class interests, racial attributes, political and social affinities, and superior culture. This was of course not exactly true, but given that the differences between white skin and black skin were more noticeable than many of the differences among Europeans themselves, and given that whites were in dominant positions politically and socially, it could easily *seem* to be true.

Slave families often resisted the oppressive workloads by banding together to help one another in the fields and to lessen the workloads of older, weaker, or sicker workers. The extended family was of vital importance under the slave system. African American mothers labored most of the day, some of then caring for white women's families, while their own children were left under the care of grandmothers and old or disabled slaves. While the two-parent, nuclear family may have been the most typical form of slave cohabitation, close relatives were often very much involved in family life. Stevenson's study suggests that in colonial and antebellum Virginia, the slave family was a "malleable extended family that, when possible, provided its members with nurture, education, socialization, material support, and recreation in the face of the potential social chaos that the slaveholder imposed."

Even though African American men were unable to own property, to provide protection and support for their children, or to work within the public sphere, there was a sexual division within the slave household. Men collected the firewood and made furniture—beds, tables, chairs—and other articles of wood, such as animal traps, butter paddles, and ax handles. They also wove baskets and made shoes. African American women grew, prepared, and preserved foods; spun thread, wove and dyed cloth, and sewed clothes; and made soap and candles.

In the North, while slavery was an accepted practice, it was not nearly as widespread. Many African American women worked as free laborers as domestic servants; others worked as spinners, weavers, and printers.

Native American Women

The work and family life experience of Native American women prior to European colonization differed depending on the region of the country and the type of tribal society. But in every Native American nation, women played very important roles in the economic life of their communities:

> They had to be resourceful in utilizing every aspect of the environment to sustain life and engaging in cultural exchanges to incorporate new productive techniques. They gathered wild plants for food, herbs for medicines and dyes, clay for pottery, bark and reeds for weaving cloth. In many nations, they also tilled the soil and sowed the seeds, cultivated and harvested, made cloth and clothing, dried vegetables, and ground grains for breads. In hunting societies, they cured the meats and dried the skins. They also assisted in the hunt in some cultures.

As a general rule, men hunted and women engaged in agricultural work. The more important hunting was to a community's survival, the more extensive the male power within the community; the greater the dependence on agriculture, the greater the power and independence of women. Women had the responsibility for raising children and maintaining hearth and home. Men engaged in hunting, fishing, and warfare.

In the East especially, many Indian communities were predominantly agricultural. Women constituted the agricultural labor force within these communities. An English woman who was held captive by a Seneca tribe observed that

> Household duties were simple and Seneca women, unlike English wives and daughters, were not slaves to the spinning wheel or the needle. In the summer, the women went out each morning to the fields, accompanied by their children, to work cooperatively and in the company of friends and relatives, planting and tending the corn, beans, and squash at a pace to their individual rhythms and skills rather than to the demands of an overseer. They moved from field to field, completing the same tasks in each before returning to the first.

Women within agricultural communities would often maintain control over tools and land—as well as any surplus foods they gathered from the land. This often enabled them (especially elderly women who were heads of households) to garner some political clout within their tribal communities. For instance, if Iroquois women opposed war on certain occasions, they might refuse to let the men have the cornmeal they would have needed to feed their raiding parties or armies. These communities often had a matrilineal family structure (inheritance and family name were through the female line, with family connections through the mother) and matrilocal residence (upon marriage a man lived with his mother-in-law's relatives).

Through the lens of the white colonist, the work roles and family structure of Native American society appeared deviant and, in some cases, perverse. After all, English society was characterized by a patriarchal family structure with patrilocal residence:

> To Europeans, Indian family patterns raised the specter of promiscuous women, freed from accountability to their fathers and husbands for the offspring they produced. . . . Equally incomprehensible—and thus perverse—to many Europeans were the work roles accepted by Indian men and women. In the world the English knew, farming was labor and farmers were male. Masculinity was linked, inexorably, to agriculture: household production and family reproduction defined femininity. That Indian men hunted was not a sufficient counterpoise, for, in the England of the seventeenth

century, hunting was a sport, not an occupation. Many concluded that Indian men were effeminate, lazy; Indian women were beasts of burden, slaves to unmanly men.

European colonization and conquest pushed Native Americans off their land, depriving them of food and livelihood, culture and traditions. Disease or warfare demolished whole societies. Others were radically transformed, especially with regard to the traditional gender and work roles. Having used military force to remove Native Americans from their lands onto reservations, the U.S. government "began a systematic effort to destroy their cultures and replace them with the values and practices of middle-class whites."

Confined to relatively small reservations, Native American men could no longer hunt as extensively as before (nor, defeated by U.S. forces, could they any longer carry on warfare). They therefore needed to redefine their social roles and to find new economic activities. In many a Native American tribe, the men took over agriculture, traditionally the women's work. Family structure also changed, at the prompting of missionaries and others including government officials, to become more like that of the Europeans, with less emphasis on the matrilineal extended family and more on the nuclear family and the husband-wife relationship.

The Arrival of Industrialization

The transformation from an agrarian rural economy to an urban industrial society ushered in a new era in women's work. With the advent of industrialization, many of the products women made at home—clothes, shoes, candles—gradually came to be made instead in factories. For a while, women still performed the work at home, using the new machines. Merchants would contract for work to be done, supplying women with the machines and the raw materials to be made into finished articles. The most common of these manufacturing trades for women was sewing for the newly emerging clothing industry. Since women had always sewn for their families, this work was considered an extension of women's traditional role, and therefore a respectable activity. As the demand for goods increased, however, home production declined and gave way to the factory system, which was more efficient in meeting emerging needs.

The rise of factory production truly separated the home from the workplace. With the decline of the household unit as the center of industrial and economy activity, the importance of women's economic role also declined. Male and female spheres of activity became more separated, as did the definitions of men's and women's roles. Man's role continued to be primarily that of worker and provider; woman's role became primarily supportive. She was to maintain a smooth and orderly household, to be cheerful and warm, and thus to provide the husband with the support and services he needed to continue his work life. The industrial revolution created a set of social and economic conditions in which the basic lifestyle of white middle-class women more nearly approached society's expectations concerning woman's role. More and more middle-class women could now aspire to the status formerly reserved for the upper classes—that of "lady." The nineteenth-century concept of a lady was that of a fragile, idle, pure creature, submissive and subservient to her husband and to domestic needs. Her worth was based on her decorative value, a quality that embraced her beauty, her virtuous character, and her temperament. She was certainly not a paid employee. This ideal was later referred to as the "cult of true womanhood" because of its rigid, almost religious standards.

Biological and social arguments were also often used to justify women's exclusion from the labor force. Women were seen as too weak and delicate to participate in the rough work world of men. It was believed they lacked strength and stamina, that their brains were small, that the feminine perspective and sensitivity were liabilities in the marketplace. Such arguments rationalized women's accepting the roles of homemaker and mother almost exclusively, as the industrial revolution spread across the country.

During the early years of industrialization, however, because many men were still primarily occupied with agricultural work and were unavailable or unwilling to enter the early factories, male laborers were in short supply. American industry depended,

then, on a steady supply of women workers. Yet how could society tolerate women's working in the factories, given the dominant ideology of the times, which dictated that a woman's place was at home? Single white women provided one answer. Their employment was viewed as a fulfillment of their family responsibilities, during an interlude before marriage.

The employment of young, single women in the early Lowell (Massachusetts) mills is a prime example of the reconciliation of ideology with the needs of industry. Francis Cabot Lowell devised a respectable route into employment for such women. Recruiting the daughters of farm families to work in his mill, which opened in 1821 in Lowell, he provided supervised boardinghouses, salaries sufficient to allow the young women to offer financial aid to their families or to save for their own trousseaux, and assurances to their families that the hard work and discipline of the mill would help prepare them for marriage and motherhood.

In the early industrial era, working conditions were arduous and hours were long. By the late 1830s, immigration began to supply a strongly competitive, permanent workforce willing to be employed for low wages in the factories, under increasingly mechanized and hazardous conditions. By the late 1850s, most of the better-educated, single, native-born women had left the mills, leaving newly immigrated women (both single and married) and men to fill these positions.

While women thus played a crucial role in the development of the textile industry, the first important manufacturing industry in America, women also found employment in many other occupations during the process of industrialization. As railroads and other business enterprises expanded and consolidated, women went to work in these areas as well. In fact, the U.S. Labor Commissioner reported that by 1890 only 9 out of 360 general groups to which the country's industries had been assigned did not employ women.

By 1900, more than five million women or girls, or about one in every five of those 10 years old and over, had become a paid employee. The largest proportion (40%) remained close to home in domestic and personal service, but domestic service was on the decline for white working-class women at the turn of the century. About 25 percent (1.3 million) of employed women worked in the manufacturing industries: in cotton mills, in the manufacture of woolen and worsted goods, silk goods, hosiery, and knit wear. The third largest group of employed women (over 18%) were working on farms. Women in the trade and transportation industries (about 10%) worked as saleswomen, telegraph and telephone operators, stenographers, clerks, copyists, accountants, and bookkeepers. Women in the professions (about 9 percent, and typically young, educated, and single, of native-born parentage) were employed primarily in elementary and secondary teaching or nursing. Other professions—law, medicine, business, college teaching—tended to exclude women. The fastest growing of these occupational groups were manufacturing, trade, and transportation. In the last thirty years of the nineteenth century, the number of women working in trade and transportation rose from 19,000 to over half a million. These women also tended to be young, single, native-born Americans; immigrants and minority women were excluded from these white-collar positions.

. . .

By the turn of the century, the labor market had become clearly divided according to gender, race, and class. Fewer manufacturing jobs were being defined as suitable for white women, especially with the rising dominance of heavy industry employment for which female workers were considered too delicate. Working-class women were increasingly devalued by their continued participation in activities men had primarily taken over (such as factory work), because these activities were regarded as lacking in the Victorian virtue and purity called for by the "cult of true womanhood." As the economy expanded and prosperity came to more and more white middle-class families, middle-class women could "become ladies." A "woman's place" was still defined as at home. If these women did work outside the home, the appropriate occupation was a white-collar job (sales, clerical, and professional occupations). White women's occupations shifted from primarily domestic service—which became increasingly identified as "black women's work"—and from light manufacturing to the rapidly growing opportunities in office and sales work. These jobs were also considered more

appropriate for feminine roles as defined by the cult of true womanhood. Women of color did not share in this occupational transformation. In 1910, for example, 90.5 percent of African American women worked as agricultural laborers or domestics, compared with 29.3 percent of white women.

The Legacy of Slavery

African American women were not part of the "cult of true womanhood." They were not sheltered or protected from the harsh realities, and "while many white daughters were raised in genteel refined circumstances, most black daughters were forced to deal with poverty, violence and a hostile outside world from childhood on." After emancipation, their employment and economic opportunities were limited, in part because the skills they had learned on the plantation transferred to relatively few jobs, and those only of low pay and status.

African American women's concentration in service work—especially domestic work—was largely a result of limited opportunities available to them following the Civil War. The only factory employment open to them was in the Southern tobacco and textile industries, and until World War I most African American working women were farm laborers, domestics, or laundresses. . . .

Despite the limited range of job opportunities, a relatively large proportion of African American women were employed. The legacy of slavery may partly account for the relatively high labor-force participation rate of African American women. Although women's labor-force participation rate is generally lower than men's, African American women's participation rate was historically much higher than that of white women. Thus, for example, white women's labor-force participation in 1890 was 16.3 percent, while African American women's rate was 39.7 percent.

World War I and the Depression

World War I accelerated the entry of white women into new fields of industry. The pressure of war production and the shortage of male industrial workers necessitated the hiring of women for what had been male-dominated occupations. Women replaced men at jobs in factories and business offices, and, in general, they kept the nation going, fed, and clothed. The mechanization and routinization of industry during this period enabled women to quickly master the various new skills. For the most part, this wartime pattern involved a reshuffling of the existing female workforce, rather than an increase in the numbers of women employed. Although the popular myth is that homemakers abandoned their kitchens for machine shops or airplane hangars, only about 5 percent of women workers were new to the labor force during the war years. . . .

Thus the wartime labor shortage temporarily created new job opportunities for women workers, and at higher wages than they had previously earned. This was not necessarily the case for African American women, however. Although World War I opened up some factory jobs to them, these were typically limited to the most menial, least desirable, and often the most dangerous jobs—jobs already rejected by white women. These jobs included some of the most dangerous tasks in industry, such as carrying glass to hot ovens in glass factories and dyeing furs in the furrier industry.

World War I produced no substantial or lasting change in women's participation in the labor force. The employment rate of women in 1920 was actually a bit lower (20.4%) than in 1910 (20.9%). The labor unions, the government, and the society at large were not ready to accept a permanent shift in women's economic role. Instead, women filled an urgent need during the wartime years and were relegated to their former positions as soon as peace returned. As the reformer Mary Von Kleeck wrote, "When the immediate dangers . . . were passed, the prejudices came to life once more."

When the men returned from the war, they were given priority in hiring, and although a number of women left the labor force voluntarily, many were forced out by layoffs. Those remaining were employed in the low-paying, low-prestige positions women had always occupied and in those occupations that had become accepted as women's domain. . . .

The Great Depression of the 1930s threw millions out of work. The severe employment problems during this period intensified the general attitude that a woman with a job was taking that job away from a male breadwinner. Yet during the 1930s, an increasing number of women went to work for the first time. The increase was most marked among younger, married women, who worked at least until the first child, and among older, married women, who reentered the marketplace because of dire economic need or in response to changing patterns of consumer demand. Most jobs held by women were part-time, seasonal, and marginal. Women's labor-force participation increased slowly throughout this period and into the early 1940s . . ., except in the professions (including feminized professions such as elementary teaching, nursing, librarianship, and social work). The proportion of women in all professions declined from 14.2 percent to 12.3 percent during the Depression decade.

World War II

The ordeal of World War II brought about tremendous change in the numbers and occupational distribution of working women. As during World War I, the shortage of male workers, who had gone off to fight, coupled with the mounting pressures of war production brought women into the workforce. A corresponding shift in attitudes about women's aptitudes and proper roles resulted. Women entered the munitions factories and other heavy industries to support the war effort. The War Manpower Commission instituted a massive advertising campaign to attract women to the war industries. Patriotic appeals were common.

. . .

Equal work did not mean equal pay for the women in these varied wartime occupations. Although the National War Labor Board issued a directive to industries that stipulated equal pay for equal work, most employers continued to pay women at a lower rate. Furthermore, women had little opportunity to advance in their new occupations.

World War II marked an important turning point in women's participation in the paid labor force. The social prohibition concerning married women working gave way under wartime pressure, and women wartime workers demonstrated that it was possible for women to maintain their households while also assuming the role of breadwinner with outside employment. More women than ever before learned to accommodate the simultaneous demands of family and work. The experience "pointed the way to a greater degree of choice for American women."

However, at the war's end, with the return of men to civilian life, there was a tremendous pressure on women to return to their former positions in the home. During this time, a new social ideology began to emerge; Betty Friedan later called it "the feminine mystique." This ideology drew in social workers, educators, journalists, and psychologists, all of whom tried to convince women that their place was again in the home. It was not until the "cult of true womanhood" advanced in the late 1800s to differentiate middle-class women from working-class women. As Friedan notes, in the fifteen years following World War II, the image of "women at home" rather than "at work" became a cherished and self-perpetuating core of contemporary American culture. A generation of young people were brought up to extol the values of home and family, and woman's role was defined as the domestic center around which all else revolved. Women were supposed to live like those in Norman Rockwell *Saturday Evening Post* illustrations. The idealized image was of smiling mothers baking cookies for their wholesome children, driving their station wagons loaded with freckled youngsters to an endless round of lessons and activities, returning with groceries and other consumer goods to the ranch houses they cared for with such pride. Women were supposed to revel in these roles and gladly leave the running of the world to men.

. . .

Yet, unlike the post-World War I period, after World War II women did not go back to the kitchens. Instead, women's labor-force participation continued to increase throughout the post-World War II decades, so that by the late 1960s, 40 percent of American women were in the labor force, and by the late 1990s, 60 percent were. Who were the women most likely to be part of this "new majority" of women at work?

After World War II: The Rise of the Married Woman Worker

Between 1890 and the beginning of World War II, single women comprised at least half the female labor force. The others were mostly married African American, immigrant, or working-class women.

The decade of the 1940s saw a change in the type of woman worker, as increasing numbers of married women left their homes to enter the world of paid work. . . . Although single women continued to have the highest labor-force participation rates among women, during the 1940s the percentage of married women in the workforce grew more rapidly than any other category. Between 1940 and 1950, single women workers were in short supply because of low birthrates in the 1930s. Furthermore, those single women available for work were marrying at younger ages and leaving the labor market to raise their families. On the other hand, ample numbers of older, married women were available, and these women (who had married younger, had had fewer children, and were living longer) were eager for paid employment.

In 1940, about 15 percent of married women were employed; by 1950, 24 percent. This increase has continued: by 1960, 32 percent of married women; in 1970, over 41 percent; in 1980, 50 percent; and by 1995, 61 percent. Indeed, as the twentieth century comes to a close, we can see that labor-force participation rates of single and married women have become almost identical. . . .

During the 1940s, 1950s, and 1960s, it was mainly older, married women entering the workforce. In 1957, for example, the labor-force participation rate among women aged forty-five to forty-nine years exceeded the rate for twenty- to twenty-four-year-old women. During the 1960s, young married mothers with preschool- or school-age children began to enter the workforce. This trend continued for the next three decades; by 1995, more than three-quarters of married women with children between six and seventeen years of age were employed, and, most significantly, almost two-thirds of those women with children under the age of six were in the labor force. . . . In short, whereas before 1970 the overwhelming majority of married women stopped working after they had children, today the overwhelming majority of married women do not.

Women of Color

Denied entrance to the factories during the rise of industrialization and, for much of the twentieth century, facing discriminatory hiring practices that closed off opportunities in the newly expanded office and sales jobs, many women of color entered domestic service. From 1910 to 1940, the proportion of white women employed in clerical and sales positions almost doubled, and there was a decline in the numbers of white women in domestic work. Private household work then became the province of African American women: the percentage of African American household workers increased from 38.5 percent in 1910 to 59.9 percent in 1940. . . . For the next three decades, African American women remained the single largest group in domestic service.

African American women's economic status improved dramatically from 1940 through the 1960s, as a result of an increase in light manufacturing jobs, as well as changes in technology. African American women moved from private household work into manufacturing and clerical work, and made significant gains in the professions. Whereas in 1940, 60 percent of employed African American females worked in private households, by the late 1960s only 20 percent did. Their job prospects continued to improve, and by the 1980s, almost half of all working African American women were doing so in "white collar" jobs—clerical and sales positions, as well as professional jobs in business, health-care, and education. Through the 1990s, the historic, job-prestige gap between African American and white working women continued to close. Almost two-thirds of working African American women had jobs in the white-collar world by 1996, compared with nearly three-quarters of working white women. . . .

Other Women of Color at Work

Each minority group has had a different experience in American society and has faced different opportunities and obstacles. Women in each group share with African American women the concerns of all minority women; they share with the men of their ethnic groups the problems of discrimination against that particular ethnic minority.

Native American Women.   As we noted earlier, gender roles in Native American communities were disrupted during the conquest and oppression by whites. For example, Navajo society was traditionally matrilineal, with extended families the norm; Navajo women owned property and played an important role in family decisions. But beginning in the 1930s, government policy disrupted this system by giving land only to males. As they could no longer make a sufficient living off the land, more and more Navajo men had to seek employment off the reservations. Nuclear families became the norm. Navajo women became dependent on male providers. With the men away much of the time, these women are often isolated and powerless. They often face divorce or desertion and thus economic difficulties, because the community frowns on women seeking work off the reservation.

Such disruption of the traditional Native American society left Native American women in very grim economic circumstances. But in recent decades, more and more of them have gotten jobs. Native American women's labor-force participation rate in 1970 was 35 percent (compared to 43% for all women). This rate rose sharply to 55 percent by the early 1990s and is now within a few percentage points of the rate for all women.

Like their African American counterparts over the past half century, Native American women have gradually moved out of low-skill farm and nonfarm work and domestic jobs into clerical, sales, professional, technical, and other "white-collar" jobs. In 1960, one in six working Native American women was employed as a domestic household worker; by the early 1990s only one in a hundred was. During the same period, the proportion of Native American women involved in agricultural work also went from ten to one in a hundred. Manufacturing work was increasingly replaced by white-collar work, reflecting the overall trends in the occupational structure; more specifically, while the percentage involved in factory work (much of it in textiles and traditional crafts) fell from 18.1 to 14.2, the percentage doing white-collar work soared from 28.9 to 61.3. Although many of these white-collar jobs are classified as "professional" (15.7% of all working Native American women) or "managerial" (9.4%), two-thirds of Native American women are still concentrated in the "secondary" sector of the labor market—which is characterized by low wages, few or no benefits, low mobility, and high instability. They are kept there because of the "stagnation of the reservation economy," discrimination, and their relatively low level of educational attainment. A significant number do not have a high school diploma (in 1990, more than one-third of all those over the age of 25, compared to one-fifth of white women).

Latina [Chicana] Women. . . . Large numbers of Chicanas migrated, usually with husband and children, from Mexico to the United States during the 1916–1920 labor shortage created by World War I. They found work in the sprawling "factory farms" of the Southwest, harvesting fruits, vegetables, and cotton in the Imperial and San Joaquin valleys of California, the Salt River valley of Arizona, and the Rio Grande valley of Texas. They also went to the Midwest, for instance to Michigan and Minnesota, to harvest sugar beets. Such migrant workers typically were exploited, spending long, tedious, and physically demanding hours in the fields for very low pay. Some became tenant farmers, which might seem a step up, except too often this system "created debt peonage; unable to pay the rent, tenants were unable to leave the land and remained virtually permanently indebted to their landlords."

During the 1920s, with a shortage of European immigration, new job opportunities opened up for Mexican Americans, and they began to migrate from rural, farm country to the urban, industrial centers, where they found work as domestics and factory workers. By 1930, one-third of working Chicanas were domestics and a quarter worked in manufacturing; at the time, the share employed in agriculture, forestry, and mining had fallen to 21 percent. Wage scales varied according to ethnicity, however. It was not uncommon to pay Chicana workers lower wages than "Anglo" (whites of European descent) women for doing the same job, whether as domestics, laundresses, or workers in the food-processing industries of the West and Southwest. Then the Depression years of the 1930s, with the general shortage of jobs, brought a backlash against Mexican American labor, and thousands of Mexicans were deported or pressured to leave.

World War II once again opened up the American labor market for Mexican migrants, as their labor was needed to offset wartime labor shortages. However, their treatment was deplorable by modern standards. In short, Mexican workers comprised a "reserve army" of exploited labor. Through the government-sponsored Bracero or "Manual Workers" program, Mexican workers were granted temporary work visas so that they could be employed on large corporate farms and elsewhere, but too often they were treated like slaves or prisoners.

World War II and the years following saw a massive shift in the occupational and geographical distribution of Chicana workers:

> Many left Texas for California, and the population became increasingly more urban. Women continued their move from the fields into garment factories throughout the Southwest. . . . [A] comparison of the 1930 and 1950 [census] data shows the magnitude of these shifts. For instance, the share of employed southwestern Chicanas working on farms dropped from 21 percent in 1930 to 6 percent in 1950, while the percentage in white-collar work doubled.

By the 1960s, the largest occupational category for Chicana workers was operatives, followed by clerical and service work. Chicanas became concentrated in particular industries—food processing, electronics (including telecommunications), and garments. Like their Native American counterparts, Chicana women have made some progress in entering professional and managerial occupations (primarily noncollege teaching, nursing, librarianship, and social work). In 1960, 8.6 percent were in these occupations; by 1980, 12.6 percent, and by the early 1990s 17.5 percent.

However, like the Native Americans, Chicana women are still overwhelmingly found in the secondary labor market (75%); much more so than women (60%) and men (32%) of white European heritage.

The dominant reasons behind the low occupational prestige of all minority groups are the same: discrimination and low educational attainment. In the case of Chicana women, over 15 percent "are illiterate by the standard measure (completion of less than five years of schooling)," but studies of functional illiteracy during the 1970s and 1980s suggest "much higher rates—perhaps as high as 56 percent." At the other end of the educational attainment spectrum, only 8.4 percent of Latina women have completed four or more years of college—compared with 21.0 percent of white women and 12.9 percent of blacks. However, education is only part of the formula for success in the U.S. occupational system: for when education is held constant, Latina women only make between 84 and 90 percent of what white women do.

Beyond lack of education, Chicana women face other important obstacles in the labor market. They have high rates of unemployment and underemployment. Many of the jobs they hold are seasonal and often nonunionized. This lack of advancement translates into higher poverty rates (23% for Chicana/os in the early 1990s). The median income for full-time Chicana workers is lower than that of any other U.S. racial-ethnic group. For Latina women (in general) with children and no husband present, the poverty rate is even worse: 49.4 percent compared with 26.6 percent of white women in this situation.

Increasingly, Chicana women, like many female workers of color around the globe, are doing service or assembly work for multi-national corporations, especially in the apparel, food-processing, and electronics industries. These women have often displaced men in assembly work because they can be paid less and many do not receive job benefits. The work hours are long, and women are often assigned monotonous tasks that are dangerous to their health.
. . .

Asian-American Women. . . . Asian Americans are considered to be the "model minority," . . . However, this is as much myth as fact. While many among both the native-born and the recent arrivals have high levels of education and professional skills and can readily fit into the labor market, others lack such advantages, often finding work only as undocumented laborers in low-paying jobs with long work days, little or no job mobility, and no benefits.

> We are told we have overcome our oppression, and that therefore we are the model minority. Model refers to the cherished dictum of capitalism that "pulling hard on your bootstraps" brings due rewards. . . . Asian American success stories . . . do little to illuminate the actual conditions of the majority of Asian Americans. Such examples conceal the more typical Asian American experience of unemployment, underemployment and struggle to survive. The model minority myth thus classically scapegoats Asian Americans. It labels us in a way that dismisses the real problems that many do face, while at the same time pitting Asians against other oppressed people of color.

In 1996, 37.3 percent of Asian women who were 25 years and over had at least a bachelor's degree, compared with 23.2 percent of non-Latina whites. Filipina American women secured the highest college graduation rate of all women, a rate 50 percent greater than that of white males. Following closely behind are Chinese American and Japanese American women, who exceed both the white male and female college graduation rates. Yet, these educational achievements bring lower returns for Asian women than for whites. Census data reveal a gap between achievement and economic reward for Asian American women, who suffer from both race and sex discrimination within the labor market. . . .

And it would be wrong to equate "Asian" with "well educated," because the majority of Asian women immigrating to the United States since 1980 have low levels of education. Though, as just noted, Asian women are much more likely to be college-educated than non-Latina white women, they are also much more likely—two and a half times more likely—to be grade-school drop outs: in 1996, 12.5 percent of Asian women had not gone beyond the eighth grade, compared to only 5.2 percent of their non-Latina white counterparts. This fact is linked to the other most obvious difference between Asian and white women . . . —the proportions working as "operators, fabricators, and laborers," where we find significantly more Asian women.

These women are most commonly employed as sewing machine operators at home or in small sweatshops in the Chinatowns of New York and San Francisco. Asian immigrant women are also heavily employed in the microelectronics industry. Women in general comprise 80 to 90 percent of assembly workers in this industry, and approximately "half of these assembly workers are recent immigrants from the Philippines, Vietnam, Korea, and South Asia." Within the microelectronics industry jobs are often "structured along racial and gender lines, with men and white workers earning higher wages and being much more likely to be promoted than women and workers of color." Karen Hossfeld's research on relationships between Third World immigrant women production workers and their white male managers in the high-tech Silicon Valley of California relates how immigrant women of color negotiate and often employ resistance to primarily white, middle-class management demands. One Filipina circuit board assembler in Silicon Valley puts it this way:

The bosses here have this type of reasoning like a see-saw. One day it's "you're paid less because women are different than men," or "immigrants need less to get by." The next day it's "you're all just workers here—no special treatment just because you're female or foreigners."

Well, they think they're pretty clever with their doubletalk, and that we're just a bunch of dumb aliens. But it takes two to use a seesaw. What we are gradually figuring out here is how to use their own logic against them.

As clerical or administrative support workers, Asian American women are disproportionately represented as cashiers, file clerks, office machine operators, and typists. They are less likely to obtain employment as secretaries or receptionists. Noting that there is an "overrepresentation of college-educated women in clerical work," Woo suggests that education functions less as a path toward mobility into higher occupational categories, and more as "a hedge against jobs as service workers and as machine operatives or assembly workers."

Asian American women with a college education who obtain professional employment are often restricted to the less prestigious jobs within this category. Asian American women "are more likely to remain marginalized in their work organization, to encounter a 'glass ceiling', and to earn less than white men, Asian American men, and white women with comparable educational backgrounds." They are least represented in those male-dominated positions of physician, lawyer, and judge, and are heavily concentrated in the more female-dominated occupations of nursing and teaching.

Asian women have been subjected to a range of stereotypes. The "Lotus Blossom" stereotype depicts them as submissive and demure sex objects: "good, faithful, uncomplaining, totally compliant, self-effacing, gracious servants who will do anything and everything to please, entertain, and make them feel comfortable and carefree." At the opposite extreme, the Dragon Lady stereotype portrays Asian women as "promiscuous and untrustworthy,"

as the castrating Dragon Lady who, while puffing on her foot-long cigarette holder, could poison a man as easily as she could seduce him. "With her talon-like six-inch fingernails, her skin-tight satin dress slit to the thigh," the Dragon Lady is desirable, deceitful and dangerous.

Asian American feminist Germaine Wong notes how stereotypes concerning Asian women operate in the workplace, serving to deter their advancement into leadership roles and to increase their vulnerability to sexual harassment. Additionally, these stereotypes have fostered a demand for "X-rated films and pornographic materials featuring Asian women in bondage, for 'Oriental' bathhouse workers in U.S. cities, and for Asian mail-order brides."

In sum, the notion of Asian Americans as the "model minority" deviates considerably from sociological reality. While Asian American women as a group have achieved some "success" in terms of high educational attainment, they receive lower returns on this investment compared to the white population. They have not "escaped the stigmatization of being minority and recent immigrants in a discriminatory job market."

READING 56

Living in McJobdom:
Third Wave Feminism and Class Inequity

Michelle Sidler

. . .

It occurred to me that when I entered graduate school in 1991, I did not anticipate gender barriers, partially because of my own naïveté, but also because of an undergraduate experience within an English department almost exclusively made up of women. It was at this moment that I realized to the fullest my indebtedness to second wave feminism—all of the female instructors of undergraduates whose brilliance and support fostered my eventual career in English studies were part of the second wave feminist movement. If not for the vital social and political work of these women, I might not have been in a position to consider even the possibility of obtaining a doctoral degree.

But looking closer at my reason for entering graduate school directly after receiving my bachelor's degree, I must confess that my decision had less to do with an overwhelming desire to study Milton or Joyce or even Welty than with my fear of facing a bleak job market holding, as I did, few technical skills and a liberal arts degree. Too many friends before me had fallen into McJobs,[1] working in part-time or temporary positions with no benefits and no hope of advancement. If I can just make it through graduate school, I thought, I will have it all—job security, benefits, great working hours, and an academic position that will allow me to engage in two of my favorite activities, teaching and writing. In a time when temporary employment agencies such as Manpower are among the most prosperous American companies, such economic concerns loom large.[2] My choices were discouragingly simple: either survive graduate school and work in academia, or risk being swallowed up into the black hole of McJobdom and losing the security and prospects of my middle-class upbringing. Indeed, going to graduate school seemed the only foreseeable alternative to what Jeff Giles in *Newsweek* magazine called, "for newly minted grads, arguably the worst job market since World War II" (1994, 65).

Many second wave feminists were faced with an either/or dilemma also: either get (or stay) married and sacrifice their own professional ambitions, or follow their desires as self-sustaining, intelligent women. . . . She, like other second wave feminists, found herself torn between two conflicting messages: raise a family or be economically self-sufficient. Second wave feminists, driven by a sense of independence and a need for equality, struggled to break down that either/or dilemma.

For many young women now, the choice whether or not to work is no longer an either/or proposition. Most twentysomething women do not question the possibility of work, and not necessarily because we feel particularly empowered or independent. With stagnant wages in many fields, women often must work just to stay afloat, even if they are married to working husbands. Generally, women no longer feel trapped into housekeeping and motherhood; on average, we are waiting later and later to have children. Since women's liberation, more women than ever are entering the professional workplace. According to Robert Reich in *Rolling Stone,* "In 1973, 57 percent of women in their 20's were in the workforce. Twenty years later, the figure had climbed to 73 percent" (1994, 119). However, many young women do not view this new presence in the workforce as an opportunity. Many, like myself, feel trapped by lower wages for all workers and know that even for married couples, two incomes are quickly becoming a necessity.

Second wave feminism helped bring about professional self-sufficiency for women, and their work paved the way for new feminisms, such as that being constructed by young women of the post–baby boom generation. But postmodernism and the new global economy have brought on concerns about the homogeneity of the so-called bourgeois white feminism of the second wave. Who has reaped the benefits of the women's movement of the 1960s and 1970s? To what extent did second wave feminism help the rise of women in *all* classes, including those outside privileged classes, and to what extent must feminism revamp itself in the wake of the new global economy? What can we learn from second wave feminism as we face an economy driven by profits, with workers edged out by technology and global competition?

The rise of women in the workplace sounds like bright news, but it begins to take on a new face when I consider again my own shaky job dilemma. Like many other twentysomethings, I feel job security slipping out from under me. Economic restructuring has destabilized employment for both men and women. Women can no longer depend on the security of a husband's income (or their own, for that matter). Nor can they assume that jobs are available; often women just have not had access to them. Even young working men are finding more McJobs and lower salaries. Third wave feminism will have to face these harsh economic conditions.

Academia itself poses an excellent example of this new destabilization. Women (and men) in academia have less encouraging economic prospects than did second wave feminists. Since my entrance into graduate school, I have found that most of the academic perks I once looked forward to are not guaranteed. Due to budget crunching and an overabundance of out-of-work academics, many universities have turned to hiring professors part-time or temporarily, thus eliminating higher salaries, benefits, and the security of tenure. In the new restructuring of faculty, many professors are paid by each course hour they teach, prompting them to teach heavy loads and leaving little time for professional development. The shortage of positions was a minor problem when most second wave feminists looked for their first academic appointments. As second waver Elizabeth Ermath writes, "When I began looking for a tenure-track job in 1969–70 the job market was just beginning to get pinched" (1993, 227). After twenty-five years, that pinch has become a painful squeeze. Doctoral students feel the economic pressure even before they graduate. While they pursue degrees, most endure their own versions of McJobs —teaching assistantships with salaries so low (and often few benefits) that many are forced to take out even more student loans, thus increasing their postdoctoral debt. . . .

. . . I have seen many of my college friends (most of whom have four-year degrees) bounce from one McJob to another. And the financial situation continues to look as grim for women as it did in the past. . . . [W]omen between twenty-five and thirty-four are still making an average salary only 82 percent that of their male counterparts. In *Working Woman,* Pamela Krueger notes that for college-educated women, future finances are even more complicated by the desire to have a family (1994, 62). The best-educated and most-skilled young women are demanding flexibility in the workplace. This goal will be difficult, if not impossible, to achieve, even for professionally prepared women, in the current economic instability.

Further, the situation is particularly drastic for young Americans with little education or professional skills. Reich notes that women and men ages twenty-five to thirty-four without a high school diploma make less than half the income of their counterparts with a college education—"the largest gulf between high earners and low earners in our nation's history" (1994, 119). This statistic is no surprise to those who observed the shrinkage of the middle class throughout the 1980s. The *Economist* agrees: "In an economy where earnings are tied ever more tightly to skills, and where employers use education as a proxy for such skills when hiring young workers, the 75% of Americans who do not graduate from college face a grim future of stagnant or falling real wages" (Generation 1994, 27–28). With fewer jobs to go around, most Americans without enough skills or education will find themselves in an economic crisis, creating a new class of the impoverished. Due to technology and global competition, downsizing and reduction of jobs remain the trend. Even for those with skills, competition for jobs will continue to tighten.

Annette Fuentes and Barbara Ehrenreich recognize the motivating force behind the worldwide employment crisis—multinational corporations guided by the "profit motive" (1983, 57). They argue that we must create a global network among working women for support and recognition. Although such a goal is an essential first step, much more needs to be done, and soon. Women, men, and feminism must redirect the profit motive, confront the widening gap between the wealthy and the underclasses, and produce options beyond the present corporate model. To prepare for such a challenge, women of all classes must familiarize themselves with economics as an integral part of feminism and of their daily lives. This need has never been greater or clearer than it is now in my generation. We can expect little improvement in these economic conditions as long as corporations value profit more than workers.

Marxist feminists argue that the union of capitalism and patriarchy leads to the domestic oppression of women.[3] These feminists have exposed the oppression of women, through domestic labor, as the reproducers of the capital workforce. However, the image of women as domestic servants to patriarchy first and capitalism second is quickly becoming outdated. Many families cannot afford the traditional family structure of the domestic mother when one-third of all men from twenty-five to thirty-four years of age earn less than what is needed to keep a family of four out of poverty (Thurow 1996, 31). Men do not have the luxury of an unemployed wife. Most women of my generation must work, whether we have families or not, to survive economically. Feminism can use the experience of resisting the oppressive yet ingrained patriarchal system to fight capitalism, but we must begin to move away from viewing patriarchy as the immediate cause of oppression and try to combat the even larger threat of American and worldwide economic hardship.

Without a new economic theory and political mission, feminism risks alienating this new generation of women, many of whom experience economic instability and, in some cases, a drop in class status. With the added insecurity of McJobs comes the decline of raw salary figures: between 1973 and 1992, real wages dropped for people at all levels of income except those in the top 20 percent (Rifkin 1995, 23). If this trend continues (and it most certainly will

with the rising of corporate downsizing and global job competition), only women in the top 20 percent will have a choice about working. . . . Women's oppression must be seen as, first, a function of wage earning and, second, a result of domestic servitude, because soon there will be few homes without working mothers. Second wave feminists did not enter an economic forecast so grim; they had no way of knowing that my generation would need their help to counter the raw face of global profit-driven capitalism.

So how can a new feminist political agenda work to relieve the economic disparity facing twenty-somethings? First, we must recognize that gender equality in the workforce does not automatically bring economic progress. Feminism in the 1960s and 1970s worked toward giving women the same economic opportunities as men. Now, however, there will be fewer economic opportunities for either gender, so we have to broaden our concerns to include issues previously viewed as gender neutral. In "The Long Goodbye," Linda Kauffman calls for a renewed sense of a feminist project that will readdress the current state of affairs, with its list of injustices that goes beyond those tackled by second wave feminism. She proposes a women's movement that addresses "injustices that might not normally be regarded as specifically feminist concerns because it is precisely the interconnection of feminist issues with other injustices that urgently needs our attention in the '90's" (1993, 141). This interconnection involves not just recognizing the plight of others but also learning how all injustices are an integral part of feminism itself.

Feminism can begin interconnecting by addressing at least three areas: academics, the media, and technology. These structures function broadly on economic, social, and cultural levels, and they have all been important in the progression of feminism. They also work on a personal level for me, as a teacher of using computers for writing. In my experience, academics, the media, and technology usually exist as contradictory forces. Feminists have been actively trying to usurp these structures as places of empowerment and change for women. But these areas have proved detrimental to twentysomethings, women, and workers. In many ways academics, the media, and technology are complicit in the workings of corporate oppression and the profit motive.

A new agenda must include mobility between the academic politics of second wave feminism and young workers both in and out of the academy. The academy is, after all, no less susceptible to economic adversity than is any other profession or institution. New doctoral graduates, especially those in the liberal arts, are facing a horrible job market as colleges and universities give in to the pressure of a technologically based economy, hiring full-time tenured faculty mostly in only those fields that will give students skills for professionalization. Higher education's need to compete in the corporate marketplace has taken priority before less economically tangible areas of study, such as the liberal arts. The academy presents a representative case of the current economic crisis and can act as a starting point, like the informant of a joint movement, one that recognizes mutual oppression where binaries such as academic/popular and man/woman still take prevalence.

At the scholarly level, we can begin by looking for theorists' discussions of the current economy that have immediate implications for twentysomething workers. Jacques Derrida recognizes injustices created by the current economy in his *Specters of Marx*. He lists ten "plagues of the new world order," the social, political, and economic structures created by multinational markets and the "New International Law" (1994, 81–84). Changing conditions in late capitalism are leading to global abuse of human rights, and the first of these on Derrida's list is unemployment. . . . Through the creation of a global pool of workers, capitalism has constructed joblessness on a grand scale. No longer can we consider unemployment a fluctuating curve in the economy; we have entered an era of chronic work shortage and poverty. Neither women nor men can assume that jobs are out there to be had and that economic stability is a function of gender equality. We must overhaul feminism to operate within this "new world order," recognizing not just the absence of work equality for women, but the absence of work for *everyone*. We need, as Derrida states, a new concept of sustained unemployment. Academics like me who face job shortages have a vested interest in addressing the theoretical issues behind our employment

crisis and in translating those issues into a new feminist agenda.

The economic adversity of young workers can also be transformed on political and social levels, particularly through the media. The women's movement of second wave feminism learned hard lessons that can aid in this struggle. One way is to stop the cycle of blame on twentysomethings. As Susan Faludi spells out so effectively in *Backlash* (1991), feminism was reflected back onto the women's movement when much popular press in the 1980s claimed that feminism was its own worst enemy. A similar backlash has begun in response to reports of the economic plight of twentysomethings. Exploiting the false stereotypes about my generation, some members of the popular press blame young workers for their financial problems. David Martin, for example, labels twentysomethings "the Whiny Generation" and argues, "Instead of blaming everyone for this state of [economic] affairs, the Whiners should acquire more skills, education and specialized knowledge for the careers of the 21st century" (1993). Of course, Martin is mistaken about the possibilities for careers of the next century; with fewer jobs even for the educated, many skilled workers will be underemployed. In addition, as technology speeds up the progression of the market, many skills acquired now by young people will be obsolete soon.

Further, Martin's statement presents a problem facing twentysomethings that feminism also faces. Martin blames young workers themselves for their dissatisfaction, asserting that they were spoiled by privileged childhoods with high standards of living and economic prosperity. Ignoring for the moment Martin's obvious overgeneralizations about the standards of living for all postboomer youth, his blame tactics echo those chronicled in Faludi's book. Such reports targeted the "triumph of women's equality" as the cause of reports of increased stress and unhappiness among women (Faludi 1991, xiii). Feminism learned valuable lessons from this type of conservative media reaction, lessons that could now be used to counter backlash in the popular press concerning economic inequality for young men and women. Such lesson sharing is a realization of the interconnectedness between feminism and other movements that Kauffman identifies.

Moving again to the theoretical level, a surprising connection can be drawn between Martin's comments and Donna Haraway's calls for a new feminism (Haraway 1990, 211). Haraway advocates using the power of technology in the postmodern era to promote a new feminist agency. Although her theory concerns the economic disadvantage of women specifically, it applies equally well to twentysomething workers—both men and women—who are in positions of economic disadvantage. She argues that "we are living through a movement from an organic, industrial society to a polymorphous, information system" that posits great power in the knowledge of technology (203). Haraway asserts that unemployment itself stems from the new technologies but that women can learn to use technology to create new, empowering social realities. Haraway believes that the forces of capitalism can be fought through the tools of technology: "An adequate socialist-feminist politics should address women in the privileged occupational categories and particularly in the production of science and technology that constructs scientific-technical discourse, processes, and objects" (211). Haraway argues that a new feminist agenda should support and encourage women who are in positions of technological power. Her feminist agenda assumes that we can use the tools of technology to fight oppression, but this approach seems simplistic. Haraway's theory sounds much like Martin's advice to young workers—just get the right kind of technical and communicative skills, and you will get the right kind of economic power.

The current economic plight of twentysomethings complicates Martin's and Haraway's insistence on the power of technology. Haraway and Martin simplify the privilege of class as a basis for acquiring knowledge of technology, particularly for young workers. As the importance of technology rises, so does the pay gap between those with and those without the economic means to attend college. The 1980s brought on a shrinking middle class and an increased necessity for a college education, but that education has gotten more and more expensive, even for those left in the middle class. As John Heilemann notes in the *Washington Monthly,* the rise in tuition for higher education is outrageous: "Between 1980 and 1990 the cost of attending the average college soared

by an astonishing 126 percent—way ahead of inflation and, more importantly, way ahead of the median family income" (1993, 43). Acquiring the necessary skills and knowledge costs more now than ever, making it more difficult for those in lower classes to obtain gainful employment, and sustaining higher education as an institution predominantly for the privileged classes. With the shrinkage in the 1980s of federal grant funds for higher education, students without the means from their families and/or scholarships find themselves taking out large student loans to finance their education (Heilemann 1993, 43). Martin and Haraway address the advantages of technology from different perspectives, but both sustain its position as powerful for those with privilege.

This brings the discussion back to the personal level, to my stake in this economic inequity as a member of the twentysomething workforce. I am looking for a new feminism that tackles the issue of affording an education that will lead to economic prosperity, a struggle that parallels the employment equality sought by second wave feminists. I am personally invested in this problem not only as a student in higher education but also as a teacher in higher education. As a student, I have had to contend with the rising cost of my studies, at both the undergraduate and the graduate levels. I have already superseded the average $35,000 debt incurred by students seeking graduate degrees (Heilemann 1993, 42). And I am not alone—as of the 1991–92 school year, student loans overtook grants as the largest source of federal educational funds that college and graduate students receive (Financial 1993). This is no surprise as I consider my college classmates, some of whom graduated from our private, four-year university with debts totaling $5,000, $20,000, even $40,000. And with direct student loan dispersal (through increased technology, students can receive their checks as soon as seventy-two hours after applying), this trend will no doubt continue to rise (Wilkinson 1994).

Whereas many women in second wave feminism faced difficult decisions between family or school, or family or work, twentysomethings have little choice in these matters. First, higher education is quickly becoming a necessity; we are told there is no longer a job for us on the factory floor, so we must incur heavy debt to obtain a degree. Second, we must put off decisions such as having children for five, ten, maybe even twenty years because of the financial burden left by our education. This too is a feminist concern. Young women may not feel as much pressure to have children as did the previous generation of women, but their decision has become even more complicated by debt.

As an instructor in academia, I bring these concerns to my classroom and discuss them with my students. Teaching technical writing to seniors, I empathize with them as they surf the Internet desperately for the job that will take them out of this debt cycle. Some succeed; many do not. And my students are the ones on "the right path," obtaining the technical degrees touted as the promise of the twenty-first century. What of those students, like me, who did not choose "the right path," who obtained liberal arts degrees not for the money expected after graduation but for the desire to learn, to teach, and, in my case, to write? As I watch my students, I often wonder, if I had the chance to go back, would I choose a different direction, perhaps one with a more promising economic outlook?

And so I return again to those undergraduate English professors who supplied me with strong female role models in academic positions of power, juggling families and careers so skillfully. Their stories echo those told in *Changing Subjects* (Greene and Kahn 1993), as many of those women also came to grips with their own sexuality, independence, and social power through second wave feminism. But even with the professional and personal barriers they overcame, there were lessons that my professors did not know to teach me, struggles they had not faced as women pursuing careers. Mass job shortage was not a hardship they had needed to overcome; neither was oppressive, lingering debt. These conditions must be concerns of a third wave feminism. Yet we can learn from the struggles fought by second wavers against oppression, transforming the aggressor from patriarchy to capitalism.

Many boomer feminists found that patriarchy could be fought not on a mass level (the bitter defeat of the Equal Rights Amendment attests to that), but in smaller, more localized ways over a long period of time. Whereas their activism took the shape of hard work in positions that pushed on the glass ceiling, a third wave activism might take the form of denying or resisting corporate America by starting worker-friendly businesses or by helping employees unite to buy out their companies, thus returning the wealth and capital of the company to those who fostered it. Whereas second wave feminists strove for equality with men, third wave feminists cannot reasonably expect equality from capitalism. But we can fight to preserve basic rights and decent working conditions for people.

Another concern—another connection and contradiction—will be the importance placed on technology. Who will benefit from a feminism that finds its economic (as well as social and political) answers in the power of or power over technology? Personal computers and instant information did not influence the economy for second wave feminists as it does now. Whereas my undergraduate professors completed their dissertations on typewriters, I am learning the Internet in graduate school and submitting papers through E-mail. Although a new feminist agenda must keep up with the changes in technology, we must not lose sight of the economic privilege required and sustained by these machines. Technologies are, after all, the master's tools, created by men for the advancement of capitalism. Haraway argues that we must usurp those tools and use them for our benefit, but I am more skeptical about our chances. The Internet, for example, should be a place for open, global discussion and organization, much along the lines that Fuentes and Ehrenreich describe (1983). However, it is quickly becoming a place of commodification, a quick and easy instrument for corporations. We cannot turn our backs on this powerful medium, but we must understand its contradictions and limitations as well.

The McJobdom inhabited by so many twenty-somethings is but a local manifestation of a growing economic condition. The condition is so subtle and pervasive that women and men of my generation do not know how to fight it. We have to recognize that global capitalism is overtaking many of the social structures under which second wave feminists operated. Academia is no longer a place of support for critically conscious scholars, media representations of the underprivileged and marginalized are often suspect, and technology is as much a hindrance to women and workers as it is an empowering tool. Leaving domestic roles to pursue a career is no longer a political statement either; it is a necessity that does not constitute activism for twentysomething women. A new, third wave feminism must combine our forces in the areas of academia, the media, and technology, constructing alliances against the profit motive and looking for the interconnection Kauffman describes. Such connections now supersede the traditional academic/popular, male/female binaries, providing the opportunity to explore injustice and inequity in new ways. But we also have to understand the contradictions inherent in many of the areas available for connection. We have to create an agenda with skepticism, looking closely and critically at the avenues we choose. Second wave feminism's identity politics gave twentysomething women the opportunity to enter the workforce and empowered us to create our own agenda, but with the rise of class instability we face a new playing field complicated by factors such as unemployment, debt, and technology. In short, third wave feminism needs a new economy.

NOTES

1. Douglas Coupland describes "McJobs" as "Low pay, low prestige, low benefits, low future" (1991, 5).
2. Jeremy Rifkin describes the magnitude of Manpower: "Manpower, the nation's largest temp agency, is now the country's single largest employer, with 560,000 workers" (1995, 190).
3. Barbara Hartmann provides an excellent discussion of the theoretical bases for the primacy of patriarchy (1981).

WORKS CITED

Coupland, Douglas. 1991. *Generation X: Tales for an Accelerated Culture.* New York: St. Martin's.

Derrida, Jacques. 1994. *Specters of Marx.* Translated by Peggy Kamuf. New York: Routledge.

Ermath, Elizabeth. 1993. "On Having a Personal Voice." In *Changing Subjects: The Making of Feminist Literary Criticism,* edited by Gayle Greene and Coppelia Kahn, 226–39. London: Routledge.

Faludi, Susan. 1991. *Backlash.* New York: Crown.

"Financial Need and Loans Soar." 1993. *USA Today,* April, 10.

Fuentes, Annette, and Barbara Ehrenreich. 1983. *Women in the Global Factory.* Boston: South End.

Generation X-onomics. 1994. *Economist,* 19 March, 27–28.

Giles, Jeff. 1994. "Generalizations X." *Newsweek,* 6 June, 62–72.

Greene, Gayle, and Coppelia Kahn, eds. 1993. *Changing Subjects: The Making of Feminist Literary Criticism.* London: Routledge.

Haraway, Donna. 1990. "A Manifesto for Cyborgs." In *Feminism/Postmodernism,* edited by Linda J. Nicholson, 190–231. London: Routledge.

Hartmann, Barbara. 1981. "The Unhappy Marriage of Marxism and Feminism." In *Women and Revolution: A Discussion of the Unhappy Marriage of Marxism and Feminism,* edited by Lydia Sargent, 1–41. Boston: South End.

Heilemann, John. 1993. "Debt 101." *Washington Monthly,* March, 42–44.

Kauffman, Linda S. 1993. "The Long Goodbye: Against the Personal Testimony or, An Infant Grows Up." In *Changing Subjects: The Making of Feminist Literary Criticism,* edited by Gayle Greene and Coppelia Kahn, 129–46. London: Routledge.

Krueger, Pamela. 1994. "Superwoman's Daughters." *Working Woman,* May.

Martin, David. 1993. "The Whiny Generation." *Newsweek,* 1 November, 10.

Reich, Robert. 1994. "Hire Education." *Rolling Stone,* 20 October, 119–25.

Rifkin, Jeremy. 1995. *The End of Work: The Decline of the Global Labor Force and the Dawn of the Post-Market Era.* New York: Tarcher/Putnam.

Thurow, Lester C. 1996. *The Future of Capitalism: How Today's Economic Forces Shape Tomorrow's World.* New York: Morrow.

Wilkinson, Francis. 1994. "Clinton's Credit: The 72-Hour Student Loan." *Rolling Stone,* 25 August, 53.

READING 57

"Hey, Why Don't You Wear a Shorter Skirt?":
Structural Vulnerability and the Organization of
Sexual Harassment in Temporary Clerical Employment

Jackie Krasas Rogers and Kevin D. Henson

Sexual Harassment in the Workplace

A large portion of the social research devoted to sexual harassment has focused on documenting the extent of sexual harassment: what percentage of women are sexually harassed (MacKinnon 1979); which women are sexually harassed and in what jobs (Carothers and Crull 1984); and who are the harassers (Gruber and Bjorn 1982; Gutek 1985). Other research categorizes types of sexual harassment (Fitzgerald 1990; MacKinnon 1979), delineates responses to sexual harassment (Gruber 1989; Maypole 1986), determines who labels which experiences as sexual harassment (Giuffre and Williams 1994; Schneider 1982), and asks the question "What factors contribute to sexual harassment?" Answers to this question have included sex-role spillover (Gutek 1985; Ragins and Scandura 1995), patriarchy (MacKinnon 1979), and compulsory heterosexuality (Giuffre and Williams 1994; Schneider 1982, 1985).

Gutek (1985) describes sexual harassment as a result of the inappropriate spillover of gender roles to the work environment. Sex-role spillover theory, while still widely employed in some fields such as social psychology, assumes that organizations are gender-neutral, asexual environments; gender and sexuality are "smuggled" into organizations by gendered workers. Women workers, in this light, are seen as women first, workers second. In female-dominated jobs, feminine role attributes such as nurturance and (hetero)sexuality spill over into the workplace. When combined with a workplace that emphasizes sexuality, men who interact with women in female-dominated jobs take on the sexual aggressor role, and the result is often sexual harassment.

There are several problems with spillover theory, most of which derive from critiques of sex-role theory in general (Connell 1987; Segal 1990). A sex role is conceptualized as something that exists outside work, a characteristic of individuals, and spills over inappropriately to the workplace. Therefore, sexual harassment is a matter of unprofessional or inappropriate behavior of individuals in the workplace. Organizational responsibility for sexual harassment, then, extends only to punishing the occasional harasser. Consequently, sex-role spillover theory identifies the sex ratio of an occupation as a key contributing factor; jobs that are highly sex segregated are fertile ground for sexual harassment.

However, gender and sexuality construct and are constructed by work relations (see, for example, Acker 1990; Hall 1993; Hochschild 1983; Lorber 1994; Pierce 1995). . . . Schneider (1982, 1985) notes how workers are obligated to enact female receptivity to heterosexual advances, which, in conjunction with their relative lack of power in the work context, creates sexual harassment. . . . A fruitful analysis would use a labor process theory approach to gendered organizations (see West 1990) including a systematic analysis of power and control in the employment relationship as it derives from and results in gender inequality.

In this light, sexual harassment is about the control of women workers, of women as workers and workers as women. Sexual harassment is about particular constructions of gender, especially organizational imperatives to "do gender" in a particular manner (Lorber 1994; West and Zimmerman 1987). Many have implicitly if not explicitly recognized the role of asymmetrical power relations in creating sexual harassment (Fiske and Glicke 1995; Gutek 1985; MacKinnon 1979).

This research explores a form of employment that ties together these themes. Temporary workers are a growing, highly feminized, and relatively powerless group in today's workplace. In the office, temporary workers are often treated as nonpersons, as passive recipients of orders (Henson 1996; Rogers 1995b), much like wait persons or even children. They find themselves interactionally invisible as they do inconspicuous work in conspicuous places, such as filing for hours in a busy hallway (Rogers 1995b). In addition, temporary workers are generally considered to hold the lowest rank in the office, as they are given work and orders by supervisors and coworkers alike. In fact, it is not unusual for permanent coworkers to participate in "dumping" undesirable work on temporary employees (Henson 1996; Rogers forthcoming).

While their low status leaves temporary workers open for many types of workplace abuse, the transitory nature of much temporary work further intensifies this vulnerability. Temporary workers report that people seldom remember their names (referring to them simply as "the temp"), isolate them from office sociability, and often treat them as a piece of furniture (Henson 1996; Rogers 1995b). Thus, temporary workers are objectified and stripped of their personhood, paving the way for poor treatment, including sexual harassment.

Understanding the interplay of gender, sexuality, and power as it relates to the organization of temporary work will enable us to gain a better understanding of some of the shortcomings in theories of sexual harassment. We address the sexual harassment of these workers and attempt to locate structural influences that affect their workplace experience as well as their opportunities for resistance. . . .

It is our contention that temporary work arrangements create an environment that both fosters and tolerates sexual harassment, frequently punishing the harassed rather than the harasser even to a greater extent than in traditional employment relationships. . . . [I]f we consider that temporaries are likely to have the lowest status in an office (virtually everyone is superior to a temporary worker) and to work in a largely female occupation (63 percent of all temporary workers are clerical), it is conceivable that they would be even more likely to be harassed than permanent workers.

Method

This research is based on in-depth interviews and extensive participant observation from two broader studies on temporary clerical work. One of the studies was conducted in Chicago in 1990–91, while the other was conducted in Los Angeles; in 1993–94. In these studies, the subject of sexual harassment was not initially included in the interview guides; both researchers, however, found it to be of concern to the interview subjects. As a research focus, sexual harassment was emergent from the data and gained in importance throughout the course of the research process. In both studies, the researcher questioned the interview subjects about their relationships with coworkers. For example, general questions such as "Who did you work with and what were those relationships like?" elicited stories of sexual harassment. . . . [A]pproximately 40 percent of the respondents found it troublesome enough to mention without being prompted to do so. It is likely that more direct questioning would have uncovered even more sexual harassment.

Together, these two studies yielded 68 in-depth interviews (35 in Chicago and 33 in Los Angeles) ranging from one to three hours in length. Interview subjects included temporary agency personnel and client company representatives, but the majority were temporary clerical workers. All interviews were tape-recorded, transcribed, coded, and analyzed. All names indicated in the body of this article are pseudonyms.

. . . Collectively, the interview subjects had worked in over 40 temporary agencies, with individual tenure in temporary employment ranging from a few months to over 10 years. The data represent a diverse group of African American, Latino, Asian American, and white men and women ranging in age from 20 to 60 years old. . . .

Gendered Worker in a Gendered Job

The clerical sector of temporary employment, like the general full-time clerical sector, is predominantly composed of women (Bureau of Labor Statistics [BLS] 1995; Howe 1986). Historically, this association of temporary work with women's work was reflected in the common inclusion of the infantilizing term *girl* in the names of the earliest temporary agencies (e.g., Kelly Girl, Western Girl, Right Girl). While temporary agencies have formally modernized their names (i.e., Kelly Girl became Kelly Services), the continued popular usage of the outdated names accurately reflects the gendered composition of the temporary workforce. Although more men have been seeking employment through temporary agencies, particularly as industrial temporary workers (Parker 1994), they still make up a relatively small proportion of the clerical temporary workforce. Indeed, a recent survey by the National Association of Temporary Services (1992) estimated that 80 percent of member agency temporaries were women; Belous (1989) estimated that more than 64 percent of the entire temporary workforce are women, and more than 20 percent of the temporary workforce is Black. Furthermore, a recent government survey concluded that "Workers paid by temporary agencies were more likely than workers in traditional arrangements to be women, young, and black" (BLS 1995, 4).

In fact, the gender composition of the temporary workforce leads to the expectation, often the assumption, that temporary workers (as secretaries) are women; the job, in other words, is gendered. . . . Furthermore, the feminized nature of the work is particularly highlighted when others fail to even recognize a male temporary as the secretary, mistaking him for someone with higher organizational status. . . .

The feminized nature of the job, shaped in part by sexualized cultural images of temporary workers, actually requires temporary workers to enact a particular construction of femaleness as part of the job. In addition, temporary agencies' demands for particular physical presentations and requirements for doing deference further highlight the gendered, racialized, and sexualized nature of temporary work.

Doing Difference

West and Fenstermaker (1995) invoke the concept of *doing difference* to explain the production of social inequalities; some of their critics argue that the notion of doing difference, with its emphasis on interaction, obfuscates power relations and relegates structures of inequality to the realm of performance (Collins 1995). . . . We attempt here to forge some of these links through an empirical examination of the structures of inequality in temporary employment and the ways in which temporary workers' interactions are shaped by the gendered expectations of their clients, their agencies, and even themselves.

Although temporary agencies are legally required to operate under equal opportunity employer legislation (i.e., to hire workers without regard to race, sex, or age), temporaries are nevertheless often hired or placed for personal characteristics other than their jobs skills. Even some of the more specific and egregious requests (e.g., for a young, blond woman with great legs) are often honored. One temporary worker overheard the following exchange:

> One guy had gone through like five secretaries in that year and he had temps, different temps, every couple of weeks. And the office manager asked him if he wanted that temp back the following week because she had to contact the agency to arrange it. And I remember he looked out of his office and kind of looked at her legs and [said], "No, she's kind of on the heavy side." So that was it. (Ludy Martinez, 36-year-old Filipina American)

The temporary industry reinforces this emphasis on physical appearance. A 1986 study of the temporary industry reported a disproportionate emphasis on temporaries' physical appearance or "femininity"; a receptionist at one temporary agency reported filing "evaluation cards of temporary worker applicants that had comments like 'homely' and 'stunning' written on them with virtually no mention of office skills" (National Association of Working Women 1986, 28). Occasionally, . . . clients assert their right to control a temporary's personal appearance by filing a formal complaint with the agency. The agency then "counsels" the errant temporary about her or his appearance (or removes her or him from the job):

> And you're expected to dress like Christie Brinkley! Oh, it's ridiculous. I wear nice clean clothes. I'm clean. My body is clean. I have good breath. I mean, I try to look as good as I possibly can. So I get a call from the temp agency at home at seven thirty at night. . . . I was just mortified. Like, "What is it?!" I felt like I was on death row for temps! So she says, "Well, it seems that you're not dressing profession- ally enough. Laura gave me a call." And of course I feel horrible. (Helen Weinberg, 24-year-old white woman)

The demands for a particular gendered (even sexy) physical presentation are not freely chosen based on the personal tastes of the temporary worker; rather, they are recognized as a right of the employer (see also Hall 1993: Paules 1991).

The depoliticized managerial prerogative to con- trol the appearance of temporary workers can also be used to justify racial bias in placing temporary workers.

> Nine out of ten times it's a little blond girl with col- ored eyes. Or somebody with an English accent. Nobody overweight. And if it's a person of color, she's gotta be drop-dead gorgeous. Not just pretty —drop-dead gorgeous. (Regina Mason, 44-year- old Latina)

"Gorgeous" women of color (those beautiful enough to be receptionists) must conform to white notions of female beauty.

Clients and temporary help service personnel also employ racialized notions about workers' capa- bilities: "articulate" workers are white. This racial logic (Hossfeld 1990) reproduces and naturalizes ra- cial inequality.

> I think "articulate" is a code word [for racial prefer- ence] that you can't ever really get called on. You can't say, "Oh you were discriminating." You were just telling them what you need. It's kind of a fine line. There's a lot of clients who are like that. Especially a lot for reception people. (Sonja Griffin, 31-year-old white woman)

Closely related is the tendency to assign back-office temporary assignments to women of color. This ar- rangement shapes interaction and then uses those very interactions to justify the view that people of color cannot "do" front-office work (i.e., white, middle-class sociability).

> But there was one Black woman in our group. And she was sent to like way in the back room on some top floor. Which was not like the corporate floor or whatever. She was put in the back. And she said she gets a lot of crappy . . . gets asked to do things that she doesn't think other people would be asked to do. I was put up front. . . . And then there was a very large white woman who was there. And she, too, was sort of hidden in the back so people wouldn't see her. I'm no beauty queen. But they put me in front, I guess, because I was the white woman. (He- len Weinberg, 24-year-old white woman)

It quickly becomes apparent that the type of femi- ninity one must do in temporary work is white, middle-class, heterosexual femininity. While certain exceptions are made, it is nearly impossible to do this brand of femininity if you are a woman of color. The consequences of the gendered/raced/classed or- ganization of temporary work are a lower paid, back- office job or no job.

Men pose an especially interesting case concern- ing the gendered nature of temporary work. Their presence in female-dominated work has the poten- tial to disrupt gender categories because men who are temporaries fail to live up to normative concep- tions of masculinity by not having a "real job." Therefore, they risk gender assessment. One accom- modation that underscores the gendered nature of temporary work is the popular construction of male temporaries as gay, which neither disrupts the essen- tial nature of gender for the observer nor challenges the dominant/subordinate statuses of male/female. Male temporary workers, heterosexual and gay, were very aware of this construction. . . . As with other men who cross over into women's work (see also Pringle 1988; Williams 1989, 1995), male temporar- ies risk their status as "real" (or at least heterosexual) men. In everyday practice, these gender crossings are assumed to say more about the essential nature of the individual men than the gendered organization of the work.

Male temporary workers' individual failings, when faced with the gender assessment of others, do not stop with questioning their sexual orientation. In addition, their drive, motivation, and competence for (male) career success may be questioned—that is, these are dead-end jobs that no "self-respecting" man would accept. Ironically, the dead-end nature of these jobs is rarely seen as problematic for women.

> I think men get a little less respect if they're temp-
> ing. There's that expectation that they should be like
> career oriented and like moving up in the world and
> being a businessman and moving himself forward
> in business. Where women can do that but it's not
> an expectation. And so I think that, I think that's
> where that Kelly Girl image, that temporaries are
> women, is. I have noticed that there is a certain
> amount, looking down upon. I think that's true of
> temps in general. They're somewhat looked down
> upon. I think the men maybe more. (Albert Baxter,
> 31-year-old white man)

The discussions of male temporaries' masculinity highlight the gendered nature of the work as they struggle with maintaining masculinity in an organizational environment that requires doing femininity.

Doing Deference

Doing deference is a special case of doing gender that demonstrates how organizational imperatives shape interaction that becomes essentialized. Temporaries, like many women workers, . . . are also expected to enact a submissive, deferential, even solicitous stance toward management, coworkers, and clients (Henson 1996). Indeed, temporary agencies demanded that their workers adopt a pleasing demeanor while on the client company's premises. Thus, the proper enactment of gender (even an institutionalized *job flirt* [see Hall 1993]) was conflated with proper job performance and monitored by the temporary agency.

Temporaries, like many service workers, were expected to smile whether or not they were particularly happy. . . . Indeed, temporary workers at an agency

that one of the researchers worked through were instructed to think of themselves as guests rather than laborers engaged in a primarily economic transaction. . . . Drawing on their personal knowledge of behavior appropriate to a well-behaved guest, temporaries were reminded that a polite guest neither challenges nor otherwise risks offending his or her host.

This guest metaphor, however, also enforces passivity by rendering any complaining or self-assertion by temporary workers on assignment as inappropriate: "Please do . . . observe the hours, procedures, and work methods of the customers without criticism" (Welcome to Right Temporaries, Inc. 1989). As the commercial nature of the relationship is obscured by the personal relations fiction, criticisms of the work, including those about abusive or disrespectful treatment, are defined as illegitimate. . . .

Being on one's best behavior, or doing good work, may be interpreted as responding to flirtatious behavior on the job, to perform a kind of job flirt (Hall 1993; MacKinnon 1979). . . . Mary LeMoine described putting up with the "flirtatious" (even harassing) behavior of a client on the job to be gracious:

> And then on the phone I've had men ask me out af-
> ter talking to me. I'm a temporary. And they start
> talking to me. They start these entire conversations.
> I had one man at the bank offer to fly me to San
> Diego to spend the weekend with him. . . . I felt very
> bad about that because in my normal situation . . . if
> someone called me at school and did that, if some-
> one called me at home and did that . . . I wouldn't
> talk to you. You know, you have no place doing this
> to me. *[So why didn't you say that there?]* Because it
> was a bank. Because it was my job. And when I got
> home I felt very bad about it. I should have just said
> that anyway. I just kind of ignored it. And I don't
> think I handled it as well as I should have. (Mary Le-
> Moine, 27-year-old white woman; emphasis added)

Temporary workers, in an effort to conform to the requirements of doing deference, may accept treatment on the job that they would not tolerate in another context.

The extent to which deference was conflated with proper job performance is highlighted by the negative reactions of male temporaries to these demands for subservience and its implicit threat to their sense of masculinity.

> It's a manly thing to be in charge. And men should want to be, supposedly in charge and delegating things. If you're a man and you're being delegated to, it somehow makes you less manly. You know what I'm saying? Whereas it seems to be okay for the person delegating to women. They seem to be okay with that relationship. And the women, maybe they're just projecting that to get by. It seems that they're more okay with that than men are. I guess I'm saying that it makes me feel less of the manly kind of qualities, like I'm in charge, you know. And men should be like takin' meetings and barking orders instead of just being subservient. (Harold Koenig, 29-year-old heterosexual white man)

. . .

Reviewing how the organization of temporary work operates in the daily work lives of temporaries provides us with the opportunity to evaluate the usefulness of sex-role spillover theories. In these examples, gendered (or sexualized) work behavior is not something temporaries freely choose to enact based on their own tastes and preferences. Rather, the low status of temporaries (as secretaries, but lower than secretaries) and the expectations of temporary agencies and clients (which quickly become job requirements) help shape temporary workers' interactions in such a way that their gender (and sexuality) is prominently featured as an aspect of the work. The emphasis placed on temporary workers' physical presentation as well as requirements for doing deference coincides with a particular construction of gender, including heterosexuality and whiteness.

. . . The organization of temporary work, in other words, helps create the gendered workplace. This theoretical stance resonates closely with the gendered organization perspective holding that gender is not something that comes from outside organizations but is constructed and reproduced within them (Acker 1990; Ferguson 1984; Lorber 1994; Williams 1995). Therefore, gendered work behavior (even that which results in sexual harassment) should be understood as constructed within and by gendered workplaces rather than the result of inappropriate sex-role spillover.

. . . We now turn to an analysis of the factors that constrain temporary workers in reporting sexual harassment and the range of temporary workers' responses to sexual harassment.

Factors That Constrain Reporting: The Organization of Vulnerability

The organization of temporary work has a tremendous impact on the extent to which temporary workers find opportunities for resistance. Chief among the organizational constraints are the institutionalization and magnification of asymmetrical power relationships between the agency, client, and temporary worker. These asymmetrical power relationships are exacerbated for temporary workers by the fear of downtime (i.e., inadequate income) and uncertainty about the actual scheduling practices of their agencies.

As employers, most temporary agencies tell their workers to report any kind of problem (such as sexual harassment) to the agency rather than handle it at the work site. At first glance this would seem to benefit the temporary workers, and indeed there is that potential. However, temporary agencies are also supposed to represent the interests of their (paying) clients. One Los Angeles agency counselor, in fact, portrayed these relationships as completely "equal" and "fair": "You have an . . . allegiance not only to the person who's paying you, but you have an allegiance as a responsibility for the applicant that you're sending out" (Sandy Mathers, 28-year-old African American woman).

However, even the agencies themselves recognize that their "natural" alignment is with the client rather than the worker. . . . [A] temporary agency counselor who reported "going to bat" for his temporary felt constrained by the need to maintain client relationships: "But you have to be very careful. This one [incident], I didn't lose a client, but there's been others where you do lose a client" (Manny Avila, 28-year-old Latino). It is almost always easier to replace a complaining temporary worker than an offended client. Therefore, in almost all conflictual circumstances, the client company is favored. . . .

Temporary workers are often very much aware of where their agency's interests lie and their own ultimate dispensability: "You don't have an alliance. If you're a temp you don't have an alliance. And I'm afraid if I complain [to my agency], they'll just throw me off the assignment" (Cindy Carson, 38-year-old white woman).

The agency and the client have tremendous power to determine the terms of work, and the relationship ranges from asymmetrical to unilateral. For example, while client companies enjoy staffing flexibility, terminating the assignment at will and often without notice, individual workers are often at the mercy of both their agency and client assignment supervisors (Henson 1996; Rogers 1995a). Neither the company nor the agency need justify these work schedule changes to temporary workers. In some cases temporaries are replaced rather than just having the assignment cut short. They are seldom advised of the reason for such decisions and may, in fact, not even know that they were replaced.

Temporaries, then, willing and eager to work, often find themselves with time off instead, time off that can be financially catastrophic. This uncertain environment led temporaries to believe that any transgression they committed against their agency, including complaining about abusive treatment, would result in punishment—primarily work deprivation.

> I should have vocalized that [displeasure] more, but I didn't feel like I was really in a position to even say that. Because underneath it all is, if they get pissed at you, they can just not give you work and say, "Oh there's no jobs." (Don Birch, 24-year-old white man)

Temporary workers' fears regarding loss of access to work assignments were not mere paranoia. As we discovered, some temporary agencies do keep records of temporaries who declined assignments to better "direct" work flow. Indeed, one agency counselor said that she gave her temporary workers only "one strike" before they were no longer considered for assignments. The definition of a strike was considerably broad including lateness, asking for higher wages, or complaining about an assignment. More than one agency counselor said that they would not

send out any "prima donnas," and this was defined as people who had complaints about any aspect of the job. . . .

. . . It was not uncommon for temporaries to report tolerating offensive jokes and patently hostile environments to maintain their "steady" assignments:

> I didn't walk out on it and I wish I would have. I was really strapped for money. And that was the office where everybody smoked. And everybody was like, I don't know how to put it . . . constantly making like racial jokes, sexist jokes. There was this guy who was like just this really sleazy sales guy. Like a stereotype. He wore like a plaid suit and slicked-back hair. He smoked a cigar. Hairbrush mustache. And he would come over and he'd just be so rude and so sexist. . . . And I was like, "Oh this is horrible! This is so humiliating! I can't take it anymore." But I stayed . . . I had to. Two weeks. It was a drag. (Pamela O'Connor, 26-year-old white woman)

Regardless of how unpleasant, any work is often better than no work at all to a temporary worker at the limits of his or her budget and without access to traditional social safety nets (e.g., unemployment benefits). As marginal workers with an unsteady flow of income from one week to the next, temporary workers feel financial constraints keenly and make decisions regarding their reactions to harassment in light of those constraints. Any behavior that has the real or perceived potential to displease the agency, including reporting legitimate problems with the assignment, is seen as putting the temporary's future prospects for work in jeopardy.

In this context, it is evident that the reporting of any difficulties, like sexual harassment, can work against a temporary worker's economic interests. . . .

Dilemmas of Resistance

Not surprisingly, most women do not report incidents of sexual harassment. . . . This research draws on an institutional understanding of women's responses to sexual harassment, but more specifically, it examines how a particular organization of work configures power relations to the detriment of sexual harassment victims. Thus, we view the range of responses to sexual harassment as they are shaped by organizational constraints rather than as individual strategies or coping behaviors.

Complain to the Agency

Temporaries are instructed to bring any work-related problems, including sexual harassment, to the attention of their agency rather than the client company. The position of the agency, however, makes bringing complaints directly to the temporary counselors a risky move. Agencies' responses can range from support to passive complicity and even overt complicity:

> They flirt with the applicant . . . oh . . . sexual harassment. I've had applicants call me in tears saying, "This man won't leave me alone. I don't know what to do. He's lookin' down my blouse. He wants to sit next to me and show me how to use the phone. I don't know what to do." Yeah, and it's difficult to say, "Well, grab your purse and leave." Because then your client's calling you and saying, "How dare you." [*What do you tell them?*] It all depends. It all depends. (Sandy Mathers, 28-year-old African American woman)

Agency representatives often infantilize the workers (Rogers 1995a), diminishing the significance of their complaints, their capability to read situations correctly, and their ability to take constructive action. They are seen as hysterical, overreacting, or oversensitive women. . . .

Most temporary workers are keenly aware (or suspect) that their complaints will not be successfully mediated or dealt with by temporary agencies. Even if they have not experienced it directly, many temporaries are able to relay stories about those they know who were not supported by their agency.

With the allegiance of the agency more closely aligned with the client than the temporary worker, . . . [w]hen they recast sexual harassment as flirting or a minor nuisance, they are clearly acting in the interests of their clients. The organization of the relationship among temporaries, clients, and agencies provides the impetus to downplay sexual harassment.

Confront the Harasser

The most direct, but least used, avenue of recourse that the women we interviewed followed was to confront the harasser. Although only one woman reported this type of resistance, it is important to note because she was able to use her position as a higher paying executive temporary secretary as well as her personal connections to the temporary agency to her benefit:

> I know one instance I had to tell the guy, "If you do that to me again, not only will your wife and human resources know, but I think I will have to tell the chairman." . . . I told the guy I was gonna tell his wife because she and I had become quite chatty friends on the phone. (Ludy Martinez, 36-year-old Filipina American)

In this case, the harassment stopped before the assignment ended. . . . Ludy was partly successful because this was a longer term executive secretarial assignment in which she had the opportunity to get to know her supervisor's wife and was able to use that relationship as a threat. Such opportunities for resistance are less likely to occur in the lower paying filing or data entry positions in which temporaries are more isolated. Even more important, at this assignment, Ludy was working through an agency managed and owned by a personal friend. This personal connection gave her more assurance that if she were to make a complaint, she would not be risking her job and the complaint would be taken seriously. However, Ludy's situation is unique, and as the exception, her experience further demonstrates the unequal alignment of power in temporary employment.

Ignore the Harasser

The most common response of temporaries to sexual harassment, like other women workers, was to ignore the harasser, take no action at all, and put up with it (Gruber 1989; Schneider 1991). For example, Kara Wallace and Pamela O'Connor described experiencing patently offensive workplace behavior that many would define as hostile environment sexual harassment, yet they chose to reframe it as "nothing major":

> Well, nobody actually physically . . . sexual harassment like that. But I would always bump into, "Honey, Baby, Sweetheart." And that place that the sleazy sales guy was . . . he would like come over and tell me dirty jokes and stuff. And I was like, "My life sucks" at that point. (Pamela O'Connor, 26-year-old white woman)

Particularly with verbal or hostile environment harassment, temporary workers were likely to ignore the harassment or fail to label it as sexual harassment at all.

Temporary workers who ignored the sexual harassment frequently explained their response (or lack thereof) in terms of the transitory nature of the work. In other words, while they noted that their temporary status may have contributed to or fostered the harassment, they also ignored it because "it's only temporary." The time required to file a complaint and procedurally follow through on it would exceed the time of the assignment:

> He'd say, "Hey, why don't you wear a shorter skirt and that would make it more interesting for us." And then later he offered me breakfast . . . and some other things. And I thought, you know, I just don't think this is the way I want to go. And it's because you're a temp. (Cheryl Hansen, 23-year-old white woman)

> There has been the usual harassment type stuff that they figure it's a temp. She'll be gone next week. And I didn't make the typical woman-type fuss . . . and that was due to temping more than anything else. . . . It wasn't worth my time filing a complaint anymore because I was a temp and I was gonna be out of there and could refuse to work for that man and everything. (Ludy Martinez, 36-year-old Filipina American).

By focusing on the short duration of the assignment, temporary workers down-play the meaning of sexual harassment. The result is that none of the women we interviewed filed a formal complaint about the sexual harassment they experienced on their assignments. These women's status as temporary seemed to work against filing a formal complaint. They felt that people would see them as making a big deal out of nothing or making the "typical woman-type fuss"; after all, it's only temporary.

While this strategy may help individual temporaries in individual situations, when we consider that several of our interview subjects were sexually harassed on a number of assignments, this strategy seldom works in the long run. . . . Being sexually harassed seems to be a routine part of being a temporary worker. Furthermore, chronic harassers have easy access to a supply of potential victims in the event the person they are harassing decides to leave the assignment.

Abandon the Assignment or Agency

One way that temporaries have resisted abusive treatment, including sexual harassment, is by finding an "acceptable" reason to leave or not renew a particular assignment. For instance, several of our subjects acknowledged that once they had a difficult assignment, they turned down further assignments at that company. . . . A second acceptable reason for refusing work was that they had something else to do other than work that week. Here, temporary workers play on the misconception that most temporaries are seeking flexible hours to combine either work and family or work and some other interest. . . . These strategies, however, can have serious financial repercussions for temporary workers who, contrary to industry propaganda, are unlikely to be working for pin money (Henson 1996; Martella 1991; Parker 1994). Furthermore, an unfortunate side effect of co-opting the flexibility myth is that it perpetuates the misconception.

Another avenue of recourse is for the temporary worker to move to another agency. . . . This strategy seems to be reserved for extreme circumstances because leaving one agency may require developing relationships with new agencies (Henson 1996; Rogers 1995a). . . . Once the switch is made, there is no guarantee that problems will not arise with the new agency since the structure of the relationships between temporary worker, agency, and client favors the link between the agency and the client.

Conclusions and Suggestions

Temporary clerical work is a highly feminized and disempowering form of employment. The low status, depersonalization, and objectification of temporary workers fosters an environment in which poor treatment including sexual harassment is likely. The gendered (raced, classed, and even heterosexualized) organization of the work is highlighted in numerous ways. . . . Therefore, the metaphor of doing gender (or race or class) can speak to oppression and exploitation when combined with a gendered organizations approach. Similarly, sexual harassment can now be seen as an outgrowth of the organization of work rather than merely the result of individual actions or even sex-role spillover in the workplace.

Possibilities for resistance to sexual harassment are severely constrained (although not eliminated) as temporary clerical work shifts more power to the employers. Judith Lorber (1994) notes that economically marginal women and men cannot be the ones to solve the problem of constant sexual harassment. The temporary employment relationship creates marginal workers as it aligns the agencies' interests with the clients' interests while pushing the demands and rights of the worker into the background. In this environment, proving harassment, damages, or even that the agency had knowledge of the harassment becomes quite difficult. Many workers tolerate harassment or other abuses rather than risk losing access to future assignments and income through the agency.

. . . Temporaries must be provided with more power, either through industry regulation or worker-owned agencies, to address sexual harassment problems without fearing economic reprisals. Yet, this would not eliminate sexual harassment from temporaries' workplaces. Organizational imperatives to do gender contribute to the problems of sexual harassment, and at the same time, they naturalize and solidify inequalities.

REFERENCES

Acker, Joan. 1990. Hierarchies, jobs, bodies: A theory of gendered organizations. *Gender & Society* 4:139–58.

Alliance Against Sexual Coercion. 1981. Organizing against sexual harassment. *Radical America* 15 (July): 17–34.

Belous, Richard S. 1989. *The contingent economy: The growth of the temporary, part-time and subcontracted workforce.* Washington, DC: National Planning Association.

Benet, Mary Kathleen. 1972. *Secretary: Enquiry into the female ghetto.* London: Sidgwick & Johnson.

Benson, Donna J., and Gregg E. Thompson. 1982. Sexual harassment on a university campus: The confluence of authority relations, sexual interest and gender stratification. *Social Problems* 29:236–51.

Bureau of Labor Statistics (BLS). 1995. *Handbook of labor statistics.* Washington, DC: U.S. Government Printing Office.

Callaghan, Polly, and Heidi Hartmann. 1991. *Contingent work.* Washington, DC: Economic Policy Institute.

Carothers, Suzanne C., and Peggy Crull. 1984. Contrasting sexual harassment in female- and male-dominated occupations. In *My troubles are going to have trouble with me,* edited by Karen Brodkin Sacks and Dorothy Remy. New Brunswick, NJ: Rutgers University Press.

Castro, June 1993. Disposable workers. *Time,* 29 March, 43–7.

Collins, Patricia Hill. 1995. Symposium on West and Fenstermaker's "Doing Difference." *Gender & Society* 4:491–4.

Connell, R. W. 1987. *Gender and power.* Stanford, CA: Stanford University Press.

Crull, Peggy. 1987. Searching for the causes of sexual harassment: An examination of two prototypes. In *Hidden aspects of women's work,* edited by Christine Bose, Roslyn Feldberg, and Natalie Sokoloff. New York: Praeger.

Ferguson, Kathy E. 1984. *The feminist case against bureaucracy.* Philadelphia: Temple University Press.

Fiske, Susan T., and Peter Glicke. 1995. Ambivalence and stereotypes cause sexual harassment: A theory with implications for organizational change. *Journal of Social Issues* 1:97–115.

Fitzgerald, L. F. 1990. Sexual harassment: The definition and measurement of a construct. In *Ivory power: Sexual harassment on campus,* edited by M. A. Paludi. Albany: State University of New York Press.

Giuffre, Patti A., and Christine Williams. 1994. Boundary lines: Labeling sexual harassment in restaurants. *Gender & Society* 8:378–401.

Golden, Lonnie, and Eileen Appelbaum. 1992. What was driving the 1982–88 boom in temporary employment: Preferences of workers or decisions and power of employers? *Journal of Economics and Society* 51: 473–94.

Gottfried, Heidi. 1991. Mechanisms of control in the temporary help service industry. *Sociological Forum* 6:699–713.

Gruber, James E. 1989. How women handle sexual harassment: A literature review. *Sociology and Social Research* 74 (October): 3–7.

Gruber, James E., and Lars Bjorn. 1982. Blue collar blues: The sexual harassment of women autoworkers. *Work and Occupations* 9:271–98.

Gutek, Barbara. 1985. *Sex and the workplace: The impact of sexual behavior and harassment on women, men, and organizations.* San Francisco: Jossey-Bass.

Hall, Elaine J. 1993. Smiling, deferring, and flirting: Doing gender by giving "good service." *Work and Occupations* 20:452–71.

Henson, Kevin D. 1996. *Just a temp.* Philadelphia: Temple University Press.

Hochschild, Arlie Russell. 1983. *The managed heart: Commercialization of human feeling.* Berkeley: University of California Press.

Hossfeld, Karen. 1990. Their logic against them: Contradictions in sex, race, and class in Silicon Valley. In *Women workers and global restructuring,* edited by Kathryn Ward, Ithaca, NY: ILR.

Howe, Wayne J. 1986. Temporary help workers: Who they are, what jobs they hold? *Monthly Labor Review* 109 (November): 45–7.

Jensen, Inger W., and Barbara A. Gutek. 1982. Attributions and assignment of responsibility in harassment. *Sex Roles* 25:19–23.

Kanber, Rosabeth Moss. 1977. *Men and women of the corporation.* New York: Basic Books.

Kilborn, Peter T. 1993. New jobs lack the old security in time of "disposable workers": The 40-hour week, with benefits, is in decline. *New York Times,* 15 March.

Leidner, Robin. 1993. *Fast food, fast talk: Service work and the routinization of everyday life.* Berkeley: University of California Press.

Livingston, Joy A. 1982. Responses to sexual harassment on the job: Legal, organizational, and individual actions. *Journal of Social Issues* 38:5–22.

Lorber, Judith. 1994. *Paradoxes of gender.* New Haven, CT: Yale University Press.

MacKinnon, Catharine A. 1979. *Sexual harassment of working women: A case of sex discrimination.* New Haven and London: Yale University Press.

———. 1987. *Feminism unmodified: Discourses on life and law.* Cambridge, MA: Harvard University Press.

Martella, Maureen. 1991. *Just a temp: Expectations and experiences of women clerical temporary workers.* Washington, DC: U.S. Department of Labor Women's Bureau.

Maypole, D. 1986. Sexual harassment of social workers at work: Injustice within? *Social Work* 31 (1): 29–34.

Morrow, Lance. 1993. The temping of America. *Time,* 29 March, 40–1.

National Association of Temporary Services. 1992. *Report on the temporary help services industry.* Alexandria, VA: DRI/McGraw Hill.

National Association of Working Women. 1986. *Working at the margins: Part-time and temporary workers in the United States.* Cleveland, OH: National Association of Working Women.

Paludi, Michele A., and Richard B. Barickman. 1991. *Academic and workplace sexual harassment: A resource manual.* Albany: State University of New York Press.

Parker, Robert E. 1994. *Flesh peddlers and warm bodies: The temporary help industry and its workers.* New Brunswick, NJ: Rutgers University Press.

Paules, Greta Foff. 1991. *Dishing it out: Power and resistance among waitresses in a New Jersey restaurant.* Philadelphia: Temple University Press.

Pierce, Jennifer. 1995. *Gender trials: Emotional lives in contemporary law firms.* Berkeley: University of California Press.

Pringle, Rosemary. 1988. *Secretaries talk: Sexuality, power, and work.* New York: Verso.

Ragins, Belle Rose, and Teri A. Scandura. 1995. Antecedents and work-related correlates of reported sexual harassment: An empirical investigation of competing hypotheses. *Sex Roles* 7/8:429–55.

Right Temporaries, Inc. 1989. *Welcome to Right Temporaries, Inc.* Organizational brochure. Chicago.

Rogers, Jackie Krasas. 1995a. It's only temporary?: The reproduction of race and gender inequality in temporary clerical employment. Ph.D. diss., University of Southern California, Los Angeles.

———. 1995b. Just a temp: Experience and structure of alienation in temporary clerical employment. *Work and Occupations* 2:137–66.

———. Forthcoming. Deskilled and devalued: Changes in the labor process in temporary clerical work. In *Rethinking the labor process,* edited by M. Wardell, P. Meiksins, and T. Steiger. Albany: State University of New York Press.

Rollins, Judith. 1985. *Between women: Domestics and their employers.* Philadelphia: Temple University Press.

Romero, Mary. 1992. *Maid in the U.S.A.* New York: Routledge.

Schneider, Beth E. 1982. Consciousness about sexual harassment among heterosexual and lesbian women workers. *Journal of Social Issues* 38 (4): 75–98.

———. 1985. Approaches, assaults, attractions, affairs: Policy implications of the sexualization of the workplace. *Population Research and Policy Review* 4:93–113.

———. 1991. Put up and shut up: Workplace sexual assaults. *Gender & Society* 5:533–48.

Segal, Lynne. 1990. *Slow motion: changing men, changing masculinities.* New Brunswick, NJ: Rutgers University Press.

West, Candace, and Sarah Fenstermaker. 1995. Doing Difference. *Gender & Society* 1:8–37.

West, Candace, and Don H. Zimmerman. 1987. Doing Gender. *Gender & Society* 1:125–51.

West, Jackie. 1990. Gender and the labor process. In *Labor process theory,* edited by D. Knights and H. Willmott. London: Macmillan.

Williams, Christine. 1989. *Gender differences at work: Women and men in nontraditional occupations.* Berkeley: University of California Press.

———. 1995. *Still a man's world: Men who do women's work.* Berkeley: University of California Press.

Woods, James. 1993. *The corporate closet: The professional lives of gay men in America.* New York: Free Press.

READING 58

Maid to Order
The Politics of Other Women's Work

Barbara Ehrenreich

In line with growing class polarization, the classic posture of submission is making a stealthy comeback. "We scrub your floors the old-fashioned way," boasts the brochure from Merry Maids, the largest of the residential-cleaning services that have sprung up in the last two decades, "on our hands and knees." This is not a posture that independent "cleaning ladies" willingly assume—preferring, like most people who clean their own homes, the sponge mop wielded from a standing position. In her comprehensive 1999 guide to homemaking, *Home Comforts,* Cheryl Mendelson warns: "Never ask hired housecleaners to clean your floors on their hands and knees; the request is likely to be regarded as degrading." But in a society in which 40 percent of the wealth is owned by 1 percent of households while the bottom 20 percent reports negative assets, the degradation of others is readily purchased. Kneepads entered American political discourse as a tool of the sexually subservient, but employees of Merry Maids, The Maids Interna-

tional, and other corporate cleaning services spend hours every day on these kinky devices, wiping up the drippings of the affluent.

I spent three weeks in September 1999 as an employee of The Maids International in Portland, Maine, cleaning, along with my fellow team members, approximately sixty houses containing a total of about 250 scrubbable floors—bathrooms, kitchens, and entryways requiring the hands-and-knees treatment. It's a different world down there below knee level, one that few adults voluntarily enter. Here you find elaborate dust structures held together by a scaffolding of dog hair; dried bits of pasta glued to the floor by their sauce; the congealed remains of gravies, jellies, contraceptive creams, vomit, and urine. Sometimes, too, you encounter some fragment of a human being: a child's legs, stamping by in disgust because the maids are still present when he gets home from school; more commonly, the Joan & David–clad feet and electrolyzed calves of the female homeowner. Look up and you may find this person staring at you, arms folded, in anticipation of an overlooked stain. In rare instances she may try to help in some vague, symbolic way, by moving the cockatoo's cage, for example, or apologizing for the leaves shed by a miniature indoor tree. Mostly, though, she will not see you at all and may even sit down with her mail at a table in the very room you are cleaning, where she would remain completely unaware of your existence unless you were to crawl under that table and start gnawing away at her ankles.

Housework, as you may recall from the feminist theories of the Sixties and Seventies, was supposed to be the great equalizer of women. Whatever else women did—jobs, school, child care—we also did housework, and if there were some women who hired others to do it for them, they seemed too privileged and rare to include in the theoretical calculus. All women were workers, and the home was their workplace—unpaid and unsupervised, to be sure, but a workplace no less than the offices and factories men repaired to every morning. If men thought of the home as a site of leisure and recreation—a "haven in a heartless world"—this was to ignore the invisible female proletariat that kept it cozy and humming. We were on the march now, or so we imagined, united against a society that devalued our labor even as it waxed mawkish over "the family" and "the home." Shoulder to shoulder and arm in arm, women were finally getting up off the floor.

In the most eye-catching elaboration of the home-as-workplace theme, Marxist feminists Maria Rosa Dallacosta and Selma James proposed in 1972 that the home was in fact an economically productive and significant workplace, an extension of the actual factory, since housework served to "reproduce the labor power" of others, particularly men. The male worker would hardly be in shape to punch in for his shift, after all, if some woman had not fed him, laundered his clothes, and cared for the children who were his contribution to the next generation of workers. If the home was a quasi-industrial workplace staffed by women for the ultimate benefit of the capitalists, then it followed that "wages for housework" was the obvious demand.

But when most American feminists, Marxist or otherwise, asked the Marxist question *cuibono?* they tended to come up with a far simpler answer—men. If women were the domestic proletariat, then men made up the class of domestic exploiters, free to lounge while their mates scrubbed. In consciousness-raising groups, we railed against husbands and boyfriends who refused to pick up after themselves, who were unaware of housework at all, unless of course it hadn't been done. The "dropped socks," left by a man for a woman to gather up and launder, joined lipstick and spike heels as emblems of gender oppression. And if, somewhere, a man had actually dropped a sock in the calm expectation that his wife would retrieve it, it was a sock heard round the world. Wherever second-wave feminism took root, battles broke out between lovers and spouses over sticky countertops, piled-up laundry, and whose turn it was to do the dishes.

The radical new idea was that housework was not only a relationship between a woman and a dust bunny or an unmade bed; it also defined a relationship between human beings, typically husbands and wives. This represented a marked departure from the more conservative Betty Friedan, who, in *The Feminine Mystique,* had never thought to enter the male sex into the equation, as either part of the housework problem or part of an eventual solution. She raged against a society that consigned its educated women to what she saw as essentially janitorial chores, beneath "the abilities of a woman of average or normal human intelligence," and, according to unidentified studies she cited, "peculiarly suited to the capacities of feeble-minded girls." But men are virtually exempt from housework in *The Feminine Mystique*—why drag them down too? At one point she even disparages a "Mrs. G.," who "somehow couldn't get her housework done before her husband came home at night and was so tired then that he had to do it." Educated women would just have to become more efficient so that housework could no longer "expand to fill the time available."

Or they could hire other women to do it—an option approved by Friedan in *The Feminine Mystique* as well as by the National Organization for Women, which she had helped launch. At the 1973 congressional hearings on whether to extend the Fair Labor Standards Act to household workers, NOW testified on the affirmative side, arguing that improved wages and working conditions would attract more women to the field, and offering the seemingly self-contradictory prediction that "the demand for household help inside the home will continue to increase as more women seek occupations outside the home." One NOW member added, on a personal note: "Like many young women today, I am in school in order to develop a rewarding career for myself. I also have a home to run and can fully conceive of the need for household help as my free time at home becomes more and more restricted. Women know [that] housework is dirty, tedious work, and they are willing to pay to have it done. . . ." On the aspirations of the women paid to do it, assuming that at least some of them were bright enough to entertain a few, neither Friedan nor these members of NOW had, at the time, a word to say.

So the insight that distinguished the more radical, post-Friedan cohort of feminists was that when we talk about housework, we are really talking, yet again, about power. Housework was not degrading because it was manual labor, as Friedan thought, but because it was embedded in degrading relationships and inevitably served to reinforce them. To make a mess that another person will have to deal with—the dropped socks, the toothpaste sprayed on the bathroom mirror, the dirty dishes left from a late-night snack—is to exert domination in one of its more silent and intimate forms. One person's arrogance—or indifference, or hurry—becomes another person's occasion for toil. And when the person who is cleaned up after is consistently male, while the person who cleans up is consistently female, you have a formula for reproducing male domination from one generation to the next.

Hence the feminist perception of housework as one more way by which men exploit women or, more neutrally stated, as "a symbolic enactment of gender relations." An early German women's liberation cartoon depicted a woman scrubbing on her hands and knees while her husband, apparently excited by this pose, approaches from behind, unzipping his fly. Hence, too, the second-wave feminists'

revulsion at the hiring of maids, especially when they were women of color: At a feminist conference I attended in 1980, poet Audre Lorde chose to insult the all-too-white audience by accusing them of being present only because they had black housekeepers to look after their children at home. She had the wrong crowd; most of the assembled radical feminists would no sooner have employed a black maid than they would have attached Confederate flag stickers to the rear windows of their cars. But accusations like hers, repeated in countless conferences and meetings, reinforced our rejection of the servant option. There already were at least two able-bodied adults in the average home—a man and a woman—and the hope was that, after a few initial skirmishes, they would learn to share the housework graciously.

A couple of decades later, however, the average household still falls far short of that goal. True, women do less housework than they did before the feminist revolution and the rise of the two-income family: down from an average of 30 hours per week in 1965 to 17.5 hours in 1995, according to a July 1999 study by the University of Maryland. Some of that decline reflects a relaxation of standards rather than a redistribution of chores; women still do two thirds of whatever housework—including bill paying, pet care, tidying, and lawn care—gets done. The inequity is sharpest for the most despised of household chores, cleaning: in the thirty years between 1965 and 1995, men increased the time they spent scrubbing, vacuuming, and sweeping by 240 percent—all the way up to 1.7 hours per week—while women decreased their cleaning time by only 7 percent, to 6.7 hours per week. The averages conceal a variety of arrangements, of course, from minutely negotiated sharing to the most clichéd division of labor, as described by one woman to the *Washington Post:* "I take care of the inside, he takes care of the outside." But perhaps the most disturbing finding is that almost the entire increase in male participation took place between the 1970s and the mid-1980s. Fifteen years after the apparent cessation of hostilities, it is probably not too soon to announce the score: in the "chore wars" of the Seventies and Eighties, women gained a little ground, but overall, and after a few strategic concessions, men won.

Enter then, the cleaning lady as *dea ex machina,* restoring tranquillity as well as order to the home. Marriage counselors recommend her as an alternative to squabbling, as do many within the cleaning industry itself. A Chicago cleaning woman quotes one of her clients as saying that if she gives up the service, "my husband and I will be divorced in six months." When the trend toward hiring out was just beginning to take off, in 1988, the owner of a Merry Maids franchise in Arlington, Massachusetts, told the *Christian Science Monitor,* "I kid some women. I say, 'We even save marriages. In this new eighties period you expect more from the male partner, but very often you don't get the cooperation you would like to have. The alternative is to pay somebody to come in. . . .'" Another Merry Maids franchise owner has learned to capitalize more directly on housework-related spats; he closes between 30 and 35 percent of his sales by making follow-up calls Saturday mornings, which is "prime time for arguing over the fact that the house is a mess." The micro-defeat of feminism in the household opened a new door for women, only this time it was the servants' entrance.

In 1999, somewhere between 14 and 18 percent of households employed an outsider to do the cleaning, and the numbers have been rising dramatically. Mediamark Research reports a 53 percent increase, between 1995 and 1999, in the number of households using a hired cleaner or service once a month or more, and Maritz Marketing finds that 30 percent of the people who hired help in 1999 did so for the first time that year. Among my middle-class, professional women friends and acquaintances, including some who made important contributions to the early feminist analysis of housework, the employment of a maid is now nearly universal. This sudden emergence of a servant class is consistent with what some economists have called the "Brazilianization" of the American economy: We are dividing along the lines of traditional Latin American societies—into a tiny overclass and a huge underclass, with the latter available to perform intimate household services for the former. Or, to put it another way, the home, or at least the affluent home, is finally becoming what radical feminists in the Seventies only imagined it was—a true "workplace" for women and a tiny, though in-creasingly visible, part of the capitalist economy. And the question is: As the home becomes a workplace for someone else, is it still a place where you would want to live?

. . .

The trend toward outsourcing the work of the home seems, at the moment, unstoppable. Two hundred years ago women often manufactured soap, candles, cloth, and clothing in their own homes, and the complaints of some women at the turn of the twentieth century that they had been "robbed by the removal of creative work" from the home sound pointlessly reactionary today. Not only have the skilled crafts, like sewing and cooking from scratch, left the home but many of the "white collar" tasks are on their way out, too. For a fee, new firms such as the San Francisco–based Les Concierges and Cross It Off Your List in Manhattan will pick up dry cleaning, baby-sit pets, buy groceries, deliver dinner, even do the Christmas shopping. With other firms and individuals offering to buy your clothes, organize your financial files, straighten out your closets, and wait around in your home for the plumber to show up, why would anyone want to hold on to the toilet cleaning?

Absent a major souring of the economy, there is every reason to think that Americans will become increasingly reliant on paid housekeepers and that this reliance will extend ever further down into the middle class. For one thing, the "time bind" on working parents shows no sign of loosening; people are willing to work longer hours at the office to pay for the people—house-cleaners and baby-sitters—who are filling in for them at home. Children, once a handy source of household help, are now off at soccer practice or SAT prep classes; grandmother has relocated to a warmer climate or taken up a second career. Furthermore, despite the fact that people spend less time at home than ever, the square footage of new homes swelled by 33 percent between 1975 and 1998, to include "family rooms," home entertainment rooms, home offices, bedrooms, and often bathrooms for each family member. By the third quarter of 1999, 17 percent of new homes were larger than 3,000 square feet, which is usually considered the size threshold for household help, or the point at which a house becomes unmanageable to the people who live in it.

One more trend impels people to hire outside help, according to cleaning experts such as Aslett and Mendelson: fewer Americans know how to clean or even to "straighten up." I hear this from professional women defending their decision to hire a maid: "I'm just not very good at it myself" or "I wouldn't really know where to begin." Since most of us learn to clean from our parents (usually our mothers), any diminution of cleaning skills is transmitted from one generation to another, like a gene that can, in the appropriate environment, turn out to be disabling or lethal. Upper-middle-class children raised in the servant economy of the Nineties are bound to grow up as domestically incompetent as their parents and no less dependent on people to clean up after them. Mendelson sees this as a metaphysical loss, a "matter of no longer being physically centered in your environment." Having cleaned the rooms of many overly privileged teenagers in my stint with The Maids, I think the problem is a little more urgent than that. The American overclass is raising a generation of young people who will, without constant assistance, suffocate in their own detritus.

If there are moral losses, too, as Americans increasingly rely on paid household help, no one has been tactless enough to raise them. Almost everything we buy, after all, is the product of some other person's suffering and miserably underpaid labor. I clean my own house (though—full disclosure—I recently hired someone else to ready it for a short-term tenant), but I can hardly claim purity in any other area of consumption. I buy my jeans at The Gap, which is reputed to subcontract to sweatshops. I tend to favor decorative objects no doubt ripped off, by their purveyors, from scantily paid Third World craftspersons. Like everyone else, I eat salad greens just picked by migrant farm workers, some of them possibly children. And so on. We can try to minimize the pain that goes into feeding, clothing, and otherwise provisioning ourselves—by observing boycotts, checking for a union label, etc.—but there is no way to avoid it altogether without living in the wilderness on berries. Why should house-

work, among all the goods and services we consume, arouse any special angst?

And it does, as I have found in conversations with liberal-minded employers of maids, perhaps because we all sense that there are ways in which housework is different from other products and services. First, in its inevitable proximity to the activities that compose "private" life. The home that becomes a workplace for other people remains a home, even when that workplace has been minutely regulated by the corporate cleaning chains. Someone who has no qualms about purchasing rugs woven by child slaves in India or coffee picked by impoverished peasants in Guatemala might still hesitate to tell dinner guests that, surprisingly enough, his or her lovely home doubles as a sweatshop during the day. You can eschew the chain cleaning services of course, hire an independent cleaner at a generous hourly wage, and even encourage, at least in spirit, the unionization of the housecleaning industry. But this does not change the fact that someone is working in your home at a job she would almost certainly never have chosen for herself—if she'd had a college education, for example, or a little better luck along the way—and the place where she works, however enthusiastically or resentfully, is the same as the place where you sleep.

It is also the place where your children are raised, and what they learn pretty quickly is that some people are less worthy than others. Even better wages and working conditions won't erase the hierarchy between an employer and his or her domestic help, because the help is usually there only because the employer has "something better" to do with her time, as one report on the growth of cleaning services puts it, not noticing the obvious implication that the cleaning person herself has nothing better to do with her time. In a merely middle-class home, the message may be reinforced by a warning to the children that that's what they'll end up doing if they don't try harder in school. Housework, as radical feminists once proposed, defines a human relationship and, when unequally divided among social groups, reinforces preexisting inequalities. Dirt, in other words, tends to attach to the people who remove it— "garbagemen" and "cleaning ladies." Or, as cleaning entrepreneur Don Aslett told me with some bitterness—and this is a successful man, chairman of the board of an industrial cleaning service and frequent television guest—"The whole mentality out there is that if you clean, you're a scumball."

One of the "better" things employers of maids often want to do with their time is, of course, spend it with their children. But an underlying problem with post-nineteenth-century child-raising, as Deirdre English and I argued in our book *For Her Own Good* years ago, is precisely that it is unmoored in any kind of purposeful pursuit. Once "parenting" meant instructing the children in necessary chores; today it's more likely to center on one-sided conversations beginning with "So how was school today?" No one wants to put the kids to work again weeding and stitching; but in the void that is the modern home, relationships with children are often strained. A little "low-quality time" spent washing dishes or folding clothes together can provide a comfortable space for confidences—and give a child the dignity of knowing that he or she is a participant in, and not just the product of, the work of the home.

There is another lesson the servant economy teaches its beneficiaries and, most troubling, the children among them. To be cleaned up after is to achieve a certain magical weightlessness and immateriality. Almost everyone complains about violent video games, but paid housecleaning has the same consequence-abolishing effect: you blast the villain into a mist of blood droplets and move right along; you drop the socks knowing they will eventually levitate, laundered and folded, back to their normal dwelling place. The result is a kind of virtual existence, in which the trail of litter that follows you seems to evaporate all by itself. Spill syrup on the floor and the cleaning person will scrub it off when she comes on Wednesday. Leave *The Wall Street Journal* scattered around your airplane seat and the flight attendants will deal with it after you've deplaned. Spray toxins into the atmosphere from your factory's smokestacks and they will be filtered out eventually by the lungs of the breathing public. A servant economy breeds callousness and solipsism in the served, and it does so all the more effectively when the service is performed close up and routinely in the place where they live and reproduce.

Individual situations vary, of course, in ways that elude blanket judgment. Some people—the elderly and disabled, parents of new babies, asthmatics who require an allergen-free environment—may well need help performing what nursing-home staff call the "ADLs," or activities of daily living, and no shame should be attached to their dependency. In a more generous social order, housekeeping services would be subsidized for those who have health-related reasons to need them—a measure that would generate a surfeit of new jobs for the low-skilled people who now clean the homes of the affluent. And in a less gender-divided social order, husbands and boyfriends would more readily do their share of the chores.

However we resolve the issue in our individual homes, the moral challenge is, put simply, to make work visible again: not only the scrubbing and vacuuming but all the hoeing, stacking, hammering, drilling, bending, and lifting that goes into creating and maintaining a livable habitat. In an ever more economically unequal culture, where so many of the affluent devote their lives to such ghostly pursuits as stock-trading, image-making, and opinion-polling, real work—in the old-fashioned sense of labor that engages hand as well as eye, that tires the body and directly alters the physical world—tends to vanish from sight. The feminists of my generation tried to bring some of it into the light of day, but, like busy professional women fleeing the house in the morning, they left the project unfinished, the debate broken off in midsentence, the noble intentions unfulfilled. Sooner or later, someone else will have to finish the job.

READING 59

Prostitution
A Difficult Issue for Feminists

Priscilla Alexander

Why Prostitution?

Prostitution exists, at least in part, because of the subordination of women in most societies. This subordination is reflected in the double standard of sexual behavior for men and women, and is carried out in the discrepancy between women's and men's earning power.

. . .

The specific reasons that prostitutes have given for choosing their work, as revealed in the studies of Dr Jennifer James in Seattle, have included money, excitement, independence, and flexibility, in roughly that order. First person accounts by women in the sex industry often mention economics as a major factor, coupled with rebellion at the restricted and tedious jobs available to them.[1] Dr James and others have also revealed a high incidence of child sexual abuse in the life histories of prostitutes: around fifty percent for adult prostitutes; seventy-five to eighty percent for juvenile prostitutes.[2] The traditional psychoanalytic explanation for the relationship between childhood sexual abuse and later involvement in prostitution is that the child has come to view sex as a commodity, and that she is masochistic. The connection many prostitutes report, however, is that the involvement in prostitution is a way of taking back control of a situation in which, as children, they had none. Specifically, many have reported that the first time they ever felt powerful was the first time they 'turned a trick.'[3] . . . It is important to remember that many women with no history of sexual assault become prostitutes (and many survivors of child sexual abuse never work as prostitutes), so the relationship between prostitution and early sexual trauma is far from clear.

A number of authors have also looked at the fact that men and women do not appear to view sex in the same way and that men as a class seem to view sex as power, with rape being the most extreme form of the use of sex as power. Women as a class tend to see sex as nurture, and this generalization is subject to great individual differences. Prostitution also involves an equation of sex with power: for the man / customer, the power consists of his ability to 'buy' access to any number of women; for the woman / prostitute, the power consists of her ability to set the terms of her sexuality, and to demand substantial payment for her time and skills. Thus, prostitution is one area in which women have traditionally and openly viewed sex as power.

. . .

The Law

. . . In 1949, the United Nations passed a convention paper that called for the decriminalization of prostitution and the enforcement of laws against those who exploit women and children in prostitution. The paper, which was read to the United Nations General Assembly by Eleanor Roosevelt, has been ratified by more than fifty countries, but not the United States. Most European countries have 'decriminalized' prostitution by removing laws which prohibit 'engaging' in an act of prostitution; although most have retained the laws against 'soliciting' 'pimping' 'pandering' 'running a disorderly house' and 'transporting a woman across national boundaries for the purposes of prostitution.' The United States, on the other hand, has retained the laws prohibiting the act of prostitution as well (except in rural counties in the state of Nevada with populations less than 250,000, which have the option of allowing legal, regulated brothels). Prostitution is also prohibited outright in Japan, and in many Asian countries, including those in which 'sex tourism' is a major including. It is decriminalized in the [former] Soviet Union, but women who work as prostitutes there are arrested for violating the law against being a parasite (i.e., not having a legally-recognized job).

In addition to laws prohibiting soliciting or engaging in an act of prostitution, and the related issues of pimping and pandering, or procuring, the United States has laws that bar anyone who has ever been a prostitute from entering this country, remaining in this country as a resident, or becoming a citizen. Deportation proceedings on those grounds were instituted in the early 1980s against a French woman who managed a brothel in Nevada, even though the business was perfectly legal.

[Former] West Germany, in addition to decriminalizing the act itself, has developed a variety of approaches ranging from a tightly controlled, single-zone brothel system in Hamburg, to a laissez-faire, open-zone system in [former] West Berlin. Denmark has repealed most of the laws restricting the right of prostitutes to work, and has passed laws designed to help women who want to get out of prostitution.

In Holland, after a prostitute was murdered a few years ago, the government decided it might be a good idea to examine the laws and to see if there weren't ways to reduce the isolation of prostitutes. The government has been working closely with the feminist prostitutes' rights movement—the Red Thread, an organization of prostitutes and ex-prostitutes, and the Pink Thread, a feminist solidarity group. In late 1986, the Dutch government allocated funds to provide the Red Thread with three employees and an office.

The countries with the most restrictive legal systems, including the United States and many countries in Southeast Asia, have the most problems with violence against prostitutes (and women perceived to be *like* prostitutes), thefts associated with prostitution, pimping (especially brutal pimping), and the involvement of juveniles. Conversely, the countries with the least restrictive measures, including the Netherlands, [former] West Germany, Sweden and Denmark, have the least problems. No country, however, is totally safe for prostitutes. The stigma still isolates the women, and the remaining laws still serve to perpetuate that stigma, rather than to dispel it and truly legitimize the women who work as prostitutes.
. . .

Who Benefits from the System

It is difficult to see how anyone benefits from the present system. At the time the United States prohibition was enacted, it was at least partly in response to feminist concerns about the abuse of women and children involved in prostitution. After an extensive muckraking campaign in the press, exposing the 'horrors' of brothel prostitution, there was much pressure to close brothels.

. . .

While the enactment of laws before World War I prohibiting prostitution, pimping, running brothels, transporting women across state lines for 'immoral' purposes, etc., did nothing to reduce prostitution, it did have other effects. Before prohibition, most brothels were owned and managed by women, most of whom had been prostitutes themselves. After the legal brothels were closed, the brothel business went underground and was headed by a male, criminal hierarchy that continues. Most massage parlors and escort services today are owned by men. Closing the brothels also forced many women to work on the streets, subjecting them to greater risks of violence. The basic conditions of women's lives, which caused some of them to choose to work as prostitutes, did not change.

For most of recorded history, prostitution has been set up for the benefit of the customer, no matter what system was in place. The stigma enforced by the prohibition in America is also enforced by systems of regulation that require prostitutes to dress differently or to live and work in special districts, or deny them the right to relationships. The health schemes that require prostitutes to have weekly checks for sexually transmitted diseases are similarly designed to benefit the customer, since there is no equivalent requirement that customers be checked to protect the prostitute, or regulation requiring brothels to provide condoms, disability insurance, workers' compensation, or health insurance. What constantly amazes me is that there is so little variation in the way nations deal with prostitution, under the law, even where there is enormous variation in just about every other aspect of society.

. . .

Options for Change

. . .

There are two main alternatives to prohibition, generally termed decriminalization and legalization. In Europe, decriminalization is sometimes referred to as abolition, and refers to the abolition or repeal of the prostitution laws. However, the term abolition is also used by some activists, including Kathleen Barry in the United States, and The Abolitionist Society in Europe, to refer to the long-term goal of eliminating all prostitution.

Ideally, decriminalization would mean the repeal of all existing criminal codes regarding voluntary prostitution, per se, between consenting adults, including mutually voluntary relationships between prostitutes and agents or managers (pimp/prostitute relationships), and non-coercive pandering (serving as a go-between). It could involve no new legislation to deal specifically with prostitution, but merely leave the businesses which surround prostitution subject to general civil, business, and professional codes that exist to cover all businesses. Such problems as fraud, theft, negligence, collusion, and force would be covered by existing penal code provisions. Alternatively, existing sections of the penal code could be modified to specifically address the issue of coercion, and business codes could be enacted to require management to provide sick leave and vacation, as well as disability, workers' compensation, and health insurance. Decriminalization of prostitution and the regulation of pimping and pandering, it seems to me, offers the best chance for women who are involved in prostitution to gain some measure of control over their work. It would make it easier to prosecute those who abuse prostitutes, either physically or economically, because the voluntary, non-abusive situations would be left alone.

Decriminalization allows for the possibility that the lives of prostitutes can become less dangerous.

For one thing, under a comprehensive decriminalization scheme, it would be possible for prostitutes to join unions and engage in collective bargaining in order to improve their working conditions. It would also be possible for prostitutes to form professional associations, and develop codes of ethics and behavior designed to reduce the problems involved in prostitution as it now exists. Finally, it would be possible for experienced prostitutes to train new prostitutes, so that their first experiences would be less dangerous.

Legalization, on the other hand, has generally meant a system of control of the *prostitute,* with the state regulating, taxing, and/or licensing whatever form of prostitution is legalized, leaving all other forms illegal, without any concern for the prostitute herself. Traditional regulation has often involved the establishment of special government agencies to deal with prostitution.

The brothels in Nevada, for example, are licensed and regulated by the government, and the women who work in them are registered as prostitutes with the sheriff. As discussed earlier, they are severely restricted in their movements outside of the brothel. Independent prostitution is illegal, as is prostitution in massage parlors, for escort services, and of course, street prostitution. The women generally work fourteen-hour shifts, on three-week (seven days a week) tours of duty, during which they may see ten or fifteen customers a day, or more. They have little or no right to refuse a customer (although the management tries to keep out potentially dangerous customers), and they have not been allowed to protect themselves from sexually transmitted diseases by using condoms (although at least two houses in Nevada are now all-condom houses, to prevent AIDS). Because of the grueling aspects of the long work shifts, many of the women use drugs (to help them stay awake and alert or to help them sleep) supplied by the same doctor who performs regular health checks.

Before much can be done to help prostitutes, the laws must be changed. The transaction between prostitute and client must be removed from the purview of the law, and the other laws dealing with prostitution must be reevaluated, and repealed or changed as necessary. Since street prostitution is singled out as 'the problem' it is important for residents, business people, and prostitutes to get together to iron out compromises that take into consideration the right of prostitutes to work without harassment, and the right of other residents and businesses to go about their lives and work without harassment.

In the meantime, until prostitution has been decriminalized, the non-coercive managers regulated, and those who use fraud and force prosecuted, pressure must be put on police and sheriff's departments, district attorneys, public defenders, bail bondspeople, judges, and pretrial diversion and probation programs to improve the treatment of persons arrested under these archaic and oppressive laws.

Should the laws in this country be changed as a result of pressure from men, including well-intentioned civil liberties attorneys, or pornographers with their own motives, there is a good chance that a brothel system will be imposed or that high-class prostitution will be decriminalized and working class prostitution (i.e., street prostitution) will remain a crime, as was proposed by the New York Bar Association in 1985. Unless there is a strong voice pointing out the oppressiveness of brothel systems, both to the women in such a system and to their sisters outside, most people in this country will assume that such a system works to the benefit of all concerned. In a brothel system, prostitution will be kept off the street, and out of the sight of children, they assume, and all in all, it would just be better, safer, and cleaner. The problem is that none of those assumptions are correct, and in exchange for a false sense of security, we would get a punitive system.

Whatever you or I think of prostitution, women have the right to make up their own minds about whether or not to work as prostitutes, and under what terms. They have the right to work as freelance workers, as do nurses, typists, writers, doctors, and so on. They also have the right to work for an employer, a third party who can take care of administration and management problems. They have the right to relationships outside of work, including relationships in which they are the sole support of the other person, so long as the arrangement is acceptable to both parties. They have the right to raise children. They have the right to a full, human existence. As feminists, we have to make that clear. We have to end separation of women into whores and madonnas.

Our experience with the Equal Rights Amendment and with abortion—not to mention sexual assault, domestic violence, sexual harassment, sex discrimination, lesbian/gay rights, and the rest of the issues on our agenda—should tell us that if we leave the issues up to male legislators and pressure groups, the resulting legislation will not be in our interests. The same is true with prostitution.

Finally, the onus for the abuses that co-exist with illegal prostitution must be put on the system that perpetuates those abuses, and no longer on the prostitutes who are abused. If we ensure that prostitution remains under the control of the prostitutes—and not in the hands of pimps, customers, and police—then we will have given the prostitutes the power, and the support, to change that institution. We will all benefit.[4]

NOTES

1. See Claude Jaget, *Prostitutes, Our Life*, Bristol, Eng.: Falling Wall Press, 1980.
2. See Jennifer James, 'Prostitutes and prostitution', in Edward Sagarin and Fred Montanino (eds), *Deviants: Voluntary Actors in a Hostile World*, General Learning Press, Scott, Foresman & Co., 1977; Mimi H., Silbert, PhD, principal investigator, *Sexual Assault of Prostitutes*, San Francisco: Delancey Street Foundation, 1981.
3. See Millet, *The Prostitution Papers*, Jaget, *Prostitutes*.
4. In 1984, the total number of arrests declined, for the first time since COYOTE began keeping track in 1973, to 112,200. There are many possible explanations: unemployment reached its peak in 1982, and has been declining ever since; heavy crackdowns in most cities have encouraged those who could move their business off the street or, retire; fear of AIDS may be discouraging new women from beginning to work as prostitutes. Gloria Lockett, Co-Director of COYOTE, who worked on the street for many of the seventeen years she was a prostitute, says that the percentage of street prostitutes in San Francisco who use IV drugs has increased sharply, which may mean that it is women who don't use drugs who have been able to leave the street or change their occupation.

READING 60

The Globetrotting Sneaker

Cynthia Enloe

Four years after the fall of the Berlin Wall marked the end of the Cold War, Reebok, one of the fastest growing companies in United States history, decided that the time had come to make its mark in Russia. Thus it was with considerable fanfare that Reebok's executives opened their first store in downtown Moscow in July 1993. A week after the grand opening, store managers described sales as well above expectations.

Reebok's opening in Moscow was the perfect post-Cold War scenario: commercial rivalry replacing military posturing; consumerist tastes homogenizing heretofore hostile peoples; capital and managerial expertise flowing freely across newly porous state borders. Russians suddenly had the "freedom" to spend money on U.S. cultural icons like athletic footwear, items priced above and beyond daily subsistence: at the end of 1993, the average Russian earned the equivalent of $40 a month. Shoes on display were in the $100 range. Almost 60 percent of single parents, most of whom were women, were living in poverty. Yet in Moscow and Kiev, shoe promoters had begun targeting children, persuading them to pressure their mothers to spend money on stylish, Western sneakers. And as far as strategy goes, athletic shoe giants have, you might say, a good track record. In the U.S. many inner-city boys who see basketball as a "ticket out of the ghetto" have become convinced that certain brand-name shoes will give them an edge.

But no matter where sneakers are bought or sold, the potency of their advertising imagery has made it easy to ignore this mundane fact: Shaquille O'Neal's Reeboks are stitched by someone; Michael Jordan's Nikes are stitched by someone; so are your roommate's, so are your grandmother's. Those someones are women, mostly Asian women who are supposed to believe that their "opportunity" to make sneakers for U.S. companies is a sign of their country's progress—just as a Russian woman's chance to spend two month's salary on a pair of shoes for her child allegedly symbolizes the new Russia.

As the global economy expands, sneaker executives are looking to pay women workers less and less, even though the shoes that they produce are capturing an ever-growing share of the footwear market. By the end of 1993, sales in the U.S. alone had reached $11.6 billion. Nike, the largest supplier of athletic footwear in the world, posted a record $298 million profit for 1993—earnings that had nearly tripled in five years. And sneaker companies continue to refine their strategies for "global competitiveness" —hiring supposedly docile women to make their shoes, changing designs as quickly as we fickle customers change our tastes, and shifting factories from country to country as trade barriers rise and fall.

The logic of it all is really quite simple; yet trade agreements such as the North American Free Trade Agreement (NAFTA) and the General Agreement of Tariffs and Trade (GATT) are, of course, talked about in a jargon that alienates us, as if they were technical matters fit only for economists and diplomats. The bottom line is that all companies operating overseas depend on trade agreements made between their own governments and the regimes ruling the countries in which they want to make or sell their products. Korean, Indonesian, and other women workers around the world know this better than anyone. They are tackling trade politics because they have learned from hard experience that the trade deals their governments sign do little to improve the lives of workers. Guarantees of fair, healthy labor practices, of the rights to speak freely and to organize independently, will usually be left out of trade pacts—and women will suffer. The recent passage of both NAFTA and GATT ensures that a growing number of private companies will now be competing across borders without restriction. The result? Big business will step up efforts to pit working women in industrialized countries against much lower-paid working women in

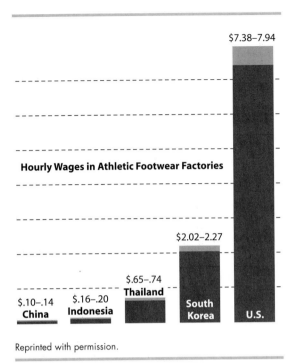

$7.38–7.94

Hourly Wages in Athletic Footwear Factories

$2.02–2.27

$.65–.74
Thailand

$.10–.14
China

$.16–.20
Indonesia

South Korea

U.S.

Reprinted with permission.

"developing" countries, perpetuating the misleading notion that they are inevitable rivals in the global job market.

All the "New World Order" really means to corporate giants like athletic shoemakers is that they now have the green light to accelerate long-standing industry practices. In the early 1980s, the field marshals commanding Reebok and Nike, which are both U.S.-based, decided to manufacture most of their sneakers in South Korea and Taiwan, hiring local women. L. A. Gear, Adidas, Fila, and Asics quickly followed their lead. In short time, the coastal city of Pusan, South Korea, became the "sneaker capital of the world." Between 1982 and 1989 the U.S. lost 58,500 footwear jobs to cities like Pusan, which attracted sneaker executives because its location facilitated international transport. More to the point, South Korea's military government had an interest in suppressing labor organizing, and it had a comfortable military alliance with the U.S. Korean women also seemed accepting of Confucian philosophy, which measured a woman's morality by her willingness to work hard for her family's well-being and to

acquiesce to her father's and husband's dictates. With their sense of patriotic duty, Korean women seemed the ideal labor force for export-oriented factories.

U.S. and European sneaker company executives were also attracted by the ready supply of eager Korean male entrepreneurs with whom they could make profitable arrangements. This fact was central to Nike's strategy in particular. When they moved their production sites to Asia to lower labor costs, the executives of the Oregon-based company decided to reduce their corporate responsibilities further. Instead of owning factories outright, a more efficient strategy would be to subcontract the manufacturing to wholly foreign-owned—in this case, South Korean—companies. Let them be responsible for workers' health and safety. Let them negotiate with newly emergent unions. Nike would retain control over those parts of sneaker production that gave its officials the greatest professional satisfaction and the ultimate word on the product: design and marketing. Although Nike was following in the footsteps of garment and textile manufacturers, it set the trend for the rest of the athletic footwear industry.

But at the same time, women workers were developing their own strategies. As the South Korean prodemocracy movement grew throughout the 1980s, increasing numbers of women rejected traditional notions of feminine duty. Women began organizing in response to the dangerous working conditions, daily humiliations, and low pay built into their work. Such resistance was profoundly threatening to the government, given the fact that South Korea's emergence as an industrialized "tiger" had depended on women accepting their "role" in growing industries like sneaker manufacture. If women reimagined their lives as daughters, as wives, as workers, as citizens, it wouldn't just rattle their employers; it would shake the very foundations of the whole political system.

At the first sign of trouble, factory managers called in government riot police to break up employees' meetings. Troops sexually assaulted women workers, stripping, fondling, and raping them "as a control mechanism for suppressing women's engagement in the labor movement," reported Jeong-Lim Nam of Hyosung Women's University in Taegu. It didn't work. It didn't work because the feminist activists in groups like the Korean Women Workers Association

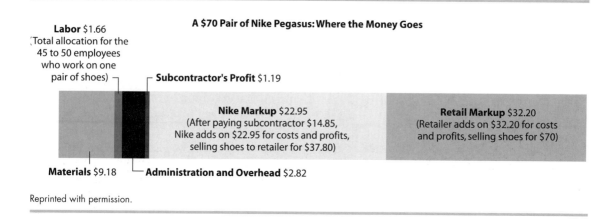

A $70 Pair of Nike Pegasus: Where the Money Goes

Labor $1.66
(Total allocation for the 45 to 50 employees who work on one pair of shoes)

Subcontractor's Profit $1.19

Nike Markup $22.95
(After paying subcontractor $14.85, Nike adds on $22.95 for costs and profits, selling shoes to retailer for $37.80)

Retail Markup $32.20
(Retailer adds on $32.20 for costs and profits, selling shoes for $70)

Materials $9.18

Administration and Overhead $2.82

Reprinted with permission.

(KWWA) helped women understand and deal with the assaults. The KWWA held consciousness-raising sessions in which notions of feminine duty and respectability were tackled along with wages and benefits. They organized independently of the male-led labor unions to ensure that their issues would be taken seriously, in labor negotiations and in the pro-democracy movement as a whole.

The result was that women were at meetings with management, making sure that in addition to issues like long hours and low pay, sexual assault at the hands of managers and health care were on the table. Their activism paid off: in addition to winning the right to organize women's unions, their earnings grew. In 1980, South Korean women in manufacturing jobs earned 45 percent of the wages of their male counterparts; by 1990, they were earning more than 50 percent. Modest though it was, the pay increase was concrete progress, given that the gap between women's and men's manufacturing wages in Japan, Singapore, and Sri Lanka actually *widened* during the 1980s. Last but certainly not least, women's organizing was credited with playing a major role in toppling the country's military regime and forcing open elections in 1987.

Without that special kind of workplace control that only an authoritarian government could offer, sneaker executives knew that it was time to move. In Nike's case, its famous advertising slogan—"Just Do It"—proved truer to its corporate philosophy than its women's "empowerment" ad campaign, designed to rally women's athletic (and consumer) spirit. In re-

sponse to South Korean women workers' new-found activist self-confidence, the sneaker company and its subcontractors began shutting down a number of their South Korean factories in the late 1980s and early 1990s. After bargaining with government officials in nearby China and Indonesia, many Nike subcontractors set up shop in those countries, while some went to Thailand. China's government remains nominally Communist; Indonesia's ruling generals are staunchly anti-Communist. But both are governed by authoritarian regimes who share the belief that if women can be kept hard at work, low paid, and unorganized, they can serve as a magnet for foreign investors.

Where does all this leave South Korean women—or any woman who is threatened with a factory closure if she demands decent working conditions and a fair wage? They face the dilemma confronted by thousands of women from dozens of countries. The risk of job loss is especially acute in relatively mobile industries; it's easier for a sneaker, garment, or electronics manufacturer to pick up and move than it is for an automaker or a steel producer. In the case of South Korea, poor women had moved from rural villages into the cities searching for jobs to support not only themselves, but parents and siblings. The exodus of manufacturing jobs has forced more women into the growing "entertainment" industry. The kinds of bars and massage parlors offering sexual services that had mushroomed around U.S. military bases during the Cold War have been opening up across the country.

But the reality is that women throughout Asia are organizing, knowing full well the risks involved. Theirs is a long-term view; they are taking direct aim at companies' nomadic advantage, by building links among workers in countries targeted for "development" by multinational corporations. Through sustained grassroots efforts, women are developing the skills and confidence that will make it increasingly difficult to keep their labor cheap. . . .

Indonesian workers' efforts to create unions independent of governmental control were a surprise to shoe companies. Although their moves from South Korea have been immensely profitable [see chart], they do not have the sort of immunity from activism that they had expected. In May 1993, the murder of a female labor activist outside Surabaya set off a storm of local and international protest. Even the U.S. State Department was forced to take note in its 1993 worldwide human rights report, describing a system similar to that which generated South Korea's boom 20 years earlier: severely restricted union organizing, security forces used to break up strikes, low wages for men, lower wages for women—complete with government rhetoric celebrating women's contribution to national development.

Yet when President Clinton visited Indonesia last November, he made only a token effort to address the country's human rights problem. Instead, he touted the benefits of free trade, sounding indeed more enlightened, more in tune with the spirit of the post-Cold War era than do those defenders of protectionist trading policies who coat their rhetoric with "America first" chauvinism. But "free trade" as actually being practiced today is hardly *free* for any workers—in the U.S. or abroad—who have to accept the Indonesian, Chinese, or Korean workplace model as the price of keeping their jobs.

The not-so-new plot of the international trade story has been "divide and rule." If women workers and their government in one country can see that a sneaker company will pick up and leave if their labor demands prove more costly than those in a neighbor country, then women workers will tend to see their neighbors not as regional sisters; but as competitors who can steal their precarious livelihoods. Playing women off against each other is, of course, old hat. Yet it is as essential to international trade politics as is the fine print in GATT.

But women workers allied through networks like the Hong Kong-based Committee for Asian Women are developing their own post-Cold War foreign policy, which means addressing women's needs: how to convince fathers and husbands that a woman going out to organizing meetings at night is not sexually promiscuous; how to develop workplace agendas that respond to family needs; how to work with male unionists who push women's demands to the bottom of their lists; how to build a global movement.

These women refuse to stand in awe of the corporate power of the Nike or Reebok or Adidas executive. Growing numbers of Asian women today have concluded that trade politics have to be understood by women on their own terms. . . . If women in Russia and Eastern Europe can challenge Americanized consumerism, if Asian activists can solidify their alliances, and if U.S. women can join with them by taking on trade politics—the post-Cold War sneaker may be a less comfortable fit in the 1990s.

NOTE

This article draws from the work of South Korean scholars Hyun Sook Kim, Seung-kyung Kim, Katherine Moon, Seungsook Moon, and Jeong-Lim Nam.

DISCUSSION QUESTIONS FOR CHAPTER EIGHT

1. How are systems of inequality evident in women's work inside the home?

2. How do women experience sexism in the paid labor force? How does racism shape the ways women experience sexism in the paid labor force? Have you had experiences of discrimination in the workplace?

3. Why has legislation requiring equal pay and prohibiting discrimination failed to bring about equality for women in the workforce?

4. How has the perception of certain work as feminine affected women's work, both inside and outside the home?

5. What changes do you think need to occur to create equitable systems of work for all women?

SUGGESTIONS FOR FURTHER READING

Fletcher, Joyce K. *Disappearing Acts: Gender, Power, and Relational Practice at Work.* Cambridge, MA: MIT Press, 1999.

Hertz, Rosanna, and Nancy L. Marshall, eds. *Working Families: The Transformation of the American Home.* Berkeley: University of California Press, 2001.

Meyer, Madonna Harrington. *Care Work: Gender, Labor, and the Welfare State.* New York: Routledge, 2000.

Neville, Kathleen. *Internal Affairs: The Abuse of Power, Sexual Harassment, and Hypocrisy in the Workplace.* New York: McGraw-Hill, 1999.

Williams, Joan. *Unbending Gender: Why Family and Work Conflict and What to Do About It.* New York: Oxford University Press, 1999.

CHAPTER NINE

Women Confronting and Creating Culture

Although literature and the arts remain important cultural forms in the twenty-first century, various forms of popular culture—television, movies, rock music, magazines, the Internet—also play a significant role in reflecting, reinforcing, and sometimes subverting the dominant systems and ideologies that help shape gender. Popular cultural forms in particular are very seductive; they reflect and create societal needs, desires, anxieties, and hopes through consumption and participation. As emphasized in Chapter 5, popular culture plays a huge role in setting standards of beauty and encouraging certain bodily disciplinary practices. Popular culture *is* culture for many people; the various forms pop culture takes help shape identity and guide people's understandings of themselves and one another.

Popular culture provides stories and narratives that shape our lives and identities. They give us pleasure at the end of a long day and enable us to take our minds off work or other anxieties. In this regard, some scholars have suggested that popular culture regulates society by "soothing the masses," meaning that energy and opposition to the status quo is redirected in pursuit of the latest in athletic shoes or tickets to an award-winning movie. Of course, popular culture creates huge multi-million-dollar industries that themselves regulate society by providing markets for consumption, consolidating power and status among certain groups and individuals. For example, in 1999, the world's largest media company, Time Warner, was acquired by the largest online company, America Online (AOL), for $162 billion in stock. Time Warner owns CNN, HBO, *Time, People,* and *Sports Illustrated* magazines, and the Warner Bros. movie, television, and music properties. This came after another merger of CBS Corporation and Viacom Inc. These mergers consolidate resources across various technologies and help form powerful conglomerates that control the flow of information to the public.

The Internet is also transforming society, making personal computers a necessity for communication and entertainment. Also increasing at a tremendous rate is the amount of pornography available on the Internet. Although providing new opportunities for making money and helping people connect across wide geographical expanses, the Internet has also encouraged a further widening of the gap between the "haves" (those with the wealth to acquire the necessary computer, modem, Internet service provider, high-speed or wireless connection, DVD player, rewritable CD-ROM, and the list goes on) and the "have-nots" (those who, due to lack of access to the technology, are further disadvantaged). When it comes to new electronic technologies, we find that, again, it is a field overwhelmingly dominated by men, illustrating how the tangle of various privileges works to encourage and maintain power in society. Although there are exceptions, women generally have been less interested in those technologies and fields of expertise that have been coded as masculine. With the increased number of computers in the school and in the home, however, many girls are growing up expecting to use computers and these technologies in their environments. There will most likely be very interesting developments in this area as the century progresses.

TELEVISION

Television is one of the most influential forms of media because it is so pervasive and its presence is taken for granted in most households in the United States. Television has changed family life because it encourages passive interaction, replacing alternative family interaction. In addition, television is a visual medium that broadcasts multiple images on a continual basis. These images come to be seen as representing the real world and influence people's understanding of others and the world around them. This is especially significant for children because it is estimated that most children, on the average, watch far more television than is good for them. Of course, the range and quality of television shows vary, and a case can be made for the benefits of educational television. Unfortunately, educational programming is only a small percentage of television viewing. It is estimated, for example, that by the time children reach their mid-teens, they might have watched more than 13,000 violent deaths on television. They learn messages about gender, about race, about class, and certainly about looks. Television is one of the major ways that children learn social norms, roles, and values.

Advertising sponsors control the content of most commercial television. During male sporting events, for example, there are commercials for beer, cars, electronic products, Internet commerce, and other products targeted at a male audience. During daytime soap operas or evening family sitcoms, on the other hand, commercials are aimed at women and focus on beauty and household products. As a result, commercial sponsors have enormous influence over the content of television programming. If they want to sell a certain product, they are unlikely to air the commercial during a feature that could be interpreted as criticizing such products or consumerism generally. In this way, commercial sponsors shape television content.

Television messages about gender tend to be very traditional. In fact, the assumed differences between the genders very often drive the plot of television programming. The format of shows is also gendered. For example, daytime soap operas focus on relationships and family and employ rather fragmented narratives with plots weaving around without closure

LEARNING ACTIVITY:
TALKING ABOUT TALK SHOWS

Watch several television talk shows. Keep a journal describing the topic of the show, the guests, and the commercial sponsors. How would you characterize the host? What do you notice about the interactions among host, guests, and audience? In what ways does gender operate in the shows? Do you think the shows are in any way empowering for the guests, audience members, or television viewers? How do you think these shows reflect either dominant or subordinate American cultures? How do you think these shows contribute to public discourse?

Reprinted with permission.

or resolution, enabling women to tune in and out as they go about multiple tasks. Scholars have pointed out that these shows reconcile women to the fragmented nature of their every-day lives and to male-dominated interpersonal relationships generally. In other words, soap operas, produced with a female viewing audience in mind, help enforce gendered social re-lations. Other scholars argue that these shows enable women viewers to actively critique bla-tant male-dominated situations in ways that help them reflect on their own lives. Jane M. Shattuc makes this point in "The Oprahification of America" by claiming that daytime tel-evision talk shows are both sensational commercialism and a new forum for political de-bate, especially for women.

A similar analysis can be made of evening family sitcoms. These shows are funny and entertaining because they are relatively predictable. The family or work group is made up of characters with distinct personalities and recognizable habits; each week this family is thrown into some kind of crisis, and the plot of the show is to resolve that crisis back to situ-ation as usual. For the most part, the messages are typical in terms of gender, race, class, and other differences, and they often involve humor that denigrates certain groups of people and ultimately maintains the status quo. Some sitcoms, however, do revolve around conflict between groups. These include social classes in the *Beverly Hillbillies* or *Frasier,* between women and men in *I Love Lucy, Home Improvement, Seinfeld,* or *Friends,* and between chil-dren and adults in *Family Ties* or *Growing Pains.* Although these shows model the status quo, they also offer opportunities for modeling critique and resistance. When Ellen De-Generes's lesbianism became an issue for viewers and sponsors of her show *Ellen,* people be-gan addressing the issue, and many criticized the homophobic reactions of some sponsors.

Increasingly, we are seeing shows and advertisements that resist the usual gendered representations, or at least show them with a new twist. Changes in society's views of gen-der have made sponsors realize that they have a new marketing niche. Often, unfortunately, these new representations involve the same old package tied up in new ways; typically they involve women and men resisting some of the old norms while keeping most intact. For example, although women are starting to be shown as competent, strong, athletic, and in control of their lives rather than ditsy housewives or sex symbols, they still are very physically attractive and preoccupied with men and relationships. An increased visibility of larger-sized women in some advertising and in catalogs (although often "large" is size 12 or 14: a very "normal" size for U.S. women) has come about as a result of the capitalist-driven need to create a new marketing niche and sell clothing to large women as well as from pressures from fat women and the women's movement. In addition, there are performers such as Roseanne Barr who actively resist gendered expectations and cultural constructions of "appropriate" body size in their work. Jennifer Reed writes about Roseanne in her essay, "Roseanne: A 'Killer Bitch' for Generation X."

THE MOVIES

In her groundbreaking work on cinema, Laura Mulvey identifies the "male gaze" as a primary motif for understanding gender in filmmaking. Mulvey argues that movies are essentially made through and for the male gaze and fulfill a voyeuristic desire for men to look at women as objects. Viewers are encouraged to "see" the movie through the eyes of the male protagonist who carries the plot forward. Some feminist scholars have suggested the possibility for "subversive gazing" by viewers who refuse to gaze the way filmmakers expect and by making different kinds of movies.

Probably the best genre of film in which to observe gender is the romantic comedy or romantic drama. These films are packed with subtle and not too subtle notions of gender, and they are very seductive in the way that they offer fun entertainment. For example, *Pretty Woman* is a contemporary retelling of the Cinderella story, in which a young woman waits for her Prince Charming to rescue her from her undesirable situation. In this case, the prostitute-with-a-heart-of-gold is swept away in a white limousine by the older rich man who procured her services and then fell in love with her. Other types of films are also revealing in terms of norms about gender. Slasher films and horror movies are often spectacular in terms of their victimization of women. The killers in these movies, such as Norman Bates in the classic *Psycho,* are often sexually disturbed and hound and kill women who arouse them. In Norman Bates's case, it was his dysfunctional, demanding mother who pushed him into such psychosis. This is also the subtext of other films like *The Texas Chainsaw Massacre* movies and *Motel Hell.* Often it is sexually active couples who are killed, either after sex or in anticipation of it. The killer usually watches, as in *Halloween II,* as he impersonates the male lover before he then kills the female partner. Although both women and men claim to be entertained by these films, it is important to talk about the messages they portray about men, about women, and about the normalization of violence.

Pornography is an extreme example of the male gaze and the normalization of violence against women (discussed in Chapter 10). With its print media counterpart, pornography extends the sexualization and objectification of women's bodies for entertainment. In pornographic representations, women are often reduced to body parts and are shown deriving pleasure from being violated and dominated. Additionally, racism intersects with sexism in pornography, and African American women in particular are often portrayed in especially demeaning and animalistic ways. Although many feminists, ourselves included, oppose

JANET AND SUSAN'S CHICK FLICK PICKS

One of the results of the feminist movement has been the growing number of films about women that do not follow the same old scripts about women either falling in love (as do the usual and popular romantic comedy "chick flicks") or being killed. These films explore women's lives and relationships more realistically or at least posit resourceful women who do not need to be rescued by a man. Very often these films are made by independent producers, and rarely do they achieve the commercial success of standard-script movies. Here we've listed some of our favorite "chick flicks" that you may not have seen. In these movies, women are strong, smart, and independent, and, if they do "get a man," it's on their own terms. Watch at least one of these movies and compare its representation of women to the representation of women in the recent blockbusters you've seen.

• *Thelma & Louise* The first of the "feminist-buddy" films, *Thelma & Louise* follows the journey of two friends who start out for a fun weekend vacation and end up dealing with the ugly consequences of unexpected violence.

• *Strangers in Good Company* A busload of elderly women get stranded in the Canadian wilderness. As they work out their own rescue, they get to know one another as complex, fascinating individuals.

• *I've Heard the Mermaids Singing* A klutzy "person-Friday" gets a part-time job as a clerical worker in an art gallery run by a lesbian, on whom she develops a crush. Through her misadventures, she and the gallery director gain entry into each other's worlds.

• *Bagdad Café* A German businesswoman finds herself stranded in the Mojave Desert after her husband leaves her beside the road. She stumbles upon a run-down café, where she becomes involved with its offbeat patrons.

• *Shirley Valentine* A middle-aged English housewife travels to Greece without her husband and finds a new lease on life and on her relationship.

• *The Incredibly True Adventures of Two Girls in Love* Two high school girls come together across social classes to experience first love. This funny, gentle movie very effectively normalizes relationships between women.

• *Antonia's Line* On the day she decides to die, 90-year-old Antonia recalls her unconventional life and the wide variety of relationships between women that have characterized it.

• *Bhaji on the Beach* A group of ethnic Indian women living in England take a bus outing to the seaside resort of Blackpool. Their differences and their bonding are focal as they spend their day at the beach.

• *Women on the Verge of a Nervous Breakdown* This comedy of errors follows the intersecting lives of a film dubber, her ex-lover, his crazed ex-mistress, his new lover, his son, and his son's girlfriend, who find the importance of love in the midst of misadventure.

LEARNING ACTIVITY:
WOMEN MAKE MOVIES

Very often the subjects that are important to women are ignored in popular filmmaking or are distorted by stereotypes or the male gaze. Despite lack of funding and major studio backing, independent women filmmakers worldwide persist in documenting the wide range of women's lives and experiences.

Visit the website of Women Make Movies at *www.wmm.com.* Browse the catalog and identify movies made by filmmakers outside the United States. What themes do they pursue? Are these themes also common in American women filmmakers' movies? In what ways do they also express cultural distinctions? How do these films differ from mainstream box office releases? Why is an organization like Women Make Movies important?

pornography, others, especially those described as "sex radicals," feel that pornography can be a form of sexual self-expression for women. They argue that women who participate in the production of pornography are taking control of their own sexuality and are profiting from control of their own bodies. In "Confessions of a Feminist Porno Star," Nina Hartley argues that as a porn star she is challenging dominant social norms that restrict women's sexuality.

Some of the more pervasive and lasting gender images in American culture derive from Walt Disney feature films such as *Cinderella, Sleeping Beauty,* and *The Little Mermaid.* Disney heroines live, however, not only on the big screen but also as dolls in little girls' rooms, on their sheets and curtains, on their lunchboxes, and even on their t-shirts. In "Construction of the Female Self: Feminist Readings of the Disney Heroine," Jill Henke, Diane Umble, and Nancy Smith argue that, on the whole, Disney characters reflect White, heterosexual, middle-class, patriarchal norms. Later representations, such as Pocahontas, still rely on these norms, even as they attempt to be more inclusive of diversity.

As women have made societal gains, Hollywood filmmaking has also changed and become more inclusive of new norms about gender. In some instances, as in *Terminator 2: Judgment Day* and *Aliens,* women are shown to be powerful, although in both movies the heroines are beautiful, fit, and often scantily clad. In other instances, especially when women have more control over the film as in a number of independent movies, films become more reflective of women's actual lives and concerns.

CONTEMPORARY MUSIC AND MUSIC VIDEOS

Popular music like rock, grunge, punk, heavy metal, techno, and rap are contemporary cultural forms targeted at youth. Often this music offers resistance to traditional cultural forms and contains a lot of teenage angst attractive to young people who are figuring out who they are in relation to their parents and other adults in positions of authority in their lives. In this way, such music serves as contemporary resistance and can work to mobilize people politically. Certainly music functions to help youth shape notions of identity. The various musi-

TEST YOUR KNOWLEDGE OF
WOMEN AND ROCK 'N' ROLL

1. Who first recorded "Hound Dog"?
   a. Elvis Presley b. Big Mama Thornton c. Billie Holiday d. Hank Williams

2. Who made the first blues recording ("Crazy Blues" and "That Thing Called Love")
   in 1920?
   a. B. B. King b. Bo Diddley c. Ma Rainey d. Mamie Smith

3. Who was given the title "The Matriarch of Rock"?
   a. Bonnie Raitt b. Ma Rainey c. Bessie Smith d. Memphis Minnie

4. Who was the original "bad girl" of rock?
   a. Etta James b. Madonna c. Cher d. Mary Wells

5. Who performed at the inauguration of Franklin Delano Roosevelt?
   a. Georgia Tom Dorsey b. Mahalia Jackson c. Sister Rosetta Tharpe d. Elvis Presley

6. By the mid-1940s who was one of the highest paid Black entertainers in the United
   States?
   a. B. B. King b. Billie Holiday c. Koko Taylor d. Nina Simone

7. Who wrote "Ball and Chain," a song made famous by Janis Joplin in the 1960s?
   a. Big Mama Thornton b. Joan Baez c. Janis Joplin d. Ira Gershwin

8. Who pioneered an innovative guitar technique in which the melody is played on
   the bass string with the thumb, while rhythmically strumming with the other fingers?
   This technique influenced the guitar's shift from a rhythm to a lead instrument.
   a. B. B. King b. Bo Diddley c. Bonnie Raitt d. Maybelle Carter

9. What was the first Country-Western number one by a woman?
   a. Kitty Wells's "It Wasn't God Who Made Honky Tonk Angels" b. Loretta Lynn's
   "Coal Miner's Daughter" c. Tammy Wynette's "Stand by Your Man" d. Dolly
   Parton's "I Will Always Love You"

10. Who was the only female band to tour with the Beatles?
    a. The Supremes b. The Chiffons c. The Ronettes d. The Shangri-Las

11. Who was the first woman inducted into the Rock and Roll Hall of Fame (1987)?
    a. Diana Ross b. Janis Joplin c. Martha Reeves d. Aretha Franklin

12. Who is Aretha Franklin's favorite singer?
    a. Little Richard b. Mahalia Jackson c. Janet Jackson d. Michael Jackson

13. What Los Angeles band created the reproductive rights organization Rock for
    Choice?
    a. X b. The Bangles c. The Go-Gos d. L7

14. Who was the first pop singer who did not base her work in the realm of the love
    song, preferring to write and sing about masturbation, incest, and infant sexuality?
    a. Amy Ray b. Patti Smith c. Donna Summer d. Kate Bush

15. Who heads Elektra Entertainment Record Company?
    a. David Geffen b. Sylvia Rhone c. Ted Turner d. Barbra Streisand

(continued)

16. Who had eight songs banned from various radio stations?
    a. Madonna b. Cher c. Loretta Lynn d. Tina Turner

17. Who started Righteous Babe Records?
    a. Ani DiFranco b. Natalie Merchant c. Joni Mitchell d. Liz Phair

18. Who was the highest paid woman in rock in 1978?
    a. Cher b. Stevie Nicks c. Linda Ronstadt d. Chrissie Hynde

19. Who wrote or co-wrote "Will You Love Me Tomorrow?" "The Loco Motion," "Up on the Roof," "One Fine Day," "I'm into Something Good," and "A Natural Woman"?
    a. Diana Ross b. Carole King c. Aretha Franklin d. Laura Nyro

20. Who won best rhythm and blues solo vocal performance, female (a category created especially for her) 8 years in a row?
    a. Aretha Franklin b. Whitney Houston c. Diana Ross d. Mariah Carey

21. Who had their own brand of white bread?
    a. The Chiffons b. The Shirelles c. The Supremes d. The Shangri-Las

22. Who was the first artist to place seven top-five singles from one album on *Billboard's* pop singles chart?
    a. Madonna b. Janet Jackson c. Michael Jackson d. Prince

23. How many times has Jewel's CD "Pieces of You" gone platinum?
    a. Twice b. Three times c. Four times d. Five times

24. Who cofounded RAIN (Rape, Abuse, and Incest National Network), a hotline for victims of abuse or violence?
    a. Emily Saliers b. Tori Amos c. Sarah McLachlan d. Bjork

25. Who were the first hip-hop artists to set rhymes to a go-go beat?
    a. Run DMC b. N.W.A c. Salt-N-Pepa d. BWP

26. Who simultaneously promoted pro-woman activism and pro-Black consciousness in hip-hop?
    a. Queen Latifah b. M.C. Lyte c. Yo Yo d. Salt-N-Pepa

27. Who earned her first Grammy in a Country-Western category and then followed with a Grammy in pop vocals?
    a. Patsy Cline b. Whitney Houston c. k. d. lang d. Tracy Chapman

28. Who is the biggest-selling female group of all time?
    a. The Supremes b. TLC c. En Vogue d. The Runaways

29. Which Latino/a artist has reached the greatest level of mass-market success?
    a. Selena b. Gloria Estefan c. Tito Puente d. Julio Iglesias

30. Which group set up female-only areas at stage front and sent boys to the back of the mosh pit?
    a. Frightwig b. Bikini Kill c. Hole d. Babes in Toyland

Answers: 1. b 2. d 3. b 4. a 5. c 6. b 7. a 8. d 9. a 10. c 11. d 12. b 13. d 14. d 15. b 16. c 17. a 18. c 19. b 20. a 21. c 22. b 23. d 24. b 25. c 26. a 27. c 28. b 29. a 30. b cal forms offer different kinds of identities from which young people can pick and choose to sculpt their own sense of self. In this way, music has, and continues to play, a key role in the consolidation of youth cultures in society. There is a huge music industry in the United States, and it works in tandem with television, film, video, and radio.

Just as rock music was an essential part of mobilizing the youth of the 1960s to rebel against traditional norms, oppose the war, and work for civil rights, rap music (and hip-hop culture generally) has been influential in recent decades as a critique of racial cultural politics. Originating in African American urban street culture of the late 1970s, rap was influenced by rhythm and blues and rock and quickly spread beyond its roots into television (like the sitcom *Living Single*), fashion, film, and, in particular, music videos. At the same time that the rap music industry has been able to raise the issue of racism, poverty, and social violence in the context of its endorsement of Black nationalism, rap has also perpetuated misogyny and violence against women in its orientation and musical lyrics. Although there are Black women performers in hip-hop and new female rappers are receiving much more attention, their status in the industry is far below the male bands. In "From Fly-Girls to Bitches and Hos," Joan Morgan argues that although feminists rightly critique the misogyny of much rap music, they must also address the racist contexts that give rise to the music and create such anger in young Black men.

About 30 years after the advent of rock music, the combination of music with visual images gave rise to the music video genre, which gained immense popularity with the prominence of MTV, a 24-hour music video station. Music videos are unique in blending television programming with commercials such that while the viewer is actually watching a commercial, the illusion is of programmatic entertainment. Music videos are essentially advertisements for record company products and focus on standard rock music, although different musical genres like Country-Western also have their 24-hour video formatting. Most music videos are fairly predictable in the ways they sexualize women, sometimes in violent ways. As in movies, women are generally present in music videos to be looked at. In fact, music videos featuring male musicians are aired in greater numbers than those featuring female musicians.

Nonetheless, we could also argue that the music video industry has allowed women performers to find their voice (literally) and to script music videos from their perspective. This opportunity has given women audience recognition and industry backing. Music videos have also helped produce a feminine voice that has the potential to disrupt the traditional gendered perspective. At its peak in the mid-1980s, MTV helped such women as Tina Turner, Cyndi Lauper, and Madonna find success. Madonna is especially interesting because she has been cast simultaneously as both a feminist nightmare perpetuating gendered stereotypes about sexualized women and an important role model for women who want to be active agents in their lives. On the latter, she has been regarded as someone who returns the male gaze by staring right back at the patriarchy.

PRINT MEDIA

No discussion of popular culture is complete without a discussion of the print media. These mass media forms include magazines, newspapers, comic books, and other periodicals. Like other media, they are a mix of entertainment, education, and advertising. Fashion magazines are heavy on advertising, whereas comic books tend to be geared toward entertainment and rely more on product sales of the comic books themselves. Newspapers fall somewhere in between.

Women's magazines are an especially fruitful subject of study for examining how gender works in contemporary U.S. society. As discussed in Chapter 5, women's magazines are a central part of the multi-billion-dollar industries that produce cosmetics and fashion and help shape the social construction of beauty. Alongside these advertising campaigns are bodily standards against which women are encouraged to measure themselves. Because almost no one measures up to these artificially created and often computer-generated standards, the message is to buy these products and your life will improve.

Generally, women's magazines can be divided into three distinct types. First are the fashion magazines that focus on beauty, attracting and satisfying men, self-improvement, and (occasionally) work and politics. Examples of these are *Vogue* (emphasizing fashion and makeup), *Cosmopolitan* (emphasizing sexuality and relationships with men), and *Self* (emphasizing self-improvement and employment), although the latter two are also heavy on beauty and fashion and the former is also preoccupied with sex. Most of these magazines have a White audience in mind; *Ebony* is one similar kind of magazine aimed at African American women. Note that there are a whole series of junior magazines in this genre, such as *Seventeen,* aimed at teenage women. However, although its title suggests the magazine might be oriented toward 17-year-olds, it is mostly read by younger teenagers and even preadolescent girls. Given the focus of teen magazines on dating, fashion, and makeup, the effects of such copy and advertisements on young girls are significant.

The second genre of women's magazines includes those oriented toward the family, cooking, household maintenance and decoration, and keeping the man you already have. Examples include *Good Housekeeping, Redbook,* and *Better Homes and Gardens.* These magazines (especially those like *Good Housekeeping*) also include articles and advertising on fashion and cosmetics, although the representations of these products are different. Instead of the seductive model dressed in a shiny, revealing garment (as is usually featured on the cover of *Cosmo*), *Redbook,* for example, features a more natural-looking woman (although still very beautiful) in more conservative clothes, surrounded by other graphics or captions featuring various desserts, crafts, and so forth. The focus is off sex and onto the home.

The third genre of women's magazines is the issue periodical that focuses on some issue or hobby that appeals to many women. *Parents* magazine is an example of an issue periodical aimed at women (although not exclusively). *Ms.* magazine is one aimed at feminists. Examples of hobby-type periodicals include craft magazines on needlework or crochet and

IDEAS FOR ACTIVISM

- Write letters to encourage networks to air television shows that depict the broad diversity of women.
- Write letters to sponsors to complain about programs that degrade or stereotype women.
- Form a reading group to study novels by female authors.
- Sponsor a media awareness event on campus to encourage other students to be aware of media portrayals of women.

LEARNING ACTIVITY: LOOKING GOOD, FEELING SEXY, GETTING A MAN

Collect a number of women's magazines, such as *Cosmopolitan, Vogue, Elle, Mirabella, Redbook,* and *Woman's Day.* Read through the magazines and fill in the chart listing the number of articles you find about each topic. What do you observe from your analysis? What messages about gender are these magazines presenting?

MAGAZINE TITLE	MAKEUP	CLOTHES	HAIR	SEX/ DATING	DIETING	FOOD/ RECIPES	HOME DECORATION	WORK	POLITICS

fitness magazines. There are many specialized issue periodicals aimed at men (such as hunting and fishing and outdoor activities periodicals, computer and other electronic-focused magazines, car and motorcycle magazines, and various sports periodicals). The best known of the latter is *Sports Illustrated,* famous also for its swimsuit edition that always produces record sales. This magazine has been described as ultra-soft pornography because of its sexualization of female athletes' bodies. That there are more issue periodicals for men reflects the fact that men are assumed to work and have specialized interests, and women are assumed to be preoccupied with looking beautiful, working on relationships, and keeping a beautiful home.

LITERATURE AND THE ARTS

In "Thinking About Shakespeare's Sister," Virginia Woolf responds to the question, Why has there been no female Shakespeare? Similarly, in the early 1970s, Linda Nochlin wrote a feminist critique of art history that sought to answer the question, Why have there been no great women artists? Woolf and Nochlin reached very similar conclusions. According to Nochlin, the reason there had been no great women artists was not because no woman had been capable of producing great art but because the social conditions of women's lives prevented such artistic endeavors.

Woolf wrote her essay in the late 1920s, but still today many critics and professors of literature raise the same questions about women's abilities to create great literature. Rarely, for example, does a seventeenth- or eighteenth-century British literature course give more than a passing nod to women authors of the periods. Quite often, literature majors graduate having read perhaps only Virginia Woolf, George Eliot, Jane Austen, or Emily Dickinson. The usual justification is that women simply have not written the great literature that men have or that to include women would mean leaving out the truly important works of the literary canon (those written by White men).

© 2000 Sylvester

In her essay, Woolf argues that it would have been impossible due to social constraints for a woman to write the works of Shakespeare in the age of Shakespeare. Although women did write, even in the time of Shakespeare, their works were often neglected by the arbiters of the literary canon because they fell outside the narrowly constructed definitions of great literature. For example, women's novels often dealt with the subjects of women's lives—family, home, love—subjects not deemed lofty enough for the canon of literature. Additionally, women often did not follow accepted forms, writing in fragments rather than unified texts. As the canon was defined according to White male norms, women's writing and much of the writing of both women and men of color were omitted.

Yet, toward the end of the twentieth century, more women began to publish novels and poetry, and these have been slowly introduced into the canon. These works have dealt with the realities of women's lives and have received wide acclaim. For example, writers such as Toni Morrison (who received the Nobel Prize for literature), Alice Walker, and Maya Angelou have written about the dilemmas and triumphs faced by Black women in a White, male-dominated culture. Annie Dillard won a Pulitzer Prize at the age of 29 for her nature essays about a year spent living by Tinker Creek. Rita Mae Brown, May Sarton, Gloria Anzaldúa, Dorothy Allison, and Audre Lorde write about lesbian lives and the confluences of sexism, heterosexism, racism, and classism. These writers have been joined by feminist playwrights such as Wendy Wasserstein, feminist performance artists such as Lily Tomlin and Lori Anderson, and feminist comedians such as Suzanne Westenhoffer, Tracey Ullman, and

Margaret Cho. In the readings, Audre Lorde and Gloria Anzaldúa write about the importance of literature for women.

Just as female writers have been ignored, misrepresented, and trivialized, so too female artists and musicians have faced similar struggles. Women's art has often been labeled "crafts" rather than art. This is because women, who were often barred from entering the artistic establishment, have tended to create works of art that were useful and were excluded from the category of art. Often, female artists, like their sisters who were writing novels and poetry, used a male pen name and disguised their identity in order to have their work published or shown. With the influence of the women's movement, women's art is being re-

ACTIVIST PROFILE:
MAXINE HONG KINGSTON

As a young girl, Maxine Hong Kingston could not find herself in the images in the books she read. The public library in her hometown of Stockton, California, had no stories of Chinese Americans and very few that featured girls. For Kingston, this meant a significant need and open space for the telling of her stories.

Kingston was born in Stockton in 1940 to Chinese immigrant parents. Her mother was trained as a midwife in China, and her father was a scholar and teacher. Arriving in the United States, Tom Hong could not find work and eventually ended up working in a gambling business. Maxine was named after a successful blonde gambler who frequented her father's establishment.

Growing up in a Chinese American community, Kingston heard the stories of her culture that would later influence her own storytelling. By earning 11 scholarships, she was able to attend the University of California at Berkeley, where she earned a B.A. in literature. She married in 1962, and she and her new husband moved to Hawaii, where they both taught for the next 10 years.

In 1976, Kingston published her first book, *The Woman Warrior: Memoirs of a Girlhood Among Ghosts.* This story of a young Chinese American girl who finds her own voice won the National Book Critic's Circle Award. Kingston's portrayal of the girl's struggle with silence was met with a great deal of criticism from many Chinese men who attacked Kingston's exploration of critical gender and race issues among Chinese Americans.

Kingston followed *Woman Warrior* with *China Men* in 1980, which also won the National Book Critic's Circle Award. This book explored the lives of the men in Kingston's family who came to the United States, celebrating their achievements and documenting the prejudices and exploitation they faced. Her 1989 novel, *Tripmaster Monkey: His Fake Book,* continued her explorations of racism and oppression of Chinese Americans. Although some critics have accused Kingston of selling out because her stories have not reflected traditional notions of Chinese culture, she has maintained her right to tell her story in her own words with her own voice.

■ JANET AND SUSAN'S MUST-READ NOVELS

A lot of great literature has been produced by women, especially in the last 30 years. Here are some of our favorites. We recommend that you add these to your summer reading list! You may also want to consider subscribing to the *Women's Review of Books*.

- Isabel Allende, *House of the Spirits* and *Eva Luna*
- Dorothy Allison, *Bastard Out of Carolina*
- Maya Angelou, *I Know Why the Caged Bird Sings*
- Margaret Atwood, *The Handmaid's Tale*
- Rita Mae Brown, *Rubyfruit Jungle*
- Sandra Cisneros, *The House on Mango Street*
- Annie Dillard, *Pilgrim at Tinker Creek*
- Marilyn French, *The Women's Room*
- Mary Gordon, *The Company of Women*
- Kaye Gibbons, *Ellen Foster*
- Ursula Hegi, *Stones from the River* and *Floating in My Mother's Palm*
- Zora Neale Hurston, *Their Eyes Were Watching God*
- Barbara Kingsolver, *The Bean Trees*
- Toni Morrison, *Sula* and *The Bluest Eye*
- Gloria Naylor, *The Women of Brewster Place*
- Marge Piercy, *The Longings of Women* and *Gone to Soldiers*
- May Sarton, *The Education of Harriet Hatfield*
- Amy Tan, *The Joy Luck Club,The Hundred Secret Senses*, and *The Bonesetter's Daughter*
- Alice Walker, *The Color Purple* and *The Temple of My Familiar*

■ HISTORICAL MOMENT: THE NEA FOUR

Chartered by the U.S. Congress in 1965, the National Endowment for the Arts (NEA) provides funding for artists to develop their work. In 1990 Congress passed legislation that forced the NEA to consider "standards of decency" in awarding grants. Four performance artists—Karen Finley, Holly Hughes, John Fleck, and Tim Miller—had been selected to receive NEA grants, but following charges by conservatives, particularly Senator Jesse Helms (R–North Carolina), that the artists' works were obscene, the NEA denied their grants. All but Finley are gay, and Finley herself is an outspoken feminist.

Finley's work deals with raw themes of women's lives. She gained notoriety for a performance in which she smeared herself with chocolate to represent the abuse of women. Latching onto this image, conservatives referred to Finley as "the chocolate-smeared woman." Her work is shocking, but she uses the shocking images to explore women's horrific experiences of misogyny, and she uses her body in her performances in ways that reflect how society uses her body against her will.

Hughes' work explores lesbian sexuality, and, in revoking her NEA grant, then-NEA chairman John Frohnmeyer specifically referenced Hughes's lesbianism as one of the

(continued)

reasons she had lost her grant. Some of her performances have included "Well of Horniness," "Lady Dick," and "Dress Suits to Hire."

Following the revocation of their grant, the four sued the U.S. government, and in 1992 a lower court ruled in favor of the plaintiffs, reinstating the grants. The government appealed in 1994 and lost again. Then, in a surprise move, the Clinton administration appealed the decision to the U.S. Supreme Court. In 1998, the Supreme Court overturned the lower court rulings and held that the "standards of decency" clause is constitutional. Since the ruling, the budget and staff of the NEA have been slashed, and, artists like Finley and Hughes must seek funding from other sources to continue their performances.

If you're interested in finding out more about feminism and censorship, visit the website of Feminists for Free Expression at *www.ffeusa.org*.

claimed and introduced into the art history curriculum, although it is often taught in the context of "women's art." This emphasizes the ways the academy remains androcentric with the contributions of "others" in separate courses. Female artists such as Georgia O'Keeffe and Judy Chicago have revitalized the art world by creating women-centered art and feminist critiques of masculine art forms.

The works of female composers and musicians have also been ignored, and very few women have been given the opportunity to conduct orchestras until recently. In fact, through the nineteenth century, only certain instruments such as the keyboard and harp were considered appropriate for women to play, and, even today, women are still directed away from some instruments and toward others. Women continue to produce literature and art and to redefine the canon. As in other male-dominated arenas, women have had to struggle to create a place for themselves. But, as a keen observer once quipped, "Ginger Rogers did everything Fred Astaire did, only backwards and in heels."

READING 61

Thinking About Shakespeare's Sister

Virginia Woolf (1929)

. . . [I]t is a perennial puzzle why no woman wrote a word of extraordinary literature when every other man, it seemed, was capable of song or sonnet. What were the conditions in which women lived, I asked myself; for fiction, imaginative work that is, is not dropped like a pebble upon the ground, as science may be; fiction is like a spider's web, attached ever so lightly perhaps, but still attached to life at all four corners. Often the attachment is scarcely perceptible; Shakespeare's plays, for instance, seem to hang there complete by themselves. But when the web is pulled askew, hooked up at the edge, torn in the middle, one remembers that these webs are not spun in midair by incorporeal creatures, but are the work of suffering human beings, and are attached to grossly material things, like health and money and the houses we live in.

I went therefore, to the shelf where the stories stand and took down one of the latest, Professor Trevelyan's *History of England.* Once more I looked up Women, found "position of," and turned to the pages indicated. "Wifebeating," I read "was a recognized right of man, and was practiced without shame by high as well as low. . . . Similarly," this historian goes on, "the daughter who refused to marry the gentleman of her parents' choice was liable to be locked up, beaten and flung about the room, without any shock being inflicted on public opinion. Marriage was not an affair of personal affection, but of family avarice, particularly in the 'chivalrous' upper classes. . . . Betrothal often took place while one or both of the parties was in the cradle, and marriage when they were scarcely out of the nurses' charge." That was about 1470, soon after Chaucer's time. The next reference to the position of women is some two hundred years later, in the time of the Stuarts. "It was still the exception for women of the upper and middle class to choose their own husbands, and when the husband had been assigned, he was lord and master, so far at least as law and custom could make

him. Yet even so," Professor Trevelyan concludes, "neither Shakespeare's women nor those of authentic seventeenth-century memoirs, like the Verneys and the Hutchinsons, seem wanting in personality and character." Certainly, if we consider it, Cleopatra must have had a way with her; Lady Macbeth, one would suppose, had a will of her own; Rosalind, one might conclude, was an attractive girl. Professor Trevelyan is speaking no more than the truth when he remarks that Shakespeare's women do not seem wanting in personality and character. Not being a historian, one might go even further and say that women have burnt like beacons in all the works of all the poets from the beginning of time—Clytemnestra, Antigone, Cleopatra, Lady Macbeth, Phèdre, Cressida, Rosalind, Desdemona, the Duchess of Malfi, among the dramatists; then among the prose writers: Millamant, Clarissa, Becky Sharp, Anna Karenine, Emma Bovary, Madame de Guermantes—the names flock to mind, nor do they recall women "lacking in personality and character." Indeed, if woman had no existence save in fiction written by men, one would imagine her a person of the utmost importance, very various; heroic and mean; splendid and sordid; infinitely beautiful and hideous in the extreme; as great as a man, some think even greater. But this is woman in fiction. In fact, as Professor Trevelyan points out, she was locked up, beaten and flung about the room.

A very queer, composite being thus emerges. Imaginatively she is of the highest importance; practically she is completely insignificant. She pervades poetry from cover to cover; she is all but absent from history. She dominates the lives of kings and conquerors in fiction; in fact she was the slave of any boy whose parents forced a ring upon her finger. Some of the most inspired words, some of the most profound thoughts in literature fall from her lips; in real life she could hardly read, could scarcely spell, and was the property of her husband.

. . .

Be that as it may, I could not help thinking, as I looked at the works of Shakespeare on the shelf . . . it would have been impossible, completely and entirely, for any woman to have written the plays of Shakespeare in the age of Shakespeare. Let me imagine, since facts are so hard to come by, what would have happened had Shakespeare had a wonderfully gifted sister, called Judith, let us say. Shakespeare himself went, very probably—his mother was an heiress—to the grammar school, where he may have learnt Latin—Ovid, Virgil and Horace—and the elements of grammar and logic. He was, it is well known, a wild boy who poached rabbits, perhaps shot a deer, and had, rather sooner than he should have done, to marry a woman in the neighbourhood, who bore him a child rather quicker than was right. That escapade sent him to seek his fortune in London. He had, it seemed, a taste for the theatre; he began by holding horses at the stage door. Very soon he got work in the theatre, became a successful actor, and lived at the hub of the universe, meeting everybody, knowing everybody, practising his art on the boards, exercising his wits in the streets, and even getting access to the palace of the queen. Meanwhile his extraordinarily gifted sister, let us suppose, remained at home. She was as adventurous, as imaginative, as agog to see the world as he was. But she was not sent to school. She had no chance of learning grammar and logic, let alone of reading Horace and Virgil. She picked up a book now and then, one of her brother's perhaps, and read a few pages. But then her parents came in and told her to mend the stockings or mind the stew and not moon about with books and papers. They would have spoken sharply but kindly, for they were substantial people who knew the conditions of life for a woman and loved their daughter—indeed, more likely than not she was the apple of her father's eye. Perhaps she scribbled some pages up in an apple loft on the sly, but was careful to hide them or set fire to them. Soon, however, before she was out of her teens, she was to be betrothed to the son of a neighbouring wool-stapler. She cried out that marriage was hateful to her, and for that she was severely beaten by her father. Then he ceased to scold her. He begged her instead not to hurt him, not to shame him in this matter of her marriage. He would give her a chain of beads or a fine petticoat, he said; and there were tears in his eyes. How could she disobey him? How could she break his heart? The force of her own gift alone drove her to it. She made up a small parcel of her belongings, let herself down by a rope one summer's night and took the road to London. She was not seventeen. The birds that sang in the hedge were not more musical than she was. She had the quickest fancy, a gift like her brother's, for the tune of words. Like him, she had a taste for the theatre. She stood at the stage door; she wanted to act, she said. Men laughed in her face. The manager—a fat, loose-lipped man—guffawed. He bellowed something about poodles dancing and women acting—no woman, he said, could possibly be an actress. He hinted—you can imagine what. She could get no training in her craft. Could she even seek her dinner in a tavern or roam the streets at midnight? Yet her genius was for fiction and lusted to feed abundantly upon the lives of men and women and the study of their ways. At last—for she was very young, oddly like Shakespeare the poet in her face, with the same grey eyes and rounded brows—at last Nick Greene the actor-manager took pity on her; she found herself with child by that gentleman and so—who shall measure the heat and violence of the poet's heart when caught and tangled in a woman's body?—killed herself one winter's night and lies buried at some cross-roads where the omnibuses now stop outside the Elephant and Castle.

That, more or less, is how the story would run, I think, if a woman in Shakespeare's day had had Shakespeare's genius . . . .

This may be true or it may be false—who can say?—but what is true in it, so it seemed to me, reviewing the story of Shakespeare's sister as I had made it, is that any woman born with a great gift in the sixteenth century would certainly have gone crazed, shot herself, or ended her days in some lonely cottage outside the village, half witch, half wizard, feared and mocked at. For it needs little skill in psychology to be sure that a highly gifted girl who had tried to use her gift for poetry would have been so thwarted and hindered by other people, so tortured and pulled asunder by her own contrary instincts, that she must have lost her health and sanity to a certainty. No girl could have walked to London and stood at a stage door and forced her way into the presence of actor-managers without doing herself a violence and suffering an anguish which may have been irrational—for chastity may be a fetish invented by certain societies for unknown reasons—but were none the less inevitable . . . .

But for women, I thought, looking at the empty shelves, these difficulties were infinitely more formidable. In the first place, to have a room of her own, let alone a quiet room or a sound-proof room, was out of the question, unless her parents were exceptionally rich or very noble, even up to the beginning of the nineteenth century. Since her pin money, which depended on the good will of her father, was only enough to keep her clothed, she was debarred from such alleviations as came even to Keats or Tennyson or Carlyle, all poor men, from a walking tour, a little journey to France, from the separate lodging which, even if it were miserable enough, sheltered them from the claims and tyrannies of their families. Such material difficulties were formidable; but much worse were the immaterial. The indifference of the world which Keats and Flaubert and other men of genius have found so hard to bear was in her case not indifference but hostility. The world did not say to her as it said to them, Write if you choose; it makes no difference to me. The world said with a guffaw, Write? What's the good of your writing? . . .

READING 62

Poetry Is Not a Luxury

Audre Lorde

The quality of light by which we scrutinize our lives has direct bearing upon the product which we live, and upon the changes which we hope to bring about through those lives. It is within this light that we form those ideas by which we pursue our magic and make it realized. This is poetry as illumination, for it is through poetry that we give name to those ideas which are—until the poem—nameless and formless, about to be birthed, but already felt. That distillation of experience from which true poetry springs births thought as dream births concept, as feeling births idea, as knowledge births (precedes) understanding.

As we learn to bear the intimacy of scrutiny and to flourish within it, as we learn to use the products of that scrutiny for power within our living, those fears which rule our lives and form our silences begin to lose their control over us.

For each of us as women, there is a dark place within, where hidden and growing our true spirit rises, "beautiful/and tough as chestnut/stanchions against (y)our nightmare of weakness/"[1] and of impotence.

These places of possibility within ourselves are dark because they are ancient and hidden; they have survived and grown strong through that darkness. Within these deep places, each one of us holds an incredible reserve of creativity and power, of unexamined and unrecorded emotion and feeling. The woman's place of power within each of us is neither white nor surface; it is dark, it is ancient, and it is deep.

When we view living in the european mode only as a problem to be solved, we rely solely upon our ideas to make us free, for these were what the white fathers told us were precious.

But as we come more into touch with our own ancient, noneuropean consciousness of living as a situation to be experienced and interacted with, we learn more and more to cherish our feelings, and to respect those hidden sources of our power from where true knowledge and, therefore, lasting action comes.

At this point in time, I believe that women carry within ourselves the possibility for fusion of these two approaches so necessary for survival, and we come closest to this combination in our poetry. I speak here of poetry as a revelatory distillation of experience, not the sterile word play that, too often, the white fathers distorted the word *poetry* to mean—in order to cover a desperate wish for imagination without insight.

For women, then, poetry is not a luxury. It is a vital necessity of our existence. It forms the quality of the light within which we predicate our hopes and dreams toward survival and change, first made into language, then into idea, then into more tangible action. Poetry is the way we help give name to the nameless so it can be thought. The farthest horizons of our hopes and fears are cobbled by our poems, carved from the rock experiences of our daily lives.

As they become known to and accepted by us, our feelings and the honest exploration of them become sanctuaries and spawning grounds for the most radical and daring of ideas. They become a safe-house for that difference so necessary to change and the conceptualization of any meaningful action. Right now, I could name at least ten ideas I would have found intolerable or incomprehensible and frightening, except as they came after dreams and poems. This is not idle fantasy, but a disciplined attention to the true meaning of "it feels right to me." We can train ourselves to respect our feelings and to transpose them into a language so they can be shared. And where that language does not yet exist, it is our poetry which helps to fashion it. Poetry is not only dream and vision; it is the skeleton architecture of our lives. It lays the foundations for a future of change, a bridge across our fears of what has never been before.

Possibility is neither forever nor instant. It is not easy to sustain belief in its efficacy. We can sometimes work long and hard to establish one beachhead of real resistance to the deaths we are expected to live, only to have that beachhead assaulted or threatened by those canards we have been socialized to fear, or by the withdrawal of those approvals that we have been warned to seek for safety. Women see ourselves diminished or softened by the falsely benign accusations of childishness, of nonuniversality, of changeability, of sensuality. And who asks the question: Am I altering your aura, your ideas, your dreams, or am I merely moving you to temporary and reactive action? And even though the latter is no mean task, it is one that must be seen within the context of a need for true alteration of the very foundations of our lives.

The white fathers told us: I think, therefore I am. The Black mother within each of us—the poet—whispers in our dreams: I feel, therefore I can be free. Poetry coins the language to express and charter this revolutionary demand, the implementation of that freedom.

However, experience has taught us that action in the now is also necessary, always. Our children cannot dream unless they live, they cannot live unless they are nourished, and who else will feed them the real food without which their dreams will be no different from ours? "If you want us to change the world someday, we at least have to live long enough to grow up!" shouts the child.

Sometimes we drug ourselves with dreams of new ideas. The head will save us. The brain alone will set us free. But there are no new ideas still waiting in the wings to save us as women, as human. There are only old and forgotten ones, new combinations, extrapolations and recognitions from within ourselves—along with the renewed courage to try them out. And we must constantly encourage ourselves and each other to attempt the heretical actions that our dreams imply, and so many of our old ideas disparage. In the forefront of our move toward change, there is only poetry to hint at possibility made real. Our poems formulate the implications of ourselves, what we feel within and dare make real (or bring action into accordance with), our fears, our hopes, our most cherished terrors.

For within living structures defined by profit, by linear power, by institutional dehumanization, our feelings were not meant to survive. Kept around as unavoidable adjuncts or pleasant pastimes, feelings were expected to kneel to thought as women were expected to kneel to men. But women have survived. As poets. And there are no new pains. We have felt them all already. We have hidden that fact in the same place where we have hidden our power. They surface in our dreams, and it is our dreams that point the way to freedom. Those dreams are made realizable through our poems that give us the strength and courage to see, to feel, to speak, and to dare.

If what we need to dream, to move our spirits most deeply and directly toward and through promise, is discounted as a luxury, then we give up the core—the fountain—of our power, our womanness; we give up the future of our worlds.

For there are no new ideas. There are only new ways of making them felt—of examining what those ideas feel like being lived on Sunday morning at 7 A.M., after brunch, during wild love, making war, giving birth, mourning our dead—while we suffer the old longings, battle the old warnings and fears of being silent and impotent and alone, while we taste new possibilities and strengths.

NOTE

1. From "Black Mother Woman," first published in *From A Land Where Other People Live* (Broadside Press, Detroit, 1973), and collected in *Chosen Poems: Old and New* (W.W. Norton and Company, New York, 1982) p. 53.

READING 63

The Path of the Red and Black Ink

Gloria Anzaldúa

*"Out of poverty, poetry;
out of suffering, song."*

—*a Mexican saying*

When I was seven, eight, nine, fifteen, sixteen years old, I would read in bed with a flashlight under the covers, hiding my self-imposed insomnia from my mother. I preferred the world of the imagination to the death of sleep. My sister, Hilda, who slept in the same bed with me, would threaten to tell my mother unless I told her a story.

I was familiar with *cuentos*—my grandmother told stories like the one about her getting on top of the roof while down below rabid coyotes were ravaging the place and wanting to get at her. My father told stories about a phantom giant dog that appeared out of nowhere and sped along the side of the pickup no matter how fast he was driving.

Nudge a Mexican and she or he will break out with a story. So, huddling under the covers, I made up stories for my sister night after night. After a while she wanted two stories per night. I learned to give her installments, building up the suspense with convoluted complications until the story climaxed several nights later. It must have been then that I decided to put stories on paper. It must have been then that working with images and writing became connected to night.

Invoking Art

In the ethno-poetics and performance of the shaman, my people, the Indians, did not split the artistic from the functional, the sacred from the secular, art from everyday life. The religious, social and aesthetic purposes of art were all intertwined. Before the Conquest, poets gathered to play music, dance, sing and read poetry in open–air places around the *Xochicuahuitl, el Árbol Florido,* Tree-in-Flower. (The *Coaxihuitl* or morning glory is called the snake plant and its seeds, known as *ololiuhqui,* are hallucinogenic.) The ability of story (prose and poetry) to transform the storyteller and the listener into something or someone else is shamanistic. The writer, as shape-changer, is a *nahual,* a shaman.

In looking at this book that I'm almost finished writing, I see a mosaic pattern (Aztec-like) emerging, a weaving pattern, thin here, thick there. I see a preoccupation with the deep structure, the underlying structure, with the gesso underpainting that is red earth, black earth. I can see the deep structure, the scaffolding. If I can get the bone structure right, then putting flesh on it proceeds without too many hitches. The problem is that the bones often do not exist prior to the flesh, but are shaped after a vague and broad shadow of its form is discerned or uncovered during beginning, middle and final stages of the writing. Numerous overlays of paint, rough surfaces, smooth surfaces make me realize I am preoccupied with texture as well. Too, I see the barely contained color threatening to spill over the boundaries of the object it represents and into other "objects" and over the borders of the frame. I see a hybridization of metaphor, different species of ideas popping up here, popping up there, full of variations and seeming contradictions, though I believe in an ordered structured universe where all phenomena are interrelated and imbued with spirit. This almost finished product seems an assemblage, a montage, a beaded work with several leitmotifs and with a central core, now appearing, now disappearing in a crazy dance. The whole thing has had a mind of its own, escaping me and insisting on putting together the pieces of its own puzzle with minimal direction from my will. It is a rebellious, willful entity, a precocious girl-child forced to grow up too quickly, rough, unyielding, with pieces of feather sticking out here and there, fur, twigs, clay. My child, but not for much longer. This female being is angry, sad, joyful, is *Coatlicue*, dove, horse, serpent, cactus. Though it is a flawed thing—a clumsy, complex, groping blind thing—for me it is alive, infused with spirit. I talk to it; it talks to me.

I make my offerings of incense and cracked corn, light my candle. In my head I sometimes will say a prayer—an affirmation and a voicing of intent. Then I run water, wash the dishes or my underthings, take a bath, or mop the kitchen floor. This "induction" period sometimes takes a few minutes, sometimes hours. But always I go against a resistance. Something in me does not want to do this writing. Yet once I'm immersed in it, I can go fifteen to seventeen hours in one sitting and I don't want to leave it.

My "stories" are acts encapsulated in time, "enacted" every time they are spoken aloud or read silently. I like to think of them as performances and not as inert and "dead" objects (as the aesthetics of Western culture think of art works). Instead, the work has an identity; it is a "who" or a "what" and contains the presences of persons, that is, incarnations of gods or ancestors or natural and cosmic powers. The work manifests the same needs as a person, it needs to be "fed," *la tengo que bañar y vestir.*

When invoked in rite, the object\event is "present;" that is, "enacted," it is both a physical thing and the power that infuses it. It is metaphysical in that it "spins its energies between gods and humans" and its task is to move the gods. This type of work dedicates itself to managing the universe and its energies. I'm not sure what it is when it is at rest (not in performance). It may or may not be a "work" then. A mask may only have the power of presence during a ritual dance and the rest of the time it may merely be a "thing." Some works exist forever invoked, always in performance. I'm thinking of totem poles, cave paintings. Invoked art is communal and speaks of everyday life. It is dedicated to the validation of humans; that is, it makes people hopeful, happy, secure, and it can have negative effects as well, which propel one towards a search for validation.

The aesthetic of virtuosity, art typical of Western European cultures, attempts to manage the energies of its own internal system such as conflicts, harmonies, resolutions and balances. It bears the presences of qualities and internal meanings. It is dedicated to the validation of itself. Its task is to move humans by means of achieving mastery in content, technique, feeling. Western art is always whole and always "in power." It is individual (not communal). It is "psychological" in that it spins its energies between itself and its witness.

Western cultures behave differently toward works of art than do tribal cultures. The "sacrifices" Western cultures make are in housing their art works in the best structures designed by the best architects; and in servicing them with insurance, guards to protect them, conservators to maintain them, specialists to mount and display them, and the educated and upper classes to "view" them. Tribal cultures keep art works in honored and sacred places in the home and elsewhere. They attend them by making sacrifices of blood (goat or chicken), libations of wine. They bathe, feed, and clothe them. The works are treated not just as objects, but also as persons. The "witness" is a participant in the enactment of the work in a ritual, and not a member of the privileged classes.

Ethnocentrism is the tyranny of Western aesthetics. An Indian mask in an American museum is transposed into an alien aesthetic system where what is missing is the presence of power invoked through performance ritual. It has become a conquered thing, a dead "thing" separated from nature and, therefore, its power.

Modern Western painters have "borrowed," copied, or otherwise extrapolated the art of tribal cultures and called it cubism, surrealism, symbolism. The music, the beat of the drum, the Blacks' jive talk. All taken over. Whites, along with a good number of our own people, have cut themselves off from their spiritual roots, and they take our spiritual art objects in an unconscious attempt to get them back. If they're going to do it, I'd like them to be aware of what they are doing and to go about doing it the right way. Let's all stop importing Greek myths and the Western Cartesian split point of view and root ourselves in the mythological soil and soul of this continent. White America has only attended to the body of the earth in order to exploit it, never to succor it or to be nur-

tured in it. Instead of surreptitiously ripping off the vital energy of people of color and putting it to commercial use, whites could allow themselves to share and exchange and learn from us in a respectful way. By taking up *curanderismo*, Santeria, shamanism, Taoism, Zen and otherwise delving into the spiritual life and ceremonies of multi-colored people, Anglos would perhaps lose the white sterility they have in their kitchens, bathrooms, hospitals, mortuaries and missile bases. Though in the conscious mind, black and dark may be associated with death, evil and destruction, in the subconscious mind and in our dreams, white is associated with disease, death and hopelessness. Let us hope that the left hand, that of darkness, of femaleness, of "primitiveness," can divert the indifferent, right-handed, "rational" suicidal drive that, unchecked, could blow us into acid rain in a fraction of a millisecond.

READING 64

Construction of the Female Self
Feminist Readings of the Disney Heroine

Jill Birnie Henke, Diane Zimmerman Umble, and Nancy J. Smith

Disney's early heroines, Cinderella and Aurora, are portrayed as helpless, passive victims who need protection. Indeed, Cinderella is the quintessential "perfect girl," always gentle, kind, and lovely. Their weaknesses are contrasted with the awesome and awful power of the evil women with whom they struggle. However, later Disney films shift from simple stories of passive, young virgins in conflict with evil, mature women to more complex narratives about rebellion, exploration, and danger. Heroines Ariel, Belle, and Pocahontas display an increasingly stronger sense of self, of choice, and of voice.

This growing empowerment of Disney heroines is reflected in shifting depictions of their intimate relationships. While early heroines fall in love at first sight and easily marry to live happily ever after, love relationships for the later heroines come at a cost. Ariel temporarily gives up her voice and ultimately

relinquishes her cultural identity. Belle discovers love only through trials, sacrifice, and learning to look beneath the surface. Ultimately, though, her love releases the Beast from the bonds of his own selfishness so they, too, are "empowered" to live happily ever after together.

Of all of Disney's characters, Pocahontas seems to break new ground. The narrative begins with her as a young woman in possession of a strong, well-developed sense of self, and a conviction that her destiny only remains to be discovered. Unlike other Disney heroines, she resists losing her identity to another for the sake of a marriage relationship. Her position and value in her community, her relationships with other females, and her understanding of her interdependence with the earth provide the most holistic picture yet of a co-actively empowered character in Disney animated films.

. . .

The five films we examine situate the central female character—who is portrayed as gentle, kind, beautiful, and virginal—in an oppressive social milieu where mothers or other sources of female guidance and wisdom are largely absent. Until *Pocahontas,* in fact, these young heroines faced the challenges of their lives without the benefit of other women's support, nurturance, or guidance.

Cinderella, Aurora, Ariel, Belle, and Pocahontas also share another quality: they all have dreams. Each differs, however, in her power to make that dream come true. The conventional Disney tale introduces the heroine near the film's beginning through a song in which she expresses these dreams. For example, viewers first meet Cinderella when she awakens from a dream and sings, "No matter how your heart is grieving, if you keep on believing, the dream that you wish will come true." Minutes later, viewers discover that her daily reality is anything but dreamy. Supported by an army of mice and barnyard animals who come to her aid, Cinderella is continuously reminded by humans in the household that she is unworthy of their "refined" company. Cinderella's stepmother and stepsisters control Cinderella, keeping her locked away from both society and opportunity. Cinderella is portrayed as powerless to act on her own behalf. Hence, she can only dream.

Perhaps Cinderella best illustrates the Disney pattern of subjugating and stifling heroines' voices and selfhood. Her gentleness and goodness are defined by her lack of resistance to abuse by her stepfamily in the film's world. She never disobeys an order, never defends her rights, and never challenges their authority over her. She rarely eats, seldom sleeps, and receives not even the simplest of courtesies, except from her animal friends. Her father's fortune is squandered for the benefit of her stepsisters. She is powerless to control her own fate in her own home. Unable to control her own time, she also is unable to control her own destiny. Cinderella does not act, she only reacts to those around her, a sure sign of both external and internalized oppression. In the face of all this abuse, she somehow remains gentle, kind and beautiful— the perfect girl.

Similarly, *Sleeping Beauty*'s Aurora is a playful teenager whose friends are forest animals, and whose dream is expressed in the song "Some day my prince will come." Aurora is on the verge of celebrating her sixteenth birthday—the day her identity will be revealed to her. At this point she has no knowledge that she really is a princess who was betrothed at birth. Her parents' choices for her define Aurora's destiny; and she has no voice in shaping that destiny.

Like Cinderella, Aurora is obedient, beautiful, acquiescent to authority, and essentially powerless in matters regarding her own fate. Furthermore, there is no one Aurora can trust. Although the fairies "protect" her from the truth about her identity and the curse on her future "for her own good," Aurora can take no action on her own behalf. Passively, she is brought back to the castle where she falls under the spell of Maleficent, touches the spinning wheel, and sleeps through most of the film while others battle to decide her future. When she awakens, she finds her "dream come true," a tall, handsome prince who rescues her from an evil female's curse.

Beginning with *The Little Mermaid,* however, the female protagonist shows signs of selfhood. Near the beginning of the film, Ariel sings of her dream to explore and her feelings of being misunderstood. She also expresses frustration and resistance: "Betcha on land they understand. Bet they don't reprimand their daughters. Bright young women, sick of swimmin', ready to stand." She asks, "When's it my turn?"

In contrast to the two previous demure female protagonists, Ariel is characterized as willful and disobedient. She follows her dreams even though she knows her actions run counter to the wishes of her father, King Triton. As a result, Triton charges the crab, Sebastian, with chaperoning his daughter "to protect her from herself." One might also read his actions as patriarchy's efforts to prevent her from achieving an independent identity. However, despite Triton's efforts to control Ariel, she explores, she asks questions, she makes choices, and she acts. For example, she rescues the human, Prince Eric, from the sea. She strikes a bargain with the sea witch, Ursula, to trade her voice for legs. Additionally, she prevents Eric's marriage to Ursula and protects him from Ursula's attack in the film's final battle. Nevertheless, it is Eric who finally kills the sea witch and it is Triton whose power enables Ariel to return to the human world by transforming her permanently into a human. Thus, while Ariel chooses to leave her own people for a life with Eric, it is still not her power but her father's power which enables her dreams to come to fruition.

Articulating one's own dreams and wishes—possessing an autonomous voice—is a strong indicator of the development of selfhood. Little wonder, then, that alarms sound for feminists concerned with the psychological development of girls and women's sense of self when Ariel literally sacrifices her voice and mermaid body to win Eric's love. What is gained by females who silence themselves in a masculinist society? What are the costs to their psychic selves for not doing so? Scholars in feminist psychological development describe the seductiveness of external rewards by denying one's selfhood. Having a voice, a sense of selfhood, is risky because it is inconsistent with images of the "perfect girl" or the true woman. When one's loyalty is not to the "masculinist system," one can end up on the margins at best and at worst socially "dead." Ultimately, Ariel's voice is silenced and she sacrifices her curiosity to gain the love of a man.

Reality for Belle in *Beauty and the Beast* means being female and wanting to experience adventure in the "great wide somewhere." Like the earlier Disney heroines, Belle dreams of having "so much more than they've got planned." Belle is the first of the Disney heroines to read, but her reading also alienates her from others in the community. She experiences herself as an "other." Townspeople call her peculiar and say that "she don't quite fit in." While Belle is aware of their opinions of her, and understands that she is supposed to marry a villager, raise a family, and conform, she also knows that she *is* different and *wants* something different—something "grand." Although Belle is unsure about how to attain her dreams, she does refuse to marry Gaston, the community "hunk" and its most eligible bachelor. She reads rather than socialize with the villagers, and she accepts that she can be nothing other than different from them. Belle likes herself and trusts her own judgment. Nevertheless, Belle is marginalized by the community for her uniqueness, for her sense of self.

Unlike her counterparts in *Cinderella* and *Sleeping Beauty*, Belle is no damsel in distress. Neither

is she a helpless witness to the film's action nor removed from it. Belle occupies double the screen time of any other character in the film, and Belle acts for herself. She dreams of more than a "provincial life" she wants adventure and, as she sings, "for once it might be grand, to have someone understand, I want so much more than they've got planned." The line might have continued, "for a girl!"

Gaston, the village brute, is attracted to Belle because of her appearance not her brain. He sings that she's "the most beautiful, so that makes her the best." He offers her a place in the community with his marriage proposal. While other women swoon for his attention, Belle rejects him: "His little wife. No, sir. Not me!" Belle's sense of self is strong enough that she refuses to settle for less than a relationship which acknowledges and values her mind, in essence, her self. However, when her father is captured by the Beast, Belle comes to his rescue and offers herself in his place. By trading her life for her father's, she seems to have relinquished her selfhood. Once a prisoner in the Beast's castle, she laments to Mrs. Potts, a kind teapot, that she has lost her father, her dreams, "everything." However, this lament suggests that she still has dreams of her own and a sense of identity apart from that of a dutiful daughter.

Belle's dilemma occurs in part because she has a caring, co-active power relationship with her father. Decision making undertaken by women who attempt to maintain selfhood but also exist in a power-with relation to others becomes much more complex, as Gilligan notes. This complexity is further illustrated by the choices that Belle subsequently makes in her relationship with the Beast. Belle negotiates the conflict she feels between freedom from the Beast and her growing affection for him. She decides not to leave him in the woods after he rescues her from wolves. Although she could escape, she chooses to help him instead. Later in the film, she again chooses to return to the Beast's castle to warn him of the impending mob, even though the Beast has released her from her promise to stay in his castle.

Like Ariel, Belle has freedom to make choices and to act on her own behalf as well as on the behalf of others; and she exercises that freedom. However, whereas Ariel at least initially seems to act out of a sense of rebellion, Belle's motivation appears to come from a craving for intellectual engagement. A simple masculinist interpretation might be that Belle acts out of a sense of personal honor or duty (to sacrifice her freedom first to help her father and later to keep the Beast). A more feminist interpretation based on Gilligan's psychoanalytic development work and standpoint theory might be that Belle acts as a result of the tension from seeking selfhood and relationships with others simultaneously. Thus, Belle's actions can be read as a series of complex decisions about when to act, and when to care for someone, how to administer comfort, when to take matters into her own hands, when to risk her personal safety. She is concerned not only with others but with herself as well, and her actions speak to both needs.

No victim, Belle sets the terms for the bargains she makes. In this sense, she exercises more power on her own behalf than previous Disney heroines. For Cinderella, Aurora, and Ariel, someone in power established the conditions within which their dreams could be realized. For example, Cinderella's fairy godmother gave her only until midnight to make her dream come true. At Aurora's christening, the good fairy Merryweather saved Aurora from Maleficent's death curse by decreeing that Aurora would sleep until awakened by a prince's kiss. And when Ariel gave her voice to Ursula in return for the sea witch's magical ability to transform Ariel into a human, Ursula placed a three day time limit on Ariel's pursuit to win Eric's love. Unlike Belle, these females have limited and tenuous opportunities to achieve their dreams. In contrast, Belle exercises substantial control over setting the terms of her own fate. She preserves her own options—by refusing Gaston's overtures and brushing off the villagers' criticisms, and she gives others options—by freeing her father from the Beast's prison, becoming a prisoner herself, and saving the Beast from the wolves. *She* holds *their* futures in her hands. Yet, ironically, one reading of the narrative conclusion is that Belle's liberation of the Beast from his spell ends with her becoming yet another "perfect girl" who marries the prince and lives happily ever after.

Another theme introduced in *Beauty and the Beast* —heroine as teacher—is expanded in *Pocahontas*. Just as Belle teaches the Beast how to be civil, gentle, and caring, Pocahontas teaches John Smith, her tribe,

and the Englishmen about nature, power, and peace. Like Belle, Pocahontas exercises power over her future. Viewers first are introduced to Pocahontas going where the wind (the spirit of her mother) leads her; as the chief's daughter, however, she knows that she must take "her place" among her people. Her father tells her, "Even the wild mountain stream must someday join the big river." She sings, "We must all pay a price. To be safe, we lose our chance of ever knowing what's around the river bend. . . . Why do all my dreams stand just around the river bend. . . . Is all my dreaming at an end!"

Like Ariel, Pocahontas defies her father in exploring the world. Like Belle, she is an active doer, not a passive victim. She also has a savage to tame in the form of an Englishman. Pocahontas introduces John Smith to the colors of the wind and to the mysteries of the world of nature. She takes political stances such as advocating alternatives to violence, and she makes choices about her life. For example, Pocahontas' decision to reject both her father's wish that she marry Kocoum, the Powhatan warrior, and John Smith's plea to go with him back to England signify that the power to control her actions is in her hands. Pocahontas' choices reflect a sense of selfhood that is a bold stroke for a Disney heroine. A feminist psychological reading might see in her decision to embrace her cultural roots an alternative to Disney's typical heterosexual narratives in which the "perfect girl's" destiny is a monogamous relationship with a (white) man. Indeed, far more than Belle, Pocahontas finds power within to express a self which is separate from that defined through relationships to a father or love interest.

Our reading of Pocahontas implies that she is clearly the most elaborate and complex character in this group of heroines. Her dreams direct her choices. She weighs the risks of choosing a smooth course versus seeking the unknown course to see what awaits her just around the river bend. With counsel from female mentors, Grandmother Willow and the spirit of the wind that symbolizes her mother, Pocahontas finds the strength to listen to her own inner voice, and to choose the less safe, uncharted course of autonomous womanhood. When confronted with the option of leaving her community in order to accompany her love interest, John Smith, she rejects his offer and instead takes her place as an unattached female leader of her people.

Pocahontas brings to the forefront the absence of diversity among Disney's previous female characters. From Cinderella through Belle, Disney's female protagonists easily could be the same characters with only slight variations in hair color. Pocahontas, too, varies only slightly in skin color, but she is the first non-Anglo heroine who is the subject of a Disney animated film. Furthermore, although some of the women may not have difficult family circumstances, (e.g., Cinderella), as Caucasians, they all belong to the privileged class in their societies, as daughters of kings, Indian chiefs, and educated inventors.

As this examination of Cinderella, Aurora, Ariel, Belle, and Pocahontas demonstrates, over time Disney's female protagonists have begun to look beyond home, to practice resistance to coercion, and to find their own unique female voices. Indeed, in Pocahontas Disney offers an adventurous female who develops a sense of self in a culture other than the dominant Anglo culture, and who chooses a destiny other than that of heterosexual romantic fulfillment.

READING 65

From Fly-Girls to Bitches and Hos

Joan Morgan

Any feminism that fails to acknowledge that black folks in nineties America are living and trying to love in a war zone is useless to our struggle against sexism. Though it's often portrayed as part of the problem, rap music is essential to that struggle because it takes us straight to the battlefield.

My decision to expose myself to the sexism of Dr. Dre, Ice Cube, Snoop Dogg, or the Notorious B.I.G. is really my plea to my brothers to tell me who they are. I need to know why they are so angry at me. Why is disrespecting me one of the few things that make them feel like men? What's the haps, what are you going through on the daily that's got you acting so foul?

As a black woman and a feminist I listen to the music with a willingness to see past the machismo in order to be clear about what I'm *really* dealing with. What I hear frightens me. On booming track after booming track, I hear brothers talking about spending each day high as hell on malt liquor and Chronic. Don't sleep. What passes for "40 and a blunt" good times in most of hip-hop is really alcoholism, substance abuse, and chemical dependency. When brothers can talk so cavalierly about killing each other and then reveal that they have no expectation to see their twenty-first birthday, that is straight-up depression *masquerading* as machismo.

Anyone curious about the process and pathologies that form the psyche of the young, black, and criminal-minded needs to revisit our dearly departed Notorious B.I.G.'s first album, *Ready to Die.* Chronicling the life and times of the urban "soldier," the album is a blues-laden soul train that took us on a hustler's life journey. We boarded with the story of his birth, strategically stopped to view his dysfunctional, warring family, his first robbery, his first stint in jail, murder, drug-dealing, getting paid, partying, sexin', rappin', mayhem, and death. Biggie's player persona might have momentarily convinced the listener that he was livin' phat without a care in the world but other moments divulged his inner hell. The chorus of "Everyday Struggle": *I don't wanna live no more / Sometimes I see death knockin' at my front door* revealed that "Big Poppa" was also plagued with guilt, regret, and depression. The album ultimately ended with his suicide.

The seemingly impenetrable wall of sexism in rap music is really the complex mask African-Americans often wear both to hide and express the pain. At the close of this millennium, hip-hop is still one of the few forums in which young black men, even surreptitiously, are allowed to express their pain.

When it comes to the struggle against sexism and our intimate relationships with black men, some of the most on-point feminist advice I've received comes from sistas like my mother, who wouldn't dream of using the term. During our battle to resolve our complicated relationships with my equally wonderful and errant father, my mother presented me with the following gems of wisdom, "One of the most important lessons you will ever learn in life and love, is that you've got to love people for what they are—not for who you would like them to be."

This is crystal clear to me when I'm listening to hip-hop. Yeah, sistas are hurt when we hear brothers calling us bitches and hos. But the real crime isn't the name-calling, it's their failure to love us—to be our brothers in the way that we commit ourselves to being their sistas. But recognize: Any man who doesn't truly love himself is incapable of loving us in the healthy way we need to be loved. It's extremely telling that men who can only see us as "bitches" and "hos" refer to themselves only as "niggas."

In the interest of our emotional health and overall sanity, black women have got to learn to love brothers realistically, and that means differentiating between who they are and who we'd like them to be. Black men are engaged in a war where the real enemies—racism and the white power structure—are masters of camouflage. They've conditioned our men to believe the enemy is brown. The effects of this have been as wicked as they've been debilitating. Being in battle with an enemy that looks just like you makes it hard to believe in the basics every human being needs. For too many black men there is no trust, no community, no family. Just self.

Since hip-hop is the mirror in which so many brothers see themselves, it's significant that one of the music's most prevalent mythologies is that black boys rarely grow into men. Instead, they remain perpetually post-adolescent or die. For all the machismo and testosterone in the music, it's frighteningly clear that many brothers see themselves as powerless when it comes to facing the evils of the larger society, accepting responsibility for their lives, or the lives of their children.

So, sista friends, we gotta do what any rational, survivalist-minded person would do after finding herself in a relationship with someone whose pain makes him abusive. We've gotta continue to give up the love but *from a distance that's safe.* Emotional distance is a great enabler of unconditional love and support because it allows us to recognize that the attack, the "bitch, ho" bullshit—isn't personal but part of the illness.

And the focus of black feminists has got to change. We can't afford to keep expending energy on banal discussions of sexism in rap when sexism is only part of a huge set of problems. Continuing on our previous path is akin to demanding that a fiending, broke crackhead not rob you blind because it's *wrong* to do so.

If feminism intends to have any relevance in the lives of the majority of black women, if it intends to move past theory and become functional it has to rescue itself from the ivory towers of academia. Like it or not, hip-hop is not only the dominion of the young, black, and male, it is also the world in which young black women live and survive. A functional game plan for us, one that is going to be as helpful to Shequanna on 142nd as it is to Samantha at Sarah Lawrence, has to recognize hip-hop's ability to articulate the pain our *community* is in and use that knowledge to create a redemptive, healing space.

Notice the emphasis on "community." Hip-hop isn't only instrumental in exposing black men's pain, it brings the healing sistas need right to the surface. Sad as it may be, it's time to stop ignoring the fact that rappers meet "bitches" and "hos" daily—women who reaffirm their depiction of us on vinyl. Backstage, the road, and the 'hood are populated with women who would do anything to be with a rapper sexually for an hour if not a night. It's time to stop fronting like we don't know who rapper Jeru the Damaja was talking about when he said:

> Now a queen's a queen but a stunt's a stunt
> You can tell who's who by the things they want

Sex has long been the bartering chip that women use to gain protection, material wealth, and the vicarious benefits of power. In the black community, where women are given less access to all of the above, "trickin'" becomes a means of leveling the playing field. Denying the justifiable anger of rappers—men who couldn't get the time of day from these women before a few dollars and a record deal—isn't empowering or strategic. Turning a blind eye and scampering for moral high ground diverts our attention away from the young women who are being denied access to power and are suffering for it.

It might've been more convenient to direct our sista-fied rage attention to "the sexist representation of women" in those now infamous Sir Mix-A-Lot videos, to fuss over *one* sexist rapper, but wouldn't it have been more productive to address the failing self-esteem of the 150 or so half-naked young women who were willing, unpaid participants? And what about how flip we are when it comes to using the b-word to describe each other? At some point we've all been the recipients of competitive, unsisterly, "bitchiness," particularly when vying for male attention.

Since being black and a woman makes me fluent in both isms, I sometimes use racism as an illuminating analogy. Black folks have finally gotten to the point where we recognize that we sometimes engage in oppressive behaviors that white folks have little to do with. Complexion prejudices and classism are illnesses which have their *roots* in white racism but the perpetrators are certainly black.

Similarly, sistas have to confront the ways we're complicit in our own oppression. Sad to say it, but many of the ways in which men exploit our images and sexuality in hip-hop is done with our permission and cooperation. We need to be as accountable to each other as we believe "race traitors" (i.e., 100 or so brothers in blackface cooning in a skinhead's music video) should be to our community. To acknowledge this doesn't deny our victimization but it does raise the critical issue of whose responsibility it is to end our oppression. As a feminist, I believe it is too great a responsibility to leave to men.

A few years ago, on an airplane making its way to Montego Bay, I received another gem of girlfriend wisdom from a sixty-year-old self-declared non-feminist. She was meeting her husband to celebrate her thirty-fifth wedding anniversary. After telling her I was twenty-seven and very much single, she looked at me and shook her head sadly. "I feel sorry for your generation. You don't know how to have relationships, especially the women." Curious, I asked her why she thought this was. "The women of your generation, you want to be right. The women of my generation, we didn't care about being right. We just wanted to win."

Too much of the discussion regarding sexism and the music focuses on being right. We feel we're *right* and the rappers are wrong. The rappers feel it's their *right* to describe their "reality" in any way they see fit. The store owners feel it's their *right* to sell whatever the consumer wants to buy. The consumer feels it's his *right* to be able to decide what he wants to listen to. We may be the "rightest" of the bunch but we sure as hell ain't doing the winning.

I believe hip-hop can help us win. Let's start by recognizing that its illuminating, informative narration and its incredible ability to articulate our collective pain is an invaluable tool when examining gender relations. The information we amass can help create a redemptive, healing space for brothers and sistas.

We're all winners when a space exists for brothers to honestly state and explore the roots of their pain and subsequently their misogyny, sans judgment. It is criminal that the only space our society provided for the late Tupac Shakur to examine the pain, confusion, drug addiction, and fear that led to his arrest and his eventual assassination was in a prison cell. How can we win if a prison cell is the only space an immensely talented but troubled young black man could dare utter these words: "Even though I'm not guilty of the charges they gave me, I'm not innocent in terms of the way I was acting. I'm just as guilty for not doing things. Not with this case but with my life. I had a job to do and I never showed up. I was so scared of this responsibility that I was running away from it." We have to do better than this for our men.

And we have to do better for ourselves. We desperately need a space to lovingly address the uncomfortable issues of our failing self-esteem, the ways we sexualize and objectify ourselves, our confusion about sex and love and the unhealthy, unloving, unsisterly ways we treat each other. Commitment to developing these spaces gives our community the potential for remedies based on honest, clear diagnoses.

As I'm a black woman, I am aware that this doubles my workload—that I am definitely going to have to listen to a lot of shit I won't like—but without these candid discussions, there is little to no hope of exorcising the illness that hurts and sometimes kills us.

READING 66

Roseanne:
A "Killer Bitch" for Generation X

Jennifer Reed

In an interview in the *Advocate*, the longest-running national lesbian and gay magazine of American culture, Roseanne marks herself as a cultural worker who speaks to Generation X feminists. Like many Generation X women (women who grew up with the second wave of feminism), Roseanne eschews the label "feminist" and says she prefers instead "killer bitch." She goes on: "It's women's self-hatred that doesn't allow us to be fighters or artists. It's the same way for black people and gay people."[1] Not only does Roseanne make explicit connections between sexist, racist, and heterosexist oppressions—a project central to third wave feminist organizing—she positions herself as an unequivocal, if irreverent, feminist activist. Although Roseanne is not a part of the Generation X age group, her work exemplifies and shapes third wave feminist sensibilities. Although Generation X feminists have been represented as the logical inheritors and creators of third wave feminism, Roseanne demonstrates that third wave feminism can be described as a discourse, a sensibility, and a politics that transcends strict generational lines. Roseanne, then, is a third wave feminist who speaks to and offers herself to Generation X feminists.

Roseanne's third wave cultural work, not to mention her irreverence, owes a debt to a solid history of feminist organizing, theorizing, and activism. She is not doing the reparative groundwork that earlier feminists had to do—the work of proving women's humanity. So much of that early activism concentrated on developing a cultural conversation that had to begin with defining and articulating "the problem." Early second wave feminists carried the weight of establishing a discourse, a burden that shaped their focus on reclaiming women's identities, researching histories, validating perceptions, and creating forums for emerging voices. Roseanne takes that work as her foundation and runs with it. Roseanne's anger is also the legacy of second wave feminism. Twenty-five years of feminist activism have raised expectations among women, and we are often disappointed. Roseanne voices the inevitable rage that comes when the knowledge created by feminist thinking and action encounters the intractability of oppressive forces. This encounter between feminist progress and ongoing feminist struggle in the context of backlash constitutes third wave feminist subjectivity.

Roseanne has made her reputation in mass culture as a loud, aggressive, overweight, working-class woman who always says what is on her mind, who will not be pushed around, who tells her own uncomfortable truths. She is particularly known for exposing the secrets of the bourgeois family by telling her own story and making public her own healing process. In her most recent autobiography, *My Lives*, published and publicized in early 1994 (and which already seems outdated), Roseanne discusses the parental abuse she suffered as a child and the enormous toll it has taken on her life.[2] As an explicit and articulate feminist, she is extremely critical of (among other things) the Hollywood establishment, the business of television, and the mainstream press. Her book is at least in part a response to journalists' portrayal of her as a woman impossible to work for and explosively moody, capriciously firing employees from her show and suing her closest associates. *My Lives* did not endear her to those who already hated her, because it is strongly and unambiguously worded, it is a direct confrontation of those who have hurt her, and it offers an unapologetic version of her own vision and truth.

Since the publication of her book, Roseanne's life has changed dramatically. In the publicity following her divorce from Tom Arnold, her subsequent marriage to her one-time chauffeur Ben Thomas, and the birth of their child Buck, Roseanne's image in dominant culture became increasingly precarious, even (maybe especially) among feminists. Some of my friends and I jokingly lamented that Roseanne was getting more difficult to hold up as a feminist icon. She didn't seem to mind. It is clear that Rose-anne is in charge of the creation, if not the reception, of her image. In many ways she is a second wave poster girl living a second wave feminist success story: she is financially independent, makes her own choices and relationships, does the work she loves, and controls that work in ways unprecedented for women. Roseanne creates her own life in a very public way, although not as a role model for anyone. She says she has no interest in being a role model. In fact, she has this to say about role models in the *Advocate* interview: "That's such a bogus concept. People use role models to not get off their asses. If you have to find somebody to copy, you have a serious problem."[3]

This sentiment points to Roseanne's third wave sensibilities. For third wave feminists, there is no one right way to be: no role, no model. One of the strengths of third wave feminism is its refusal of a singular liberal-humanist subjectivity. With no utopic vision of the perfectly egalitarian society or the fully realized individual, third wave feminists work with fragmentation of existing identities and institutions. If third wave feminism distinguishes itself from the second wave in any definable way, it is in its emphasis on making room for contradictions. We struggle to accommodate the differences and conflicts *between* people as well as *within* them. Third wave feminism looks for, ferrets out, and defines our contradictions—which ones we can live with, which ones we cannot, in ourselves, in our society—and these depend on the context. If we are trying to figure out how to use differences dynamically, creating alternative families and connections, surviving a capitalist society without exploiting others, minimizing our own exploitation and that of other women and men, we can take our role models only from the audacity and tenacity we see modeled in a world that makes no room for us. Roseanne models the courage we need. . . .

. . .

. . . [E]xcess is Roseanne's signature transgressive strategy. Roseanne's fat body is among the most immediately visible and radically destabilizing forces she uses. Rosalind Coward makes the point that in dominant U.S. culture, the ideal feminine body is that of an adolescent, a slight and immature body that connotes powerlessness. In contrast, Coward writes, "Fat women can be extremely imposing. A large woman who is not apologizing for her size is certainly not a figure to invite the dominant meanings to which our culture attaches to femininity."[4] By performing her fat body unapologetically, Roseanne breaks one of the cardinal rules of "woman." In the words of Rowe, "For women, excessive fatness carries associations with excessive willfulness and excessive speech."[5] Roseanne does not hope we do not notice her fat body. She foregrounds her body throughout the show, drawing attention to her weight with jokes that are not at all self-deprecating or apologetic. She doesn't try to explain away her weight, she doesn't make the jokes at her own expense, she doesn't use them for pity, she doesn't use them to say that she is not attractive, and she doesn't allow a fat body to desexualize her. By talking about her fat body, she refuses to erase it or hide it.

Early in the show, in a medley of old jokes, Roseanne says, "Well, I'm fat. I thought I'd point that out." She then gives an example of how fat people think differently than thin people, by imitating how a fat person would give directions. All of the markers in the directions are fast-food restaurants, ending with, "It's that chocolate brown building over there on the left, you can't miss it." In another bit, about gay men, she says, "I thank God for gay men. If not for them, us fat women would have no one to dance with." Comments about her fat body are interspersed throughout the show and combined with a sarcastic, unapologetic, loud style that links fat voice to fat body. She swears and she uses incorrect grammar. Her voice is uncontrolled, unmodulated, often shrill. She yells and screeches with abandon. Such bigness of both movement and speech is integral to the unruly woman's performance.

Sandra Lee Bartky writes that "women are far more restricted than men in their movement and in their spatiality."[6] Feminine movement and gesture are confined and constricted. Women learn to take up as little room as possible, staying within a narrow range of distance from the body's center, moving tensely and carefully. In contrast, Roseanne plays the "loose woman." Bartky writes, "The 'loose woman' violates these norms: her looseness is manifest not only in her morals, but in her manner of speech and quite literally in the free and easy way she moves."[7] Clearly, Roseanne plays the "loose woman" in every sense of the term, but two moments in particular illustrate the ways in which she combines that style with explicit social and political critique. Speaking about how "men only want one thing," she says: "Can you imagine what it was like, that meeting that men had to decide what that one thing that men want out of life was going to be?" In a very gruff voice, she takes on the persona of the man in charge of the meeting: "All right, listen fellas, I call this meeting to order. Can I have your attention? Shut up. All right. I got two votes over here for power tools. The chair recognizes Hiram." Now, as Hiram, in a gentle, lilting voice: "What if the one thing we wanted out of life was to nurture the life force in every living thing?" As the chair: "Yeah, uh, the chair says Hiram is a fag and doesn't deserve to have a penis. The chair recognizes Tony." As Tony, spitting on the floor and grabbing his crotch, burping, and snorting: "All right, now this may sound a little old-fashioned, guys, but what if the one thing we wanted out of life was pussy?" As chair: "Well, the chair likes pussy. All those in favor say 'aye.' . . .All right, so whaddya say, guys, well all get outta here, we go try to find some pussy, and if we can't find any, we come back here and beat the shit outta Hiram?"

Especially in her enactment of Tony, Roseanne here performs the excess of bodies: it is excessive because most often in hegemonic culture, we are trained not to notice anything about the body that calls attention to itself. Just as Roseanne does not allow her own body to be invisible, she does not allow other bodies or bodily processes to be erased, and she plays an exaggerated male body so as to make an oppressive masculinity visible. . . . In the same vein, she performs a lengthy piece on women's experiences of menstruation. She says, "It's hard being a woman. . . . It's harder for us than it is for you men. Maybe it would be easier for us if we were only one woman, but no, we have to have that twenty-eight-day cycle, and during that twenty-eight days, at least that many personalities come and inhabit your body, and you're helpless." Roseanne goes on to enact, in an exaggerated manner, several of the personalities she experiences as part of her "normal" cycle. She uses her face, voice, and body in an uninhibited way to express her hostility and moodiness, her desire for control of her life, and her ambitions to be better and to work out. She becomes the exhausted woman who feels guilt for not taking good enough care of the kids, the woman who is awestruck by life itself, and the horny woman who says, "I just want to be and get fucked. I want it one time in the morning to open my eyes, then I want it one time at night just to close 'em. Then I want it one more time during the day, just 'cause I know he don't want to. And then I want . . . chocolate." She becomes the self-pitying woman, the victim, the eager-to-please woman, and the angry woman.

Both of these multiplicity monologues exemplify Roseanne's exposure of bodily processes, by enacting them and talking about them, as a strategy not to be "gross" or "crass" for its own sake, but to make larger political points. In the first monologue she confronts heterosexual, heterosexist, and homophobic assumptions of a masculinity that objectifies women, abhors what and who it labels "feminine," and embraces violence as a form of self-expression. And in the second, she makes visible and audible and funny a common women's experience, one that historically has been taboo to mention and, thus, instilled with shame and embarrassment, or that has been the object of misogynist derision, dismissal, and derogation. Roseanne talks about menstruation here like she talks about fat: it is a biological fact that requires no apology, embarrassment, or explanation. This piece in particular demonstrates Roseanne's use of the multiplicity and fragmentation of her selves to *describe* her experience of herself. And by making her own fat and her own menstrual cycle visible in her own words, she works to wrest female bodies from the control of misogynist discourse that makes fatness and menstruation shameful for women.

Roseanne marks herself as an unruly or loose woman through her performance of excess, her loud voice, her aggressive posture, her working-class syntax, her nonconstricted, abundant body, and her observations and opinions (that is, what she says). Mary Russo would call Roseanne's performance that of a "grotesque body," because she does what is particularly dangerous for women: she "makes a spectacle of herself." For a woman, Russo writes, this has "to do with a kind of inadvertency and loss of boundaries. . . . [Such women step] into the limelight out of turn—too young, too old, too early or too late— and yet anyone, any woman, could make a spectacle out of herself if she was not careful."[8] Russo argues that the grotesque woman, marked by a performance of parody, excess, and gender masquerade, is a potentially productive strategy for feminist intervention into the category "woman." It offers the possibility to go beyond the critique of what-is-always-there, "woman," to a counterhegemonic re-performance of gender, a radicalization of heterogender.

Negotiating the possibilities and limitations of gender roles has been a particularly accessible strategy for the third wave, and is a luxury provided by the groundwork done by second wave feminists. That work created the space for the irreverence, parody, dissonance, and irony that Roseanne uses to create a new subjective space for women. This, then, is a subjective space that negotiates the ambivalence inherent in the use of these strategies. This construction of "woman" both parodies and embraces glamour, the trappings of high femininity, and the very performance of gender and of heterorelating. In other words, it is a construction committed to working with the contradictions and the irreconcilability that constitute any attempt at carving out subjective space for women. This is one of the primary offerings the third wave makes to feminism.

NOTES

1. Roseanne, "Her Life Was a Woman," interview by Peter Galvin, *Advocate,* 24 January 1995, 54.
2. Roseanne Arnold, *My Lives* (New York: Ballantine, 1994).
3. Roseanne, "Her Life as a Woman."
4. Rosalind Coward, *Female Desires: How They Are Sought, Bought, and Packaged* (New York: Grove, 1985), 41.
5. Rowe, "Roseanne," 410.
6. Sandra Lee Bartky, "Foucault, Femininity, and the Modernization of Patriarchal Power," in *Feminism and Foucault,* ed. Irene Diamond and Lee Quinby (Boston: Northeastern University Press, 1988), 66. Bartky, building on a Foucauldian analysis, makes the point that feminine bodies are produced by a myriad of modern cultural practices. The body constructed to be feminine is a body made to be deferential, subordinate. The feminine body's subordinate status is manifested in any number of narrowly defined behaviors. Feminine bodies must be small, thin, hairless, circumscribed in their movements, and decorated.
7. Ibid.
8. Mary Russo, "Female Grotesques: Carnival and Theory," in *Feminist Studies/Critical Studies,* ed. Teresa de Lauretis (Bloomington: Indiana University Press, 1986), 213.

READING 67

The Oprahification of America
Talk Shows and the Public Sphere

Jane M. Shattuc

Today I am sitting between two people who have never been this close face to face since one very unforgettable night two years ago. Debbie says that the man sitting across from her locked her in a closed room, held a gun to her, and violently raped her. Jawah says Debbie is lying.

—*Oprah Winfrey,* The Oprah Winfrey Show, *May 3, 1994*

Are daytime TV talk shows simply sensational commercialism, or could they be a new form of political debate? Oprah Winfrey's visceral description from her May 3, 1994, show seemingly relegates the social issues involved in rape to the realm of cheap thrills. But on another level, the program's dramatic and individualized account allows ordinary citizens—in the studio and at home—to enter into a debate about sexual power in their everyday lives, a rare moment on network television.

Traditionally, democratic thought assumes that there must be an independent public arena where political opinion can be formed freely. The arena should be entirely free of the taint of government control as well as that of corporation capitalism. For many Americans, the town meeting is the ideal of participatory democracy: the citizen takes part in the politics of the local community by standing up and speaking up. But such direct communication is becoming less tenable in the age of information technology and global communication.

If TV has become the central communicator of information in late capitalist America, no other public forum replicates the town meeting's democratic sensibility better than the first generation of daytime TV talk shows born in the 1970s and 1980s: *The Oprah Winfrey Show, Sally Jessy Raphael, Donahue,* and even *Geraldo*.[1] Here, "average" Americans debate important, albeit sensationalized, issues that are central to their political lives: racism, sexuality, welfare rights, and religious freedom. Would Jürgen Habermas have included the American talk show as part of the public sphere when he defined the latter as "the realm of our social life in which something approaching public opinion can be formed. . . . A portion of the public sphere comes into being in every conversation in which private individuals assemble to form a public body"?[2] The answer depends on whose definition of politics one invokes.

The concept of the public sphere—the place where public opinion can be formed—looms over all analyses of talk shows. From "The Talk Show Report" in *Ladies Home Journal* to think pieces about tabloid culture in the *New York Times* to a Marxist collective analysis of the genre in *Sociotext* to an article on talk and female empowerment in *Genders,* our culture is hyperconscious that daytime TV talk shows are involved in the political arena.[3] They are a rare breed: highly popular programs that depend on social topics and participation from average citizens. However, there is a fear that the programs may be trivializing "real" politics by promoting irrational, victimized, and anomalous individuals as represen-

tative of the citizenry. The print press often has pejoratively alluded to the "Oprahification" of America. Yet the popularity of the shows continually highlights two questions: Can the content of talk shows be defined as "political"? And, more important, can the shows—the children of corporate media interests—be considered public arenas where the "people" form opinion freely?

Even though the women's movement has shown that politics in the late twentieth century includes the personal, American culture still is uncomfortable with describing the content of daytime talk shows as political. The term *political* is derived from the Latin *politicus,* which means relating to a citizen.[4] A citizen is defined by her or his allegiance to a state, which in return offers protection to the citizen. Obviously, the shows, with their dependence on spectacle, individualism, and sensation, deviate radically from the traditional political discussions about social policy that define citizenship—such as Oxford debates, congressional deliberations, union hall meetings, and even network news, which all emphasize established political institutions. Although the practice of debate has shifted from the Aristotelian model of speaker and listener to the coordinated discussion, the shows are more personal and emotional in content and vertiginous in structure, breaking with traditional structures in political discussion. Here, American politics moves from the "analytical is political" tradition to "the personal as political" in the latter half of the century.[5]

No other TV genre—not news, prime-time drama, or soap opera—generates more ongoing social controversy than daytime talk shows. Beyond the headline-grabbing *Jenny Jones* murder or Winfrey's cocaine confession, the shows provoke endless debates about everyday experience.[6] Not only does viewer give-and-take occur as part of the shows, but discussions continue on the news, in the workplace, and at home: the popularization of current political, social, and theoretical topics. The shows raise questions about fact versus fiction as the audience tests the credibility of the stories presented. (In the common vernacular: "Are those people for real?") They test the demarcation between entertainment and news, as they mix political issues and personal drama. Finally, the programs use ordinary people to stage social issues that are infrequently discussed elsewhere on television: homosexuality, familial conflict, sexual relations, and racial divisions. As the events of the 1990s bring into the political arena an angry African American underclass, gay activists, and working women, might the *Oprah* audience be the newest incarnation of the public sphere?

Even though Habermas concedes that, historically, the public sphere has been more an ideal than a fact, the concept still influences the assumptions of capitalist democracy. Hopes of a public sphere are evoked whenever a writer bemoans the passing of considered discussion of current events where the commercial pressures for "entertainment" have destroyed objectivity and truth. The *New York Times* represents this stance as the principal defender of "real" news when John J. O'Connor, the paper's TV critic, warns against "trash TV" and talk show sensation:

> There's a battle being waged in television these days and broadly speaking, it's taking place along "us versus them" cultural lines. Depending on your vantage point, the results so far could be interpreted as either democracy taking the offensive or the barbarians . . . are in the business of inventing emotional "wallops," and are openly contemptuous of what they like to refer to as "pointy-headed" journalists, meaning for the most part the college-educated kind that works in non-tabloid print.[7]

Here a newspaperman who writes about television for a traditional news medium suppresses questions about the objectivity in news reporting in favor of charges that tabloid or talk shows are manipulative or promote what another *New York Times* reporter calls "the new kind of dumbness."[8] This nostalgia for the loss for the bourgeois public sphere is deeply intertwined with a kind of politics in which clear categories of power are maintained: a class, culture, and gender hierarchy based on the centrality of the educated white bourgeois male.[9] Not surprisingly, Phil Donahue is often nominated by the written press as the most "responsible" or "trusted" of hosts.[10]

The talk show industry self-consciously trades on the concept of "the people speaking." But when cultural studies critics speak of it as "an active audience," other critics have decried the concept as a "naive, unattainable ideal."[11] Within this pessimistic perspective, the problem of active viewers is twofold. Under a veneer of participation the talk show audience is a passive mass led by commercial interests and self-promoting hosts. The active audience of the shows can also be a forum for social control when the audience taunts, shouts down, and demands conformity of the "guest deviants."

Nevertheless, the feminist movement has launched a thoroughgoing critique of the public sphere and the dichotomy of a serious/trivial split that underpins the discussion about daytime talk shows.[12] From a feminist point of view, the problem lies in the fact that the public sphere is contrasted to the private sphere and therefore produces a not-so-subtle division between masculine and feminine realms: men participate in the serious realm of politics and rational debate; women govern the realm of the domestic arena and emotionalism.[13]

As a result, many feminists have come to champion talk shows as a new public sphere or counter-public sphere. Talk shows not only promote conversation and debate, they break down the distance between the audience and the stage. They do not depend on the power of expertise or bourgeois education. They elicit common sense and everyday experience as the mark of truth. They confound the distinction between the public and the private. Talk shows are about average women as citizens talking about and debating issues and experience.

. . .

. . . *Oprah* does challenge the supposed objectivity of traditional patriarchal power. The host—a big, black woman—undercuts the authority of the talk show debate format with her self-confessional style; she routinely admits her early sexual and drug abuse and a chronic struggle with weight loss. Her program also represents a potentially radical public sphere that privileges process over a single truth or closure.

Yet the structure of an *Oprah* program is typical of most daytime talk shows: problem/solution. Most often, the problem is introduced as a personal problem (for example, obesity, HIV positive, a bisexual spouse), but then is generalized to a larger social issue. For instance, an April 15, 1994, program on mothers who want to give up their violent children was generalized by Winfrey as "what really makes a child act this way." Either by taking the opposite side or by teasing out the other view, Winfrey questions the guest to flesh out the problem. The ubiquitous guest labels or "I.D.s" (in production parlance) underline the social representativeness of the guests; for example, one is a "mother who wants to give away a violent child," another is a "convicted woman who plotted her husband's death." The labeling offers a popularized version of the logic of identity politics, which attempts to break down the hegemonic notion of homogeneity or that "we all are one." Yet not all social divisions are represented; talk shows favor gender, sexual preference, familial, and criminal labels. Race and class remain structuring absences. The audience intuits these categories through the guest's appearance, words, and actions.

After establishing the guest's problem and social representativeness, Winfrey directs the debate through her selection of questioners and specifically through the rhetorical use of the pronouns *you, I,* and *we.* She invokes the audience as a larger social collectivity: "I am sure what mothers out there are thinking"; or "When I first heard about this, like everybody, I wondered what the big deal is"; or (my favorite, because it's Winfrey at her most self-aggrandizing) "The question we all have, I am speaking for the audience here and the audience around the world listening to you." As these quotations reveal, Winfrey engages an audience that actively thinks and adjudicates. It is also important that she positions herself with the audience as one of many outside observers/judges who have a social/personal stake in the issue.

Even though the host changes alignment from being sole authority to being a member of the audience, her/his authority is never relinquished. What many observers celebrate as Winfrey's debunking of her authority—she will even sit in the audience—also can be seen as a subtle move that allows her to orchestrate a collective response from the audience. When Wendy Kaminer in *I'm Dysfunctional, You're Dysfunctional* laments about her experience on *Oprah:* "If all issues are personalized, we lose our ca-

pacity to entertain ideas, to generalize from our own or someone else's experiences, to think abstractly," she has missed the point.[14] Such shows continually move from personal identification to larger group identification in order to be popular as a broad commercial medium. The host generalizes the particular experience into a larger social frame to capture the interest of a large audience. For all their individualized narratives, the shows speak in social generalities. They just do not speak about or advocate changing specific social and political institutions.

. . .

In general, talk shows do not offer traditional political topics. Rather, they translate politics into the everyday experience of the political. So the shows are rarely overtly "political." They are ultimately feminist not because they say they are but because they are populated by women and they discuss domestic and everyday experience as social problems. They do not follow the classical tradition of the bourgeois public sphere, where, J. B. Thompson maintains, "the authority of the state could be criticized by an informed and reasoning public or 'publicness.'"[15] The audience may or may not connect the discussion of abuse, sexual partners, and interracial conflict to legislation, elections, and news stories.

However, talk shows do offer proof that social experience is not a matter of ideology or false consciousness but, rather, has demonstrable consequences that can be proven through the physical and emotional evidence of its victims. Although the program and the experts establish and resolve the debate, the distant evidence of expert knowledge alone is no longer valid. Nor are the synthetic spectacles of commercial television programming acceptable. Rather, the talk show relies on the tangible or physical signs of the society: testimonials, emotions, and the body as well as laughter, facial expression, and tears. These are forms of argument and evidence available to the nonexperts or underclasses. And they are gaining acceptance as talk shows test the centrality of the educated bourgeoisie to define politics and debate.

Oddly enough, in this age of postmodern simulation, talk shows demand a belief in the authenticity of lived experience as a social truth. Perhaps, this belief is what the "Oprahification" of America really is. As one *Oprah* audience member stated on April 14, 1994: "Don't tell me how to feel. I am my experience."

NOTES

1. I want to separate this first generation of talk shows of the 1970s and 1980s from the second generation of the 1990s hosted by Ricki Lake, Richard Bev, Gordon Elliot, Jenny Jones, and Jerry Springer. The phenomenal financial success of *The Oprah Winfrey Show* by 1990 spawned numerous new talk shows. Under the competition, the new programs changed the format considerably by removing the expert and social issues, emphasizing the implicit excess and sensation, and adding a campy or more tongue-in-cheek style. For further discussion of this generic shift, see my book, *The Talking Cure: Women and Talk Shows* (New York: Routledge, 1996).

2. "The Public Sphere: An Encyclopedia Article," *New German Critique* (autumn 1984): 49. For a more thorough discussion of the relation of talk shows to Habermas's public sphere, see Sonia Livingston and Peter Lunt, *Talk on Television: Audience Participation and Public Debate* (London: Routledge, 1994).

3. Barbara Lippert, "The Talk Show Report," *Ladies' Home Journal*, April 1994, 154–56, 210; John Corry, "A New Age of Television Tastelessness?" *New York Times*, 29 May 1988, 1; John J. Connor, "Defining What's Civilized and What's Not," *New York Times*, 25 April 1989, C18; Paolo Carpignano, Robin Andersen, Stanley Aronowitz, and William Difazio, "Chatter in the Age of Electronic Reproduction: Talk Television and the 'Public Mind,'" *Sociotext* 25–26 (1990): 33–55; Gloria-Jean Masciarotte, "C'mon Girl: Oprah Winfrey and the Discourse of Feminine Talk," *Genders* 11 (fall 1991): 81–110.

4. *Webster's New World Unabridged Dictionary*, 2d ed. (New York: Simon and Schuster, 1983), 1392.

5. Masciarotte, "C'mon Girl: Oprah and the Discourse of Feminine Talk," 89.

6. On March 6, 1995, during a taping of a Jenny Jones show on secret admirers, a Michigan man Scott Amedure surprised a male friend, Jon Schmitz, by admitting that he had a crush on him. The next day, Schmitz murdered Amedure, alleging that he had been "humiliated" by the exposure on national television. Jenny Jones and talk shows in general were blamed in the press for being irresponsible for misleading guests. See the cover story, Michelle Green, "Fatal Attraction," *People*, 27 March 1995, 40–44.

Oprah Winfrey, host of *The Oprah Winfrey Show*, "confessed" her use of cocaine in front of a live audience during the taping of a program in late January 1995. The statement was reported on the evening news as well as the printed press. For the tabloid coverage, see cover stories, Jim Nelson, "Oprah and Cocaine: The Shocking Story She Didn't Tell You on TV," *National Inquirer*, 31 January 1995, 5; and Ken Harrell, "Oprah: 'How a Man Made Me Slave to Cocaine,'" *Globe*, 31 January 1995, 37.

7. O'Connor, "Defining What's Civilized and What's Not," C18.

8. Corry, "A New Age of Television Tastelessness?" sec. 2, 1.

9. Consider how a series of binary oppositions surface in these discussions of the liberal news tradition and the exploitative talk show genre: democratic versus biased, independent versus profit-oriented, serious versus trivial, educated versus uneducated, and masculine versus feminine.

10. For an example, see Eric Sherman, "Who's the Best? Donahue? Oprah? Someone Else?" *TV Guide*, 26 March 1986, 26. *Newsweek* describes Phil Donahue as "America's most trusted tour guide across today's constantly shifting social and cultural terrain" (*Newsweek*, 29 October 1979, 78).

11. Michael Schudsen, "Was There Ever a Public Sphere? If So, When? Reflections on the American Case," in *Habermas and the Public Sphere*, ed. Craig Calhoun (Cambridge, Mass.: MIT Press, 1992), 143–63.

12. See Nancy Fraser, *Unruly Practices: Power, Discourse, and Gender in Contemporary Social Theory* (Minneapolis: University of Minnesota Press, 1989), 113–43; Masciarotte, "C'mon Girl: Oprah and the Discourse of Feminine Talk," 81–110; and Patricia Mellencamp *High Anxiety: Catastrophe, Scandal, Age, and Comedy* (Bloomington: Indiana University Press, 1990), 194–229.

13. In *Unruly Practices*, Nancy Fraser outlines this debate: "Consider, first, the relations between (official) private economy and private family as mediated by the roles of worker and consumer. These roles, I submit, are gendered roles. And the links they forge between family and (official) economy are effected as much in the medium of gender identity as in the medium of money" (Fraser, *Unruly Practices*, 124). According to Fraser, one should also consider how the concept of the "citizen" is one associated with men: "as Habermas understands it, the citizen is centrally a participant in political debate and public opinion formation. This means that citizenship, in his view, depends cru-

cially on the capacities for consent and speech, the ability to participate on a par with others in dialogue. But these are capacities connected with masculinity in a male-dominated, classical capitalism; they are in ways denied women and deemed at odds with femininity" (ibid.). As further evidence, Fraser cites studies on the inequalities in male/female dialogues and the lack of respect women have over consent in marital rape. She concludes by quoting Carole Pateman: "If

women's words about consent are consistently reinterpreted, how can they participate in the debate among citizens?" (ibid.).

14. Wendy Kaminer, *I'm Dysfunctional. You're Dysfunctional: The Recovery Movement and Other Self-Help Fashions* (New York: Vintage, 1993), 38.

15. J. B. Thompson, *Ideology and Modern Culture: Critical Social Theory* (Cambridge: Polity Press, 1990), 112.

READING 68

Confessions of a Feminist Porno Star

Nina Hartley

"A feminist porno star?" Right, tell me another one, I can hear some feminists saying. I hear a chorus of disbelief, a lot like the two crows in the Disney movie "Dumbo"— "I thought I'd seen everything till I saw an elephant fly." On the surface, contradictions seem to abound. But one of the most basic tenets of feminism, a tenet with which I was inculcated by the age of ten, was the *right* to sexual free expression, without being told by society (or men) what was right, wrong, good, or bad. But why porno? Simple— I'm an exhibitionist with a cause: to make sexually graphic (hard core) erotica, and today's porno is the only game in town. But it's a game where there is a possibility of the players, over time, getting some of the rules changed.

As I examine my life, I uncover the myriad influences that led me to conclude that it was perfectly natural for me to choose a career in adult films. I find performing in sexually explicit material satisfying on a number of levels. First, it provides a physically and psychically safe environment for me to live out my exhibitionistic fantasies. Secondly, it provides a surprisingly flexible and supportive arena for me to grow in as a *performer*, both sexually and non-sexually. Thirdly, it provides me with erotic material that I like to watch for my own pleasure. Finally, the medium allows me to explore the theme of celebrating a positive female sexuality—a sexuality that has heretofore been denied us. In choosing my roles and characterizations carefully, I strive to show, always,

women who thoroughly enjoy sex and are forceful, self-satisfying and guilt-free without also being neurotic, unhappy or somehow unfulfilled.

. . .

Once I passed puberty, two books in particular were very influential in the continuing development of my personal sexual philosophy: *Our Bodies, Ourselves* and *The Happy Hooker*. The former taught me that women deserved to be happy sexually, that their bodies were wonderful and strong, and that all sexual fantasies were natural and okay as long as coercion was not involved. The latter book taught me that an intelligent, sexual woman could choose a job in the sex industry and not be a victim, but instead emerge even stronger and more self-confident, with a feeling, even, of self-actualization.

High school was uneventful—I became deeply involved in the excellent drama department at Berkeley High, exploring a long-standing interest in the theater arts. Contrary to a lot of adolescents' experiences with peer pressure in the realm of sex and drugs, I was lucky to have no pressure placed on me one way or another. . . . Consequently, I had a more active fantasy life than sex life, and was very ripe when I lost my virginity at eighteen to a man with whom I had my first long term relationship. This, unfortunately, had more forgettable moments than memorable ones. The sex and intimacy were mediocre at best, and I realized that my libido was not to have a good future with this man. My present husband is just the opposite. He gave full support for my long-dormant lesbian side; for the past four years I have lived with him and his long term woman lover in a close-knit, loving, supportive and intellectually stimulating *menage-a-trois.*

I stripped once a week while getting my bachelor's degree in nursing, magna cum laude, enjoying it to the fullest and using the performance opportunity to develop the public side of my sexuality. I went into full time movie work immediately following graduation, having done a few movies while still in school.

I know there are people who wonder, "Is she naive or something? What kind of a cause is porno?" But let's face it, folks: while the sex drive may be innate, modes of sexual behavior are learned. . . . If the media can have an effect on people's behavior, and I believe it does, why is it assumed that sex movies must always reinforce the most negative imagery of women? That certainly isn't what I'm about. From my very first movie I have always refused to portray rape, coercion, pain-as-pleasure, woman-as-victim, domination, humiliation and other forms of nonconsensual sex.

I can look back on all of my performances and see that I have not contributed to any negative images or depictions of women; and the feedback I get from men and women of all ages supports my contention. I get a lot of satisfaction from my job—for me it is a job of choice. As feminists, we must all fight to change our society so that women who don't want to do gender-stereotyped jobs can be free to work, support their families decently, and fulfill their potential in whatever job they choose. This includes not feeling compelled to do sex work because other well-paying options are severely limited.

Each of us has some idea or action that we hate but that is still protected by the First Amendment. I consider myself a reformer, and as a reformer I need a broad interpretation of the First Amendment to make my point. As a feminist I have principles that won't allow me to take license with that precious right to free speech. There have always been, and to some degree will always be, extremists who see the First Amendment as their license to do or say whatever, and not as a right which has implied responsibilities. Of course the sexual entertainment medium is no exception to this. I say censure them, but do not censor me.

DISCUSSION QUESTIONS FOR CHAPTER NINE

1. How do you think cultural forms shape gender? How might cultural forms function subversively to challenge traditional gender norms?

2. How do some television shows reflect changing gender norms while at the same time keeping most other norms intact? Can you name some examples?

3. What are some recent movies you've seen? How are women depicted in these movies? How is the gaze constructed in these movies?

4. How does pornography as a cultural form influence gender norms in U.S. society?

5. Why do you think some critics suggest there has never been a female Shakespeare or a female da Vinci? Do you agree with this assessment? Why or why not?

SUGGESTIONS FOR FURTHER READING

Brunsdon, Charlotte. *The Feminist, the Housewife, and the Soap Opera.* New York: Oxford University Press, 2000.

Hollows, Joanne. *Feminism, Femininity, and Popular Culture.* Manchester, England: Manchester University Press, 2000.

Meyers, Marian, ed. *Mediated Women: Representations in Popular Culture.* Bridgehampton, NY: Hampton Press, 1999.

Pollock, Griselda. *Differencing the Canon: Feminist Desire and the Writing of Art's Histories.* New York: Routledge, 1999.

Roberts, Robin. *Sexual Generations: 'Star Trek, the Next Generation' and Gender.* Champaign: University of Illinois Press, 1999.

Valdivia, Angharad N. *A Latina in the Land of Hollywood and Other Essays on Media Culture.* Tucson: University of Arizona Press, 2000.

Whiteley, Sheila. *Women and Popular Music: Sexuality, Identity, and Subjectivity.* New York: Routledge, 2000.

CHAPTER TEN

Resisting Violence Against Women

Sexual, verbal, and physical abuse of women in the United States occurs at an alarming rate. About 2,000 rapes are committed daily at the rate of about one every 5 minutes. One out of every four women on college campuses has experienced sexual violence, and about one in three women will experience such violence in their lifetime. A woman is battered every 15 seconds, more than 4 million U.S. women are physically assaulted by their partners each year, and about 1,500 women are murdered every year by their partners. In 90 percent of cases where children are raped, it is by someone they know, and almost 30 percent of all rape victims are under the age of 11.

Violence against girls and women is a persistent problem all over the world, with some countries condoning or legalizing such crimes. The reading "Violence Against Women: An Issue of Human Rights" explains how violence against girls and women is the most pervasive form of human rights abuse in the world today. When the United Nations World Conference on Women met in Beijing, China, in 1995, the Platform for Action gave priority to addressing global violence against women as a human rights issue. Historically violence against women has also been a central aspect of wars and military occupation. Fiona Lee's article, "Militarism and Sexual Violence," explores the ways various military forces have encouraged the sexual exploitation of women.

What do you think would be the societal response if men and boys routinely were victimized in these ways by women and girls? As discussed in Chapter 2, because these crimes are against a whole group of people whose only connection is that they are female, it is appropriate to consider these abuses crimes of hate and misogyny. Although violence against women is not generally understood as a hate crime, there are various laws that have helped in this struggle. These include rape shield laws, which prevented a victim's sexual history from being used by defense attorneys, and various state rape reform laws. Mandatory arrest procedures in cases of domestic violence and the creation of protective or temporary restraining orders have helped survivors of domestic abuse. In addition, the 1994 Violence Against Women Act provides some legal protections for women, although currently this act is under review.

Any discussion attempting to address the issue of violence against women must involve several key points. First, violence against women must be understood in the context of socially constructed notions of gender. If boys are raised to hide emotion, see sensitivity as a weakness, and view sexual potency as wound up with interpersonal power, and girls are raised to be dependent and support masculine entitlement, then interpersonal violence should be no surprise. Second, violence by men is a power issue and must be seen as related to masculine dominance in society generally. Indeed, entitlements associated with mascu-

HISTORICAL MOMENT: THE VIOLENCE AGAINST WOMEN ACT OF 1994

For decades feminist activists had worked to gain recognition of the extent and severity of violence against women in the United States. On the whole, violence against women had not been fully recognized as a serious crime within the criminal justice system.

Often reports of sexual assault were greeted with skepticism or victim-blaming. Prior to feminist activism in the 1970s, women had to present evidence of resistance to sexual assault; rules of evidence allowed consideration of a victim's entire sexual history; and husbands were exempt from charges of raping their wives. Following the opening of the first rape crisis centers in 1972, grassroots advocacy managed to not only provide care and services to victim, but also change these laws.

Generally, domestic violence was considered by law enforcement to be a "family matter," and so police, prosecutors, and judges were often reluctant to "interfere." The first domestic violence shelters opened in the mid-1970s, but not until the 1980s did this problem receive widespread attention. Thanks to activists, laws did change in the 1980s to codify domestic violence as criminal conduct, to provide increased penalties, to create civil protection orders, and to mandate training about domestic violence for law enforcement.

Following a Washington, DC, meeting of representatives from various groups advocating for victims of sexual assault and domestic violence in the 1980s, activists turned their attention to ensuring federal legislation to protect women through interstate enforcement of protection orders, to provide funding for shelters and other programs for victims, and to provide prevention efforts. By demonstrating the need for these protections and programs, grassroots advocates and the National Organization for Women (NOW) Legal Defense Fund were able to develop bipartisan support in Congress and to pass the Violence Against Women Act (VAWA) in 1994. The four subtitles of the Act describe the target areas of concern: Safe Streets, Safe Homes for Women, Civil Rights for Women and Equal Justice for Women in the Courts, and Protections of Battered Immigrant Women and Children. VAWA changed rules of evidence, police procedures, penalties, and court procedures. It also authorized funding for prevention, education, and training.

Since 1994, VAWA has been reauthorized and modified several times. To find out more about VAWA, visit the website of the U.S. Department of Justice's Violence Against Women Office at *www.ojp.usdoj.gov/vawo*.

linity produce a range that some scholars term the *rape spectrum*. This means that all sexist behaviors are arranged along a continuum from perhaps unexamined feelings of superiority over women on one end to rape on the other. In this sense, all these behaviors, even though they are so very different in degree, are connected at some level. Male domination of the political systems that address these crimes is also an issue. In "Supremacy Crimes," Gloria Steinem explains this relationship between privilege and violence against others.

Third, male sexual violence is related to the ways violence is eroticized and sexuality is connected to violence. Although pornography is the best example of this problem, women's

RACE, CLASS, SEXUAL ORIENTATION, AND VIOLENCE AGAINST WOMEN

- Among Asian/Pacific Islander women, 6.8 percent reported being raped at some point in their lifetime; 17.7 percent of White women, 18.8 percent of African American women, 24.4 percent of mixed race women, and 34.1 percent of Native American/Native Alaskan women reported being raped. Among Hispanic women, 19.6 percent reported being raped.[*]
- Among Asian/Pacific Islander women, 49.6 percent reported being physically assaulted at some point in their lifetime; 51.3 percent of White women, 52.1 percent of African American women, 57.5 percent of mixed race women, and 61.4 percent of Native American/Native Alaskan women reported physical assault. Among Hispanic women, 53.2 percent reported physical assault.[*]
- Native American/Native Alaskan women were most likely to report rape and physical assault. Asian/Pacific Islander women were least likely to report victimization, although many did talk about violence as a significant concern.[*]
- Women of all races and Hispanic and non-Hispanic women were about equally vulnerable to violence by an intimate.[†]
- Rape/sexual assault rates increased as household income decreased.[†]
- Battering occurs in lesbian relationships at the same rate as in heterosexual relationships.

[*] Statistics are from the National Violence Against Women Survey.
[†] Statistics are from the National Crime Victimization Survey.

magazines and advertising generally are rampant with these themes. Finally, we must understand violence against women in terms of the normalization of violence in society. We live in a society where violence is used to solve problems every day.

Consider the following story told to us. The woman, a White professional in her early 30s, had been having a drink with her colleagues one early evening after work. A well-dressed man struck up a conversation with her, and they chatted a while. When she was leaving with her colleagues, the man asked if he could call her sometime, and she gave him her business card that listed only work information. He called her at work within the next week and asked her to have dinner with him, and, seeing no reason not to, she agreed to meet him at such-and-such a restaurant after work. She was careful to explain to us that both times she saw this man she was dressed in her professional work clothes and it was early evening in a public space. There was nothing provocative, she emphasized, about her clothes or her demeanor. At some point during the meal she started feeling uncomfortable. The man was very pushy; he chose and ordered her food for her and started telling her that if she wanted to date him, he had certain requirements about how his girlfriends dressed and acted. She panicked and felt a strong need to get away from him, so, at some point she quietly excused herself saying she needed to visit the ladies' room. She then did a quick exit and did not return to the table. Unfortunately, this was not the end of the story. The man found out where her home was and started to stalk her. One evening he forced his way into her apartment and beat her very badly. Fortunately, he did not rape her. Although she took

ACTIVIST PROFILE: DEL MARTIN

In the 1950s, few lesbians were able to be out about their sexual identity. In fact, in most places homosexual sex was illegal, and lesbians and gay men were easy targets for violence, even by police. Nonetheless, in 1955 Del Martin (left), her partner Phyllis Lyon, and six other women co-founded the Daughters of Bilitis. The group started as a social club for lesbians seeking to meet and socialize with other lesbians, but before long it expanded its mission to include social reform, and chapters of the organization were launched around the country. Martin was president of the national organization from 1957 to 1960.

Martin became involved in the feminist movement in the early 1970s, and in 1976 wrote *Battered Wives*, a revolutionary examination of the experiences of victims of domestic violence. One of the most significant contributions of the book was identifying the origins of domestic violence in the patriarchal structure of the nuclear family. She wrote, "The nuclear family is the building block of American society, and the social, religious, educational and economic institutions of society are designed to maintain, support and strengthen family ties even if the people involved can't stand the sight of one another." Martin advocated collective thinking among members of government, social agencies, religious institutions, and political action groups. Her vision led to the creation of a movement addressing the problem of battered women.

In 1975, she helped found the Coalition for Justice for Battered Women. She also co-founded *La Casa de las Madres,* a refuge for battered women in San Francisco. She helped write the protocol for the San Francisco criminal justice system and served 3 years on the California Commission on Crime Control and Violence Prevention.

Partners since 1953, in the late 1990s, Martin and Lyons continued to work for issues of justice, particularly those related to aging. In 1995, they were appointed delegates to the White House Conference on Aging. For nearly 50 years they have worked tirelessly on behalf of marginalized people in order to bring about a more just world. Read "A Letter from a Battered Wife," shared by Del Martin in this volume.

KEY FINDINGS OF THE NATIONAL VIOLENCE AGAINST WOMEN SURVEY

Analysis of survey data on the prevalence, incidence, and consequences of violence against women produced the following results:

• Physical assault is widespread among adults in the United States: 51.9 percent of surveyed women and 66.4 percent of surveyed men said they were physically assaulted as a child by an adult caretaker and/or as an adult by any type of attacker. An estimated 1.9 million women and 3.2 million men are physically assaulted annually in the United States.

• Many American women are raped at an early age: Of the 17.6 percent of all women surveyed who said they had been the victim of a completed or attempted rape at some time in their life, 21.6 percent were younger than age 12 when they were first raped, and 32.4 percent were ages 12 to 17. Thus, more than half (54 percent) of the female rape victims identified by the survey were younger than age 18 when they experienced their first attempted or completed rape.

• Stalking is more prevalent than previously thought: 8.1 percent of surveyed women and 2.2 percent of surveyed men reported being stalked at some time in their life; 1.0 percent of women surveyed and 0.4 percent of men surveyed reported being stalked in the 12 months preceding the survey. Approximately 1 million women and 371,000 men are stalked annually in the United States.

• American Indian/Alaska Native women and men report more violent victimization than do women and men of other racial backgrounds: American Indian/Alaska Native women were significantly more likely than white women, African-American women, or mixed-race women to report they were raped. They also were significantly more likely than white women or African-American women to report they were stalked. American Indian/Alaska Native men were significantly more likely than Asian men to report they were physically assaulted.

• Rape prevalence varies between Hispanic and non-Hispanic women: Hispanic women were significantly less likely than non-Hispanic women to report they were raped at some time in their life.

• There is a relationship between victimization as a minor and subsequent victimization: Women who reported they were raped before age 18 were twice as likely to report being raped as an adult. Women who reported they were physically assaulted as a child by an adult caretaker were twice as likely to report being physically assaulted as an adult. Women who reported they were stalked before age 18 were seven times more likely to report being stalked as an adult.

• Women experience more intimate partner violence than do men: 22.1 percent of surveyed women, compared with 7.4 percent of surveyed men, reported they were physically assaulted by a current or former spouse, cohabiting partner, boyfriend or girlfriend, or date in their lifetime; 1.3 percent of surveyed women and 0.9 percent of surveyed men reported experiencing such violence in the previous 12 months. Approximately 1.3 million women and 835,000 men are physically assaulted by an intimate partner annually in the United States.

- Violence against women is primarily intimate partner violence: 64.0 percent of the women who reported being raped, physically assaulted, and/or stalked since age 18 were victimized by a current or former husband, cohabiting partner, boyfriend, or date. In comparison, only 16.2 percent of the men who reported being raped and/or physically assaulted since age 18 were victimized by such a perpetrator.

- Women are significantly more likely than men to be injured during an assault: 31.5 percent of female rape victims, compared with 16.1 percent of male rape victims, reported being injured during their most recent rape; 39.0 percent of female physical assault victims, compared with 24.8 percent of male physical assault victims, reported being injured during their most recent physical assault.

- The risk of injury increases among female rape and physical assault victims when their assailant is a current or former intimate: Women who were raped or physically assaulted by a current or former spouse, cohabiting partner, boyfriend, or date were significantly more likely than women who were raped or physically assaulted by other types of perpetrators to report being injured during their most recent rape or physical assault.

Source: National Violence Against Women Survey, National Institute of Justice and Center for Disease Control and Prevention, July 2000.

out a restraining order on him, he managed to gain entrance into her apartment building again and beat her senseless one more time in the hallway outside her apartment.

This story is a tragic illustration of misogyny and masculine entitlement. The man felt he had the right to define the reality of women in his life and expected them to be subordinate. He believed it was his entitlement. He was so full of rage that when a woman snubbed him, he would have to subdue her. In addition, the woman's telling of the story is illustrative of societal norms that blame women for their own victimization. When tearfully sharing her story, she had felt the shame and humiliation that comes with such an experience; she wanted it to be known that she had not been "asking for it": He had given no indication that he was anything but clean-cut and upstanding, she was dressed appropriately, she took no risks other than accepting a date, she gave him only her work numbers, and she agreed to meet him in a public place. What more could she have done except be wary of all men she might meet?

Men are also survivors of sexual abuse, especially childhood sexual abuse. They are most likely to have been hurt by an older boy or man, although sometimes by women or older female family members. Given the norms in our society about masculine invulnerability, it is often hard for men to talk about such abuse and to seek help. As a result, men are more likely than women to be in denial about such experiences. Sometimes men who have been abused react by trying to master the abuse, identifying with the source of their abuse to avoid the weakness associated with being a victim.

Sexual harassment at school, in the street, in public places, and in the workplace is also a form of sexual violence. Sexual violence can occur online or in an Internet chat room. In this chapter we discuss sexual assault and rape, physical abuse, and incest and end with a discussion of pornography as a form of violence against women. Because many forms of

Reprinted with permission.

pornography are legal, some object to thinking about pornography in the context of sexual violence and claim instead that it is a legitimate type of entertainment. Despite these concerns, we have decided to discuss it in the context of sexual violence because pornography eroticizes unequal power relations between women and men and often involves representations of coercive sex. Men are the major consumers of pornography, and women's bodies tend to be the ones on display. Pornography thus represents a particular aspect of gender relations that reflects the issue of male sexual violence against women.

RAPE

Although rape can be defined as sex without consent, it is understood as a crime of aggression because the focus is on hurting and dominating. More specifically, it is the penetration of any bodily orifice by a penis or object without consent. Someone who is asleep, passed out, or incapacitated by alcohol or drugs cannot give consent. Silence, or lack of continued resistance, does not mean consent. Likewise, consent is not the same as giving in to pressure and intimidation. Consent is a freely made choice that is clearly communicated. Consensual sex is negotiated through communication where individuals express their feelings and desires and are able to listen to and respect others' feelings and desires. Rape can happen to anyone—babies who are months old to women in their 90s, people of all races, ethnicities, and socio-economic status. Both women and men are raped, and, as already discussed, overwhelmingly it is a problem of men raping women and other men. Rape occurs relatively frequently in prisons where dominant men rape men they perceive as inferior. Often dominant inmates refer to these men as "women." In this way, rape is about power, domination, and humiliation and must be understood in the context of male dominance and power in gender relations.

Individuals may be sexually assaulted without being raped. Sexual assault can be defined as any sexual contact without consent and/or that involves the use of force. Like rape, sexual assault is an act of power, control, and domination. The terms can get confusing because sexual assault, sexual abuse, and rape are often used interchangeably. Basically, rape is a form of sexual assault or sexual abuse, but sexual assault or abuse do not necessarily imply rape. The sexual abuse of children is often termed *molestation,* which may or may not involve rape. When children are molested or raped by family members, it is termed *incest.* Although the rates of rape are very high, sexual assault rates generally (which include but are not limited to rape) are even higher.

In addition to the rape figures given at the beginning of the chapter, only about 1 in every 10 rapes is ever reported and less than 5 percent of perpetrators or fewer than 5 in 100 are ever convicted. Acquaintance rape, often termed *date rape,* where each person is known to the other, is the most frequent form of rape, and it is the most underreported. Among college women, more than 80 percent report that the assault involved someone the survivor knew. Women are more likely to report a rape if the perpetrator is someone they did not know. Seventy to 80 percent of campus rapes involve drugs and alcohol. A 2000 national study for the U.S. Department of Justice on the sexual victimization of college women found that almost 3 percent *reported* experiencing a completed and/or attempted rape (about 350 women on a campus with 10,000 female students). Over 15 percent were sexually victimized during the current academic year, 5 percent had someone expose their sex-

LEARNING ACTIVITY:
HOW SAFE IS YOUR CAMPUS?

Investigate the safety and security of your campus by asking these questions:

- How many acts of violence were reported on your campus last year?
- Does your campus have a security escort service?
- What resources does your campus provide to ensure safety?
- What training and educational opportunities about safety does your college provide?
- What specialized training about violence is offered to fraternities and sports teams on your campus?
- How does your school encourage the reporting of violence?
- What support services does your school offer to victims of violence?
- What is your school administration's official protocol for dealing with complaints of violence?
- How does your school's code of conduct address violence?
- Are there dark areas of your campus that need additional lighting?
- Are emergency phones available around your campus?

ual organs to them, and over 2 percent were observed naked without their consent. Thirteen percent reported being stalked. It is important to note that most of these victims knew their offender (*www.ncjrs.org*). High rates of rape on college campuses (especially gang rapes) tend to occur by fraternity members, often as part of male bonding rituals. The differences between high- and low-risk fraternities as potentially dangerous places for women are discussed in the reading "Fraternities and Collegiate Rape Culture" by A. Ayres Boswell and Joan Z. Spade.

Very often women realize that a past sexual encounter was actually a rape, and, as a result, they begin to think about the experience differently. They may have left the encounter hurt, confused, or angry but without being able to articulate what happened. Survivors need to talk about what occurred and get support. It is never too late to get support from people who care. Feeling ashamed, dirty, or stupid is a typical reaction for those who have experienced sexual assault. It is not their/your fault.

Societal myths about rape include the following:

- *Rapes happen less frequently in our society than women believe. Feminists in particular blow this out of proportion by focusing on women's victimization.* This is false; rape happens at an alarming rate. We do not know the actual rate because so much rape goes unreported. Although feminists care about the victimization of women, we focus on surviving, empowerment, and making changes to stop rapes from happening.
- *Women are at least partly responsible for their victimization in terms of their appearance and behavior (encouraging women to feel guilty when they are raped).* This is false; rape is the only violent crime when the victim is not de facto perceived as innocent. Consider the suggestion that a man who has just been robbed was asking to have his wallet stolen.
- *Men are not totally responsible for their actions. If a woman comes on to a man sexually, it is impossible for him to stop.* This is false; men are not driven by uncontrollable biological urges, and it is insulting to men to assume that this is how men behave. Note how this myth is related to the previous one that blames the victim.

These myths not only support masculine privilege concerning sexuality and access to women and therefore support some men's tendency to sexually abuse women, but also are important means for controlling women's lives. Recall again the discussion of sexual terrorism in Chapter 2. Such terrorism limits women's activities and keeps us in line by the threat of potential sexual assault. Research on rapists in the early 1980s revealed that, although there are few psychological differences between men who have raped and those who have not, the former group were more likely to believe in the rape myths, were more tolerant of interpersonal domination of women generally, and showed higher levels of sexual arousal around depictions of rape.

As will be discussed in Chapter 11, political institutions have historically supported men's access to women as sexual property and therefore have been slow to respond to women's rights in this arena. For example, there are still some states with marital exemption policies that do not characterize the rape of wives as crimes because wives are characterized as the sexual property of husbands. The history of racism in the South and the lynching of Black men for fabricated rapes of White women have influenced how society and the courts deal with the interaction of race and sexual violence. Men of color get longer sentences when they are convicted of rape than do White men, just as women of color have less credibility in the courtroom than White women.

BATTERING AND PHYSICAL ABUSE

There are several terms for the physical abuse of women in relationships and in the home: domestic abuse, spouse abuse, dating abuse or violence, wife battering, or wife abuse. The first three terms have been rejected by some scholars and activists in this area because these terms imply that women and men perpetrate violence at the same rate. The objection to this is similar to the one against "school violence" or "teen shootings" to which Steinem refers in the reading "Supremacy Crimes." Popular understanding of school and street violence avoids the fact that primarily males are the perpetrators of violence. Although there are some women who physically abuse men and some girls who bring handguns to school, overwhelmingly this is a problem of men hitting women and boys shooting other children in schools. Similarly, in the home most violent crimes are committed by men against women. Again, consider the response if it were girls and women who were the major perpetrators of violence. We believe that society would make note of the gendered nature of these acts if the situation were reversed.

Women who are physically abused are also always emotionally abused because they experience emotional abuse by virtue of being physically terrorized. Emotional abuse, however, does not always involve physical abuse. A man, for example, who constantly tells his partner that she is worthless, stupid, or ugly can emotionally abuse without being physically abusive. Sometimes the scars of emotional abuse take longer to heal than physical abuse. Del Martin's "A Letter from a Battered Wife" poignantly expresses the situation of an abused woman.

Why do some men physically abuse women or abuse other men? They abuse because they have internalized sexism and the right to dominate women (or others they perceive as subordinate) in their lives, have learned to use violence as a way to deal with conflict, and have repressed anger. Given this, how is it possible to explain why some women abuse men or abuse other women? Abusive behavior is an act of domination. Women too can internalize domination and can see men in their interpersonal relationships as subordinate to them, even though there is little support for that in society generally. Women in romantic relationships with other women can likewise negotiate dominance and subordination in their relationships and act this out. Battering is a problem in the lesbian community.

Another question is why do women so often stay in abusive relationships? The research on this suggests that when women leave abusive relationships they return about five to seven times before actually leaving for good. There are several complicated and interconnected reasons that women stay. First, emotional abuse often involves feelings of shame, guilt, and

■ ## IDEAS FOR ACTIVISM

- Volunteer at a local domestic violence shelter.
- Organize a food, clothing, and toiletries drive to benefit your local domestic violence shelter.
- Interrupt jokes about violence against women.
- Organize Domestic Violence Awareness Month (October) activities on your campus.
- Create and distribute materials about violence against women on your campus.

CHECK UP ON YOUR RELATIONSHIP

DOES YOUR PARTNER

Constantly put you down?

Call you several times a night or show up to make sure you are where you said you would be?

Embarrass or make fun of you in front of your friends or family?

Make you feel like you are nothing without him/her?

Intimidate or threaten you? "If you do that again, I'll . . . "

Always say that it's your fault?

Pressure you to have sex when you don't want to?

Glare at you, give you the silent treatment, grab, shove, kick, or hit you?

DO YOU

Always do what your partner wants instead of what you want?

Fear how your partner will act in public?

Constantly make excuses to other people for your partner's behavior?

Feel like you walk on eggshells to avoid your partner's anger?

Believe if you just tried harder, submitted more, that everything would be okay?

Stay with your partner because you fear what your partner would do if you broke up?

These indicators suggest potential abuse in your relationship. If you've answered yes to any of these questions, talk to a counselor about your relationship. Remember, when one person scares, hurts, or continually puts down the other person, it's abuse.

Created by the President's Commission on the Status of Women, Oregon State University.

low self-esteem. Women in these situations (like rape survivors generally) often believe that the abuse is their fault. They may see themselves as worthless and have a difficult time believing that they deserve better. Low self-esteem encourages women to stay and to return to abusive men. Second, some women who are repeatedly abused become desensitized to the violence; they may see it as a relatively normal aspect of gender relationships and therefore something to tolerate.

A third reason women stay in abusive relationships is that men who abuse women tend to physically isolate them from others. This often involves a pattern where women are prevented from visiting or talking to family and friends, are left without transportation, and/or have no access to the telephone. Notice how, when women are abused, the shame associated with this situation can encourage women to isolate themselves. An outcome of this isolation is that women do not get the reality check they need about their situation. Isolation thus helps keep self-esteem low, prevents support, and minimizes women's options in terms of leaving the abusive situation.

A fourth reason women stay is that they worry about what people will think, and this worry keeps them in abusive situations as a consequence of the shame they feel. Most women in abusive relationships worry about this to some extent, although middle-class women probably feel it the most. The myth that this is a lower-class problem and that it does not happen to "nice" families who appear to have everything going for them is part of the problem. And, indeed, the question about what people will think is a relevant one: Some churches tell abused women to submit to their husbands and hide the abuse, neighbors often look the other way, mothers worry about their children being stigmatized at school, and certainly there is embarrassment associated with admitting your husband or boyfriend hits you. For men this issue is even more pertinent, and the shame and embarrassment may be even greater for abused men.

A fifth reason women stay is that they cannot afford to leave. Women in this situation fear for the economic welfare of themselves and their children should they leave the abusive situation. These women tend to have less education and to have dependent children. They understand that the kind of paid work they could get would not be enough to support the family. Reason six is that some survivors believe that children need a father—and even a bad father might be better than no father. Although this belief is erroneous in our view, it does keep women in abusive situations "for the sake of the children." Interestingly, the primary reason women do permanently leave an abusive relationship is also the children: When women see that their children are being hurt, this is the moment when they are most likely to leave for good.

THE CYCLE OF VIOLENCE

Domestic violence may seem unpredictable, but it actually follows a typical pattern no matter when it occurs or who is involved. Understanding the cycle of violence and the thinking of the abuser helps survivors recognize they are not to blame for the violence they have suffered—and that *the abuser is the one responsible.*

1. *Tension building* The abuser might set up the victim so she is bound to anger him. The victim, knowing her abuser is likely to erupt, is apologetic. She may even defend his actions.
2. *The abuse* The batterer behaves violently, inflicting pain and abuse on the victim.
3. *Guilt and fear of reprisal* After the violence, the abuser may have feelings of "guilt" —not normal guilt, in which he'd feel sorry for hurting another person, but actually a fear of getting caught. He might blame alcohol for his outburst.
4. *Blaming the victim* The abuser can't stand any kind of guilt feeling for long, so he quickly rationalizes his actions and blames the victim for causing him to hurt her. He might tell her that her behavior "asked for it."
5. *"Normalcy"* At this point, the batterer exhibits kind and loving behavior. Welcomed by both parties, an unusual calm will surround the relationship. He may bring gifts and promise the violence will never happen again.
6. *Fantasy/set-up* Batterers and abusers fantasize about their past and future abuses. These fantasies feed the abuser's anger. He begins to plan another attack by placing his victim in situations that he knows will anger him.

Reprinted from *Take Care: A Guide for Violence-Free Living,* a publication of Raphael House of Portland.

Another reason women stay is that there is often nowhere to go. Although the increase in the numbers of crisis lines and emergency housing shelters is staggering given their absence only a few decades ago, some women still have a difficult time imagining an alternative to the abusive situation. This is especially true of women who live in rural areas and who are isolated from friends and family. Reason eight is that battered women often believe their partner will change. Part of the cycle of violence noted by scholars in this area is the "honeymoon phase" after the violent episode. First comes the buildup of tension when violence is brewing, second is the violent episode, and third is the honeymoon phase when men tend to be especially remorseful—even horrified that they could have done such a thing—and ask for forgiveness. Given that the profile of many batterers is charm and manipulation, such behavior during this phase can be especially persuasive. Women are not making it up when they think their partner will change.

Finally, women stay because they believe their partner might kill them—or hurt or kill the children—should they leave. Again, his past violence is often enough to make her realize this is no idle threat. Men do kill in these situations and often after wives and girlfriends have fled and brought restraining orders against them.

INCEST

This topic is especially poignant as the poem by Grace Caroline Bridges, "Lisa's Ritual, Age 10," demonstrates. Incest is the sexual abuse (molestation, inappropriate touching, rape, being forced to watch or perform sexual acts on others) of children by someone significant to the child. "Significant" might include such people as, for example, a baby-sitter, Boy Scout leader, boyfriend of an older sister, as well as immediate family members, friends, and relatives. We started this chapter with the statistic that in 90 percent of cases where children are raped it is by someone they know. Studies suggest that one in every three to five girls have experienced some kind of childhood sexual abuse by the time they are 16 years old. For boys this number is one in eight to ten, although this may be underestimated because boys are less likely to admit that they are survivors. Again, like other forms of abuse, this crosses all ethnic, class, and religious lines. Power is always involved in incest, and, because children are the least powerful group in society, the effects upon them can be devastating. Children who are abused often have low self-esteem and may find it difficult to trust.

Incest can be both direct and indirect. Direct forms include vaginal, oral, and rectal penetration; sexual rubbing; excessive, inappropriate hugging; body and mouth kissing; bouncing a child on a lap against an erection; and sexual bathing. Direct incest also includes forcing children to watch or perform these acts on others. Indirect incest includes sexualizing statements or joking, speaking to the child as a surrogate spouse, inappropriate references to a child's body, or staring at the child's body. Other examples involve intentionally invading children's privacy in the bathroom or acting inappropriately jealous when adolescents start dating. These indirect forms of incest involve sexualizing children and violating their boundaries.

Often siblings indulge in relatively normal uncoerced sexual play with each other that disappears over time. When this involves a child who is several years older or one who uses threats or intimidation, however, then the behavior can be characterized as incestuous. Indicators of abuse in childhood include excessive crying, anxiety, night fears and sleep disturbances, depression and withdrawal, clinging behaviors, and physical problems like urinary tract infections and trauma to the perineal area. Adolescent symptoms often include

VIOLENCE AGAINST WOMEN:
SELECTED HUMAN RIGHTS DOCUMENTS

International human rights documents encompass formal written documents, such as conventions, declarations, conference statements, guidelines, resolutions and recommendations. Treaties are legally binding to those States which have ratified or acceded to them, and their implementation is observed by monitoring bodies, such as the Committee on the Elimination of Discrimination Against Women (CEDAW).

GLOBAL DOCUMENTS

The Universal Declaration of Human Rights (1948) has formed the basis for the development of international human rights conventions. Article 3 states that everyone has the right of life, liberty and security of the person. According to article 5, no one shall be subjected to torture or to cruel, inhuman or degrading treatment or punishment. Therefore, any form of violence against women which is a threat to her life, liberty or security of person or which can be interpreted as torture or cruel, inhuman or degrading treatment violates the principles of this Declaration.

The International Covenant on Economic, Social and Cultural Rights (1966), together with the *International Covenant on Civil and Political Rights,* prohibits discrimination on the basis of sex. Violence detrimentally affects women's health, therefore, it violates the right to the enjoyment of the highest attainable standard of physical and mental health (article 12). In addition, article 7 provides the right to the enjoyment of just and favourable conditions of work which ensure safe and healthy working conditions. This provision encompasses the prohibition of violence and harassment of women in the workplace.

The International Covenant on Civil and Political Rights (1966) prohibits all forms of violence. Article 6.1 protects the right to life. Article 7 prohibits torture and inhuman or degrading treatment or punishment. Article 9 guarantees the right to liberty and security of person.

The Convention against Torture and Other Cruel, Inhuman or Degrading Treatment or Punishment (1984) provides protection for all persons, regardless of their sex, in a more detailed manner than the International Covenant on Civil and Political Rights. States should take effective measures to prevent acts of torture (article 2).

The Convention on the Elimination of All Forms of Discrimination against Women (1979) is the most extensive international instrument dealing with the rights of women. Although violence against women is not specifically addressed in the Convention, except in relation to trafficking and prostitution (article 6), many of the anti-discrimination clauses protect women from violence. States Parties have agreed to a policy of eliminating discrimination against women, and to adopt legislative and other measures prohibiting all discrimination against women (article 2). In 1992, the Committee on the Elimination of Discrimination Against Women (CEDAW) which monitors the implementation of this Convention, formally included gender-based violence under gender-based discrimination. General Recommendation No. 19, adopted at the 11th session (June 1992), deals entirely with violence against women and the measures taken to eliminate such violence. As for health issues, it recommends that States should provide support services for all

(continued)

victims of gender-based violence, including refuges, specially trained health workers, and rehabilitation and counselling services.

The *International Convention on the Elimination of All Forms of Racial Discrimination* (1965) declares that States Parties undertake to prohibit and to eliminate racial discrimination in all its forms and to guarantee the enjoyment of the right to security of the person and protection by the State against violence or bodily harm, whether inflicted by government officials or by any individual group or institution (article 5).

The four *1949 Geneva Conventions* and two additional Protocols form the cornerstone of international humanitarian law. The Geneva Conventions require that all persons taking no active part in hostilities shall be treated humanely, without adverse distinction on any of the usual grounds, including sex (article 3). They offer protection to all civilians against sexual violence, forced prostitution, sexual abuse and rape.

Regarding international armed conflict, *Additional Protocol I* to the 1949 Geneva Conventions creates obligations for parties to a conflict to treat humanely persons under their control. It requires that women shall be protected against rape, forced prostitution and indecent assault. *Additional Protocol II*, applicable during internal conflicts, also prohibits rape, enforced prostitution and indecent assault.

The *Convention on the Rights of the Child* (1989) declares that States Parties take appropriate legislative, administrative, social and educational measures to protect the child from physical or mental violence, abuse, maltreatment or exploitation (article 19). States shall act accordingly to prevent the exploitative use of children in prostitution or other unlawful sexual practices, and the exploitative use of children in pornographic performances and materials (article 34).

The *International Convention on the Protection of the Rights of All Migrant Workers and Members of Their Families* (adopted by the General Assembly in 1990, not yet in force) contains the right of migrant workers and their family members to liberty and security of person as proclaimed in other international instruments. They shall be entitled to effective protection by the State against violence, physical injury, threats and intimidation, whether by public officials or by private individuals, groups or institutions (article 16).

eating disorders, psychosomatic complaints, suicidal thoughts, and depression. Survivors of childhood sexual violence may get involved in self-destructive behaviors like alcohol and drug abuse or cutting on their bodies as they turn their anger inward, or they may express their anger through acting out or promiscuous behavior. In particular, girls internalize their worthlessness and their role as sexual objects used by others; boys often have more anger because they were dominated, an anger that is sometimes projected onto their future sexual partners as well as onto themselves. Although it takes time, we can heal from being sexually violated.

PORNOGRAPHY

Pornography involves the sexualization and objectification of women's bodies and parts of bodies for entertainment value. According to Catherine MacKinnon, who has written on and debated the issue of pornography at length, pornography can be defined as the graphic, sexually explicit subordination of women through pictures and/or words. She says pornography includes one or more of the following: women presented as dehumanized sexual objects, things, or commodities; shown as enjoying humiliation, pain, or sexual assault; tied up, mutilated, or physically hurt; depicted in postures or positions of sexual submission or servility; shown with body parts—including though not limited to vagina, breasts, or buttocks—exhibited such that women are reduced to those parts; women penetrated by animals or objects; and women presented in scenarios of degradation, humiliation, torture, shown as filthy or inferior, bleeding, bruised, or hurt in a context that makes these conditions sexual. MacKinnon adds that the use of men, children, or transsexuals in the place of women is also pornography. Note the definition includes the caveat that because a person has consented to being harmed, abused, or subjected to coercion does not alter the degrading character of the behavior.

Just as there are degrees of objectification and normalization of violence in pop culture forms, so too in pornography there is a continuum from the soft porn of *Playboy* to the hard-core *Hustler* and along to illegal forms of representation like child pornography and snuff films. Snuff films are illegal because women are actually murdered in the making of these films. The Internet is one of the largest sites for pornography. There are thousands of pornography sites on the Web, including those of "fantasy rape" that depict women being raped, and "sex" is still the top search word. In addition to Internet pornography there is the problem of Internet prostitution since this technology is utilized for the global trafficking and the sexual exploitation of women and children. The reading by Donna Hughes, "The Internet and the Global Prostitution Industry," explains this important social problem.

Many people do not oppose pornography because they feel that it represents free speech, or because they feel that the women have chosen to be part of it, or because they like the articles in these magazines. This is especially true of soft porn like *Playboy.* Some see pornography as a mark of sexual freedom and characterize those who would like to limit pornography as prudish. In the reading "Pornography and Freedom," John Stoltenberg explains how sexual freedom requires sexual justice and suggests that pornography is a violation of this justice rather than an expression of it. He writes about pornography in the context of gender and male domination in society.

Some make a distinction between hard core and soft porn and feel that the former is harmful and the latter relatively harmless. Others oppose pornography entirely as a violation of women's rights against objectification and sexualization for male pleasure and believe that people's rights to consume such materials are no longer rights when they violate the rights of others. This is an important debate that has brought some interesting coalitions that normally do not work together, such as feminists and conservative religious groups.

In this way acts of violence and the threat of violence have profound and lasting effects on all women's lives. We tend to refer to those who have survived violence as "survivors" rather than "victims" to emphasize that it is possible to go on with our lives after such experiences, difficult though that might be. Understanding and preventing violence against women has become a worldwide effort, bringing women and men together to make this a safer place for everyone.

READING 69

Violence Against Women
An Issue of Human Rights

Women in Action

Violence against women is the most pervasive form of human rights abuse in the world today. It includes assault, battery, rape, sexual slavery, mutilation, and murder. It is not a new phenomenon. It is not tied to poverty or economic upheaval. It is not related to the social displacement of peoples. Instead, it cuts across social and economic situations and is deeply embedded in cultures around the world—so much so that millions of women consider it a way of life.

Over the past decade, national and international groups have turned a spotlight on the hidden brutality of violence against women. They have called on the international community to value a woman's right to be free from violence as a human right. This focus on violence against women has spurred the development of strategies and programs to address the problem. Still, efforts to eradicate violence remain in their infancy and most societies continue to consider violence against women a private, so-called "family" matter.

Abused at Home

The highest percentage of violence against women occurs at home. A recent World Bank analysis indicates that one-quarter to one-half of all the world's women have been battered by an intimate partner. Regional studies confirm the level of violence. Statistics from Latin America show that between 26 and 60 percent of adult women have been beaten at least once in their lives. In Asia, 60 percent of all women have been assaulted. In sub-Saharan Africa, approximately 42 percent of women report being battered regularly by an intimate partner.

Victims of Rape

Data on rape provides another chilling picture: One out of five women worldwide is a victim of rape.

Most of them know their attackers. Young girls are the most frequent targets. Forty to 60 percent of all known sexual assaults are committed against girls aged 15 years and younger.

And although rape as a weapon of war has been internationally condemned since the Nuremberg trials following World War II, armies continue to use it in conflicts around the world. In 1992, as many as 20,000 women were raped in the first months of the war in Bosnia-Herzegovina. In Rwanda, between 2,000 and 5,000 rape-related pregnancies were reported in 1994. Over the past 10 years, mass rape has been documented in Peru, Myanmar, Liberia, Cambodia, Somalia, and Uganda.

Other Forms of Violence

Female infanticide and sex-selective abortions are also forms of violence against women. Demographers estimate that 60 million women are "missing" from the populations of South and West Asia, China, and North Africa, as a result. In India, particularly the northern regions, and in China and the Republic of Korea, genetic testing for sex has grown into a booming business. A recent study of amniocentesis procedures in a Bombay hospital found that 95.5 percent of aborted fetuses are female. UNICEF reports anecdotal evidence of the practice of female infanticide in some Asian communities.

Another fatal practice, "dowry killing," occurs in India. There, women are killed because they cannot meet the dowry demands of husbands' families. More than a dozen women are reported killed each day in dowry-related incidents—higher than 5,000 per year.

Female genital mutilation, practiced in at least 28 countries, mainly in Africa, is another form of violence against women. Considered a rite of passage for young girls, an estimated 130 million women and girls alive today have undergone a procedure in which all or part of the outer genitalia is removed. Two million girls each year undergo the operation, which is not only painful but also often results in a lifetime of health-related problems.

Responding to the Violence: The Role of the International Community

The international community has a role to play in reducing the violence against women. The 1979 approval by the United Nations of the Convention on the Elimination of Forms of Discrimination Against Women (CEDAW) marked a significant beginning in addressing the problem. Today, 160 countries have ratified the convention. Although it is a milestone in international efforts to reduce violence against women, nearly one-third of the signatory countries have declared that they will not be subject to several CEDAW provisions. These include equal rights to nationality and citizenship, equal ownership of family property, and an equal role in marriage and family life.

National Constitutions and Criminal Codes

At the national level, many countries have constitutions and laws intended to protect women against violence. Constitutions include bans on violence against human beings and the right to the integrity of the body and the right of life. Most prohibit discrimination against citizens.

Brazil's new constitution requires the state to combat violence against women. Colombia declares violence in the family destructive and provides for penalties by law. Equality under the law is written into most constitutions. Some refer specifically to women, like the constitutions of China, Greece, and Poland. These types of provisions are important because, in the absence of other laws or regulations, they can be used to protect women from violence.

National laws that protect against violence are usually part of the penal code. However, only 44 countries worldwide have laws that specifically protect women against domestic violence. Of these, some have expanded the law to cover cultural practices. For example, 12 countries have now criminalized the practice of female genital mutilation.

Most countries have laws against sexual assault and rape. The problem lies, however, in the level of protection guaranteed by the law. Efforts to reform rape law have been ongoing for decades and have centered on determining what constitutes rape. Only 17 countries now consider marital rape to be a criminal offense. Twelve Latin American countries still allow a rapist to escape prosecution if he marries his victim.

READING 70

Supremacy Crimes

Gloria Steinem

You've seen the ocean of television coverage; you've read the headlines: "How to Spot a Troubled Kid," "Twisted Teens," "When Teens Fall Apart."

After the slaughter in Colorado that inspired those phrases, dozens of copycat threats were reported in the same generalized way: "Junior high students charged with conspiracy to kill students and teachers" (in Texas); "Five honor students overheard planning a June graduation bombing" (in New York); "More than 100 minor threats reported statewide" (in Pennsylvania). In response, the White House held an emergency strategy session titled "Children, Violence, and Responsibility." Nonetheless, another attack was soon reported: "Youth With 2 Guns Shoots 6 at Georgia School."

I don't know about you, but I've been talking back to the television set, waiting for someone to tell us the obvious: it's not "youth," "our children" or "our teens." It's our sons—and "our" can usually be read as "white," "middle class," and "heterosexual."

We know that hate crimes, violent and otherwise, are overwhelmingly committed by white men who are apparently straight. The same is true for an even higher percentage of impersonal, resentment-driven, mass killings like those in Colorado; the sort committed for no economic or rational gain except the need to say, "I'm superior because I can kill." Think of Charles Starkweather, who reported feeling powerful and serene after murdering ten women and men in the 1950s; or the shooter who climbed the University of Texas Tower in 1966, raining down death to gain celebrity. Think of the engineering student at the University of Montreal who resented females' ability to study that subject, and so shot to death 14 women students in 1989, while saying, "I'm against feminism." Think of nearly all those who have killed impersonally in the workplace, the post office, McDonald's.

White males—usually intelligent, middle class, and heterosexual, or trying desperately to appear so —also account for virtually all the serial, sexually motivated, sadistic killings, those characterized by stalking, imprisoning, torturing, and "owning" victims in death. Think of Edmund Kemper, who began by killing animals, then murdered his grandparents, yet was released to sexually torture and dismember college students and other young women until he himself decided he "didn't want to kill *all* the coeds in the world." Or David Berkowitz, the Son of Sam, who murdered *some* women in order to feel in control of *all* women. Or consider Ted Bundy, the charming, snobbish, young would-be lawyer who tortured and murdered as many as 40 women, usually beautiful students who were symbols of the economic class he longed to join. As for John Wayne Gacy, he was obsessed with maintaining the public mask of masculinity, and so hid his homosexuality by killing and burying men and boys with whom he had had sex.

These "senseless" killings begin to seem less mysterious when you consider that they were committed disproportionately by white, non-poor males, the group most likely to become hooked on the drug of superiority. It's a drug pushed by a male-dominant culture that presents dominance as a natural right; a racist hierarchy that falsely elevates whiteness; a materialist society that equates superiority with possessions, and a homophobic one that empowers only one form of sexuality.

As Elliott Leyton reports in *Hunting Humans: The Rise of the Modern Multiple Murderer,* these killers see their behavior as "an appropriate—even 'manly' —response to the frustrations and disappointments that are a normal part of life." In other words, it's not their life experiences that are the problem, it's the impossible expectation of dominance to which they've become addicted.

This is not about blame. This is about causation. If anything, ending the massive cultural cover-up of supremacy crimes should make heroes out of boys and men who reject violence, especially those who reject the notion of superiority altogether. Even if one believes in a biogenetic component of male aggression, the very existence of gentle men proves that socialization can override it.

Nor is this about attributing such crimes to a single cause. Addiction to the drug of supremacy is not their only root, just the deepest and most ignored one. Additional reasons why this country has such a high rate of violence include the plentiful guns that make killing seem as unreal as a video game; male violence in the media that desensitizes viewers in much the same way that combat killers are desensitized in training; affluence that allows maximum access to violence-as-entertainment; a national history of genocide and slavery; the romanticizing of frontier violence and organized crime; not to mention extremes of wealth and poverty and the illusion that both are deserved.

But it is truly remarkable, given the relative reasons for anger at injustice in this country, that white, non-poor men have a near-monopoly on multiple killings of strangers, whether serial and sadistic or mass and random. How can we ignore this obvious fact? Others may kill to improve their own condition —in self-defense, or for money or drugs; to eliminate enemies; to declare turf in drive-by shootings; even for a jacket or a pair of sneakers—but white males addicted to supremacy kill even when it worsens their condition or ends in suicide.

Men of color and females are capable of serial and mass killing, and commit just enough to prove it. Think of Colin Ferguson, the crazed black man on the Long Island Railroad, or Wayne Williams, the young black man in Atlanta who kidnapped and killed black boys, apparently to conceal his homosexuality. Think of the Aileen Carol Wuornos, the white prostitute in Florida, who killed abusive johns "in self-defense," or Waneta Hoyt, the upstate New York woman who strangled her five infant children between 1965 and 1971, disguising their cause of death as sudden infant death syndrome. Such crimes are rare enough to leave a haunting refrain of disbelief as evoked in Pat Parker's poem "jonestown": "Black folks do not/Black folks do not/Black folks do not commit suicide." And yet they did.

Nonetheless, the proportion of serial killings that are not committed by white males is about the same as the proportion of anorexics who are not female. Yet we discuss the gender, race, and class components of anorexia, but not the role of the same factors in producing epidemics among the powerful.

The reasons are buried deep in the culture, so invisible that only by reversing our assumptions can we reveal them.

Suppose, for instance, that young black males—or any other men of color—had carried out the slaughter in Colorado. Would the media reports be so willing to describe the murderers as "our children"? Would there be so little discussion about the boys' race? Would experts be calling the motive a mystery, or condemning the high school cliques for making those young men feel like "outsiders"? Would there be the same empathy for parents who gave the murderers luxurious homes, expensive cars, even rescued them from brushes with the law? Would there be as much attention to generalized causes, such as the dangers of violent video games and recipes for bombs on the Internet?

As for the victims, if racial identities had been reversed, would racism remain so little discussed? In fact, the killers themselves said they were targeting blacks and athletes. They used a racial epithet, shot a black male student in the head, and then laughed over the fact that they could see his brain. What if *that* had been reversed?

What if these two young murderers, who were called "fags" by some of the jocks at Columbine High School, actually had been gay? Would they have got the same sympathy for being gay-baited? What if they had been lovers? Would we hear as little about their sexuality as we now do, even though only their own homophobia could have given the word "fag" such power to humiliate them?

Take one more leap of the imagination: suppose these killings had been planned and executed by young women—of any race, sexuality, or class. Would the media still be so disinterested in the role played by gender-conditioning? Would journalists assume that female murderers had suffered from being shut out of access to power in high school, so much so that they were pushed beyond their limits? What if dozens, even hundreds of young women around the country had made imitative threats—as young men have done—expressing admiration for a well-planned massacre and promising to do the same? Would we be discussing their youth more than their gender, as is the case so far with these male killers?

I think we begin to see that our national self-examination is ignoring something fundamental, precisely because it's like the air we breathe: the white male factor, the middle-class and heterosexual one, and the promise of superiority it carries. Yet this denial is self-defeating—to say the least. We will never reduce the number of violent Americans, from bullies to killers, without challenging the assumptions on which masculinity is based: that males are superior to females, that they must find a place in a male hierarchy, and that the ability to dominate *someone* is so important that even a mere insult can justify lethal revenge. There are plenty of studies to support this view. As Dr. James Gilligan concluded in *Violence: Reflections on a National Epidemic,* "If humanity is to evolve beyond the propensity toward violence . . . then it can only do so by recognizing the extent to which the patriarchal code of honor and shame generates and obligates male violence."

I think the way out can only be found through a deeper reversal: just as we as a society have begun to raise our daughters more like our sons—more like whole people—we must begin to raise our sons more like our daughters—that is, to value empathy as well as hierarchy; to measure success by other people's welfare as well as their own.

But first, we have to admit and name the truth about supremacy crimes.

READING 71

Fraternities and Collegiate Rape Culture
Why Are Some Fraternities More Dangerous Places for Women?

A. Ayres Boswell and Joan Z. Spade

Date rape and acquaintance rape on college campuses are topics of concern to both researchers and college administrators. Some estimate that 60 to 80 percent of rapes are date or acquaintance rape (Koss et al. 1988). Further, 1 out of 4 college women say they were raped or experienced an attempted rape, and 1 out of 12 college men say they forced a woman to have sexual intercourse against her will (Koss, Gidycz, and Wisniewski 1985).

Although considerable attention focuses on the incidence of rape, we know relatively little about the context or the *rape culture* surrounding date and acquaintance rape. Rape culture is a set of values and beliefs that provide an environment conducive to rape (Buchwald, Fletcher, and Roth 1993; Herman 1984). The term applies to a generic culture surrounding and promoting rape, not the specific settings in which rape is likely to occur. We believe that the specific settings also are important in defining relationships between men and women.

Some have argued that fraternities are places where rape is likely to occur on college campuses (Martin and Hummer 1989; O'Sullivan 1993; Sanday 1990) and that the students most likely to accept rape myths and be more sexually aggressive are more likely to live in fraternities and sororities, consume higher doses of alcohol and drugs, and place a higher value on social life at college (Gwartney-Gibbs and Stockard 1989; Kalof and Cargill 1991). Others suggest that sexual aggression is learned in settings such as fraternities and is not part of predispositions or preexisting attitudes (Boeringer, Shehan, and Akers 1991.) To prevent further incidences of rape on college campuses, we need to understand what it is about fraternities in particular and college life in general that may contribute to the maintenance of a rape culture on college campuses.

Our approach is to identify the social contexts that link fraternities to campus rape and promote a rape culture. Instead of assuming that all fraternities provide an environment conducive to rape, we compare the interactions of men and women at fraternities identified on campus as being especially *dangerous* places for women, where the likelihood of rape is high, to those seen as *safer* places, where the perceived probability of rape occurring is lower. Prior to collecting data for our study, we found that most women students identified some fraternities as having more sexually aggressive members and a higher probability of rape. These women also considered other fraternities as relatively safe houses, where a woman could go and get drunk if she wanted to and feel secure that the fraternity men would not take advantage of her. We compared parties at houses identified as high-risk and low-risk houses as well as at two local bars frequented by college students. Our analysis provides an opportunity to examine situations and contexts that hinder or facilitate positive social relations between undergraduate men and women.

The abusive attitudes toward women that some fraternities perpetuate exist within a general culture where rape is intertwined in traditional gender scripts. Men are viewed as initiators of sex and women as either passive partners or active resisters, preventing men from touching their bodies (La-Plante, McCormick, and Brannigan 1980). Rape culture is based on the assumptions that men are aggressive and dominant whereas women are passive and acquiescent (Buchwald et al. 1993; Herman 1984). What occurs on college campuses is an extension of the portrayal of domination and aggression of men over women that exemplifies the double standard of sexual behavior in U.S. society (Barthel 1988; Kimmel 1993).

Sexually active men are positively reinforced by being referred to as "studs," whereas women who are sexually active or report enjoying sex are derogatorily labeled as "sluts" (Herman 1984; O'Sullivan 1993). These gender scripts are embodied in rape myths and stereotypes such as "She really wanted it; she just said no because she didn't want me to think she was a bad girl" (Burke, Stets, and Pirog-Good 1989; Jenkins and Dambrot 1987; Lisak and Roth 1988; Malamuth 1986; Muehlenhard and Linton 1987; Peterson and Franzese 1987). Because men's sexuality is seen as more natural, acceptable, and uncontrollable than women's sexuality, many men and women excuse acquaintance rape by affirming that men cannot control their natural urges (Miller and Marshall 1987).

Whereas some researchers explain these attitudes toward sexuality and rape using an individual or a psychological interpretation, we argue that rape has a social basis, one in which both men and women create and re-create masculine and feminine identities and relations. Based on the assumption that rape is part of the social construction of gender, we examine how men and women "do gender" on a college campus (West and Zimmerman 1987). We focus on fraternities because they have been identified as settings that encourage rape (Sanday 1990). . . .

Gender Relations

Relations between women and men are shaped by the contexts in which they meet and interact. As is the case on other college campuses, *hooking up* has replaced dating on this campus, and fraternities are places where many students hook up. Hooking up is a loosely applied term on college campuses that had different meaning for men and women on this campus.

Most men defined hooking up similarly. One man said it was something that happens

> when you are really drunk and meet up with a woman you sort of know, or possibly don't know at all and don't care about. You go home with her with the intention of getting as much sexual, physical pleasure as she'll give you, which can range anywhere from kissing to intercourse, without any strings attached.

The exception to this rule is when men hook up with women they admire. Men said they are less likely to press for sexual activity with someone they know and like because they want the relationship to continue and be based on respect.

Women's version of hooking up differed. Women said they hook up only with men they cared about and described hooking up as kissing and petting but not sexual intercourse. Many women said that hooking up was disappointing because they wanted longer-term relationships. First-year women students realized quickly that hook-ups were usually one-night stands with no strings attached, but many continued to hook up because they had few opportunities to develop relationships with men on campus. One first-year woman said that "70 percent of hook-ups never talk again and try to avoid one another; 26 percent may actually hear from them or talk to them again, and 4 percent may actually go on a date, which can lead to a relationship." Another first-year woman said, "It was fun in the beginning. You get a lot of attention and kiss a lot of boys and think this is what college is about, but it gets tiresome fast."

Whereas first-year women get tired of the hook-up scene early on, many men do not become bored with it until their junior or senior year. As one upperclassman said, "The whole game of hooking up became really meaningless and tiresome for me during my second semester of my sophomore year, but most of my friends didn't get bored with it until the following year."

In contrast to hooking up, students also described monogamous relationships with steady partners. Some type of commitment was expected, but most people did not anticipate marriage. The term *seeing each other* was applied when people were sexually involved but free to date other people. This type of relationship involved less commitment than did one of boyfriend/girlfriend but was not considered to be a hook-up.

The general consensus of women and men interviewed on this campus was that the Greek system, called "the hill," set the scene for gender relations. The predominance of Greek membership and subsequent living arrangements segregated men and women. During the week, little interaction occurred between women and men after their first year in college because students in fraternities or sororities live and dine in separate quarters. In addition, many non-Greek upper-class students move off campus into apartments. Therefore, students see each other in classes or in the library, but there is no place where students can just hang out together.

Both men and women said that fraternities dominate campus social life, a situation that everyone felt limited opportunities for meaningful interactions. One senior Greek man said,

> This environment is horrible and so unhealthy for good male and female relationships and interactions to occur. It is so segregated and male dominated. . . . It is our party, with our rules and our beer. We are allowing these women and other men to come to our party. Men can feel superior in their domain.

. . .

Treatment of Women

Not all men held negative attitudes toward women that are typical of a rape culture, and not all social contexts promoted the negative treatment of women. When men were asked whether they treated the women on campus with respect, the most common response was "On an individual basis, yes, but when you have a group of men together, no." Men said that, when together in groups with other men, they sensed a pressure to be disrespectful toward women. A first-year man's perception of the treatment of women was that "they are treated with more respect to their faces, but behind closed doors, with a group of men present, respect for women is not an issue." One senior man stated, "In general, college-aged men don't treat women their age with respect because 90 percent of them think of women as merely a means to sex." Women reinforced this perception. A first-year woman stated, "Men here are more interested in hooking up and drinking beer than they are in getting to know women as real people." Another woman said, "Men here use and abuse women."

Characteristic of rape culture, a double standard of sexual behavior for men versus women was prevalent on this campus. As one Greek senior man stated, "Women who sleep around are sluts and get bad reputations; men who do are champions and get a pat on the back from their brothers." Women also supported a double standard for sexual behavior by criticizing sexually active women. A first-year woman spoke out against women who are sexually active: "I think some girls here make it difficult for the men to respect women as a whole."

. . .

Fraternity men most often mistreated women they did not know personally. Men and women alike reported incidents in which brothers observed other brothers having sex with unknown women or women they knew only casually. A sophomore woman's experience exemplifies this anonymous state: "I don't mind if 10 guys were watching or it was videotaped. That's expected on this campus. It's the fact that he didn't apologize or even offer to drive me home that really upset me." . . .

Attitudes Toward Rape

The sexually charged environment of college campuses raises many questions about cultures that facilitate the rape of women. How women and men define their sexual behavior is important legally as well as interpersonally. We asked students how they defined rape and had them compare it to the following legal definition: the penetration of an act of sexual intercourse with a female against her will and consent, whether her will is overcome by force or fear resulting from the threat of force, or by drugs or intoxicants; or when, because of mental deficiency, she is incapable of exercising rational judgment. (Brownmiller 1975, 368)

When presented with this legal definition, most women interviewed recognized it as well as the complexities involved in applying it. A first-year woman said, "If a girl is drunk and the guy knows it and the girl says, 'Yes, I want to have sex,' and they do, that is still rape because the girl can't make a conscious, rational decision under the influence of alcohol." Some women disagreed. Another first-year woman stated, "I don't think it is fair that the guy gets blamed when both people involved are drunk."

The typical definition men gave for rape was "when a guy jumps out of the bushes and forces himself sexually onto a girl." When asked what date rape was, the most common answer was "when one person has sex with another person who did not consent." Many men said, however, that "date rape is when a woman wakes up the next morning and regrets having sex." Some men said that date rape was too gray an area to define. "Consent is a fine line," said a Greek senior man student. For the most part, the men we spoke with argued that rape did not occur on this campus. One Greek sophomore man said, "I think it is ridiculous that someone here would rape someone." A first-year man stated, "I have a problem with the word rape. It sounds so criminal, and we are not criminals; we are sane people."

Whether aware of the legal definitions of rape, most men resisted the idea that a woman who is intoxicated is unable to consent to sex. A Greek junior man said, "Men should not be responsible for women's drunkenness." One first-year man said, "If that is the legal definition of rape, then it happens all the time on this campus." A senior man said, "I don't care whether alcohol is involved or not; that is not rape. Rapists are people that have something seriously wrong with them." A first-year man even claimed that when women get drunk, they invite sex. He said, "Girls get so drunk here and then come on to us. What are we supposed to do? We are only human."

Discussion and Conclusion

These findings describe the physical and normative aspects of one college campus as they relate to attitudes about and relations between men and women. Our findings suggest that an explanation emphasizing rape culture also must focus on those characteristics of the social setting that play a role in defining heterosexual relationships on college campuses (Kalof and Cargill 1991). The degradation of women as portrayed in rape culture was not found in all fraternities on this campus. Both group norms and individual behavior changed as students went from one place to another. Although individual men are the ones who rape, we found that some settings are more likely places for rape than others. Our findings suggest that rape cannot be seen only as an isolated act and blamed on individual behavior and proclivities, whether it be alcohol consumption or attitudes. We also must consider characteristics of the settings that promote the behaviors that reinforce a rape culture.

Relations between women and men at parties in low-risk fraternities varied considerably from those in high-risk houses. Peer pressure and situational norms influenced women as well as men. Although many men in high- and low-risk houses shared similar views and attitudes about the Greek system, women on this campus, and date rape, their behaviors at fraternity parties were quite different.

Women who are at highest risk of rape are women whom fraternity brothers did not know. These women are faceless victims, nameless acquaintances—not friends. Men said their responsibility to such persons and the level of guilt they feel later if the hook-ups end in sexual intercourse are much lower if they hook up with women they do not know. In high-risk houses, brothers treated women as subordinates and kept them at a distance. Men in high-risk houses actively discouraged ongoing heterosexual relationships, routinely degraded women, and participated more fully in the hook-up scene; thus, the probability that women would become faceless victims was higher in these houses. The flirtatious nature of the parties indicated that women go to these parties looking for available men, but finding boyfriends or relationships was difficult at parties in high-risk houses. However, in the low-risk houses, where more men had long-term relationships, the women were not strangers and were less likely to become faceless victims.

. . .

Alcohol consumption was a major focus of social events here and intensified attitudes and orientations of a rape culture. Although pressure to drink was evident at all fraternity parties and at both bars, drinking dominated high-risk fraternity parties, at which nonalcoholic beverages usually were not available and people chugged beers and became visibly drunk. A rape culture is strengthened by rules that permit alcohol only at fraternity parties. Under this system, men control the parties and dominate the men as well as the women who attend. As college administrators crack down on fraternities and alcohol on campus, however, the same behaviors and norms may transfer to other places such as parties in apartments or private homes where administrators have much less control. At commercial bars, interaction and socialization with others were as important as drinking, with the exception of the nights when the bar frequented by under-class students became crowded. Although one solution is to offer nonalcoholic social activities, such events receive little support on this campus. Either these alternative events lacked the prestige of the fraternity parties or the alcohol was seen as necessary to unwind, or both.

. . .

Students on this campus were aware of the contexts in which they operated and the choices available to them. They recognized that, in their interactions, they created differences between men and women that are not natural, essential, or biological (West and Zimmerman 1987). Not all men and women accepted the demeaning treatment of women, but they continued to participate in behaviors that supported aspects of a rape culture. Many women participated in the hook-up scene even after they had been humiliated and hurt because they had few other means of initiating contact with men on campus. Men and women alike played out this scene, recognizing its injustices in many cases but being unable to change the course of their behaviors.

. . .

Our findings indicate that a rape culture exists in some fraternities, especially those we identified as high-risk houses. College administrators are responding to this situation by providing counseling and educational programs that increase awareness of date rape including campaigns such as "No means no." These strategies are important in changing attitudes, values, and behaviors; however, changing individuals is not enough. The structure of campus life and the impact of that structure on gender relations on campus are highly determinative. To eliminate campus rape culture, student leaders and administrators must examine the situations in which women and men meet and restructure these settings to provide opportunities for respectful interaction. Change may not require abolishing fraternities; rather, it may require promoting settings that facilitate positive gender relations.

REFERENCES

Barthel, D. 1988. *Putting on Appearances: Gender and Advertising.* Philadelphia: Temple University Press.

Boeringer, S. B., C. L. Shehan, and R. L. Akers. 1991. "Social Contexts and Social Learning in Sexual Coercion and Aggression: Assessing the Contribution of Fraternity Membership." *Family Relations* 40: 58–64.

Brownmiller, S. 1975. *Against Our Will: Men, Women and Rape.* New York: Simon & Schuster.

Buchwald. E., P. R. Fletcher, and M. Roth (eds.). 1993. *Transforming a Rape Culture.* Minneapolis, MN: Milkweed Editions.

Burke, P., J. E. Stets, and M. A. Pirog-Good. 1989. "Gender Identity, Self-Esteem, Physical Abuse and Sexual Abuse in Dating Relationships." In M. A. Pirog-Good and J. E. Stets (eds.), *Violence in Dating Relationships: Emerging Social Issues.* New York: Praeger.

Gwartney-Gibbs, P., and J. Stockard. 1989. "Courtship Aggression and Mixed-Sex Peer Groups." In M. A. Pirog-Good and J. E. Stets (eds.), *Violence in Dating Relationships: Emerging Social Issues.* New York: Praeger.

Herman, D. 1984. "The Rape Culture." In J. Freeman (ed.), *Women: A Feminist Perspective.* Mountain View, CA: Mayfield.

Jenkins, M. J., and F. H. Dambrot. 1987. "The Attribution of Date Rape: Observer's Attitudes and Sexual Experiences and the Dating Situation." *Journal of Applied Social Psychology* 17: 875–895.

Kalof, L., and T. Cargill. 1991. "Fraternity and Sorority Membership and Gender Dominance Attitudes." *Sex Roles* 25: 417–423.

Kimmel, M. S. 1993. "Clarence, William, Iron Mike, Tailhook, Senator Packwood, Spur Posse, Magic . . . and Us." In E. Buchwald, P. R. Fletcher, and M. Roth (eds.), *Transforming a Rape Culture.* Minneapolis, MN: Milkweed Editions.

Koss, M. P., T. E. Dinero, C. A. Seibel, and S. L. Cox. 1988. "Stranger and Acquaintance Rape: Are There Differences in the Victim's Experience?" *Psychology of Women Quarterly* 12: 1–24.

Koss, M. P., C. A. Gidycz, and N. Wisniewski. 1985. "The Scope of Rape: Incidence and Prevalence of Sexual Aggression and Victimization in a National Sample of Higher Education Students." *Journal of Consulting and Clinical Psychology* 55: 162–170.

LaPlante, M. N., N. McCormick, and G. G. Brannigan. 1980. "Living the Sexual Script: College Students' Views of Influence in Sexual Encounters." *Journal of Sex Research* 16: 338–355.

Lisak, D., and S. Roth. 1988. "Motivational Factors in Nonincarcerated Sexually Aggressive Men." *Journal of Personality and Social Psychology* 55: 795–802.

Malamuth, N. 1986. "Predictors of Naturalistic Sexual Aggression." *Journal of Personality and Social Psychology* 50: 953–962.

Martin, P. Y., and R. Hummer. 1989. "Fraternities and Rape on Campus." *Gender and Society* 3: 457–473.

Miller, B., and J. C. Marshall. 1987. "Coercive Sex on the University Campus." *Journal of College Student Personnel* 28: 38–47.

Muehlenhard, C. L., and M. A. Linton. 1987. "Date Rape and Sexual Aggression in Dating Situations: Incidence and Risk Factors." *Journal of Counseling Psychology* 34: 186–196.

O'Sullivan, C. 1993. "Fraternities and the Rape Culture." In E. Buchwald, P. R. Fletcher, and M. Roth (eds.), *Transforming a Rape Culture.* Minneapolis, MN: Milkweed Editions.

Peterson, S. A., and B. Franzese. 1987. "Correlates of College Men's Sexual Abuse of Women." *Journal of College Student Personnel* 28: 223–228.

Sanday, P. R. 1990. *Fraternity Gang Rape: Sex, Brotherhood, and Privilege on Campus.* New York: New York University Press.

West, C., and D. Zimmerman. 1987 "Doing Gender." *Gender and Society* 1: 125–151.

READING 72

A Letter from a Battered Wife

Del Martin

A friend of mine received the following letter after discussing wife-beating at a public meeting.

I am in my thirties and so is my husband. I have a high school diploma and am presently attending a local college, trying to obtain the additional education I need. My husband is a college graduate and a professional in his field. We are both attractive and, for the most part, respected and well-liked. We have four children and live in a middle-class home with all the comforts we could possibly want.

I have everything, except life without fear.

For most of my married life I have been periodically beaten by my husband. What do I mean by "beaten"? I mean that parts of my body have been hit violently and repeatedly, and that painful bruises, swelling, bleeding wounds, unconsciousness, and combinations of these things have resulted.

Beating should be distinguished from all other kinds of physical abuse—including being hit and shoved around. When I say my husband threatens me with abuse I do not mean he warns me that he may lose control. I mean that he shakes a fist against my face or nose, makes punching-bag jabs at my shoulder, or makes similar gestures which may quickly turn into a full-fledged beating.

I have had glasses thrown at me. I have been kicked in the abdomen when I was visibly pregnant. I have been kicked off the bed and hit while lying on the floor—again, while I was pregnant. I have been whipped, kicked and thrown, picked up again and thrown down again. I have been punched and kicked in the head, chest, face, and abdomen more times than I can count.

I have been slapped for saying something about politics, for having a different view about religion, for swearing, for crying, for wanting to have intercourse. I have been threatened when I wouldn't do something he told me to do. I have been threatened when he's had a bad day and when he's had a good day.

I have been threatened, slapped, and beaten after stating bitterly that I didn't like what he was doing with another woman.

After each beating my husband has left the house and remained away for a few days.

Few people have ever seen my black and blue face or swollen lips because I have always stayed indoors afterwards, feeling ashamed. I was never able to drive following one of these beatings, so I could not get myself to a hospital for care. I could never have left my young children alone, even if I could have driven a car.

Hysteria inevitably sets in after a beating. This hysteria—the shaking and crying and mumbling—is not accepted by anyone, so there has never been anyone to call.

My husband on a few occasions did phone a day or so later so we could agree on an excuse I would use for returning to work, the grocery store, the dentist appointment, and so on. I used the excuses—a car accident, oral surgery, things like that.

Now, the first response to this story, which I myself think of, will be "Why didn't you seek help?"

I did. Early on in our marriage, I went to a clergyman who, after a few visits, told me that my husband meant no real harm, that he was just confused and felt insecure. I was encouraged to be more tolerant and understanding. Most important, I was told to forgive him the beatings just as Christ had forgiven me from the cross. I did that, too.

Things continued. Next time I turned to the doctor. I was given little pills to relax me and told to take things a little easier. I was just too nervous.

I turned to a friend, and when her husband found out, he accused me of either making things up or ex-aggerating the situation. She didn't, but she could no longer really help me. Just by believing me she was made to feel disloyal.

I turned to a professional family guidance agency. I was told there that my husband needed help and that I should find a way to control the incidents. I couldn't control the beatings—that was the whole point of my seeking help. At the agency I found I had to defend myself against the suspicion that I wanted to be hit, that I invited the beatings. Good God! Did the Jews invite themselves to be slaughtered in Germany?

I did go to two more doctors. One asked me what I had done to provoke my husband. The other asked if we had made up yet.

I called the police one time. They not only did not respond to the call, they called several hours later to ask if things had "settled down." I could have been dead by then!

I have nowhere to go if it happens again. No one wants to take in a woman with four children. Even if there were someone kind enough to care, no one wants to become involved in what is commonly referred to as a "domestic situation."

Everyone I have gone to for help has somehow wanted to blame me and vindicate my husband. I can see it lying there between their words and at the end of their sentences. The clergyman, the doctor, the counselor, my friend's husband, the police—all of them have found a way to vindicate my husband.

No one has to "provoke" a wife-beater. He will strike out when he's ready and for whatever reason he has at the moment.

I may be his excuse, but I have never been the reason.

I know that I do not want to be hit. I know, too, that I will be beaten again unless I can find a way out for myself and my children. I am terrified for them also.

As a married woman I have no recourse but to remain in the situation which is causing me to be painfully abused. I have suffered physical and emotional battering and spiritual rape because the social structure of my world says I cannot do anything about a man who wants to beat me. . . . But staying with my husband means that my children must be subjected to the emotional battering caused when they see their mother's beaten face or hear her screams in the middle of the night.

I know that I have to get out. But when you have nowhere to go, you know that you must go on your own and expect no support. I have to be ready for that. I have to be ready to support myself and the children completely, and still provide a decent environment for them. I pray that I can do that before I am murdered in my own home.

I have learned that no one believes me and that I cannot depend upon any outside help. All I have left is the hope that I can get away before it is too late.

I have learned also that the doctors, the police, the clergy, and my friends will excuse my husband for distorting my face, but won't forgive me for looking bruised and broken. The greatest tragedy is that I am still praying, and there is not a human person to listen.

Being beaten is a terrible thing; it is most terrible of all if you are not equipped to fight back. I recall an occasion when I tried to defend myself and actually tore my husband's shirt. Later, he showed it to a relative as proof that I had done something terribly wrong. The fact that at that moment I had several raised spots on my head hidden by my hair, a swollen lip that was bleeding, and a severely damaged cheek with a blood clot that caused a permanent dimple didn't matter to him. What mattered was that I tore his shirt! That I tore it in self-defense didn't mean anything to him.

My situation is so untenable I would guess that anyone who has not experienced one like it would find it incomprehensible. I find it difficult to believe myself.

It must be pointed out that while a husband can beat, slap, or threaten his wife, there are "good days." These days tend to wear away the effects of the beating. They tend to cause the wife to put aside the traumas and look to the good—first, because there is nothing else to do; second, because there is nowhere and no one to turn to; and third, because the defeat is the beating and the hope is that it will not happen again. A loving woman like myself always hopes that it will not happen again. When it does, she simply hopes again, until it becomes obvious after a third beating that there is no hope. That is when she turns outward for help to find an answer. When that help is denied, she either resigns herself to the situation she is in or pulls herself together and starts making plans for a future life that includes only herself and her children.

For many the third beating may be too late. Several of the times I have been abused I have been amazed that I have remained alive. Imagine that I have been thrown to a very hard slate floor several times, kicked in the abdomen, the head, and the chest, and still remained alive!

What determines who is lucky and who isn't? I could have been dead a long time ago had I been hit the wrong way. My baby could have been killed or deformed had I been kicked the wrong way. What saved me?

I don't know. I only know that it has happened and that each night I dread the final blow that will kill me and leave my children motherless. I hope I can hang on until I complete my education, get a good job, and become self-sufficient enough to care for my children on my own.

READING 73

Lisa's Ritual, Age 10

Grace Caroline Bridges

Afterwards when he has finished
lots of mouthwash helps
to get rid of her father's cigarette taste.
She runs a hot bath
   to soak away the pain
     like red dye leaking from her
      school dress in the washtub.

She doesn't cry
When the bathwater cools she adds more hot.
She brushes her teeth for a long time.

Then she finds the corner of her room,
curls against it. There the wall is
hard and smooth
as teacher's new chalk, white
as a clean bedsheet. Smells
fresh. Isn't sweaty, hairy, doesn't stick
to skin. Doesn't hurt much
when she presses her small backbone
into it. The wall is steady
while she falls   away:
   first the hands   lost

arms dissolving   feet gone
   the legs   dis-   jointed
     body cracking down
       the center like a fault
        she falls inside
         slides down like
dust   like kitchen dirt
        slips off
the dustpan into
         noplace
a place where
nothing happens,
nothing ever happened.

When she feels the cool
wall against her cheek
she doesn't want to
come back. Doesn't want to
think about it.
The wall is quiet, waiting.
It is tall like a promise
only better.

READING 74

Pornography and Freedom

John Stoltenberg

There is a widespread belief that sexual freedom is an idea whose time has come. Many people believe that in the last few decades we have gotten more and more of it—that sexual freedom is something you can carve out against the forces of sexual repressiveness, and that significant gains have been won, gains we dare not give up lest we backslide into the sexual dark ages, when there wasn't sexual freedom, there was only repression.

Indeed many things seem to have changed. But if you look closely at what is supposed to be sexual freedom, you can become very confused. Let's say, for instance, you understand that a basic principle of sexual freedom is that people should be free to be sexual and that one way to guarantee that freedom is to make sure that sex be free from imposed restraint. That's not a bad idea, but if you happen to look at a magazine photograph in which a woman is bound and gagged and lashed down on a plank with her genital area open to the camera, you might well wonder: Where is the freedom from restraint? where's the sexual freedom?

Let's say you understand that people should be free to be sexual and that one way to guarantee that freedom is to make sure people can feel good about themselves and each other sexually. That's not a bad idea. But if you happen to read random passages from books such as the following, you could be quite perplexed:

> "Baby, you're gonna get fucked tonight like you ain't never been fucked before," he hissed evilly down at her as she struggled fruitlessly against her bonds. The man wanted only to abuse and ravish her till she was totally broken and subservient to him. He knelt between her widespread legs and gloated over the cringing little pussy he was about to ram his cock into.

. . .

After reading that, you might well ask: Where's the freedom from hatred? where's the freedom from degradation? where's the sexual freedom?

Let's say you understand people should be free to be sexual and that one way to guarantee that freedom is to make sure people are not punished for the individuality of their sexuality. And then you find a magazine showing page after page of bodies with their genitals garroted in baling wire and leather thongs, with their genitals tied up and tortured, with heavy weights suspended from rings that pierce their genitals, and the surrounding text makes clear that this mutilation and punishment are experienced as sex acts. And you might wonder in your mind: Why must this person suffer punishment in order to experience sexual feelings? why must this person be humiliated and disciplined and whipped and beaten until he bleeds in order to have access to his homoerotic passion? why have the Grand Inquisitor's most repressive and sadistic torture techniques become what people do to each other and call sex? where's the sexual freedom?

If you look back at the books and magazines and movies that have been produced in this country in the name of sexual freedom over the past decade, you've got to wonder: *Why has sexual freedom come to look so much like sexual repression? why has sexual freedom come to look so much like unfreedom?* The answer, I believe, has to do with the relationship between freedom and justice, and specifically the relationship between *sexual* freedom and *sexual* justice. When we think of freedom in any other sense, we think of freedom as *the result* of justice. We know that there can't truly *be* any freedom until justice has happened, until justice exists. For any people in history who have struggled for freedom, those people have understood that their freedom exists on the future side of justice. The notion of freedom *prior to* justice is understood to be meaningless. Whenever people do not have freedom, they have understood freedom to be that which you arrive at by achieving justice. If you told them they should try to have their freedom without there being justice, they would laugh in your face. Freedom *always* exists on the far side of justice. That's perfectly understood—except when it comes to sex.

The popular concept of sexual freedom in this country has never meant sexual justice. Sexual-freedom advocates have cast the issue only in terms of having sex that is free from suppression and restraint. Practically speaking, that has meant advocacy of sex that is free from institutional interference; sex that is free from being constrained by legal, religious, and medical ideologies; sex that is free from any outside intervention. Sexual freedom on a more personal level has meant sex that is free from fear, guilt, and shame—which in practical terms has meant advocacy of sex that is free from value judgments, sex that is free from responsibility, sex that is free from consequences, sex that is free from ethical distinctions, sex that is essentially free from any obligation to take into account in one's consciousness that the other person is a *person*. In order to free sex from fear, guilt, and shame, it was thought that institutional restrictions on sex needed to be overthrown, but in fact what needed to be overthrown was any vestige of an interpersonal ethic in which people would be real to one another; for once people are real to one another, the consequences of one's acts matter deeply and personally; and particularly in the case of sex, one risks perceiving the consequences of one's acts in ways that feel *bad* because they do not feel *right*. This entire moral-feeling level

454   *Chapter Ten* | Resisting Violence Against Women

of sexuality, therefore, needed to be undone. And it was undone, in the guise of an assault on institutional suppression.

Sexual freedom has never really meant that individuals should have sexual self-determination, that individuals should be free to experience the integrity of their own bodies and be free to act out of that integrity in a way that is totally within their own right to choose. Sexual freedom has never really meant that people should have absolute sovereignty over their own erotic being. And the reason for this is simple: Sexual freedom has never really been about *sexual justice between men and women.* It has been about maintaining men's superior status, men's power over women; and it has been about sexualizing women's inferior status, men's subordination of women. Essentially, sexual freedom has been about preserving a sexuality that preserves male supremacy.

. . .

Pornography and Male Supremacy

Male-supremacist sexuality is important to pornography, and pornography is important to male supremacy. Pornography *institutionalizes* the sexuality that both embodies and enacts male supremacy. Pornography says about that sexuality, "Here's how": Here's how to act out male supremacy in sex. Here's how the action should go. Here are the acts that impose power over and against another body. And pornography says about that sexuality, "Here's who": Here's who you should do it to and here's who she is: your whore, your piece of ass, yours. Your penis is a weapon, her body is your target. And pornography says about that sexuality, "Here's why": Because men are masters, women are slaves; men are superior, women are subordinate; men are real, women are objects; men are sex machines, women are sluts.

Pornography institutionalizes male supremacy the way segregation institutionalizes white supremacy. It is a practice embodying an ideology of biological superiority; it is an institution that both expresses that ideology and enacts that ideology— makes it the reality that people believe is true, keeps it that way, keeps people from knowing any other

possibility, keeps certain people powerful by keeping certain people *down.*

Pornography also *eroticizes* male supremacy. It makes dominance and subordination feel like sex; it makes hierarchy feel like sex; it makes force and violence feel like sex; it makes hate and terrorism feel like sex; it makes inequality feel like sex. Pornography keeps sexism sexy. It keeps sexism *necessary* for some people to have sexual feelings. It makes reciprocity make you go limp. It makes mutuality leave you cold. It makes tenderness and intimacy and caring make you feel like you're going to disappear into a void. It makes justice the opposite of erotic; it makes injustice a sexual thrill.

Pornography exploits every experience in people's lives that *imprisons* sexual feelings—pain, terrorism, punishment, dread, shame, powerlessness, self-hate —and would have you believe that it *frees* sexual feelings. In fact the sexual freedom represented by pornography is the freedom of men to act sexually in ways that keep sex a basis for inequality.

You can't have authentic sexual freedom without sexual justice. It is only freedom for those in power; the powerless cannot be free. Their experience of sexual freedom becomes but a delusion borne of complying with the demands of the powerful. Increased sexual freedom under male supremacy has had to mean an increased tolerance for sexual practices that are predicated on eroticized injustice between men and women: treating women's bodies or body parts as merely sexual objects or things; treating women as utterly submissive masochists who enjoy pain and humiliation and who, if they are raped, enjoy it; treating women's bodies to sexualized beating, mutilation, bondage, dismemberment. . . . Once you have sexualized inequality, once it is a learned and internalized prerequisite for sexual arousal and sexual gratification, then anything goes. And that's what sexual freedom means on this side of sexual justice.

Pornography and Homophobia

Homophobia is absolutely integral to the system of sexualized male supremacy. Cultural homophobia expresses a whole range of antifemale revulsion: It expresses contempt for men who are sexual with men because they are believed to be "treated like a woman" in sex. It expresses contempt for women who are sexual with women just *because* they are women and also because they are perceived to be a rebuke to the primacy of the penis.

But cultural homophobia is not merely an expression of woman hating; it also works to protect men from the sexual aggression of other men. Homophobia keeps men doing to women what they would not want done to themselves. There's not the same sexual harassment of men that there is of women on the street or in the workplace or in the university; there's not nearly the same extent of rape; there's not the same demeaned social caste that is sexualized, as it is for women. And that's thanks to homophobia: Cultural homophobia keeps men's sexual aggression directed toward women. Homophobia keeps men acting in concert as male supremacists so that they won't be perceived as an appropriate target for male-supremacist sexual treatment. Male supremacy *requires* homophobia in order to keep men safe from the sexual aggression of men. Imagine this country *without* homophobia: A woman raped every three minutes *and a man* raped every three minutes. Homophobia keeps that statistic at a "manageable" level. The system is not foolproof, of course. There are boys who have been sexually molested by men. There are men who have been brutalized in sexual relationships with their male lovers, and they too have a memory of men's sexual violence. And there are many men in prison who are subject to the same sexual terrorism that women live with almost all the time. But for the most part—happily—homophobia serves male supremacy by protecting "real men" from sexual assault by other real men.

Pornography is one of the major enforcers of cultural homophobia. Pornography is rife with gay-baiting and effemiphobia. Portrayals of allegedly lesbian "scenes" are a staple of heterosexual pornography: The women with each other are there for the male viewer, the male voyeur; there is not the scantest evidence that they are there for each other. Through so-called men's-sophisticate magazines—the "skin" magazines—pornographers outdo one another in their attacks against feminists, who are typically derided as lesbians—"sapphic" at best, "bulldykes" at worst. The innuendo that a man is a "fairy" or a "faggot" is, in pornography, a kind of dare or a challenge to prove his cocksmanship. And throughout pornography, the male who is perceived to be the passive orifice in sex is tainted with the disdain that "normally" belongs to women.

. . .

Pornography and Men

Now this is the situation of men within male supremacy: Whether we are straight or gay, we have been looking for a sexual freedom that is utterly specious, and we have been looking for it through pornography, which perpetuates the very domination and subordination that stand in the way of sexual justice. Whether we are straight or gay, we have been looking for a notion of freedom that leaves out women; we have been looking for a sexuality that preserves men's power over women. So long as that is what we strive for, we cannot possibly feel freely, and no one can be free. Whatever sexual freedom might be, it must be after justice.

I want to speak directly to those of us who live in male supremacy as men, and I want to speak specifically to those of us who have come to understand that pornography does make sexism sexy; that pornography does make male supremacy sexy; and that pornography does define what is sexy in terms of domination and subordination, in terms that serve *us as men*—whether we buy it or not, whether we buy into it or not—because it serves male supremacy, which is exactly what it is for.

I want to speak to those of us who live in this setup as men and who recognize—in the world and in our very own selves—the power pornography can have over our lives: It can make men believe that our penises are like weapons. It can make men believe—for some moments of orgasm—that we are just like the men in pornography: virile, strong, tough, maybe cruel. It can make men believe that if you take it away from us, we won't have sexual feelings.

. . .

We've got to be telling our sons that if a man gets off by putting women down, *it's not okay.*

We've got to be telling merchants that if they peddle women's bodies and lives for men's consumption and entertainment, *it's not okay.*

We've got to be telling other men that if you let the pornographers lead you by the nose (or any other body part) into believing that women exist to be tied up and hung up and beaten and raped, *it's not okay.*

We've got to be telling the pornographers—Larry Flynt and Bob Guccione and Hugh Hefner and Al Goldstein and all the rest—that whatever they think they're doing in our names as men, as entertainment for men, for the sake of some delusion of so-called manhood . . . well, it's not okay. It's not okay with *us.*

READING 75

The Internet and the Global Prostitution Industry

Donna M. Hughes

The Internet has become the latest place for promoting the global trafficking and sexual exploitation of women and children. This global communication network is being used to promote and engage in the buying and selling of women and children. Agents offer catalogues of mail order brides, with girls as young as 13. Commercial prostitution tours are advertised. Men exchange information on where to find prostitutes and describe how they can be used. After their trips men write reports on how much they paid for women and children and give pornographic descriptions of what they did to them. New technology has enabled an online merger of pornography and prostitution, with videoconferencing bringing live sex shows to the Internet.

Sexual Exploitation on the Internet

Global sexual exploitation is on the rise. The profits are high, and there are few effective barriers at the moment. Because there is little regulation of the Internet, the traffickers and promoters of sexual exploitation have rapidly utilised the Internet for their purposes.

Traffickers and pornographers are the leading developers of the Internet industry. *PC Computing* magazine urges entrepreneurs to visit pornography Web sites. "It will show you the future of on-line commerce. Web pornographers are the most innovative entrepreneurs in the Internet." The pornographers and other promoters of sexual exploitation are the Internet leaders in the developing privacy services, secure payment schemes and online data base management.

The development and expansion of the Internet is an integral part of globalisation. The Internet sex industry has made local, community and even, national standards obsolete. Nichols Negroponte, Director of the Media Laboratory at the Massachusetts Institute of Technology, and founder of *Wired* magazine said, "As we interconnect ourselves, many of the values of a nation-state will give way to those of both larger and smaller electronic communities." The standards and values on the Internet are being set by the sex industry and its supporters and users. This has meant that women are increasingly "commodities" to be bought, sold, traded and consumed.

Newsgroups and Web Sites for Men Who Buy Women and Children

The oldest forum on the Internet for promoting the sexual exploitation of women is the alt.sex .prostitution. Its "aim is to create market transparency for sex-related services." Postings from this newsgroup are archived into a site called The World Sex Guide which provides "comprehensive, sex-related information about every country in the world."

The guide includes information and advice from men who have bought women and children in prostitution. They tell others where and how to find and buy prostituted women and children in 110 countries. . . .

The men buying women and posting the information see and perceive the events only from their self-interested perspective. Their awareness of racism, colonisation, global economic inequalities, and of course, sexism, is limited to how these forces benefit them. A country's economic or political crisis and the accompanying poverty are advantages, which produce cheap readily available women for the men. Often men describe how desperate the women are and how little the men have to pay.

The postings also reveal that men are using the Internet as a source of information in selecting where to go and how to find women and children to buy prostitution. Men describe taking a computer print out of hotels, bar addresses and phone numbers with them on their trips, or describe how they used the Internet search engines to locate sex tours. . . .

This rapid publishing electronic medium has enabled men to pimp and exploit individual women. Now, men can go out at night, buy a woman, go home, and post the details on the newsgroup. By morning anyone in the world with an Internet connection can read about it and often have enough information to find the same woman. For example, in Nevada, one man bought a woman called "Honey" and named the brothel where she could be found. Within a couple of weeks other men went and bought "Honey" themselves and posted their experiences to the newsgroup. Within a short period of time men were having an orgy of male bonding by describing what each of them did to this woman. The men are keeping a special Web site on the Internet for men to post their experiences of buying this one woman. Additional sites have been created for other identifiable women. To my knowledge this is completely unprecedented. The implications for this

type of public exchange in a fast-publishing easily accessible medium like the Internet are very serious for the sexual exploitation of women in the future. . . .

Prostitution Tours

Centers for prostitution tourism are also the sources of women trafficked for purposes of sexual exploitation to other countries. For centers of prostitution in European countries, women from poor countries are imported legally and illegally to fill the brothels. Among the largest sources of trafficked women today are the countries of the former Soviet Union. Advertisements for prostitution tours to these sites appear on the Internet, usually described as "romance tours" or "introduction tours."

Prostitution tours enable men to travel to "exotic" places and step outside whatever community bounds may constrain them at home. In foreign cities they can abuse women and girls in ways that are more risky or difficult for them in their hometowns.

As prostitution has become a form of tourism for men, it has become a form of economic development for poor countries. Tourism was recommended by the United States advisory boards as a way to generate income and repay debts. Nation-states set their own tourist policies and could, if they chose to do so, prevent or suppress the development of prostitution as a form of tourism. Instead, communities and countries have to rely on the sale of women and children's bodies as their cash crop. As the prostitution industry grows, more girls and women are turned into sexual commodities for sale to tourists. In the bars of Bangkok, women and girls don't have names —they have numbers pinned to their skimpy clothes. The men pick them by numbers. They are literally interchangeable sexual objects.

Prostitution tourism centers in industrialised countries are receiving sites for trafficked women from poor countries. The Netherlands is the strongest international proponent for legalised prostitution. Its capital, Amsterdam, is the leading prostitution tourism center in Europe. In 1997 the Netherlands legalized brothels. The result has been increased trafficking to Amsterdam from all over the world.

. . .

Bride Trafficking

Mail order bride agents have moved to the Internet as their preferred marketing location. The Internet reaches a prime group of potential buyers—men from Western countries with higher than average incomes. The new technology enables Web pages to be quickly and easily updated; some services claim they are updating their selection of women weekly. The Internet reaches a global audience faster and less expensively than any other media.

The agents offer men assistance in finding a "loving and devoted" woman whose "views on relationships have not been ruined by unreasonable expectations." The agencies describe themselves as "introduction services," but a quick examination of many of the Web sites reveals their commercial interests in bride trafficking, sex tours and prostitution.

The catalogues offer women mostly from Asia, Eastern Europe and Latin America, although in mid-1998 special catalogues of women from Africa appeared. They are called "African Queens," and "Brides of Nubia." Pictures of the women are shown with their names, height, weight, education and hobbies. Some catalogues include the women's bust, waist and hip measurements. The women range in age from 13 to 50. One of the commonly promoted characteristics of women from Eastern Europe is that they "traditionally expect to marry gentlemen that are 10 to 20 years older." The women are marketed as "pleasers," who will make very few demands on the men, and will not threaten them with expectations in their relationships, as women from the U.S. and Western Europe do.

In 1990 the Philippine government banned the operation of prostitution tour and mail order bride agencies in the Philippines. One trafficker lamented this new law, and told his customers that now he was operating out of the United States with his computer. He sent his own Filipina wife back to the Philippines to make contact and recruit women and adolescent girls for his Web site. Another com-plained that with the ban, the Philippine government is "definitely working against the interests of their own people. These girls want and need to leave that country." The same agent also complained that the U.S. government will not allow his youngest "brides" on offer into the country. "The service itself is not restricted by the American government, although they are real picky about getting your bride into the United States—they won't give a visa to a bride under sixteen." In his catalog of potential brides 19 girls are aged 17 or younger.

The bride traffickers sell addresses to men. Later they offer to arrange tours for the men to go to meet the woman with whom they have been corresponding, or to meet as many women as possible. Men pay for these services over the Internet with their credit cards.

. . .

Live Video Conferencing

The most advanced technology on the Internet is live video conferencing, in which live audio and video are transmitted over the Internet from video recorder to computer. This advanced technology is being used to sell live sex shows over the Internet. Real time communication is possible, so the man can personally direct the live sex show as he is viewing it on his computer.

The only limitation on this type of global sex show is the need for high-speed transmission, processing and multimedia capabilities. The software required is free, but the most recent versions of Web browsers have these capabilities built into them. As more men have access to high-speed multimedia computer and transmission equipment, this type of private sex show will grow. There are no legal restrictions on live sex shows that can be transmitted over the Internet. As with all Internet transmissions, there are no nation-state border restrictions. With Internet technology a man may be on one continent, while directing and watching a live strip show, a live sex show, or the sexual abuse of a child on another continent. There have been several documented cases of live transmission of the sexual abuse of children through live video conferencing.

. . .

Who buys women over the Internet? According to the Internet Entertainment Group (EIG), the largest pimp on the Web, the buyers for live strip shows are 90 percent male, 70 percent are between the ages of 18 and 40. The buyers are young men in college, and businessmen and professionals who log on from work. This information was obtained from analysis of credit card usage.

Growth of the Commercial Prostitution Industry on the Internet

. . .

The estimated number of pornographic Web sites varies widely. In late 1997, according to Naughty Linx, an online index, there were 28,000 "sex sites" on the Web with about half of them trying to make money selling pornography, videos, or live sex shows. Another study estimated that there were 72,000 pornographic Web sites on the Internet. At the end of 1997, Leo Preiser, the Director of the Center for Technology at National University estimated that 60 percent of the electronic commerce on the Web was pornography.

At the end of 1997, the online sex industry was estimated to be making US$1 billion a year, just in the United States. In findings from a 1997 survey, *Inter@ctive Week* magazine reported that 10,000 sex industry sites were bringing in approximately US$1 billion per year. A midsize site that was accessed 50,000 times per day made approximately US$20,000 each month. Established sex industry sites could expect to make 50 to 80 percent profits. Forrester Research, an Internet analyst firm, estimated that the Internet sex industry would make close to US$1 billion in 1998. "We know of at least three sites doing more than US$100 million a year. And there are hundreds of sites out there."

Regulation

The new technologies of the Internet have leapt over national borders and have left lawmakers scrambling to catch up. Internet users have adopted and defend an unbridled libertarianism. Any kind of regulation or restriction is met with hysterics and predictions of a totalitarian society. Even the most conservative restrictions on the transmission of child pornography are greeted with cries of censorship. The December 1996 issue of *Wired,* the leading professional publication on the Internet, stated that a new law in the United States, which made it illegal to transmit indecent materials to minors, was censorship. Internet libertarianism coupled with United States free speech absolutism is setting the standard for Internet communications.

Expressions of concern or condemnation of forms of sexual exploitation of women and children on the Internet are minimized by claims that pornographers have always been the first to take advantage of new technology—first photography, then movies, then VCRs, now the Internet. Those concerned about the use of the Internet for sexual exploitation are chastened with history lectures on new technology and pornography.

The solution that is being promoted is software programs that will screen out sexually explicit material. U.S. President Bill Clinton . . . supported a rating system on the Internet, so pornography would be rated and software programs will screen it out. This is seen as a way to protect children. Most adults are only concerned that their children may see pornography on the Internet. They aren't concerned about the women who are being exploited in the making of the pornography. In any search for a solution to pornography and prostitution it is crucial to remember, that sexual exploitation starts with real people and the harm is to real people.

We need international judicial and police cooperation in regulating the Internet and ending the trafficking and prostitution of women and the girls. If it is illegal to run a prostitution tour agency or mail order bride agency in the Philippines, then it should be illegal to advertise these services on a computer in the USA. The countries that send the men on tours and receive the mail order brides should also ban the operation of such agencies and prohibit the advertisement of these services from computer servers in their country.

The European Union defines trafficking as a form of organised crime. It should be treated the same way on the Internet. All forms of sexual exploitation should be recognised as forms of violence against women and human rights violations, and governments should act accordingly. Although the Internet offers open communication to people throughout the world, it should not be permitted to be dominated and controlled by men's interests or the interests of the prostitution industry, at the expense of women and children.

READING 76

Militarism and Sexual Violence

Fiona Lee

Throughout history women have been fundamental to the military's ability to operate successfully. While women have worked as soldiers, nurses, and support staff, they have also played other roles. In particular, women have been used as a form of recreation at the same time that the torture and rape of enemy women has functioned to humiliate and demonstrate power over the enemy.

The military uses a social construction of masculinity that relies on the objectification of women in order to sustain soldiers' morale and discipline. Military personnel are trained to dehumanize as a part of preparation for war. Often the easiest way to achieve this is to teach men to exercise their power over women. Ordinary training ditties often compare guns to penises and war to sex; men are called pussies and sissies and quickly learn that the definition of masculine is "not feminine." During the Vietnam War, "rest and recreation," or "R and R," was frequently re-labeled "I and I" for "intercourse and intoxication," clearly establishing the fact that military leave was analogous to the sexual violation of women (Enloe 1990).

Prostitution and various forms of sexual slavery have been among the spoils of military conquest for as long as war has existed (Elshtain 1989; Leuchtag 1995). Military prostitution has been justified by the theory that soldiers need an outlet for sexual energy. It is argued that if prostitution is not provided, soldiers will inevitably go out and rape civilian women due to the fact that they are men, and men need sex. Thus, the atrocities of military prostitution are hidden under the guise of protecting "innocent" women: daughters, sisters and wives. Yet, despite the guise of protection, military prostitution has resulted in a huge increase in local violence directed towards women. Incidents of domestic violence, sexual harassment and rape increase in communities of military occupation (Enloe 1990). In this way, prostitution is used by militaries as a tool, a tactic, and a strategy for the domination of whole communities.

The close relationship between militarism and the commodification of women's bodies and militarism as a masculinized concept encourages international prostitution. Such prostitution, in effect, depends on a concept of global patriarchy that encourages male sexual prerogatives (Watanabe 1995). Current levels of local prostitution in Saigon, Thailand, Vietnam and the Philippines are a direct result of U.S. military bases in these areas (Sturdevant and Stoltzfus 1992). It is difficult to argue that these women are making conscious choices to sell sex; economic situations drive them to support themselves and their families in this way. Most come from poor families and have little education. A prostitute in Nepal was quoted as commenting, "If I were a man, maybe I would have committed murder to fill my stomach. But as a woman, I became a prostitute" (Hornblower and Morris 1993: 44). This illustrates the dire circumstances in which many of these women find themselves. A similar situation has occurred in more recent times in Bosnia. When a merchant was asked how the people of Kapsovar would greet the Americans, he replied that the building of brothels was underway (Raymond 1999).

The rape of enemy women has also been recorded as a by-product of military action throughout history. It is a well-known fact that rape is one of the most effective strategies to "drive a wedge through a community, to shatter a society, and to destroy a people" (MacKinnon 1994: 190). In effect, rape of this kind results in the "castration" or de-masculinization of enemy men. This tactic has been used in conjunction with other forms of "ethnic cleansing" in Bosnia (Rejali 1998). Thousands of Croatian women have been raped and forced to bear children of Serbian descent.

While prostitution and rape were tactics used by both sides of the conflict during World War II, it is especially the plight of the "comfort women" that illustrates the complex relationship between prostitution and rape in wartime. During this war the Japanese government sanctioned a system of sexual slavery and enslaved thousands of comfort women as prostitutes for the Japanese Imperial army. These were young Chinese, Korean, and Philippino women who were deceived or abducted and forced into prostitution (Dolgopol 1995; Lord 1999). The first woman to break the comfort women's fifty year silence of shame that followed the sexual atrocities in World War II was Kim Haku in 1990: "When I was seventeen years old, the Japanese soldiers came along in a truck, beat us and dragged us into the back. . . . I was told that if I were drafted, I would earn lots of money at the textile company. . . . The first day I was raped and the rapes never stopped" (Watanabe 1995: 505). Her story is not unusual. It is estimated that approximately 150,000 to 200,000 women were forced into sexual slavery between 1928 and 1945. Often just 1,000 women would be forced to serve approximately 50,000 soldiers. The young women, sometimes as young as 14 and 15 years old, were made to perform sexually up to 20 and 30 times a day; one source says 80 times a day (anon. 1992: 32). These "prostitutes" were, in effect, raped over and over again.

The aftermath of the war was equally painful for these women. Fewer than 30% survived to the end of the war. Many died during the course of service, felled by disease or abuse, slain by fleeing troops, left to starve in the jungle, or killed by the Japanese to prevent them from telling their stories. Those who did survive suffered an acute sense of shame and worthlessness, and were often faced with sexually transmitted diseases or sterility (Watanabe 1995; anon. 1992).

In this way, since militaries are built on the solid foundation of patriarchal cultures that encourage the subordination and dehumanization of women, sexual violence has established itself as an inevitable accompaniment to war. Indeed, it could be maintained that it is essential to war: a concern for all those who seek equality, peace, and freedom.

REFERENCES

Anonymous. 1992. "Comfort Without Joy." *Economist* 322: 32.

Dolgopol, Ustina. 1995. "Women's Voices, Women's Pain." *Human Rights Quarterly* 17, 1: 127–154.

Elshtain, Jean Bethke. 1989. *Women and War.* (New York: Basic Books).

Enloe, Cynthia. 1990. *Bananas, Beaches and Bases: Making Feminist Sense of International Politics.* (Berkeley: University of California Press).

Hornblower, Margot and Morris, Nomi. 1993. "The Skin Trade." *Time* June 21: 44.

Leuchtag, Alice. 1995. "Merchants of Flesh." *Humanist* 55: 11.

Lord, Mary. 1999. "The Comfort Woman's Cry." *US News and World Report* December 16: 26.

MacKinnon, Catharine. 1994. "Rape, Genocide, and Women's Human Rights" in *Mass Rape: The War Against Women in Bosnia-Herzegovi,* edited by Alexandra Stiglmayer (Lincoln: University of Nebraska Press).

Raymond, Janice G. "Prostitution Is Rape That Is Paid For" *http://www.uvi.edu/artsci/wms/hughes/catw/kinrap.html.* Viewed 2/11/99.

Rejali, Darius M. 1998. "After Feminist Analyses of Bosnian Violence." Pp. 26–32 in *The Women and War Reader,* edited by Lois Ann Lorentzen and Jennifer Turpin (New York: New York University Press).

Sturdevant, Saundra Pollock and Stoltzfus, Brenda. 1992. *Let the Good Times Roll: Prostitution and the U.S. Military in Asia* (New York: New York Press).

Watanabe, Kazuko. 1995. "Trafficking in Women's Bodies: Then and Now." *Peace and Change* 20: 501–151.

DISCUSSION QUESTIONS FOR CHAPTER TEN

1. How do violence and the threat of violence exert social control on women? Do you ever fear gender-based violence? How do you think your gender affects your answer to this question?

2. Why do you think many feminists suggest that acts of violence against women are actually hate crimes? Do you think these acts should be classified as hate crimes?

3. Why do you think violence against women is so prevalent in society? Why do you think violence against women is primarily perpetrated by men?

4. How do myths about violence against women silence women and perpetuate sexist systems of oppression?

5. What steps do you believe need to be taken in order to address the problem of violence against women?

SUGGESTIONS FOR FURTHER READING

Bass, Ellen, and Laura Davis. *The Courage to Heal: A Guide for Women Survivors of Child Sexual Abuse,* rev. ed. New York: Harperperennial, 1994.

Evans, Patricia. *The Verbally Abusive Relationship: How to Recognize It and How to Respond.* Holbrook, MA: Adams Media Corp., 1996.

Jones, Ann. *Next Time, She'll Be Dead: Battering & How to Stop It,* rev. ed. Boston: Beacon, 2000.

Raine, Nancy Venable. *After Silence: Rape and My Journey Back.* New York: Three Rivers Press, 1999.

Ristock, Janice L. *No More Secrets: Violence in Lesbian Relationships.* New York: Routledge, 2002.

Smith, Merril D. *Sex Without Consent: Rape and Sexual Coercion in America.* New York: New York University Press, 2002.

Warshaw, Robin. *I Never Called It Rape: The Ms. Report on Recognizing, Fighting, and Surviving Date and Acquaintance Rape.* New York: Harperperennial, 1994.

CHAPTER ELEVEN

State, Law, and Social Policy

As we have noted in earlier chapters, societal institutions are established patterns of social behavior organized around particular needs and purposes. Gender, race, class, and other systems of inequality structure social institutions, creating different effects on different people. The state, the institution explored in this chapter, is a major social institution organized to maintain systems of legitimized power and authority in society. The state plays an important role in both teaching and enforcing social values. It is a very powerful institution that has profound implications for women's everyday lives.

The *state* is an abstract concept that refers to all forms of social organization representing official power in society: the government, law and social policy, the courts and the criminal system, the military, and the police. The state determines how people are selected to govern others and controls the systems of governance they must use. With considerable authority in maintaining social order, the state influences how power is exercised within society. The definition of *state* here is different from state as a geographic region, such as California or Ohio.

Because the state is a conduit for various patterns of social inequity, it does not always fairly regulate and control social order. Historically, women and people of color have been treated very poorly by the state, and there are still many problems and challenges at all levels of the political system. However, the state has also been a tool for addressing historical forms of social, political, and economic inequalities (as evidenced by civil rights and affirmative action legislation). Many people are involved in the struggle to effect change through laws and social policies. A key focus of this chapter is the interaction between the state and gender relations in society.

The state provides basic institutional structure in the sense that it regulates other institutions—for instance, the family (such as the Family Leave Act or considering some families to be illegitimate and thus ineligible for state benefits), education (such as Title IX), the economic system (such as antitrust laws that prevent monopolies), and religion (such as state rules for the separation of church and state). In this way, the state is a very powerful regulator of society.

GOVERNMENT AND REPRESENTATION

Although the terms *government* and *state* tend to be used interchangeably, the government is actually one of the institutions that make up the state. The government creates laws and procedures that govern society and is often referred to as the political system. Although the U.S. government or political system is purported to be a democracy based on the principle

LEARNING ACTIVITY: WOMEN IN LEADERSHIP AROUND THE WORLD

Visit the website of the "Worldwide Guide to Women in Leadership" at *www.guide2 womenleaders.com.* Follow the link to "Women Heads of Governments and Ministers by Country" to discover how many women are leading world governments and where. Find out if a woman has ever served as governor or lieutenant governor of your state by following the link to "Women Local Leaders." To find out what women other than Shirley Chisholm have run for the Presidency of the United States, follow the link to "Women Presidential Candidates."

of equal representation, the government is not representative of all people, and those who participate as elected officials do not necessarily represent all interests equitably.

The U.S. Constitution was formed at a time when White men were regarded as the only legal entity; women or people of color were not considered equal before the law. As a result, these individuals have had a complicated relationship with the Constitution. In the early formation of the republic, women were excluded because it was assumed that politics and citizenship were purely masculine domains. The founding fathers believed that women's political identity should be restricted because their presence in politics was immoral, corruptive, and potentially disruptive. Instead it was believed that women should be confined to the private sphere of the home where they would be dependent upon men (fathers, husbands, brothers) to represent them. Therefore, because women had no separate legal identity and were legal beings only through their relationship to a man, they had no claims to citizenship rights as women.

As you know from Chapter 1, the Seneca Falls convention in 1848 produced the Declaration of Sentiments and Resolutions that aimed to ensure citizenship rights for women. Women would have to wait until 1920 with the passage of the Nineteenth Amendment to the U.S. Constitution to receive the vote. In 1868, however, the Fourteenth Amendment was ratified, asserting that no state shall "make or enforce any law which will abridge the privileges or immunities of citizens of the United States, nor . . . deprive any person of life, liberty, or property without due process of law, nor deny to any person within its jurisdiction the equal protection of laws." This "person" was assumed to be male, and, as a result, women could still not vote, and the government did not (and, many would argue, still does not) extend the same protection of the law to women as it does to men. Susan B. Anthony, one of the first feminists who helped write the Declaration of Sentiments and Resolutions, wanted to test her belief that the Fourteenth Amendment should give women, as citizens, the right to vote. She voted in an election in Rochester, New York, and was fined. Hoping to push the case to the Supreme Court, Anthony refused to pay the fine. The case, however, was dropped in order to avoid this test of law. In the Anthony reading "Constitutional Argument," she argues her right to vote as a citizen under the terms guaranteed by the Fourteenth Amendment. This excerpt is from a speech Anthony gave in 1873.

In 1923 the Equal Rights Amendment was introduced into Congress to counter the inadequacies of the Fourteenth Amendment concerning women and citizenship. It was rewritten in the 1940s to read: "Equality of rights under the law shall not be denied or abridged by the United States or by any state on account of sex"; and it eventually passed Congress (almost 50 years later) in 1972. Unfortunately, it failed to be ratified by the states and suffered a serious defeat in the early 1980s.

An illustration of how the government has handled women and citizenship concerns the treatment of women who have married non-U.S. citizens. Prior to the mid-1920s, non-native-born women who married U.S. citizens automatically became American, and native-born women who married non-U.S. citizens automatically lost their citizenship and were expected to reside in their husband's country. They also lost their right to vote, once women had been given the vote in 1920. When laws were passed to retain women's citizenship in the mid-1920s, still only men were able to pass on citizenship to their children. Laws equalizing citizenship on these issues were eventually passed in the mid-1930s.

In addition to rights, citizenship also entails such obligations as taxation, jury duty, and military service. Although women have shared taxation with men, in the past they have been prevented from service and/or exempted from jury duty because of their role as mothers and housewives. It was not until the 1970s that the Supreme Court declared that juries had

Reprinted with permission from Nicole Hollander.

LEARNING ACTIVITY:
THE LEAGUE OF WOMEN VOTERS

The League of Women Voters was founded by Carrie Chapman Catt in 1920 during the convention of the National American Woman Suffrage Association, just 6 months before the Nineteenth Amendment was ratified. In its early years, the league advocated for collective bargaining, child labor laws, minimum wage, compulsory education, and equal opportunity for women in government and industry. Today the league is still involved in advocacy for justice, working on such issues as Medicare reform, campaign finance reform, and environmental preservation, as well as continuing the work begun over 80 years ago to encourage women to use their political voices. To learn more about the League of Women Voters or to join the league, visit their website at *www.lwv.org*.

ACTIVIST PROFILE: WILMA MANKILLER

With her election as chief of the Cherokee Nation, Wilma Mankiller took both a step forward and a step backward. Although Mankiller was the first woman to serve as chief of a major Native American tribe in modern times, her election recalled the importance women had among the Cherokee before colonization by Europeans. Precontact Cherokee society was matrifocal and matrilineal. Women owned the property and maintained the home and were intimately involved in tribal governance.

Mankiller first became committed to involvement in Native American rights in 1969 when Native activists, including some of her own siblings, occupied Alcatraz island in San Francisco Bay. The 19-month occupation became a turning point in Mankiller's life. She became director of the Native American Youth Center in Oakland, California, and in 1973 she watched as her brother joined other Native American activists as they held off FBI agents for 72 days at Wounded Knee, South Dakota.

Following a divorce, Mankiller returned to her family's land in Oklahoma and began to work for the Cherokee Nation; as an economic stimulus coordinator, she had the task of encouraging Cherokee people to train in environmental health and science and then return to their communities to put their knowledge to use. In 1981, she became director of the Cherokee Nation Community Development Department, and her work was so successful that she attracted the attention of Chief Ross Swimmer, who asked her to run as his deputy chief in 1983.

Despite sexist rhetoric and verbal threats from opponents, Swimmer and Mankiller won. In 1985, Swimmer was named head of the Bureau of Indian Affairs by President Ronald Reagan, and Mankiller became chief of the Cherokee Nation. In 1987, Mankiller ran on her own and was elected chief in her own right. That year, *Ms.* magazine named her Women of the Year. She was re-elected in 1991, winning by 83 percent of the vote.

During her tenure as chief, Mankiller focused on addressing high unemployment and low education rates among Cherokee people, improving community health care, implementing housing initiatives and child and youth projects, and developing the economy of northeastern Oklahoma. She created the Institute for Cherokee Literacy, emphasizing the need for Cherokee people to retain their traditions. She did not run for re-election in 1995. In 1998 President Bill Clinton awarded her the Presidential Medal of Freedom.

to be representative of the community. Even then juries were often racially biased such that it was not unusual for an African American to face a White jury. A 1986 Supreme Court ruling stated that juries could not be constituted on the basis of race, and a 1994 ruling declared that gender too could not be used as a basis for jury competence. The obligation for military service, which many women have wanted to share with men, is outlined in more detail later in the chapter. Of course, women have served in auxiliary roles as nurses, transport drivers, and dispatchers for many years and are now able to participate in combat positions within some divisions of the armed services.

Although women tend to be as involved as men in electoral politics (and sometimes even more involved) in terms of voting, showing support, and volunteering for campaigns, there are markedly fewer women involved in official political positions associated with campaigns. Women still constitute a relatively small number of candidates for local, state, and national offices, and their presence is greater at the local rather than national levels. As political offices get more visible, higher level, better paid, and more authoritative or powerful, there are fewer women in these positions. Several explanations may explain this gap. Although some suggest that women are just not interested and that they lack the credentials, the main reasons are conflict between family and work roles, lack of political financing, and discrimination and sexist attitudes toward women in politics.

The 107th Congress of the year 2001–2003 includes 60 women or almost 14 percent in the House of Representatives, 13 women or 13 percent in the Senate, and 13.6 percent overall in Congress. Of these 73 women in Congress, 20 or 27.4 percent are women of color. These figures, although much improved compared to pre-1990s statistics, are still alarming; they illustrate male and White domination in society and challenge the extent to which women and people of color are represented. However, remember that females do not necessarily represent women's interests, just as people of color do not necessarily support issues that improve the status of non-White groups. Many feminists vote for men in political office over opposing women candidates because they understand that being a female does not necessarily mean that her politics, or those of the party she represents, are pro-women. In terms of the gender gap in voting, on the average women tend to lean toward the Democratic Party more than men do and are more likely to be concerned about such issues as education, welfare, health care, and the environment. For example, during the 2000 presidential election a majority of women voted Democrat for Al Gore while a majority of men voted Republican for George W. Bush. This can be explained by the fact that while there are exceptions, men are more likely as a group to vote for a strong defense, anti-welfare, and anti–affirmative action policies: the stance of the Republican party. This does not of course imply that all men are Republican, only that as a group, they are more likely to favor the issues put forward by this political party.

HISTORICAL MOMENT:
SHIRLEY CHISHOLM FOR PRESIDENT

Shirley Chisholm was born to a mother from Barbados and a father from British Guiana. She grew up in Barbados and Brooklyn and graduated with honors from Brooklyn College with a major in sociology. Following graduation, she worked at the Mt. Calvary Childcare Center in Harlem and became active in local politics. She completed a master's in education at Columbia University in 1952 and then managed daycare centers.

Chisholm ran for a state assembly seat in 1964 and won, serving in the New York General Assembly until 1968. While in the New York legislature, she focused on issues of education and daycare. In 1968, she ran for and won a seat in the U.S. Congress representing New York's Twelfth Congressional District, becoming the first Black woman in the House of Representatives. Chisholm quickly distinguished herself as an outspoken advocate for the poor and for women's and civil rights and against the war in Vietnam.

During a speech on equal rights for women before the House of Representatives in 1969, Chisholm pointed out, "More than half of the population of the United States is female. But women occupy only 2 percent of the managerial positions. They have not even reached the level of tokenism yet. No women sit on the AFL-CIO council or Supreme Court. There have been only two women who have held Cabinet rank, and at present there are none. Only two women now hold ambassadorial rank in the diplomatic corps. In Congress, we are down to 1 senator and 10 representatives. Considering that there are about 3½ million more women in the United States than men, this situation is outrageous."

In January 1972, Chisholm announced her candidacy for the Democratic nomination for the presidency: "I stand before you today as a candidate for the Democratic nomination for the Presidency of the United States. I am not the candidate of Black America, although I am Black and proud. I am not the candidate of the women's movement of this country, although I am a woman, and I am equally proud of that. I am not the candidate of any political bosses or special interests. I am the candidate of the people."

Chisholm became the first woman considered for the presidential nomination. Although she was defeated, she did garner more than 150 votes from the delegates to the Democratic National Convention in Miami. She continued to serve in Congress until 1982. She has written two books: *Unbossed and Unbought* and *The Good Fight*.

WOMEN AND THE LAW

The United States inherited British common law that utilized the doctrine of *femme couverte* or covered women: Husband and wife were one person under law, and she was his sexual property. As a result, married women could not seek employment without the husband's consent, keep their own wages, own property, sue, exercise control over their children, and control their reproductive lives. The reading by Margaret Conway and others, "Women and Family Law: Marriage and Divorce," explains laws and public policies governing marriage under British common law. Because husbands and wives were "one" in marriage, wives were sexual property of husbands, and rape within marriage was legally condoned. It was legally impossible to charge a husband with raping his wife because it would imply that the husband was raping himself. The phrase "rule of thumb" meant that it was okay to beat a woman so long as an implement no wider than the thumb was used. Although the Married Women's Property Act of 1848 allowed women to own and inherit property, the other constraints on their lives remained intact through the twentieth century. Even with the passage of these property acts, however, the law allowed the husband to control community property (jointly owned legally by husband and wife) until the 1970s.

Prior to the 1960s most states decriminalized violence in the family and operated marital rape exemption laws. It was not until the 1980s and 1990s that women had legal protections against violence; these protections include legislation such as the rape shield laws, mandatory arrest procedures in cases of domestic violence, public notification programs about convicted sex offenders in communities, the creation of protective or temporary restraining orders, state rape reform laws, and the 1994 Violence Against Women Act. As the reading by Conway explains, although most states have abolished marital rape exemptions, there are states that retain these laws in some fashion today. And, certainly, as the readings in Chapter 10 suggest, violence against women is increasing rather than decreasing in contemporary society.

Also prior to the 1960s, women's reproductive lives were a function of state control because the state had criminalized access to contraceptive information and procedures. As discussed in Chapter 6, before the passage of *Griswold v. Connecticut* in 1965, women had no

■   WOMEN IN ELECTIVE OFFICE

Visit the site of the Center for American Women in Politics at *www.rci.rutgers.edu/~ cawp*. Follow the link to "Facts and Findings" and select "Women in Statewide Elective Office" from the pull-down menu to discover which women currently hold elective office in the United States. Next use the pull-down menu to discover who are the women of color currently in elective office. What elective positions do women in your state hold?

■   IDEAS FOR ACTIVISM

- Visit the homepage for Women Leaders Online at *www.wlo.org*. Women Leaders Online (WLO) is the first and largest women's activist group on the Internet. WLO provides action alerts to make people aware of issues that need activism. The organization also promotes voter education and facilities email access to your U.S. senators and representatives.
- For more information about political issues of concern to women, visit the homepage of the Feminist Majority Foundation at *www.feminist.org*. Follow the link to "Take Action" for ideas about what you can do to make a difference.

legal right to contraceptives, and before the early 1970s with the passage of state abortion rulings and *Roe v. Wade,* they had no legal right to an abortion. The issue of reproductive rights is still controversial, and the legal arena is the site for many of these battles today.

In terms of work and employment, *Muller v. Oregon* in 1908 reaffirmed the state's justification for limiting women's employment. This legislation approved Oregon's right to prevent women from working in factories or similar facilities for more than 10 hours a day based upon the state's interest in protecting the reproductive functions of women. It was considered important for the "well-being of the race" that women's ability to contract freely be limited. As discussed in Chapter 8, by the 1960s various civil rights legislation was passed including the Equal Pay Act and Title VII, preventing employers from discriminating against women and people of color in employment. Affirmative action legislation of the 1970s and sexual harassment legislation of the 1980s further attempted to dismantle gender- and race-based inequities in the labor force. Challenges remain in this area, however, as systems of inequality still shape labor force experiences.

The state also affects women through the institution of marriage. Women had access to divorce in the nineteenth century, although divorce was much more difficult to obtain. In addition, divorce carried a considerable stigma, especially to the divorced wife. Prior to the advent of no-fault divorce in the 1970s (divorce on demand by either or both parties), partners had to sue for divorce. Grounds to sue were based on a spouse's violation of the marriage contract such as by cruelty, abandonment, or adultery, and the courts needed to prove that someone had committed a crime. This procedure was difficult and expensive for women; it also tended to involve a double standard of behavior based upon gender. Nonetheless, because this procedure allowed wives to show that husbands were "guilty," wives

■ AFFIRMATIVE ACTION: MYTH VERSUS REALITY

Myth: Women don't need affirmative action any more.

Reality: Though women have made gains in the last 30 years, they remain severely underrepresented in most nontraditional professional occupations as well as blue-collar trades. The U.S. Department of Labor's Glass Ceiling Commission Report (1995) states that although White men are only 43 percent of the Fortune 2000 workforce, they hold 95 percent of the senior management jobs.

Myth: Under affirmative action, minorities and women receive preferences.

Reality: Affirmative action does not require preferences, nor do women and minorities assume that they will be given preference. Race, gender, and national origin are factors that can be considered when hiring or accepting qualified applicants, which is similar to the preferences given to veterans in hiring and to children of alumni in college admissions.

Myth: Affirmative action is really quotas.

Reality: Affirmative action provides women and minorities with full educational and workplace opportunities. Race, national origin, and gender are among several factors to be considered, but relevant and valid job or educational qualifications are not to be compromised. Further, the Supreme Court has made clear that affirmative action or programs that claim to be affirmative action are illegal if: (1) an unqualified person receives benefits over a qualified one; (2) numerical goals are so strict that the plan lacks reasonable flexibility; (3) the numerical goals bear no relationship to the available pool of qualified candidates and could therefore become quotas; (4) the plan is not fixed in length; or (5) innocent bystanders are impermissibly harmed.

Myth: Affirmative action leads to reverse discrimination.

Reality: Evidence demonstrates that reverse discrimination is rare. For example, of the 91,000 employment discrimination cases before the Equal Employment Opportunities Commission, approximately 3 percent are reverse discrimination cases. Further, a study conducted by Rutgers University and commissioned by the U.S. Department of Labor (1995) found that reverse discrimination is not a significant problem in employment and that a "high proportion" of claims brought by White men are "without merit."

Myth: Affirmative action programs that aid the economically disadvantaged—needs-based programs—are enough to address discrimination.

Reality: Women and minorities face discrimination as they climb the corporate ladder and bump up against the glass ceiling.

Myth: Unqualified individuals are being hired and promoted for the sake of diversity/affirmative action.

Reality: Only affirmative action plans that do not compromise valid job or educational qualifications are lawful. Plans must be flexible, realistic, reviewable, and fair. The Supreme Court has found that there are at least two permissible bases for voluntary affirmative action by employers under Title VII: (1) to remedy a clear and convincing history of past discrimination by the employer or union, and (2) to cure a manifest imbalance in the employer's workforce.

(continued)

Myth: Affirmative action does not have a place in government contracts.

Reality: Congress has created federal procurement programs to counter the effects of discrimination that have raised artificial barriers to the formation, development, and utilization of businesses owned by disadvantaged individuals, including women and minorities. Only qualified businesses can participate in these procurement programs. These programs are still needed because although minorities own almost 9 percent of all businesses and women own 34 percent of all businesses, together minorities and women receive only about 8.8 percent of the over $200 billion in federal contract awards.

Myth: Title VII alone is sufficient to address discrimination.

Reality: Affirmative action means taking positive, proactive, and preemptive steps to root out discrimination, rather than waiting for after-the-fact litigation. Title VII addresses discrimination, but it does so only after an instance of discrimination has been claimed. Affirmative action policies are a means to end discrimination in a far less costly and disruptive way than protracted litigation.

Myth: Underrepresentation of minorities and women in the corporate world (or other high-paying jobs) is not due to discrimination.

Reality: Although discrimination is not the sole reason for the lack of women and minorities in the corporate world, we must still deal with past and present discrimination. A study of the 1982 Standard MBA graduating class found that in 1992, 16 percent of the men held CEO titles compared to 2 percent of the women. Twenty-three percent of men become corporate vice presidents, but only 10 percent of the women, whereas 15 percent of men served as directors, compared to 8 percent of the women.

Myth: The so-called earnings gap between men and women has closed significantly in recent years; therefore, affirmative action is no longer needed to achieve pay equity.

Reality: In 1993, the total amount of wages women lost due to pay inequity was nearly $100 billion. The average woman loses approximately $420,000 over a lifetime due to unequal pay practices. Working women still earn just 76 cents for every dollar men earn. Much of this wage gap is due to the fact that women are still segregated into traditionally female-dominated jobs where wages are low. Further, the pay gap exists even within the same occupation. In 86 occupations tracked by the Bureau of Labor Statistics, women earn 20 to 35 percent less than men.

Myth: Most analyses that point to wage differentials between men and women do not take into account differences in hours worked and years of uninterrupted work experience between the sexes. Female earnings are depressed because women work, on average, fewer hours per week than men and have more interruptions over their working lives than do men.

Reality: The wage inequities most often cited are based on Department of Labor and Census Bureau data on year-round, full-time workers who have a permanent attachment to the workforce. These data do not compare full-time male workers to part-time female workers, nor do they compare permanent workers to part-time and contingent workers.

Source: www.civilrights.org/aa/mythreal.html.

might receive relatively generous compensation. With the advent of no-fault divorce, this has changed because no one is charged with blame.

Likewise *alimony,* the payment that women have traditionally received as compensation for their unpaid roles as wives and mothers, has been reduced or eliminated through various legislation since 1970. Although eliminating alimony indicates a more gender-neutral situation where women are not simply viewed as dependent wives and mothers and may even have higher earnings than the husband, it has caused problems. This is because despite the gender-neutral language and intentions, society is stratified along gender, and women still tend to be financially subordinate to men. For example, the reading by Conway reports a California study that showed the living standard of wives and children decreased by 73 percent whereas that of men increased by 42 percent after divorce. This financial hardship is often exacerbated by court-mandated child support that does not get paid to women. Some states have enforced legislation to track errant child support monies and enforce payment.

PUBLIC POLICY

State policies determine people's rights and privileges, and, as a result, the state has the power to exclude groups, discriminate against groups, and create policies in favor of groups. By maintaining inequality, the state reflects the interests of the dominant groups in society and supports policies that work in their interests and reinforce their power. Native Americans, for example, have suffered because of state policies that required relocation, and African Americans have been harmed by Jim Crow laws that helped enforce segregation in the South and prevented African Americans from voting. There were miscegenation laws in the United States that prevented interracial marriage and aimed to maintain racial purity and superiority, and many states instigated laws that prevented African Americans from residing in certain communities and/or being in a town after sundown. Some of these laws were still on the books into the late twentieth century.

An example of how policy reinforces systems of inequality is seen in lesbian and gay plaintiffs who are in the court system for child custody, contract, or property disputes. It is also evident in current discussions concerning gay marriage. Homophobia in the system tends to work against gays and lesbians. The Defense of Marriage Act (DOMA), which allows states not to recognize gay unions performed in other states, is a current piece of legislation that attempts to prevent lesbians and gay men from enjoying the privilege of state recognition of marriage. In "The Crime That Had No Name," Mary Frances Berry reports that "new stories" are infiltrating the justice system in ways that offer hope for lesbians and gay men.

Welfare policy is especially illustrative of the ways the state is a conduit for the perpetuation of systems of inequality. Ideologies (recall from Chapter 2 that these are sets of beliefs that support institutions in society) about who is deserving of wealth rely on the individualistic notion that success is a result of hard work and ambition; thus, anyone who works hard and pushes him- or herself will succeed economically. The corollary of this, of course, is that the fault associated with lack of economic success rests with the individual. This was referred to in Chapter 2 as the bootstrap myth. This myth avoids looking at structural aspects of the labor force and social systems that perpetuate classism and instead focuses on the individual. It helps explain the stigma associated with welfare in the United

States and the many stereotypes associated with women on welfare—that they are lazy, cheat the system, and have babies to increase their welfare check. Women on welfare often face a triple whammy: they are women facing lower-paid work, they are mothers and have domestic responsibilities and childcare expenses, and they are single with only one pay check. Indeed, if women earned as much as comparable men, then single women generally would see a rise in their incomes and a substantial drop in poverty rates. If we applied this comparable situation to single mothers, poverty rates would be cut almost in half, from 25 percent to 13 percent. Having a job does not necessarily lift women out of poverty.

Critics of the Welfare Reform policies of the 1990s have argued that not only have such policies failed to make low-income families self-sufficient, but they have kept wages low and undermined women's independence. The Welfare Reform Bill of 2002 raises the number of hours mothers receiving welfare have to work outside the home, study, or be involved in training, from 30 to 40 hours at the same time that daycare in most states is totally inadequate. President Bush has also attempted to provide incentives for women to marry as a strategy for reducing welfare costs. Heidi Hartmann and Hsiao-ye Yi write about welfare reform with a focus on single-mother families in "The Rhetoric and Reality of Welfare Reform."

A most obvious example of policies working to favor dominant groups is the practice often called "wealthfare" or "welfare for the rich." These policies reflect the ties political leaders have to the economic system and the ways the government subsidizes corporations and reduces taxes and other payments to the state for some corporations and businesses. Wealthfare involves five major types: direct grants; allowing publicly funded research and development to be used free by private for-profit corporations; discounted fees for public resources (such as grazing fees on public land); tax breaks for the wealthy; and corporate tax reductions and loopholes. It has been estimated that more than $200 billion in corporate welfare could be saved over the next 5 years if policies reining in these favors were instigated. Neither Republican nor Democratic lawmakers want to do this because they fear losing donations to their respective parties.

THE CRIMINAL JUSTICE SYSTEM

The law can be defined as formal aspects of social control that determine what is permissible and what is forbidden in a society. The courts are created to maintain the law through adjudicating conflicts that may be unlawful and deciding punishments for people who have broken the law. The role of the police is to enforce these laws and keep public order. Prisons are responsible for punishing those who have broken the law and protecting society from people who have committed crimes. All these fit together to maintain the control of the state.

Although women are especially likely to be victims of certain crimes, such as rape and battering, they constitute a small proportion of people arrested for crimes (about 20 percent) and a smaller number of those who are sent to prison. It is important to understand that about 44 percent of women in correctional facilities have been sexually assaulted some time in their lives and in almost 70 percent of these cases the abuse occurred before the women were 18 years old. Women of color are more likely to be incarcerated than White women; the group with the highest levels of incarceration is young African American males. These figures are related to gendered forms of behavior that encourage more males into violence and risk-related activities as well as the perception by criminal justice officials that

WOMEN IN POLICING

- Women constitute 14.3 percent of all sworn law enforcement positions among municipal, county, and state law enforcement agencies in the United States, with 100 or more sworn officers. Women of color hold 6.8 percent of these positions.
- Women are 14.2 percent of all federal officers.
- From 1990 to 1999, the representation of women in sworn law enforcement increased by only 5.3 percent.
- Women hold 5.6 percent of sworn Top Command law enforcement positions. Women of color hold only 1.1 percent of Top Command positions.
- In state agencies, women constitute only 6.2 percent of officers, compared with 16.6 percent in municipal agencies and 11.1 percent in county agencies.
- Women hold 66.1 percent of lower-paid civilian law enforcement positions. Women of color hold 25.7 percent of civilian positions.

Source: National Center for Women & Policing, "Equality Denied: The Status of Women in Policing:1999," *www.feminist.org.*

WOMEN IN PRISON

- In 1998, 3.2 million women were arrested, accounting for 22 percent of all arrests.
- The per capita rate of arrest among juvenile women was nearly twice the adult rate.
- Nearly 952,000 women were under the care, custody, or control of correctional agencies. Eighty-five percent of these women were under the supervision of probation or parole agencies.
- These women were the mothers of about 1.3 million minor children.
- Nearly two-thirds of the women confined in jails and prisons were women of color. Nearly two-thirds of the women under probation supervision were White.
- Nearly 6 out of 10 women in state prisons had experienced sexual or physical abuse in the past. About a third of imprisoned women had been abused by an intimate; just under a fourth had been abused by a family member.
- Eleven women out of 1,000 will be incarcerated in their lifetime: 5 out of 1,000 White women; 15 out of 1,000 Hispanic women; and 36 out of 1,000 African American women.
- In 2001, 93,031 women were inmates under the jurisdiction of state or federal correctional authorities.

Source: Bureau of Justice Statistics Special Report, "Women Offenders," December 1999.
Note: Unless otherwise noted, statistics are for 1998.

women (especially White women) are less dangerous than men. Among men, poor men and men of color are more likely to be considered a danger to society and tend to receive the longest sentences.

Nonetheless, the rate of crime committed by women has increased in recent years with the largest increase being drug-related criminal behavior. Most of the homicides enacted by women involve male victims, and they are most likely to have taken place in the home. Women are more likely to be first-time offenders than men, are less likely to use firearms, and are more likely to use kitchen knives and other household implements. This evidence suggests that much female homicide is done in self-defense. Although prior to the 1980s women who killed in self-defense almost always lost their plea, today juries are more understanding of the experiences of battered women. Even so, it is still very difficult for women to convince a jury that they were being abused, and there are many women in prison suffering very long sentences for these acts. Defendants must meet two criteria for claiming justifiable homicide as self-defense that include reasonable fear or perception of danger such that killing was the only course of action to protect the defendant's life and the confrontation of the defendant with deadly force by the assailant. In addition, among men and women who kill in self-defense during a rape where the assailant is a man, men who kill are more likely to be acquitted than women who kill. Likewise the crimes of passion that men commit on discovering an adulterous wife are viewed more sympathetically than when women kill adulterous men. The reading by Nina Siegal, "Stopping Abuse in Prison," explores the inhumane treatment of some women prisoners and the widespread sexual abuse that they experience.

Another example of the double standard concerning women as victims is U.S. asylum law that provides protection for immigrants fleeing their country if they are being persecuted because of race, religion, nationality, political opinion, or membership in a social group. As the reading by Anna Shelton "Battered Women: A New Asylum Case" explains, although there have been important advancements in asylum law that have protected women fleeing abusive husbands and gays and lesbians who fear persecution in their country, protection for battered women under these circumstances is still difficult to obtain. Finally, all marginalized people (women and men) are at risk of being victimized by hate crimes. Helen Zia focuses on hate crimes, pornography, and the abuse of Asian American women in her article, "Where Race and Gender Meet: Racism, Hate Crimes, and Pornography."

THE MILITARY

The military, a branch of government that is constituted to defend against foreign and domestic conflict, is a central component of the state and political system. As mentioned in Chapter 2, the military has strong ties to the economic system through a military-industrial complex that supports industries that manufacture weapons. Military presence overseas, as well as wars fought in the United States, tend to be related to U.S. economic interests like the need for oil. The Pentagon has connections to other branches of the state, especially the government and its representatives. The military is a very male-dominated arena, not only in terms of actual personnel who serve but in terms of the ways it is founded upon so-called masculine cultural traits like violence, aggression, hierarchy, competition, and conflict. The military uses misogynistic and homophobic attitudes to enforce highly masculine codes of behavior. In the mid-1990s women made up about 12 percent of active military forces.

Throughout most of history, women were not allowed to serve in the military except in such auxiliary forces as nursing. It was not until World War II that women who served in any military capacity were given formal status and not until 1976 that women were allowed into the military academies. In terms of race, the armed forces were officially segregated until 1948. Currently about 30 percent of the armed forces are people of color, and

WOMEN IN THE MILITARY

Women have served in the U.S. armed forces since 1901, when the Army Nurse Corps was established. About 6,000 have been involved in the war in Afghanistan. Milestones affecting women:

1967	Military abolishes 2% cap on women serving in the armed forces.
1973	Draft ends. Armed forces seek more women.
1976	Women admitted to service academies.
1978	Women allowed permanent assignment to Navy support ships.
1981	U.S. Supreme Court rules that excluding women from the draft is constitutional.
1991	About 41,000 women are sent to the Gulf War. Five die from hostile fire.
1993	Defense Secretary Les Aspin orders combat aviation and combat surface ships opened to women.
1994	Rule changes open more than 80,000 Army and Marine positions to women. Combat assignments to infantry, armor, artillery and special operations remain off-limits.
1999	Kosovo war sees female pilots and other crewmembers fly first wartime combat missions.
2000	Two of 17 sailors killed in bombing of USS Cole in Yemen are women.

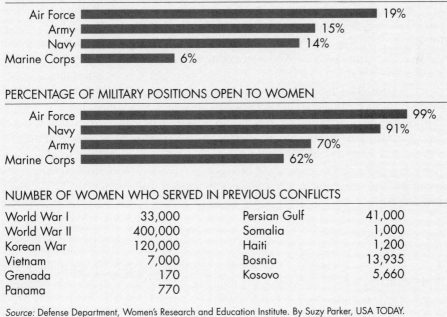

PERCENTAGE OF WOMEN IN MILITARY BRANCHES

Air Force	19%
Army	15%
Navy	14%
Marine Corps	6%

PERCENTAGE OF MILITARY POSITIONS OPEN TO WOMEN

Air Force	99%
Navy	91%
Army	70%
Marine Corps	62%

NUMBER OF WOMEN WHO SERVED IN PREVIOUS CONFLICTS

World War I	33,000	Persian Gulf	41,000
World War II	400,000	Somalia	1,000
Korean War	120,000	Haiti	1,200
Vietnam	7,000	Bosnia	13,935
Grenada	170	Kosovo	5,660
Panama	770		

Source: Defense Department, Women's Research and Education Institute. By Suzy Parker, USA TODAY.

about 14 percent are women (with the Air Force having the highest proportion of women at 19 percent). Of women who serve, 38 percent are women of color. These figures are disproportionate compared to the general population and reflect the lack of opportunities for people of color in the civilian realm. Despite their relative high numbers of service, people of color are less likely than Whites proportionately to be found in leadership positions. This is true for women of all races as well.

In 1981 the Supreme Court reaffirmed that it is constitutional to require registering men but not women for the draft. Men at this point are subject to conscription if a draft is in process and women are not, although women are allowed to serve if they wish. The rationale for the 1981 decision centered on the fact that women were not allowed in combat positions, although it also involved the notion that women have responsibilities in the home and family. After women's service in the Gulf War in 1991, the pressure was on for President Clinton in 1993 to order a repeal of the ban on women in combat positions, and now most Navy and Air Force positions are open to women. The Army and Marines still prevent women from combat positions in field artillery, armor, and infantry.

In recent years the treatment of women in the military has received considerable public attention. Take, for example, the story of Shannon Faulkner who attempted to attend the all-male military academy the Citadel. Even though a court demanded the Citadel accept women, it still is a very inhospitable place for women cadets. Similarly, in 1991 the Tailhook scandal revealed that in this gathering of high-ranking Navy flying personnel, considerable sexual harassment had been an ongoing practice. The report from the Defense Department described men wearing t-shirts with inscriptions like "Women Are Property" as well as engaging in rowdy and misogynous behavior. A 1997 Army report found widespread harassment aimed at women personnel.

Finally, the military has a long history of homophobia that has included the execution, persecution, and dismissal of gay soldiers. Arguments in favor of such prejudice mirror those proposing racial segregation in earlier times: The morale and fighting spirit of military personnel will drop if openly gay and lesbian personnel are present, and gays and lesbians pose a national security threat. Through the 1980s, more than 15,000 military personnel were discharged because of homosexuality. By the mid-1990s President Clinton had created the "don't ask, don't tell" policy, which was supposed to be a compromise, although it has few supporters. Discharges are still allowed under the policy, and, as one study reports, dismissals increased after the initiation of the policy. In addition, lesbians were disproportionately discharged. In this way, the government policy on lesbians and gays in the military illustrates how the state has differential effects on some groups compared to others.

The state is a very powerful institution that has enormous effects upon women's everyday lives. It is important to understand how gender, race, and class mold and shape government, law, and policy and how these institutions reflect and promote the needs of some groups over others.

READING 77

Constitutional Argument

Susan B. Anthony

Friends and Fellow-Citizens:—I stand before you under indictment for the alleged crime of having voted at the last presidential election, without having a lawful right to vote. It shall be my work this evening to prove to you that in thus doing, I not only committed no crime, but instead simply exercised my citizen's right, guaranteed to me and all United States citizens by the National Constitution beyond the power of any State to deny.

Our democratic-republican government is based on the idea of the natural right of every individual member thereof to a voice and a vote in making and executing the laws. We assert the province of government to be to secure the people in the enjoyment of their inalienable rights. We throw to the winds the old dogma that government can give rights. No one denies that before governments were organized each individual possessed the right to protect his own life, liberty and property. When 100 or 1,000,000 people enter into a free government, they do not barter away their natural rights; they simply pledge themselves to protect each other in the enjoyment of them through prescribed judicial and legislative tribunals. They agree to abandon the methods of brute force in the adjustment of their differences and adopt those of civilization. Nor can you find a word in any of the grand documents left us by the fathers which assumes for government the power to create or to confer rights. The Declaration of Independence, the United States Constitution, the constitutions of the several States and the organic laws of the Territories, all alike propose to *protect* the people in the exercise of their God-given rights. Not one of them pretends to bestow rights.

> All men are created equal, and endowed by the Creator with certain inalienable rights. Among these are life, liberty and the pursuit of happiness. To secure these, governments are instituted among men, deriving their just powers from the consent of the governed.

Here is no shadow of government authority over rights, or exclusion of any class from their full and equal enjoyment. Here is pronounced the right of all men, and "consequently," as the Quaker preacher said, "of all women," to a voice in the government. And here, in this first paragraph of the Declaration, is the assertion of the natural right of all to the ballot; for how can "the consent of the governed" be given, if the right to vote be denied? Again:

> Whenever any form of government becomes destructive of these ends, it is the right of the people to alter or abolish it, and to institute a new government, laying its foundations on such principles, and organizing its powers in such form, as to them shall seem most likely to effect their safety and happiness.

Surely the right of the whole people to vote is here clearly implied; for however destructive to their happiness this government might become, a disfranchised class could neither alter nor abolish it, nor institute a new one, except by the old brute force method of insurrection and rebellion. One-half of the people of this nation today are utterly powerless to blot from the statute books an unjust law, or to write there a new and a just one. The women, dissatisfied as they are with this form of government, that enforces taxation without representation—that compels them to obey laws to which they never have given their consent—that imprisons and hangs them without a trial by a jury of their peers—that robs them, in marriage, of the custody of their own persons, wages and children—are this half of the people who are left wholly at the mercy of the other half, in direct violation of the spirit and letter of the declarations of the framers of this government, every one of which was based on the immutable principle of equal rights to all. By these declarations, kings, popes, priests, aristocrats, all were alike dethroned and placed on a common level, politically, with the lowliest born subject or serf. By them, too, men, as such, were deprived of their divine right to rule and placed on a political level with women. By the practice of these declarations all class and caste distinctions would be abolished, and slave, serf, plebeian, wife, woman, all alike rise from their subject position to the broader platform of equality.

The preamble of the Federal Constitution says:

We, the people of the United States, in order to form a more perfect union, establish justice, insure domestic tranquillity, provide for the common defence, promote the general welfare and secure the blessings of liberty to ourselves and our posterity, do ordain and establish this Constitution for the United States of America.

It was we, the people, not we, the white male citizens, not we, the male citizens; but we, the whole people, who formed this Union. We formed it not to give the blessings of liberty but to secure them; not to the half of ourselves and the half of our posterity, but to the whole people—women as well as men. It is downright mockery to talk to women of their enjoyment of the blessings of liberty while they are denied the only means of securing them provided by this democratic-republican government—the ballot. . . .

READING 78

Women and Family Law
Marriage and Divorce

M. Margaret Conway, David W. Ahern, and Gertrude A. Steuernagel

Laws and Public Policies Governing Marriage

American public policy regarding marriage is rooted in English common law. The common law doctrine that had the most serious economic and legal consequences for women was coverture; by the act of marriage, a woman in effect committed legal suicide. Under this doctrine, a woman's legal identity was suspended during marriage. As Supreme Court Justice Hugo Black aptly but disapprovingly described coverture, the husband and wife became one, but the husband was the one.[1]

When her legal identity merged with that of her husband (symbolized by the assumption of his surname), the wife's ownership and control of her property, including her earnings, passed to him. She lost the right to enter into contracts; without it, she could not engage in a business or profession. Nor could she bring suit.

At various times throughout the second half of the nineteenth century, state legislators removed many of these disabilities stemming from coverture. These statutes, which were collectively known as the Married Women's Acts, varied in content from state to state, but most conferred on wives the right to own and control property, to conduct a business, to enter into contracts, and to sue. The acts were egalitarian in theory, and were an improvement over the common law doctrine of coverture, but they did not make married women their husbands' equals. If a woman followed tradition and worked inside the home (as an unpaid housekeeper and childbearer) rather than outside the home, her new right to own property, for example, had little practical significance because few women had money or property of their own. Even if a woman worked outside the home, her wages were likely to be a small fraction of her husband's. More fundamentally, coverture had reflected society's attitude that women were subordinate socially, economically, and legally, and that attitude was affected by the Married Women's Acts. Nonetheless, they represented the most important changes that would be made in the status of married women until the 1970s.

As noted, most family law in the United States is state law. States establish the conditions for the legal recognition of a marriage. Currently, fifteen states and the District of Columbia recognize common law marriage, sometimes referred to as nonceremonial marriage. Although the definition of common law marriage varies among those states that recognize it, in general a common law marriage occurs between two individuals of the opposite sex who live together for a significant period of time and represent themselves as a married couple or who intend to be married. Couples within a common law marriage can file joint tax returns and enjoy all of the benefits of a conventional marriage. A formal divorce is needed to end a common law marriage.[2]

Marital Property Law

Two kinds of marital property law govern spousal rights of ownership, control, and disposition of property acquired during marriage: separate property law and community property law. *Separate property law* is derived from English common law; its fundamental principle is that each spouse owns and controls all property that he or she acquires during the marriage. *Community property law* is derived from the civil law of France and Spain; its principal tenet is that the "community," consisting of husband and wife, owns everything acquired during the marriage. Forty-two states are separate property law states; the other eight (Arizona, California, Idaho, Louisiana, Nevada, New Mexico, Texas, and Washington) are community property law states.

With passage of the Married Women's Acts in the nineteenth century, married women in separate property law states acquired the right to own and control the property they brought to the marriage and that which they acquired during marriage. The husband would, as before, own what he brought to the marriage as well as that which he acquired during the marriage. And because the husband owned his earnings and everything bought with his money, he had the legal right to control the family assets, since the wife, in her traditional role, had no assets. Many separate property law states offered some legal protection to the non-wage-earning spouse, however; they prohibited either spouse from selling the family home without the consent of the other. Further, most of these states gave a widow (or widower) a share one-third to one-half) of the estate of a deceased spouse. In addition, the law in these states permitted joint ownership of property. If spouses chose joint ownership, each had equal control over the assets of both.

In community property law states, property acquired during marriage is considered to belong to the community and thus to both spouses; a bank account in the name of one spouse belongs to the community and thus to both. Until the reforms of the 1970s, however, the law authorized the husband to control the assets of the community.

Beginning in the 1970s, the community property law states experimented with various techniques to increase the wife's managerial control. One technique was to give each spouse control over his or her earnings; control over the remaining property resided with both. Another was to permit each spouse to manage the community property, subject to the restriction that neither could commit more than one-half of that property without the consent of the other.

. . .

Marital Rape

Traditionally, a husband was immune from prosecution for raping his wife. One justification for this exemption stems from the pronouncement of the seventeenth-century English jurist Lord Chief Justice Matthew Hale that marriage implies consent to sexual intercourse. According to this theory, marriage is a contract, under the terms of which a husband has the absolute power to determine the time, place, and manner of sexual intercourse. The husband is authorized to enforce the contract unilaterally, by force if he deems that necessary.

In the 1970s, some states either modified the marital exemption rule or abolished it. Whereas the exemption traditionally was absolute, these states denied immunity if the parties were divorced, living apart, or legally separated; if force was used; if there was fear of bodily harm; or if physical injury was inflicted.[3] By the late 1990s, most states had abolished the marital defense in rape cases, although variations among the states remained. Two states, for example, continue a marital exception for lesser cases but deny it for forcible rape. Two other states retain a spousal exception for rape but have adopted new spousal sexual assault laws.[4]

Social Security Benefits

The social security retirement benefits received by women, on average, are lower than those received by men. The disparities are both long-term and contemporary.[5] In part, the reason is simply that women earn less than men. . . . Because benefits are related to earnings, the benefits received by working women who are now of retirement age are lower than those received by working men of retirement age. Indeed, many married retired women workers have chosen to receive spousal benefits rather than benefits on the basis of their earnings alone because the former are higher.

Many women receive retirement benefits that are lower than those received by men because they never held a paying job; their benefits are thus dependent upon their husband's earnings. Spousal benefits, however, do not equal those of the retired wage earner. A retired wage earner receives 100 percent of the benefits to which he or she is entitled, but the dependent spouse over the age of sixty-five receives an amount equal to 50 percent of those benefits. Widows over the age of sixty-five receive the 100 percent to which their husbands would have been entitled. If widows start receiving benefits before age sixty-five, however, the amount is 71.5 percent. An older

nonworking woman whose husband dies before she reaches age sixty-five frequently has little choice but to accept the lower benefit at an earlier age. Divorced older women who never worked outside the home during marriage receive retirement benefits that are equal to or less than spousal benefits. If the marriage lasted less than ten years (the requirement was less than twenty years until 1979), she receives no benefits on the basis of her husband's earnings; now she receives 50 percent if the marriage lasted more than ten years.

The social security system offers no protection to widowed homemakers under the age of sixty unless they are disabled or have minor children. Benefits cease when the child reaches the age of eighteen. The widow is not entitled to receive benefits again until age sixty. This "widow's gap" leaves many middle-aged dependent homemakers who lack job skills or work experience with no source of income. If the widowed homemaker is disabled, there are no benefits until she reaches age fifty.

One proposal aimed at reducing the economic insecurity of older married women who never worked outside the home is to assign a monetary value to homemaking and child rearing. To finance such a program, either homemakers would pay taxes on the assigned value of their services in the home, or paid workers would pay more taxes. Another suggestion intended to protect married women is an "earnings sharing" plan under which each person's benefits would be based on his or her earnings when single plus one-half of the total earnings of the married couple. For a one-income family, the worker's earning on which benefits would be based would be split 50-50; the earnings credits would be divided if the couple were to divorce or when one spouse reached age sixty-two.

Most of the economic disadvantages suffered by married women under the social security system are unrelated to specific gender-based distinctions but are rather a result of the different economic and domestic roles and pay scales of men and women. The Social Security Act was replete with such distinctions, but the most obvious ones have been changed by Congress or invalidated by the Supreme Court—although those that were invalidated by the Court discriminated primarily against men, not women. In

1975, for example, the Supreme Court invalidated a provision authorizing benefits for widows with minor children but denied benefits to similarly situated widowers.[6] In 1977 it invalidated a provision that authorized benefits for surviving widows over the age of sixty but denied benefits to similarly situated widowers unless they had received at least one-half of their support from their wives.[7]

Neither judicial nor legislative changes in social security legislation provide economic security for women who had spent most or all of their adult lives as homemakers or in low-paying or part-time jobs. The social security system was not originally intended to be the sole source of retirement income; it was designed to supplement other resources, including private pension plans provided by employers. But married women fare no better under these plans for much the same reason that they suffer under the social security system. As a result of the efforts of such groups as the Older Women's League, the plight of older women is beginning to receive the attention of the nation's lawmakers. The proposed economic equity act, which deals with a variety of issues of interest to women (such as child care), seeks greater equity in both the social security system and private pension plans. Until both married and single women routinely enter the work force and earn as much as men, older women who have to rely on their own pensions are likely to continue to be economically insecure.

Laws and Public Policies Governing Divorce

Public policy regarding divorce was traditionally based on the assumption that marriage is a lifelong arrangement. Grounds for divorce were both limited and gender based. Almost 50 percent of all marriages now end in divorce. In the 1970s, most states moved toward acceptance of divorce on demand. In 1970, California inaugurated no-fault divorce when it adopted an "irreconcilable differences" standard. Irreconcilable differences are those which a court determines "to be substantial reasons for not continuing the marriage and which make it appear that the marriage should be dissolved." No-fault divorce is now available in some form in all of the states. Whatever grounds are statutorily specified, most states in effect allow unilateral divorce on demand. Although no-fault divorce was initially viewed as benefiting both men and women because it would lessen the recriminations associated with divorce, the reform may have further disadvantaged economically dependent women because they can no longer use the refusal to agree to a divorce as a bargaining chip to obtain a larger property settlement or alimony payment.[8]

A state's interest in the preservation of marriage may have dwindled, but its interest in related problems (property division, alimony, child custody, child support) certainly has not. Changes in these areas in the name of equality were precipitated by the no-fault movement. Early indications are that the newer egalitarian reforms, like the nineteenth-century Married Women's Property Acts, when superimposed on the unchanged social and economic roles of husbands and wives, will fail to bring about the equality sought by their advocates. On the basis of an in-depth ten-year study (1974–1984) of the post-reform status of women and children in California, one scholar concluded that California's no-fault divorce, in combination with changed rules governing property division and spousal support, accounted for a post-divorce decline of 73 percent in the living standard of women and children and a rise of 42 percent in that of men.[9]

Some states, including Idaho, Michigan, and Iowa, are considering what supporters see as "pro-family" changes in divorce law. These range from extending the waiting period for the divorce to become finalized to educating parents concerning the effects of divorce on children to a return to fault-based divorces. In 1997, Louisiana enacted a law giving couples the option of "covenant marriage." If couples choose a covenant marriage—and they are not required to do so—they agree to seek counseling if problems develop in their marriage and are entitled to seek divorce or legal separation for a very limited set of reasons, including adultery, abandonment, and physical or sexual abuse of the spouse or children. Couples may petition to have their marriages retroactively designated as covenant marriages.

Interestingly, 84 percent of attorneys responding to an American Bar Association survey indicated they do not favor a return to fault-based divorces. The attorneys did not see fault-based divorce as a solution to the problems of no-fault, including the financial disparity between husbands and wives that often leads to women faring poorly in divorce.[10]

Property Division

Lorna Jorgenson Wendt and Gary Wendt, childhood sweethearts, were married thirty-two years. While Gary advanced in his career, eventually becoming chairman of GE Capital Services, Lorna stayed home with the couple's two daughters. Lorna became the quintessential "corporate wife." She entertained her husband's business associates, traveled with him on business trips, and represented him in a number of community and charitable groups. Although Lorna had studied to become a teacher and had taught while Gary went to Harvard Business School, she gave this up to become a full-time wife and mother. The couple prospered financially and went from very few assets to a marital estate worth as much as $100 million. Unfortunately, the marriage did not last. Gary offered Lorna an $11 million settlement, but she refused it, arguing that she was entitled to not only half of what they had accumulated during their marriage, but also half of what Gary would receive when he retired. This would include stock options, bonuses, and unvested pension benefits. Gary claimed Lorna had not contributed to his successes; she claimed she did. The judge ruled in Lorna's favor, and argued that the marriage was indeed a partnership. Lorna and Gary were divorced in Connecticut, a state that does not have community property laws but does give judges latitude in deciding who gets what in divorce cases.[11]

The basic issues to be decided in dividing property are which property is to be divided, how it is to be divided, and what factors are to be considered in making the division. Historically, in most states the title and acquisition source have been decisive in determining which property acquired during marriage is subject to division. The law itself was gender neutral; however, in a traditional marriage in which the husband worked outside the home for money and the wife worked either inside the home without monetary compensation or outside the home as well, at a lower paying job, the wife was clearly at a disadvantage.

In separate property law states, titled property (such as a house or a car) acquired by the husband with his earnings and held in his name belonged to him; it was not subject to division, even if the wife contributed financially to the acquisition of property held in his name. He could take it with him when he left the marriage. The court might order him to pay alimony, but the property remained his. The acquiring spouse—usually presumed to be the husband—also owned untitled family assets such as household goods. Further, the husband's earning capacity and his retirement benefits—frequently a family's most valuable assets—were considered his alone and thus not subject to division. Even if the wife worked in the home as well as at a low-paying job to help support the family and to put her husband through school, she traditionally would not reap any benefit from her labors if the couple divorced. The husband took his earning capacity, as well as any pension rights he acquired during the marriage, with him when he left the marriage. If the wife were the innocent party, that fact might enable her to obtain some of what the law deemed to be her husband's property. Nonetheless, for traditional homemakers, termination of a long marriage could spell economic disaster.

Responding to the organized efforts of women's groups, legislatures began to reform marital property laws in the 1970s. As a result, title and monetary contribution to the acquisition of family assets in separate property law states have been of decreasing importance with regard to property division at the time of divorce. Instead, most of these state legislatures have expanded the definition of marital property subject to division to include all property acquired during the marriage regardless of title or whose income paid for such property. Property acquired by gift or inheritance is still not subject to division nor, in some states, is property that the couple agrees to exclude by prenuptial agreement.

. . .

Formal equality of property division, whether in a separate property law state or a community property law state, might not achieve real equality. Since few couples amass many divisible assets (the average has been estimated to be $20,000, usually a house), equal division frequently requires sale of the house and the award of one-half of the proceeds to the husband and one-half to the wife. Eminently fair on its face, such a division might be unequal in fact if one-half goes to the husband and one-half goes to the wife and the children, for whom she must provide primary care in addition to perhaps finding a low-paying job with flexible hours while she prepares to move from the family home. If she is not awarded, or cannot collect, child support, her descent into poverty is not forestalled by equal property division. For an older traditional housewife without minor children but with few job prospects, equal property division rarely permits continuation of the living standard she enjoyed during marriage because that standard was dependent on her former husband's earnings, which he takes with him.

. . .

Award and Payment of Alimony

Historically, payment of alimony was based on the common law duty of a husband to support his wife. In theory, this obligation continued after divorce if the husband was at fault. In fact, the award of alimony has been the exception, not the rule. From the late nineteenth century to the early 1970s, alimony was awarded in only 10 to 15 percent of all divorces.

In the 1970s, states began revising their alimony laws. Alimony statutes were made gender neutral, thus permitting awards to husbands. Short-term "rehabilitative" awards (temporary payments to permit acquisition of job skills) began to replace long-term alimony obligations. The enactment of no-fault divorce laws meant that the "guilty" party was no longer required to pay alimony to the "innocent" party. In determining whether and how much alimony is to be awarded, courts consider such factors as the dependent spouse's need (alimony is usually not awarded if the judge decides that the dependent spouse is able to work; a short-term award is made to those without job skills), the wage earner's ability to pay, the length of the marriage (an award of alimony is rare in short-term marriages), the age of the partners (alimony is usually not awarded to a young or middle-aged spouse if the judge decides that he or she is capable of self-support), and the contributions (including homemaking activities) of the dependent spouse. Whether the dependent or lower-paid spouse receives alimony or a sufficient amount depends on whether the judge makes a realistic assessment of such factors as the ability of a traditional housewife to enter or reenter the job market and earn a living wage if she does. Frequently both are overestimated, with the result that the dependent spouse's income and living standard decline.

The anti-alimony trend of the 1970s has perhaps worked to the disadvantage of a few women; it probably has had little effect on most of the others, who, under the old, for-cause-only divorce laws, would have received little or nothing—although wives of "guilty" well-to-do men who wanted a divorce might have been able to extract alimony from them. About 15 percent of all divorced women are awarded alimony.

Today, many states use the Uniform Marriage and Divorce Act (UMDA) as a model for alimony awards. But the award of alimony and its payment are two different things. In 1978, only two-thirds of the women awarded alimony actually received some payment. The average amount received was only $2,850. In the 1980s, the average amount was not even $4,000—less than half the poverty level. In 1981, the figure was $3,000; in 1983, it was $3,980; and in 1985, it was $3,733. Of the 19.1 million divorced and separated women in 1985, 840,000 were entitled to alimony but 616,000 actually received payment.[12]

The infrequency of alimony awards and the small amounts that are awarded and received account for some of the poverty faced by traditional housewives who become divorced in middle age and by young custodial parents who receive little or no child support yet have responsibility for child care. The seemingly exorbitant alimony extracted from a few wealthy men, such as in the case of Gary and Lorna Wendt, grabs the public's attention, but the reality is that just as few men are rich, few women are awarded alimony and fewer still receive alimony payments above the poverty level. If the partners are economic and domestic equals (they divide responsibilities for child care and housework), elimination of a long-term alimony obligation is simply an acknowledgement of an egalitarian marriage and does not spell economic hardship. But because roles continue to differ in many marriages, many spouses who were dependent during marriage become poorer after divorce if alimony is not ordered or received.

Child Support

Change is the only constant in descriptions of America's families. American households are becoming more and more diverse, requiring us to rethink the meaning of "family." In 1970, for example, there were 5.6 million families maintained by women with no husband present. By 1995, that number had more than doubled to 12.2 million.[13] The reasons for this jump include increases in divorce, separation, and out-of-wedlock births. What is important to remember, however, is that many children residing in female-headed households live in poverty. Indeed, a child living in a single-parent household—be that parent a mother, father, or some other adult—is much more likely than a child in a two-parent household to be poor. Today, almost 25 percent of American children live in poverty. Policy makers agree that nonpayment of child support is a major contributing factor to childhood poverty. Many also feel that parents, rather than the government, should be responsible for children's financial situation. To that effect, Congress created in 1975 the Child Support Enforcement (CSE) program. This program is charged with establishing and enforcing support obligations of noncustodial parents.[14] The Office of Child Support Enforcement within the Administration for Children and Families of the Department of Health and Human Services oversees the program. Although it does succeed in collecting some child support, the program has not been an unqualified success. In its first year, it collected $700,000, and by 1996 the program had secured more than $12 billion.[15] Yet many children continued to receive little

or no support. In 1991, for example, payments were awarded to only 46 percent of custodial parents, and only 75 percent of those actually received payment.[16] In 1991, the most recent year for which comprehensive data are available on both paid and unpaid support, a total of $11.9 billion was paid in child support. This was $5.8 billion less than what was owed.[17] As a result, Congress took action. The welfare reform act known as the Personal Responsibility and Work Opportunity Reconciliation Act of 1996 provided for a major overhaul of the CSE program. Under the revised program, there are now a number of state and federal databases available to those trying to locate noncustodial parents, an important first step in collecting child support. CSE staff also has access to motor vehicle databases, public utilities records, and state and local tax records. In addition, access to IRS information has been simplified. The new law also increases the tools available to those responsible for collecting child support. For example, drivers licenses and professional, occupation, and recreational licenses may be revoked for nonpayment of child support. There are also provisions in the new law to help correct the problem of a parent moving to a different state to avoid payment.

It is too early to determine the effectiveness of these reforms. Some of the issues surrounding child support, however, may be beyond the scope of what public policy can do, and some policies intended to correct a problem may actually make it worse or result in undesirable consequences. Those who work in the domestic abuse area, for example, fear that increased pressure on women to name fathers and pursue child support collection may result in more violence against these women. Ironically, then, welfare reform designed to help women and children may actually place them at greater risk of physical assault.[18] There are also problems with implementation. Computerization, the so-called "magic bullet" of child support enforcement, has not proceeded smoothly. In 1988 a law was passed that required states to computerize child support collection; the 1996 welfare law called for enhancement of these systems. Unfortunately, as of July 1997 only fifteen states, comprising just 14 percent of the child support caseload, were certified or conditionally certified as having met the computerization requirements contained in the original 1988 law. Congress has continually extended the deadline for computerization, and only one state met the original 1995 target date.[19] There was little for the 1996 welfare reform requirements to build on.

Child Custody

On July 5, 1991, Sharon Lynne Bottoms gave birth to a baby boy she named Kenneth Tyler Doustou. "Tyler," as he came to be known, was naturally unaware he would soon become the center of a heated court battle between his mother and his grandmother, Pamela Key Bottoms. When Tyler was two years old, his grandmother learned that her daughter was a lesbian. As a result, she sought legal custody of the boy, and in 1993 a county court in Virginia ruled in her favor. This decision was subsequently upheld by the circuit court, with the judge in that case stating that lesbians are never fit to be parents. Sharon was permitted only limited visitation with Tyler and never in the presence of her partner, April Wade. In 1994 the Virginia court of appeals ruled that Sharon was a fit parent, but a subsequent 1995 decision by the Virginia Supreme Court returned custody to Tyler's grandmother. The decision, although not equating lesbianism with unfitness to parent, did claim that Tyler would be stigmatized if raised by a lesbian mother. Legal battles continue over Sharon's visitation arrangements with her son.[20]

The case of Sharon Bottoms is one example of the emotional, legal, and financial costs of child custody issues, all of which are complicated by the fact that Sharon Bottoms is a lesbian. Each year, more than one million children are affected by their parents' divorce.[21] They join the swelling ranks of children who are living with the impact of divorce. Even children whose parents never married can find themselves affected by custody issues.

In the matter of child custody, changes in public policy have kept pace with cultural changes. Under the common law that prevailed in the early days of this country, fathers automatically received custody of children. Since most family law, including questions of custody, is determined by individual states, changes in this practice began to occur on a state-by-

state basis. In the early to middle nineteenth century, courts began to award custody of young children to mothers. This came to be known as the "tender years doctrine," referring to the age of the children in question. In the 1970s, some states abandoned the tender years doctrine in favor of a gender neutral standard, although many courts continued to award custody of very young children to mothers.[22] Today, courts in twenty states award sole or joint legal custody and sole or joint physical custody. Courts in most states favor joint legal custody, while joint physical custody continues to be unusual.[23]

. . .

Conclusion

The common law doctrine of coverture established the legal inferiority of married women to their husbands. By the end of the nineteenth century, state legislatures had removed many of the disabilities stemming from coverture. Married women acquired the rights to own property, to sue, and to enter into contracts. Such legal changes did not bring about equality, however. If a woman played the traditional role of wife and mother, she had few legally enforceable rights. If the marriage ended, the law tended to favor men in all areas other than child custody. A lower standard of living, if not poverty, awaited many divorced women. Not only did they emerge from marriage with few of the assets acquired during marriage, they either were not awarded or did not receive alimony or child support payments.

As a result of the women's movement, legislatures began to increase married women's rights. The new legislation directed judges to divide marital property equally or equitably. Both Congress and the states have concentrated their efforts on forcing the noncustodial parent to make child support payments. In many states, the female partner in a nonmarital relationship has been given the opportunity to prove that she is entitled to some of the property acquired during cohabitation.

Because many of these changes are relatively recent, their long-term effect is difficult to assess, but there is some indication that they have not improved the status of women, particularly those whose marriages end in divorce. Even no-fault divorce and equal or equitable property division, which seemed to hold so much promise, have rebounded to the disadvantage of some, especially women who receive little or no alimony or child support and have a lower earning capacity because they have been restricted to childbearing and housekeeping roles. Whether women will in fact become equal partners in a marriage as well as after its dissolution will depend in part on judicial and legislative capacity to adapt the new laws to these realities and to change the laws found wanting.

NOTES

1. Dissenting in *United States v. Yazell,* 382 U.S. 341, 361 (1966).

2. The states that recognize common law marriage are Alabama, Colorado, Georgia, Idaho (if created before January 1, 1996), Iowa, Kansas, Montana, New Hampshire (for inheritance purposes only), Ohio (if created before October 10, 1991), Oklahoma, Pennsylvania, Rhode Island, South Carolina, Texas, and Utah.

3. See Leigh Bienen, "Rape III: National Developments in Rape Reform Legislation," *Women's Rights Law Reporter* 6 (Spring 1980): 170–213. See also Dennis Drucker, "The Common Law Does Not Support a Marital Exception for Forcible Rape," *Women's Rights Law Reporter* 5 (Winter–Spring 1979): 181–200.

4. Neil Miller, "Domestic Violence Legislation Affecting Policy and Prosecutor Responsibilities in the United States: Inferences from a Fifty-State Review of State Statutory Codes," presented to the Fifth International Family Violence Conference, University of New Hampshire, June 30, 1997 (revised September 2, 1997), available at the Institute for Law and Justice web site at http://www.ilj.org/dv/vawa.htm (July 1998).

5. U.S. Department of Health, Education, and Welfare, *Social Security and the Changing Roles of Men and Women* (Washington, D.C.: Government Printing Office, 1979). For an overview of the variations, see U.S. Department of Commerce, Bureau of the Census, "Social Security (OASI) Retirement Benefits, by Sex: 1960 to 1981"; and U.S. Department of Commerce, Bureau of the Census, *Statistical Abstract of the United States, 1996* (Washington, D.C.: Government Printing Office, 1997), 374.

6. *Weinberger v. Wiesenfeld,* 420 U.S. 655 (1975).

7. *Califano v. Goldfarb,* 430 U.S. 199 (1977).

8. Lenore J. Weitzman, *The Divorce Revolution: The Unexpected Social and Economic Consequences for Women and Children in America* (New York: Free Press, 1985).

9. Ibid., 323. Although few dispute that the economic status of most divorced women has declined, not everyone attributes that decline to no-fault divorce. See, for example, Annamay T. Sheppard, "Women, Families, and Equality," *Women's Rights Law Reporter* 12 (Fall 1990): 143–152.

10. For a discussion of the survey results, see "Family Law Attorneys Reject Return to Fault-Based Divorce Finds ABA Survey," the American Bar Association web site at http://www.abanet.org/media/oct96/faulrrel.html (July 1998). For a discussion of Louisiana's covenant marriage law, see "Louisiana's Covenant Marriage Law" at Bob Walker's Official New Orleans Area Wedding Guide at http://206.104.52.1/walker/ covenant _marriage.html (July 1998).

11. Sharon Walsh and Devon Spurgeon, "Divorce Means an Equal Split, Judge Rules in Big-Money Case." *Washington Post,* December 4, 1997, E1.

12. Stuart S. Nagel and Lenore J. Weitzman, "Women as Litigants," *Hastings Law Journal* 23 (November 1971): 171–198. See also U.S. Department of Commerce, Bureau of the Census, *Divorce, Child Custody, and Child Support* (Washington, D.C.: Government Printing Office, 1979); *Child Support and Alimony: 1981* (1983), *Child Support and Alimony: 1983* (1986), and *Child Support and Alimony: 1985* (1987); Weitzman, *The Divorce Revolution;* citizens Advisory Council on the Status of Women, *The ERA and Alimony and Child Support Laws,* CACSQ 23-N-1972 (Washington, D.C.: Department of Labor, 1972); Andrea H. Beller, "Trends in Child Support Payments," *Proceedings, First Annual Women's Policy Research Conference,* Washington, D.C., May 19, 1989, 52–57; Demie Kurz, "Divorce and Inequality: The Case of Child Support," *Proceedings, Second Annual Women's Policy Research Conference,* Washington, D.C., June 1–2, 1990, 32–39; Mimi Hall, "Child Support: States Pay If Parents Don't," *USA Today,* March 28, 1994, 10A; J. Hanna, "Divorce Law: A Debate About to Happen Again," *Chicago Tribune,* January 7, 1996, sec. 2, 1.

13. "Changing Family Composition," the Administration for Children and Families, Department of Health and Human Services at http://www.acf.dhhs.gov/ACF Programs/CSE/new/magazine.html#9708h.

14. Ibid.

15. Ibid.

16. U.S. Department of Commerce, Bureau of the Census, *Statistical Abstract of the United States, 1996* (Washington, D.C.: Government Printing Office, 1997), 385.

17. "Who Receives Child Support?" Economics and Statistics Administration. U.S. Department of Commerce, at http://www.census.gov/socdemo/www/chldsupp .html (May 1995).

18. See Paula Roberts, "Pursuing Child Support: More Violence?" the Electronic Policy Network at http://epn .org/clasp/970916.html (May 1997).

19. Center for Law and Social Policy, "Child Support: Computer Systems Snags" at http://www.handsnet .org/handsnet2/Articles/art.876165029.html (October 6, 1997).

20. "ACLU Fact Sheet: Chronology of Bottoms v. Bottoms, A Lesbian Mother's Fight for Her Son" at the American Civil Liberties web site at http://www.aclu .org/news/n050797c.html (July 1998). In a few states, including Alaska, California, New Mexico, and Pennsylvania, a parent's sexual orientation cannot technically be used to deny custody. See the 'Lectric Law Library web site at http://www.lectlaw.com/files/fam08 (July 1998).

21. U.S. Department of Commerce, Bureau of the Census, *Statistical Abstract of the United States, 1996*, p. 105.

22. Anne P. Mitchell, "The Hypocrisy of 'Equality' in a Family Law Context" at her web site at http://central .co.nz/~stokem/fare/dads.html (1991).

23. "Types of Child Custody" at the DivorceSource web site at http://www.divorcesource.com/AL/info/ cctypes.html (July 1998). States that don't distinguish between legal and physical custody use "custody" to refer to both sets of arrangements. See the Nolo Press web site at http://www.nolo.com/ChuckPC/PC.index .html#2 (July 1998).

CHRONOLOGY

1881 In *Chapman v. Phoenix National Bank,* a New York state court interprets common law as requiring a married woman to adopt her husband's surname as her own.

1945 In *People ex. rel. Rago v. Lipsky,* an Illinois state court rules that under common law, a married woman's legal surname is that of her husband.

1952 In *Hill v. Estate of Westbrook,* a California court dismisses a dependent cohabitant's attempt to obtain a share of the estate of her deceased partner on the grounds that a nonmarital sexual union confers no rights on the dependent partner.

1966 In *United States v. Yazell,* the Supreme Court recognizes the power of a state to restrict the right of married women to enter into contracts regarding their separate property.

1971, 1972 In *Forbush v. Wallace,* a federal district court holds that Alabama can constitutionally require a married woman to adopt her husband's surname as her legal name. The Supreme Court affirms that holding.

1972 In *Stuart v. Board of Supervisors of Elections for Howard County,* Maryland's highest court holds that the common law rule that individuals have the right to choose their own legal name applies to married women; thus, a married woman has the legal right to be known by her maiden name rather than the surname of her husband.

1972 In *Sillery v. Fagan and Fagan,* New Jersey's highest court throws out the common law rule that a husband is legally obligated to support his wife on the grounds that it is an unconstitutional gender distinction and holds that both the wife and the husband are legally liable for debts incurred by the wife.

1973 In *Green v. Commissioner,* a Massachusetts state court holds that the old common law rule that a wife's domicile follows that of her husband is outmoded and therefore will no longer be enforced.

1975 In *Weinberger v. Wiesenfeld,* the Supreme Court invalidates a provision of the Social Security Act that provides benefits for widows, but not widowers, with minor children.

1976 In *Marvin v. Marvin,* the California Supreme Court holds that property division agreements between cohabitants are judicially enforceable.

1977 In *Califano v. Goldfarb,* the Supreme Court invalidates a provision in the Social Security Act that authorizes retirement benefits for surviving widows, but not widowers.

1979 In *Kozlowski v. Koslowski,* the New Jersey Supreme Court upholds a lower court's enforcement of an agreement between cohabitants concerning financial support when the relationship ends.

1979 In *Hewitt v. Hewitt,* Illinois's highest court refuses to permit judicial enforcement of property division agreements between cohabitants.

1980 In *Trammel v. United States,* the Supreme Court abandons the traditional rule in federal courts that a person cannot testify against his or her spouse without the consent of the defendant spouse.

1981 In *Condore v. Prince George's General Hospital,* Maryland's highest court holds that the common law rule requiring a husband to support his wife violates the state's equal rights amendment.

1981 In *McCarty v. McCarty,* the Supreme Court holds that military pensions are not community property subject to division at the time of divorce. Congress rejects this interpretation and enacts legislation permitting states to consider such retirement benefits to be divisible at the time of divorce.

1982   In *Artiss v. Artiss,* a Hawaii court awards a dependent cohabitant a share of property acquired during cohabitation.

1993   In *Bottoms v. Bottoms,* the Virginia Supreme Court grants custody of a lesbian mother's son to the boy's grandmother.

1996   The Personal Responsibility and Work Opportunity Reconciliation Act (P.L. 104–193), popularly known as "welfare reform," provides for more aggressive collection of child support.

1996   The Defense of Marriage Act (P.L. 104–199) allows states not to recognize same sex marriages if legalized by another state.

1997   Louisiana enacts its Covenant Marriage Law aimed at making divorce more difficult to obtain.

READING 79

The Crime That Had No Name

Mary Frances Berry

When lesbians and gay men began to disclose their relationships in child custody, contract, and property disputes, they asked the public and the courts to adopt the new stories of acceptance to displace the old stories of sickness and sin. They wanted not only to redefine sex, . . . but also to redefine the family— the gateway to acceptance in civil society—to gradually include homosexual relationships. The courts recognized that a redefinition of acceptable sex involved a redefinition of the family. Judges interpreted standard legal doctrines and chose between the old and evolving stories in deciding the issues.

In child custody cases, early gay claimants were summarily rejected. In 1952, the same year in which the Pennsylvania legislature made homosexuality eligible for psychiatric treatment as an alternative to incarceration, a gay father's suit to remove conditions on his joint custody of his children came before the state supreme court. Luther Bachman and Catherine Bachman, of Lehigh County, divorced in 1946 after nine years of marriage and the birth of two children. Catherine and the children continued to live in the same house where she and Bachman had resided; he paid child support. Bachman was a businessman and active in community affairs. She was "a devoted mother," but Luther received shared custody after the divorce, which continued during Catherine's remarriage. Three years after the divorce, Bachman tried to eliminate a restriction on his custody that

forbade anyone except his mother from being present with him and the children. He claimed the condition was "impractical," "embarrassing" to him, and "perplexing" to the children. At the hearing concerning his request, Catherine told the judge that she objected to the children staying with Bachman overnight because they were "too young" and because, since he "admitted his homosexual tendencies," she did not want the children exposed to his gay acquaintances.

At trial, Bachman admitted only that he was "bi-erotic" and he was "as much attracted to male friendships" as to "female friendships." The trial court found that he lived in a newly built, "pretentious" house with his mother and a male friend. The friend could have afforded his own apartment but, after moving from New York City, had lived with Bachman since about six months before the hearing. The friend also appeared "qualified and capable," but had no job, other than employment by Bachman. The court thought Bachman's "propensities were abnormal and his conduct immoral." Furthermore, a "convicted sodomist" formerly in Bachman's employ "testified that he had had relations with him on four occasions." Bachman had not remarried and displayed his gay lifestyle openly.

The trial court left the shared custody arrangements intact. However, the state supreme court decided to make a change in "the best interests and permanent welfare of the children." Although no "untoward incidents involving the children [had] occurred," the judges thought "harmful influences" might be met with. Because of Bachman's homosexuality, the justices awarded full custody to their mother. She could grant him "such limited visitation" as she thought in the best interests of the children. Bachman essentially lost even shared custody because, in the view of the court, he wanted more than toleration; he wanted acceptance of his homosexual lifestyle.

Judges in *Bachman* and other child custody disputes involving gays reflected the public's adherence to the old story of appropriate family behavior. In this old story, homosexuality remained a perversion. In 1980, the Kentucky appellate court, finding a homosexual parent's behavior too open and threatening, agreed to consider a father's suit to void a custody order granted to his wife when they divorced. The court noted that the couple's daughter was less than a year old at the time of the divorce. Soon the father learned that the mother had begun a lesbian relationship and worked at a lesbian bar. Her lover lived with her and the child, and the two women had exchanged vows and rings in a commitment ceremony. The court agreed that the mother's new lifestyle could harm the infant. The evidence included a court-appointed psychologist's opinion that "there is a social stigma attached to homosexuality," so the child would "have additional burdens to bear in terms of teasing, possible embarrassment and internal conflicts." Also, research on the effects of parental modeling on children indicated that she might "have difficulties in achieving a fulfilling heterosexual identity of her own in the future." The court, still enmeshed in the old story, perceived the possibility of positive attitudes toward homosexual relationships as too far removed to counter any negative effects on children.

In the same year, however, a Massachusetts court decided to develop a new legal narrative about sexual orientation. The new story treated homosexual and heterosexual families as similar: both faced difficulties, but could function equally well.

Brenda King Bezio was a lesbian who, admittedly, had led an unstable life and had suffered longstanding financial and physical problems. A trial court decided that a permanent guardian should keep her children, because of her lesbianism and her former inability to care for them. The appellate judges disagreed, finding no evidence that the sexual preference of adults in the home had "any detrimental impact on children," and concluding that her earlier problems were resolved. Furthermore, the record included no proof that children "who are raised with a loving couple of the same sex are any more disturbed, unhealthy, maladjusted than children raised with a loving couple of mixed sex." Therefore, the state could not take children away from their parents "simply because their households fail to meet the ideals approved by the community . . . [or] simply because the parents embraced ideologies or pursue life-styles at odds with the average." Dr. Alexandra Kaplan, a clinical psychologist and professor of psychology at the University of Massachusetts, testified: "There is no evidence at all that sexual preference of adults in the home has any detrimental impact on children." Many factors influence child rearing, and "sexual preference per se is typically not one of them." Dr. Kaplan also testified that a parent's homosexual relationship would not necessarily cause a child to become a homosexual instead of a heterosexual: "Most children raised in a homosexual situation become heterosexual as adults." Furthermore, she explained, the sexual orientation of the parent "is irrelevant to [the child's] mental health." Psychologist David Johnson, a defense witness who had seen the children in play therapy, concurred with Dr. Kaplan. The Massachusetts court accepted the new stories gays and lesbians had been telling for nearly a decade, and also acknowledged the evidence provided for those new stories. The court rejected as unfounded the myths of the past.

However, the work of undermining the stories of danger to children and perversion in a homosexual family was not yet done. Proof of this lay in the decisions of other courts that rejected the *Bezio* decision. The conflicting perspectives in the Kentucky and Massachusetts cases were at issue in Virginia's disposition of Sharon Bottoms's fight for custody of her three-year-old son. One court, adopting the Massachusetts view, found no evidence that the child would be harmed if Bottoms was awarded custody. The Virginia Supreme Court overturned the decision in 1995, preferring the rationale of harm and confused identity used in the Kentucky decision. Professor Nancy Polikoff, of the American University law school, argued that the court had given a "blueprint to any judge who wants to deny custody to a gay or lesbian parent." All such a judge had to do was selectively quote expert opinion and emphasize the stigma attached to homosexuality.

Homosexual-parent custody disputes remain caught between new and old stories. By 1995, eight states had denied custody to a homosexual parent and five had not. In 1996, the Washington State Supreme Court extended the new positive stories. On the basis of expert testimony, the justices concluded that restrictions on either parent's sexual behavior with partners other than the former spouse were inappropriate: "Problems with adjustment are the normal response to any breakup of a family. But restrictions on a parent's conduct designed to artificially ameliorate changes in a child's life are not permissible. If the problem is adjustment, the remedy is counseling."

Courts in child custody cases could not avoid considering whether an acceptable family meant only a family that practiced heterosexual sex. To decide property and contract disputes between gays, the courts had to acknowledge the reality of a same-sex relationship; however, they could avoid confronting directly whether the relationship constituted a family. Much like courts that relied on due process concerns in deciding sodomy cases, they took refuge in legal stories. They upheld the validity of standard contract and property rules, so important to every enterprise in society, without regard to the parties' sexuality. In Arkansas, Benjamin Selman bought a house in the name of his companion, James Bramlett, with an oral agreement that Bramlett would transfer it to Selman once he obtained his divorce. Selman and Bramlett had been lovers and lived together for about a year. In 1980, the state supreme court concluded that Bramlett knew the title was temporary and must convey it back to Selman. He could not gain a "windfall" by taking advantage of their relationship, "by claiming the stigma of homosexuality." According to this and other decisions, to reinforce standard contract doctrines did not undermine family values.

Similarly, a dispute between tennis champion Martina Navratilova and her lover Judy Nelson was interpreted so as to require no sanction of their lesbian relationship. The matter, the parties agreed, rested solely on the validity of a contract. Nelson, a forty-five-year-old divorced mother of two, began living with Navratilova in July 1984, and traveled with her to tournaments around the world. Nelson and Navratilova signed a "non-marital cohabitation agreement" in 1986. Nelson sued Navratilova upon receiving formal notification from her in April 1991 that their relationship was over. Nelson wanted to enforce the cohabitation agreement, which provided that if they parted they would divide assets accrued since they began living together. Nelson's lawsuit was settled out of court in 1992. However, despite the public awareness of the affair, the legal result avoided sanction of homosexuality and relied solely on contract law.

The law punished homosexual behavior when it became categorized as homosexuality. As gays sought public recognition they became a threat to gender prescriptions. Judicial opinions mirrored public concern about gender roles and were influenced by race and class narratives. Gay men, lesbians, and African American homosexuals were regarded very differently. Gay males evoked a negative response because they represented the dominant group. Gay male sex was a threat to the image of males as patriarchs and heads of families, who exercised power over women and children. Lesbians were harassed in bars and on the streets, but sex between women was not the target of the sodomy statutes. Further, lesbians did not solicit sex from strangers in public restrooms and other venues, behavior that exposed men to criminal charges. African American men were peripheral to power. However, African American gays faced homophobia within the black community, because of widely accepted fundamentalist religious stories. They also were harassed by the legal system because they defied the image of the sexually consumed African American man. This image was important to white men who defined themselves as the opposite, a civilized other.

Homosexuality in the courts traveled a long and convoluted route, from being an outlawed offense with no story to tell, to being an outlawed offense enveloped in medical stories of sin and illness, to become a story in itself, one of affirming relationships and positive values. Gays and lesbians are still elaborating newer stories in an attempt to gain societal acceptance and displace the old ones that linger in the public mind. Because the old stories change, homosexuals' experiences and self-images change, and hence so do the stories they tell. Languages, stories, and identities are protean dynamic forces, just like the society they reflect or tell about. Indeed, the story about gay men and lesbians has changed enough for a federal Employer Non-Discrimination Act to re-

ceive serious consideration. It has also changed sufficiently for domestic partnerships to gain recognition from a few employers. The old story still protects the definition of marriage as a union of one man and one woman, and still appears in child custody arrangements. The work of imprinting new stories has yet to be fully accomplished. Until the work is done, gay and lesbian relationships will be regarded as a major challenge to gender roles—just as interracial marriage was considered a major challenge to racial subordination before the 1960s.

READING 80

The Rhetoric and Reality of Welfare Reform

Heidi Hartmann and Hsiao-ye Yi, with Megan DeBell and Jacqueline Chu

In recent years, we have witnessed a major shift in the poverty debate, away from the Great Society ideal of providing relief for the poor, toward the "New Federalism" vision of smaller government and reduced dependence on government. The rhetoric has also shifted from alleviating or eliminating poverty to reducing illegitimacy and "ending welfare as we know it." Despite these changes, women have remained at the center of the poverty debate, and public assistance programs, formerly Aid to Families with Dependent Children (AFDC) and its current replacement, Temporary Assistance to Needy Families (TANF), which provides assistance primarily to single-parent families, are the focus of copious media attention. The Clinton Administration, the Congress, and the National Governors Association all offered welfare reform proposals to end the safety net features of AFDC and decrease dependency on federal public assistance. With the passage of the Personal Responsibility and Work Opportunity Reconciliation Act of 1996 (which provides block grants to the states of fund TANF), each individual state is now developing its own welfare programs in response to the federal time limit on benefit receipt and the requirement to participate in the labor force.

[Here] we take a closer look at the subpopulation of the poor that currently preoccupies policymakers —single-mother families. One reason this group is central to the poverty debate is their sizeable presence among the poor. Single-mother families make up 60 percent of all poor families with children, and people living in these families make up 22 percent of all poor people. Single-mother families are more likely to experience poverty than almost any other group. For example, in 1994, 44 percent of single-mother families were poor, compared with 8 percent of married-couple families with children and 12 percent of people over age sixty-five (U.S. Bureau of the Census 1995). Over the past two decades, the number of poor female-headed households grew by 45 percent, faster than all poor families and poor married-couple families (which grew by 39 and 24 percent, respectively). The higher incidence of poverty among single mothers results from several causes: (a) single mothers lack access to the income stabilizing effect of an additional earner that many married-couple families enjoy, (b) they receive only small amounts of child support from the absent fathers, and (c) they earn substantially less than male breadwinners.

Since former President Reagan's characterization of welfare mothers as "Welfare Queens," poverty has come to be viewed as the result of pathological behavior of individuals rather than as the result of structural flaws in the economic system or even simply misfortune or bad luck. Those who received AFDC benefits were viewed as lazy, preferring to sit at home and have more babies instead of acquiring the skills they need to obtain jobs to lift them out of poverty. And welfare benefits themselves were seen as encouraging this pathological behavior. According to one opinion poll, more than two-thirds of Americans believe that welfare does more harm than good (Davidson 1995). Because of this perception, the dominant theme of the 1996 federal welfare legislation and the state programs being implemented now is to put the able-bodied to work. No one argues against the value of work: in fact, another poll shows that fully 94 percent of Americans believe welfare mothers will gain self-respect by working.

If policies requiring work are to succeed, policymakers must look realistically at two assumptions underlying the new programs: (a) single mothers who are the primary caretakers of their children can work outside the home and (b) they will find work that enables them to support themselves and their children. Policymakers newly charged with getting women off welfare and into work must also deal with the legacy of the bad rap these women had while on welfare. If they were such pathological people, how will they be able to work now?

. . .

The Myth That Welfare Breeds Dependence and Fertility

[The Institute for Women's Policy Research] IWPR . . . using the first four panels of the SIPP and covering the years 1984 through 1989 found that only a minority, 26 percent, of single-mother families who receive welfare are totally dependent on welfare.[1] Three-quarters of the single mothers had substantial income either from their own earnings or from their families or both. Moreover, of those who appear to depend exclusively on welfare (because they report no other substantial income source), virtually all (98%) have family incomes that fall below the fed-

eral poverty line. Far from supporting welfare recipients at a "queenly" level, welfare provides only the barest subsistence. It should not be surprising, therefore, that welfare mothers package income from as many sources as possible in an effort to increase their well-being. More than half (57 percent) of single mothers are helped financially by their families. Of these, 26 percent work for pay as well, while 31 percent receive only family help to supplement their AFDC benefits. In addition to those who receive help from their families, another 17 percent who receive little family help work outside the home to bring in earnings to supplement their welfare benefits. Those mothers who have additional sources of income are substantially less likely to be poor (see Table 1). It can hardly be said, then, that welfare mothers are actually dependent on welfare in the sense of total dependence that the critics of welfare seem to take for granted.[2] Research also shows that women who receive welfare benefits are no more fertile than other women are. In fact, at least one study (Rank 1989) found that women receiving welfare have fewer children than similarly situated women not receiving welfare benefits. It is therefore extremely unlikely that either of the widely held beliefs that welfare mothers have babies in order to collect welfare or that they have one baby after another to increase their welfare benefits could be true. In the IWPR study sample, the average number of children for each welfare mother is 2.1, slightly below the average for all U.S. Women (Spalter-Roth et al. 1995).

The Myth of the Lazy Welfare Mother

Despite the popular perception that welfare mothers do not work, half of all single mothers who spend any time on welfare also work in the labor market (at least 300 hours, over a two-year period): 20 percent combined work and welfare; 23 percent cycled between work and welfare; and another 7 percent worked limited hours, spending more time looking for work than actually working. An additional 23 percent were not employed but spent substantial time looking for work. In other words, more than seven out of ten AFDC recipients spent significant time in the labor force, either working or looking for work, but not finding it. Severe disabilities prevent

Table 1 Types and Impact of Income Packages Among AFDC Recipients

	TOTAL NUMBER	AFDC ONLY *	FAMILY AND AFDC **	EMPLOYED AND AFDC ***	EMPLOYMENT, FAMILY, AND AFDC
Total	2,797,285	732,335	865,995	484,511	714,444
As Percent of Total	100%	26%	31%	17%	26%
Total in Poverty	2,027,494	716,9837	634,878	372,565	303,114
Percent in Poverty	72%	98%	73%	77%	42%

*To be included in this study of AFDC recipients, a woman must receive AFDC for at least 2 months out of the 24-month study period.
**To be included in this category, recipients must live with relatives contributing at least $1,500 in family income over the 24-month study period.
***To be considered employed, a welfare recipient must work at least 300 hours during the 24-month study period.
Source: IWPR calculations based on the Survey of Income and Program Participation, 1984 and 1986–1988 panels.
From: Spalter-Roth, Burr, Hartmann, and Shaw (1995).

nearly one in ten welfare mothers from working or seeking work—these women compose one-quarter of welfare mothers who neither work nor look for work (Spalter-Roth et al. 1995).

Table 2 shows that only 9 percent of the time spent on AFDC during the two-year study period is spent by able-bodied mothers who are neither working at paid employment, looking for work, attending school, nor caring for babies or preschoolers year-round or pre-teens during the summer. Few welfare dollars are "wasted" on able-bodied women who are not caring for children too young to care for themselves. These data suggest that the AFDC system achieved its original goal of enabling women without other means of support to care for their own children (rather than send them to orphanages while the mothers worked). But they also suggest that if all these mothers are required to work, a great deal of childcare will need to be done by others.

What Factors Increase the Likelihood of Working for Single Welfare Mothers?

While most of the single mothers in IWPR's study participated in the labor force, many spent their time unsuccessfully looking for work or experienced periods of unemployment between spells of welfare receipt and work. IWPR research suggests that employment at stable and long-term jobs provides the greatest likelihood of escaping poverty, although the odds of escaping poverty by work alone are small for

Table 2 Welfare Mothers' Time Use Over a Two-Year Period

Percent of time receiving welfare	77%
Percent of time not receiving welfare	23%
Percent of time receiving welfare	100%
Working	13%
Looking for Work	18%
In School	8%
Caring for baby (under two years)	18%
Caring for preschool children (ages 2–5)	22%
Caring for children (ages 6–12) during summer months	4%
Disabled, doing none of the above	8%
Able-bodied, doing none of the above	9%

Source: IWPR calculations based on the Survey of Income and Program Participation, 1984 and 1986–1988 panels.
From: Spalter-Roth, Burr, Hartmann, and Shaw (1995).

this group of women. Generally, as noted above, earnings from employment are packaged together with other income sources such as AFDC and income from other family members. Nonetheless, paid employment does improve the economic wellbeing of these single mothers and their families.

Not surprisingly, the factors that predict whether an AFDC recipient works are the same factors that predict employment for most women, regardless of

Table 3 Results from Multivariate Logistics Models

FACTORS THAT SIGNIFICANTLY IMPROVE THE CHANCES THAT AN AFDC RECIPIENT WORKS	FACTORS THAT SIGNIFICANTLY IMPROVE THE CHANCES THAT AN AFDC RECIPIENT ESCAPES POVERTY
Human Capital	**Human Capital**
Able-bodied	Has completed high school
Has completed high school	Has work experience
Has work experience	Has had job training
Has had job training	
Additional Income	**Additional Income**
Another earner in household	Income from other family members
Gets married	
Receives child support	
Children	**Children**
Fewer children	Fewer children
No infants or toddlers	
State-of-Residence Characteristics	**State-of-Residence Characteristics**
Low unemployment rate (3.5%)	High welfare benefit per person per month
	Low unemployment rate
	Employment Conditions
	Stable work
	Union coverage

Source: IWPR calculations based on the Survey of Income and Program Participation, 1984 and 1986–1988 panel.
From: Spalter-Roth, Burr, Hartmann, and Shaw (1995).

income level: such as not having a disability; the availability of jobs; not having infants or toddlers in their care; access to family supports (i.e., child care or earnings from other family members); and greater levels of accumulated human capital including high school education, job training, and past work experience (see table 3). For instance, having a work-preventing disability makes it seven times more likely that these single mothers will not find employment. AFDC recipients are more likely to find work if more jobs are available (i.e., if they live in states with low unemployment rates), while mothers with older children who have lower childcare costs and fewer demands on their time are much more likely to work. Additionally, family supports ease the costs of working, which significantly increases the likelihood of working. Obtaining more work experience or job training and completing high school makes the mothers more attractive to employers and more likely to find work—these factors double the chances of finding work.

Contrary to stereotypes, average state benefit levels, the amount of time spent looking for work, the mother's age, and the mother's welfare history were insignificant in distinguishing between mothers who engage in paid employment and those who do not. And being African American had little bearing on predicting whether an AFDC mother engages in paid work.

Job Prospects of Mothers Receiving Welfare

Low-Wages and Unstable Jobs: Can Single Mothers Rely on the Low-Wage Labor Market?

If low-income single mothers succeed in finding work, do their jobs provide sufficient earnings to raise their families out of poverty? Tables 4 and 5 compare single mothers who receive AFDC with

Table 4 Characteristics of Low Income* Single Mothers

| | | AFDC Recipients | | |
	TOTAL	WELFARE RELIANT	WORK/ WELFARE PACKAGERS	NON-AFDC WORK RELIANT
Sample Size (Unweighted)	2,554	688	474	1,392
Sample Size (Weighted)	5,735,793	1,536,332	1,117,029	3,082,432
Percent (Weighted)	100.00%	26.80%	19.50%	53.70%
Demographic				
Age (mean years)	32.2	30.3	29.3	34.3
Teenage (Age 19 or less)	9.70%	11.40%	10.70%	8.50%
Youth (Age 20–24)	16.40%	20.60%	24.50%	11.50%
Young (Age 25–34)	38.10%	40.70%	40.90%	35.90%
Prime (Age 35+)	35.60%	37.30%	23.90%	44.10%
Percent Recently Married	57.10%	44.10%	49.90%	66.20%
Race and Ethnicity				
White	43.20%	32.50%	42.10%	48.90%
African-American	40.70%	48.70%	44.00%	35.50%
Hispanic	13.90%	16.90%	11.20%	13.40%
Other	2.40%	2.80%	2.60%	2.20%
Family and Household Structure				
Number of Children	1.6	2.0	1.8	1.4
Age of Children (monthly average)				
Percent of Children under Age 3	24.30%	29.90%	30.70%	19.20%
Percent of Children Age 3 to 5	16.30%	20.30%	18.20%	13.60%
Percent of Children Age 6 to 12	34.00%	32.00%	33.80%	35.00%
Percent of Children Age 13 to 17	25.40%	17.90%	17.20%	32.20%
Number of People in Household	3.7	4.1	3.9	3.5
Human Capital				
Education and Job Training				
Years of Schooling	11.3	10.6	11.4	11.6
Educational Attainment				
Percent High School Diploma Only	41.00%	31.80%	43.40%	44.70%
Percent Some College	17.70%	11.40%	18.80%	20.50%
Percent 4 Year College or More	3.10%	1.30%	1.80%	4.60%
Percent Enrolled in School During Survey	26.10%	32.70%	32.70%	22.10%
Percent Ever Received Job Training	27.10%	22.50%	33.30%	27.10%
Percent Ever Received Federal Job Training	9.70%	11.00%	15.20%	7.10%
Work Experience				
Years of Work Experience	7.2	3.7	5.8	9.4
Current Job Tenure (Years)	3	1.3	2.1	4.2
Physical Limitation on Work				
Percent Disabled	17.00%	27.20%	13.90%	13.00%

*Family income is less than 200 percent of the federal poverty line.
Source: IWPR calculations based on the Survey of Income and Program Participation 1986, 1987, 1988, and 1990 panels.
From: IWPR (forthcoming).

Table 5 Poverty and Employment Characteristics of Low-Income Single Mothers (Over the 24-Month Study Period)

	Single Mothers		
	AFDC Recipients		Non-AFDC
	WELFARE RELIANT[a]	WORK/WELFARE PACKAGERS[b]	WORK RELIANT[c]
Sample size (Unweighted)	688	474	1,392
Sample size (Weighted)	1,536,332	1,117,029	3,082,432
Poverty (modified definition)[d]			
Percent in Poverty	79.1%	52.7%	29.2%
Months in Poverty	19.8	14.7	8.4
Labor Force Participation			
Percent in the Labor Force (monthly average)	11%	65%	74%
Percent Ever Worked During the Survey	11%	100%	84%
Weeks of Employment	8.5	53.5	84.1
Weeks of Unemployment	20.3	14.1	5.9
Total Hours Worked	140	1,862	3,232
Number of Jobs per Recipient	1.09	1.71	1.69
Earnings (in 1994 dollars)			
Total Annual Earnings	$327	$5,419	$11,134
Annual Earnings in Primary Job	$309	$4,713	$9,955
Hourly Wage Rate at Primary Job	$4.42	$5.29	$6.60
Work Experience			
Total Weeks Worked	9	54	84
Weeks in Primary Job	9	47	77
Weeks in full-time at the primary job	1	29	57
Weeks part-time at the primary job	8	18	20

[a] Welfare Reliants received AFDC for at least two months during the 24-month survey period but had less than 300 hours of paid work.
[b] Work/Welfare packagers received AFDC for at least two months during the survey but had over 300 hours of paid work.
[c] Work Reliants received AFDC for fewer than two months. Only 1 percent of these women received AFDC during the 24-month survey period, for spells of a maximum of one month.
[d] Includes the cash value of Food Stamps and Women, Infants, and Children (WIC).
Source: IWPR calculations based on the Survey of Income and Program Participation, 1986, 1987, 1988, and 1990 panels.
From: IWPR (forthcoming).

low-income employed mothers who do not receive AFDC (whom we call the "work reliants").[3] The work-reliant group represents a best case scenario for what we can expect to happen to welfare recipients who, because of time limits and work requirements, will likely rely more on the labor market for their livelihood. Given the often inadequate wages and intermittent work that characterize the low-wage labor market, however, it is unlikely that single mothers can achieve above-poverty incomes based on their earnings alone. Moreover, the work reliants,

who by definition have incomes up to 200 percent of the poverty level and receive welfare for one month or less, have demographic and human capital characteristics that enable them to work more hours and earn more per hour than those women still receiving welfare assistance.

The work reliants are the most likely of the low-income single mothers in our study to have a high school diploma; only 30 percent of the work reliants lack a high school diploma compared with 36 percent of the work/welfare packagers (those who both receive welfare and work) and 56 percent of those who rely mainly on welfare. As table 4 shows, work-reliant single mothers have more work experience and more years on their current jobs. They are also older, have fewer children, and have older children. They and the work/welfare packagers are much less likely than the welfare reliants to have a physical work-limiting disability. As table 5 shows, the work reliants work substantially more hours than the work/welfare packagers, for a total of 3,232 hours, or about three-quarters time, over the two-year study period. They have the highest hourly wages among low-income single mother—an average of $6.60 per hour and total annual earnings of $11,134 (in 1994 dollars). Although low-wage service jobs constitute the largest source of employment for both the work reliants and the work/welfare packagers, a comparison of tables 6 and 7 shows that the work-reliant mothers are more likely to be in better jobs (managerial, professional, technical or precision production jobs).[4] (Of work-reliant single mothers, 33 percent work in the service occupations and 14 percent work in the higher-

skilled occupations, while for the packagers, 38 percent work in the service occupations and 11 percent work in the higher-skilled technical, professional and managerial occupations.) Work-reliant single mothers earn more per hour in each occupation than do work/welfare packagers—an average of $7.43 per hour versus $5.96 per hour (in January 1997 dollars), consistent with their higher levels of human capital. For welfare mothers who work, the most common occupations are domestic workers, cashiers, nursing aides, childcare workers, and wait persons (data not shown).

Despite their greater work effort and slightly better occupational status, work-reliant single mothers experience significant levels of job instability, holding an average of 1.7 jobs during the two-year survey period, the same as work/welfare packagers (see table 5). Though work-reliant single mothers spend significantly fewer months in poverty than other low-income single mothers, they still earn less than the $14,916 that Edin and Lein (1997) estimate is necessary for working single mothers to survive at a minimal standard of decency.

Table 6 Jobs and Wages of Work/Welfare Packagers
(average hourly wages in January 1997 dollars [a])

	% IN OCCUPATION	HOURLY RATE [b]
Service	37.80%	$5.86
Administrative Support	19.00%	$6.69
Operator/Laborer/Farming [c]	18.50%	$4.90
Sales	14.30%	$5.67
Managerial	3.80%	$7.39 [d]
Professional	3.70%	
Technicians/Related Support	1.90%	
Precision Production	1.10%	
Total	100.10%	$5.96

[a] Wage rates were CPI-adjusted to the January 1997 dollar value from their original amount in the current dollar value at the time of the survey.
[b] The wage rates are for the primary jobs held by the respondents during the two-year survey period. A primary job is the job at which the respondent worked the longest hours, including wage, salary, and self-employed jobs. The hourly wage rate is calculated from total earnings and total hours worked at the primary job.
[c] Including 2.1% in farming and forestry.
[d] Average for four occupations: managerial, professional, technicians and related support, and precision production, due to small case numbers.
Source: IWPR calculations based on the Survey of Income and Program Participation, 1990 and 1991 panels.

Table 7 Jobs and Wages of Market Reliant Single Mothers in Low-Income Families (average hourly wages in January 1997 dollars[a])

	% IN OCCUPATION	HOURLY RATE[b]
Service	33.00%	$6.60
Administrative Support	22.30%	$8.39
Operator/Laborer/Farming[c]	17.10%	$7.05
Sales	13.40%	$6.49
Professional	5.30%	$9.17
Managerial	3.40%	$9.55
Technicians/Related Support	2.50%	$10.63
Precision Production	3.00%	$7.41
Total	100.00%	$7.43

[a] The amount of the wage rates were CPI-adjusted to the January 1997 dollar value from their original amount in the current dollar value at the time of the survey.
[b] The wage rates are for the primary jobs held by the respondents during the two-year survey period. A primary job is the job at which the respondent worked the longest hours, including wage, salary, and self-employed jobs. The hourly wage rate is calculated from total earnings and total hours worked at the primary job.
[c] Including 0.7% in farming and forestry.
Source: IWPR calculations based on the Survey of Income and Program Participation, 1990 and 1991 panels.

What Factors Increase the Chances of Escaping Poverty for AFDC Single Mothers?

Stable jobs, more human capital, union membership, and access to means- and non-means-tested benefits increase the chances of escaping poverty (see table 3). Among all single mothers who package work and welfare, the more months during which a mother pools income with other family members, the more likely she is to escape poverty. Single mothers who have access to income from family members on a continuous basis are eight times more likely to escape poverty than women who do not have this steady income source.

The majority of working welfare mothers lack access to significant family resources—for these mothers, earnings from employment and stable jobs become a more important ingredient of an antipoverty strategy. Of primary importance is job volatility (the number of times they change jobs). Regardless of the reasons for job loss, the more times the mother starts and stops working, the more likely she is to be poor. Mothers whose jobs are covered by union contracts generally enjoy more job stability—union coverage triples these mothers' chances of escaping poverty.

Working welfare mothers with a high school education and job training are more likely to escape poverty. Although previous work experience is also significant, it takes ten years of work experience to raise a family's chances of escaping poverty by two-thirds. Living in states with higher AFDC benefits is also a significant antipoverty factor, as is receiving non-means-tested benefits, such as unemployment compensation, social security, or worker's compensation.

How Significant Are Childcare Costs for Single Mothers?

As noted earlier (table 7.3), the presence of young children is an important factor in reducing the likelihood of a low-income single mother's employment. Underlying this negative association is the lack of affordable, quality childcare (Kimmel 1995). Recent research at IWPR has analyzed childcare usage among working mothers in low-income families

Table 8 Child Care Arrangements of Children Under Six for Low-Income *
Single Working Mothers

	AFDC MOTHERS	NON-AFDC MOTHERS
Sample Size (Unweighted)	78	208
Sample Size (Weighted)	306,007	799,579
Average Number of Children Under Age 6	1.3	1.2
Primary Care Arrangements (percent of total children)		
Relative Care	53.40%	36.70%
Other Parent	10.40%	8.90%
Siblings	0.60%	1.50%
Grandparents	25.70%	17.50%
Other Relatives	16.70%	8.80%
Non-Relative Family-Based Care	16.50%	20.90%
Center-Based Care	19.80%	30.00%
Other Care **	10.20%	12.40%
Percent of Children in Paid Care	46.70%	52.90%
Percent of Children with More than One Arrangement	19.10%	30.50%

* Family income is less than 200 percent of the federal state poverty line.
** Other care includes child in school, child caring for self, and child care by mother while mother is working.
Source: IWPR Calculations based on the 1998 and 1990 panels and Topical Module 3 of the Survey of Income and Program Participation.

(those within 200 percent of the poverty line) with children under thirteen to investigate both what type of childcare these families use and how much they pay for it.[5]

Both working single mothers who receive welfare and those who do not use relative care most often, followed by center-based care and non-relative family-based care. Working single mothers who receive welfare are considerably poorer than those who do not; they use much more care provided by grandmothers and other relatives than do the work-reliant mothers, who use more center-based care (see table 8). Despite their greater use of relatives, AFDC working mothers and work-reliant mothers pay for childcare about half the time. Among AFDC working mothers, 33 percent who use grandparent care, 71 percent who use other relatives, 83 percent who use family care by nonrelatives, and 68 percent who use center-based care pay for it. Among the work-reliant single mothers, lower proportions pay for relative care but higher proportions pay for nonrelative and center-based care (data not shown).[6]

To determine the burden of cost to single working mothers, the childcare cost in relation to mother's earnings, to total family incomes, and to the families' poverty status (see table 9) was analyzed. Both AFDC and non-AFDC single working mothers are about equally likely to pay for childcare (ranging from 38.6 to 40.9 percent; these proportions are lower than those noted earlier for children under six, because children up through age twelve are included in this analysis—it is easier to find unpaid care for older children). Furthermore, low-income non-AFDC mothers and AFDC mothers paid about the same amount for childcare monthly, with the AFDC mothers paying slightly more ($222 per month versus $204 per month). Since the AFDC working mothers earn substantially less, the cost of childcare is a much higher burden for these mothers than it is for the non-AFDC working mothers. AFDC mothers spend $1.72 per hour of employment on childcare, amounting to 34 percent of the mother's earnings overall. Work-reliant mothers pay $1.36 per hour of employment and 19 percent of their earn-

Table 9 Child Care Costs for Single Mothers with Children Under Age 13 in Low-Income Families, 1994 Dollars

	Working Mothers [a]			
	AFDC [b]		Non-AFDC	
	PAYING	NOT PAYING	PAYING	NOT PAYING
Sample Size (Unweighted)	70	49	234	160
Sample Size (Weighted)	272,000	180,000	868,000	601,000
Average Number of Children	1.7	1.9	1.5	1.6
Average Size of Household	4.5	4.1	3.6	3.4
Distribution of Families by Paying and Not-Paying	60.20%	39.80%	59.10%	40.90%
Monthly Child Care Cost		$222		$204
Mother's Hourly Wage Rate [c]	$5.81	$5.92	$6.81	$0.79
Mother's Hours Worked	132	141	161	164
Cost per Mother's Employment Hour		$1.72		$1.36
Mother's Monthly Earnings	$735	$813	$1,088	$1,281
Cost as a Percent of Mother's Earnings		34.30%		19.20%
Monthly Family Income	$1,491	$1,586	$1,089	$1,881
Cost as a Percent of Family Income		19%		13%
Percent in Poverty [d]	48.70%	51.50%	28.40%	15.10%
Percent in Poverty if Child Care Costs are Subsidized		34.50%		8.10%

[a] Mothers who were working as well as enrolled in school are not included in this table to avoid over-estimating childcare costs in relation to mother's earnings and family income. All data are for Month 12 in the 24-month study period.
[b] Women in the AFDC group may or may not be on AFDC in Month 12, but receive AFDC for at least two months of the 24-month study period.
[c] Mother's hourly wage rate is for her primary job (the job at which she worked the most hours) during Month 12.
[d] A modified poverty measure, which includes the cash value of food stamps and WIC in family income for Month 12 is used.
Source: IWPR calculations based on the 1988 and 1990 panels and Topical Module 3 of the Survey of Income and Program Participation.

ings overall on childcare. Work-reliant mothers have lower childcare costs (per working hour) because, among other reasons, they have older children and fewer children. Their lower childcare costs undoubtedly contribute to their greater work effort.

To what degree would childcare subsidies help poor employed mothers escape poverty? These findings suggest that about one-third of the below-poverty AFDC families would benefit from childcare subsidies (up to the amount of their current childcare cost, $214 monthly, on average) and escape poverty, that is, their poverty rate would decrease by one-third (from 52 to 34 percent). The poverty rate for families of low-income, non-AFDC, single mothers would decrease by nearly half (from 15.1 to 8.1 percent). Along with this simple effect on family well-being, childcare subsidies might have further positive effects that would help mothers stabilize their employment and improve their earning capacity in the long run.

Conclusions

Continuing research at IWPR strongly suggests that welfare recipients required to work as a result of welfare reform will likely do worse in the labor market than those already working. They have less education and work experience, which are likely to lead to lower earnings and higher childcare costs per employment hour because they have more and younger children. Their earnings will be low, well below the poverty level, and their childcare costs will be high. They will therefore need considerable ongoing financial assistance to enable them to work and maintain their current standard of living, which is already quite low. It appears from this analysis that when conditions improve for single mothers on welfare, when they have completed their schooling and their children are older, they begin to work and increase their work hours over time. These are the women who have been most able to leave welfare, and many have done so. The welfare reforms underway amount to pushing women off welfare before these basic, work-enabling conditions have been met.

Government data for 1996 saw no change in overall poverty rates but a large increase in the proportion of families living below 50 percent of the poverty standard. It is possible that this is an early result of welfare reform. The welfare rolls have fallen quite dramatically in many states, frequently by 40 to 60 percent, in the past several years. According to the President's Council of Economic Advisors, reduced rolls are a result of state-based welfare reforms undertaken under the previous waiver programs (which allowed states to experiment with AFDC eligibility rules and benefit levels), the 1996 welfare reform, the strong economy which has provided many new jobs, and decreased applications for welfare assistance even among those eligible (possibly as a result of the intense public discussion about changes in the welfare system).

Currently, because the strong economy is providing employment opportunities and because the federal block grant funds to the states, which are based on previous caseloads, are high relative to current caseloads, many states have large budget surpluses. Some states, not all, are spending increased amounts on childcare, job placement, and job training to facilitate the transition of these prejob-ready single mothers from welfare to work. Few are saving for a rainy day, raising great concerns for what might happen to poor families when the economy turns downward again.

As Nancy Fraser has pointed out, the United States is nearly unique among advanced industrial countries in having no ongoing financial support for mothers, either in the form of paid maternity leave for workers (which is strictly voluntary in all but five states in the United States) or in the form of child allowances. While most industrial nations have both maternity/child rearing financial aid and poor relief, the United States rolls both programs into one, providing maternal support only for those women who are desperately poor and lack other resources. Consequently, there is a stigma attached to the poor stay-at-home mom, the only mom who is obviously subsidized by taxpayers.

Policy Recommendations

Policymakers must recognize that there are no simple or inexpensive ways to make welfare mothers more self-sufficient over the long term. Not investing in these women now will likely doom most of them to more intense and long lasting poverty, even if more of them are working.

The five-year lifetime limit on benefit receipt will work against enabling women to complete high school or enter college, education they sorely need to increase their earnings capacity. Time limits may also make it difficult for these women to use welfare as unemployment insurance: given the instability in the low-wage labor market most of them will likely enter, income to fill the gaps between jobs will be necessary. While unemployment insurance should theoretically cover them in between jobs, in many states, low-wage workers who have not been able to work full-time for enough weeks of the year will not qualify for benefits; benefits are likely to be low for low-wage workers and may not be high enough to tide a mother with children over a jobless period. IWPR research has shown that when women who had left welfare lost their jobs, they were more likely to go back on welfare than on unemployment insurance.

Also, mothers who care for children will continue to have the kinds of family emergencies that put many of them on welfare in the first place. Lacking any other source of income in periods when they cannot work because of family needs, women who have exhausted their time limits will likely suffer great hardship. Expanding Temporary Disability Insurance programs, now required for workers in five states, to the rest of the states and enhancing them to provide paid family leaves would help women at all income levels, but would be especially important for low-income women. Alternatively, unemployment insurance could be expanded to provide paid family leave.

Finally, the presence or threat of domestic violence often prevents these women from entering the workforce or completing job-training programs. Women suffering from domestic violence will often need more than five years of benefits. Though states can exempt such women from the time limit, they are not required to do so. Recent estimates show that from one-fifth to over one-half of all AFDC recipients are current victims of domestic violence (Raphael 1996). Time limits on benefits will be especially difficult for this group of women, since repeated attempts to leave abusive relationships are usually needed. For many reasons, the issue of time limits in benefit receipt should be reexamined.

Efforts to increase single mothers' earnings in the labor market are also needed. A higher federal minimum wage (even with the recent increase, the minimum wage is still below its historic relative average), greater support for unionization among low-wage workers, and discouragement of the contingent work phenomenon would all improve the earnings prospects of welfare mothers. Stronger enforcement of antidiscrimination laws and new laws requiring pay equity would also help. In the interim, welfare reform should encourage welfare recipients, who already exhibit substantial work and job search effort, to package earnings along with their benefits so that they can stabilize their family income at a higher level. Given low wages and low benefits, the average single-mother family needs both to survive. Although many states have liberalized their welfare programs in this way, these work/welfare packagers could face hardship when their five-year lifetime limits have been reached if, in the interim, they have not been able to find higher wage jobs that allow them to survive without welfare.

Childcare and healthcare are especially important for this group of newly working mothers who will lose welfare benefits. By providing childcare subsidies to low-income mothers and mothers who formerly relied on AFDC, policymakers could improve the likelihood that low-income families could work their way out of poverty. Recent Congressional action has provided more funding for health insurance for the children of the working poor, but has done little to provide it for their mothers (and fathers).

Reforms such as childcare and healthcare subsidies for the working poor, higher wages, more unionization, reduced contingent work, improved unemployment insurance, and paid family leave would help all working women, though they would help the poor disproportionately more. The only potentially good thing about welfare reform is that it could lead to a changed perception of welfare mothers as working mothers, enabling them to have more in common with all mothers. Cross-class coalitions in support of these workplace reforms could become more possible. Alternatively, competition for scarce resources, such as subsidized daycare slots, might intensify between the welfare working poor and the working poor not moving off welfare and opportunity for unity could be lost.

Despite the prevailing perception that social policies have failed to achieve their goals, federal programs for the elderly have resulted in dramatic improvements in their economic status, primarily because of increases in real Social Security benefits (which grew by 57 percent between 1970 and 1986; Moon and Juster 1995) and Medicare and Medicaid programs, which cover more of the costs of medical care for the elderly. The poverty rate for the elderly in the United States fell from a high of 30 percent in 1967 to 12 percent in 1994 (U.S. Bureau of the Census 1996). These programs, which have broad benefits, also have broad support. They help all the elderly, but they help the poor elderly more.

While it is unlikely that programs targeted only at poor single mothers and their families will ever achieve the scale of the Social Security programs, current reforms and cutbacks will almost certainly result in *increased* poverty for many single mothers and their children. Sensible policies, targeted at increasing education and training, providing subsidized childcare and healthcare, establishing paid family leave, and reforming the low-wage labor market should be designed to help a broad group of women workers. Such programs could help poor single mothers lengthen and strengthen their labor market participation, improve their earnings, and perhaps, eventually, move beyond the need for welfare assistance from the public.

NOTES

1. The sample size for this study was 1,181 single mothers who received welfare for at least two months of the twenty-four-month study period. They represented about 2.8 million women in the U.S. population, or 80 percent of all adult AFDC recipients; see Spalter-Roth et al. (1995).
2. It should be noted that the percentages of women identified as working or receiving help in the EWPR study are higher than those so identified in administrative data. The administrative data are generally cross sectional and refer to a given point in time, for example, a single month. Although in any one month the average percentage receiving income from other family members may be small, the proportion receiving substantial family help over the twenty-four-month study period is much larger.
3. The data for these comparisons are drawn from an as yet unpublished IWPR study of the 1986 through 1990 SIPP panels, which includes analysis of all low-income families with minor children at home.
4. These data are from a recent unpublished analysis of SIPP data from the 1990 and 1991 panels (containing data up through 1992).
5. The 1988 and 1990 SIPP panels were used in this analysis.
6. All data in this paragraph pertain to children under age six.

REFERENCES

Davidson, Joe. Welfare mothers stress importance of building self-esteem if aid system is to be restructured. *Wall Street Journal,* 12 May 1995.

Edin, Kathryn J. and Laura Lein. 1997. *Making ends meet: How single mothers survive welfare and low-wage work.* New York: Russell Sage Foundation.

Kimmel, J. 1995. The effectiveness of child care subsidies in encouraging the welfare to work transitions of low-income single mothers. *The American Economics Review* 85: 271–275.

Rank, Mark R. 1989. Fertility among women on welfare. *American Sociological Review* 54, 2: 296–304.

Raphael, Jody. 1996. *Prisoners of abuse: Domestic violence and welfare recipients.* A second report of the Women, Welfare and Abuse Project. Chicago: Taylor Institute.

Spalter-Roth, Roberta M., Beverly Burr, Heidi Hartmann, and Lois Shaw. 1995. *Welfare that works: The working lives of AFDC recipients.* A Report to the Ford Foundation, Washington D.C.: Institute for Women's Policy Research.

U.S. Bureau of the Census. 1996. Income, poverty, and valuation of noncash benefits: 1994. *Current Population Reports,* Series P60–189. Washington D.C.: GPO

READING 81

Where Race and Gender Meet
Racism, Hate Crimes, and Pornography

Helen Zia

There is a specific area where racism, hate crimes, and pornography intersect, and where current civil rights law fails: racially motivated, gender-based crimes against women of color. This area of bias-motivated sexual assault has been called "ethno-rape"; I refer to it as "hate rape."

I started looking into this issue after years of organizing against hate killings of Asian Americans.

After a while, I noticed that all the cases I could name concerned male victims. I wondered why. Perhaps it was because Asian-American men came into contact with perpetrator types more often or because they are more hated and therefore more often attacked by racists. But the subordination and vulnerability of Asian-American women, who are thought to be sexually exotic, subservient, and passive, argued against that interpretation. So where were the Asian-American women hate-crime victims?

Once I began looking, I found them, in random news clippings, in footnotes in books, through word of mouth. Let me share with you some examples I unearthed of bias-motivated attacks and sexual assaults:

- . . . Ly Yung Cheung, a nineteen-year-old Chinese woman who was seven months pregnant, was pushed in front of a New York City subway train and decapitated. Her attacker, a white male high school teacher, claimed he suffered from "a phobia of Asian people" and was overcome with the urge to kill this woman. He successfully pleaded insanity. If this case had been investigated as a hate crime, there might have been more information about his so-called phobia and whether it was part of a pattern of racism. But it was not investigated.
- . . . Fifty-two-year-old Japanese-American Helen Fukui disappeared in Denver, Colorado. Her decomposed body was found weeks later. Her disappearance on Pearl Harbor Day, when anti-Asian speech and incidents increase dramatically, was considered significant in the community. But the case was not investigated as a hate crime and no suspects were ever apprehended.
- . . . An eight-year-old Chinese girl named Jean Har-Kaw Fewel was found raped and lynched in Chapel Hill, North Carolina—two months after *Penthouse* featured pictures of Asian women in various poses of bondage and torture, including hanging bound from trees. Were epithets or pornography used during the attack? No one knows—her rape and killing were not investigated as a possible hate crime.
- Recently a serial rapist was convicted of kidnapping and raping a Japanese exchange student in Oregon. He had also assaulted a Japanese woman in Arizona, and another in San Francisco. He was sentenced to jail for these crimes, but they were never pursued as hate crimes, even though California has a hate statute. Was hate speech or race-specific pornography used? No one knows.

- At Ohio State University, two Asian women were gang raped by fraternity brothers in two separate incidents. One of the rapes was part of a racially targeted game called the "Ethnic Sex Challenge," in which the fraternity men followed an ethnic checklist indicating what kind of women to gang rape. Because the women feared humiliation and ostracism by their communities, neither reported the rapes. However, campus officials found out about the attacks, but did not take them up as hate crimes, or as anything else.

All of these incidents could have been investigated and prosecuted either as state hate crimes or as federal civil rights cases. But they were not. To have done so would have required one of two things: awareness and interest on the part of police investigators and prosecutors—who generally have a poor track record on race and gender issues—or awareness and support for civil rights charges by the Asian-American community—which is generally lacking on issues surrounding women, gender, sex, and sexual assault. The result is a double-silencing effect on the assaults and deaths of these women who become invisible because of their gender and their race.

Although my research centers on hate crimes and Asian women, this silence and this failure to provide equal protection have parallels in all of the other classes protected by federal civil rights and hate statutes. That is, as other communities of color have a similar prosecution rate for hate crimes against the women in their communities—namely, zero. This dismal record is almost as bad in lesbian and gay antiviolence projects: the vast preponderance of hate crimes reported, tracked, and prosecuted concern gay men—very few concern lesbians. So where are all the women?

The answer to this question lies in the way our justice system was designed, and the way women are mere shadows in the existing civil rights framework. But in spite of this history, federal and state law do offer legal avenues for women to be heard. Federal civil rights prosecutions, for example, can be excellent platforms for high-visibility community education on the harmful impact of hate speech and behavior. When on June 19, 1982, two white auto workers in Detroit screamed racial epithets at Chinese-American Vincent Chin and said, "It's because of you motherfuckers that we're out of work," a public furor followed, raising the level of national discourse on what constitutes racism toward Asian Americans. Constitutional law professors, and members of the American Civil Liberties Union and the National Lawyers Guild had acted as if Asian Americans were not covered by civil rights law. Asian Americans emphatically corrected that misconception.

Hate crimes remedies can be used to force the criminal justice bureaucracy to adopt new attitudes. Patrick Purdy went to an elementary school in Stockton, California, in which 85 percent of the students came from Southeast Asia. When he selected that school as the place to open fire with his automatic weapon and killed five eight-year-olds and wounded thirty other children, the police and the media did not think it was a bias-motivated crime. Their denial reminds me of the response by the Montreal officials to the anti-feminist killings of fourteen women students there. But an outraged Asian-American community forced a state investigation into the Purdy incident and uncovered hate literature in the killer's effects. As a result, the community was validated, and, in addition, the criminal justice system and the media acquired a new level of understanding.

Imagine if a federal civil rights investigation had been launched in the case of the African-American student at St. John's University who was raped and sodomized by white members of the school lacrosse team, who were later acquitted. Investigators could have raised issues of those white men's attitudes toward the victim as a black woman, found out whether hate speech or race-specific pornography was present, investigated the overall racial climate on campus, and brought all of the silenced aspects of the incident to the public eye. Community discourse could have been raised to a high level.

Making these investigations happen will not be an easy road. Hate crimes efforts are generally expended on blatant cases, with high community con-sensus, not ones that bring up hard issues like gender-based violence. Yet these intersections of race and gender hatred are the very issues we must give voice to.

There is a serious difficulty with pushing for use of federal and state hate remedies. Some state statutes have been used against men of color: specifically, on behalf of white rape victims against African-American men. We know that the system, if left unchecked, will try to use antihate laws to enforce unequal justice. On the other hand, state hate statutes could be used to prosecute men of color who are believed to have assaulted women of color of another race—interminority assaults are increasing. Also, if violence against women generally were made into a hate crime, women of color could seek prosecutions against men in their own community for their gender-based violence—even if this would make it harder to win the support of men in communities of color, and of women in those communities who would not want to be accused of dividing the community.

But at least within the Asian-American antiviolence community, this discourse is taking place now. Asian-American feminists in San Francisco have prepared a critique of the Asian movement against hate crimes and the men of that movement are listening. Other communities of color should also examine the nexus between race and gender for women of color, and by extension, for all women.

The legal system must expand the boundaries of existing law to include the most invisible women. There are hundreds of cases involving women of color waiting to be filed. Activists in the violence-against-women movement must reexamine current views on gender-based violence. Not all sexual assaults are the same. Racism in a sexual assault adds another dimension to the pain and harm inflicted. By taking women of color out of the legal shadows, out of invisibility, all women make gains toward full human dignity and human rights.

READING 82

Battered Women
A New Asylum Case

Anna Shelton

A battered immigrant from the Congo calls collect from a pay phone at the 300-bed detention center in Elizabeth, New Jersey. She has been waiting there since March 1998 to be granted asylum in the United States. She goes only by her initials, D. K. In hurried French, she describes the history of her relationship with her abusive husband in her home country. She says she endured threats and harassment from the beginning of their marriage twenty-five years ago. After twenty-one years together, she claims, her husband began to abuse her physically in front of her four children.

"He beat me," she says. "He kicked me. He dragged me on the ground. He threatened me with a gun." Once she had an operation on her eye after he beat her badly, she says. Her husband is a major in the military and has friends among the police. These connections, she says, "made it difficult for me to do anything."

Then, in January 1998, her husband beat her almost to death, she says. Her son saved her, dragging her out of the house and taking her to the home of her brother. She was unconscious for four days.

While she recovered, her brother and a friend began making plans to send her to the United States, where they understood she would be protected. Using her sister's passport, she left the Congo in March 1998.

"My brother told me that when I got to the United States, I just needed to explain my story and they would understand," she says. "So I explained it to somebody in the airport, and they saw my face, which was deformed after the beating and was sort of twisted. My cheek was sagging a little bit." Instead of gaining protection, D. K. was taken to Manchester, Massachusetts, where she was processed as an illegal immigrant because she had used her sister's passport.

"I would like for the United States to protect women like me," she says. "Neither my family nor my government can protect me in my country. There are women who die because of these things. I lived it—I saw it with my own eyes. There was one policeman whose wife wanted to leave him, and so he killed her. I just want to emphasize that if I go back to the Congo, I cannot divorce my husband because he'll never agree to it. He'll kill me. I'm absolutely positive he'll kill me."

D. K. is not alone. Dozens of battered women from around the world have applied for asylum in the United States, but they are finding it much more difficult to obtain than they ever anticipated.

Under current U.S. law, you can gain asylum only if you have a "credible fear" of persecution because of your race, religion, nationality, political opinion, or membership in a social group. Advocates for battered women argue that some women fleeing domestic violence should be granted asylum as well. Canada began offering protection to battered women seeking asylum in 1993.

In 1994, U.S. Immigration Judge Paul Nejelski granted protection to a Jordanian woman who was fleeing thirty years of domestic violence in her home country. It was the first time an immigration judge granted asylum for someone fleeing spousal abuse. "The respondent has been harmed and threatened on account of two of the five grounds," Nejelski ruled, "political opinion and membership in a particular social group." He determined that "these two grounds are not mutually exclusive. The respondent believes in Western values. The respondent's social group consists of those women who espouse Western values and who are unwilling to live their lives at the mercy of their husbands, their society, their government."

The next big step forward occurred in 1995, when the Immigration and Naturalization Service (INS) issued gender guidelines for asylum officers considering the cases of women who have been persecuted because of their sex. The guidelines state that "rape (including mass rape in, for example, Bosnia), sexual abuse and domestic violence, infanticide, and genital mutilation are forms of mistreatment primarily directed at girls and women, and they may serve as evidence of past persecution on account of one or more of the five grounds."

In 1997, Fauziya Kassindja of Togo was the first to file a successful claim, citing fear of genital mutilation. Adelaide Abankwah of Ghana was the second. Her similar claim was just granted on August 13.

Asylum guidelines have also been broadened in recent years to grant protection to gays and lesbians who fear persecution in their home countries. Dusty Aráujo, asylum program coordinator at the International Gay and Lesbian Human Rights Commission in San Francisco, says that the commission knows of about 250 cases of asylum granted in the United States on the basis of sexual orientation since 1994. "Around the world, gays, lesbians, transgendered, and HIV-positive people are denied their rights on a daily basis," says Aráujo. "In many countries, people are jailed just because someone thinks they are gay, and are tortured, blackmailed, and threatened with psychiatric treatment." People persecuted because of their sexual orientation should be regularly granted asylum in the United States, Aráujo says.

Despite these landmark extensions of asylum, protection in the United States for women fleeing domestic violence is hard to come by. In late June, the Board of Immigration Appeals, which is part of the Department of Justice, denied asylum to a Guatemalan woman who said she was seeking protection from an abusive husband in her home country.

Rodi Alvarado Peña, now thirty-three years old, told authorities she was kicked, pistol-whipped, and raped by her husband until she hemorrhaged, *The Washington Post* reported. Like D. K., Alvarado said that she was beaten by her husband so badly she lost consciousness. Alvarado told the *Post* that when she sought protection from police, they told her "they couldn't insert themselves in the matter of a couple." After years of abuse, Alvarado fled to the United States to seek help.

Originally, Alvarado was told that she could stay. In 1996, Immigration Judge Mimi Yam granted her

asylum claim. But the INS appealed the decision, and the Board of Immigration Appeals overturned Yam 10 to 5. The majority stated that her claim "does not lie in our asylum laws as they are currently formulated." That decision sets a bad precedent for pending domestic-violence-related cases, including D. K.'s. Alvarado is appealing the decision.

Congressman Luis Gutierrez, Democrat of Illinois, is leading a campaign to draw attention to Alvarado's case. The Congressional Hispanic Caucus, with Gutierrez as chairman of its task force on immigration, presented a letter to Attorney General Janet Reno in July asking her to step in and reverse the Alvarado ruling.

"We are deeply troubled by this decision and find it to be inconsistent with a growing body of precedent in the U.S.," the letter says, calling the decision "a wrong and unacceptable step backwards."

Neil Nolen, staff attorney with Ayuda, a nonprofit advocacy organization for refugees and victims of domestic violence, was also outraged by the denial. "This decision seems to be in direct conflict with INS's own instructions," he says. "As national advocates, we're demanding that both the INS and the Clinton Administration be consistent in their defense of women's rights."

But INS spokesman Daniel Kane contends that the Board acted appropriately. "Although gender-related claims can raise hard questions, the INS remains committed to their fair adjudication and to seeing the law surrounding them develop in a fair way," he said. "Gender guidelines are one manifestation of this commitment."

Advocates for battered immigrants are trying to seek relief not just for the women who come to the United States, but for those undocumented and abused women who are already living here. The Violence Against Women Act, passed in 1994, makes it possible for battered immigrants living within the United States to petition for residency status by themselves. Usually, U.S. citizens and permanent residents must file for a visa in order for their spouses to gain status in America. But abusive husbands who are working legally in the United States sometimes refuse to file for their spouses in order to maintain control over them. The option that allows these battered wives to gain status is called the self-petition. Since the processing system was established in September 1996, says Violence Against Women Act program officer Karen FitzGerald, the INS has received 8,080 self-petitions and has approved 4,323.

"Jennifer" came to the United States from Mexico when she was ten years old, she says, crossing the border illegally to join her mother. When she was fifteen, she "got kind of in love" with a twenty-one-year-old man who was renting a room in her mother's house. He had a green card. The two were married when she was sixteen years old. The abuse started, she says, with what she thought were playful pinches and little punches on her arm. But one evening, she says, he slapped her on the face because she could not get their baby daughter to stop crying. Another day, when he was drunk, he beat her savagely, she says. "He got on top of me, and he got a perfume bottle and smashed it on my head. He wouldn't stop. I said, 'What are you doing? You don't even know who I am! I'm your wife. Don't do this. Love me better.' And then he got a brass knob that was on the bedpost and he smashed it, first on my face and second on my head." Jennifer ran outside as he threatened to beat her with a belt, and someone in the neighborhood called the police, she says.

When she finally did manage to leave him, he found her, kidnapped her and their three children, and took them to Mexico. Once across the border, he put them in an isolated house with dirt floors. He kept them there for eight months without letting them out, she says. But one morning, she managed to flee with her children.

Jennifer took a taxi to Tijuana, where she stayed in a homeless shelter and worked as a cashier for six months. This spring, she returned illegally to the United States with her children. Her self-petition is pending.

But because of defects in the Violence Against Women Act, some abused immigrant women find it difficult to self-petition.

Currently, the law requires women to return to their home countries for final processing. This may sound like an innocuous requirement, but it can lead to a disastrous outcome for women who lived illegally in the United States with their partners. Once these women leave the United States, they could be barred from reentering because they were at one time unlawfully present. The irony is that in order to be eligible to petition in the first place, they must have been undocumented.

Congress has the opportunity to pass the Violence Against Women Act II, which would correct the defect and make the petitioning process more flexible for women seeking protection.

Those who oppose broader immigration fear the floodgates will open by extending asylum to abused women and by expanding the self-petitioning process. They also contend that we are losing sight of the original reasons for an established set of international asylum laws.

"Asylum law was written to prevent genocide and ethnic cleansing of large groups of people based on race, ethnicity, or national origin," says David Ray, associate director of the anti-immigration group Federation for American Immigration Reform. "Asylum law was certainly never written to address domestic inequalities or problems such as abuse in marriages. If you make family problems one of the reasons to qualify for asylum, you would completely undermine the program. If you encourage addressing domestic problems by mass exodus, you're going to be creating more problems on top of it."

But Shirley Tang, D. K.'s pro bono attorney at the New Jersey-based law firm Friedman Siegelbaum, disagrees.

"We're not asking that every battered women apply for asylum in the United States," she says. "We're not asking that at all. What we're asking for is that very small sliver of the world population where the woman is beaten by her husband; where there are no mechanisms within the country that provide for women's groups, shelters, or safe houses; where the law of the country itself prohibits the woman from free access to go on with her life and start over. That's when the United States should be the safe haven that it represents itself to be."

"Isabel" is a teacher from Guatemala who is currently seeking asylum in the United States on the basis of domestic abuse. She married her boyfriend when she was just sixteen and very much in love. One night in 1982, when she was seven months pregnant with their first child, her husband got drunk and threw her on the bed, breaking her arm, she says. He proceeded to rape her.

Isabel wanted to get a divorce, but that can take a long time in Guatemala, and her husband would not agree to it. She says he called and threatened to kill her and their three children: "He said, 'You know who this is. If you go to court, when you come back to your house, you'll find your children dead. You'll have to pick up the pieces, and you'll have to put the pieces in different boxes because they won't be recognizable or identifiable.'"

The death threats continued. In October 1996, her husband told her mother that Isabel would be killed the following March. She left her children with her mother and fled to the United States that fall.

"In my country," Isabel says, "when you seek help, when you are a married woman and you are abused, it doesn't matter what kind of education you have. When one looks for help, the police say, 'This is a domestic problem. Go home and solve it.' Even if they see the man killing his wife, they tell you, 'Go home and solve your problem there.'"

Domestic violence is widespread in Guatemala, Isabel says, and the effects are devastating. "In my country, many women choose the quick way out, the shortcut—they are committing suicide. They can no longer put up with it, and this is their only way out.

Isabel was lucky and escaped. But it has been three years since she last saw her children, who are now ten, fifteen, and seventeen years old. They are living with their grandmother, yet they see their father sometimes, and they say that he has been treating them badly, hitting them and insulting them. Her husband sends messages to Isabel through her children, saying he knows where she is and could hurt her.

When her kids ask when they will be able to see her again, she doesn't know how to answer. She has not heard whether she will be granted asylum, and she is worried, especially in light of the Alvarado decision.

"Sometimes I think I will be able to accomplish it, bringing my children here," she says. "But now, with this decision, I feel that at any moment, this will all end with a letter that says that I have to return to my country."

READING 83

Stopping Abuse in Prison

Nina Siegal

Widespread abuses of women behind bars barely received notice until seven or eight years ago. Across the country, there were incidents of prison or jail staff sexually molesting inmates with impunity. Slowly but surely, the nation's correctional facilities are responding to this abuse.

"Ten years ago, I think we knew it was going on, but we hadn't named it," says Brenda Smith, a Practitioner-in-Residence at Washington College of Law at American University. "Until you raise it as a problem, and until people start coming forward and talking about it, it is not perceived as a problem."

The changes are the result of several landmark legal cases, a shift in government policy, and the attention of human-rights groups. Still, problems remain. Guards continue to rape women inmates. But now there's a process to bring them to justice.

The stories were too consistent to be ignored. Numerous female inmates in three Washington, D.C., prison and jail facilities said they had been awakened at two or three in the morning for a "medical visit" or a "legal visit" only to be led into the kitchen, the clinic, the visiting hall, or a closet to have sex. Many inmates were becoming pregnant in a system that allowed no conjugal visits.

"There were a lot of places where people could have sex," says Smith. "A lot of it was in exchange for cigarettes." Prison employees offered other deals: "'I will give you phone calls, I will make sure you get a better job assignment, I'll give you drugs if you have sex with me.' The sex involved not just correctional officers. It involved chaplains, administration, deputy wardens, contractors, and food-service workers. It involved not just male staff but female staff as well," Smith says.

In 1993, the National Women's Law Center and a District of Columbia law firm filed a class-action suit, *Women Prisoners vs. District of Columbia Department of Corrections,* in U.S. District Court. The suit alleged a pattern of discrimination against women in the jail, the Correctional Treatment Facility, and the Lorton Minimum Security Annex, a D.C. facility in Lorton, Virginia. A large portion of the case focused on issues of sexual misconduct, based on evidence that the law firm had collected during an investigation. The following year, a judge found that there was a pattern of practice of misconduct so severe that it violated the Eighth Amendment protection against cruel and unusual punishment. The decision was appealed and is still in court.

As extreme as the D.C. situation was, it was not unique.

Lawyers in Georgia had been preparing a class-action suit on behalf of men and women in the state's prisons for almost ten years when they began to come across striking charges of sexual misconduct in the Georgia Women's Correctional Facility in Milledgeville and the nearby camp, Colony Farm. The alleged activities included rape, criminal sexual contact, leering, and abusive catcalling of inmates. One lieutenant had sex with at least seven prisoners from 1987 to 1991, directing women to meet him in various locations in the prisons for sex.

In 1992, the lawyers for the suit, *Cason v. Seckinger,* amended their complaint to add allegations of sexual abuse that had taken place over a period of fourteen years. Seventeen staff members were indicted. None were convicted, though several were dismissed from their jobs as a result of the lawsuit. The suit resulted in a number of federal court orders requiring the department to rectify many of its practices. It also influenced the department to close Milledgeville and move all the female inmates to a different facility.

These two suits—and the criminal prosecutions that ensued—were the first major legal attempts to address a problem that had been plaguing the criminal justice system for decades.

One of the biggest cases for the rights of women prisoners was settled last year. The case (*Lucas vs. White*) involved three inmates of a federal facility in Pleasanton, California, called FCI Dublin, who were sold as sex slaves to male inmates in an adjoining facility. Inmates paid guards to allow them into the cells of female inmates who were being held in the men's detention center, which is across the street from Dublin.

The plantiffs settled their civil suit against the Federal Bureau of Prisons for $500,000 and forced the agency to make dramatic changes in the way it handles allegations of misconduct. According to the settlement, the Bureau of Prisons was to set up a confidential hotline, or some other reporting mechanism, so that inmates and staff can inform the authorities of problems inside. It was also supposed to provide medical and psychological treatment for inmates who have been victimized and establish new training programs for staff and inmates.

Geri Lynn Green, one of the two attorneys for the Lucas case, has been monitoring the changes at the prison since the case settled. After the lawsuit and the subsequent training, she says, "it appears there was a tremendous impact."

Brett Dignam, clinical professor of law at Yale University, agrees that the *Lucas* case made a big difference: "More prison staff members are resigning over issues of sexual misconduct."

Human rights advocates, too, have taken up the cause. In 1996, the Women's Rights Project at Human Rights Watch issued "All Too Familiar: Sexual Abuse of Women in U.S. Prisons."

The 347-page report detailed problems in California, Washington, D.C., Michigan, Georgia, and New York. "We have found that male correctional employees have vaginally, anally, and orally raped female prisoners and sexually assaulted and abused them," says the report. "We found that in the course of committing such gross misconduct, male officers have not only used actual or threatened physical force, but have also used their near total authority to provide or deny goods and privileges to female prisoners to compel them to have sex, or, in other cases, to reward them for having done so."

In June, 1998, the United Nations sent a special rapporteur, Radhike Coomaraswamy, to the United States to investigate sexual misconduct in the nation's women's facilities. She argued that stronger monitoring was needed to control widespread abuses.

"We concluded that there has been widespread sexual misconduct in U.S. prisons, but there is a diversity—some are dealing with it better than others," Reuters reported her saying in December. "Georgia has sexual misconduct but has set up a very strong scheme to deal with it. In California and Michigan, nothing has been done and the issue is very prevalent." In April, Coomaraswamy will give a final report to the U.N. Commission on Human Rights.

In March of 1999, Amnesty International released its own report, " 'Not Part of My Sentence': Violations of the Human Rights of Women in Custody," which includes a section on sexual abuse. "Many women inmates are subjected to sexual abuse by prison officials, including: sexually offensive language, observation by male officers while showering and dressing, groping during daily pat-down searches, and rape." In addition to the problems detailed in the Human Rights Watch report, Amnesty investigators found problems in Illinois, Massachusetts, New Hampshire, Texas, West Virginia, and Wyoming.

Lawyers and human rights groups have won some important reforms. In 1990, only seventeen states had a law on the books defining sexual misconduct in prisons as either a misdemeanor or a felony offense. Today, there are only twelve states left that do not criminalize sexual relations between staff and inmates—Alabama, Kentucky, Massachusetts, Minnesota, Missouri, Montana, Nebraska, Oregon, Utah, Vermont, West Virginia, and Wisconsin—according to Amnesty International, which is campaigning to get all these states to pass their own laws.

The U.S. Justice Department is also taking a more active role. It has filed two suits charging that the correctional systems in Michigan and Arizona were responsible for violations of prisoners' constitutional rights. The suits cite numerous allegations of abuse, including rape, lack of privacy, prurient viewing, and invasive pat searches. Both cases are still pending.

Meanwhile, state prison systems are training personnel. Andie Moss was a project director with the Georgia Department of Corrections in 1992 when the department was asked to help interview inmates for the class-action lawsuit. She ended up culling information from women who said they had been subjected to misconduct over a fourteen-year period. Today, Moss works with the National Institute of Corrections, part of the Bureau of Prisons. Her primary responsibility is to develop training programs to educate both staff and inmates about sexual misconduct, the new laws, and their rights.

Since her program, "Addressing Staff Sexual Misconduct," was initiated in early 1997, Moss and her team have provided training for more than thirty state correctional systems, and she expects to complete training for all fifty states by the end of 1999.

The training involves four basic elements: clarifying the departments' sexual misconduct policy, informing inmates and staff of the law in their state, telling inmates and staff how to report abuse that they witness, and giving examples of how people have intervened in the past.

"We know it's still an issue. We know corrections departments still need to work diligently on this," says Moss. "It's a constant effort because it is a cultural change. But if you could follow the change in the law, the change in policy and practice, there's been an amazing effort in the last three years."

Despite all the positive steps, however, women are still being abused in America's prisons and jails. Investigators from a number of California-based law firms who recently visited the Valley State Prison for Women in Chowchilla, California, heard stories of at least a dozen assaults by specific guards. They also found "a climate of sexual terror that women are subjected to on a daily basis," says Ellen Barry, founding director of Legal Services for Prisoners with Children, based in San Francisco.

"The instances of both physical and sexual abuse are much higher than any other institution where I've interviewed women," she says. "The guards are really brutalizing women in a way that we really haven't seen before."

Valley State Prison inmate Denise Dalton told investigators that a doctor at the facility groped her and conducts inappropriate pelvic exams. "If I need Tylenol, all I need to do is ask him for a pelvic and he will give me whatever I want," she said.

But most of the abusive conduct was of the type that, Barry says, made for "a climate of sexual terror" in the prison. Coreen Sanchez, another inmate, said that in December, she entered the dayroom at the facility and asked a correctional officer if the sergeant had come in, and he responded by saying, "Yeah, he came in your mouth." She also reported seeing correctional officers flaunt their erections in front of inmates.

Advocates of prisoners say there still needs to be a dramatic cultural shift within the system before women are safe from the people who guard them behind bars.

"I think we have to keep in perspective the limitations of litigation and advocacy work for truly making a change in this arena," says Barry.

One problem that advocates cite is the recalcitrance of the unions that represent prison guards. "The people we really have to win over are not legislators, but the unions," says Christine Doyle, research coordinator for Amnesty International U.S.A. "Guards look at this as a workplace violation, as something fun to do on the job. They don't look at these women as human beings. The message that these are human beings they are exploiting isn't getting through."

For them to get that message, says Doyle, corrections officers will have to hear it from within the unions, and not from any set of codes, procedures, or laws. "We have states that have legislation, and some of them are just as bad, if not worse, than states without legislation," Doyle says. "So, obviously, that doesn't work. If it comes from within, and the unions

themselves say, 'We can do this internally,' workers will respond better."

Human rights groups, for now, are focusing on legislative solutions. In 1996, Human Rights Watch recommended that Congress require all states, as a precondition of receiving federal funding for prisons, criminalize all sexual conduct between staff and inmates. It also urged the Department of Justice to establish secure toll-free telephone hotlines for reporting complaints.

Amnesty International's new report takes an additional step, arguing that the role of male staff be restricted in accordance with the United Nations' Standard Minimum Rules for the Treatment of Prisoners, which state that "women prisoners shall be attended and supervised only by women officers."

Debra LaBelle, a civil rights attorney who filed a class-action suit on behalf of abused women inmates in Michigan, says she would like to see men taken out of women's institutions altogether.

"I resisted going there for a long time, but I don't know another solution," she says. "When we started out, they didn't do any training, much supervision, investigation. In the last three years, they've changed countless policies and yet it is still happening. Get them out of there. It's not like they're losing employment opportunities. There are, unfortunately, many more facilities that men can work in."

Sheila Dauer, director of the Women's Human Rights Program for Amnesty International, says the group's report aims to persuade the final thirteen states without laws against sexual misconduct to initiate legislation, starting with eight state campaigns this year. She says the campaign will also lend support to a federal bill that would do the same thing.

Amnesty's report, she says, is designed to "wake up the American public to the horrible abuses that women inmates are suffering in prison and stop the suffering."

■
_____

DISCUSSION QUESTIONS FOR CHAPTER ELEVEN

1. What are some of the ways the state maintains social inequality? Have you experienced discrimination by the state in any way?

2. How does the early American assumption that citizens were White men perpetuate contemporary social inequities?

3. Do you believe that full equality can be achieved under our present system of democracy and capitalism? Why or why not?

4. What myths that maintain inequity do you see operating in the state, the law, and social policies?

5. What changes do you believe should be made in order to create a more just state?

SUGGESTIONS FOR FURTHER READING

Arneil, Barbara. *Politics and Feminism: An Introduction.* Malden, MA: Blackwell, 1999.

Baer, Judith A. *Our Lives Before the Law: Constructing a Feminist Jurisprudence.* Princeton, NJ: Princeton University Press, 1999.

Enloe, Cynthia. *Maneuvers: The International Politics of Militarizing Women's Lives.* Berkeley: University of California Press, 2000.

Forrell, Caroline, and Donna Matthews. *A Law of Her Own: The Reasonable Woman as a Measure of Man.* New York: New York University Press, 2000.

Katzenstein, Mary Fainsod, and Judith Reppy, eds. *Beyond Zero Tolerance: Discrimination in Military Culture.* Lanham, MD: Rowman and Littlefield, 1999.

LaDuke, Winona. *The Winona LaDuke Reader: A Collection of Essential Writings.* Stillwats, MN: Voyageur, 2002.

Woods, Harriet. *Stepping Up to Power: The Political Journey of American Women.* Boulder, CO: Westview, 2000.

CHAPTER TWELVE

Religion and Spirituality in Women's Lives

Religion is a complex and complicating feature of many women's lives. Although many women feel empowered by religion because it offers them a place of belonging, comfort, acceptance, and encouragement, others feel oppressed by religion because it excludes and sometimes denigrates women. In this way, as this chapter will explore, religion remains a significant personal and political force in women's lives. Many of the social and cultural battles raging in American society are cast in religious terms—abortion, gay marriage, sex education, racial violence, domestic violence, to name a few—and many women organize their lives around their religious convictions.

The Southern Baptist controversy illustrates the experiences of many women in religious traditions. Throughout the 1980s and early 1990s, Southern Baptists, the nation's largest Protestant denomination with more than 14 million members, were embroiled in a controversy between fundamentalist and moderate leaders. The Baptist battles began over the issue of inerrancy (the notion that the Bible is without error in history, science, or doctrine) but quickly expanded to include, and then emphasize, social issues such as abortion, homosexuality, and the role of women in the home and church. As the fundamentalists grew in political power, they led the Southern Baptist Convention to pass resolutions excluding women from pastoral leadership in the churches and encouraging wives to submit to their husbands. Fundamentalist victory, however, did not come without a long, bitter conflict in which many women, particularly women in ministry, left the denomination. Other women decided to stay and focus their efforts on the autonomous local churches that carried on in the Baptist tradition of dissent, unbound by convention resolutions. Many became involved in alternative Baptist organizations that grew out of the controversy and promised women more visibility, opportunity, and support as seminary professors and denominational leaders. The women who found positions as seminary professors often faced resistance from students and misunderstanding from colleagues. Numbers of women became associate pastors in moderate Baptist churches, but very few were offered senior pastor positions. Women in the pews heard the rhetoric of equality, but it came from the lips of the men who held the top positions in the churches and newly formed Baptist organizations.

The willingness of so many moderate Southern Baptist women to stay in Baptist churches despite the anti-woman actions of the Southern Baptist Convention indicates the powerful pull of religion. Even women who strongly opposed the policy of the Southern Baptist Convention often became active participants in other Christian denominations: few left Christianity entirely. This simultaneous push and pull of religion, as exemplified by the experience of Southern Baptist women, merits careful feminist analysis. As both a force that can oppress and empower, religion has a dramatic potential to work politically—either to continue women's oppression or to support women's liberation. Understanding this complex dynamic involves a close reading of the discourse of religion.

RELIGION AS OPPRESSIVE TO WOMEN

Southern Baptists are not alone in Christianity, nor is Christianity alone in world religions, in functioning as an oppressive force to women. This section discusses four ways that religion as belief and institutional practice has helped subordinate women. First, central to religion's oppressive function is the notion of a divinely ordained order of creation in many religions in which woman is deemed inferior. This notion is often supported by creation myths that embed woman's inferior status in the religious community's narrative of identity; these are the stories a religious community tells about itself in order to make itself known to both members and the outside community. For example, a common interpretation of the second Hebrew myth of creation (although feminist biblical scholars take issue with this interpretation) is that Eve is created after Adam because she is to serve him and be his inferior. Later in the Christian testament, one writer argues that woman's secondary status is a result of Eve's role as temptress in the fall of humanity. As Elizabeth Cady Stanton pointed out in her "Introduction to *The Woman's Bible*" over a hundred years ago, the Bible has most often been used to maintain the oppression of women by excluding them from particular roles in church, family, and society.

Second, women's lower status is further maintained by excluding women from sacred rituals. Women have not been allowed to celebrate the Eucharist, pray in public, dance sacred dances, hear confession, make sacrifices, baptize, enter the holy of holies, read sacred scriptures aloud in public, preach, or teach men. One argument for the exclusion of women from priesthood has been that the priest stands as a representative of God, and a woman cannot represent God because she is female. The underlying assumption is that men are more Godlike than women. When worshippers see only men as representatives of God, it reinforces the notion that men are more Godlike, and women's exclusion continues.

Third, religions maintain women's oppression very directly through church laws that require wives to submit to their husbands, that regulate women's sexuality, and that create highly defined gender roles for women and men. For example, these laws may keep women in abusive relationships. Women are often told by church authorities that their role in the home is to be the support person for the husband and to submit to his divinely ordained authority in the home. Then, when abuse occurs, a woman may be told that she is to continue to submit because that is her role, and God will change her husband because of her obedience to God's commandments. The husband's abusive behavior then becomes the wife's responsibility because his changing is contingent upon her submission. This situation is exacerbated by a prohibition on divorce in some denominations, which prevents women from permanently leaving abusive marriages.

Finally, historically and currently, religions also exercise power over women through church and state sanctioned control. In the "burning times" (between the eleventh and fourteenth centuries) millions of women in Europe were murdered as witches. For many of these women, "witchcraft" was simply the practice of traditional healing and spirituality and the refusal to profess Christianity. For other women, the charge of witchcraft had nothing to do with religious practices and everything to do with accusations rooted in jealousy,

IDEAS FOR ACTIVISM

- Invite a group of women pastors, ministers, priests, and rabbis to participate in a panel discussion of women in ministry.
- Organize a women's spirituality group.
- Organize an educational event to explore women in the world's religions. If possible, invite practitioners of various faiths to speak about women in their religious tradition.
- Investigate the official stance of your own religious tradition on women's roles and women's issues. Where there is room for improvement, write religious leaders to express your opinion.
- Organize an event to commemorate the women who died in the "burning times."

LEARNING ACTIVITY:
THAT OLD-TIME TV RELIGION

Watch several episodes of religious programming on television, such as the *700 Club* and two or three televised worship services. Who are the key personalities? What is their message? In the worship services, who is speaking? Who is singing? Who is leading? What messages about gender are conveyed, not only in the words themselves but also in the roles played by different people? What messages about race, class, sexual orientation, and/or ability are conveyed? Do you think these shows are helpful to people? Why or why not? Are they helpful to women? Who do you think benefits from these shows? Are there ways in which these shows reinforce the subordination of women and other nondominant groups? Keep a log of your observations to share with your classmates.

greed, and fear of female sexuality. But in the frenzy of the times, defending oneself against an accusation of witchcraft was practically impossible, and an accusation alone generally meant death.

Other examples include the ways Christian imperialism has proved destructive for women and men of color and reinforced racism and ethnocentrism. The genocide of Native Americans was conducted with the underlying belief that it was the God-given destiny of Europeans to conquer the native peoples of the Americas. Without understanding African cultures, Christian missionaries insisted indigenous African peoples adopt Western ways. The legacy of Christian racism continued in the American South, where many Christians defended slavery based on their reading of scripture. Following reconstruction, hate groups such as the Ku Klux Klan arose, calling for the continued dominance of the White, anglo, Christian race. In Germany, thousands of Christians joined in Hitler's plan to build a master race and contributed directly to the genocide of 6 million Jews. In the 1950s and 1960s, while many Christians worked tirelessly for the civil rights movement and African American churches in particular became sites of resistance to racism, many others defended segregation and participated in acts of racial hatred. Only in 2000 did Bob Jones University, a fundamentalist institution of higher education in South Carolina, repeal its rule against interracial dating. Despite the many advances in the twentieth century, the twenty-first century began with the continuing problems of racism and intolerance by many who profess Christianity. But, as Elizabeth Cook-Lynn suggests in "A Visit from Reverend Tileston," Christian inability to listen to others may ultimately prove harmful to Christianity itself.

In India, many Hindu women are raised to see self-immolation as a high form of religious commitment. *Sati,* the act by which a wife throws herself on the burning pyre with her dead husband, was considered a great act of honor by the codifiers of Hindu law and became glorified in Hindu legends told to little girls. In the nineteenth century, the British who occupied and colonized India outlawed sati. Nonetheless, as recently as 1987, 18-year-old Roop Kanwar was burned alive on her husband's funeral pyre. Karen McCarthy Brown relates the story of Roop Kanwar to fundamentalism in her essay titled "Fundamentalism and the Control of Women."

Currently the Religious Right, a political movement of religious ultraconservatives in the United States, is attempting to exert control over women by influencing the American legal system. Already the Religious Right has managed to chip away at abortion rights by convincing lawmakers to pass various restrictions on abortion. At the end of the twentieth century and the beginning of the twenty-first, the Religious Right's agenda began to focus on the gains made by the gay and lesbian rights movement. A particularly telling example of the power of the Religious Right to influence American politics came in the Defense of Marriage Act (DOMA), mentioned in Chapter 11, which allows states not to recognize gay unions performed in other states. At the time the law passed, no state even allowed gay marriage. DOMA was a significant departure from precedent in which every state recognized the legal contracts entered into by other states. By mid-2000, more than two-thirds of the states had passed state laws refusing to recognize gay marriages performed in other states.

The Muslim practice of wearing the veil (*hijab*) presents an especially complex example of the simultaneously oppressive and empowering role of religion in women's lives. From a Western perspective, the practice of veiling is often viewed as absolutely oppressing. Although many Muslim women criticize the coercion exercised in Afghanistan, they also see choosing to wear the veil as an empowering practice of ethnic and cultural identity in the face of Western influence. Nadia Hijab argues this point in "Islam, Social Change, and the Reality of Arab Women's Lives." Muslim women often explain that they feel safer when veiled in public. The veil indicates that a woman is devout and virtuous, and therefore Muslim men will not objectify and sexualize a veiled woman. In fact, very often these women express sympathy for American women who must constantly fear sexual assault in public places. The veil, they claim, protects them and therefore allows them the freedom to move about publicly without fear.

RELIGION AS EMPOWERING TO WOMEN

Despite religion's long history of oppressing women, women have also experienced profound support, encouragement, and satisfaction in religion. This section focuses on those aspects of empowerment. First, for many women religion provides an environment in which they experience real community with other women. Women in traditional marriages who work in the home may find their only real social outlet in the church. Here they build

HISTORICAL MOMENT:
BECOMING A BISHOP

Until 1984, no Black woman had been elected bishop of a major religious denomination in the United States, but in that year, the Western Jurisdictional Conference of the United Methodist Church elected Leontine Kelly its first African American woman bishop and only the Church's second female bishop.

Both Kelly's father and brother were Methodist ministers. Kelly married and had three children but divorced in the early 1950s. She remarried a Methodist minister in 1956 and returned to college to earn a bachelor's degree and become a social studies teacher. Kelly was drawn to preaching and became a certified lay preacher. When her husband died in 1969, she accepted the church's invitation for her to become pastor. She earned a master of divinity (MDiv) from Wesley Theological Seminary in 1976 and became an ordained minister in the Methodist Church. From 1977 to 1983 she was pastor of Asbury-Church Hill United Methodist Church in Richmond, Virginia, and then became assistant general secretary of evangelism for the United Methodist General Board of Discipleship.

Kelly's nomination to the post of bishop by a group of California clergywomen was not without controversy. Some thought her unfit for the position because she was a Black woman. Others opposed her nomination because she was divorced. Nonetheless, she was elected and then named bishop for the San Francisco Bay area, making her the chief administrator and spiritual leader for more than 100,000 United Methodists in Northern California and Nevada. She remained at that post for 4 years until her retirement in 1988.

In the fall of 2000, the United Methodist Church elected three African American women as bishops, the first since Leontine Kelly: Violet Fisher, Linda Lee, and Beverly Shamana. Kelly commented, "I will always be the first African American woman bishop of the United Methodist Church, but praise God I am no longer the only."

connections with other women and participate in personally meaningful experiences in a community context.

Second, religion may provide women with opportunities for building and exercising leadership skills within religious organizations. Particularly for women in traditional families, this allows them to develop skills they might not learn otherwise. For example, although Southern Baptists have generally excluded women from pastoral leadership in the churches, the Woman's Missionary Union (WMU), auxiliary to the Southern Baptist Convention, has provided thousands of women with the opportunity to become lay leaders in their churches, as well as in associational, state, and national WMU organizations. WMU is a missions education organization for women. In local church WMU organizations, women plan, budget, and implement programs for education and action. WMU curriculum materials teach young girls that they can do anything God calls them to do. The subversive power of this message is clear in talking to Southern Baptist women in ministry. Many of them report first experiencing their call to ministry in a WMU organization. Similarly, Catholic

LEARNING ACTIVITY: WOMEN OF FAITH

Interview three women who actively participate in a religious community. Ask about their experiences as women in their faith. Use the following questions or develop your own interview protocol.

- What is your religious community's stance on women's roles in home, society, and the religious community itself?
- What roles do women fulfill in your religious community?
- In what activities do you participate in your religious community?
- In what ways has your religious community been empowering for you as a woman? Has your religious community ever been oppressive to you as a woman?
- What do you gain by your participation in your religious community?
- How might your religious community better serve women?

Gather the data obtained by several other students in your class and examine your findings. Do you see any common themes arising from your interviews? What do your data suggest about these women's experiences in their faith communities? Can you make any generalizations from the data about how women experience religion as both empowering and oppressive?

ACTIVIST PROFILE:
NANNIE HELEN BURROUGHS

Nannie Helen Burroughs was only 21 years old when she delivered her stirring speech, "How the Sisters Are Hindered from Helping" at the 1900 National Baptist Convention in Richmond, Virginia. This speech proved to be instrumental in the formation of the Women's Convention Auxiliary to the National Baptist Convention, the largest African American women's organization in the country at that time. The Women's Convention promptly elected Burroughs its corresponding secretary and continued to re-elect her every year from 1900 to 1948. In 1948, she became the convention's president and served in that role until her death in 1961.

Burroughs was also a tireless activist—challenging lynching and segregation, denouncing employment discrimination, opposing European colonization of Africa, and promoting women's suffrage. After the Nineteenth Amendment was passed, she founded the National League of Republican Colored Women and worked to encourage African American women to become politically involved. She also established the Women's Industrial Club, which offered short-term housing to African American women and taught them basic domestic skills. The club also offered moderately priced lunches for downtown office workers. During the Depression, Burroughs formed Cooperative Industrial, Inc., which provided free facilities for a medical clinic, hair salon, and variety store.

One of Burroughs's driving passions was the education of African American women. In 1909, with the support of the National Baptist Convention, she opened the National Trade and Professional School for Women and Girls in Washington, DC, and served as the institution's president. The school emphasized a close connection between education and religion. Its curriculum focused on the development of practical and professional skills and included a program in Black history in which every student was required to take a course. Burroughs's motto for the school was "We specialize in the wholly impossible." In 1964, the school was renamed the Nannie Burroughs School. In 1975 Mayor Walter E. Washington proclaimed May 10 Nannie Helen Burroughs Day in the District of Columbia in recognition of Burroughs's courage in advocating for education for African American women despite societal norms.

women have been empowered through convent experiences, in which they exercise leadership and enjoy community with other women.

Third, leadership within the church or religious organization may facilitate women's power within their local or regional communities as well as encourage their participation in various forms of social activism. For example, in Santeria, a Caribbean religion, women who are healers or *santeras* have great personal power and hold immense social power in their communities. These women willingly enter into altered states of consciousness and allow the spirits to use them to bring about healing. When a person visits a *santera*, the *santera* sees all the spirits with that person, and the *santera* is often able to reveal to the person

LEARNING ACTIVITY: HOW WELL DO YOU KNOW THE GODDESS?

Match the Goddess to her name.

_____ 1. Odudua

a. Egyptian mother Goddess and Goddess of the underworld, the queen of heaven and mother of light.

_____ 2. Coatlicue

b. "Queen of Heaven." Assyrian creator of life, mother and guardian. Goddess of fertility, love, sexuality, and justice.

_____ 3. Izanami-no-kami

c. Celtic creator of life. Mother Goddess of the earth and moon. The mother of all heroes or deities.

_____ 4. Demeter

d. Scandinavian creator of life. Leader of the Valkyries.

_____ 5. Tho-og

e. "Great, Invincible, and Magnificent Founder and Savior, Commander and Guide, Legislator and Queen." Creator and mother Goddess of Anatolia.

_____ 6. Kali

f. The mother of Hawaii. Mother and guardian, mother of Pele and the Hawaiian people.

_____ 7. Astarte

g. Creator of life who brings fertility and love. Goddess of the Yoruba people of Nigeria.

_____ 8. Kokyan Wuhti

h. Tibetan primordial being. The eternal mother who is self-formed. She is the preexisting space.

_____ 9. Freyja

i. "The Great Mother Goddess." Mesopotamian Goddess of justice, earth, nature, and goodness.

_____ 10. Haumea

j. Hindu Goddess. She who gives life and also destroys it. The symbol of eternal time.

_____ 11. Po Ino Nogar

k. "Spider Grandmother." Hopi creator of life. Benificent deity who created humans, plants, and animals.

_____ 12. Hathor

l. "Serpent Skirt." Mother Goddess of all Aztec deities of Mexico, the ruler of life and death.

_____ 13. Anu

m. Greek mother and guardian. One of the twelve great Greek Olympian deities. She has power over the productivity of the earth and the social order of humans.

_____ 14. Asherah

n. "Female-Who-Invites." Japanese creator of life, earth and nature, heaven and hell.

_____ 15. Artemis Ephesus

o. "Great One." Vietnamese creator of life. World fertility Goddess who brings rice to the people and protects the fields and harvests.

Answers: 1. g 2. l 3. n 4. m 5. h 6. j 7. b 8. k 9. d 10. f 11. o 12. a 13. c 14. i 15. e

Source: Martha Ann and Dorothy Myers Imel. _Goddesses in World Mythology: A Biographical Dictionary._ New York: Oxford University Press, 1993.

what she or he needs to do. This ability puts the *santera* in an extremely powerful position, especially when the person consulting her is a politician or government official, as is often the case. Furthermore, as Caribbean women visit *santeras,* they see women who wield power in their culture and who can act as role models for them.

Another example of the role of religion in encouraging social activism is that of Jesse Daniel Ames who helped organize the antilynching movement in the early part of the twentieth century. She worked through women's missions organizations in Methodist and Baptist churches in the South. Black churches were at the heart of the 1950s and 1960s civil rights movement in which many early leaders of second wave feminism had their first experiences of political organizing. A key component of Judaism is social justice, and Jewish women have long been actively involved in anti-Semitic, anti-racist, anti-sexist, and anti-heterosexist work. Ernestine Louise Rose, who fought for women's rights and against slavery during the 1840s and 1850s, challenged New York state lawmakers in 1854 to allow women to retain their own property and have equal guardianship of children with their husbands. When male politicians urged women to postpone their quest for suffrage and focus on the rights of former slaves, Rose declared, "Emancipation from every kind of bondage is my principle." She also spoke out against anti-Semitism and set the tone for twentieth-century Jewish feminists' critique of Judaism's traditional attitudes toward women.

Finally, for many women, religion provides a place in which they find a sense of worth as a valued person. In the late twentieth century, many women participated in revivals of ancient woman-centered religions and have become empowered through the revaluing of the feminine implicit in this spirituality. Wicca, or witchcraft, is a Goddess and nature-oriented religion whose origins pre-date both Judaism and Christianity. Current Wiccan practice involves the celebration of the feminine, connection with nature, and the practice of healing. As Starhawk suggests in "Witchcraft and Women's Culture," witchcraft encourages women to be strong, confident, and independent and to love the Goddess, the earth, and other human beings. This notion of witchcraft is very different from the cultural norms associated with witches that are propagated at Halloween.

WOMEN AND GOD-LANGUAGE

Many theorists contend that one of the most powerful influences in molding gender and maintaining gender oppression is language. The language religions use to talk about God is especially powerful in shaping the ways we think about men and women. Any language we use to talk about God is of necessity metaphorical. We create images that can only partially represent the full reality of the concept of God. Unfortunately, those images sometimes become understood in literal rather than metaphorical ways. So instead of thinking of God *as* Father, we may come to think God *is* Father. Throughout Jewish and Christian history, the preponderance of images for God have been masculine—Father, King, Lord, Judge, Master—and the effect has been that many people believe that God is male.

In ancient times, the image of the Great Mother Goddess was primary in many cultures, but as war-centered patriarchal cultures developed, the life-giving Goddess had to be defeated by the warring God. In ancient Babylonian mythology, Tiamat was the Great Mother, but she was eventually slaughtered by her son Marduk, the God of war. Yahweh, the God of the ancient Israelites, was originally a consort of the Canaanite Mother Goddess, but, as the Israelites moved toward a patriarchal monotheism (belief in just one God), Yah-

LEARNING ACTIVITY:
EXPLORING NEW METAPHORS FOR DEITY

Metaphors are images drawn from familiar human experiences, used in fresh ways to help explore realities that are not easily accessible in our everyday experience. All language about deity is metaphorical because no one image or analogy can capture the essence of deity. Throughout the history of Jewish and Christian faiths, in particular, deity has been variously imaged as Father, Shepherd, King, Lord, and Master. Originally, these metaphors helped many people explore and grapple with different aspects of the nature of deity. Many contemporary theologians, however, suggest the need for new metaphors for deity, shocking metaphors that will cause people to think about deity in new ways. Theologian Sallie McFague contends, "The best metaphors give both a shock and a shock of recognition." In good metaphors, we see something about reality, and we see it in new ways.

What are some of the metaphors for deity with which you are familiar? In what ways have those metaphors been helpful? In what ways are those metaphors limiting? What do you perceive as the consequences of taking these metaphors literally? Are there some metaphors you think have outlived their usefulness?

Following are a number of new metaphors for deity that are being utilized in current theological discussion. What do you think of these metaphors? In what new ways do they cause you to think about deity? What new ideas about deity do they suggest to you? In what ways do they call you to reappraise images of deity?

- God as mother
- God as lover
- God as companion
- God as gambler
- The earth and God's body

Can you think of any shocking new metaphors that help you think about deity in original ways?

weh became prominent as the Great Father God, and worship of the Goddess was harshly condemned by Yahweh's priests. The prominence of a single masculine image of deity then became reflected in the exclusion of women from the priesthood and eventually from the concept of Israel itself.

In response to the hegemony of masculine images of God, feminist theologians have constructed alternative feminine images of deity. Some theologians, such as Virginia Mollenkott, have returned to the Jewish and Christian testaments to point out the existence of feminine images within scripture. Other theologians, such as Sallie McFague, have challenged people to develop new models of God such as God as mother, God as love, and God as companion. And yet other women have returned to the ancient images of the Goddess herself. In "Grandmother of the Sun: The Power of Woman in Native America," Paula Gunn Allen explains Native American feminine images of deity.

The political nature of the decision to challenge normative God-language does not go unnoticed by traditionalists wishing to cling to male images. The Southern Baptist Convention issued a statement declaring that God is not *like* a father, but God *is* Father. And a group of mainline churchwomen created a furor within their denominations when at a conference they chose to call God "Sophia," a biblical, but feminine, name for deity.

REINTERPRETING AND RECONSTRUCTING TRADITIONS

For those feminist women who have chosen to remain in religious traditions, the task of reworking oppressive elements has been great. Theology itself has been constructed with male experience as normative and has not taken into account the experiences of both men and women. Since the 1960s, feminist theologians have undertaken the task of rethinking traditional theological notions from the perspective of women's experiences. For example, the traditional notion of sin expressed in the story of the Fall in Genesis is that of pride and the centrality of the self. Redemption in the Christian testament then involves the restoration of what man lacks—sacrificial love. Yet the normative experience for women is not pride and self-centeredness, given that women are generally socialized to be self-negating for the sake of their families, and, in fact, encouraging women to be self-sacrificing as a form of redemption simply exacerbates women's situation. Feminist theology, as Alicia Ostriker suggests in her poem "Everywoman Her Own Theology," brings women's experiences to the center and reconstructs theological concepts in keeping with those experiences.

Because of the predominance of Christianity in the United States, the Bible and its various interpretations play a large role in shaping women's lives. Given this importance, feminist re-examinations of religion are on a continuum from reinterpretation to reconstruction. *Reinterpretation* involves recognizing the passages that are particularly problematic for women and highlighting and reintegrating the passages that extol equality between women and men. Proponents of such reinterpretation include Christian feminists who maintain a positive view of scripture as they continue to accept scripture as an authority in their lives. The goal of *reconstruction,* however, is to move beyond reinterpretation and recognize the patriarchal underpinnings of various interpretations and the ways they have been used to oppress women.

As an example of a reconstructionist account, Christian testament scholar Elisabeth Schüssler Fiorenza encourages readers of scripture to look for the presence of women in the margins and around the edges of the text. She calls for biblical readers to re-create the narratives of women that were left out of but hinted at in the text. In a similar fashion, the reading "Standing Again at Sinai" by Jewish feminist scholar Judith Plaskow calls for a reconceptualization of notions of God, Torah, and Israel that are inclusive of women. Other reconstructions of scripture include "womanist" biblical interpretations of women of color that analyze the Bible in light of both sexism and racism. In these accounts the Bible itself is subject to scrutiny in terms of its expressions of justice and injustice. Readers of the Bible with this perspective focus on the moral and ethical imperatives of justice contained therein and with an eye toward struggle for liberation for women of color.

Women have begun to challenge and reconstruct religious traditions as well as scripture. For example, Jewish women have developed feminist haggadahs, texts containing the ritual for celebrating the Passover seder. These feminist haggadahs commemorate the women of the Exodus, the liberation of the Israelites from slavery in Egypt. In one haggadah, the four sons of the traditional ceremony become four daughters, and the lives of the women celebrating Passover are inserted in the ceremony to create a living history and a new story.

"... and so, then I said, 'You think that just because I'm a woman I can't preach, just because I'm a woman I can't hold office in the convention, just because I'm a woman I can't do evangelism, just because I'm a woman I can't teach theology!' And he said, 'Yes.'"

Reprinted with permission from Norma Young

Perhaps one of the most contentious reconstructions of religious traditions is the ordination of women. Although feminist church historians have recovered a long tradition of women as rabbis, priests, pastors, bishops, and evangelists, most Christian denominations did not ordain women until the latter part of the twentieth century. Many still do not. One exception to this is the Quakers. Quakers have a long and unique history of women's equality in the congregation. Although Quakers do not ordain anyone, some groups of Quakers do record ministers, and women have always been among the recorded. In silent Quaker meetings, women as well as men are assumed to be able to receive and speak a word from God. Beginning in the 1960s, many mainline Protestant churches began to ordain women ministers, although men still make up the larger percentage of senior pastors in almost every denomination. Roman Catholics still prohibit women from becoming priests, although there is a growing movement within Catholicism, particularly American Catholicism, to change this policy. Only the United Church of Christ ordains openly gay and lesbian people, as does the Unitarian Universalist Association.

CREATING NEW SPIRITUAL TRADITIONS

Although some feminists believe in the reinterpretation and reconstruction of scriptures and choose to work within existing denominations, others prefer to create their own empowering religious texts and organizations. For some, traditional religious scriptures are so essentially androcentric that they can only reproduce patriarchal social relations. They see no possibility of liberation for women in scripture because even reconstruction of biblical texts cannot change the patriarchal core of, for example, the Bible. Rather, these reconstructions simply perpetuate the patriarchal order. Feminist philosopher Mary Daly argues that patriarchal language is not accidental or incidental to the Bible but is an essential element of it, rendering the Bible useless in the liberation of women. These women look beyond traditional scripture for their spiritual insights and understandings.

In this way, although many women have expressed their spirituality within formal religious traditions, many others have created forms of spiritual expression outside churches, synagogues, and mosques. Women's spirituality is an empowering force that has taken such various forms as meditation, poetry, art, prayer, ritual, and social action. Spirituality enables women to experience connection with creation, with other human beings, and with the divine within themselves.

For many feminists, spirituality is a central force in their politics. The awareness of the interconnectedness of all things motivates feminist action toward justice and peace and encourages women to work together across differences. Nature-based spiritualities affirm the connections among all living things and seek to protect the natural environment on which we all depend. Feminist spirituality values and affirms the diversity that makes up the unity of creation, and it challenges women to restructure the systems of power that create and maintain injustice. As Marge Piercy writes:

Praise our choices, sisters, for each doorway
open to us was taken by squads of fighting
women who paid years of trouble and struggle,
who paid their wombs, their sleep, their lives
that we might walk through these gates upright.
Doorways are sacred to women for we
are the doorways of life and we must choose
what comes in and what goes out. Freedom
is our real abundance.*

---

* "The Sabbath of Mutual Respect," *The Moon Is Always Female.* New York: Knopf, 1980.

READING 84

Introduction to *The Woman's Bible*

Elizabeth Cady Stanton (1895)

From the inauguration of the movement for woman's emancipation the Bible has been used to hold [woman] in the "divinely ordained sphere," prescribed in the Old and New Testaments.

The canon and civil law; church and state; priests and legislators; all political parties and religious denominations have alike taught that woman was made after man, of man, and for man, an inferior being, subject to man. Creeds, codes, Scriptures and statutes, are all based on this idea. The fashions, forms, ceremonies and customs of society, church ordinances and discipline all grow out of this idea.

. . .

The Bible teaches that woman brought sin and death into the world, that she precipitated the fall of the race, that she was arraigned before the judgment seat of Heaven, tried, condemned and sentenced. Marriage for her was to be a condition of bondage, maternity a period of suffering and anguish, and in silence and subjection, she was to play the role of a dependent on man's bounty for all her material wants, and for all the information she might desire on the vital questions of the hour, she was commanded to ask her husband at home. Here is the Bible position of woman briefly summed up.

. . .

These familiar texts are quoted by clergymen in their pulpits, by statesmen in the halls of legislation, by lawyers in the courts, and are echoed by the press of all civilized nations, and accepted by woman herself as "The Word of God." So perverted is the religious element in her nature, that with faith and works she is the chief support of the church and clergy; the very powers that make her emancipation impossible. When, in the early part of the Nineteenth Century, women began to protest against their civil and political degradation, they were referred to the Bible for an answer. When they protested against their unequal position in the church, they were referred to the Bible for an answer.

This led to a general and critical study of the Scriptures. Some, having made a fetish of these books and believing them to be the veritable "Word of God," with liberal translations, interpretations, allegories and symbols, glossed over the most objectionable features of the various books and clung to them as divinely inspired. Others, seeing the family resemblance between the Mosaic code, the canon law, and the old English common law, came to the conclusion that all alike emanated from the same source; wholly human in their origin and inspired by the natural love of domination in the historians. Others, bewildered with their doubts and fears, came to no conclusion. While their clergymen told them on the one hand, that they owed all the blessings and freedom they enjoyed to the Bible, on the other, they said it clearly marked out their circumscribed sphere of action: that the demands for political and civil rights were irreligious, dangerous to the stability of the home, the state and the church. Clerical appeals were circulated from time to time conjuring members of their churches to take no part in the anti-slavery or woman suffrage movements, as they were infidel in their tendencies, undermining the very foundations of society. No wonder the majority of women stood still, and with bowed heads, accepted the situation.

READING 85

Fundamentalism and the Control of Women

Karen McCarthy Brown

Religious fundamentalism is very difficult to define; yet many of us—scholars and journalists in particular—think we know it when we see it. For those attuned to gender as a category of analysis, a stab of recognition is often occasioned by the presence of high degrees of religiously sanctioned control of women. In conservative religious movements around the world, women are veiled or otherwise covered; confined to the home or in some other way strictly limited in their access to the public sphere; prohibited from testifying in a court of law, owning property, or initiating divorce; and they are very often denied the authority to make their own reproductive choices.

I propose to take up the thread of the control of women and follow it into the center of the maze of contemporary fundamentalism. Yet I will not argue, as might be expected, that the need to control women is the main motivation for the rise of fundamentalism, but rather that aggravation of this age-old, widespread need is an inevitable side effect of a type of stress peculiar to our age.

I will suggest that the varieties of fundamentalism found throughout the world today are extreme responses to the failed promise of Enlightenment rationalism. Fundamentalism, in my view, is the religion of the stressed and the disoriented, of those for whom the world is overwhelming. More to the point, it is the religion of those at once seduced and betrayed by the promise that we human beings can comprehend and control our world. Bitterly disappointed by the politics of rationalized bureaucracies, the limitations of science, and the perversions of industrialization, fundamentalists seek to reject the modern world, while nevertheless holding onto its habits of mind: clarity, certitude, and control. Given these habits, fundamentalists necessarily operate with a limited view of human activity (including religious activity), one confined largely to consciousness and choice. They deny the power of those parts of the human psyche that are inaccessible to consciousness yet play a central role in orienting us in the world. Most of all they seek to control the fearsome, mute power of the flesh. This characteristic ensures that fundamentalism will always involve the control of women, for women generally carry the greater burden of human fleshliness.

This essay is an exploratory one. Its topic is huge and it ranges widely, crossing over into several academic disciplines other than my own. Occasionally I am forced to paint with a broad stroke and a quick hand. Writing that is preliminary and suggestive can be risky, but the connections I see between religious fundamentalism and other, larger aspects of our contemporary world seem compelling enough to lead me to take that risk. My argument begins close to home, in the United States, with Christian anti-abortion activism.

The Anti-Abortion Movement in the United States

The "pro-life movement" emerged in the 1970s as a new type of religio-political organization. It was a bottom-up movement that used sophisticated, top-down technology. In the early stages of the movement, the organizing work was done around kitchen tables. But the envelopes stuffed at those tables were sent to addresses on computer-generated mailing lists, the product of advanced market-research techniques. This blend of grass-roots organization and advanced technology quickly brought a minority movement[1] to a position of significant political power. The combination of traditional and modern methods also reveals an ambivalence toward the ways of the modern world that I will later argue is characteristic of fundamentalist movements.

Many observers have noted an inconsistency in the pro-life position. The very groups who launch an emotional defense of the fetus's right to life are curiously indifferent to children outside the womb. As a rule pro-lifers do not support social programs focused on issues such as child abuse, day care, foster care, or juvenile drug use. They oppose welfare programs in general and have taken no leadership in educational reform beyond concern with sex education, public school prayer, and the theory of evolution. Furthermore, their so-called pro-life argument is deeply compromised by staunch support for increased military spending and for the death penalty. It seems clear that the pro-life position is not a consistent theological or philosophical stance. A quite different kind of consistency emerges from the full range of this group's social policy positions. Their overriding concern is that of maintaining strong and clear social boundaries—boundaries between nation-states, between law-abiding citizens and criminals, between the righteous and the sinful, between life and death, and not coincidentally, between men and women. This is a group centrally concerned with social order and social control.

Beyond the trigger of the 1973 Supreme Court decision in *Roe v. Wade,* stresses with a broader historical range have contributed to a focus on boundary maintenance in the anti-abortion movement. The upheavals of the 1960s created the immediate historical context of the anti-abortion movement of the 1970s. Student activists of the 1960s questioned the authority of parents, educators, and politicians. Black activists challenged the cherished American myths of equal opportunity and equal protection under the law. And the Vietnam War not only raised questions about U.S. military prowess but also planted doubts about the moral valence of the international presence and policy of the United States. These are very specific reasons why Americans in the 1970s might have felt that the social and moral orders were becoming dangerously befuddled.

. . .

A World Suddenly Too Big

From the mid-nineteenth century into the early decades of the twentieth, the writings of travelers, missionaries, and, eventually, anthropologists were popular bedside reading materials in the United States.

Americans were fascinated by exotic "others." They were concerned about their own place in this expanding, newly complex world. Most of these books did more than titillate. With their implicit or explicit social Darwinism, they also carried deeply comforting messages of progress and of Western superiority. Such messages, coming from many sources, infused an air of optimism into an otherwise disorienting age. During the same general time span, the seeds of American fundamentalism were sown and came to fruition.

Some of the social forces that shaped this period —expanding knowledge of and contact with the larger world, and increased communication—had emerged over a relatively long period of time. Others, such as the burgeoning of cities, the dramatic increase in immigrant populations, and a series of shifts in women's roles, had occurred more recently.[2] All of these forces came together in the second half of the nineteenth century to contribute to a general sense of vertigo; the world was becoming too big, too complicated, and too chaotic to comprehend. Most important, each individual's own place in it was uncertain. Religion, given its basic orientational role in human life, emerged as a natural arena for dealing with the resulting stress.

From that period until this in the United States, conservative Christians have come under a double attack. On one level, they have had to deal with the general stress of the times; and on the other, with the direct challenge of Enlightenment rationalism in the form of biblical higher criticism and evolutionary theory. The reaction of some groups of Christians has been ironic: they have responded to the threat by mimicking Enlightenment rationalism. The religion-versus-science debate pits against one another groups who share a common intellectual style: each claims to possess the truth. Believers, like rationalists, stress consciousness, clarity, and control.[3] Morality is codified; sacred narratives are taken literally and sometimes attempts are made to support them with "scientific evidence"; all sorts of truths are listed and enumerated; scripture becomes inerrant. Furthermore conscious consent to membership in the community of belief, on the model of "making a decision for Christ," becomes increasingly important.

These are the religious groups we call fundamentalists. Their central aim is to make of their religion an Archimedean point in the midst of a changing world. But to do so, they must limit their religion's responsiveness to its social environment; and as a result they are left with little flexibility to respond to the complexity of their own feelings or to the challenge of a changing world. Sometimes they fall into aggressively defending brittle truths. This is what makes fundamentalism in the contemporary world problematic and, in some cases, dangerous.

. . .

Fundamentalism Cross-Culturally

Up to this point, I have been concerned with Christian fundamentalism in the United States, but in the process I have focused on dimensions of the story that serve, without denying the significance of local variations, to characterize fundamentalism around the globe. Religious fundamentalism is born in times and places where, for a variety of reasons, the world suddenly seems too complex to comprehend; and one's place in it, too precarious to provide genuine security.

One example is modern India, where the cult that developed around the recent immolation of a young woman on her husband's funeral pyre has been described as an instance of fundamentalism. John Hawley demonstrates that the background for the *sati* of Roop Kanwar was emerging Hindu nationalism in India augmented by a multitude of local destabilizing forces in Deorala, the site of the immolation. Furthermore, as Hawley and other authors have pointed out, Deorala is not a truly deprived area, and its residents are not traditionalists out of contact with the larger realities of modern India. I would therefore suggest, along with Hawley, that fundamentalism is not primarily a religion of the marginalized, as some have argued. Its more salient feature is that it develops among people caught off balance. Hence, fundamentalist groups often arise in situations where social, cultural, and economic power is up for grabs; many, like these groups now being referred to as Hindu fundamentalists, arise in postcolonial situations. Far from being essentially marginal to the societies in which they exist, fundamentalists are often directly involved in the political and economic issues of their time and place. And they often have a significant, if precarious, stake in them.

For the Rajputs in Deorala, traditional sources of pride and authority are being challenged by increasing contact with the cities of Jaipur and Delhi, and through them, all of India. These Rajputs are experiencing the disorientation of having to depend on economic and political systems beyond their control. Marwari merchants and industrialists, financial backers of the cult of the goddess Sati, are destabilized in another way. As their economic role expands throughout India, they risk their livelihood in a wider, less familiar, and less predictable world than the one in which earlier generations operated. The Marwari focus on the district around Jhunjhunu with its important Sati shrine gives them their emotionally saturated Archimedean point. The case of the Marwari businessmen suggests, even more directly than does that of the Rajputs, that fundamentalism is not a religion of the marginalized, but of the disoriented.

In the contemporary Indian context, rallying around the *sati* of Roop Kanwar (like anti-abortion activity in the United States) reasserts social control and demonstrates moral worth. It strengthens gender boundaries and provides an example of undiluted, innocent virtue that vicariously underwrites the virtue of Rajputs and Marwaris in general. Furthermore, as in the United States, insecurity about social control and moral rectitude is displaced onto the body of a woman. But in the *sati* ritual described by Hawley, the drive to kill the devouring, fleshly goddess and to enshrine the pure, spiritual one is much more painfully literal.

Both men and women attended the *sati* of Roop Kanwar, and both men and women subsequently revere her. At first glance this may seem difficult to understand, but the complicity of Indian women in the practice of *sati* has to be considered on more than one level. At the deepest level its explanation lies in the fear of women's will and women's flesh that men and women share, and in the relief that both feel when these forces are kept in check. But on another level there are explanations of a much more practical nature. Most Indian women's economic security heavily depends on marriage. A woman doing homage at a Sati shrine thus signals to her husband and to the world at large, as well as to herself, that she intends to be good and to do good, according to her society's standards. Thus she chooses to ignore any anger or fear she might feel about the practice, in the name of living a secure and ordered life. It is a herculean task for women to try to define the meaning and worth of their lives in terms different from those that prevail in their community. So some security can always be found in surrendering to, and even helping to strengthen, the accepted gender norms.

. . .

The Failed Promise of Enlightenment Rationalism

Modern communications, transnational economic pressures, and wars waged from the opposite side of the globe have brought many populations intimate knowledge of the vastness and complexity of their worlds. In the late twentieth century, the others in relation to whom we must define ourselves are more available to our experience and imagination than ever before; yet few if any of us have a satisfactory model for understanding ourselves within this complex, stressful world.

We all live in and are defined by a world too big and unstable for intellect or belief to comprehend, and we all react to intimations—as well as a few pieces of hard evidence[4]—of the failed promise of the Enlightenment. Academics, politicians, and ordinary folk the world over are immersed in this challenge and most commonly react to it (as fundamentalists do) by assuming that, with sufficient effort, the chaos can be first comprehended and then managed. In this way fundamentalists are simply extreme versions of the rest of us.

An emphasis on the control of women is characteristic of fundamentalism, but there is some of it everywhere in the world. The anti-abortion movement in the United States arises out of a much broader context in which, among other signals of misogyny, public power and authority have been denied to women for centuries. And the Sati cult could

not have become an issue in Indian nationalism if in general Indian women were not seen as sources of pollution as well as of blessing—as a result of which they have been subject to a variety of social controls through the ages. When the mind and the spirit are cut off from the body, women become magnets for the fear raised by everything in life that seems out of control. The degree to which control is exercised over women is therefore a key to the profundity of stresses felt by most persons and groups. Fundamentalism is a product of extreme social stress.

Religion, whose primary function is to provide a comprehensible model of the world and to locate the individual safely and meaningfully within it, is an obvious place for this type of stress to express itself and seek redress. But as long as religions deal with this stress by positing a world that can be directly known, and in which it is possible to determine one's own fate, they only reinforce the controlling tendencies of enlightenment rationalism and do nothing to move us beyond it to whatever comes next. We should be suspicious of any religion that claims too much certainty or draws the social boundaries too firmly. In this period marked by the gradual breakdown of Enlightenment rationalism and Euro-American hegemony in the world, something more is necessary. We need help in accepting ourselves as organic creatures enmeshed in our world rather than continuing to posture as cerebral masters granted dominion over it. This requires that we learn to trust the wisdom of our mute flesh and accept the limitations inherent in our humanity. If we could do this, it would radically diminish our scapegoating of women and all the other "others" who provide a convenient screen on which to project fears.

The resurgence of religion that we are experiencing at the turn of this millennium should not be viewed in an entirely negative light. If any system of orientation in the world can help us now, it seems likely to be a religious one. There is no small comfort in knowing that, as the grand ambitions spawned by the Enlightenment falter in the present age, what is likely to emerge is not what several generations of social scientists predicted. It is not civilization marching toward increasing secularization and rationalization. What is slowly being revealed is the hubris of reason's pretense in trying to take over religion's role.

NOTES

1. From the beginning of the anti-abortion movement to the present, opinion polls have consistently shown that the majority of people in the United States favor a woman's right to have an abortion.

2. Betty A. DeBerg, *Ungodly Women: Gender and the First Wave of American Fundamentalism* (Minneapolis: Fortress Press, 1990), has an excellent discussion of the general changes—and particularly the changes in women's roles—attendant to the formation of fundamentalism in the United States. . . .

3. Often the only kind of control that fundamentalists can exercise over a chaotic and threatening world rests in their claim to have a privileged understanding of the deeper meaning of the chaos. Fundamentalists who engage in "end-time" thinking thus sometimes find themselves in the position of welcoming the signs of modern social decay because these signal the approach of the time when God will call home the chosen few.

4. The growing ecological crisis is one of the most tangible pieces of this evidence; it also reinforces the point that reason alone is an insufficient problem-solving tool, because we are incapable of holding in consciousness the full range of the interconnectedness of things.

READING 86

Grandmother of the Sun
The Power of Woman in Native America

Paula Gunn Allen

There is a spirit that pervades everything, that is capable of powerful song and radiant movement, and that moves in and out of the mind. The colors of this spirit are multitudinous, a flowing, pulsing rainbow. Old Spider Woman is one name for this quintessential spirit, and Serpent Woman is another. Corn Woman is one aspect of her, and Earth Woman is another, and what they together have made is called Creation, Earth, creatures, plants, and light.

At the center of all is Woman, and no thing is sacred (cooked, ripe, as the Keres Indians of Laguna Pueblo say it) without her blessing, her thinking.

> . . . In the beginning Tse che nako, Thought Woman finished everything, thoughts, and the names of all things. She finished also all the languages. And then our mothers, Uretsete and Naotsete said they would make names and they would make thoughts. Thus they said: Thus they did.[1]

This spirit, this power of intelligence, has many names and many emblems. She appears on the plains, in the forests, in the great canyons, on the mesas, beneath the seas. To her we owe our very breath, and to her our prayers are sent blown on pollen, on corn meal, planted into the earth on feather-sticks, spit onto the water, burned and sent to her on the wind. Her variety and multiplicity testify to her complexity: she is the true Creatrix for she is thought itself, from which all else is born. She is the necessary precondition for material creation, and she, like all of her creation, is fundamentally female—potential and primary.

She is also the spirit that informs right balance, right harmony, and these in turn order all relationships in conformity with her law.

To assign to this great being the position of "fertility goddess" is exceedingly demeaning: it trivializes the tribes and it trivializes the power of woman. Woman bears, that is true. She also destroys. That is true. She also wars and hexes and mends and breaks. She creates the power of the seeds, and she plants them. As Anthony Purley, a Laguna writer, has translated a Keres ceremonial prayer, "She is mother of us all, after Her, mother earth follows, in fertility, in holding, and taking again us back to her breast."[2]

The Hopi account of their genatrix, Hard Beings Woman, gives the most articulate rendering of the difference between simple fertility cultism and the creative prowess of the Creatrix. Hard Beings Woman (Huruing Wuhti) is of the earth. But she lives in the worlds above where she "owns" (empowers) the moon and stars. Hard Beings Woman has solidity and hardness as her major aspects. She, like Thought Woman, does not give birth to creation or to human beings but breathes life into male and female effigies that become the parents of the Hopi—in this way she "creates" them. The male is Muingwu, the god of crops, and his sister-consort is Sand Altar Woman who is also known as Childbirth Water Woman. In Sand Altar Woman the mystical relationship between water, worship, and woman is established; she is also said to be the mother of the katsinas, those powerful messengers who relate the spirit world to the world of humankind and vice versa.[3]

Like Thought Woman, Hard Beings Woman lived in the beginning on an island which was the only land there was. In this regard she resembles a number of Spirit Woman Beings; the Spirit genatrix of the Iroquois, Sky Woman, also lived on an island in the void which only later became the earth. On this island, Hard Beings Woman is identified with or, as they say, "owns" all hard substances—moon, stars, beads, coral, shell, and so forth. She is a sea goddess as well, the single inhabitant of the earth, that island that floats alone in the waters of space. From this meeting of woman and water, earth and her creatures were born.[4] . . .

Contemporary Indian tales suggest that the creatures are born from the mating of sky father and earth mother, but that seems to be a recent interpolation of the original sacred texts. The revision may have occurred since the Christianizing influence on even the arcane traditions, or it may have predated Christianity. But the older, more secret texts suggest that it is a revision. It may be that the revision appears only in popular versions of the old mythic cycles on which ceremony and ritual are based; this would accord with the penchant in the old oral tradition for shaping tales to reflect present social realities, making the rearing and education of children possible even within the divergent worlds of the United States of America and the tribes.

According to the older texts (which are sacred, that is, power-engendering), Thought Woman is not a passive personage: her potentiality is dynamic and unimaginably powerful. She brought corn and agriculture, potting, weaving, social systems, religion, ceremony, ritual, building, memory, intuition, and their expressions in language, creativity, dance, human-to-animal relations, and she gave these offerings power and authority and blessed the people with the ability to provide for themselves and their progeny.

Thought Woman is not limited to a female role in the total theology of the Keres people. Since she is the supreme Spirit, she is both Mother and Father to all people and to all creatures. She is the only creator of thought, and thought precedes creation.[5]

Central to Keres theology is the basic idea of the Creatrix as She Who Thinks rather than She Who Bears, of woman as creation thinker and female thought as origin of material and nonmaterial reality. In this epistemology, the perception of female power as confined to maternity is a limit on the power inherent in femininity. But "she is the supreme Spirit, . . . both Mother and Father to all people and to all creatures."[6] . . .

In Keres theology the creation does not take place through copulation. In the beginning existed Thought Woman and her dormant sisters, and Thought Woman thinks creation and sings her two sisters into life. After they are vital she instructs them to sing over the items in their baskets (medicine bundles) in such a way that those items will have life. After that crucial task is accomplished, the creatures thus vitalized take on the power to regenerate themselves—that is, they can reproduce others of their kind. But they are not in and of themselves self-sufficient; they depend for their being on the medicine power of the three great Witch creatrixes, Thought Woman, Uretsete, and Naotsete. The sisters are not related by virtue of having parents in common; that is, they are not alive because anyone bore them. Thought Woman turns up, so to speak, first as Creatrix and then as a personage who is acting out someone else's "dream." But there is no time when she did not exist. She has two bundles in her power, and these bundles contain Uretsete and Naotsete, who are not viewed as her daughters but as her sisters, her coequals who possess the medicine power to vitalize the creatures that will inhabit the earth. They also have the power to create the firmament, the skies, the galaxies, and the seas, which they do through the use of ritual magic.

. . .

The Heart of Power

. . .

Pre-Conquest American Indian women valued their role as vitalizers. Through their own bodies they could bring vital beings into the world—a miraculous power whose potency does not diminish with industrial sophistication or time. They were mothers, and that word did not imply slaves, drudges, drones who are required to live only for others rather than for themselves as it does so tragically for many modern women. The ancient ones were empowered by their certain knowledge that the power to make life is the source of all power and that no other power can gainsay it. Nor is that power simply of biology, as modernists tendentiously believe. When Thought Woman brought to life the twin sisters, she did not give birth to them in the biological sense. She sang over the medicine bundles that contained their potentials. With her singing and shaking she infused them with vitality. She gathered the power that she controlled and focused it on those bundles, and thus they were "born." Similarly, when the sister goddesses Naotsete and Uretsete wished to bring forth some plant or creature they reached into the basket (bundle) that Thought Woman had given them, took out the effigy of the creature, and thought it into life. Usually they then instructed it in its proper role. They also meted out consequences to creatures (this included plants, spirits, and katsinas) who disobeyed them.

The water of life, menstrual or postpartum blood, was held sacred. Sacred often means taboo; that is, what is empowered in a ritual sense is not to be touched or approached by any who are weaker than the power itself, lest they suffer negative consequences from contact. The blood of woman was in and of itself infused with the power of Supreme Mind, and so women were held in awe and respect. The term *sacred,* which is connected with power, is similar in meaning to the term *sacrifice,* which

means "to make sacred." What is made sacred is empowered. Thus, in the old way, sacrificing meant empowering, which is exactly what it still means to American Indians who adhere to traditional practice. Blood was and is used in sacrifice because it possesses the power to make something else powerful or, conversely, to weaken or kill it.

Pre-contact American Indian women valued their role as vitalizers because they understood that bearing, like bleeding, was a transformative ritual act. Through their own bodies they could bring vital beings into the world—a miraculous power unrivaled by mere shamanic displays. They were mothers, and that word implied the highest degree of status in ritual cultures. The status of mother was so high, in fact, that in some cultures Mother or its analogue, Matron, was the highest office to which a man or woman could aspire.

The old ones were empowered by their certain knowledge that the power to make life is the source and model for all ritual magic and that no other power can gainsay it. Nor is that power really biological at base; it is the power of ritual magic, the power of Thought, of Mind, that gives rise to biological organisms as it gives rise to social organizations, material culture, and transformations of all kinds—including hunting, war, healing, spirit communication, rain-making, and all the rest. . . .

A strong attitude integrally connects the power of Original Thinking or Creation Thinking to the power of mothering. That power is not so much the power to give birth, as we have noted, but the power to make, to create, to transform. Ritual means transforming something from one state or condition to another, and that ability is inherent in the action of mothering. It is the ability that is sought and treasured by adepts, and it is the ability that male seekers devote years of study and discipline to acquire. Without it, no practice of the sacred is possible, at least not within the Great Mother societies.

And as the cultures that are woman-centered and Mother-ritual based are also cultures that value peacefulness, harmony, cooperation, health, and general prosperity, they are systems of thought and practice that would bear deeper study in our troubled, conflict-ridden time.

NOTES

1. Anthony Purley, "Keres Pueblo Concepts of Deity," *American Indian Culture and Research Journal* 1 (Fall 1974): 29. The passage cited is Purley's literal translation from the Keres Indian language of a portion of the Thought Woman story. Purley is a native-speaker Laguna Pueblo Keres.
2. Ibid., 30–31.
3. Hamilton A. Tyler, *Pueblo Gods and Myths,* Civilization of the American Indian Series (Norman, OK: University of Oklahoma Press, 1964), 37. Evidently, Huruing Wuhti has other transformative abilities as well. Under pressure from patriarchal politics, she can change her gender, her name, and even her spiritual nature.
4. Ibid., 93.
5. Purley, "Keres Pueblo Concepts," 31.
6. Ibid.

READING 87

Islam, Social Change, and the Reality of Arab Women's Lives

Nadia Hijab

For more than a hundred years, Arab women have been engaged in the public debate on their role in a rapidly changing society. Both women and men have conducted the debate within an Islamic framework; they have turned to the Quran, the sharia (Islamic law), the sayings of the Prophet Muhammad, and the lives of his companions to define women's rights in the modern age. While modernists have argued for the most liberal interpretation of Islam possible, the conservatives have used the same sources to argue for restrictions on women's roles.

Social Change

The debates make frequent references to the centrality of Arab women in maintaining family ties and community solidarity and in transmitting cultural values across generations. This was best captured in the document prepared by the Economic and Social Commission for Western Asia for the 1985 United Nations World Conference on Women, which was held in Nairobi. The document declared:

> Constitutions, charters, and legislation in the region have asserted the role of the family as the nucleus of social organization in Arab societies. It is necessary, therefore, to make available to the family the economic, social, cultural, and psychological conditions that would ensure its stability and satisfy its needs.

Therefore, the document accorded "priority to the work of women who devote their time to family and home affairs and hence ensure the continuity of generations, the cultivation of values, and the transmittal of knowledge and expertise from one generation to another."

Hitherto, Arab women themselves have assigned a great deal of value to their traditional roles within the family. This is partly because they are accorded a great deal of respect. As the social scientist Nadia Haggag Youssef noted, women's status can be seen as having two different components:

> the *rights* given to women and the *respect* given to them. Confusion ensues because the two distinct factors are erroneously used interchangeably, when in reality they are often inversely correlated. Thus, women receive great respect in certain societies that give them few rights; they receive equality of rights in societies in which they compete with men but have relatively low respect.

Today, Arab women are in the unenviable position of having to choose between rights and respect.

Neither women nor men want to lose the warmth and security that the extended Arab family traditionally provided, particularly at a time of rapid social and economic change. However, modernization efforts by the state have steadily eroded traditional support and mediation systems, and women now are increasingly reliant on state legislation and institutions to protect their rights. Yet in the crucial area of relations within the family, the law in the Arab world does not provide for equal rights between men and women. This has occurred because the debate on women's roles has been conducted within the Islamic framework.

Law and the Islamic Framework

The constitutions of the Arab nations, in those countries that have them, provide for nondiscrimination based on race, sex, or creed as called for in international law and United Nations conventions. Thus they provide equal political rights for Arab women, who can vote and stand for election in all the Arab countries that have parliaments (except in Kuwait). Arab labor laws that have been legislated during this century also compare well to international standards.

However, family laws, which regulate rights and responsibilities in marriage, divorce, child custody, and inheritance, do not provide for equality between the sexes because they have been developed within the Islamic framework in all Arab countries. Because the legislation has been developed independently, there is a wide range in interpretation. While Tunisia has almost achieved equality between men and women within the Islamic framework, Egyptian law provides for "equivalence" rather than equality. In Bahrain, which has not passed a state law regulating family relations, the disposition of legal opinion has been delegated to the judges to interpret the sharia directly as they see fit.

Thus, in effect, most family laws, as they currently stand, contradict the provisions of the constitutions and labor laws that have been decreed. For instance, in some Arab countries the constitution may guarantee the right to work and the labor law may be fair, yet the family law may allow a husband to stipulate

that his wife must have his consent to work outside the home.

Egypt is one of the Arab countries that has ratified the United Nations Convention on the Elimination of All Forms of Discrimination Against Women (CEDAW), which is the most far-reaching international instrument providing for equality between men and women. Such ratification of a United Nations convention is seen as the governments' commitment to bring their national laws into line with the convention, unless they have stipulated reservations to specific articles. As was the case with many other countries around the world, Egypt had reservations. These included the following reservation to Article 16:

> concerning the equality of men and women in all matters relating to marriage and family relations during marriage and upon its dissolution. This must be without prejudice to the Islamic sharia provisions whereby women are accorded rights equivalent to those of their spouses so as to ensure a just balance between them. This is out of respect for the sanctity deriving from firm religious beliefs which govern marital relations in Egypt and which may not be called in question.

The reservation explained that, in the Egyptian context, the husband was obliged to support the wife financially and to provide support in case of divorce, while the wife had no such obligation; "the sharia therefore restricts the wife's rights to divorce by making it contingent on a judge's ruling, whereas no such restriction is laid down in the case of the husband." Thus, on the one hand, women should be entitled to full equality with men since Egypt has ratified the Convention. On the other hand, when it comes to the detailed application of the Convention, women's rights are restricted on grounds that no one "may call into question." In effect, the fact that family law has evolved within an Islamic framework means that Arab women can be equal outside the home but not within it.

This is being increasingly questioned by Arab feminists, who hold Tunisia up as a model, noting that it has evolved its family law within an Islamic framework, but has interpreted sharia law in such a way that it provides for equality between men and women.

Islam and Identity

It is clear that the Islamic framework continues to be of great importance and to have a strong hold when it comes to defining women's roles within the family. This attitude is reinforced by the fact that the region is still engaged in shaping its identity vis-à-vis other parts of the world, an exercise that has proven to be quite painful because memories of Western colonialism in the region are still fresh. In many Arab countries, independence was only won in the 1950s or 1960s—and in the case of the Palestinians it has yet to be achieved. The quest for independence was charged by the desire to express national identity without external interference. Thus the contentious question of what constituted an authentic Arab identity surfaced after independence. To date, it has not been satisfactorily resolved, nor have other questions that were a by-product of colonialism, such as how independent Arab state systems should relate to non-Arabs living within their societies.

The effort to define an authentic identity in postcolonial societies gave culture and heritage a more important and prominent role than they might otherwise have had. The extreme example is Algeria, perhaps one of the most harshly colonized Arab countries, where the French sought to stamp out Islamic religion and culture. After independence in 1962, therefore, there was great emphasis on defining Algerian identity in terms of the country's "Arab–Islamic heritage." This had an appreciable impact on defining women's rights and responsibilities. Indeed, one reason why it took the country nearly twenty years to pass a family law at all was because of the complexity (if not impossibility) of forging consensus on what an "Arab–Islamic heritage" is and how this translates into rights and responsibilities for men and women. The family law that was eventually passed was much closer to the conservative interpretation of Islamic law than the liberal one enshrined in Tunisian law.

The question of identity is thus complicated by the need to define "the self" in opposition to the former colonialists, which is, in the final analysis, a defensive position. As Leila Ahmed has pointed out:

> the Islamic civilisation is not only a civilisation unambiguously on the defensive, emphasizing and reaffirming old values, but also a civilisation that finds itself reaffirming them the more intransigently and dogmatically and clinging to them perhaps the more obstinately because it is reaffirming them against [an old enemy—the West].

What makes the challenge even more acute is the fact that, in the postindependence era, many Arabs feel that economic and cultural colonialism has replaced political colonialism, and that there is all the more reason to adhere to indigenous culture and tradition in response. Efforts to redefine women's roles in society are often seen, rightly or wrongly, as an extension of Western efforts at cultural domination. During the Lebanese civil war (1975–1990), a Lebanese woman writer, Mona Fayyad Kawtharani, argued strongly that the *hijab* (Islamic headcovering) was a form of resistance to cultural and by extension economic domination. In an article in the daily newspaper *As Safir* in 1985, she said that the West had found that:

> [the] best way to control us was by destroying our cultural and religious beliefs, so that the believer came to be defined as a "fanatic." And this was done to enable the West to invade our lands and to penetrate with its consumer commodities, to transform our countries into markets. This led to political and economic dependency, and to loss of cultural identity, which was replaced by "modernisation." The Easterner would not buy these diverse commodities—clothes, cars, electrical appliances, processed foods, furniture, etc.—unless he was convinced that he was in need of a culture other than his own, and that this culture represented "modernity" whereas his own represented backwardness.

Kawtharani went on to defend the veil as a symbol of opposition to political, economic, and cultural domination. In fact, the notable increase in the use of the veil over the last decade is a multifaceted phenomenon. Some people support it for reasons of cultural authenticity, others for reasons of piety, and still others because it enables them to study and work outside the home without fear of harassment.

The search for an authentic (Arab–Islamic) identity, the incomplete separation of religion and state (particularly when it comes to family law), and the sense that the West continues to dominate cultural and economic development, all mean that it is wiser —indeed safer—to articulate proposals for change in Islamic rather than Western terms. This is why, as Ahmed pointed out:

> reformers and feminists repeatedly try to affirm (with remarkable tenacity and often too with inge-

nuity) that the reforms they seek involve no disloyalty to Islam, that they in fact are in conformity with it, and if not in conformity with the letter and actual text of the culture's central formulation, then in conformity with what nevertheless is still there somehow, in the spirit not quite caught by the words.

Thus, the debate on women's roles in the Arab world is not only a debate about women's roles within the family. It is also linked to the debate on the role of Islam in the state, and is closely bound with the Arab search for political independence, economic self-reliance, and an authentic identity. . . .

READING 88

Standing Again at Sinai

Judith Plaskow

Exploring the Terrain of Silence

. . . The central Jewish categories of Torah, Israel, and God are all constructed from male perspectives. Torah is revelation as men perceived it, the story of Israel told from their standpoint, the law unfolded according to their needs. Israel is the male collectivity, the children of a Jacob who had a daughter, but whose sons became the twelve tribes. God is named in the male image, a father and warrior much like his male offspring, who confirms and sanctifies the silence of his daughters. Exploring these categories, we explore the parameters of women's silence.

In Torah, Jewish teaching, women are not absent, but they are cast in stories told by men. As characters in narrative, women may be vividly characterized, as objects of legislation, singled out for attention. But women's presence in Torah does not negate their silence, for women do not decide the questions with which Jewish sources deal. When the law treats of women, it is often because their "abnormality" demands it. If women are central to plot, the plots are not about them. Women's interests and intentions must be unearthed from texts with other purposes, for both law and narrative serve to obscure them.

The most striking examples of women's silence come from texts in which women are most central, for there the normative character of maleness is especially jarring. In the family narratives of Genesis, for example, women figure prominently. The matriarchs of Genesis are all strong women. As independent personalities, fiercely concerned for their children, they often seem to have an intuitive knowledge of God's plans for their sons. Indeed, it appears from the stories of Sarah and Rebekah that they understand God better than their husbands. God defends Sarah when she casts out Hagar, telling Abraham to obey his wife (Gen. 21:12). Rebekah, knowing it is God's intent, helps deceive Isaac into accepting Jacob as his heir (Gen. 25:23; 27:5–17). Yet despite their intuitions, and despite their wiliness and resourcefulness, it is not the women who receive the covenant or who pass on its lineage. The establishment of patrilineal descent and the patriarchal family takes precedence over the matriarch's stories. Their relationship to God, in some way presupposed by the text, remains an undigested element in the narrative. What was the full theophany to Rebekah, and how is it related to the covenant with Isaac? The writer does not tell us; it is not sufficiently important. And so the covenant remains the covenant with Isaac, while Rebekah's experience floats at the margin of the story.

The establishment of patrilineal descent and patriarchal control, a subtext in Genesis, is an important theme in the legislation associated with Sinai. Here again, women figure prominently, but only as objects of male concerns. The laws pertaining to women place them firmly under the control of first fathers, then husbands, so that men can have male heirs they know are theirs. Legislation concerning adultery (Deut. 22:22, also Num. 5:11–31) and virginity (Deut. 22:13–21) speaks of women, but only to control female sexuality to male advantage. The *crime* of adultery is sleeping with another man's wife, and a man can bring his wife to trial even on suspicion of adultery, a right that is not reciprocal. Sleeping with a betrothed virgin constitutes adultery. A man who sleeps with a virgin who is not betrothed must simply marry her. A girl whose lack of virginity shames her father on her wedding night can be stoned to death for harlotry. A virgin who is raped must marry her assailant. The subject of these laws is women, but the interest behind them is the purity of the male line.

The process of projecting and defining women as objects of male concerns is expressed most fully not in the Bible, however, but in the Mishnah, an important second-century legal code. Part of the Mishnah's Order of Women (one of its six divisions) develops laws discussed in the Torah concerning certain problematic aspects of female sexuality. The subject of the division is the transfer of women—the regulation of women who are in states of transition, whose uncertain status threatens the stasis of the community. The woman who is about to enter into a marriage or who has just left one requires close attention. The law must regularize her irregularity, facilitate her transition to the normal state of wife and motherhood, at which point she no longer poses a problem. . . .

Thus Torah—"Jewish" sources, "Jewish" teaching—puts itself forward as *Jewish* teaching but speaks in the voice of only half the Jewish people. This scandal is compounded by another: The omission is neither mourned nor regretted; it is not even noticed. True, the rabbis were aware of the harshness

of certain laws pertaining to women and sought to mitigate their effects. They tried to find ways to force a recalcitrant husband to divorce his wife, for example. But the framework that necessitated such mitigations went unquestioned. Women's Otherness was left intact. The Jewish passion for justice did not extend to Jewish women. As Cynthia Ozick puts it, one great "Thou shalt not"—"Thou shalt not lessen the humanity of women"—is missing from the Torah.

For this great omission, there is no historical redress. Indeed, where one might expect redress, the problem is compounded. The prophets, those great champions of justice, couch their pleas for justice in the language of patriarchal marriage. Israel in her youth is a devoted bride, subordinate and obedient to her husband/God (for example, Jer. 2:2). Idolatrous Israel is a harlot and adulteress, a faithless woman whoring after false gods (for example, Hos. 2,3). Transferring the hierarchy of male and female to God and his people, the prophets enshrine in metaphor the legal subordination of women. Those who might have named and challenged women's marginalization thus ignore and extend it.

The prophetic metaphors mark an end and a beginning. They confront us with the injustice of Torah; they link that injustice to other central Jewish ideas. If exploring Torah means exploring a terrain of women's silence, this is no less true of the categories of Israel or God.

Israel, the bride, the harlot, the people that is female (that is, subordinate) in relation to God is nonetheless male in communal self-perception. The covenant community is the community of the circumcised (Gen. 17:10), the community defined as male heads of household. Women are named through a filter of male experience: that is the essence of their silence. But women's experiences are not recorded or taken seriously because women are not perceived as normative Jews. They are part of but do not define the community of Israel.

The same evidence that speaks to women's silence in the tradition, to the partiality of Torah, also reflects an understanding of Israel as a community of males. In the narratives of Genesis, for example, the covenant moves from father to son, from Abraham to Isaac to Jacob to Joseph. The matriarchs' relation to their husbands' God is sometimes assumed, sometimes passed over, but the women do not constitute the covenant people. Women's relation to the community is also ambiguous and unclear in biblical legislation. The law is couched in male grammatical forms, and its content too presupposes a male nation. "You shall not covet your neighbor's wife" (Ex. 20:17). Probably we cannot deduce from this verse that women are free to covet! Yet the injunction assumes that women's obedience is owed to fathers and husbands, who are the primary group addressed.

The silence of women goes deeper, however, than who defines Torah or Israel. It also finds its way into language about God. Our language about divinity is first of all male language; it is selective and partial. The God who supposedly transcends sexuality, who is presumably one and whole, comes to us through language that is incomplete and narrow. The images we use to describe God, the qualities we attribute to God, draw on male pronouns and experience and convey a sense of power and authority that is clearly male. The God at the surface of Jewish consciousness is a God with a voice of thunder, a God who as lord and king rules his people and leads them into battle, a God who forgives like a father when we turn to him. The female images that exist in the Bible and (particularly the mystical) tradition form an underground stream that occasionally reminds us of the inadequacy of our imagery without transforming its overwhelmingly male nature.

This male imagery is comforting and familiar—comforting because familiar—but it is an integral part of a system that consigns women to the margins. Since the experience of God cannot be directly conveyed in language, imagery for God is a vehicle that suggests what is actually impossible to describe. Religious experiences are expressed in a vocabulary drawn from the significant and valuable in a particular culture. To speak of God is to speak of what we most value. In attributing certain qualities to God, we both attempt to point to God and offer God's qualities to be emulated and admired. To say that God is just, for example, is to say both that God acts justly and that God demands justice. Justice belongs to God but is also ours to pursue. Similarly with maleness, to image God as male is to value the quality and those who have it. It is to define God

in the image of the normative community and to bless men—but not women—with a central attribute of God.

But our images of God are not simply male images; they are images of a certain kind. The prophetic metaphors for the relation between God and Israel are metaphors borrowed from the patriarchal family —images of dominance softened by affection. God as husband and father of Israel demands obedience and monogamous love. He repays faithfulness with mercy and loving-kindness, but punishes waywardness, just as the wayward daughter can be stoned at her father's door (Deut. 22:21). When these family images are combined with political images of king and warrior, they reinforce a particular model of power and dominance. God is the power over us, the One out there over against us, the sovereign warrior with righteousness on his side. Family and political models of dominance and submission are recapitulated and rendered plausible by the dominance and submission of God and Israel. The silence and submission of women becomes part of a greater pattern that makes it appear fitting and right.

. . .

Clearly, the implications of Jewish feminism reach beyond the goal of equality to transform the bases of Jewish life. Feminism demands a new understanding of Torah, Israel, and God. It demands an understanding of Torah that begins by acknowledging the injustice of Torah and then goes on to create a Torah that is whole. The silence of women reverberates through the tradition, distorting the shape of narrative and skewing the content of the law. Only the deliberate recovery of women's hidden voices, the unearthing and invention of women's Torah, can give us Jewish teachings that are the product of the whole Jewish people and that reflect more fully its experiences of God.

Feminism demands an understanding of Israel that includes the whole of Israel and thus allows women to speak and name our experience for ourselves. It demands we replace a normative male voice with a chorus of divergent voices, describing Jewish reality in different accents and tones. Feminism impels us to rethink issues of community and diversity, to explore the ways in which one people can acknowledge and celebrate the varied experiences of its members. What would it mean for women *as women* to be equal participants in the Jewish community? How can we talk about difference without creating Others?

Feminism demands new ways of talking about God that reflect and grow out of the redefinition of Jewish humanity. The exclusively male naming of God supported and was rendered meaningful by a cultural and religious situation that is passing away.

The emergence of women allows and necessitates that the long-suppressed femaleness of God be recovered and explored and reintegrated into the Godhead. But feminism presses us beyond the issue of gender to examine the nature of the God with male names. How can we move beyond images of domination to a God present *in* community rather than over it? How can we forge a God-language that expresses women's experience?

READING 89

Everywoman Her Own Theology

Alicia Ostriker

I am nailing them up to the cathedral door
Like Martin Luther. Actually, no,
I don't want to resemble that *Schmutzkopf*
(See Erik Erikson and N. O. Brown
On the Reformer's anal aberrations,
Not to mention his hatred of Jews and peasants),
So I am thumbtacking these ninety-five
Theses to the bulletin board in my kitchen.

My proposals, or should I say requirements,
Include at least one image of a god,
Virile, beard optional, one of a goddess,
Nubile, breast size approximating mine,
One divine baby, one lion, one lamb,
All nude as figs, all dancing wildly,
All shining. Reproducible
In marble, metal, in fact any material.

Ethically, I am looking for
An absolute endorsement of loving-kindness.
No loopholes except maybe mosquitoes.
Virtue and sin will henceforth be discouraged,
Along with suffering and martyrdom.
There will be no concept of infidels;
Consequently the faithful must entertain
Themselves some other way than killing infidels.

And so forth and so on. I understand
This piece of paper is going to be
Spattered with wine one night at a party
And covered over with newer pieces of paper.
That is how it goes with bulletin boards.
Nevertheless it will be there.
Like an invitation, like a chalk pentangle,
It will emanate certain occult vibrations.

If something sacred wants to swoop from the
            universe
Through a ceiling, and materialize,
Folding its silver wings,
In a kitchen, and bump its chest against mine,
My paper will tell this being where to find me.

READING 90

Witchcraft and Women's Culture

Starhawk

From earliest times, women have been witches, *wicce*, "wise ones"—priestesses, diviners, midwives, poets, healers, and singers of songs of power. Woman-centered culture, based on the worship of the Great Goddess, underlies the beginnings of all civilization. Mother Goddess was carved on the walls of paleolithic caves, and painted in the shrines of the earliest cities, those of the Anatolian plateau. For her were raised the giant stone circles, the henges of the British Isles, the dolmens and cromlechs of the later Celtic countries, and for her the great passage graves of Ireland were dug. In her honor, sacred dancers leaped the bulls in Crete and composed lyric hymns within the colleges of the holy isles of the Mediterranean. Her mysteries were celebrated in secret rites at Eleusis, and her initiates included some of the finest minds of Greece. Her priestesses discovered and tested the healing herbs and learned the secrets of the human mind and body that allowed them to ease the pain of childbirth, to heal wounds and cure diseases, and to explore the realm of dreams and the unconscious. Their knowledge of nature enabled them to tame sheep and cattle, to breed wheat and corn from grasses and weeds, to forge ceramics from mud and metal from rock, and to track the movements of moon, stars, and sun.

Witchcraft, "the craft of the wise," is the last remnant in the west of the time of women's strength and power. Through the dark ages of persecution, the covens of Europe preserved what is left of the mythology, rituals, and knowledge of the ancient matricentric (mother-centered) times. The great centers of worship in Anatolia, Malta, Iberia, Brittany, and Sumeria are now only silent stones and works of art we can but dimly understand. Of the mysteries of Eleusis, we have literary hints; the poems of Sappho survive only in fragments. The great collections of early literature and science were destroyed by patriarchal forces—the library of Alexandria burnt by Caesar, Charlemagne's collection of lore burnt by his son Louis "the Pious," who was offended at its "paganism." But the craft remains, in spite of all efforts to stamp it out, as a living tradition of Goddess-centered worship that traces its roots back to the time before the triumph of patriarchy.

The old religion of witchcraft before the advent of Christianity was an earth-centered, nature-oriented worship that venerated the Goddess, the source of life, as well as her son-lover-consort, who was seen as the Horned God of the hunt and animal life. Earth, air, water, fire, streams, seas, wells, beasts, trees, grain, the planets, sun, and most of all, the moon, were seen as aspects of deity. On the great seasonal festivals—the solstices and equinoxes, and the eves of May, August, November, and February,—all the countryside would gather to light huge bonfires, feast, dance, sing, and perform the rituals that assured abundance throughout the year.

When Christianity first began to spread, the country people held to the old ways, and for hundreds of years the two faiths coexisted quite peacefully. Many people followed both religions, and country priests in the twelfth and thirteenth centuries were frequently upbraided by church authorities for dressing in skins and leading the dance at the pagan festivals.

But in the thirteenth and fourteenth centuries, the church began persecution of witches, as well as Jews and "heretical" thinkers. Pope Innocent the VIII, with his Bull of 1484, intensified a campaign of torture and death that would take the lives of an estimated 9 million people, perhaps 80 percent of whom were women.

The vast majority of victims were not coven members or even necessarily witches. They were old widows whose property was coveted by someone else, young children with "witch blood," midwives who furnished the major competition to the male-dominated medical profession, free-thinkers who asked the wrong questions.

An enormous campaign of propaganda accompanied the witch trials as well. Witches were said to have sold their souls to the devil, to practice obscene and disgusting rites, to blight crops and murder children. In many areas, the witches did worship a Horned God as the spirit of the hunt, of animal life and vitality, a concept far from the power of evil that was the Christian devil. Witches were free and open about sexuality—but their rites were "obscene" only to those who viewed the human body itself as filthy and evil. Questioning or disbelieving any of the slander was itself considered proof of witchcraft or heresy, and the falsehoods that for hundreds of years could not be openly challenged had their effect. Even today, the word *witch* is often automatically associated with "evil."

With the age of reason in the eighteenth century, belief in witches, as in all things psychic and supernatural, began to fade. The craft as a religion was forgotten; all that remained were the wild stories of broomstick flights, magic potions, and the summoning of spectral beings.

Memory of the true craft faded everywhere except within the hidden covens. With it, went the memory of women's heritage and history, of our ancient roles as leaders, teachers, healers, seers. Lost, also, was the conception of the Great Spirit, as manifest in nature, in life, in woman. Mother Goddess slept, leaving the world to the less than gentle rule of the God-Father.

The Goddess has at last stirred from sleep, and women are reawakening to our ancient power. The feminist movement, which began as a political, economic, and social struggle, is opening to a spiritual dimension. In the process, many women are discovering the old religion, reclaiming the word *witch* and, with it, some of our lost culture.

Witchcraft, today, is a kaleidoscope of diverse traditions, rituals, theologies, and structures. But underneath the varying forms is a basic orientation common to all the craft. The outer forms of religion—the particular words said, the signs made, the names used—are less important to us than the inner forms, which cannot be defined or described but must be felt and intuited.

The craft is earth religion, and our basic orientation is to the earth, to life, to nature. There is no dichotomy between spirit and flesh, no split between Godhead and the world. The Goddess is manifest in the world; she brings life into being, *is* nature, *is* flesh. Union is not sought outside the world in some heavenly sphere or through dissolution of the self into the void beyond the senses. Spiritual union is found in life, within nature, passion, sensuality—through being fully human, fully one's self.

Our great symbol for the Goddess is the moon, whose three aspects reflect the three stages in women's lives and whose cycles of waxing and waning coincide with women's menstrual cycles. As the new moon or crescent, she is the Maiden, the Virgin—not chaste, but belonging to herself alone, not bound to any man. She is the wild child, lady of the woods, the huntress, free and untamed—Artemis, Kore, Aradia, Nimue. White is her color. As the full moon, she is the mature woman, the sexual being, the mother and nurturer, giver of life, fertility, grain, offspring, potency, joy—Tana, Demeter, Diana, Ceres, Mari. Her colors are the red of blood and the green of growth. As waning or dark moon, she is the old woman, past menopause, the hag or crone that is ripe with wisdom, patroness of secrets, prophecy, divination, inspiration, power—Hecate, Ceridwen, Kali, Anna. Her color is the black of night.

The Goddess is also earth—Mother Earth, who sustains all growing things, who is the body, our bones and cells. She is air—the winds that move in the trees and over the waves, breath. She is the fire of the hearth, of the blazing bonfire and the fuming volcano; the power of transformation and change. And she is water—the sea, original source of life; the rivers, streams, lakes and wells; the blood that flows in the rivers of our veins. She is mare, cow, cat, owl, crane, flower, tree, apple, seed, lion, sow, stone, woman. She is found in the world around us, in the cycles and seasons of nature, and in mind, body, spirit, and emotions within each of us. Thou art Goddess. I am Goddess. All that lives (and all that is, lives), all that serves life, is Goddess.

Because witches are oriented to earth and to life, we value spiritual qualities that I feel are especially important to women, who have for so long been conditioned to be passive, submissive and weak. The craft values independence, personal strength, *self*—not petty selfishness but that deep core of strength within that makes us each a unique child of the Goddess. The craft has no dogma to stifle thought, no set of doctrines that have to be believed. Where authority exists, within covens, it is always coupled with the freedom every covener has, to leave at any time. When self is valued—in ourselves—we can see that self is everywhere.

Passion and emotion—that give depth and color and meaning to human life—are also valued. Witches strive to be in touch with feelings, even if they are sometimes painful, because the joy and pleasure and ecstasy available to a fully alive person make it worth occasional suffering. So-called negative emotion—anger—is valued as well, as a sign that something is wrong and that action needs to be taken. Witches prefer to handle anger by taking action and making changes rather than by detaching ourselves from our feelings in order to reach some nebulous, "higher" state.

Most of all, the craft values love. The Goddess' only law is "Love unto all beings." But the love we value is not the airy flower power of the hippies or the formless, abstracted *agape* of the early Christians. It is passionate, sensual, personal love, *eros,* falling in love, mother-child love, the love of one unique human being for other individuals, with all their personal traits and idiosyncrasies. Love is not something that can be radiated out in solitary meditation—it manifests itself in relationships and interactions with other people. It is often said "You cannot be a witch alone"—because to be a witch is to be a lover, a lover of the Goddess, and a lover of other human beings.

READING 91

A Visit from Reverend Tileston

Elizabeth Cook-Lynn

Fifty miles from the nearest town of any size, deep in the Bend of the Missouri River where the Dakotapi had made history for generations, lived the Family: Father, a first-born son whose eyes bore the immutable and unspoken agony of his generation, handsome and strong, a cattleman not so much from choice as from necessity; Mother, a fine quill artist, small boned and stout, a woman with one crooked elbow caused by a childhood accident, a good cook, accomplished at the piano, guitar and harmonica, talents she had learned at the government boarding school; Uncle, the Mother's younger brother, a truck driver sometimes, a drunk increasingly often whenever those inexplicable waves of grief washed over him; Grandmother, Grandfather and five children ranging in ages from 3 to 15 years. Uncle's son often lived with the Family as did the Grandmother's half sister and her husband and their two granddaughters. The Family was part of a small community

which has reassembled itself at this place after the violent Diaspora and Displacement which was endured by this ancient tribe for several generations, the Family all the more closely knit because of this tragedy of recent history as well as the more practical problem of long distances to the few sparse surrounding towns settled a hundred years before by whites anxious to possess land and become rich. The year was 1935 and this was a place where strangers, though alien and undesirable, even called *to' ka,* were largely unthreatening and often ignored, and where strange events were witnessed with inexplicable but characteristic tolerance.

From the gravelled road which followed the course of the river, the small three-room frame house in which the Family now lived, built by the U.S. Government for Bureau of Indian Affairs employees in early reservation days and abandoned in later times, looked strangely remote and ageless. It seemed to stare listlessly toward the river's loop, and in winter its long-windowed eyes would be the first to catch a glimpse of the landing of the Canadian geese on the cold shores of the whitened, timeless river. It turned its back on the ludicrously inexpedient pyramid-shaped, steel-roofed ice-house which had once afforded Bureau employees from the East the luxury of iced drinks in the summer as they came to this blistering Dakotah prairie to work "in the Indian Service." The ice-house was abandoned now, also, too big and deep to be of any use to the Family except for the summer drying of the pounded meat and berry patties, *wasna,* which would be laid out upon its roof in the sun. During this drying process the children would be set to fanning the flies away with long willows, a task which held attention a surprisingly brief time. Bored, they would run off in pursuit of more imaginative pastimes only to be called back as soon as Grandmother discovered their absence.

Also at the rear of the house was a large tipi, the color of smoke at the top, streaked with rain, lined with cow hides, comfortable, shaded in late afternoon by the lone pine tree which was, itself, a stranger to the hot plains country of the Dakotah, itself a survivor of the days when Bureau employees lived there. The children imagined that the tree was brought there by a medicine man and was used in his cures but it was not a cedar, just a scraggly pine tree which had barely survived hard times. There was a tall hand pump set in the middle of the yard where Grandmother would kneel to wash the paunch during butchering times and also a corral set some distance away in the tall pasture grass at the foot of a small rise in the prairie landscape. A huge mound of earth covered a man-made cave which was complete with wooden steps and a slanting door which had to be picked up and drawn aside. A very large bull-snake often found refuge from the blistering sun under one of the wooden steps, stretching himself full length in the soft, cool black earth.

Just beyond the cave was the small white outdoor toilet, another survivor of former times, a product of imaginative Public Health Service officials who set about dotting Indian reservations with these white man's conveniences during the early part of the cen-

tury. Across the road from the house a gray stuccoed Catholic church, St. Anne's, sat with a closed, tight-lipped visage as though shielding itself from the violent summer prairie storms which came intermittently, pounding the gravel and the stucco, flattening the prairie grass. To the rear of the church lay the remains of the ancestors in a cemetery which, years later, was said to be occupied by a den of rattlesnakes.

In summer evenings, the air was often still and quiet, heavy with moisture. After a late meal, the quiet deepened. The only sound was Grandmother's soft footsteps as she went back and forth to the kitchen carrying dishes from the table. Her ankle length black dress hid her bowed legs and her head was covered, always, with a black scarf, her long white braids lying on her breast. Every now and then she stopped to wipe her smooth face with a white cloth, breathlessly.

"Grandmother, we should cook outside, tomorrow," said the Youngest Daughter, disheveled and hot, bearing a load too heavy for her to the kitchen.

The Mother simply sat, one arm outstretched on the table, the crooked one fanning her face and hair with a handkerchief. For her it had been a long day as she and her sister had spent the afternoon picking wild plums and buffalo berries along the river.

As the evening came on, the children could be heard outside running and chasing one another around the house and yard, trying to touch each other on the back, stretching away, laughing, now and again falling and crashing into the bushes near the pump. The dogs barked loudly. It was a game the boys never seemed to tire of even as the sun started to glow in the west and Uncle went outside to begin his nightly summer ritual of starting a smoke-fire, a smudge, to keep the mosquitoes away for the evening.

"*Hoksila kin tuktel un he?*" muttered Uncle as he looked around for one of his nephews to help him gather firewood. "He's never around when you need him."

"Go get some of that wood over there by the back porch," he directed his voice toward the hapless Youngest Daughter who wrinkled up her nose, but went, dutifully, to get the wood. Uncle bent down on one knee to place the sticks and dead leaves just right to produce a heavy smoke. He carefully touched a match to the soft underbrush and as the smoke rose he watched, one thumb hooked in his belt. In a few moments smoke filled the air and members of the Family began to gather for the evening.

They might even see man-being-carried in the sky, thought Uncle, and then he could tell a story if the children felt like listening and could stay awake long enough for the stars to show themselves clearly.

When he straightened up, he was surprised to see a small black sedan some distance down the road, making its way slowly toward them. He kept his eyes on the road to see if he could recognize in the dusk who its occupants were. He stepped up on the porch and lit a cigarette, the match illuminating the fine, delicate bones of his deeply pocked, scarred face.

Holding the match close for a moment, Uncle said, to no one in particular, "A car's coming."

Cars were rarely seen here on this country road this late in the evening.

As Uncle stood watching, he heard church music, faintly at first, and later, blaring, and he realized after a few long moments that it was coming from the loudspeaker positioned on top of the sedan.

"On-ward, Christian so-o-o-l-diers," sang the recorded voices of an entire church choir into the quiet evening light as the car came slowly into the river's bend, "with the cross of J-e-e-e-sus going on before."

Uncle stood with the cigarette in his mouth, his hands in his pockets as his brother-in-law came out of the house and sat down on the porch step with a cup of coffee. They watched the car approach and listened to the music, now blaring loud enough to get the attention of the children who stopped running and stood gazing at the strange-looking vehicle.

They stood, transfixed, as the car approached slowly and came to a stop. The loudspeaker fell silent as the driver of the sedan parked the car on the side of the road near the mailbox and, with great cheer, stepped from the car, waving and smiling. He was a man of about forty with a broad, freckled face. He was perspiring heavily and he made his way down the short path from the road to the house. Behind him came two women dressed in blue white-

flowered dresses, brown stockings and flat brown shoes; their faces, like pale round melons, were fixed with broad smiles. They all carried black leather-bound Bibles, the kind with red-tipped pages.

"Boy, it's hot!" said the fortyish freckled man as he held out his hand in greeting. The Father did not look at him nor did he get up. He put the cup to his lips and sipped coffee quietly, ignoring the intrusion with sullen indifference. Uncle kept his hands in his pockets and with his tongue he shifted his cigarette to the other side of his mouth.

Ignoring what was clearly a personal affront by the two men on the steps, the freckled man said, "Say, that's a good trash burning operation there," turning to the children standing beside the smudge. The children looked first at the smudge and then back at the perspiring man and, silently, they shook hands with him. Grasping the unwilling hand of the Youngest Daughter standing a few feet away, the man, in a loud voice asked, "Is your mommy home, honey?" Nearly overcome with embarrassment she said, "Yeh, she's in there," and gestured toward the door.

"Well," the man said as he turned and walked up the steps slowly, avoiding the Father and the Uncle still mutely positioned there, "we've come a long way with the message of hope and love we've got right here," and he patted the black leather-bound book he carried. As he tapped on the screen door, the Mother appeared and the freckled man quickly opened the door, stepped inside and held it open for the two smiling women who accompanied him to squeeze inside and in front of him.

"I'm Sister Bernice," began the plumper of the two women, "and this is Sister Kate . . . ?" Her voice trailed off as if she had asked a question. When there was no response, she turned to the freckled man and, putting her hand on his elbow she said, "And we're here with Reverend Tileston."

Taking a deep breath, the Reverend said to the Mother in his kindliest voice, "Ma-a'aam, we'd like to pray with you," and there in the middle of the room he knelt and began paging through his Bible, motioning for the women to join him as he knelt. His two companions quickly dropped to their knees and the plump one said to the Mother, "Please pray with us, sister," and the Mother, after a brief, uncertain moment, also knelt. Espying the Grandmother and her half sister peering at them curiously from the kitchen doorway, the Reverend quickly got up and led them to the middle of the room saying, "Come on with us, Granny, pray with us," and the two old women, too, with great effort, got to their knees. The Youngest Daughter, having followed the astonishing trio into the house, stood beside her Grandmother and looked expectantly at the perspiring freckled man as he fell to reading from the leather-bound book:

"With ALL our energy we ought to lead back ALL men to our most MER-ci-ful Re-DEEE-mer," he read. His voice rose:

"He is the Divine Conso-o-o-oler of the afflicted"; Youngest Daughter hung her head, copying the attitude of the visitors.

"To rulers and subjects alike He teaches lessons of true holiness,"
the Reverend sucked in air:

"unimpeachable justice and,"
he breathed again,

"generous charity."
The Reverend's voice seemed to fill the cramped little room and Sisters Bernice and Kate, eyes tightly closed, murmured "Amen" louder and louder with each breath the minister took.

Youngest Daughter glanced first at her Mother, then her Grandmothers who were kneeling shoulder to shoulder, faces impassive, eyes cast to the floor. Then, the Reverend closed the book, raised his arms and recited from memory, PROVERBS:

"Hear, O Children, a father's instruction," he shouted. "Be attentive, that you may gain understanding! Yea, excellent advice I give you; my teaching do not forsake."

One of the dogs, hunching itself close to the screen door, began to whine.

The Reverend continued to shout: "When I was my father's child, frail, yet the darling of my mother, he taught me, and said to me: 'Let your heart hold fast my words! Keep my commands, do not forget; go not astray from the words of my mouth.'"

His arms fell and his voice softened as he uttered the last phrase, opened his eyes and looked, unsee-

ing, at the little girl, his gaze moist and glittering. The dog's whine became more persistent, his tone now pitched higher to match the Reverend's and he began to push his nose against the screen door, causing it to squeak loudly.

The Reverend Tileston looked into the passive faces of the Mother and the Grandmothers and he said, "The beginning of wisdom is: get wisdom; at the cost of ALL-L-L-L you have," his arm swung dangerously close to the unfortunate dog who flattened his ears and pushed himself closer to the door.

"Get understanding," Reverend Tileston urged. "Forsake her not and she will preserve you; love her, and she will safeguard you; extol her, and she will exalt you; she will bring you honors if you embrace her; she will put on your head a graceful diadem; a glorious crown will she bestow upon you."

The words seemed to roll from his tongue and Youngest Daughter imagined shining crowns placed upon the heads of her Mother and her Grandmothers still kneeling stiffly and impassively. She was thrilled with the sound of the English words though she knew she didn't comprehend their meaning. It was like the time when Felix Middle Tent, the well-known Dakotah orator, made his speeches at the tribal council meeting she sometimes attended with her father, when he used his most eloquent and esoteric Dakotah vocabulary, oftentimes derisively referred to by Uncle as "jawbreakers."

As the Reverend's hefty arm again swept the room, the whining dog lurched backward and fell against a large pail of buffalo berries which Mother had left on the porch that late afternoon. Terrified, the dog leapt into the second pail of plums, scattering them wildly, then he dashed under the porch where he set up a mournful howl. The boys who had been listening at the side window fled into the bushes, laughing and screaming.

The Mother and Grandmothers, surprised and shocked at this turn of events but bent upon retrieving the day's pickings, swept past the astonished, speechless minister, shouting abuse at the now thoroughly miserable dog, and the screen door slammed behind them. Youngest Daughter was left looking into the disappointed faces of the Reverend and his companions. She smiled.

Forced by these circumstances to admit that the spiritual moment was lost, the Reverend Tileston got to his feet and ushered Sisters Bernice and Kate out of the house, carefully picking a path through the berries covering the porch. He was relieved that the Father and Uncle were nowhere to be seen and he turned at the last step and made a final effort, saying, "Meditate, Mothers, on the Scriptures, have knowledge of them for they are the food which sustains men during times of strife."

The women, engrossed in saving the berries, didn't hear him.

His final proselytical gesture, the attempted distribution of printed pamphlets, was also ignored.

Their composure now completely shattered, the trio which bore God's word into this obscure bend in the river found its way, falteringly, to the sedan, switched on the loudspeaker, and drove slowly away.

Youngest Daughter looked after them as they ventured deeper into the curve along the river and the faint echo of "With the Cross of Jee-e-sus . . . " rang in her ears. After a moment she went to find Uncle who would tell her a story about the star people and how the four blanket carriers once helped him find his way home from a long and difficult journey.

She hoped that the Reverend knew about the blanket carriers.

DISCUSSION QUESTIONS FOR CHAPTER TWELVE

1. Why do you think the control of women is a central component in many religions?

2. How do you think religion has been both empowering and oppressive for women?

3. How do you think the availability of a greater variety of images of God might impact religion and religion's influence on social life?

4. How might women work toward reform from within religious traditions? Why might some women feel the need to abandon religious traditions completely?

5. How have negative stereotypes of witchcraft served to perpetuate the oppression of women? Why do you think practices of women's spirituality were (and still are) perceived as such a threat?

6. How do nondominant religious traditions challenge the influence of hegemonic Christianity in U.S. society?

SUGGESTIONS FOR FURTHER READING

Christ, Carol, and Judith Plaskow, eds. *Womanspirit Rising: A Feminist Reader in Religion.* San Francisco: HarperCollins, 1992.

Gross, Rita M. *Feminism and Religion: An Introduction.* Boston: Beacon, 1996.

Isasi-Diaz, Ada Maria, and Yolanda Tarango. *Hispanic Women: Prophetic Voice in the Church.* San Francisco: Harper & Row, 1988.

King, Ursula, ed. *Women in the World's Religions: Past and Present.* New York: Paragon, 1987.

Mollenkott, Virginia. *Sensuous Spirituality: Out from Fundamentalism.* New York: Crossroad, 1992.

Reis, Elizabeth, ed. *Spellbound: Women and Witchcraft in America.* Wilmington, DE: Scholarly Resources, 1998.

Spretnak, Charlene. *The Politics of Women's Spirituality: Essays by Founding Mothers of the Movement.* New York: Anchor, 1982.

CHAPTER THIRTEEN

Activism, Change, and Feminist Futures

THE PROMISE OF FEMINIST EDUCATION

In Chapter 1 we discussed the objectives of women's studies as a discipline. These objectives include, first, an understanding of the social construction of gender and the intersection of gender with other systems of inequality in women's lives; second, a familiarity with women's status, contributions, and individual and collective actions for change; and third, an awareness of ways to improve women's status. A fourth objective of women's studies is that you will start thinking about patterns of privilege and discrimination in your own life and understand your position vis-à-vis systems of inequality. We hope you will learn to think critically about how societal institutions affect individual lives—especially your own. We hope you will gain new insights and confidence and that new knowledge will empower you.

Feminist educators attempt to give students more inclusive and socially just forms of knowledge and to support teachers using their power in nonexploitive ways. Women's studies usually involve nonhierarchical, egalitarian classrooms where teachers respect students and hope to learn from them as well as teach them. The focus is on the importance of the student voice and experience and encouraging both personal and social change. Most women's studies classes, however, are within colleges that do not necessarily share the same goals and objectives. Many feminist educators operate within the social and economic constraints of educational institutions that view "counter-hegemonic" education—that is, education that challenges the status quo—as problematic and/or subversive. Despite these constraints, feminist education, with its progressive and transformative possibilities, is an important feature on most campuses.

For many students, and perhaps for you too, the term *feminism* is still problematic. Many people object to the political biases associated with feminist education and believe knowledge should be objective and devoid of political values. It is important to emphasize that all knowledge is associated with power, as knowledge arises from communities with certain positions, resources, and understandings of the world. This means that all knowledge (and not just feminist knowledge) is ideological in that it is in some way associated with history and politics. To declare objectivity or value-neutrality is to mask the workings of power within knowledge. Although feminist education is more explicit than other forms of knowledge in speaking of its relationship to power in society, this does not mean it is more biased or ideological than other forms of knowledge. As civil rights activists declared, "If you're not part of the solution, then you're part of the problem." In other words, whether you are part of the problem or part of the solution (however you define problem and solution), you are equally political.

Many people support the justice-based goals of feminism but do not identify with the label. The reading by Lisa Maria Hogeland titled "Fear of Feminism: Why Young Women Get the Willies" addresses this issue. She also looks in depth at continuing resistance to feminism as politics and as a way of life. She makes the important distinction between *gender consciousness* and *feminist consciousness,* explains why one does not necessarily imply the other, and discusses the fear of reprisals and consequences associated with a feminist consciousness.

ACTIVISM

We live in a complex time. White women have made significant progress over the past decades and have begun the twenty-first century integrated into most societal institutions. Although the progress of women of color lags behind the gains made by White women, they too are beginning to be heard. Yet, the big picture is far from rosy, as society has not been transformed in its core values as feminists throughout the last century would have wanted. An equitable sharing of power and resources in terms of gender, race, class, and other differences has not been actualized. In addition, as women receive more public power, they are encouraged to internalize more private constraints concerning the body and sexuality.

These times at the turn of the century have been touted as prosperous even while the gap between the rich and the poor in the United States is the largest among industrialized nations and is increasing. Most people are working harder than ever so that they may enjoy this prosperity, and large numbers of people (especially non-White children) are living in poverty. Violence is increasing in our society in all walks of life; women, people of color, and gays and lesbians are frequently the target of hate and hostility; and the balance of power in the world seems fragile and in the hands of relatively few (often egocentric, delusional) men. Wars surround us. The picture is one of great optimism and yet simultaneous despair.

In the reading "Taking the High Road," Suzanne Pharr writes that violence, bigotry, and hatred are related in important ways to the alienation and disconnection felt by some people in contemporary society. She encourages us to address the rage, cynicism, and meanspiritedness of this historical moment and come up with a transformational politics that encourages a consciousness shift and extends generosity and compassion toward others. In other words, any movement for justice-based equalities must have a strong moral foundation based upon love and human dignity, and community.

As Audre Lorde, one of the most eloquent writers of the feminist second wave, once declared, "Silence will not protect you." Lorde wrote about the need to be part of social change efforts, and she encouraged us to speak out and address the problems in our lives and communities. And, as the reading by Michael Kimmel, "Real Men Join the Movement," implies, speaking out and addressing inequities involves learning how to be an ally to people who are different from you and who do not enjoy the privileges you enjoy. Kimmel emphasizes the necessity of men joining with women to make this world better for everyone. In this sense, coalitions are a central aspect of social change efforts.

In the past four decades there has been significant resistance to the status quo in U.S. society, despite enormous backlash from the conservative right and other groups. Response to this backlash is the focus of Ruth Rosen's article in the readings, "Epilogue: Beyond Backlash." The strength of justice-based resistance has been its multiissue and multistrategic approach. *Multiissue* means organizing on many fronts over a variety of different issues that include political, legal, and judicial changes; educational reform; welfare rights; eliminating

SIZE DOES MATTER AND
▇ NINE OTHER TIPS FOR EFFECTIVE PROTEST

- *Size does matter.* The most memorable protests—and the ones the media tends to cover—are the big ones: Think of the 1968 March on Washington and the Million Man March in 1995. The best way to put masses of people on the streets? Forge coalitions in order to broaden your base of potential protesters.
- *Get organized.* A large crowd is not, ipso facto, an effective performance. In November 1997, the Disney/Haiti Justice Campaign pulled together a sizable number of protesters outside the Disney Store in Times Square to denounce the company's Haitian sweatshops, but organizers failed to start a picket line or lead energetic chants. Many in the crowd simply milled around with their hands in their pockets or sipping coffee.
- *Location, location, location.* Many large, well-organized protests happen outside corporate headquarters or foreign consulates. Unfortunately, those tend to be on side streets with little pedestrian traffic and no adjoining public spaces. Simply relocating the event to a busy nearby corner can increase the audience tenfold.
- *Distinguish yourself.* In December 1997, the East Timor Action Network marched up Madison Avenue to the Indonesian Consulate to protest the occupation of East Timor. Only a few carried signs; the rest were indistinguishable from other pedestrians on the crowded street. Solution? Form a picket line or sit down en masse on the busy sidewalk.
- *Get the crowd involved.* Successful protests encourage audience participation—appearing exclusive is a sure way to alienate onlookers from your cause. At a 1997 World AIDS Day vigil in New York, for example, organizers handed out chalk to passersby and asked them to write on a nearby fountain the names of loved ones who had died of AIDS.
- *Put it down on paper.* A simple, clearly written leaflet that explains who is protesting, why, and how to get involved is crucial. Sure, it may end up in the nearest trash can, but some people will read it, and a few might show up at the next event.
- *Manage the media.* Of course, the biggest prize for any protest is media coverage. Inform local newspapers and TV and radio stations (not just "progressive" media) a few days in advance.
- *Above all, be spectacular.* Eye-catching costumes, a sea of candles in a dark plaza, limp bodies being carried from a street to a police van—these telegenic images make for good press. At an August 1997 march prompted by the police beating of Haitian immigrant Abner Louima, many waved toilet plungers—the tool with which Louima was allegedly beaten and sodomized—transforming an ordinary object into an unforgettable symbol of violent racism.
- *Meteorology matters.* A wet and cold protester is usually a demoralized one. Plan for foul weather by establishing an alternative day; if timing is critical, find a nearby indoor or protected space to which protesters can retreat. To be sure, there are exceptions: A dedicated group braving the elements can convey a profound sense of commitment to a cause—assuming, of course, that someone's watching.
- *Use protest to beget protest.* Any single march or demonstration should be one link in a larger chain. Most political movements, after all, must endure for years to attain their goals. So think about the morning after: How can the momentum generated (if any) be maintained? How soon is too soon for the next protest? What worked, what

didn't? Protests should be carefully crafted performances designed to be unforgettable and moving for audiences and participants alike. Only meaningful and memorable protests can effectively challenge people to think differently and motivate still further protest in the days and years ahead.

Source: Jeff Goodwin, *Mother Jones*, March/April 1990.

violence; reproductive issues; and workplace reform. *Multistrategic* means relying on working coalitions that mobilize around certain shared issues and involve different strategies toward a shared goal.

As discussed in Chapter 1, some liberal or moderate activists have worked within the system and advocated change from within. Their approach locates the source of inequality in barriers to inclusion and advancement and has worked to change women's working lives through comparable worth, sexual harassment policy, and parenting leaves. Legal attacks on abortion rights have been deflected by the work of liberal feminists working within the courts, and affirmative action and other civil rights legislation have similarly been the focus of scholars, activists, and politicians working in the public sphere. These organizations tend to be hierarchical with a centralized governing structure (president, advisory board, officers, and so forth) and local chapters around the country. Other strategies for change take a more radical approach (for example, radical or cultural feminism) and attempt to *transform* the system rather than to adapt the existing system. Together these various strategies work to advocate justice-based forms of equality.

Although differences in strategy are sometimes a source of divisiveness among activists and feminists, they are also a source of strength in being able to work on multiple issues from multiple approaches. Indeed, any given issue lends itself to both reformist and radical approaches. Lesbian and gay rights, for example, is something that can be tackled in the courts and in the voting booths as organizations work toward legislation to create domestic partner legislation or community civil protections. At the same time, consciousness-raising activities and grassroots demonstrations, such as candlelight vigils for victims of hate crimes and Queer Pride parades, work on the local level. As the reading by Marj Schneider on the movement for disability rights, "From Personal Tragedy to Group Consciousness," explains, change occurs as a result of group consciousness that challenges old ways of thinking as well

■ LEARNING ACTIVITY: FEMINIST.COM

Visit the website of feminist.com at *www.feminist.com* and follow the link to the activism page. There you'll find links to action alerts and legislative updates for a number of feminist organizations, including the National Organization for Women (NOW), Sisterhood Is Global, Women Organizing for Change, and Planned Parenthood. Follow these links to learn what actions you can take. The website also offers links to government resources and voter education and other activist resources.

IDEAS FOR ACTIVISM

- Organize an activism awareness educational event on your campus. Invite local activists to speak about their activism. Provide opportunities for students to volunteer for a wide variety of projects in your area.
- Find out about your school's recycling program. If there's not one in place, advocate with administrators to begin one. If one is in place, try to find ways to help it function more effectively and to encourage more participation in recycling. If recycling services are not provided in your local community, advocate with city and county officials to begin providing these services.
- Find out what the major environmental issues are in your state and what legislative steps need to be taken to address these concerns. Then organize a letter-writing campaign to encourage legislators to enact laws protecting the environment.
- Identify a major polluter in your community and organize a nonviolent protest outside that business demanding environmental reforms.
- Sponsor a workshop on conflict management and nonviolence for campus and community members.

as laws and institutional reforms (such as the Americans with Disabilities Act). Together, the different strategies improve the quality of life.

One important aspect to consider is that simply increasing women's participation and leadership does not necessarily imply a more egalitarian or feminist future. As you know, there are women and people of color who are opposed to strategies for improving the general well-being of disenfranchised peoples. Changing the personnel—replacing men with women, for example—does not necessarily secure a different kind of future. Although in practice liberal feminism is more sophisticated than, for example, simply considering female candidates merely because they are women, it has been criticized for promoting women into positions of power and authority irrespective of their stance on the social relations of gender, race, class, and other differences.

Contemporary feminism is concerned with issues that are increasingly global. These concerns have resulted in the sponsorship of numerous international conferences and have promoted education about women's issues all over the world. And, as communication technologies have advanced, the difficulties of global organization have lessened. International feminist groups have worked against militarism, global capitalism, and racism, as well as supporting issues identified by indigenous women around the world. This activism culminated in 1995 with the United Nations Fourth World Conference on Women held in Beijing, China (the first conference was held in Mexico City in 1975, the second in Copenhagen in 1980, and the third in Nairobi in 1985). More than 30,000 women attended the Beijing conference and helped create the internationally endorsed Platform for Action. This platform is a call for concrete action involving human rights of women and girls as part of universal human rights, the eradication of poverty of women, the removal of obstacles to women's full participation in public life and decision making, the elimination of all forms of violence against women, the assurance of women's access to educational and health services, and actions to promote women's economic autonomy. The text of the Platform for Action is included in the readings and also discussed in the reading by Ruth Rosen.

UN MILLENNIUM DEVELOPMENT GOALS

1. Eradicate extreme poverty and hunger
   - Reduce by half the proportion of people living on less than a dollar a day
   - Reduce by half the proportion of people who suffer from hunger

2. Achieve universal primary education
   - Ensure that all boys and girls complete a full course of primary schooling

3. Promote gender equality and empower women
   - Eliminate gender disparity in primary and secondary education preferably by 2005, and at all levels by 2015

4. Reduce child mortality
   - Reduce by two thirds the mortality rate among children under five

5. Improve maternal health
   - Reduce by three quarters the maternal mortality ratio

6. Combat HIV/AIDS, malaria and other diseases
   - Halt and begin to reverse the spread of HIV/AIDS
   - Halt and begin to reverse the incidence of malaria and other major diseases

7. Ensure environmental sustainability
   - Integrate the principles of sustainable development into country policies and programmes; reverse loss of environmental resources
   - Reduce by half the proportion of people without sustainable access to safe drinking water
   - Achieve significant improvement in lives of at least 100 million slum dwellers, by 2020

8. Develop a global partnership for development
   - Develop further an open trading and financial system that is rule-based, predictable and non-discriminatory. Includes a commitment to good governance, development and poverty reduction—nationally and internationally
   - Address the least developed countries' special needs. This includes tariff- and quota-free access for their exports; enhanced debt relief for heavily indebted poor countries; cancellation of official bilateral debt; and more generous official development assistance for countries committed to poverty reduction
   - Address the special needs of landlocked and small island developing States
   - Deal comprehensively with developing countries' debt problems through national and international measures to make debt sustainable in the long term
   - In cooperation with the developing countries, develop decent and productive work for youth
   - In cooperation with pharmaceutical companies, provide access to affordable essential drugs in developing countries
   - In cooperation with the private sector, make available the benefits of new technologies—especially information and communications technologies

By the year 2015 all 189 United Nations Member States have pledged to meet the above goals.

Source: http://www.un.org/millenniumgoals/index.html.

ACTIVIST PROFILE: INDIGO GIRLS, EMILY SALIERS AND AMY RAY

In many ways Indigo Girls Emily Saliers and Amy Ray exemplify contemporary feminist activism. With a comprehensive understanding of injustice and a commitment to work for equality on all fronts, Saliers and Ray have consciously worked to make a difference in the world, using their status as rock stars to advocate for the world's disadvantaged.

The duo started playing together in high school as the B Band and then Saliers and Ray, becoming Indigo Girls in 1985 while at Emory University in Atlanta. They were signed by Epic Records in 1988 and released their self-titled album to critical acclaim. By September 1989, the album had gone gold, and Indigo Girls was nominated for a Grammy as Best New Artist and won a Grammy for the Best Contemporary Folk Recording of 1989. Since then, Indigo Girls has released eight albums. They have sold over 7 million albums worldwide, including one double platinum disc, three platinum, and four gold, and have earned six Grammy nominations.

Beyond their talent as musicians, Saliers and Ray stand out because of their integrity and the way they have lived their convictions. Although many of their songs deal with relationships and heartbreak, many also deal with political issues such as poverty, homelessness, discrimination, and homophobia. More importantly, Saliers and Ray have used their wealth and influence to bring about change in the music industry and in the world at large. In 1990, in appreciation for the help provided to Indigo Girls by other Atlanta and Athens musicians, Ray founded Daemon Records, an independent label focusing on Atlanta-area bands. Indigo Girls has participated in three Lilith Fair concert series (initiated by musician Sarah McLachlan to highlight women musicians), and in 1998 they started the Suffragette Sessions Tour, described by Ray as "a socialist experiment in rock and roll—no hierarchy, no boundaries."

In 1995 and 1997, Indigo Girls headlined a series of concerts called Honor the Earth to benefit indigenous activists. They have also been involved in supporting a number of other justice causes such as Greenpeace; the Zapatistas in Chiapas, Mexico; and AIDS research.

In 1994, both Ray and Saliers openly acknowledged their sexuality. In 1999, five high schools in South Carolina and Tennessee canceled scheduled Indigo Girls concerts. But the shows were rebooked in clubs, and the students came anyway.

The activism of Indigo Girls Amy Ray and Emily Saliers offers a powerful model for feminist activism. Recognizing the adage "injustice anywhere is a threat to justice everywhere," Ray and Saliers practice a multifaceted activism, challenging oppression wherever it is found. As their song "Hammer and a Nail" states, "Now I know a refuge never grows from a chin in a hand in a thoughtful pose, gotta tend the earth if you want a rose."

FUTURE VISIONS

How might the future look? How will our knowledge of gender, race, and class-based inequalities be used? Does our future hold the promise of prosperity and peace or economic unrest and increased militarization? Will technology save us or quicken our destruction? Will feminist values be a part of future social transformation? Jennifer Baumgardner and Amy Richards imagine such a feminist future. Chapter 1 started out with their essay "A Day without Feminism"; now we can explore what their idea of "A Day with Feminism" looks like. Many who write about the future also emphasize that future visions are metaphors for the present; we anticipate the future in light of how we make sense of the present and have come to understand the past. This approach encourages us to look at the present mindfully, so that we are aware of its politics, and creatively, so that we can see the possibility for change. In her playful poem "Warning," Jenny Joseph looks to the future to offer some guidance in the present.

There are some social trends that have implications for the future. Given the higher fertility rates among the non-White population as well as immigration figures, Whites will eventually become a relatively smaller percentage of the population until they are no longer a majority in the United States. In addition, the rise in births between 1946 and 1960 (the baby boomer cohort) and the decline through the 1970s will mean a large percentage of the population will be over 65 years old within the next couple of decades. The 2000 Census suggests that by 2030 there will be about 70 million older persons (65 years and older), more than twice their number in 1999 and reaching approximately 20 percent of the population. Currently, persons 65 years and older represent about 13 percent of the population. And, although some people have always lived to be 80, 90, and 100 years old, this number will grow in response to better nutrition and health care among certain segments of the population. As the baby boomers age, they will create stress on medical and social systems. They might also influence family systems as several generations of aged family members could require care at the same time. This is complicated by the fact that families are becoming

■ PRINCIPLES OF ENVIRONMENTAL JUSTICE

1. Environmental justice affirms the sacredness of Mother Earth, ecological unity and the interdependence of all species, and the right to be free from eclogical destruction.
2. Environmental justice demands that public policy be based on mutual respect and justice for all peoples, free from any form of discrimination or bias.
3. Environmental justice mandates the right to ethical, balanced, and responsible uses of land and renewable resources in the interest of a sustainable planet for humans and other living things.
4. Environmental justice calls for universal protection from nuclear testing, extraction, production and disposal of toxic/hazardous wastes and poisons that threaten the fundamental right to clean air, land, water, and food.
5. Environmental justice affirms the fundamental right to political, economic, cultural, and environmental self-determination of all peoples.
6. Environmental justice demands the cessation of the production of all toxins, hazardous wastes, and radioactive materials, and that all past and current producers be held strictly accountable to the people for detoxification and containment at the point of production.
7. Environmental justice demands the right to participate as equal partners at every level of decision making, including needs assessment, planning, implementation, enforcement, and evaluation.
8. Environmental justice affirms the right of all workers to a safe and healthy work environment, without being forced to choose between an unsafe livelihood and unemployment. It also affirms the right of those who work at home to be free from environmental hazards.
9. Environmental justice protects the right of victims of environmental injustice to receive full compensation and reparations for damages as well as quality health care.
10. Environmental justice considers governmental acts of environmental injustice a violation of international law, the Universal Declaration on Human Rights, and the United Nations Convention on Genocide.
11. Environmental justice must recognize a special legal and natural relationship of Native Peoples to the U.S.government through treaties, agreements, compacts, and covenants affirming sovereignty and self-determination.
12. Environmental justice affirms the need for urban and rural ecological policies to clean up and rebuild our cities and rural areas in balance with nature, honoring the cultural integrity of all our communities, and providing fair access for all to the full range of resources.
13. Environmental justice calls for the strict enforcement of principles of informed consent and a halt to the testing of experimental reproductive and medical procedures and vaccinations on people of color.
14. Environmental justice opposes the destructive operations of multinational corporations.
15. Environmental justice opposes military occupation; repression and exploitation of lands, peoples and cultures, and other life forms.

16. Environmental justice calls for the education of present and future generations that emphasizes social and environmental issues, based on our experience and an appreciation of our diverse cultural perspectives.
17. Environmental justice requires that we, as individuals, make personal and consumer choices to consume as little of Mother Earth's resources and to produce as little waste as possible; and make the conscious decision to challenge and reprioritize our lifestyles to ensure the health of the natural world for present and future generations.

Source: People of Color Environmental Leadership Summit, 1991. *www.umich.edu/˜jrazer/nre/whatis.html.*

smaller, and divorce and remarriage rates will probably continue at current rates. Ties between stepfamilies and other nonfamilial ties are most likely going to become more important in terms of care and support.

In our society where the profit motive runs much of our everyday lives, where citizens have lost respect for political and governmental institutions, and where people are working longer hours and becoming more disconnected from families and communities, the issue of integrity is something to consider. The definition of integrity is two part: one, a moral positioning about the distinction between right and wrong, and two, a consistent stance on this morality such that we act out what we believe and attempt to live our ideals. "Do as I say and not as I do" is an example of the very opposite of integrity. What might it mean to live with feminist-inspired integrity as well as envision a future where feminist integrity is central? We'll discuss seven implications here.

First, it is important to set feminist priorities and keep them. In a society where sound bytes and multiple, fragmented pieces of information vie to be legitimate sources of knowledge, we must recognize that some things are more important than others. Priorities are essential. Postmodernism might have deconstructed notions of truth to the point where some argue that there is no such thing as the truth; yet, some things are truer than others. Figure out your truths and priorities based upon your own values, politics, and/or religion.

Second, it is important that we live and envision a society that balances personal freedom and identity with public and collective responsibility. Suzanne Pharr writes about this in "Taking the High Road" when she says that transformational politics calls for living with communal values by which we learn how to honor the needs of the individual as well as the group. The United States is a culture that values individualism very highly and often forgets that although the Constitution says you have the right to do something, I also have the right to criticize you for it. Similarly, we must question the limitations associated with certain rights. Is your right still a right if it violates my rights or hurts a community? And, just because the Constitution says something is your right, that does not necessarily make that act a moral choice. Although the Constitution exists to protect choices and rights, it does not tell us which choices and rights are best.

Third, recognize that corporate capitalism does not function in everybody's interests. In this sense, *economic* democracy must not be confused with *political* democracy. Many of us have learned that capitalist societies are synonymous with democracies and that other economic systems are somehow undemocratic in principle. We live in a society that attempts a political democracy at the same time that economic democracy, or financial equity

WOMEN WORKING FOR PEACE

The International Peace Bureau (IPB) is the world's oldest and most comprehensive international peace federation. Founded in 1892, the organization won the Nobel Peace Prize in 1910. Its role is to support peace and disarmament initiatives. Current priorities include the abolition of nuclear weapons, conflict prevention and resolution, human rights, and women and peace. To learn more about the IPB, visit the website at *www.ipb.org.*

The Women's International League for Peace and Freedom (WILPF), founded in 1915 to protest the war in Europe, suggests ways to end war and to prevent war in the future; as well, it seeks to educate and mobilize women for action. The goals of the WILPF are political solutions to international conflicts, disarmament, promotion of women to full and equal participation in all society's activities, economic and social justice within and among states, elimination of racism and all forms of discrimination and exploitation, respect of fundamental human rights, and the right to development in a sustainable environment. For more information, including action alerts and readings, visit the WILPF homepage at*www.wilpf.org.*

FEMALE NOBEL PEACE LAUREATES

Ten women have been honored with the Nobel Peace Prize for their work for justice. They are:

Baroness Bertha Von Suttner (1905) Austrian honored for her writing and work opposing war.

Jane Addams (1931) International President, Women's International League for Peace and Freedom.

Emily Greene Balch (1946) Honored for her pacifism and work for peace through a variety of organizations.

Betty Williams and Mairead Corrigan (1976) Founders of the Northern Ireland Peace Movement to bring together Protestants and Catholics to work for peace together.

Mother Teresa (1979) Honored for her "work in bringing help to suffering humanity" and her respect for individual human dignity.

Alva Myrdal (1982) Honored with Alfonso Garcia Robles for their work with the United Nations on disarmament.

Aung San Suu Kyi (1991) Burmese activist honored for nonviolent work for human rights in working for independence in Myanmar.

Rigoberta Menchú Tum (1992) Honored for her work for "ethno-cultural reconciliation based on respect for the rights of indigenous peoples."

Jody Williams (1997) Honored for her work with the International Campaign to Ban Landmines.

Source: http://womenshistory.about.com/education/womenshistory/msubnobelpeace.htm.

for all peoples, is limited. Unfortunately, capitalism has had deleterious effects on both physical and human environments, and consumerism has changed families and communities by encouraging people to accumulate material possessions beyond their immediate needs. Perhaps a motto for the future might be "pack lightly."

Fourth, a present and future with a core value of feminist integrity is one that understands the limitations of technology as well as its liberating aspects. This means being in control of technology so that it is used ethically and productively. This is related to the previous point about capitalist expansion. Corporations have invested heavily in new technologies that do not always work for the collective good.

Fifth, feminist integrity requires advocating a sustainable physical environment. There is only one world and we share it; there is an interdependence of all species. Given this, it makes no sense to destroy our home through such behaviors as global climate change, environmental pollution, and species eradication. Sustainable environmental practices start with addressing issues associated with capitalist global expansion and technological development, as discussed previously. Also associated is the need for environmental justice because the poor and communities of color have suffered disproportionately in terms of environmental pollution and degradation. Environmental justice calls for protection from nuclear testing, extraction, production, and disposal of toxic and hazardous wastes and poisons that threaten the fundamental right to clean air, land, water, and food. It also demands that workers have the right to safe and healthy work environments without being forced to choose between unsafe livelihood and unemployment.

Sixth, a peaceful and sustainable future is one that respects human dignity, celebrates difference and diversity, and yet recognizes that diversity does not necessarily imply equality. It is not enough to be tolerant of the differences among us, although that would be a good start; it is necessary to recognize everyone's right to a piece of the pie and work toward equality of outcome and not just equality of access. We believe we must create social movements that derive from an ethic of caring, empathy, and compassion.

Seventh and finally, we believe it is important to have a sense of humor and to take the time to play and celebrate. As socialist labor reformer Emma Goldman once said, "If I can't dance, I don't want to be part of your revolution."

A justice-based politics of integrity embraces equality for all peoples. It is an ethic that has the potential to help create a peaceful and sustainable future, improving the quality of our lives and the future of our planet. An ethic that respects and values all forms of life and seeks ways to distribute resources equitably is one that moves away from dominance and uses peaceful solutions to environmental, societal, and global problems. As a blueprint for the future, a focus on justice and equality has much to offer. As Rosen writes in the reading "Epilogue: Beyond Backlash," in her reference to the movement for women's human rights, the struggle has begun and there is no end in sight!

READING 92

Fear of Feminism
Why Young Women Get the Willies

Lisa Maria Hogeland

I began thinking about young women's fear of feminism, as I always do in the fall, while I prepared to begin another year of teaching courses in English and women's studies. I was further prodded when former students of mine, now graduate students elsewhere and teaching for the first time, phoned in to complain about their young women students' resistance to feminism. It occurred to me that my response—"Of course young women are afraid of feminism"—was not especially helpful. This essay is an attempt to trace out what that "of course" really means; much of it is based on my experience with college students, but many of the observations apply to other young women as well.

Some people may argue that young women have far less to lose by becoming feminists than do older women: they have a smaller stake in the system and fewer ties to it. At the same time, though, young women today have been profoundly affected by the demonization of feminism during the 12 years of Reagan and Bush—the time when they formed their understanding of political possibility and public life. Older women may see the backlash as temporary and changeable; younger women may see it as how things are. The economic situation for college students worsened over those 12 years as well, with less student aid available, so that young women may experience their situation as extremely precarious—too precarious to risk feminism.

My young women students often interpret critiques of marriage—a staple of feminist analysis for centuries—as evidence of their authors' dysfunctional families. This demonstrates another reality they have grown up with: the increased tendency to pathologize any kind of oppositional politics. Twelve years of the rhetoric of "special interests versus family values" have created a climate in which passionate political commitments seem crazy. In this climate, the logical reasons why all women fear feminism take on particular meaning and importance for young women.

To understand what women fear when they fear feminism—and what they don't—it is helpful to draw a distinction between gender consciousness and feminist consciousness. One measure of feminism's success over the past three decades is that women's gender consciousness—our self-awareness as women—is extremely high. Gender consciousness takes two forms: awareness of women's vulnerability and celebration of women's difference. Fear of crime is at an all-time high in the United States; one of the driving forces behind this fear may well be women's sense of special vulnerability to the epidemic of men's violence. Feminists have fostered this awareness of violence against women, and it is to our credit that we have made our analysis so powerful; at the same time, however, we must attend to ways this awareness can be deployed for nonfeminist and even antifeminist purposes, and most especially to ways it can be used to serve a racist agenda. Feminists have also fostered an awareness of women's difference from men and made it possible for women (including nonfeminists) to have an appreciation of things pertaining to women—perhaps most visibly the kinds of "women's culture" commodified in the mass media (soap operas and romance, self-help books, talk shows, and the like). Our public culture in the U.S. presents myriad opportunities for women to take pleasure in being women—most often, however, that pleasure is used as an advertising or marketing strategy.

Gender consciousness is a necessary precondition for feminist consciousness, but they are not the same. The difference lies in the link between gender and politics. Feminism politicizes gender consciousness, inserts it into a systematic analysis of histories and structures of domination and privilege. Feminism asks questions—difficult and complicated questions, often with contradictory and confusing answers—about how gender consciousness can be used both for and against women, how vulnerability and difference help and hinder women's self-determination and freedom. Fear of feminism, then, is not a fear of gender, but rather a fear of politics. Fear of politics can be understood as a fear of living in consequences, a fear of reprisals.

The fear of political reprisals is very realistic. There are powerful interests opposed to feminism—let's be clear about that. It is not in the interests of white supremacy that white women insist on abortion rights, that women of color insist on an end to involuntary sterilization, that all women insist on reproductive self-determination. It is not in the interests of capitalism that women demand economic rights or comparable worth. It is not in the interests of many individual men or many institutions that women demand a nonexploitative sexual autonomy —the right to say and mean both no and yes on our own terms. What would our mass culture look like if it didn't sell women's bodies—even aside from pornography? It is not in the interests of heterosexist patriarchy that women challenge our understandings of events headlined MAN KILLED FAMILY BECAUSE HE LOVED THEM, that women challenge the notion of men's violence against women and children as deriving from "love" rather than power. It is not in the interests of any of the systems of domination in which we are enmeshed that we see how these systems work—that we understand men's violence, male domination, race and class supremacy, as systems of permission for both individual and institutional exercises of power, rather than merely as individual pathologies. It is not in the interests of white supremacist capitalist patriarchy that women ally across differences.

Allying across differences is difficult work, and is often thwarted by homophobia—by fears both of lesbians and of being named a lesbian by association. Feminism requires that we confront that homophobia constantly. I want to suggest another and perhaps more subtle and insidious way that fear of feminism is shaped by the institution of heterosexuality. Think about the lives of young women—think about your own. What are the arenas for selfhood for young women in this culture? How do they discover and construct their identities? What teaches them who they are, who they want to be, who they might be? Our culture allows women so little scope for development, for exploration, for testing the boundaries of what they can do and who they can be, that romantic and sexual relationships become the primary, too often the only, arena for selfhood.

Young women who have not yet begun careers or community involvements too often have no public life, and the smallness of private life, of romance as an arena for selfhood, is particularly acute for them. Intimate relationships become the testing ground for identity, a reality that has enormously damaging consequences for teenage girls in particular (the pressures both toward and on sex and romance, together with the culturally induced destruction of girls' self-esteem at puberty, have everything to do with teenage pregnancy). The feminist insistence that the personal is political may seem to threaten rather than empower a girl's fragile, emergent self as she develops into a sexual and relational being.

Young women may believe that a feminist identity puts them out of the pool for many men, limits the options of who they might become with a partner, how they might decide to live. They may not be wrong either: how many young men feminists or feminist sympathizers do you know? A politics that may require making demands on a partner, or that may motivate particular choices in partners, can appear to foreclose rather than to open up options for identity, especially for women who haven't yet discovered that all relationships require negotiation and struggle. When you live on Noah's ark, anything that might make it more difficult to find a partner can seem to threaten your very survival. To make our case, feminists have to combat not just homophobia, but also the rule of the couple, the politics of Noah's ark in the age of "family values." This does not mean that heterosexual feminist women must give up their intimate relationships, but it does mean that feminists must continually analyze those pressures, be clear about how they operate in our lives, and try to find ways around and through them for ourselves, each other, and other women.

For women who are survivors of men's violence —perhaps most notably for incest and rape survivors—the shift feminism enables, from individual pathology to systematic analysis, is empowering rather than threatening. For women who have not experienced men's violence in these ways, the shift to a systematic analysis requires them to ally themselves with survivors—itself a recognition that *it could happen to me.* Young women who have not been victims of men's violence hate being asked to identify with it; they see the threat to their emergent sense of autonomy and freedom not in the fact of men's violence, but in feminist analyses that make them identify with it. This can also be true for older women, but it may be lessened by the simple statistics of women's life experience: the longer you live, the more likely you are to have experienced men's violence or to know women who are survivors of it, and thus to have a sense of the range and scope of that violence.

My women students, feminist and nonfeminist alike, are perfectly aware of the risks of going unescorted to the library at night. At the same time, they are appalled by my suggesting that such gender-based restrictions on their access to university facilities deny them an equal education. It's not that men's violence isn't real to them—but that they are unwilling to trace out its consequences and to understand its complexities. College women, however precarious their economic situation, and even despite the extent of sexual harassment and date rape on campuses all over the country, still insist on believing that women's equality has been achieved. And, in fact, to the extent that colleges and universities are doing their jobs—giving women students something like an equal education—young women may experience relatively little overt or first-hand discrimination. Sexism may come to seem more the exception than the rule in some academic settings— and thus more attributable to individual sickness than to systems of domination.

Women of all ages fear the existential situation of feminism, what we learned from Simone de Beauvoir, what we learned from radical feminists in the 1970s, what we learned from feminist women of color in the 1980s: feminism has consequences. Once you have your "click!" moment, the world shifts, and it shifts in some terrifying ways. Not just heterosexism drives this fear of political commitment—it's not just fear of limiting one's partner-pool. It's also about limiting oneself—about the fear of commitment to something larger than the self that asks us to examine the consequences of our actions. Women fear anger, and change, and challenge—who doesn't? Women fear taking a public stand, entering public discourse, demanding—and perhaps getting— attention. And for what? To be called a "feminazi"? To be denounced as traitors to women's "essential nature"?

The challenge to the public-private division that feminism represents is profoundly threatening to young women who just want to be left alone, to all women who believe they can hide from feminist issues by not being feminists. The central feminist tenet that the personal is political is profoundly threatening to young women who don't want to be called to account. It is far easier to rest in silence, as if silence were neutrality, and as if neutrality were safety. Neither wholly cynical nor wholly apathetic, women who fear feminism fear living in consequences. Think harder, act more carefully; feminism requires that you enter a world supersaturated with meaning, with implications. And for privileged women in particular, the notion that one's own privilege comes at someone else's expense— that my privilege *is* your oppression—is profoundly threatening.

Fear of feminism is also fear of complexity, fear of thinking, fear of ideas—we live, after all, in a profoundly anti-intellectual culture. Feminism is one of the few movements in the U.S. that produce non-academic intellectuals—readers, writers, thinkers, and theorists outside the academy, who combine and refine their knowledge with their practice. What other movement is housed so substantially in bookstores? All radical movements for change struggle against the anti-intellectualism of U.S. culture, the same anti-intellectualism, fatalism, and disengagement that make even voting too much work for most U.S. citizens. Feminism is work—intellectual work as surely as it is activist work—and it can be very easy for women who have been feminists for a long time to forget how hard-won their insights are, how much reading and talking and thinking and work produced them. In this political climate, such insights may be even more hard-won.

Feminism requires an expansion of the self—an expansion of empathy, interest, intelligence, and responsibility across differences, histories, cultures, ethnicities, sexual identities, othernesses. The differences between women, as Audre Lorde pointed out over and over again, are our most precious resources in thinking and acting toward change. Fear of difference is itself a fear of consequences: it is less other women's difference that we fear than our own implication in the hierarchy of differences, our own accountability to other women's oppression. It is easier to rest in gender consciousness, in one's own difference, than to undertake the personal and political analysis required to trace out one's own position in multiple and overlapping systems of domination.

Women have real reasons to fear feminism, and we do young women no service if we suggest to them that feminism itself is safe. It is not. To stand opposed to your culture, to be critical of institutions, behaviors, discourses—when it is so clearly *not* in your immediate interest to do so—asks a lot of a young person, of any person. At its best, the feminist challenging of individualism, of narrow notions of freedom, is transformative, exhilarating, empowering. When we do our best work in selling feminism to the unconverted, we make clear not only its necessity, but also its pleasures: the joys of intellectual and political work, the moral power of living in consequences, the surprises of coalition, the rewards of doing what is difficult. Feminism offers an arena for selfhood beyond personal relationships but not disconnected from them. It offers—and requires—courage, intelligence, boldness, sensitivity, relationality, complexity, a sense of purpose, and, lest we forget, a sense of humor as well. Of course young women are afraid of feminism—shouldn't they be?

■ # READING 93

Real Men Join the Movement

Michael Kimmel

Cory Shere didn't go to Duke University to become a profeminist man. He was going to be a doctor, covering his bets with a double major in engineering and premed. But his experiences with both organic chemistry and feminist women conspired to lead this affable and earnest 20-year-old Detroit native in a different direction. Now in his junior year, he still has a double major—women's studies and psychology. And he works with a group of men to raise awareness about sexual assault and date rape.

Eric Freedman wasn't profeminist either, when he arrived at Swarthmore College three years ago. A 20-year-old junior literature major from Syracuse, New York, he became involved in a campus antiracism project, and began to see the connections among different struggles for equality. At an antiracism workshop he helped organize, he suddenly found himself speaking about male privilege as well as white privilege. This fall, he's starting a men's group to focus on race and gender issues.

Who are these guys? And what are they doing in the women's movement?

They are among a growing number of profeminist men around the country. These aren't the angry divorcés who whine about how men are the new victims of reverse discrimination, nor are they the weekend warriors trooping off to a mythopoetic retreat. They're neither Promise Keepers nor Million Man Marchers vowing to be responsible domestic patriarchs on a nineteenth-century model.

You might think of profeminist men as the "other" men's movement, but I prefer to consider it the "real" men's movement, because by actively supporting women's equality on the job or on the streets and by quietly changing their lives to create that equality at home, profeminist men are also transforming the definition of masculinity. Perhaps this is the movement about which Gloria Steinem rhapsodized when she wrote how women "want a men's movement. We are literally dying for it."

Profeminist men staff the centers where convicted batterers get counseling, organize therapy for rapists and sex offenders in prison, do the workshops on preventing sexual harassment in the workplace, or on confronting the impact of pornography in men's lives. On campus, they're organizing men's events during Take Back the Night marches; presenting programs on sexual assault to fraternities, dorms, and athletic teams; taking courses on masculinity; and founding campus groups with acronyms like MAC (Men Acting for Change), MOST (Men Opposed to Sexist Tradition), MASH (Men Against Sexual Harassment), MASA (Men Against Sexual Assault), and, my current favorite, MARS (Men Against Rape and Sexism). Maybe John Gray was right after all—real men *are* from Mars!

Feminism and Men's Lives

I first met Cory, Eric, and about a dozen other young profeminist men in April at the Young Feminist Summit, organized by NOW, in Washington, D.C. They were pretty easy to spot among the nearly one thousand young women from colleges all over the country. As we talked during an impromptu workshop, I heard them describe both the exhilaration and isolation of becoming part of the struggle for women's equality, the frustrations of dealing with other men, the active suspicions and passive indifference of other students.

It felt painfully familiar. I've spent nearly two decades in feminist politics, first as an activist in antirape and antibattery groups, and later helping to organize the National Organization for Men Against Sexism (NOMAS), a network of profeminist men and women around the country. More recently, I've tried to apply the insights of academic feminist theory to men's lives, developing courses on men, debating with Robert Bly and his followers, and writing a history of the idea of manhood in the United States.

Of course, men like Cory and Eric are a distinct minority on campus. They compete with the an-

gry voice of backlash, those shrill interruptions that scream "Don't blame me, I never raped anyone! Leave me alone!" They compete with that now familiar men-as-victims whine. Men, we hear, are terrified of going to work or on a date, lest they be falsely accused of sexual harassment or date rape; they're unable to support their scheming careerist wives, yet are vilified as bad fathers if they don't provide enough child support to keep their ex-wives in Gucci and Donna Karan after the divorce.

In the public imagination, profeminist men also compete with the mythopoetic vision of the men's movement as a kind of summer-camp retreat, and the earnest evangelical Promise Keepers with their men-only sports-themed rallies, and the Million Man March's solemn yet celebratory atonement. All offer men solace and soul-work, and promise to heal men's pain and enable them to become more nurturing and loving. All noble goals, to be sure. But to profeminist men, you don't build responsibility and democracy by exclusion—of women, or of gays and lesbians.

And profeminist men compete with the most deafening sound coming from the mouths of American men when the subject is feminism: silence. Most men, on campus and off, exude an aura of studied indifference to feminism. Like the irreverent second child at the Passover seder, they ask, "What has this to do with me?"

A lot. Sure, feminism is the struggle of more than one half of the population for equal rights. But it's also about rethinking identities, our relationships, the meanings of our lives. For men, feminism is not only about what we *can't* do—like commit violence, harassment, or rape—or *shouldn't* do, like leave all the child care and housework to our wives. It's also about what we *can* do, what we *should* do, and even what we *want* to do—like be a better father, friend, or partner. "Most men know that it is to all of our advantage—women and men alike—for women to be equal," noted NOW President Patricia Ireland, in her Summit keynote address. Far from being only about the loss of power, feminism will also enable men to live the lives we say we want to live.

This isn't the gender cavalry, arriving in the nick of time to save the damsels from distress. "Thanks for bringing this sexism stuff to our attention, ladies," one might imagine them saying. "We'll take it from here." And it's true that some men declare themselves feminists just a bit too effortlessly, especially if they think it's going to help them get a date. (A friend calls it "premature self-congratulation," and it's just as likely to leave women feeling shortchanged.)

In part, this explains why I call them "profeminist men" and not "feminist men" or "male feminists." As an idea, it seems to me, feminism involves an empirical observation—that women are not equal—and the moral position that declares they should be. Of course, men may share this empirical observation and take this moral stance. And to that extent men support feminism as an ideal. But feminism as an identity also involves the felt experience of that inequality. And this men do not have, because men are privileged by sexism. To be sure, men may be oppressed—by race, class, ethnicity, sexuality, age, physical ability—but men are not oppressed *as men*. Since only women have that felt experience of oppression about gender, it seems sensible to make a distinction in how we identify ourselves. Men can support feminism, and can call ourselves "antisexist" or "profeminist." I've chosen profeminist because, like feminism, it stresses the positive and forward-looking.

In a sense, I think of profeminist men as the Gentlemen's Auxiliary of Feminism. This honorable position acknowledges that we play a part in this social transformation, but not the most significant part. It's the task of the Gentlemen's Auxiliary to make feminism comprehensible to men, not as a loss of power—which has thus far failed to "trickle down" to most individual men anyway—but as a challenge to the false sense of entitlement we have to that power in the first place. Profeminism is about supporting both women's equality and other men's efforts to live more ethically consistent and more emotionally resonant lives.

. . .

The routes taken by today's profeminist men are as varied as the men themselves. But most do seem to have some personal experience that made gender inequality more concrete. For some, it involved their

mother. (Remember President Clinton describing how he developed his commitment to women's equality when he tried to stop his stepfather from hitting his mother? Of course, one wishes that commitment had facilitated more supportive policy initiatives.) Max Sadler, a 17-year-old senior at Trinity High School in New York City, watched his professional mother hit her head on the glass ceiling at her high-powered corporate job—a job she eventually quit to join a company with more women in high-level positions. Max shared her frustration, and also felt ashamed at the casual attitudes of her male colleagues.

Shehzad Nadeem, a 19-year-old student at James Madison University in Virginia, remembered the way his older sister described her experiences. "I could barely believe the stories she told me, yet something deep inside told me that they were not only true, but common. I realized that we men are actively or passively complicit in women's oppression, and that we have to take an active role in challenging other men." Shehzad joined MOST (Men Opposed to Sexist Tradition), which has presented workshops on violence and sexual assault at Madison dorms.

. . .

Or perhaps it was having a feminist girlfriend, or even just having women friends, that brought these issues to the fore for men. "I grew up with female friends who were as ambitious, smart, achieving, and confident as I thought I was—on a good day," recalls Jason Schultz, a founder of MAC at Duke, who now organizes men's programs to combat campus sexual assault. "When I got to college, these same women began calling themselves feminists. When I heard men call women 'dumb chicks' I knew something was wrong."

. . .

The Profeminist "Click!"

But there has to be more than the presence of feminist role models, challenges from girlfriends, brilliant assignments, or challenging support from professors. After all, we all have women in our lives, and virtually all of those women have had some traumatic encounter with sexism. There has to be something else.

Feminists call it the "click!"—that moment when they realize that their pain, fears, confusion, and anger are not theirs alone, but are shared with other women. Do profeminist men have "clicks!"? Yes, but they don't typically come from righteous indignation or fear, but rather from guilt and shame, a gnawing sense of implication in something larger and more pervasive than individual intention. It's that awful moment when you hear women complain about "men" in general and realize, even just a little bit, that you are what they're talking about. (Much of men's reactive defensiveness seems to be a hedge against these feelings of shame.)

Suddenly, it's not those "bad" men "out there" who are the problem—it's all men. Call it the Pogo revelation: "We have met the enemy, and he is us."

That's certainly the way it felt for Jeff Wolf (not his real name). A sexually naive college sophomore, he found himself growing closer and closer to a woman friend, Annie, during a study date. They talked long into the night, and eventually kissed. One thing began to lead to another, and both seemed eager and pleased to be with the other. Just before penetration, though, Jeff felt Annie go limp. "Her eyes glazed over, and she went kind of numb," he recalled, still wincing at the memory.

This is the moment that many a college guy dreams of—her apparent surrender to his desire, even if it was induced by roofies or alcohol. It's a moment when men often space out, preferring to navigate the actual encounter on automatic pilot, fearing that emotional connection will lead to an early climax.

As Annie slipped into this mental coma, though, Jeff stayed alert, as engaged emotionally as he was physically. "What had been so arousing was the way we had been connecting intellectually and emotionally," he said. After some patient prodding, she finally confessed that she'd been raped as a high school sophomore, and ever since, had used this self-protective strategy to get through a sexual encounter without reliving her adolescent trauma. Jeff, it seemed, was the first guy who noticed.

. . .

Others say their "click!" experience happened later in life. In the 1970s, psychologist David Greene was deeply involved in political activism, when he and his wife had a baby. "Not that much changed for me; I still went around doing my thing, but now there was a baby in it." On the other hand, his wife's life was totally transformed by the realities of round-the-clock child care. She'd become a mother. "After several weeks of this, she sat me down and confronted me," he recalls. "The bankruptcy of my politics quickly became clear to me. I was an oppressor, an abuser of privilege—I'd become the enemy I thought I was fighting against." The couple meticulously divided housework and child care, and David learned that revolutions are fought out in people's kitchens as well as in the jungles of Southeast Asia. Terry Kupers, a 54-year-old psychiatrist, and author of *Revisioning Men's Lives,* remembers his first wife initiating some serious talks about the "unstated assumptions we were making about housework, cooking, and whose time was more valuable." Not only did Kupers realize that his wife was right, "but I also realized I liked things better the new way."

. . .

Profeminism Today— and Tomorrow

And just as sisterhood is global, so too are profeminist men active around the world. Men from nearly 50 countries—from Mexico to Japan—regularly contribute to a newsletter of international profeminist scholars and activists, according to its editor, Oystein Holter, a Norwegian researcher. Scandinavian men are working to implement a gender equity mandated by law. Liisa Husu, a senior advisor to Finland's gender equity commission, has developed a parliamentary subcommittee of concerned men. (When I met with them last fall, we spent our day discussing our mutual activities, after which they whisked me off to an all-male sauna resort on the shore of an icy Baltic Sea for a bit of male-bonding as a follow-up to all that equity work.) Scandinavian men routinely take parental leave; in fact, in Sweden and Norway they've introduced "Daddy days," an additional month of paid paternity leave for the men to have some time with their newborns after the mothers have returned to work. About half of Swedish men take paternal leave, according to fatherhood expert Lars Jalmert at the University of Stockholm.

The world's most successful profeminist organization must be Canada's White Ribbon Campaign. Begun in 1991 to coincide with the second anniversary of the Montreal Massacre—when a young man killed 14 women engineering students at the University of Montreal on December 6, 1989—its goal was to publicly and visibly declare opposition to men's violence against women by encouraging men to wear a white ribbon as a public pledge. "Within days, hundreds of thousands of men and boys across Canada wore a ribbon," noted Michael Kaufman, one of the campaign's founders. "It exceeded our wildest expectations—even the prime minister wore a ribbon." This year, WRC events are also planned for Norway, Australia, and several U.S. colleges; in Canada, events include an Alberta hockey team planning a skating competition to raise money for a local women's shelter. WRC organizers have also developed curricula for secondary schools to raise the issue for boys.

But just as surely, some of the most important and effective profeminist men's activities are taking place in American homes every day, as men increasingly share housework and child care, reorganize their schedules to be more responsive to the needs of their families, and even downsize their ambitions to develop a family strategy that does not revolve exclusively around *his* career path. "Housework remains

the last frontier" for men to tame, argues sociologist Kathleen Gerson in her book *No Man's Land*. . . .

But the payoff is significant. If power were a scarce commodity or a zero-sum game, we might think that women's increased power would mean a decrease in men's. And since most men don't feel very powerful anyway, the possibilities of further loss are rather unappealing. But for most men, all the power in the world does not seem to have trickled down to enable individual men to live the lives we say we want to live—lives of intimacy, integrity, and individual expression. By demanding the redistribution of power along more equitable lines, feminism also seeks a dramatic shift in our social priorities, our choices about how we live, and what we consider important. Feminism is also a blueprint for men about how to become the men we want to be, and profeminist men believe that men will live happier, healthier, and more emotionally enriched lives by supporting women's equality.

Part of profeminist men's politics is to visibly and vocally support women's equality, and part of it is to quietly and laboriously struggle to implement that public stance into our own lives. And part of it must be to learn to confront and challenge other men, with care and commitment. "This cause is not altogether and exclusively woman's cause," wrote Frederick Douglass in 1848. "It is the cause of human brotherhood as well as human sisterhood, and both must rise and fall together."

◼ READING 94

From Personal Tragedy to Group Consciousness
The Movement for Disability Rights

Marj Schneider

For over 30 years the disability rights movement has pushed for equal treatment and opportunities in education, employment and community life. In recent years, the situation faced by disabled people has changed dramatically. Prior to the 1970s, there was little legal recourse for a disabled person denied ed-

ucation, housing or a job, and no laws mandating that buildings and public transit systems be usable by people in wheelchairs (Johnson, 1988: 46). Many states had large institutions that passed for home for thousands of people labeled mentally retarded. During the seventies and eighties, most of these warehousing institutions were closed. Residents moved into smaller facilities or group homes, allowing some developmentally disabled people to participate more in their communities (Trent, 1994: 264–65). Today, most disabled children are educated in regular classrooms along with their peers (Kerzner Lipsky & Gartner, 1989: 3–24). Computers adapted for use by blind, learning disabled and physically disabled persons, and faster, light-weight wheelchairs are examples of technological advancements, unavailable in the past, that promote independence (Shapiro, 1993: 211–236).

A new group consciousness on the part of disabled people challenges old ways of thinking about disability, but long-held, unexamined beliefs and attitudes of nondisabled society are slow to change. Disabled people have long maintained that societal fears, prejudices and stereotypes often present more problems than the limitations imposed by the disability itself (Shapiro, 1993: 9).

. . .

The Medical Model

During the twentieth century, increasing numbers of nondisabled professionals have promoted a medicalized view of disability, casting the disabled individual into the perpetual role of patient. In this role, patients depend upon professionals rather than participate in decision-making regarding their physical care and other needs (Funk, 1987: 13).

Historian Paul Longmore (1992) says that the goal of professional intervention has been, if not to cure people, then at least to correct the functional consequences of a disability enough to enable them to participate in society. The emphasis is on "normalization," to try to be as much like nondisabled people as possible. Longmore (1992) states: "Within this medical model lurks considerable ambivalence about people who look different or function differently. . . . Fundamentally, this is a paternalistic ideology that regards the objects of its concern as incompetent to manage their own lives, sometimes as even dangerous to society and as needing supervision."

. . .

Early Activism

Challenges to the medical model began when blind and deaf people founded their own organizations to advocate for legislation and policies to address their particular needs (Funk, 1987: 13). The development of a broader disability rights movement started in the 1960s, and was profoundly influenced by the black civil rights and women's movements. Ideas such as integration and equality of opportunity took hold among disabled people who began talking about how society needed to change rather than how they as individuals needed to "overcome their handicaps." There was a growing comprehension that they had rights, could make their own choices and could be full and equal participants in society.

In 1972, the incorporation of the Berkeley Center for Independent Living was the first instance of severely disabled individuals designing a program to meet their own needs as they saw them. Over the next decade, more than 200 programs run by disabled people were established throughout the country modeled on the Berkeley Center. These centers created services to facilitate disabled people's living in the community, giving hope and dignity. The new concept of independent living had a tremendous impact on disability professionals, law makers and disabled people around the world (Funk, 1987: 15).

Other coalitions and organizations evolved as well that cut across differing disabilities to focus on issues of common concern. The decades of the sixties and seventies saw significant growth in organizing and advocacy efforts by disabled people and parents of disabled children. Traditional disability programs and policies were challenged in the courts and legislatures, based on constitutional rights. By 1979, there were class action suits on behalf of institutionalized mentally disabled people in 17 states. Advocates demanded that individuals be provided with alternatives for living in the community (Funk, 1987: 15–16).

In 1973, Congress passed a Rehabilitation Act that included Section 504, which banned discrimination against disabled people by programs receiving federal funds. However, Section 504 wasn't implemented until 1977 when activists occupied the offices of the Department of Health Education and Welfare for 28 days, demanding that the rules governing this law be signed. Since Section 504 affected only programs getting federal dollars, activists began working for passage of state access laws and adding disabled people as a protected group under state civil rights statutes. Some communities with active disability organizations slowly became more accessible, but it was rare to find one being totally barrier-free (Johnson, 1988: 47).

In 1975, the Education for All Handicapped Children Act (today called the Individuals with Disabilities Education Act, IDEA) mandated that all children, regardless of the severity of their disabilities, receive a free appropriate public education. The word *appropriate* in the law means that a child's needs should be met in ways that work best for the individual, not on the basis of category of disability. The law reflected the belief that a disability didn't necessarily mean a child should be removed from the regular classroom, though some children might require specialized services (Kerzner Lipsky & Gartner, 1989: 5).

. . .

The Current Situation

In the late eighties, disability activism reemerged on the national level when advocates drafted and began lobbying for the passage of the Americans with Disabilities Act (ADA). The ADA is a comprehensive piece of civil rights legislation extending the provisions of Section 504 to cover all businesses and public facilities. Activists organized a grassroots campaign that included visits to every member of Congress from constituents with compelling stories of discrimination (Shapiro, 1994: 125). But opposition to the proposed act came from transportation and business groups resulting in compromises before the bill was passed and signed into law on July 26, 1990 (Dardick, 1993: 99).

The ADA has four titles that cover employment, government programs, public accommodations, transportation and telecommunications. Civil rights protection for other minorities also entails expense to implement and enforce, but they do not require the obvious financial outlay of making busses and subways physically accessible, or providing disability-related accommodations on the job or in government services. Some businesses resist complying with the law, assuming costs will be prohibitive, and that only a few people will benefit.

. . .

The public accommodations provisions of Title III of the ADA require that businesses building new, or remodeling old facilities must make them physically accessible. Businesses cannot discriminate in providing goods or services to patrons with disabilities. Implementation of this part of the act has had the most visible impact on all Americans. These access requirements have provided needed impetus in communities that had no building access codes prior to the ADA. Curb-cuts are now common-place. Malls and hotels are built with access in mind. Old, heavy doors are being replaced with light-weight or automatic ones. Of course thousands of older buildings still only have steps leading to them, or remain difficult to negotiate inside for mobility-impaired people. Even completed modifications may still be inadequate, poorly designed or broken (Woodward, 1995: 28).

Title I prohibits discrimination in employment for businesses with 15 or more employees. An employer cannot refuse to hire an otherwise qualified disabled person, and employers must make "reasonable accommodations" so a disabled person can perform a job. This could mean putting an amplifier on a telephone, lowering a desk or modifying a work schedule. Employers aren't required to hire disabled persons over other applicants, nor are they required to provide accommodations if the cost would pose an "undue hardship." There are incentives in the law to encourage businesses to comply with the ADA such as tax deductions for the removal of architectural barriers (Dardick, 1993: 100). According to the University of West Virginia's Jobs Accommodation Network, 69% of accommodations cost $500 or less (Johnson, 1993: 102).

However, John Woodward, writing in the *Disability Rag* (1995: 28), believes that Title I is not serving the long-term unemployed disabled population it was supposed to benefit. This section of the law is enforced by the Equal Employment Opportunity Commission (EEOC), an agency of the Federal government that makes determinations on all types of discrimination claims related to employment. Since Title I of the ADA went into effect, 50% of the 34,877 complaints filed with the EEOC were from individuals with back injuries. A much smaller number of claims came from persons with other kinds of conditions covered under the law such as emotional/psychological impairment, neurological impairments or mobility impairments. Some 89% of discrimination claims are over issues of firing, benefits and promotions, rather than the refusal to hire disabled applicants.

. . .

Legislative and policy changes are not the only arenas where disabled activists push for social change. However, under the current anti–big government political climate, the ADA has come under attack, and supporters must not only work to ensure its enforcement, but must also monitor attempts to amend or repeal the act. The ADA has become a favorite target of conservatives who want to see government stop protecting civil rights.

. . .

Other Key Issues

Many disabled individuals are living successful, fulfilling lives because of the progress that has been made in building and transportation access, medical treatment and technology, education, and opportunities to participate in work and community life. Yet there are crucial needs that continue to be unmet for many, and each disability group has particular issues of concern.

The United States is almost the only industrialized country in the world that does not have a national health insurance program. According to the US Census Bureau's 1993 Population Survey, 39.7 million Americans have no insurance to cover the high cost of doctors visits or hospital stays. When Congress debated health care reform in 1993 and 1994, the voices of disabled people were part of the discussion. This issue is more compelling for us because many of us confront medical problems and daily living situations that neither private insurance nor the government's medicare/medicaid programs deal with adequately. Writing in *Mainstream,* William Stothers says, "Those of us with disabilities are

at greatest risk, not because we're sick, most of us aren't, but because we're at the edge. A common cold or flu can create serious ramifications quickly. Our need for health care services keeps many of us dependent upon government support programs" (Stothers, 1994: 46). Congress has failed to pass any health care reform measures, in part due to vehement opposition from the powerful insurance industry that wants to keep its profits high. This issue hasn't gone away. The crisis is deepening despite its becoming a dead issue for the media.

Assistance from a personal care attendant is essential for individuals who need help with activities of daily living like getting in and out of bed, dressing, bathing, eating, going to the bathroom, shopping, and cleaning. Some states have programs to provide attendant care to those who need it for at least a few hours each day. But other states have no attendant services at all, and older people as well as young people and children with severe disabilities are forced to live in nursing homes or other large institutions. The World Institute on Disability estimates that 7.7 million people in the US require assistance from another person to accomplish everyday tasks. Three million of these people are not getting the help they need and must rely on volunteers. About one third of these live in institutions and could live in the community if support services were available. On the average, nursing home care costs $30,000 per person per year. Attendant care costs half this much or less (ADAPT, 1995). Currently, most long-term care funds through Medicaid are funneled into nursing homes and are not being directed into more cost-efficient attendant programs. ADAPT (Americans Disabled for Attendant Programs Today) holds highly visible protest actions around the country against this practice. They are demanding that 25% of Medicaid money that goes to nursing homes be redirected to community-based alternatives.

. . .

Conclusion

Before the beginning of the movement for disability rights, disabled people wouldn't have been part of the decision-making process about attendant services or health care reform. For the first time, we are present at the table, advocating for ourselves on the issues that affect our lives. At times we still aren't invited, but we make a place at the table for ourselves, sharing knowledge gained through personal experience. Even though advocates repeat the advantages of programs that meet people's disability-related needs and laws that create opportunities, many politicians refuse to notice and continue to discredit and slash resources for human services.

The support of nondisabled allies who have learned from disabled people is crucial to hold on to our gains and continue to make progress. Anyone can become disabled either through accident or illness. Then questions about rights and choices become immediate and very real. It's not just those who are disabled now who benefit from opportunities for education and jobs. It's not just those who are disabled now who benefit from inclusion in family and community life. All of us benefit when disabled people are participants, not burdens who've been locked away and forgotten.

The disability-rights movement is challenging priorities in American society: promoting passage and enforcement of laws like the ADA; protesting and lobbying for adequate health care and attendant services; and demanding public resources go to individuals not institutions. The needs are so obvious and the benefits so clear.

REFERENCES

ADAPT. (1995, May). Facts Sheet.

Dardick, G. (1993) "Moving Towards Independence: The Americans with Disabilities Act and What It Means." *The Whole Earth Review,* Fall, 1992, reprinted in the *Utne Reader,* March/April, issue 56, pp. 98–100.

Funk, R. J. "Disability Rights: From Caste to Class in the Context of Civil Rights." (1987). In Gartner, A. & Joe, T. (Eds.), *Images of the Disabled, Disabling Images.* pp. 7–339. New York: Praeger.

Johnson, M. (1988). "Disability Rights Movement: Overcoming the Social Barriers." *The Nation Magazine,* April 9, reprinted in *Reporting on Disability: Approaches and Issues.* Johnson and Elkins. (Eds.), pp. 46–48.

Johnson, M. (1993). "Pushing for Access: Loopholes in the ADA Present Continuing Obstacles." *The Progressive,* August 1991, reprinted in the *Utne Reader.* March–April 56, pp. 101–103.

Kerzner Lipsky, D. & Gartner, A. "The Current Situation." (1989) in Kerzner Lipsky D. & Gartner A. (eds.), *Beyond Separate Education: Quality Education for All.* Baltimore, Paul H. Brooks, pp. 3–24.

Longmore, P. (1992). "Subverting the Dominant Paradigm." Lecture, University of Minnesota, October 5.

Shapiro, J. P. (1994). "Disability Policy and the Media: A Stealth Civil Rights Movement Bypasses the Press and Defies Conventional Wisdom." *Journal of Social Policy,* 22(1) pp. 123–133.

Shapiro, J. P. (1993). *No Pity: People with Disabilities Forging a New Civil Rights Movement.* New York: Times Books.

Stothers, W. G. (1994, April). "There's a Crisis All Right and It's Bad for Our Health." *Mainstream,* p. 46.

Trent, J. W. (1994). *Inventing the Feeble Mind: A History of Mental Retardation in the United States.* Berkeley: University of California Press.

Woodward, J. R. (1995, July–August). "The ADA at 5." *Disability Rag,* pp. 27–31.

READING 95

The Beijing Declaration and Platform for Action

Beijing Declaration

1. We, the Governments participating in the fourth World Conference on Women,

2. Gathered here in Beijing in September 1995, the year of the fiftieth anniversary of the founding of the United Nations,

3. Determined to advance the goals of equality, development and peace for all women everywhere in the interest of all humanity,

4. Acknowledging the voices of all women everywhere and taking note of the diversity of women

and their roles and circumstances, honouring the women who paved the way and inspired by the hope present in the world's youth,

5. Recognize that the status of women has advanced in some important respects in the past decade but that progress has been uneven, inequalities between women and men have persisted and major obstacles remain, with serious consequences for the well-being of all people,

6. Also recognize that this situation is exacerbated by the increasing poverty that is affecting the lives of the majority of the world's people, in particular women and children, with origins in both the national and international domains,

7. Dedicate ourselves unreservedly to addressing these constraints and obstacles and thus enhancing further the advancement and empowerment of women all over the world, and agree that this requires urgent action in the spirit of determination, hope, cooperation and solidarity, now and to carry us forward into the next century.

We reaffirm our commitment to:

8. The equal rights and inherent human dignity of women and men and other purposes and principles enshrined in the Charter of the United Nations, to the Universal Declaration of Human Rights and other international human rights instruments, in particular the Convention on the Elimination of All Forms of Discrimination against women and the Convention on the Rights of the Child, as well as the Declaration on the Elimination of Violence against Women and the Declaration on the Right to Development.

9. Ensure the full implementation of the human rights of women and of the girl child as an inalienable, integral and indivisible part of all human rights and fundamental freedoms;

10. Build on consensus and progress made at previous United Nations conferences and summits—on women in Nairobi in 1985, on children in New York in 1990, on environment and development in Rio de Janeiro in 1992, on human rights in Vienna in 1993, on population and development in Cairo in 1994 and on social development in Copenhagen in 1995 with the objective of achieving equality, development and peace;

11. Achieve the full and effective implementation of the Nairobi Forward-looking Strategies for the Advancement of Women;

12. The empowerment and advancement of women, including the right to freedom of thought, conscience, religion and belief, thus contributing to the moral, ethical, spiritual and intellectual needs of women and men, individually or in community with others and thereby guaranteeing them the possibility of realizing their full potential in society and shaping their lives in accordance with their own aspirations.

We are convinced that:

13. Women's empowerment and their full participation on the basis of equality in all spheres of society, including participation in the decision-making process and access to power, are fundamental for the achievement of equality, development and peace;

14. Women's rights are human rights;

15. Equal rights, opportunities and access to resources, equal sharing of responsibilities for the family by men and women, and a harmonious partnership between them are critical to their well-being and that of their families as well as to the consolidation of democracy.

16. Eradication of poverty based on sustained economic growth, social development, environmental protection and social justice requires the involvement of women in economic and social development, equal opportunities and the full and equal participation of women and men as agents and beneficiaries of people-centered sustainable development;

17. The explicit recognition and reaffirmation of the right of all women to control all aspects of their health, in particular their own fertility, is basic to their empowerment;

18. Local, national, regional and global peace is attainable and is inextricably linked with the advancement of women, who are a fundamental force for leadership, conflict resolution and the promotion of lasting peace at all levels.

19. It is essential to design, implement and monitor, with the full participation of women, effective, efficient and mutually reinforcing gender-sensitive

policies and programmes, including development policies and programmes, at all levels that will foster the empowerment and advancement of women;

20. The participation and contribution of all actors of civil society, particularly women's groups and networks and other non-governmental organizations and community-based organizations, with full respect for their autonomy, in cooperation with Governments, are important to the effective implementation and follow-up of the Platform for Action;

21. The implementation of the Platform for Action requires commitment from Governments and the international community. By making national and international commitments for action, including those made at the Conference, Governments and the international community recognize the need to take priority action for the empowerment and advancement of women.

We are determined to:

22. Intensify efforts and actions to achieve the goals of the Nairobi Forward-looking Strategies for the Advancement of Women by the end of this century;

23. Ensure the full enjoyment by women and the girl child of all human rights and fundamental freedoms and take effective action against violations of these rights and freedoms;

24. Take all necessary measures to eliminate all forms of discrimination against women and the girl child and remove all obstacles to gender equality and the advancement and empowerment of women;

25. Encourage men to participate fully in all actions toward equality;

26. Promote women's economic independence, including employment, and eradicate the persistent and increasing burden of poverty on women by addressing the structural causes of poverty through changes in economic structures, ensuring equal access for all women, including those in rural areas, as vital development agents, to productive resources, opportunities and public services;

27. Promote people-centered sustainable development, including sustained economic growth, through the provision of basic education, lifelong education, literacy and training, and primary health care for girls and women;

28. Take positive steps to ensure peace for the advancement of women and, recognizing the leading role that women have played in the peace movement, work actively towards general and complete disarmament under strict and effective international control, and support negotiations on the conclusion, without delay, of a universal and multilaterally and effectively verifiable comprehensive nuclear-test-ban treaty which contributes to nuclear disarmament and the prevention of the proliferation of nuclear weapons in all its aspects;

29. Prevent and eliminate all forms of violence against women and girls;

30. Ensure equal access to and equal treatment of women and men in education and health care and enhance women's sexual and reproductive health as well as education;

31. Promote and protect all human rights of women and girls;

32. Intensify efforts to ensure equal enjoyment of all human rights and fundamental freedoms for all women and girls who face multiple barriers to their empowerment and advancement because of such factors as their race, age, language, ethnicity, culture, religion, or disability, or because they are indigenous people;

33. Ensure respect for international law, including humanitarian law, in order to protect women and girls in particular;

34. Develop the fullest potential of girls and women of all ages, ensure their full and equal participation in building a better world for all and enhance their role in the development process.

We are determined to:

35. Ensure women's equal access to economic resources, including land, credit, science and technology, vocational training, information, communication and markets, as a means to further the advancement and empowerment of women and girls, including through the enhancement of their capacities to enjoy the benefits of equal access to these resources, *inter alia,* by means of international cooperation;

36. Ensure the success of the Platform for Action, which will require a strong commitment on the part of Governments, international organizations and institutions at all levels. We are deeply convinced that economic development, social development and environmental protection are interdependent and mutually reinforcing components of sustainable development, which is the framework for our efforts to achieve a higher quality of life for all people. Equitable social development that recognizes empowering the poor, particularly women living in poverty, to utilize environmental resources sustainably is a necessary foundation for sustainable development. We also recognize that broad-based and sustained economic growth in the context of sustainable development is necessary to sustain social development and social justice. The success of the Platform for Action will also require adequate mobilization of resources at the national and international levels as well as new and additional resources to the developing countries from all available funding mechanisms, including multilateral, bilateral and private sources for the advancement of women; financial resources to strengthen the capacity of national, subregional, regional and international institutions; a commitment to equal rights, equal responsibilities and equal opportunities and to the equal participation of women and men in all national, regional and international bodies and policy-making processes; and the establishment or strengthening of mechanisms at all levels for accountability to the world's women;

37. Ensure also the success of the Platform for Action in countries with economies in transition, which will require continued international cooperation and assistance;

38. We hereby adopt and commit ourselves as Governments to implement the following Platform for Action, ensuring that a gender perspective is reflected in all our policies and programmes. We urge the United Nations system, regional and international financial institutions, other relevant regional and international institutions and all women and men, as well as non-governmental organizations, with full respect for their autonomy, and all sectors of civil society, in cooperation with Governments,

to fully commit themselves and contribute to the implementation of this Platform for Action.

. . .

Platform for Action
Critical Areas of Concern

41. The advancement of women and the achievement of equality between women and men are a matter of human rights and a condition for social justice and should not be seen in isolation as a women's issue. They are the only way to build a sustainable, just and developed society. Empowerment of women and equality between women and men are prerequisites for achieving political, social, economic, cultural and environmental security among all peoples.

42. Most of the goals set out in the Nairobi Forward-looking Strategies for the Advancement of Women have not been achieved. Barriers to women's empowerment remain, despite the efforts of Governments, as well as non-governmental organizations and women and men everywhere. Vast political, economic and ecological crises persist in many parts of the world. Among them are wars of aggression, armed conflicts, colonial or other forms of alien domination or foreign occupation, civil wars and terrorism. These situations, combined with systematic or de facto discrimination, violations of and failure to protect all human rights and fundamental freedoms of all women, and their civil, cultural, economic, political and social rights, including the right to development and ingrained prejudicial attitudes towards women and girls are but a few of the impediments encountered since the World Conference to Review and Appraise the Achievements of the United Nations Decade for Women: Equality, Development and Peace, in 1985.

43. A review of progress since the Nairobi Conference highlights special concerns—areas of particular urgency that stand out as priorities for action. All actors should focus action and resources on the strategic objectives relating to the critical areas of concern which are, necessarily, interrelated, interdependent and of high priority. There is a need

for these actors to develop and implement mechanisms of accountability for all the areas of concern.

44. To this end, Governments, the international community and civil society, including non-governmental organizations and the private sector, are called upon to take strategic action in the following critical areas of concern:

- The persistent and increasing burden of poverty on women
- Inequalities and inadequacies in and unequal access to education and training
- Inequalities and inadequacies in and unequal access to health care and related services
- Violence against women
- The effects of armed or other kinds of conflict on women, including those living under foreign occupation
- Inequality in economic structures and policies, in all forms of productive activities and in access to resources
- Inequality between men and women in the sharing of power and decision-making at all levels
- Insufficient mechanisms at all levels to promote the advancement of women
- Lack of respect for and inadequate promotion and protection of the human rights of women
- Stereotyping of women and inequality in women's access to and participation in all communication systems, especially in the media
- Gender inequalities in the management of natural resources and in the safeguarding of the environment
- Persistent discrimination against and violation of the rights of the girl-child

READING 96

Taking the High Road

Suzanne Pharr

In the mid-1990s, we are seeing a rapid rise of mean-spiritedness, fed by radio and television, the rhetoric of cynical politicians, and the embittered disillusionment of people whose hopes and dreams have been destroyed and whose lives feel threatened. It is a mean-spiritedness that seems to feed upon itself, seeking everywhere someone to blame, someone who is the cause of this pain, this disappointment, this failure to succeed. The airwaves are filled with rancor and anger, cynicism and accusation. Recently, I have been asking people to describe the mood of the country. They respond, "depressed, angry, overwhelmed, feeling isolated and cut off, mistrustful, mean, hurt, fearful." To succeed, our organizing must address these feelings.

As progressive and moderate voices are excluded or silenced or mimic this rage and cynicism, I worry about our better selves diminishing from lack of nurturance and support. I think of our better selves as that place where compassion, sympathy, empathy, tolerance, inclusiveness, and generosity reside.

All of our strategies for social change will mean very little if we do not have access to that place inside us where generosity, for example, lives. Much of our work has to be focused on nurturing the life of the spirit, on keeping the door to our better selves as wide open as possible.

Cultural work offers one of our best means of nurturing the individual spirit and our sense of connection to others. It is through the creation of art and culture that the spirit is fed and kept alive and our common humanity is expressed and exposed.

Yet in much of our social change work, we incorporate art and culture only as "add-ons"—the concert after a conference, the song or poem at the beginning of the meeting. We rarely see cultural organizing as social change work. One reason is that we are often stuck in the same old methods of organizing and do not question how people learn, what moves us to change. Another reason is that we can sometimes become too focused on a single goal or issue and do not consider the wholeness of ourselves and our constituency. In building a movement, eating and singing together may be as important as handing out leaflets. Being able to involve our families with us in our work may be as important as recruiting new members. The basis for successful organizing work is people who are connected, not separated, people who feel whole, not fragmented.

Storytelling is one of the strongest cultural expressions; it helps us feel whole and connected. Nothing is more critical than storytelling to defining our humanity. When telling our stories, we assert both our individuality and our connection to others, and we make others aware of our identity and history. What better way to counter gross stereotyping, demonizing, and dehumanization than by presenting a multiplicity of voices and experiences, each individualized, each unique, and each connected to a common history?

In the early days of the women's antiviolence movement, women met in groups to tell the story of the violence that had occurred in their lives. For many, it was the first time they had told anyone what happened—the rape, incest, battering, torture—and telling the story to others brought them out of isolation and gave them connection to a group. But what followed next was the foundation for a women's antiviolence movement: after women heard each others stories, they came to recognize the great similarities among them. Through discussing these commonalities, they created an analysis of the relationship between the perpetrator of violence and its target, and they recognized that though the victim is frequently blamed for the violence, the fault lies with the perpetrator and the society that accepts the violence. Those desiring to end violence against themselves and other women then moved to take action: creating safe homes and battered women's shelters, hotlines and support groups, working with police, changing laws, confronting batterers and rapists, providing political education and changing public policy.

For whatever reasons, progressive people have not always talked a great deal about the strong moral convictions underlying why we do this work of social justice: *it is because we believe every person counts, has human dignity, and deserves respect, equality, and justice.* This morality is the basis for our vision, and all our work flows from this basic belief.

We are living in a time in which people are crying out for something to believe in, for a moral sense, for purpose, for answers that will bring some calm to the chaos they feel in their lives. I believe it is our moral imperative to help each other make connections, to show how everyone is interrelated and belongs in community. It is at our peril if we do work that increases alienation and robs meaning from life. Today's expressions of violence, hatred, and bigotry are directly related to the level of alienation and disconnection felt by people. For our very survival, we must develop a sense of common humanity.

It may be that our most important political work is figuring out how to make the full human connection, how to engage our hearts as well as our minds, how to heal the injuries we have suffered, how to do organizing that transforms people as well as institutions.

We have to think about our vision of change.

I am not arguing that we should give up direct action, civil disobedience, issue campaigns, political education, confrontation, membership and voter drives, et cetera. We need to do these things and much more. I am suggesting that we rethink the meaning of social change and learn how to include the long-term work of transforming people as we work for social justice. We must redefine "winning." Our social change has to be more than amassing resources and shifting power from the hands of one group to another. We must seek a true shift in consciousness, one that forges vision, goals, and strategies from belief, not just from expediency, and allows us to become a strong political force.

The definition of transformational politics is fairly simple: it is political work that changes the hearts and minds of people; supports personal and group growth in ways that create healthy, whole people, organizations, and communities; and is based on a vision of a society where people—across lines of race, gender, class, and sexuality—are supported by institutions and communities to live their best lives.

It calls for living with communal values. We face a daunting challenge here because our culture glorifies individualism. Creating community requires seeing the whole, not just the parts, and understanding how they interrelate. However, the difficult part is learning how to honor the needs of the individual as well as those of the group, without denying the importance of either. It requires a balance between identity and freedom on the one hand and the collective good and public responsibility on the other. It requires ritual and celebration and collective ways to grieve and show anger; it requires a commitment to resolve conflict.

Building connection and relationship demands that we give it time, not just in meetings but in informal opportunities surrounding meetings, structured and unstructured. Our communities are where our moral values are expressed. It is here that we are called upon to share our connection to others, our interdependence, our deepest belief in what it means to be part of the human condition, where people's lives touch one another, for good or for bad. It is here where the rhetoric of belief is forced into the reality of living. It is from this collection of people, holding within it smaller units called families, that we build and live democracy—or, without care and nurturance, where we detach from one another and destroy our hope for survival.

It is one thing for us to talk about liberation politics; it is of course another to live it. We lack political integrity when we demand liberation for one cause or one group of people and act out oppression or exploitation toward others. In our social change organizations in particular we can find ourselves in this dangerous position: where we are demanding, for example, liberation from sexism but within the organization we act out racism, economic injustice, and homophobia. Each is reflected in who is allowed to lead, who makes the highest and lowest salaries, who is allowed to participate in the major decision-making, who decides how resources are used. If the organization does not have a vision and a strategy

that also include the elimination of racism, sexism, economic injustice, and homophobia (as well as oppressions relating to age, physical ability, et cetera), then internal conflict is inevitable.

. . .

I believe that all oppressions in this country turn on an economic wheel; they all, in the long run, serve to consolidate and keep wealth in the hands of the few, with the many fighting over crumbs. Without work against economic injustice, against the dehumanizing excesses of capitalism, there can be no deep and lasting work on oppression. The theocratic Right has been successful in driving wedges between oppressed groups because there is little common understanding of the linkages common to all oppressions. Progressives have contributed to these divisions because, generally, we have dealt only with single pieces of the fabric of injustice. Often we have no knowledge of a shared history. We stand ready to be divided. Our challenge is to learn how to use the experiences of our many identities to forge an inclusive social change politics. The question that faces us is how to do multi-issue coalition-building from an identity base. The hope for a multiracial, multi-issue movement rests in large part on the answer to this question.

If women are treated as people undeserving of equality within civil rights organizations, or lesbians and gay men are, how can those organizations demand equality? If women of color and poor women are marginalized in women's rights organizations, how can those organizations argue that women as a class should be moved into full participation in the mainstream? If lesbian and gay organizations are not feminist and antiracist in all their practices, what hope is there for the elimination of homophobia and heterosexism in a racist, sexist society? It is an issue of integrity.

When we grasp the value and interconnectedness of our liberation issues, then we will at last be able to make true coalition and begin building a common agenda that eliminates oppression and brings forth a vision of diversity that shares both power and resources.

READING 97

Epilogue
Beyond Backlash

Ruth Rosen

"If you're on the right track, you can expect some pretty savage criticism," veteran feminist Phyllis Chesler warned young women at the close of the twentieth century. "Trust it. Revel in it. It is the truest measure of your success." Words of wisdom from one of the pioneer activists who understood the meaning of a fierce backlash.

No movement could have challenged so many ideas and customs without threatening vast numbers of women and men. Some activists viewed the backlash as either a political conspiracy or a media plot hatched to discredit feminists. But the backlash, in fact, reflected a society deeply divided and disturbed by rapid changes in men's and women's lives, at home and at work.

Abortion genuinely polarized American women. Working women, as sociologist Kristin Luker discovered, tended to support abortion rights, while homemakers, who depended on a breadwinner's income, were more likely to regard children as a means of keeping husbands yoked to their families and so opposed it. The backlash, which had grown alongside the women's movement, gained strength in 1973 after the Supreme Court, in its *Roe v. Wade* decision, made abortion legal. The Catholic Church—and later the evangelical Christian Right—quickly mobilized to reverse that decision. By 1977, Congress had passed the Hyde Amendment, which banned the use of taxpayers' money to fund abortions for poor women. By 1980, the New Right had successfully turned abortion into a litmus test for political candidates, Cabinet officials, and Supreme Court justices. By 1989, the Supreme Court's *William L. Webster v. Reproductive Health Services* decision began the process of chipping away at women's right to abortion.

A long, drawn-out struggle over the Equal Rights Amendment also helped consolidate opposition to the women's movement. Passed quickly by Congress in a burst of optimism in 1972, the ERA needed to be ratified by thirty-eight state legislatures in order to become a part of the Constitution. Within a year, the ERA received swift ratification or support from thirty states, but then it stalled, and in 1978, proponents extracted a reluctant extension from Congress. By 1982, the ERA, unable to gain more state ratifications, had been buried, a victim of the rising symbolic politics of a triumphant political movement of the Right.

The ten-year battle over the ERA and the escalating struggle over abortion helped mobilize conservative women. Ironically, women of the Right learned from the women's movement, even if in opposition to it. In a kind of mirror-image politicking, they began to form their own all-female organizations, including Happiness of Motherhood Eternal (HOME), Women Who Want to Be Women (WWWW), American Women against the Ratification of the ERA (AWARE), Females Opposed to Equality (FOE), and the Eagle Forum. Soon, they engaged in their own kinds of local and national consciousness-raising activities. Their tactics, like those of the women's movement, included polite protest and lobbying in Washington, as well as more militant rallies and protests. But unlike the women's movement, the fringes engaged in actual terrorism at abortion clinics.

The political struggle also catapulted several conservative women to national prominence. Among them was Phyllis Schlafly, a shrewd attorney who nonetheless—like Betty Friedan almost two decades earlier—described herself as "just a housewife," and founded Stop ERA, which she credited with defeating the ERA. An influential if little-known member of the conservative Right, Schlafly had written a book, *The Power of the Positive Woman*

(1977), which attacked feminists for their negative assessments of women's condition in the United States. Schlafly also blamed "limousine liberals," "the cosmopolitan elite," and "chic fellow travelers" for living in a rarefied world that cared little about the traditional family and its values. Schlafly used her antifeminism as a vehicle for reinventing herself as a national celebrity. Thanks to the media, her name soon became a household word.

The growing engagement of women in the religious and secular New Right legitimated an increasing fusillade of attacks on feminism by right-wing male religious and political leaders. In *The New Right: We're Ready to Lead*, Richard Viguerie, one of those leaders, announced that the New Right had to fight "anti-family organizations like the National Organization for Women and to resist laws like the Equal Rights Amendment that attack families and individuals." Schlafly, Viguerie, and other leaders of the New Right blamed the hedonistic values of American culture on feminists. For them, an independent woman was by definition a selfish, self-absorbed creature who threatened the nation's "traditional values."

Support for the growing backlash came from many directions, including many women who were not members of any New Right organization. Some of those disgruntled women now felt overwhelmed by the double responsibilities they bore at home and at work; they blamed feminism for their plight. The media took its cue from such women. A new formulaic narrative appeared in the print media, that of the repentant career woman who finally realizes that feminism had very nearly ruined her life. Editors began to dispatch reporters in search of professional women who had quit their high-status jobs and returned home with great sighs of relief to care for their husbands and children.

Like the "first woman" stories of the 1970s, these cautionary tales of the 1980s obscured the actual lives of the vast majority of women in the labor force, for whom there was no choice but to get up every morning and go to work. Most working mothers labored at low-paid jobs, and husbands generally avoided even a reasonable share of the housework from their now-employed spouses. So women daily returned home to what sociologist Arlie Hochschild

dubbed the "second shift." Even successful professional women were discovering that they, too, had no choice but to enter careers on men's terms. Their new employers expected them to be available "25 hours a day, seven days a week" and their husbands, too, expected the same services they would have received from an unemployed wife. To secure promotions, career women—but not men—felt compelled to choose whether to dedicate their prime child-bearing years to their careers and remain childless, or to face the daunting prospect of trying to do it all.

Despite the difficulties women and men experienced as they tried to adjust to this newly configured home life, it's important to recognize that the women's movement did not invariably pit men against women. This was not a battle between the sexes; it was part of the highly gendered and racialized cultural wars that polarized Americans in the wake of the 1960s. Men and women fought *together* on both sides of the divide, for this was a struggle between social and cultural ideals.

. . .

Feminist responses to the backlash began to appear in literature as well. During the heady years of the 1970s, feminist utopian novels had become the *genre du jour*. Some of the most prominent novels—Marge Piercy's *Woman on the Edge of Time* or Ursula Le Guinn's *The Left Hand of Darkness*—had played with gender and sexual identity and optimistically imagined new ways of achieving gender equality. In the wake of the backlash, the Canadian novelist Margaret Atwood published a bleak dystopian novel, *The Handmaid's Tale* (1986), which quickly became a best-seller. This chilling novel took the destructive potential of the religious backlash seriously and offered a scary answer to the question: "What if the religious Right actually gained political power?"

Despite the sense of gloom and defeat that many feminists experienced at the time, American women were, in fact, increasingly embracing the goals of the women's movement. Reasons were not hard to fathom. Growing numbers of women were falling into poverty. Diana Pearce's 1978 phrase "the feminization of poverty" caught a startling and unexpected reality of American life. Divorce rates, which had doubled since 1965, had created a new cohort of women who joined the poor when their marriages ended. By 1984, working women began to outnumber women who worked at home and the glamorization of the superwoman and her career choice had eroded the prestige of homemaking. The growing tendency of middle-class women to postpone marriage and motherhood, combined with an increase in single mothers and divorced mothers, created a critical mass of women who now wondered how they were going to support themselves and their children. Polls steadily revealed what the much-publicized backlash obscured, that a majority of women now looked favorably upon the goals of the women's movement.

Women's attitudes had, in fact, changed rapidly. In a 1970 Virginia Slims opinion poll, 53 percent of women cited being a wife and mother as "one of the best parts of being a woman." By 1983, that figure had dropped to 26 percent. In 1970, very few women expressed concern over discrimination. By 1983, one-third of women agreed that "male chauvinism, discrimination, and sexual stereotypes ranked as their biggest problem"; while 80 percent agreed that "to get ahead a woman has to be better at what she does than a man." Nor did women still believe they lived privileged lives, as they had in 1975, when one-third of Americans viewed men's lives as far more difficult. By 1990, nearly half of all adults assumed that men had the easier life.

At the height of the backlash, in short, more American women, not fewer, grasped the importance of the goals of the women's movement. In 1986, a Gallup poll asked women, "Do you consider yourself a feminist?" At a time when identifying yourself as a feminist felt like a risky admission, 56 percent of American women were willing to do so (at least privately to Gallup's pollsters). Women of all classes were also becoming aware of the ways in which gender shaped their lives. Sixty-seven percent of all women, including those who earned under $12,500 *and* those who made more than $50,000, favored a strong women's movement. Pollsters consistently found that more African-American women approved of the goals of the women's movement than did white women. A 1989 poll found that 51 percent of all men, 64 percent of white women, 72 percent of Hispanic women, and 85 percent of African-American women agreed with the statement: "The United States continues to need a strong women's movement to push for changes that benefit women."

In 1989, *Time* magazine ushered in a new decade with yet one more pronouncement of the death of feminism. Its cover story, "Women Face the '90s," bore the subtitle "During the '80s, they tried to have it all. Now they've just plain had it. Is there a future for feminism?" But, inside, the reader discovered quite a different story. Feminism was endangered, *Time* magazine suggested, not because it had failed, but precisely because it had been so successful. "In many ways," the article declared,

> feminism is a victim of its own resounding achievements. Its triumphs—in getting women into the workplace, in elevating their status in society and in shattering "the feminine mystique" that defined female success only in terms of being a wife and a mother—have rendered it obsolete, at least in its original form and rhetoric.

The growth of gender consciousness had, in fact, altered society and culture in countless ways. In August 1980, a *New York Times* editorial declared that the women's movement, once viewed as a group of "extremists and troublemakers," had turned into an "effective political force." The editorial concluded that "the battle for women's rights is no longer lonely or peripheral. It has moved where it belongs; to the center of American politics." In 1984, commenting on legislation that would grant child support for all families and give wives access to their husbands' pensions, the *Times* editorialized that "'Women's Issues' have already become everyone's." And so they had. Perhaps the important legacy was precisely that "women's issues" had entered mainstream national politics, where they had changed the terms of political debate.

Everyday life had changed in small but significant ways. Strangers addressed a woman as Ms.; meteorologists named hurricanes after *both* men and women; schoolchildren learned about sexism before they became teenagers; language became more gender-neutral; popular culture saturated society with comedies, thrillers, and mysteries that turned on changing gender roles; and two decades after the movement's first years, the number of women politicians doubled. Even more significantly, millions of women had entered jobs that had once been reserved for men.

Although women had not gained the power to change institutions in fundamental ways, they had joined men in colleges and universities in unprecedented numbers. In the 1950s, women had constituted only 20 percent of college undergraduates, and their two most common aspirations, according to polls of the time, were to become the wife of a prominent man and the mother of several accomplished children. By 1990, women constituted 54 percent of undergraduates and they wanted to do anything and everything. Women had also joined men in both blue collar and professional jobs in startling numbers. In 1960, 35 percent of women had worked outside the home; by 1990, that figure had jumped to 58 percent. During the same period, the number of female lawyers and judges leaped from 7,500 to 108,200; and female doctors from 15,672 to 174,000.

The cumulative impact of decades of revelations, education, debates, scandals, controversies, and high-profile trials raised women's gender consciousness, which in turn eventually showed up in a long-awaited political "gender gap." In 1871, Susan B. Anthony had prematurely predicted that once women got the right to vote, they would vote as a bloc. A gender gap did not appear until 1980, when more men than women voted for Ronald Reagan, whose opposition to the Equal Rights Amendment and abortion may have moved some women into the Democratic column. More important was Reagan's pledge to dismantle the welfare state, which nudged even more women toward the Democrats, the party more likely (theoretically) to preserve the safety net. Eventually, the gender gap would cause at least a temporary realignment of national politics. In 1996, 16 percent more women than men voted for Bill Clinton for president. Some political analysts now believed that women were voting their interests as workers, family caregivers, or as single or divorced mothers.

Gender gap or not, the rightward tilt of American politics led to the demonization of poor women and their children. As some middle-class women captured meaningful and well-paid work, ever more women slid into poverty and homelessness, which,

on balance, the women's movement did too little, too late, to change. On the other hand, the lives of many ordinary working women, who had not become impoverished, improved in dramatic ways. In 1992, a *Newsweek* article described how twenty years of the women's movement had changed Appleton, Wisconsin (the hometown of Joseph McCarthy and the John Birch Society). Women, the magazine reported, had taken on significant roles in local politics. In addition, the article observed,

> There are women cops and women firefighters, and there are women in managerial jobs in local business and government. There is firm community consensus, and generous funding with local tax dollars, for Harbor House, a shelter for battered women. And there is an active effort, in the Appleton public schools, to eliminate the invidious stereotyping that keeps young women in the velvet straitjacket of traditional gender roles.

Global Feminism

As ideas from the Western women's movement traveled across the Atlantic, American feminists learned more than they taught. On October 25, 1985, President Vigdis Finnbogadottir of Iceland joined tens of thousands of women who had walked off the job in a twenty-four-hour protest against male privilege on the island. She also refused to sign a bill that would have ordered striking flight attendants back to work. Iceland's telephone system collapsed, travel came to a halt, and groups of men crowded into hotels for the breakfast their wives refused to cook for them.

As feminism began spreading beyond industrialized nations, American feminists also encountered new definitions of "women's issues." Sometimes "freedom" meant better access to fuel and water, toppling a ruthless dictator, or ending a genocidal civil war. The gradual emergence of global women's networks made such encounters and confrontations inevitable.

Many of these networks grew out of the United Nation's 1975 International Women's Year. At the first World Conference on Women in Mexico, delegates urged the UN to proclaim the years between 1975 and 1985 "The Decade for Women." At each subsequent UN conference, there were two parallel meetings—one for delegates who represented their governments and another for women who participated in the nongovernmental organization (NGO) meetings. The numbers of NGO participants mushroomed. Six thousand women participated in the second conference, held in 1980 at Copenhagen; fourteen thousand attended the third in 1985 in Nairobi; and a startling thirty thousand arrived in Huairou, China, for the fourth in 1995.

What President Kennedy's Commission on the Status of Women had done for American women activists, the UN's World Conferences now did at a global level. Proximity bred intimacy and spread knowledge. The thousands of women rubbing shoulders or debating in Mexico, Denmark, Kenya, or China were learning from and teaching each other about their lives. Aside from their differences, they were also discovering the ubiquity of certain kinds of shared oppression—violence and poverty that had once seemed local, rather than global. And, in the process, they were nurturing and legitimating a global feminism, which was quite literally being born at UN conferences as they watched.

That didn't mean that women everywhere interpreted the information newly available to them in the same way. From the start, the NGO forum meetings witnessed serious clashes between "First" and "Third" World women, and between women whose nations were at war. Over time, the atmosphere began to improve. Western feminists began to *listen,* rather than *lecture,* and women from developing countries, who had formerly viewed Western concerns over clitoridectomies, dowry deaths, wife-beatings, and arranged marriages as so many instances of cultural imperialism—the urge of developed countries to impose their values and customs on underdeveloped nations—began the painful process of redefining their own customs as crimes.

Here was the essence of global feminism—addressing the world's problems *as if women mattered.* Human rights organizations, for instance, had traditionally focused exclusively on state-sanctioned violence against political activists. But most women encountered violence not in prison or at protests, but in their homes and communities. Viewed as customs rather than crimes, wife-beating, rape, genital exci-

sion, dowry deaths, and arranged marriages had never been certified as violations of women's human rights.

At a 1993 UN World Conference on Human Rights in Vienna, women from all over the globe movingly testified to the various forms of violence that had devastated their lives. Feminists successfully made their case; the conference passed a resolution that recognized violence against women and girls as a violation of their human rights. One immediate consequence of this historic redefinition of human rights was that Western nations could now grant *political* asylum to women fleeing certain violence or death from husbands or other relatives.

Two years later, at a 1995 UN Conference on Development and Population in Cairo, feminists criticized accepted development policies that promoted massive industrial or hydroelectric projects as *the* way to improve the standard of living of developing nations. Such projects, they argued, irreversibly damaged the human and natural ecology, provided work for indigenous men, but not for women, and undermined women's traditional economic role and social authority. Instead, they advocated small-scale cottage industries, through which women could earn money for their education. They also attacked those population experts who took it, as an article of faith, that population growth automatically declined when industrial development lifted people out of poverty. Citing the failure of such policies, feminists countered that educating women and giving them control over their reproductive decisions was a far more effective way of controlling population growth. As one reporter wrote, "The deceptively simple idea of a woman making a decision about her future is one of the cornerstones of the emerging debate on global population policy."

The "Platform for Action," the document that emerged from the Beijing conference in 1995, asked the nations of the world to see social and economic development through the eyes of women. Although the "Platform" recognized the differences that separated women, it also emphasized the universal poverty and violence that crippled the lives of so many of the world's women. In addition to affirming women's rights as human rights, the conference also declared three preconditions for women's advancement; equality, development, and peace. To many participants, the event seemed like a miracle, a moment existing out of time, when the world's women imagined a different kind of future, even if they had little power to implement it.

By publicizing even more gender consciousness, the 1995 Fourth World Conference on Women probably encouraged greater numbers of the world's women to challenge traditional forms of patriarchal authority. In the years following the conference, feminist activists and scholars began the process of redefining rape (when it occurred during a military conflict) as a war crime, publicizing the particular plight of refugees (most of whom were women), and rethinking the role women might play in reconstructing societies ravaged by war.

At the same time, women in both developed and developing nations began debating the impact of feminism itself on global culture and economics. Was feminism yoked only to concepts of individual rights? Was it simply an inevitable by-product of Western consumer capitalism, whose effects would rupture the ties that bound families and communities together—and to the land? Or could feminism help protect the rights of women as they left family and land behind and entered the global wage economy? Could women's rights, redefined as human rights, provide a powerful new stance from which to oppose totalitarian societies of both the Right and the Left? Many theories proliferated, heated debates took place, but the answers—even many of the questions—lay in the future.

There is no end to this story. Over a hundred years ago, the suffragist Matilda Gage turned her gaze toward the future. The work of her generation of activists, she wrote, was not for them alone,

> nor alone for the present generation, but for all women of all time. The hopes of posterity were in their hands, and they were determined to place on record for the daughters of 1976, the fact that their mothers of 1876 had thus asserted their equality of rights, and thus impeached the government of today for its injustice towards women.

Nearly a century later, veteran feminist Robin Morgan, along with thousands of other twentieth-century "daughters," took up the unfinished agenda left by the suffrage movement. Morgan, too, realized that she struggled for future daughters and worried that her generation might squander precious opportunities.

> I fear for the women's movement falling into precisely the same trap as did our foremothers, the suffragists: creating a bourgeois feminist movement that never quite dared enough, never questioned enough, never really reached out beyond its own class and race.

As women in developing countries become educated and enter the marketplace as wage-earners, they will invariably intensify existing cultural conflicts between religious and secular groups, and between those sectors of society living under preindustrial conditions and those who connect through cyberspace in a postmodern global society. Like small brushfires, these cultural wars may circle the globe, igniting a wild and frightening firestorm. Inevitably, some women will feel defeated as they encounter wave after wave of backlash. But in the darkness of their despair, they should remember that resistance is not a sign of defeat, but rather evidence that women are challenging a worldview that now belongs to an earlier era of human history.

Each generation of women activists leaves an unfinished agenda for the next generation. First Wave suffragists fought for women's citizenship, created international organizations, dedicated to universal disarmament, but left many customs and beliefs unchallenged. Second Wave feminists questioned nearly everything, transformed much of American culture, expanded the idea of democracy by insisting that equality had to include the realities of its women citizens, and catapulted women's issues onto a global stage. Their greatest accomplishment was to change the terms of debate, so that women mattered. But they left much unfinished as well. They were unable to change most institutions, to gain greater economic justice for poor women, or to convince society that child care is the responsibility of the whole society. As a result, American women won the right to "have it all," but only if they "did it all."

It is for a new generation to identify what they need in order to achieve greater equality. It may even be their solemn duty. In the words of nineteenth-century suffragist Abigail Scott Duniway:

> The young women of today, free to study, to speak, to write, to choose their occupation, should remember that every inch of this freedom was bought for them at a great price. It is for them to show their gratitude by helping onward the reforms of their own times, by spreading the light of freedom and truth still wider. The debt that each generation owes to the past it must pay to the future.

The struggle for women's human rights has just begun. As each generation shares its secrets, women learn to see the world through their own eyes, and discover, much to their surprise, that they are not the first, and that they are not alone. The poet Muriel Rukeyser once asked, "What would happen if one woman told the truth about her life?" Her answer: "The world would split open." And so it has. A revolution is under way, and there is no end in sight.

READING 98

Warning

Jenny Joseph

When I am an old woman I shall wear purple
With a red hat which doesn't go, and doesn't suit me.
And I shall spend my pension on brandy and summer gloves
And satin sandals, and say we've no money for butter.
I shall sit down on the pavement when I'm tired
And gobble up samples in shops and press alarm bells

And run my stick along the public railings
And make up for the sobriety of my youth.
I shall go out in my slippers in the rain
And pick the flowers in other people's gardens
And learn to spit.

You can wear terrible shirts and grow more fat
And eat three pounds of sausages at a go
Or only bread and pickle for a week
And hoard pens and pencils and beermats and things in boxes.

But now we must have clothes that keep us dry
And pay our rent and not swear in the street
And set a good example for the children.
We must have friends to dinner and read the papers.
But maybe I ought to practise a little now?
So people who know me are not too shocked or surprised
When suddenly I am old, and start to wear purple.

READING 99

A Day with Feminism

Jennifer Baumgardner and Amy Richards

Women and men are paid equal wages for work of comparable value, as is every race and ethnic group, co-parenting is a given, men lengthen their lives by crying and otherwise expressing emotion, and women say "I'm sorry" only when they truly should

be. To the extent that we can imagine this even now, this is the equality feminists have been working for since that day in Seneca Falls in 1848. With each generation, the picture will get bigger and at the same time more finely detailed.

When Elizabeth Cady Stanton and her crew wrote the Declaration of Sentiments, they knew that this nation's Declaration of Independence would have no justice or power unless it included the female half of the country. For these women, equality was being full citizens who were able to own and inherit property, just as men were, to have the right to their own children, and the ability to vote. In 1923, Alice Paul had the vision to write the Equal Rights Amendment so that laws could not be made based on sex, any more than they could be made based on race, religion, or national origin. By the 1970s, Betty Friedan, Audre Lorde, Gloria Steinem, and Shirley Chisholm could imagine women's equality in the paid workforce, a new vision of family and sexuality, and legislative bodies that truly reflected the country. They could not have foreseen a twenty-three-year-old White House intern who owned her own libido and sexual prowess the way Monica Lewinsky did. (They certainly wouldn't have imagined that a woman with that much access to power would just want to blow it.)

Now, at the beginning of a new millennium, we have witnessed a woman running for President who has a chance of winning, a first lady who translates that unparalleled Washington experience into her own high-flying political ambitions, easily reversible male birth control, gay parenting, a women's soccer team that surpasses the popular appeal of men's, and parental leave for both parents. And we can imagine more: federally subsidized child-care centers for every child and legalized gay marriage in all fifty states. A number of leaps are still needed to bring us to a day of equality, but at least we can begin to picture what such a future might hold.

Whether children are born to a single mother, a single father, two mothers, two fathers, or a mother and a father, a family is defined by love, commitment, and support. A child who has two parents is just as likely to have a hyphenated last name, or choose a whole new name, as she or he is to have a father's or birth mother's name. Carrying on a lineage is an individual choice, not the province of the father or the state.

Men work in child-care centers and are paid at least as well as plumbers, sanitation workers, or firefighters. When kids sit down to their breakfast Wheaties, they are as likely to confront a tennis star like Venus Williams as a golf pro like Tiger Woods. On TV, the male and female newscasters are about the same age and, whether black or white, are as likely to report foreign policy as sports. In general, people on camera come in all shapes and sizes. If you are watching drama, women are just as likely to be the rescuers as the rescued, and men are just as likely to ask for help as to give it. Women are as valued for their sense of humor as men are for their sex appeal. On Monday-night television, women's soccer or basketball is just as popular as men's basketball or football. Barbie no longer has feet too tiny to stand on or finds math hard; nor do girls. G. I. Joe, now a member of a peacekeeping force, likes to shop at the mall. In grade school, boys and girls decorate their bedrooms with posters of female athletes.

By the time girls hit junior high, they have already had the opportunity to play sports, from soccer to Little League, hockey to wrestling, and they share gymnastics and ballet classes with boys. Boys think ballet and gymnastics are cool. Kids hit puberty fully aware of how their bodies work: erections, nocturnal emissions, periods, cramps, masturbation, body hair —the works. These topics still cause giggling, curiosity, and excitement, but paralyzing shame and utter ignorance are things of the past. In fact, sweet-sixteen birthdays have given way to coming-of-age rituals for both genders, and don't assume that the birthday kid has never been kissed. Around the time that girls and boys are learning how to drive, both have mastered manual stimulation for their own sexual pleasure.

In high school, many varsity teams have coed cheerleaders, athletes all, but mostly cheering is left to the fans. Differences in girls' and boys' academic performance are as indistinguishable as differences in their athletic performance though they are very different as unique individuals. Some girls ask other girls to the prom, some boys ask boys, and that is as okay as going in as a mixed couple. Some go alone or not at all, and that's okay, too. Athletic scholarships have no more prestige or funding than arts scholarships.

Students take field trips to local museums where women are the creators of the art as often as they are its subjects. In preparation for this trip, students study art history from Artemisia Gentileschi to Mark Rothko, from Ndebele wall paintings to Yayoi Kusama. The museums themselves were designed by architects who may have been among the 11 percent of architects who were female in the 1990s. Military school is open to everyone and teaches peacekeeping as much as defense. Women's colleges no longer exist, because women to longer need a compensatory environment, and women's history, African-American history, and all those remedial areas have become people's and world history.

Women achieved parity long ago, so the idea of bean counting is irrelevant. At Harvard, 75 percent of the tenured professors are women, and at nearby Boston College, 30 percent of the tenured faculty is female. History courses cover the relevance of a movement that ended sexual violence against women. Though there is still a throwback incident now and then, men are even more outraged by it than women are. Once a year, there is a party in the quad to commemorate what was once called Take Back the Night.

Women walking through a park at night can feel just as safe as they do during the day, when kids play while white male nannies watch over them, right along with women and men of every group. In fact, it's as common to see a white man taking care of a black or a brown baby as it is to see a woman of color taking care of a white baby.

Sex is separate from procreation. Because there is now a national system of health insurance, birth control and abortions are covered right along with births, and the Hyde Amendment's ban of federal funding for abortions is regarded as a shameful moment in history, much like the time of Jim Crow laws. A judicial decision known as *Doe v. Hyde* effectively affirmed a woman's right to bodily integrity, and went way past the right to privacy guaranteed by *Roe v. Wade*. Abortion isn't morally contested territory because citizens don't interfere with one another's life choices, and women have the right to determine when and whether to have no children, a single child, or five children.

Environmentally sound menstrual products are government-subsidized and cost the same as a month's worth of shaving supplies. After all, women's childbearing capacity is a national asset, and young,

sexually active men often opt for freezing their sperm or undergoing a simple vasectomy to control their paternity. Many men choose vasectomies, given that it's the least dangerous and most foolproof form of birth control—as well as the easiest to reverse. Men are screened for chlamydia, human papilloma virus, herpes, and other sexually transmitted diseases during their annual trip to the andrologist. Doctors learn how to detect and treat all of the above, in both men and women. Although the old number of three million or so new cases of STDs each year has dropped to half that amount, STDs are still as common (and about as shameful) as the common cold—and are finally acknowledged as such.

The Equal Rights Amendment has put females in the U.S. Constitution. There are many women of all races in fields or institutions formerly considered to be the province of men, from the Virginia Military Institute and the Citadel to fire departments and airline cockpits. Women are not only free to be as exceptional as men but also as mediocre. Men are as critiqued or praised as women are. Women's salaries have jumped up 26 to 40 percent from pre-equality days to match men's. There are no economic divisions based on race, and the salary categories have been equalized. This categorization is the result of legislation that requires the private sector—even companies that employ fewer than 50 people—to report employees' wages. Many older women are averaging half a million dollars in back pay as a result of the years in which they were unjustly underpaid. Women and men in the NBA make an average of $100,000 per year. Haircuts, dry cleaning, and clothes for women cost the same as they do for men.

The media are accountable to their constituency. Magazines cover stories about congressional hearings on how to help transition men on welfare back into the workforce. Many of these men are single fathers—by choice. Welfare is viewed as a subsidy, just as corporate tax breaks used to be, and receiving government assistance to help rear one's own child is as destigmatized as it is to be paid to rear a foster child. Howard Stern, who gave up his declining radio show to become a stay-at-home granddad, has been replaced on radio by Janeane Garofalo, who no longer jokes primarily about her "back fat" and other perceived imperfections. (Primary caregiving has humanized Stern so that people no longer have to fear for his influence on his offspring.) Leading ladies and leading men are all around the same age. There is always fanfare around *Time* magazine's Person of the Year and *Sports Illustrated*'s coed swimsuit issue. *Rolling Stone* covers female pop stars and music groups in equal numbers with male stars, and women are often photographed for the cover *with* their shirts on. Classic-rock stations play Janis Joplin as often as they play Led Zeppelin.

Women who choose to have babies give birth in a birthing center with a midwife, a hospital with a doctor, or at home with a medicine woman. Paid childcare leave is for four months, and it is required of both parents (if there is more than one). Child rearing is subsidized by a trust not unlike Social Security, a concept pioneered by the welfare-rights activist Theresa Funiciello and based on Gloria Steinem's earlier mandate that every child have a minimum income. The attributed economic value of housework is figured into the gross national product (which increases the United States' GNP by almost 30 percent), and primary caregivers are paid. Whether you work in or out of the home, you are taxed only on your income; married couples and people in domestic partnerships are taxed as individuals, too. When women retire, they get as much Social Security as men do, and all people receive a base amount on which they can live.

The amount of philanthropic dollars going to programs that address or specifically include women and girls is now pushing 60 percent, to make up for all the time it was about 5 percent.[1] More important, these female-centered programs no longer have to provide basic services, because the government does that.[2] All school meals, vaccinations, public libraries, and museums are government-funded and thus available to everybody. Taxpayers have made their wishes clear because more than 90 percent of the electorate actually votes.

"Postmenopausal zest" is as well documented and as anticipated as puberty. Women in their fifties— free from pregnancy, menstruation, and birth control—are regarded as sexpots and envied for their wild and free libidos. "Wine and women," as the saying goes, "get better with age."

Every man and woman remembers exactly where they were the moment they heard that the Equal Rights Amendment passed. The President addressed the nation on the night of that victory and said, "Americans didn't know what we were missing before today . . . until we could truly say that all people are created equal." The first man stood at her side with a tear running down his face.

The social-justice movement, formerly known as feminism, is now just *life*.

NOTES

1. In 1997, according to research undertaken by Women and Philanthropy, only 5.7 percent of philanthropic dollars went to programs specifically benefiting women and girls.
2. At present, some of life's basic necessities are either not available to those who need them or must be paid for with private funding. For example, between 21 and 23 percent of U.S. adults are functionally illiterate, according to the Literacy Volunteers of America. Yet this organization, the largest literacy-training initiative in America, does not get a dime from the government and is funded almost exclusively by individual donors and corporations.

DISCUSSION QUESTIONS FOR CHAPTER THIRTEEN

1. How has your experience in a feminist classroom had on impact on you?
2. What do you consider important factors for building a "beloved community"?
3. How do you envision a just future? How do you think we can get there?
4. What does integrity mean to you? How does integrity affect your work for justice?

5. What impact might a "transformational politics" have on our society?

6. Why are peace and the environment important women's issues?

7. What will you take away from this class to help you make your way in the world?

SUGGESTIONS FOR FURTHER READING

Clare, Eli, and Suzanne Pharr. *Exile and Pride.* Boston: South End, 1999.

Daly, Mary. *Quintessence . . . Realizing the Archaic Future: A Radical Elemental Feminist Manifesto.* Boston: Beacon, 1999.

Mellor, Mary. *Feminism & Ecology.* New York: New York University Press, 1998.

Naples, Nancy A. *Community Activism and Feminist Politics: Organizing Across Race, Class, and Gender.* New York: Routledge, 1997.

———. *Grassroots Warriors: Activist Mothering, Community Work, and the War on Poverty.* New York: Routledge, 1998.

Ryan, M. J., ed. *The Fabric of the Future: Women Visionaries of Today Illuminate the Path to Tomorrow.* Berkeley: Conari, 2000.

Credits

from The National Women's Health Resource Center, Inc. **Page 237** "10 Things You Can Do to Protect Choice," CARAL Pro-Choice Education Fund. Reprinted by permission of CARAL, San Francisco, CA. **Page 404** Reprinted from TAKE CARE: A GUIDE FOR VIOLENCE-FREE LIVING, a publication of Raphael House of Portland. **Page 443** "Affirmative Action: Myth vs. Reality," February 1997. Copyright © 1997. Reprinted by permission of American Association of University Women. **Page 522** "Size does matter and nine other tips for effective protest," MOTHER JONES. March/April 1999, pp. 58–59, © 1999, Foundation for National Progress. Reprinted by permission of Mother Jones. **Page 528** "Principles of Environmental Justice" reprinted by permission of UCC Commission for Racial Justice. **Page 156** From "Lesbian, Gay, Bisexual and Transgender Rights" from HUMAN RIGHTS WATCH WORLD REPORT 2002. Used with permission of Human Rights Watch. **Page 240** The United Nations is the author of the original material. Reprinted by permission from The World's Women 2000: Health in THE WORLD'S WOMEN 2000 at *www.un.org.* **Page 557** The United Nations is the author of the original material. Reprinted by permission from UN MILLEN-NIUM DEVELOPMENT GOALS at www.un.org. **Page 65** From *www.undp.org/unifem/brights.htm.* Reprinted by permission. **Page 17** From "US Suffrage Movement Timeline" at *www.rochester.edu/sba/timeline1.html.* Prepared by Mary Hugh, Rare Books and Special Collections Department. **Page 4** The United Nations is the author of the original material. Reprinted by permission from The World's Women 2000: Women and Men in Families in THE WORLD'S WOMEN 2000 at www.un.org. **Page 325** Reprinted by permission of the Food and Agriculture Organization of the United Nations. **Page 288** The United Nations is the author of the original material. Reprinted by permission from THE WORLD'S WOMEN 2000 at www.un.org. **Page 562** Female Nobel Peace Laureates from *http://womenshistory.about.com/education/womenshistory/msubnobelpeace.htm.* **Page 14** From "Yes, I Am a Feminist," MS, September/October 1997, pp. 49–42. Copyright © 1997 MS.

PHOTO CREDITS

p. 3, Courtesy Susan E. Cayleff, San Diego State University; p. 6, © Corbis; p. 17, © Bettmann/Corbis; p. 68, © Bettmann/Corbis; p. 119, © Yellow Dog Productions/Getty Images/The Image Bank; p. 122, © AP/Wide World Photos; p. 159, © Corbis; p. 202, 205, © Bettmann/Corbis; p. 251, © AP/Wide World Photos; p. 289, © Ronnie Kaufman/Corbis; p. 293, Courtesy National Council of Jewish Women; p. 326, © Bill Aron/PhotoEdit; p. 334, Courtesy Dawn M.C. Cuellar; p. 387, © AP/Wide World Photos; p. 397, © Jane Scherr; p. 427, Photo © J. Cleland, Courtesy of Phyllis Lyon and Del Martin; p. 430, © Dwayne Newton/PhotoEdit; p. 466, © Peter Turnley/Corbis; p. 468, © AP/Wide World Photos; p. 521, © Rachel Epstein/PhotoEdit; p. 522, Library of Congress; p. 558, © AP/Wide World Photos

Index